D1566834

LAW AND THE MENTAL HEALTH SYSTEM

CIVIL AND CRIMINAL ASPECTS

Fifth Edition

By

Christopher Slobogin
Professor of Law
Vanderbilt University

Arti Rai
Elvin R. Latty Professor of Law
Duke Law School

Ralph Reisner
Professor of Law, Emeritus,
University of Illinois–Champaign
Visiting Professor,
University of California–San Diego

AMERICAN CASEBOOK SERIES®

Mat # 40618929

American Casebook Series and West Group are trademarks registered in the U.S. Patent and Trademark Office.

COPYRIGHT © 1985, 1990 WEST PUBLISHING CO.
© West, a Thomson business, 1999, 2004
© 2009 THOMSON/WEST
      610 OPPERMAN DRIVE
      ST. PAUL, MN 55123
      1–800–313–9378

Printed in the United States of America

ISBN: 978–0–314–18364–4

TEXT IS PRINTED ON 10% POST
CONSUMER RECYCLED PAPER

LAW AND THE MENTAL HEALTH SYSTEM

CIVIL AND CRIMINAL ASPECTS

Fifth Edition

By

Christopher Slobogin
Professor of Law
Vanderbilt University

Arti Rai
Elvin R. Latty Professor of Law
Duke Law School

Ralph Reisner
Professor of Law, Emeritus,
University of Illinois–Champaign
Visiting Professor,
University of California–San Diego

AMERICAN CASEBOOK SERIES®

Mat # 40618929

American Casebook Series and West Group are trademarks registered in the U.S. Patent and Trademark Office.

COPYRIGHT © 1985, 1990 WEST PUBLISHING CO.
© West, a Thomson business, 1999, 2004
© 2009 THOMSON/WEST
      610 OPPERMAN DRIVE
      ST. PAUL, MN 55123
      1–800–313–9378

Printed in the United States of America

ISBN: 978–0–314–18364–4

 TEXT IS PRINTED ON 10% POST CONSUMER RECYCLED PAPER

To Danute
　　— *Ralph Reisner*

————————

To Cindy
　　— *Christopher Slobogin*

————————

To Stuart, Sophia and Anna
　　— *Arti Rai*

*

Preface

This fifth edition of Law and the Mental Health System continues to pursue the objectives of the first four editions. First, we want to give the student a clear picture of past, present and possible future legal doctrine, as well as some feel for the most significant clinical and empirical literature, relating to three major topics: the delivery of mental health services, the regulation of the mental health professions, and the relationship between society and people with mental disability. Second, in each of these areas, we try to provide insights into how and to what degree the legal system can be used to implement desired social objectives. Third, this book attempts to sensitize the student to the (often very different) perspectives of the mental health professions on these issues.

The book continues to be divided into three parts, all of which have been significantly updated in this edition with new legal, empirical and critical material. Part I, "Mental Health Treatment and the Patient-Therapist Relationship," focuses primarily on the patient-therapist relationship and in that context examines the role of the legal system in promoting the quality of services, the protection of patient autonomy and privacy, and similar values. Chapter One provides important background information concerning the nature and characteristics of mental disorders, the diagnostic process, the modalities of mental health treatment, the mental health professions, and the economics of mental health care; the chapter thus serves as an important backdrop not only to the chapters in Part I but also to the other chapters of the book. The remaining chapters in Part I explore administrative licensing and regulation (Chapter Two), the application of malpractice law (Chapter Three), informed consent doctrine (Chapter Four), and confidentiality (Chapter Five).

Part II, "Deprivations of Liberty and Property," switches the focus to state intervention into the lives of people with mental disability. Chapter Six examines the preliminary issue of the extent to which the mental health professions are able to identify disability and its consequences. The next three chapters provide materials on laws affecting mentally disabled individuals who are charged with or convicted of crime (Chapter Seven), who are thought to be in need of hospitalization (Chapter Eight) and who are believed to be incompetent to exercise control over their property or person (Chapter Nine). Chapter Ten ends Part II with an exploration of issues that arise in treating persons with mental disability who have been the subject of state intervention.

Part III, "Benefits Eligibility and Legal Protection Against Discrimination," examines a number of laws meant to benefit all people with mental disability, whether or not the state has acted to deprive them of liberty or property. Chapter Eleven looks at federal benefit programs connected with education and social security. Chapter Twelve discusses laws that attempt to prevent discrimination against people with mental disability, including the Americans with Disabilities Act.

v

For their help on the book, the authors wish to acknowledge several individuals. As in the instance of earlier editions, Ralph Reisner was the beneficiary of help, counsel and advice from many quarters. In particular, he is deeply indebted to Lee Wong, a recent graduate of the University of California-San Diego, who in her last two years at the university assisted him on various projects. Her skill, dedication, and enthusiasm in all endeavors related to the revision of this book were invaluable. Hopefully, her involvement in the project will also prove to be of some benefit to her in her future career as a physician. Particular thanks are also due to Dr. John R. Kelsoe of the Department of Psychiatry, University of California at San Diego, for his invaluable help and review of the section in Chapter One pertaining to organic therapies. His extraordinary knowledge of the field helped the author sift through a complex and rapidly changing area of law. For help on the fifth edition, Professor Reisner is also deeply indebted to Cindy Ly, a recent graduate of the University of California, San Diego, who in her last two years at the university assisted him in various writing projects including the updating and revisions of the chapters in this book for which he was responsible. Her skill, dedication, and enthusiasm were invaluable. Ralph Reisner also wishes to extend his thanks to Dr. Paula Johnson, Senior Deputy Director, State Affairs; Department of Government Relations, American Psychiatric Association for providing invaluable information on the state of current legislation. Also, he is grateful to Barbara Holthaus Esq. and Priscilla Lozano Esq. of the Office of General Counsel, University of Texas System, for their help in clarifying some of the perplexing issues associated with the Virginia Tech shooting case that are treated in Chapters 3 and 5. Finally Professor Reisner expresses his gratitude and appreciation to his wife Danute, for the encouragement and support that she has graciously and unstintingly provided over the many years that he has been involved in this writing project.

For their comments on earlier versions of Part II of the book, Professor Slobogin continues to be indebted to a number of individuals: Professor Richard Bonnie of the University of Virginia Law School; Professor Nancy Ehrenreich of Denver Law School; Professor Gary Melton of the University of South Carolina; Professor John Monahan of the University of Virginia Law School; Professor Stephen Morse, University of Pennsylvania Law School; Professor Michael Perlin of New York Law School; John Petrila, University of South Florida; Professor Elyn Saks of the University of Southern California; Professor Elizabeth Scott of the University of Virginia Law School; and Professor David Wexler of Arizona Law School.

Professor Rai continues to be indebted to Professor Clark Havighurst of Duke Law School and Professor Mark Hall of Wake Forest University Law School for insights on the subject of health care finance. Professor Amy Wax of the University of Pennsylvania Law School provided valuable insights into the law and economics of disability-based discrimination.

CHRISTOPHER SLOBOGIN
ARTI RAI
RALPH REISNER

October 1, 2008

Acknowledgments

The authors wish to acknowledge, with gratitude, permission to reprint the following copyrighted materials.

A New Intellectual Framework of Psychiatry, by Eric R. Kandel, AMERICAN JOURNAL OF PSYCHIATRY, vol. 155(4), p. 460, 1998. Copyright 1998, the American Psychiatric Association. Reprinted by permission.

From DIAGNOSTIC AND STATISTICAL MANUAL, 4TH EDITION—TEXT REVISED 2000. Reprinted with permission from the Diagnostic and Statistical Manual of Mental Disorders, Fourth Edition. Washington, DC, American Psychiatric Association, 2000.

From THE PSYCHIATRIC THERAPIES, T.B. Karasu, ed., Copyright © 1984 by the American Psychiatric Association. Reprinted by permission of the American Psychiatric Publishing Group, Inc.

From THE PSYCHIATRISTS, by Arnold A. Rogow, Copyright © 1970 by Arnold A. Rogow. Used by permission of G.P. Putnam's Sons, a division of Penguin Group (USA) Inc.

From THE CENTER CANNOT HOLD: My Journey Through Madness, by Elyn R. Saks. Copyright © 2007 Elyn R. Saks. Reprinted by permission of Hyperion. All rights reserved.

Managed Care and the Evolving Role of the Clinical Social Worker in Mental Health, by Jeffrey Cohen, 48 SOCIAL WORK 34 (2003). Copyright © 2003, National Association of Social Workers, Inc. Reprinted by permission of the National Association of Social Workers.

From MANAGEMENT OF MENTAL HEALTH AND SUBSTANCE ABUSE SERVICES: STATE OF THE ART AND EARLY RESULTS, by David Mechanic, Mark Schlesinger, and Donna D. McAlpine, 3/22/95. Reprinted by permission of Blackwell Publishers.

Licensing Mental Therapists, by D. Hogan, from The New York Times, July 18, 1979. Copyright © 1979 by The New York Times Company. Reprinted by permission of the New York Times, Inc.

Occupational Licensing: A Framework for Analysis, by Jonathon Rose, 1979 ARIZONA STATE LAW JOURNAL 189 (1979). Copyright © 1979 by Arizona State University College of Law. Reprinted by permission of the Arizona State Law Journal and the author.

The Politics of Hysteria, by Joan Acocella, from THE NEW YORKER, April 6, 1998, p. 64, 66. Copyright © 1998. Reprinted by permission of Joan Acocella.

FORNIA LAW REVIEW 693 (1974). Copyright © 1974 by California Law Review, Inc. Reprinted by permission.

The Role of Mental Health Professionals in the Criminal Process: The Case for Informed Speculation, by Richard Bonnie and Christopher Slobogin, from 66 VIRGINIA LAW REVIEW, 427 (1980). Reprinted with permission from the Virginia Law Review Association.

To Have and Have Not: Assessing the Value of Social Science to the Law as Science and Policy, by David Faigman, from 38 EMORY LAW JOURNAL 1005 (1989). Reprinted with permission.

Myself Alone: Individualizing Justice Through Psychological Character Evidence, by Andrew Taslitz, from 52 MARYLAND LAW REVIEW 1 (1993). Reprinted with permission.

Sex Offender Civil Commitments: Scientists Or Psychics?, by Donna Cropp Bechman, from 16 CRIMINAL JUSTICE MAGAZINE 24 (2001). Reprinted with permission from the American Bar Association.

From COMPETENCY TO STAND TRIAL, by Ronald Roesch and Stephen Golding (1980). Reprinted with permission from Ronald Roesch.

From PSYCHOLOGICAL EVALUATIONS FOR THE COURTS: A HANDBOOK FOR MENTAL HEALTH PROFESSIONALS AND LAWYERS, by Gary Melton, John Petrila, Norman Poythress, Christopher Slobogin (second edition, 1997). Reprinted with permission granted by Guilford Press.

Psychiatry and the Dangerous Criminal, by Norval Morris, from 41 SOUTHERN CALIFORNIA LAW REVIEW 514 (1968). Reprinted with the permission of the Southern California Law Review.

Book review of Abraham Goldstein's THE INSANITY DEFENSE, by Lady Wooton (1968). Reprinted by permission of the Yale Law Journal Company and Fred B. Rothman & Company, Vol. 77, pp. 1019–1051.*

From THE INSANITY DEFENSE, by David Hermann (1983). Courtesy of Charles C. Thomas, Publisher, Springfield, Illinois.

Dangerousness as a Criterion in the Criminal Process, by Christopher Slobogin, from Bruce Sales & Daniel Shuman, eds., LAW, MENTAL HEALTH & MENTAL DISORDER (1996). Reprinted with permission.

The Constitutionality and Morality of Civilly Committing Violent Sexual Predators, by Alexander Brooks, from 15 U. PUGET SOUND LAW REVIEW 709 (1992). Reprinted with permission.

Washington's Sexually Violent Predator Law: A Deliberate Misuse of the Therapeutic State for Social Control, by John LaFond, from 15 U. PUGET SOUND LAW REVIEW 655 (1992). Reprinted with permission.

Acute Psychiatric Hospitalization of the Mentally Ill in the Metropolis: An Empirical Study, by George Dix, from 1968 WASHINGTON UNIVERSITY LAW QUARTERLY 485 (1968). Reprinted with permission from the Washington University Law Quarterly.

Developments in the Law—Civil Commitment of the Mentally Ill, from 87 HARVARD LAW REVIEW 1190 (1974). Reprinted with permission from the Harvard Law Review.

A Preference for Liberty: The Case Against Involuntary Commitment of The Mentally Disordered, by Stephen Morse, from 70 CALIFORNIA LAW REVIEW 54 (1982). Copyright © 1982 by California Law Review, Inc. Reprinted by permission of California Law Review, Inc. and the author.

Assessing and Predicting Violence: Research, Law, and Applications, by T. Litwack and L. Schlesinger, in HANDBOOK OF FORENSIC PSYCHOLOGY 205 (Weiner, Hess, eds. 1987). Copyright © 1987 by John Wiley & Sons, Inc.

Dangerousness Defined, from LAW, PSYCHIATRY & MENTAL HEALTH SYSTEMS, by Alexander Brooks. Copyright © 1974 by Little, Brown. Reprinted with permission of Little, Brown and author.

Dangerousness as a Criterion for Confinement, by Alan Dershowitz, from 11 BULLETIN OF AMERICAN ACADEMY OF PSYCHIATRY AND LAW 172 (1974). Copyright © 1974 by American Academy of Psychiatry and Law. Reprinted by permission.

Where Involuntary Commitment, Civil Liberties, and the Right to Mental Health Care Collide: An Overview of California's Mental Illness System, by Meredit Karasch, from 54 HASTINGS L.J. 493 (2003). Reprinted with permission.

From OFFENSE TO OTHERS, by Joel Feinberg (1985). Reprinted by permission of Oxford University Press.

Involuntary Psychiatric Commitments to Prevent Suicide, by David Greenberg. 49 N.Y.U.L.REV. 227, 257–58 (1974). Reprinted with permission granted from the New York University Law Review.

From MENTAL HEALTH LAW, by David Wexler. Copyright © 1981. Reprinted with permission granted by Plenum Publishing Corporation and the author.

Least Restrictive Treatment of the Mentally Ill: A Doctrine in Search of Its Senses, by Browning Hoffman and Larry Foust, from 14 SAN DIEGO LAW REVIEW 1100 (1977). Reprinted with permission from the San Diego Law Review.

The Therapeutic Significance of the Civil Commitment Hearing: An Unexplored Potential, by John Ensminger and Thomas Liguori, from 6 JOURNAL OF PSYCHIATRY AND LAW 5 (1978). Reprint permission granted by the Federal Legal Publications.

Guidelines for Involuntary Civil Commitment, by the National Center for State Courts, from 10 MENTAL DISABILITY LAW REPORTER 409

(1986). Reprint permission granted by Ingo Keilitz, Director, Institute of Mental Disability and Law, National Center for State Courts.

Institutionalization, Deinstitutionalization, and the Adversary Process, by Judge David Bazelon, from 75 COLUMBIA LAW REVIEW 897 (1975). Copyright © 1975 by the Directors of the Columbia Law Review Association, Inc. All rights reserved. Reprinted by permission.

Of Rights Lost and Rights Found: The Coming Restoration of the Right to a Jury Trial in Minnesota Civil Commitment Proceedings, by C. Peter Erlinder, from 29 WILLIAM. MITCHELL LAW REVIEW 1269 (2003). Reprinted with permission.

Litigiousness as a Resistance to Therapy, by Robert Miller et al., from David Wexler, ed., THERAPEUTIC JURISPRUDENCE: THE LAW AS THERAPEUTIC AGENT (1991). Reprinted with permission.

A Model State Law on Civil Commitment of the Mentally Ill, by Clifford Stromberg and Alan Stone, from 20 HARVARD JOURNAL OF LEGISLATION 274 (1983). Copyright © 1983 by the President and Fellows of Harvard College. Reprinted by permission of the Harvard Journal of Legislation.

The Waivability of Recommitment Hearings, by David Wexler, from 20 ARIZONA LAW REVIEW 175 (1978). Copyright © 1978 by the Arizona Board of Regents. Reprinted by permission of the Arizona Law Review and the author.

Voluntary Hospitalization of the Mentally Ill, by Janet Gilboy and John Schmidt, from 66 NORTHWESTERN LAW REVIEW 429 (1971). Reprinted with permission.

The Negotiation of Voluntary Admission in Chicago State Mental Hospitals, by Susan Reed & Dan Lewis, from 18 JOURNAL OF PSYCHIATRY & LAW 137 (1990). Reprinted with permission.

The Consequences of the Insanity Defense: Proposals to Reform Post-Acquittal Commitment Law, by James Ellis, from 35 CATHOLIC UNIVERSITY LAW REVIEW 961 (1986). Reprinted by permission of Catholic University Law Review.

REINVENTING JUSTICE: THE AMERICAN DRUG COURT MOVEMENT, by James L. Nolan, Jr. Copyright © 2001. Reprinted by permission of Princeton University Press.

Distributive and Paternalist Motives in Contract and Tort Law, With Special Reference to Compulsory Terms and Unequal Bargaining Power, by Duncan Kennedy, from 41 MARYLAND LAW REVIEW 563 (1982). Reprinted with permission from the Maryland Law Review.

Competency to Consent to Research: A Psychiatric Overview, by Paul Appelbaum and Loren Roth, from 39 ARCHIVES OF GENERAL PSYCHIATRY 951 (1982). Copyright © 1982 by American Medical Association. Reprinted by permission.

The Side Effects of Incompetency Labeling and the Implications for Mental Health Law, by Bruce Winick, from 1 PSYCHOLOGY, PUBLIC POLICY & LAW 6 (1995). Reprinted with permission.

Competency to Refuse Treatment, by Elyn Saks, from 69 NORTH CAROLINA LAW REVIEW 945 (1991). Reprinted with permission of the North Carolina Law Review.

Sterilization of Mentally Retarded Persons: Reproductive Rights and Family Privacy, by Elizabeth Scott, from 1986 DUKE LAW JOURNAL 806 (1986). Reprinted with permission from the Duke Law Journal.

The Right to Refuse Antipsychotic Medications: Law and Policy, by Alexander Brooks, from 39 RUTGERS LAW REVIEW 339 (1987). Reprinted with permission of the author.

Unbuckling the "Chemical Straitjacket:" The Legal Significance of Recent Advances in the Pharmacological Treatment of Psychosis, by Douglas Mossman, from 39 SAN DIEGO LAW REVIEW 1033 (2002). Reprinted with the permission of the San Diego Law Review.

Awakenings with the New Antipsychotics, by Kenneth Duckworth, from PSYCHIATRIC TIMES, May, 1998. Reprinted with permission.

Legal Regulation of Applied Behavior Analysis in Mental Institutions and Prisons, by Paul Friedman, from 17 ARIZONA LAW REVIEW 61 (1975). Copyright © 1975 by Arizona Board of Regents. Reprinted by permission.

The Role of the Criminal Defense Lawyer in Representing the Mentally Impaired Defendant: Zealous Advocate of Office of the Court?, by Rodney Uphoff, from 1988 WISCONSIN LAW REVIEW 65. Copyright © by Wisconsin Law Review. Reprinted by permission.

Incompetency to Stand Trial: As Assessment of Costs and Benefits, and a Proposal for Reform, by Bruce Winick, from 39 RUTGERS LAW REVIEW 243 (1987). Reprinted with permission of Rutgers Law Review and the author.

Insight into Schizophrenia: Anosognosia, Competency, and Civil Liberties, by Xavier F. Amador & Andrew A. Shiva, from 11 GEORGE MASON CIVIL RIGHTS LAW JOURNAL 24 (2000). Reprinted with permission.

Voluntariness, Free Will and the Law of Confessions, by Joseph Grano, from 65 VIRGINIA LAW REVIEW 859 (1979). Reprinted with permission from the Virginia Law Review Association and Fred B. Rothman & Co.

Words Without Meaning: The Constitution, Confessions, and Mentally Retarded Suspects, by Morgan Cloud et al., from 69 UNIVERSITY OF CHICAGO LAW REVIEW 495 (2002). Reprinted with permission.

The Long Lonesome Road, by Joseph Nocera, from THE TEXAS MONTHLY, November, 1986. Copyright © 1987 by Texas Monthly. Reprinted with permission.

Note: The Supreme Court: 1981 Term, from 96 HARVARD LAW RE-VIEW 62 (1982). Copyright © 1982 by the Harvard Law Review Association. Reprinted with permission.

Leaving Civil Rights to the "Experts": From Defense to Abdication Under the Professional Judgment Standard, by Susan Stefan, from 102 YALE LAW JOURNAL 639 (1992). Reprinted by permission of the Yale Law Journal Company and Fred B. Rothman & Company.

Mental Hospitals and the Civil Liberties Dilemma, by H. Davidson, from 31 MENTAL HYGIENE 371 (1967). Reprinted with permission of the National Mental Health Association, Alexandria, Va.

Note: The *Wyatt* Case: Implementation of a Judicial Decree Ordering Institutional Change, from 84 YALE LAW JOURNAL 1338 (1975). Reprinted by permission of The Yale Law Journal Company and Fred B. Rothman & Company.

Beyond Least Restrictive Alternative Doctrine: A Constitutional Right to Treatment for Mentally Disabled Persons in the Community, by Jan Costello and James Preis, from 20 LOYOLA LOS ANGELES LAW REVIEW 1527 (1987). Reprinted with permission of the Loyola L.A. Law Review.

Federal Power, Segregation, and Mental Disability, by John V. Jacobi, from 39 HOUSTON LAW REVIEW 1231 (2003). Reprinted with permission.

Treatment of the Mentally Disabled: Rethinking the Community–First Idea, from 69 UNIVERSITY NEBRASKA LAW REVIEW 413 (1990). Reprinted with permission.

The Role of Cost in Educational Decisionmaking for the Handicapped Child, by Katharine T. Bartlett, from 48 LAW & CONTEMPORARY PROBLEMS 7 (1985). Reprinted with permission.

*

*

Table of Contents

PART II.   DEPRIVATIONS OF LIBERTY AND PROPERTY

*

Table of Cases

The principal cases are in bold type. Cases cited or discussed in the text are roman type. References are to pages. Cases cited in principal cases and within other quoted materials are not included.

*

LAW AND THE MENTAL HEALTH SYSTEM

CIVIL AND CRIMINAL ASPECTS

Fifth Edition

*

Part I

MENTAL HEALTH TREATMENT AND THE PATIENT–THERAPIST RELATIONSHIP

1

Chapter One

MENTAL DISORDERS AND THEIR TREATMENT, THE MENTAL HEALTH PROFESSIONS, AND MENTAL HEALTH CARE FINANCE

Table of Sections

I. INTRODUCTION

This book is about law and the mental health system. The "mental health system" is that constellation of services, institutions, and personnel involved in diagnosis, assessment, and treatment of emotional, psychological, or psychiatric disorders. It includes both public and private treatment and diagnostic services, carried out not only in mental hospitals, community mental health centers, and private offices, but in institutions such as schools, prison, and drug rehabilitation centers.

The mental health system has undergone many profound changes in the last several decades, four of which will be mentioned here. First, the percentage of the population utilizing the mental health system has increased substantially due to a number of factors, including improvements in mental health treatment, the decreased stigma associated with such treatment, federal and state statutes that provide entitlements to care, and the expansion of the definition of "mental disorder." Second, pharmacological advances have fundamentally altered the treatment of serious mental illnesses by medicalizing the nature of psychiatric practice, reducing the importance and the duration of institutionalization, and fueling ethical debates over how much control patients should have over their treatment. Third, where pharmacological treatment is not needed, non-medical personnel, most prominently psychologists and social workers, are taking the place of psychiatrists as the primary care providers, for reasons that are at least partially economic. Fourth, just as it has with medical care generally, the advent of managed care has greatly influenced the types and duration of mental health treatment and the identity of those who provide it.

This chapter discusses several key matters that are related to these four developments and that form the backdrop for the rest of this book. It first examines the concept of mental disorder, which is a crucial concept for many of the laws and legal rules discussed in the following chapters. It then describes current knowledge about treatment of mental problems, a subject that is important both in determining the degree to which the mental health professions can be held legally responsible for helping people, and in assessing the extent to which coerced treatment intervention is warranted. Next it describes the most prominent mental health professions—psychiatrists, psychologists, and social workers—all of whom play a role in the legal system as litigants, experts and occasionally even legal decisionmakers. Finally, it examines the way in which mental health care is financed, because economic concerns often exert significant influence on law and policy in the mental health system.

II. PERSPECTIVES ON MENTAL DISORDER

A. THE INTERFACE OF LAW AND MENTAL DISORDER

Most of the laws we will be examining in this book require a finding of "mental disorder." Insurance compensation for mental health treatment will generally be dependent on such a finding (see section V of this chapter). Some knowledge about the nature of mental disorder is important in determining the scope of the mental health professions' authority and liability in connection with diagnosis and treatment (Chapters Two through Five). A mental disorder finding is often crucial in many types of criminal and civil litigation involving the government: for example, mental disorder may establish an excuse or mitigation for crime (Chapter Seven); form the predicate for involuntary civil commitment (Chapter Eight); or lead to a finding of incompetency (Chapter Nine). A finding of mental disorder is also generally required in order for individuals to qualify for various entitlements and protections against discrimination (Chapters Eleven and Twelve). Typically, as detailed in Chapter Six, these and numerous other issues involving the mental status of a litigant will be resolved on the basis of the testimony of mental health experts.

In all of these contexts, the expectations and requirements of the legal system will often be in tension with the diagnostic paradigm of the mental health professions. Although, as Sections II–IV of this chapter indicate, there are significant differences in the conceptual models and treatment choices chosen by mental health clinicians, the diagnostic scheme contained in the latest version of American Psychiatric Association's Diagnostic and Statistical Manual (DSM) is widely accepted. This diagnostic scheme is based on a number of underlying precepts, two of which are particularly important to fashioning mental health law. One is that, in general, mental pathologies are not susceptible to precise definition. The other is that, because abilities within a given diagnostic category may vary widely, a particular clinical diagnosis is not sufficient to establish a mental disorder, disability, disease, or defect for legal purposes. In the words of the fourth and latest edition of the DSM (labeled DSM–IV–TR, for fourth edition, text revised):

> When the DSM–IV categories, criteria, and textual descriptions are employed for forensic purposes, there are significant risks that diagnostic information will be misused or misunderstood. These dangers arise because of the imperfect fit between the questions of ultimate concern to the law and the information contained in a clinical diagnosis. In most situations, the clinical diagnosis of a DSM–IV mental disorder is not sufficient to establish the existence for legal purposes of a "mental disorder," "mental disability," "mental disease," or "mental defect." . . . It is precisely because impairments, abilities, and disabilities vary widely within each diagnostic category that assignment of a particular diagnosis does not imply a specific level of impairment or disability. [Moreover,] a diagnosis does not carry any necessary implications regarding the causes of the individual's mental disorder or its associated impairments [such as] the degree of control over the behaviors that may be associated with the disorder.

DSM–IV–TR at xxxii–xxxiii.

The imprecision inherent in the diagnostic approach taken by the mental health professions reflects the reality that the symptoms of a person suffering from a particular mental disorder are both changeable over time and frequently overlap with the symptoms of other mental disorders. Moreover, unlike most physical illnesses, physiologically detectible signs that are susceptible to clinical measurement often do not accompany mental disorders. In contrast, fair and predictable adjudication requires legal standards that are relatively clear and unambiguous. For this reason, legal standards often do not have a counterpart in the psychiatric diagnostic paradigm. The interface of law and the mental health system is also complicated by the divergence in the predictive capacities of mental health experts and the requirements of the legal system. Various laws, such as those governing criminal sentencing or civil commitment, require judgments as to the future actions of a particular defendant or patient. As discussed further in Chapter 6, the accuracy of this predictive testimony is highly contested.

The discrepancy between what the legal system requires and what mental health professionals can deliver reflects the current level of development of the behavioral sciences. In the meantime, there is likely to exist an uneasy alliance between law and the mental health professions, particularly in the adjudication context. Most of the chapters in this book highlight these interface issues.

B. WHAT IS MENTAL DISORDER?

The American Psychiatric Association's Diagnostic and Statistical Manual states that a "mental disorder" is:

a clinically significant behavioral or psychological syndrome or pattern that occurs in an individual and that is associated with present distress (e.g., a painful symptom) or disability (i.e., impairment in one or more important areas of functioning) or with a significantly increased risk of suffering death, pain, disability, or an important loss of freedom.

DSM–IV–TR, at xxx–xxxii. Furthermore, DSM–IV states, the syndrome or pattern cannot be "an expectable and culturally sanctioned response to a particular event" (such as death of a loved one). Id. Although this language does impose some limits, many have noted that terms such as "distress," "disability," "loss of freedom," and "expectable and culturally sanctioned" are hugely value-laden and still permit a wide amount of leeway in defining specific disorders. The drafters of DSM–IV admit as much, stating "that no definition adequately specifies precise boundaries for the concept of 'mental disorder.' " Id.

The ambiguous boundaries of mental disorder have caused a few commentators to question whether the concept of mental disorder makes sense. Most famously, the "radical psychiatrist" Thomas Szasz's has argued that, for most of what we call mental disorder, "[t]he norm from which deviation is measured is a psychosocial and ethical standard," not a physical one. Thomas S. Szasz, Ideology and Insanity 12 (1970). To Szasz, either a person has a brain disease, in which case the appropriate intervention is neurological, or he or she has a "problem in living," which is not an illness but a social condition. Id. at 21. A modern version of Szasz's view, which some label "radical consumerism" (to be distinguished from the "consumer movement," which attempts to empower patients by increasing their involvement in treatment decision-making and increasing funding for mental health care) claims "that psychiatrists make [patients] sick" and attempts to "restrict the work of psychiatrists and care for the seriously mentally ill [through] laws restricting involuntary treatment and electro-convulsive therapy." Sally L. Satel & Richard E. Redding, "Sociopolitical Trends in Mental Health Care: The Consumer/Survivor Movement and Multiculturalism," Kaplan & Sadock's Comprehensive Textbook of Psychiatry 644 (8th ed. 2005). A related movement, which advocates multi-cultural therapy, fosters "the patient's understanding of how his or her psychological distress is due to oppression and social injustice." Members of this movement "see themselves as the 'last minority.' " Id.

Critics of radical psychiatry have taken issue with Szasz' and radical consumerism's claim that "mental illness" is merely a subjective psychosocial and ethical valuation. Michael Moore, for example, argues that mental illness signifies something quite objective and concrete, namely irrationality.

"'Insanity' and 'mental illness' mean, and historically have meant, 'irrational'; to be insane, or to be mentally ill, is to fail to act rationally often enough to have the same assumption of rationality made about one as is made of most of humanity . . . Unless we can perceive another being as acting for intelligible ends in light of rational beliefs, we cannot understand that being in the same fundamental way that we understand each other's actions in daily life."

Michael Moore, "Some Myths about Mental Illness," 18 Inquiry 233 (1975).

Another critic of radical psychiatry, Robert Evan Kendell, argues that mental illness should be defined with reference to whether "the abnormality place[s] the individual at a 'biological disadvantage.'" According to Kendell, this notion "[p]resumably ... must embrace both increased mortality and reduced fertility." Relying on empirical research with respect to the mortality and fertility of various groups, he concludes that there is adequate evidence that schizophrenia, manic-depressive illness, some sexual disorders (including homosexuality), and some forms of drug dependence "carry with them an intrinsic biological disadvantage, and on these grounds are justifiably regarded as illness." See Robert Evan Kendell, "The Concept of Disease and Its Implications for Psychiatry," 127 Brit.J.Psychiat. 305 (1975).

There are problems with both of these latter approaches. The fact that Kendell would call homosexuality a mental disorder while apparently excluding many mental conditions that can shorten life calls his approach into question. Moore's theory is, of course, subject to the criticism that it is difficult to formulate an adequate definition of rationality. In subsequent work, Moore has constructed an elaborate, multi-level definition that looks at the intelligibility, consistency, and coherence of a person's motivating desires and beliefs. See Michael Moore, Law and Psychiatry: Rethinking the Relationship 100–08 (1984). However, even Moore's elaborate definition relies at its foundational (and least demanding) level on social context—whether someone's desires and beliefs are "intelligible" depends on whether they are coherent in the context of the society in which one lives. Christopher Slobogin, "A Rational Approach to Responsibility," 83 Mich. L. Rev. 820, 830–31 (1985) (reviewing Law and Psychiatry).

Another important prism through which mental disorder can be viewed (if not necessarily defined precisely) is etiology, or cause. The ascendant etiological approach, particularly given recent advances in brain imaging, genetics, and psychopharmacology, is the *medical* or biological model. This model posits that abnormal mental states result from abnormal physiological or chemical conditions within the body. Moreover, contrary to Szasz's assertions, biologically abnormal correlates have been found for a substantial portion of what we label mental disorder. For example, individuals with schizophrenia, who suffer from hallucination and delusions, have enlarged brain ventricles (i.e. irregularities in the ratio of brain tissue to fluid in the brain); decrements in portions of the brain responsible for memory, attention, emotional expression, and information integration; and deficiencies in those areas of the brain associated with self-awareness (as shown through brain imaging). See Benedicto Crespo–Faccorro et al., "Neuropsychological Functioning and Brain Structure in Schizophrenia," 19 Int'l Rev. Psychiatry 325 (2007); Douglas Mossman, "Unbuckling the 'Chemical Straightjacket': The Legal Significance of Recent Advances in the Pharmacological Treatment of Psychosis," 39 San Diego L. Rev. 1033, 1049–56 (2002). Similarly, researchers have discovered abnormal biological correlates to such mood disorders as bipolar affective disorder (swings between severe depression and mania) and unipolar severe depression. See Brian Shannon, "The Brain Gets Sick, Too—The Case for Equal Insurance Coverage of Serious Mental Illness," 24 Mary's L.J. 365, 369 (1993). Even certain mental disorders that might be viewed as less severe—for example, personality disorders, such as anti-social personality disorder ("ASPD") and conduct disorder (roughly speaking, a failure to conform to social norms)—have been linked with abnormal biological correlates. ASPD has been linked with frontal lobe dysfunction and conduct disorder with various neurochemical abnormalities. See 2 Psychiatry 1299–1300 (Allan Tasman et al., eds. 1997).

Other etiological approaches focus on environmental factors. These include *psychodynamic/psychoanalytic* models and *behavioral* models of mental disorder, to be described further below. It should be emphasized, however, that the many of the most current versions of the medical/biological model incorporate the importance of psychodynamic and behavioral factors. Eric Kandel, a prominent Nobel prize-winning psychiatrist and exponent of the medical model, has argued that environmental factors, both positive and negative, can produce significant alterations in the expression of relevant genes and hence in the function of nerve cells. For example, psychotherapy and behavioral counseling can be effective because they produce advantageous changes in gene expression and hence in neuronal interconnections. Conversely, a negative environment produces disadvantageous changes in gene expression. Similarly, the Surgeon General's 1999 report on Mental Health observes that "mental illness appears to result from the interaction of multiple genes that confer risk, and this risk is converted into illness by the interaction of genes with environmental factors." Mental Health: Report of the Surgeon General 53 (1999). Finally, the American Psychiatric Association has noted that the term mental disorder "implies a distinction between 'mental' disorders and 'physical' disorders that is a reductionistic anachronism of mind/body dualism. A compelling literature documents that there is much 'physical' in mental disorders and much 'mental' in 'physical' disorder." See DSM–IV–TR, at xxx. The following materials explore the medical, psychodynamic and behavioral models in more detail. The materials on the latter two models are taken from the Surgeon General's Report on Mental Health, supra, at 55–56.

1. *The Medical Model*

The following statement of principles, taken from an article by Eric Kandel, is representative of current approaches to the medical model.

As a result of advances in neural science in the last several years, both psychiatry and neural science are in a new and better position for a rapprochement, a rapprochement that would allow the insights of the psychoanalytic perspective to inform the search for a proper understanding of the biological basis of behavior. As a first step towards such a rapprochement, I here outline an intellectual framework designed to align current psychiatric thinking and the training of future practitioners with modern biology.

This framework can be summarized in five principles, that constitute, in simplified form, the current thinking of biologists about the relationship of mind to brain.

Principle 1. All mental processes, even the most complex psychological processes, derive from operations of the brain. The central tenet of this view is that what we commonly call mind is a range of functions carried out by the brain. The actions of the brain underlie not only relatively simple motor behaviors, such as walking and eating, but all of the complex cognitive actions, conscious and unconscious, that we associate with specifically human behavior, such as thinking, speaking, and creating works of literature, music, and art. As a corollary, behavioral disorders that characterize psychiatric illness are disturbances of the brain function, even in those cases where the causes of the disturbances are clearly environmental in origin.

Principle 2. Genes and their protein products are important determinants of the pattern of interconnections between neurons in the brain and the details of their functioning. Genes, specifically combinations of genes, therefore exert a significant control over behavior. As a corollary, one component contributing to the development of major mental illnesses is genetic.

Principle 3. Altered genes do not, by themselves, explain all the variance of a given major mental illness. Social or developmental factors also contribute very importantly to behavior, including social behavior, so behavior and social factors can exert actions on the brain by feeding back upon it to modify the expression of genes and thus the function of nerve cells. Learning, including learning that results in dysfunctional behavior, produces alterations in gene expression. Thus all of "nurture" is ultimately expressed as "nature".

Principle 4. Alterations in gene expression induced by learning give rise to changes in patterns of neuronal connections. These changes not only contribute to the biological basis of individuality but presumably are responsible for initiating and maintaining abnormalities of behavior that are induced by social contingencies.

Principle 5. Insofar as psychotherapy or counseling is effective and produces long-term changes in behavior, it presumably does so through learning, by producing changes in gene expression that alter the strength of synaptic connections and structural changes that alter the anatomical pattern of interconnections between nerve cells of the brain. As the resolution of brain imaging increases, it should eventually permit quantitative evaluation of the outcome of psychotherapy.

Eric R. Kandel, "A New Intellectual Framework for Psychiatry," 155(4) Am J Psychiatry 457, 460 (1998).

2.   *Psychodynamic Theories*

Psychodynamic theories of personality assert that behavior is the product of underlying conflicts over which people often have scant awareness. Sigmund Freud (1856–1939) was the towering proponent of psychoanalytic theory, the first of the 20th-century psychodynamic theories. Many of Freud's followers pioneered their own psychodynamic theories, but this [discussion] covers only psychoanalytic theory. A brief discussion of Freud's work contributes to a historical perspective of mental health theory and treatment approaches.

Freud's theory of psychoanalysis holds two major assumptions: (1) that much of mental life is unconscious (i.e., outside awareness), and (2) that past experiences, especially in early childhood, shape how a person feels and behaves throughout life. Freud's structural model of personality divides the personality into three parts—the id, the ego, and the superego. The id is the unconscious part that is the cauldron of raw drives, such as for sex or aggression. The ego, which has conscious and unconscious elements, is the rational and reasonable part of personality. Its role is to maintain contact with the outside world in order to help keep the individual in touch with society. As such, the ego mediates between the conflicting tendencies of the id and the superego. The latter is a person's conscience that develops early in life and is learned from parents, teachers, and others. Like the ego, the superego has conscious and unconscious elements.

When all three parts of the personality are in dynamic equilibrium, the individual is thought to be mentally healthy. However, according to psychoanalytic theory, if the ego is unable to mediate between the id and the superego, an imbalance would occur in the form of psychological distress and symptoms of mental disorders. Psychoanalytic theory views symptoms as important only in terms of expression of underlying conflicts between the parts of personality. The theory holds that the conflicts must be understood by the individual with the aid of the psychoanalyst who would help the person unearth the secrets of the unconscious. This was the basis for psychoanalysis as a form of treatment. . . .

3.   *Behaviorism and Social Learning Theory*

Behaviorism (also called learning theory) posits that personality is the sum of an individual's observable responses to the outside world. As charted by J. B. Watson and B. F. Skinner in the early part of the 20th century, behaviorism stands at loggerheads with psychodynamic theories, which strive to understand underlying conflicts. Behaviorism rejects the existence of underlying conflicts and an unconscious. Rather, it focuses on observable, overt behaviors that are learned from the environment. Its application to treatment of mental problems, which is discussed later, is known as behavior modification.

Learning is seen as behavior change molded by experience. Learning is accomplished largely through either classical or operant conditioning. Classical conditioning is grounded in the research of Ivan Pavlov, a Russian physiologist. It explains why some people react to formerly neutral stimuli in their environment, stimuli that previously would not have elicited a reaction. Pavlov's dogs, for example, learned to salivate merely at the sound of the bell, without any food in sight. Originally, the sound of the bell would not have elicited salvation. But by repeatedly pairing the sight of the food (which elicits salvation on its own) with the sound of the bell, Pavlov taught the dogs to salivate just to the sound of the bell by itself.

Operant conditioning, a process described and coined by B. F. Skinner, is a form of learning in which a voluntary response is strengthened or attenuated, depending on its association with positive or negative consequences. The strengthening of responses occurs by positive reinforcement, such as food, pleasurable activities, and attention from others. The attenuation or discontinuation of responses occurs by negative reinforcement in the form of removal of a pleasurable stimulus. Thus, human behavior is shaped in a trial and error way through positive and negative reinforcement, without any reference to inner conflicts or perceptions. What goes on inside the individual is irrelevant, for humans are equated with "black boxes." Mental disorders represented maladaptive behaviors that were learned. They could be unlearned through behavior modification (behavior therapy).

The movement beyond behaviorism was spearheaded by Albert Bandura, the originator of social learning theory (also known as social cognitive theory). Social learning theory has its roots in behaviorism, but it departs in a significant way. While acknowledging classical and operant conditioning, social learning theory places far greater emphasis on a different type of learning, particularly observational learning. Observational learning occurs through selectively observing the behavior of another person, a model. When the behavior of the model is rewarded, children are more likely to imitate the behavior. For example, a child who observes another child receiving candy for a particular behavior is more likely to carry out similar behaviors. Social learning theory asserts that people's cognitions—their views, perceptions, and expectations toward their environment—affect what they learn. Rather than being passively conditioned by the environment, as behaviorism proposed, humans take a more active role in deciding what to learn as a result of cognitive processing. Social learning theory gave rise to cognitive-behavioral therapy. . . .

Questions and Comments

1. *The relationship between etiology and disorder.* Etiological approaches can help us understand the boundaries of disorder. However,

etiology does not necessarily correspond precisely with what we as a society might want to consider a disorder. In other words, social considerations necessarily influence the parameters of disorder. Consider, for example, the biological approach to etiology. If unusual mathematical ability were correlated with an abnormal level of a particular neurochemical, would/should such ability be considered a disorder? Under the behaviorist/social learning approach, the importance of social influence in determining what is considered disorder is even more obvious. What constitutes "maladaptive behavior that is learned" (the behaviorist definition of mental disorder) is obviously influenced to some extent by the requirements of the society in which one lives.

2. *The relative contributions of heredity and environment.* Some of the most interesting work in the area of mental disorder has attempted to track the relative contributions of heredity and environment. For example, the heritability of bipolar disorder, according to the most rigorous twin study, is about 59 percent. Twin studies indicate that schizophrenia has a somewhat higher rate of heritability. Mental Health: Report of the Surgeon General 54 (1999). Other disorders, including several in the huge category known as personality disorders, are not as clearly linked to heredity. For instance, one prominent psychiatric textbook states that there is "only limited support" for a hereditary link with paranoid personality disorder, and speculates that "[p]aranoid belief systems could develop through parental modeling, a history of discriminatory exploitation or abandonment, and the isolation of anger, resentment, and bitterness onto a group that is external to and distinct from oneself." 2 Psychiatry 1293 (Allan Tasman et al., eds. 1997). Similarly, the introversion associated with schizoid personality disorder may be heritable, but it is "likely that a sustained history of isolation during infancy and childhood with encouragement and modeling of interpersonal withdrawal, indifference, and detachment by parental figures contributes to the development of schizoid personality traits." Id. at 1295–96. On the other hand, "there is considerable support from twin, family, and adoption studies for a genetic contribution to the etiology of the criminal, delinquent tendencies of persons with ASPD [anti-social personality disorder]." Id. at 1299. At the same time, "[m]odeling by parental figures and peers; excessively harsh, lenient, or erratic discipline; and a tough, harsh environment in which feelings of empathy and warmth are discouraged (if not punished) and tough-mindedness, aggressiveness, and exploitation are encourage (if not rewarded) have all been associated with the development of ASPD." Id. at 1300.

3. *Legal implications of etiology.* The law has tended to prefer traditional versions of the medical/ biological model of mental disorder over the psychodynamic and behavioral/social learning models. To some extent, this preference is probably an accident of history. The medical tradition preceded the other two (for example, Hippocrates theorized that depression was caused by black bile and hence could be cured by purgatives) and thus was the first one encountered by the law. But there is also a philosophical reason for the law's attraction to the medical model, particularly in the context of the criminal justice and civil commitment systems discussed in Part II. The psychodynamic and behavioral/social learning models tend to focus more on factors external to the individual as causes of behavior and thus threaten the

current foundations of the legal system. For example, imagine the impact abandonment of the medical model might have on the theory of criminal responsibility. Because the behavioral or social models suggest that mental disorder can result from exogenous factors, such as rewards for aggressive behavior, certain types of parents, or poverty, endorsement of these models could broaden enormously the scope of defenses based on lack of criminal responsibility. See, e.g., David Bazelon, "The Morality of the Criminal Law," 49 S.Cal.L.Rev. 385, 396 (1976)(arguing that social background, including poverty, should be considered in evaluating criminal responsibility). Similarly, to the extent that the law allows coercive treatment to ameliorate mental disorder associated with dangerousness or incompetency, allegiance to the exogenous models of mental disorder might permit state intervention into the lives of persons other than the mentally disordered individual; according to the non-medical models, especially the social one, these other persons are contributors to the disorder. See David Wexler, Mental Health Law 22 (1981)(noting this possibility). It bears emphasis, however, that to the extent the medical model is expanding to show that heredity influences a greater range of criminal behavior (cf. the research on anti-social personality disorder discussed above), and to incorporate the importance of environmental factors (cf. the Kandel excerpt), the medical model may also expand the scope of defenses available.

Etiology can be important in other areas of the law as well. As discussed in Section IV of this chapter, the blurring of the distinction between mental and physical becomes particularly salient in the context of insurance coverage. This is because coverage for "mental illness" is typically much less generous than coverage for "physical illness"; plaintiffs who have been denied coverage on the grounds that they have exhausted their mental health coverage have brought suits arguing that their illness (for example, bipolar disorder) is actually a physical disease of the brain. The suits have had varying degrees of success.

4. *The Surgeon General's discussion of mental disorder.* In 1999, the Surgeon General of the United States issued an informative report on mental health and treatment that discussed the science of mental disorder. The drafters of the Report focused on three types of "mental disorder"—anxiety, psychosis and mood disorders—that they considered the most serious and most prevalent. These three conditions also figure in many of the legal issues to be discussed in this book.

> **Anxiety**: [T]he mechanisms that regulate anxiety may break down in a wide variety of circumstances, leading to excessive or inappropriate expression of anxiety. Specific examples include phobias, panic attacks, and generalized anxiety. In phobias, high-level anxiety is aroused by specific situations or objects that may range from concrete entities such as snakes, to complex circumstances such as social interactions or public speaking. Panic attacks are brief and very intense episodes of anxiety that often occur without a precipitating event or stimulus. Generalized anxiety represents a more diffuse and nonspecific kind of anxiety that is most often experienced as excessive worrying, restlessness, and tension occurring with a chronic and sustained pattern. In each case, an anxiety disorder may be said to exist if the anxiety experienced is disproportion-

ate to the circumstance, is difficult for the individual to control, or interferes with normal functioning.

In addition to these common manifestations of anxiety, obsessive-compulsive disorder and post-traumatic stress disorder are generally believed to be related to the anxiety disorders.... In the case of obsessive-compulsive disorder, individuals experience a high level of anxiety that drives their obsessional thinking or compulsive behaviors. When such an individual fails to carry out a repetitive behavior such as hand washing or checking, there is an experience of severe anxiety.... Post-traumatic stress disorder is produced by an intense and overwhelmingly fearful event that is often life-threatening in nature. The characteristic symptoms that result from such a traumatic event include the persistent reexperience of the event in dreams and memories, persistent avoidance of stimuli associated with the event, and increased arousal.

Psychosis: Disturbances of perception and thought process fall into a broad category of symptoms referred to as psychosis.... One of the most common groups of symptoms that result from disordered processing and interpretation of sensory information are the hallucinations ... A more complex group of symptoms resulting from disordered interpretation of information consists of delusions. A delusion is a false belief that an individual holds despite evidence to the contrary. A common example is paranoia, in which a person has delusional beliefs that others are trying to harm him or her. Attempts to persuade the person that these beliefs are unfounded typically fail and may even result in the further entrenchment of the beliefs.

... In addition to hallucinations and delusions, patients with psychotic disorders such as schizophrenia frequently have marked disturbances in the logical process of their thoughts. Specifically, psychotic thought processes are characteristically loose, disorganized, illogical, or bizarre ...

However, in addition to positive symptoms, patients with schizophrenia and other psychoses have been noted to exhibit major deficits in motivation and spontaneity that are referred to as negative symptoms ... Positive symptoms such as hallucinations are responsible for much of the acute distress associated with schizophrenia, but negative symptoms appear to be responsible for much of the chronic and long-term disability associated with the disorder.

...

Disturbances of Mood: Disturbances of mood characteristically manifest themselves as a sustained feeling of sadness or sustained elevation of mood. As with anxiety and psychosis, disturbances of mood may occur in a variety of patterns associated with different mental disorders. The disorder most closely associated with persistent sadness is major depression, while that associated with sustained elevation or fluctuation of mood is bipolar disorder.... Along with the prevailing feelings of sadness or elation, disorders of mood are associated with a host of related symptoms that include disturbances in appetite, sleep patterns, energy level, concentration, and memory.

Mental Health: A Report of the Surgeon General 39–43 (1999).

5. *Epidemiology of mental disorder*. The Surgeon General's Report estimates that 28 to 30% of the American population suffers from a mental or addictive disorder. About 9% of the population suffers *significant* impairment from these disorders. The Report also summarizes the available data about the prevalence of mental disorder among various ethnic and cultural groups. According to the Report, socioeconomic differences account for a higher prevalence of mental disorder among African Americans than among whites. Moreover, even accounting for prevalence rates, African Americans are overrepresented in psychiatric hospitals. The Report suggests that poverty, a disinclination to seek help, and lack of outpatient services that are deemed appropriate may lead African Americans to delay seeking treatment until symptoms become sufficiently severe to warrant inpatient care. As for Hispanic Americans, those born in the U.S. appear to have rates of mental disorder similar to U.S. whites. The prevalence of mental illness among Asian Americans (and among different groups of Asian Americans) has not been studied thoroughly, but one study suggests that Asian Americans are only a quarter as likely as whites, and half as likely as African Americans and Hispanic Americans to seek outpatient treatment. Like studies on Asian Americans, studies on American Indians/Alaska Natives are limited. Depression and suicide appear to be significant problems. Alcohol abuse and dependence is particularly problematic, with rates of occurrence twice that found in any other population group. Among Native American veterans, post-traumatic stress disorder is more prevalent than in white veterans. Native Americans are also overrepresented in public psychiatric hospital in relation to whites. Id. at 83–86.

6. *Public perception of mental disorder*. The Surgeon General's Report observes that, by the 1990s, Americans had achieved greater scientific understanding of mental illness. While distinguishing mental illness from ordinary worry and unhappiness, the public also expanded its definition of mental illness to encompass anxiety, depression, and other mental disorders. The public attributed mental illness to a mix of biological abnormalities and vulnerabilities to social and psychological stress. On the other hand, the public's perception of mental illness today more frequently incorporates violent behavior than it did fifty years ago. Thirty-one percent of the group that associated mental illness with psychosis (i.e. disturbance of perception and thought process) mentioned violence in its descriptions of mental illness, in comparison with 13 percent in the 1950s. Id. at 7–8.

7. *Case studies*. In the following eight cases, do the people evidence symptoms of "mental disorder" or "mental illness"? Why or why not? In answering this question, consider (1) the DSM's definition of mental disorder (as well as specific diagnostic categories, found in Appendix A); (2) Moore's irrationality approach and Kendell's biological disadvantage approach; (3) the different etiological approaches to mental disorder; (4) Szasz' critique of the mental disorder concept; and (5) the descriptions of mental disorder in the Surgeon General's Report on Mental Health. Are there other variables that should be considered as well?

Case 1. John works at a 7–11; he is very quiet. One of his co-workers discovers that, each day after work, John spends several hours in the closet.

When questioned about this, John says: "I've been doing it for three or four months, you know, it's where my mother used to put me." When asked what he does there, he explains: "I'm talking with Martians. They left me here to teaching Earthlings about Mars. I'm also a rock star you know, but I'm getting smaller every day and pretty soon you won't be able to see me."

Case 2. Sam wants to set the world record for number of days on top of a flag pole. At the present time, he has been on a platform on top of a pole for 33 days. Although he is malnourished and dizzy from lack of food and sleep, he says he will not come down until he has stayed on the pole a total of 73 days, which will be a new record.

Case 3. Alyson, 55, lives in the country. She has drunk heavily for years. Recently she has become convinced that the cropdusters flying over her house are government airplanes bombarding her house with electronic particles. As evidence of this, she points to several places in her house where the foundations are weakened and notes the fact that her dog has mysteriously died. She also believes her house is being bugged by the government.

Case 4. Cecelia goes to all-night worship services at her fundamentalist church. During the services, she claims to hear voices talking to her, often speaking tongues, and occasionally behaves in a wild way so that others have to restrain her. The monthly meetings are the only times she acts like this.

Case 5. Jimmy is a member of an ashram, a commune centered around Eastern religious beliefs. Since joining the ashram, Jimmy has been required to participate every day in strenuous series of classes, meditation, and prayer sessions, as well as street solicitations. He is constantly fatigued, has lost all sexual desire and sense of humor, and goes into trances quite frequently. He says he has found the true answer to "Life's Questions" and wants to continue at the ashram.

Case 6. Mary, a lawyer, says she feels hopeless and worthless. When asked why, she says she is single, has no good friends and no family, and thinks her work is meaningless. She is barely able to go to the office in the morning and in the evening she goes straight home, watches TV and falls asleep by 8 p.m. She cries frequently and sometimes wishes she were dead. She resists any efforts to "cheer her up" or get her involved socially.

Case 7. Sarah is 21 and lives with her parents. She says she has no idea what she wants to do with her life. She has been put on probation for shoplifting. She will hole up in her room with piles of junk food for days. When her mother or father tries to talk to her, Sarah often explodes with anger and usually retreats to her room. Recently, she has taken to sticking safety pins in her skin and letting them hang.

Case 8. As a child, Donald would torture small animals. He was always getting in fights with other children. By the time he was 25, he had been charged with several crimes, and convicted of burglary, two assaults and arson. When asked about these events, he merely states that they seemed like the thing to do at the time; he is only sorry that he got caught.

Now consider the eight cases "contextually." If the people described sought treatment, should "mental health insurance" cover the treatment? Assume instead that (1) none of these people want treatment; (2) that the relevant civil commitment law permits forcible treatment if the person suffers from mental disorder and is dangerous to self or others; (3) that the requisite danger has been proven; and (4) that effective treatment is available. Is there enough evidence of mental disorder to justify intervention? More is said about insurance and commitment law elsewhere in this book. The effort here is to stimulate initial thoughts about the contextual nature of mental disorder. It may be defined differently depending on whether a mental health professional, insurance company, or judge is making the decision.

C. DIAGNOSING MENTAL DISORDER (DSM)

DSM–IV includes in its listing of "mental disorders" an enormous number of syndromes and psychological patterns (over three hundred in the fourth edition). In the approximate hierarchy likely to occur to a layperson asked to define "mental illness," the major DSM categories might be organized as follows:

- Psychoses (e.g., schizophrenia, manifested by hallucinations and delusions);
- Dementias (involving a significant loss of consciousness and memory);
- Mood disorders (e.g., depression; the bipolar disorders, manifested by swings between severe depression and mania);
- Dissociative disorders (including dissociative identity disorder, formerly known as multiple personality disorder);
- Mental retardation;
- Anxiety disorders (including post-traumatic stress disorder);
- Personality disorders (a large category that is meant to encompass "an enduring pattern of inner experience and behavior that deviates markedly from the expectations of the individual's culture" and that includes paranoid personality disorder; schizoid personality disorder (detachment from social relationships and a restricted range of emotional expression), schizotypal personality disorder (odd beliefs or magical thinking; unusual perceptual experiences including bodily illusions; excessive social anxiety); antisocial personality disorder (disregard for and violation of the rights of others); borderline personality disorder (impulsivity; inappropriate, intense anger or difficulty controlling anger); histrionic personality disorder (excessive emotionality and attention seeking); narcissistic personality disorder (grandiosity, need for admiration, and lack of empathy); avoidant personality disorder (feelings of inadequacy and hypersensitivity to negative evaluation); dependent personality disorder (submissive and clinging behavior related to an excessive need to be take care of); and obsessive-compulsive personality disorder (preoccupation with orderliness, perfectionism, and control));
- Sexual disorders (including pedophilia) and impulse disorders (including pyromania and kleptomania);

- Eating and sleeping disorders and disorders that feature exaggerated symptoms (somatoform and factitious disorders);

- Substance abuse disorders that do not result in dementia, including not just alcohol and drug-related disorders but caffeine and nicotine-related disorders.

Appendix A to this book contains DSM–IV diagnostic criteria for a variety of commonly diagnosed mental disorders (e.g. mental retardation, attention-deficit/hyperactivity disorder, various psychotic disorders, and various mood and personality disorders).

As noted earlier, the American Psychiatric Association's Diagnostic and Statistical Manual is the best known taxonomy of mental disorder. It is now in its fourth edition. In 2000, that edition was revised significantly. As a result, the current version of the manual is referred to as DSM–IV–TR (for text revised).

The first edition of the DSM, DSM–I, was published in 1952. DSM–I and the second edition (DSM–II), which was published in 1958, were dominated by psychoanalytic thinking (as was organized psychiatry generally at the time). Because of the nature of psychoanalytic practice, in which a small number of patients are treated intensively over a period of years, DSM–I and DSM–II did not build on a large data set. As a result, the probability that two clinicians examining the same patient would arrive at the same diagnosis was low. DSM–II's lack of reliability led to criticism from a number of different quarters: from researchers who were interested in the biological basis of mental illness and thus needed to conduct their research on comparable populations of patients; from legal scholars, who argued that unreliable diagnoses should not be admissible in court; and from health insurance providers who were concerned about providing coverage for diseases that were vaguely defined. See Robert D. Miller, "History of Psychiatric Diagnosis: A Guidebook for Nonclinicians," 23 Colo. Law. 39, 40 (1994).

In response to these criticisms, the APA appointed a task force in 1974 to revise DSM–II. From 1975 through 1979, successive Task Force Drafts of DSM–III were considered at the annual meeting of the APA, as well as at a special meeting in 1976 that focused entirely on DSM–III. Throughout that period, critiques were solicited from the rest of the psychiatric profession and from groups of psychoanalysts, psychologists, and social workers.

DSM–III, which emerged in 1980, replaced the subjective approach of DSM–I and DSM–II with a more descriptive and objective approach. DSM–III also represented a significant expansion in the enterprise of classification: while DSM–II was only about 150 pages long, DSM–III was more than 500 pages in length. Between 1977 and 1980, the DSM–III diagnostic scheme was subjected to field trials to determine the extent to which different clinicians arrived at the same diagnosis using the DSM–III categories. In general, the tests revealed that interrater agreement for the major diagnostic categories (e.g., schizophrenia, manic-depressive psychosis) was quite high (between 69% and 85%). For other diagnostic categories, the rate of agreement was lower (often below 50%), but was still a marked improvement over the reliability of DSM–II.

A substantially revised version of DSM–III (DSM–III–R) came out in 1988. With DSM–IV, the research process became even more exhaustive. In addition to the clinical experience of task force members, large literature searches were incorporated into the reviews. Published in 1994, DSM–IV is over 900 pages long and contains over 300 diagnoses, organized under 16 diagnostic categories (e.g., schizophrenia and other psychotic disorders; mood disorders; anxiety disorders; dissociative disorders; childhood disorders; personality disorders; mental retardation). DSM–IV–TR is somewhat longer, but with the same number of diagnoses as DSM–IV. DSM–V is projected for publication in 2012.

The DSM's diagnostic labels are meant to be used in connection with a "multi-axial system" consisting of five axes. Axis I is for reporting all of the major diagnostic classes of disorder, except for personality disorders and mental retardation (which are reported on Axis II). Axis III is for reporting general medical conditions that may bear upon the individual's mental disorder. Axis IV is for reporting psychosocial and environmental problems that may affect the diagnosis and treatment of the mental disorder. These may include problems with the individual's primary support group, social environment, educational problems, and economic problems. Finally, Axis V is for reporting global assessment of functioning (GAF), which is calculated on a scale of 1 to 100. Below is an example of how the multi-axial system might work in a given case, taken from DSM–IV (the numbers in Axes I and II are the DSM–IV diagnostic codes):

Axis 1	296.23	Major Depressive Disorder, Single Episode, Severe Without Psychotic Features
	305.00	Alcohol Abuse
Axis II	301.6	Dependent Personality Disorder Frequent Use of Denial
Axis III		None
Axis IV		Threat of job loss
Axis V		GAF=35 (current)

Mental health professionals, and occasionally this book, often speak in terms of "Axis I" or "Axis II" diagnosis, with the latter usually connoting a less serious (personality) disorder.

The introduction to DSM–IV expresses several caveats about its use, three of which will be noted here. First, it states, "[a] common misconception is that a classification of mental disorders classifies people, when actually what is being classified are disorders that people have." Thus, the drafters note, DSM–IV "avoids the use of such expressions as 'a schizophrenic' or 'an alcoholic' and uses the more accurate, but admittedly more cumbersome, 'an individual with Schizophrenia' or 'an individual with Alcohol Dependence' " (a convention this book will try to adhere to as well). DSM–IV–TR, at xxxi. Second, "there is no assumption that each category of mental disorder is a completely discrete entity with absolute boundaries dividing it from other mental disorders or from no mental disorder. There is also no assumption that all individuals described as having the same mental disorder are alike in all important ways." Id. Finally, as discussed earlier in this chapter, the DSM–IV emphasizes that the clinical diagnosis of a DSM–IV mental disorder is not sufficient to establish the existence for legal purposes of a "mental disorder," "mental disability," "mental disease," or "mental defect." Id. at xxxiii.

Questions and Comments

1. *Social and political influences on the DSM–IV.* Political and social forces have strongly influenced the DSM system. Probably the most prominent example is the APA's treatment of homosexuality. Prior to the 1960's, homosexual activity was a crime in most states. The psychiatric community considered homosexuality a "disease," and it was classified as such in the DSM system. Beginning in the early 1960's, many states either repealed such laws or stopped enforcing them as society's attitudes toward homosexuality changed. In 1973, in response to widespread criticism on the part of various lobbying groups, the APA "delisted" homosexuality as a disease classification (although "transvestic fetishism" and "gender identity disorder," involving strong desires to be the other sex, remain in DSM–IV). For a detailed discussion of the events surrounding the delisting of homosexuality, see Herb Kutchins & Stuart Kirk, Making Us Crazy 55–99 (1997).

Other examples of diagnostic definitions that reflect political influence abound. For example, in 1980, in response to pressure from Vietnam veterans groups, the APA added a Posttraumatic Stress Disorder categorization to the DSM. More recent still is the social and political controversy associated with the condition popularly known as multiple personality disorder ("MPD"). According to proponents of the diagnosis, MPD is closely associated with childhood sexual abuse that is generally not remembered until adulthood. The MPD diagnosis was not included in the DSM system until 1980. After its inclusion in the DSM–III, however, the diagnosis took on a life of its own. According to one estimate, almost 40,000 new cases of MPD were diagnosed between 1985 and 1995. See Joan Acocella, "The Politics of Hysteria," The New Yorker, April 6, 1998, at 66. The MPD movement was endorsed not only by some feminist writers and child protection advocates but also by a variety of culturally conservative organizations. By the early 1990's, however, there had been a significant backlash: patients who had been diagnosed with MPD were suing therapists and winning multi-million dollar awards. *Id.* at 71–72. The DSM–IV no longer includes an MPD diagnosis; the new term for MPD is "dissociative identity disorder" (see Appendix A). The litigation engendered by MPD is discussed more fully in Chapter Three.

2. *Criticism of modern versions of the DSM.* Perhaps the most widespread criticism of the modern DSM system (i.e., the third and fourth editions) is that the diagnostic criteria are often still too broad and/or vague, making their application by mental health professionals a self-serving "pathologizing" of everyday behavior. See Herb Kutchins & Stuart Kirk, Mak-

ing Us Crazy 21–54 (1997). Critics have pointed to studies showing that, in representative samples of adults, 50% of respondents reported at least one lifetime disorder and about 30% reported at least one 12–month disorder as defined by the DSM. See R.C. Kessler et al., "Lifetime and 12–month Prevalence of DSM–III–R Psychiatric Disorders in the United States," 51 Archives of General Psychiatry 8 (1994). The Surgeon General's estimate of a 28–30% prevalence of mental disorder noted previously was also based on DSM criteria.

Criticisms about overly broad diagnostic criteria have been particularly pointed in the case of DSM–IV diagnoses that apply to children and adolescents. For example, in the mid–1990's, over two and a half million people, mostly children between the ages of 5 and 12, were taking medication for attention-deficit/hyperactivity disorder (ADHD). See Lawrence Diller, "The Run of Ritalin: Attention Deficit Disorder and Stimulant Treatment in the 1990s," Hastings Center Report, March 1996. One of the reasons for the large number of ADHD diagnoses was the significant liberalization in the diagnostic criteria under DSM–IV: hyperactivity is no longer a requirement and the person need display ADHD in only two environments, not every environment (see Appendix A). Professor Diller catalogues some of the consequences of this liberalization:

> The increasing numbers of children and adults who meet the broader ADHD criteria are beginning to have an impact in the classroom and workplace. Parents find the only way to get extra help for their children is to have them labeled with a disorder. The Individuals with Disabilities Education Act of 1990 and recent interpretations of Section 504 of the 1973 Rehabilitation Act have become broad and potent legal tools for families of children with ADHD seeking special services from their school districts.... In the workplace more and more employers are being asked to make changes for their workers who are affected with ADHD.... Attention–Deficit Hyperactivity Disorder has contributed to a crisis in the disability insurance industry. Claims have soared for a host of ill-defined conditions. Insurers have fled the business of providing disability insurance, making it prohibitively expensive or impossible to obtain. As more people meet diagnostic criteria, many will attempt to gain services. It remains to be seen whether broadly defined disabilities ultimately trivialize suffering or make it more difficult for the more severely impaired person to obtain urgently needed recognition and service.

Lawrence Diller, *supra*. The issues Diller raises applies to many mental disorders with broadly defined diagnostic criteria. Cf. Kelli Schmidt, " 'Who are you to say what my best interest is?' Minors' Due Process Rights When Admitted By Parents for Inpatient Mental Health Treatment," 71 Wash. L. Rev. 1187, 1209 (1996)(arguing that the diagnosis of "conduct disorder," which DSM–IV states is typified by "repetitive and persistent pattern of behavior in which the basic rights of other or major age-appropriate societal norms or rules are violated," is applied too frequently to adolescents).

Similar criticisms have been levied at the DSM's criteria for depression. Allen Horwitz and Jerome Wakefield have argued that the DSM conflates normal sadness with true depressive disorder. In their view, normal sadness, including sadness resulting from various life events, can be intense; be accompanied by sleeplessness, lack of concentration, and changed appetite; cause impairment or distress; and last for 2 weeks, as required by DSM's definition of depression (see Appendix A). But, they contend, true depression should be diagnosed only when these symptoms result "from failure of a person's internal mechanisms to perform their functions as designed by nature," a distinction which they argue will ensure better prognosis, appropriate treatment, efficient use of resources, avoidance of stigma and the "conceptual integrity of psychiatry." Allan v. Horwitz & Jerome C. Wakfield, The Loss of Sadness: How Psychiatry Transformed Normal Sorrow into Depressive Disorder 15–22 (2007).

Others critics have claimed that DSM's comprehensiveness will harm treatment efficacy. The DSM–IV covers so many conditions, they argue, that it may lead to situations in which the diagnosis, not the patient, is treated. Gary Tucker, "Putting DSM–IV in Perspective," 155 Am. J. Psychiatry 159 (1998). The result may also be a more boring profession, where psychiatrists "grind out" patients based on their diagnosis rather than individualized assessment. Id.

Finally, the DSM–IV has been criticized for bias against non-Western and minority culture. Only a small percentage of disorder descriptions include cultural information. Even its critics note, however, that the DSM–IV is more sensitive in this regard than its predecessors. For example, 14 of the 16 major diagnostic classes include some discussion of cultural issues. In addition, an appendix entitled "Outline for Cultural Formulation and Glossary of Culture–Bound Syndromes" describes "recurrent, locality-specific patterns of aberrant behavior and troubling experience that may or may not be linked to a particular DSM–IV diagnostic category." These include *amok* (a period of brooding followed by violent outbursts, observed in Malaysia, Laos, Philippines and other Pacific nations), *ataque de nervios* (a syndrome of "uncontrollable shouting, crying, trembling, and aggression typically triggered by a stressful event involving family" observed in Latino groups), and *ghost sickness* (anxiety, hallucination, loss of consciousness and/or other symptoms associated with a preoccupation with death, observed in Native American cultures). DSM–IV–TR, at 898–903.

III. TREATMENT OF MENTAL DISORDER

A. INTRODUCTION

"Deranged states", what today would probably be diagnosed as schizophrenia, have been a part of social history since earliest recorded times. Societal reaction to afflicted individuals ranged from exclusion from the community to the punitive. In both Greece and Rome the seriously ill were kept under restraints by their families or imprisoned or exiled. In medieval times and during the Renaissance, mental illness was though to result from possession by demons or witchcraft that could only be expunged by torture or exorcism.

As early as the fourteenth century, mental institutions took the place of prisons as a place to confine the mentally ill. The regimen in asylums was generally harsh, with an emphasis on restraint. Early in the 19th century reformers starting with Pinel, the author of an influential book published in 1801, began to advocate the "humane treatment" of the mentally ill. Since effective forms of treatment had not been developed at the time, this goal simply meant the operation of asylums in a more humane manner. It was not until the end of the 19th century that psychiatry, which at the time was a relatively new field, began its search for ways to treat mental illness. The approaches taken were highly experimental and focused in the main on patients who had been committed to asylums. These therapies–including "malarial fever therapy" (inducing, then curing, malaria), lobotomies (excision of the frontal lobes), coma therapy, and electro-convulsive therapy (ECT)–achieved only marginal beneficial results. Among these only ECT, which provided relief to individuals suffering from psychotic depression, is still employed today, though the application techniques have undergone material change.

Psychiatric drugs (often called psychotropic medication) were first introduced in the late 1940s and have revolutionized the treatment of serious disorders. The first breakthrough came in 1949, with the discovery that lithium could be used to treat bipolar affective disorders. The success of lithium hastened the development of many other drugs. In the 1950s, a variety of antidepressant drugs such as monoamine oxidase inhibitor (MAOIs) and tricyclics/heterocyclics were introduced. In 1955, the antipsychotic chlorpromazine was introduced in the United States: chlorprozamine ultimately played a significant role in the reduction of state mental hospital populations. During the 1970s and 1980s, many pharmacologic agents were developed to address anxiety. And finally, in the late 1980s and early 1990s, selective serotonin reuptake inhibitors (SSRIs) emerged to treat depression. A number of psychoanalytically oriented therapies also developed during the early 20th century, spurred by the theory of Sigmund Freud and others.

Today, the treatment of various mental disorders relies on either biological (primarily psychopharmacology) or non-biological treatment techniques (psychotherapy), or sometimes the two in combination. Psychopharmacology, which has advanced markedly since its initial development, is now used to treat not only psychotic conditions, but also a broad range of less serious disorders. While the psychiatric profession, together with other biological scientists, has been primarily responsible for research leading to the development of these drugs, it is family practitioners and internists rather than psychiatrists who write the majority of psychotropic prescriptions. According to one survey, general practitioners and internists rather than psychiatrists are responsible for writing three-quarters of the psychotropic medications that are prescribed annually. See Wall Street Journal, April 10, 1998, at B–1. Alternatives to pharmacology are electroconvulsive therapy (ECT) and phototherapy. ECT is generally used when a patient is unresponsive to or cannot tolerate pharmacological treatment.

Non-biological treatment methods include a range of what are referred to as "psychosocial" therapies. These therapies encompass a variety of techniques, all of which rely basically on verbal communications between the therapist and the patient. The choice between a biological form of treatment and psychotherapy is determined by the nature of the disorder and its severity. Generally, the more severe disorders, such as psychotic depression and schizophrenia, are treated pharmacologically, though the pharmacology is often supplemented by some form of psychosocial therapy. The treatment of less severe disorders, on the other hand, is likely to rely more on some form of psychotherapy, though psychotropic medication is sometimes employed as an adjunct.

The type of therapy chosen by the public and the duration of various therapeutic interventions has been influenced both by advances in psychopharmacology and the impact of managed care programs. Recent studies indicate that over a ten-year span—1987 to 1997—various changes have occurred in the choice of therapy, the duration of therapy and the diagnosis of those seeking psychotherapeutic treatment. While the percentage of the population receiving psychotherapy increased only slightly over the ten-year period (3.2 percent of the population in 1987 versus 3.6 percent in 1997), the number of treatment sessions received by patients dropped significantly. Specifically, the percentage of patients who received more than 20 therapeutic sessions dropped from *circa* 16% in 1987 to 10% in 1997. In fact, nearly a third of the patients involved in psychotherapy in 1997 attended only one or two sessions. The diagnosis of patients undergoing psychotherapy also changed markedly over the ten-year span. Almost 40% of the patients surveyed in one of the studies were listed on insurance forms as suffering from depression or other mood disorders compared with 19.5% ten years earlier. Finally, there was a dramatic increase in the percentage of patients receiving psychotherapy who also received psychotropic medication. By 1997, 61.5% of patients undergoing psychotherapy were also treated with psychotropic medication, compared to only 31.5% a decade earlier. See Erica Goode, 'Psychotherapy Shows a Rise Over Decade, But Time Falls,' N.Y. Times, Nov. 20, 2002 at A19.

The following materials briefly summarize the principal characteristics of the various biological and non-biological therapies that are currently employed in the treatment of selected mental disorders. The attention given to the biological therapies and their associated side effects in the material which follow is motivated by the following considerations: (1) As noted in Chapter 2, the exclusive *legal right*, until recently, of physicians and psychiatrists to prescribe psychotropic medication is being challenged by non-physician mental health professionals such as psychologists. Presumably the complexities involved in the selection of specific medications and the serious side effects associated with their use will have a bearing on the formulation of public policy concerning the prescription privileges of non-physicians; (2) As detailed in Chapter 3, the growing use of psychotropic medication in the treatment of mental disorders coupled with the potential for adverse side effects raises complex issues in the application of malpractice law; (3) Application of the law of informed consent, which is treated in Chapter 4, presupposes that basic information concerning treatment and associated risks will be communicated to the patients who have the capacity to comprehend the data provided. The range and complexity of the side effects associated with various psychotropic medications, may be relevant to how the doctrine of informed consent should be applied in this context; (4) An understanding of psychotropic medication, particularly the subcategory of drugs known as antipsychotic medication, is an important predicate to analyzing the scope of the constitutional right to refuse medication, which has occasioned a significant amount of litigation in the past several decades (as discussed in Chapter Nine).

B. BIOLOGICAL THERAPIES

As noted, advances in psychopharmacology have provided caregivers with powerful tools to treat a range of mental disorders. Yet some of these drugs have side effects that can impair normal functions, or permanently damage organs. Given the significance of these negative outcomes in a variety of legal contexts, such as in actions for malpractice or where the lawfulness of involuntary medication is an issue, the following materials, in addition to describing some of the most commonly used psychopharmacological drugs, seek to highlight the side effects that are associated with their use.

1. *Treatment of Depression*

a. *Pharmacological Therapy*

Anti-depressant drugs can be roughly classified under four major categories: (1) a group of newly-developed miscellaneous drugs known as Selective Serotonin Reuptake Inhibitors (SSRIs), which include fluoxetine (Prozac), sertraline (Zoloft), paroxetine (Paxil), fluvoxamine (Luvox), citalopram (Celexa), escitalopram (Lexapro), and the most popular of the SSRI type of medication, flouxetine (Prozac); (2) Monoamine Oxidase Inhibitors (MAOIs); (3) the tricyclic antidepressants, and; (4) a group of miscellaneous drugs, which include bupropion (Wellbutrin), mirtazepine (Remeron) and trazodone (Desyrel).

The four categories of anti-depressant drugs differ in both their level of effectiveness and side-effects. The SSRIs were developed in a search for anti-depressants with lower levels of toxicity and fewer side effects than the older medications such as the MAOIs and tricyclics. The most successful of these is Prozac, which was introduced in 1987, and is effective in the treatment of most depressive conditions, except perhaps severe or psychotic depression. Some estimates suggest that upward of 10 million persons are regular users of Prozac in the United States. Prozac and the other medications in this group are relatively free of serious side effects. Nevertheless, common side effects can include sexual dysfunctions and particularly decreased libido and anorgasmia in both men and women. Also, a small proportion (10–15%) of patients taking these drugs manifest increased anxiety, nervousness, and insomnia. Delusional hallucinations and paranoid reactions occur in *circa* one percent of patients taking Prozac. Some studies, though inconclusive, have suggested that Prozac may be loosely linked with the development of suicidal preoccupation and violence. See Vale, "The Rise and Fall of Prozac: Products Liability Cases and 'The Prozac' Defense in Criminal Litigation," 1993 St. Louis U. Pub. L. Rev. 525, 527–29 (1993). See also Benedict Carey, "Antidepressant Studies Unpublished," N.Y. Times, Jan. 27, 2008 (noting that, according to a meta-review in the New England Journal of Medicine, when unpublished studies withheld by drug companies are included in the analysis, Prozac and Paxil outperform placebos only by a modest margin).

The high level of toxicity and side effects of MAOIs have limited their use, though they are sometimes employed in the treatment of "atypical depression," characterized by symptoms such as oversleeping, anxiety, panic attacks, and phobias. Side-effects of MAOIs include severe elevation of blood pressure, headaches, nausea, vomiting, possible confusion, and even psychotic symptoms. Additionally, they do not interact well with certain foods items and various over-the-counter medications. SSRIs, because of their similar efficacy profile and greater safety, have largely supplanted the use of MAOIs in recent years.

Tricyclic antidepressants such as amitriptyline (Elavil), imiprimine (Tofranil) and nortryptiline (Pamelor) are the agents most commonly used for the treatment of major depression. The side effects of tricyclics include blurred vision, weight gain, constipation, dizziness, fainting (from lower blood pressure), muscle twitches, fatigue, and decreased sexual energy. However, not all patients experience these side effects and the side effects that are likely to be encountered by a particular patient are unpredictable. For some patients, tricyclics are not a feasible treatment modality since they interact with other medications.

The fourth category of antidepressants drugs includes a group of miscellaneous drugs each of which has somewhat different properties and side effects. These include buproprion (Wellbutrin), trazadone (Desyrel), mirtazapine (Remeron). Bupropion, which has a different mode of action from the others (a reliance on dopamine or norepinephrine rather than serotonin), has anxiety and insomnia as a possible side effect, but avoids the sexual dysfunction associated with SSRIs. Nefazadone has a serotonin-based mode of action and also avoids the sexual dysfunction risk of SSRIs. Remeron has a novel mode of action that is somewhat sedating.

b.   Electroconvulsive Therapy ("ECT")

Electroconvulsive therapy, or ECT, (which was formerly known as electro-shock therapy) is used to treat severe depression, particularly when the patient does not respond to anti-depressant medication. ECT involves the application of electric pulses (100–300 V) to the brain in order to induce a seizure, which for unknown reasons has proved effective in the treatment of depression. Unlike medication, ECT can produce beneficial results fairly rapidly, which is an advantage when the patient is suicidal or cannot, because of side effects, tolerate antidepressant medication. See 9 Mental Health Disorders Sourcebook 469–70 (Karen Bellenir, ed. 1996). While ECT was fairly widely used in earlier years, particularly in psychiatric hospitals, it is far less frequently used today, primarily because of the development of anti-depressant medications.

Formerly, ECT was associated with two major problems: the patient's discomfort caused by the procedure and the bone fractures resulting from the motor activity of the induced seizures. Today, these side effects have been largely eliminated by the use of general anesthetics and pharmacological muscle relaxants during treatment. Estimates place the number of patients who annually received ECT treatment in the early 1990s at 50,000 to 100,000. See Herrold G. Bernstein, Drug Therapy in Psychiatry 186 (3rd ed., 1995). When properly administered, the primary side effect of ECT is a loss of memory formation during the time that the patient is receiving treatment. However, studies indicate that the patient's ability to store memories in the future is unaffected. Hence typically the patient is able to recall everything in the past and to learn and remember things in the future without any change. However, they may never clearly recall what occurred during the period in which they were receiving ECT.

2.   *Treatment of Bipolar Disorders*

"Bipolar" disorders are characterized by episodes of depression and "highs," the latter corresponding to what is known as the "manic" phase. The depressive phases of bipolar disorders tend to be treated by the same medications that are employed for unipolar depression. The treatment of choice for many decades for the manic phase is Lithium. Lithium, which is taken orally, has been found to significantly diminish severe manic symptoms in five to fourteen days, though it may take several months of medication until the condition is fully controlled. Lithium treatment is sometimes supplemented by antipsychotic medication (neuroleptics) particularly in the first several days of treatment.

Lithium treatment poses the danger of numerous side effects, some of which are serious and even life threatening. Even in the absence of lithium toxicity, which can have serious health consequences, normal symptoms may include drowsiness, nausea, vomiting, fatigue, hand tremors, or urinary problems. Since excess lithium in the system can be life threatening, use of this drug requires regular blood tests throughout the course of treatment. Mental Health Disorders Sourcebook, Vol. 9, Karen Bellenir, ed. at 422–423 (1996).

More recently, several drugs originally developed to treat epilepsy have been shown to be effective for bipolar disorder. These include valproic acid (Depakote), carbamazepine (Tegretol), lamotragine (Lamictal), gabapentin (Neurontin) and topiramate (Topamax). Valproic acid has been shown to have equal efficacy to lithium in the treatment of acute mania, and has become the drug of choice because of its favorable side effect profile. Lamictal recently has been shown to have particular efficacy in the depressed phase of bipolar disorder. However, lithium has the strongest data for the long term reduction of the risk of suicide. Each of these drugs are used not only for the treatment of acute mania but also for prophylactic treatment. Among the serious side effects associated with the use of Tegretol is liver dysfunction and complications affecting the immune system. Depakote also is associated with liver dysfunction, and Lamictal with rare occurrence of a toxic rash.

3. *Treatment of Schizophrenia*

Schizophrenia, a severe mental disorder characterized by psychotic symptoms (thought disorder hallucinations, delusion, paranoia) and impairment in job and social functioning, affects more than two million Americans. The primary medications used to treat schizophrenic disorders are the antipsychotic medications, also called neuroleptics. Although these medications are not a cure for schizophrenia, they are effective in alleviating or reducing symptoms. Chlorpromazine (Thorazine), the first medication of this kind, became available for use in the United States in the 1950s. See 9 Mental Health Disorders Sourcebook, *supra* at 87–88. Since its discovery, a dozen or so other classes of antipsychotic medications have been developed.

Other anti-psychotic medications used for the treatment of schizophrenia include fluphenazine (Prolixin), haloperidol (Haldol) and a number of new drugs classified as "atypicals." Symptom reduction, in the case of all neuroleptics, is believed to result from the capacity of these agents to block binding sites (receptors) for the neurotransmitter, dopamine, found in the brain. The neuroleptic of choice for any given patient must be determined to a considerable degree by trial and error. According to one authority: "[p]rior drug effectiveness [for a particular patient] is often the best predictor of current response." See W. Reid et al., The Treatment of Psychiatric Disorders 191(Brunner & Mazel eds., 3d ed.,1997) [hereinafter Reid et al.].

Since schizophrenia, which tends to be a chronic condition, is characterized by episodic psychotic episodes, initiation of a medication regime is usually in response to an acute phase of the disease, where the symptomatology is particularly pronounced. For that reason, once emergency treatment is called for, the neuroleptic drug is given in doses sufficient to control the acute psychosis. Once the patient has stabilized, initial dose levels of most neuroleptics can usually be reduced by up to fifty percent. See id. at 190. Thereafter, patients are frequently kept on maintenance dosage to prevent relapse. In general, neuroleptics are taken orally on a daily basis. However, neuroleptics may also be administered by injection, particularly in a crisis situation where the patient will not cooperate taking oral medication. A second form of injectable medication is long-acting and therefore is used when a patient is incapable of adhering to a regular maintenance dosage regime. When taken by injection and of the long-acting variety, the drug can be administered on a weekly or semi-weekly basis, rather than daily as in the case of medication, which is taken orally. The dosage for individual patients will vary depending on a variety of factors, including the severity of the illness, the rate at which the patient metabolizes the medication and the manifestation of negative side effects.

The older neuroleptic medications are associated with several severe side effects which may or may not become manifest in a particular patient. Among the most common side effects are dystonia (involuntary contraction or muscle spasm) and akathisia (feeling of restlessness sometimes associated with continuous leg movement). Approximately ten to fifteen percent of the patients treated with neuroleptics develop one or both of these symptoms. Both conditions, however, are reversible when anti-psychotic medication is lowered or terminated and both can be counteracted by anti-cholinergic medication. See Harold I. Kaplan & Benjamin J. Sadock, Synopsis of Psychiatry 1031 (8th ed., 1996) [hereinafter Kaplan & Sadock].

Neuroleptics can also produce tremors and slowed or stiff movements resulting in a condition resembling Parkinson's disease (called Pseudoparkinsonism.) Approximately fifteen percent of the patients who are treated by neuroleptics develop this reaction. Pseudoparkinsonism resulting from anti-psychotic medication is reversible when medication is lowered or terminated. See Kaplan & Sadock, *supra*, at 1031.

Tardive dyskinesia is the most serious and sometimes irreversible side effect resulting from prolonged use of neuroleptic medications. The disorder consists of abnormal, involuntary, irregular movements of the muscles of the head, limbs, and trunk. The severity of movements ranges from minimal to grossly incapacitating. All neuroleptics currently on the market have been associated with tardive dyskinesia though clozapine (Clozaril) and the other atypical medications are less likely to produce tardive dyskinesia than other neuroleptics. About ten to twenty percent of patients who are treated for more than one year with neuroleptics develop tardive dyskinesia. To some extent, the incidence is affected not only by the length of treatment, but also by the dosage. The remission rate of tardive dyskinesia varies depending on the severity of the symptoms. In mild cases, the remission rate is fifty to ninety percent, whereas in severe cases, the remission rate is five to forty percent. See Kaplan & Sadock, *supra*, at 1133. Approaches to minimizing tardive dyskinesia risk include prevention, diagnosis, and management. Prevention can, in part, be achieved by the use of dopamine receptor antagonist medications, though the use of these drugs poses other risks. The risk can also be reduced by careful management of the medication involving a close monitoring of dosages and possible changes in the class of medication that is employed.

Other possible side effects of some anti-psychotic medications include skin rashes, cholestatic jaundice, sun sensitivity, and a lowering of the white blood cell count. Except for clozapine, the risk of a lowered white blood cell count is extremely small. With clozapine, there is a one to two percent risk, which in turn requires that those on this medication undergo weekly blood cell monitoring.

Since the early 1990s several new drugs have joined clozapine in the category of atypical antipsychotics. These drugs include risperidone (Risperdal), olanzepine (Zyprexa), quitiapine (Seroquel), and ziprasadone (Geodon). The advantages of this class of medication have been described as follows:

> The January 1994 entrance of risperidone into the U.S. pharmacopeia dramatically altered treatment prospects for patients with psychotic disorders and initiated a change in the drugs that U.S. psychiatrists selected to treat psychoses.... Olanzapine, quetiapine, risperidone, and ziprasidone all appear to have several advantages over older neuroleptics: (1) The novel agents all treat positive symptoms at least as effectively as conventional neuroleptics, but they accomplish this with a much lower frequency and intensity of the noxious neuromotor side effects caused by the older D2 blockers.... (2) Not only is the level of extrapyramidal side effects much lower with newer agents, but the risk of developing tardive dyskinesia is lower as well. (3) Available evidence suggests that patients who need antipsychotic medication prefer the novel agents and may be better off taking them than the older D2–blockers. (4) One reason for this preference may be that atypical agents leave patients less burdened with negative symptoms than they would be were they to take neuroleptics, possibly because the newer drugs induce less motor slowing. (5) A growing number of studies suggest that the atypical antipsychotics are better than the older drugs at ameliorating cognitive deficits that characterize schizophrenia.

Douglas Mossman, "Unbuckling the 'Chemical Straightjacket': The Legal Significance of Recent Advances in the Pharmacological Treatment of Psychosis," 39 San Diego L. Rev. 1033, 1062–81 (2002).

While this new class of medication appears to reduce the risk of various side effects, they are not risk-free. For instance, one study found that Zyprexa, Risperdal, and Seroquel increased patients' risk of developing diabetes and rapid weight gain. "Schizophrenia Drugs May Raise Diabetes Risk, Study Says," N.Y. Times, August 25, 2003. Risperdal has been found to cause a higher incidence of Parkinsonian symptoms than Haldol, one of the older neuroleptics, Michael B. Knable et al., "Extrapyramidal Side Effects with Risperidone and Haloperidol at Comparable D2 Receptor Levels," 75 Psychiatry Res. 91, 98 (1997) and has also been associated with a chewing disorder of the mouth known as "rabbit syndrome". Tomar Levin & Uriel Heresco-Levy, "Risperidone-Induced Rabbit Syndrome," 9 Eur. Neuropsychopharmacology 137, 137 (1999). In an FDA-reviewed study, twenty-two percent of Zyprexa patients suffered a "serious" adverse event, compared to eighteen percent of the Haldol patients. Robert Whitaker, Mad in America: Bad Science, Bad Medicine and the Enduring Mistreatment of the Mentally Ill 281 (2002). A recent study also found that schizophrenia patients had a better quality of life when using the old drugs than when taking the new ones. L.M. Davies et at., "Cost-Effectiveness of First v. Second-Generation Antipsychotic Drugs," 191 Brit. J. Psychiatry 14, 16–17 (2007).

4. *Treatment of Neuro-behavioral and Attention Deficit Hyperactivity Disorders (ADHD)*

Ritalin, which is produced by Ciba–Geigy Pharmaceutical Co., and has been on the market since the mid–1960's, is currently the drug of choice for the treatment of hyperactivity associated with ADHD. It may be administered to school-age children over the age of six and has generally been found to be effective in reducing hyperactivity associated with ADHD. Use of the drug, which acts as a mild central nervous system stimulant, is generally coupled with other remedial measures, including some form of psychosocial therapy. While relatively free of negative side-effects, its use is contraindicated in the case of children with a psychotic condition, since Ritalin may aggravate some of the symptomotology associated with such disorders as major anxiety and agitation. Additionally, in some patients, Ritalin may result in hypersensitivity to the drug itself. See Richard Welke, "Litigation Involving Ritalin and the Hyperactive Child," Det. C.L. Rev. 125 (1990).

5. *Treatment of Anxiety, Panic Disorders, and Phobias*

Various medications are available for the treatment of severe anxiety and panic disorders. The preferred medication for most anxiety disorders are a class of tranquilizers known as benzodiazepines and buspirone (Buspar). Antidepressants are also sometimes prescribed for the more generalized forms of anxiety, especially when the anxiety is accompanied by depression.

The most commonly used benzodiazepines are diazepam (Valium) and alprazolam (Xanax). Benzodiazepines have few side effects, except for drowsiness and some loss of coordination. These effects however, result in some risks in the operation of motor vehicles or other machinery. Also, benzodiazepines, when taken in combination with other substances such as alcohol, can lead to severe complications including cardiac arrest. See 9 Mental Health Disorders Sourcebook, *supra*, at 428–429. An additional side effect is the risk of tolerance and addiction, which can occur with extended use at higher dosages.

Questions and Comments

1. *Incidence of prescription of atypical anti-psychotic medications.* The growing trend towards the new class of anti-psychotic medication is suggested by a report that more than 15 million prescriptions were written in 2002 for two of the leading atypical anti-psychotic medications (Zyprexa and Risperdal). Erica Goode, "Three Schizophrenia Drugs May Raise Diabetes Risk," N.Y. Times, August 25, 2003, at A–8.

2. *Cost factors influencing choice of medication over psychotherapy.* The current trend in favor of biological treatment is largely the consequence of advances in psychopharmacology. It is also influenced, however, by the fact that many insurance companies will reimburse the full cost of treatment with medication but only part of the cost of psychotherapy. See "Managed Care's Focus On Psychiatric Drugs Alarms Many Doctors: Talk Therapy is Discouraged," Wall St. J., Dec. 1 1995, at A–1 and A–4.

3. *Cost factors in the selection of medication.* A choice of one drug over another may, in some instances, be influenced by cost factors, particularly where there is a third party payer, i.e. a state agency or an HMO. For instance, the acquisition cost of the newer class of atypical drugs for the treatment of schizophrenia is sometimes 70–100 times higher than the older class of neuroleptics. For a patient with schizophrenia taking one of the atypical classes of drugs rather than one of the older drugs, this might entail an added cost of $3,000–4,000 per year.

4. *Cosmetic psychopharmacology.* Drugs such as Ritalin (for ADHD) or Prozac (for depression) are being prescribed not only to address serious mental disorder but also simply to enhance mood or improve behavior. Peter Kramer, a psychiatrist at Brown University, has coined the term "cosmetic psychopharmacology" to describe the use of drugs to improve mental agility. See Peter Kramer, Listening to Prozac 246 (1993). In the view of critics like Kramer, the prescription of these drugs raises ethical issues, since demand for their use is largely in response to societal pressures on the individual to appear socially adept and integrated.

5. *Psychosurgery.* Psychosurgery represents another biological therapy, though it is not widely used today and is generally restricted to psychiatrically hospitalized patients with serious disorders that have not responded to other forms of treatment. Generally referred to as "stereotactic" procedures, including subcaudate tractotomy, anterior cingulotomy, limbic leukotomy and anterior capsulotomy, these procedures involve creating very small lesions in various areas of the brain. Nonetheless, given their intrusiveness, they are usually reserved for persons with very serious depressive, obsessive-compulsive or other anxiety disorders, after all other treatments have failed. Various studies have shown that these types of psychosurgery bring benefits for 25 to 70% of those treated, with about 25% showing "outstanding improvement." Kaplan & Sadock, *supra*, at 2520. Minor short-term side effects such as confusion, headaches, and nausea are common; severe and enduring effects are rare, although seizures occur in approximately 1 to 3% of the cases. Suicide rates also appear to be reduced, and intelligence may be enhanced. Id. However, according to one critic, "virtually all studies of psychosurgery have been retrospective anecdotal reports by proponents of the technique, rather than prospective control studies; therefore, … the evaluative literature in this area is seriously flawed." Bruce Winick, The Right to Refuse Mental Health Treatment 109 (1998).

C. NON–BIOLOGICAL TREATMENTS (PSYCHOTHERAPY)

Psychotherapy is a treatment intervention that relies on communication rather than biological or physical modalities; hence it is often called "talk therapy." As noted earlier, it includes psychoanalysis, behavior therapy, cognitive therapy and simple "counseling." It is the most common outpatient treatment for mental disorders and other mental problems. A 1990's study of 500 persons who sought psychotherapy found that the most common patient complaints were interpersonal problems, depression, uncontrolled behavior, and anxiety. Kaplan & Sadock, *supra*, at 2217–18. The following report describes some of the most common psychotherapies.

MENTAL HEALTH: REPORT OF THE SURGEON GENERAL
pp. 65–67.
(1999).

... Participants in psychotherapy can vary in age from the very young to the very old, and problems can vary from mental health problems to disabling and catastrophic mental disorders. Although people often are seen individually, psychotherapy also can be done with couples, families, and groups.... Estimates of the number of orientations to psychotherapy vary from a very small number to well over 400. The larger estimate generally refers to all the variations of the three major orientations, that is, psychodynamic, behavioral, and humanistic. Each orientation falls under the more general conceptual category of either action or reflection.

Psychodynamic orientations are the oldest. They place a premium on self-understanding, with the implicit (or sometimes explicit) assumption that increased self-understanding will produce salutary changes in the participant. Behavioral orientations are geared toward action, with a clear attempt to mobilize the resources of the patient in the direction of change, whether or not there is any understanding of the etiology of the problem. Humanistic orientations aim toward increased self-understanding, often in the direction of personal growth, but use treatment techniques that often are much more active than are likely to be employed by the psychodynamic clinician. While the following paragraphs focus on psychodynamic, behavioral, and humanistic orientations, they also discuss interpersonal therapy and cognitive-behavioral therapy as outgrowths of psychodynamic and behavioral therapy, respectively....

1. *Psychodynamic Therapy*

The first major approach to psychotherapy was developed by Sigmund Freud and is called psychoanalysis. Since its origin more than a century ago, psychoanalysis has undergone many changes. Today, Freudian (or classical) psychoanalysis is still practiced, but other variations have been developed—ego psychology, object relations theory, interpersonal psychology, and self-psychology, each of which can be grouped under the general term "psychodynamic". The psychodynamic therapies, even though they differ somewhat in theory and approach, all have some concepts in common. With each, the role of the past in shaping the present is emphasized, so it is important, in understanding behavior, to understand its origins and how people come to act and feel as they do. A second critical concept common to all psychodynamic approaches is the belief in the unconscious, so that there is much that influences our behavior of which we are not aware. This makes the process of understanding more difficult, as we often act for reasons that we cannot state, and these reasons often are linked to previous experiences. Thus, an important part of psychodynamic psychotherapy is to make the unconscious conscious or to help the patient understand the origin of actions that are troubling so that they can be corrected.

For some psychodynamic approaches, such as the classical Freudian approach, the focus is on the individual and the experiences the person had in the early years that give shape to current behavior, even beyond the awareness of the patient. For other, more contemporary approaches, such as interpersonal therapy, the focus is on the relationship between the person and others. First developed as a time-limited treatment for midlife depression, interpersonal therapy focuses on grief, role disputes, role transitions, and interpersonal deficits. The goal of interpersonal therapy is to improve current interpersonal skills. The therapist takes an active role in teaching patients to evaluate their interactions with others and to become aware of self-isolation and interpersonal difficulties. The therapist also offers advice and helps the patient to make decisions.

2. *Behavior Therapy*

A second major approach to psychotherapy is known as behavior modification or behavior therapy. It focuses on current behavior rather than on early patterns of the patient. In its earlier form, behavior therapy dealt exclusively with what people did rather than what they thought or felt. The general principles of learning were applied to the learning of maladaptive as well as adaptive behaviors. Thus, if a person could be conditioned to act in a functional way, there was no reason why the same principles of conditioning could not be employed to help the person unlearn dysfunctional behavior and learn to replace it with more functional behavior. The role of the environment was very important for behavior therapists, because it provided the positive and negative reinforcements that sustained or eliminated various behaviors. Therefore, ways of shaping that environment to make it more responsive to the needs of the individual were important in behavior therapy.

More recently, there has been a significant addition to the interests and activities of behavior therapists. Although behavior continued to be important in relation to reinforcements, cognitions—what the person thought about, perceived, or interpreted what was transpiring—were also seen as important. This combined emphasis led to a therapeutic variant known as cognitive-behavioral therapy, an approach that incorporates cognition with behavior in understanding and altering the problems that patients present.

Cognitive-behavioral therapy draws on behaviorism as well as cognitive psychology, a field devoted to the scientific study of mental processes, such as perceiving, remembering, reasoning, decision making, and problem solving. The use of cognition in cognitive-behavioral therapy varies from attending to the role of the environment in providing a model for behavior, to the close study of irrational beliefs, to the importance of individual thought processes in constructing a vision of the surrounding world. In each case, it is critical to study what the individual in therapy thinks and does and less important to understand the past events that led to that pattern of thinking and doing. Cognitive-behavioral therapy strives to alter faulty cognitions and replace them with thoughts and self-statements that promote adaptive behavior. For instance, cognitive-behavioral therapy tries to replace self-defeatist expectations ("I can't do anything right") with positive expectations ("I can do this right"). Cognitive-behavioral therapy has gained such ascendancy as a means of integrating cognitive and behavioral views of human functioning that the field is more frequently referred to as cognitive-behavioral therapy rather than behavior therapy.

3. *Humanistic Therapy*

The third wave of psychotherapy is referred to variously as humanistic, existential, experiential, or Gestalt therapy. It owes its origins as a treatment to the client-centered therapy that was originated by Carl Rogers, and the theory can be traced to philosophical roots beginning with the 19th century philosopher, Soren Kierkegaard. The central focus of humanistic therapy is the immediate experience of the client. The emphasis is on the present and the potential for future development rather than on the past, and on immediate feelings rather than on thoughts or behaviors. It is rooted in the everyday subjective experience of the person seeking assistance and is much less concerned with mental illness than it is with human growth.

One critical aspect of humanistic treatment is the relationship that is forged between the therapist, who in some ways serves as a guide in an exploration of self-discovery, and the client, who is seeking greater knowledge of the self and an expansion of inherent human potential. The focus on the self and the search for self-awareness is akin to psychodynamic psychotherapy, while the emphasis on the present is more similar to behavior therapy.

Although it is possible to describe distinctive orientations to psychotherapy, as has been done above, most psychotherapists describe themselves as eclectic in their practice, rather than as adherents to any single approach to treatment. As a result, there is a growing development referred to as "psychotherapy integration". It strives to capture what is best about each of the individual approaches.

Questions and Comments

1. *Duration of therapy and managed care.* Talk therapies can vary in intensity and duration. Classical psychoanalysis requires "free association"—the reporting all that comes to mind, including dreams—while in the presence of the analyst, who then interprets this information to promote a

"regressive transference neurosis" in which the early years of childhood are re-created in the doctor-patient relationship. American Psychiatric Association, The Psychiatric Therapies 834 (T.B. Karasu ed., 1984). As practiced by Freud, this process involved daily sessions of one hour each over a period of several years, and even today anything less than three hours a week "would not entitle the procedure to be called analysis even if other technical procedures were maintained." Id. Psychoanalytic psychotherapy, a newer version of Freud's approach, involves one or two hours a week, again for a number of years. Id. The average "dosage" of "brief" psychotherapies (which de-emphasize free association in favor of more direct questioning), and of interpersonal, behavioral and cognitive therapies is not as high, but can still be anywhere from several weeks to over a year, depending on the problem being treated.

For patients who are dependent on third party payer insurance benefits with caps, long-term therapies are not a feasible alternative since they will frequently not be authorized by the managed care organization. The cost implications of long-term therapies has led "[m]anaged care companies [to] focus on resolving patients' acute symptoms, rather than ridding them of their mental health conditions ... [leading] to the gradual disappearance of the use of the psychodynamic model as the dominant framework in the treatment of individuals suffering from mental illness." Jeffrey Cohen, "Managed Care and the Evolving Role of the Clinical Social Worker in Mental Health," 48 Social Work 34 (2003).

2. *Educational background and choice of treatment by therapist.* For some diagnostic categories such as schizophrenia, there is a consensus that the treatment of choice involves psychopharmacology. However, for some other disorders such as moderate depression or anxiety reactions, the health professions are split, with some advocating psychotherapy as the preferred treatment and others advocating the use of psychopharmacology. To some extent, the advocacy of a particular therapeutic approach will reflect the training of the therapist or his or her professional category, i.e. psychiatrist or psychologist. Also, between psychiatrists and psychologists, the latter will be more inclined to pursue psychotherapy for the treatment of various disorders in part because as psychologists, they are generally excluded by law from prescribing psychotropic medication and therefore cannot direct this form of treatment. The emerging drive by organized psychology to change state laws to acquire prescription privileges for psychologists is treated in Chapter 2.

3. *Psychotherapy for people with psychosis.* Although medication is the preferred treatment for the most serious disorders, other treatments can be effective. Below is an excerpt from Elyn Saks' autobiography, The Center Cannot Hold 89–100 (2007), which provides an example of such therapy and also paints a searing picture of a person with mental illness.

> I stumbled into Elizabeth Jones's office in a desperate lunge for salvation, and in the process began one of the most extraordinary experiences of my life. At the time it was often unmitigated hell. The work I was beginning with Mrs. Jones was not "counseling" or "therapy" as many Americans think of it or experience it themselves. No, this was talk therapy of the densest, most intellectually rigorous, challeng-

ing, and unsettling sort: Kleinian analysis, a treatment method that found its origins in the work of Sigmund Freud.

Freud built his theory of mind and method of treatment upon the concept of the human "unconscious"—the idea that we all think, feel, and do what we do for reasons that we are not entirely aware of. He believed that the unconscious was a "seething cauldron," filled with primitive forces at war with one another, forces that literally drove us to act. Central to Freud's thinking about psychoanalysis was the powerful relationship between the analyst and the patient, or analysand. From that relationship developed the "transference"—the name Freud gave to the intense feelings, beliefs, and attitudes the patient unconsciously recalls from early life and then directs toward the analyst. It was the transference itself that was the thing to be analyzed; it provided the raw material that would then be mined by the analyst and analysand for many years.

Freud had many reservations, however, about what could be accomplished with a psychotic analysand. He believed that psychosis was too narcissistic, too inward-looking, to allow the patient to develop a transference relationship with the analyst, and without that transference, there would be no grist for the psychoanalytic mill. Now, no one had diagnosed me as schizophrenic; indeed, even the work "psychosis" hadn't yet been mentioned. Still, I was depressed, I was behaving oddly, and people had a strong suspicion that I was delusional. I'd read enough Freud at this point to know that with this new psychoanalytic relationship, I was about to launch into uncharted and potentially troubling waters.

Elizabeth Jones, however, was a "Kleinian"—she practiced an offshoot of Freudian analysis developed by Melanie Klein, an Austrian psychoanalyst who immigrated to London in the late 1920s. Unlike Freud (and later, his daughter Anna), Klein believed that people with psychosis could benefit from analysis and that the necessary transference would develop. It was her theory that psychotic individuals are filled with (even driven by) great anxiety, and that the way to provide relief is to focus directly on the deepest sources of that anxiety.

Because most human anxiety stems from very primitive (read: infantile) fantasies about bodily parts and bodily functions, the direct nature of Kleinian interpretation calls for using the same kind of language that the patient's fantasies are couched in. To do this, Kleinian analysts employ the same words and images that the analysand uses—and as a consequence, Kleinian analysts can sometimes sound just as crazy as their patients do. These simple yet often startling exchanges between doctor and patient operate something like arrows shot directly at whatever it is that's upsetting the person being analyzed. If the arrow hits, it punctures the target; what results is something like a valve opening and long-pent-up steam being released.

A central tenet of both classical and Kleinian analysis is that the treater must remain fairly anonymous to her patient—she does not answer questions about herself, have pictures of her family on the wall, tell you where she went to school or where she is going on vacation.

Indeed, you don't even see your analyst during your sessions—how she looks as she reacts to you and what you are saying. You're on the couch. There is a simple reason for this: If the analyst is a so-called blank slate, the traits the patient attributes to her come primarily from the patient rather than the analyst. That's where transference develops, and the patient becomes better able to see how her mind works. And it was that process—and, ideally, reaping the fruit of it—that Elizabeth Jones and I embarked upon.

Though I never knew much about Mrs. Jones's life, I came to know her well from the way she reacted to me in the consulting room: with tolerance, patience, and understanding. Her voice was calm and soothing; she clearly didn't frighten easily. At the same time she was both extremely empathic and rigorously honest. She was also the first accomplished professional woman I had come to know.

During my sessions with Mrs. Jones, I whispered—because I was convinced that people in the house next door or across the street were able to hear what I was saying. Soon, some of the beliefs that had begun at the Warneford (for example, that beings in the sky controlled my thoughts and were poised to hurt me) took center stage in my thinking again. I would mutter complete nonsense, disconnected words and rhymes, which even as I whispered them out loud gave me great shame. I didn't want Mrs. Jones to hear them, in spite of her absolute "tell everything" rule.

Me: "They're messing with fetuses. They think it's us whereas the truth is God. Voices went, tabernacle, out to the edge of time. Time. Time is too low. Lower the boom. The TV is making fund of me. The characters are laughing at me. They think I am a failure and deserve to suffer. Everyone watching knows. The TV is telling the story of my life."

The doctors in the hospital had been stiff and formal when they dealt with me, seemingly more interested in giving me advice—"Eat more, Elyn!"—than in figuring out what was going on inside my head. Mrs. Jones was different. Her training had prepared her well for me, and she went directly to the heart of the matter, in the process sparing neither my feelings nor my assumptions about how a proper British matron should speak.

Mrs. Jones: "Tell me about your difficulties at university."

Me: "I'm not smart enough. I can't do the work."

Mrs. Jones: "You were first in your class at Vanderbilt. Now you're upset about Oxford because you want to be the best and are afraid you can't be. You feel like you are a piece of shit from your mother's bottom."

Me: "I'm closing the curtains from now on because people across the street are looking at me. They can hear what I'm saying. They are angry. They want to hurt me."

Mrs. Jones: "You are evacuating your angry and hostile feelings onto those people. It is you who are angry and critical. And you want to control what goes on in here."

Me: "I *am* in control. I control the world. The world is at my whim. I control the world and everything in it."

Mrs. Jones: "You want to feel in control because in fact you feel so helpless."

Me: "I had a dream. I was making golf balls out of fetuses."

Mrs. Jones: "You want to kill babies, you see, and then make a game out of it. You are jealous of the other babies. Jealous of your brothers, jealous of my other patients. You want to kill them. And then you want to turn them into a little ball so you can smack them again. You want your mother and me to love only you."

While the content of what Mrs. Jones said to me was not always a comfort (more often than not, it was startling, and had the effect of catching me up short), her presence in the room was. So calm, so reasonable, no matter what bizarre words and images she or I used. No matter what I said to her, no matter how disgusting or horrible, she never recoiled from what I said. To her, my thoughts and feelings were not right or wrong, good or bad; they just were.

I must have looked an odd sight around the Oxford campus, making my appointed rounds in solitude, still occasionally muttering to myself, still lapsing (badly) in self-care, forgetting to eat, thin enough for a good strong wind to blow me away, and always, always, burdened with a large bag of books. In the bag were the texts I needed for my academic studies, of course, but others as well: psychiatry books; abnormal psychology books; a book on suicide that Dr. Hamilton had recommended months before; a book by Dr. Storr on the personality types that often were the underpinnings of actual mental illness ("depressive" and "paranoid" were two that particularly resonated with me).

Because the odd thing was, I didn't think I was particularly crazy, or that what I often thought or felt was unique to me. Instead, I had come to believe that everyone had these thoughts or feelings, this sense of a force or evil energy pushing on them to do evil or be destructive. The difference was, they all knew how to manage it, how to hide it, how to control it, because that was the socially appropriate thing to do. They had stronger wills, and better coping skills, than I did. They knew how to keep their demons in check; I did not. But perhaps I could learn.

As my sessions with Mrs. Jones increased, and I became accustomed to spooling out the strange products of my mind, my paranoia began to shift. Although the nameless, faceless creatures from the sky had no less power over my fears and thoughts, the actual human people in my daily comings and goings seemed less scary and more approachable. No longer a faceless, threatening mass, existing only to judge or possibly harm me (or be targets for me to harm), they were becoming individual persons— human beings, as I was—vulnerable, and interesting, perhaps with something in common with me, possibly even friendship. Slowly, I made one friend, and then two. One evening, I had a companion for a lecture; a few days later, I went to a small dinner party. Blinking and shaky (as though I'd been in a cave, and the light, as welcome as it was, was something I'd have to get used to), I began to move back into the world again.

* * *

As helpful as my relationship with Mrs. Jones was proving to be, the intensity of what I was feeling for her opened some kind of door, and the psychotic thoughts marched right through it, growing more and more violent every session.

Me: "I had a dream. My mother and I are standing outside. We hear an explosion and look off into the distance. We see a mushroom cloud. My mother and I embrace, crying, telling each other that we love each other. Then we both killed."

Mrs. Jones: "You rage is so great that you destroy the planet. And your mother—and I—we do not protect you. You hate us for that. Your hateful feelings cause the world to explode. You tell your mother that you love her, and you want to make contact with her and with me. But then your rage kills everyone off."

Soon, Mrs. Jones herself became the overt object of my fantasies. Notwithstanding Freud, my psychosis had not gotten in the way of my developing an intense transference to her, and that transference was not pretty. "I know you say you are my analyst," I snarled at her one afternoon. "But I also know the truth. You are an evil monster, perhaps the devil. I won't let you kill me. You are evil, a witch. I'll fight."

She never even stirred in her chair, and her reply was measured in tone. "You have hateful feelings toward me, Elyn. You hate that I know things that you don't know. You hate that you feel you need me. You put your hateful feelings in me and that's why you think I am dangerous. You fear that bad part of yourself."

"Are you trying to kill me?" I hissed. "I know about the bombs. I can make a bomb, too. You are the devil. You are trying to kill me. I am evil. I've killed you three times today. I can do it again. Don't cross me. I've killed hundreds of thousands of people with my thoughts."

Psychotic people who are paranoid do scary things because they are scared. And when you're both psychotic and paranoid, it's like that sweaty midnight moment when you sit bolt upright in your bed from a nightmare that you don't yet know isn't real. But this nightmare went on all through the daylight as well. The closer I felt to Mrs. Jones, the more terrified I became: She was going to hurt me. Maybe she was even going to attempt to kill me. I needed to take steps to prevent that from happening.

Walking by kitchen stores, I stared through the display windows at the knives, thinking that I should buy one and take it to my next session. Once, I even went into a hardware store to look at the axes, wondering which one, if any, might protect me. For a while, I carried a serrated kitchen knife and a box cutter in my purse to my sessions—just in case. She is evil and she is dangerous. She keeps killing me. She is a monster. I must kill her, or threaten her, to stop her from doing evil things to me. It will be a blessing for all the other people she is hurting.

At the very same time I was terrified of Mrs. Jones, I was equally terrified I was going to lose her, so much so that I could barely tolerate weekends when I would not see her for two days. I'd start to unravel on Thursday and be nearly inconsolable until Tuesday. In the intervening time, it took everything I had to protect myself—and my friends—from what was going on in my head: "Yes, of course, let's get a hamburger, OK, let's discuss that book we both read," all the while plotting ways to keep Mrs. Jones from abandoning me: I will kidnap her and keep her tied up in my closet. I will take good care of her. I will give her food and clothes. She will always be there when I need her to give me psychoanalysis.

And then, once back in her office again, I'd tell her every single evil thing.

Me: "I will not let you go on vacation this year. I have a weapon. I will take you to my room and put you in my closet. You will stay with me. You will not have a choice. I won't let you go. Throw. So."

Her: "You feel absolutely dependent on me, like a baby, and that makes you angry. You imagine ways to keep me near you, and some of these ways have violence in them, so that you will show me that you are stronger than I am."

Her tolerance and understanding seemed endless, and her steady and calm presence contained me, as if she were the glue that held me together. I was falling apart, flying apart, exploding—and the gathered my pieces and held them for me.

Psychosis is like an insidious infection that nevertheless leaves some of your faculties intact; in a psychiatric hospital, for example, even the most debilitated schizophrenic patients show up on time for meals, and they evacuate the ward when the firm alarm goes off. So it was for me. Completely delusional, I still understood essential aspects of how the world worked. For example, I was getting my schoolwork done, and I vaguely understood the rule that in a social setting, even with the people I most trusted, I could not ramble on about my psychotic thoughts. To talk about killing children, or burning whole worlds, or being able to destroy cities with my mind was not part of polite conversation.

At times, though, I was so psychotic that I could barely contain myself. The delusions expanded into full-blown hallucinations, in which I could clearly hear people whispering. I could hear my name being called when no one was physically around—in a corner of the library, or late at night, in my bedroom where I slept alone. Sometimes, the noise I heard was so overwhelming it drowned out almost all other sound. Stop, stop, stop. No. Stop. Days went by when I simply could not bear to be around anyone; unless I was with Mrs. Jones, I stayed alone in my room, with the door locked and my lights out.

"Elyn, are you angry with me?" asked Sam one afternoon.

"No," I said. "Why?"

"Because you're avoiding me. You didn't come out to dinner with us, you didn't answer your door last night or the night before, and right now, you're scowling at me."

It's because I can't hear you, I wanted to tell him. It's louder than you, and if my energy goes to you, I won't have any left to fight it. I will not be able to keep it at bay. You will be in danger. We will all be in terrible danger. I was just enough in the real world to know that what I was thinking much of the time wasn't real—or at least it wouldn't be real to him.

Think about having a bad flu, on a day when you can't stay home huddled under the covers. You have business, you have responsibilities. And so, summoning up reserves you didn't know you had, you somehow make it through the day, sweating, shaking, nodding politely to colleagues while barely controlling the nausea—because you know that if you can just pull it off, then you can go home, where your couch (or your bed, or a hot bath, or whatever you define as comfort and safety) is waiting. You hold it together, and then, once you're home, you collapse. For two straight years, I did my work, met my obligations, made it through the day as best I could, and then fled to Mrs. Jones, where I promptly took the chains off my mind and fell apart.

D. TREATMENT OUTCOMES

The determination of treatment efficacy is obviously a critical one for both the patient and society. The efficacy of biological treatments has been studied in greater detail than the efficacy of the non-biological therapies. In part this is because the federal Food and Drug Administration has to review all drugs, including psychotropic drugs, for safety and efficacy before they can be marketed. The section that follows summarizes a series of studies of the efficacy of various modalities used to treat the most common mental disorders. Some compare the relative benefits and downsides of two different therapies—either two psychotherapies or one psychotherapeutic technique compared to a medication regime. As you will note, some of the cited studies come to diametrically different results when comparing the same two modalities. The essential reason for these differences is the inherent limitations of the evaluation process when it involves mental disorder treatment methodologies.

The investigation of a treatment modality ideally involves the use of a double blind experimental design. Typically this entails randomly dividing the research subjects who manifest the same disorder into two separate groups. One group is administered the treatment modality being tested, another group does not receive the investigational treatment (the control group). At the conclusion of the test period the groups are compared with respect to positive and negative reactions to the intervention. The double blind design can only be employed reliably when (1) all the test subjects have the same symptoms at the start; (2) each therapy being studied is standardized so it can be consistently applied within the study groups; and (3) there are clear and unambiguous outcome markers. The latter refers to outcome features—for instance, a reduction of fever or white cell count or any other characteristic that is unambiguous and will be judged the same way by any qualified evaluator.

In the absence of a double blind methodology, authoritative evaluation of mental disorder therapies is problematic. At the same time, for mental disorder therapies, the double blind research design is not generally achievable. For one thing, as elaborated in Part II of this chapter, except for a limited number of severe disorders such as schizophrenia, there is all too often little agreement among experts as to a diagnosis. Very frequently the range of symptoms exhibited by an individual makes it difficult to assign a particular diagnosis. As a result the cohorts being tested lack the precise common characteristics needed for a reliable double blind test procedure.

The second requirement—uniformity of the treatment modality—is difficult to achieve in the case of psychotherapies. As previously noted, there are significant variations in the way individual therapists use and apply a particular therapeutic technique. As a result the evaluation of a particular psychotherapy will lack reliability since it will sometimes be difficult to match a particular outcome with a specific therapeutic approach. This problem is not likely to present itself where the therapy being evaluated is a psychopharmacological agent since the "input" is a standardized one.

Finally, any evaluation of the curative effects on a mental disorder of a particular intervention will encounter an unavoidable methodological problem in that the measurement of outcome (no effect, improvement, or negative impact) is complicated by the lack verifiable indices of amelioration or improvement. With few exceptions mental disorders have no physiologically verifiable symptoms. Any assessment of an individual's condition must therefore depend entirely on self-reporting by the patient or observations of behavioral signs by the researcher. However, both of these indices will have a subjective element, which will limit the reliability of any finding or conclusion. Any self reporting reaction or feeling by the research subject is inherently subjective. Also, given the subtleties of behavior it will generally be difficult, if not impossible, to develop rating scales of observable behavior that are methodologically rigorous. For instance, if the item to be observed is the mood of the subject at a given point of time on some sort of a scale, different evaluators are likely to reach variable conclusions. This is because mood will be manifested by subtle outward signs that defy clear categorization in terms of a rating scale. It is only when the behavioral signs are extreme such as, for instance, wild gesticulations or verbal expressions not directed to any person in the immediate area that the behavioral evaluation by different evaluators will achieve a reasonable level of uniformity.

In spite of these challenges in the evaluation process, researchers have sought over the years to evaluate both individual therapies and groups of competing therapies. As might be expected given the methodological limitations described above the studies do not reach consistent result in some instances. Nevertheless, as a group they may provide general guidance as to the utility of various therapeutic approaches for the treatment of particular mental disorders.

1. *Psychotropic Medication*

Studies indicate that when effectiveness is defined as a greater than 50% decrease in the Hamilton Rating Scale for Depression, antidepressant medications are effective in about two-thirds of the patient population. Depending on the specific antidepressant used, tricyclics have effectiveness rates of between 60–68% and SSRIs of between 45–79%. MAOIs have an effectiveness rate of about 65%. See generally Jan Fawcett & Robert Barkin, "Efficacy Issues With Antidepressants," 58 J. Clin Psychiatry Supp. (6)32 (1997). Compliance with the drug regimen is important: 65% of patients who stop treatment relapse within a year compared with 15% of those who continue with drug treatment. See Somitra Pathare & Carol Paton, "Psychotropic Drug Treatment," 315 British Medical Journal 661 (1997).

Pharmacological treatment for other conditions also shows promise. It is estimated that 70 to 90% of individuals with severe panic disorder will respond to either benzodiazepines or antidepressants. Benzodiazepines have been shown to be effective in treating not only panic disorder but also generalized anxiety. Jacques Bradwein, "Benzodiazepines for the Treatment of Panic Disorder and Generalized Anxiety Disorder: Clinical Issues and Future Directions," 38 Can. J. Psychiatry Supp. (4) S109 (1993). As for bipolar disease, approximately 75% of sufferers respond to lithium, carbemazepine, or a combination of ancillary medications. E. Fuller Torrey, Out of the Shadows 5–6 (1997). And stimulant drugs as a treatment for ADHD produce a response rate of about 70%. It is not clear, however, whether pharmacotherapy alone produces long-term improvement in any domain of functioning with ADHD. Larry Goldman et al., "Diagnosis and Treatment of Attention–Deficit/Hyperactivity Disorder in Children and Adolescents," 279 JAMA 1100 (1998).

Finally, antipsychotic medications mitigate symptoms in about 75% of people with schizophrenia. But 15–20% of these individuals experience a relapse within any given year. Margie Patlak, "Schizophrenia: Real Lives, Imaginary Terror," 31(6) FDA Consumer 23 (1997). Indeed, some evidence suggests that the drugs make patients more likely to have psychotic episodes over the long term. John R. Bola et al., "Treatment of Acute Psychosis Without Neuroleptics: Two-Year Outcomes from the Soteria Project, 191 J. Nerv. & Men. Dis. 219, 224–25 (2003). The efficacy of the atypical drugs has also been questioned. A review of 52 studies involving 12,649 patients concluded that "[t]here is no clear evidence that atypical antipsychotics are more effective or are better tolerated than conventional antipsychotics." John Geddes et al., "Atypical Antipsychotics in the Treatment of Schizophrenia: Systematic Overview and Meta-Regression Analysis," 321 Brit. Med. J. 1371 (2000). Another review concluded that "[f]irst generation antipsychotics were associated with lower total mental health care costs in 2 of 3 studies on chronically ill patients, but were also associated with more ... side effects." Erik Johnsen & Hugo A. Jorgensen, "Effectiveness of Second Generation Antipsychotics: A Systematic Review of Randomized Trials," www.medscape.com/viewarticle/575468_1 (2008).

2. Non-biological Therapies

As noted earlier, efficacy of evaluations of psychotherapies confronts special methodological problems that generally will preclude definitive assessments. At the same time, these studies may point to patterns that in the aggregate may have probative value. The following excerpt from a leading psychiatric textbook summarizes a number of efficacy studies:

EFFICACY ISSUES

Many people identify the beginning of the critical evaluation of psychotherapy outcome research with the review by Eysenck (1952), which was based on 24 reports that he collected from various sources, most of which did not describe any controlled investigations of psychotherapy. [Eysenck concluded that the effectiveness of psychotherapy did not exceed the spontaneous remission rate.—Ed.] The arguments were indirect and inferential, and statistics were uncritically pooled. Instead of being ignored, the review, which threw doubt on the efficacy of psychotherapy, stimulated despair, anger, criticism, and rebuttals. Despite the belief of some that Eysenck's arguments have been undermined and defeated, it is interesting to note that a paper published in 1980 in a prestigious psychological journal has essentially resurrected Eysenck's critique and argued that his claims have never been adequately dealt with.

To illustrate some of the diversity of opinion resulting from the various reviews of the literature, a number of authors may be quoted or cited. In 1964, Cross stated that the "efficacy [of psychotherapy] has not been scientifically demonstrated beyond a reasonable doubt." In 1966, after reviewing 14 controlled studies of psychotherapy, Dittman stated that his own "conclusions are modest, and are, moreover, diluted by confusion." On a more optimistic note, Meltzoff and Kornreich (1970) concluded that "controlled research has been notably successful in demonstrating more behavioral change in treated patients than in untreated controls." More cautiously, Bergin (1971) stated that "psychotherapy, as practiced over the last 40 years, has had an average effect that is modestly positive." Malen (1973) arrived at a mixed conclusion after his review of the literature. He stated that "there is considerable evidence that dynamic psychotherapy is effective in psychosomatic conditions; but, that the evidence in favor of dynamic psychotherapy * * * [for] neurosis and character disorders * * * is weak * * *."

The review by Luborsky et al. (1975) concludes that "everyone has won and all must have prizes," meaning that no one psychotherapy is more effective than any other. Frank (1979) concludes from his review of the literature that "psychotherapy * * * [is] more effective than informal, unplanned help."

Controlled Studies

Over the years, the general trend has been for the recent and more comprehensive reviews to conclude that psychotherapy is effective for a variety of symptomatic and behavioral problems, i.e., chronic moderate anxiety states, simple phobias, depressive symptoms, sexual dysfunctions, adjustment disorders, family conflicts, and communication difficulties.

A large number of studies have been concerned with combined treatment for various diagnostic conditions. Research on schizophrenia has not shown that traditional psychotherapies significantly enhance the benefit of pharmacotherapy, but the effects of the psychotherapy are much more difficult to quantify than are the drug effects. However, token economy therapies and psychosocial rehabilitation are valuable as an adjunct treatment for schizophrenics. Studies of drug/psychotherapy interactions for major affective disorders reveal that psychotherapy for some depressed patients produced better results and that the effects of psychotherapy plus drugs are basically additive in treating depression. Studies of psychotherapy for medically ill patients suggest that psychotherapy plus a medical regimen is more effective in influencing some of the target symptoms for certain medical illnesses than is medical treatment alone. Psychotherapy is especially useful for post-illness psychosocial rehabilitation. A general conclusion about interaction effects is that drugs affect symptoms relatively early whereas psychotherapy has an influence on interpersonal relations and social adjustment, especially at a later stage of treatment.

* * *

Although a number of papers have proposed the possibility of deterioration effects due to psychotherapy and anecdotes on this topic have been reported by clinicians, research data on the subject are limited. In addition, the idea of negative effects is fraught with conceptual as well as research problems. The most extensive review of this literature comes to the conclusion that about five percent of patients in psychotherapy get worse (Sloane et al., 1975).

* * *

Controversy still reigns over the question of whether certain types of therapy are more effective than other types for certain kinds of problems. Another issue that also has not been adequately studied is what aspects or elements of the complex therapeutic interaction are relatively the most effective. Then there is the question of spontaneous remission, which may be high in certain conditions.

In addition, the comparability of therapies bearing the same generic labels has been challenged, and many investigators have noted that relatively little is known about the actual process of psychotherapy and about the degree of variation that exists in the way it is carried out. Attempts are now being made to create manuals designed to provide guidelines for the therapist on the conduct of different modes of therapy. Such guidelines may be useful in controlled research settings but are believed by many clinicians to be largely unsuitable to the operation of their day-to-day practice. It is unclear at the present time whether this apparent conflict between the research demands of reproducibility and standardization will ever be reconciled with the clinicians' need for flexibility, creativity, and sensitivity to the uniqueness of individual patients.

The Psychiatric Therapies 834–36, T.B. Karasu, ed. (1984).

Questions and Comments

1. *Effectiveness of psychotherapy compared to no treatment.* The Luborsky survey cited in the material excerpted above reviewed 33 different studies. Sixty percent of these studies indicated that psychosocial therapies were superior to no treatment, while 40% found no significant difference. See Luborsky et al., "Comparative Studies of Psychotherapies, 'Is it True that Everyone Has Won and All Must Have Prizes?'" 32 Arch. Gen. Psych. 995 (1975).

2. *Comparison of efficacy of psychotherapy and medication.* A number of studies have attempted to quantify the efficacy of the non-biological therapies. In 1989, the National Institute of Mental Health conducted the first comprehensive federally funded effort to investigate the efficacy of various mental health treatment modalities for depression. The study, which randomized depressed subjects to short-term psychotherapy (both behavior therapy and more traditional interpersonal psychotherapy), pharmacotherapy, and a control group found that depressed patients who saw a trained psychotherapist were better off 18 months later than those who didn't receive psychotherapy. The group treated with psychotherapy did not, however, do as well as the group given standard anti-depressant drug treatment. Jerry E. Bishop, "Psychotherapy Has Measurable Effect On Depression in Closely Watched Test," Wall St. J., Nov. 13, 1989, at B4. However, a more recent study found that cognitive-behavior therapy is at least as effective in treating depression as medication This study of 240 moderately to severely depressed people found that, after two months, improvement occurred in 47% of the group receiving cognitive therapy (16 weeks of weekly two-hour sessions), 50% of the group receiving medication (Paxil), and 25% of the placebo patients. After four months the response rates of the first two groups were identical (57%), and after 16 weeks only 25% of the first group (which received "booster" sessions) relapsed, compared to 40% of those on medication. Sharon Beglely, "In NIMH Study, Therapy Works as Well as Drugs for Depression," N.Y. Times, May 24, 2002 at B1. See also Steven D. Hollon, "Psychotherapy and Pharmacotherapy: Efficacy, Generalizability, and Cost–Effectiveness," in Cost–Effectiveness of Psychotherapy: A Guide for Practitioners, Researchers and Policymakers 14, 17 (Nancy E. Miller & Kathryn M. Magruder eds., 1999).

3. *Comparison of various psychotherapies.* Some recent studies have sought to compare the relative efficacy of behavioral therapy with other psychosocial interventions. Unlike earlier studies, some of this recent research suggests that behavioral oriented therapies have a longer lasting effect than other psychosocial interventions. See Steven Hollon & Aaron Beck, "Cognitive and Cognitive–Behavioral Therapies," in Handbook of

Psychotherapy and Behavior Change 428 (A. Bergen and S. Garfields eds., 4th ed., 1994).

4. *Efficacy of combined biological and psychotherapies.* A number of studies have compared the relative efficacies of psychotherapy and "combined therapy" (psychotherapy teamed with pharmacotherapy) in treating mental illness. A meta-analysis of six such studies in the area of depression found that while combined therapy is not significantly more effective than psychotherapy alone for milder depression, it is much more effective than psychotherapy alone for treating more severe recurrent depression. Michael Thase et al., "Treatment of Major Depression with Psychotherapy or Psychotherapy–Pharmacotherapy Combinations," 54 Arch. Gen. Psych. 1009 (1997).

5. *Efforts to reconcile biological and psychoanalytic models of mental processes and treatment.* Psychoanalysts, once vocal critics of psychopharmacology, increasingly rely on a combination of medication and psychoanalytically oriented therapy. According to one survey, 90% of the psychoanalysts who responded commonly prescribed psychotropics. Kaplan & Sadock, *supra*, at 2227. At the same time, psychoanalysts usually do not consider medication to be the primary treatment. Consider this brief description of "neuropsychoanalysis," a discipline that tries to integrate psychoanalytic insights and brain research:

> Neuropsychoanalysts ... are not trying to demonstrate that all (or even most) of Freud's ideas were right. A dream doesn't necessarily represent a repressed wish, and no one thinks brain imaging will find evidence for penis envy or even the existence of an ego, id, and superego locked in an unending tug-of-war. But neuropsychoanalysts contend that Freud's view of the mind, despite its many flaws, remains the richest one yet developed. And even as they welcome advances in neuroscience, they are also wary of the field's impact. Like psychotherapists of all stripes, [neuropsychoanalysts are] worry that brain research is encouraging a biological reductionism in which psychiatrists focus exclusively on neurotransmitters and drugs. "The structure of the human personality has not traditionally been on the agenda of most neuroscientists," says [one neuropsychoanalyst].

Joshua Kendall, "Managed Care Tried to Kill Off Freud: Can Tony Soprano Help Revive Him?" Boston Globe, Feb. 9, 2003, at D1.

IV. THE MENTAL HEALTH PROFESSIONS

A. OVERVIEW

The purveyors of mental health treatment can be classified into three primary groups—psychiatrists (including psychoanalysts), psychologists, and clinical social workers. Until the 1970s, psychiatrists were the dominant providers of mental health care, including both psychosocial therapies and treatments involving the use of psychopharmacology. Today, according to one report, clinical social workers alone account for as much as 65% of all psychotherapy and mental health services. See Jeffrey Cohen, "Managed Care and the Evolving Role of the Clinical

Social Workers in Mental Health," *infra*. Within the mental health treatment system, psychiatrists have increasingly been relegated to the supervision and management of psychopharmacological treatment.

The reasons for these changes in the respective roles of the various professions are complex. In part, they are economically driven, representing a shift of consumers from the more highly priced service provided by medically trained psychiatrists to lower priced service providers. At the same time, as detailed in Chapter 2, these changes also have been affected by court decisions and legislation that have reduced the medical profession's control over the provision of mental health services.

The materials that follow describe the education, training, and general functions of the three primary categories of mental health professionals. It then recounts recent trends that have brought about significant changes in the roles of these professions.

B. PSYCHIATRISTS

1. *Development of the Profession*

The origins of psychiatry lie in the practice of medicine within asylums for the insane where, during the 19th century, physicians attributed the deviant behavior of inmates to diseases of the mind. However, as the following excerpt indicates, psychiatric practice as we know it today is a more recent phenomenon:

> Psychiatry, unlike psychoanalysis, did not begin in the twentieth century, but its influence and eminence are of relatively recent origin. If we view 1844, the founding year of what later became the American Psychiatric Association, as the official birthdate of American psychiatry, it is possible to suggest that psychiatry did not come of age until World War II, when, quite apart from its usefulness in the war, psychiatry became an accepted part of the American scene and even achieved a certain fashionableness. Since this development owes so much to the impact upon psychiatry of Freudian psychoanalysis—one is tempted to credit Freud with both the birth of psychoanalysis and the rebirth of psychiatry—it is conceivable that psychiatry without psychoanalysis would have taken quite a different direction, perhaps back toward the mental hospital from which it emerged more than a century ago, or toward an easier synthesis with other behavioral sciences.

Arnold A. Rogow, The Psychiatrists at 31–32 (1970).

2. *Education and Training*

The definition of who is a psychiatrist or, more important, who is qualified to practice psychiatry is determined at least on a formal level by state law. Under the law of most states *any licensed physician* can practice and render psychiatric treatment. As a practical matter, however, norms imposed by the medical profession itself serve to ensure that the practice of psychiatry is restricted to those physicians who have completed a psychiatric residency program, which is a requirement for membership in the American Psychiatric Association. These informal methods of control are normally exercised at the local level. Thus, only physicians who have completed the residency program and are members of the American Psychiatric Association will receive referrals from other physicians in the community. Similarly, only physicians who are members of the American Psychiatric Association will be accorded hospital privileges which enable them to function as psychiatrists in a hospital setting.

Since only licensed physicians are qualified to become psychiatrists, the training of a psychiatrist necessarily begins with medical school. The psychiatric residency which follows the completion of medical school is normally of three years duration. Residency programs may be either of a generalized nature or specialized in such fields as child or juvenile psychiatry. Residency programs also differ in terms of their theoretical orientation. Some are primarily organically oriented and therefore emphasize biological treatment approaches, principally psychopharmacology. Other programs lean towards psychoanalytic theory, and therefore give more emphasis to treatment that incorporates the analytical model of human behavior. In between are programs which seek to strike a balance between different therapeutic orientations in terms of curriculum and treatment approaches. In spite of some differences in the orientation of particular programs all will normally have a curriculum which includes formal courses and seminars combined with clinical training. As described by one commentator:

> The central core of the curriculum ... usually consists of a didactic program focused on the principles and techniques of psycho-therapy and somato-therapy (shock treatment and drug therapy). Residents generally are involved with patients from the start of training and in addition take courses and seminars concerned with the psychopathology of neuroses and psychoses, clinical neurology, personality development, personality assessment, child psychiatry, psychopharmacology, research problems, and other topics. Much attention is given to interviewing techniques and the skills involved in probing a patient's history and accurately diagnosing his problems * * *.

Arnold A. Rogow, The Psychiatrists at 48 (1970).

As in the cases of other medical specialties psychiatry is subject to an accreditation procedure established under the auspices of relevant medical professional groups. In the case of psychiatry it is the American Board of Psychiatry and Neurology, whose membership is drawn from the American Medical Association, which certifies candidates in either general psychiatry, child psychiatry or neurology. Certification in one of these fields is available to any candidate who passes a rather rigorous examination and has completed a psychiatry residence. Significantly, most practicing psychiatrists are not board certified (the percentage of "board certified" psychiatrists has been variously estimated at between

33 and 48 percent). In fact, certification is only a practical necessity for those psychiatrists who frequently serve as expert witnesses or act as consultants to agencies that require board certification.

In common parlance psychiatrists are frequently confused with psychoanalysts. While these two professional groups overlap in many ways, they are distinct professional categories. Psychoanalysts tend to be psychiatrists who have additional specialized training provided by one of the institutes of the American Psychoanalytic Association. The present structure of the American Psychoanalytic Institute was established in 1933 and is at present a federation of 29 societies and 20 training institutions. Each of these institutes operates its own training program, which is of six to ten years duration. Admission into a training program is decided by an institute committee. Admission generally requires a medical background, though decisions as to admissibility also take into account the personality characteristics of the applicant in terms of his or her suitability for analytic training. The following excerpt describes a typical training program.

> Once admitted for training, the candidate must undergo the preparatory analysis previously noted "four or more times a week" and also carry through a program of assigned reading, lectures, and supervised clinical experience, all of which is designed to provide him with a thorough knowledge of Freud's theories and other relevant psychoanalytic contributions. He is further required to analyze under supervision at least two adult cases, devoting to each a minimum of 150 hours of analysis and "carrying at least one of them through the terminal phase of analysis." It is expected that material from these analyses will be presented by him "in no less than three extended presentations" at clinical conferences, of which he is required to attend at least fifty during his training. At each stage of training his progress is determined by the institute's educational committee. * * * If the candidate successfully completes the training program, he is given a written statement to that effect by the institute, and he may then apply for membership in the American Psychoanalytic Association.

Arnold A. Rogow, The Psychiatrists at 49 (1970).

3. Function

The role and function of a psychiatrist today varies substantially, depending on the professional setting and the theoretical orientation of the psychiatrist. Practice settings range from private office practice to employment within a public or private hospital whose clientele are inpatients. Psychiatric practice may also involve full or part-time affiliation with a community mental health center or general medical group practice (or managed care organization) which offers specialized psychiatric treatment or counseling among other medical services. Psychiatrists practicing in a private office setting will most commonly use a combination of treatment methods, depending on the severity and nature of the disorder. Moreover, psychiatrists engaged in private practices are increasingly affiliating with nonmedical professionals, such as psychologists and psychiatric social workers. In these group practice situations, the treatment function is divided between psychiatrists and non-physicians psychotherapists, with the former having responsibility for initial diagnosis and the management of the medication regime, and the latter involved primarily in supportive psychotherapy. Under this model, psychologists and psychiatric social workers are part of a treatment team with primary responsibility for psychotherapy. Psychiatrists operating as staff members in a psychiatric hospital tend to be primarily be engaged in diagnosis and medication management.

The function of psychiatrists is also significantly influenced by their theoretical orientation. While the division is today less distinct than in earlier times, psychiatrists continue to be divided between two theoretical orientations: those that emphasize the psychoanalytic model, and those who have more of an organic orientation as to the etiology of mental disorders. See Eric Kandel, "A New Intellectual Framework for Psychiatry," 155 Am. J. Psychiatry 457–458 (1998). This theoretical orientation, in turn, influences the type of treatment that is utilized by psychiatrists. Those adhering to the psychoanalytic model are more inclined to favor long-term psychotherapy and somewhat less reliance on psychotropic medication, particularly for the treatment of the nonmajor mental disorders. Psychiatrists who are more organically oriented, on the other hand, tend to favor short-term directive psychotherapy with greater reliance on organic treatment modalities such as psychopharmacology.

C. PSYCHOLOGISTS

1. *Development of the Profession*

The emergence of psychology as one of the treating professions is a relatively recent phenomenon. In fact, from the mid-nineteenth century to the middle 1940's, psychology essentially was an academically based discipline. The following excerpt traces the developments leading to the profession's eventual emergence as a major presence in the psychotherapy field:

> Pre–1940, the bulk of psychologists were employed in institutions of higher learning where they engaged in teaching and conducting research in animal learning behavior and brain behavior relations. It was in the mid–1940s that the psychologist practitioner role within the health field began to emerge in a significant manner. The large-scale employment of clinical and counseling psychologists by the Veterans Administration during the World War II era is widely accepted as providing a significant impetus to the emergence of psychologists as practitioners in the health area. In the mental health area, the initial functioning of the psychologist was within the framework of the mental health team. This was particularly the case within health service delivery systems such as hospitals and

mental health clinics. Such teams usually were comprised of a psychiatrist (who was frequently the team leader), a social worker, a nurse (whose special interest and training were in psychiatric nursing), and usually a clinical psychologist.

Francis R.J. Fields & Rudy J. Horwitz, Psychology and Professional Practice at xi (1982).

Clinical psychology has, since 1950, become a dominant force in the mental health treatment field. In most states, as detailed below, the practice of psychology is open to those holding a doctorate as well as those holding only a Master's degree in psychology. Omitting clinical psychologists who hold only a Master's degree, the number of psychologists (Ph.D. and Psy.D) exceeds the number of practicing psychiatrists by more than 2 to 1. The numerical balance in favor of clinical psychologists is even greater if clinical psychologists who hold only a Master's degree are included.

2. *Education and Training*

There are a number of different types of psychologists, including clinical psychologists, counseling psychologists, industrial psychologists, social psychologists and experimental/research psychologists. The category of most relevance to this book is clinical psychology, which is the largest specialty and is most directly involved in helping people with mental and emotional problems.

Any description of the educational background of clinical psychologists is complicated by the fact that there are no national standards governing the qualifications needed to practice as a clinician. While in most states the practice of psychology is the subject of some form of regulation (see Chapter 2), the licensing criteria differ from state to state. In some, a Ph.D. or Psy.D. degree may be a requisite, while in others a masters degree in psychology is a sufficient credential. Whatever the degree requirement states have not sought to evaluate the sufficiency of individual educational programs. Unlike the formal accreditation criteria that are applied by state licensing agencies to medical schools, there have, up to now, been no comparable efforts to apply accreditation standards to psychology programs. See Introduction to Clinical Psychology 57 (Lynda A. Heiden & Michel Hersen, eds., 1995) [hereinafter Heiden & Hersen]. Any generalization concerning the curricular content of program in psychology is also complicated by the sheer number of programs being offered throughout the country. For instance, there are currently over 200 psychology departments offering a master's degree in psychology which annually award upward of 8,000 Master's degrees. By far the greatest number (80%) of these are in clinical psychology. Heiden & Hersen at 54.

Until 1950, an academic background, and specifically a Ph.D. in psychology, was the primary educational criterion for entry into clinical practice. The Ph.D. programs, at least until 1947, tended to include three major subject areas: diagnostics and testing, research and therapy. Heiden & Hersen, *supra*, at 48. Those in the clinical psychology track were required to complete a one year clinical internship following satisfaction of the general Ph.D. psychology requirements. In response to charges that the traditional Ph.D. programs in psychology were too research oriented, a number of universities, in the early 70's, established a separate Doctorate in Psychology (Psy.D.) This new degree program had a curriculum which emphasized the development of clinical practice skills. Thus, there are today two doctoral routes to the practice of psychology. Though both generally take four years to complete (and sometimes longer), the Psy.D. curriculum is generally more focused on clinical training than the Ph.D. degree, which remains somewhat more research oriented. The 1970's also witnessed an expansion of Master's level psychology programs leading to clinical practice. As described in greater detail in Chapter 2, the scope of practice authorized by law to those holding a Master's degree varies from state to state.

States that regulate the practice of psychology, either by licensing or certification, frequently establish specific educational requirements such as the holding of either a Master's or Doctorate degree. At the same time, as noted above, state regulatory agencies do not attempt to provide any accreditation standards for degree programs. As a consequence, the only educational credentials issue is whether the applicant for licensing or certification in fact holds the requisite degree. While there is no official accreditation of educational programs by the states, professional organizations such as the American Psychological Association (A.P.A.) have adopted an accreditation process with specific requirements. The A.P.A.'s accreditation of programs, while not legally binding for purposes of regulation, does influence an applicant's job prospects. For instance, the Veterans Administration, which is the largest employer of psychologists in the United States, will only employ psychologists who have earned a Ph.D. or Psy.D. from a program accredited by the A.P.A.

3. *Function*

While a primary function of psychologists in earlier years was psychological assessment and diagnosis, psychologists today are increasingly engaged in psychotherapy either as part of a team or independently. Even today, however, an important part of the work of psychologists involves psychological assessment. The assessment process typically involves the administration and interpretation of standardized tests such as the MMPI (Minnesota Multi-phasic Personality Inventory) and intelligence tests as well as diagnosis based on more subjective impressions.

These assessment functions are not necessary performed in a context of mental health treatment and therapy. For instance, personality assessments and intelligence tests administered by psychologists are also utilized as a screening device by employers or by domestic relations courts when child custody is an issue. Nevertheless, as noted, the traditional function of psychologists as diagnosticians is giving way to a greater role in the provision of psychotherapy.

As in the case of psychiatrists, different theoretical orientations lead to differences among psychologists in their treatment approaches. For instance, those who adhere to the Freudian model tend to rely on psychoanalytic techniques or "dynamically oriented" psychotherapy. Others may employ "cognitive" therapy approaches. Those who are behaviorally oriented tend to focus on specific abnormal patterns, and use learning theory to "decondition" maladaptive behavior.

D. CLINICAL SOCIAL WORKERS

1. *Education and Training*

Psychiatric social work is a subspeciality of social work and, as such, developed later than either psychiatry or clinical psychology. A psychiatric social worker typically will have a Master of Social Work (M.S.W.) from an accredited school of social work. The degree requires a minimum of two years graduate study after college, including a field placement in the community. The focus of study includes individual development and behavior, the dynamics of families, the techniques of individual, group and family therapy, and the use of community resources for disturbed patients.

2. *Function*

As this curriculum suggests, psychiatric social workers are often concerned with the relationship of people to their family and community. They are usually heavily involved in evaluation, treatment, and monitoring of people with mental problems. They often operate as part of a treatment team, although increasingly they function independently in private practice, with over 20% now engaged in such practice.

The primary reason for the latter development has been states' willingness to license social workers. Licensure gave social workers credibility and entitlement to third-party reimbursement. A second reason social workers have become more independent is explored in the next section.

E. THE INTERACTION OF THE PROFESSIONS IN AN ERA OF MANAGED CARE

Managed care, which is discussed in detail in the next section of this chapter, is the provision of health services that are paid for by a third party (either the government or an insurance company) and that are ultimately governed by the third party rather than the mental health professional and the patient. The following excerpt explores some of the effects managed care has had on the three professions just described.

JEFFREY COHEN

Managed Care and the Evolving Role of the Clinical
Social Worker in Mental Health.
48 Social Work 34 (2003).

... As recently as 1960, before the onset of managed mental health care, the roles of psychiatrists, psychologists, and clinical social workers tended to be distinct. Psychiatrists had the overall responsibility of patient care, conducted psychotherapy, prescribed medication, and supervised hospital care. Clinical psychologists conducted testing and provided group therapy and other therapeutic modalities in institutions and hospitals. Clinical social workers performed comprehensive psychosocial assessments, counseled regarding family issues, and created discharge plans for patients in social services agencies. At that time, the mental health field was far from overcrowded.

By the mid–1970s the number of clinical social workers providing mental health treatment in the United States had grown, almost equaling the number of psychiatrists. Both professions had almost twice the number of clinical psychologists. In the subsequent 15 years, clinical social workers and clinical psychologists tripled their numbers, while the number of psychiatrists grew by less than 40 percent. With the increased number of nonpsychiatric practitioners, along with the introduction of psychotropic medication, the role of the psychiatrist shifted. As psychopharmacology, biology, genetics, and hard science influenced psychiatry, psychiatrists began to withdraw from psychotherapy. Psychiatric practice instead shifted its primary focus to patients in need of psychopharmacological agents, with psychiatrists prescribing and monitoring medication use and administering medical procedures such as electroconvulsive therapy (ECT).

With psychiatrists' shift in emphasis, clinical social workers and clinical psychologists assumed more responsibility in mental health treatment, and psychotherapy, in particular. The proliferation of managed care companies during the 1980s furthered the increased involvement of clinical social workers and clinical psychologists. Because of improved training and the less-expensive nature of their services, clinical social workers and clinical psychologists were more involved in providing psychotherapy to patients suffering from mental illness.... For some time, clinical social workers have performed the largest portion of psychotherapeutic work done in the United States. Clinical social workers provide as much as 65 percent of all psychotherapy and mental health services.

... With managed care's influence, psychiatrists are being replaced by nonmedical practitioners in many domains of mental health treatment in which they once predominated. Psychiatrists are being forced into new practice arrangements and roles, such as consultants for multidisciplinary groups. Psychiatrists are also increasingly being limited to dealing with patients with the most severe mental disorders, which tend to involve the use of medication and need for prescription privilege. Past responsibilities of long-term therapy and treatment aimed at overcoming problems that diminish patients' quality of life have given way to treatment of such cases as serious psychotic disorders, with threat to life and risk of decompensation deemed the main reasons for their involvement.

The new trend of using clinical social workers in place of clinical psychologists and psychiatrists by managed care companies has touched off territorial disputes among practitioners in the mental health field. As the mental health professions compete for the same health care dollars, each profession guards its turf, protecting itself by defining responsibilities it is uniquely qualified to perform, and, at the same time, vying for the right to expand services. For example, as the number of clinical social workers has grown in the area of psychotherapeutic treatment, clinical psychologists have lobbied for prescription and full hospital privileges, which historically have been reserved for psychiatrists. Clinical psychologists reason that they could serve as a less-expensive replacement for psychiatrists, or even provide both psychotherapeutic and psychopharmacological treatment to patients [prescription privileges for psychologists is discussed in detail in Chapter 2, Prescription Privileges]. As managed care companies pass psychologists over for less-expensive clinical social workers, the lack of differentiation among mental health professionals by managed care companies undoubtedly frustrates clinical psychologists.

. . . As managed care companies continue to reduce reimbursement dollars, changes in multidisciplinary team structures are inevitable, with even more reliance on master's-level service providers. Practitioner distinctions already have begun to diminish in favor of more team-oriented models, with the boundaries between the uniqueness of the individual disciplines beginning to blur. Psychiatrists often head the team, coordinating services in conjunction with psychotherapists and other mental health care providers on the treatment team. However, it is not unusual for a clinical psychologist or even a clinical social worker to lead the team, with the psychiatrist relegated to the role of psychopharmacology consultant rather than an active team member.

. . . In the future, indicators suggest that nonpsychiatric practitioners will emerge as the dominant providers of treatment. . . . [M]anaged care companies will expect nonmedical practitioners, such as clinical social workers to provide the bulk of outpatient care in the mental health care field. . . . Distinctions between master's-level and doctoral-level providers will become more evident as master's-level practitioners assume primary responsibility for direct mental health services, and doctoral-level providers assume more administrative, supervisory, and research-oriented roles. The rapid increase in managed care's influence, accompanied by the reduction of referrals to more expensive specialists, suggests that demand for clinical psychologists will continue to diminish. As managed health care organizations restrict consumer choice of providers, many mental health professionals, such as clinical psychologists, may have difficulty joining reimbursement plans.

Despite the shift away from doctoral-level providers and the narrowing role of the medical practitioner in the treatment regime of managed care companies, psychiatrists will likely have an essential and continuing role in the mental health care system. [M]anaged mental health care still needs medical practitioners for their knowledge of psychopharmacology and experience in prescribing medications. . . . The distance between the domains of psychotherapists and psychopharmacologists will continue to widen, however, as psychiatrists undoubtedly will continue to be the most-expensive mental health professionals. Psychotherapy has already become a predominantly nonmedical activity, and there is every indication that this trend will continue until the medically trained therapist becomes rare. Some practitioners (for example, psychiatric nurses) who are not psychiatrists can circumvent the barrier to their prescribing drugs through an alliance with a psychiatrist. This practice is likely to increase in frequency, further narrowing the role of the psychiatrist and widening the gap between the medical and nonmedical mental health practitioner. . . .

Questions and Comments

1. *Pay scales.* The excerpt notes that psychiatrists are the most expensive type of mental health care provider. According to the 2002–03 edition of the U.S. Labor Department's Occupational Outlook Handbook, the average annual salary of psychiatrists is $130,000, while psychologists average $50,000 and social workers $30,000.

2. *Other clinical disciplines.* Mental health services are also provided to limited extent by psychiatric nurses. Under the law of some states, psychiatric nurses have limited prescription privileges.

Additionally, clergy, school counselors, and marriage and family counselors provide counseling that, to some extent, could be considered mental health treatment. As far back as 1985, one commentary suggested that the latter group was challenging social workers in their field of specialty, noting that, in California, there were already 16,000 marriage and family counselors. See "Social Workers Vault into a Leading Role in Psychotherapy," N.Y. Times, April 30, 1985, at 20, col. 4.

3. *Patient's choice of professions.* The discussion in the preceding section is based upon the premise that the mental health field is made up of different professional categories and that the consumer need only elect the one that most closely fits his needs. In reality, however, prospective patients may have their choice circumscribed by economic or related factors. For instance, state licensing laws have had a significant influence on the public's use of one rather than another category of professional. There has been an increasing tendency on the part of the disfavored professions to seek relief through legislative or judicial channels. The nature of these initiatives is considered in Chapter Two, part II (Issues in the Allocation of Function Among the Mental Health Professions). In addition, as discussed in the section which follows, if a patient is enrolled in a managed care organization

("MCO"), the MCO will most likely dictate the professional category of the therapist. In general, MCOs are likely to authorize the use of high-cost psychiatrists only for biological therapies.

Aside from insurance considerations, the choice of a therapist will be influenced by the overall economic circumstances of the patient. Those of limited means are likely to be more sensitive to differences in the fee structure of the respective professions and consequently are more likely to seek the services of auxiliary mental health professionals rather than psychiatrists or certified psychologists.

Those who do not qualify under any insurance program and do not have private resources may need to rely on the subsidized services provided by community mental health centers. Here, the patients' opportunity to select a particular professional category to provide treatment may be restricted by staff availability or by the assignment practices of the center.

4. *Legal system influence on the allocation of function.* The role of the respective mental health professions has also been influenced by the action of state legislatures and courts. The legislation and court decisions affecting these changes are detailed in Chapter 2, part II (Issues in the Allocation of Function Among Professions).

V. MENTAL HEALTH CARE FINANCE: THE PROBLEMS OF COST AND COVERAGE

A. AN OVERVIEW OF MENTAL HEALTH CARE FINANCE

The subject of how mental health treatment is financed is a complex one. In part, this is because mental health services are provided by a tremendous variety of different institutions, both public and private. These institutions include: psychiatric hospitals, both public and private; general hospitals; community-based supported living arrangements; private office-based practices; nursing homes; correctional facilities; and school-based counseling services. A 1999 report issued by the U.S. Surgeon General termed this collection of loosely coordinated facilities and services the "de facto mental health service system." The Surgeon General's report estimated that 15% of U.S. adults and 21% of U.S. children and adolescents use the de facto system every year.

During the period from 1986 to 2003, the average annual nominal growth in mental health treatment expenditures was 6.7%. In comparison, total health care expenditures increased by 8.0% annually. Because of the slower growth rate of mental health expenditures, mental health spending fell from 8% of the total health care budget in 1986 to 6% in 2003. During this time period, the mix of services also changed, with more care provided in outpatient settings and through the administration of prescription drugs. Tami Mark et al., Mental Health Treatment Expenditure Trends, 1986–2003, 58 Psychiatric Services 1041 (2007).

1. *Public Finance*

One notable feature of mental health care finance is the predominance of the public sector—that is, federal, state, and local government funding—particularly for individuals with serious mental illness. In 2003, the public sector paid for 58% of all mental health costs. The centrality of the public sector is unsurprising, given that many individuals with serious mental illness often incur high medical costs and are unable to secure private sector health insurance through a full-time job.

Through much of the 20th century, individuals with serious mental illness were institutionalized in state mental hospitals. (For a discussion of the legal standards used for civil commitment in the early to mid 20th century, see Chapter 8.) In 1955, for example, state psychiatric hospitals housed more than half a million individuals with serious mental illness. Although these hospitals were intended to be an improvement over the 19th century practice of housing the mentally ill in prisons and jails, conditions in these hospitals were generally abysmal. See Albert Deutsch, The Shame of the States 41–42 (1948). By the early 1960s, reform-oriented activists had attracted national political attention to the concept of a community-based model for delivery of mental health services. In 1963, Congress passed the Community Mental Health Centers (CMHC) Act. Until it was substantially revised during the Reagan Administration, this Act made federal funds for community mental health centers directly available to non-profit community groups. The move away from state psychiatric hospitals was substantially accelerated by the 1965 passage of Medicaid and Medicare.

From the outset, both Medicaid and Medicare have imposed significant restrictions on their coverage of services at so-called "institutions for mental disease" (IMDs)—that is, hospitals or nursing facilities of more than 16 beds that are "primarily engaged in providing diagnosis, treatment, or care of persons with mental diseases . . . " Medicaid will cover inpatient services at IMDs only if the recipient is under 21 or over 65. 42 U.S.C. § 1396d(a)(xi)(1), 4(A), (14), (16). Medicare has a 190–day lifetime maximum limitation on inpatient coverage in an IMD. 42 U.S.C. § 1395d(b)(3). The legislative history of the Medicaid statute indicates that Congress considered inpatient psychiatric care to be a state function. In addition, Congress was suspicious of the efficacy of large, state-funded psychiatric hospitals. Schweiker v. Wilson, 450 U.S. 221, 241–42, 101 S.Ct. 1074, 67 L.Ed.2d 186 (1981) (Powell, J., dissenting).

The coverage restrictions in Medicaid and Medicare greatly influenced the way mental health care was delivered. In order to transfer the fiscal burden of treating the mentally ill to the federal government, states quickly reduced their state hospital populations. From 1970 to 1975, for example, state hospital populations fell at a rate of 11% a year. See Joanmarie Davoli, "No Room at the Inn: How the Federal Medicaid Program Created Inequities in Psychiatric Hospital Access for the Indigent Mentally Ill," 29 Am.J.L.Med. 159, 170 (2003). In contrast, the advent of effective antipsychotic medicines in the decade between 1955 and 1965 had only reduced state hospital populations by about 1.75% annually. *Id.* Many commentators also argue that civil libertarian concerns—specifically, elevated legal requirements for civil commitment, see Chapter 8—were less important in reducing state hospital populations than was the monetary incentive. See, e.g., Clifford J. Levy, "Ingredients of a Failing System: A Lack of State Money, a Group Without a Voice," N.Y. Times, April 28, 2002, at A32; E. Fuller Torrey, Out of the Shadows 91–140 (1997). Currently, only about 70,000 patients remain in state psychiatric hospitals.

To the extent that individuals with serious mental illness receive treatment, they typically receive such treatment in nursing homes, general hospitals with psychiatric beds, or community-based facilities. Some of this health expenditure—primarily treatment in nursing homes and general hospitals—is covered by Medicaid or Medicare. Those who are seriously mentally ill are able to obtain coverage through Medicare or Medicaid because they are considered disabled. Federal law provides that persons with disabilities who have the appropriate work history are eligible for Social Security Disability Insurance ("SSDI") and therefore for Medicare. In 2001, about 28% of SSDI-qualified individuals had a mental disorder. Disabled individuals who do not have the requisite work history can be eligible for Supplemental Security Income (SSI) and thus for Medicaid. In 2001, 35.4% of SSI-qualified individuals had a mental disorder other than mental retardation. (For further discussion of the SSDI and SSI programs, see Chapter 11, Section II.)

In part because of rapid growth in SSI coverage of individuals with mental disorder, Medicaid has emerged as the largest public funder of mental health services. By 2003, Medicaid funded about 26% of total U.S. mental health expenditures, and Medicare funded about 7%. Tami Mark et al., Mental Health Treatment Expenditure Trends, 1986–2003, 58 Psychiatric Services 1041 (2007).

Significantly, however, just as Medicaid does not cover most mental health treatment provided at IMDs, it also does not cover community-based living arrangements for most individuals with mental illness. (Medicaid makes an exception for developmental disabilities such as mental retardation.) To the extent that states provide such community-based treatment, they must generally pay for it entirely through state and local funds. The dearth of federal funding for community-based services and IMDs has led to widespread concern that individuals with serious mental illness are either not being treated at all or are being housed in nursing homes, general hospitals, or other facilities that have limited ability to care for their needs.

When public funds are unavailable, individuals with serious mental illness may also be incarcerated temporarily, even in the absence of criminal charges. More generally, although the prevalence of mental disorder among incarcerated individuals is difficult to estimate precisely, studies indicate that this prevalence is higher in correctional institutions than in the general public. Lita Jans et al., Chartbook on Mental Health and Disability in the United States 39 (2004).

2. *Private Finance*

In 2003, the private sector paid for approximately 42% of all mental health care costs. Historically, many private insurers have placed strict limits on mental health care coverage. Some insurers have not covered mental health care at all. Others have limited annual inpatient hospital days and outpatient visits. Still others have imposed annual or lifetime caps on mental health expenditures. Significantly, these limits have often been much more stringent in the mental health context than in the physical health context. *See* 142 Cong. Rec. S3589 (daily ed. Apr. 18, 1996) (statement of Sen. Wellstone).

In 1996, Congress attempted to address some of these disparities by passing the Mental Health Parity Act (MHPA). The MHPA provides that insurance plans offering both mental health benefits and medical/surgical benefits may not impose annual or lifetime dollar limits on mental health benefits that are lower than comparable limits on medical/surgical benefits. The MHPA has many limitations, however. It does not place any limitations on the co-payments or deductibles a plan can charge for mental health services. Further, it does not forbid plans from restricting the number of visits or inpatient days they will cover. Indeed, under the MHPA, plans are not required to offer *any* mental health benefits. In addition, a plan is exempted from the MHPA's requirements if it can prove that the result of compliance would be an increase of at least 1% in the cost of the plan. Finally, treatment for substance abuse or chemical dependency is not covered by the MHPA's provisions. Although the MPHA was originally set to expire in 2001, the sunset provision has been extended seven times. The MHPA is currently scheduled to expire at the end of 2008.

At the time of the MHPA's enactment, some estimates suggested that as many 30,000 covered entities would qualify for the 1% percent exemption. These estimates appear to have been based on the assumption that it is more difficult to control moral hazard (the tendency to overuse services when one is insured for those services) in the context of mental health than physical health. See David Mechanic, "Mental Health Services in the Context of Health Insurance Reform," 71 Milbank Q. 349, 352–53 (1993). As of September 2001, however, fewer than twenty covered entities had claimed the exemption. John Jacobi, "Parity and Difference: The Value of Parity Legislation for the Seriously Mentally Ill," 29 Am.J.L. & Med. 185, 193–94 (2003). The MHPA's limited scope probably reduces its impact of costs. In addition, the aggressive rise of managed mental health care in the early 1990s has assisted cost control efforts.

The next section discusses the rise of managed care and the effect this rise has had on coverage and quality of care. Section C then discusses mechanisms, both legislative and judicial, to expand mental health care coverage.

B. THE ROLE OF MANAGED BEHAVIORAL HEALTH CARE

Mental health care is now provided to the majority of individuals under the age of 65 through some type of managed care organization ("MCO"). Defined broadly, managed care is any system of health care payment or delivery where the health plan attempts to control the use of health services by its enrollees in order to contain health costs. *See* Physician Payment Review Commission, Annual Report (1996). MCOs control costs through a variety of mechanisms. One arrangement is capitation; under capitation, the clinician is paid a fixed amount of money for all services provided to the patient. In contrast with fee-for-service payment, where there is an incentive to deliver as much care as possible, capitation discourages the use of services. Other MCOs try to control costs through prospective utilization review or case management. Before a clinician undertakes an intervention, the utilization reviewer or case manager for the managed care plan makes a determination about whether the plan will cover the intervention. In addition, MCO contracts often limit explicitly the scope and duration of coverage. For example, many MCOs impose limits on how many inpatient psychiatric hospital days or outpatient visits they will pay for in a given year. (In contrast, fee-for-service plans typically impose annual or lifetime caps on mental health care expenditures.) Finally, MCOs often cut costs by relying on social workers (and other relatively inexpensive personnel) rather than psychiatrists or psychologists for much of the therapy they provide.

These cost-control techniques are typically applied not by the MCO that covers the enrollees' physical health care but, rather, by specialized, for-profit behavioral health MCOs. In most cases, the behavioral health MCO contracts directly with the employer or state. The MCO may assume the insurance risk by agreeing to provide care for a predetermined price per enrollee. Alternatively, the behavioral health MCO administers the plan but does not assume insurance risk. The variety of different contractual arrangements is large, and these arrangements are often quite complex.

Numerous studies of managed mental health care support the proposition that it is effective at containing costs. See David Shern et al., "Medicaid Managed Care and the Distribution of Societal Costs for Persons With Severe Mental Illness," 165 Am. J. Psychiatry 254 (2008) (noting studies). However, cost-containment in the sector specifically covered by managed strategies can result in additional use of services in other sectors (e.g. the criminal justice system, friends and family). See id. (providing evidence for this phenomenon and citing other studies). Additionally, in both the private and public sector, there are concerns that the cost-cutting spurred by managed care will result in inadequate treatment, particularly for those with serious mental illness. Various studies of this question are discussed below.

1. *Private Sector*

One large study of private sector managed care involving 50,000 patients found that managed care cost-cutting often works by strictly limiting hospital stays. The study found that while patients with mental illness constituted only 5.7% of inpatient cases that were reviewed, they accounted for 55% of the gap between the total number of inpatient days requested and number of days approved. Moreover, the gap between bed days requested and bed days approved did not vary by the seriousness of the mental health diagnosis. Denials of requested days were as large and frequent for patients with psychoses as for patients with less serious mental disorders. See T.M. Wickizer and D. Lessler, "Effects of Utilization Management on Patterns of Hospital Care Among Privately Insured Patients," 36(11) Medical Care 1545 (1998). Most other studies in the private sector confirm that the advent of managed care results in substantial decreases in inpatient admissions and length of stay. See David Mechanic and Donna McAlpine, "Mission Unfulfilled: Potholes on the Road to Mental Health Parity," 18(5) Health Affairs 7 (Sept/Oct. 1999) (summarizing studies).

As Mechanic and McAlpine point out, if managed care is functioning properly, reductions in inpatient care should be accompanied by increases in claims for substitute services, such as outpatient treatment. Some studies show such substitution, but other studies indicate little substitution. Id. In addition, the study by Wickizer and Lessler indicates that reduced length of stay resulting from utilization management makes it more likely that patients will be readmitted to the hospital within 60 days.

Other data on quality are available from the Rand Medical Outcomes Study (MOS), a large observational study involving more than 12,000 group practice patients and almost 10,000 solo practice patients. The purpose of this study was to examine differences in care of chronic conditions, including depression, among various types of provider organizations, including HMOs, varying types of multispecialty groups, and single-specialty small groups and solo practices. In all settings psychiatrists treated patients with more serious depression. However, those who initially received prepaid care from psychiatrists developed new limitations in role and physical functioning over time while those treated by fee-for-service ("FFS") psychiatrists showed no such deterioration. The different outcomes of prepaid and FFS practice that were noted among psychiatrists did not apply to other therapists or general clinicians, who did equally well in both settings. Because psychiatrists treat the sickest patients, however, these results raise concerns about the quality of care of those with the most serious mental illnesses within HMOs. For an extended discussion of the results of the RAND study, see David Mechanic, Mark Schlesinger, and Donna D. McAlpine, "Management of Mental Health and Substance Abuse Services: State of the Art and Early Results," Milbank Quarterly, 3/22/95.

2. *Public Sector*

Public sector experimentation with capitation and other forms of managed care has also been studied. Although critics worry that capitation amounts are inadequate, and that there is too great an emphasis on cost containment, gaps in evidence preclude any definitive conclusions. The following excerpt from the Mechanic, Schlesinger, and McAlpine article summarizes the results of some early studies.

Manning and his colleagues (1993) analyzed the first year of experience of Medicaid beneficiaries with a diagnosis of schizophrenia who were enrolled in the Utah Prepaid Mental Health Plan compared with those in an FFS plan ... Although patients were not randomized between prepaid and FFS plans, and there were major selection effects, the capitated patients at baseline were sicker and had higher prior inpatient and outpatient utilization. Using pre-and post-respondent interview data on mental health status, functioning, satisfaction with care and utilization, the researchers compared the two groups, adjusting for baseline demographic characteristics and other baseline measures. There were no significant differences, although the lack of precision makes it difficult to reject the hypothesis of no difference ...

Thus, for the severely mentally ill covered by Medicaid, prepayment appears associated with few significant changes in outcomes, with some modest evidence of improvements in a few dimensions and hints of problems in others. All the studies, however, are limited, and a convincing demonstration and evaluation is yet to be carried out.

Questions and Comments

1. *Other public sector outcomes studies.* Some studies that are not mentioned in the Mechanic article support its tentative suggestions that publicly funded managed care is not necessarily associated with a decline in access or quality. A March 1993 U.S. General Accounting Office ("GAO") study of six states that used managed mental health care concluded that managed care plans provided access to services that was at least as good as or better than the access provided by fee-for-services plans. See U.S. Gen. Acct. Off., Medicaid: States Turn to Managed Care to Improve Access and Control (1993). The study also found that the states' decision to adopt a prepaid system had not diminished quality of care. Id. More recent studies of the Medicaid managed care experience in Colorado and Massachusetts also indicate that managed care can reduce costs without impairing quality. B.J. Cuffel et al., "Two–Year Outcomes of Fee-for-Service and Capitated Medicaid Programs for People With Severe Mental Illness," 37 Health Services Research 341 (2002) (discussing clinical outcomes in Colorado); R. G. Frank and T.G. McGuire, "Savings from a Medicaid Carve–Out for Mental Health and Substance Abuse Services in Massachusetts," 48 Psychiatric Services 1147 (1997).

On the other hand, a study of the Medicaid managed care in Tennessee determined that the process of implementation not only reduced services overall but directed resources away from the most severely ill individuals. C.F. Chang et al., "Tennessee's Failed Managed Care Program for Mental Health and Substance Abuse Services," 279 JAMA 868 (1998). A more limited study of individuals receiving anti-psychotic medication through the Tennessee Medicaid program similarly found that the transition to managed care was associated with an 18% reduction in adherence to therapy. W.A. Ray et al., "Effect of a Mental Health "Carve–Out" Program on the Continuity of Anti–Psychotic Therapy," 348 New Engl J Med 1885 (2003).

Moreover, longer term follow-up of the Utah managed care plan indicated that, for enrollees with schizophrenia, the Utah prepaid plan was ultimately associated with poorer outcomes, as measured by termination of treatment, excessive reliance on crisis intervention, poor medication management, and reduced use of psychotherapy. Michael Popkin et al., "Changes in Process of Care for Medicaid Patients with Schizophrenia in Utah's Prepaid Mental Health Plan," 49 Psychiatric Services 518 (1998).

2 .. *Performance standards for behavioral health care.* The National Committee for Quality Assurance ("NCQA"), a private non-profit organization that accredits health plans, has developed accreditation standards for managed behavioral healthcare companies. One of the standards requires that these companies demonstrate "well-established lines of communication between primary-care physicians and their behavioral health care practitioners." Other standards address quality improvement, accessibility of services, utilization review, credentialing, and preventive services.

3. *Criteria for allocating care.* One way to allocate a limited pool of societal resources for mental health services would be to give priority to coverage of serious mental illness. The argument in favor of this method would be that serious illness interferes much more profoundly with an individual's life than illness that is less serious. In addition, focusing resources on serious illness would address the worry that expansive DSM–IV diagnostic criteria have resulted in money and attention being diverted towards relatively ordinary behavior. See pp. 31, 37. For a famous argument that societal resources should preferentially be allocated towards the least well-off, *see* John Rawls, A Theory of Justice 302–03 (1971); for an application of this argument in the health care arena, *see* Norman Daniels, Just Health Care 35 (1985). Other mechanisms for allocating scarce mental health resources might focus on those interventions that were most cost-effective—in other words, those interventions that had, relative to their cost, proven most efficacious in treating mental illness. The effectiveness of any given intervention could be measured in terms of the percentage of patients who had their symptoms alleviated. Alternatively, it could be measured in terms of the average amount by which the intervention improved patients' quality-of-life. For a discussion of cost-effectiveness as an allocation criterion, see Arti K. Rai, "Rationing Through Choice: A New Approach to Cost–Effectiveness Analysis in Health Care," 72 Ind.L.J. 1015 (1997).

What advantages or disadvantages can you see to each of these approaches? Are there alternative approaches to allocation/rationing that might be preferable? To what extent, if any, does our current system of mental health care finance follow a systematic approach to allocation? The next section considers various strategies for improving coverage. In evaluating these strategies, consider whether they reflect a particular theoretical stance towards allocation. Will some of these strategies (e.g. strategies that require parity with respect to all conditions listed in the DSM–IV) be too costly?

C. IMPROVING COVERAGE

As indicated above, even with the 1996 enactment of the MHPA, insurance coverage of mental health in both the public and private sectors is significantly less generous than coverage of physical health. Legislative and judicial efforts to expand mental health coverage have thus focused on achieving parity between physical and mental health benefits. These efforts have been launched at both the state and federal level.

1. *State Statutes Addressing Private Insurance*

Approximately 42 states have now enacted some form of legislation mandating that insurers offer mental health benefits comparable to their physical health benefits. Most of these laws go beyond the MHPA in that they require parity not only in annual and lifetime dollar limits but also in co-payments and deductibles. Because of cost concerns, however, state parity laws have generally focused on serious mental illness. For example, California law requires that disability insurers that offer any coverage for disorders of the brain offer comparable coverage for severe mental disorders that have a biological origin. Cal. Ins. Code § 10123.15. Texas law requires plans for government employees to have parity in coverage for serious mental illnesses. Serious mental illness is defined to include eight specific disorders. A few states have passed laws that require parity for all conditions covered by the DSM, excluding substance abuse.

One very significant limitation of these state mandates is that they do not apply to a large category of plans, namely self-insured employee benefits plans that are governed by the Employee Retirement Income Security Act of 1974 ("ERISA"). ERISA has a broad preemption clause (Section 514(a)) that preempts any state statutory or common law that "relates to" an ERISA governed plan. 29 U.S.C.A. § 1144(a). Although the preemption provision is subject to a savings clause that exempts from preemption those state laws that regulate the "business of insurance," Congress has determined that self-insured employee benefits plans are *not* insurance plans for the purposes of the savings clause. 29 U.S.C.A. § 1144(b)(2)(B). Because many large companies are self-insured, about 40% of Americans who receive insurance coverage through a private employer are not covered by state mandates.

2. *Federal Parity Measures*

As was noted earlier, Congress responded to the limitations ERISA places on state legislative efforts by passing a federal law, the Mental Health Parity Act of 1996 ("MHPA"). Ever since the MHPA was passed, however, analysts have emphasized that it leaves untouched most restrictions on mental health coverage. As a consequence, plans often limit mental health treatment to as few as 30 outpatient visits and 30 days of hospital care.

For the last ten years, Congress has been debating legislation that would implement more comprehensive versions of parity. In March 2008, the House passed legislation that would prohibit health insurers that provide mental health coverage from setting lower limits of any kind on such coverage than they set for physical health services. The legislation would also prohibit higher co-payments for mental health services. Additionally, under the House bill, insurers that chose to provide mental health coverage would have to "include benefits" for any mental health condition listed in the DSM–IV. Insurers could still deny coverage if they determined a service was not "medically necessary." The House bill continues to exempt employers with 50 or fewer employees. As of July, 2008, the bill had yet to pass in the Senate.

Relevant to this debate is research on the costs of parity mental health care. Two studies have found that, because of efficiencies of scale and the expertise of MCOs (which require pre-approval of care at small increments), the extra costs of such care are not significant. H.H. Goldman et al., "Behavioral Health Insurance Parity for Federal Employees," 354 N. Engl. J. Med. 1378 (2006); "The Costs of Covering Mental Health and Substance Abuse Care at the Same Level as Medical Care in Private Insurance Plans," Testimony Presented to the Health Insurance Committee, National Conference of Insurance Legislators, July 13, 2001, by Roland Sturm, Ph.D. RAND Health, *available at* www.rand.org/pubs/testimonies/2005/CT180.pdf

3. *Medicaid and Medicare Reform*

Various policy analysts and advocacy groups, including President's George W. Bush's Commission on Mental Health and the National Alliance for the Mentally Ill, have urged that reform of Medicaid and Medicare be considered. In particular, these commentators suggest revisiting the exclusion of IMDs from Medicaid coverage as well as Medicaid's failure to cover most community-based care.

4. *Litigation Under the Americans with Disabilities Act*

The Rehabilitation Act of 1973 and the Americans with Disabilities Act of 1990 ("ADA") are parallel federal statutes that respectively bar discrimination against disabled persons in federally funded programs and non-federally funded programs. Individuals with mental disabilities have tried to use the ADA in particular as a mechanism by which to improve access to mental health services. The ADA extends protection against discrimination "on the basis of disability" to the following areas relevant to mental health care finance: private employment (Title I), public services and programs provided by state and local governments (Title II), and "public accommodations" (Title III), a broadly defined category that includes insurance offices.

a. *Challenges to Private Insurance Plans*

ADA challenges to private insurance plans have focused on claims that plans with mental health benefits less generous than their physical health benefits violate Titles I and III of the ADA.

Title I challenges are based on a provision in the title which bars employers from discriminating against individuals with disabilities with respect to the "terms, conditions, and privileges of employment." 42

U.S.C. § 12112(a). Plaintiffs who invoke this provision argue that unfavorable treatment for mental illnesses is discrimination based on disability. Unfavorable treatment of mental illness can occur both in ordinary health insurance and in long-term disability insurance. In the context of ordinary health insurance, however, the Equal Employment Opportunity Commission ("EEOC"), which has authority to promulgate regulations under Title I, has taken the position that insurance coverage restrictions that specifically target mental illness do not necessarily represent distinctions based on disability within the meaning of the ADA. As discussed further in Chapter 12, infra, the ADA requires that a disability "substantially limit[ ] one or more life activities." Thus, according to the EEOC, restrictions on mental health coverage can apply to, and affect adversely, not only individuals with disabilities but also individuals without disabilities. See generally EEOC Interim Guidance on Application of ADA to Health Insurance, Daily Lab. Rep. (BNA) No. 109, at E1–E3 (June 9, 1993). Under the EEOC position, in order for a restriction in an ordinary health insurance plan to be disability-based, it would have to target a particular disability or set of disabilities (e.g. schizophrenia, mood disorders). Id. at E–2.

Because of the EEOC position, most lawsuits that have challenged unfavorable treatment of mental illness have arisen in the context of long-term disability insurance. In the context of long-term disability insurance, the EEOC argument that distinctive treatment of mental illness affects both individuals with disabilities and individuals without disabilities does not apply: this is because all individuals who qualify for such long-term insurance are disabled. Indeed, the EEOC itself brought one of the most first, and most influential, lawsuits challenging under Title I of the ADA a long-term insurance plan's treatment of mental illness. The disability plan at issue in *EEOC v. CNA Insurance*, 96 F.3d 1039 (7th Cir.1996) provided two years of benefit for those with mental disabilities. In contrast, the plan had no such restriction for those with physical disabilities. The Seventh Circuit rejected the EEOC argument, holding that so long as all employees, "the perfectly healthy, the physically disabled, and the mentally disabled" had access to the same set of benefits at the same price, there was no discrimination. In reaching this conclusion, the Seventh Circuit relied on a Supreme Court case interpreting the Rehabilitation Act, *Alexander v. Choate*, 469 U.S. 287, 105 S.Ct. 712, 83 L.Ed.2d 661 (1985). In that case, the Court held that so long as a facially neutral limitation on insurance coverage (in that case, 14 days of coverage for inpatient hospital care) provided "meaningful access" to individuals with disabilities, the fact that the limitation had a disparate impact on such individuals did not create a Rehabilitation Act violation.

It could be argued that the Seventh Circuit's extrapolation from the *Alexander v. Choate* line of argument is misplaced. The coverage restriction at issue was not facially neutral but, rather, was specifically targeted towards mental health care. Nonetheless, most other circuit courts that have addressed challenges to restrictions on mental health coverage in long-term disability policies have rejecting such challenges by following some version of the Seventh Circuit's reasoning. See, e.g., *Parker v. Metropolitan Life Insurance Co.*, 121 F.3d 1006 (6th Cir.1997); *Ford v. Schering–Plough Corp.*, 145 F.3d 601 (3d Cir.1998); *Kimber v. Thiokol Corp.*, 196 F.3d 1092 (10th Cir.1999); *Lewis v. Kmart Corp.*, 180 F.3d 166 (4th Cir.1999); *Weyer v. Twentieth Century Fox Film Corp.*, 198 F.3d 1104 (9th Cir.2000); *EEOC v. Staten Island Savings Bank*, 207 F.3d 144 (2d Cir.2000). Some of these courts have also indicated that a former employee on long-term disability is not eligible to sue for employment discrimination in the first instance because Title I of the ADA only covers those who are *currently* able to hold an employment position. EEOC v. CNA Insurance, *supra* ; Weyer, *supra*; *but see* Ford v. Schering–Plough (rejecting this argument). Finally, a number of these circuit court decisions (e.g. *EEOC v. CNA Insurance*) have noted that Congress' decision to pass the Mental Health Parity Act of 1996 implied that it did not expect the ADA to mandate equal insurance treatment of mental and physical disabilities.

On occasion, plaintiffs have tried to use Title III of the ADA to challenge restrictions on mental health coverage in long-term disability policies. The Sixth Circuit has held that the same arguments that preclude application of the ADA in the Title I context also apply in Title III cases. See *Parker v. Metropolitan Life Insurance Co.*, 121 F.3d 1006, 1015–1010 (6th Cir.1997) (arguing in Title III context that the ADA does not prohibit the unfavorable treatment of mental disabilities vis à vis physical disabilities). Courts have also rejected Title III suits on the theory that the Title's prohibition against discrimination by public accommodations like insurance offices concerns only physical access to the public accommodation's facilities and does not extend to the content of the goods and services provided by the accommodation. See, e.g., *Parker v. Metropolitan Life Insurance Co.*, 121 F.3d 1006 (6th Cir.1997); *Weyer* (2000); but see *Carparts Distribution Center v. Automotive Wholesaler's Association of New England, Inc.*, 37 F.3d 12 (1st Cir.1994) (Title III protection *does* extend to the content of the public accommodation's goods and services).

Finally, it should be emphasized that all ADA-based discrimination claims brought against insurance plans are vulnerable to defenses based on the ADA's very significant "safe harbor" provision. Under this provision, if a defendant insurance company can demonstrate that its coverage restrictions are based on sound actuarial principles, then the company can not be held liable for discrimination. 42 U.S.C. § 12201(c). The safe-harbor defense is subject to the caveat that the coverage restrictions can not be used as a "subterfuge" to evade the purposes of Title I or Title III. Courts have, however, interpreted the subterfuge language narrowly, to hold that unless the employers intended to discriminate in a non-fringe benefit related aspect of the employment relation, the coverage restriction can not be a subterfuge. *Krauel v. Iowa Methodist Medical Center*, 95 F.3d 674 (8th Cir. 1996).

b. Challenges to Public Insurance Programs

The major ADA-based challenge to a public sector program was a Title II challenge brought by two women in a Georgia psychiatric institution. This case, *Olmstead v. L.C. by Zimring*, was decided by the Supreme Court in 1999. In *Olmstead* (discussed further in Chapter 10), the Court held that the state of Georgia had an obligation under the ADA to provide community-based treatment for persons with mental disabilities "when the State's treatment professionals determine that such placement is appropriate, the affected persons do not oppose such treatment, and the placement can be reasonably accommodated, taking into account the resources available to the State and the needs of others with mental disabilities."

As discussed further in Chapter 12, however, since *Olmstead*, the availability of monetary damages against state defendants who violate the ADA has been called into question by the Supreme Court's sovereign immunity jurisprudence. To the extent that federal funding is involved, however, the inability to secure monetary damages under the ADA may lead to more frequent challenges under the Rehabilitation Act. Although the Supreme Court has not addressed the issue directly, most circuit courts have held that a state's acceptance of federal funding under the Rehabilitation Act constitutes a waiver of sovereign immunity.

5. Challenges Based on the Blurred Line Between Mental and Physical Disorder

Plaintiffs have sometimes challenged an insurance contract's mental health coverage restrictions by arguing that, because their mental illnesses have a biological basis, they should be allowed to invoke the more generous physical illness provisions of the insurance contract. Because many of these cases involve insurance plans governed by ERISA, courts have had to address not only the terms of the insurance contract but also how the standard of review may be altered by the application of ERISA. The following case provides a comprehensive discussion of these issues.

PHILLIPS v. LINCOLN NATIONAL LIFE INSURANCE COMPANY

United States Court of Appeals, Seventh Circuit, 1992.
978 F.2d 302.

COFFEY, CIRCUIT JUDGE.

Gordon B. Phillips ("Phillips"), as guardian for his dependent son, James G. Phillips ("James"), brought this action in the district court under the Employee Retirement Income Security Act of 1974 (ERISA), 29 U.S.C. §§ 1001–1461, against Lincoln National Life Insurance Company ("Lincoln") seeking recovery of benefits under an employee welfare benefit plan ("the Plan") established by his employer, Seedboro Equipment Company ("Seedboro"), pursuant to its purchase of an insurance policy from Lincoln. Both parties agree that the Plan is an employee welfare benefit plan governed by ERISA. Phillips argued in the district court that Lincoln erroneously applied the Plan's mental illness benefit limitation to Phillips' benefits claim for expenses incurred in the treatment of James' illness. The district court entered summary judgment in favor of Phillips, and Lincoln appeals. We affirm.

I.   BACKGROUND

On November 1, 1984, Seedboro established a benefit plan for its employees through its purchase of a group health insurance policy from Lincoln. The Plan defined the health insurance benefits available for eligible employees of Seedboro and their dependents. Phillips, who is Seedboro's president, and his dependent son James were eligible participants in the Plan. The Plan provisions relevant to the instant dispute are as follows:

MAJOR MEDICAL BENEFITS

Maximum Benefit (Lifetime Aggregate) $1,000,000

Except that, the Maximum Benefit (Lifetime Aggregate) for charges for mental illness(es) is $25,000

* * *

MAJOR MEDICAL LIMITATIONS

The maximum payment for care of mental illness or care of nervous conditions of any type or cause by a doctor will not be more than:

1. $20.00 for each visit; and
2. one visit on any one day; and
3. 50 visits during any calendar year.

(A "visit" occurs each time the doctor provides care to the patient).

* * *

DEFINITIONS

Illness-means:

1. A disorder or disease of the body or mind . . . .

* * *

The Plan provided no definition of the term "mental illness."

In December, 1981, when he was 16 years old, James was diagnosed as suffering from what doctors call "congenital encephalopathy." Congenital encephalopathy is a brain malfunction, manifested by neurological defects, whose exact location in the brain cannot be pinpointed. James' condition was diagnosed through extensive neuropsychological testing measuring language ability, motor and perceptual skills, visual and verbal memory, and intelligence. In addition, a brain scan performed in 1989 revealed that a portion of James' brain was "not putting out the electrical impulses or processing electrical stimuli and impulses the way it would normally." In James' case, his neurological defect has given rise to a cluster of behavioral disorders. * * * James has what his doctors describe as "horrible" social skills and is "often very loud and obnoxious." James frequently inappropriately touches others and engages in "repetitive mannerisms" such as rocking back and forth. James can be hyperactive, hyperexcitable, "extremely self abusive" and "physically abusive to [others]." At times he is psychotic, suffers from periods of compulsive eating, and has rapid mood swings. James also has significant difficulties processing visual information. Although he is not mentally retarded, he does have a learning disability. * * *

According to the record, medical science has been unable to implement a treatment program to successfully attack and contain the mental affliction from which James suffers. Therefore, doctors are forced to confine their efforts to helping James control and function with the behavioral manifestations of his illness. Under Dr. Bateman's care, James is treated with medications to control his neurological problems and lives in a monitored environment where he is hopefully learning how to cope with his condition. James is also given low dosages of medications to ameliorate some of the behavioral manifestations of his illness, such as irritability and extreme anxiety. * * *

From the effective date of the Plan in 1984 until October, 1987, Lincoln paid $25,000 in Plan benefits for the expenses Phillips incurred in the treatment of James' illness. Having reached the Plan's mental illness limitation cap, Lincoln refused to reimburse Phillips for any of the subsequent expenses arising from his son's treatment. In early 1990, Phillips appealed Lincoln's determination to the Lincoln National Appeals Committee, arguing that James' illness was a physical condition which gave rise to certain mental deficiencies and thus fell outside the scope of the Plan's mental illness limitation. The Appeals Committee affirmed the original claim determination.

Following the decision of the Lincoln Appeals Committee, Phillips filed a complaint in the district court. * * *

In a published opinion, the district court explained that Phillips and Lincoln advanced "competing reasonable interpretations" of the Plan term "mental illness". *Phillips v. Lincoln National Life Insurance Company*, 774 F.Supp. 495, 499 (N.D.Ill.1991). The court noted that Phillips argued in his summary judgment motion that the term "mental illness" referred only to those illnesses with non-physical causes, "such as illnesses traceable to abuse suffered in one's childhood or to other types of traumatic experiences. According to [Phillips], behavioral problems traceable to an organic or physical cause are other than 'mental illnesses.' "*Id.* Lincoln's summary judgment motion took issue with Phillips' definition of mental illness, arguing that the cause of a behavioral illness does not determine whether it is a mental illness. Id. at 500. In Lincoln's view, an illness is a mental illness if its symptoms include extremely abnormal behavior. *Id.* * * *

[T]he district court found that both definitions "have intuitive appeal and partially describe the qualities of a mental illness." *Id.* Since the Plan offered no definition of the term "mental illness," the district court concluded that the term as used in the Plan was ambiguous because it was susceptible to more than one reasonable interpretation. *Id.*

Faced with this ambiguity, the district court adopted the state law rule of contract interpretation contra proferentem in fashioning the federal common law governing the ERISA dispute between Lincoln and Phillips. *Id.* at 502. The rule of contra proferentem dictates that ambiguities in a contract be construed against the drafter. The district court thought this case presented an appropriate instance for the application of contra proferentem * * * Accordingly, the district court read the ambiguity in the Plan in Phillips' favor, ruling that, as a matter of law, the Plan's mental illness limitation did not apply to James' condition. * * * Lincoln appealed the summary judgment order * * *

II. Standard of Review

Phillips brought his suit against Lincoln under 29 U.S.C. § 1132(a)(1)(B) of ERISA which authorizes a plan participant to bring a civil action "to recover benefits due to him under the terms of his plan. . . . " The Supreme Court has made clear that "a denial of benefits challenged under § 1132(a)(1)(B) is to be reviewed under a de novo standard unless the benefit plan gives the administrator or fiduciary discretionary authority to determine eligibility for benefits or to construe the terms of the plan." *Firestone Tire & Rubber Company v. Bruch*, 489 U.S. 101, 115, 109 S.Ct. 948, 956, 103 L.Ed.2d 80 (1989). The district court action in reviewing Lincoln's denial of Phillips' benefits claim de novo was proper as neither of these exceptions apply here.

* * *

III. Analysis

In *Hammond v. Fidelity and Guaranty Life Insurance Company*, 965 F.2d 428 (7th Cir.1992), we considered several of the issues raised by this appeal. Hammond centered around the interpretation of the term "totally disabled" in an employee benefit life insurance plan governed by ERISA. Id. at 428. In determining the law applicable to the dispute, we noted that

> "ERISA explicitly states that it 'shall supersede any and all State laws insofar as they may now or hereafter relate to any employee benefit plan.' 29 U.S.C. § 1144(a). However, Congress also enacted an 'insurance savings clause' in § 1144(b)(2) which provides that a state law is not preempted if it regulates insurance; that is, if it 'has the effect of transferring or spreading a policyholder's risk, . . . is an integral part of the policy relationship between the insurer and the insured, and . . . the practice is limited to entities within the

insurance industry.' *Pilot Life Ins. Co. v. Dedeaux,* 481 U.S. 41, 48–49, 107 S.Ct. 1549, 1553–54 [95 L.Ed.2d 39] (1987). . . . "

Id. at 430. The question we faced in Hammond reappears in the instant case: whether "state laws governing insurance policy interpretation [are] preserved under ERISA." *Id.* We decided that they were not so preserved because "state rules of contract interpretation" did not "regulate insurance" within the meaning of ERISA § 1144(b)(2) and because Congress intended "uniformity of decisions under ERISA." *Id.* "We therefore conclude[d] that ERISA preempts state decisional rules [of contract interpretation], and that any ambiguities in ERISA plans and insurance policies should be resolved by referring to the federal common law rules of contract interpretation." *Id.* * * * In *Hammond*, we summarized the relevant rules of federal common law contract interpretation as follows:

> "[W]e interpret the terms of the [ERISA-governed] policy 'in an ordinary and popular sense as would a [person] of average intelligence and experience.' * * * "

Hammond, 965 F.2d at 430.

* * *

[W]e turn now to the crux of Lincoln's position: its contention that a mental illness ought to be defined as a condition whose primary observable symptoms are behavioral. This view was adopted by a panel of the Eighth Circuit in *Brewer v. Lincoln National Life Insurance Company,* 921 F.2d 150 (8th Cir.1990), cert. denied, 501 U.S. 1238, 111 S.Ct. 2872, 115 L.Ed.2d 1038 (1991). *Brewer* presented facts similar to the instant case: a father, as guardian for his son, sued an insurance company for its refusal to reimburse the full costs of his son's treatment for affective mood disorder, a condition which had been successfully treated with a combination of drugs and psychotherapy. *Id.* at 152. The *Brewer* court, citing ERISA's directive, contained in 29 U.S.C. § 1022(a)(1), that summary plan descriptions "be written in a manner calculated to be understood by the average plan participant," stated that terms in insurance policies governed by ERISA "should be accorded their ordinary, and not specialized, meanings." *Id.* at 154. The court then applied that interpretive rule to the case at hand:

> "[t]he cause of a disease is a judgment for experts, while laymen know and understand symptoms. Laymen undoubtedly are aware that some mental illnesses are organically caused while others are not; however, they do not classify illnesses based on their origins. Instead, laypersons are inclined to focus on the symptoms of an illness; illnesses whose primary symptoms are depression, mood swings and unusual behavior are commonly characterized as mental illnesses regardless of their cause.
>
> "Neither policy in this case limited the definition of 'mental illness' to only those illnesses that have a non-organic origin, and the district court should not have adopted a definition that effectively

imposed such a limitation. By focusing upon the disease's etiology, the district court considered factors that are important to experts but not to laypersons. The court thus failed to examine the term 'mental illness' as a layperson would have, which is the examination we concluded ERISA and federal common law require."

Id.

* * *

[T]he appellant's main argument is that we, like the *Brewer* court, ought to conclude that the term "mental illness" can only be understood as a description of the symptoms of a condition, and that a condition's cause is irrelevant to its classification. *See also Equitable Life Assurance Society v. Berry*, 212 Cal.App.3d 832, 260 Cal.Rptr. 819, 824 (1989) (manifestation (i.e., symptoms) of a condition, not the cause of the condition, is the appropriate "yardstick" to use in determining whether a condition is a mental illness). * * *

Moreover, like Lincoln, Phillips is able to point to a federal court of appeals decision approving its preferred definition of "mental illness." A panel of the Ninth Circuit, in *Kunin v. Benefit Trust Life Insurance Company*, 910 F.2d 534 (9th Cir.), *cert. denied*, 498 U.S. 1013, 111 S.Ct. 581, 112 L.Ed.2d 587 (1990), upheld a finding of the district court that autism was not a mental illness under an ERISA employee welfare benefit plan because "mental illness refers to a behavioral disturbance with no demonstrable organic or physical basis.... [I]t stems from reaction to environmental conditions as distinguished from organic causes." *Id.* at 538 (citation to district court opinion omitted). Since autism has an organic cause, it did not qualify as a mental illness. *Id.* * * *

Faced with these competing definitions of "mental illness" which have divided not only the litigants but also federal and state courts, we have no trouble agreeing with the district court's finding that the term "mental illness" as used in the Plan is ambiguous. As in *Kunin*, where the Ninth Circuit found the term "mental illness" in a welfare benefit plan ambiguous, here the Plan "contains no definition or explanation of the term 'mental illness,' and offers no illustration of the conditions that are included or excluded. Nor does the policy contain any language suggesting whether the cause or the manifestation [of an illness] determines whether an illness is covered...." 910 F.2d at 541. We thus hold that the Plan term "mental illness" is ambiguous as applied to individuals like James who have mental disorders caused by organic illnesses.

Following *Hammond*, which states that federal common law rules of contract interpretation require us to construe "[a]mbiguous terms in an insurance contract ... strictly ... in favor of the insured," 965 F.2d at 430, we hold that the district court correctly ruled that the Plan's mental illness limitation does not apply to James' condition. The adoption by the district court of the state law rule of contract interpretation contra proferentem as part of the federal common law of ERISA was proper. * * *

Lincoln argues that the application of the rule of contra proferentem in the ERISA context was foreclosed by the Supreme Court in *Firestone*. We disagree. In *Firestone*, the Court considered the question of the appropriate standard of review for ERISA actions brought under 29 U.S.C. § 1132(a)(1)(B), challenging denials of benefits by ERISA plan administrators. 489 U.S. at 108, 109 S.Ct. at 952. The Court concluded that de novo review was required also making clear that principles of trust law are useful guides in the development of federal common law in ERISA cases. *Id.* at 108, 111, 109 S.Ct. at 952, 954. In its discussion of relevant trust law principles, the Court stated that as "they do with contractual provisions, courts construe terms in a trust agreement without deferring to either party's interpretation." *Id.* at 112, 109 S.Ct. at 955. The Court also noted that in actions challenging an employer's denial of benefits before the enactment of ERISA "[i]f the plan did not give the employer or administrator discretionary or final authority to construe uncertain terms, the court reviewed the employee's claim as it would have any other contract claim—by looking to the terms of the plan and other manifestations of the parties' intent." *Id.* at 112–13, 109 S.Ct. at 955 (citations omitted).

Lincoln argues that this language in *Firestone* precludes application of the rule of contra proferentem in ERISA actions because that rule is inconsistent with the Supreme Court's instruction that the intent of the parties to an ERISA plan should be the focus of the inquiry. We disagree for the reasons articulated by the *Kunin* court in rejecting this reading of *Firestone*'s dicta:

> "In [Firestone], . . . the Supreme Court was discussing the standard according to which courts should review a plan administrator's interpretation of plan provisions. The Court held that reviewing courts should interpret disputed provisions de novo, not defer to the administrator's interpretation. The Court said nothing whatsoever about ordinary principles of construction according to which courts and administrators alike should arrive at their interpretations. . . . [A distinction exists] between (1) using certain presumptions, including presumptions in favor of a party, in order to arrive at the correct interpretation, and (2) deferring to a particular party's interpretation. Rejecting (2) obviously does not undermine the soundness of (1). We might say, for example, that a jury should not defer to a defendant's plea of "not guilty"—we want the jury to determine his guilt or innocence de novo. However, this in no way implies that the jury, in making this determination, is not required to presume innocence—and indeed, to presume it quite strongly. Again, we might say that a baseball umpire should not defer to a baserunner's claim that he is safe; but this proposition is fully consistent with the separate rule that ties go to the runner. Likewise, while we may not defer to an insured's construction, we must

not fail to indulge in a presumption that ambiguous language favors the insured. * * * "

Kunin, 910 F.2d at 541. *But see Allen v. Adage*, 967 F.2d 695, 701 (1st Cir.1992) (relying on *Firestone* to hold that, in most ERISA cases, contra proferentem contradicts the combined principles of the law of trusts and de novo review); *Brewer*, 921 F.2d at 153–54 (state law rule of contra proferentem is preempted by ERISA, 29 U.S.C. § 1144(a) and was rejected in ERISA context by *Firestone*); *Finley v. Special Agents Mutual Benefit Association*, Inc., 957 F.2d 617, 619–20 (8th Cir.1992) (same). *Cf. Delk v. Durham Life Insurance Company*, 959 F.2d 104, 105–06 (8th Cir.1992) (contra proferentem is applicable in the ERISA context when an ambiguity cannot be resolved by interpreting the language as would an average plan participant). * * *

IV.

* * * We hold that the Plan's mental illness limitation does not apply to James' condition, and therefore the district court's entry of summary judgment in favor of Phillips is AFFIRMED.

BAUER, CHIEF JUDGE, dissenting.

I respectfully dissent. The majority opinion does an outstanding job of covering the issues involved. What it comes down to, in my opinion, is the acceptance or rejection of the rationalization and imperatives set out in *Brewer v. Lincoln National Life Insurance Company*, 921 F.2d 150 (8th Cir.1990), cert. denied, 501 U.S. 1238, 111 S.Ct. 2872, 115 L.Ed.2d 1038 (1991). That case is well discussed in the majority opinion and I shall not waste any more forest land with further development; suffice to say that I agree that insurance coverage and exclusions must be "written in a manner calculated to be understood by the average plan participant." And this policy clearly limits the coverage "for care of mental illness or care of nervous conditions of any type or cause.... "

I believe that any fair reading of the problems facing James inescapably lead to the conclusion that he suffers from "a mental illness" or "nervous disorder." The cause, as the policy clearly states, is not controlling. "Mixed organic brain syndrome" with the manifestations exhibited by James that require the present hospitalization and treatment is a "mental illness."

Questions and Comments

1. *Contract Language.* If you were drafting an insurance contract, could you include language that would get around the problems faced by the defendant in the *Phillips* case? What would this language look like? For a discussion of the contractual language issue, see Paul S. Appelbaum, "Litigating Insurance Coverage for Mental Disorders," 40 Hosp. & Community Psychiatry 993, 993 (1989).

2. *The Role of ERISA.* The *Phillips* case includes an extended discussion of how insurance contracts governed by ERISA should be interpreted. As the *Phillips* court notes, courts are divided as to whether ordinary common law rules of insurance contract interpretation—in particular the

contra proferentum rule—apply to ERISA-governed contracts. This issue is an important one because many insurance contracts covering mental health are ERISA-governed and will, at least arguably, be ambiguous.

3. *Challenges to Medicaid and Medicare Coverage of Mental Health Services.* As noted, both Medicaid and Medicare place significant restrictions on the types of mental health services they will cover. Could these restrictions be challenged as discriminatory under the Rehabilitation Act? Note that although Medicaid does not cover community-based mental health services, states can petition the Secretary of Health and Human Services for a waiver that would allow such coverage. The waiver application must demonstrate, however, that the state's request will be "budget-neutral."

Problem: Public Sector Mental Health Service Provision

Imagine that you are a policy assistant to a recently elected member of the U.S. Senate. She asks you to review the current system of public sector mental health coverage (i.e. Medicaid, Medicare, direct state and local government funding) and to come up with a proposal that would improve the current system. What would your proposal envision? What would be the respective roles of the federal and state governments? Would your proposal provide recipients with any judicially enforceable rights?

Which interest groups do you expect to be most supportive of, or opposed to, your proposal? Are the members of these groups major contributors to your Senator?

Chapter Two

REGULATION OF THE MENTAL HEALTH PROFESSIONS

I. ADMINISTRATIVE REGULATION

A. INTRODUCTION

Legislatures and the courts have long recognized the state's interest in assuring the quality of professional services, that address the health needs of the public. The legal system has relied on two basic approaches to safeguard adequate standards in the rendering of health services. One is the torts system, which subjects professionals who fail to meet basic quality standards to monetary liability for injuries resulting from their malfeasance. The emphasis of the torts system, which is addressed in

Chapter Three, is on remediation designed to both provide compensation to injured parties and deter future injurious conduct. Institutionally, this approach relies on enforcement of rights within the court system.

The other approach to quality assurance in the rendering of professional health services relies on administrative regulation, which is either preventive or remedial. In the case of the former, the emphasis is on either direct or indirect "entry" criteria intended to reduce the risk that those rendering health services lack the necessary qualifications. Administrative regulation can also be remedial. Here, the emphasis is on the application of administrative sanctions, involving either de-licensing or fines where there has been a departure from accepted professional standards. The materials which follow describe the systems of administrative regulation that are typically employed to promote quality assurance in the rendering of mental health services.

B. REGULATION OF ENTRY AND CERTIFICATION

1. *Perspectives on Occupational Licensing*

Regulation, whatever its form, is presumably designed to promote some legitimate governmental purpose. The following excerpt summarizes the rationale for occupational regulation, noting particularly the ostensible justification for such regulation in the health field:

> Consumer protection is the rationale most commonly advanced as a justification for occupational licensing. In particular it is believed that control of entry and regulation of the practice are necessary to protect consumers from incompetent, dishonest, financially irresponsible, unsafe, and unsanitary provision of various services.

> Such a broad consumer protection rationale is incomplete and deficient. First and foremost, government intervention to protect consumers is only necessary when the market fails to perform that function. A market solution is preferable to an administrative solution unless the latter facilitates the transaction more efficiently than the market. While the market may fail to produce competitive results because the firms engage in anticompetitive conduct or because an industry is not competitively structured, the type of market failure that is particularly relevant here involves that caused by transaction costs. * * * [T]he question is whether consumers of a particular service are able to make informed and intelligent selections of various service providers, free from undue exploitation by the latter. If the market failure is significant, [e.g., because of failure by the industry to provide adequate information or inability of the consumer to comprehend available information], consumers will not be able to make such a selection. Consequently they will have difficulty determining their needs, evaluating the quality of the alternatives or the services rendered, and judging the price and other characteristics of the transaction. Thus the market will not permit consumers quickly to detect and avoid incompetent, fraudu-

lent, or financially irresponsible providers. On the other hand, if there is no significant market failure, a consumer will be able to choose those service providers who, in the mind of the consumer, represent the best combination of high quality service and cost. Such a process will adequately protect consumers from incompetency, dishonesty, and the other problems mentioned above.

Thus in examining occupational licensing the critical question is which types of service transactions are likely to be characterized by sufficient market failure to warrant governmental intervention. In many situations an administrative solution seems unnecessary. For example, in the case of barbers, cosmetologists, funeral homes, taxidermists, driver training schools, private investigators, and probably contractors, architects, and engineers, to name a few, a priori reasoning suggests that the market functions adequately. In fact in such areas it is doubtful that consumers of the services know or care whether the provider is licensed. * * * In some areas it is difficult to generalize, particularly since the nature and sophistication of all consumers are not equivalent. The health field, and perhaps lawyers, present the most difficult questions. Market failure may be more likely in these areas. * * * Moreover one may be influenced by the fact that the potential for serious harm from an incorrect decision is greater in these areas, and by a fear that consumers of these services may be insufficiently risk-adverse. In any event, some licensing seems warranted with doctors, dentists, other providers of health services, and lawyers.

J. Rose, Occupational Licensing: A Framework For Analysis, 1979 Ariz. St.L.J. 189, 190–192.

While licensing seems to be an established part of the regulatory landscape, a vocal minority contends that licensing is contrary to the public interest. In this connection, consider the merits of the arguments against licensing advanced by one commentator:

* * * Invariably, the rationale advanced for restricting the right to practice is protection of the public. But a strong case can be made that the only ones really being protected are the professionals themselves. First, psychotherapy is nearly incapable of definition, and regulations invariably encroach on such related fields as education. Second, academic credentials and written examinations are worthless as measures of therapeutic effectiveness. * * * [One researcher] has concluded that neither criteria predicts anything but future grades and test scores, no matter what the profession. * * *

* * *

* * * Moreover, there are so many negative side effects to licensing that it is hard to imagine when it would be a useful means of regulation: Evidence is accumulating that licensing significantly increases the cost of professional services, decreases the supply of practitioners, inhibits improvements in the organization and deliv-

ery of services, stifles innovative training programs, and is discriminatory.

* * *

The question is whether alternatives exist. Major improvements could obviously be gained by small changes in existing laws. For instance, statutes might only restrict the right to use certain titles while basing the requirements for licensing on competency, not credentials. Such changes, however, don't go far enough. Since we know so little about therapeutic effectiveness, we need regulations that encourage responsible experimentation and diversity, but also protect the public from incompetence and unethical conduct.

All practitioners should be required to register with the state but not to make academic or other credentials a prerequisite to practice. Laws should, however, require therapists to disclose their training and techniques to all clients. An active, powerful and well-financed disciplinary board, a variety of nongovernment certification organizations, and a comprehensive campaign to educate the public are necessary, if this system is to work properly. There are certainly risks involved in this approach, but I believe they are fewer than if we continue on our current path. The fact is that the only sure losers in today's continuing war among the mental-health professions will ultimately be their patients.

Daniel B. Hogan, Licensing Mental Therapists, N.Y. Times, July 18, 1979, at A23.

2. *Forms of Regulation of Entry*

a. *Licensing of Psychiatrists*

Like professional licensing generally, the licensing of psychiatrists is a state rather than federal function. Thus, psychiatrists, like other physicians, must be licensed in whatever state they wish to practice. The licensing requirements applicable to physicians generally include graduation from an accredited medical school, satisfactory completion of a series of standardized examinations, and at least one year of post graduate medical education in the form of residency training. More specifically, the licensing of physicians and by implication psychiatrists entails the following:

"Each state has is own board of medical examiners and each individual board of medical examiners selects the criteria it will require for licensure of physicians in its state. The individual states rely on the approval of various national organizations with specialized expertise to satisfy certain state licensure criteria. For example, the Liaison Committee of Medical Education (LCME) of the American Medical Association accredits medical schools, guaranteeing that they provide the recognized four-year medical school curriculum containing the required academic and clinical elements. Generally, boards of medical examiners across the nation will accept candidates with medical degrees from schools accredited by the LCME, thus avoiding the need of each state to independently develop criteria for medical education.

In order to obtain initial licensure, states generally require candidates to present evidence of graduation from an accredited medical school having successfully received an M.D. (doctor of medicine) or D.O. (doctor of osteopathy) in a four-year program. The candidate also must have passed a proficiency examination; currently, that is the United States Medical Licensing Exam (USMLE), or other combination of older tests, such as that formerly given by the National Board of Medical Examiners (NBME).

The Federation of State Medical Boards (FSMB) and the NBME have collaborated in establishing a single, three-step examination for medical licensure. Step 1 of the exam process tests the examinee's knowledge of basic biomedical sciences, with an emphasis on principles and mechanisms of health, disease, and modes of therapy. Step 2 assesses whether an examinee can apply the medical knowledge and understanding of clinical science considered essential for the provision of patient care. Step 3 assesses the physician's ability to apply biomedical and clinical sciences, emphasizing patient management in ambulatory settings. Most state licensing authorities require completion of Steps 1, 2 and 3 within a seven-year period. Licensing boards also set a limit on the number of attempts allowed to pass each step and have established, as an eligibility requirement for Step 3, the completion or near completion of at least one postgraduate training year.

Physicians seeking initial licensure must have successfully completed 'postgraduate' medical education in the form of residency training . . . . . . All state licensing authorities require at least one year of postgraduate training; ten states require two years and one, Nevada, requires three years."

Kenneth Wing & Patricia Kuzler, Law and the American Health System, 462–63 (1998).

While the practice of psychiatry requires a medical license, completion of a psychiatric residency is not legally mandated. Nevertheless a psychiatric residency is likely to be a practical necessity for any physician functioning as a psychiatrist. For instance, most hospitals accord admissions privileges to the psychiatric wing of a hospital only to those physicians who have completed a psychiatric residency.

b. Licensing of Psychologists

Regulation usually takes one of two basic forms—licensing or certification. A license grants a special privilege, by allowing the holder to engage in activities otherwise proscribed by law. Licensing statutes contain two essential aspects: (1) they limit the performance of certain activities or the rendition of specified services to a designated class of persons; and (2) they restrict the acquisition of a license to those who meet established qualifications and follow certain procedures. For instance, the practice of medicine is restricted to those holding a medical license.

Certification or "title licensing" as it is sometimes referred to, does not seek to reserve certain functions or activities to a specifically designated class of individuals, i.e., those holding a license, but rather limits the use of a designated *title* to those who meet specified training and experience requirements. A certification or title licensing statute may provide, for example, that only those who have completed a Ph.D. or Psy.D. in psychology may describe themselves as "certified psychologists" or "psychologists," or use any other title incorporating the term "psychology" or similar phraseology.

i. Licensing Mode of Regulation

In contrast to psychiatry, the practice of psychology is subject to a licensing requirement in only about three-quarters of the states. In those states that utilize a licensing scheme, anyone not licensed is prohibited from practicing or performing the services normally rendered by a psychologist. The effectiveness of such a form of regulation is thus dependent on the clarity by which the functions and activities which require licensing can be defined.

California employs fairly typical language in its licensing statutes. It stipulates that anyone who is not a licensed psychologist cannot render "psychological services" for a fee. The key phrase, "psychological services," is in turn defined as "the application of psychological principles, methods, and procedures of understanding, predicting, and influencing behavior, such as the principles pertaining to learning, perception, motivation, emotions, and interpersonal relationships; and the methods and procedures of interviewing, counseling, psychotherapy, behavior modification, and hypnosis; and of constructing, administering, and interpreting tests of mental abilities, aptitudes, interests, attitudes, personality characteristics, emotions, and motivations" (California Business and Professions Code § 2903 [1978]).

At the same time, the statute exempts from coverage, those "doing work of a psychological nature," so long as the services they provide are "consistent with the laws governing their respective professions [and] they do not hold themselves out to the public by any title or description of services incorporating the words 'psychological,' 'psychologist,' 'psychology,' 'psychometrist,' 'psychometrics,' or 'psychometry,' or that they do not state or imply that they are licensed to practice psychology ..." id.

ii. Certification or Title Licensing

The remaining states that regulate psychological practice adhere to the certification or title licensing model. States that rely on certification as a regulatory technique typically provide for the issuance of a license to persons who meet specified educational requirements (usually a PhD or in some states, a Masters Degree) and successful completion of a state administered examination. In this respect, states utilizing this certification model are not substantially different from those that rely on a straight licensing scheme. However, unlike states that utilize the licensing mode of regulation, those that utilize the certification model do not prohibit unlicensed persons from performing various functions associated with the practice of psychology. Instead, title licensing generally makes it a criminal offense for anyone not licensed to use various titles such as "psychologist", "psychotherapist", "mental health counselor" or similar titles. Thus, in a title licensing state, non-licensed individuals can, in theory, perform the functions of a psychologist, so long as they do not hold themselves out or advertise as being psychologists.

In contrast to general licensing statutes, the certificate form of licensing avoids the need to define the precise functions that are prohibited to all but those holding a license. Title licensing, however, may encounter legal challenge on other grounds. For instance, one appellate court held that a title licensing statute that made it a criminal offense for an unlicensed psychologist to hold himself or herself out or use the title of "psychologist" was a violation of the petitioners' commercial speech rights under the first amendment. In *Abramson v. Gonzalez*, 949 F.2d 1567 (11th Cir. 1992), the majority concluded that the State's interest in protecting its citizens from incompetent health professionals could be achieved by less restrictive means than the blanket prohibition on non-licensed psychologists to advertise themselves as psychologists. In reaching this result, the court found that such advertising by non-licensed psychologists was not misleading. The dissenting opinion would have sustained the Florida statute as an appropriate exercise of the State's police power to protect the health and safety of its citizens. Except for the decision in *Gonzalez*, no other reported appellate decision has struck down a state title licensing statute.

As suggested by the above materials, professional licensing, in contrast to the certification mode of regulation, enables states to exercise greater control over designated professional functions. However, outright licensing schemes frequently encounter problems of definition that may hamper their enforcement.

c. *Clinical Social Workers*

As noted in Chapter 1, the clinical social worker profession has emerged as one of the major providers of psychotherapeutic treatment. In fact, some estimates suggest that clinical social workers today account for more than half of all psychotherapy services. "Licensure laws governing clinical social workers vary widely in requirements, scopes of practice, ethical standards, governing bodies, levels of licensure, right of privilege, continuing education requirements, and other areas." Model Licensure Law for Clinical Social Workers, Clinical Social Work Federation Memorandum, May, 2002.

Clinical social work licensure laws either fall within the title protection system or the regulation of function, which precludes the performance of specified tasks by anyone other than the license profession. According to data collected by the Clinical Social Work Federation, as of July 2003, at least 41 states have some sort of licensing scheme for clinical social workers. In most instances, state regulation of clinical social workers relies on the certification or title licensing model. Those that meet the certification requirements, receive the imprimatur of the state, which tends to be a precondition to both employment by mental health centers and a condition of reimbursement under either public or private insurance programs. See, 'Summary of States with Practice and Title Protection for Clinical Social Workers', Clinical Social Workers Federation Memorandum, July 23, 2003.

A common adjunct of state regulation of entry or certification for all of the health professions is the establishment of a disciplinary system designed to ensure adherence to a professional mode of conduct. This function is usually undertaken by an administrative body, which has the authority to promulgate rules of conduct and to conduct disciplinary proceedings where there has been a breach of professional standards. This aspect of state regulation is treated in subsection C, which follows.

Questions and Comments

1. *Questions.* What are the relative advantages and disadvantages of standard licensing models in contrast to certification or title licensing? Which is more likely to promote the provision of quality care to members of the public? Which form of regulation is easier to enforce?

2. *Administration of licensing laws.* While licensing laws are products of state legislative action, the standards established by the legislature are typically fairly general and relegate to administrative bodies the task of developing specific standards for the issuance of a license. The appointees to these administrative boards are frequently the representatives of the various professional groups and organizations that represent the profession within the state. Thus, professional organizations such as local chapters of either the American Psychiatric Association or the American Psychological Association have a considerable influence on the standards that are adopted by the regulatory boards.

3. *Enforcement of licensing laws.* Despite the fact that approximately three-quarters of the states license psychologists, and a violation of the licensing act is usually a criminal misdemeanor, very few cases charging unauthorized practice of psychology are ever brought.

4. *Indirect effects of licensing.* State licensing serves not only to provide an imprimatur of competency, but may be a pre-condition to qualifying services rendered by that profession for reimbursement under either publicly financed health services such as Medicare or private health insurance plans. See, Social Workers Vault Into a Leading Role in Psychotherapy, N.Y. Times, Apr. 30, 1985 at 17.

5. *Application of licensing laws to "unconventional" therapy providers.* What obstacles, if any, are there to the use of licensing laws to regulate the

provision of counseling or treatment services by ostensibly religious affiliated entities? Consider in this connection the excerpt from the obituary of L. Ron Hubbard, founder of the Church of Scientology:

> Clients paid Scientology up to $300 an hour for a one-on-one counseling process, known as auditing. To monitor a client's responses to questions, church staff members use an electrical instrument on the client's skin.

> The goal of "auditing," which can go on for years and cost clients hundreds of thousands of dollars, is to increase control over thought processes in a portion of the mind where, Scientologists assert, emotional problems and psychosomatic illnesses are born.

N.Y. Times, Jan. 29, 1986 at 22.

Could standard licensing laws be applied to prevent the rendering of counseling services by the Church of Scientology where the auditor has not been licensed by the state as a psychotherapist? Would there be any First Amendment problems in such regulation?

6. *Retroactive effect of regulation.* Can newly enacted state licensing and certification statutes operate to exclude established therapists from continuing to provide mental health services? Frequently newly enacted statutes and regulations will include "grandfather clauses," under which persons who do not meet the statutory criteria but who had practiced before the statute took effect nonetheless may be licensed. If grandfather clauses are not provided, does the practitioner have any legal remedies? In *Berger v. Board of Psychologist Examiners*, 521 F.2d 1056 (D.C.Cir.1975), the court found a rather restrictive grandfather clause to be unconstitutional. The clause in question permitted the substitution of a master's degree or 24 credit hours of psychology taken subsequent to a bachelor's degree and seven years practice for a doctorate degree and passage of an examination. Berger, a practicing psychologist for 14 years, received his training through apprenticeships with several psychiatrists. The court found that the statute's irrebuttable presumption of appellant's incompetence to practice psychology violated the Due Process Clause of the Fifth Amendment. The court remanded to the licensing board to determine whether Berger's experience was commensurate with that of licensed psychologists.

C. ADMINISTRATIVE REGULATION OF PROFESSIONAL STANDARDS

A common adjunct of state regulation of the professions is the establishment of a disciplinary system designed to ensure adherence to a professional code of conduct. This function is usually undertaken by an administrative body which has the authority to both promulgate rules of conduct and to conduct disciplinary proceedings where there has been a breach of professional conduct. The governing boards of such administrative bodies charged with regulating a particular professional group tend to largely be composed of members of the regulated profession acting as representatives of relevant professional organizations (i.e. The American Medical Association [AMA], The American Psychiatric Association [APA], or The American Psychological Association [Apa]). These boards are generally responsible for both developing practice standards for the particular profession and supervising a disciplinary system, which investigates complaints of professional misconduct and imposes appropriate sanctions on wrongdoers. Permissible sanctions include license revocation or suspension or the imposition of a fine. In a case of alleged professional misconduct, the accused practitioner is entitled to a hearing on the charges. The primary purpose of that hearing is to provide the accused an opportunity to be heard, to present evidence, and to challenge the testimony of adverse witnesses. The hearing need not be a formal trial before a judge or jury; rather, it is usually relatively informal, conducted by an individual member of a panel or by the full board of the regulatory agency. An accused practitioner has various procedural rights, including the right to prior notice of and to be present at the hearing. While the assistance of legal counsel is usually permitted, it has not been viewed as a constitutional right of an individual facing a disciplinary board. Witnesses may present testimony in an informal narrative fashion, rather than in accordance with rules of evidence at trials.

Despite its informality, a disciplinary hearing must, as a matter of constitutional doctrine, comport with basic notions of fairness. The tribunal must reach a decision of guilt or innocence on the basis of probative evidence, and not on the basis of unsupported allegations or prejudice. Normally, an accused practitioner may obtain judicial review of an adverse agency decision. The scope of review is, however, limited. Typically, a court will confine its inquiry to determining whether the accused received a fair hearing, and whether the tribunal based its decision upon substantial probative evidence and not upon speculation, bias, or other arbitrary factors.

The case set forth below illustrates both the legal issues that are commonly raised in these types of proceedings and the role of courts in reviewing the administrative decisions.

MISSISSIPPI STATE BOARD OF PSYCHOLOGICAL EXAMINERS v. HOSFORD

Supreme Court of Mississippi, 1987.
508 So.2d 1049.

ROBERTSON, JUSTICE, for the Court:

I.

This case presents sensitive questions regarding the authority of a state-created board, charged with the governance of a learned profession, to interpret the canons of ethics of that profession and in accordance therewith to discipline a member of that profession. The case also presents questions regarding the scope of appellate judicial review of such disciplinary action.

Substantially, the case involves a charge that a psychologist disclosed patient confidences without the patient's consent and in violation of his profession's confidentiality principles. The state board found that the violation had occurred and suspended the psychologist's license for ninety days. The Chancery Court reversed. As we regard the action taken within the authority and discretion of the Board, we reverse and reinstate the order of suspension.

II.

A.

Robert L. Hosford, Ph.D., holds a license issued by the Mississippi State Board of Psychological Examiners to engage in the professional practice of psychology in this state. Dr. Hosford maintains his offices in Jackson, Mississippi, and exercises his license by practicing in the field of clinical psychology. Dr. Hosford was the Respondent below and is the Appellee here.

The Mississippi State Board of Psychological Examiners (the Board) is the Appellant here.

This case has its genesis in the psychologist-patient relationship between Dr. Hosford and Patricia F. Lindsey and her former husband, Jimmy G. Lindsey. That relationship came into being on December 31, 1981, when the Lindseys, then husband and wife, consulted Dr. Hosford in his professional capacity and sought counseling and advice regarding difficulties they were experiencing in their marital relationship. These consultations continued for a little over two months. During their course, from time to time Patricia Lindsey would meet with Dr. Hosford privately, at other times Jimmy Lindsey would meet with Dr. Hosford privately, and on still other occasions the Lindseys would jointly consult with Dr. Hosford.

In March of 1982 the Lindseys' marriage was clearly on the rocks as Patricia filed in the Chancery Court of Madison County, Mississippi, an action for divorce. Of immediate concern was the temporary custody of the parties' six-year-old son, Jon D. Lindsey. A temporary custody hearing was scheduled in Chancery Court for March 19, 1982. At that hearing Jimmy Hosford [sic] submitted an affidavit made by Dr. Hosford, dated March 18, 1982, setting forth the background of his professional relationship with the Lindseys and giving his opinion that temporary custody of the child should be placed with his father, Jimmy G. Lindsey. The giving of this affidavit has given rise to the present proceedings.

At some time prior to the temporary hearing Dr. Hosford talked with the attorney representing Jimmy G. Lindsey and furnished certain information to the attorney who then prepared a draft of the proposed affidavit. Dr. Hosford then reviewed the affidavit and made editing changes and corrections. The affidavit was then retyped in final form and was executed by Dr. Hosford on March 18, 1982, in the presence of a notary public.

In relevant part the affidavit states that Dr. Hosford counseled with Patricia Lindsey and Jimmy Lindsey both together and separately concerning their personal relationship as well as their respective relationships with their son; that during the course of these consultations Dr. Hosford reached conclusions regarding the "psychological traits of the parties including those which have a bearing on or relate to their respective concepts of parenthood in general and their respective responsibilities and roles as parents to their child in particular." The affidavit continued, making clear that the opinion to be given was "based upon his [Dr. Hosford's] counseling with the parties, his observations of them...." In the affidavit Dr. Hosford then gave rather specific opinions regarding the parenting skills of the two parties, the details of which need not be recounted, except to say that the opinion of Patricia F. Lindsey was quite unfavorable. In the final analysis, Dr. Hosford gave his "professional opinion that the interest and welfare of the child will be best served and promoted by placing his care, custody and control with Jimmy G. Lindsey,...."

Patricia Lindsey did not consent to the giving of this affidavit. If we understand the record correctly, Dr. Hosford stipulated before the Board that he "did not receive a signed waiver of the psychologist-patient privilege."

B.

On March 9, 1983, Patricia F. Lindsey filed with the Mississippi State Board of Psychological Examiners a complaint against Dr. Robert L. Hosford wherein she charged Dr. Hosford with unauthorized, unprofessional and illegal disclosure of matters communicated to him and protected from disclosure by the psychologist-patient privilege. The matter came on for hearing before the Board on November 30, 1984. At that hearing Patricia and Dr. Hosford appeared personally and testified. Patricia established her prima facie case as recited above. Dr. Hosford defended on the alternative grounds that he disclosed no matters the confidentiality of which was protected or, in the alternative, that there was a "clear danger" to the child which created an exception to his profession's confidentiality principle and necessitated disclosure.

In due course on January 22, 1985, the Board rendered its final decision finding that Dr. Hosford had violated Principle 5 of the American Psychological Association's Ethical Principles of Psychologists[1] and further that this violation could not be excused under the clear danger principle, the Board finding "that the clear danger exception to Principle 5 pertains to only life and death situations." The Board exonerated Dr. Hosford from violation of the Mississippi statutory psychologist-patient

---

1. Principle 5, considered by the Board under the authority of Miss.Code Ann. § 73–31–21(a)(1) (1972), reads as follows:
CONFIDENTIALITY
Psychologists have a primary obligation to respect the confidentiality of information obtained from persons in the course of their work as psychologists. They reveal such information to others only with the consent of the person or the person's legal representa- *tive, except in those unusual circumstances in which not to do so would result in clear danger to the person or to others. Where appropriate, psychologists inform their clients of the legal limits of confidentiality.*

* * *

d. *See* Ethical Principles of Psychologists, as printed in 'American Psychologist,' Vol. 36, No. 6 at 633, 635–36 (June 1981).

privilege. Miss.Code Ann. § 73–31–29 (1972). By reason of Dr. Hosford's violation of APA Principle 5, the Board ordered Dr. Hosford's license to practice psychology in the State of Mississippi suspended for a period of ninety days.

Thereafter Dr. Hosford perfected his appeal to the Chancery Court of the First Judicial District of Hinds County, Mississippi. [the Chancery Court reversed the Board's decision] and ordered Dr. Hosford's license reinstated and all proceedings pertaining to the matter expunged.

The Board now appeals to this Court and asks reinstatement of its order of suspension.

* * *

IV.

Proceedings seeking suspension or termination of the license of a professional are serious matters. Quite literally one's ability to earn a living is at stake. Balanced against the professional's legitimate self-interest is the interest of the profession and the consumers of its services in honesty, competency and the observance of reasonable ethical principles.

In a variety of contexts we have held that disciplinary charges against a professional must be proved by clear and convincing evidence. [T]his burden of proof rule applies as well to disciplinary proceedings before the State Board of Psychological Examiners.

Board decisions affecting the license of a psychologist are appealable. In such case the Chancery Court sits as an appellate court, as do we. The Chancery Court has no authority to proceed de novo. Put otherwise, only where the decision is arbitrary and capricious may a court on appeal intervene.

The Chancery Court violated this premise with regard to the issue of consent. The record before the Board reflects that Patricia Lindsey gave no consent or otherwise waived her right to confidentiality. * * *

We emphasize further the role of the Board. It consisted at the time of six members, five of whom were licensed psychologists. One Board member was a person not a psychologist but who has expressed a continuing interest in the field of psychology. Its members are selected by the governor from a list of nominees submitted by the Mississippi Psychological Association. Ordained by statute, the Board is the keeper of the conscience of those who engage in the professional practice of psychology in this state. From this it follows that the Board be the primary interpreter of the ethical principles to which psychologists in this state are subject.

V.

At all times relevant hereto, the Board had authority to suspend the license of one subject to its jurisdiction where that individual "has violated the current code of ethics of the American Psychological Association." One provision of that code regards patient confidences. Principle 5 of the Ethical Principles of Psychologists requires respect for "the confidentiality of information obtained from persons in the course of their work as psychologists." Only two exceptions to the principle of confidentiality are found. The first, of course, is where the patient consents to the disclosure. In the second, even though no consent be given, the psychologist may disclose otherwise confidential information where "not to do so would result in clear danger to the person or to others."

Having well in mind our limited scope of review in matters such as this, there can be little doubt but that the matters disclosed in Dr. Hosford's affidavit were protected from disclosure by the confidentiality strictures of Principle 5. Indeed, we perceive nothing in this appeal which turns upon disputed facts. All agree what happened. At issue is the Board's authority and the propriety of the sanction it has imposed.

* * *

VI.

The Board does not have carte blanche authority to say that Principle 5 means anything it wishes.[2] Yet we do not consider it appropriate that we interject ourselves between the Board and Dr. Hosford regarding its interpretation of the clear danger exception. The Board construes the exception narrowly to apply only to cases where "life and limb" were in danger. Dr. Hosford would have us read it more broadly, to cover situations where the best interest[s] of the child are at stake. In the context of this case, the danger at issue is that without the disclosure temporary custody of the child may not be placed with the parent better suited to exercise such custody in the child's best interest. The Board has considered this danger as one not within the scope of the ethical principle.While today's opinion should not be read as suggesting that we will sanction any reading the Board may give to the language of the APA Ethical Principles, the reading the Board has given these principles in the case at bar is not one that is so arbitrary or unreasonable that we should intervene. It may be true that placement of temporary custody within the wrong parent may result in some emotional or psychological damage to the child. And, indeed, where that issue is presented to a Chancery Court and the issue and facts fully fleshed out, we are by no means prepared to say that the psychologist's lips will be forever sealed

2. The record is not clear whether the Board considered Dr. Hosford's transgression to have been at the point of disclosure of the affidavit to the Chancery Court or at the earlier point of disclosure to Jimmy Lindsey's attorney of the information necessary for preparation of the affidavit. We will proceed here on the assumption that the violation of Principle 5 occurred when the affidavit was filed with the court. Because Dr. Hosford also had a professional relationship with Jimmy Lindsey, he was to some extent empowered to communicate otherwise confidential information to Jimmy's attorney. The ultimate dimensions of this "some extent" need not be addressed as the point was not directly presented below nor is it before us this day.

by the privilege (although we do not decide that point today as the matter is not before us).[3]

In the context of this record we recognize the Board's authority, in the construction of the clear danger exception to Principle 5, to determine that the requirement of confidentiality is paramount to the danger that temporary custody of the child might be placed with the wrong parent. Put otherwise, it is within the Board's authority, as the keeper of the conscience of the psychologists of this state, to consider the requirement of confidentiality of sufficient strength and importance that the clear danger exception should be read narrowly and limited to cases involving imminent danger to life and limb.

Reversed and Rendered.

Questions and Comments

1. *Question.* How explicit must ethical standards be before sanctions are applied? Was the ethical principle which the Board found Dr. Hosford had violated drawn clearly enough for Dr. Hosford to know whether or not he could disclose the information be obtained from Mrs. Lindsey? Did he have adequate notice that "the clear danger exception * * * pertains to only life and death situations" and does not encompass a custodial placement that could adversely affect the child?

2. *Hypothetical.* How would you, as an attorney, advise your client, a psychologist, who tells you that one of his patients, while not an abusive parent, fantasizes about abusing her child because she does not like the child and does not like parenthood? Would disclosure in the course of a custody proceeding violate Principle 5 of the APA's Ethical Principles of Psychologists? Could such information be subpoenaed by a court in a child custody proceeding under most state laws? For further discussion of confidentiality between patient and therapist, see *infra* Chapter 5.

3. *Effectiveness of administrative remediation.* How effective are disciplinary hearings as a remedial device? Is the public interest likely to be adequately protected by hearings conducted and controlled by members of the profession of the accused? Is there any significant risk that leaving the control of discipline to representatives of the profession will lead to policies that are overly protective of the profession and individual practitioners? Any definite answer to these questions is difficult to come by since there have been no systematic studies gauging the efficacy of state disciplinary boards. However, occasional media reports suggest that administrative panels have at times been duly lax in the administration of the disciplinary system.

4. *Self regulation by the professions.* In addition to state regulation, local chapters of each the major mental health professions has adopted an internal regulatory system that supervises the ethical standards of its members. Thus, most professional organizations in addition to stipulating the specific educational requirements for membership also promulgate their

3. We are aware that there is authority in other jurisdictions that the best interest of the child does override the psychologist-patient privilege in a child custody proceeding. * * *

own codes of ethics that frequently influence, at least indirectly, the development of standards applicable to the whole profession. For instance, while psychiatrists, as physicians, must adhere to the ethical standards of the medical profession, the American Psychiatric Association in addition has adopted the American Medical Association *Principles of Medical Ethics With Annotations Especially Applicable to Psychiatry*. Promulgated by the APA Ethics Committee, the annotations are intended to assist psychiatrists in dealing with the "special ethical problems in psychiatric practice that differ in coloring and degrees from ethical problems in other branches of medical practice, even though the basic principles are the same." 'Foreword', APA Principles of Medical Ethics With Annotations Especially Applicable to Psychiatry (1986 ed.). Similarly, ethical standards for psychologists and social workers are provided, respectively, by the American Psychological Association's *Ethical Principles of Psychologists* and the *Code of Ethics* of the National Association of Social Workers.

The professional organizations also perform a policing function in that they may investigate allegations of a member's misconduct or malpractice. The organization's peer group review committees may censure a member or even withdraw membership upon a finding of misconduct. In addition to individual disciplinary action, these organizations have attempted to take more pervasive measures to solve profession-wide problems. For example, in the face of growing evidence of sexual exploitation of patients by therapists, both the American Psychological Association and the American Psychiatric Association have directly addressed the problem by adopting ethics codes that forbid intimate relations between therapists and their patients. See Susan Diesenhouse, 'Therapists Start to Address Damage Done by Therapists', N.Y. Times, Aug. 20, 1989, at E5.

5. *Administrative response to malpractice.* The inability of the states' disciplinary process to control highly unconventional therapies and/or professional misconduct is highlighted by a widely publicized case involving the suicide of Paul Lozano, a Harvard medical student. See, 'Paths of Patient and His Therapist Cross on Dark Journey Leading to Death?' N.Y. Times, Apr. 22, 1992, at 22, and 'Did His Doctor Love Him to Death?' Time, Apr. 13, 1992, at 61.

As reported in the media, Lozano had, for more than two years, intermittently been under the care of a Harvard psychiatrist, Dr. Margaret Bean–Bayog. The therapy, which Dr. Bean–Bayog herself acknowledged as "somewhat unconventional" involved her playing the role of a "nonabusive mom." Among the techniques utilized by Dr. Bean–Bayog was the preparation of flash cards which the patient was to use repeatedly. These cards were inscribed with messages such as "I'm your mom and I love you and you love me very, very much. Say that 10 times." and "I'm going to miss so many things about you, the closeness and the need and the phenomenal sex." Aside from the unconventionality of the therapy, there were allegations that Lozano and the psychiatrist had been sexually involved.

The nature of the therapy that Lozano had undergone with Dr. Bean–Bayog came to light in the fall of 1990 when Lozano consulted another psychiatrist, Dr. William Barry Gault. In spite of Dr. Gault's complaint to the Massachusetts Board of Registration in Medicine, no action was taken by the board and, in fact, the Board is reported as having "lost the [Dr. Gault's] letter". N.Y. Times, Apr. 12, 1992, at 22. Moreover, "even after being given a long file about the case in March 1991" (following Lozano's suicide) by a lawyer for the Lozano family, the board did not, according to news reports, begin a serious investigation until April of 1992 nearly a year after the suicide of Paul Lozano. *Id.*

6. *Regulation of sexual misconduct.* There exists a broad-based professional consensus that sexual relations between a psychotherapist and the patient are likely to be damaging to the patient. Support for this view is provided by studies showing that such "intimacy is damaging to at least 90 percent of the patients involved, sometimes resulting in despondency, loss of motivation, exacerbation of the patient's alcoholism or other drug dependency, hospitalization, and even suicide." 'Sex With Therapists Said to Harm Clients', N.Y. Times, Aug. 29, 1981, at 7. See also, 'Study Examines Adverse Effects of Psychotherapist–Patient Affairs', N.Y. Times, Feb. 4, 1985, at 9, col. 1.

Professional recognition of the harms flowing from sexual encounters between therapist and patients finds expression in the canons of ethics of both the American Psychiatric Association and the American Psychologist Association which proscribe intimate relations between therapist and patient. Notwithstanding these injunctions, various studies suggest that sexual misconduct by mental health professionals remains a significant problem. The findings of one study suggests that between five and six percent of male psychotherapists (including psychiatrists, psychologists, and psychiatric social workers) become sexually involved with their patients. In some cases, the therapists were found to have been involved with 20 to 30 patients at a time. 'Sex With Therapists Said to Harm Clients', N.Y. Times, Aug. 29, 1981, at 7. The magnitude of the problem is also suggested by the incidence of legal actions brought by patients charging their therapist with sexual misconduct. Such actions constituted 17 percent of the malpractice actions filed throughout the country in the mid 1980s. 'Study Examines Adverse Effects of Psychotherapist–Patient Affairs,' N.Y. Times, Feb. 4, 1985, at 9, col. 1. A 1986 survey of psychiatrists found that, of 1,423 respondents, 7 percent of male and 3 percent of female psychiatrists reported having sexual contact with patients. See, 'Therapists Start to Address Damage Done by Therapists,' N.Y. Times, Aug. 20, 1989, at E5.

A variety of legal mechanisms exist that have the potential of discouraging sexual relations between therapist and patient. In states where mental health professionals are licensed, licensing agencies are typically empowered to establish professional standards and impose sanctions in the event that these standards are violated. The effectiveness of this regulatory mode, however, depends very much on the extent to which state licensing agencies are willing to vigorously investigate complaints and impose meaningful legal sanctions. There are seemingly significant differences in the capacity or willingness of different state licensing agencies to deal with this particular problem. In at least one state, California, psychologists who engage in sexual relations with patients may also confront the possibility of criminal sanctions. See, West's Ann.Cal.Bus. & Prof.Code §§ 2960(n) and 2970, which on their face make sexual relations between a psychologist and the patient a criminal offense punishable by imprisonment for up to six months or a fine not exceeding $2,000. But see, *Peer v. Municipal Court of South Bay Jud. Dist.*, 128 Cal.App.3d 733, 180 Cal.Rptr. 137 (1982), where the court found it unnecessary to decide whether such conduct stated a criminal offense under the Business and Professions Code.

The tort system may also deter sexual relations between therapist and patient by exposing the therapist to civil liability for damages. As noted, sexual misconduct at one point accounted for 17 percent of the malpractice actions brought by patients. A number of problems, however, limit the effectiveness of the tort system as a deterrent. For one thing, some patients are deterred from suing by the publicity and exposure of confidential matters that may accompany a law suit. Any patient who sues must disclose not only the details of the sexual relations but also the fact that he or she had been undergoing treatment from a therapist. Beyond this are the costs of a law suit and the uncertainty of damages that will be recovered even if the plaintiff prevails.

The deterrent potential of the tort system may also be limited by the availability of malpractice insurance which tends to shield the therapist from economic loss. However, some insurance programs such as that managed by the American Psychiatric Association have restricted coverage for sexual misconduct, thereby presumably enhancing the deterrent value of the tort system. See, 'Study Examines Adverse Effects of Psychotherapist–Patient Affairs', N.Y. Times, Feb. 4, 1985, at 9, col. 1.

7. *Administrative remediation versus the tort system.* What are the advantages, if any, of administratively conducted disciplinary hearings over other remedial actions such as private suits for malpractice or criminal prosecution? To what extent will the monetary costs and other burdens of litigation discourage an injured or aggrieved patient from pursuing his or her private remedies? Are administrative disciplinary proceedings a good substitute? Does the patient obtain relief in this system, even if the disciplinary proceeding results in a sanction against the practitioner?

Note in this connection that one of the possible advantages of disciplinary proceedings is that the patient or witnesses can frequently avoid the publicity that is invariably connected with a public law suit. Under the law of some states, a disciplinary hearing may be closed to the public and the press. Could this be a significant advantage to a complaining witness? To what extent is the accused practitioner prejudiced by a closed hearing if he is represented by counsel?

8. *Right to counsel.* State law inevitably allows professionals facing disciplinary proceedings before a regulatory agency to have legal representation. The right to have the assistance of counsel is generally discretionary where the disciplinary hearings are conducted through the self-regulation mechanisms of professional organizations. For example, the American Psy-

chiatric Association's *Recommended Procedures for District Branch Ethics Committee Hearings* provide for notice of the complaint, legal counsel at the discretion of the hearing panel, informal hearing at which both the complainant and the accused may present evidence, non-adversarial questioning by the hearing panel, and a decision based upon a preponderance of the evidence. In addition to creating an atmosphere of fairness to the accused, such procedures may help to reduce the risk of erroneous disciplinary action by the hearing panel, for which the accused may choose to file a civil suit for damages. See, APA Ethics Newsletter, Vol. I, No. 3, September 1985.

9. *Violations under federal law.* A psychotherapist's breach of duty may also violate a federal law or regulation. In a somewhat unusual case, the Securities and Exchange Commission charged a psychiatrist who had traded shares based on insider information. The information had been acquired by the therapist in the course of treating a patient who was a senior executive of a company involved in a merger. The psychiatrist, who had been charged under the fraud provisions of the federal securities law, agreed to pay a civil penalty of $27,000 plus any illegal profits he had earned as a result of the insider training. See, 'Insider Trading By Psychiatrist Is Charged By SEC,' Wall St.J., Mar. 4, 1986 at 10.

II. ISSUES IN THE ALLOCATION OF FUNCTION AMONG THE MENTAL HEALTH PROFESSIONS

As noted in Chapter 1, prior to the 1940's, the treatment of mental disorders was primarily the domain of psychiatrists and to a lesser extent, family-care physicians. It is only within the past 50 years that psychology which previously had been associated with academic research moved into patient treatment. In the interim, psychologists, along with clinical social workers, have become a dominant force in mental health treatment and counseling.

This change in the allocation of functions among mental health professionals can be traced to a number of factors. Among these are the changing economics of health care, coupled with structural changes in the way that health services are delivered. Clearly, the growth of managed care systems has stimulated the trend towards the utilization of less costly non-medically trained professionals such as psychologists and psychiatric social workers. At the same time, signals emanating from the legal system by way of legislation and court decisions have served to remove barriers that had previously served to solidify the dominant position of the medical profession in the rendering of mental health services. The materials which follow examine the role of the legal system in reallocating functions among the professions. A concluding section will focus on a key emerging issue: the legislative efforts by psychologists to gain prescription privileges for the treatment of mental disorders.

A. INDEPENDENT BILLING AUTHORITY

VIRGINIA ACADEMY OF CLINICAL PSYCHOLOGISTS v. BLUE SHIELD OF VIRGINIA

United States Court of Appeals, Fourth Circuit, 1980.
624 F.2d 476.

K.K. HALL, CIRCUIT JUDGE:

This controversy arises over the refusal by defendants Blue Shield of Virginia and Blue Shield of Southwestern Virginia to pay for services rendered by clinical psychologists unless such services are billed through a physician. Plaintiffs Virginia Academy of Clinical Psychologists and Dr. Robert J. Resnick, a practicing clinical psychologist, claim that this policy violates Section 1 of the Sherman Act. 15 U.S.C. § 1. The district court found no violation.

We affirm in part and reverse in part.

Since 1962, Blue Shield of Virginia [BSV or the Richmond Plan] and Blue Shield of Southwestern Virginia [BSSV or the Roanoke Plan] have included outpatient coverage for mental and nervous disorders and for psychotherapy as a method of treating those disorders. Between 1962 and 1972, Richmond Plan coverage included direct payment to psychologists for psychotherapy rendered to subscribers. In 1972, this policy was revised to allow payment only when the services were billed through a physician.

The revised policy of the Richmond Plan was announced after consultation with various provider groups, including the American Psychological Association and the defendant Neuropsychiatric Society of Virginia [NSV]. Contact between the Richmond Plan and NSV, however, was particularly close.

Beginning in 1971, Dr. Levi Hulley, M.D., the head of the Plan's professional relations committee, met several times with NSV's president, Dr. Terrell Wingfield, M.D., over the question of payment for psychotherapy. Cooperation between the two groups followed: NSV, at the Plan's request, conducted a survey of Virginia psychiatrists on various aspects of psychiatric practice and later passed a resolution recommending, inter alia, that the Richmond Plan terminate direct payment to clinical psychologists. Immediately prior to adopting its policy, Richmond Plan officials met with a special NSV committee to discuss the scope of mental health coverage. The Plan adopted some of NSV's recommendations, including that of refusing to cover services rendered by psychologists unless billed by a physician.

* * *

[The court first reversed the district court's holding that the challenged activity was entitled to First Amendment protection. It then rejected the district court's alternative holding that the defendant's agreement was protected by the McCarran–Ferguson Act, which exempts from antitrust liability all state regulated "business of insurance." 15 U.S.C. § 1913(b) (1976)].

The final, critical issue is whether these combinations were "in restraint of trade." 15 U.S.C. § 1. The district court held that under the rule of reason, no violation was established. We disagree.

The district court began: "[t]he starting point in deciding the proper factual context for this case is deciding what sector of the economy is affected. * * * In other words, the court looks to see who is competing with whom." 469 F.Supp. at 560. The court found that clinical psychologists are not equal providers of therapy with psychiatrists because they do not render medical treatment and are not qualified to diagnose nervous and mental disorders or ascertain their source. The court further found that medical necessity in most, if not all cases requires regular contact between the psychologist's patient and a medical doctor.

The district court concluded that the clinical psychologist is not competitive with the psychiatrist unless the clinical psychologist is working under the "supervision" of a medical doctor. A psychologist working with a physician, the court continued, is paid by the Plans on an equal basis with a psychiatrist, except that the psychologist must bill through a physician.

> The court can well understand that plaintiffs do not like to bill through a physician as a matter of professional pride. The evidence shows that billing through a medical doctor is a requirement of the Blue Shield plan as a means of ascertaining that the treatment given and billed for was medically necessary. This procedure also tends to promote contact between the clinical psychologists and the physicians at all stages of treatment, and thus enhances the supervisory process.

469 F.Supp. at 561.

Appellants assert that the evidence establishes a boycott and therefore their exclusion from direct Blue Shield coverage is illegal *per se.* We agree that the challenged policy closely resembles that alleged in *Ballard v. Blue Shield of Southern West Virginia,* 543 F.2d 1075 (4th Cir.1976), which we found to be a boycott. Nor does the comparison necessarily fail because the concerted refusal to deal is conditional, rather than absolute.

The "boycott" characterization, however, avails us little in determining whether an agreement such as this is *per se* illegal. Because of the special considerations involved in the delivery of health services, we are not prepared to apply a *per se* rule of illegality to medical plans which refuse or condition payments to competing or potentially competing providers.

While we agree with the district court's rejection of a *per se* rule in this case, we think the court's analysis was misdirected. The rule of reason looks to the impact of the challenged practice upon competitive conditions.

The district court's finding that "the clinical psychologist is not competitive with the psychiatrist in treating nervous and mental disorders unless the clinical psychologist is working under the supervision of a medical doctor" reflects a value judgment, rather than an evaluation of anticompetitive effects.

The record demonstrates that psychologists and psychiatrists do compete; indeed it is susceptible to judicial notice. Both provide psychotherapy, and are licensed to do so by State law. Competition in the health care market between psychologist and M.D. providers of psychotherapy is encouraged by the legislature, and its existence is well documented.

The Blue Shield Plans are a dominant source of health care coverage in Virginia. Their decisions as to who will be paid for psychotherapy necessarily dictate, to some extent, which practitioners will be chosen from among those competent under the law to provide such services.

Whether the "medical necessity" of referral and close contact between the therapist and a physician satisfies the rule of reason, as a cost control measure, is a matter not before us. The Plan's requirement that the psychologists' fee be billed through a physician, however, cannot stand.

The issue is more than one of professional pride. State law recognizes the psychologist as an independent economic entity as it does the physician. The Blue Shield policy forces the two independent economic entities to act as one, with the necessary result of diminished competition in the health care field. The subscriber who has a need for psychotherapy must choose a psychologist who will work as an employee of a physician; a psychologist who maintains his economic independence may well lose his patient. In either case, the psychologist ceases to be a competitor.

* * * [W]e are not inclined to condone anticompetitive conduct upon an incantation of "good medical practice." Moreover, we fail to see how the policy in question fulfills that goal. Any assertion that a physician must actually *supervise* the psychologist to assure the quality of the psychotherapy treatment administered is refuted by the policy itself. The Blue Shield policy provides for payment to psychologists for psychotherapy if billed through *any* physician—not just those who regularly treat mental and nervous disorders. It defies logic to assume that the average family practitioner can supervise a licensed psychologist in psychotherapy, and there is no basis in the record for such an assumption.

There are, of course, procompetitive reasons for requiring examination and consultation by a physician in order to assure that psychotherapy is not needlessly performed to treat a problem with physical etiology, but such safeguards must be accomplished in ways which do not sacrifice the economic independence of the psychologist.

The elimination of the bill-through provision does not preclude a variety of other cost control and quality control measures by Blue Shield.

It does, however, expand consumer and provider alternatives. In addition, competition from licensed non-M.D. providers is likely to result in lower costs and the elimination of needless duplication of administrative costs created by the bill-through requirement.

Affirmed in Part, Vacated and Remanded in Part.

Comments

1.   *Comment.* The *Blue Shield of Virginia* case illustrates the use of the federal antitrust laws to prevent insurance companies from limiting coverage and reimbursement for psychotherapy unless the services were rendered under the aegis of a licensed physician. However, because the rule applied in the *Blue Shield of Virginia* case stems from the antitrust laws, a violation occurs only when the insurance carrier's policy is the product of an agreement by the carrier with another entity. Thus, the decision would not preclude an individual company from unilaterally adopting a policy limiting reimbursement for clinical services performed under the supervision of a psychiatrist unless such restrictions are prohibited by state law (*See,* Note 2 infra.)

2.   *Freedom of choice laws.* A number of states have adopted what are known as freedom of choice laws [FOC]. These laws limit the authority of private insurance companies to condition reimbursement for psychotherapy to services that are prescribed and billed through a physician. A report summarizes the trend over the past twenty years:

> 40 states now have "freedom of choice" laws that require insurance companies to reimburse psychologists for therapy if patients prefer them to psychiatrists. The psychological association is lobbying for similar laws in those states that do not have such laws.

> Social workers are following in the psychologists' footsteps, but are meeting with more opposition, both from insurance companies and psychiatrists. Social work associations have managed to get laws passed in 35 states licensing social workers, but have persuaded only 14 to pass laws requiring insurers to reimburse social workers for psychotherapy.

"Social Workers Vault Into a Leading Role in Psychotherapy," N.Y. Times, Apr. 30, 1985, at 17, col. 5.

B.   AUTHORITY WITHIN THE PSYCHIATRIC HOSPITAL

CALIFORNIA ASSOCIATION OF PSYCHOLOGY PROVIDERS v. RANK

Supreme Court of California, 1990.
51 Cal.3d 1, 270 Cal.Rptr. 796, 793 P.2d 2.

BROUSSARD, JUSTICE.

The issue before us is whether a hospital may permit clinical psychologists to take primary responsibility for the diagnosis and treatment of their hospitalized patients. Prior to 1978, regulations of the Department of Health Services (hereafter Department) declared that a psychiatrist must take charge of the diagnosis and treatment of all patients admitted to psychiatric wards or hospitals. In 1978, however, the Legislature enacted Health and Safety Code section 1316.5, which after confirming that hospitals could admit psychologists to their staffs, provided that such psychologists may, subject to the rules of the hospital, "carry professional responsibilities consistent with the scope of their licensure and competence." In 1980 the Legislature added language declaring that if such a hospital offered services that both physicians and psychologists could perform, "such service may be performed by either, without discrimination."

When the Department in 1983 reissued its 1975 regulations prohibiting hospitals from permitting a psychologist to carry primary responsibility for the diagnosis and treatment of patients, plaintiffs sued for declaratory relief. The trial court granted their motion for summary judgment, declared the regulations invalid, and directed the Department to issue new regulations permitting psychologists to take primary responsibility for the diagnosis and treatment of hospitalized patients. After a complex procedural history, . . . the Court of Appeal reversed the trial court and found that the Legislature intended clinical psychologists to have the right to diagnose and treat their hospitalized patients without supervision from a physician "only in those instances where a physician has initially ruled out a medical basis for the patient's mental disorder and determined that it is not subject to medical treatment, and where the patient's mental disorder does not subsequently become susceptible to medical treatment after admission to the *health* facility." The statutory prohibition against discrimination, it said, prohibits requiring supervision by a psychiatrist, but only "after a medical diagnosis and medical treatment have been ruled out. . . ." We granted review, and now uphold the ruling of the trial court, which we believe conforms to the language and carries out the purpose of the 1978 and 1980 legislation.

Diagnosis and Treatment of Hospitalized Patients

The Department's 1983 regulations, by providing that a psychiatrist must be responsible for diagnosis and treatment of all mental patients, prohibited a hospital from permitting a clinical psychologist to take responsibility for diagnosis and treatment of his own patients. The Court of Appeal opinion went halfway, permitting the psychologist to exercise that responsibility only after a physician has ruled out a medical cause for the patient's condition or medical treatment of that condition. We explain that neither the Department's regulations nor the limitations in the Court of Appeal opinion conforms to the language of section 1316.5.

(a) The Scope of Review

* * *

"[W]hile the construction of a statute by officials charged with its administration . . . is entitled to great weight, nevertheless," "[w]hatever the force of administrative construction . . . final responsibility for the interpretation of the law rests with the courts. Administrative regulations that alter or amend the statute or enlarge or impair its scope are void and courts not only may, but it is their obligation to strike down such regulations."

(b) *The Plain Meaning of Section 1316.5.*

[The majority opinion reached the following conclusions. First, it determined that the clear intent of § 1316.5 that governs the diagnosis and treatment of patients who have been *admitted into a hospital* on psychiatric grounds is to *equalize* the authority of psychiatrists and psychologist to diagnose and treat hospitalized patients the majority opinion relied primarily on an analysis of an related provision pertaining generally to the practice of psychology.

Second, it found that § 2903 of the Business and Professions Code that antedated enactment of § 1316.5 and which, according to the majority was drafted primarily to regulate outpatient practice, authorizes psychologist to diagnose and treat mental disorders *without* the involvement of any other professionals. While acknowledging that § 2903 pertained to the authority of psychologists in the outpatient context, the majority nevertheless found that § 2903 to be relevant to the interpretation of the key phrase of § 1316.5 that gives equal authority to physicians, psychiatrists and clinical psychologists as to those functions that each profession is "authorized by law to perform". Finally, it concluded that it would be would be anomalous to construe § 1316.5 giving psychologists who practice in hospital and institutions *less* authority than they would have in outpatient settings, the majority held that the legislature intended that "psychologists may [like psychiatrists] carry the responsibility of diagnosing and treating the psychological problems of patients in hospitals" without the involvement or supervision of other professional.]

I

We conclude that section 1316.5 means what the trial court said it meant: that a hospital may permit clinical psychologists or its staff to "provide psychological services within the legal scope of their licensure, without physician supervision and without discriminatory restrictions."
* * *

We perceive no statutory basis for this distinction between hospital practice and outpatient practice. . . .

Appellants contend that hospital practice is different because hospitalized patients generally have more serious disorders. It is up to the Legislature, however, to decide whether and how to distinguish between outpatient and hospital practice, and whether any restrictions on the psychologist's hospital practice should take the form of law, administrative regulation, or hospital rule. The Legislature here has chosen to leave the matter to the discretion of each hospital. By authorizing hospitals to permit psychologists to carry responsibilities consistent with their licensors, it has given hospitals discretion to allow psychologists to assume the same responsibilities vis-a-vis their hospitalized patients as in an outpatient setting. Under section 1316.5, hospitals may also adopt non-discriminatory rules that may restrict the psychologist's scope of practice. Section 1316.5 does not permit the courts, or the Department, to enact such restrictions themselves.

Moreover, the first condition laid down by the Court of Appeal opinion—that before a psychologist may take responsibility for a hospitalized patient it must be determined the patient's disorder has no "medical basis"—appears to mistake the distinction between psychology and medicine. That distinction turns on the nature of the treatment each can provide, not the origin of the condition treated. Medical methods, especially medication, are commonly used to treat mental conditions of no known organic origin. Conversely, psychological methods, including testing, counseling, and psychotherapy, are commonly used to treat organic disorders. Psychological tests, for example, are frequently used to diagnose the existence and extent of brain damage resulting from physical injury or disease and, depending on the nature of the damage, psychological methods may be the best or only way to treat the condition.

There is no bright line distinguishing conditions of physical from those of psychological origin. The ultimate cause of a patient's condition may be uncertain or unknown, and in some cases it may be unnecessary to determine that cause to treat him. Indeed, depending on one's view of theories concerning the possible genetic or chemical origin of various disorders, it may be impossible for a physician ever to "rule out" the possibility of an organic basis of the patient's condition. Thus, the authority of the psychologist cannot hinge upon a requirement that the patient's condition derive from a nonorganic cause.

* * *

CONCLUSION

* * *

We conclude that under California law a hospital that admits clinical psychologists to its staff may permit such psychologists to take primary responsibility for the admission, diagnosis, treatment, and discharge of their patients. The 1983 Department regulations requiring a psychiatrist to supervise, diagnosis and treatment of all admitted mental patients are therefore invalid. The judgment of the Court of Appeal is reversed, and the case is remanded for further proceedings consistent with this opinion.

MOSK AND EAGLESON, JJ., STEVEN J. STONE, J. PRO TEM, concurring.

KENNARD, JUSTICE, dissenting.

I dissent.

In granting plaintiff psychologists primary responsibility for the admission, diagnosis, treatment and discharge of hospitalized patients, the majority grants by litigation what could not be achieved by legislation. In doing so, the majority fails to adhere to established standards of judicial review; disregards an eminently reasonable interpretation of the governing statute by the agency charged with its enforcement; and, through a strained interpretation of legislative history, converts legislative rejection into implied legislative acceptance.

Fidelity to established standards of judicial review, a fair reading of statutory language, and an analysis of legislative history, compel the conclusion that the Department of Health Services (Department) did not act in excess of its authority when it promulgated the challenged regulations.

* * *

The standard governing our review of the Department's regulations in this case is unambiguous. The regulations are not alleged to be arbitrary, capricious or wholly lacking in evidentiary support; the only question before this court is whether the regulations "transgress statutory power." . . .

The majority invokes this legal standard but ignores its application. The majority accords no deference whatsoever to the Department's interpretation of the statutes it is charged with implementing and enforcing. Disregarding the Department's reasonable interpretation of the law, the majority substitutes its judgment for that of the rule making agency—in violation of Government Code section 11340.1

Statutory Analysis

The statute contains no express language granting clinical psychologists primary responsibility for hospitalized patients. The majority, however, insists that such a grant is implied in the statute's references to (1) the performance of services by clinical psychologists within "the scope of their licensure" and "without discrimination," and (2) their eligibility for membership on a hospital's medical staff. I disagree.

Scope of Licensure

* * *

Patients do not necessarily enter hospitals with psychological conditions neatly divorced from biological, neurological, physiological or genetic disorders. The nature of an illness cannot be ascertained prior to diagnosis by a legally authorized professional. Physicians are legally qualified to provide comprehensive diagnosis and treatment; psychologists are not.

Unlike psychologists, physicians possess the legal authority to consider all possible causes of an illness. The State Medical Practice Act, which governs physicians, defines diagnosis as including "any undertaking by any method, device, or procedure whatsoever . . . to ascertain or establish whether a person is suffering from any physical or mental disorder. In contrast, the diagnostic authority granted psychologists is severely limited. The scope of their licensure limits psychologists to the diagnosis of *psychological* problems." Unlike physicians, psychologists are not allowed to "use any method, device, or procedure" or determine whether a person is suffering from "any physical or mental disorder." Psychologists are limited to the application of psychological principles to psychological disorders. Thus, they may not diagnose an illness caused or complicated by nonpsychological factors.

Unlike psychologists, physicians are authorized to use "any and all ... methods," including drugs and devices, in the treatment of physical and mental conditions. Psychologists, on the other hand, are statutorily prohibited from prescribing drugs, performing surgery, or administering electro-convulsive therapy. Nor may they use biofeedback instruments that pierce or cut the skin; the law restricts them to the use of psychological principles. Thus, psychologists may not provide treatment that would require more than the application of psychological principles.

* * *

As demonstrated above, the authority of a physician to diagnose and treat is different and much broader than that granted psychologists. Because the concept of primary responsibility includes the ability to evaluate a hospitalized patient's *overall* condition and to select the most appropriate methods of treatment, the Legislature's grant of limited authority to psychologists cannot be equated with *primary* responsibility. Nothing in the statutory scheme suggests otherwise.

* * *

Prohibition Against Discrimination

Section 1316.5 prohibits discrimination between physicians and clinical psychologists with respect to the health services *both* are authorized to perform. As shown above, the health services psychologists are authorized to provide and the health services physicians are authorized to provide are not coextensive.

The antidiscrimination clause does not address the issue of who has primary responsibility for a patient. It simply requires that when psychologists and physicians are *both authorized* to provide the health service, one may not be preferred over the other. Thus, if *psychological* services are required as part of the treatment of a patient, a physician may not be selected to perform the services over a psychologist. The clause neither says nor implies that psychologists are to be given overall primary responsibility for the admission, diagnosis, treatment, and discharge of hospitalized patients.

Legislative History

[A review of the legislative-history of section 1316.5 indicates that the] Legislature specifically considered and *rejected* giving clinical psychologists the very expansion of authority that the majority grants them.

CONCLUSION

Section 1316.5 does not expressly give clinical psychologists authority to assume primary responsibility for hospitalized patients. The statute is, at best, ambiguous and its legislative history strongly suggests that the Legislature had no intention to confer such authority. The regulations the Department enacted were within the scope of its statutory authority and consistent with the language and legislative history of section 1316.5. In disregarding the reasonable interpretation of the administrative agency charged with responsibility for enforcing the statute, and possessed of the expertise necessary to assess the practical impact of alternative interpretations, the majority has succumbed to the temptation to substitute its judgment for that of the Legislature and the Department.

LUCAS, C.J., and PANNELLI, J., concur.

Questions and Comments

1. *Question.* Was California Health and Safety Code section 1316.5 unambiguous? Is the dissent correct that Sec. 1316.5 was inherently ambiguous as to whether the legislature intended to give psychologists co-equal responsibility for intake diagnosis? If the dissent is correct, is it possible that the proponents of the legislation, which broadened the rights of psychologists, intentionally supported a bill which was ambiguous as to its scope? That might be the case, if the proponents of the legislation felt that clarity in the bill (particularly a clear expansion of the rights of psychologists to make them co-existent with those of psychiatrists) would prevent its adoption. Under this strategy, the proponents of the legislation might have foreseen the courts as a more favorable battle ground. In light of the issues posed in question two, are courts really the appropriate forum for resolving these issues?

2. *Primary responsibility for treatment.* The majority's opinion characterizes the Court of Appeals decision as having conferred "primary responsibility for treatment" on psychiatrists. The dissent claims that the Court of Appeals decision did not allocate primary responsibility for *treatment* to psychiatrists, but rather allocated only *initial diagnostic* responsibility. Is it, in fact, possible to bifurcate the diagnostic process from subsequent treatment, with the result that psychiatrists have primary diagnostic responsibility but co-equal treatment responsibility?

3. *Implications of the decision on choice of treatment modality.* Does the majority's decision in striking down the Department of Health services regulation likely to affect the kind of treatment that psychiatric patients will receive? In this connection, consider that generally psychologists are not authorized by law to prescribe psychotropic medication. Since the decision will permit psychologists to have primary treatment responsibility, including diagnosis and the charting of a treatment plan, is this likely to have an impact on the choice of treatment selected by the psychologists? Does this mean that whenever a psychologist is the attending or admitting clinician that the patient is likely to be offered psychotherapy rather than more medically-oriented therapies, such as psychotropic medication? Conversely,

would the allocation of primary responsibility exclusively to psychiatrists result in far greater use of psychotropic medication?

4. *Non-extension of special privileges of psychiatrists to psychologists.* While the court in *Rank* interprets California law as indicative of a legislative intent to equalize the status of psychiatrists and psychologists with respect to providing of services in psychiatric facilities, courts in other contexts have been unwilling to imply a legislative intent to equalize. For instance, an appellate California decision refused to interpret a California law granting immunity to institutional psychiatrists who erroneously order the release of a dangerous patient as covering institutional psychologists. See *Ford v. Norton*, 89 Cal.App.4th 974, 107 Cal.Rptr.2d 776 (2001). Is there a justification for this distinction other than statutory language?

5. *Restrictive practices in education.* Challenges to the dominance of the medically trained therapist have also been pressed in the field of education. For instance, psychoanalytic institutes which are the primary training base for psychoanalysts had traditionally excluded non-medically trained applicants. Thus, training institutes would normally only accept applicants who held a medical degree. In 1985 a group of non-physician mental health professionals brought suit against the American Psychoanalytic Association [APA], challenging on antitrust grounds their exclusion from affiliated the training institutes. While denying the motions by both plaintiffs and defendants for summary judgment, the court rejected the argument that defendant's actions were protected by the First Amendment. *Bryant Welch, Ph.D. et al. v. American Psychoanalytic Association*, 1986 WL 4537 (S.D.N.Y.1986). The case was subsequently settled under an agreement reached by the parties in which the APA agreed to admit non-physicians into the association's training institutes. As noted in the commentary which follows, the result in *Welch v. APA* was applauded not only by psychologists but also by other non-medical mental health professionals.

To the Editor:

Millions of Americans have undergone, or will undergo, psychoanalysis. All of us, therefore, should applaud the legal settlement of a lawsuit brought by four psychologists against the American Psychoanalytic Association and the International Psychoanalytical Association to get them to open the doors of their major training institutes to therapists who do not hold medical degrees (Health pages, Oct. 20).

Before this case, the American Psychoanalytic Association and the International Psychoanalytical Association restricted admission to their training institutes to psychiatrists, barring clinical social workers, psychologists and other mental-health professionals who are not psychiatrists. This policy disregarded the basic reality that nonmedical therapists now perform most of this country's therapy.

That this is so was documented in a May 1, 1985 article, according to which the number of social workers offering psychotherapy in the United States more than doubled between 1975 and 1985, rising from 25,000 to 60,000. During the same period, the number of clinical psychologists doubled from 15,000 to slightly more than 30,000. In comparison, the total number of psychiatrists increased by only one-third, from 26,000 to 38,000.

In addition, as your report on the successful suit noted, competent provision of psychotherapy and psychoanalysis does not require medical training. In the event that a client needs drug therapy or other medical care, he or she can be referred to a psychiatrist or other physician for treatment.

That clinical social workers and psychologists can now attend American Psychoanalytic and International Psychoanalytical Association institutes is not a crucial victory. They have long studied side by side with psychiatrists in the many psychoanalytical institutes that are not affiliated with those organizations. It is, however, a gain for simple fairness. The majority of this country's therapists will no longer be subject to arbitrary restrictions on their training.

ROBERT J. EVANS

[President, New York State Society
of Clinical Social Work Psychotherapists]

N.Y. Times, Nov. 12, 1988, at 14.

6. *Perspectives on the allocation of responsibility among the professions.* As noted, the past 30 years has witnessed a significant reallocation of functions among the primary mental health professions. The perspectives of the respective professions to these changes are captured by the two commentaries set out below:

To the Editor:

The growth of lay psychotherapy in the United States ("Social Workers Vault Into a Leading Role in Psychotherapy" by Daniel Goleman, Science Times, April 30) threatens to denude the country of its only wholly qualified line of defense against mental and emotional illness: the physician trained both in biological and psychodynamic psychiatry. Behind this growth are historical, economic and social reasons.

For decades, social workers, psychologists, nurses and others were brought into the herculean task of dealing with mental illness in hospitals and outpatient clinics. All originally had other tasks, but were permitted, under supervision, to assume some treatment with certain patients. They were essentially "barefoot doctors" in this struggle.

The development of Medicaid and Medicare furthered the process. It became very profitable for hospitals and clinics to use salaried nonmedical personnel to treat patients, since the hourly rates for reimbursement were identical whether treatment was by physician-psychiatrists or others.

Many of these barefoot doctors jumped to the erroneous conclusion that they were fully competent to do what they had been encouraged to do in an emergency, and now present themselves as independent practitioners capable of treating all patients for all conditions. They left salaried positions, where there was at least a semblance of medical and psychiatric supervision, for the marketplace.

They are often either unaware, or will deny, that they lack the essential medical and psychiatric training that is the only basis for diagnosis and treatment. The result is malpractice.

Depression, for instance, is not diagnosed or is misdiagnosed, and the wrong kind of treatment is then prescribed; a patient is given psychotherapy for a type of phobia that responds well to other treatment; physical symptoms are misinterpreted as "psychosomatic." Since patients rarely complain or sue, this has not caught the public attention.

A preliminary physical examination by a physician; getting a psychiatrist or general physician who will agree to "cover" by prescribing antianxiety or antidepressant medication; "supervision" of cases by a psychiatrist—none of these suffice to prevent serious errors of diagnosis and treatment by a lay therapist in independent private practice. Every patient is, in effect, unwittingly playing Russian roulette. And fees by all who entered the market have risen quickly to a common level.

Psychiatrists are not blameless. Heads of department are reluctant to antagonize professional blocs within their administrations. * * * Absence of criticism has emboldened lay therapists.

The extent to which they are emboldened is indicated by lawsuits entered or pending against the American Psychoanalytic Association and the American Academy of Psychoanalysis, major educational bodies that train physician-psychiatrists. The suits seek to force these organizations to train nonphysicians. The suits will not be won because these organizations have the right to set the standards they consider proper for the public health, but the suits will affect public opinion and serve to harass those organizations.

Will the barefoot doctors drive out the doctors? Will treatment of mental and emotional illness sink to the lowest common denominator? Since anyone can claim competence, is it likely, by a Gresham's Law, that there will be no truly competent medical specialists to treat mental or emotional illness? The implication for the public health is not good.

SEYMOUR C. POST, M.D.
Assoc. Clinical Professor of
Psychiatry
College of Physicians and
Surgeons of Columbia University
New York, May 15, 1985

N.Y. Times, May 19, 1985, at 20, col. 3.

To the Editor:

Dr. Seymour C. Post's letter ("And Now the Age of the Barefoot Psychotherapist," May 19), in response to Daniel Goleman's article on the growing psychotherapeutic role of social workers (Science Times, April 30) was, sadly, further evidence of the elitist attitude American psychiatry has toward the treatment of mental illness. One need only look at the shrinking therapy dollar in terms of third-party unwillingness to underwrite lengthy treatment to understand American Psychiatric Association rationalizations for its "closed-shop" attitude.

Dr. Post's choice of the "barefoot doctor" metaphor is interesting in light of differences in medical versus graduate training within psychology. While most medical schools offer a four-to six-week course in behavioral science in addition to several weeks' rotation through a psychiatric unit, graduate programs in clinical and service-oriented psychology provide four years of academic and specialized training in psychopathology and its treatment in addition to a year's internship, usually in a hospital or an outpatient setting.

While a newly graduated physician entering a psychiatric residency knows little about psychopathology, a newly graduated psychologist already possesses specialized graduate training. It is common practice in many medical centers for psychologists to participate in the training of psychiatry residents.

Dr. Post does, however, have a valid point in emphasizing that a medical background is necessary in dealing with specific psychiatric disorders. Most psychologists would agree that there are subgroups of psychiatric disorders that require medication. Despite this, there are psychological disorders that do not require medication and that respond favorably to drug-free psychotherapy. Since most hospital-based staff psychiatrists rarely carry regular therapy cases within the hospital, a task usually relegated to psychologists, it is difficult not to wonder who the most experienced and specialized individual is.

Let us propose a truce, with medication issues and medically oriented diagnoses within the purview of psychiatry and behavioral psychodiagnostics and psychotherapy as the domain of psychologists and others licensed to practice. "The implication for the public health," of which Dr. Post speaks, is certainly "not good," given the unfortunate animosity these fields have toward one another, and taking potshots at each other is not conducive to the cooperation necessary to provide quality mental-health care.

PAUL MICHAEL RAMIREZ
Clinical Neuropsychologist
Bronx Psychiatric Center
Bronx, May 21, 1985

N.Y. Times, May 29, 1985, at 20, col. 3.

* * *

C. PRESCRIPTION PRIVILEGES

1. Overview

As noted in Chapter 1, advances in neural science coupled with the development of a range of psychotropic medications that can be used to treat a variety of mental disorders have fundamentally transformed the delivery of mental health services. Treatment is increasingly relying on psychopharmacology either by itself or in conjunction with psychotherapy.

While federal law regulates the dispensing and distribution of a limited class of pharmaceuticals, it is state legislatures that authorize prescription privileges for designated professional classes. The legal authority to write prescriptions has, with limited exceptions, been the exclusive province of those holding a medical license. Thus, the use of psychopharmacology in the treatment of patients has generally been restricted to medical practitioners, which includes those holding an M.D. or similar degree and, by definition, psychiatrists who must be medically trained and licensed.

Since legal authority to prescribe has largely been confined to the medical profession, psychologists are in effect barred from using psychopharmacology as a treatment tool. As a consequence, under current law, the role of psychologists in all states but one is limited to the use of psychotherapy, which involves only oral communications between the patient and the therapist.

The economic implications for clinical psychologists of these trends, which are likely to continue with future advances in psychopharmacology, led the Council of the American Psychological Association (hereinafter "Apa" to distinguish it from the American Psychiatric Association which goes under the acronym "APA"), the principal organization representing psychologists, to adopt a resolution in 1995 making "the pursuit of prescription privileges an official objective of the organization."[4] As a result, the Apa and its local affiliates have pressed for changes in state law designed to extend to psychologists, who have undergone additional training in psychopharmacology, authority to write prescriptions for psychotropic medications.[5]

Four arguments have been advanced to support the Apa's policy of seeking prescription privileges for psychologists. First, its advocates have argued that cost factors serve to limit access to mental health care, which would be mitigated if psychologists were allowed to prescribe. Second, organized psychology contends that the scarcity of psychiatrists in some rural areas means that the mental health treatment needs of these communities are not being met. Extending prescription privileges to psychologists would, it is argued, alleviate the gap.[6] Third, Apa points to the fact that the "bulk of psychotropic medications are in fact" not being prescribed by psychiatrists, but instead "are being prescribed by

---

4. Robiner, Bearman, and Berman, 'Prescription Authority for Psychologists: A Looming Health Hazard?', 9 Clinical Psychology: Science and Practice, 231 (2002) [hereinafter Robiner] at 232.

5. The 1997 Physicians Desk Reference (PDR) lists *circa* 80 medications that fall under the category of psychotropic drugs.

6. Those challenging prescription privilege for psychologists contend that there is no shortage of mental health care in rural areas since primary care physicians, and not psychiatrists, are responsible for at least 50% of all prescriptions for psychiatric medication written throughout the country. Thus, under their view the shortage of psychiatrists does not, as contended, support the conclusion that the population in these areas do not have access to mental health treatment involving psychopharmacology. Robiner at 241.

primary care physicians who have no extensive training in the treatment of mental disorders." See J. Scotti and B. Elelstein, *Education* in Introduction to Clinical Psychology, ed. L. Heiden and M. Hersen, Plenum Press, (1995), 313. Finally, advocates for the Apa's position point to the fact that other non-physician health care professionals currently have full or partial prescription privileges.[7] For instance, podiatrists are able to prescribe in all 50 states; optometrists have limited prescription privileges in most states; advanced nurse practitioners have partial or complete prescription privileges in 47 states; and 40 states allow physicians' assistants to prescribe. See Cullen, "In Pursuit of Prescription Privileges," 28 Professional Psychology: Research and Practice, 101, 102 (1997).

The extension of prescription privileges to psychologists is vigorously opposed by various organizations representing the medical profession, including the American Psychiatric Association (APA) and the American Medical Association (AMA). This opposition is grounded on the contention that the risks and possible complications associated with the use of prescription drugs requires specialized training education that psychologists do not generally possess. Specifically, opponents point out that while covered drugs (i.e. those required by federal law to be dispensed only by prescription) have potential curative powers, their use presents very substantial side effect risks and possibly adverse interaction with other medications that the patient may be taking to treat other conditions. Under this view, those prescribing a drug must not only be aware of the potential side effects, but also be able to balance the beneficial effects against the possible risks. It is argued that such balancing of risks and benefits requires not only a thorough knowledge of the biological effects on the system of various pharmaceutical agents, but also the underlying chemistry of the reactions that they may produce. In the words of one commentator, "a competent prescriber must understand not only the particular medication but also other drugs, treatments and potential chemical interactions, as well as possible physical and emotional side effects on each patient." Coleman & Shellow, "Prescribing Privileges for Psychologists: Should Only 'Medicine Men' Control the Medicine Cabinet?," 1990 Journal of Psychiatry and Law, Fall–Winter, 269, 276 (1990) [hereinafter Coleman & Shellow]. The exercise by psychologists of independent prescription privilege will, it is argued, "undermine patient care and contribute to medication errors."[8]

2. *Legislative Initiatives and Developments*

The model legislation for prescription privileges endorsed by the Apa would grant psychopharmacology prescription privileges to psychologists

---

7. The relevance of prescription authority by non-physician professional such as dentists, optometrists, podiatrists and nurse practitioners is challenged by opponents of psychologist prescription privilege. According to some commentators, "[Their] train- ing models are much closer to that of physicians than those of psychologists and their clinical practice is more focused on physical functions including medication effects." Robiner at 241.

8. Robiner at 242–243.

who meet the requirements for prescription privileges under state law. Licensing to prescribe would be tied to a series of specific requirements, including the holding of a doctorate level psychology degree, completion of specialized psychopharmacology training programs, and passage of a certifying examination. Thus, the certification to prescribe would have requirements in addition to those needed to qualify for a license to practice psychology.

Since 1995, bills patterned on the Apa model legislation have been introduced in 16 states. These legislative initiatives failed to gain approval at either the committee or full chamber stage in all but two states. New Mexico became the first state in 2002 to enact legislation enabling psychologists who meet specified requirements to qualify for a prescription license. N.M. Stat. 1978 § 61–9–17. More recently, Louisiana added the category of "medical psychologist" who upon meeting various qualifications is permitted to prescribe pharmaceutical medication for the treatment of mental or emotional disorders. La.Stat. Title 28, § 58–1.

The New Mexico legislation establishes a three-stage procedure whereby doctorate-level (Ph.D. or doctorate in clinical psychology) psychologists who fulfill various conditions may be licensed to prescribe psychotropic medications. An initial stage leading to a *conditional* license requires an application to satisfy various conditions. Among the conditions are the following: (1) completion of a doctorate program in psychology from an accredited institution of higher learning; (2) the holding of a license to practice as a psychologist in the state of New Mexico; (3) successful completion of 450 hours of an approved "organized program of education" pertaining to psychopharmacology;[9] (4) completion of an approved 80–hour supervised practicum in clinical assessment and pathophysiology; (5) completion under the supervision of a psychiatrist *or medically trained physician* (italics added) the treatment of no less than 100 patients; and (6) passage of an approved (by the Board of Psychologist Examiners and the Board of Medical Examiners) national certification examination that tests the applicant's knowledge of pharmacology in the diagnosis, care and treatment of mental disorders.

Upon satisfactorily completing the above requirements in phase one, an applicant is eligible apply for a phase two *conditional* prescription certificate. Those holding a conditional certificate, which is valid for two years, may prescribe psychotropic medication "under the supervision of a licensed physician."

At the end of the two-year supervised prescription period, an applicant may apply for a phase three full prescription certificate. Such certificate will be issued subject to an applicant providing evidence that he or she has: (1) successfully completed a two-year period of prescribing psychotropic medication as certified by a supervising licensed physician;

---

9. Consisting of the following core areas of instruction: (a) neuroscience; (b) pharmacology; (c) psychopharmacology; (d) physiology; (e) pathophysiology; (f) appropriate and relevant physical and laboratory assessment; and (g) clinical pharmacotherapeutics.

(2) successfully completed a process of independent peer review; (3) hold a valid psychologist license; and (4) adequate malpractice insurance coverage.

The Louisiana legislation is somewhat more restrictive than New Mexico's. Persons licensed as medical psychologists may only prescribe in consultation and collaboration with the patient's primary or attending physician. Also, medical psychologists must re-consult with the patient's physician prior to making a change in the patient's medication regime.

3. *Educational Requirements for Competency to Prescribe*

A key issue in the debate concerning prescription privileges for psychologists is the length and type of education and training needed for the exercise of prescription authority in a manner beneficial to patients while avoiding undue health risks. Clearly, the delineation of educational prerequisites for prescription authority needs to take into account both the diagnostic complexities associated with the prescription function and the risks that can result from prescription errors.

a. *Risk Factors Associated with the Prescription Function*

As detailed in chapter 1, various classes of psychotropic drugs pose serious side effects risks, that in some instances can be life threatening, For instance, psychotropics can lead to or exacerbate kidney disease or result in permanent neurological damage. Antidepressants can cause cardiac arrhythmias. Moreover, "[a]lthough newer psychoactive medications such as SSRIs, have a more favorable side effect profile than previous generations of medications, they are still powerful drugs that can yield serious adverse side effects[10] ..." Minimization of such outcomes is likely to require close monitoring and continuous evaluation of a patient's blood chemistry or anatomical functions including, in particular, neurological responses.

A further complication associated with the use of psychotropic medication is the potential of adverse effects due to the drug interactions. Psychotropic drugs interact not only with each other but with drugs prescribed for other medical conditions. In fact, [p]sychoactive medications have been described as presenting more complex drug interactions and adverse effects than any other class of drugs[11]. For instance, according to one author:

> "psychotropics can affect the blood level of drugs prescribed for other medical conditions compromising the treatment of conditions such as AIDS. Moreover, the potential of adverse drug interactions is not insignificant in the light of statistics indicating that "[m]any people who take psychoactive medications also take other medications that complicate their care[12] ..." In fact, one study has found that "[i]n primary care and psychiatric settings, more than 70% of

10. Robiner at 242.

12. *Id* at 242.

11. *Id* at 242.

patients prescribed an antidepressant take at least one other drug and a third take at least three other drugs[13]."

The complexities associated with the prescription of psychotropic medications are exacerbated by the constant expansion of medication options. For instance, in 1998, the new Food and Drug Administration "approved 90 new drugs, 30 new molecular entities, 124 new or expanded use of agents, and 344 generic drugs".[14] Moreover, "nearly half of the drugs currently marketed have become available only with the past decade".[15] This phenomenon, it has been argued, increases the need for those prescribing mediations to have a knowledge of the full pharmaceutical spectrum and a sufficient science background to understand the chemistry of drug interaction.[16]

b. Educational Requirements

As might be expected, organized psychology and the medical/psychiatric establishment have very different conceptions concerning the educational experience that is required to exercise the prescriptive function in an effective and safe manner. The model legislation endorsed by the Apa would require, in addition to a doctorate degree in psychology, a post-doctorate training program of psychopharmacology-related instruction with a minimum of 300 contact hours taken either full or part-time. The subject matter to be covered in this 300–hour instructional component is not specified. Additionally, the Apa model would also require supervised practice of 100 patients over an unspecified amount of time.

As previously noted, the New Mexico educational requirements exceed those proposed by the Apa. In place of the 300–hour Apa proposed requirement, New Mexico stipulates 450 hours of psychopharmacology-related instruction. Additionally, the New Mexico legislation imposes an 80–hour supervised practicum in clinical assessment and psychophysiology. Also, the New Mexico certification requirements, while adopting the Apa model calling for the supervised treatment of 100 patients, imposes a 400–hour requirement for this segment. Finally, the New Mexico legislation imposes a two-year conditional permit period during which the prescribing psychologist must be supervised by a licensed physician.

The medical/psychiatric establishment has not articulated the educational requirements that might substitute for a medical education for qualifying other mental health professionals, such as psychologists, to exercise a prescription function. However, the literature reflecting the view point of the psychiatric/medical professions seems to universally reject the educational proposals backed by the organized psychology as grossly inadequate in achieving minimum levels of prescription competence. Moreover, the differences that exist between the professions seem fundamental and therefore are unlikely to be bridged by nuanced

13. *Id* at 242.

14. Robiner at 242.

15. Id.

16. Id.

changes in the requirements that have been set forth by the Apa or its affiliates.

Basically, the medical/psychiatric community takes the view that the overall educational experience of doctoral graduates in psychology does not provide an adequate basis for the prescription of medications. From the perspective of organized psychiatry"[t]he biological sciences and related course work is the educational foundation for knowledge and conceptual understanding related to prescription safety[17]". Under this view, both the undergraduate and doctoral level education of psychologists are severely deficient in the biological sciences. Reference is made to the fact that the undergraduate preparation for entry into medical school typically requires one or more courses in biology, physics, inorganic and organic chemistry, microbiology, genetics and human physiology. By comparison, the undergraduate psychology curriculum has a social science or behavioral focus with only a minimum of biological or science courses being required. As a consequence, one study found that only 7% of doctoral graduates in psychology have a significant undergraduate biology or chemistry course background.[18]

At the graduate level the discrepancies between the curricula of medical schools and those of doctoral programs in psychology are even wider in the view of those questioning the sufficiency of the educational requirements proposed by organized psychology. As described by one critic of the Apa's proposal:

> The [graduate] training of physicians and other doctoral providers (e.g., dentists) entails [extensive] coursework in anatomy, biochemistry, cell biology, immunology, microbiology, pathology, pharmacology, physiology, as well as laboratory experiences in the biological and physical sciences and physical, clinical training. . . . [By comparison, doctoral level psychology education] never has required extensive training in the biological sciences Programs vary in how much training is provided in the biological and physical sciences, but it is generally quite limited for degrees in professional psychology. If anything, the training of psychologists is moving away from the "scientist-practitioner" model to other models that de-emphasize scientific background and activities.[19]

The Apa's licensing proposal presumes that any deficiencies in basic science and biology in the previous educational experience of psychologists can be rectified by *post doctoral* education and training Thus, the Apa's model legislation contemplates a special *post doctoral* training program of 300 contact hours of didactic instruction in pharmacology supplemented by a period of supervised practice involving at least 100 patients. This approach underlies the New Mexico prescription licensing legislation which however, has increased the educational requirements from those recommended by the Apa to 450 hours of training in

17. Robiner at 236.
18. *Id.*

19. Robiner at 242.

pharmacology related subjects and an 80 hour psycho-pharmacology practicum.

Clearly, a key issue dividing the medical and psychologist professions is the adequacy of the specialized post graduate education and training under either the Apa or the New Mexico models. From the standpoint of the medical profession the presumed deficiencies in science and biology in the undergraduate and graduate level curricula of psychologists cannot be made up by relatively concentrated post doctoral educational experience. Simply in terms of the number of contact hours of class room instruction, the 300 or 450 hours contemplated by the models being put forth by the psychologist profession compare unfavorably, it is asserted, with the *circa* 1800 hours of medical school classroom instruction[20] and the more than 1500 hours of classroom instruction in relevant clinical and biologically based subjects in the psychiatry residency programs.[21] Moreover, the argument is made that there are equally wide discrepancies in the extent of supervised clinical training. In contrast to the 80 hour practicum and 450 hours of supervised treatment required under the New Mexico psychologist prescription legislation, medical students are required to devote much of their second and third year of medical school to supervised clinical work with patients. Moreover, to be licensed a medical school graduate must complete a one year internship following medical school. However, since physicians are called upon to do much more than write prescriptions the medical school paradigm in not necessarily the appropriate one for judging the scope and depth of training that is needed for a reasonable level of prescription competency.

As suggested by the section that follows, resolution of the educational requirements issue is not likely to be decided by legislatures only on the basis of what is the *optimum* level of care in the mental health treatment context. While public health considerations are likely to be a primary consideration other factors including financial ones will undoubtedly influence how the educational issue is legislatively resolved. Nevertheless, one may question whether existing undergraduate and graduate programs in psychology provide an adequate educational experience in the biological sciences if the nature of psychological practice is to expand to include a prescription function.

4. *Economic Dimension of the Debate*

Since 1984, organized psychology has floated legislative prescribing proposals in some 20 states, and has had legislation introduced in 16, While the proposed legislation has been adopted in the only one state, the Apa's legislative initiatives in this area are continuing and various state legislative committees are likely to confront the issue in the coming years. As a consequence, the legislatures of various states are likely to be faced with having to decide whether to authorize or withhold psycholo-

20. Id.

21. "Psychologists Prescription Authority, Memo with Chart Issued by the American Psychiatric Association (Undated)."

gist prescription privileges and in that connection weigh both the health-safety and *economic* implications of the proposal.

How these varying considerations may come into play is illustrated by the following hypothetical fact situation: Assume a legislative finding that the extension of the privilege to psychologists and primary care physicians will lead to a 30% increased error rate[22] than that of either primary care physicians or psychiatrists. At the same time, there is a legislative finding that the current billing rates for psychiatrists average $200 per session, compared to $100 per session for licensed doctoral level psychologists. Thus, under these hypothetical facts, the extension of a prescription privilege to psychologists would lead to a projected cost saving in the operation of the mental health system of some estimated amount though this would be accompanied by some reduction in the overall quality of health care due to the hypothetical greater error rate in prescriptions written by psychologists.

But a legislature's calculation of cost/benefits would also need to take into account a number of related variables including the effect of any system wide cost savings or increased access to mental health care due to the reduction in cost. For instance if the per unit cost of prescription related mental health care is reduced by the utilization of less costly professionals, would this lead to greater access, either because more non-insured individuals could now afford care, or because existing insurance limits of insured patients would allow an increase in the number of covered sessions with prescription authority therapists? Given these decision variables, it seems evident that the way the issue is legislatively resolved would affect the interests of not only the respective professions but also that of insurers and other agencies whose economic exposure would be affected by the outcome.

Questions and Comments

1. *Review of Chapter One materials on psychopharmacology.* The range of psychopharmacological medications currently being utilized is described in Chapter 1. As indicated by these materials, psychopharmacological medications potentially have very serious side effects, and sometimes interact negatively with other medications that the patient may be taking for non-psychiatric disorders.

2. *Alternative educational models.* The Apa's emphasis on post-doctoral training rather than modification of the undergraduate and graduate education requirements to prepare psychologists for a medication prescribing role undoubtedly reflects the need of the organization to accommodate the interests of psychologists who are already established in their careers. In the absence of such consideration, what educational requirements at the under-

---

22. "Error rate" as used here means prescriptions that are either contra-indicated because of the patient's condition or because the prescription will interact adversely with other medications that the patient is taking.

The assumed greater error rate for psychologists is simply a hypothetical fact assumption and is not based on any empirical evidence, though if the New Mexico legislation is in operation for a period of time, estimates of error rates for the various professions may be ascertainable.

graduate and graduate level should be imposed as a minimum condition for qualifying as a prescribing psychologist? Presumably, the prescription function involving psychotropic medications can be exercised in a safe and proper manner without a medical degree. However, since medications can have a profound effect on not only the nervous system, but also the entire biological state of the patient, some background in physiology and the biological sciences would seem to be indicated. Moreover, it could be argued that it would be rational to modify both the undergraduate and graduate curricula for those students aspiring to a clinical psychology practice with prescription authority. Should legislative committees considering prescription privileges for psychologists therefore stipulate a set of undergraduate and graduate requirements in the biological sciences, at least for those who have not yet completed their training in psychology? Moreover, if such requirements were established at the state legislative level, is it likely that institutions of higher learning would in turn modify their programs in psychology to incorporate the required courses?

3. *Hypothetical*. Henry Helper has a practice as a clinical psychologist in Small Gulch, New Mexico. Two years ago, Dr. Helper satisfactorily completed all requirements stipulated by New Mexico law for being licensed as a prescribing psychologist. As a result, he has been able to acquire a number of new patients whose disorders require prescription of psychotropic medication. Ten months ago, a new patient, Luna Loop, came to see him with a variety of complaints including a feeling of depression accompanied by constant fatigue, low energy, and forgetfulness. During the initial two sessions, Dr. Helper sought to diagnose Ms. Loop's condition. Based on the symptoms that she relayed and the disclosure that earlier in her life, she had been briefly hospitalized for a severe depressive episode, Dr. Helper diagnosed her as suffering from depression and prescribed Tofranil, a tricyclic antidepressant. Over the next two months, Ms. Loop's condition did not change and she continued to suffer from the original symptoms, which, if anything, had become more pronounced. Since she was not responding to the Tofranil, Dr. Helper changed her medication to Wellbutrin, another antidepressant. Five months after she had started seeing Dr. Helper, Ms. Loop was involved in a vehicular accident, which resulted from momentary confusion leading her to step on the accelerator rather than the brake. Following the accident, she was taken to the local emergency room by ambulance where she was found to have fractures of the femur and the collarbone. Additionally, tests of her blood chemistry disclosed that she had a severe thyroid condition. In the view of the attending physicians, her thyroid condition had developed to the point that she either had suffered or was about to suffer a myxedema coma, which is a condition associated with severe thyroid deficiencies. Moreover, the physicians at the hospital informed her that her thyroid condition, which can have symptoms similar to those of depression, was probably responsible for the symptoms that led her to consult Dr. Helper five months earlier. She also learned that had her thyroid condition could easily have been diagnosed by a simple blood test and could readily have been treated with TSH (thyroid stimulating hormone) medication.

In view of the substantial medical bills and claims for damages by the driver of the other vehicle, Ms. Loop consults Sam Bailey, a personal injury lawyer. Upon reviewing the case, Lawyer Bailey advises Ms. Loop to file a malpractice action against Dr. Helper on the basis that he both failed to properly diagnose her condition and prescribed the wrong medication, which in combination worsened her condition ultimately leading to the vehicular accident.

At the trial, the defense did not attempt to refute any of the facts. However, as a matter of law, the defense asserted that Dr. Helper's actions had not deviated from the "degree of skill and care ordinarily employed under similar circumstances by members of the psychology profession in good standing". Lawyer Bailey, however, argued that the standard of care should be based on the skill and care ordinarily exercised by "all classes of health practitioners legally authorized to prescribe medication." and not limited to the skill and care of "psychologists in good standing who hold a prescription license".

Which standard of care should be applied to determine the liability of Dr. Helper for misdiagnosing Ms. Loop's condition and the associated prescription errors?

4. *Apa proposal governing the standard of care for prescribing psychologists.* The Apa takes the position that psychologists who acquire independent prescriptive authority should not "stand in the shoes" of other health care professionals, such as psychiatrists or primary care physicians. Instead, their performance should be compared to that of other psychologists. The Apa's draft legislation on this point would be as follows:

"Psychologist's Standard of Care:

Any licensed psychologist authorized under this act to prescribe shall be held to that degree of skill and care ordinarily employed, under similar circumstances by members of the psychology profession in good standing, and using reasonable care and diligence in the exercise of this authority."

See 'The Legal and Legislative Considerations of Prescription Privileges for Psychologists', American Psychological Association, Office of Legal & Regulatory Affairs, Practice Directorate, Jan. 11, 1994, at 20.

5. *Psychologist opposition to prescription privileges.* Not all psychologists and organizations representing psychologists concur with the Apa's policy of seeking prescription privileges for psychologists. For instance, the American Association of Applied and Preventive Psychology has come out against prescription privileges. See Press Release of the American Association of Applied and Preventive Psychology, Jan. 11, 1995. See also Adams and Bieliauskas, 'On Perhaps Becoming What You Had Previously Despised: Psychologists as Prescribers of Medication', 1 Journal of Clinical Psychology in Medical Settings, 189 (1994); Moyer, 'An Opposing View on Prescription Privileges for Psychologists', 26 Professional Psychology: Research and Practice, 586 (1995).

Chapter Three

PROFESSIONAL LIABILITY FOR MALPRACTICE

Table of Sections

I. INTRODUCTION

As noted in Chapter Two, the public interest in protecting the consumers of mental health services has led to a system of state regulation that seeks to ensure the quality of services by limiting entry into the various mental health fields to those who meet certain minimum qualifications. The emphasis of this approach is prospective in the sense that prevention of injury is the main objective. In contrast, the legal system has established a malpractice liability scheme which is remedial in nature. Its emphasis is on furnishing those injured by substandard professional care with opportunities for obtaining judicial relief. Both systems, however, are designed to induce conformity to professional norms in the delivery of treatment services.

The term "malpractice" is something of a catchall, and encompasses all actions for substandard professional care regardless of the specific doctrinal basis of the claim. Private actions for malpractice may be based on any of several legal grounds. Most actions are grounded in negligence doctrine, but some malpractice claims rest on the intentional tort doctrines of assault and battery, invasion of privacy, or breach of confidentiality. Additionally, occasional malpractice suits are based on principles of contract law.

While malpractice claims have reached critical proportions for some medical specialties, mental health professionals have to date escaped extensive malpractice liability exposure. Data provided by the insurance industry shows that claims filed against psychiatrists in earlier years constituted less than one-half of one percent of all medical malpractice claims. See Bonnie, 'Professional Liability and the Quality of Mental Health Care,' 16 Law Medicine and Health Care 229 (1988).

A number of factors account for the relative paucity of malpractice actions against mental health professionals. The primary reason pertains to the nature of the therapeutic interventions that are normally employed. Except for biologically based treatments such as ECT and psychopharmacology, other treatment modalities generally involve some form of psychotherapy. Even if improperly employed, psychotherapy will generally not result in demonstrable physical harm (excluding patient suicide), which is the most common basis for major jury awards. Additionally, it may be difficult for a patient-plaintiff to establish that an adverse, psychological reaction was the result of malpractice, rather than merely a symptom of the disorder for which the patient was being treated.

Also, the range of psychotherapeutic treatment modalities that are employed, coupled with the lack of consensus among mental health professionals as to the most appropriate approach for a given case, creates problems of proof for patient-plaintiffs. Finally, many former psychiatric patients undoubtedly choose to avoid litigation rather than face public disclosure of the fact that they have undergone treatment.

While these factors appear to have deterred lawsuits in the past, there are indications that the relative immunity enjoyed by mental health professionals over the years may be ending. Changes in the methods of treatment, and particularly the increased use of psychophar-macology for the treatment of mental disorders, have resulted in a substantial rise in malpractice actions against psychiatrists. In fact, claims based on improper psychopharmacological treatment today consti-tute the largest category of malpractice claims in the mental health field. While a clear majority of malpractice suits have in the past involved psychiatrists, other mental health professionals, such as psychologists and psychiatric social workers, are increasingly the target of lawsuits by former patients. This expansion is in part attributable to changes in the law which have broadened the basis for malpractice liability to cover a variety of circumstances where physical injury is not necessarily present. For instance, courts and juries have become increasingly willing to assign liability when therapists have breached their duty of trust by engaging in sexual intimacies with patients. Similarly, courts have become more receptive to claims based on unorthodox treatment tech-niques, such as those involving the use of recovered memory.

Other doctrinal changes, such as those that have expanded the class of persons to whom a therapist owes a duty of care, have also served to increase psychiatrists' exposure to malpractice actions. The scope of this change and its impact on the mental health profession will be explored more fully in Section II.C. [Liability to Third Parties] of this chapter.

The materials that follow will first consider the elements of negli-gence, particularly as they apply to cases in the mental health field. Thereafter, the chapter will examine in greater detail three issues that are in the forefront of litigation involving mental health professions. A final section of the chapter will examine certain non-negligence remedies available to plaintiffs who have been injured in the mental health treatment context. Malpractice cases alleging invasion of privacy or breach of confidentiality are considered in Chapter Five. The doctrine of informed consent, which has developed as a separate theory of recovery, is dealt with in Chapter Four.

Comments

1. *Effect of tort law on professional standards.* The extent to which malpractice law actually serves to induce adherence to professional stan-dards of care has been the subject of considerable debate among torts experts. The impact of malpractice liability on mental health professionals is the subject of the following excerpt:

> . . . "By imposing liability for breaches of this socially defined standard of care, the tort system might be expected to induce the health

care professions to design 'safer' clinical practices, just as manufacturers of consumer products supposedly are induced to design safer products."

However, malpractice law is not analogous to the law of products liability because the standard of care in malpractice actions is defined by professional custom. The legal system does not purport to substitute a societal norm for the prevailing professional norm; instead it serves primarily as a mechanism of enforcing the professional norm. Thus, if malpractice law has a beneficial impact on the quality of care, the anticipated effect would be found primarily in the degree to which it induces conformity to the prevailing practice.

This is not the entire story, however. The prevailing custom or practice is rarely prescribed by a professional standard-setting body. Instead, it must be "discovered," *ex post,* through a survey of expert opinion. In situations where the prevailing standard of care is not easily ascertained, it becomes defined in the courtroom. Thus, as a result of the pro-compensation bias that seems to characterize modern tort litigation, an indeterminate standard may become transmuted into a standard which is higher than that employed by most practitioners. To this extent, the law might be expected to have a more pronounced impact on the quality of care by pushing clinical practice toward the practice of the most informed practitioners. Certainly this was one of the expected effects of the shift from a "locality rule" to a national standard of care.

The question, yet unanswered, is whether the malpractice liability system has these favorable effects on clinical practice. Does it help to induce conformity to prevailing professional standards? Does it help to elevate those standards?

Richard Bonnie, Professional Liability and Quality of Health Care, 16 Law, Medicine and Health Care, 229, 234 (1988).

2. *Proposed federal caps on non-economic damages for medical malpractice.* Dramatic increases in the size of medical malpractice awards in recent years has, in some jurisdictions, led to extraordinary increases in the cost of medical malpractice insurance. In some states, such as California, caps on non-economic damages for pain and suffering have been legislatively mandated. However, currently only a minority of states have limitations on damages for pain and suffering. This has resulted in calls for federal legislation mandating limits on the non-economic damages that can be awarded in medical malpractice cases. In the spring of 2003, separate bills were introduced to both the House of Representatives and the Senate to cap medical malpractice damages for pain and suffering (HR5, the "HEALTH Act" and S.11, the "Patients First Act of 2003"). These respective bills had different provisions, though both would have established limits on non-economic damages. On March 13, 2003, the House of Representatives passed the HEALTH Act by a vote of 229–196. In the Senate, on a procedural vote, a majority voted to block the bill from being debated by a vote of 49–48. Various commentators expect that the issue will be revisited in a subsequent session of the Congress.

II. CLAIMS BASED ON NEGLIGENCE

A. THE DOCTRINE: AN OVERVIEW

The unique characteristics of a therapist's work pose a particular challenge to legal institutions when the quality of the services rendered must be judged. For one thing, psychiatry has been described as both a science, requiring technical skills, and an art, dependent upon the personal relationship between the psychiatrist and his patient. In addition, even experts frequently have difficulty in assessing whether the therapy has been successful. The changes in the patient may be so subtle as to be imperceptible. Moreover, it is sometimes difficult to attribute a particular outcome, be it negative or positive, to the therapeutic intervention.

In spite of these complications, decisions as to the quality of care which was rendered in a particular instance cannot be avoided. The doctrinal framework under which these claims are measured is the law of negligence. In general terms this means that any professional who renders services has a legal duty to perform his professional functions in a manner comporting with the skill and technical proficiency normally exercised by other professionals in the same field. A professional's failure to meet this legal standard when rendering services establishes the key element of a claim of negligence. But to be successful in a law suit a patient-plaintiff must be able to prove more than that the services were of substandard quality. In fact, negligence has at least four distinct elements, each of which must be established by the plaintiff. These elements have been described in the following terms by one noted commentator:

1. A duty, or obligation, recognized by the law, requiring the person to conform to a certain standard of conduct, for the protection of others against unreasonable risks.

2. A failure on the person's part to conform to the standard required: a breach of the duty. * * *

3. A reasonably close causal connection between the conduct and the resulting injury. * * *

4. Actual loss or damage resulting to the interests of another. Prosser and Keeton, On the Law of Torts, § 30 (5th ed., 1984).

The application of these elements to real cases in the face of a technologically changing society remains one of the major challenges faced by the legal system. In the mental health field it is not only changes in methods of treatment, and particularly the growing emphasis on the use of psychotropic medication, but structural changes in the way that health services are delivered, i.e., managed care systems, that complicates the development of coherent legal standards. Nevertheless, it is in this context that courts are being called upon to shape and apply professional negligence standards. The following materials explore the special problem raised in the adjudication of malpractice claims against mental health professionals.

Comments

1. *Drugs and psychiatric malpractice.* The three most common claims in psychiatric malpractice suits have involved mistakes in diagnosis, improper treatment, and drug reactions. See Perr, "Psychiatric Malpractice Issues", in S. Rabkin (Ed.) Legal Encroachment on Psychiatric Practice, New Dimensions for Mental Health Services, No. 25 at 47 (1985). The rising use of drugs that affect mood or behavior makes increasingly likely suits related to adverse drug reactions. In fact, claims arising from treatment involving psychopharmacology today constitute the single largest category of malpractice actions brought against psychiatrists.

The serious side effects associated with the use of some psychotropic medications, such as the neuroleptics, are described at pp. 28–31. The dilemma confronting psychiatrists and other physicians is that for some disorders, such as schizophrenia, there is no other therapy currently available. Thus, the choice is between prescribing neuroleptics (which, in all likelihood, will reduce or even eliminate the most pronounced symptoms of the disease with their attendant side-effect risks) or doing nothing, which means that the patient will need to contend with the debilitating effects of the disease. Given this situation, the cases that impose liability on the prescribing physician generally involve a failure on the part of the psychiatrist to monitor the medication regime and terminate it or substitute another medication when adverse side effects appear. The other major category of claims is based on the improper choice of a particular medication where another medication might have been more effective or carry fewer side effects.

2. *Relationships creating a duty of care.* A threshold question in any case alleging professional negligence is whether the injured party is a member of the class of persons legally protected under the law of negligence. Traditionally, the answer to this question was relatively clear cut. No duty of care was owed except to those with whom the professional had established a contractual relationship. Thus, if the plaintiff had not been the professional's patient, the case was dismissed, unless the plaintiff alleged more than mere negligence. However, the existence of a professional relationship, establishing what is called privity between the patient-claimant and therapist-defendant, is no longer the dispositive factor in professional negligence cases. An increasing number of jurisdictions have modified or repudiated the privity doctrine. The circumstances under which a therapist may be held liable to persons with whom he has no professional relationship are elaborated in subsection C, *infra*.

3. *Liability for diagnostic functions carried out at request of third party.* A related question concerns the liability of a therapist for negligence when he or she is performing a diagnostic service at the request of a third party. Here the individual being evaluated is not technically a patient for purposes of treatment and is not in contractual privity with the therapist. This situation arises most commonly in the employment context when an employer requires an employee or an applicant for employment to submit to a

psychological evaluation. May the clinician or physician be held liable to the employee if he is negligent in carrying out the diagnostic evaluation and, consequently, misdiagnoses the employee's condition? See *Hoesl v. United States of America, Dr. David Allen Kasuboski,* 629 F.2d 586 (9th Cir.1980) (where the court did not reach the claim of negligence but held that misdiagnosis was actionable as defamation). But see *Hammer v. Polsky,* 36 Misc.2d 482, 233 N.Y.S.2d 110 (1962) (traditional view that action for malpractice for misdiagnosis will only lie where complaint alleges that defendant was plaintiff's physician).

1. The "Ordinary Standard of Care" Element

a. Introduction

As noted, a key requirement for the imposition of liability is the failure to exercise the required "standard of care" in the particular circumstances under which treatment was rendered. A departure from the applicable standard of care can come about from actions initiated by the therapist, as well as those that should have been taken. In the case of the former a departure from the standard of due care may also result from either the election of an inappropriate therapy or improper *implementation* of the therapy. The improper use of a treatment modality might involve either its use when no beneficial result could reasonably be expected or its use when one could reasonably anticipate exacerbation of the condition or some other side effect. Because, for example, the administration of thorazine is contraindicated in the case of an individual suffering from depression, its administration to a depressed patient who subsequently commits suicide might result in liability. See, e.g., *Brandt v. Grubin,* 131 N.J.Super. 182, 329 A.2d 82 (1974). An example of improper implementation of a customary therapeutic modality would be the administration of ECT without the administration of the muscle relaxant. It might also include the uninterrupted and prolonged administration of psychotropic medication coupled with a failure to terminate treatment upon the appearance of symptoms of tardive dyskinesia. See, e.g. *Clites v. State,* 322 N.W.2d 917 (Iowa App.1982).

A departure from standards of due care may also occur where the therapist is charged with having failed to take protective actions that could have averted injury. Claims of this nature most commonly arise where the therapist is alleged to have failed to prevent a patient's suicide by initiating civil commitment or some other action that might have averted the suicide. Here, liability might come about because a therapist failed to recognize or underestimated the risk of suicide and the precautions needed to counter it.

Application of the standard of care element in the mental health treatment context is complicated by a number of factors. As noted in Chapter One, conceptual differences among professionals result in a lack of consensus as to both the etiology of psychiatric disorders and the appropriate method of treatment. Secondly, the diagnostic process is frequently compromised by the lack of clear, *physical* symptoms that are associated with most mental disorders. In general medicine, the diagnosis process relies primarily on the presentation of physical symptoms and laboratory tests such as x-ray, ultrasound, blood chemistry analysis and CAT scans. The diagnosis of mental disorders, on the other hand, must depend mostly on somewhat subjective evaluations of behavioral traits and the symptoms verbally articulated by the patient. The lack of objectively verifiable symptomatology in the case of most mental disorders means that there is likely to be far less agreement among mental health professionals as to a particular diagnosis. The degree of uncertainty that permeates the diagnostic process in turn will affect the outcome of malpractice litigation where the allegation concerns diagnostic error (generally to the benefit of the defense).

Finally, studies have shown that exceptional behaviors such as suicide or extreme violence towards others are extremely difficult to predict with any degree of certainty, even by trained behavioral specialists such as psychologists and psychiatrists. At the same time, the failure to prevent such occurrences is a common basis for malpractice claims against mental health professionals.

The materials that follow address the challenges that confront the legal system when applying the doctrine of negligence in a variety of mental health treatment contexts. As an initial matter, the materials focus on the legal criteria pertaining to the standard of care element.

   b.   *Defining the Standard*

STEPAKOFF v. KANTAR

Supreme Judicial Court of Massachusetts, 1985.
393 Mass. 836, 473 N.E.2d 1131.

O'CONNOR, JUSTICE.

Helen J. Stepakoff, widow of Gerald Stepakoff (Stepakoff) and executrix of his estate, brought this action in the Superior Court against William G. Kantar, Stepakoff's psychiatrist. The plaintiff alleged that, although the defendant either knew or reasonably should have known that Stepakoff was suicidal, he negligently failed to inform her of that fact or to make appropriate arrangements for Stepakoff's protection, as a result of which Stepakoff committed suicide. The plaintiff seeks damages for Stepakoff's conscious suffering and wrongful death.

The case was tried to a jury. The trial judge directed a verdict for the defendant on the claim for conscious suffering, and the jury found for the defendant on the claim for wrongful death. Judgment was entered, and the plaintiff appealed. We transferred the appeal to this court on our own motion.

The plaintiff argues that the judge erred by refusing to instruct the jury that a psychiatrist who knows or reasonably should know that his patient is likely to harm himself has a duty to take reasonable precautions to prevent such harm, and by refusing to instruct the jury regarding a psychiatrist's statutory authority to hospitalize a patient involuntarily. The plaintiff also claims that the judge improperly instructed the jury concerning the burden of proof, and that he erroneously directed a verdict for the defendant on the claim for conscious suffering. We conclude that the judge did not commit reversible error, and we affirm the judgment for the defendant.

The jury could have found the following facts. Stepakoff began to see the defendant in November of 1973, and the two established a relationship as psychiatrist and patient that lasted until Stepakoff's death on or about February 16, 1975. The defendant diagnosed Stepakoff as a manic-depressive psychotic, and he formed the opinion that Stepakoff was "potentially suicidal." The defendant thought, however, that Stepakoff had a defense mechanism that rendered him less able to take decisive action as his predicament worsened. Furthermore, the defendant thought that he had a "solid pact" with Stepakoff that Stepakoff would contact him if Stepakoff felt suicidal.

During 1974 and early 1975, the plaintiff and Stepakoff had marital difficulties. On February 13, 1975, the plaintiff went to Florida. Before going, she told Stepakoff to be out of the house when she returned. She telephoned the defendant to express her concern about the situation, but he assured her that she should feel free to go.

The defendant planned to spend the weekend that began on Saturday, February 15, in Maine. Before his departure, he prepared Stepakoff for his absence. He gave Stepakoff the name and telephone number of another psychiatrist who had agreed to cover for him. He developed with Stepakoff a plan for the weekend, and he told Stepakoff that he would call him each night that he remained away. On Friday, February 14, the defendant and Stepakoff had an "emergency" meeting. During that meeting, the defendant considered involuntarily hospitalizing Stepakoff, but decided against it. After the meeting, he dictated a note for his files that included the following sentence: "There is a question of whether he will make it over the weekend."[1] The defendant also called the covering psychiatrist and described Stepakoff's situation.

On Saturday, February 15, Stepakoff called the covering psychiatrist, and the two met. Stepakoff reassured the doctor that he did not intend to commit suicide. That night, as planned, the defendant called Stepakoff. Based on that conversation, the defendant formed a favorable diagnostic impression of Stepakoff's condition. The defendant hung up after agreeing with Stepakoff that they would talk again the next night, but on Sunday, February 16, the police found Stepakoff in his garage, dead from carbon monoxide inhalation.

---

1. At trial, the defendant testified that when he used those words he meant: "Whether he would be able to carry out the activities that he and I outlined, or whether the type of thing that happened to him just preceding his psychiatric admission to Newton–Wellesley [in 1974] would occur, in which he seemed to be paralyzed in his capacities to function, to—at that time, he couldn't get up out of the chair in my office and drive his car home. And it was that type of regression and inability to function that I was questioning."

The jury heard the testimony of two psychiatrists. One of them expressed the opinion that the defendant's treatment of Stepakoff did not conform to good medical practice. He testified that the defendant should have involuntarily hospitalized Stepakoff. The other disagreed. In his opinion, Stepakoff did not meet the requirements for involuntary hospitalization set forth in G.L. c. 123, § 12. Over the plaintiff's objection, the judge allowed the witness to testify as to what those requirements were.

1.   *Instructions as to the Defendant's Duty.*

The plaintiff argues that the trial judge committed reversible error by failing to give the jury her requested instructions, numbered 10, 11, and 12, regarding a psychiatrist's duty to his patient. We reprint those requested instructions in the margin.[2] After the judge's charge, the plaintiff objected, by number, to the judge's failure to give those instructions.

* * *

The plaintiff concedes that the judge correctly instructed the jury concerning the defendant's "general medical malpractice duty to exercise the care and skill of the average psychiatrist," but she contends that the judge should *also* have instructed the jury that if, under that general malpractice standard, the defendant knew or should have known that Stepakoff presented a serious danger to himself, the defendant owed Stepakoff a specific legal duty to safeguard him from that danger, or at least to use reasonable care to do so. We will assume that requests 10, 11, and 12 fairly presented that instruction to the judge, but we conclude that the judge correctly refused to give it.

"Negligence, without qualification and in its ordinary sense, is the failure of a responsible person, either by omission or by action, to exercise that degree of care, vigilance and forethought which, in the discharge of the duty then resting on him, the person of ordinary caution and prudence ought to exercise under the particular circumstances." [Citation] Negligence of a physician who practices a specialty consists of a failure to exercise the degree of care and skill of the average qualified physician practicing that specialty, taking into account the advances in the profession and the resources available to the physician. [Citation] The rule with respect to the physician-patient relationship is an adaption of the broader negligence principle. In the context of that relationship,

2. "10. A treating psychiatrist owes to his patient a duty to safeguard the patient from danger due to mental incapacity where that incapacity is known, or ought to have been known, to the psychiatrist through the exercise of ordinary care.... "11. If Dr. Kantar knew of facts from which he could have reasonably thought that the patient was likely to harm himself in the absence of protective measures, then Dr. Kantar had a duty to use reasonable care under the circumstances to prevent such harm and to safeguard the patient from self-inflicted injury or death.... "12. This duty is proportionate to the patient's needs, that is, such reasonable care and attention as the patient's known mental condition requires.... "(Citations omitted.)

the law views the care and skill commonly exercised by the average qualified physician as the equivalent of the "care, vigilance and forethought which ... the person of ordinary caution and prudence ought to exercise under the particular circumstances." *Altman v. Aronson, supra.*

The judge instructed the jury: "[I]f you find that the care and treatment given by Dr. Kantar to Gerald Stepakoff from December of 1973 to February of 1975 was not in accordance with good medical practice and in violation or breach of the standard of care and skill of the average member of the medical profession practicing his specialty of psychiatry between December '73 and February of 1975, and that, if as a direct and proximate result of that negligence, Gerald Stepakoff died, the plaintiff, Helen Stepakoff, would be entitled to recover...." " That instruction fully and accurately stated the law. The plaintiff was not entitled to further instructions relative to the reasonableness of the defendant's acts or failures to act. The plaintiff has not directed our attention to any case in which a court has bifurcated the duty owed by a psychiatrist to a suicidal patient by declaring that, when diagnosing a patient, the psychiatrist must exercise the care and skill customarily exercised by an average qualified psychiatrist, while, after diagnosing a patient as suicidal, the psychiatrist's duty to take preventive measures becomes one of "reasonableness." We are unwilling to disturb our longstanding rule that a physician, practicing a specialty, owes to his or her patient a duty to comply in all respects with the standard set by the average physician practicing that specialty.

We are not moved to a different conclusion * * * by cases from other jurisdictions cited by the plaintiff in support of the proposition that a hospital and its staff must exercise reasonable care for the safety of confined patients likely to harm themselves. Even if those cases support the proposition that hospitals must meet an ordinary negligence standard, as distinguished from a good medical practice standard, they do not persuade us that the duty owed by a psychiatrist to a suicidal outpatient should differ from that imposed by this court on physicians to other patients.

* * *

Judgment affirmed.

Questions and Comments

1. *The ordinary negligence standard compared to the good medical practice standard.* In Kantar, the plaintiff unsuccessfully sought instructions that would have the jury measure liability in terms of the "reasonableness" of the physician's suicide prevention measures. Would the standards sought by the plaintiff result in elevating the standard of care ordinarily applicable to physicians and other health professionals, namely, the "degree of care and skill of the average qualified physician practicing that specialty, taking into account the advances in the profession and resources available to the physician?"

2. *Standards generated by the professions.* Professional organizations, such as the American Psychiatric Association, the American Psychological Association, and combinations of medical centers sometimes formulate practice guidelines which set out protocols to the treatment of various disorders. For example, in 1996, the medical centers at Duke, Colombia and Cornell Universities together issued "Recommended Guidelines for the Treatment of Bipolar Disorders and Schizophrenia." These guidelines were subsequently published in the *Journal of Clinical Psychiatry.*

Such guidelines generated by professional organizations or institutions can be introduced by plaintiffs or defendants to establish either adherence to or a lack of due care. Thus, such guidelines are likely to be highly influential in establishing professional standards and influencing the outcome of litigation.

3. *Which standard applies?* The liability of a therapist for negligence may turn on the expertise and knowledge of those in a particular profession. Thus, a psychologist, unlike a medically trained psychiatrist, would generally not be liable for a failure to diagnose an *organic* disorder presented by the patient. On the other hand, a therapist who holds himself out as having the expertise of another specialized profession may be held to have the knowledge and expertise of that profession.

2. Defenses and Limitations

a. Professional Judgment Rule

SCHREMPF v. STATE

Court of Appeals of New York, 1985.
66 N.Y.2d 289, 496 N.Y.S.2d 973, 487 N.E.2d 883.

OPINION OF THE COURT

WACHTLER, CHIEF JUDGE.

Claimant's husband was stabbed and killed by Joseph Evans, a mental patient who had been released from a State institution and was still receiving outpatient care from that facility. In a suit for wrongful death the Court of Claims found the State liable for negligently failing to have the assailant committed as an inpatient sometime prior to the assault. The Appellate Division affirmed, with one justice dissenting.

On this appeal, the State of New York urges that the claim be dismissed * * * it is urged that the decisions of the State psychiatrist fell within the area of professional medical judgment and thus cannot serve as a basis for a negligence or malpractice award. For the reasons that follow, we agree with the State's * * * contention and reverse the Appellate Division's order.

In December 1981 claimant's husband, Albert Schrempf, was employed at Consolidated Industries of Greater Syracuse, Inc., a private nonprofit organization which provides vocational rehabilitation for outpatients from mental institutions. On December 9, 1981 he was stabbed to death at his place of employment by Joseph Evans, a 27–year–old outpatient from Hutchings Psychiatric Institute, a State mental facility.

Evans had been admitted for treatment at Hutchings on six occasions beginning in May 1979. The admissions usually followed violent altercations with members of his family and involved some property damage and attempted assaults, but not the infliction of personal injury. On these occasions he claimed that he was prompted by inner voices commanding him to act. He was generally diagnosed as a manic depressive hypomanic type or, more rarely, as a paranoid schizophrenic, which were described at trial as degrees of the same general condition. * * * Several of the admissions were voluntary. Evans generally resented the involuntary commitments and sometimes responded with threats against staff members or resorted to violent resistance. On one occasion, he broke the jaw of another patient.

Evans' condition was generally improved or stabilized by psychotherapy and medication which could be provided on an outpatient basis. However, he was a difficult outpatient because he had an erratic attendance record and did not regularly take prescribed medications. He was sensitive to, and had an adverse reaction to, certain drugs and sometimes stated that he would not take his medication because it was against his religion.

Evans' last involuntary commitment as an inpatient ended in January of 1981. In the summer of that year, he broke windows in his mother's house and subsequently pleaded guilty to criminal mischief. He was sentenced to probation and his probation officer suggested that he seek psychiatric treatment.

On September 28, 1981 he returned to Hutchings and was voluntarily admitted. He was examined on that occasion by the psychiatrist who had first admitted him in 1979 and who had also treated him on most of his subsequent admissions. She found that he was experiencing "persecutory delusions" that he was possessed and might be changing into a homosexual. However, she noted that he was calm and remained cooperative. Based on the examination and her knowledge of his psychiatric history, she determined that he was again suffering from manic depression and that at that time he did not pose a risk to himself or others. She placed him on outpatient status but assigned him to a special clinic for recalcitrant outpatients so that his use of the medication could be monitored.

In October Evans worked at a part-time job, without apparent incident. In November he was referred by his probation officer to Consolidated Industries for vocational rehabilitation. He participated in that program on a trial basis for approximately 10 days over the next three or four weeks.

Throughout this period his participation in the outpatient program diminished. In October he said he did not want to come any more because he had a job. He rarely met with his psychiatrist in October and did not see her after November 1. He did not regularly go to the clinic for his medication in October, and in November only appeared on two dates, November 9 and November 30.

His psychiatrist encouraged him to continue in the outpatient program and to take his medication. When he complained that the drugs made him drowsy at work, she reduced the dosage and directed him to take the medicine at night. On November 17 she informed his probation officer that he was not taking his medication. She also monitored his behavior through the probation officer and others and found no evidence that his condition was deteriorating. On the contrary, she was informed that he appeared to be polite and cooperative by all who observed him at the clinic, the probation office and Consolidated Industries. Indeed he was being considered for permanent membership at Consolidated at the time of the assault on December 9, 1981.

At the trial, the claimant urged that the State had been negligent in the care and treatment of Evans by releasing him and permitting him to remain on outpatient status in 1981, particularly after his psychiatrist had reason to believe he was not taking his medication as prescribed. The Court of Claims held that the decision to release Evans in January 1981 involved a medical judgment for which the State could not be held liable. However, the court concluded that the State was negligent in admitting Evans to outpatient care, instead of confining him as an inpatient in September 1981. The court also held that the State psychiatrist should have done "something more" when it became evident that the patient was not taking his prescribed medication.

The Appellate Division affirmed, without opinion. * * *

* * *

A physician's duty is to provide the level of care acceptable in the professional community in which he practices [Citation]. He is not required to achieve success in every case and cannot be held liable for mere errors of professional judgment. * * * The "line between medical judgment and deviation from good medical practice is not easy to draw" particularly in cases involving psychiatric treatment. * * *

Although in the past, the care of those suffering from mental infirmities was generally limited to confinement, the modern and more humane policy of the medical profession and the law contemplates returning the mental patient to society, if he does not pose an immediate risk of harm to himself or others. * * * This [decision], we have noted, requires a sensitive appraisal of competing interests: "(1) the State's duty to treat and care for its mental defective wards, with an eye toward returning them to society more useful citizens, and (2) the State's concern that the inmates in its institutions cause no injury or damage to the property of those in the vicinity." * * * Because psychiatry is not an exact science, decisions with respect to the proper course of treatment often involve a calculated risk and disagreement among experts as to whether the risk was warranted or in accord with accepted procedures. * * * These circumstances necessarily broaden the area of professional judgment to include treatments tailored to the particular case, where the "accepted procedure" does not take into account factors which the treating physician could reasonably consider significant. * * *

The only remaining question is whether the treating physician was negligent in failing to intervene in some manner once she had reason to believe that Evans was not taking his medication as prescribed. In view of the fact that Evans was a voluntary outpatient, the State's control over him, and consequent duty to prevent him from harming others, is more limited than in cases involving persons confined to mental institutions. Even the claimant's experts did not agree as to what should and could be done with such a patient. They variously proposed compelling or coercing him to resume medication, changing the medication to a drug with longer lasting effects, conducting a full reexamination of him, initiating involuntary commitment proceedings or threatening him with commitment if he did not cooperate. The court held that the treating psychiatrist should have done "something more", and suggested that "at the very least, an in-depth psychiatric evaluation should have been conducted to determine Evans' level of functioning." The court did not indicate what should have been done had Evans refused to cooperate.

One point on which all the experts agreed was that the patient's failure to take his medication did not necessarily mean that his condition was deteriorating or that he would become dangerous. That would largely depend on his behavior and, again, there was agreement that his outward appearance and behavior did not show any "warning signs" indicative of this kind of change. Although claimant's experts ignored or discounted these factors, they played a significant role in the attending physician's assessment. They indicated to her that there was a chance that his condition was improving as it appeared to be, and suggested a corresponding risk that intervention by resort to aggressive measures might disrupt the process. As noted, she knew from past experience that he resented involuntary treatment and often responded violently in that setting. Thus, there were risks either way. The treating physician, as she testified at trial, simply attached greater significance to those factors which seemed most promising and chose the course which appeared to offer the best opportunity for long-term rehabilitation. We know with hindsight that it was a mistaken impression. However, under the circumstances, it must be recognized as an exercise of professional judgment for which the State cannot be held responsible.

Accordingly, the order of the Appellate Division should be reversed and the claim dismissed.

JASEN, MEYER, KAYE, ALEXANDER and TITONE, JJ., concur.

SIMONS, J., taking no part.

Order reversed, with costs, and claim dismissed.

Questions and Comments

1. *Significance of Professional Judgment Rule.* The risk that a professional will be held liable for malpractice is obviously influenced by the

standard governing the finding of malpractice. Thus, the professional judgment rule should at least in theory carry with it a lesser level of risk of liability than a standard formulated in terms of whether the car or treatment conformed to the "care and skill exercised by the average qualified medical [or other health care] professional". The latter tends to shift the inquiry away from the individualized perceptions of the professional being charged with malpractice to professional of that class in general.

2. *Absence of liability as a matter of law.* Note that the Court of Appeals holds that in spite of a finding of negligence by the trial court, application of the professional judgment role requires a judgment for the defendant as a matter of law. On what basis does the Court reach the conclusion that the circumstances were such that the decision taken by the physician of necessity had to involve a significant element of guesswork and thus within the professional judgment rule? Is the rule, as applied by the Court of Appeals, simply a way of trumping the imposition of liability at the trial level, because of its conclusion that liability is not justified in view of the uncertainties of predicting suicide or other extraordinary behaviors?

3. *Recognition of doctrine in other jurisdictions.* The professional judgment rule which, when applicable, calls for appropriate instructions to the jury, has not been universally adopted. In fact, to date, it has been expressly recognized by only a minority of jurisdictions and has been rejected by at least one state. See, *Ouellette v. Subak,* 391 N.W.2d 810 (Minn.1986). The rule seems to have had its origins in New York where it has been applied to all phases of malpractice, including psychiatry. See, *Littleton v. Good Samaritan Hospital,* 39 Ohio St.3d 86, 529 N.E.2d 449 (1988). The "best judgment rule" shields a physician from liability "for mere errors of judgment provided he does what he thinks best after careful examination." *Littleton v. Good Samaritan Hospital,* 39 Ohio St.3d 86, 529 N.E.2d 449, 457 (1988).

In the mental health context it has most commonly been applied to exculpate psychiatrists for their decision to not seek a patient's involuntary hospitalization. As explained by the Supreme Court of Ohio:

> "Under such a 'psychotherapist judgment rule,' the court would not allow liability to be imposed on therapists for simple errors in judgment. Instead, the court would examine the 'good faith, independence and thoroughness' of a psychotherapist's decision not to commit a patient. * * * Factors in reviewing such good faith include the competence and training of the reviewing psychotherapists, whether the relevant documents and evidence were adequately, promptly and independently reviewed, whether the advice or opinion of another therapist was obtained, whether the evaluation was made in light of the proper legal standards for commitment, and whether other evidence of good faith exists." (Citation omitted).

Id. at 458.

4. *Sub silentio adoption.* The courts of some jurisdictions have without expressly relying on the professional judgment doctrine refused to assign liability where the psychiatrist failed to commit and the patient subsequently injured a third party. For instance, in *Soutear v. United States,* 646 F.Supp. 524 (E.D.Mich.1986) in holding against a claimant who asserted that the

facility's failure to psychiatrically commit the patient constituted negligence, the court observed:

> "Psychiatry * * * is not an exact science. Medical doctors cannot predict with perfect accuracy whether or not an individual will do violence to himself or to someone else. Thus, we hold a psychiatrist to only the standard of care of his profession. That standard 'must take into consideration the uncertainty which accompanies psychiatric analysis * * *.' The concept of 'due care' in appraising psychiatric problems, assuming proper procedures are followed, must take account of the difficulty often inevitable in definitive diagnosis." *Lipari v. Sears, Roebuck & Co.*, [497 F.Supp. 185, 192 (D.Neb.1980)] quoting *Hicks v. United States*, * * * 511 F.2d 407, 417 (D.C.Cir.1975). *Thus, a psychiatrist will not be held liable for his patient's violent behavior simply because he failed to predict it accurately.*

Id. at 536, quoting *Davis v. Lhim*, 124 Mich.App. 291, 301, 335 N.W.2d 481 (1983) (emphasis added by the court).

5. *Limitations on the professional judgment rule.* Note that the professional judgment rule only applies where the decision taken has been preceded by a "careful examination" of the patient. *Littleton*, 529 N.E.2d at 457.

b. Respectable Minority Doctrine

A patient who has received treatment involving the use of a particular technique may, if the outcome is not satisfactory, claim that the physician or therapist was negligent in not utilizing a more effective treatment modality. Such claim of negligence in the selection of treatment may be advanced, moreover, even where the physician or therapist has obtained the informed consent of the patient. (The doctrine of informed consent is treated in Chapter Four).

Generally, claims that physicians or therapists have utilized the wrong therapeutic technique or failed to use the most effective one will, as with all other aspects of performance, be measured by the standard of due care, i.e., what members of the profession would customarily do under the circumstances. While a finding that the therapeutic approach used was not "customary" does not necessarily lead to liability, proof of conformity to custom generally precludes a finding of liability. Thus, whether a particular treatment is "customary" or "accepted" by the profession may well be dispositive of the issue of liability.

Proof that a particular procedure is customary does not, however, require that it be used by a majority of practitioners. In fact, in a number of jurisdictions, a defense is established by a showing that a particular treatment approach is supported by a "respectable minority" of those in the field. As described by one court the "respectable minority" rule means that "[W]here two or more schools of thought exist among competent members of the medical profession concerning proper medical treatment for a given ailment, each of which is supported by responsible medical authority, it is not malpractice to be among the minority * * * [of those following] one of the accepted schools." *Chumbler v. McClure*, 505 F.2d 489, 492 (6th Cir.1974). There remain, however, some unresolved questions as to the scope of the doctrine. For instance, does the doctrine immunize a practitioner from liability upon a showing that a particular treatment technique is used by a "respectable minority", even though the therapy used is on the average likely to be less effective than an alternate treatment modality? In the treatment of mental disorders, this question is likely to arise with increasing frequency as new treatment techniques based on biological precepts compete with traditional forms of psychotherapy. The case of *Osheroff v. Chestnut Lodge* which follows is illustrative of the context in which cases of this type are likely to arise.

Osheroff v. Chestnut Lodge, Inc.

[Since the action was initially brought in 1982 as an arbitration proceeding before the Maryland Health Care Arbitration Panel, no official report of the case exists. The facts set out below are based on several secondary sources and the decision of the Maryland court of special appeals, 62 Md.App. 519, 490 A.2d 720 (1985), which affirmed the arbitral award on procedural grounds.]

Summary of Legal Proceedings

In 1982, Dr. Rafael Osheroff initiated a lawsuit against Chestnut Lodge, Inc. claiming that Chestnut Lodge negligently misdiagnosed his condition and negligently failed to utilize psychopharmacological treatment. This, he alleged, prevented him from returning promptly to normal functioning, with the consequential loss of a lucrative medical practice, and his standing in the medical community.

As required under Maryland law, Dr. Osheroff's suit was submitted to the Maryland Health Care Arbitration Panel (HCAP) which held extended hearings at which numerous experts were called to testify. In his review of the case, Professor Gerald L. Klerman summarized the events leading up to the settlement:

> The Arbitration Panel found for the plaintiff and awarded him financial damages [in the amount of $250,000]. This was not a majority decision, however, and the director of the Arbitration Panel sent the panel back for an amended decision, which reduced the award. Under Maryland statute, once an arbitration process is concluded, any party to the proceedings may reject the panel's arbitration and call for court review. Both sides appealed. The claimant, Dr. Osheroff, requested a jury trial, which was to have taken place in October, 1987. However, before any action was taken by the court, a settlement was agreed upon by both parties.

Klerman, 'The Psychiatric Patient's Right to Effective Treatment: Implications of Osheroff vs. Chestnut Lodge', 147 Am.J. of Psychiatry 409, 410–411 (Apr. 1990)* [hereinafter Klerman]. See also, *Osheroff v. Chest-*

* American Journal of Psychiatry, vol. 147, pp. 409–418 (1990). Copyright © 1990 by The American Psychiatric Association. All excerpts from Dr. Klerman's article have been reprinted by permission of the American Psychiatric Association.

nut Lodge, 62 Md.App. 519, 490 A.2d 720 (Md.App.1985) (challenge to procedures followed by the Maryland Health Claims Arbitration office).

Factual Background

The medical social history of Dr. Osheroff prior to his hospitalization has been summarized by one commentator:

> "The patient, Dr. Rafael Osheroff, a 42–year–old, white male physician, was admitted to Chestnut Lodge in Maryland . . . on Jan. 2, 1979. His history included brief periods of depressive and anxious symptoms as an adult; these had been treated on an outpatient basis. He had completed medical school and residency training, was certified as an internist and became a sub-specialist in nephrology.
>
> Before his 1979 hospitalization, Dr. Osheroff had been suffering from anxious and depressive symptoms for approximately two years, and had been treated as an outpatient with individual psychotherapy and tricyclic antidepressant medications. Dr. Nathan Kline, a prominent psychopharmacologist in New York, had initiated outpatient treatment with tricyclic medication, which, according to Dr. Kline's notes, produced moderate improvement. The patient, however, did not maintain the recommended dose, his clinical condition gradually worsened and hospitalization was recommended."

Klerman, p. 411.

In January 1979, Dr. Osheroff admitted himself into Chestnut Lodge which, for over forty years, had been one of the major centers devoted to "a clinical practice in intensive individual psychotherapy based on psychoanalytic and interpersonal paradigms". Klerman, p. 411. A number of prominent American psychiatrists had been trained at Chestnut Lodge, many of whom subsequently became leaders in psychoanalytically oriented clinical psychiatry.

Upon admission, Dr. Osheroff was diagnosed as suffering from "psychotic reaction, agitated type and narcissistic personality disorder". Malcolm, 'Treatment Choices and Informed Consent in Psychiatry: Implications of the Osheroff Case for the Profession', 14 J. Psychiatry & Law, 9, 16 (1986). [hereinafter Malcolm]. Both following his admission and throughout his stay in Chestnut Lodge, the treatment program for Dr. Osheroff consisted of four sessions of individual psychotherapy per week and group therapy. Malcolm, pp. 17–18. At no time was he given antidepressive medication because of the facility's decision to "attempt a 'more ambitious treatment goal' of dealing with the long range difficulties of the underlying personality disorder." Malcolm, p. 17.

Although the hospital records indicate that at various times the staff felt that Dr. Osheroff was making progress, it seems evident that Dr. Osheroff did not noticeably improve during his seven months stay at Chestnut Lodge. In fact the patient "lost 40 pounds, experienced severe insomnia, and had marked psychomotor agitation. His agitation, manifested by incessant pacing, was so extreme that his feet became swollen and blistered, requiring medical attention." Klerman, p. 409.

The circumstances leading to Dr. Osheroff's release and admission into another facility are also described in Professor Klerman's study:

"The patient's family became distressed by the length of the hospitalization and by his lack of improvement. They consulted a psychiatrist in the Washington, D.C., area, who spoke to the hospital leadership on the patient's behalf. In response, the staff at Chestnut Lodge held a clinical case conference to review the patient's treatment. They decided not to make any major changes—specifically not to institute any medication regimen but to continue the intensive individual psychotherapy. Dr. Osheroff's clinical condition continued to worsen. At the end of 7 months, his family had him discharged from Chestnut Lodge and admitted to Silver Hill Foundation in Connecticut.

On admission to Silver Hill Foundation, Dr. Osheroff was diagnosed as having a psychotic depressive reaction. His treating physician began treatment with a combination of phenothiazines and tricyclic antidepressants. Dr. Osheroff showed improvement within 3 weeks and was discharged from Silver Hill Foundation within 3 months.

* * *

Following his discharge from Silver Hill Foundation in the summer of 1979, the patient resumed his medical practice. He has been in outpatient treatment, receiving psychotherapy and medication. He has not been hospitalized and has not experienced any episodes of depressive symptoms severe enough to interfere with his professional or social functioning. He has resumed contact with his children and has also become active socially."

Klerman, p. 410.

IMPACT OF PRACTITIONER ORIENTATION ON DIAGNOSIS AND TREATMENT

A useful starting point in considering the diagnostic and treatment issues raised by the Osheroff case are the observations of Professor Klerman as to the theoretical divisions which characterize psychiatry in the country:

"Resolution of both the clinical and scientific issues is made difficult by the divisions within psychiatry in the United States, where psychiatry is divided theoretically and clinically into different schools—biological, psychoanalytic, and behavioral. * * * Various terms have been used to describe these divisions and splits—schools, movements, ideologies, and paradigms. * * * Whatever term is used, there is agreement that these differences in theory and practice involve controversies over the nature of mental illness [and] the appropriateness of different forms of treatment * * * ".

Klerman, p. 411.

Chestnut Lodge, where Dr. Osheroff was initially admitted is, as noted previously, one of the leading psychoanalytically oriented in-patient treatment centers in the country. There is a general consensus that the theoretical orientation of the treating therapist is likely to significantly influence both the diagnostic process and the choice of treatment. In the case of Dr. Osheroff, the admitting psychiatrist at Chestnut Lodge made a *primary* diagnosis of "major narcissistic person-ality disorder". A diagnosis of "manic-depressive illness, depressed type" was entered as a secondary diagnosis. Malcolm, p. 16. While the exis-tence of "personality disorder"[a] as a diagnostic category is not necessari-ly rejected by biologically oriented psychiatrists, it is far more central to the psychoanalytic paradigm. As in the case of other similar psychopa-thologies a "narcissistic personality disorder" is seen as derivative of an early childhood development crisis. Malcolm, pp. 17–18. Thus, under one prevalent hypothesis the disorder results because during childhood the affected individual "failed to internalize an idealized parental image because he either lost or was traumatically disappointed in idealized objects. This idealized image is a forerunner of the superego. Because this idealized image is missing, certain superego functions are missing." Malcolm, p. 17.

Not only is the diagnostic approach likely to be influenced by the theoretical orientation of the therapist, but so is the choice of treatment. Adherence to the psychoanalytic model is likely to influence the thera-peutic approach in three ways. First, there is a general consensus on the part of those adhering to the psychoanalytic model that many disorders can only be treated through long term psychoanalysis. Second, and of equal significance, certain forms of depression are perceived as being derived from, and associated with a psychopathology whose origin is in early childhood development. Klerman, p. 412. As a consequence whatev-er treatment program is undertaken must address the underlying root causes of the disorder rather than the surface symptomatology. In the case under consideration this meant that the staff of Chestnut Lodge placed emphasis on the treatment of the narcissistic personality disorder rather than the depression which was seen as a derivative symptom. Finally, a psychoanalytic orientation leads many therapists to avoid the use of psychotropic medication during the course of therapy, "because of the possible adverse effects of the pharmacotherapy". Klerman, p. 413.

a. "The essential feature is a Personali-ty Disorder in which there are a grandiose sense of self-importance or uniqueness; preoccupation with fantasies of unlimited success; exhibitionistic need for constant attention and admiration; characteristic re-sponses to threats to self-esteem; and char-acteristic disturbances in interpersonal re-lationships, such as feelings of entitlement, interpersonal exploitativeness, relationships that alternate between the extremes of ov-eridealization and devaluation, and lack of empathy. The exaggerated sense of self-importance may be manifested as extreme self-cen-teredness and self-absorption. Abilities and achievements tend to be unrealistically ov-erestimated. Frequently the sense of self-importance alternates with feelings of spe-cial unworthiness * * *." Diagnostic and Statistical Manual of Mental Disorders, 3rd ed., American Psychiatric Association, 1980, pp. 315–316.

The Silver Hill Foundation where Dr. Osheroff was admitted following his release from Chestnut Lodge, entered a diagnosis of severe depressive reaction. In this respect, the diagnosis of the two institutions were in accord. However, unlike Chestnut Lodge, the psychiatrist at Silver Hill did not diagnose the patient as suffering from a narcissistic personality disorder.[b]

Silver Hill's diagnosis of "psychotic depression" led to a treatment program of psychotropic medication combined with "supportive therapy" rather than analytical therapy. This choice of treatment would be regarded as standard by those in the biologically oriented schools of psychiatry. Klerman, p. 412.

The Efficacy of Alternate Treatment Modalities

A court hearing on an Osheroff type of claim could be expected to admit evidence relevant to the efficacy of the treatment modalities that were used or could have been used. The state of evidence relevant to this issue has been summarized by Professor Klerman:

> With regard to all kinds of therapeutics—pharmacotherapy, surgery, radiation, psychotherapy—the most scientifically valid evidence as to the safety and efficacy of a treatment comes from randomized controlled trials when these are available. Although there may be other methods of generating evidence, such as naturalistic and follow-up studies, the most convincing evidence comes from randomized controlled trials.

> There have been many controlled clinical trials of psychiatric treatments; most have been conducted to evaluate psychopharmacological agents.

> * * *

> Research on the efficacy of psychotherapy has lagged behind that of psychopharmacology, but has, nevertheless, been extensive. * * * Specific reviews of the evidence have appeared with regard to psychotherapy of neurosis, schizophrenia, depression, and obsessive-compulsive disorders.

> * * *

> With regard to the treatment of the patient's diagnosis of *narcissistic personality* [emphasis added] disorder, there were no reports of controlled trials of any pharmacological or psychotherapeutic treatment for this condition at the time of his hospitalization. The doctors at Chestnut Lodge decided to treat Dr. Osheroff's personality disorder with intensive individual psychotherapy based on psychodynamic theory.

b. In subsequent testimony the admitting psychiatrist at Silver Hill stated that while she considered a diagnosis of personality disorder, she did not enter the diagnosis because it was "not preeminent" at the time. Malcolm at 22.

With regard to the treatment of the patient's DSM–II diagnosis of psychotic depressive reaction, there was very good evidence at the time of his hospitalization for the efficacy of two biological treatments—ECT and the combination of phenothiazines and tricyclic antidepressants. The combination pharmacotherapy was the treatment later prescribed at Silver Hill Foundation.

There are no reports of controlled trials supporting the claims for efficacy of psychoanlytically-oriented intensive individual psychotherapy of the type advocated and practiced at Chestnut Lodge and administered to Dr. Osheroff.

* * *

It should not be concluded there is no evidence for the value of any psychotherapy in the treatment of depressive states. Depressive states are heterogeneous and there are many forms of psychotherapy. There is very good evidence from controlled clinical trials for the value of a number of brief psychotherapies for nonpsychotic and nonbipolar forms of depression in ambulatory patients. The psychotherapies for which there is evidence include cognitive-behavioral therapy, interpersonal psychotherapy, and behavioral therapy. However, no clinical trials have been reported to support the claims for efficacy of psychoanalysis of intensive individual psychotherapy based on psychoanalytic theory for any form of depression.

* * *

Even if we assume that the personality disorder was correctly diagnosed in Dr. Osheroff's case, there is no evidence to support the premise that the presence of a narcissistic personality disorder militates against the use of antidepressant medication.

* * *

A related therapeutic issue raised by the case has to do with the possible negative interactions between psychotherapy and pharmacotherapy for depression. Many psychoanalytically oriented psychotherapists have argued against the use of medication in patients receiving psychotherapy because of the possible adverse effects of the pharmacotherapy on the conduct of the psychotherapy, although there is evidence that the combination of drugs and psychotherapy does not interfere with the psychotherapy of depression. Moreover, findings from controlled trials suggest the combination of drugs and psychotherapy may have beneficial additive effects in the treatment of depression.

Klerman, p. 412–413.

Questions and Comments

1.   *Question.* What was the ostensible negligence in Osheroff? Was it an erroneous diagnosis, wrong treatment, or both?

2. *The relationship of diagnosis to treatment.* In his complaint, Dr. Osheroff alleged negligence both as to diagnosis, i.e., narcissistic personality disorder, and as to choice of treatment. To what extent is a decision of the second issue dependent on the resolution of the first?

3. *Question.* Is the theoretical orientation of the therapist relevant to the question of liability, in the sense that diagnosis is to some extent influenced by the particular school to which the therapist adheres? For instance, the diagnosis of narcissistic personality is closely associated with psychoanalytic concepts pertaining to ego formation. In other words, if the analytic model is applied, the diagnosis in Osheroff may not have been far afield, at least for those who adhere to the psychoanalytic model. Apparently, such a defense is losing currency with the development of psychopharmacology, which in the case of some disorders, promises a fairly rapid recovery.

4. *Application of the respectable minority doctrine.* Should disposition of an Osheroff type case take into account the existence of a minority view made up of traditional psychoanalytically oriented psychiatrists who tend to avoid the use of psychotropic medication on the grounds that it interferes with the classical analytic course of treatment?

5. *Effect of informed consent.* Should it be relevant in assessing liability whether the patient was informed of the relative lengths of treatment and the conceivable advantages under each? If so, does this suggest that the doctrine of informed consent, which will be treated in Chapter Four, may have some relevance in assessing liability for alleged negligence in selection of a course of treatment? In other words, why should a patient who has made an informed choice after being presented with all the relevant facts be allowed to pursue a claim for negligence if the outcome is disappointing? Doesn't the answer here depend on whether a patient can, at the outset, contractually exempt the therapist from liability? The enforceability of covenants not to sue in the context of medical treatment is in some doubt. In some instances, particularly as to standardized treatment, such contractual limitations from liability have been held to violate public policy. However, where the procedure is experimental and the patient has been informed of the alternatives and risks, such provisions are usually enforced. See, *Schneider v. Revici,* 817 F.2d 987 (2d Cir.1987).

6. *Question.* Could a case with facts identical to those of Osheroff be decided on a narrower ground than negligence in the *initial* choice of therapy? Could it be argued that the Chestnut Lodge facility was not necessarily negligent in its initial use of intensive individual psychotherapy but that it became negligent when it persisted in the use of this technique over the period of several months even though the patient's condition did not improve but, in fact, deteriorated?

7. *Effect on the development of new treatment modalities.* Is there any danger that diversity in treatment would be stifled if the immunity normally provided by the respectable minority rule could be overridden by evidence that the challenged treatment is demonstratively less effective on the average than an alternative form? What degree of proof as to superiority in efficacy should be required? Would this standard have been met in the instant case?

8. *Duty to refer.* What would be the implications for mental health professionals who are not psychiatrists of a holding that the staff of Chestnut Lodge was negligent in not using antidepressants to treat Dr. Osheroff. Recall, in this connection, that non-psychiatrists do not have the legal authority to prescribe psychotropic medication. Would a finding that Chestnut Lodge was negligent in not using psychotropic medication suggest that a non-psychiatrist dealing with a depressed patient has a duty to refer the patient to a psychiatrist so that the patient may receive psychopharmacological treatment?

9. *Treatment "beyond the pale".* Treatment techniques may be used which do not meet the respectable minority level. This may occur either where the treatment is explicitly experimental, or where it is simply the product of an idiosyncratic treatment approach. Sometimes it may be a combination of the two. There are two earlier reported cases imposing liability on mental health professionals who used non-biologically based "innovative" therapy. One such case is *Hammer v. Rosen,* 7 N.Y.2d 376, 198 N.Y.S.2d 65, 165 N.E.2d 756 (1960), where the psychiatrist, Dr. John Nathaniel Rosen, "had developed immediately after World War II a reputation for dramatic success in treatment and cure of schizophrenic patients (those suffering from a serious mental disorder marked by a loss of contact with reality).

Dr. Rosen treated schizophrenics rather than neurotics. To bridge the communication gap which treating persons of this much lower mental level posed, Dr. Rosen, after ascertaining his patient's mental level and before attempting to raise the mental level of his patient, attempted to project himself on the communicable mental plateau of his patient in order to establish mental contact and eventually rapport and trust. "In executing this technique, which of course was highly personalized, but which was consented to by the spouse, next of kin, or legal guardian of each patient, it would certainly be presumed that Dr. Rosen might touch certain patients from time to time with differing degrees of force, depending upon the mental condition and needs of the patient, in order to effectively and fully explore and utilize the possibilities and potentialities which his method offered." Morse, 'The Tort Liability of the Psychiatrist,' 18 Syracuse L.R. 691, 704–707 (1967). In reversing the trial court's dismissal of the plaintiff's claim for malpractice, the appellate court held that the plaintiff's case could, in view of the "fantastic" nature of the treatment, be submitted to the jury without any expert testimony that the treatment constituted malpractice. Significantly, at the trial neither the plaintiff nor the defense introduced any evidence either as to the reasonableness or acceptability to the psychiatric profession of the experimental therapy developed by Dr. Rosen. It is unclear how the case might ultimately have been decided had Dr. Rosen introduced testimony attesting to the efficacy of his therapeutic approach or introduced evidence that the therapy was viewed as promising by some accepted segment of the psychiatric profession.

The use of "innovative" therapy also led to a finding of liability in *Abraham v. Zaslow* (San Francisco, Cy.Sup.Ct.1972) reported in N.Y. Times, Jul. 5, 1972, at 27 and APA Monitor, March 1973. The therapy in question was called "Rage Reduction Therapy or Z–Process." This involved breaking down the patient's resistance, by applying extensive physical stimulation to an immobilized patient in order to reduce the repressed compulsion to escape. The process was originally developed for use on autistic children, but Dr. Zaslow expanded it for use with disturbed adults. At trial the plaintiff testified, "I was tortured, including choking, beating, holding and tying me down and sticking fingers in my mouth." Ralph Slovenko, Psychiatry and Law, at 428, n. 39 (1973).

10. *Criminal liability for therapy "Beyond the Pale"*. Treatment by two unlicensed psychotherapists of a ten-year-old child who died in the course of the treatment resulted in a conviction for reckless child abuse in a 2001 Colorado case. The victim was being treated for "reactive detachment disorder," which presumably involved an inability to form a loving relationship because of early trauma. As part of the treatment, she was "wrapped in a sheet to simulate a womb while four adults pushed against her with pillows." The aim of the treatment was to have her "emerge 'reborn' " and be able to bond with her adoptive mother. The child died of asphyxiation leading to the charges and conviction. Publicity concerning the case resulted in the adoption by the Colorado legislature of a law outlawing rebirthing therapy. N.Y. Times, April 21, 2001, p. A–7.

11. *Evolving standards governing innovative therapy*. The standards governing the liability of physicians undertaking experimental or innovative therapy have undergone a marked change in recent years. As noted by one commentator, "The rule to be extracted from the early cases involving human experimentation is that physicians vary from established treatment at their own peril." Michael H. Shapiro & Roy G. Spence, Bioethics and Law, at 871 (1981). "The more modern courts take a less restrictive view of untried medical treatment and surgical procedures; and several decisions establish the right of the general field of medicine and surgery to progress and advance to some experimentation." Id. While this may be the trend for biologically based treatments it may, as suggested by the following note, be less true in the case of psychotherapy.

12. *Controversial psychotherapy*. No form of psychotherapy in recent years has been as controversial as a technique known as Recovered Memory therapy (R.M.). Over an eight year span starting in 1990 the use of this technique led to 105 malpractice suits by former patients against their therapists. Of this number, 42 were settled out of court with one settlement leading to the payment of 10.2 million dollars to the patient and her family. Of the nine cases that went to trial, all resulted in a verdict for the plaintiff. Forty-three cases were still pending as of July 1998. E. Loftus, 'The Price of Bad Memories', 22 Skeptical Inquirer 22, 24 (1998). In all of these cases, the plaintiff alleged that the treatment involving R.M. was not a legitimate form of therapy. The defense, on the other hand, has generally taken the position that R.M. is an innovative and state-of-the-art treatment for Multiple Personality Disorder. The section which follows provides a more detailed discussion of these cases and the issues they raise.

B. SELECTED MALPRACTICE ISSUES

1. *Recovered Memory Therapy*

a. *Prologue*

The idea that childhood events may be repressed from consciousness and recalled through therapy has been a fundamental tenet of Freudian psychoanalytic theory. However, until the mid–1970's, the notion that childhood memories could be repressed served more as a theoretical abstraction than the central focus of a treatment regime. Its acceptance as a treatment technique by a committed minority of therapists is closely associated with developments on the diagnostic front that gave special prominence to a disorder known as "Multiple Personality Disorder" (M.P.D.).

Even before the mid–1970's there was some recognition within the psychiatric community that some individuals might develop distinct multiple personalities, although this disorder was generally regarded as being fairly esoteric and rare. Nevertheless, it gained a certain prominence among the public as a result of a best-selling book, "The Three Faces of Eve," which was followed by an award-winning movie by the same title. The disorder gained additional prominence with the 1973 publication of the highly publicized book, "Sybil," which subsequently became a TV movie. Like Eve, Sybil would spontaneously lapse into multiple personalities, or "alters" (alternate personalities). Notwithstanding these popular depictions, the disorder was generally viewed by the psychiatric profession as an extremely rare one. A 1964 study of the medical literature up to that time yielded only six reported cases of the disorder.

In contrast with this earlier period, by 1990, M.P.D. had become a commonly diagnosed disorder. One estimate suggests that between 1985 and 1995, an M.P.D. diagnosis had been ascribed to 40,000 patients. The factors leading to the increased use of an M.P.D. diagnosis have been outlined by one commentator:

"Until about 1975, there had been no M.P.D. specialty. Multiple-personality disorder had no separate listing in the American Psychiatric Association's 'Diagnostic and Statistical Manual of Mental Disorder,' or D.S.M., the guidebook to diagnosis. But in 1980, after vigorous lobbying by interested therapists, the new edition of D.S.M. gave M.P.D. a primary-level listing among the dissociative disorders—conditions in which some part of mental functioning splits off from consciousness. In 1984, the new M.P.D. enthusiasts founded an organization of their own, the International Society for the Study of Multiple Personality and Dissociation (I.S.S.M.P. & D.), and began holding annual conferences, co-sponsored by Rush–Presbyterian–St. Luke's Medical Center, in Chicago. That hospital subsequently set up the country's first dissociative-disorders unit, under the M.P.D. expert Bennett Braun. Other units followed. Between 1970 and 1990, the average annual output of publications on M.P.D. increased 6000 percent."

Among those publications were two 1989 textbooks: "Diagnosis and Treatment of Multiple Personality Disorder," by Frank Putnam, and "Multiple Personality Disorder," by Colin Ross. Both offered treatment plans focusing on presumed childhood abuse. Using hypnosis, the therapist was instructed to flush out the alters and get them to divulge their secrets, a process that often involved protracted reenactments called "abreactions."

Acocella, Joan, "The Politics of Hysteria", The New Yorker, Apr. 6, 1998, at 66.

M.P.D. also gained prominence as a consequence of media attention.

[Throughout the 1980's] magazines and newspapers were retailing utterly credulous stories about M.P.D. And then there was television. Phil Donahue was apparently the first talk-show host to present a program on M.P.D.; he was followed by Sally Jessy Raphael, Larry King, Leeza Gibbons, and Oprah Winfrey. Meanwhile, celebrities were coming forward with tales of childhood abuse: Roseanne, La Toya Jackson, Oprah herself. Some claimed to be multiples. Roseanne, for example, had unearthed 21 personalities in herself, including Piggy, Bambi, and Fucker. M.P.D. experts also went on TV. Bennett Braun appeared on the Chicago evening news with his star patient, who switched personalities on camera. Again and again, on the talk shows it was stressed that M.P.D. was not rare, it was common.

Id. at 68.

The recovered memory movement was also spread by several best-selling manuals on the subject, such as "The Courage to Heal," which in its two editions, sold over three quarter of a million copies. These publications promulgated the notion that M.P.D. was primarily a disorder of women who had been sexually abused as children.

M.P.D. rests on the following set of fundamental assumptions: "[t]hat people routinely banish traumatic experiences from consciousness because they are too horrifying to contemplate; that these forgotten experiences cannot be recalled by any normal process but only by special techniques; that these techniques produce reliable recovery of memory; that before such recovery, these forgotten experiences cause miserable symptoms; that healing is possible only by digging out and reliving the forgotten experiences." See E. Loftus, "Memory Distortions and False Memory Creation," 24 Bulletin of the American Academy of Psychiatry and the Law, 281–85 (1996) [hereinafter, Loftus, Memory Distortions].

The recovery of early childhood memories, which is a central feature of M.P.D. treatment, relies on a variety of techniques, such as "age regression and guided visualization" (where a patient is talked through an imagined scene to awaken repressed memories). Repressed Memory (R.M.) therapy also frequently utilizes hypnosis and sodium amytal (truth serum) for the ostensible purpose of removing barriers to the recovery of forgotten or repressed experiences. In any event, the primary purpose of such therapeutic sessions is presumably to uncover traumatic childhood events, particularly involving sexual abuse by an adult. Not infrequently, the offending adult is identified as a member of the patient's family, and most commonly, a parent. Other less common "discovered" traumatic experiences may include satanism, torture, ritual murder, and cannibalism.

The number of patients that underwent R.M. therapy in the 80's and 90's cannot be estimated with any degree of certainty. It is clear, however, that a relatively small but committed group of mental health professionals, including psychiatrists and psychologists, at one point subscribed to M.P.D. and R.M. therapy. Moreover, the proposition that memories elicited under hypnosis were more accurate than non-hypnotic recall seemingly had fairly widespread support among most mental health professionals.

For many patients and their families, the effects of M.P.D. therapy were devastating. Charges of sexual abuse by parents and other relatives were a common outcome of therapy. Litigation by patients to recover damages from sexual abuse uncovered in the course of R.M. therapy became a fairly common phenomenon.

The tide changed, however, in the early 1990's, as cases of false recall (and the devastating consequences on parents and families) were publicized in professional journals and the media. For instance, a 1993 issue of the Harvard Mental Health Letter called for an immediate end to M.P.D. treatment. The popular press followed suit with articles in magazines such as *Time* and TV expose programs questioning the reliability of R.M. therapy. The controversy surrounding M.P.D. soon made its way through the legal system, as numerous former patients came to believe that the memories of sexual abuse had been falsely implanted by their therapists. By December of 1997, at least 105 former patients had filed malpractice suits against their former therapists. See E. Loftus, "The Price of Bad Memories," 22 Skeptical Inquirer, 23–24, (1998) [hereinafter Loftus, Price of Bad Memories]. Overall, the plaintiffs in these cases prevailed; a verdict in favor of the plaintiffs was obtained in all of the nine cases that had come to trial, 42 resulted in settlements involving some payment of damages and 53 were still pending as of December 1997. Id. at 24.

b. *Anatomy of Recovered Memory Malpractice Law Suit*

[The Facts set out below have been abstracted from various secondary sources and the plaintiff's complaints in *Burgus v. Rush Presbyterian St. Luke's Medical Center et al.* (Cir. Ct. of Cook County, IL., No. 91L8394 and 93L14050.)]]

In early spring of 1986, Patricia Burgus was referred to the psychiatric trauma section of Rush–Presbyterian–St. Luke's Hospital in Chicago [Hereinafter "St. Luke's"]. The basis for the referral was severe, postpartum depression. At the time, St. Luke's had established a Disassociate Disorder unit headed by Dr. Bennett Braun.

Following her admission as a voluntary patient on March 5, 1986, Ms. Burgus who was diagnosed as suffering from mental illness, including M.P.D. remained continually hospitalized for the next 27 months as a patient in the hospital's Dissociative Disorder Program. According to her complaint, throughout her hospital stay, and in the three years that she was treated as an outpatient following discharge in June of 1988, she received R.M. therapy in addition to various medications, including sedatives, hypnotics, and psychotropic drugs such as Inderal, Halcion, and Xanax.

The R.M. treatment regime that Burgus underwent involved the use of techniques intended to bring to the surface "repressed memories." Aided by hypnosis, she developed numerous "alters" (alternate personalities), which led her to uncover supposedly "repressed memories" including membership in a satanic cult, abuse by numerous men during childhood, abuse of her children, and cannibalism.

Approximately one week following Ms. Burgus' hospitalization, she and her husband were asked to agree to the psychiatric hospitalization (also in St. Luke's) of their two children, John and Mikey, who at the time of their admission were four and five years old, respectively. In the course of their hospitalization, which lasted approximately three years, the children were subjected to various therapies, including extensive psychotropic medication and psychotherapy which in part relied on R.M. techniques. The complaint alleged that in some such sessions, the children were "encouraged" to develop "alter" personalities and were exposed to suggestive techniques including being shown handguns and handcuffs.

During her treatment, Ms. Burgus apparently accepted various memories of traumatic events as true. But she eventually concluded that the memories were false and had been implanted by her psychiatrist in the course of treatment, which on occasion involved hypnosis. She subsequently filed a lawsuit against St. Luke's and Dr. Braun and another psychiatrist who had treated her and her two sons. Her complaint alleged misdiagnosis and lack of due care in the selection and application of treatment. She also alleged a lack of informed consent to the treatment, namely that she had not been informed of the risks and the psychiatric trauma associated with R.M. therapy.

A separate complaint on behalf of the children alleged that while both children were diagnosed as suffering from M.P.D., neither child was in fact afflicted with this disorder. The complaint further alleged that neither child suffered from any kind of disorder to which psychiatric hospitalization for a period of three years was medically justified.

The plaintiffs' claim for damages included medical expenses in excess of 2.8 million dollars, lost earnings resulting from a permanent disability occasioned by the failed therapy, and unspecified damages for mental suffering.

In defending against Ms. Burgus' lawsuit, Dr. Braun asserted that the memories had not been implanted but were generated by the patient herself. He was quoted as having stated: "She just spit it out ...... all of the cult stuff that she was talking about I learned from her. The idea to bring the meat in was hers. I merely said if he [her husband] does bring it in, I will try to get it analyzed for human protein [for the purpose of establishing whether it was human flesh]. Yes, the kids did see the handcuffs. They did see a gun. But it was for therapeutic reasons." See "Memory Therapy Leads to a Lawsuit And Big Settlement," The N.Y. Times, Nov. 5, 1997, at 1 [hereinafter N.Y. Times, *Lawsuit*].

The Burgus case was settled shortly before it was scheduled to go to trial. Under the terms of the settlement, Patricia Burgus and her two children received 10.6 million dollars from the insurance companies of the two defendant psychiatrists and St. Luke's hospital. After the settlement, which Dr. Braun opposed, both psychiatrists denied any malpractice. Dr. Elva Poznanski, the section chief of child and adolescent psychiatry was quoted as stating: "On the basis of the knowledge available at that time, I would not change the treatment of these boys." See N.Y. Times, Lawsuit. The defendant, Dr. Braun, called the settlement "a travesty" and was quoted as stating: "A patient comes into the hospital doing so bad that she belongs in the hospital, and after several serious events in the hospital which I can't disclose because of patient confidentiality, she was discharged and is doing much better ... Where's the damage?" See N.Y. Times, Lawsuit.

c.   *Legal Issues Raised in M.P.D. Litigation Cases*

i.   M.P.D. as a Diagnostic Category

A threshold question relates to the validity of M.P.D. as a diagnostic category. Arguably, if the diagnostic category does not exist, in the sense that the primary characteristics ascribed to the disorder do not accord with empirical fact, its use in diagnosis may not be warranted. Under this view, therapists using this diagnostic category could be found to have deviated from the standard of care applicable to the diagnostic function. While the M.P.D. classification has been subject to attack, there appears to be a general consensus among the psychiatric profession that in rare cases a patient may suffer from a disorder characterized by the manifestation of distinct alternate personalities. At the same time, according to one report, "[while] most psychiatric professionals do seem to believe that multiple-personality disorder is real ... it rarely occurs spontaneously and therefore does not deserve to be a primary-level diagnosis." See Acocella, The New Yorker, Hysteria, at 71. Moreover, "[l]ike the majority of psychiatric patients, people diagnosed with M.P.D. tend to be 'co-morbid'; that is, they meet the diagnostic criteria for more than one disorder ... [T]he average M.P.D. patient qualifies for three or four other psychiatric diagnoses ... typical accompaniment being depression, antisocial personality disorder, and borderline personality disorder." Id. at 72. Some have therefore questioned whether therapists are justified in labeling a patient as suffering from M.P.D. when the dominant symptomology is chronic depression or borderline personality.

However, the primary significance of mislabeling is that it is likely to trigger the selection of an inappropriate therapy, which either harms the patient or, at the very least, does not improve their condition. For instance, placing an M.P.D. diagnosis on a patient whose major symptomology is depression may constitute a departure from an ordinary standard of care, particularly if the subsequent treatment is inappropriate for a person suffering from depression.

ii. Method of Treatment

Regardless of diagnosis, the most controversial issue concerns the method of therapy advocated by proponents of M.P.D. theory (the flushing out of the "alter" for the purpose of having them reveal their secrets). As noted, the theory behind R.M. treatment rests on several assumptions, including (1) a patient's psychopathology, and specifically M.P.D., is caused by trauma and in most cases sexual abuse during childhood; (2) traumatic events are frequently repressed; (3) repressed trauma can be brought to the surface by the use of various techniques, including "abreaction," (a process that involves a reenactment of prior events), regressed memory processes and hypnosis; (4) memories elicited by hypnosis or the application of sodium amytal have a high likelihood of being accurate, and (5) the recovery of forgotten traumatic experiences can provide relief from the symptoms associated with M.P.D.

Successful plaintiffs in malpractice action against therapists for the use of R.M. therapy have been able to establish a lack of due care by expert testimony challenging the scientific validity of several of the assumptions underlying R.M. For instance, one leading expert has written, "there is no cogent scientific support for this repression folklore, and an ample reason to believe that extraordinarily suggestive prolonged searches for hidden memories can be harmful . . . This is not to say that people cannot forget horrible things that have happened to them; most certainly they can. But there is virtually no extensive histories of abuse of which they are completely unaware. Yet an unfounded faith in the repressed memory ideology has lead some clinicians to engage in practices that are risky if not dangerous in terms of their potential for creating false beliefs and memories." Loftus, "Memory Distortions," at 282–283. See also E. Loftus, "Creating False Memories," Scientific American, Sept. 1997, at 71.

Successful cases have also challenged the reliability of memories elicited through hypnosis. In this regard, plaintiffs have relied on a body of recent research indicating that post-event information often becomes incorporated into memory, supplementing or altering a person's recollection. Evidence that hypnotically induced recall is not necessarily reliable has in turn allowed plaintiffs to argue that the therapist's misrepresentations to the patient concerning the accuracy of recalled memories constitutes a departure from the ordinary standard of care.

Additionally, plaintiffs have in various cases been able to establish that the recalled memories are not only inherently unreliable, but that they were moreover distorted by suggestions planted by the therapists. Again, evidence to this effect has allowed plaintiffs to assert that the therapist's misrepresentation of accuracy constituted malpractice.

Questions and Comments

1. *Other R.M. cases.* The *Burgus* case is by no means the most extraordinary of the R.M. malpractice claims that have been filed against therapists in recent years. A case involving as plaintiff, Elizabeth Carlson, is highlighted in Joan Acocella's incisive article, The Politics of Hysteria, The New Yorker, Apr. 6, 1998, at 64.

2. *Application of respectable minority rule.* Would the respectable minority rule (See pp. 139–40) be available to a therapist defending a malpractice action involving the use of R.M. therapy? Is the rule (in those jurisdictions where it is applied) limited to situations where the therapist elects one of several possible therapies and where the one selected has the potential of effectively treating the disorder? In other words, is a respectable minority defense preclude where the therapy has no realistic chance of being effective? If this is true, what is the status of R.M. therapy under the respectable minority rule?

3. *Impact of R.M. litigation.* The series of successful lawsuits against therapists employing R.M. therapy has had a number of consequences. In 1993, the American Psychiatric Association issued a circular to its members, cautioning that memories obtained through R.M. techniques are often not true and that memories obtained under hypnosis may be unreliable. Also, a number of specialized psychiatric units established for the treatment of Dissociative Disorders have closed, including Dr. Braun's unit at St. Luke's. Acocella, Hysteria at 78. Finally, the most recent edition of the American Psychiatric Association's Diagnostic and Statistical Manual IV omits the category "Multiple Personality Disorder," and in its place substituted the category "Dissociative Identity Disorder." According to one commentator, this change reflects the desire of the psychiatric profession to "shake off the scandal" associated with M.P.D. id. at 76.

4. *Changes in malpractice insurance coverage.* The legal liability associated with R.M. therapy and hypnosis has caused some insurance malpractice carriers to exclude or otherwise limit coverage involving the use of hypnosis in therapy.

5. *Legislative proposals.* Efforts to curb abuses resulting from therapies such as R.M. have led to some initiatives on the legislative front. One such proposal, advanced by an advocacy group for reform, calls for the adoption by state legislatures and Congress of a "Truth and Responsibility in Mental Health Practices Act." The proposed text of such act would read: "No tax or tax exempt monies may be used for any form of health care treatment, including any form of psychotherapy, that has not been proven safe and effective by rigorous, valid and reliable scientific investigations and accepted as safe and effective by a substantial majority of the relevant scientific community." Id. at 78. If such a proposal were adopted, how would the legislation be implemented and which entity would be empowered to determine whether a particular psychotherapy is "safe and effective?" Is the effectiveness of psychotherapy amenable to being validated by reliable scientific investigation? What is the history of past efforts to gauge the effectiveness of different forms of psychotherapy? (See pp. 45–48).

6. *Rights of third parties to maintain legal action.* The rights of *third* parties falsely accused of abuse in R.M. therapy to bring in actions against

therapists is treated at pp. 208–215. That section focuses on the case *Ramona v. Ramona*, No. Civ. 61898 (Sup.Ct. Napa County 1994) which is one of the first successful lawsuits brought by a third party (the father of the patient) against therapists who employed R.M. treatment.

7. *Question*. As suggested in the introduction of this chapter, most malpractice litigations against mental health professionals have involved the use of biological therapies (medication and ECT). Only rarely (e.g. Osheroff v. Chestnut Lodge Inc. discussed at pp. 140–46) have therapists been charged with malpractice where *psychotherapy* was the treatment of choice. What then explains the volume of litigation in the use of R.M. therapy (105 malpractice actions initiated between 1988 and 1998)? Is the reason connected to the fact that unlike psychotherapy generally, R.M. treatment frequently results in highly distressing situations for not only the patient but also third parties accused of abuse, coupled with the fact that this distress is directly traceable to the actions of the therapist?

Arguably, in more conventional psychotherapy, even if the treatment is not particularly effective, it will generally be difficult for patients to prove that the particular psychotherapeutic approach utilized (assuming it was one that is accepted by the profession) was less effective than an alternative or that the patient suffered a recognizable harm from such therapy.

8. *Patient law suits against "discovered" abusers*. Recovered R.M. therapy has led some patients to initiate lawsuits against parents, relatives, and neighbors, alleging sexual abuse during their childhood. Typically, these cases involve claims by the plaintiff, but the events upon which the suit is based were repressed or disassociated until therapeutic intervention brought to the surface repressed memories. In some cases, such suits have been based on events that occurred thirty or forty years earlier. See Loftus, "Memory Distortions and False Memory Creation", 24 Bulletin of the Academy of Psychiatry and Law, at 281–82 (1996). Some legislatures have facilitated the bringing of such suits by changing the statute of limitations so that the statute does not begin to run until a plaintiff has discovered the facts essential to the cause of action. Id. at 282. As a result, "[h]undreds of civil plaintiffs have now taken advantage of [the modified statute of limitations] ... and brought suits in which they claim that their memories surfaced in therapy. Id. at 282. However, according to one report, '[a]s the suits against therapists multiplied, suits against the alleged abusers receded and those that were filed did not fare well.' " Acocella, Hysteria at 76.

9. *Criminal prosecutions of R.M. therapists*. Litigation concerning R.M. therapy has not been confined to the civil courts. On October 29, 1998, federal authorities in Houston obtained a criminal sixty-count indictment against the administrator and four mental health professionals of the former Spring Shadows Glen Hospital (*United States v. Peterson et al.*, No. Civ. H97–237 (S.D.Tex. 1998)). The professionals named in the indictment, including two psychiatrists, a Ph.D. psychologist, and a psychiatric social worker, were charged with "exaggerating diagnosis" and overstating the need for expensive treatment in order to unjustly collect insurance payments. According to the indictment, the defendants were part of a conspiracy that "did fraudulently treat the insured patients for M.P.D. caused by unsubstantiated and unrealistic allegations and abuses, including satanic

ritual abuse and cult activity, while at the same time creating medical records to substantiate such treatment." Additionally, the indictment alleged that the defendants "did fraudulently elicit statements of satanic ritual abuse and cult activities from the admitted patients, through nontraditional treatment modalities, including the use of leading or suggestive questions during therapy sessions while the patients were: under hypnosis; under the influence of a drug or combination of drugs; isolated from their families, friends, and the outside world . . ." See Mark Smith, "Mental Health Workers Fear Indictments" Impact,' Houston Chronicle, Oct. 30, 1997, at 1.

Following the indictments, the international society for the study of Dissociative Disorders issued a news release which asserted that the indictments would have a "chilling effect" on health care delivery and indicates a willingness by the federal government to set standards for diagnosis and treatment and to decide which patient memories are "accurate." Id.

2. *Liability for Patient Suicide*

One of the more vexing issues concerns the liability of a therapist where the patient commits suicide. Suicidal impulses may, in fact, be one of the prime reasons why a patient is in therapy. Where a patient under treatment commits suicide, the next of kin may assert a claim against the therapist for malpractice, alleging, for instance, that the therapist elected an improper mode of therapy. A claim of this type might follow the treatment of a patient who entered therapy having suicidal impulses coupled with depression and where the therapist failed to consider antidepressant medication and instead relied entirely on psychotherapy. Liability may also arise from a therapist's failure to take appropriate precautions when he or she has knowledge of a patient's suicidal propensities. Needed precautions might include proper monitoring of the patient's condition or instituting civil commitment of the patient. In most instances, therapist "inaction" is the most problematic in terms of assigning liability. One reason is that suicide prediction is notoriously unreliable. Various studies have shown that suicide prediction by experts is likely to grossly overpredict suicide, resulting in numerous "false positives," i.e. prediction that individuals will commit suicide, when in fact they would not. Thus, the widespread use of civil commitment to *prevent* suicide would, as one court has noted, result in numerous patients who are not in fact suicide risks being subjected to a loss of freedom. See *Johnson v. United States*, 409 F.Supp. 1283 (M.D.Fla.1976).

Additionally, the invocation of civil commitment by a therapist where a patient has disclosed suicidal ideas poses the risk that the patient—therapist relationship, which relies on trust, may be ruptured, making it less likely that the therapist will be in a position thereafter to provide effective treatment. These considerations have made courts hesitant to assign liability in those instances where it is charged that a patient's suicide resulted from the therapist's failure to take some affirmative action, such as initiating commitment. *Weathers v. Pilkinton*, which follows, illustrates this trend, though the specific rule used by the court to limit liability on the basis that suicide is, as a matter of law, an independent intervening event is the rule in only a minority of jurisdictions.

WEATHERS v. PILKINTON
Court of Appeals of Tennessee, 1988.
754 S.W.2d 75.

Opinion

CANTRELL, JUDGE.

In this action for wrongful death against a doctor who allegedly failed to take the proper steps to prevent his patient from taking his own life, the trial judge held that the suicide of the [decedent] was an independent intervening cause and directed a verdict for the defendant. We affirm, on a related, although slightly different, ground.

* * *

[The decedent, Michael Weathers, was married in 1982 at the age of 27. His wife gave birth to a son a year later. He made the first overt reference to his death during an argument with his wife on Christmas day of 1983, when he pulled a gun from a drawer and asked her to shoot him. Three months later, after another argument with his wife, he entered a psychiatric hospital as a voluntary patient, and remained in treatment there for two months. Four months later, in August 1984, the decedent and his wife separated. Two weeks later, he took an overdose of codeine, which did not prove fatal. Some weeks later, he again had an argument with his wife, and again, asked her to kill him. This episode was followed by a two-week psychiatric hospitalization coupled with medication.

On September 14, the decedent took an overdose of Elavil and was again admitted to a regional hospital under the care of Dr. Pilkinton, a general physician. He was discharged eight days later, but was readmitted on November 7, 1984, after taking another overdose of drugs and leaving a suicide note. He was taken unconscious to the hospital, but upon his insistence he was released the next morning. Upon his release, he was urged by Dr. Pilkinton to enter outpatient therapy at a local community mental health clinic. For the next three weeks, the decedent seemed in a reasonably good mood, and was able to resume his employment. However, on November 28, after coming home from work, he called his wife and informed her that he intended to shoot himself. He carried out his threat before the arrival of the police, who had been summoned by his wife.]

* * *

The plaintiff, Ellen Weathers, brought this action against Dr. Pilkinton. The complaint contains two counts. The first count is for the wrongful death. * * * The second count is for the tort of outrageous conduct and is brought on behalf of Mrs. Weathers personally. Under the first count the plaintiff alleged that the negligence of Dr. Pilkinton was the proximate cause of Mr. Weathers' death.

At the trial the plaintiff presented two expert witnesses. They testified that to fulfill the standard of care in effect in the Nashville area, Dr. Pilkinton should have committed Mr. Weathers involuntarily on November 11, 1984 and should have ordered a psychiatric evaluation of Mr. Weathers after the three recent suicide attempts. In addition the experts testified that it was a mistake for Dr. Pilkinton to order Mr. Weathers to return to Luton Mental Health Center for outpatient care since his previous experience there had proved unsuccessful. Finally, each expert testified that in his opinion Dr. Pilkinton's negligence was the proximate cause of Mr. Weathers' death.

At the close of the plaintiff's proof the trial judge directed a verdict in favor of Dr. Pilkinton on both counts. On the negligence count the trial judge held that Mr. Weathers' suicide was an intervening intentional act that proximately caused his death. (Therefore, assuming that Dr. Pilkinton deviated from the standard of care, his negligence could not constitute the proximate cause of the death of Mr. Weathers.) On the second count, the trial judge held that there was simply no evidence of an intentional infliction of emotional distress on Mrs. Weathers which is a necessary element of the tort of outrageous conduct.

THE OUTRAGEOUS CONDUCT ACTION

We affirm the directed verdict on the outrageous conduct count.

The facts of this case simply do not warrant a finding that Dr. Pilkinton's conduct was outrageous nor a finding that as a result of his conduct Mrs. Weathers suffered the type of severe emotional distress that is a necessary element of the tort.

THE WRONGFUL DEATH ACTION

* * *

There is evidence in the record from which the jury might find that Dr. Pilkinton was negligent in treating Mr. Weathers.

If there is evidence from which the jury could have concluded that Dr. Pilkinton was negligent, the sole remaining question is whether there is evidence from which the jury could have concluded that the alleged negligence of Dr. Pilkinton was the proximate cause of the death of the decedent. As our Supreme Court said in *Lancaster v. Montesi*, 216 Tenn. 50, 390 S.W.2d 217 (1965), the cases in this jurisdiction and elsewhere have generally held that an act of suicide breaks the chain of causation unless the decedent's reason and memory were so far obscured that he did not know and understand what he was doing and was not therefore a responsible human agency.

The court quoted the following excerpt from *Daniels v. New York, N.H. & H.R. Co.,* 183 Mass. 393, 67 N.E. 424 (1903): "An act of suicide resulting from a moderately intelligent power of choice, even though the choice is determined by a disordered mind, should be deemed a new and independent, efficient cause of the death that immediately ensues." 67 N.E. at 426.

From this line of cases we conclude that where a defendant injures another either wilfully or negligently and as a result of the injury, the injured person commits suicide the act of suicide is, as a matter of law, an intervening independent cause if the decedent knew and understood the nature of his or her act or the act resulted from a moderately intelligent power of choice.

The appellant does not contest the rule established in *Jones* and *Lancaster,* but instead argues that there is a different rule where the decedent is under the care of a health care provider and consequently the health care provider has a specific duty of care to the patient. We acknowledge that there is a difference and—since proximate cause is based on forseeability—that the fact that mentally ill persons might take their lives if adequate precautions are not taken to protect them from themselves is more forseeable than the fact that a person injured by an ordinary act of negligence might become so depressed that suicide would result.

However, we must recognize that this is still an action for wrongful death and the right that survives to the widow is the same cause of action the decedent would have had had he survived. Thus, if the decedent could not have sued no right survives. [citation]

* * *

The rule is otherwise, of course, where the decedent did not know the nature or consequences of his act, or his reason and memory [were], at the time, so far obscured that he did not know and understand what he was doing and was therefore not a responsible human agency. Under those circumstances the act of suicide would not be a wilful, calculated, deliberate act that would defeat an action for wrongful death.

Therefore, we are of the opinion that the result in this case turns on the question of whether there is evidence in the record from which the jury might conclude that on the date of his death Mr. Weathers did not know and understand the nature of his suicidal act and, therefore, did not have a wilful and intelligent purpose to accomplish it. The only evidence in the record tending to show that Mr. Weathers did not know and understand the nature of his acts on November 28, 1984 is the circumstantial evidence of his history of depression, his treatment, and his prior suicide attempts. Neither of the medical experts who testified on behalf of the plaintiff testified that Mr. Weathers was bereft of reason or that he did not know and understand what he was doing.

On the other hand, the overwhelming evidence shows that from November 11 until November 28, 1984, Mr. Weathers functioned normally and lived an unremarkable life. Viewing the evidence in the light most favorable to the plaintiff, we are of the opinion that there is no evidence from which the jury could conclude that Mr. Weathers was, on November 28, 1984, in such a state of anxiety or depression that he did not know what he was doing. Therefore, the trial judge was correct in directing a verdict for the defendant.

The judgment of the court below is affirmed.

TATUM, SPECIAL JUDGE, dissenting:

I agree with the majority in the dismissal of the outrageous conduct action, but must respectfully dissent from the majority opinion affirming the action of the Trial Court in directing a verdict for the defendant in the negligence action. In my view, a jury question was presented.

I agree with the majority that there was evidence of negligence on the part of the defendant. I disagree that such negligence could not be found by a jury to be the proximate cause of the death of the decedent.

The history of the previous attempts of the decedent to commit suicide is strong evidence that he was afflicted with a mental illness that caused suicidal compulsions. It was for this reason that the decedent was placed in the care of the defendant, a health provider. It was the duty of the defendant to attempt to prevent the decedent from committing suicide.

In *Adams v. Carter County Memorial Hospital,* 548 S.W.2d 307 (Tenn.1977), our Supreme Court cited, with apparent approval, a treatise in 24 Vanderbilt Law Review, 217 (1971) entitled "Civil Liability for Causing Suicide: A Synthesis of Law and Psychiatry." I quote from this treatise:

> "Hospitals and psychiatrists with an affirmative duty to prevent their patients from committing suicide....

> First, it seems clear that liability could be imposed upon a psychiatrist for a gross error in judgment with respect to whether a patient should be confined. Giving full ambit to psychological justifications for not confining patients unless absolutely necessary, suicidal symptoms may be so apparent that confinement would be ordered by a psychiatrist of ordinary skill. For example, if an individual has made serious suicidal attempts, has been deeply depressed, has suffered loss of sleep, appetite, and in effect is almost unable to function in society, but his psychiatrist has declined to have him placed in a hospital, the psychiatrist might be held liable for the individual's subsequent suicide."

* * *

I agree with the New Jersey Superior Court in *Cowan v. Doering,* 215 N.J.Super. 484, 522 A.2d 444 (1987). In that case, a physician admitted a depressed patient to intensive care, who had taken an overdose of sleeping pills. The physician failed to take suicidal precautions. The patient subsequently attempted suicide by jumping from the hospital window. At trial, the physician took the position that the patient understood and appreciated the consequences of her acts and therefore her suicidal attempt was an independent intervening cause. In rejecting this defense and upholding a jury verdict, the New Jersey court stated:

"Observation has particular efficacy where, as here, the duty of the physician and the hospital encompasses the responsibility to safeguard the patient from the reasonably foreseeable risk of self-inflicted harm.

We find no sound reason to adopt the sterile and unrealistic approach that if a disabled plaintiff is not totally incompetent, he is fully legally accountable for his own negligence. In view of the present state of medical knowledge, it is possible and practical to evaluate the degrees of mental acuity and correlate them with legal responsibility. In our view, a patient known to harbor suicidal tendencies whose judgment has been blunted by a mental disability should not have his conduct measured by external standards applicable to a normal adult. Where it is reasonably foreseeable that a patient by reason of his mental or emotional illness may attempt to injure himself, those in charge of his care owe a duty to safeguard him from his self-damaging potential. This duty contemplates the reasonably forseeable occurrence of self-inflicted injury regardless of whether it is the product of the patient's volitional or negligent act."

* * *

In my view, suicide is not an intervening independent cause that will relieve a physician of liability or negligence when the patient had no power of choice. There was evidence in this case that the decedent acted with compulsion and not through a power of choice. * * * As stated, the history of the decedent's previous attempts to commit suicide is circumstantial evidence sufficient to make a jury question as to whether the suicide was committed by "intelligent power of choice" or by compulsion due to mental illness. I repeat that this suicidal tendency or compulsion was specifically the ailment which the defendant was entrusted to treat.

* * *

I have a high respect for the opinions of my colleagues. However, I would reverse the judgment of the trial court and remand the case for trial on the negligence issue.

Questions and Comments

1. *Questions.* The majority in *Weathers v. Pilkinton* holds that suicide is an independent intervening cause unless the patient "did not know and understand the nature of his suicidal act and, therefore, did not have willful and intelligent purpose to accomplish this." Would this include or exclude an individual suffering from psychotic depression whose basic motivation for suicide is a feeling of worthlessness and a pessimism as to the future? If such individual would be held to "understand the nature of his suicidal act" would it not preclude liability even where the patient is being treated specifically to minimize the risk of suicide?

2. *Liability for suicide of outpatient.* The old common law rule adopted by the court in *Weathers v. Pilkinton* that serves to limit a therapist's liability for the patient's suicide on the basis that suicide is an independent

intervening event is losing favor in most jurisdictions. The more modern view is illustrated by *Kockelman v. Segal,* 61 Cal.App.4th 491, 71 Cal.Rptr.2d 552 (1998). In reversing the granting of defendant's motion for summary judgment by the trial court, the appellate court explained the contemporary approach to the liability of the treating therapist in the following terms:

> "Defendant's summary judgment was based upon the single claim that as a matter of law a psychiatrist owes no duty of care to an outpatient who may be suicidal ... Under traditional tort law principles, a person is not ordinarily liable for the actions of another and is under no duty to protect another person from harm. An affirmative duty to protect another from harm may arise, however, where a "special relationship" exists. Such a special relationship is typically where the plaintiff is particularly vulnerable and dependent upon the defendant who, correspondingly, has some control over the plaintiff's welfare. '[T]he relationship between a therapist and his patient satisfies this requirement ... ' (*Tarasoff v. Regents of University of California* (1976) 17 Cal.3d 425, 435) ...
>
> ... We disagree with *Weathers.* Despite the fact that a patient is not bereft of reason and may appreciate the consequences of his actions, we recognize the fact that there are varying degrees of mental affectation. Although a patient may be in full understanding of his actions, an illness may still exist for which treatment has been requested and admission sought ... Rather than absolve the physician of liability when self-destructive conduct is reasonably foreseeable, the better approach is to require reasonable precautions in light of the special relationship between the physician and his patient ...
>
> ... Existing case law provides that a psychotherapist or other mental health care provider has a duty to use a reasonable degree of skill, knowledge and care in treating a patient, commensurate with that possessed and exercised by others practicing within that specialty in the professional community. If those who are caring for and treating mentally disturbed patients know of facts from which they could reasonably conclude that the patient would be likely to self-inflict harm in the absence of preventative measures, then those caretakers must use reasonable care under the circumstances to prevent such harm from occurring. See also *Stepakoff v. Kantar* (1985), which is set out at pp. 130–133, holding the psychiatrist liable for the suicide of the patient who was being treated on an outpatient basis.

3. *Liability for suicide of hospitalized patients.* In the case of patients who are hospitalized because of suicidal tendencies and who subsequently commit suicide while in a facility, courts have generally rejected the proximate cause limitation, which some jurisdictions apply where the patient was being treated as an outpatient. In the case of institutionalized patients, courts have generally held that both proximate cause and contributory negligence are issues to be decided by the jury. Thus, the key issue in these cases is whether the risk of suicide was reasonably foreseeable and whether the care and treatment by the institution and treating staff conformed to the ordinary standard of care. The legal principles applicable to cases of this type were expounded by the court in *Winger v. Franciscan Medical Center,* 299

Ill.App.3d 364, 233 Ill.Dec. 748, 701 N.E.2d 813 (3 Dist. 1998). In explaining why the proximate cause limitation is not applicable where the patient was institutionalized, the court noted:

> "This is an action asserting psychiatric malpractice and the failure to properly supervise; it is different from general medical malpractice actions because the negligence is not in the diagnosis or treatment but, rather, it is in the failure to carefully protect a patient from inflicting self-harm. 'There is a substantial difference between holding one liable to foresee the suicide of a person sane when injured who later commits suicide, and holding a hospital liable where it admits a psychiatric patient with known suicidal tendencies.' "

Id. at 701 N.E.2d 813, 818.

In the above excerpt, is the court's rationale persuasive in distinguishing between the liability of therapists who are treating a patient on an outpatient basis from the care of patients who are institutionalized? Is the failure to properly supervise a hospitalized patient materially different from the failure of a mental health professional exercise due care and, if necessary, initiate commitment proceedings where potentially suicidal patient is being treated on an outpatient basis? Is the duty to supervise and take precautions to safeguard the patient more easily carried out when the patient is hospitalized? Does the exercise of due care and the protection of the patient from suicide in both situations call for a prediction by the mental health professional of the likelihood that the patient is in fact suicidal? What degree of probability should trigger precautionary actions by the therapist?

4. *Proximate cause in other contexts.* The issue of proximate cause has also arisen in a different context. For instance, hospitalized psychiatric patients will sometimes wander away from the facility and die from exposure. While it may not have been negligence to permit the patient to be on the grounds unaccompanied, the question that may need to be resolved is whether the death could have been prevented by an earlier or more diligent search of the surrounding grounds. This was the basic fact situation in *Lando v. State,* 47 A.D.2d 972, 366 N.Y.S.2d 679 (1975), modified, 39 N.Y.2d 803, 385 N.Y.S.2d 759, 351 N.E.2d 426 (1976), involving a suit against a state psychiatric hospital by the administrator of the estate of a deceased mental patient. The suit alleged negligence for failure on the part of the hospital to promptly conduct a search for the patient after she disappeared from the hospital grounds. The body was not found until eleven days after her disappearance. At the trial the extent and thoroughness of the search were seriously questioned, and the testimony as to the measures taken by the hospital was sharply disputed. Reversing an award for the plaintiff administrator, the court concluded that the element of proximate cause had not been adequately proved:

> To demonstrate entitlement to an award in this situation, the claimant must establish the existence of a duty; that the duty was breached and that the breach was the proximate cause of death. Even if we assume the existence of a duty and assume but do not concede its breach, the claim here must *fail because of a lack of proof that the breach was the proximate cause of the result.* Without this connection between the duty and the result, there can be no recovery. The deceased may

have been the victim of foul play or she may have died from natural causes and the time of death is uncertain. There is no proof as to when Miss Lando's body fell or was placed or thrown into the obscuring foliage. Hence, several possibilities as to what occurred exist and, since the State would not be responsible for one or more of these possibilities, the claimant cannot recover without proving that the death was sustained wholly or in part by a cause for which the State was responsible . To conclude here that the failure to make an adequate search was the proximate cause requires speculation of the rankest sort.

Id. at 973, 366 N.Y.S.2d at 680. On review by New York's highest court the decision of the appellate division denying the claim for decedent's wrongful death was affirmed. However, the father's claim for damages for mental anguish resulting from his being "denied access and control over the body of his deceased daughter for a period of 11 days" was reinstated. 39 N.Y.2d 803, 385 N.Y.S.2d 759, 351 N.E.2d 426 (1976). See also, *Castillo v. United States of America,* 552 F.2d 1385 (10th Cir.1977).

3.   *Sexual Misconduct as a Basis for Liability*

CORGAN v. MUEHLING

Appellate Court of Illinois, First District, 1988.
167 Ill.App.3d 1093, 118 Ill.Dec. 698, 522 N.E.2d 153.

Justice Scariano delivered the opinion of the court:

In March of 1979, Penelope Corgan came under the psychological care of Conrad Muehling. She alleges in count I of her complaint that he conducted her treatment negligently, was negligent in having sexual relations with her during this treatment, and "negligently failed either to recognize the evolution of the psychotherapeutic phenomenon of transference and countertransference or deal appropriately with such evolving phenomenon," all of which caused her emotional trauma.

* * *

This appeal is taken from those orders of the trial court which dismissed counts II and IV of the plaintiff's third amended complaint . [In addition] the trial judge certified the related questions of whether *Rickey v. Chicago Transit Authority* (1983), 98 Ill.2d 546, 75 Ill.Dec. 211, 457 N.E.2d 1, bars Corgan from recovering for emotional damages under counts I and III.

Counts I, III
A.   *Introduction.*

In count I, Corgan charges Muehling with malpractice. Malpractice is a form of negligence thus the first count is in essence for negligence. Furthermore, the parties agree that count III, wherein Corgan alleges willful and wanton misconduct, also is basically an action for negligence, since this court has held that willful and wanton misconduct is an aggravated form of negligence. Count III is *not* for the intentional infliction of emotional distress; indeed, Corgan does not contend otherwise. While we must accept all well-pleaded facts as true Corgan does not plead the elements that constitute intentional infliction of emotional distress. She does not allege that Muehling's actions were calculated to cause severe emotional distress; rather, among other allegations, she claims that he was acting solely for his own sexual gratification.

B.   The Rickey Case.

Simply and briefly, the questions certified by the circuit court in this case are whether counts I and III of Corgan's third amended complaint are barred by *Rickey v. Chicago Transit Authority* (1983), 98 Ill.2d 546, 75 Ill.Dec. 211, 457 N.E.2d 1. In *Rickey,* the plaintiff was attempting to recover damages for the emotional distress he allegedly suffered as a result of the CTA's negligence when he saw his brother being injured on an escalator. The Illinois supreme court, in a unanimous opinion, framed the issue in the following manner: "The underlying question is, of course, whether any person who suffers emotional distress can recover, but the question here specifically is whether a bystander at the injury of another who, generally under the decisions, is a close relative of the bystander can recover." *Rickey,* 98 Ill.2d at 553, 75 Ill.Dec. 211, 457 N.E.2d 1.

The court then discussed the "impact rule," the governing law in Illinois at that time, which required physical impact or injury in order for a plaintiff to recover in an action for the negligent infliction of emotional distress. The *Rickey* court noted that this requirement had been frequently satisfied by trivial contacts, and that consequently the impact rule had fallen into disfavor. The court also recognized that although recovery for emotional distress should not be determined solely on the basis of whether there was any physical impact visited upon the plaintiff, the appellate court went too far in adopting a standard which "would permit recovery for emotional disturbance alone." [citation] Our supreme court acknowledged that courts were hesitant in allowing recovery for purely emotional injuries and explained such unwillingness as follows: "courts have given as reasons for this reluctance apprehensions that the door would be opened for fraudulent claims, that damages would be difficult to ascertain and measure, that emotional injuries are hardly foreseeable and that frivolous litigation would be encouraged." [citation]

The court then proceeded to announce its holding:

> "The standard that we substitute for the one requiring contemporaneous injury or impact is the standard which has been adopted in the majority of jurisdictions where this question of *recovery by a bystander* for emotional distress has been examined. [Citations.] That standard has been described as the zone-of-physical-danger rule. Basically, under it a *bystander who is in a zone of physical danger* and who, because of the defendant's negligence, has reasonable fear for his own safety is given a right of action for physical injury or illness resulting from emotional distress. *The bystander,* as stated, must show physical injury or illness as a result of the

emotional distress caused by the defendant's negligence." (Emphasis added.) (*Rickey,* 98 Ill.2d at 555, 75 Ill.Dec. 211, 457 N.E.2d 1.)

Accordingly, the supreme court remanded the cause because the complaint did allege physical manifestations, and it was unclear whether the plaintiff was endangered by the alleged negligence and had a reasonable fear for his own safety.

C. Therapist–Patient Sexual Contact.

We have long been aware that plaintiffs in other states have successfully maintained malpractice actions against their psychologist, psychiatrist, or social worker, predicated primarily on the therapist's alleged sexual contact with his patient. The leading case is from the State of New York, wherein the plaintiff alleged that she "was induced to have sexual intercourse with the defendant as part of her prescribed therapy," and was as a result "so emotionally and mentally injured that she was required to seek hospitalization on two occasions during 1971." (*Roy v. Hartogs* (1976) 85 Misc.2d 891, 381 N.Y.S.2d 587, 588.) The court in *Roy* upheld the trial court's award of damages to the plaintiff, justifying its holding as follows: "By alleging his client's mental and emotional status was adversely affected by this deceptive and damaging treatment, plaintiff's counsel asserted a viable cause of action". *Roy,* 381 N.Y.S.2d at 588.

The court of appeals in our sister state of Michigan, relying on *Roy,* held that allegations analogous to those in *Roy* were sufficient to state a cause of action for psychiatrist malpractice. (*Cotton v. Kambly* (1980), 101 Mich.App. 537, 300 N.W.2d 627.)

The United States court of appeals has upheld an award for a plaintiff who alleged that the individual treating her psychiatric problems had committed malpractice by having sexual intercourse with her. (*Simmons v. United States* (9th Cir.1986), 805 F.2d 1363.) The plaintiff contended that her therapist, employed by the United States as a social worker in the Indian Health Service, was guilty of malpractice which had caused her to attempt suicide. A doctor who gave psychiatric counseling to Simmons subsequent to her having terminated consultation with the social worker "stated that her counselor's misconduct was the cause of her psychological problems and that her problems were due essentially to his inappropriate response to the normal 'transference phenomenon' in therapy." *Simmons,* 805 F.2d at 1364.

The court, in a unanimous opinion, proceeded to analyze the plaintiff's malpractice claim. It said that "[t]ransference is the term used by psychiatrists and psychologists to denote a patient's emotional reaction to a therapist". (*Simmons,* 805 F.2d at 1364.) The court went on to explain that transference is crucial to the therapeutic process and that "[t]he proper therapeutic response is countertransference, a reaction which avoids emotional involvement and assists the patient in overcoming problems." (*Simmons,* 805 F.2d at 1365.) The court described as follows the legal consequences of a counselor's failure to properly manage the transference phenomenon: "When the therapist mishandles transference and becomes sexually involved with a patient, medical authorities are nearly unanimous in considering such conduct to be malpractice. [Citations.]" (*Simmons*, 805 F.2d at 1365.) Moreover, it recognized that "[c]ourts have uniformly regarded mishandling of transference as malpractice or gross negligence".

In a malpractice action in the State of Washington, the plaintiff alleged that she had a sexual relationship with her psychiatrist which "was the direct and proximate cause of damages to the plaintiff, including humiliation, mental anguish, shock, outrage, depression, inconvenience, medical expenses, loss of wages, marital difficulties and general deterioration of emotional well being." (*Omer v. Edgren* (1984), 38 Wash.App. 376, 685 P.2d 635, 636.) The trial court granted summary judgment to the therapist, but the appellate court reversed, holding that there was sufficient evidence for a finder of fact to determine that the defendant had committed malpractice.

The court concluded by addressing the doctor's contention that his patient had not been damaged. It noted that the plaintiff "testified in her deposition she suffered no loss with respect to medical expenses, lost earnings, or marital difficulties," but that she "claimed general as well as special damages." (*Omer*, 685 P.2d at 638.) The court, although cognizant of the difficulty articulated in *Rickey* of proving damages of this nature, nevertheless held that this problem in itself was not enough to bar the plaintiff from recovery because "[i]njury flowing from the alleged relationship, though difficult to prove, may be as real as that type of injury which can be proven with mathematical certainty." *Omer*, 685 P.2d at 638.

D. The Application of Rickey

* * *

* * * [T]here is considerable controversy and confusion over whether the zone of danger test should be used in cases involving direct victims of negligence. It is clear, however, that *Rickey* does not become inapplicable solely because a case involves a malpractice claim.

* * *

We believe that the application of the *Rickey* test in cases involving direct victims of malpractice is inappropriate. Our conclusion is supported by the decisions of courts in other jurisdictions which have awarded damages to plaintiffs who have had sexual relations with their therapists, although these plaintiffs have not alleged that they were physically injured. As we have seen, the Washington court in *Omer* directly addressed this concern, concluding that the plaintiff nevertheless deserved compensation. Moreover, were we to hold to the contrary, it would be hopelessly difficult for individuals to plead an action for psychologist malpractice which results only in emotional distress, for it seems incongruous to the point of absurdity that in cases involving malpractice by psychologists a victim should be required to demonstrate that he or she was put in fear of *physical* injury. Nor can there be any rational justification for our courts to mandate that in order to qualify for damages in a psychologist or social worker malpractice case a patient exhibit physical manifestations of his or her emotional trauma suffered at the hand of therapists who are qualified to minister to their needs only in cases of mental or emotional malaise, especially since, as the *Omer* court points out, such an injury, "though difficult to prove, may be as real as that type of injury which can be proven with mathematical certainty." (*Omer*, 685 P.2d at 638.) We do not glean from *Rickey* any overarching unitary theory that would apply to the case at bar.

Therefore, in the absence of a decision by our supreme court which mandates a clearly different result, and supported by the law of our own appellate court and other jurisdictions, we hold that the zone of danger rule enunciated in *Rickey* has no application in this case, which involves a direct victim of negligence.

* * *

In conclusion, we hold that counts I, III, and IV of the complaint state valid causes of action.

HARTMAN, P.J., and BILANDIC, J., concur.

Questions and Comments

1. *Historical perspective.* Litigation charging malpractice for sexual misconduct is of fairly recent origin. Until the 1970's such conduct rarely led to litigation. In fact, a fringe element of the psychiatric profession had, at one point, openly advocated patient/therapist sexual relations as a legitimate form of therapy. Robertson, Psychiatric Malpractice: Liability of Mental Health Professionals, at 325–326 (1988). The case of *Roy v. Hartogs,* 85 Misc.2d 891, 381 N.Y.S.2d 587 (1976), signaled a decided turn of attitude on the part of courts and the psychiatric profession. In *Hartogs,* the defendant was charged with having "induced" the plaintiff "to have sexual intercourse as a part of her prescribed therapy." The plaintiff alleged, as a result of the improper treatment, she had become "so emotionally and mentally injured that she was required to seek hospitalization on two occasions," 381 N.Y.S.2d at 588. *Roy v. Hartogs,* which resulted in a judgment for the plaintiff, received considerable publicity particularly as a result of a subsequent book, *Betrayal,* co-authored by the plaintiff and Lucy Freeman (1976).

2. *Requirement of intentional infliction or physical impact.* Some jurisdictions continue to adhere to the rule that recovery for mental suffering will not be allowed unless: a) the distress was inflicted intentionally, or b) the mental suffering is accompanied by a physical manifestation of the injury. Prosser & Keeton on Torts, 5th edition, West Publishing (1984), § 12. Since the emotional harm resulting from the sexual misconduct of the therapist cannot be said to have been *intentionally* inflicted, the plaintiff has at least a theoretical barrier to overcome in those jurisdictions which require either a physical impact or that the harms have been inflicted intentionally. *Corgan v. Muehling* is illustrative of the approach of courts in jurisdictions which require a physical impact or injury. On what basis was the court able to hold that the plaintiff had a cause of action, in spite of the fact that there was neither a physical impact or injury?

3. *Per se rule of liability.* Courts appear to be moving toward a *per se* rule in therapist sexual misconduct cases. There is an increasing tendency to permit a recovery even in the absence of proof of actual damages. Would it make sense for courts to adopt a *per se* rule that sexual misconduct is actionable as negligence even in the absence of proof of actual damages? Some cases have suggested that difficulties of proof in cases of sexual misconduct should not bar a recovery.

In *Omer v. Edgren,* 38 Wash.App. 376, 685 P.2d 635 (1984), the therapist defended on the grounds that the patient had not been damaged by the affair. As noted by the court:

> "The most elementary conceptions of justice and public policy require that the wrongdoer shall bear the risk of the uncertainty [of actual damages] which his own wrong has created.

> " 'The constant tendency of the courts is to find some way in which damages can be awarded where a wrong has been done. Difficulty of ascertainment is no longer confused with right of recovery' for a proven invasion of the plaintiff's rights."

Id. at 638.

4. *Other theories for recovery.* In jurisdictions which do not recognize a cause of action for *negligent* infliction of emotional distress the patient who has been sexually involved with the therapist may be able to rely on other theories to recover damages. Washington state courts, for instance, have allowed an action for assault against the offending therapist, even though the patient technically consented to the act of intercourse. As reasoned by the court, the fiduciary relationship that a therapist has to his patient serves to vitiate any consent that may have been given.

Aside from negligence and assault, what other theories might be used to obtain a recovery against a therapist who becomes sexually involved with his patient during the course of treatment?

5. *Punitive damages.* Punitive damages may be awarded when there are "circumstances of aggravation or outrage, such as spite or 'malice,' or a fraudulent or evil motive on the part of the defendant, or such a conscious and deliberate disregard of the interests of others that his conduct may be called willful or wanton." W. Prosser, Handbook of the Law of Torts, § 2, pp. 9–10 (4th ed. 1971), Prosser & Keeton On Torts, 5th edition, West Publishing (1984), § 2. Surprisingly, cases of sexual misconduct have generally not awarded punitive damages. For instance, in *Roy v. Hartogs,* discussed in note 1, supra, the trial judge had allowed $100,000 in punitive damages on the grounds that a "patient must not be fair game for a lecherous doctor." However, the Court of Appeals, while sustaining general damages, eliminated punitive damages altogether on the basis that actions constituting malpractice were not "wanton or reckless". Punitive damages have, however, been sustained in a few sexual misconduct cases. See, e.g., *Greenberg v. McCabe,* 453 F.Supp. 765 (E.D.Pa.1978).

6. *Non-patient claims.* Does a patient have a cause of action when the therapist has sexual relations with the patient's spouse? A recovery has been allowed to a non-participating party where both spouses were patients of the offending therapists. *Mazza v. Huffaker,* 61 N.C.App. 170, 300 S.E.2d 833

(1983), review denied, 309 N.C. 192, 305 S.E.2d 734 (1983). In sustaining a judgment in favor of a patient who discovered the therapist and the plaintiff's wife (who was also a patient) together in bed, the court relied on the theory of *de facto* abandonment. In its conventional form a cause of action for abandonment lies for the "failure by a physician to continue to provide services to a patient when it is needed in a case for which the physician has assumed responsibility and from which he has not been properly relieved." *Brandt v. Grubin,* 131 N.J.Super. 182, 329 A.2d 82 (1974) (finding no abandonment of a psychiatric patient). Aside from abandonment, could it be argued that the therapist's relations with the patient's wife also constituted negligence in the treatment of the husband?

* * *

C. LIABILITY TO THIRD PARTIES

1. *The Dangerous Patient and the Duty of Care to Third Persons*

a. *Introduction*

As mentioned in a previous section of this chapter the traditional limit on professional liability was the contractual relationship, usually called privity of contract, between the professional and his client. Thus, the threshold question in a negligence suit was always whether the plaintiff had been the defendant's client. Unless a professional relationship had existed between the two parties, the court would usually dismiss the plaintiff's negligence suit. The privity doctrine is no longer the dispositive factor in professional negligence cases. An increasing number of jurisdictions have modified or repudiated this doctrine, concluding that while the privity limit on liability provides certainty in the law, it may not promote justice or deter negligent conduct. A move away from traditional limitations on a professional's liability to third parties (those with whom no contractual relationship exists) is traceable to a 1928 decision rendered by one of the most influential state courts of the time.

In the landmark case of *Palsgraf v. Long Island Railroad,* 248 N.Y. 339, 162 N.E. 99 (1928), the New York Court of Appeals established a test of foreseeability to determine whether the actor had a duty of care to the injured party.[a] Under this test, the court asked whether the

---

a. In *Palsgraf* a passenger was attempting to board one of the defendant's trains while carrying a bulky and apparently fragile package. The defendant railroad's employees while attempting to help the passenger board the train, jostled him, and the package fell to the ground. The unmarked package contained fireworks, which exploded upon impact. The force of the explosion knocked over a platform scale thirty feet away, which in turn fell upon and injured another passenger, the plaintiff in the case. At trial the jury found the defendant's employees negligent and entered an award for the plaintiff. New York's highest court, however, reversed that decision, concluding that although the trainmen might have been negligent toward the passenger boarding the train, those trainmen could not have foreseen that their negligent actions would injure the plaintiff, who had been standing thirty feet away. The relationship between the parties, Chief Justice Cardozo said, would determine whether the defendant's actions constituted negligence toward the plaintiff.

defendant actor should have reasonably foreseen that his actions would injure the plaintiff. If that question was answered affirmatively, the defendant would be found liable.

The court characterized this limitation on the extent of liability for negligence as follows:

[T]he risk reasonably to be perceived defines the duty to be obeyed, and risk imports relation; it is risk to another or to others within the range of apprehension.

248 N.Y. at 344, 162 N.E. at 100.

Foreseeability of injury to a third person, therefore, may constitute an alternative basis of professional malpractice liability, imposing liability on a defendant-therapist who had no contractual relationship with the injured party. This foreseeability criterion, though a convenient benchmark of liability, is decidedly imprecise of measurement and extends professional liability beyond the limits set by the privity doctrine.

While foreseeability became a basis for tort liability under *Palsgraf,* malpractice cases against physicians continued to be governed by notions of privity for most circumstances. However, extension of a physician's liability to third parties was seen in the early 20's in cases involving contagious diseases. In 1919, the Supreme Court of Minnesota found a valid cause of action against a physician treating a patient for scarlet fever for failing to advise her parents that the disease was infectious and for advising them that it was safe to visit her, and even to remove her to her home without risk of the disease being communicated. *Skillings v. Allen,* 143 Minn. 323, 173 N.W. 663 (1919). The court found that the physician owed a duty of care to those who were "naturally exposed to infection to a greater degree than anyone else". Id. at 664.

In 1928, the Ohio Supreme Court held that a physician has a duty to warn persons in dangerous proximity to a smallpox patient of the infectiousness of the disease. *Jones v. Stanko,* 118 Ohio St. 147, 160 N.E. 456 (1928). The court upheld an award for the wrongful death of a man who visited the doctor's patient after being assured that the patient was not contagious. The patient died of black smallpox, as did the decedent in the case. The following materials trace the development of the third-person liability doctrine in the context of mental health treatment.

b. Foundations for Tarasoff: Institutional Liability

MERCHANTS NATIONAL BANK & TRUST CO. OF FARGO v. UNITED STATES

United States District Court, District of North Dakota, 1967.
272 F.Supp. 409.

RONALD N. DAVIES, DISTRICT JUDGE.

[An action under the Federal Torts Claim Act by the administrator of the Estate of Eloise A. Newgard against the United States for negligence in the treatment of Newgard's husband, who killed her shortly after release by a veteran's administration hospital.]

Early in the morning of January 17, 1965, Dr. Mack V. Traynor, a Fargo physician, was called to the Newgard apartment in Fargo, North Dakota, by Newgard's wife, Eloise. She was frantic-voiced and said she needed help. The doctor, promptly responding to the call, found Newgard glassy-eyed and making senseless talk about horses, cattle "and God most of the time." Dr. Traynor felt Newgard was completely psychotic.

Dr. Albert C. Kohlmeyer, a well qualified psychiatrist, saw Newgard the same day in the Neuropsychiatric Institute section of the hospital. He found him very agitated, "carrying on" about religious ideas and testified that Newgard thought "he was Christ or some representative of Christ." Because of his delusional ideas, the psychiatrist thought Newgard was psychotic and although he saw Newgard only a couple of days, it was his belief that Newgard's illness had been coming on for a long time. Dr. Kohlmeyer felt Newgard was a schizophrenic, chronic, with acute exacerbation, paranoid type.

On January 19, 1965, the Cass County, North Dakota, Mental Health Board after a hearing, ordered Newgard committed to the State Hospital at Jamestown, North Dakota. Later because he was a veteran, an amended order was issued by the board, making the commitment a dual one so that Newgard could eventually be transferred to the Veterans Administration Hospital at Fort Meade, South Dakota. Effective March 23, 1965, Newgard was transferred to Meade where he was admitted to a ward and placed under the direct supervision of Dr. Leonard S. Linnell, a medical doctor and psychiatrist.

For a number of weeks Newgard was treated with tranquilizers and saw a clinical psychologist, Dr. Jesse H. Craft, weekly, for psychotherapy and examinations. During the course of Newgard's treatment and care he was interviewed by Dr. Linnell about once a week. The psychiatrist also sent Newgard to Dr. Truman M. Cheney, a vocational psychologist, for testing and reporting his job aptitudes. Newgard was given various jobs around the hospital, a procedure followed by Meade in the treatment of hospital patients and which is followed in hospitals of a similar nature.

Sometime before July 18, 1965, Dr. Truman M. Cheney, Counseling Psychologist at Meade, had made arrangements to put Newgard on leave at the ranch owned by Mr. and Mrs. Clarence A. Davis located some ten miles north of Belle Fourche, South Dakota. Dr. Cheney told Mr. Davis that Newgard had had "a mental disturbance, a nervous breakdown" and that Newgard wanted hard work to forget some of his troubles and for rehabilitation purposes. Mr. Davis had never before had a Meade patient working on his ranch.

On July 18, 1865, Newgard was released by Dr. Linnell on work leave to rancher Davis.

It develops that on July 24, 1965, Newgard left the ranch for the weekend. He was to have returned Monday, July 26th, but Newgard went to his parents' home at Mayville, North Dakota. His wife Eloise had no idea he was in Mayville and was there herself only for a brief visit. Newgard wanted his wife to return with him to Fargo but she declined. Newgard got possession of a car and ultimately drove to his mother-in-law's home in Detroit Lakes, Minnesota, where on July 31, 1965, he first attempted to run Eloise Newgard down with the car and failing that, got out of the vehicle, shot and killed her.

* * *

[The court reviewed evidence which showed that in arranging for Newgard's placement on the ranch, no one at Meade took any steps to inform Rancher Davis of Newgard's condition or the conditions governing his release. It was also shown that the Meade staff made no attempt to monitor Newgard from the time he was placed on the ranch up to the time he shot his wife.]

Dr. Linnell ignored and rejected every warning signal that Newgard was delusional at Meade and every warning signal that Eloise A. Newgard had every reason to be in mortal fear of her husband because of his prior conduct and the nature of some of the letters he wrote her while a patient at Meade.

The plaintiff alleges that the Government, acting through its duly authorized agents employed by the Veterans Administration, undertook the custody, care and treatment of Newgard, knowing him to be an insane and incompetent person with homicidal tendencies, and that the Government's inexcusable negligence was the proximate cause of Eloise A. Newgard's death on July 31, 1965, at the hands of her husband.

* * *

Considering the circumstances under which Newgard was placed on leave of absence at the Davis ranch, as disclosed by the credible evidence, the Government's agents and employees not only did not exercise due care; in the view of this Court they exercised no care at all.

This Court is of the opinion that in the case of Newgard the defendant's agents were tortiously negligent both in the matter of substandard professional conduct on the part of Dr. Linnell, and because of gross negligence on the part of Dr. Linnell and Dr. Cheney in the careless custodial care of Newgard. . . .

The Court concludes that plaintiff is entitled to recover the sum of Two Hundred Thousand Dollars ($200,000.00) from the defendant, as compensatory damages, arising out of and from the gross negligence of the defendant, acting by and through its agents and employees, which was the sole and proximate cause of the death of Eloise A. Newgard.

Questions and Comments

1. *Restatement of Torts.* While the court in *Merchants National Bank* did not rely on the Second Restatement of Torts, § 319 of the Restatement does provide a basis for the imposition of liability on institutions:

§ 319 One who takes charge of a third person whom he knows or should know to be likely to cause bodily harm to others if not controlled is under a duty to exercise reasonable care to control the third person to prevent him from doing such harm.

The commentaries to this section of the Restatement make clear that the institution may be liable to a third party who is injured by a patient if:

1. A patient is released when the facility knew or had reason to know of the patient's dangerous proclivities;

2. The institution fails to conduct an adequate predischarge examination of a patient with a history of violent behavior; or

3. The institution's failure to take adequate precautions allows a patient to escape.

2. *Liability for release of dangerous patients.* A number of cases have imposed liability on psychiatric facilities for the release of patients that the institution knew or should have known to be dangerous. See, *Estate of Mathes v. Ireland,* 419 N.E.2d 782 (Ind.App.1981); *Semler v. Psychiatric Institute of Washington, D.C.,* 538 F.2d 121 (4th Cir.1976). In *Semler* the psychiatric facility had custody of a convicted felon, who, without court authorization, was placed on outpatient status. The patient killed an individual, and in a subsequent wrongful death suit the institution was found liable to the victim's parents.

Liability may also attach where the psychiatric institution due to negligence permits a foreseeably dangerous patient to escape. For instance, in *Tamsen v. Weber,* 166 Ariz. 364, 802 P.2d 1063 (App. 1990), the court held that a cause of action was stated where the psychiatric facility had given the escaped patient, who subsequently injured a third, person unsupervised ground privileges.

3. *Voluntary patients.* Should it make a difference for purposes of assigning liability if the patient is voluntarily admitted, rather than involuntarily committed? Voluntary patients have the right to be released upon their request unless civilly committed. Some courts have adopted the position that a different standard will apply where the patient who causes the injury was in the institution on a voluntary status. See e.g., *Sellers v. United States,* 870 F.2d 1098, 1104 (6th Cir.1989), in which the court stated:

[T]here are additional reasons why Sellers cannot succeed on his claim of negligent discharge.... Firestine was admitted to the VAH voluntarily. A review of the case law will demonstrate that this fact is central to a determination of the VAH's duty regarding the length of Firestine's commitment. An analysis of this issue centers on the question of whether a "special relationship" exists between the patient and the hospital.

In *Hinkelman v. Borgess Medical Center,* 157 Mich.App. 314, 403 N.W.2d 547 (1987), the court specifically addressed the issue of when a special relationship should be found to exist. The court explained that the existence of a special relationship, such as that between a physician and patient, is premised on the notion of control over the patient. *Id.* at 550. In *Hinkelman,* the court found that there was no special relationship between the patient and the hospital when the patient had been admitted voluntarily, had not stayed more than a few days, and had left before he could be treated. *Id.* at 551. The court placed great weight on the fact that the duty imposed on mental hospitals is "based on the control vested by *involuntary* commitment." *Id.* at 552 (emphasis added). "In contrast, where a patient's hospitalization was voluntary, no duty has been imposed due to the facility's inability to compel patient confinement."

4. *Statutory immunity.* Some states have enacted laws that specifically grant immunity to institutions that improvidently release a patient or prisoner who subsequently injures a third party. For instance, California's civil commitment statute (the Lanterman–Petris–Short Act) grants immunity from all criminal and civil liability to any psychiatrist responsible for evaluating an involuntarily committed patient in an initial 72–hour treatment and evaluation period. If the treating psychiatrist, based on his or her personal observation, authorizes the release of the patient within the initial 72–hour period, the psychiatrist is immune from all liability even if the patient later causes harm to a third person or him or herself. Such immunity granted by statute reflects "the legislature's determination that the goal of ending indefinite confinement outweighs the early release potential for harm". *Ford v. Norton*, 89 Cal.App.4th 974, 107 Cal.Rptr.2d 776 (2001)

c. *The Tarasoff Doctrine*

TARASOFF v. REGENTS OF UNIVERSITY OF CALIFORNIA

Supreme Court of California, 1976.
17 Cal.3d 425, 131 Cal.Rptr. 14, 551 P.2d 334.

TOBRINER, JUSTICE.

On October 27, 1969, Prosenjit Poddar killed Tatiana Tarasoff. Plaintiffs, Tatiana's parents, allege that two months earlier Poddar confided his intention to kill Tatiana to Dr. Lawrence Moore, a psychologist employed by the Cowell Memorial Hospital at the University of California at Berkeley. They allege that on Moore's request, the campus police briefly detained Poddar, but released him when he appeared rational. They further claim that Dr. Harvey Powelson, Moore's superior, then directed that no further action be taken to detain Poddar. No one warned plaintiffs of Tatiana's peril.

Concluding that these facts set forth causes of action against neither therapists and policemen involved, nor against the Regents of the University of California as their employer, the superior court sustained defendants' demurrers to plaintiffs' second amended complaints without leave to amend.[3] This appeal ensued.

---

3. The therapist defendants include Dr. Moore, the psychologist who examined Poddar and decided that Poddar should be committed; Dr. Gold and Dr. Yandell, psychiatrists at Cowell Memorial Hospital who concurred in Moore's decision; and Dr. Powelson, chief of the department of psychiatry, who countermanded Moore's decision and directed that the staff take no action to confine Poddar.

Plaintiffs' complaints predicate liability on two grounds: defendants' failure to warn plaintiffs of the impending danger and their failure to bring about Poddar's confinement pursuant to the Lanterman–Petris–Short Act. Defendants, in turn, assert that they owed no duty of reasonable care to Tatiana.

We shall explain that defendant therapists cannot escape liability merely because Tatiana herself was not their patient. When a therapist determines, or pursuant to the standards of his profession should determine, that his patient presents a serious danger of violence to another, he incurs an obligation to use reasonable care to protect the intended victim against such danger. The discharge of this duty may require the therapist to take one or more of various steps, depending upon the nature of the case. Thus it may call for him to warn the intended victim or others likely to apprise the victim of the danger, to notify the police, or to take whatever other steps are reasonably necessary under the circumstances.

In the case at bar, plaintiffs admit that defendant therapists notified the police, but argue on appeal that the therapists failed to exercise reasonable care to protect Tatiana in that they did not confine Poddar and did not warn Tatiana or others likely to apprise her of the danger.

* * *

1. PLAINTIFFS' COMPLAINTS

Plaintiffs, Tatiana's mother and father, filed separate but virtually identical second amended complaints. The issue before us on this appeal is whether those complaints now state, or can be amended to state, causes of action against defendants. We therefore begin by setting forth the pertinent allegations of the complaints.

Plaintiffs' first cause of action, entitled "Failure to Detain a Dangerous Patient," alleges that on August 20, 1969, Poddar was a voluntary outpatient receiving therapy at Cowell Memorial Hospital. Poddar informed Moore, his therapist, that he was going to kill an unnamed girl, readily identifiable as Tatiana, when she returned home from spending the summer in Brazil. Moore, with the concurrence of Dr. Gold, who had initially examined Poddar, and Dr. Yandell, assistant to the director of the department of psychiatry, decided that Poddar should be committed for observation in a mental hospital. Moore orally notified Officers Atkinson and Teel of the campus police that he would request commitment. He then sent a letter to Police Chief William Beall requesting the assistance of the police department in securing Poddar's confinement.

Officers Atkinson, Brownrigg, and Halleran took Poddar into custody, but, satisfied that Poddar was rational, released him on his promise to stay away from Tatiana. Powelson, director of the department of psychiatry at Cowell Memorial Hospital, then asked the police to return Moore's letter, directed that all copies of the letter and notes that Moore had taken as therapist be destroyed, and "ordered no action to place Prosenjit Poddar in 72–hour treatment and evaluation facility."

Plaintiffs' second cause of action, entitled "Failure to Warn Of a Dangerous Patient," incorporates the allegations of the first cause of action, but adds the assertion that defendants negligently permitted Poddar to be released from police custody without "notifying the parents of Tatiana Tarasoff that their daughter was in grave danger from Posenjit Poddar." Poddar persuaded Tatiana's brother to share an apartment with him near Tatiana's residence; shortly after her return from Brazil, Poddar went to her residence and killed her.

2. PLAINTIFFS CAN STATE A CAUSE OF ACTION AGAINST DEFENDANT THERAPISTS FOR NEGLIGENT FAILURE TO PROTECT TATIANA

The second cause of action can be amended to allege that Tatiana's death proximately resulted from defendants' negligent failure to warn Tatiana or others likely to apprise her of her danger. Plaintiffs contend that as amended, such allegations of negligence and proximate causation, with resulting damages, establish a cause of action. Defendants, however, contend that in the circumstances of the present case they owed no duty of care to Tatiana or her parents and that, in the absence of such duty, they were free to act in careless disregard of Tatiana's life and safety.

In analyzing this issue, we bear in mind that legal duties are not discoverable facts of nature, but merely conclusory expressions that, in cases of a particular type, liability should be imposed for damage done.

* * *

* * *[Duty] is not sacrosanct in itself, but only an expression of the sum total of those considerations of policy which lead the law to say that the particular plaintiff is entitled to protection.

* * *

We depart from "this fundamental principle" only upon the "balancing of a number of considerations"; major ones "are the foreseeability of harm to the plaintiff, the degree of certainty that the plaintiff suffered injury, the closeness of the connection between the defendant's conduct and the injury suffered, the moral blame attached to the defendant's conduct, the policy of preventing future harm, the extent of the burden to the defendant and consequences to the community of imposing a duty to exercise care with resulting liability for breach, and the availability, cost and prevalence of insurance for the risk involved."

The most important of these considerations in establishing duty is foreseeability. As a general principle, a "defendant owes a duty of care to all persons who are foreseeably endangered by his conduct, with respect to all risks which make the conduct unreasonably dangerous." As we shall explain, however, when the avoidance of foreseeable harm requires a defendant to control the conduct of another person, or to warn of such conduct, the common law has traditionally imposed liability only if the defendant bears some special relationship to the dangerous person or to the potential victim. Since the relationship between a therapist and his patient satisfies this requirement, we need not here decide whether foreseeability alone is sufficient to create a duty to exercise reasonable care to protect a potential victim of another's conduct.

Although, as we have stated above, under the common law, as a general rule, one person owed no duty to control the conduct of another nor to warn those endangered by such conduct, the courts have carved out an exception to this rule in cases in which the defendant stands in some special relationship to either the person whose conduct needs to be controlled or in a relationship to the foreseeable victim of that conduct (see Rest.2d Torts, supra, §§ 315–320). Applying this exception to the present case, we note that a relationship of defendant therapists to either Tatiana or Poddar will suffice to establish a duty of care; as explained in section 315 of the Restatement Second of Torts, a duty of care may arise from either ''(a) a special relation between the actor and the third person which imposes a duty upon the actor to control the third person's conduct, or (b) a special relation between the actor and the other which gives to the other a right of protection.''

Although plaintiffs' pleadings assert no special relation between Tatiana and defendant therapists, they establish as between Poddar and defendant therapists the special relation that arises between a patient and his doctor or psychotherapist. Such a relationship may support affirmative duties for the benefit of third persons. Thus, for example, a hospital must exercise reasonable care to control the behavior of a patient which may endanger other persons. A doctor must also warn a patient if the patient's condition or medication renders certain conduct, such as driving a car, dangerous to others.

Although the California decisions that recognize this duty have involved cases in which the defendant stood in a special relationship *both* to the victim and to the person whose conduct created the danger, we do not think that the duty should logically be constricted to such situations. Decisions of other jurisdictions hold that the single relationship of a doctor to his patient is sufficient to support the duty to exercise reasonable care to protect others against dangers emanating from the patient's illness. The courts hold that a doctor is liable to persons infected by his patient if he negligently fails to diagnose a contagious disease or, having diagnosed the illness, fails to warn members of the patient's family.

Since it involved a dangerous mental patient, the decision in *Merchants Nat. Bank & Trust Co. of Fargo v. United States* comes closer to the issue. The Veterans Administration arranged for the patient to work on a local farm, but did not inform the farmer of the man's background. The farmer consequently permitted the patient to come and go freely during nonworking hours; the patient borrowed a car, drove to his wife's residence and killed her. Notwithstanding the lack of any ''special relationship'' between the Veterans Administration and the wife, the court found the Veterans Administration liable for the wrongful death of the wife.

* * *

Defendants contend, however, that imposition of a duty to exercise reasonable care to protect third persons is unworkable because therapists cannot accurately predict whether or not a patient will resort to violence. In support of this argument amicus representing the American Psychiatric Association and other professional societies cites numerous articles which indicate that therapists, in the present state of the art, are unable reliably to predict violent acts; their forecasts, amicus claims, tend consistently to overpredict violence, and indeed are more often wrong than right. Since predictions of violence are often erroneous, amicus concludes, the courts should not render rulings that predicate the liability of therapists upon the validity of such predictions.

The role of the psychiatrist, who is indeed a practitioner of medicine, and that of the psychologist who performs an allied function, are like that of the physician who must conform to the standards of the profession and who must often make diagnoses and predictions based upon such evaluations. Thus the judgment of the therapist in diagnosing emotional disorders and in predicting whether a patient presents a serious danger of violence is comparable to the judgment which doctors and professionals must regularly render under accepted rules of responsibility.

We recognize the difficulty that a therapist encounters in attempting to forecast whether a patient presents a serious danger of violence. Obviously we do not require that the therapist, in making that determination, render a perfect performance; the therapist need only exercise "that reasonable degree of skill, knowledge, and care ordinarily possessed and exercised by members of [that professional specialty] under similar circumstances."

Within the broad range of reasonable practice and treatment in which professional opinion and judgment may differ the therapist is free to exercise his or her own best judgment without liability; proof, aided by hindsight, that he or she judged wrongly is insufficient to establish negligence.

In the instant case, however, the pleadings do not raise any question as to failure of defendant therapists to predict that Poddar presented a serious danger of violence. On the contrary, the present complaints allege that defendant therapists did in fact predict that Poddar would kill, but were negligent in failing to warn.

Amicus contends, however, that even when a therapist does in fact predict that a patient poses a serious danger of violence to others, the therapist should be absolved of any responsibility for failing to act to protect the potential victim. In our view, however, once a therapist does in fact determine, or under applicable professional standards reasonably should have determined that a patient poses a serious danger of violence to others, he bears a duty to exercise reasonable care to protect the foreseeable victim of that danger. While the discharge of this duty of due care will necessarily vary with the facts of each case, in each instance the adequacy of the therapist's conduct must be measured against the traditional negligence standard of the rendition of reasonable care under the circumstances.

* * *

* * * In sum, the therapist owes a legal duty not only to his patient, but also to his patient's would-be victim and is subject in both respects to scrutiny by judge and jury.

The risk that unnecessary warnings may be given is a reasonable price to pay for the lives of possible victims that may be saved. We would hesitate to hold that the therapist who is aware that his patient expects to attempt to assassinate the President of the United States would not be obligated to warn the authorities because the therapist cannot predict with accuracy that his patient will commit the crime.

Defendants further argue that free and open communication is essential to psychotherapy that "Unless a patient is assured that information [revealed by him] can and will be held in utmost confidence, he will be reluctant to make the full disclosure upon which diagnosis and treatment depends." The giving of a warning, defendants contend, constitutes a breach of trust which entails the revelation of confidential communications.

We recognize the public interest in supporting effective treatment of mental illness and in protecting the rights of patients to privacy and the consequent public importance of safeguarding the confidential character of psychotherapeutic communication. Against this interest, however, we must weigh the public interest in safety from violent assault. The Legislature has undertaken the difficult task of balancing the countervailing concerns. In Evidence Code section 1014, it established a broad rule of privilege to protect confidential communications between patient and psychotherapist. In Evidence Code section 1024, the Legislature created a specific and limited exception to the psychotherapist-patient privilege: "There is no privilege if the psychotherapist has reasonable cause to believe that the patient is in such mental or emotional condition as to be dangerous to himself or to the person or property of another and that disclosure of the communication is necessary to prevent the threatened danger."

We realize that the open and confidential character of psychotherapeutic dialogue encourages patients to express threats of violence, few of which are ever executed. Certainly a therapist should not be encouraged routinely to reveal such threats; such disclosures could seriously disrupt the patient's relationship with his therapist and with the persons threatened. To the contrary, the therapist's obligations to his patient require that he not disclose a confidence unless such disclosure is necessary to avert danger to others, and even then that he do so discreetly, and in a fashion that would preserve the privacy of his patient to the fullest extent compatible with the prevention of the threatened danger.

The revelation of a communication under the above circumstances is not a breach of trust or a violation of professional ethics; as stated in the

Principles of Medical Ethics of the American Medical Association (1957), section 9: "A physician may not reveal the confidence entrusted to him in the course of medical attendance * * * *unless he is required to do so by law or unless it becomes necessary in order to protect the welfare of the individual or of the community.*" (Emphasis added.) We conclude that the public policy favoring protection of the confidential character of patient-psychotherapist communications must yield to the extent to which disclosure is essential to avert danger to others. The protective privilege ends where the public peril begins.

Our current crowded and computerized society compels the interdependence of its members. In this risk-infested society we can hardly tolerate the further exposure to danger that would result from a concealed knowledge of the therapist that his patient was lethal. If the exercise of reasonable care to protect the threatened victim requires the therapist to warn the endangered party or those who can reasonably be expected to notify him, we see no sufficient societal interest that would protect and justify concealment. The containment of such risks lies in the public interest. For the foregoing reasons, we find that plaintiffs' complaints can be amended to state a cause of action against defendants Moore, Powelson, Gold, and Yandell, and against the Regents as their employer, for breach of a duty to exercise reasonable care to protect Tatiana.

[The court went on to reject a claim by the defendants that release of information obtained from Poddar would violate a state statute governing the disclosure of confidential information in the possession of state officials. The court also held that the plaintiffs' claim was not barred by the state's governmental immunity statute in so far as it related to the psychiatrist's failure to warn third persons.]

WRIGHT, C.J., and SULLIVAN and RICHARDSON, JJ., concur.

MOSK, JUSTICE (concurring and dissenting).

I concur in the result in this instance only because the complaints allege that defendant therapists did in fact predict that Poddar would kill and were therefore negligent in failing to warn of that danger. Thus the issue here is very narrow: we are not concerned with whether the therapists, pursuant to the standards of their profession, "should have" predicted potential violence; they allegedly did so in actuality. Under these limited circumstances I agree that a cause of action can be stated.

* * *

I would restructure the rule designed by the majority to eliminate all reference to conformity to standards of the profession in predicting violence. If a psychiatrist does in fact predict violence, then a duty to warn arises. The majority's expansion of that rule will take us from the world of reality into the wonderland of clairvoyance.

CLARK, JUSTICE (dissenting).

Until today's majority opinion, both legal and medical authorities have agreed that confidentiality is essential to effectively treat the mentally ill, and that imposing a duty on doctors to disclose patient threats to potential victims would greatly impair treatment. Further, recognizing that effective treatment and society's safety are necessarily intertwined, the Legislature has already decided effective and confidential treatment is preferred over imposition of a duty to warn.

The issue whether effective treatment for the mentally ill should be sacrificed to a system of warnings is, in my opinion, properly one for the Legislature, and we are bound by its judgment. Moreover, even in the absence of clear legislative direction, we must reach the same conclusion because imposing the majority's new duty is certain to result in a net increase in violence.

The majority rejects the balance achieved by the Legislature's Lanterman–Petris–Short Act. (Welf. & Inst.Code, § 5000 et seq., hereafter the act.) In addition, the majority fails to recognize that, even absent the act, overwhelming policy considerations mandate against sacrificing fundamental patient interests without gaining a corresponding increase in public benefit.

* * *

COMMON LAW ANALYSIS

Entirely apart from the statutory provisions, the same result must be reached upon considering both general tort principles and the public policies favoring effective treatment, reduction of violence, and justified commitment.

Generally, a person owes no duty to control the conduct of another. Exceptions are recognized only in limited situations where (1) a special relationship exists between the defendant and injured party, or (2) a special relationship exists between defendant and the active wrongdoer, imposing a duty on defendant to control the wrongdoer's conduct. The majority does not contend the first exception is appropriate to this case.

* * *

Overwhelming policy considerations weigh against imposing a duty on psychotherapists to warn a potential victim against harm. While offering virtually no benefit to society, such a duty will frustrate psychiatric treatment, invade fundamental patient rights and increase violence.

The importance of psychiatric treatment and its need for confidentiality have been recognized by this court.

"It is clearly recognized that the very practice of psychiatry vitally depends upon the reputation in the community that the psychiatrist will not tell." (Slovenko, *Psychiatry and a Second Look at the Medical Privilege* (1960) 6 Wayne L.Rev. 175, 188.)

Assurance of confidentiality is important for three reasons.

DETERRENCE FROM TREATMENT

First, without substantial assurance of confidentiality, those requiring treatment will be deterred from seeking assistance. It remains an unfortunate fact in our society that people seeking psychiatric guidance tend to become stigmatized. Apprehension of such stigma—apparently increased by the propensity of people considering treatment to see themselves in the worst possible light—creates a well-recognized reluctance to seek aid. This reluctance is alleviated by the psychiatrist's assurance of confidentiality.

FULL DISCLOSURE

Second, the guarantee of confidentiality is essential in eliciting the full disclosure necessary for effective treatment. The psychiatric patient approaches treatment with conscious and unconscious inhibitions against revealing his innermost thoughts. "Every person, however well-motivated, has to overcome resistances to therapeutic exploration. These resistances seek support from every possible source and the possibility of disclosure would easily be employed in the service of resistance."

Until a patient can trust his psychiatrist not to violate their confidential relationship, "the unconscious psychological control mechanism of repression will prevent the recall of past experiences."

SUCCESSFUL TREATMENT

Third, even if the patient fully discloses his thoughts, assurance that the confidential relationship will not be breached is necessary to maintain his trust in his psychiatrist—the very means by which treatment is effected.

* * * All authorities appear to agree that if the trust relationship cannot be developed because of collusive communication between the psychiatrist and others, treatment will be frustrated.

Given the importance of confidentiality to the practice of psychiatry, it becomes clear the duty to warn imposed by the majority will cripple the use and effectiveness of psychiatry. Many people, potentially violent—yet susceptible to treatment—will be deterred from seeking it; those seeking it will be inhibited from making revelations necessary to effective treatment; and, forcing the psychiatrist to violate the patient's trust will destroy the interpersonal relationship by which treatment is effected.

VIOLENCE AND CIVIL COMMITMENT

By imposing a duty to warn the majority contributes to the danger to society of violence by the mentally ill and greatly increases the risk of civil commitment—the total deprivation of liberty—of those who should not be confined. The impairment of treatment and risk of improper commitment resulting from the new duty to warn will not be limited to a few patients but will extend to a large number of the mentally ill. Although under existing psychiatric procedures only a relatively few receiving treatment will ever present a risk of violence, the number making threats is huge, and it is the latter group—not just the former—whose treatment will be impaired and whose risk of commitment will be increased.

Both the legal and psychiatric communities recognize that the process of determining potential violence in a patient is far from exact, being fraught with complexity and uncertainty. In fact precision has not even been attained in predicting who of those having already committed violent acts will again become violent, a task recognized to be of much simpler proportions.

This predictive uncertainty means that the number of disclosures will necessarily be large. As noted above, psychiatric patients are encouraged to discuss all thoughts of violence, and they often express such thoughts. However, unlike this court, the psychiatrist does not enjoy the benefit of overwhelming hindsight in seeing which few, if any, of his patients will ultimately become violent. Now, confronted by the majority's new duty, the psychiatrist must instantaneously calculate potential violence from each patient on each visit. The difficulties researchers have encountered in accurately predicting violence will be heightened for the practicing psychiatrist dealing for brief periods in his office with heretofore nonviolent patients. And, given the decision not to warn or commit must always be made at the psychiatrist's civil peril, one can expect most doubts will be resolved in favor of the psychiatrist protecting himself.

Neither alternative open to the psychiatrist seeking to protect himself is in the public interest. The warning itself is an impairment of the psychiatrist's ability to treat, depriving many patients of adequate treatment. It is to be expected that after disclosing their threats, a significant number of patients, who would not become violent if treated according to existing practices, will engage in violent conduct as a result of unsuccessful treatment. In short, the majority's duty to warn will not only impair treatment of many who would never become violent but worse, will result in a net increase in violence.

The second alternative open to the psychiatrist is to commit his patient rather than to warn. Even in the absence of threat of civil liability, the doubts of psychiatrists as to the seriousness of patient threats have led psychiatrists to overcommit to mental institutions. This overcommitment has been authoritatively documented in both legal and psychiatric studies.

Given the incentive to commit created by the majority's duty, this already serious situation will be worsened, contrary to Chief Justice Wright's admonition "that liberty is no less precious because forfeited in a civil proceeding than when taken as a consequence of a criminal conviction."

CONCLUSION

* * *

The tragedy of Tatiana Tarasoff has led the majority to disregard the clear legislative mandate of the Lanterman–Petris–Short Act. Worse, the majority impedes medical treatment, resulting in increased violence from—and deprivation of liberty to—the mentally ill.

We should accept legislative and medical judgment, relying upon effective treatment rather than on indiscriminate warning.

The judgment should be affirmed.

McComb, J., concurs.

Questions and Comments

1. *Scope of holding.* Note that the *Tarasoff* opinion does not decide whether Dr. Moore or the University of California outpatient clinic was negligent. The case merely holds that the plaintiff has stated a cause of action that, if proved at trial, would entitle the plaintiff to relief. On remand to the lower court, the trier of fact would have had to decide whether Dr. Moore's failure to notify the victim or her family did in fact constitute a breach of his duty to the third-party victim. A jury might also have found that by notifying the police Dr. Moore had exercised due care and thus was not negligent. (The *Tarasoff* case was settled by the parties out of court prior to retrial.)

2. *Comment on* Tarasoff. The majority decision in *Tarasoff* strives to make the formulation of new doctrine appear as a natural and logical extension of existing doctrine. In reaching its conclusion that the therapist has a duty to third parties, the majority pursues three lines of analysis. First, it cites earlier medical cases from other jurisdictions that imposed a duty on physicians to notify third parties who are likely to come into contact with a patient suffering from a contagious disease. The majority opinion, however, fails to distinguish imposing a duty when there is a clearly diagnosable and invariably contagious disease from the facts of *Tarasoff*, where the duty was triggered not by a clearly diagnosible condition, but by a clinical prediction of probable future conduct on the part of the patient.

Second, the majority opinion looks to Section 315 of the Restatement of Torts Second, which provides:

> There is no duty so to control the conduct of a third person as to prevent him from causing physical harm to another unless
>
> > (a) a special relation exists between the actor and the third person which imposes a duty upon the actor to control the third person's conduct, or
> >
> > (b) a special relation exists between the actor and the other which gives to the other a right to protection.

Although the wording of Section 315 seems compatible with the majority's holding in *Tarasoff*, the commentaries to this section should not be overlooked. They emphasize that the duty attaches only in certain enumerated "special relations," when, for example, the defendant is an innkeeper, common carrier, or landowner. Presumably, therefore, the drafters of the Restatement Second did not intend to include the psychiatrist-patient relationship in Section 315.

The third part of the court's opinion was a policy analysis. Here the court addressed the competing interests of affording protection to persons who may be endangered by a patient against the interest of protecting the integrity of the therapist-patient relationship. The court concluded as a matter of policy that the need to protect persons from serious harm outweighed the possibly destructive effects on the patient-therapist relationship that might be caused from a rule requiring disclosure to third parties.

3. *Tarasoff and the ability to predict.* To what extent are the divergent conclusions of the majority as expressed by Justice Tobriner's opinion and the dissenting opinion of Justice Clark founded on different perceptions as to the ability of clinicians to predict dangerous or abnormal behavior? Do any policy considerations support the imposition of a duty to warn if, in fact, the ability of the therapist to predict dangerous behavior correctly is very limited? In this context, see the discussion in Chapter Six pp. 468–88 on the problem of predicting dangerous behavior.

Regarding clinicians' abilities to predict dangerousness, consider Givelber, et al., "Tarasoff, Myth and Reality: An Empirical Study of Private Law in Action," 1984 Wis.L.Rev. 443 (1984). The authors asked a group of psychiatrists, psychologists, and social workers to gauge their own ability to predict dangerous behavior. Over seventy-five percent of the clinicians responded that they could make firm predictions ranging from probable violence to certain violence. Only five percent suggested that violence is impossible to predict.

4. *An alternative approach.* In his concurring opinion Justice Mosk would limit the duty to warn to those cases in which the "psychiatrist does in fact predict violence." Presumably this means that liability cannot be imposed unless the psychiatrist has actually concluded that the patient is likely to be violent. One commentator has praised this approach:

> Making the legal duty dependent on the therapist's subjective determination of the patient's dangerousness would of course extremely limit the number of instances in which suit could successfully be brought. In the usual case, once the therapist has convinced himself that a patient is certainly dangerous, he will take some action. Only where he has reached this conclusion—and made it clear in records or consultation—and then failed to act would liability be imposed. Unlike the *Tarasoff* standard, then, this formulation would provide no incentive to the therapist to overpredict dangerousness early in the treatment process and to act to warn potential victims who might or might not be in serious danger. It seems to me quite clear that both the public interest and the patient's needs are better served by a legal standard which does not serve to discourage or undermine the effective treatment of potentially dangerous individuals. Moreover, the safety of the potential victims may well be more successfully promoted by such a standard, since premature action by the therapist is likely to terminate the therapeutic relationship, with the result that patients whose illnesses might have been successfully treated would remain a source of danger to those they originally threatened.

Alan Stone, "The Tarasoff Decisions: Suing Psychotherapists to Safeguard Society," 90 Harv.L.Rev. 358, 375–376 (1976).

How practical is Justice Mosk's standard? Are the arguments in favor of it convincing? What evidence would a plaintiff have to introduce to establish the existence of a duty? Would this approach in effect permit the psychiatrist to insulate himself from liability? In other words, would not any psychiatrist be able to avoid liability for failure to warn by merely refusing to formulate predictions?

5. *Influence of Tarasoff.* The *Tarasoff* duty to warn foreseeable victims has been widely adopted by courts in numerous other jurisdictions. However, the doctrine has been explicitly rejected by the courts of at least two states. See *Nasser v. Parker*, 249 Va. 172, 455 S.E.2d 502 (1995); *Thapar v. Zezulka*, 994 S.W.2d 635 (Tex. 1999).

6. *Hypothetical.* Assume the same basic fact situation as in Tarasoff except that the psychiatrist, Dr. Kareful, upon learning of the patient's intent to murder the supervisor at his place of work, immediately initiates emergency commitment proceedings [emergency admissions procedures are considered in Chapter 8]. However, he does not notify the intended victim (the supervisor). The patient is hospitalized but a week later is released at which point he goes to the place where he previously worked and murders the intended victim. Under these circumstances could Dr. Kareful be held liable under California law in an action by the victim's next of kin? What legal standard should be applied to determine liability in this situation?

7. *Statutory limitations on Tarasoff.* Several states have enacted statutes which restrict psychotherapists' liability to third parties. Colorado has restricted the duty to warn to situations where the patient has made specific threats. Colo.Rev.Stat. 13–21–117. Louisiana has created a specific duty to warn third parties who have been specifically threatened. La.Stat.Ann.–R.S. 2800.2. In some states the duty to warn is not expressly imposed by statute but may be implied by specific limitations in their requirements of confidentiality. (See, e.g., West's Fla.Stat. § 456.059).

California now exempts psychiatrists from liability under certain involuntary treatment situations. For example, psychiatrists cannot be held liable for "any action by a person released" from a facility offering 72–hour treatment and evaluation at or before the end of 72 hours. (West's Ann.Cal. Welf & Inst.Code § 5173). Other statutes address facilities specifically treating suicidal patients (§ 5267) and facilities offering 90–day involuntary treatments of "imminently dangerous persons" (§ 5306).

California modified the *Tarasoff* duty in 1985 by adopting Section 43.92 of the Civil Code, West's Ann.Cal.Civ.Code § 43.92. Section 43.92 immunizes therapists from liability except where the patient "has communicated to the psychotherapist a serious threat of physical violence against a reasonably identifiable victim or victims." Governor Deukemejian had vetoed a similar measure in 1984, claiming that the bill increased the danger to the public by limiting the *Tarasoff* duty. Does Section 43.92 embrace a standard even narrower than that advocated by Justice Mosk? Suppose that in *Tarasoff*, Poddar, during therapy sessions, made numerous statements exhibiting extreme hostility toward Tatiana but never explicitly threatened to kill her. If the defendants nevertheless concluded that Poddar evinced a threat to Tatiana, would the *Tarasoff* majority find a duty to warn? Would there be a duty under Justice Mosk's formulation? How explicit must the communication be before liability will be found under Section 43.92?

8. *Criminal liability after Tarasoff.* Assume a psychiatrist fails to take steps to prevent a patient from killing another after the patient specifies the victim, in contravention of the California law described above. Could the doctor be found liable not only in tort, but criminally as well, on an accomplice or omission theory? Under the Model Penal Code, an individual who purposely fails to perform a duty (here, the one created by *Tarasoff*) and is aware of a substantial risk that the failure to perform this duty will lead to death of another can be liable for manslaughter. See Model Penal Code § 2.06(3) & (4). Furthermore, a breach of a duty toward another that causes a reasonably foreseeable death can amount to negligent or reckless homicide. Model Penal Code §§ 2.01(3); 210.3 & 210.4. If, as under California law, the duty is triggered merely by hearing an individual threaten to harm a specified individual and a breach of duty is established merely by failing to warn the specified individual, could *anyone* (a teacher, lawyer or lay person) be liable, both civilly or criminally, for a subsequent death caused by the person who threatened the harm? What special expertise is needed under such a legal regime? See generally, Christopher Slobogin, "Tarasoff as a Duty to Treat: Insights from Criminal Law," 75 U. Cin. L. Rev. 645 (2006). Liability of non-professionals under *Tarasoff* is considered again in later materials.

9. *Use of patient disclosures in criminal prosecutions.* Essentially, the Tarasoff doctrine and its later permutations represent a decision by courts that the protection of individuals and the public outweighs the benefits of enforcing the traditional privileged status of patient-psychotherapist communications. While the privilege is thus overridden where the psychotherapist fails to either warn potential victims or take other actions to protect the public such as notifying the police, the use of such otherwise confidential communications may have limits where the confidential communications are used in a criminal prosecution based essentially on the disclosures to the psychotherapist. In *United States v. Glass*, 133 F.3d 1356 (10th Cir.1998), the defendant, while hospitalized, disclosed to the psychotherapist his intent to shoot President Clinton since "he wanted to get into the history books like Hinckley". Several days later, upon agreeing to participate in outpatient treatment and reside in his father's home, he was released. Ten days later, upon discovering that the patient had left the father's home, a hospital staff member notified the police, which referred the matter to the Secret Service. Secret Service agents then interviewed the psychotherapist who had been treating the defendant at the hospital and were told of the threat made by the defendant. The defendant was subsequently indicted for knowingly and willfully making a "threat to take the life of, to kidnap, or to inflict bodily harm against the President of the United States". In reversing the trial court's introduction of the otherwise privileged communications between the patient and the psychotherapist, the appellate court remanded the case to the trial court to "determine whether, in context of this case, the threat was serious when it was uttered and whether its disclosure was the only means of averting harm to the President when the disclosure was made." While the court, thus, did not hold that the privileged information was inadmissible, it did place limits on its submission by requiring the prosecution to show that the disclosure at the time it was made to the police "was the only means of averting harm to the President."

In the *United States v. Hayes*, 227 F.3d 578 (2000) the Sixth Circuit took a more restrictive view of the admissibility of patient disclosures as a basis for criminal prosecution. The opinion of the court in *Hayes* and a contra opinion by the Florida Supreme Court are treated at pp. 405–413.

d.   Later Applications of Tarasoff

BRADY v. HOPPER

United States District Court, District of Colorado, 1983.
570 F.Supp. 1333.

I.

ALLEGATIONS OF THE COMPLAINT

Plaintiffs James Scott Brady, Timothy John McCarthy, and Thomas K. Delahanty were all shot and seriously injured by John W. Hinckley, Jr. ("Hinckley") in his attempt to assassinate President Reagan on March 30, 1981, in Washington, D.C. The defendant, Dr. John J. Hopper, Jr., is the psychiatrist who had been treating Hinckley from late October, 1980, until March, 1981.

Plaintiffs' complaint alleges that Dr. Hopper was negligent in examining, diagnosing, and treating Hinckley in conformity with reasonable standards of psychiatric care. According to the complaint, Hinckley was brought to Dr. Hopper in late October, 1980, by Hinckley's parents because the parents were concerned about their son's behavior, including a purported suicide attempt by drug overdose. Plaintiffs allege despite Hinckley's attempted suicide on at least one if not several occasions, Dr. Hopper negligently formed the opinion that Hinckley was not seriously ill. Dr. Hopper proceeded to treat Hinckley and and prescribed valium and biofeedback therapy. Dr. Hopper also recommended to Hinckley's parents that Hinckley be on his own by the end of March, 1981. Plaintiffs assert that Dr. Hopper's treatment was not only ineffective, but that it actually aggravated Hinckley's mental condition, and made him more aggressive and dangerous, thereby creating an unreasonable risk of harm to others.

The complaint alleges that Dr. Hopper knew or should have known that Hinckley was a danger to himself or others, and that Dr. Hopper either possessed or had access to, information which would have indicated that Hinckley identified with the assassin in the movie "Taxi Driver"; that he was collecting books and articles on political assassination; and that Hinckley possessed guns and ammunition. According to the complaint, Hinckley's parents were aware of and concerned about their son's worsening condition, and contacted Dr. Hopper and recommended that their son be hospitalized. Despite the possibility Hinckley might have been amenable to that idea, Dr. Hopper recommended that Hinckley not be hospitalized, and that treatment continue on an outpatient basis.

The rest of Hinckley's strange story is well known. In March, 1981, Hinckley left Denver and traveled across the country to Washington,

D.C. On March 30, 1981, he attempted to assassinate President Reagan, and, in the process, shot and injured plaintiffs. Hinckley was subsequently tried for these crimes and found not guilty by reason of insanity. He is currently confined to St. Elizabeth's Hospital where he is receiving medical and psychiatric care.

The gravamen of plaintiffs' complaint is that if Dr. Hopper had properly performed his professional duties, he would have controlled Hinckley's behavior; therefore, Hinckley would not have made the presidential assassination attempt. Specifically, plaintiffs assert that the prescription of valium and biofeedback therapy, coupled with the advice that Hinckley's parents "cut him off", aggravated Hinckley's condition and actually contributed to his dangerous propensity. Further, plaintiffs assert that Dr. Hopper should have consulted with another psychiatrist regarding his form of treatment, and that Dr. Hopper should have taken steps to have Hinckley confined. Finally, plaintiffs allege that Dr. Hopper should have warned Hinckley's parents of their son's extremely dangerous condition, and that he should have warned law enforcement officials of Hinckley's potential for political assassination.

II.

Summary of the Arguments

The primary issue raised by defendant's motion is whether the relationship between therapist and patient gives rise to a legal duty such that Dr. Hopper can be held liable for the injuries caused to plaintiffs by Hinckley. The Restatement (Second) of Torts § 315 states as follows:

> There is no duty so to control the conduct of a third person as to prevent him from causing physical harm to another unless
>
> (a) a special relation exists between the actor and the third person which imposes a duty upon the actor to control the third person's conduct, or
>
> (b) a special relation exists between the actor and the other which gives to the other a right to protection.

The thrust of defendant's argument is that the relationship between Dr. Hopper and Hinckley, that of a therapist and outpatient, is not a "special relationship" which gives rise to a duty on the part of the therapist to control the actions of the patient. In other words, defendant asserts that the therapist-outpatient relationship lacks sufficient elements of control required to bring the therapist within the language of § 315.

* * *

Defendant next argues that the duty to control the violent acts of another does not arise absent specific threats directed to a reasonably identifiable victim. The leading case on a therapist's liability for the violent actions of a patient is *Tarasoff v. Regents of University of California,* 17 Cal.3d 425, 131 Cal.Rptr. 14, 551 P.2d 334 (1976).

* * *

In *Thompson v. County of Alameda,* 27 Cal.3d 741, 167 Cal.Rptr. 70, 614 P.2d 728 (1980), the California Supreme Court again faced the question of the extent of liability to a third party for the dangerous acts of another. In *Thompson,* a juvenile offender known to have dangerous propensities was confined in a county institution. This patient had made generalized threats regarding his intention to kill, but had made no specific threats regarding any identifiable person. The county institution released the patient on temporary leave, and, within a day, the patient killed a young boy in his neighborhood. The court refused to extend *Tarasoff* to a setting where there was no identifiable victim. Instead, it took a more limited approach to the duty to warn, and concluded that even in the case of a person with a history of violence, no duty existed when the person had made only nonspecific threats of harm directed at nonspecific victims. *Id.* at 614 P.2d 735. *See also, Doyle v. United States,* 530 F.Supp. 1278 (C.D.Cal.1982); *Furr v. Spring Grove State Hospital,* 53 Md.App. 474, 454 A.2d 414 (1983).

* * *

III.

DISCUSSION

In my opinion, the main issue raised by the pleadings and briefs is not simply whether the therapist-outpatient relationship is a "special relationship" which gives rise to a legal duty on the part of the therapist; rather the key issue is to what extent was Dr. Hopper obligated to protect these particular plaintiffs from this particular harm?[4] It is implicit in the majority of cases in this area that the therapist-patient relationship is one which under certain circumstances will give rise to a duty on the part of the therapist to protect third persons from harm. *Tarasoff v. Regents of University of California, supra.* However, the existence of a special relationship does not necessarily mean that the duties created by that relationship are owed to the world at large. It is fundamental that the duty owed be measured by the foreseeability of the risk and whether the danger created is sufficiently large to embrace the specific harm. *Palsgraf v. Long Island R. Co.,* 248 N.Y. 339, 162 N.E. 99 (1928).

It is this requirement of foreseeability which has led numerous courts to conclude that a therapist or others cannot be held liable for injuries inflicted upon third persons absent specific threats to a readily identifiable victim. *Thompson v. County of Alameda,* supra; *Doyle v. United States,* 530 F.Supp. 1278 (C.D.Cal.1982); *Furr v. Spring Grove Hospital, supra; Megeff v. Doland, supra; see also Hasenei v. United*

---

4. Definition of the scope of the defendant's duty is a question of law for the court. *Metropolitan Gas Repair Serv., Inc. v.* *Kulik, Colo.,* 621 P.2d 313 (1980). *See also, Sanchez v. United States,* 506 F.2d 702 (10th Cir.1974).

States, supra at 1012, n. 22; *cf. Jablonski v. United States,* 712 F.2d 391 (9th Cir.1983) (hospital liable for acts of outpatient where victim was foreseeable object of patient's violence). Unless a patient makes specific threats, the possibility that he may inflict injury on another is vague, speculative, and a matter of conjecture. However, once the patient verbalizes his intentions and directs his threats to identifiable victims, then the possibility of harm to third persons becomes foreseeable, and the therapist has a duty to protect those third persons from the threatened harm.

For purposes of this motion only, it must be assumed that Dr. Hopper's treatment and diagnosis of Hinckley fell below the applicable standard of care. Moreover, the doctor-patient relationship between Dr. Hopper and Hinckley was one which gave rise to certain duties on the part of Dr. Hopper. The real question, however, is whether that duty encompasses the injuries of which plaintiffs complain. In other words, was there a foreseeable risk that Hinckley would inflict the harm that he did?

Accepting as true the facts alleged in the complaint and viewing them in a light most favorable to plaintiffs, it is my conclusion that plaintiffs' injuries were not foreseeable; therefore, the plaintiffs fall outside of the scope of defendant's duty. Nowhere in the complaint are there allegations that Hinckley made any threats regarding President Reagan, or indeed that he ever threatened anyone. At most, the complaint states that if Dr. Hopper had interviewed Hinckley more carefully, he would have discovered that Hinckley was obsessed with Jodie Foster and the movie "Taxi Driver", that he collected books on Ronald Reagan and political assassination, and that he practiced with guns. According to plaintiffs, if Dr. Hopper had properly performed his professional duties, he would have learned that Hinckley suffered from delusions and severe mental illness, as opposed to being merely maladjusted. Even assuming all of these facts and many of plaintiffs' conclusions to be true, the allegations are still insufficient to create a legal duty on the part of Dr. Hopper to protect these plaintiffs from the specific harm.

The parties have for the most part cast their arguments in terms of whether the relationship between Dr. Hopper and *Hinckley* gave rise to a particular duty on the part of Dr. Hopper. However, the legal obstacle to the maintenance of this suit is that there is no relationship between Dr. Hopper and *plaintiffs* which creates any legal obligation from Dr. Hopper to these plaintiffs. As explained by Justice Cardozo, negligence is a matter of relation between the parties, and must be founded upon the foreseeability of harm to the person in fact injured. *Palsgraf v. Long Island R. Co.,* 162 N.E. at 101. *See also, Taitt v. United States of America,* Civil Action No. 82–M–1731 (D.Colo.1983) (Matsch, J.).

In essence, defendant argues that the instant case presents an even clearer basis than *Thompson* for a finding of no duty. It is argued that even according to the allegations in the complaint, Hinckley had no history of violence directed to persons other than himself; he had no history of arrests; no previous hospitalizations arising from any violent episodes; and in fact, he did not appear to be a danger to others. Thus, defendant asserts, this case involves, and plaintiffs have pled, none of the "warning signs" by which Hinckley's conduct or mental state would give rise to a duty on the part of Dr. Hopper.

The question of whether a legal duty should be imposed necessarily involves social policy considerations. See *Prosser, Law of Torts* § 43, 257 (4th Ed. 1971). In the present case, there are cogent policy reasons for limiting the scope of the therapist's liability. To impose upon those in the counseling professions an ill-defined "duty to control" would require therapists to be ultimately responsible for the actions of their patients. Such a rule would closely approximate a strict liability standard of care, and therapists would be potentially liable for all harm inflicted by persons presently or formerly under psychiatric treatment. Human behavior is simply too unpredictable, and the field of psychotherapy presently too inexact, to so greatly expand the scope of therapists' liability. In my opinion, the "specific threats to specific victims" rule states a workable, reasonable, and fair boundary upon the sphere of a therapist's liability to third persons for the acts of their patients.

The present case is one which makes application of the previously stated rules and policy considerations particularly difficult. Plaintiffs' injuries are severe and their damages extensive. Their plight as innocent bystanders to a bizarre and sensational assassination attempt is tragic and evokes great sympathy. Nevertheless, the question before the Court is whether Dr. Hopper can be subjected to liability as a matter of law for the injuries inflicted upon plaintiffs by Hinckley. I conclude that under the facts pleaded in the complaint, the question must be answered in the negative.

Accordingly, it is

ORDERED that defendant's motion to dismiss is granted.

Comments

The *Brady* court requirement of a readily identifiable victim tracks the standard established by the California Supreme Court. Three years after *Tarasoff*, the court in *Thompson v. County of Alameda*, 27 Cal.3d 741, 167 Cal.Rptr. 70, 614 P.2d 728 (1980), held that a general threat that the patient would kill some child in his neighborhood precluded the imposition of liability for failure to warn because of the lack of a clearly identifiable victim. The requirement of a readily identifiable victim has been followed by most jurisdictions at least with respect to a possible duty to warn a potential victim. However, as illustrated by *Hamman v. County of Maricopa*, which follows, the absence of a readily identifiable victim does not necessarily relieve the therapist of liability to third parties who are injured by a predictably dangerous patient.

HAMMAN v. COUNTY OF MARICOPA

Supreme Court of Arizona, 1989.
161 Ariz. 58, 775 P.2d 1122.

HOLOHAN, JUSTICE (Retired).

We granted the plaintiffs' petition for review to determine the nature and extent of a psychiatrist's duty to third parties injured by the psychiatrist's patient. The plaintiffs filed a tort action against the defendants for injuries inflicted on Robert Hamman by John Carter, a patient of the defendant, Dr. Manuel Suguitan. The superior court granted the defendants' motion for summary judgment, and the Court of Appeals affirmed the judgment of the lower court in part and reversed in part. 161 Ariz. 53, 775 P.2d 1117 (App.1987).

* * *

John Carter is the son of plaintiff Alice Hamman, and stepson of plaintiff Robert Hamman. On January 5, 1982, the Hammans brought Carter to the Maricopa County Hospital emergency psychiatric center because Carter had been exhibiting strange behavior. Dr. Suguitan, a psychiatrist who had previously admitted Carter to the hospital in August, 1981, interviewed Carter for about five minutes and noted the following symptoms: (1) anxious but cooperative, (2) fear and apprehension about a place to live, (3) loose associations and blocking,[5] (4) inappropriate affect,[6] (5) tries to conceal depression by grimacing, and (6) employs denial[7] and projection.[8] Dr. Suguitan did not review the medical records of Carter's 1981 hospitalization.

After interviewing Carter, Dr. Suguitan had a discussion with Mrs. Hamman, the specifics of which are disputed by the parties. Mrs. Hamman stated in her deposition that she told Dr. Suguitan the details of Carter's abnormal behavior since his hospitalization in August 1981. She described various incidents of strange behavior, a few instances of violent conduct, and a recent incident in which Carter was discovered to be carrying photos of animals with their heads cut off. Mrs. Hamman also testified in her deposition that she told Dr. Suguitan that she and Mr. Hamman feared that Carter would either be killed or kill somebody and that they never turned their backs on Carter. Mrs. Hamman further

---

5. " 'Loose associations' occur when a person starts talking on one subject and going on a tangent and continues on another subject unrelated to the first topic...."
" 'Blocking' is when a person starts to say something and in midsentence he stops and he is unable to proceed to complete that sentence or statement that he intended to make." (Deposition of Manuel G. Suguitan, M.D., March 7, 1984, at 21).

6. "Affect" is "a freudian term for the feeling of pleasantness or unpleasantness evoked by a stimulus; also the emotional

complex associated with a mental state...." Dorland's Illustrated Medical Dictionary 44 (25th ed. 1974).

7. " 'Denial' is manifestations when the patient does not want to talk about what is bothering them." (Deposition of Manuel G. Suguitan, M.D. at 34).

8. "Projection" is "a mental mechanism by which a repressed complex is disguised by being regarded as belonging to the external world or to someone else." Dorland's Illustrated Medical Dictionary at 1262.

testified that Dr. Suguitan told her that Carter was schizophrenic and psychotic, but that he was "harmless." Dr. Suguitan denied in his deposition that Mrs. Hamman told him about the specific details of the patient's conduct, and he denied that he ever told her that Carter was "harmless."

Dr. Suguitan did not refer to Carter's medical records from his previous hospitalization at Maricopa County. Those records would have shown among other things that Carter expressed jealousy of his stepfather and that the treatment plan had been to "seclude and restrain" the patient from agitation, assaultive, or dangerous behavior. Carter had also been examined and treated in the past at Desert Samaritan Hospital. Dr. Suguitan did not review the patient's medical records from that hospital. Those records would have revealed that Carter had a history of drug abuse and violent behavior, and he had made statements that he wanted to punish someone.

On January 5, 1982, as Mrs. Hamman discussed Carter's behavior and the Hammans' fear of him, she repeatedly begged Dr. Suguitan to admit Carter to the hospital. Dr. Suguitan refused to admit Carter. Instead, he wrote a prescription for Navane, gave it to Mrs. Hamman, and instructed her to give Carter 10 milligrams of Navane each morning and night. Dr. Suguitan admits he ordered this treatment knowing that Carter had not been taking the Navane which had been previously prescribed for him in August, 1981. Mrs. Hamman stated that Dr. Suguitan then told her to call him again in one week. Dr. Suguitan states that he advised Mrs. Hamman to take Carter to Tri–City Medical Center for follow-up care.

Upon being denied admission, Carter fled down the street brushing his teeth. The Hammans eventually persuaded him to get in their truck and go home. They gave him the medication as prescribed that night and again the following morning and night on January 6.

Although Mrs. Hamman tried to give Carter his medication on the morning of January 7, Carter refused to take it. At approximately 11:00 a.m. that day, Mr. Hamman while working on a home project with an electric drill, was attacked without warning by Carter. He repeatedly beat Hamman over the head with wooden dowels. Mr. Hamman suffered a heart attack during the beating as well as severe brain damage from the blows to his head. Carter later stated he believed Mr. Hamman was going to physically attack Mrs. Hamman with the drill, and that he (Carter) reacted as he did to protect his mother. Carter was later criminally charged for the beating, but found not guilty by reason of insanity.

The Hammans subsequently filed this civil action. The complaint contained three counts charging medical malpractice by Dr. Suguitan while employed by Maricopa County, general negligence, and a claim against Maricopa County for negligent training and supervision of psychiatric personnel.

The defendants filed a motion for summary judgment, essentially contending Dr. Suguitan owed no duty to the Hammans because Carter had never communicated to Suguitan any specific threat against the Hammans. The trial court granted the defendants' motion, and entered judgment against the plaintiffs dismissing all their claims for relief.

On appeal, the Court of Appeals divided the plaintiffs' claims into two separate theories of liability: (1) that Dr. Suguitan owed them a duty not to negligently diagnose and treat Carter's condition, and (2) that they reasonably relied upon Dr. Suguitan's advice that Carter was harmless. Regarding the first theory, the majority of the Court of Appeals followed the "specific threats to specific victims" approach. *See Brady v. Hopper,* 570 F.Supp. 1333 (D.Colo.1983), *aff'd,* 751 F.2d 329 (10th Cir.1984). Under this view, a psychiatrist incurs no duty to any third party unless his patient communicates to the psychiatrist a specific threat against a specific person.

* * *

We approve of the ruling of the Court of Appeals that the alleged negligent representation by Dr. Suguitan that Carter was "harmless" stated a valid claim. The issue taken for review is whether Dr. Suguitan and Maricopa County owed a duty to the Hammans, absent a specific threat by the patient against them, properly to diagnose, treat or control the patient.

ANALYSIS

A negligence action may be maintained only if there is a duty or obligation, recognized by law, which requires the defendant to conform to a particular standard of conduct in order to protect others from unreasonable risks of harm. The issue of duty is usually one for the court as a matter of law. The danger reasonably to be perceived defines the duty to be obeyed.

* * *

Tarasoff and its progeny

The landmark case regarding the duty of a psychiatrist to protect others against the conduct of a patient is *Tarasoff v. Regents of Univ. of Cal.,* The *Tarasoff* court held that the psychiatrist-patient relationship was sufficient under [Restatement of Torts, Second] § 315 to support the imposition of an affirmative duty on the defendant for the benefit of third persons. The court ruled that when a psychiatrist determines or, pursuant to the standards of the profession, should determine that a patient presents a serious danger of violence to another, the psychiatrist incurs an obligation to use reasonable care to protect the intended victim against such danger. According to the *Tarasoff* court, discharge of that duty may require the psychiatrist to warn the intended victim or others reasonably likely to notify the victim, to notify the police, *"or to take whatever other steps are reasonably necessary under the circumstances."* (Emphasis added).

Although the *Tarasoff* decision did not state that a psychiatrist's duty to third parties arises only when his patient communicates a specific threat concerning a specific individual, numerous subsequent decisions interpret *Tarasoff*. For example, in *Brady, supra,* John W. Hinckley, Jr. injured the plaintiffs in his attempt to assassinate President Reagan. The suit alleged, in part, that Hinckley's psychiatrist had negligently diagnosed and treated him. The *Brady* court held that the psychiatrist owed no duty to the plaintiffs because Hinckley had not made specific threats against a readily identifiable victim. 570 F.Supp. at 1339.

Similarly, in *Thompson v. County of Alameda,* 27 Cal.3d 741, 614 P.2d 728, 167 Cal.Rptr. 70 (1980), the parents of a young child sued the county for the wrongful death of their son. The juvenile offender, James F., killed the child within 24 hours of his release from confinement into the temporary custody of his mother. James stated he would kill a child in the community at random, and the county knew it. Nonetheless, county officials released him without warning local police, parents, or James' mother. Distinguishing *Thompson* from *Tarasoff,* the majority of the California Supreme Court refused to impose "blanket liability." The court stated that liability may be imposed only in those instances in which the released offender posed a predictable threat of harm to a named or readily identifiable victim. James made a generalized threat to a segment of the population. Consequently, the majority refused to impose upon the psychiatrist a duty to protect such a large group in the community.

Other courts, however, have not required a specific threat as a prerequisite for liability. Instead, they require that the psychiatrist reasonably foresee that the risk engendered by the patient's condition would endanger others. For example, in *Petersen v. State,* 100 Wash.2d 421, 671 P.2d 230 (1983), a patient was hospitalized for several weeks and treated with Navane after his psychiatrist diagnosed him as having schizophrenic and hallucinogenic symptoms. The hospital allowed the patient to go home for Mother's Day, but required him to return that night. Upon his return, hospital personnel observed the patient driving recklessly and spinning his car in circles on hospital grounds. The psychiatrist nevertheless released the patient the following morning and continued to prescribe Navane even though he knew of the patient's reluctance to take such medication. Five days later, the patient drove through a red light at 50–60 miles per hour, striking plaintiff's car and injuring her. The *Petersen* court emphasized the importance of foreseeability in defining the scope of a person's duty to exercise due care. In affirming plaintiff's claim based on negligent treatment of the patient, the court ruled that the psychiatrist had a duty to protect any person foreseeably endangered by the patient.

* * *

In the present case, the Court of Appeals would limit a psychiatrist's duty and liability to cases in which there are specific threats against third parties, *i.e.,* the *Brady* approach. The plaintiffs concede that Carter never made any specific threats against Mr. Hamman.

STANDARD

We believe the *Brady* approach is too narrow. *Tarasoff* envisioned a broader scope of a psychiatrist's duty when the court stated: "[O]nce a therapist does in fact determine, or under applicable professional standards reasonably should have determined, that a patient poses a serious danger of violence to others, he bears a duty to exercise reasonable care to protect the foreseeable victim of that danger." Additionally, we agree with those cases interpreting *Tarasoff* which state that a psychiatrist should not be relieved of this duty merely because his patient never verbalized any specific threat. We recognize the concern about adopting a rule which would be too inclusive, subjecting psychiatrists to an unreasonably wide range of potential liability. However, we believe that the approach used by the Ninth Circuit in *Jablonski*, 712 F.2d 391 (9th Cir.1983) allays such fears and represents a sound analytical foundation for the facts before us. In holding that Jablonski's girlfriend (Kimball) was a foreseeable victim, the court stated:

> Unlike the killer in *Tarasoff,* Jablonski made no specific threats concerning any specific individuals. Nevertheless, Jablonski's previous history indicated that he would likely direct his violence against Kimball. He had raped and committed other acts of violence against his wife. His psychological profile indicated that his violence was likely to be directed against women very close to him. This, in turn, was borne out by his attack on Pahls. Thus, Kimball was specifically identified or "targeted" to a much greater extent than were the neighborhood children in *Thompson.*

712 F.2d at 398.

Dr. Suguitan was aware that schizophrenic-psychotic patients such as Carter are prone to unexpected episodes of violence. He knew that Carter was living with and being cared for by the Hammans. Dr. Suguitan, in denying Carter's admission to the hospital, released the patient into the care of the Hammans. If indeed Dr. Suguitan negligently diagnosed Carter as harmless, the most likely affected victims would be the Hammans. Their constant physical proximity to Carter placed them in an obvious zone of danger. The Hammans were readily identifiable persons who might suffer harm if the psychiatrist was negligent in the diagnosis or treatment of the patient. The fact that Carter never verbalized any specific threats against the Hammans does not change the circumstances that, even without such threats, the most likely victims of the patient's violent reaction would be the Hammans. We reject the notion that the psychiatrist's duty to third persons is limited to those against whom a specific threat has been made. We hold that the standard originally suggested in *Tarasoff* is properly applicable to psychiatrists. When a psychiatrist determines, or under applicable professional standards reasonably should have determined, that a patient poses a serious danger of violence to others, the psychiatrist has a duty to exercise reasonable care to protect the *foreseeable victim* of that danger. The foreseeable victim is one who is said to be within the zone of danger, that is, subject to probable risk of the patient's violent conduct.

CONTROL

The defendants contend that Dr. Suguitan did not fail in any obligation to protect the Hammans. They point out that any duty by the psychiatrist to control his patient is limited by statute. Unless a patient meets the statutory criteria, the psychiatrist cannot involuntarily admit a patient into the hospital.

The defendants argue if the patient was not dangerous, there could be no involuntary commitment. Dr. Suguitan found Carter not dangerous, therefore, he could not be committed and the defendant could not control him.

The plaintiffs, however, submitted evidence from two psychiatrists in opposition to the defendants' motion for summary judgment. The plaintiffs' psychiatrists, in their affidavits, stated that a competent examination and proper diagnosis would have disclosed that Carter was a person suffering from a mental illness which made him dangerous to others. He was, therefore, admittable to the hospital on an involuntary basis under the statutes. They further stated that the defendant's examination of the patient fell below the acceptable standard for psychiatrists. The issue of ability to control is one which must be decided at trial.

The plaintiffs' experts in their affidavits also stated that even if Carter was not admittable as an emergency patient, there were numerous other acceptable medical procedures and precautions which Dr. Suguitan should have taken to lessen the danger posed to the Hammans. Some of these other steps include not only warning the Hammans of Carter's potential for danger, but also providing detailed instructions to follow should Carter's condition deteriorate. The doctor should have provided for outpatient follow-up care which would take into consideration the risk inherent in Carter's medical condition. Thus, the discharge of the defendant psychiatrist's duty is not limited to instances when the psychiatrist can control a patient by commitment to a hospital. The psychiatrist to fulfill his duty to those within the zone of risk must take the action reasonable under the circumstances.

CONCLUSION

The rule which we adopt does not impose upon psychiatrists a duty to protect the public from all harm caused by their patients. We do not, however, limit the duty of the psychiatrist to third parties only in those instances in which a specific threat is made against them. We hold that the duty extends to third persons whose circumstances place them within the reasonably foreseeable area of danger where the violent conduct of the patient is a threat.

That part of the Court of Appeals' opinion which is inconsistent with views expressed herein is vacated. The judgment of the trial court is reversed, and the case is remanded for further proceedings consistent with this opinion.

Questions and Comments

1. *Scope of holding.* Note that the *Hamman* decision does not establish liability, but simply holds that the trial court improperly granted the defendant's motion for summary judgment. The plaintiff's action charging malpractice had asserted that the defendant's psychiatrist was negligent in not anticipating that the patient was dangerous. Under the plaintiff's theory, once dangerousness is determined, the psychiatrist was under a duty to protect potential victims. Such duty could presumably be discharged *either* by warning the family with whom the patient was living (whose members were ultimately the victims of the assault) or by initiating commitment proceedings.

2. *Courts v. the legislature.* In response to the Arizona Supreme Court's holding in the *Hamman* case, the Arizona legislature enacted A.R.S. Sec. 36–517.02 which provided that "There shall be no cause of action" nor any "legal liability" against a mental health provider unless "the patient [had] communicated to the mental health provider an explicit threat of imminent serious harm to a *clearly identified or identifiable victim* [emphasis added]." Subsequently, however, the Arizona Supreme Court in *Little v. All Phoenix South Community Mental Health Center*, 186 Ariz. 97, 919 P.2d 1368 (App.1995) held that the legislature's enactment violated a provision of the state's constitution, which bars the abrogation of the "right of action to recover damages for injuries." Id. at 1375. According to the court, the *Hamman* decision created a common law cause of action, which once established, could not be legislatively restricted. Thus, the only way the reach of *Hamman* could be contained would be by an amendment of the state's constitution.

The expansion of third party liability, which eliminates the need for a clearly identifiable victim, obviously has serious financial implications for health providers, since it significantly enlarges their potential liability. Are courts or legislatures better equipped to determine the allocation of financial risk resulting from injuries caused by mental patients who subsequently cause harm to others? What information gathering resources are available to a court to make the necessary economic judgments implicit in a decision which significantly expands the liability of health providers? What resources are generally available to legislatures?

3. *Construction of the "identifiable victim" standard.* The identifiable victim requirement has been broadly construed in a number of jurisdictions. For instance, in *Jablonski v. United States,* 712 F.2d 391 (9th Cir.1983), the patient who had served a five year prison term for raping his wife subsequently killed his girlfriend after attempting to rape her mother. In holding the psychiatrist liable, the court ruled that although the patient had not made a *specific* threat "[h]is psychological profile indicated that his violence was likely to be directed against women very close to him." Id. at 398. Similarly, in *Davis v. Lhim,* 124 Mich.App. 291, 335 N.W.2d 481 (1983), where the patient shot and killed his mother during a scuffle, the psychiatrist was found liable. The mother was found to be a foreseeable victim on

the basis of evidence that two years before the homicide the patient had acted "strangely" and had threatened her for money. This together with the fact that the therapist had knowledge that the patient was a drug addict and would need money to obtain drugs was "sufficient to support a jury finding that defendant [the psychiatrist] should have known that [the patient] posed a serious threat to his mother." Id. at 490.

4. *Non-professionals and the duty to warn.* Should the duty to warn apply to a non-professional? In *Rozycki v. Peley,* 199 N.J.Super. 571, 489 A.2d 1272 (1984), a group of neighborhood children were sexually assaulted by Arthur Peley in 1981. Their parents sued on the children's behalf, naming Peley's wife, Catherine, as a defendant. Peley had been previously arrested in 1977 on a morals charge involving a minor. At that time he was placed in a diversion program in which he, accompanied by Catherine, received psychiatric treatment. The plaintiffs alleged that Catherine knew of her husband's pedophilia and thus had a duty to warn the children of the potential danger. The New Jersey court declined to extend its prior holding in *McIntosh v. Milano,* 168 N.J.Super. 466, 403 A.2d 500 (1979) (adopting the *Tarasoff* doctrine), to include non-professionals. The court reasoned that lay persons are not experts and could not be expected to assess another person's dangerousness. The court added that in this particular case the public interest in protecting the marital relationship also counseled against imposing such a duty on the defendant.

If liability is limited only to psychotherapists, which professions should fall into the category of "therapists"? A licensed marriage counselor? An unlicensed marriage counselor? A marriage counselor in a state which does not require a license?

5. *Contributory negligence.* Should liability attach to the psychotherapist when the victim was aware of the danger posed by the patient? At least one court has held that knowledge by the victim forecloses liability on the part of the psychotherapist to warn. In *Matter of Votteler's Estate,* 327 N.W.2d 759 (Iowa 1982), a psychiatric patient seriously injured plaintiff by intentionally running over her with a car. Although the patient had attempted to run her down twice before, plaintiff nevertheless argued that the defendant psychiatrist had a duty to warn her about his patient's violent nature. Plaintiff insisted that she would have appreciated the seriousness of the danger only if warned by a professional. Without deciding whether it would embrace the *Tarasoff* doctrine, the Iowa Supreme Court held that in any case the duty would not extend to situations where the foreseeable victim knew of the danger.

6. *Liability in absence of "foreseeable victim".* While most jurisdictions have adhered to the clearly identifiable victims standard, a minority of courts have held that a cause of action is stated even where the injured third party was not a particularized potential victim. For instance, *Currie v. United States,* 644 F.Supp. 1074 (M.D.N.C.1986), the patient, who was being seen on an outpatient basis for "post traumatic stress disorder" had originally sought psychiatric help from the VA staff for "rage attacks", which caused him to fear "losing control" due to anger at fellow employees. The treating psychiatrist was aware that the patient, at times, carried a gun and had "thoughts of hurting anyone who would take his property". The

disclosure by the patient that he had hostility towards IBM, his former employer that had recently discharged him led the psychiatrist to call representatives at IBM to notify them of the possibility of violent action by the patient. Additionally, both the police and FBI were informed by the VA staff of the patient's condition and potential for harm. At the same time, the VA treating staff concluded that while the patient was probably dangerous, he did not have a "mental disease", which was a necessary condition for involuntary commitment under state law.

While granting the defendant's motion to dismiss, the court nevertheless opined that a treating psychiatrist could be liable even in the absence of a clearly foreseeable victim. In these circumstances, the basis for an action would be the failure to initiate commitment proceedings or to take some other action such as notifying the police. In holding that a cause of action does not require a foreseeable victim the court tempered the scope of liability by imposing a "good faith" test under which liability would attach only where the psychiatrist's decision lacked "good faith, independence, and thoroughness". Thus, simple errors of judgment would not, as a matter of law, lead to liability. In applying this announced standard to the uncontested facts, the court concluded that the psychiatrist's decision to not initiate commitment proceedings showed good faith and therefore warranted summary judgment.

7. *Liability for unintentional injuries.* The Supreme Court of one state has extended the duty of care to non-foreseeable victims for the *unintentional* acts of a patient, which caused injury to third persons. In *Schuster v. Altenberg*, 144 Wis.2d 223, 424 N.W.2d 159 (1988), the plaintiffs were the relatives of a patient who were injured in an accident in a car that was driven by the patient who, at the time, was being treated for manic depressive illness on an outpatient basis by the defendant psychiatrist. The cause of action was based on the defendant's failure to properly diagnose and treat the patient or alternatively, on the failure to either warn the victims of the risk posed by the patient driving or in taking steps to have the patient either voluntarily or involuntarily committed. In holding that the pleadings stated a legally cognizable claim, the Wisconsin Supreme Court concluded that there is no "legitimate policy reason which could operate to support a distinction between a psychotherapist's duty to warn on the basis of whether the patient particularizes potential victims of his or her violent tendencies or makes generalized statements of dangerous intent". Discharge of the duty, according to the majority, did not necessarily require the notification of a potential victim, but depending on the circumstances of the case, could be discharged by taking other steps such as contacting the police or initiating commitment proceedings.

8. *Questions concerning Schuster v. Altenberg.* Do you agree with the conclusion of the court's majority that there is no significant policy reason to distinguish between the imposition of liability where a psychiatrist treats a patient on an outpatient basis and fails to initiate commitment from the liability that may attach to the decision to release an institutionalized patient who subsequently injures a third person? Are the predictive capacities of mental health professionals likely to be the same in these two circumstances?

Is it significant that a patient who has been involuntarily committed may have been found to be both mentally ill and dangerous to either self or others? Once such finding has been made in a judicial or administrative proceeding, should it have any continuing evidentiary weight so that a decision to release requires an affirmative determination by the caregiver that the patient is no longer mentally ill or dangerous or both? Should a therapist who is treating a patient on an outpatient basis be under the same duty to affirmatively establish the dangerousness or non-dangerousness of the patient? These issues are discussed further in Chapter Eight.

9. *Liability for acts of institutionalized patients.* As noted in note 2, p. 175, the tendency, even before *Tarasoff*, had been to hold institutions and key personnel liable to third persons where a psychiatric facility negligently released a dangerous patient. Liability in these cases, however, was not based on a failure to warn a particular foreseeable victim, but rather a general duty to protect the public from the release of dangerous patients or prisoners.

e. *Perspectives on Tarasoff*
Capacity to predict dangerousness

From the dissenting opinion of Justice Mosk in *Hedlund v. Superior Court of Orange County*, 34 Cal.3d 695, 194 Cal.Rptr. 805, 669 P.2d 41 (1983).

"The majority opinion unfortunately perpetuates the myth that psychiatrists and psychologists inherently possess powers of clairvoyance to predict violence. There is no evidence to support this remarkable belief, and, indeed, all the credible literature in the field discounts the existence of any such mystical attribute in those who practice the mind-care professions.

The serious flaw in the majority opinion is its acceptance of the claim that a failure to diagnose "dangerousness" may be a basis for liability. In its text, the opinion employs such terms as failure to "predict" behavior, and flatly declares that a negligent act occurs "when the therapist has, or *should have* diagnosed dangerousness" (italics added), as if that subjective characteristic would be revealed through a stethoscope or by an X-ray.

In *People v. Burnick* (1975) 14 Cal.3d 306, 121 Cal.Rptr. 488, 535 P.2d 352, we discussed at considerable length the virtually unanimous authorities in the field of psychiatry who concede their inability to predict violence. "In light of recent studies it is no longer heresy to question the reliability of psychiatric predictions. Psychiatrists themselves would be the first to admit that however desirable an infallible crystal ball might be, it is not among the tools of their profession. It must be conceded that psychiatrists still experience considerable difficulty in confidently and accurately *diagnosing* mental illness." Yet those difficulties are multiplied manyfold when psychiatrists venture from diagnosis to prognosis and undertake to predict the consequences of such illness: "A diagnosis of mental illness tells us nothing about whether the person so diagnosed is or is not dangerous. Some mental patients are dangerous, some are not. Perhaps the psychiatrist is an expert at deciding whether a person is mentally ill, but is he an expert at predicting which of the persons so diagnosed are dangerous? Sane people, too, are dangerous, and it may legitimately be inquired whether there is anything in the education, training or experience of psychiatrists which renders them particularly adept at predicting dangerous behavior. Predictions of dangerous behavior, no matter who makes them, are incredibly inaccurate, and there is a growing consensus that psychiatrists are not uniquely qualified to predict dangerous behavior and are, in fact, less accurate in their predictions than other professionals.''

''During the past several years further empirical studies have transformed the earlier trend of opinion into an impressive unanimity: 'The evidence, as well as the consensus of opinion by responsible scientific authorities, is now unequivocal.' (Diamond, 'The Psychiatric Prediction of Dangerousness' (1975) 123 U.Pa.L.Rev. 439, 451.) In the words of spokesmen for the psychiatric profession itself, 'Unfortunately, this is the state of the art. Neither psychiatrists nor anyone else have reliably demonstrated an ability to predict future violence or ''dangerousness.'' Neither has any special psychiatric ''expertise'' in this area been established.' And the same studies which proved the inaccuracy of psychiatric predictions have demonstrated beyond dispute the no less disturbing manner in which such prophecies consistently err: they predict acts of violence which will not in fact take place ('false positives'), thus branding as 'dangerous' many persons who are in reality totally harmless.''

Because of the inherent undependability of such predictions, we adopted in *Burnick* the beyond-a-reasonable-doubt standard for commitment to mental facilities.

Unfortunately a year later in *Tarasoff v. Regents of University of California* a thin majority of this court employed a loose and ill-conceived dictum that encourages a dilution of *Burnick*. Although the case involved *actual* knowledge of planned violence, the four-to-three majority spoke expansively in terms of what the doctor "knew or should have known." My separate opinion pointed out that there are no professional standards for forecasting violence and concluded that any rule should "eliminate all reference to conformity to standards of the profession in predicting violence. If a psychiatrist does in fact predict violence, then a duty to warn arises. The majority's expansion of that rule will take us from the world of reality into the wonderland of clairvoyance."

* * *

Id. at 48–49.

RICHARD BONNIE, PROFESSIONAL LIABILITY AND QUALITY OF HEALTH CARE

16 Law, Medicine, and Health Care, 229, 234 (1988).

"[H]ospitals and individual practitioners might respond to the perceived threat of litigation by taking steps to reduce the risk of liability. But the impact on clinical practice may not necessarily be favorable. Indeed, it is possible that the threat of liability, however remote, actually has had an adverse effect in recent years on the costs of medical services and perhaps on the quality of care as well."

The argument runs something like this: Because many practitioners actually exaggerate the relatively low risk of liability, they will be led to take "defensive" measures that either make no real contribution to the patient's care or are not cost-effective from a purely clinical standpoint. These so-called "defensive" practices increase the cost of care and, to the extent that the entire cost cannot be passed on to consumers, they have a regressive effect on the quality of care by diverting professional energies from their best clinical use.

In economic terms, it is said that the practitioner, by overreacting to the threat of malpractice liability, increases the preventive costs without a corresponding reduction in injury costs.

Examples of purely defensive practices, with little clinical utility, are often said to include unnecessary diagnostic tests.

* * *

I am not inclined to believe that mental health practitioners are led to engage in what they believe to be clinically useless practices solely to reduce the risk of liability.... [For example] good record keeping in mental health has considerable clinical utility, and any additional documentation that is provided "purely" for legal purposes exacts no significant incremental cost.

* * *

Another feature of the defensive medicine argument should be taken more seriously, however. Exaggerated fear of malpractice liability may generate disincentives for adopting practices that, while clinically preferable entail a higher risk of bad outcomes than would less preferable modes of treatment. Hypothetically, practitioners may avoid procedures thought to be associated with high legal risks even though they may be in the patients' best interests. Even worse, defensive practices induced by the threat of liability may actually reduce the quality of care available to patients.

These defensive practices have been observed, though not definitively proven, in studies of professional responses to the doctrine announced in *Tarasoff v. Board of Regents of the University of California.* Because treatment of the potentially violent patient in the "community is perceived to be a high-risk endeavor, one response to the prospect of *Tarasoff* liability for failing to take adequate precautions has been a lowered thresh old for hospitalizing these patients and a tendency to prolong the period of hospitalization. There is also some evidence that senior clinicians in hierarchical practice settings avoid treating potentially violent patients, leaving the care of such patients in the hands of junior, less adequately trained colleagues.

Similarly, one empirical investigation of clinical practice in the wake of the *Tarasoff* decision found that almost one-fifth of the responding clinicians reported having decided to avoid asking their patients questions that could yield information bearing on the likelihood of violent behavior. Even more reported that they had changed their record-keeping practices in an effort to reduce the risk of liability-some by keeping more detailed records, echoing the response to the Duke survey, but others by refraining from keeping detailed records. Obviously the failure to inquire about, or to record, clinically relevant material could seriously compromise the quality of care in this clinical context."

SCHOPP & WEXLER, "SHOOTING YOURSELF IN THE FOOT WITH DUE CARE:" PSYCHOTHERAPISTS AND CRYSTALLIZED STANDARDS OF TORT LIABILITY IN PSYCHIATRIC JURISPRUDENCE

17 J. Psychiatry & Law 163 (1989).

Under certain conditions, relatively fixed rules of liability regarding identified types of professional practice can crystallize in the law of negligence. * * * Courts may treat violations of these statutes as negligence per se as presumptive evidence of negligence, or merely as relevant evidence regarding the appropriate standard of care. When rules of reasonable care crystallize into relatively fixed standards of negligence per se or presumptive negligence, actors may be able to select with more confidence behavior that will constitute due care.

* * *

While the crystallized duties described above elicit relatively little dissent, the *Tarasoff* court's duty to protect has been much more controversial. In *Tarasoff*, the court found the therapists liable for failing to warn their patient's victim that the patient presented a threat to her safety. The court did not merely find that this particular failure to warn was negligent under the circumstances. Rather, the court articulated a crystallized duty to protect potential victims when the therapist determines or should have determined that the patient presents a danger to others. . . .

* * *

Brown, an outpatient at a community mental health center, attends weekly therapy due to periodic episodes of anxiety and depression and his life-long inability to maintain a job or a relationship. Recently he has spoken of another patron at a neighborhood bar who has insulted and pushed him. This week Brown states, "but now I got some brass knuckles, so if he pushes me again, I'll cave his face in." When the therapist suggests that she might have to warn the potential victim, Brown pounds his fist on the table, yelling, "if you ever tell anyone I come here, I'll never come back." The therapist believes from past experience with Brown that she can best serve his interests and those of the public by maintaining therapeutic contact, calming him down, and talking him into leaving the weapon at home, but she also believes that she can best avoid liability under *Tarasoff* by warning the potential victim.

[In Brown] a clinician encounters circumstances in which the interests of the patient and the community diverge from the clinician's, and this divergence is a product of a crystallized legal standard that defines the clinician's potential liability, at least as he or she understands it, in a manner that conflicts with the patient's interests or those of the community. The clinicians in these cases *believe* that they can best protect themselves from liability under these standards by practicing in a manner other than that which would promote the interests of their patients or of society.

2. *Third Party Recovery Under Alternate Theories: Negligent Infliction of Emotional Distress*

As noted in the preface to this section, liability to third persons in the event of physician or therapist malpractice has traditionally been confined to a very limited number of circumstances. For instance, *Tarasoff* and its progeny were careful to limit such liability to treatment situations involving patients who were foreseeably dangerous to identified individuals. Recently, an expansion of the doctrine of third party liability emerged in litigation brought before a California state trial court. That case, *Ramona v. Ramona,* No. Civ. 61898 (Sup.Ct. Napa County 1994), which involved repressed memory therapy, led to a $475,000 judgment against the therapist (a licensed marriage and family counselor), a consulting psychiatrist, and the facility where the treatment took place.

In August, 1989, Holly Ramona disclosed to her mother, Stephanie, that she had an eating disorder and that she felt she needed professional help. Mrs. Ramona put Holly in touch with Dr. Barry Grundlin, the Ramona family psychiatrist. Dr. Grundlin diagnosed Holly as suffering from bulimia.

Through a referral, Mrs. Ramona obtained the name of Marche Isabella, a licensed Marriage Family and Child Counselor (MFCC), whose practice concentrated on the treatment of eating disorders. Holly, then a student at the University of California at Irvine, began individual psychotherapy sessions with Isabella in September, 1989 which lasted through the fall semester. According to the therapist, Holly, on her own, began to vaguely recall having been sexually abused by her father, Gary, when she was between 5 and 8 years old. Subsequent sessions dealt with these "nascent memories". At some point, these recollections were communicated to Holly's mother, Stephanie. Having reached the tentative conclusion that Holly's condition was attributable to having been sexually abused as a child, Ms. Isabella arranged to have Holly seen by a psychiatrist, Dr. Richard Rose, for the purpose of administering sodium amytal, which she believed would lead to the recovery of Holly's repressed memories. During the sodium amytal treatment, Holly purportedly recalled episodes of sexual abuse by her father during childhood.

Subsequently, Isabella arranged for a meeting of the family, including Holly, her father Gary Ramona, and his wife Stephanie. At the March 21, 1990 meeting, Gary was for the first time told of the diagnosis of childhood sexual abuse and of Holly's recollections that he had abused her. At the same time, those present at the meeting were informed that the diagnosis of sexual abuse had been verified during sodium amytal session. They were also informed that sodium amytal acts like a truth serum, and that someone under the influence of sodium amytal cannot lie unless trained to do so.

After hearing these revelations at the family meeting, Stephanie Ramona file for divorce from Gary. Information pertaining to the charges of sexual abuse also reached Gary's employer, who initially placed Gary on leave of absence and sometime thereafter terminated his employment.

Gary subsequently filed suit in state court against Ms. Isabella, Dr. Rose, and Western Medical Center, where the sodium amytal therapy was administered.the suit sought damages for negligent infliction of emotional distress. Plaintiff's cause of action for negligent infliction of emotional distress was based on an established California Supreme Court precedent, *Molien v. Kaiser Foundation Hospitals*, 27 Cal.3D 916, 167 Cal.Rptr. 831, 616 P.2d 813 (1980). In *Molien*, a physician misdiagnosed a married female patient as having a sexually transmitted disease. She was then advised by the physician to inform her husband in order that he could receive testing and, if necessary, treatment. It later turned out that the diagnosis was wrong and that the patient did not have a sexually transmitted disease. The husband subsequently brought suit under a third party liability theory of negligence. In finding for the husband, the California Supreme Court noted:

> In the case at bar the risk of harm to plaintiff was reasonably foreseeable to defendants. It is easily predictable that as erroneous diagnosis of syphilis and its probable source would produce marital discord and resultant emotional distress to a married patient's spouse, Dr. Kilbridge's advice to Mrs. Molien to have her husband examined for the disease confirms that plaintiff was a foreseeable victim of the negligent diagnosis. Because the disease is normally transmitted only by sexual relations, it is rational to anticipate that both husband and wife would experience anxiety, suspicion, and

hostility when confronted with what they had every reason to believe was reliable medical evidence of a particularly noxious infidelity.

We thus agree with plaintiff that the alleged tortious conduct of defendant was directed to him as well as to his wife. Because the risk of harm to him was reasonably foreseeable we hold, in negligence parlance, that under these circumstances defendants owed plaintiff a duty to exercise due care in diagnosing the physical condition of his wife.

Id. at 835.

The basic principle underlying *Molien* was reaffirmed by the California Supreme Court in *Burgess v. Superior Court,* 2 Cal.4th 1064, 9 Cal.Rptr.2d 615, 831 P.2d 1197 (1992). In *Burgess,* the plaintiff was a pregnant woman who went into labor, and because of the physician's malpractice, delivered a child born with brain damage. She subsequently filed suit in her own behalf against the physician on a theory of negligent infliction of emotional distress. In affirming a judgment in favor of the plaintiff, the court reviewed the dimensions of the doctrine of negligent infliction of emotional distress:

> The law of negligent infliction of emotional distress in California is typically analyzed ... by reference to two "theories" of recovery: the "bystander" theory and the "direct victim" theory. In cases involving family relationships and medical treatment, confusion has reigned as to whether and under which "theory" plaintiffs may seek damages for negligently inflicted emotional distress.
>
> Because the use of the "direct victim" designation has tended to obscure rather than illuminate the relevant inquiry in cases such as the one at hand, we briefly turn our attention to the present state of the law in this area before proceeding to apply this law to the facts that confront us.
>
> We have repeatedly recognized that "[t]he negligent causing of emotional distress is not an independent tort, but the tort of negligence. The traditional elements of duty, breach of duty, causation, and damages apply. Whether a defendant owes a duty of care is a question of law. Its existence depends upon the foreseeability of the risk and a weighing of policy considerations for and against imposition of liability."
>
> The distinction between the "bystander" and "direct victim" cases is found in the source of the duty owed by the defendant to the plaintiff. The "bystander" cases.... culminating in *Thing v. La Chusa,* 48 Cal.3d 644, 257 Cal.Rptr. 865, 771 P.2d 814 (1989), address "the question of duty in circumstances in which a plaintiff seeks to recover damages as a percipient witness to the injury of another." These cases "all arise in the context of physical injury or emotional distress caused by the negligent conduct of a defendant with whom the plaintiff *had no* preexisting relationship, and to

whom the defendant *had not* previously assumed a duty of care *beyond that* owed to the public in general." (emphasis added).

In other words, bystander liability is premised upon a defendant's violation of a duty not to negligently cause emotional distress to people who observe conduct which causes harm to another.

Because in such cases the class of potential plaintiffs could be limitless, resulting in the imposition of liability out of all proportion to the culpability of the defendant, this court has circumscribed the class of bystanders to whom a defendant owes a duty to avoid negligently inflicting emotional distress. These limits are set forth in *Thing* as follows: "In the absence of physical injury or impact to the plaintiff himself, damages for emotional distress should be recoverable only if the plaintiff: (1) is closely related to the injury victim, (2) is present at the scene of the injury-producing event at the time it occurs and is then aware that it is causing injury to the victim and, (3) as a result suffers emotional distress beyond that which would be anticipated in a disinterested witness."

In contrast, the label "direct victim" arose to distinguish cases in which damages for serious emotional distress are sought as a result of a breach of duty owed the plaintiff that is "assumed by the defendant or imposed on the defendant as a matter of law, or that arises out of a relationship between the two." In these cases, the limits set forth in *Thing, supra,* have no direct application. Rather, well-settled principles of negligence are invoked to determine whether all elements of a cause of action, including a duty of care, are present in a given case.

Much of the confusion in applying rules for bystander and direct victim recovery to the facts of specific cases can be traced to this court's decision in *Molien,* which first used the "direct victim" label. In that case, we answered in the affirmative the question of whether, in the context of a negligence action, damages may be recovered for serious emotional distress unaccompanied by physical injury.

In so holding, we found that a hospital and a doctor owed a duty directly to the husband of a patient, who had been diagnosed incorrectly by the doctor as having syphilis and had been told to so advise her husband in order that he could receive testing and, if necessary, treatment. We reasoned that the risk of harm to the husband was reasonably foreseeable and that the "alleged tortious conduct of the defendant was directed to him as well as to his wife." Under such circumstances we deemed the husband to be a "direct victim" and found the criteria for bystander recovery not to be controlling.

The broad language of the *Molien* decision coupled with its perceived failure to establish criteria for characterizing a plaintiff as a "direct victim" rather than a "bystander," has subjected *Molien* to criticism from various sources, including this court. (E.g., *Thing, supra*). The great weight of this criticism has centered upon the perception that

Molien introduced a new method for determining the existence of a duty, limited only by the concept of foreseeability. To the extent that *Molien* stands for this proposition, it should not be relied upon and its discussion of duty is limited to its facts. As recognized in *Thing*, "[It] is clear that foreseeability of the injury alone is not a useful 'guideline' or a meaningful restriction on the scope of [an action for damages for negligently inflicted emotional distress.]"

Nevertheless, other principles derived from *Molien,* are sound: (1) damages for negligently inflicted emotional distress may be recovered in the absence of physical injury or impact, and (2) a cause of action to recover damages for negligently inflicted emotional distress will lie, notwithstanding the criteria imposed upon recovery by bystanders, in cases where a duty arising from a preexisting relationship is negligently breached. In f act, it is this later principle which defines the phrase "direct victim." That label signifies nothing more.

Id. at 617–19.

In *Ramona*, the plaintiff introduced compelling evidence that the therapist had committed malpractice by erroneously representing to the patient, Holly; her mother, Stephanie; and the father plaintiff, Gary, that sodium amytal was, in effect, a truth serum, and that recollections made under the influence of sodium amytal therapy were completely reliable. The plaintiff also introduced evidence that repressed memory therapy coupled with the use of sodium amytal to enhance recall was not an appropriate therapy for the treatment of bulimia.

The existence of malpractice alone, however, would not allow the plaintiff to recover, since an action for malpractice is ordinarily only maintainable by the patient. As a third party, the plaintiff had to predicate his action on another ground, and in the case at hand, the selected basis was negligent infliction of emotional distress. Under *Molien* and *Burgess,* supra, such third party actions could be maintained as long as the plaintiff was a "direct victim." Throughout the proceeding, the defendants took the position that *Burgess* had limited the reach of *Molien*, with the result that the plaintiff in *Ramona* did not have the status of a direct victim.

In denying a motion for non-suit at the close of the plaintiff's case, the *Ramona* trial court addressed the policy questions involved as follows:

The third issue that was raised, the one which no counsel really spent a lot of time on now because it's been argued before me twice and before other judges twice before that, is frankly the most interesting and compelling and difficult one in this case. And it's the most interesting one because it is the issue that brings in to conflict with one another several really important policies in the law. And this is the question of whether a father may maintain a lawsuit against the therapists or other health care providers of his daughter alleging that he was damaged by their negligent treatment of her.

Through counsel he diligently tried to argue again and again that he was a patient and I have found that no duty arose. I found that he was not a patient for purposes of the assessment of whether a duty existed. And that's a legal determination that the Court makes, whether a duty existed. I have found that a duty did not exist to him by reason of the circumstances of the case under Supreme Court law that has been existent for some time and which I have found still exists.

What's going on in a lawsuit of this sort, as I say, is the conflict of policies. And on the one hand, the defendants argue if you allow nonpatients to sue health care providers, it will have a terrible, chilling effect upon the ability of any health care provider to do what his or her patient needs. . . .

How, they ask, is a health care provider to know what to do when presented with a patient who recalls or thinks he or she is recalling the sorts of things that are presented by this lawsuit. . . . That's an argument that has significant social implications attendant to it.

Of equal significance, however, and with equal social implications, is the question of what is somebody who, for the sake of this point we will presume to be factually innocent of having engaged in misconduct with respect to his daughter, to do if confronted with the unfounded and incorrect accusation of having molested her which results in his loss of everything?

It's as unpalatable to some to have health care providers put in the impossible situation of dealing with a patient presenting real problems but knowing that the health care providers might be subjected to liability as it is to others to have a falsely accused parent lose everything and have no recourse in court.

Those are the kinds of policy issues that the courts are called upon to resolve, because in the area of tort law, and this is a tort action, there's very little statutory law. There's very little law created by the legislature that creates norms. Probably because the situations giving rise to tort actions are so fluid and so changing and so we have generalized concepts of law that are handed down through cases and through traditions, through precedents, according to which we regulate ourselves as a society.

And the purposes of tort law are twofold; to provide redress for people who are injured in some way or another; and to mediate, to control, to direct the conduct of other people. And these are the kinds of difficult conflicts that the court [sic] are called upon to resolve.

Ramona v. Ramona, No. Civ. 61898 (Sup.Ct. Napa County 1994).

Ultimately, the trial court held that the plaintiff had met the legal standards of *Molien* and *Burgess*, and permitted the case to go to the jury, which found for the plaintiff and awarded him $475,000. No appeal was taken from this judgment.

Questions and Comments

1. *"Direct victim"*. As the excerpts from *Molien* and *Burgess* indicate, a mere "bystander" cannot generally recover for negligent infliction of emotional distress. However, according to *Burgess,* one who is a "direct victim" of the negligent act can recover so long as there is a "duty arising from a pre-existing relationship [which] is negligently breached". *Burgess v. Superior Court*, 2 Cal.4th 1064, 1074, 9 Cal.Rptr.2d 615, 831 P.2d 1197 (1992) . It is not clear from Burgess whether the pre-existing relationship must be between the victim and the defendant rather than simply between any two parties, such as a therapist and the patient. However, the trial court in *Ramona* apparently took the view that the pre-existing relationship need not be between the plaintiff and the therapist, but could be satisfied by a relationship between the therapist and the patient, Holly. Is this an appropriate reading of the rule announced by *Burgess*?

2. *Must falsity be proven?* In order to prevail in a *Ramona*-type case, must the plaintiff prove that the recalled memory of abuse is false? Note in this connection that in *Ramona* the jury specifically found that the defendants had implanted or reinforced "false memories that plaintiff had molested her as a child". What is the doctrinal connection of the falsity of the recall to the negligent infliction of emotional distress? Is the reason falsity must be proved simply that it is a common sense predicate to recovery?

3. *Scope of disclosure needed to maintain action.* What would have been the result in *Ramona* had the facts been different, and the only communication that the father had as to the false recall was from the daughter? In other words, had there been no communication between the father and the therapist, would recovery have been possible? Would the answer be the same had the daughter also made a disclosure to a friend who then informed the father's employer?

4. *Definition of who is a patient.* The plaintiff originally pleaded the case on the theory that he could maintain the action as a patient of the therapists, since he had participated in a meeting of the family members (father, mother, and daughter) with the therapist. However, the trial court dismissed this theory of recovery, finding that the meeting which the father attended did not make him a patient of the therapist.

5. *Plaintiff's election of theory.* The plaintiff could theoretically have elected to sue on a defamation theory. Why didn't he? Under California Civil Code § 47 there is a conditional privilege granted to therapists. Thus, the only individual whom the father might successfully have been able to sue on a defamation theory would have been the daughter and other nonprofessionals who may have communicated the allegations concerning the alleged abuse.

6. *Legitimacy of recovered-memory therapy.* As recounted in Section B.1, there exists a significant difference of opinion among professionals as to the effectiveness and appropriateness of recovered memory therapy. Various authorities have criticized recovered-memory therapy on the basis that it is unreliable and, further, is of no therapeutic value. *See* Ofshee and Singer, 'Recovered–Memory Therapy and Robust Repression–Influence and Pseudomemories,' 42 International Journal of Clinical & Experimental hypnosis 391–410 (1994); Spiegel and Scheflin 'Dissociated or Fabricated—Psychiatric

Aspects of Repressed Memory in Criminal and Civil Cases,' 42 International Journal of Clinical & Experimental Hypnosis, 411–432 (1994); Yapko, 'Suggestibility and Repressed Memories of Abuse—A Survey of Psychotherapists' Beliefs, 36 American Journal of Clinical Hypnosis 163–171 (1994).

7. *Malpractice Litigation.* As detailed at note 3, p. 155. R.M. Therapy has generated numerous successful lawsuits by former patients against their therapists.

D. LIABILITY OF PARTICULAR DEFENDANTS

1. *Liability of Non–Clinician Therapists*

NALLY v. GRACE COMMUNITY CHURCH OF THE VALLEY

Supreme Court of California, 1988.
47 Cal.3d 278, 253 Cal.Rptr. 97, 763 P.2d 948.

Lucas, Chief Justice.

I. Introduction

On April 1, 1979, 24–year–old Kenneth Nally (hereafter Nally) committed suicide by shooting himself in the head with a shotgun. His parents (hereafter plaintiffs) filed a wrongful death action against Grace Community Church of the Valley (hereafter Church), a Protestant Christian congregation located in Sun Valley, California, and four Church pastors: MacArthur, Thomson, Cory and Rea (hereafter collectively referred to as defendants), alleging "clergyman malpractice," i.e., negligence and outrageous conduct in failing to prevent the suicide. (See Code Civ.Proc., § 377.) Nally, a member of the Church since 1974, had participated in defendants' pastoral counseling programs prior to his death.

II. Facts

A. Background

In 1973, while attending University of California at Los Angeles (hereafter UCLA), Nally became depressed after breaking up with his girlfriend. He often talked about the absurdity of life, the problems he had with women and his family, and he occasionally mentioned suicide to his friends. Though Nally had been raised in a Roman Catholic household, he converted to Protestantism while he was a student at UCLA, and in 1974 he began attending the Church, the largest Protestant church in Los Angeles County. Nally's conversion became a source of controversy between him and his family. During this time, Nally developed a close friendship with defendant Pastor Cory, who was responsible for overseeing the ministry to the collegians attending the Church. On occasion, Nally discussed his problems with Cory, but the two never established a formal counseling relationship. Between 1974 and 1979, Nally was active in defendants' various Church programs and ministries.

Defendants offered pastoral counseling to church members in matters of faith, doctrine and the application of Christian principles. During 1979, defendant Church had approximately 30 counselors on its staff, serving a congregation of more than 10,000 persons. Defendants taught that the Bible is the fundamental Word of God containing truths that must govern Christians in their relationship with God and the world at large, and in their own personal lives. Defendant Church had no professional or clinical counseling ministry, and its pastoral counseling was essentially religious in nature. Such counseling was often received through instruction, study, prayer and guidance, and through mentoring relationships called "discipleships."

* * *

In essence, defendants held themselves out as *pastoral* counselors able to deal with a variety of problems—not as professional, medical or psychiatric counselors.

In 1975, Nally was seeing a secular psychologist to discuss problems he was having with his girlfriend. After graduating from UCLA in 1976, he spent one semester at Biola College in La Mirada and was enrolled in the Talbot Theological Seminary's extension on defendants' church grounds. During this time, Nally became involved in a relationship with a girlfriend who was a fellow Bible student. In January 1978, he established a "discipling relationship" with Pastor Rea with whom he often discussed girlfriend and family problems. They met five times in early 1978, but when Nally lost interest in "discipling," the meetings were discontinued.

Following the breakup with his girlfriend in December 1978, Nally became increasingly despondent. Pastor Cory encouraged him to seek the counsel of either Pastor Thomson or Rea. The friendship with Cory and the five discipling sessions with Rea in early 1978, constituted the full extent of the "counseling" Nally received from defendants before the spring of 1979.

In February 1979, Nally told his mother he could not "cope." She arranged for him to see Dr. Milestone, a general practitioner, who prescribed Elavil, a strong anti-depressant drug, to relieve his depression.

* * *

B. The Events Preceding Nally's Suicide

On March 11, 1979, Nally took an overdose of the antidepressant prescribed by Dr. Milestone. Plaintiffs found him the following day and rushed him to a hospital. At the hospital, Dr. Evelyn, Nally's attending physician, advised plaintiffs that because their son "was actually suicidal," she could not authorize his release from the hospital until he had seen a psychiatrist. The record indicates that plaintiffs, concerned about their friends' reactions to their son's suicide attempt, asked Dr. Evelyn to inform other persons that Nally had been hospitalized only for the aspiration pneumonia he suffered after the drug overdose rendered him unconscious.

On the afternoon of March 12, Pastors MacArthur and Rea visited Nally at the hospital. Nally, who was still drowsy from the drug overdose, separately told both pastors that he was sorry he did not succeed in committing suicide. Apparently, MacArthur and Rea assumed the entire hospital staff was aware of Nally's unstable mental condition, and they did not discuss Nally's death-wish comment with anyone else.

Four days later, Dr. Hall, a staff psychiatrist at the hospital, examined Nally and recommended he commit himself to a psychiatric hospital. When both Nally and his father expressed reluctance at the thought of formal commitment, Hall agreed to release Nally for outpatient treatment, but warned Nally's father that it would not be unusual for a suicidal patient to repeat his suicide attempt. Nally was released from the hospital by Drs. Hall and Evelyn the next day.

On his release from the hospital on March 17, 1979, Nally arranged to stay with Pastor MacArthur, because he did not want to return home. MacArthur encouraged Nally to keep his appointments with Dr. Hall, and arranged for him to see Dr. John Parker, a physician and Church deacon, for a physical examination.

* * *

Eleven days before his suicide, Nally met with Pastor Thomson for spiritual counseling. According to the record, Nally asked Thomson whether Christians who commit suicide would nonetheless be "saved." Thomson referred Nally to his training as a seminary student and acknowledged "a person who is once saved is always saved," but told Nally that "it would be wrong to be thinking in such terms." Following their discussion, Thomson made an appointment for Nally to see Dr. Bullock for a physical examination but did not refer Nally to a psychiatrist.

* * *

The day after his visit with Bullock, Nally encountered Pastor Thomson in the Church parking lot. Nally told Thomson that he was thinking of seeing a psychologist. Thomson recommended Nally contact Dr. Mohline, Director of the Rosemead Graduate School of Professional Psychology. The following day, Nally spent approximately 90 minutes with Mohline, who in turn referred him to the Fullerton Psychological Clinic. Nally and his father went to the clinic the next day, and Nally discussed possible therapy with Mr. Raup, a registered psychologist's assistant. Raup testified he believed that Nally was "shopping for a therapist or counselor or psychologist" and that he was not going to return to the clinic. At the end of the week, Nally met with a former girlfriend. She turned down an apparent marriage proposal by telling Nally, "I can't marry you when you are like this. You have got to pull yourself together. You have got to put God first in your life." The next day, Nally left plaintiffs' home following a family disagreement. Two days later, he was found in a friend's apartment, dead of a self-inflicted gunshot wound.

III. PROCEDURAL BACKGROUND

A. ALLEGATIONS OF THE COMPLAINT

* * * In the first two counts of the complaint, alleging wrongful death based on "clergyman malpractice" and negligence, plaintiffs asserted that defendant Church was negligent in the training, selection and hiring of its spiritual counselors. Plaintiffs also claimed that following Nally's suicide attempt by drug overdose, defendants failed to make themselves available to Nally for counseling and "actively and affirmatively dissuaded and discouraged [Nally] from seeking further professional psychological and/or psychiatric care."

* * *

In ruling [affirmatively] on the nonsuit motion, the trial court noted that Nally voluntarily sought defendants' counsel and that the court had no compelling reason to interfere in defendants' pastoral activities. * * *

The Court of Appeal * * * reversed, holding that although the "clergyman malpractice" count failed to state a cause of action separate from the "negligence" count, both could be construed as stating a cause of action for the "negligent failure to prevent suicide" by "nontherapist counselors." In this context, the Court of Appeal held that nontherapist counselors—*both religious and secular*—have a duty to refer suicidal persons to psychiatrists or psychotherapists qualified to prevent suicides. Moreover, the court held, imposition of a negligence standard of care on pastoral counselors does not impinge on the free exercise of religion guaranteed by the First Amendment, because the state's compelling interest in the preservation of life justifies the narrowly tailored burden on religious expression imposed by such tort liability.

* * *

Our review of the record reveals the trial court correctly granted a nonsuit as to plaintiffs' causes of action. Neither the evidence adduced at trial nor well-established principles of tort law support the Court of Appeal's reversal of nonsuit in this case. As we explain below, we need not address the constitutional issues posed by defendants.

* * *

1. Legal Requirements for Imposing a Duty of Care

a) Creation of a Duty

"A tort, whether intentional or negligent, involves a violation of a *legal duty,* imposed by statute, contract or otherwise, owed by the defendant to the person injured. Without such a duty, any injury is 'damnum absque injuria'—injury without wrong. [Citations.]" Thus, in order to prove facts sufficient to support a finding of negligence, a plaintiff must show that defendant had a duty to use due care, that he breached that duty, and that the breach was the proximate or legal cause of the resulting injury.

* * *

b) Special Relationship

Although we have not previously addressed the issue presently before us, we have imposed a duty to prevent a foreseeable suicide only when a special relationship existed between the suicidal individual and the defendant or its agents. For example, two cases imposed such a duty in wrongful death actions after plaintiffs proved that the deceased committed suicide in a hospital or other in-patient facility that had accepted the responsibility to care for and attend to the needs of the suicidal patient. * * * In *Meier,* a cause of action for negligence was held to exist against both the treating psychiatrist and the hospital, and in *Vistica,* liability was imposed on the hospital alone, the only named defendant in the case.

The Court of Appeal here would extend the previously carefully limited precedent, relying initially for the creation of a duty of care (on defendants and other nontherapist counselors) in the foregoing *Meier* and *Vistica* cases. Indeed, the Court of Appeal specifically stated that ''Logic and policy both dictate the duty announced in those cases applies to non-therapist counselors as well.'' We disagree. As defendants and amici curiae point out, *Meier* and *Vistica* are readily distinguishable from the facts of the present case and, as we explain, severely circumscribe the duty they create.

Both *Meier* and *Vistica* address the issue of a special relationship, giving rise to a duty to take precautions to prevent suicide, in the limited context of hospital-patient relationships where the suicidal person died while under the care and custody of hospital physicians who were aware of the patient's unstable mental condition. In both cases, the patient committed suicide while confined in a hospital psychiatric ward. Liability was imposed because defendants failed to take precautions to prevent the patient's suicide even though the medical staff in charge of the patient's care knew that the patient was likely to attempt to take his own life.

Neither case suggested extending the duty of care to personal or religious counseling relationships in which one person provided nonprofessional guidance to another seeking advice and the counselor had no control over the environment of the individual being counseled. In sharp contrast, Nally was not involved in a supervised medical relationship with defendants, and he committed suicide well over two weeks after he was released from the hospital against the advice of his attending psychiatrist and physician.

* * *

Thus, contrary to the Court of Appeal's interpretation, none of these cases supports the finding of a special relationship between Nally and defendants, or the imposition of a duty to refer a suicidal person to a professional therapist as urged in the present case. Indeed, on their limited facts, *Bellah, Vistica* and *Meier* weigh against creating such a duty. With the foregoing in mind, we now turn to other considerations and explain further why we should not impose a duty to prevent suicide on defendants and other nontherapist counselors.

c) The Connection Between Defendants' Conduct and Nally's Suicide and the Foreseeability of Harm

Other factors to consider in determining whether to impose a duty of care on defendants include the closeness of the causal connection between defendants' conduct and the injury suffered, and the foreseeability of the particular harm to the injured party. * * *

Plaintiffs argue that Nally's statement to Pastors Rea and MacArthur (while he was recovering from his suicide attempt at the hospital), "that he was sorry he wasn't successful and that he would attempt suicide after his release from the hospital," were "hidden dangers" that would have affected his prognosis and treatment. Accordingly, plaintiffs reason that Rea and MacArthur should have warned the hospital staff and plaintiffs that Nally was still contemplating suicide after his initial attempt. We disagree.

The closeness of connection between defendants['] conduct and Nally's suicide was tenuous at best. As defendants observe, Nally was examined by five physicians and a psychiatrist during the weeks following his suicide attempt. Defendants correctly assert that they "arranged or encouraged many of these visits and encouraged Nally to continue to cooperate with all doctors." In addition, as stated above, following Nally's overdose attempt Dr. Evelyn warned plaintiffs that Nally remained suicidal and that they should encourage him to see a psychiatrist on his release from the hospital. Plaintiffs also rejected both Dr. Hall's and Dr. Parker's suggestion that Nally be institutionalized because, according to plaintiffs, their son was "not crazy."

Nevertheless, we are urged that mere knowledge on the part of the defendants that Nally may have been suicidal at various stages in his life should give rise to a duty to refer. Imposition of a duty to refer Nally necessarily would imply a general duty on all nontherapists to refer all potentially suicidal persons to licensed medical practitioners.

One can argue that it is foreseeable that if a nontherapist counselor fails to refer a potentially suicidal individual to professional, licensed therapeutic care, the individual may commit suicide. While under some circumstances counselors may conclude that referring a client to a psychiatrist is prudent and necessary, our past decisions teach that it is inappropriate to impose a duty to refer—which may stifle all gratuitous or religious counseling—based on foreseeability alone. Mere foreseeability of the harm or knowledge of the danger, is insufficient to create a legally cognizable special relationship giving rise to a legal duty to prevent harm.

d) Public Policy Considerations

Imposing a duty on defendants or other nontherapist counselors to, in the Court of Appeal's words, "insure their counselees [are also] under the care of psychotherapists, psychiatric facilities, or others authorized and equipped to forestall imminent suicide," could have a deleterious effect on counseling in general. Although both plaintiffs and the present Court of Appeal, in dictum, exempt services such as "teen hotlines" which offer only "band aid counseling," from a newly formulated standard of care that would impose a "duty to refer," the indeterminate nature of liability the Court of Appeal imposes on nontherapist counselors could deter those most in need of help from seeking treatment out of fear that their private disclosures could subject them to involuntary commitment to psychiatric facilities.

As defendants, amici curiae, and the Court of Appeal dissenter observe, neither the Legislature nor the courts have ever imposed a legal obligation on persons to take affirmative steps to prevent the suicide of one who is not under the care of a physician in a hospital. * * * Indeed, for all practical purposes, a doctor to whom a nontherapist counselor refers a suicidal person may refuse to take the patient. Furthermore, under the Lanterman–Petris–Short Act (Welf. & Inst.Code, §§ 5200, 5201), "[a]ny individual may" but is not required to institute involuntary commitment proceedings.

We also note that the Legislature has exempted the clergy from the licensing requirements applicable to marriage, family, child and domestic counselors (Bus. & Prof.Code, § 4980 et seq.) and from the operation of statutes regulating psychologists (id., § 2908 et seq.). In so doing, the Legislature has recognized that access to the clergy for counseling should be free from state imposed counseling standards, and that "the secular state is not equipped to ascertain the competence of counseling when performed by those affiliated with religious organizations."[Cite]

Furthermore, extending liability to voluntary, noncommercial and noncustodial relationships is contrary to the trend in the Legislature to encourage private assistance efforts. This public policy goal is expressed in the acts of the Legislature abrogating the "Good Samaritan" rule. Statutes barring the imposition of ordinary negligence liability on one who aids another now embrace numerous scenarios. (See, e.g., Gov.Code, § 50086 [exempting from liability first aid volunteers summoned by authorities to assist in search or rescue operations]; Health & Saf. Code, §§ 1799.100, 1799.102 [exempting from liability nonprofessional persons giving cardiopulmonary resuscitation].)

* * *

Even assuming that workable standards of care could be established in the present case, an additional difficulty arises in attempting to identify with precision those to whom the duty should apply. Because of the differing theological views espoused by the myriad of religions in our state and practiced by church members, it would certainly be impractical, and quite possibly unconstitutional, to impose a duty of care on pastoral counselors. Such a duty would necessarily be intertwined with the religious philosophy of the particular denomination or ecclesiastical teachings of the religious entity. * * * We have previously refused to impose a duty when to do so would involve complex policy decisions, and we are unpersuaded by plaintiffs that we should depart from this policy in the present case. * * *

e) Availability of Insurance

As several commentators observe, although lawsuits stemming from spiritual counseling are few, a new type of "clergyman malpractice" insurance has been offered to religious organizations to protect against potential liability for spiritual counseling that causes injury. Apparently, such insurance provides coverage to religious congregations and their pastors for damages caused by the counseling activities of the pastors while acting within the scope of their duties. The value of such insurance, however, is unknown and difficult to determine because few cases have been filed against the clergy.

f) Conclusion

For the foregoing reasons, we conclude that plaintiffs have not met the threshold requirements for imposing on defendants a duty to prevent suicide. Plaintiffs failed to persuade us that the duty to prevent suicide (heretofore imposed only on psychiatrists and hospitals while caring for a suicidal patient) or the general professional duty of care (heretofore imposed only on psychiatrists when treating a mentally disturbed patient) should be extended to a nontherapist counselor who offers counseling to a potentially suicidal person on secular or spiritual matters.

* * * Accordingly, we conclude the trial court correctly granted defendants' nonsuit motion as to the "clergyman malpractice" or negligence causes of action.

* * *

The judgment of the Court of Appeal is reversed and the Court of Appeal is directed to enter judgment affirming the judgment of nonsuit and dismissing the action.

MOSK, PANELLI, ARGUELLES and EAGLESON, JJ., concur.

KAUFMAN, JUSTICE, concurring.

I concur in the judgment that nonsuit was properly granted, but disagree with the majority's holding that defendants owed no duty of care to the plaintiffs.

The majority appears to reject the proposition that defendants in this matter, or "nontherapist counselors in general," have a duty to advise potentially suicidal counselees to seek competent medical care. (Maj. opn. at p. 105 of 253 Cal.Rptr., at p. 956 of 763 P.2d.) Yet the majority does not purport to "foreclose imposing liability on nontherapist counselors, who hold themselves out as professionals, for injuries related to their counseling activities." (Maj. opn. at p. 110, fn. 8 of 253 Cal.Rptr., at p. 961, fn. 8 of 763 P.2d.)

In view of the majority's suggestion that a nontherapist counselor who holds himself out as competent to treat a suicidal person owes a duty of care to that person, I am baffled as to the basis or the *necessity* of the majority's broad conclusion that "nontherapist counselors in general" do *not* owe such a duty. The evidence in the record, viewed—as the law requires—in *plaintiffs'* favor, demonstrates that defendants (1) expressly held themselves out as fully competent to deal with the most severe psychological disorders, including major depression with suicidal symptoms, (2) developed a close counseling relationship with Kenneth Nally for that very purpose, and (3) realized that Nally's suicide was at least a possibility. Thus, the evidence was more than sufficient, in my view, to trigger a minimal duty of care to Nally. What was fatally *absent* from plaintiffs' case was not evidence of duty, but proof that defendants breached that duty, and that such breach constituted a proximate cause of Nally's suicide. Therefore, while I concur in the decision to reverse the judgment of the Court of Appeal and to reinstate the judgment of nonsuit and dismissal of the action, I strongly disagree with the conclusion that defendants owed no duty of care in this matter.

BROUSSARD, J., concurs.

Questions and Comments

1. *Questions.* Which view is more compelling, that of the majority or that of Justice Kaufman, who would not foreclose the imposition of liability on non-therapist counselors if they "hold themselves out as professionals, for injuries related to their counseling activities"? What might be the negative consequences of adopting the dissent's position? Would it necessarily cut down on religious counseling opportunities or would it simply tend to encourage religious counselors to make referrals where they are in doubt as to the condition or prognosis of the person they are counseling?

If liability were imposed on religious counselors who purport to deal with mentally distressed parishioners, is there any way of distinguishing "teen hotlines" or other telephone hotlines which offer only "band aid counseling"? Does the majority opinion speak to this?

2. *Liability of unlicensed therapists.* Persons who hold themselves out as mental health professionals, even though they are not licensed under state law, will generally be held to the standard of care of the profession that they are purporting to practice. For instance, in *Horak v. Biris,* the defendant, a certified social worker who operated a "center for psychotherapy", was charged with malpractice (having engaged in sexual relations with a patient) and defended on the grounds that he should not be held to a standard of care of a psychologist. In rejecting this defense, the court made the following observation:

> The field of practice engaged in by defendant here more closely resembles the practice of psychology rather than social work, as those two practices are currently defined in the Illinois Revised Statutes. (See Ill.Rev.Stat.1979, ch. 111, pars. 5304 and 6302.) Because of the apparent

overlapping of these two fields, we think the proofs may well reveal that defendant possessed or should have possessed a basic knowledge of fundamental psychological principles which routinely come into play during marriage and family counseling. The "transference phenomenon" is apparently one such principle, and has been defined in psychiatric practice as "a phenomenon * * * by which the patient transfers feelings towards everyone else to the doctor, who then must react with a proper response, the counter transference, in order to avoid emotional involvement and assist the patient in overcoming problems." (*Aetna Life & Casualty Co. v. McCabe* (E.D.Pa.1983), 556 F.Supp. 1342, 1346.) The mishandling of this phenomenon, which generally results in sexual relations or involvement between the psychiatrist or therapist and the patient, has uniformly been considered as malpractice or gross negligence in other jurisdictions, whether the sexual relations were prescribed by the doctor as part of the therapy, or occurred outside the scope of treatment.

Horak v. Biris, 130 Ill.App.3d 140, 85 Ill.Dec. 599, 474 N.E.2d 13, 18 (1985). See also, *Corgan v. Muehling,* 167 Ill.App.3d 1093, 118 Ill.Dec. 698, 522 N.E.2d 153 (1988) (non-licensed psychologist was held to the standard of care of licensed professional psychologists).

3. *Liability of clergymen counselors for sexual misconduct.* The tendency to shield clergy-counselors from malpractice liability has also been extended to claims based on sexual misconduct, where, for instance, a clergyman who acted as a marriage counselor had sexual relations with the advisee wife. In *Bladen v. First Presbyterian Church of Sallisaw*, 857 P.2d 789 (Okl.1993). The Oklahoma Supreme Court refused to apply malpractice liability concepts to clergy-counselors because unlike psychologists and psychiatrists, they "do not use the transference mechanism" in carrying out their counseling functions. Id. at 794. However, this broad exemption from liability may be changing. Recently, the court of appeals for the Fifth circuit sustained a jury award of $100,000 against a minister who, while rendering marital and mental health counseling, engaged in sexual relations with the women he was counseling. *Mullanix v. Baucum*, 134 F.3d 331 (5th Cir.1998). See also Wall Street Journal, Feb. 12, 1998, p. B12. In rejecting the defendant's constitutional defense, the court held that the First Amendment does not categorically insulate religious relationships from judicial scrutiny.

2. *Liability of Health Care Institutions*

As discussed in Chapter One, Section IV, *supra*, health care institutions—in particular managed care organization—play an important role in mental health treatment decisions. As a consequence, they are often named as defendants in malpractice suits. These actions seek to hold the institution directly or vicariously liable for allegedly negligent treatment or coverage decisions. The institution that is sued may be the insurer (typically a managed care organization), an outside entity that conducts utilization review for the insurer, or a hospital. The case that follows is illustrative of claims of this type involving a patient who was allegedly discharged prematurely from a hospital.

MUSE v. CHARTER HOSPITAL OF WINSTON–SALEM, INC.

Court of Appeals of North Carolina 1995.
117 N.C.App. 468, 452 S.E.2d 589.

LEWIS, JUDGE.

This appeal arises from a judgment in favor of plaintiffs in an action for the wrongful death of Delbert Joseph Muse, III (hereinafter "Joe"). Joe was the son of Delbert Joseph Jr., (hereinafter "Mr. Muse") and Jane K. Muse (hereinafter "Mrs. Muse"), plaintiffs. The jury found that defendant Charter Hospital of Winston–Salem, Inc. (hereinafter "Charter Hospital" or "the hospital") was negligent in that, inter alia, it had a policy or practice which required physicians to discharge patients when their insurance expired and that this policy interfered with the medical judgment of Joe's treating physician, Dr. L. Jarrett Barnhill, Jr. The jury awarded plaintiffs compensatory damages of approximately $1,000,000. The jury found that Mr. and Mrs. Muse were contributorily negligent, but that Charter Hospital's conduct was willful or wanton, and awarded punitive damages of $2,000,000 against Charter Hospital. Further, the jury found that Charter hospital was an instrumentality of defendant Charter Medical Corporation (hereinafter "Charter Medical") and awarded punitive damages of $4,000,000 against healthcare Charter Medical.

The facts on which this case arose may be summarized as follows. Joe, who was sixteen years old at the time, was admitted to Charter Hospital for treatment related to his depression and suicidal thoughts. On 12 June 1986, Joe's treatment team consisted of Dr. Barnhill, as treating physicians, Fernando Garzon, as nursing therapist, and Betsey Willard, as social. During his hospitalization, Joe experienced auditory hallucinations, suicidal and homicidal thoughts major depression. Joe's insurance coverage was set to expire on 12 July 1986. As that date neared, Dr. Barnhill decided that a blood test was needed to determine the proper dosage of a drug he was administering to Joe. The blood test was scheduled for 13 July, the day after Joe's insurance was to expire. Dr. Barnhill requested that the hospital administrator allow Joe to stay at Charter Hospital two more days, until 14 July, with Mr. and Mrs. Muse signing a promissory note to pay for the two extra days. The test results did not come back from the lab until 15 July. Nevertheless, Joe was discharged on 14 July and was referred by Dr. Barnhill to the Guilford County Area Mental Health, Mental Retardation and Substance Abuse Authority (hereinafter "Mental Health Authority") for outpatient treatment. Plaintiffs' evidence tended to show that Joe's condition upon discharge was worse than when he entered the hospital. Defendants' evidence, however, tended to show that while his prognosis remained guarded, Joe's condition at discharge was improved. Upon his discharge, Joe went on a one week family vacation. On 22 July he began outpatient treatment at the Mental Health Authority, where he was seen by Dr.

David Slonaker, a clinical psychologist. Two days later, Joe again met with Dr. Slonaker. Joe failed to show up at his 30 July appointment, and the next day he took a fatal overdose of Desipramine, one of his prescribed drugs.

On appeal, defendants present numerous assignments of error. We find merit in one of defendants' arguments.

II.

Defendants next argue that the trial court submitted the case to the jury on an erroneous theory of hospital liability that does not exist under the law of North Carolina. As to the theory in question, the trial court instructed: "[A] hospital is under a duty not to have policies or practices which operate in a way that interferes with the ability of a physician to exercise his medical judgment. A violation of this duty would be negligence." The jury found that there existed "a policy or practice which required physicians to discharge patients when their insurance benefits expire and which interfered with the exercise of Dr. Barnhill's medical judgment." Defendants contend that this theory of liability does not fall within any theories previously accepted by our courts.

* * *

Our Supreme Court has recognized that hospitals in this state owe a duty of care to their patients. Id. In *Burns v. Forsyth County Hospital Authority, Inc.*, this Court held that a hospital has a duty to the patient to obey the instructions of a doctor, absent the instructions being obviously negligent or dangerous. Another recognized duty is the duty to make a reasonable effort to monitor and oversee the treatment prescribed and administered by doctors practicing at the hospital. [ ] In light of these holdings, it seems axiomatic that the hospital has the duty not to institute policies or practices which interfere with the doctor's medical judgment. We hold that pursuant to the reasonable person standard, Charter Hospital had a duty not to institute a policy or practice which required that patients be discharged when their insurance expired and which interfered with the medical judgment of Dr. Barnhill.

III.

Defendants next argue that even if the theory of negligence submitted to the jury was proper, the jury's finding that Charter Hospital had such a practice was not supported by sufficient evidence. * * * We conclude that in the case at hand, the evidence was sufficient to go to the jury.

Plaintiffs' evidence included the testimony of Charter Hospital employees and outside experts. Fernando Garzon, Joe's nursing therapist at Charter Hospital, testified that the hospital had a policy of discharging patients when their insurance expired. Specifically, when the issue of insurance came up in treatment team meetings, plans were made to discharge the patient. When Dr. Barnhill and the other psychiatrists and therapists spoke of insurance, they seemed to lack autonomy. For example, Garzon testified, they would state, "So and so is to be discharged. We must do this." Finally, Garzon testified that when he returned from a vacation, and Joe was no longer at the hospital, he asked several employees why Joe had been discharged they all responded that he was discharged because his insurance had expired. Jane Sims, a former staff member at the hospital, testified that several employees expressed alarm about Joe's impending discharge, and that a therapist explained that Joe could no longer stay at the hospital because his insurance had expired. Sims also testified that Dr. Barnhill had misgivings about discharging Joe, and that Dr. Barnhill's frustration was apparent to everyone. One of plaintiff's experts testified that based on a study regarding the length of patient stays at Charter Hospital it was his opinion that patients were discharged based on insurance, regardless of their medical condition. Other experts testified that based on Joe's serious condition on the date of discharge, the expiration of insurance coverage must have caused Dr. Barnhill to discharge Joe. The experts further testified as to the relevant standard of care, and concluded that Charter Hospital's practices were below the standard of care and caused Joe's death. We hold that this evidence was sufficient to the jury.

Defendants further argue that the evidence was insufficient to support the jury's finding that Charter Hospital engaged in conduct that was willful or wanton. An act is willful when it is done purposely and deliberately in violation of the law, or when it is done knowingly and of set purpose, or when the mere will has free play, without yielding to reason. We conclude that the jury could have reasonably found from the above-stated evidence that Charter Hospital acted knowingly and of set purpose, and with reckless indifference to the rights of others. Therefore, we hold that the finding of willful or wanton conduct on the part of Charter Hospital was supported by sufficient evidence.

* * *

For the reasons stated, we find no error in the judgment of the trial court, except for that part of the judgment awarding punitive damages, which is reversed and remanded for proceedings consistent with this opinion.

No error in part, reversed in part and remanded.

ORR, J., dissents.

While the jury found that defendant was negligent, I find insufficient evidence to raise the defendant's conduct to the level required to submit the issue of willful and wanton conduct to the jury. A policy to terminate a patient's hospitalization based upon insurance benefits ending in and of itself is not wilful or wanton conduct. To sustain plaintiff's contention there must be, according to our law, a deliberate purpose not to discharge a duty necessary for a person's safety. If the hospital had simply discharged the patient with no referral to another physician or medical facility, then a cognizable claim for wilful or wanton conduct would have been established. Such was not the case here, as I read the record, and although Dr. Barnhill's care in discharging the patient may well have been negligent, there is nothing to suggest that the hospital's policy or its implementation by Dr. Barnhill was done with reckless or deliberate disregard for the patient's safety. Therefore, I concluded that the trial court erred in submitting the issue of wilful and wanton conduct to the jury and would accordingly vote to reverse.

Questions and Comments

1. *Law in other jurisdictions.* The *Muse* case is the first reported appellate decision imposing liability on a hospital under similar circumstances. In other cases where liability has been imposed, the defendant hospital was a publicly designated provider of emergency room services.

2. *Implications of the Muse decision.* Can the *Muse* decision be read as holding that contractual limitations notwithstanding, the hospital may not discharge a patient where the discharge holds the potential of serious injury? If this is the basis of the holding, it can have very substantial implications for the hospital or health care organizations. In fact, if gratuitous services must be provided to the public on any extended basis, the provider could confront serious financial difficulties, including insolvency. Are courts in a better position than legislatures to make basic policy decisions that have very significant financial implications for industries such as the health care industry? What kinds of fact-gathering should be the basis of these kinds of economic decisions which reallocate financial burdens outside of the private ordering process (e.g. normal contracts between parties)?

3. *Physicians' duty to contest reimbursement limits.* In the *Muse* case, the decedent's treating physician, Dr. Barnhill, did make some efforts to get him extra time in the hospital. Ultimately, however, he did not contest the reimbursement limit. Some courts have held that physicians have a duty to contest reimbursement limits and may be held liable for violations of that duty. In *Wickline v. State*, 192 Cal.App.3d 1630, 239 Cal.Rptr. 810 (1986), the California Supreme Court held that a physician could be held liable in negligence for not contesting vigorously a reimbursement decision made by Medi–Cal (California's version of Medicaid). As a consequence of the reimbursement decision, the plaintiff, Mrs. Wickline, was discharged early after her operation; her leg subsequently became gangrenous and had to be amputated.

4. *Managed care organizations as defendants.* Managed care organizations (MCOs), have also been sued under various theories. They have been held vicariously liable for the negligent behavior of the physicians with whom they contract, see, e.g., *Boyd v. Albert Einstein Medical Center*, 377 Pa.Super. 609, 547 A.2d 1229 (1988). But see *Jones v. U.S. Healthcare*, 282 A.D.2d 347, 723 N.Y.S.2d 478, 478 (2001) (MCO cannot be held vicariously liable where the documentary evidence clearly states that doctors and hospitals are independent contractors). MCOs have also been held directly liable for negligence in setting up a financial incentive scheme that encourages physicians to refrain from providing care, see, e.g., *Bush v. Dake*, File No. 86–85767 NM–2 (1989). In addition, the California Supreme Court has held that a utilization reviewer can be held liable for "tortious inducement of breach of contract". *Wilson v. Blue Cross of Southern California*, 222

Cal.App.3d 660, 271 Cal.Rptr. 876 (1990) (premature discharge of patient who subsequently committed suicide; insurance coverage covered 30 days of hospitalization, though patient was discharged after 10 days). Finally, in the largest and most significant number of cases, plaintiffs have challenged the MCO utilization review process, arguing that the MCO owed the plaintiff a duty of care and was negligent in prospectively denying coverage for a particular intervention. See, e.g., *Andrews–Clarke v. Travelers Insurance Co.*, 984 F.Supp. 49 (D.Mass.1997) (suit against insurance company and utilization reviewer, where defendants denied coverage for admission to 30–day private detoxification program and plaintiff's husband subsequently committed suicide). As discussed in note 5, however, suits that allege direct wrongdoing by health plans have had mixed success when brought against employer-sponsored health plans, primarily because of the preemptive role of the federal Employee Retirement Income Security Act ("ERISA").

Since 1997, eleven states have passed laws explicitly authorizing patients to sue their health plans directly. Texas was the first to enact right-to-sue legislation. Under the Texas law, which was passed in 1997, a managed care organization can be sued for failure to exercise ordinary care in making a "health care treatment decision." Health plans can be held directly liable for coverage decisions; they can also be held vicariously liable for the negligence of their employees or agents in making coverage decisions. Tex. Civ. Prac. & Rem. Sections 88.001–88.003 (1997). Once again, however, as discussed in note 5, the validity of these laws as applied to employer-sponsored health plans has been challenged under ERISA.

5. *The role of ERISA*. ERISA governs the vast majority of *employer-sponsored* insurance plans. Because of this fact, and because of ERISA's broad preemption clauses, ERISA plays an important role in negligence-based challenges to insurers' denials of coverage. ERISA's preemption clauses displace any state statute or common law that implicates the administration or structure of the plan benefit. ERISA beneficiaries who want to contest benefits determinations are supposed to utilize the remedial scheme provided by ERISA; this scheme limits recovery to the value of the benefits denied. Compensatory and consequential damages are not available under ERISA's remedial scheme.

Many courts have held that because negligence-based challenges to coverage denials are really benefits determination disputes, they are preempted by ERISA. See, e.g., *Andrews–Clarke v. Travelers Insurance Co.*, 984 F.Supp. 49 (D.Mass.1997); *Jass v. Prudential Health Care Plan*, 88 F.3d 1482 (7th Cir.1996); *Corcoran v. United HealthCare, Inc.*, 965 F.2d 1321 (5th Cir.1992); *Tolton v. American Biodyne*, 48 F.3d 937 (6th Cir. 1995). In *Aetna Health Inc. v. Davila*, 542 U.S. 200 (2004), the Supreme Court similarly held that two challenges brought under the Texas statute discussed in note 4 were challenges to benefits denials and hence entirely preempted by ERISA.

The Third Circuit has tried to draw a distinction between negligence challenges that involve "quantity" of care and those that involve "quality" of care, arguing that only the former type of challenge is preempted by ERISA. See *Dukes v. U.S. Healthcare, Inc.*, 57 F.3d 350 (3d Cir.1995). In *Pegram v. Herdrich*, 530 U.S. 211, 120 S.Ct. 2143, 147 L.Ed.2d 164 (2000), the U.S. Supreme Court appeared to support the Third Circuit's position to some extent by indicating that, given the states' historic obligation to regulate health care quality, state law-based challenges to coverage decisions that raise *both* eligibility and quality of treatment questions may not be preempted by ERISA. The Pennsylvania Supreme Court had an immediate opportunity to apply *Pegram* when the U.S. Supreme Court vacated and remanded the state court's opinion in *Pappas v. Asbel* for reconsideration in light of Pegram. 530 U.S. 1241, 120 S.Ct. 2686, 147 L.Ed.2d 959 (2000). The Pennsylvania Supreme Court held that an MCO's denial of permission to use a hospital outside its network was a mixed eligibility and treatment decision and hence subject to challenge under state law. The state court focused on the fact that the utilization reviewer, a physician employed by the MCO, "rejected another medical doctor's opinion based on his clinical judgment." *Pappas v. Asbel*, 564 Pa. 407, 768 A.2d 1089, 1096 (2001). Do you see any problems with a preemption analysis that turns on whether a particular benefits decision can be characterized as "purely" involving eligibility questions? The 2004 Supreme Court decision in Aetna v. Davila, supra, appears to narrow the scope of *Pegram* by emphasizing that, even when benefits determinations made by ERISA plan administrators are based on medical judgments, challenges to such benefits determinations are generally preempted. According to the *Aetna* court, the reasoning of *Pegram* is limited to those cases where the malfeasance in question is committed by a party who is either a treating physician or the physician's.

6. *Independent Review Provisions and ERISA.* In addition to passing right-to-sue laws, some states have pass laws requiring MCOs to provide an independent review of coverage disputes. These statutes have been challenged as preempted by ERISA. In *Rush Prudential HMO v. Moran*, 536 U.S. 355, 122 S.Ct. 2151, 153 L.Ed.2d 375 (2002), the Supreme Court determined that although such statutes did "relate to" the administration and structure of ERISA-governed plans, they were nonetheless not preempted because they fell within a savings clause that exempts from preemption laws that regulate the "business of insurance."

7. *Federal legislative proposals to impose liability on MCOs.* As various observers have pointed out, the liability gap created by ERISA preemption was probably not intended by the framers of ERISA. In the early 1970s, when ERISA was enacted (primarily as a means of ensuring that national employers were relieved of the administrative burden of complying with multiple state laws in designing their benefits plans), insurers typically did not play any role in determining whether a particular treatment would be provided. At most, insurers might contest their responsibility to provide payment after treatment had been delivered.

In 2001, the 107th Congress took its last significant step to date in the direction of amending ERISA. The Senate passed a bill that authorized liability against MCOs offered through ERISA plans if they failed to exercise "ordinary care" in making decisions about eligibility or coverage. The bill also eliminated ERISA preemption of state law causes of action challenging coverage determination based on clinical criteria. S. 1052, 107th Cong., Section 402 (2001) (amending Section 502 of ERISA). A bill passed by the House created a cause of action for ERISA plan beneficiaries similar to that provided in the Senate bill. Unlike the Senate bill, however, the House bill prohibited courts from classifying coverage disputes as challenges to the quality of medical care under state tort law. H.R. 2563, 107th Cong., Section 402 (2001). The differences between the Senate and House bills were not resolved, and the future of ERISA reform remains uncertain.

As a practical matter, what differences are there between the approach taken between the House and Senate? If you were a national employer, which approach would you favor? What if you were an MCO?

8. *Managed care limitations on types of medication.* Medical utilization review by MCOs extends to the type of medication that will be paid for under an insurance plan. Such review can sometimes lead to MCO substitution of the particular medication ordered by the physician. Generally, the substitution is designed to replace the prescribed drug by a less expensive one. In one reported case, the patient had been taking Risperdal, a new antipsychotic drug that cost $5.75 a day retail. The MCO to which he belonged, however, ordered that Navane, which costs 42 cents a day, be substituted for the higher priced Risperdal. The patient's condition deteriorated and he ultimately committed suicide.

According to one report, "with 50 million Americans already covered by restrictive drug plans under managed care, the practice of switching prescription is coming under attack from the American Medical Association and pharmacist groups as potentially dangerous interference with patient care." Freudenheim, 'Not Quite What Doctor Ordered: Drug Substitutions Add to Discord Over Managed Care,' The N.Y. Times, Oct. 8, 1996, at C1.

3. *Liability of Institutions of Higher Learning*

a. Introduction

Public attention has increasingly been drawn in recent years to the violent acts of mentally disturbed students on campuses. While the number of mass shootings on campuses remain relatively rare, some of these events have had catastrophic consequences. For instance, the April 2007 Virginia Tech shootings resulted in the death of 32 students and staff.

In some instances, these types of events have resulted in legal action against the university. Such suits have been primarily based on the alleged failure of the mental health professionals employed by the educational institution to exercise due care in the protection of students and staff.[c] In states that adhere to the *Tarasoff* doctrine liability may turn on a failure of a university therapist to take appropriate actions to prevent the imminently dangerous acts of patient such as notification of law enforcement officials, civil commitment or a warning to third persons at risk (the latter duty often limited to "identifiable" potential victims). See *Eckhardt vs. Kirts*, 179 Ill.App.3d 863, 534 N.E.2d 1339 (1989) (collecting cases).

---

c. Federal civil rights laws may in some instances provide an alternate theory of liability where the defendant institution is a public university. Specifically, an action for damages against a public university can theoretically be brought under 42 U.S.C. Section 1983.

Even where a student has not been under treatment in a university operated health facility, the institution may be charged with having failed to take appropriate action to prevent a student suicide or protect students and staff from the purposefully violent acts of a student. The legal standard that applies under these circumstances is still developing. Where a student commits suicide, a threshold issue is whether the university has a "special relationship" with the student. Under § 314A of the Restatement of Torts (Second), examples of a special relationship include "the relationship between a common carrier and its passengers, an innkeeper and his guests, a possessor of land and his invitees, and one who takes custody of another thereby depriving him of other assistance" but is not limited to these situations. In at least two cases involving student suicides, the trial court ruled that the plaintiffs' allegation of a "special relationship" with the university was sufficient to avoid dismissal. *Shin v. Massachusetts Inst. of Technology*, 19 Mass. L.Rptr. 570, 2005 WL 1869101 (Mass.Super. 2005); *Schieszler v. Ferrum College*, 236 F.Supp.2d 602 (W.D.Va. 2002). Implicit in both cases is the perception that universities have some control of the actions of students (particularly if they reside in university residence halls). Also, there may be the lingering notion that a university stands in *loco parentis* to underage students. But see *Jain v. State*, 617 N.W.2d 293 (Iowa 2000) (rejecting the notion that university student relations establish a special relationship).

The liability of universities for the violent acts of students who harm third persons is more problematic. Here § 315 of the Restatement is apposite. That section provides:

> There is no duty so to control the conduct of a third person as to prevent him from causing physical harm to another unless
>
> (a) a special relation exists between the actor and the third person which imposes a duty upon the actor to control the third person's conduct, or
>
> (b) a special relation exists between the actor and the other which gives the other a right to protection.

This provision *explicitly* requires a finding that the university had a duty to control the conduct of a third person. Given the limited control that a university has over student conduct that does not violate either the criminal law or university regulations, victims of student violence may have difficulty sustaining this burden. It also requires a "special" relationship between the university and the injured party which, in cases that don't involve university mental health professionals or arise in non-*Tarasoff* jurisdictions, can also be difficult to show. The Virginia Tech University incident, which involved a mentally disturbed student, illustrates the complexity of the issues raised in cases of this type.

b. Case Study—The Virginia Tech Tragedy of April 2007

Most of the following material is taken from the monograph, *Mass Shootings at Virginia Tech, Report of the Review Panel*, presented to

Governor Kaine and Commonwealth of Virginia (August 2007) (hereafter Review Panel Report) and the Timeline therein, available at http://www. vtreviewpanel.org/report/index.html).

Prologue

Virginia Tech University is a sprawling campus with 131 buildings on 2,600 acres in Southwest Virginia. In 2007, it had an enrollment of approximately 26,000 students. The university has its own police department of 35 officers. The campus police operate in close cooperation with the police department of the adjacent city of Blacksburg. There are no guards at any of the entrance roads leading to the campus nor are guards stationed at any university buildings.

On April 16th, 2007, a senior student, Seuong Hu Cho, shot to death 32 students and faculty and wounded or injured 17 others. These shootings were committed in two separate episodes. First, in the early hours of April 16th, Cho murdered two students in a dormitory room in west Amber Johnston presidential hall. Approximately, two and a half hours later, Cho entered Norris Hall, an engineering building, systematically went from classroom to classroom and, using automatic pistols, fatally shot 30 students and staff members.

An investigation following the events of April 16 disclosed that Cho had a history of mental problems, beginning in early childhood. For instance, immediately prior to entering high school, Cho was diagnosed by a psychiatrist as suffering from "selective mutism" and "major depression, single episode". During the nearly four years that Cho attended Virginia Tech, he also exhibited behaviors that were symptomatic of a mental disorder. Key events and Cho's behavioral history while enrolled at Virginia Tech are summarized below.

Timeline of Events During Cho's Enrollment in Virginia Tech

August 2003: Cho enters Virginia Tech as a business information systems major. He attracts little during his freshman year. He has a difficult time with his roommate over neatness issues and changes rooms. His parents make weekly trips to visit him. His grades are good. He does not see a counselor at school or home. He is excited about college.

Fall 2004: During his sophomore year, Cho moves off campus to room with a senior who is rarely at home. Cho complains that mites in the apartment are affecting his skin, but doctors tell him his facial blemishes are acne and prescribe minocycline. He becomes interested in writing and decides to switch his major to English beginning his junior year. He submits the necessary paperwork late that sophomore year. His sister notes a growing passion for writing over the summer break, though he is secretive about its content. Cho submits a book idea to a publishing house.

Spring 2005: The book proposal is rejected, an event which depresses him, according to his family. He still sees no counselor at school or home, and exhibits no behavioral problems other than extreme quietness.

Fall 2005: Cho starts junior year and moves back into the dorms. Serious problems begin to surface. His sister notes that he is writing less, and wonders if the publisher's rejection letter curbed his enthusiasm for writing and reversed his improving attitude. At school, Cho is taken to some parties by his suitemates at the start of the fall semester. At one of these parties, he stabs at the carpet in a girl's room with a knife. Professor Nikki Giovanni, Cho's poetry professor, is concerned about the violence expressed in his writing. She also asks him to stop taking pictures of classmates from a camera held under the desk. She offers to get him into another class and writes a letter to English Department Chair Lucinda Roy to accelerate that process. Dr. Roy agrees to remove Cho from the class and tutors him one-on-one with assistance from Professor Frederick D'Aguiar. When Cho refuses to go to counseling, Dr. Roy notifies the Division of Student Affairs, the University's Cook Counseling Center, the Schiffert Health Center, the Virginia Tech police, and the College of Liberal Arts and Human Sciences. Cho's problems are also discussed with the university's Care Team, a unit that reviews students with problems, but no direct action is taken.

November 27, 2005: A female resident files a report with the Virginia Tech Police Department (VTPD) indicating that Cho had made "annoying" contact with her on the Internet, by phone, and in person. The VTPD interviews Cho, but the female student declines to press charges. The investigating officer refers Cho to the school's disciplinary system, the Office of Judicial Affairs.

November 30, 2005: Cho calls Cook Counseling Center and is triaged (i.e., given a preliminary screening) by phone following his interaction with VTPD police.

December 6, 2005: E-mails among resident advisors (RAs) reflect complaints by a female resident in Cochrane residence hall regarding instant messages (IMs) from Cho sent under various strange aliases. E-mails from an R.A. also report that Cho went in disguise to a female student's room (the event of November 27).

December 12, 2005: A female student from Campbell Hall files a report with the VTPD complaining of "disturbing" IMs from Cho. She requests that Cho have no further contact with her. Cho does not keep a 2:00 p.m. appointment at Cook Counseling Center but is triaged by the Center again by phone that afternoon.

December 13, 2005: VTPD notifies Cho that he is to have no further contact with the second female student who complained. After campus police leave, Cho's suitemate receives an IM from Cho stating, "I might as well kill myself now." The suitemate alerts the VTPD, who arranges for a prescreener, a licensed clinical social worker from the New River Valley Community Services Board (the regional outpatient mental health center), to evaluate him. The prescreener concludes that Cho is "an imminent danger to self or others." She also notes that Cho was "mentally ill and was not willing to be treated voluntarily." A magistrate issues a temporary detaining order, and Cho is transported to Carilion St. Albans Psychiatric Hospital for an overnight stay and mental evaluation.

December 14, 2005:

7 a.m. The person assigned as an independent evaluator, psychologist Roy Crouse, evaluates Cho and concludes that he does *not* present an imminent danger to himself.

Before 11 a.m. During the overnight stay at Carilion, Cho received one milligram, Ativa which was administered to treat anxiety. A staff psychiatrist at Carilion evaluates Cho, concludes he is not a danger to himself or others, and recommends outpatient counseling. He gathers no collateral information.

11–11:30 a.m. Special Justice Paul M. Barnett conducts Cho's commitment hearing. Cho is represented by an attorney. After hearing evidence on Cho, the Special Justice rules, contrary to the Carilion evaluators, that "Cho presents an immediate danger to self or others as a result of mental illness" and orders outpatient treatment.

Noon. Following the hearing, the Carilion psychiatric hospital staff psychiatrist dictates in his evaluation summary that "there is no indication of psychosis, delusions, suicidal or homicidal ideation." The psychiatrist finds that "his insight and judgment are normal... Followup and aftercare to be arranged with the counseling center at Virginia Tech; medications, none." Cho is released.

No information is available concerning the interactions between Carilion's psychiatric facility and the university's Cook Center before and after Cho's psychiatric hospitalization. But shortly before Cho's discharge from Carilion's Pyschiatric Hospital on December 14th, a clinical support representative affiliated with the New River Valley Community Services Board establishes contact with the Cook Center to make an appointment for Cho. The Review Panel's Report elaborates on the events immediately prior to and following Cho's discharge.

> The clinical support representative (CSR) contacted Cook Counseling Center at Virginia Tech to make an appointment for Cho. The Cook Counseling Center required that Cho be put on the phone (a practice begun shortly before this hearing according to the CSR) to make the appointment, which he did. The appointment was scheduled for 3:00 p.m. that afternoon, December 14. The CSR does not recall whether this phone call was made prior to or following the hearing....

> Due to the rapidly approaching outpatient appointment for Cho, the CSR urged the treating psychiatrist to expedite the dictation and transcription of his discharge summary. It was transcribed shortly before noon and the physical evaluation findings and recommendation about an hour later. The clinical support representative recalls faxing the records to Cook Counseling Center, but he did not place a

copy of the transmittal confirmation in the hospital records. Cook Counseling Center, however, has no record of having received any hospital records until January 2006. The physical evaluation report indicated that Cho was to be treated by the psychiatrist at [Carilion] "and hopefully have some intervention in therapy for treatment of his mood disorder." The discharge summary, which was not part of the records received by the panel from Cook Counseling Center, indicated "followup and aftercare to be arranged with counseling center at Virginia Tech. Medications none."

Cho was discharged from [Carilion] at 2:00 p.m. on December 14. [No person that was interviewed by the Review Panel] could say how Cho got back to campus. However, the electronic scheduling program at the Cook Counseling Center indicates that Cho kept his appointment that day at 3:00 p.m. He was triaged again, this time face-to-face, but no diagnosis was given. The triage report is missing (as well as those from his two prior phone triages), and the counselor who performed the triage has no independent recollection of Cho. It is her standard practice to complete appropriate forms and write a note to document critical information, recommendations, and plans for follow-up.

It is unclear why Cho would have been triaged for a third time rather than receiving a treatment session at his afternoon appointment following release from [the Carilion inpatient psychiatric facility]. The *Collegiate Times* had run an article at the beginning of the fall semester expressing "concern about the diminished services provided by the counseling center" and the temporary loss of its only psychiatrist. It was the policy of the Cook Counseling Center to allow patients to decide whether to make a followup appointment. According to the existing Cook Counseling Center records, none was ever scheduled by Cho. Because Cook Counseling Center had accepted Cho as a voluntary patient, no notice was given to the CSB, the court, [Carilion], or Virginia Tech officials that Cho never returned to Cook Counseling Center."

January, 2006. The Cook Counseling Center receives a psychiatric summary from Carilion. No followup action is taken by Cook Counseling Center or the University's Care Team.

April 17, 2006. Cho's technical writing professor, Carl Bean, suggests that Cho drop his class after repeated efforts to address shortcomings and Cho's inappropriate choice of writing assignments. Cho follows the professor to his office, raises his voice angrily, and is asked to leave. Bean does not report this incident to university officials.

Spring, 2006. Cho writes a paper for Professor Hicok's creative writing class concerning a young man who hates the students at his school and plans to kill them and himself. The writing contains a number of parallels to the events of April 16, 2007 and the recorded messages later sent to NBC [released after Cho's death].

September 6–12, 2006. Professor Lisa Norris, another of Cho's writing professors, alerts the Associate Dean of Liberal Arts and Human Sciences, Mary Ann Lewis, about disturbing behavior by Cho, but the dean's notes make "no mention of mental health issues or police reports" on Cho. Professor Norris encourages Cho to go to counseling with her, but he declines.

Fall, 2006. Professor Falco, another of Cho's writing instructors, confers with Professors Roy and Norris, who tell him that Dr. Roy in Fall 2005 and Professor Norris in 2006 alerted the Associate Dean of Students, Mary Ann Lewis, about Cho.

February 2, 2007. Cho orders a .22 caliber Walther P22 handgun online from TGSCOM, Inc.

February 9, 2007. Cho picks up the handgun from J–N–D Pawnbrokers in Blacksburg, across the street from the university.

March 12, 2007. Cho rents a van from Enterprise Rent–A–Car at the Roanoke Regional Airport, which he keeps for almost a month. [Cho videotapes some of his subsequently released diatribe in the van.]

March 13–April 7, 2007. On March 13, having waited the 30 days between gun purchases required by Virginia law, Cho purchases a 9mm Glock 19 handgun and a box of 50 9mm full metal jacket practice rounds at Roanoke Firearms. The store initiates the required background check by police, who find no record of mental health issues. Eight days later, Cho goes to PSS Range and Training, an indoor pistol range, and spends an hour practicing. The next day he purchases two 10–round magazines for the Walther P22 on eBay, and three additional 10–round magazines from another eBay seller. In the following weeks he purchases additional ammunition magazines, ammunition, and a hunting knife from Wal–Mart and Dick's Sporting Goods and chains from Home Depot.

April 8, 2007. Cho spends the night at the Hampton Inn in Christiansburg, Virginia, videotaping segments for his manifesto-like diatribe against his fellow students and society at large [which he later sent to NBC]. He also buys more ammunition.

April 13, 2007. Bomb threats are made to Torgersen, Durham, and Whittemore halls, in the form of an anonymous note. The threats are assessed by the VTPD and the buildings evacuated. There is no lockdown or cancellation of classes elsewhere on campus. Handwriting analysis fails to link these threats to Cho.

April 14, 2007. An Asian male wearing a hooded garment is seen by a faculty member in Norris Hall. The faculty member later (after April 16) tells police that one of her students had told her the doors were chained. Cho may thus have been practicing his assault. He also buys more ammunition.

April 15, 2007. Cho places his weekly Sunday night call to his family in Fairfax County. They report the conversation as normal and that Cho said nothing that caused them concern.

April 16, 2007. Cho goes on a shooting rampage, resulting in the murder of two students in West Ambler Johnston residence hall and 30 students two and a half hours later in Norris Hall, Engineering Building.

Selected Legal/Policy Issues

The Virginia Tech tragedy raises a multiplicity of policy issues, which the Review Panel Report divided into three categories. One set of issues pertains to the institutional capacity of universities to identify at-risk students who have "problems" and to take appropriate action to channel such students into treatment. In this regard, the Report included the following finding:

> Residence Life [an administrative unit having responsibility over the resident halls] knew through their staff (two resident advisors and their supervisor) that there were multiple reports and concerns expressed over Cho's behavior in the dorm, but this was not brought before the Care Team. The academic component of the university spoke up loudly about a sullen, foreboding male student who refused to talk, frightened classmate and faculty with macabre writings, and refused faculty exhortations to get counseling. However, after Judicial Affairs and the Cook Counseling Center opined that Cho's writings were not actionable threats, the Care Team's one review of Cho [in 2005] resulted in their being satisfied that private tutoring would resolve the problem. No one sought to revisit Cho's progress the following semester or inquire into whether he had come to the attention of other stakeholders on campus.

The Review Panel Report also noted a lack of coordination between psychiatric facilities to which people have been committed and after care outpatient clinics. In particular, the panel found a lack of follow up on the part of Carilion and insufficient or non-existent communications between that facility and the university's Cook Counseling Center.

Finally, the review panel found that communications between campus units and outside agencies such as Carilion were hampered both by misinterpretations of state and federal law requirements and by defects in state and federal regulations governing when disclosures pertaining to students evidencing signs of mental abnormality and dangerousness may be made. In the words of the report:

> The Care Team was hampered by overly strict interpretations of federal and state privacy laws (acknowledged as being overly complex), a decentralized corporate university structure, and the absence of someone on the team who was experienced in threat assessment and knew to investigate the situation more broadly, checking for collateral information that would help determine if this individual truly posed a risk or not.

Issues associated with the protection of student privacy when students are either dangerous to themselves or to third persons are treated in Chapter 5 at pp. 324–25.

Questions and Comments

1. *The university's options.* As noted in the excerpt from the Review Panel's Timeline of Events, Cho's behavior and his threat to commit suicide led the university police to initiate commitment proceedings in the evening of December 13, 2005, well over a year before the shootings. Was there any other event during the nearly four years that Cho was a student that would have justified involuntary commitment? Assuming there was not, what options were open to the Virginia Tech administration? Could the university have conditioned enrollment on Cho's agreement to undergo outpatient therapy? If Cho had refused, would the risk to other students (or himself) possibly have increased?

2. *The university's response to the shootings.* There was a lapse of two and a half hours between the time of the original two shootings and Cho's murderous rampage in Norris engineering hall. Some have questioned why, during this two and a half hour period, the university did not lock down the campus or make any effort to inform students of a potential danger either by text messaging, email or phone communications.

3. *Gun control.* The most lethal school shootings over the past twenty years have involved the use of guns, more often than not by people with mental disability. The federal Gun Control Act, originally enacted in 1968, prohibits gun purchases by anyone who has been adjudicated as a "mental defective" or has been committed to a mental institution. 18 U.S.C. § 922(g)(4). In spite of this prohibition, Cho was able to purchase two automatic weapons in the months preceding his rampage.

Administration of the federal law relies on a federal registry of persons barred from purchasing guns. Gun sellers are legally required, before making a sale, to access the federal registry to ascertain that the purchaser is not a person prohibited from making a purchase. The federal data base in turn relies on reports from state agencies that under state law are charged with gathering and reporting data pertaining to psychiatric hospitalizations. The Review Panel report found that while Virginia law authorized state agencies to report involuntarily hospitalization to the federal registry, no report on Cho's *outpatient* hospitalization on December 2005 had been filed, which allowed him to purchase two automatic pistols and ammunition without hindrance. As a result, the Review Panel called for an amendment of Virginia law to "clarify... the appropriate recipients of certified copies of [psychiatric hospitalization orders... [and] the party responsible for [certifying and reporting such orders"]. Review Panel Report, p. 61. The Virginia Tech and similar episodes spurred Congress to enact the NICS (National Instant Criminal Background Check System) Improvement Act. This legislation, signed into law on January 8, 2008, provides grants to states to upgrade information and identification technologies for firearms eligibility determination.

4. *Immunity.* State operated institutions of higher learning, unlike their private counterparts, are generally covered by state sovereign immunity law. See pp. 242–244. As a result, in tragedies such as the Virginia Tech shootings, the university and its staff are covered by Virginia's governmental immunity legislation. In general, such legislation places caps on recoveries against public institutions and their staff for non-intentional torts. Addition-

ally, it imposes various procedural requirements that restrict eligibility to file a lawsuit. It also bears noting that in a number of other similar cases the state legislature adopted laws providing for compensation, bypassing the normal legal recovery procedures.

5. *Settlement in Virginia Tech case.* An $11 million settlement with the families of 24 of the victims of the Virginia Tech shootings was judicially approved on June 17th, 2008, thus avoiding "a court battle over whether anyone but the gunman was to blame." New York Times, June 18, 2008, A15. Of the remaining eight families involved, four agreed to the settlement but were not prepared to go before the judge and four did not participate. Of the latter four, two have filed notices of lawsuits and two have to date not filed any claim. The settlement also covers the claims of 17 persons who were injured in the mayhem. Id.

4. *Public Officials and Governmental Units*

a. *Introduction*

As the preceding sections make clear, a mental health professional who provides substandard care or fails to conform to legal requirements such as informed consent may be liable for damages. The employing agency also may be liable for damages caused by the mental health professional. However, when the employing agency is a governmental one, such as a public institution of higher learning or the professional is a public employee, special rules often apply to limit liability. These rules stem from the doctrines of sovereign immunity and official immunity.

The doctrine of sovereign immunity is largely historical in nature. When the United States was created from the former colonies of Great Britain, the new government inherited the sovereign immunity that had been enjoyed by the king. The doctrine was based on a monarchical semi-religious tenet that "the king can do no wrong," and its effect was to prevent the government from being sued without its consent. Justice Holmes stated the proposition in a more pragmatic way when he wrote in *Kawananakoa v. Polyblank*, 205 U.S. 349, 353, 27 S.Ct. 526, 527, 51 L.Ed. 834 (1907):

> A sovereign is exempt from suit, not because of any formal conception or obsolete theory, but on the logical and practical ground that there can be no legal right as against the authority that makes the law on which the right depends.

Sovereign immunity is rooted in social policy as well as in history. It is seen as preserving government's control over its funds, property, and instrumentalities. Without immunity, it is argued, the government would be hampered in its essential functions. In addition, some argue that a democratic society needs sovereign immunity to prevent individuals from depleting the treasury at the expense of the majority of the population.

The immunity doctrine has come under increasing criticism, however, as government has become larger and more pervasive. It is argued that injuries caused by the government should be born by the entire society as a cost of government rather than by the particular individual injured.

b. Immunity Under Federal Law

Originally the federal government alleviated this burden upon individuals on a case by case basis, allowing certain individuals to sue the government. In 1946, however, Congress passed the Federal Tort Claims Act [FTCA], which waived the federal government's immunity from suit in a broad range of circumstances. Through the FTCA, Congress intended to compensate victims of the negligent conduct of government activities in circumstances in which a victim could collect damages from a private tort feasor.

The FTCA, however, excludes some torts from coverage, and thus the immunity doctrine remains in effect for those causes of action. For example, the federal government remains immune from suit for damages resulting from combat activities in time of war. A section of the FTCA provides that the United States will not be liable for "any claim arising out of arrest, battery, false imprisonment, false arrest, malicious prosecution, abuse of process, libel, slander, misrepresentation, deceit, or interference with contract rights" except in law enforcement cases. 28 U.S.C. § 2680(b). This provision has sometimes been broadly construed to preclude recovery from the government for medical malpractice. Thus, a claim of battery for an operation performed in a Veterans Administration hospital on the wrong leg of the plaintiff was denied in *Moos v. United States,* 118 F.Supp. 275 (D.Minn.1954), *affirmed* 225 F.2d 705 (8th Cir.1955).

The FTCA also excludes the federal government from liability for acts or omissions that are within the "discretionary function or duty" of any federal agency or employee. 28 U.S.C. § 2680(a). The distinction between discretionary and non-discretionary duties is often difficult. Almost every act performed by a government official includes some discretion in the manner in which it is performed. Therefore, the discretionary function exclusion has been construed by courts to involve a planning/operational distinction. *Dalehite v. United States,* 346 U.S. 15, 73 S.Ct. 956, 97 L.Ed. 1427 (1953). Under this test, the federal government has been held to be immune from suit based on negligence in making top-level planning decisions such as whether to export fertilizer. *Dalehite, id.* In contrast, the federal government may be held liable for the negligence of federal employees in the "operational" level of government in carrying out the plans even though such actions may involve a certain amount of discretion. For example, the Supreme Court in *Indian Towing Co. v. United States,* 350 U.S. 61, 76 S.Ct. 122, 100 L.Ed. 48 (1955), found that checking the electrical system of a lighthouse was at the "operational level" and did not involve discretion within the meaning of the FTCA. The government was therefore not immune from suit to recover damages suffered by a barge that ran aground while a Coast Guard lighthouse was not operating.

The FTCA additionally places various procedural requirements on persons with claims against the government. The most important is the requirement of exhaustion of administrative remedies. The injured party must have been denied relief from the agency from which recovery is sought before suit may be brought in court. In this way Congress sought to encourage compromise and to minimize the burden added to the courts when immunity was waived.

c. Immunity Under State Law

The principle that the sovereign cannot be sued without its consent applies to the various states of the United States. Absent waiver, states, state agencies, and state officers in their official capacities are generally immune from suit. The general immunity of states from law suits is problematic where Congress has enacted legislation providing a private cause of action against private or public actors for the violation of a federally protected right. In this situation, the eleventh amendment is likely to bar the award of damages against a state though other forms of relief including injunctions may be available even when the state has not consented to be sued. The jurisprudence pertaining to the reach of the eleventh amendment as a bar to lawsuits against the states is discussed pp. 1280–82. Every state has, to at least some extent, consented to be sued by adopting legislation waiving sovereign immunity in some circumstances. These statutes, although generally not as comprehensive as the FTCA, serve much the same purpose. Immunity is waived only for those circumstances explicitly set forth in the statute and only if the prescribed procedures are followed. There are some circumstances, however, in which a state or state agency may be sued even though it has not waived its immunity. Such a circumstance arises when the state is acting not in its governmental capacity, but in a "proprietary" capacity, as when the state creates an agency to engage in a primarily commercial venture.

There is no uniform rule declaring whether state and municipal hospitals exist under the proprietary or governmental function of the state. The maintenance of a hospital for the service of the public health and to treat indigent patients is generally held to be a governmental function, and thus the hospital is immune from suit absent waiver of immunity. In contrast, the operation of a hospital for the purpose of obtaining a pecuniary profit is generally considered to be a proprietary function not immune from suit. Unfortunately, the majority of state hospitals fall within a middle category for which generalizations are impossible. See generally Annot. 25 A.L.R.2d 203, 228 (1952) and Supp. (1981).

Some cases arise in which the governmental agency is immune from suit, but the employee who actually committed the wrong is amenable to suit in his individual capacity. Additionally, a plaintiff may wish to seek recovery from both the government agency and the individual employee. However, in any suit against a government employee one must consider the doctrine of official immunity.

Government employees are not, of course, absolved from their private and personal tort liabilities merely because of their employment. When, however, a person is injured as a result of government (federal, state, or local) action, the employee causing the injury may be immune from liability under the doctrine of official immunity.

Official immunity has been recognized by the courts as a means of relieving the burden that would otherwise fall upon government officials if they were held accountable in private tort suits for every action taken or decision made. The immunity allows government employees to execute their duties without unreasonable fear of liability and prevents qualified persons from being discouraged from entering government employment out of such fear. Courts have, however, recognized that not every government employee requires the same type of protection. The scope of the immunity therefore varies among government employees.

In essence there are two types of immunity: absolute and qualified. Judges have long been granted absolute immunity for their judicial acts, even when their conduct is corrupt or malicious. Such an immunity was recognized in order to preserve an independent judiciary by eliminating the possibility of vexatious suits. Because the immunity extends to all members of the judicial branch, such mental health professionals as hearing officers in commitment proceedings and psychiatrists appointed by the court benefit from the doctrine. A doctor who signs papers in a commitment process or who testifies at a commitment hearing or child custody proceeding has "absolute immunity" from liability for actions taken in his capacity as an officer of the court. *Duzynski v. Nosal,* 324 F.2d 924 (7th Cir.1963); *Williams v. Westbrook Psychiatric Hospital,* 420 F.Supp. 322 (E.D.Va.1976); *Rogers v. Janzen,* 711 F.Supp. 306 (E.D.La. 1989).

Generally, when a defamatory statement is made during the course of a judicial proceeding it is absolutely privileged, even if made maliciously and with knowledge that it was false. So long as the act was required or permitted by law, the privilege bars a civil cause of action for libel or slander. In some jurisdictions, the privilege exists during preliminary proceedings involving pleadings, affidavits, or other papers, whereas in other jurisdictions the privilege exists only after the action has begun. The privilege also extends to post-trial motions and final judgment enforcement proceedings. However, for such immunity to attach the statement must be made with the honest belief that it was relevant or material to the litigation. Not protected are slanderous statements which were plainly irrelevant, were voluntarily made, and which the declarant could not reasonably have believed were relevant.

Outside the hearing context, decisions relating to diagnosis, care and treatment require judgment and choice and are, therefore, considered discretionary and entitled only to qualified immunity. Specifically, a decision outside the court process to detain a mentally ill patient or to release on a temporary or permanent basis is protected only by qualified immunity. See, *Porter v. Maunnangi,* 764 S.W.2d 699 (Mo.App.1988).

Similarly, an evaluation of the suitability of a mentally ill patient to participate in an outpatient versus an inpatient program is considered to be discretionary. See *Canon v. Thumudo,* 430 Mich. 326, 422 N.W.2d 688 (1988).

If qualified immunity applies, the officer cannot be held liable for any act within his governmental duties that was performed in good faith. Thus, for example, a psychiatrist employed by a state mental hospital who negligently determines that a civilly committed patient remains mentally ill and denies the patient release would be immune from liability for false imprisonment. If, however, the psychiatrist makes his report knowing that the patient is qualified for release, his/her report may have been made in bad faith, and qualified immunity will not protect him/her from liability. See e.g., *Hoffman v. Halden,* 268 F.2d 280 (9th Cir.1959); *Mierop v. State,* 22 Misc.2d 216, 201 N.Y.S.2d 2 (1960).

Actions that are wholly outside of the authority of the official are not protected by either absolute or qualified official immunity. However, courts will often extend the immunity to the officer if determination of the scope of his authority would have required a determination of legal questions that could perplex a court. Thus, if an officer acted under authority of a statute later determined to be unconstitutional, he is protected by the same immunity he would have if the statute had been valid. The immunity of public officials in actions brought under the federal Civil Rights Acts is discussed in the section which follows.

The various types of immunity recognized for governments and government employees have come under increasing attack as the role of government has increased in this country. Many have argued that liability should be borne by all as a cost of government and that government employees should not enjoy more privileges than they would have if employed in a similar function in the private sector. Certainly many of the original justifications for the immunities have changed. Courts and legislatures have therefore adjusted the immunity doctrines to try to deal with these changes by waiving or eroding immunity in some areas and extending it into others. That process continues today. Whatever the ultimate outcome, government and official immunity will undoubtedly continue to have an important place in litigation involving the mental health professions.

III. RECOVERY AND DAMAGES UNDER ALTERNATIVE THEORIES

A. MISCELLANEOUS NON–NEGLIGENCE THEORIES

A deviation from professional standards may give rise to a cause of action based on theories other than negligence. Some of these special theories, such as an action for failure to obtain the patient's informed consent or for a breach of confidentiality are treated in Chapters Three and Four, respectively. Depending on the circumstances the patient may also be able to resort to various intentional tort theories to vindicate his rights (e.g., an action for assault where the therapist has engaged in sexual relations with a patient who because of the nature of the relationship lacks effective capacity to give consent). See, *Omer v. Edgren,* 38 Wash.App. 376, 685 P.2d 635 (1984). Also, as noted, in some special circumstances, a therapist may be held liable for negligent infliction of emotional distress. See pp. 208–214.

A therapist's failure to meet professional standards may also lead to an action for breach of contract. The reason why a patient's claim will be grounded in contract will vary. At times, it may be to take advantage of a longer statute of limitations. In other instances, the plaintiff may use the contract theory to avoid problems of proof of negligence. For instance, as noted in the subsection Damages for Sexual Misconduct, supra, in some jurisdictions recovery under a negligence theory for mental distress will only be allowed where the infliction was intentional or where the mental suffering was accompanied by physical harm or injury. In these jurisdictions, a plaintiff may be more successful under a breach of contract theory which will allow at least a recovery of all fees paid to the therapist. See *Anclote Manor Foundation v. Wilkinson,* 263 So.2d 256 (Fla.App.1972).

Some courts have, however, imposed limitations on the patient's freedom to select a contractual theory of recovery over standard negligence. In *Dennis v. Allison,* 698 S.W.2d 94 (Tex.1985), for instance, the Texas Supreme Court, in holding that the plaintiff who had been sexually assaulted by her therapist could not maintain an action in breach of implied warranty, stated:

> "It is not necessary to impose an implied warranty theory as a matter of public policy because the plaintiff/patient has adequate remedies [in tort] to redress wrongs committed during treatment." Id. at 96.

B. CLAIMS BASED ON FEDERAL CIVIL RIGHTS LAWS

Certain federal statutes, collectively known as the Civil Rights Statutes, allow patients to sue mental health professionals for deprivations of their civil rights. The most widely used of these statutes provides that:

> Every person who, under color of any statute, ordinance, regulation, custom, or usage, of any State or Territory, subjects, or causes to be subjected, any citizen of the United States or other person within the jurisdiction thereof to the deprivation of any rights, privileges, or immunities secured by the Constitution and laws, shall be liable to the party injured in an action at law, suit in equity, or other proper proceeding for redress.

42 U.S.C. § 1983 (1970).

Although these statutes were originally passed after the Civil War to assure the rights of the newly emancipated slaves, since the civil rights movements of the 1960's and 70's the scope of their application has continuously expanded beyond racial discrimination. Accordingly, the number of civil rights actions filed each year has increased from 296 in 1960 to 16,332 in 1981 and to well over 50,000 today (Director, Administrative Office of the United States Courts, Annual Report [1995]). Today a mental health patient can bring a civil rights action against a mental health professional under the following circumstances: (1) the conduct complained of was committed by a person acting under color of state law; (2) this conduct deprived the patient of rights, privileges, or immunities secured by the Constitution or laws of the United States; and (3) the conduct complained of was not protected by the professional's qualified immunity.

While meeting these three requirements will often be somewhat burdensome, the advantages of the civil rights action over the traditional state tort action will often justify this effort. The most obvious advantage in seeking a federal forum is that the plaintiff-patient will be able to remove his case from the state court, which may have subtle political ties to the state agency involved. Additionally, a successful plaintiff may qualify for attorney's fees under 42 U.S.C. § 1988. Also, resort to the Civil Rights statutes allows a plaintiff to avoid state exhaustion of remedies requirements. The federal forum may also be necessary to avoid state created limitations on liability, whether it be the creation of a fixed ceiling of liability or the nonrecognition of punitive damages for particular actions. However, certain immunities may still operate to bar recovery of damages (though not necessarily injunctive relief). Where the patient seeks only relief that is equally available under state tort law, the advantages of a federal action may be outweighed by the additional elements of proof which confront a plaintiff in a federal civil rights action.

A major hurdle in every claim based on section 1983 [set out above] is the requirement that the conduct forming the basis of the action be that of one acting under color of state law. The case which follows highlights the difficult issues involved in the application of this criterion.

SPENCER v. LEE

United States Court of Appeals, Seventh Circuit, 1989.
864 F.2d 1376.

POSNER, CIRCUIT JUDGE.

Do a private physician and a private hospital act under color of state law, and therefore lay themselves open to suit under 42 U.S.C. § 1983, when they commit a mentally disturbed person? Adhering to *Byrne v. Kysar,* 347 F.2d 734 (7th Cir.1965), and *Duzynski v. Nosal,* 324 F.2d 924, 929–31 (7th Cir.1963), we hold they do not.

* * *

The plaintiff, William Spencer, appeals from the dismissal of his complaint for failure to state a claim, so we must proceed on the assumption that the facts alleged in the complaint are true. In 1982 and

1984, Spencer's physician, defendant Bumyong Lee, authorized Spencer to be involuntarily committed to St. Elizabeth Hospital. On the second of these occasions the police were called in to take Spencer to the hospital against his will, and on the fourth day of his five days of hospitalization Dr. Lee directed a nurse to inject Spencer with a drug. Spencer protested that he was allergic to the drug, but he was injected anyway and sustained bodily injury. Spencer seeks damages under 42 U.S.C. § 1983 for the deprivation of his liberty without due process of law and for the reckless infliction of injury during his second confinement. Pendent counts seek damages under the common law of Illinois for false imprisonment and malpractice. Spencer had no lawyer in the district court, and his complaint is barely coherent. The district court ordered him to furnish a more definite statement of his claim. In response, Spencer submitted medical records * * * These documents depict Spencer as a schizophrenic with suicidal tendencies who has been in and out of mental institutions many times. Among his delusions are that "all winter he was sick until this time when the police starting a kind of prostitution operation also near motel where he is staying, they have been running a chain saw, the chain saw produced hormones in his testes and he couldn't sit still." * * * However, the district judge did not rely on any of the medical records—which Spencer did not vouch for (he just produced them in response to the judge's order) and has had no chance to explain (away)—and we won't rely on them either.

The casting of this lawsuit as one for the redress of a violation of the Fourteenth Amendment's due process clause, which forbids *states* to deprive persons of life, liberty, or property without due process of law, would certainly strike the innocent eye as puzzling. The due process clause is directed to action by state government; 42 U.S.C. § 1983 creates a remedy against persons acting under color of state law, such as police officers. The defendants in this case are not public employees. They provide no services under contract to the state government or any of its subdivisions. They do not participate (so far as is relevant to this case) in any state or other governmental programs. A purely private physician and a purely private hospital are alleged to have confined the plaintiff against his will and to have injured him by improper medical treatment. These are classic allegations of false imprisonment and malpractice—torts for which the common law of Illinois provides remedies that the plaintiff does not suggest are inadequate.

In arguing that the defendants are nonetheless state actors for purposes of the Fourteenth Amendment and section 1983, the plaintiff relies on the Illinois Mental Health and Developmental Disabilities Code, which provides that "when a person is asserted to be subject to involuntary admission and in such a condition that immediate hospitalization is necessary for the protection of such person or others from physical harm, any person 18 years of age or older may present a [commitment] petition to the facility director of a mental health facility in the county where the respondent resides or is present." Ill.Rev.Stat. ch. 91½, § 3–601(a). The petition must include much factual detail and be accompanied by a certificate, signed by a physician or other qualified professional, stating that the respondent requires immediate hospitalization and that the physician has examined the respondent within the previous 72 hours, and setting forth the factual basis for the physician's opinion that immediate hospitalization is required. §§ 3–601(b), 3–602. Within 24 hours of the respondent's admission to the mental health facility, the facility must forward the relevant papers to the local state court, which must in turn hold a hearing within 5 days (exclusive of weekends and holidays—so the longest possible prehearing commitment is 8 days) on whether there are grounds for continuing to hold the respondent. § 3–611.

This complex of provisions, Spencer argues, operates to "deputize" private physicians such as Dr. Lee and private hospitals such as St. Elizabeth to carry out the exclusive state function of committing the mentally ill. For a maximum of eight days these ostensibly private actors are empowered by the Mental Health Code to hold and treat people against their will. This power, Spencer concludes, is a state power that does not cease to be such merely because delegated to private persons.

If the State of Illinois ordered or encouraged private persons to commit the mentally ill, they would indeed be state actors, for they would be doing the state's business. It would make no difference that they were not technically employees of the state. Or if the state decided to contract out the provision of state highway police or the administration of state prisons to private entrepreneurs of security and correctional services, the entrepreneurs and their employees would (we may assume) be state actors. The details of the contractual relationship between state agencies and the persons who actually implement state policy—whether those persons are state employees or independent contractors or the employees of independent contractors—are of no moment. In accordance with *Marsh v. Alabama,* 326 U.S. 501, 66 S.Ct. 276, 90 L.Ed. 265 (1946), we may further assume that if the state allowed a residential subdivision or high-rise apartment building to form its own de facto municipal government, that government would be an arm of the state for purposes of the Fourteenth Amendment, just as de jure municipal governments are; again the technicality of governmental employment would not control the case. Who does the state's business is the state's actor.

At the opposite extreme is the situation where the state decides to reduce the scope of government. Suppose the state owned a railroad, and decided to sell it to a private person. Would the new owner be deemed a state actor under the Constitution, on the ground that the state had "deputized" him to operate "its" railroad? He would not. The scope of government is not fixed; deregulation does not create a host of state actors in the private sector, like the moraine that marks the farthest advance of a glacier. Certain powers, however, are "traditionally the exclusive prerogative of the State," and their exercise by private persons is state action. *Marsh* can be understood in this light—as a case not of deregulation, but of the delegation of public powers to private actors.

We have to situate the present case in this grid. It is not a case of governmental encouragement or direction of private persons; and "a State normally can be held responsible for a private decision only when it has exercised coercive power or has provided such significant encouragement, either overt or covert, that the choice must in law be deemed to be that of the State." *Blum v. Yaretsky, supra,* 457 U.S. at 1004, 102 S.Ct. at 2786. [The plaintiff's] argument is that the commitment of the mentally ill, like the arrest of criminal suspects, is so central and traditional a function of government that the state cannot limit its responsibility for performing the function. Any private individual who is empowered to commit a person to an institution against the person's will *is* government, just as the "company town" in *Marsh* was a part of the government of Alabama, although a part that had been handed over to a private entity to administer.

Spencer is thus appealing—with support in the language of cases like *Blum* and in the outcome of *Marsh*—to the idea that governmental functions that have traditionally been the *exclusive* prerogative of government, usually because they involved a high degree of coercion, can be delegated but not abandoned. The treatment of the mentally disabled, however, as of the sick and infirm generally, is not such a function. The issue here, it is true, is involuntary commitment rather than treatment. But the analogy that Spencer seeks to draw to arrest is inapt, since a citizen's arrest is not subject to challenge under section 1983. There have been citizen arrests for as long as there have been public police—indeed much longer. In ancient Greece and Rome, and in England until the nineteenth century, most arrests and prosecutions were by private individuals. (Some crimes, e.g., shoplifting, are still privately prosecuted in England.) Arrest has never been an exclusively governmental function. Not all state-authorized coercion is government action.

* * *

The question we are trying to answer is whether a private person is doing the state's business and should be treated as an employee or other formal agent of the state. So we ask, is there a tradition of treating civil commitment of the mentally disturbed as a governmental function and, if so, how well established is it?

The specific provisions of the Mental Health Code dealing with emergency commitment by private physicians to private hospitals are not 200 years old; they are less than 50 years old. See Revised Mental Health Act, art. 5, 1945 Ill.Laws 1011. But commitment has long been a private remedy, albeit one subject (like repossession, self-defense, citizen's arrest, and other infringements on rights of liberty or property) to rigorous safeguards. Even public commitment in Illinois is private in a sense, because the state requires relatives of voluntarily and involuntarily committed mental patients alike to pay the cost of their upkeep in the state's institutions, and it allows the involuntarily committed to be placed in private homes as well as public and private hospitals. And long before the passage of the 1945 statute, the law of Illinois authorized the confinement of an insane person by private persons, for up to ten days, if he was a danger to himself or others.

Private commitment was not novel in 1893; nor was it invented in Illinois. According to Blackstone, writing in 1765, "On the first attack of lunacy, or other occasional insanity, while there may be hope of a speedy restitution of reason, it is usual to confine the unhappy objects in private custody under the direction of their nearest friends and relations." 1 Commentaries on the Laws of England 305. Histories of the treatment of the insane focus on public institutions, but involuntary extrajudicial commitment to private institutions has long been commonplace. London's notorious lunatic asylum, nicknamed "Bedlam," was originally private; it was representative of private medieval institutions to which the insane were committed to have their demons exorcised. See Albert Deutsch, The Mentally Ill in America 15, 40, 62, 418–24 (2d ed. 1949).

The reasons for private commitment, as for self-defense, citizen's arrests, and other private remedies, are intensely practical. If a person displays symptoms of acute and violent mental illness, his family or physician—in an appropriate case a passerby or other stranger—may have to act immediately to restrain him from harming himself or others, and there may be no public institution at hand. That is why the Illinois Mental Health Code allows private persons to commit to private (as well as to public) institutions. We do not know the circumstances in which Mr. Spencer was committed, but it appears that the first commitment was because he had tried to commit suicide, and let us assume this was indeed the reason. If his father and Dr. Lee and St. Elizabeth had had to initiate a judicial proceeding before committing him, he might have killed himself before they could obtain the necessary order. When family members commit a person who has just tried to kill himself, they do not, by virtue of this action, become state actors subject to suit under section 1983.

To allow family members, physicians, and other private persons to exercise the commitment power without safeguards, however, including a provision for a hearing eventually—and sooner rather than later—would be monstrous. If Spencer thinks the eight days allowed by Illinois law for confinement prior to hearing is too much, he can challenge the constitutionality of the statute. He has not done so. Indeed, he relies on the statute to make the defendants state actors. But a private commitment is no more state action than a citizen's arrest, the repossession of chattels, or the ejection of trespassers is. The statutes authorizing or constraining these private activities may or may not be constitutional; the activities themselves remain private.

We are given some pause by the allegation in Spencer's complaint of involvement by the local police: It is possible that the police were called in to assist with one of Spencer's commitments, though this does not seem to be what he is alleging. At all events, police assistance in the lawful exercise of self-help does not create a conspiracy with the private person exercising that self-help. The citizen who makes a citizen's arrest is not transformed into a state actor by handing over the arrested person to the police—indeed, if he fails to do so, the arrest is invalid and he is liable for false imprisonment.

The pressure to transform state common law torts into federal constitutional torts comes from the immunities and the damage ceilings that states frequently impose on suits against their public officials (see, e.g., *Archie v. City of Racine,* 847 F.2d 1211, 1227 (7th Cir.1988) (concurring opinion)), from a sense that state judges are sometimes unsympathetic to suits against the state, and from the availability of attorney's fee awards in civil rights suits under 42 U.S.C. § 1988. Only the last of these considerations is present in a case such as this where the only defendants are private persons (or private institutions) not acting pursuant to formal judicial order. There is neither practical nor legal basis for this suit.

Affirmed.

RIPPLE, CIRCUIT JUDGE, with whom FLAUM, CIRCUIT JUDGE, joins, concurring in part and dissenting in part.

* * *

CUMMINGS, CIRCUIT JUDGE, with whom CUDAHY, CIRCUIT JUDGE, joins, dissenting.

Disagreeing with the majority's conclusion that the actions of the defendants in committing Spencer to St. Elizabeth Hospital necessarily cannot constitute state action, I respectfully dissent from the majority's holding.

* * *

Spencer has clearly articulated a sufficient liberty interest in his allegations of involuntary commitment and treatment during his detention at St. Elizabeth Hospital. The only issue remaining is whether the actions of Dr. Lee and St. Elizabeth Hospital implicate state action.

I.   INVOLUNTARY COMMITMENT

A.   *Function of the State*

The involuntary commitment of an individual believed to be a danger to himself or others without a judicial hearing is no doubt one of the most severe infringements of personal liberty. However, the state has power to cause such a deprivation acting pursuant to its *parens patriae* power to protect and provide care for the mentally ill. *Addington v. Texas,* 441 U.S. at 426, 99 S.Ct. at 1809. Although neither Dr. Lee nor St. Elizabeth Hospital is a state employee, the state action component may be fulfilled if their actions may be "fairly attributable to the state." *Lugar,* 457 U.S. at 939, 102 S.Ct. at 2755. The test of "fair attribution" involves two elements where a private party is alleged to be a state actor: First, the deprivation must be caused by the exercise of some right or privilege created by the State or by a rule of conduct imposed by the State or by a person for whom the State is responsible. . . . Second, the party charged with the deprivation must be a person who may fairly be said to be a state actor. *Lugar* at 937, 102 S.Ct. at 2753–2754. The Supreme Court explained further that mere action by a private party pursuant to a statute without "something more" will not transform the private party into a state actor. The "something more" necessary to convert the private activity into state action varies with the factual circumstances, resulting in correspondingly varied tests: the "public function" test, the "state compulsion" test, the "nexus" test, and the "joint action" test. *Lugar* at 939, 102 S.Ct. at 2754–2755.

* * *

As support for its decision, the majority traces the historical roots of involuntary commitment, concluding that since the commitment of the mentally ill has never been the exclusive prerogative or traditional function of the state, it is not state action when performed by a private entity. However interesting this history lesson may be, the more relevant question for determining whether state action exists is not whether private citizens were capable of unilaterally committing the mentally ill in the days when Bedlam existed in England, but whether under the present law private citizens are capable of depriving individuals of their liberty to the same extent as may the state or whether the state has a superior, unique authority to deprive individuals of liberty in this manner, an authority not inured in the general citizenry. Indeed, as the majority readily concedes, every public function has an analogous private function in history. The majority's opinion, nonetheless, assumes as a premise of its argument that what constitutes a public function is relatively stagnant over time. It may have been the case that in the time of Bedlam the rights of the mentally ill were not recognized and protected to the same extent they are today, as were the rights of minorities prior to the Thirteenth and Fourteenth Amendments. Illinois has altered the course of history by affirmatively recognizing the rights of the mentally ill through its enactment of Chapter II of the Illinois Mental Health and Developmental Disabilities Code.

* * *

It is clear from the statutory framework that no private individual may commit a patient to a mental health institution for treatment on an emergency basis without a prior determination by a qualified physician or mental health facility that the patient warrants confinement. In the commitment procedure, the physician's certificate serves a quasi-judicial function correlative to an arrest warrant issued by a judge authorizing the seizure of a suspect. This Court recognized the nature of the physician's function in the commitment process in *Byrne,* 347 F.2d at 736, where doctors, who were members of a court-appointed committee, were held to have performed a quasi-judicial function in examining and recommending commitment of the patient. Under the Illinois mental health code, the state has delegated its adjudicatory determination in the emergency context to the physician, empowering the physician to use the force of state law enforcement agencies to confine any individual the physician determines to be in need of emergency commitment.

* * *

B. Participation of State Officials

* * *

In his *pro se* complaint, as indicated by the majority opinion, Spencer does not specifically allege a "conspiracy" with police officers in his emergency involuntary commitment at St. Elizabeth Hospital. Indeed, it would be surprising if a *pro se* plaintiff with a history of mental illness had sufficient working knowledge of the law to plead the legal phrases which compose the elements of a Section 1983 action. The Court should not penalize Spencer for his inartfully pleaded complaints and subsequent motions. Nonetheless, the majority summarily disposes of this claim due to Spencer's inability to name police officers as defendants or mention the involvement of the police with sufficient frequency. Given the Court's obligation to construe Spencer's complaint liberally and dismiss the complaint only if he can prove no set of facts which would entitle him to relief, Spencer has sufficiently alleged the involvement of the Danville Police Department to sustain defendants' motion to dismiss.

* * *

[T]he mere presence of the police while Spencer was detained at St. Elizabeth Hospital is sufficient participation to constitute state action.

* * *

In my opinion, the judgment should be reversed and the cause remanded for further proceedings.

Questions and Comments

1. *Other decisions. Spencer v. Lee* has been followed by the Eleventh Circuit, which also rejected the finding of state action in the context of an involuntary commitment to a private psychiatric facility. *Harvey v. Harvey*, 949 F.2d 1127 (11th Cir. 1992).

However, a Second Circuit District Court decision in *Rubenstein v. Benedictine Hospital*, 790 F.Supp. 396 (N.D.N.Y. 1992), held that the actions by a private hospital emergency room physician who involuntarily hospitalized the plaintiff constituted state action, and therefore, Section 1983 could be invoked as basis for relief. In reaching this conclusion, the court noted that the emergency room physician was a 'designee' of the county director of community services and that as a 'designee,' the physician was empowered to take custody, detain and transport a patient after signing an application for involuntary commitment as well as direct peace officer to take into custody and transport a patient.

In *Ruhlmann v. Ulster County Dept. of Social Services*, 234 F.Supp.2d 140 (N.D.N.Y. 2002), the court in denying the defendants' motion for

Summary Judgment held that the determination of whether a private physician should be characterized a "state actor" is a fact specific inquiry. In making this determination, courts "typically look at such factors as the public function of the party's conduct, where the party acted under state compulsion and whether the party's action was jointly taken with the state". Id. at 160.

2. *State funding of private facilities.* Would the "under color of law" requirement be met if the mental health professional who is the object of a § 1983 action was employed by a private non-profit mental health center which receives 85% of its funding from state agencies and the rest from fees? See, *Rendell–Baker v. Kohn,* 457 U.S. 830, 102 S.Ct. 2764, 73 L.Ed.2d 418 (1982).

3. *The deprivation of federal rights requirement.* Section 1983 is intended to protect the patient from "the deprivation of any rights, privileges, or immunities secured by the Constitution and laws" 42 U.S.C. § 1983. The statute covers only violations of rights guaranteed by the federal Constitution and federal laws and not those guaranteed by state law.

Two kinds of constitutional rights are protected by the Civil Rights Statutes: substantive rights and procedural rights. Substantive rights include those guaranteed by the Bill of Rights. Procedural rights are those protected by the due process clause of the Fourteenth Amendment. As might be expected, one of the most common procedurally grounded claims in the mental health treatment context involves irregularities in civil commitment. In fact, a violation may occur even when the psychiatric admission was ostensibly voluntary. For instance, in *Zinermon v. Burch,* 494 U.S. 113, 110 S.Ct. 975, 108 L.Ed.2d 100 (1990), the Supreme Court held that a valid § 1983 claim was stated where the claimant charged that state officials knew or should have known that he was incompetent to give informed consent to his psychiatric admission. His admission under these circumstances, according to the Court, denied him his constitutionally guaranteed procedural rights.

The imposition or the withholding of treatment may give grounds to an action under § 1983. In *Knecht v. Gillman,* 488 F.2d 1136 (8th Cir.1973) [set out at pp. 999–1002], the plaintiff had been an inmate in a mental institution where the patients were given apomorphine, a drug that induces vomiting, when they violated hospital rules by, for example, swearing or lying. The court found that this use of apomorphine was not an accepted nor recognized form of treatment and that the use of this drug on an involuntary basis was cruel and inhuman punishment. The physician responsible for its administration was held liable in a civil rights action brought by the patient. In *Philipp v. Carey,* 517 F.Supp. 513 (N.D.N.Y.1981), the plaintiffs were mentally retarded voluntary residents of a state mental health facility, who complained that they were being given debilitating psychotropic drugs as a substitute for treatment and rehabilitation. The court found a § 1983 cause of action. Based on a violation of Section 504 of the Rehabilitation Act, a federal law prohibiting the denial of benefits to handicapped persons by a facility receiving federal funding. 29 U.S.C. § 794.

A mentally ill patient may also attack the conditions of his confinement through a civil rights action. In *Jobson v. Henne,* 355 F.2d 129 (2d Cir.1966), the patient was assigned uncompensated work for up to sixteen hours a day. The work was not part of a therapy program, nor was it related to the patient's housekeeping needs. The court held that this stated a possible cause of action as a violation of the patient's Thirteenth Amendment right (freedom from involuntary servitude). *Jobson v. Henne* and related Thirteenth Amendment issues are discussed in greater detail at pp. 1158–60.

Other conditions of a patient's confinement may give rise to a civil rights action against a mental health professional. In *Gerrard v. Blackman,* 401 F.Supp. 1189 (N.D.Ill.1975), the court held that a psychiatrist who monitored an involuntary patient's calls to her attorney could be subject to a possible civil rights action. In *Jones v. Superintendent,* 370 F.Supp. 488 (W.D.Va.1974), the court refused to find a civil rights violation where the patient who was a vegetarian for religious reasons had been denied a special diet. The plaintiff was unable to show any physical injury, however, and the case suggests that an action might lie where there is such harm.

4. *Negligent deprivation of rights.* Whether negligent deprivations are actionable under § 1983 is not entirely clear. The U.S. Supreme Court has consistently rejected any state of mind requirement for section 1983. In *Daniels v. Williams,* 474 U.S. 327, 106 S.Ct. 662, 88 L.Ed.2d 662 (1986), however, the Court held that lack of due care by a state official could not "deprive" a person of life, liberty, or property under the fourteenth amendment. Thus, after *Daniels,* it is clear that a section 1983 action is not available where the plaintiff alleges only that he was negligently deprived of liberty or property without due process. The Court offered no guidance as to whether a person can be negligently deprived of a substantive right which has been incorporated into the Fourteenth Amendment. Additionally, *Daniels* leaves open the question of whether a state of mind short of intent, such as recklessness or gross negligence, is sufficient to violate the due process clause.

5. *Immunity under § 1983.* The need to give decision makers relative freedom to exercise discretionary judgment has caused the Supreme Court to interpret § 1983 to provide officials sued under the Act with qualified immunity similar to that described in section II.A.d., Sovereign Immunity, supra. As a result, a plaintiff will not prevail in a § 1983 action unless the defendant's conduct violated "clearly established statutory or constitutional rights which a reasonable person would have known". *Harlow v. Fitzgerald,* 457 U.S. 800, 818, 102 S.Ct. 2727, 2738, 73 L.Ed.2d 396 (1982).

6. *Other civil rights statutes.* Although most psychiatric civil rights actions are brought under § 1983, two other sections should be noted. The first is 42 U.S.C. § 1985. This section is very similar to § 1983, but provides a remedy for a conspiracy to violate civil rights. The second is 18 U.S.C. § 242, which provides for criminal sanctions for a violation of civil rights by one acting under color of state law. The major difference between the civil and criminal statutes is intent. Criminal law generally is based on the assumption that the wrongdoer understands that he is doing something wrong and that he should be punished. Civil law, on the other hand, is simply a method of allocating losses. The intent requirement, therefore, in a criminal civil rights action is more stringent, and, indeed, the statute itself declares that the deprivation must be "willful." The U.S. Supreme Court has

interpreted this to mean that the act must be done intentionally and with the specific intent to deprive the victim of a constitutional right. *Screws v. United States,* 325 U.S. 91, 65 S.Ct. 1031, 89 L.Ed. 1495 (1945). If, for example, the supervising psychiatrist of a mental hospital knew that a patient was sane and not dangerous, yet refused to authorize the patient's discharge, the psychiatrist could be held guilty of a criminal violation of the patient's rights.

Chapter Four

INFORMED CONSENT

I. INTRODUCTION

The fundamental principle that every person should have the right to determine what should be done with his/her body has deep-seated roots in our jurisprudence. In 1914 Justice Cardozo affirmed this basic right in *Schloendorff v. Society of New York Hospital*, 211 N.Y. 125, 129–130, 105 N.E. 92, 93 (1914), in the following terms:

> Every human being of adult years and sound mind has a right to determine what shall be done with his own body; and a surgeon who

performs an operation without his patient's consent commits an assault, for which he is liable in damages.

For many years, however, the right of self-determination was honored more in the abstract than in reality. It is only relatively recently that the right has been given meaningful expression by courts and legislatures. The Supreme Court's 1973 disposition of the abortion cases provides the most dramatic evidence of this shift. Acknowledging the primacy of a woman's right to terminate an unwanted pregnancy, the Court rested its holding on the basic principle that every person has the right to determine what happens to his or her body.

This growing recognition of the individual's right to bodily self-determination can also be seen in another line of cases, those dealing with the prerogative of self-decision as to medical treatment. A limited right to self-determination had been a traditional part of our jurisprudence for many years. Courts were quite prepared, even before the turn of the century, to classify as a battery the rendering of medical treatment that involved a touching performed without the patient's approval or consent. The consent necessary to immunize the physician from liability was, however, very limited and required nothing more than the patient's general agreement to the proposed treatment. The patient had no recognized right to receive comprehensible information about the treatment's risks. Thus, a physician would escape liability if the patient agreed to treatment, even if the patient was totally unaware of the risks it involved.

Only since 1960 has the doctrine of consent emerged as something more than a mere technicality. In a series of cases decided in the early 1960's various state courts ruled that the patient could not give meaningful consent unless he had received adequate information about the risks of the therapy and any available alternative treatments. The courts found that consent based on inaccurate or incomplete information deprived the patient of the right to charter his own course as to treatment and use of his body.

The doctrine of informed consent in its present form comprises two separate elements. One involves the duty of *disclosure* of relevant information to the patient; the other pertains to the patient's *consent* to the proposed therapy. There is disagreement, however, on both the precise doctrinal source of this right as well as its actual scope and dimension. As the materials in this chapter make clear, in some jurisdictions informed consent is subsumed under the doctrine of assault and battery. In others, violations of this right are treated as a form of professional negligence. The implications of these different approaches are explored in the materials that follow.

It is important to note that the doctrine of informed consent pertains exclusively to medical-treatment situations. Moreover, until recently, its application was limited to physically intrusive treatment modalities such as ECT or psychopharmacology. Its extension to psychotherapy is a relatively recent phenomenon, largely associated with the litigation involving recovered memory therapy, which is discussed in Chapter 3.

Two reasons may explain why the doctrine has until very recently been limited to intrusive biological therapies. One relates to the peculiarities of the law of damages. In some jurisdictions, recovery of monetary damages requires that the injured party has suffered physical injury. Such injury is, of course, a more likely outcome of surgery or psychopharmacology than of conventional psychotherapy.

Thus, in some states, absent physical injury, the lack of informed consent to psychiatric or psychological treatment precludes recovery for damages. In recent years, however, courts have demonstrated a marked tendency to expand compensation for non-physical injuries in tort law. A continuation of this trend could result in exposing psychotherapists to an increased risk of liability under the doctrine of informed consent even where the injury is not physical.

There is, however, an additional but related problem in application of the doctrine to the field of psychotherapy. A cause of action predicated on the lack of informed consent requires that the patient's injury be the direct and proximate cause of the treatment. This element of proof becomes increasingly difficult if an injury is not immediately identifiable as the direct consequence of the treatment. This point is illustrated by the following hypothetical fact situation. A patient feels that she is not advancing in her job as her intellectual potential might dictate due to excessive passivity and an inability to direct subordinates. On the therapist's recommendation, the patient agrees to undergo assertiveness training, but is not informed that such training may alter personal relationships. The training is successful to the extent that the patient has become more assertive and better able to cope in the work place; however, her husband is unable to adjust to her new and more assertive personality and tensions in the marriage cause it to break up. Theoretically, the patient could assert that she would have not consented to the therapy had she been informed of the risks. In this situation the patient faces the significant difficulty of proving both that the psychotherapy in fact led to the personality change and that this was the proximate cause of the failure of her marriage. While this burden of proof might not be altogether impossible to meet, it presents problems far more formidable than demonstrating that a particular physical injury was the direct and proximate cause of a surgical procedure. In spite of the various doctrinal and practical difficulties, it is likely that the concept of informed consent will increasingly be applied to non-biological treatment situations. The field of psychological research, which has in the past been all too often characterized by a widespread disregard of any notion of informed consent, would seem particularly vulnerable to this form of legal regulation.

For those professionals whose activities are covered by the doctrine of informed consent, the impact can be formidable. Under this doctrine the possibility of civil liability no longer hinges on a departure from the exercise of reasonable skill in providing treatment. Rather, professionals can face liability even when the treatment was flawless. Recovery for the patient or research subject is predicated solely on the lack of appropriate consent to treatment. The following materials provide an overview of the doctrine's current development. Keep in mind, however, that the doctrine is still in an evolutionary stage, and that some issues, particularly in the context of research, remain to be resolved.

II. ORIGINS OF THE DOCTRINE OF INFORMED CONSENT

The doctrine of informed consent was ushered in by two cases decided in the early 1960's. *Natanson v. Kline*, 186 Kan. 393, 350 P.2d 1093 (1960), clarified, 187 Kan. 186, 354 P.2d 670 (1960) and the more influential case of *Mitchell v. Robinson*, 334 S.W.2d 11 (Mo.1960).

In *Mitchell v. Robinson*, which involved the failure to disclose the risk of bone fractures in the use of insulin and electro-shock therapy, the court held that "a doctor owes a duty to his patient to make reasonable disclosure of all significant facts: a doctor who fails to perform this duty is guilty of malpractice." Prior to these cases, courts typically treated problems of consent as interlocked with the law of assault and battery, which insulated the physician from liability if the patient assented to a particular medical procedure. Adequate information was not a necessary component of a binding consent. The particular significance of the *Mitchell* and *Natanson* cases, and to some extent such earlier cases as *Salgo v. Leland Stanford Jr. University Board of Trustees*, 154 Cal. App.2d 560, 317 P.2d 170 (1957), is the courts' recognition that a patient's consent cannot be meaningful or binding unless it is based upon sufficient information concerning the risks of the treatment. It is important to note that while a clear majority of states have accepted the *Mitchell–Natanson* approach, it has not been universally adopted. The trend, however, is clearly toward a general recognition of the therapist's duty to provide adequate information.

Questions and Comments

1. *Battery as a basis for recovery.* Numerous cases, some decided as early as the beginning of the century, used a theory of battery to impose liability on physicians who performed medical procedures without the patient's authorization. Typically, these cases involved one of two basic fact situations. In one the physician performed a medical or surgical procedure different than the one authorized by the patient. For instance, in *Hively v. Higgs,* 120 Or. 588, 253 P. 363 (1927), a surgeon who during an operation on a patient's nose also removed the patient's tonsils was held liable for battery. Similarly, a dentist who had been authorized to extract two teeth, but removed eight while the patient was under sodium pentathol, was held liable in battery. *Moore v. Webb,* 345 S.W.2d 239 (Mo.App.1961).

The second situation leading to liability has involved the performance of a procedure consented to by the patient, but on a different part of the body than the patient had authorized. For instance, in *Mohr v. Williams,* 95 Minn. 261, 104 N.W. 12 (1905), the physician initially diagnosed the patient's right ear as requiring surgery (an ossiculectomy). The patient consented to undergo the recommended procedure, but during the operation the surgeon discovered a more serious defect in the left ear and performed an ossiculectomy on that instead. The court found that these facts established a basis for liability under a theory of battery. It is important to note, however, that in none of these early cases was liability predicated on the physician's failure to disclose information about collateral risks inherent in the treatment. Moreover, the physician could establish a complete defense with evidence that he had informed the patient of the planned procedure and that the patient had authorized the proposed treatment.

2. *Alternate theories.* The modern doctrine of informed consent has been applied under different doctrinal headings. Some courts have chosen to view the failure to inform as vitiating any technical consent which might have been given, thus rendering the physician liable for assault and battery. More commonly, however, courts have characterized violations of the duty to inform as giving rise to an action based on negligence. A few jurisdictions have permitted the plaintiff-patient to proceed on both a negligence and an assault and battery rationale. *See, e.g., Belcher v. Carter,* 13 Ohio App.2d 113, 234 N.E.2d 311 (1967).

Whether a jurisdiction appends informed consent to the doctrine of assault and battery rather than negligence is of more than theoretical interest and can have important practical implications for the litigants. At least four major consequences can follow the choice of one doctrine over the other. First, negligence actions generally are subject to a longer statute of limitations than those based on a theory of battery. A court's decision to subsume informed consent under battery may preclude a lawsuit that was still viable under the state's statute of limitations for negligence.

Second, the burden of proof imposed on the respective parties may vary with the theory chosen. For instance, when the action is based on battery, it is easier for the plaintiff to recover without introducing expert testimony to establish the prevailing medical practice as to the scope of disclosure. A full explanation of this point is provided in the notes following *Canterbury v. Spence,* 464 F.2d 772 (D.C.Cir.1972), which appears in the next section.

Third, the measure of damages may depend on which theory is utilized. Since battery is an intentional tort, the plaintiff may be able to recover punitive damages, particularly if he can show an element of malice. Also, under the battery theory the plaintiff may receive nominal damages even without a showing of actual injury. In negligence actions, on the other hand, damages are ordinarily awarded only in relation to the injuries actually suffered.

Fourth, under the terms of malpractice insurance policies, the defendant physician or therapist might not be covered if the action alleges battery, since intentional torts are specifically excluded in some policies.

III. ELEMENTS OF THE DOCTRINE OF INFORMED CONSENT

A. THE DISCLOSURE REQUIREMENT

1. *Standards Governing the Scope of Disclosure*

As indicated in the preceding section, the doctrine of informed consent requires that the therapist disclose the collateral risks of the proposed treatment. However, a rule framed in these general terms leaves two issues unanswered. First, must there be disclosure of every risk, or is it sufficient if the physician informs the patient of only the more significant and probable adverse consequences? Second, is the adequacy of disclosure to be judged by what the medical profession regards as appropriate in the particular circumstances or by some other standard? The cases which follow represent two divergent approaches to the latter question.

AIKEN v. CLARY

Supreme Court of Missouri, 1965.
396 S.W.2d 668.

FINCH, JUDGE.

Plaintiff went to trial on Count III of a malpractice action wherein he alleged negligence of defendant in failing sufficiently to advise plaintiff of the hazards and risks involved in insulin shock therapy to enable plaintiff to give an informed consent for the treatment. Plaintiff alleged that as a result of such therapy administered by defendant he was caused to lapse into a coma and to suffer organic brain damage, resulting in total disability. He sought recovery of $150,000. The jury returned a verdict for defendant. After an unavailing motion for new trial, plaintiff appealed to this court.

* * * We proceed * * * to examine the evidence, which, insofar as pertinent to this assignment and viewed most favorably to plaintiff, was as follows:

After military service from 1941 to 1945 plaintiff entered employment of the Frisco Railroad, ultimately serving as an electrician in the diesel engine department. Early in 1961 plaintiff became irritable and "changed almost his entire personality." He was cross with the children, particularly a teen-age daughter, spent money on things for which he had never spent money before, and had trouble sleeping so that he lost a great amount of sleep and rest. His wife discussed with him the matter of seeing a doctor, but he maintained that his wife needed a doctor as much as he did, and that it was she who was "way out in left field." He agreed to see a doctor if she would, and they then consulted Dr. Lewis E. Jorel of Springfield, who previously had treated their daughter.

Following conferences by the doctor with both plaintiff and his wife, plaintiff entered St. John's Hospital at Springfield, Missouri, on June 3, 1961, for a complete physical examination.

[Following the administration of various tests and procedures, the plaintiff was found to have no physical disorder. Plaintiff was referred to Dr. Clary for a psychiatric examination. Dr. Clary diagnosed plaintiff as suffering from paranoid schizophrenia, and recommended both electric and insulin shock therapy. After consulting both his wife and his family physician, plaintiff gave his consent to ECT and insulin therapy.]

With respect to the information given by Dr. Clary to plaintiff in these conversations as to the nature of the treatment and the risks involved, plaintiff offered in evidence certain statements of the defendant given in an earlier deposition. That testimony was as follows:

"Q. When you talked to him previous to the moving down to psychiatry and signing the release, did you tell him what the possible effects of insulin shock therapy might be?

"A. I told him it would put him to sleep, I told him there was risks involved, I told him the same thing about electric shock therapy. I didn't belabor the point, I told him it was risky because this guy was real shook, but I told him it was risky, and he had no questions.

"Q. Did you tell him it might possibly result in his death?

"A. I implied it. In talking about the anesthetic, I said people take anesthetic, and there are hazards. Some people over-react to anesthetics, and insulin, I told him, it is like being put to sleep, there are risks involved. In terms of specifically telling him, 'This can kill you,' no, sir, I didn't.

"Q. Did you tell him it might possibly result in a delayed awakening, possible brain damage?

"A. No, I didn't tell him that."

Dr. Clary testified that he thought the plaintiff had the mental capacity at least to understand the ordinary affairs of life, understand what the treatment really was and what it might do to him. He again related what he had told plaintiff and stated that he tried to explain it to him on a level he would understand, and he thought plaintiff knew exactly what he was getting into. At the second conference between Dr. Clary and plaintiff, the latter agreed to take whatever treatment Dr. Clary recommended.

Accordingly, on June 9, 1961, a nurse in the psychiatric ward presented to plaintiff a form of "Consent to Shock Therapy." It read as follows: "I (We) hereby request and authorize Dr. Clary and whomever he may designate to assist him, to administer insulin and/or electroshock therapy to Mr. Aiken; and to continue to administer such therapy and such other supplemental treatment as he may deem advisable from time to time. The effect and nature of shock and/or insulin treatment have been fully explained to me (us), as well as the hazards involved. Notwithstanding the fact that there are risks to the patient inherent in this treatment, I (we) voluntarily accept the risks involved. No assurance has been made by anyone with respect to the results that may be obtained. I have been given a copy of the pamphlet 'Information to Relatives.' " The nurse testified that she did not explain anything about the dangers involved in the therapy when she presented the consent for signature. The plaintiff read the consent in her presence and she asked him if he had any questions, but he had none and he signed the consent.

Beginning on June 12, 1961, and continuing through June 22, 1961, plaintiff was given a series of shock treatments which involved insulin in increasing amounts of from 40 to 260 units. On June 22, 1961, plaintiff went into a deep coma. He suffered a delayed awakening from the insulin and did not respond to the procedures used for the purpose of bringing the patient out of the coma. A specialist in internal medicine was called in and plaintiff was transferred to the intensive care unit but the coma was prolonged and as a result plaintiff suffered brain damage.

Dr. Robert L. Lam, M.D., a specialist in neurology and psychiatry, testified for plaintiff that from an examination made by him at the Veterans Hospital in Little Rock, Arkansas, on January 16, 1964, his opinion was that plaintiff had severe organic brain damage, that he was totally incapacitated in terms of employment and that his condition was permanent as a result of the prolonged insulin coma. Plaintiff was still in the Veterans Hospital at the time of trial.

Dr. Lam was interrogated as to dangers in insulin shock therapy and he testified that the possible dangers or complications thereof are coma and death or prolonged coma resulting in various degrees of brain damage, or that there might be the production of epilepsy or localized paralysis, or there might be a vascular disturbance. In addition, he said that with convulsions that may occur one could have fractures of certain types, either of the vertebrae or the extremities. The doctor was not asked and did not undertake to testify as to the frequency of occurrence of such events, or any of them, and said that no doctor could predict which patient would be the one to have trouble, saying, "So that the only thing one can say is that, when one has a patient getting deep coma insulin, that there is a possibility that this could occur." Dr. Lam also testified that there was nothing improper in the administration of the insulin shock therapy and that the administration thereof was according to good medical practice. Dr. Lam was not asked about the adequacy of defendant's disclosures to plaintiff.

* * *

Defendant first asserts that plaintiff failed to make a submissible case because he failed to offer any expert medical evidence as to what a reasonably careful and prudent physician engaged in similar practice would do under the same or similar circumstances with respect to disclosure of risks involved in the proposed therapy. There is no dispute but that plaintiff did not offer any expert testimony on this matter of what a reasonably prudent practitioner would disclose. We must determine, therefore, whether plaintiff is required to offer such proof in order to make a submissible case.

The basic philosophy in malpractice cases is that the doctor is negligent by reason of the fact that he has failed to adhere to a standard of reasonable medical care, and that consequently the service rendered was substandard and negligent. In our judgment, this is true whether the alleged malpractice consists of improper care and treatment (the usual malpractice case) or whether it is based, as here, on an alleged failure to inform the patient sufficiently to enable him to make a judgment and give an informed consent if he concludes to accept the recommended treatment.

How, then, is a jury to determine whether a physician has been negligent in failing to inform his patient adequately to enable him to make an informed decision whether to consent to recommended treatment? What proof must a plaintiff offer? Obviously, in addition to evidence as to plaintiff's condition and the treatment proposed and administered, there must be testimony as to what risks are involved and what disclosures were made by the doctor. These necessarily are a part of plaintiff's case. Such evidence was offered by plaintiff in this case. The real issue here is whether plaintiff is required to go further and as a part of his case offer evidence as to a standard of medical conduct with reference to disclosures by the physician to his patient or whether this is a matter which the jury may decide without such expert testimony. There are cases from some states which hold that such expert testimony is necessary as a part of plaintiff's case and cases from other states holding that such evidence is not required.

* * *

We have reexamined this question and have concluded that the question of what disclosure of risks incident to proposed treatment should be made in a particular situation involves medical judgment and that expert testimony thereon should be required in malpractice cases involving that issue. The question to be determined by the jury is whether defendant doctor in that particular situation failed to adhere to a standard of reasonable care. These are not matters of common knowledge or within the experience of laymen. Expert medical evidence thereon is just as necessary as is such testimony on the correctness of the handling in cases involving surgery or treatment.

* * *

[Expert testimony as to the appropriate of the level of disclosure required in a particular case would need to take into account such factors as] the state of the patient's health, the condition of his heart and nervous system, his mental state, and * * * among other things, whether the risks involved were mere remote possibilities or something which occurred with some sort of frequency or regularity. This determination involves medical judgment as to whether disclosure of possible risks may have such an adverse effect on the patient as to jeopardize success of the proposed therapy, no matter how expertly performed. (Defendant in this case testified that plaintiff was "real shook.") After a consideration of these and other proper factors, a reasonable medical practitioner, under some circumstances, would make full disclosure of all risks which had any reasonable likelihood of occurring, but in others the facts and circumstances would dictate a guarded or limited disclosure. In some cases the judgment would be less difficult than in others, but, in any event, it would be a medical judgment.

* * *

Accordingly, we hold that plaintiff, in order to sustain his burden of proof, is required to offer expert testimony to show what disclosures a reasonable medical practitioner, under the same or similar circumstances, would have made, or, stated another way, that the disclosures as made by the defendant do not meet the standard of what a reasonable medical practitioner would have disclosed under the same or similar circumstances. To whatever extent *Mitchell v. Robinson* is inconsistent with the views herein expressed, it is disapproved.

Once plaintiff has offered sufficient proof to make a submissible case, including the required expert testimony which we have discussed, then the ultimate determination of whether defendant did or did not fail to disclose to plaintiff in accordance with the standard of what a reasonable medical practitioner would have done is a jury question under proper instructions from the court.

* * *

In view of the fact that plaintiff made no offering of any expert testimony relative to the extent of disclosure a reasonable medical practitioner would have made under the same or similar circumstances, he failed to make a submissible case for the jury. However, we will not affirm this case on that basis for the reason that counsel for plaintiff asserted in the presentation of the case that in the case of Mitchell v. Robinson, supra, this court had stated that expert testimony is not necessary in cases involving extent of duty to warn, and that he relied thereon in offering no proof of that character. In the light of language used in the opinion of *Mitchell v. Robinson,* supra, it was reasonable for counsel to assume the lack of a requirement of such testimony in this case. Under those circumstances, we feel compelled to reverse and remand for a new trial in order to afford plaintiff an opportunity to offer expert testimony on the standard of disclosure required.

* * *

The judgment is reversed and the cause remanded for a new trial.

All of the Judges concur.

Questions and Comments

1. *Comment on Aiken.* Note that although the *Aiken* court sustained the defendant's legal argument, it reversed the judgment in defendant's favor and remanded the case for retrial. The court reached this unusual outcome on the basis that the plaintiff's lawyer had reasonably relied on the

Mitchell v. Robinson opinion, which did not signal any requirement that a plaintiff must present expert testimony on the question of whether medical practitioners would make disclosures in similar circumstances. Normally when an attorney errs in this way, appellate courts are less forgiving than the *Aiken* court, and the client is precluded from a second opportunity to litigate the case.

2. *Role of practitioner in determining scope of disclosure.* Under *Aiken v. Clary*, a medical practitioner, or other professional, involved in treatment are only required to disclose those risks that "a reasonable medical practitioner under the same or similar circumstances would have made". Thus, the scope of mandated disclosure is to be judged by the same standard as is applied where the medical practitioner is being charged with malpractice. The critical issue in such cases is whether the actions of the practitioner deviated from the ordinary standards of care.

Does this standard reflect an appropriate compromise between the patient's interests in receiving sufficient information upon which to base the decision to accept or reject treatment and the interest of the medical profession in being able to carry out its professional function without undue risk of liability?

3. *Need for expert testimony.* Since liability will only attach under the *Aiken v. Clary* formulation where there has been a deviation from the prevailing professional standards, in order to prevail, a plaintiff must introduce expert testimony on the question of whether medical practitioners generally would make disclosure of a particular risk in the same or similar circumstances.

4. *Privilege to withhold information.* Can a patient's fragile mental state be a legally sufficient basis for withholding information pertaining to risk from a patient? The scope of what is known as the privilege of non-disclosure is covered in greater detail in Section 2, *infra*, "Exceptions to the Duty to Disclose".

5. *Alternative to the ordinary practitioner "standard".* The case of *Canterbury v. Spence*, which follows, established an alternate test, which serves to de-emphasize the role of the medical profession in defining the boundaries of what risks must be disclosed.

CANTERBURY v. SPENCE

United States Court of Appeals, District of Columbia Circuit, 1972.
464 F.2d 772.

Spottswood W. Robinson, III, Circuit Judge:

This appeal is from a judgment entered in the District Court on verdicts directed for the two appellees at the conclusion of plaintiff-appellant Canterbury's case in chief. His action sought damages for personal injuries allegedly sustained as a result of an operation negligently performed by appellee Spence, a negligent failure by Dr. Spence to disclose a risk of serious disability inherent in the operation, and negligent post-operative care by appellee Washington Hospital Center. On close examination of the record, we find evidence which required submission of these issues to the jury. We accordingly reverse the judgment as to each appellee and remand the case to the District Court for a new trial.

[In 1958, at the age of 19, appellant sought medical attention for severe pain between his shoulder blades. After tests revealed a "filling defect" in appellant's spine, Dr. Spence told the appellant that he required surgery to repair what Dr. Spence suspected was a ruptured disc. The surgery revealed a swollen spinal cord, dilated veins, and an absence of fat surrounding the spine. Dr. Spence attempted to relieve the pressure by surgically enlarging the outer wall of the spinal cord.

The day after surgery, the appellant fell off of his bed while voiding unassisted by hospital personnel. Several hours later he was virtually paralyzed from the waist down. Dr. Spence reopened the surgical wound "to allow the spinal cord greater room in which to pulsate". At the time of his 1968 trial, the appellant required crutches to walk, and still suffered from urine incontinence and paralysis of the bowels.

The damages claimed by appellant included pain and suffering, medical expenses, and loss of earnings.]

* * *

II

Appellant filed suit in the District Court on March 7, 1963, four years after the laminectomy and approximately two years after he attained his majority. The complaint stated several causes of action against each defendant. Against Dr. Spence it alleged, among other things, negligence in the performance of the laminectomy and failure to inform him beforehand of the risk involved. Against the hospital the * * * answers denied the allegations of negligence.

* * *

Appellant introduced no evidence to show medical and hospital practices, if any, customarily pursued in regard to the critical aspects of the case, and only Dr. Spence, called as an adverse witness, testified on the issue of causality. Dr. Spence described the surgical procedures he utilized in the two operations and expressed his opinion that appellant's disabilities stemmed from his pre-operative condition as symptomized by the swollen, non-pulsating spinal cord. * * * Dr. Spence further testified that even without trauma paralysis can be anticipated "somewhere in the nature of one percent" of the laminectomies performed, a risk he termed "a very slight possibility." He felt that communication of that risk to the patient is not good medical practice because it might deter patients from undergoing needed surgery and might produce adverse psychological reactions which could preclude the success of the operation.

At the close of appellant's case in chief, each defendant moved for a directed verdict and the trial judge granted both motions. The basis of the ruling, he explained, was that appellant had failed to produce any medical evidence indicating negligence on Dr. Spence's part in diagnosing appellant's malady or in performing the laminectomy; that there was no proof that Dr. Spence's treatment was responsible for appellant's disabilities; * * * The judge did not allude specifically to the alleged breach of duty by Dr. Spence to divulge the possible consequences of the laminectomy.

We reverse. The testimony of appellant and his mother that Dr. Spence did not reveal the risk of paralysis from the laminectomy made out a prima facie case of violation of the physician's duty to disclose which Dr. Spence's explanation did not negate as a matter of law. There was also testimony from which the jury could have found that the laminectomy was negligently performed by Dr. Spence. * * * These considerations entitled appellant to a new trial.

* * *

III

Suits charging failure by a physician adequately to disclose the risks and alternatives of proposed treatment are not innovations in American law. They date back a good half-century, and in the last decade they have multiplied rapidly. There is, nonetheless, disagreement among the courts and the commentators on many major questions, and there is no precedent of our own directly in point. For the tools enabling resolution of the issues on this appeal, we are forced to begin at first principles.

The root premise is the concept, fundamental in American jurisprudence, that "[e]very human being of adult years and sound mind has a right to determine what shall be done with his own body. * * * "True consent to what happens to one's self is the informed exercise of a choice, and that entails an opportunity to evaluate knowledgeably the options available and the risks attendant upon each. The average patient has little or no understanding of the medical arts, and ordinarily has only his physician to whom he can look for enlightenment with which to reach an intelligent decision. From these almost axiomatic considerations springs the need, and in turn the requirement, of a reasonable divulgence by physician to patient to make such a decision possible.

A physician is under a duty to treat his patient skillfully but proficiency in diagnosis and therapy is not the full measure of his responsibility. The cases demonstrate that the physician is under an obligation to communicate specific information to the patient when the exigencies of reasonable care call for it.

* * *

The context in which the duty of risk-disclosure arises is invariably the occasion for decision as to whether a particular treatment procedure is to be undertaken. To the physician, whose training enables a self-satisfying evaluation, the answer may seem clear, but it is the prerogative of the patient, not the physician, to determine for himself the direction in which his interests seem to lie. To enable the patient to chart his course understandably, some familiarity with the therapeutic alternatives and their hazards becomes essential.

* * *

We now find, as a part of the physician's overall obligation to the patient, a similar duty of reasonable disclosure of the choices with respect to proposed therapy and the dangers inherently and potentially involved.[1]

* * *

IV

Duty to disclose has gained recognition in a large number of American jurisdictions, but more largely on a different rationale. The majority of courts dealing with the problem have made the duty depend on whether it was the custom of physicians practicing in the community to make the particular disclosure to the patient. If so, the physician may be held liable for an unreasonable and injurious failure to divulge, but there can be no recovery unless the omission forsakes a practice prevalent in the profession. We agree that the physician's noncompliance with a professional custom to reveal, like any other departure from prevailing medical practice, may give rise to liability to the patient. We do not agree that the patient's cause of action is dependent upon the existence and nonperformance of a relevant professional tradition.

There are, in our view, formidable obstacles to acceptance of the notion that the physician's obligation to disclose is either germinated or limited by medical practice. To begin with, the reality of any discernible custom reflecting a professional consensus on communication of option and risk information to patients is open to serious doubt. We sense the danger that what in fact is no custom at all may be taken as an affirmative custom to maintain silence, and that physician-witnesses to the so-called custom may state merely their personal opinions as to what they or others would do under given conditions. We cannot gloss over the inconsistency between reliance on a general practice respecting divulgence and, on the other hand, realization that the myriad of variables among patients makes each case so different that its omission can rationally be justified only by the effect of its individual circumstances. Nor can we ignore the fact that to bind the disclosure obligation to medical usage is to arrogate the decision on revelation to the physician alone. Respect for the patient's right of self-determination on particular

---

1. Some doubt has been expressed as to ability of physicians to suitably communicate their evaluations of risks and the advantages of optional treatment, and as to the lay patient's ability to understand what the physician tells him. We do not share these apprehensions. The discussion need not be a disquisition, and surely the physician is not compelled to give his patient a short medical education; the disclosure rule summons the physician only to a reasonable explanation. That means generally informing the patient in nontechnical terms as to what is at stake: the therapy alternatives open to him, the goals expectably to be achieved, and the risks that may ensue from particular treatment and no treatment. So informing the patient hardly taxes the physician, and it must be the exceptional patient who cannot comprehend such an explanation at least in a rough way.

therapy demands a standard set by law for physicians rather than one which physicians may or may not impose upon themselves.

* * *

V

Once the circumstances give rise to a duty on the physician's part to inform his patient, the next inquiry is the scope of the disclosure the physician is legally obliged to make. The courts have frequently confronted this problem but no uniform standard defining the adequacy of the divulgence emerges from the decisions. Some have said "full" disclosure, a norm we are unwilling to adopt literally. It seems obviously prohibitive and unrealistic to expect physicians to discuss with their patients every risk of proposed treatment—no matter how small or remote—and generally unnecessary from the patient's viewpoint as well. Indeed, the cases speaking in terms of "full" disclosure appear to envision something less than total disclosure, leaving unanswered the question of just how much.

The larger number of courts, as might be expected, have applied tests framed with reference to prevailing fashion within the medical profession. Some have measured the disclosure by "good medical practice," others by what a reasonable practitioner would have bared under the circumstances, and still others by what medical custom in the community would demand. We have explored this rather considerable body of law but are unprepared to follow it. The duty to disclose, we have reasoned, arises from phenomena apart from medical custom and practice. The latter, we think, should no more establish the scope of the duty than its existence. Any definition of scope in terms purely of a professional standard is at odds with the patient's prerogative to decide on projected therapy himself. That prerogative, we have said, is at the very foundation of the duty to disclose, and both the patient's right to know and the physician's correlative obligation to tell him are diluted to the extent that its compass is dictated by the medical profession.

In our view, the patient's right of self-decision shapes the boundaries of the duty to reveal. That right can be effectively exercised only if the patient possesses enough information to enable an intelligent choice. The scope of the physician's communications to the patient, then, must be measured by the patient's need, and that need is the information material to the decision. Thus the test for determining whether a particular peril must be divulged is its materiality to the patient's decision: all risks potentially affecting the decision must be unmasked. And to safeguard the patient's interest in achieving his own determination on treatment, the law must itself set the standard for adequate disclosure.

* * *

In broad outline, we agree that "[a] risk is thus material when a reasonable person, in what the physician knows or should know to be the patient's position, would be likely to attach significance to the risk or cluster of risks in deciding whether or not to forego the proposed therapy."

The topics importantly demanding a communication of information are the inherent and potential hazards of the proposed treatment, the alternatives to that treatment, if any, and the results likely if the patient remains untreated. The factors contributing significance to the dangerousness of a medical technique are, of course, the incidence of injury and the degree of the harm threatened. A very small chance of death or serious disablement may well be significant; a potential disability which dramatically outweighs the potential benefit of the therapy or the detriments of the existing malady may summons discussion with the patient.

There is no bright line separating the significant from the insignificant; the answer in any case must abide a rule of reason. Some dangers—infection, for example—are inherent in any operation; there is no obligation to communicate those of which persons of average sophistication are aware. Even more clearly, the physician bears no responsibility for discussion of hazards the patient has already discovered, or those having no apparent materiality to patients' decision on therapy. The disclosure doctrine, like others marking lines between permissible and impermissible behavior in medical practice, is in essence a requirement of conduct prudent under the circumstances. Whenever nondisclosure of particular risk information is open to debate by reasonable-minded men, the issue is for the finder of the facts.

* * *

The guiding consideration our decisions distill, however, is that medical facts are for medical experts and other facts are for any witnesses—expert or not—having sufficient knowledge and capacity to testify to them. It is evident that many of the issues typically involved in nondisclosure cases do not reside peculiarly within the medical domain. Lay witness testimony can competently establish a physician's failure to disclose particular risk information, the patient's lack of knowledge of the risk, and the adverse consequences following the treatment. Experts are unnecessary to a showing of the materiality of a risk to a patient's decision on treatment, or to the reasonably, expectable effect of risk disclosure on the decision. These conspicuous examples of permissible uses of nonexpert testimony illustrate the relative freedom of broad areas of the legal problem of risk nondisclosure from the demands for expert testimony that shackle plaintiffs' other types of medical malpractice litigation.

[The court next determined that the issues of whether the defendant Dr. Spence had performed the laminectomy negligently and whether the hospital was negligent in the aftercare should have been submitted to the jury.]

X

This brings us to the remaining question, common to all three causes of action: whether appellant's evidence was of such caliber as to require a submission to the jury. On the first, the evidence was clearly sufficient to raise an issue as to whether Dr. Spence's obligation to disclose information on risks was reasonably met or was excused by the surrounding circumstances. Appellant testified that Dr. Spence revealed to him nothing suggesting a hazard associated with the laminectomy. His mother testified that, in response to her specific inquiry, Dr. Spence informed her that the laminectomy was no more serious than any other operation. When, at trial, it developed from Dr. Spence's testimony that paralysis can be expected in one percent of laminectomies, it became the jury's responsibility to decide whether that peril was of sufficient magnitude to bring the disclosure duty into play.

[Reversed and remanded for new trial.]

Questions and Comments

1. *Materiality as criterion for liability. Canterbury* defines the breadth of required disclosure to include any risk which either singly or in combination with other risks would be deemed significant by the average patient in deciding whether to accept or forego the therapy. "Materiality" is the shorthand expression of this principle.

2. *Rule in other jurisdictions.* Although the *Clary* and *Spence* courts both anchor the duty of disclosure to the doctrine of negligence, the operational standard by which liability is to be determined is, as noted, very different. There is a split among jurisdictions as to the appropriate standard. As of 1998, at least 14 jurisdictions had adopted the *Canterbury v. Spence* rule. A probable majority of jurisdictions appear to adhere to the more traditional *Aiken v. Clary* standard.

Jurisdictions that have rejected the professional standards rule have done so on the basis that under this standard disclosure "is totally subject to the whim of the physicians in the particular community" and vests the physician "with virtually unlimited discretion in establishing the proper scope of disclosure" and is "inconsistent with the patient's right to self-determination." *Largey v. Rothman,* 110 N.J. 204, 540 A.2d 504 (1988).

Jurisdictions which adhere to the professional standards rule give the following justifications: only physicians can determine the effect that a risk might have on a particular patient; the physician does not have enough time to give all the information patients may request; negligence normally evaluates the conduct of a reasonable actor, not the expectations of a reasonable victim; the physician should not be subjected to the hindsight of the patient and the second guessing of the jury. See B. Furrow, et al., Health Law (1987).

3. *Need for expert testimony.* In contrast to the rule in *Aiken v. Clary,* the *Spence* court would allow a plaintiff to prevail in the absence of expert testimony as to the medical standard of disclosure of a particular risk (or alternate mode of treatment). However, expert testimony would still be necessary to establish that a particular procedure or treatment carries with

it or is associated with it a specified degree of risk. At the same time, under the *Canterbury v. Spence* formulation, a plaintiff would not need to introduce expert testimony to establish that the non-disclosed risk was material, i.e. that it was the kind of risk or cluster of risks that "a reasonable person in . . . the patient's position would be likely to attach significance . . . in deciding whether or not to forego the proposed therapy." The determination of whether a risk that was not disclosed was material would then be a question to be decided by the jury or trier of fact.

4. *Disclosure of alternatives.* To what extent does either the majority or minority view require disclosure of additional alternative therapies? Could a therapist be held liable if he has disclosed all collateral risks of the proposed therapy but has failed to point out alternatives? Does either case speak to this point?

What if the undisclosed alternative involves even greater risk than the actual procedure? Consider *Logan v. Greenwich Hospital Association*, 191 Conn. 282, 465 A.2d 294 (1983). Plaintiff underwent a needle biopsy to obtain a specimen of kidney tissue. The procedure involved inserting a surgical needle into her back, under a local anesthetic, to extract the sample. Plaintiff's gall bladder was punctured during the biopsy, and abdominal surgery was required to remove it. At the time she gave her consent, the plaintiff was unaware of an alternate procedure, an open biopsy, which required an incision under general anesthetic. The defendants testified that the plaintiff was not informed about this alternative because the risk of complications was greater than with a needle biopsy. The trial court instructed the jury that there is a duty to warn of feasible alternatives but that "an alternative that is more hazardous is not a viable alternative." The jury returned a verdict for the defendants. On appeal, the Connecticut Supreme Court reversed. The court reasoned that the instruction was inconsistent with the view that patients must be provided with sufficient information to make an intelligent choice. Connecticut follows the *Canterbury v. Spence* standard. Would the result be different under the *Aiken v. Clary* rule?

5. *Scope of duty to communicate.* What is the therapist's liability for non-disclosure of risk data not known by him/her? In the instance of established therapies, as distinguished from experimental therapies (which are considered separately in section IV, infra), the therapist has a duty to disclose only those risks known to him or that are generally known by a reasonably proficient practitioner. The *Canterbury* court defined this rule in the following terms:

> The category of risks which the physician should communicate is, of course, no broader than the complement [of risk] he could communicate. The duty to divulge may extend to any risk he actually knows, but he obviously cannot divulge any of which he may be unaware.

464 F.2d 772, 787 n. 84 (D.C.Cir.1972).

However, if the therapist is unaware of risks that are generally known by practitioners in the field, non-disclosure could give rise to a claim based on negligence. As noted by the court in *Canterbury:*

> Nondisclosure of an unknown risk does not, strictly speaking, present a problem in terms of the duty to disclose although it very well might pose

problems in terms of the physician's duties to have known of it and to have acted accordingly.

Id.

6. *Temporary aspects of materiality.* Is it possible that the materiality of the risk might change over period of time? For instance, the side effects of a particular medical drug may not be discovered until the drug has been in use for several years. When initially prescribed, the actual risks may have been unknown or perceived as less severe. To what extent does the *Canterbury* approach invite a court to gauge materiality by the state of knowledge prevailing at the time of trial rather than at the time of treatment? Would the *Aiken* requirement of expert testimony lessen this risk?

7. *Evidentiary problems.* When the parties agree on what was communicated, all that must be adjudicated is whether this quantum of information was sufficient. Not infrequently, however, the extent of disclosure will be disputed by the parties. In this situation, the trier of fact must decide what the therapist in fact disclosed by weighing the credibility of the respective parties. Once the factual questions have been resolved, application of the governing legal standard will produce the verdict. This initial stage of fact determination imposes particular stresses on the adjudicatory system. Unless the disclosure has been reduced to writing, the only evidence available is the parties' conflicting testimony. Quite apart from the risk of intentional distortion, there is the possibility of inadvertent distortion, since a witness may be required to recollect the substance of verbal communication that took place several years earlier.

Can therapists protect themselves against claims based on faulty patient recollection of what was disclosed? Is it feasible to make audio recordings of risk disclosure sessions? How long should the recordings be kept? Alternatively, is it feasible to reduce to writing a description of the risks of therapy and require the patient to read and sign such document? These issues are considered in greater detail in the subsection on The Determination of Patient Assent: Evidentiary Problems at pp. 290–97.

8. *Informed consent to psychotherapy.* The imposition of liability on psychotherapists for failure to obtain informed consent has been relatively rare. (But see, *Osheroff v. Chestnut Lodge* and *Burgus v. Rush Presbyterian St. Luke's Medical Center*, discussed *supra* at pp. 140–46, where a lack of informed consent was alleged). This result is undoubtedly explained in large part by the evidentiary problems which would generally confront the patient-plaintiff in the proof of causation and damages. Putting aside these practical difficulties, are there not numerous situations in everyday practice which at least technically violate the rights of the patient to informed consent? To what extent would the doctrine of informed consent require disclosure in the following situations?

(a) There is a substantial body of expert opinion that long-term outpatient psychotherapy involves a significant risk of "negative effects." *See* Hadley & Strupp, 'Contemporary Views of Negative Effects in Psychotherapy,' 33 Archives of General Psychiatry 1291 (1976). Is there any obligation on the part of the therapist to disclose the risks of the potentially negative effects prior to the commencement of a prolonged course of treatment?

(b) In some instances a patient who is close to decompensation may not tolerate intense psychoanalysis. In these cases the risk is that the analysis will in fact trigger decompensation. Must this risk be communicated when, in the analyst's view, there is any reasonable possibility that the analysis will result in decompensation?

(c) An established novelist has for some time suffered from intermittent bouts of anxiety and occasional episodes of depression. The novelist consults an analyst to explore the possibilities of treatment. At the initial interview the patient expresses some fear that successful treatment might detract from or at least reduce his creative abilities. In response to a direct question as to the risks of therapy the therapist answers: "To the extent that your creativity is the result of neurosis, there may be some loss, but your true creativity will be enhanced by the removal of neurotic blocks, inhibitions, and distortions." Would this reply constitute a sufficient disclosure of the risks inherent in therapy?

9. *Exceptions to the duty to disclose.* In *Canterbury v. Spence*, the court recognized a medical privilege to withhold collateral risk data. The court's discussion of this point is reprinted in the following subsection.

2. Exceptions to the Duty to Disclose

CANTERBURY v. SPENCE

United States Court of Appeals, District of Columbia Circuit, 1972.
464 F.2d 772.

(The main body of the opinion is set out in the preceding Section.)

VI

Two exceptions to the general rule of disclosure have been noted by the courts. Each is in the nature of a physician's privilege not to disclose, and the reasoning underlying them is appealing. Each, indeed, is but a recognition that, as important as is the patient's right to know, it is greatly outweighed by the magnitudinous circumstances giving rise to the privilege. The first comes into play when the patient is unconscious or otherwise incapable of consenting, and harm from a failure to treat is imminent and outweighs any harm threatened by the proposed treatment. When a genuine emergency of that sort arises, it is settled that the impracticality of conferring with the patient dispenses with need for it. Even in situations of that character the physician should, as current law requires, attempt to secure a relative's consent if possible. But if time is too short to accommodate discussion, obviously the physician should proceed with the treatment.

The second exception obtains when risk-disclosure poses such a threat of detriment to the patient as to become unfeasible or contraindicated from a medical point of view. It is recognized that patients occasionally become so ill or emotionally distraught on disclosure as to foreclose a rational decision, or complicate or hinder the treatment, or perhaps even pose psychological damage to the patient. Where that is so, the cases have generally held that the physician is armed with a privilege to keep the information from the patient, and we think it clear that portents of that type may justify the physician in action he deems medically warranted. The critical inquiry is whether the physician responded to a sound medical judgment that communication of the risk information would present a threat to the patient's well-being.

The physician's privilege to withhold information for therapeutic reasons must be carefully circumscribed, however, for otherwise it might devour the disclosure rule itself. The privilege does not accept the paternalistic notion that the physician may remain silent simply because divulgence might prompt the patient to forego therapy the physician feels the patient really needs. That attitude presumes instability or perversity for even the normal patient, and runs counter to the foundation principle that the patient should and ordinarily can make the choice for himself. Nor does the privilege contemplate operation save where the patient's reaction to risk information, as reasonably foreseen by the physician, is menacing. And even in a situation of that kind, disclosure to a close relative with a view to securing consent to the proposed treatment may be the only alternative open to the physician.

Questions and Comments

1. *Scope of the exception.* Non-disclosure, under the *Canterbury v. Spence* formulation, is justified in three instances: first, where disclosure is likely to cause the patient to become so "ill or emotionally distraught" as to "foreclose a rational decision"; second, where the disclosure will "complicate or hinder the treatment"; and third, where the disclosure will result in "psychological damage to the patient." This last standard raises at least two problems of interpretation. One is the degree of "psychological damage to the patient" that must be shown to justify non-disclosure. Would the risk of moderate to severe depression be a sufficient justification? Alternatively, would anticipation of a severe but transient anxiety reaction justify non-disclosure?

The second problem concerns the *source* or *cause* of the illness or emotional distress, which "foreclose[s] a rational decision." Should the exception be construed to preclude only those situations where the disclosure itself caused the patient to become emotionally distraught, or is the exception intended to include those patients who, because of their mental illness, already have an irrational fear of the treatment? In other words, is it sufficient if, instead of being caused by disclosure, the irrationality is an underlying feature or symptom of the mental illness?

2. *Rules in other jurisdictions.* The California Supreme Court has articulated the medical disclosure exception in somewhat different terms. In *Cobbs v. Grant,* 8 Cal.3d 229, 104 Cal.Rptr. 505, 502 P.2d 1 (1972) the court observed:

> A disclosure need not be made beyond that required within the medical community when a doctor can prove by a preponderance of the evidence he relied upon facts which would demonstrate to a reasonable man the disclosure would have so seriously upset the patient that the

patient would not have been able to dispassionately weigh the risks of refusing to undergo the recommended treatment.

Id. at 516.

A minority of courts have also allowed the privilege of nondisclosure "where an explanation of every risk attendant upon a treatment procedure may well result in alarming a patient who is already apprehensive and who may, as a result, refuse to undertake surgery or treatment in which there is minimal risk * * * ". *Woods v. Brumlop,* 71 N.M. 221, 228, 377 P.2d 520, 525 (1962). Can an exception framed in these terms be applied without devouring the disclosure rule itself?

3. *Hypothetical.* The rule permitting non-disclosure of risks appears to have particular relevance when the patient is mentally ill. Assume the following situation: A hospitalized psychiatric patient, suffering from a number of phobias and delusions, believes that death will inevitably follow any prolonged period of impotency. In addition to the psychiatric disorder, the patient also suffers from high blood pressure. A commonly used drug for the treatment of high blood pressure is Inderal. One of the possible but unlikely side effects of this drug is impotency. Would the treating physician be justified in prescribing Inderal without disclosing to the patient the risk of impotency?

4. *Misrepresentation compared to nondisclosure.* Does the privilege to withhold information also allow a therapist to misrepresent the nature of the treatment or diagnosis to an emotionally disturbed patient in order to induce the patient to undergo needed therapy? In the somewhat unusual case of *Kraus v. Spielberg,* 37 Misc.2d 519, 236 N.Y.S.2d 143 (1962), the plaintiff, who had a tuberculosis phobia, consulted a physician because of acute stomach pains. To induce the patient to agree to chemotherapy treatment, the therapist led the plaintiff to believe that the tuberculous germs had spread to her stomach. In fact, however, the doctor had not verified the exact location of the tubercular condition. The plaintiff consented to the therapy and later suffered unpleasant side effects. Finding that the misrepresentation was necessary to induce the plaintiff to undergo needed treatment, the court held for the defendant-therapist. Is it likely that the case would be decided the same way today in jurisdictions recognizing the doctrine of informed consent?

5. *Waiver of right.* May a patient waive his right to be informed, and can the therapist rely on such waiver? This issue has not been conclusively resolved; however, the California Supreme Court has stated in *dictum:*

> "[A] medical doctor need not make disclosure of risks when the patient requests that he not be informed."

Cobbs v. Grant, 8 Cal.3d 229, 104 Cal.Rptr. 505, 516, 502 P.2d 1, 12 (1972).

BARCLAY v. CAMPBELL

Supreme Court of Texas, 1986.
704 S.W.2d 8.

McGEE, JUSTICE.

This is a medical malpractice case. Milton Barclay sued Dr. W. Lawrence Campbell, alleging that the doctor negligently prescribed certain drugs for Barclay and negligently failed to disclose to Barclay certain risks associated with the drugs. The trial court granted a partial directed verdict in favor of Dr. Campbell on informed consent * * *. The court of appeals affirmed the trial court judgment, holding that the trial court did not err in directing a verdict for Dr. Campbell on the issue of informed consent. 683 S.W.2d 498. We disagree. The issue of informed consent should have been submitted to the jury. Therefore, we reverse the judgment of the court of appeals and remand the cause to the trial court.

Barclay was referred to Dr. Campbell in January of 1978 by his employer's company physician. Dr. Campbell treated Barclay for mental illness and during the course of treatment prescribed certain neuroleptic drugs for Barclay. In a small percentage of cases, these drugs produce a condition known as tardive dyskinesia. This condition is marked by involuntary muscle movements. The evidence is undisputed that Dr. Campbell did not warn Barclay of the risks associated with the neuroleptic drugs, and Barclay now suffers from tardive dyskinesia.

This cause is governed by the Medical Liability and Insurance Improvement Act, TEX.REV.CIV.STAT.ANN. art. 4590i (Vernon Supp. 1985), enacted in 1977. * * * The Texas Medical Disclosure Panel was established by the Act to determine which risks related to medical care should be disclosed. Section 6.07(a) of the Act creates a rebuttable presumption of negligence when the physician has failed to disclose a risk found on the list. Section 6.07(b) provides that if the panel has made no determination concerning the disclosure of risks attendant to a particular medical procedure in question, the physician is under the "duty otherwise imposed by law." * * * In our case, the panel has not made a determination of risk disclosure associated with neuroleptic drug ingestion. Consequently, this cause falls under section 6.07(b) of the Act.

In *Peterson v. Shields,* 652 S.W.2d 929, 931 (Tex.1983), we held that the "duty otherwise imposed by law" meant the duty imposed by section 6.02 of the Act, that is, "to disclose the risks or hazards that could have influenced a reasonable person in making a decision to give or withhold consent." * * * Thus, the focus shifts from the "reasonable medical practitioner" standard to the "reasonable person" standard which asks what risks are material to making the decision to give or withhold consent to a particular medical procedure.

If no presumption has been established by the Act, the plaintiff must prove by expert testimony that the medical condition complained of is a risk inherent in the medical procedure performed. *Id.* The expert should also "testify to all other facts concerning the risk which show that knowledge of the risk could influence a reasonable person in making a decision to consent to the procedure." *Id.*

* * *

In our case, there was expert testimony introduced at trial that tardive dyskinesia is an inherent risk associated with neuroleptic drugs.

Inherent means that the risk is one which exists in and is inseparable from the drug itself. Tardive dyskinesia arises from the use of the drug and not from any defect in the drug or negligent human intervention. Certain precautions must be taken in prescribing the drug due to the inherent risks associated with the medication.

* * * We hold that the expert testimony concerning the probabilities of contracting tardive dyskinesia is some evidence that the risk was material enough to influence a reasonable person in his decision to give or withhold consent to the procedure.

* * *

[T]he court of appeals held that the undisputed evidence established that Barclay did not have the reactions of a reasonable person. Relying on section 6.07(a)(2) of the Act, the court of appeals held that it was the legislature's intent to excuse a defendant who is negligent in failing to disclose a risk if it was not medically feasible to make the disclosure. The court of appeals concluded that even if the risk was material and, therefore, should have been disclosed, Dr. Campbell was excused from making the disclosure because it was not medically feasible. The testimony used to support this conclusion was that Barclay did not have the reactions of a reasonable person because he was suffering from schizophrenia. The consensus of the expert testimony was that had Barclay known of the risk of side effects like tardive dyskinesia, it probably would have caused him to refuse the treatment, no matter how minimal the risk and how great the counterveiling risk of refusing the medication.

While we appreciate the dilemma facing a psychiatrist in such a position, we hold that it was not the legislature's intent to take away an individual's right to make such decisions for himself just because his doctor does not believe his patient is reasonable. The court of appeals applied a subjective standard to determine if Barclay was entitled to be informed of the risk. The Act requires the application of an objective standard. The issue is not whether Barclay could have been influenced in making a decision whether to give or withhold consent to the procedure had he known of the risk. Rather, the issue is whether a "reasonable person" could have been influenced in making a decision whether to give or withhold consent to the procedure had he known of the risk. If a "reasonable person" could have been influenced, then Barclay was also entitled to be warned of the risk.

* * *

Barclay introduced the required expert testimony and, therefore, was entitled to issues on the question of informed consent. Barclay's mental illness does not foreclose his right to be informed of the risk if the jury finds the risk is material in the sense of one which could influence a reasonable person in making a decision to give or withhold consent to the procedure. We reverse the judgment of the court of appeals and remand the cause to the trial court for trial on the issue of informed consent.

B. OTHER ELEMENTS NECESSARY TO ESTABLISH A CLAIM

1. *Causation*

Mere non-disclosure of a risk is not sufficient to impose liability on the therapist. Liability results only if an *injury* occurs that would not have occurred *but for* the non-disclosure. Thus, a patient must prove that if the risk of injury had been disclosed, he would not have consented to the therapy that resulted in the injury. "Causation" is the shorthand legal term used to describe the relationship that must exist between the breach of duty (non-disclosure of a material fact) and the resulting injury.

In determining causation, the trier of fact can, in theory, either focus on an abstraction based on the likely decision of the particular plaintiff or on what patients similarly situated would ordinarily decide had full disclosure been made. The excerpt from *Canterbury v. Spence*, which follows, establishes the majority rule.

CANTERBURY v. SPENCE

United States Court of Appeals, District of Columbia Circuit, 1972.
464 F.2d 772.

[The main body of the opinion is set forth at pp. 267–73].

A causal connection exists when, but only when, disclosure of significant risks incidental to treatment would have resulted in a decision against it. The patient obviously has no complaint if he would have submitted to the therapy notwithstanding awareness that the risk was one of its perils. On the other hand, the very purpose of the disclosure rule is to protect the patient against consequences which, if known, he would have avoided by foregoing the treatment. The more difficult question is whether the factual issue on causality calls for an objective or a subjective determination.

It has been assumed that the issue is to be resolved according to whether the factfinder believes the patient's testimony that he would not have agreed to the treatment if he had known of the danger which later ripened into injury. We think a technique which ties the factual conclusion on causation simply to the assessment of the patient's credibility is unsatisfactory.

* * *

[W]hen causality is explored at a post-injury trial with a professedly uninformed patient, the question whether he actually would have turned the treatment down if he had known the risks is purely hypothetical: "Viewed from the point at which he had to decide, would the patient have decided differently had he known something he did not know?" And the answer which the patient supplies hardly represents more than a guess, perhaps tinged by the circumstance that the uncommunicated hazard has in fact materialized.

In our view, this method of dealing with the issue on causation comes in second-best. It places the physician in jeopardy of the patient's hindsight and bitterness. It places the factfinder in the position of deciding whether a speculative answer to a hypothetical question is to be credited. It calls for a subjective determination solely on testimony of a patient-witness shadowed by the occurrence of the undisclosed risk.

Better it is, we believe, to resolve the causality issue on an objective basis: in terms of what a prudent person in the patient's position would have decided if suitably informed of all perils bearing significance. If adequate disclosure could reasonably be expected to have caused that person to decline the treatment because of the revelation of the kind of risk or danger that resulted in harm, causation is shown, but otherwise not. The patient's testimony is relevant on that score of course but it would not threaten to dominate the findings.

Questions and Comments

1. *Causation vs. materiality.* Causation must be distinguished from the element of materiality. Material risks, as noted previously, are those to which the patient is "likely to attach significance * * * in deciding whether or not to forego the proposed therapy." *Canterbury v. Spence,* 464 F.2d 772, 787 (D.C.Cir.1972). Not all material risks, of course, would prompt a patient to refuse therapy. In such a case, disclosure would be irrelevant to the patient's final decision. Waltz and Schoneman provide an example of this distinction: "[I]t would be reasonable to conclude that a patient who required brain surgery to survive would not have refused it even had he known of an undisclosed risk of speech impediment. At the same time the risk of a speech impediment could well be deemed to constitute nondisclosure of a material fact". Waltz & Schoneman, 'Informed Consent to Therapy,' 64 Nw.U.L.Rev. 628, 648 (1970).

2. *Objective and subjective tests of causation.* Basically, two approaches—either the objective or subjective tests—are used to determine the element of materiality. Whichever test is applied, the determination of whether the non-disclosed information influenced the decision of the plaintiff in the case is a question for the jury or trier of fact. However, the choice of either the objective or subjective test will determine the standard by which the jury makes its determination of whether a particular fact or cluster of facts were material in terms of the patient's decision. Under the objective test adopted by the court in *Canterbury v. Spence,* the jury will be called upon to determine materiality in terms of the effect that non-disclosure of a material risk would have for a hypothetical reasonable person in the plaintiff's position. This test has been adopted by most jurisdictions.

Under the subjective test, the fact-finder focuses on the particular plaintiff to determine whether that individual would have foregone the therapy if the risk had been disclosed. Thus, the "subjective" approach is likely to focus on the plaintiff's testimony. Here, of key importance is the plaintiff's credibility as judged by the fact-finder. Only a minority of courts have adopted this approach. See *Scott v. Bradford*, 606 P.2d 554 (Okl.1979); *Arena v. Gingrich*, 84 Or.App. 25, 733 P.2d 75 (1987).

2. *Damages*

The previous subsection pointed out that a successful plaintiff must prove that a material risk of the therapy was not disclosed and that a reasonable person in the plaintiff's position would not have consented to the therapy had the risk been disclosed. What remains to be considered is the measure of damages applicable to this type of case. While few cases have addressed this question, it has generally been assumed that a successful plaintiff is entitled to damages to compensate for the loss or injury resulting from the risk that materialized. Thus, the measure of damages is generally the same as in a malpractice case. It has been argued that this rule is unduly harsh from the therapist's perspective and that the recovery should be reduced by an amount attributable to whatever injury or loss would have occurred if no therapy had been undertaken or if an alternative therapy had been adopted. Thus, under this view, if the plaintiff inevitably would have suffered physical deterioration if he had received no therapy whatsoever, that factor would reduce the amount of damages he can recover.

These general rules of damages may vary somewhat in the few jurisdictions that treat the doctrine of informed consent as a variant of an action in assault and battery. In those jurisdictions, because the basis of the claim is an "unauthorized touching," the therapist can be liable for monetary damages even if the plaintiff suffered no actual injury. Also, since battery is viewed as an intentional tort, the defendant can be assessed punitive or exemplary damages. However, most courts would not impose exemplary damages unless the physician was guilty of actual malice.

In some jurisdictions, prevailing rules on damages significantly limit the impact of the doctrine of informed consent. Unless some *physical injury* results from the treatment, it is unlikely that a patient can recover anything more than nominal damages. In a number of states, mental distress, fright, shock, humiliation, or similar violations of psychological integrity do not ordinarily constitute compensable injury unless accompanied by physical impact. As a result, conventional psychotherapists, unless they also use treatment modalities such as drugs, which have the potential of inflicting physical harm, are relatively immune from liability. Undoubtedly, this explains in part the relative absence of reported cases against non-medically trained psychotherapists for failure to secure the patient's informed consent. It also explains why behavioral science researchers, in spite of numerous reported violations of the requirements of informed consent, have escaped liability. However, the trend is clearly toward recognition of psychological harm as a sufficient basis for the recovery of monetary damages even when not associated with any physical injury. With these considerations in mind consider the following hypothetical fact situation:

A patient consults a psychotherapist to overcome his flying phobia, which in view of his occupational need to travel is proving to be an increasing handicap to his professional advancement. The therapist agrees to treat the patient, and over a period of the next three months gives him a series of desensitization procedures coupled with hypnotherapy.

The patient is informed that he has made material progress and the next step is to take a short flight. The patient is not alerted to the possibility that he will feel great anxiety during the flight. In fact, the therapist assures him that he is entirely ready to take the next step. Pursuant to the therapist's recommendations, the patient secures a ticket and boards an airline flight to the next city. Shortly after takeoff, in spite of the patient's use of a tape-recorder designed to facilitate self-hypnosis, the patient experiences a severe anxiety attack. By the time the airplane lands 30 minutes later, the patient is in a state of total collapse. He is taken by ambulance to the nearest hospital and is placed under sedation. Upon release a week later, the patient remains in a highly agitated and anxious state, which is accompanied by insomnia. As a result of this condition he is absent from work for the next three weeks. Upon his return to work, he learns that during his absence he was considered but rejected for a promotion, on the grounds that his records indicated that he had health problems. Badly shaken by the experience and somewhat angry at the therapist for having encouraged him to take the flight, he consults an attorney to inquire whether he has any basis to sue the therapist.

What is the attorney likely to advise? Would the result be different in a jurisdiction which requires physical injury?

C. ISSUES PERTAINING TO PATIENT ACKNOWLEDGMENT AND UNDERSTANDING

1. *Introduction*

In its original form, legally sufficient consent required nothing more than patient assent to the proposed treatment. Failure to obtain consent subjected the therapist to liability for assault and battery. The modern doctrine, on the other hand, requires that the consent be an *informed* one.

The elements of informed consent are twofold. First, the therapist must disclose information pertaining to the risks of the proposed therapy. Second, as under the original doctrine, the patient must agree to undergo the therapy. In law the agreement that the patient must give to authorize the therapist to start the therapy is known as consent.

Two types of problems arise in connection with the element of consent or agreement. One pertains to the evidentiary requirements imposed by the legal system. In other words, what actions or expressions on the part of the patient will suffice to establish consent? A second and more complex problem relates to the level of patient understanding that must accompany the consent or agreement. More specifically, does the legal system require that the patient understand the nature and degree of risk that was disclosed? If so, can the requisite level of understanding be presumed, or must the therapist establish its existence? These interrelated issues are explained in the materials that follow.

Both legal opinions and the writings of legal commentators have advanced the view that "[t]o establish consent to a risk it must be shown that the patient was aware of the risk and assented to the encountering of it". Jon R. Waltz & Fred E. Inbau, Medical Jurisprudence, at 164 (1971). What these assertions leave unanswered, however, is whether the patient must have actual rather than imputed knowledge. Consider for a moment the legal efficacy of a consent given by a patient who has been fully informed of all risks and alternatives but who, unknown to the physician, fails to adequately understand the information he has received. Two different approaches can be followed in dealing with this problem.

One alternative focuses on the therapist's disclosure. If that disclosure is deemed adequate, in the sense that an ordinary patient would comprehend the information transmitted, awareness will be imputed without regard to the patient-plaintiff's *actual level of comprehension*. It is this approach that the *Canterbury v. Spence* court advocated. In a footnote, the court observed that "the physician discharges the duty when he makes a reasonable effort to convey sufficient information *although the patient, without fault of the physician, may not fully grasp it*". 464 F.2d 772, 780 n. 15 (D.C.Cir.1972) [emphasis added]. Thus, under this approach, the therapist has discharged his duty when he has made full disclosure in terms that would be comprehensible to the average patient.

Under the other approach, a patient's consent would not be effective unless he had *actual* knowledge and understanding of the therapist's disclosure. In the event of litigation, then, the fact-finder would be required to determine whether the *particular* patient-plaintiff had understood what the therapist had told him. One commentator has explained the rationale for this approach:

> Even when the information presented is adequate, therefore, the consenting process may be nothing more than a "ritual" if the patient-subject remains "uneducated and uncomprehending." To avoid this result, the physician could be held responsible for taking reasonable steps to ascertain whether the information presented has been understood, so that if it has not he may supplement it as needed or may convey the same information in a manner more comprehensible to the particular patient.

Capron, "Informed Consent in Catastrophic Disease Research and Treatment," 123 U.Pa.L.Rev. 340, 414 (1974).

The weight of legal opinion has, however, rejected the "subjective" approach on a variety of grounds. As Waltz and Inbau have observed:

One difficulty with this view is that the patient's testimony, undeniably admissible at trial, in fact controls the issue of consent. And the trial lawyer's healthy cynicism tells him that a claimant's testimony is sometimes susceptible to modification based upon hindsight. Another difficulty is that it leaves no room for reasonable communication or interpretation mistakes by the physician; he assumes the risk of incorrectly concluding that the patient in fact understood and assented to the risks communicated. As the entire history of contract law attests, legal relationships based on communication cannot practicably be made to depend on the vagaries of the parties' subjective intent.

Jon Waltz & Fred Inbau, Medical Jurisprudence, at 165 (1971).

Comment

As a practical matter, the question whether the patient's awareness should be measured objectively or subjectively has only rarely arisen in modern informed consent cases. The reasons for this are twofold. First, modern cases have emphasized the element of disclosure. To the extent that the physician fails to inform the patient adequately, the question of awareness is typically never reached, since the case can be disposed of on that ground. Thus, the scope of patient awareness would only be an issue if the fact-finder determined that the therapist had given adequate disclosure, and the patient contended that he did not understand its content. Cases based on this type of contention are, however, very hard to win, which at least in part explains their absence. Moreover, a patient's case would be weakened by the dual contentions that there was insufficient disclosure and that he (she) lacked awareness because he (she) did not understand what was disclosed. While these are not necessarily inconsistent positions, the plaintiff's lawyer would be concerned that emphasis on the patient's lack of comprehension might buttress the defendant's contentions that there was full disclosure and that the patient, through no fault of the therapist, failed to understand what was said.

2. *The Determination of Patient Assent: Evidentiary Problems*

As has been noted, consent consists of the dual ingredients of awareness and assent. To establish consent to a risk it must be shown that the patient is made aware of the risk and knowingly assented to the treatment. Thus, in the event of litigation, the fact-finder must determine whether the patient's expressions in their totality (both verbal and nonverbal) support the conclusion that he assented to the treatment. The test is an objective one: intent is gauged by what is known as the reasonable person standard. Under this test the question is whether a reasonable therapist would have concluded from the patient's statements and behavior that the patient was aware of the risks that had been communicated and that he had manifested a willingness to undergo the therapy or procedure. Any other approach would, of course, subject the therapist to the unreasonable risk that a patient who manifests assent could subsequently deny it on the basis of unexpressed mental reservations.

When divorced from the question of knowledge, however, the element of assent is not likely to be an issue. The mere fact that the patient had some interaction with the therapist generally establishes assent to at least some form of treatment. But the issue is likely to be much broader. The crucial question for the fact-finder is usually not whether there was assent in the narrow sense, but whether the assent was coupled with sufficient knowledge and awareness. As might be expected, this factual determination poses problems of an evidentiary nature. Most commonly, an informed consent case will, if litigated, turn at least in part on the credibility of the parties to the action. The patient will contend that because of inadequate disclosure, he was not made aware of the risks of the treatment. The therapist, on the other hand, may have a substantially different recollection of what was disclosed. To lower the risk of erroneous recollection, a therapist would be wise to keep a written summary of the information communicated to the patient and a written record of a patient's consent.

Questions and Comments

1. *Empirical data on information recall.* What are the implications of various studies showing that within a relatively short period of time patients frequently lose recall of much of the medical data disclosed during the consent obtaining process? In one study which involved 200 cancer patients, it was found, for instance, that one day after receiving relevant information on the risks of chemotherapy, "[o]nly 60 per cent understood the purpose and the nature of the procedure, and only 55 per cent correctly listed even one major risk or complication." Cassileth, et al., "Informed Consent—Why Are Its Goals Imperfectly Realized?" 302 New. Eng. J.Med. 896 (1980). *See also* Epstein & Lasagna, 'Obtaining Informed Consent: Form or Substance?,' 123 Arch Inter.Med. 682 (1969); Schultz, et al., "Are Research Subjects Really Informed?," 123 West. J.Med. 76 (1975).

Do studies such as the one described above call into question the overall utility of the informed consent doctrine? Do they at least point to the need for those providing treatment to maintain adequate records evidencing the disclosures made to the patient?

2. *Statutory requirements.* A number of states have enacted statutes that spell out the evidentiary requirements for informed consent to medical or surgical procedures. Typically, these statutes require that the attending physician provide the patient with a document that sets forth the procedures of treatment to be undertaken and the major risks. At the same time, they require that the patient sign a document acknowledging that the disclosure of information has been made and that all of his questions pertaining to the treatment have been answered. In turn, the fulfillment of these documentary requirements constitutes either *prima facie* or conclusive evidence that informed consent to treatment has been given. The Iowa statute illustrates this approach to proof of informed consent:

A consent in writing to any medical or surgical procedure or course of procedures in patient care which meets the requirements of this section shall create a presumption that informed consent was given. A consent in writing meets the requirements of this section if it:

1. Sets forth in general terms the nature and purpose of the procedure or procedures, together with the known risks, if any, of death, brain damage, quadriplegia, paraplegia, the loss or loss of function of any organ or limb, or disfiguring scars associated with such procedure or procedures, with the probability of each such risk if reasonably determinable.

2. Acknowledges that the disclosure of that information has been made and that all questions asked about the procedure or procedures have been answered in a satisfactory manner.

3. Is signed by the patient for whom the procedure is to be performed, or if the patient for any reason lacks legal capacity to consent, is signed by a person who has legal authority to consent on behalf of that patient in those circumstances.

Iowa Code Ann. § 147.137.

Note that the Iowa statute only requires disclosure of certain major risks that are itemized in Section 1 of the statute. Also, note that the statute does not require any information on alternative treatment.

In those states with statute regulating informed consent, the question of legislative preemption arises. A court in one of those states may have to determine whether the legislature has preempted the entire area or whether there is room for judicially developed remedies to supplement the statutory provisions.

3. *Effect of written form.* Is it possible for a patient who has signed a form that exhaustively lists the risks and hazards of the therapy to contend that although he/she signed the form he/she did not, in fact, understand its content? The answer to this question would presumably turn on whether, under the law of the state controlling the disposition of the case, the signing of a statement is *conclusive* evidence of informed consent on the part of the patient. If it is only *prima facie* evidence, the patient's signature on a consent form would not preclude the contention that he was not, in fact, adequately informed. This suggests that for maximum protection the therapist should do more than obtain the patient's written consent on a form that recites the significant risks. In addition, the therapist should verbally explain the risks and alternatives and then enter a notation in the patient's file recounting the general nature of the conversation.

In *Hondroulis v. Schuhmacher*, 553 So.2d 398 (La., 1988), the court held that the Louisiana informed consent statute, which mandated that patients be provided with a written listing of all potential complications which might result from any medical procedure, which must be signed by the patient, merely creates a presumption of disclosure, which may be rebutted by proof that material facts were not adequately disclosed by the consent form.

4. *Standardized forms.* Note that standardized consent forms that merely recite that the patient has been informed of "all risks" are likely to

be of little legal protection. Valid consent requires disclosure of the specific risks and available alternative therapy.

Therefore, a summary consent form merely attesting that "all risks" have been communicated will not foreclose the admission of evidence that there was not, in fact, a sufficient disclosure. Not surprisingly, fairly detailed standardized consent forms are becoming more frequent. Illustrative of the standardized forms that have been developed is the one set out below for obtaining consent to electroshock therapy (ECT).

CONSENT TO ELECTRIC SHOCK THERAPY

A.M.

Date _____ Time _____ P.M.

1. I authorize Dr. _____, and assistants of his choice, to administer electric shock treatment, and relaxant drugs and other medication, to *(name of patient)* and to continue such treatment at such intervals as he and his assistants may deem advisable.

2. I understand that this treatment consists of passing a controlled electric current between two electrodes applied to the patient's temples. In some instances, the patient may be given medication prior to treatment to reduce tension and produce muscular relaxation. I understand that the patient will not feel the electric current and will feel no pain. When the electric current is administered, the patient becomes unconscious and has strong convulsive muscular contractions which may last from 35 to 50 seconds. The patient gradually regains consciousness and his confusion clears within 15 to 60 minutes. The patient may experience headache and nausea.

3. I understand that the treatments may cause temporary confusion and memory impairment. I also understand that certain risks and complications are involved in the treatment. The most common risk is fracture and dislocation of the limbs and vertebrae. I acknowledge that these and other risks and complications of this procedure have been explained to me.

4. In addition to the foregoing, the strict care which will be required immediately following treatment and during convalescence has been fully explained to me.

5. The alternative methods of treatment have been explained and no guarantee or assurance has been given by anyone as to the results that may be obtained.

Signed _____

Witness _____

5. *Revocation of consent.* The right to consent implies the right to revoke any consent that has been given. Thus, a patient may withdraw his consent at any time before the treatment has been concluded. However, under the law of most states this principle does not apply to the consent given by a patient entering an institution through a voluntary admission

procedure. Typically, laws governing admission to psychiatric facilities stipulate that a voluntary patient may be forcibly detained for a designated period even after he has withdrawn his voluntary admission consent.

3. *Psychiatric Patient Consent*

Recall that the doctrine of informed consent incorporates two elements: the communication of relevant information and assent predicated upon an adequate understanding of the communicated information. The application of this model in the mental health treatment context, however, raises particular problems. Psychiatric patients and those who are developmentally disabled are by definition more likely than the average population to suffer from impairments which may diminish or interfere with the requisite comprehension. In the instance of retardation, the barrier to understanding manifests itself at the cognitive level. In the case of mental illness, the impediment to informed consent is more likely to involve a distortion of the information provided or an impairment in the patient's ability to communicate his intentions. One commentator has provided the following description of the way that mental illness can interfere with the giving of informed consent:

> * * * how does one obtain consent from a severely ill catatonic schizophrenic who sits and stares at a blank wall all day, refusing to speak to anyone? Certainly if a patient is psychotic or hallucinating and cannot assimilate information about a proposed procedure, he does not have the capacity to reach a decision about the matter in question. Some mental patients are incapable of evaluating information in what most people would call a rational manner. A treatment decision might ordinarily be based on considerations of perceived personal objectives, or long-term versus short-term risks and benefits. But there are patients whose acceptance or rejection of a treatment is not made in relation to any "factual" information. To add to this dilemma, while a mental patient may refuse to give his consent to a procedure, his refusal may only be a manifestation of his illness, having little resemblance to his actual desires.

G. Annas, et al., Informed Consent to Human Experimentation: The Subject's Dilemma, at 152 (1977).

When it is clear that the patient's psychiatric condition precludes the giving of informed consent, non-emergency treatment cannot be administered without a judicial determination that the patient is legally incompetent and consent is provided by an appointed guardian. (The competency adjudication process and the mechanism for the giving of substituted consent are discussed in Chapter Nine.) Thus, unless the patient has already been adjudicated to be incompetent, any substantial doubt as to the patient's capacity to give consent would call for the initiation of competency proceedings by the physician or mental facility.

In some instances, however, the capacity of a particular patient to give informed consent will not be altogether clear. Assessments are frequently complicated by the fact that "competency is not necessarily a fixed state that can be assessed with equivalent results at any one of a number of times. Like the patient's mental status as a whole, a patient's competency may fluctuate as a function of the natural course of his or her illness, response to treatment, psychodynamic factors[,] * * * metabolic status, intercurrent illnesses, or the effects of medication." Appelbaum & Roth, 'Clinical Issues on the Assessment of Competency,' 138 Am.J. of Psychiatry, 1462–1465 (1981). The clinician's assessment may be further clouded by the lack of clear legal guidelines as to what constitutes capacity to consent (see Chapter Nine at pp. 923–32).

Except for highly generalized judicial prescriptions, there are at the present time no detailed uniform standards governing the determination of *capacity* in the treatment context. The distinction between *competency* and *capacity* have been explained by leading commentators in the field:

> "*Competence* is a legal construct: in most jurisdictions only a court can decide if a person is incompetent. Assessments of *capacity*, on the other hand, are relegated to medical or mental health professionals. Legislatures, in drafting competence statutes, may determine what type and degree of clinically assessed incapacity will allow a judge to declare an individual legally 'incompetent.' Theories of competence to make medical decisions focus on various criteria, the most common of which, and the ones adopted by the law, are cognitive. Although the law focuses on cognitive impairments, there are no uniform standards among the jurisdictions to identify the relevant abilities that, when impaired, constitute incompetence."

Berg, et al., "Constructing Competence: Formulating Standards of Legal Competence to Make Medical Decisions," 48 Rutgers L.Rev. 345, 348–349 (1996).

Whatever the governing legal standard, the determination of capacity to consent will, as a practical matter, need to be decided in most instances by the treating clinician or an institutional review board set up for such a purpose.

Exposure to liability is minimized, however, by the judicially announced rule that a "physician discharges the duty when he makes a reasonable effort to convey sufficient information although the patient, without fault of the physician, may not fully grasp it." *Canterbury v. Spence,* 464 F.2d 772, 780 n. 15 (D.C.Cir.1972). Thus if the clinical determination of capacity at the time of the giving of consent involves the exercise of due care, those providing treatment would be insulated from liability even if the assessment were subsequently deemed to have been erroneous.

Questions and Comments

1. *Judicial criteria for substituted consent.* Some courts have refused to authorize treatment for an incompetent patient where the patient, had, during a prior lucid phase, manifested an objection to a particular form of treatment. In *Conservatorship of Waltz,* 180 Cal.App.3d 722, 227 Cal.Rptr. 436 (1986), the inpatient was found unable to give informed consent because

of a psychotic fear reaction to even the discussion of the proposed ECT treatment. However, during rational periods, the patient expressed what would be considered a normal fear of ECT. The opposition to treatment manifested during a phase of competency governed. The court held that "even though he has a mental illness which causes him to be paranoid about ECT and many other things, this fact alone cannot be used to negate the presence of a rational fear of ECT which causes him to refuse treatment even during nonpsychotic moments."

The issue in *Waltz* concerned the patient's capacity to give informed consent. As elaborated in Chapter Nine, different regulatory approaches have been adopted to deal with this problem. In some states there are proceedings to determine the individual's overall competency. In the absence of competency, the power to give consent to medical treatment may be delegated to a guardian or conservator. Other states have adopted *limited* guardianship proceedings where the inquiry focuses on the individual's capacity in a particular sphere of activity. In some states, such as California, there are special provisions governing the giving of consent to intrusive psychiatric treatment modalities. Finally, New York uses non-judicial Surrogate Decision Making Committees, composed of both professionals and interested lay people, to determine the patient's capacity to give informed consent and to determine the patient's best interests by considering the patient's values and preferences.

Different procedures also have been adopted by the states to control the administration of antipsychotic medication to prisoners. The procedures mandated by the state of Washington were sustained in *Washington v. Harper*, 494 U.S. 210, 110 S.Ct. 1028, 108 L.Ed.2d 178 (1990) set out at pp. 964–80.

2. *Consent capacity of psychiatric patients.* The capacity of psychiatric patients to understand and correctly interpret medical information has been the subject of numerous empirical studies. *See* Roth, "Competency to Consent to or Refuse Treatment," in Psychiatry 1982: The American Psychiatric Annual Review, 350, L. Grinspoon, ed. (1982); Roth, *et al.*, "Informed Consent in Psychiatric Research," 39 Rutgers L.Rev. 425 (1987).

By and large, these studies indicate that psychotic patients frequently suffer severe impairment of competency to consent to medical treatment. For instance a 1978 study of hospitalized schizophrenic patients receiving antipsychotic medication included the following findings:

> "while the schizophrenic patients, as compared with medical patients, did not have defective understanding of the side effects and risks of medication, the schizophrenic patients were less knowledgeable about how their medication related to the nature of their problem. To the extent that schizophrenic patients fail to understand the nature of their problem, it may be anticipated that they will also fail to understand the risks and benefits of treatment or to weigh risks and benefits in deciding whether to accept treatment." *Id.* at 357.

Also, as reported by Roth, a study conducted in 1981 found "that even after having been carefully informed, most of the schizophrenic outpatients treated in a cognitive disorder clinic did not absorb or understand information about tardive dyskinesia." Id. On the other hand, a study of persons suffering from psychotic depression found that most patients in this category (more than 75 percent) "were able to understand the information the consent form gave about electro-convulsive treatment." Roth, 357–358.

3. *Standardized measurements of capacity to consent.* Researchers in the field have in recent years sought to standardize instruments for the measurement of capacity to consent in the treatment context. One of these is the MacArthur Treatment Competence Study tool (MacCAT–T), developed by Paul Appelbaum and Thomas Grisso. See Appelbaum and Grisso, "The MacArthur Treatment Competence Study I," 19 Law and Human Behavior 105 (1995); Grisso, et al., "The MacCAT–T: A Clinical Tool to Assess Patients' Capacities to Make Treatment Decisions," 48 Psychiatric Services 1415 (1997).

IV. RESEARCH AND INFORMED CONSENT

A. INTRODUCTION

The preceding Section considered the doctrine of informed consent in the context of treatment, including *treatment* modalities which are innovative or experimental. However, experimentation is not always limited to treatment intended to enhance the well-being of the subject. In research situations, the activities in which the experimental subject is involved are primarily or wholly designed to develop or contribute to scientific or medical knowledge. Because the interests of the researcher and the subject are thus potentially in conflict, special regulations have been developed to protect the rights of experimental subjects.

The evolution of professional and legal standards to control research involving human subjects largely parallels the development of the doctrine of informed consent in the therapeutic treatment context. Thus, it was not until the early 1960's that courts, legislatures and professional organizations began to seriously search for methods to protect research subjects. Much of the impetus for this activity came from the disclosure of abuses in various research programs. For example, during the 1960's researchers at the Tuskegee Institute began a study of black males suffering from syphilis. The Tuskegee researchers intentionally deprived the subjects of treatment in order to study the degenerative effects of syphilis, a fact that, when revealed later, led to much criticism of the study and its researchers. In the social sciences, Stanley Milgram's obedience experiments, in which subjects were given the illusion that they were administering painful electric shocks to other persons, drew considerable criticism. Although these experiments are not typical of biomedical and behavioral research, fear of such overzealousness in the cause of science has been a primary motive for the regulation of human-subject research.

The materials in this section will examine the legal regulation of both biomedical and behavioral research on human subjects. Since the risk to subjects is ordinarily greater in biomedical research, most current regulations were promulgated with that type of research in mind. Biomedical research may be defined as a scientific inquiry having a direct or immediate physical effect on the subject, which in turn produces some biological change. Biomedical research includes almost all medical research and psychiatric research aimed at the physiological origins of psychopathology.

Behavioral research is defined as a scientific inquiry into the factors determinative of human attitudes and behavior. In contrast to biomedical research, behavioral research generally involves no physical intrusion of the subject.

B. OVERVIEW OF STATUTORY AND ADMINISTRATIVE REGULATION

Congress and several state legislatures have shown their awareness of the public concern over the propriety of human-subject experimentation by enacting legislation. Congress created two regulatory mechanisms, both under the aegis of the Department of Health and Human Services (HHS), to insure the proper conduct of human-subject research. Both the Food and Drug Act of 1938 (21 U.S.C. § 355) and the National Research Act of 1974 (42 U.S.C. 2891–2892) empower the Secretary of HHS to promulgate regulations affecting human-subject research. Several states, including New York and California, have also enacted legislation which in some respects parallels the federal regulation.

Two principal checks on biomedical and behavioral research are created by the HHS regulations. First, researchers must submit detailed protocols describing their proposed research to an Institutional Review Board (IRB) made up of representatives drawn from different academic disciplines. These IRBs must be established in each HHS-funded institution and oversee the conduct of all human-subject research; they are empowered to either prohibit or modify the research being proposed. 45 C.F.R. § 46.113. In reviewing proposals, the IRBs are under a mandate to insure that risks to human subjects are minimized. Moreover, each proposal must reasonably balance the risk to human subjects against the anticipated benefit of the research. 45 C.F.R. § 46.111(a)(1), (2). Where the proposed research involves pregnant women, fetuses, children, or prisoners, additional criteria must be met.

A second feature of the regulations is the requirement of informed consent of all subjects. Thus, as in the therapy situation, researchers must disclose all appropriate alternative procedures and all foreseeable risks. The HHS regulations also impose requirements in addition to those needed where the subject's participation is solely for treatment purposes. For instance, the researcher must also inform the subject that he or she may withdraw at any time.

The Food and Drug Act of 1938 creates a second area of federal regulation of human-subject research. The act empowers the Secretary of HHS to approve the use of investigational drugs and medical devices. All researchers administering investigational drugs and devices must certify that the informed consent of either the subject or their proxies will be obtained. The regulations today require consent by the research subject or his legal representative except where four specific conditions are met, including the requirement of "a life threatening situation necessitating the use of the test article." 21 C.F.R. § 50.23.

A number of states, such as California and New York, have enacted legislation similar to the HHS regulations. *See* West's Ann.Cal.Penal Code §§ 2670–2678; N.Y.—McKinney's Pub.Health Law §§ 2440–2446. Like the HHS regulations, both New York and California require the subject's informed consent. Unlike HHS regulations, both the California and New York statutes cover all medical research conducted within the state, not just research in institutions receiving state funding. Neither the California nor the New York statutes explicitly cover behavioral research (unlike the HHS regulations, which cover all human-subject research but do explicitly exempt several categories of behavioral research including surveys, educational testing, and observation of public behavior. 45 C.F.R. § 46.101(b)).

As previously noted, neither federal nor most state regulations provides specific remedies for human subjects injured while participating in research. HHS merely denies funding to institutions with whom an offending researcher is affiliated, while California imposes criminal penalties on medical researchers who fail to obtain their subject's informed consent. West's Ann.Cal.Health & Safety Code § 21476. Some private remedy may nevertheless be available to an injured patient under state tort law or conceivably under one of the federal civil rights statutes. The scope of the Federal Civil Rights laws and their impact on the mental health treatment field is discussed in Chapter Three.

Questions and Comments

1. *Disclosure under HIPAA of PHI in research context.* A research institution is only subject to the Health Insurance Portability and Accountability Act [HIPAA] privacy rules if it is a covered entity [HIPAA privacy provisions are discussed in detail in Chapter 5]. However, if the research facility is also involved in treatment and meets HIPAA's covered entity criteria it must comply with the privacy rules. This means that it can transfer personal health information (PHI) to another covered entity without the patient's authorization. On the other hand, transfer of PHI to a non-covered entity requires the research subject's authorization. However, as a practical matter such authorization will generally have been obtained before an individual is admitted into the a research program. Such pre-admission authorization is permitted by HIPAA privacy rules. (45 CFR § 164.508(b)(4)(i)) discussed in greater detail in Chapter 5.

2. *International standards.* An important contributing factor in the movement for reform not only in the U.S. but also in other countries was the disclosure of human rights abuses carried out under the guise of scientific experimentation by Nazi scientists during World War II. *See,* Ratnoff & Smith, 'Human Laboratory Animals: Martyrs for Medicine,' 36 Ford.L.Rev. 673, 679 (1968). The World Medical Association has been at the forefront of efforts to develop international standards for the control of human experimentation. One result of these efforts is the first and second Helsinki Declaration. *See, generally,* Jon R. Waltz & Fred E. Inbau, Medical Jurisprudence, at pp. 381–383 (1971).

The Tuskegee study and other abuses which stimulated the movement towards greater regulation are discussed in Nathan Hershey and Robert D. Miller, Human Experimentation and the Law, at 153–56 (1976).

3. *HHS regulations.* The HHS regulations under the National Research Act delegate to each institution's IRB the power to review all consent forms and procedures. But the regulations do not indicate to what degree IRB representatives should intervene in the consent process to insure that subjects are truly informed. Some commentators have argued that IRBs have concentrated too heavily on the review and revision of consent forms, suggesting that subjects might receive better protection if IRB representatives more frequently intervened in the consent process itself. *See,* Robertson, "Taking Consent Seriously: IRB Intervention in the Consent Process," 4 IRB: A Review of Human Subject Research 10 (1982) (citing study by Gray (1975) in which 40% of subjects signing consent forms did not know they were involved in research).

4. *Definition of "risk of harm."* Under the HHS regulations, determinations of a subject's risks in proposed research have significant impact on whether the IRB will approve the proposed research. Accordingly, the definition of risk of harm will be pertinent to a court's determination of whether a researcher acted negligently. Neither state nor federal regulations, however, adequately define risk of harm. The HHS regulations define "minimal risk" as that risk of harm "not greater, considering probability and magnitude, than those ordinarily encountered in daily life * * *." 45 C.F.R. § 46.102. But such definitions say nothing about what kind of harm must be considered by IRBs. Risk of harm would certainly include physical harm, but what kinds of psychological harm could be included?

Some individual IRBs have sought to eliminate this uncertainty by providing a definition of "risk of harm." For example, the University of Illinois's IRB provides researchers with lists of research examples. One list covers research involving minimal risk. A second list covers research involving greater than minimal risk (e.g., studies of the effects of prescribed tranquilizers on driving skills).

5. *Self regulation.* To a certain degree, researchers police their own activities through a process of self-questioning normally a part of any legitimate scientific inquiry. That scientists are encouraged to publish the results of their studies also affects the procedures utilized in research. Individual journals, for instance, can refuse to publish results of experiments that were not conducted in conformance with guidelines established by agencies such as the Department of Health and Human Services. Also, publication itself means that both the results and the research methods become available to the research community at large, which can then offer its own critique. The ethical codes and policy statements of professional organizations have also played a part in the process of self-regulation, particularly in the area of biomedical research.

C. PEOPLE WITH MENTAL ILLNESS AS RESEARCH SUBJECTS

1. Introduction

Few issues in the mental health field are as difficult to sort out as the standards that should regulate research involving severely mentally ill subjects where the research is designed to develop new approaches to the treatment of mental disorders but where the research does not provide any immediate benefit and in fact may result in some detriment to the research subject. The dilemma posed by this type of research has been described by a leading authority in the following terms:

> Research into the etiology and treatment of severe mental disorders must often confront a difficult conundrum: persons suffering from these disorders—usually the only appropriate subjects for study—may lack the capacity to consent to research. Thus the very illnesses from which they suffer appear to throw a roadblock in the path of developing better treatments. A recent court decision in New York suggests that it may not be easy to find ways around this problem.

> Most persons with mental illness retain the capacity to make decisions, even during acute exacerbations. Patients in this group can choose for themselves whether to participate in research. However, some of the most severely affected patients—including those with treatment-resistant schizophrenia, psychotic depression, and Alzheimer's disease—lack sufficient decision-making capacity to understand, appreciate, or reason about joining a research project, or they may be unable to indicate their decision. In legal terms, they are incompetent to decide about participating in research, and they would be precluded from consenting to enter a research project.

> Researchers in New York and elsewhere have often felt frustrated by the exclusion of this group of potential subjects. Their frustration grows when the research involves innovative approaches to treatment-resistant disorders, which might not otherwise be available to patients.

P. Appelbaum, "Psychiatric Research and the Incompetent Subject," 48 Psychiatric Services, 73 (July 1997) [hereinafter Appelbaum, Psychiatric Research and the Incompetent Subject].

Under current law and regulation, such research involving mentally ill subjects may proceed so long as various standards are met, including the obtaining of conformed consent, either from the patient or his surrogate. The exposition that follows explores the issues that must be addressed, when the research subject has the capacity to consent, or, in the absence of capacity, when alternative methods of obtaining consent from a surrogate, such as a court, must be followed.

2. *Issues in Patient/Subject Consent*

Where it is the patient that is looked to for consent for participation in research, the initial issue to be addressed is the same as where the patient is being asked to consent to treatment—does the subject have sufficient capacity to provide consent? Consequently, the issue of capacity will be decided by the same criteria as discussed previously. What becomes particularly important in the research context is full disclosure of the possible short-and long-term detriment that the research subject may suffer. A recent case illustrating the issues that may be raised in this context was the subject of a commentary by Dr. Appelbaum:

In May 1994, the federal Office of Protection from Research Risks (OPRR) issued a report on its investigation of complaints against a leading group of schizophrenia researchers at the University of California at Los Angeles (UCLA) Medical School. The subjects on whose behalf complaints were filed had participated in a series of studies using Prolixin decanoate, a long-lasting, injectable form of a standard antipsychotic agent.

Subjects in the UCLA studies initially went through a one-year, fixed-dose study in which they received injections every two weeks. On the successful completion of the first study, subjects who were willing to continue in the research were enrolled in a second, more controversial protocol. Each subject was assigned, in a randomized, double-blind fashion, to continue the same dose of Prolixin or to receive a placebo injection. After twelve weeks, the groups crossed-over, with those subjects who had received active medication now getting a placebo, and vice versa. Subjects who were still stable after an additional twelve weeks were then assigned to a withdrawal protocol. The medications were stopped and subjects were followed for at least one year, or until a serious exacerbation or psychotic relapse occurred. The goal of the study was to identify predictors of successful functioning without antipsychotic medication.

Two subjects who had been enrolled in the withdrawal protocol ran into trouble. One subject committed suicide after completion of the formal one-year drug withdrawal study, while continuing to be followed by the research team in a drug-free state. A second person, a young college student, experienced a severe psychotic relapse that began not long after the medication was discontinued. During this period, he left school, began to hallucinate, and threatened to kill his parents when he became convinced that they were possessed by the devil. He and his parents alleged that, despite repeated appeals to the research team, it took nine months before he was put back on medication.

In the wake of these episodes, allegations were made to OPRR that the drug withdrawal protocols in which the subjects had been enrolled were unethical because they virtually guaranteed that subjects would relapse; that proper informed consent had not been obtained from the subjects; and that the investigators, who were also the subjects' clinicians, had not monitored their conditions closely enough and had been too slow about pulling them off the protocol and restarting medications.

OPRR's investigation concluded that the design of the research was not unethical, since it comported with current clinical and scientific standards. However, the agency determined that the informed consent obtained from subjects was inadequate, because the consent documents failed to describe clearly the differences between being in the research project and receiving ordinary clinical care. Although UCLA's monitoring of subjects' clinical status was deemed to be acceptable, OPRR also found that subjects should have been informed that their clinicians simultaneously were acting as investigators in the study.

Far from settling the controversy regarding drug-free research in schizophrenia, the OPRR report stimulated renewed consideration of the issues. The controversy was widely covered in the popular media, congressional hearings were held, and a lawsuit was filed against UCLA by the family of one of the subjects.

P. Appelbaum, "Drug–Free Research in Schizophrenia: An Overview of the Controversy," 18 IRB: A Review of Human Subjects Research (Jan.– Feb. 1996).

Questions and Comments

1. *Media Attention.* The issue of research subject consent has received widespread attention by the media. Some reports suggest that the use of research involving mentally ill patients who take part in research studies involving an occasion is not insubstantial. According to a recent New York Times report, "Federal ethics officials estimate that there have been 100 to 300 experiments in which patients were taken off their medicines when no new medicine was being tried; rather, they were taken off their medicines to observe the patients as they relapsed in order to study the illnesses." P. Hilts, "Psychiatric Researchers Under Fire", N.Y. Times, May 19, 1998, at B11.

2. *Questions.* Is there any alternative to using mentally ill research subjects where the research pertains specifically to the development of new and improved mental disorder treatment modalities? If there is any way around the use of mentally ill research subjects for this purpose? What requirements should be imposed, other than obtaining the informed consent from research subjects who, while mentally ill, may be legally competent?

3. *Adequacy of disclosure.* As the materials in the earlier part of this chapter suggest, consent cannot be effective unless they consent-giver is provided with sufficient information to make an informed decision. Some research studies have been criticized on the basis of insufficient disclosure. For instance, a research project involving the Maryland Psychiatric Research Center at the University of Maryland, was brought before the National Bioethics Advisory Commission. The study in question involved "[n]ine hospitalized schizophrenic patients [who] were recruited to participate in a study during which they were taken off their medicine and given four increasing doses of ketamine, an anesthetic related to the hallucinogen 'angel dust,' to induce psychotic symptoms." P. Hilts, "Did Consent Form Tell Enough?," N.Y. Times, May 19, 1998, at B12. According to a psychiatrist at the National Institute of Mental Health who is the editor of the institute's Schizophrenia Bulletin, "the ketamine study was important because it was probing a part of the brain, NMDA receptors, that might play a crucial role in psychotic symptoms." Id.

The issue brought before the National Bioethics Advisory Commission involved the adequacy of disclosure. The consent form stated: "You are invited to participate in a research study which will take place at the Maryland Psychiatric Research Center to test a medication named ketamine, for schizophrenia." The form also clearly stated that ketamine was not being tested "as a therapy for your illness." Id. However, the consent form went on to state: "[T]his medication, if effective, may not alter the underlying disease, but merely offer symptomatic treatment." Is this last statement misleading in view of the fact that there was general agreement among psychiatric researchers that "ketamine is not a treatment for schizophrenia, but rather induces psychotic episodes, and that was the reason researchers wanted to use it: to create symptoms." Id. Did the patients in the study give *informed* consent in the light of the statement that the medication (i.e. ketamine) might "merely offer symptomatic treatment"?

4. *Institutionalized research subjects.* While it is difficult to arrive at numerical estimates, institutionalized persons and particularly prison inmates have frequently served as experimental subjects in clinical tests conducted by pharmaceutical companies. In some instances, the research subjects who participate in a trial have a condition or illness that pertains to the drug being tested. In other cases, the research subjects have no abnormality or illness but nonetheless consent to participate in a drug testing program. In this instance, there is no therapeutic value to the research subjects who agree to participate in the clinical trial. Typically, when prison inmates serve as research subjects, they not only give their written consent but also receive some compensation from the drug company. Moreover, the consent is usually based on full disclosure of any risks associated with the drug being tested. In one case, *Bailey v. Lally*, 481 F.Supp. 203 (D.Md.1979), present and former prison inmates who had volunteered to participate in a research project involving the testing of a drug to counter malaria and other disorders brought a civil rights action asserting a violation of their constitutional rights. The plaintiff inmates had given their consent and had received compensation for participating in the clinical trial. However, they asserted that the conditions of incarceration were "so bad and the inducements to participate so great" that their participation had in fact not been voluntary. In rejecting the plaintiff's claim, the court held that the conditions of imprisonment were not so oppressive as to invalidate the consents that had been given.

3. Consent in the Absence of Patient/Subject Capacity

The considerations that ostensibly support the use of mentally ill research subjects where the research pertains specifically to the development of new treatment modalities are set out at the beginning of this section. Current regulations at both the federal and state level do not altogether preclude the use of subjects who lack the capacity to consent in this type of research. At the same time, the process for obtaining consent where the research will not directly benefit the patient in terms of treatment generally requires a formal approval process with governing standards that differ from state to state. As noted by Dr. Appelbaum,

"Legal proceedings for purposes of assigning guardianship for such patients may offer a way out in some cases, but such efforts usually depend on the presence of involved family members who are willing to spend the money required for legal representation and court fees associated with the proceedings. Even then, the power of a guardian to consent to research participation is not always clear. In practice, guardianship is rarely a viable option; incompetent patients usually end up excluded from research studies."

Appelbaum, Psychiatric Research and the Incompetent Subject.

Questions and Comments

1. *State regulation of surrogate consent.* Some states, such as New York, have sought to deal with the problem of consent of mentally ill research subjects by issuing detailed regulations governing research in psychiatric facilities owned or licensed by the state. Some of the requirements typically imposed by these types of regulations have been described as follows:

Before subjects lacking decision-making capacity could be recruited for a research project, an institutional review board was required to determine that the research could not be done without including this group. Moreover, the study had to be judged "likely to produce knowledge of overriding therapeutic importance for the understanding or treatment of a condition that is presented by the patient." Subjects could also be included when the study offered the prospect of direct benefit to them that would not be obtainable otherwise.

If patients meeting these criteria had not appointed a surrogate decision maker through a durable power of attorney—which most patients have not—the regulations offered a list of persons from whom consent for their participation in research could be obtained. These persons included the patient's spouse, parent, adult child, adult sibling, or guardian, or, in the absence of any of these, a "close friend," as defined in the regulations or by an appropriate court. Even if one of these persons consented on a patient's behalf, an objection by the patient would block his or her entry into the study, unless a court ruled that it offered the only option for direct benefit to the patient.

Appelbaum, Psychiatric Research and the Incompetent Subject at p. 73.

Notwithstanding the fact that these regulations were drafted through a process that involved patient advocates and other concerned parties, the regulations were challenged by plaintiffs who were concerned that patients might be forced into research without their consent. While not reaching the sufficiency of the regulations themselves, the New York appellate court hearing the case struck down the regulation, finding that the Office of Mental Health lacked authority to issue the regulations. At the same time, the Court suggested that the rules could be repromulgated in a technically correct fashion, which would then open the way for a substantive review. See *T.D. v. New York State Office of Mental Health*, 228 A.D.2d 95, 650 N.Y.S.2d 173 (1996).

D. SPECIAL PROBLEMS ASSOCIATED WITH BEHAVIORAL RESEARCH

In biomedical research the subject's knowledge about the research usually has little or no effect on research outcomes. In contrast, behavioral research frequently requires some deception of the subject as to the nature and purpose of the experiment. Consequently, strict imposition of the informed consent requirement would severely limit the behavioral research that could be conducted.

It has therefore been argued that some adjustment in the informed consent doctrine developed for biomedical research is called for in behavioral research. Moreover, it has been suggested that the need for strict informed consent standards is somewhat reduced by the nature of the risks posed by behavioral research, which rarely poses risk of physical harm. Some types of behavioral research, however, may expose the subject to risk of legally compensable psychological harm. Because the magnitude of these risks depends on the type of behavioral research conducted, it may be useful in evaluating current and proposed standards of informed consent to consider the legal implications associated with different types of behavioral research.

1. *Passive Observation Studies*

Passive observation of subjects in public places, without any modification of their environment, normally poses no risk of psychological harm. For example, in an experiment conducted by Bryan and Test (1967), the researchers measured the effect that the employment of black or white Santas as Salvation Army bell ringers had on frequency of donation. The mere act of giving or not giving constituted an experience of ordinary life which the researchers did not alter. Participants were completely unaware of ever having participated in the experiment.

In some instances, however, passive observation studies could subject the researcher to legal liability. For instance, in one controversial experiment by Humphreys (1970), the researcher stationed himself in public restrooms and posed as "lookout" for male homosexuals engaging in sex acts. By pretending to stand watch for intruders, the researcher was able to witness hundreds of sexual acts and sometimes follow up on these observations with interviews in which the purpose of the experiment was disclosed.

In this instance, even though the acts were committed in a public place, the nature of the activities plus the reasonable expectations of the parties would presumably give rise to protected privacy interests. Thus, by failing to inform the subjects of the true purpose of his presence, the researcher could in some jurisdictions become liable for invasion of privacy. See Fried, "Problems of Consent in Sex Research: Legal and Ethical Considerations in Ethical Issues," in Sex Therapy and Research, 31 (Masters, et al., eds., 1980).

An action for invasion of privacy can also occur when the defendant publishes a matter concerning the private life of another which is highly offensive and is not of legitimate concern to the public. Restatement (Second) of Torts § 652D (1965). Thus, if an acquaintance of one of the subjects in the Humphreys's experiment had been able to identify the subject from the information presented in the published findings, the research might have constituted an invasion of privacy.

The HHS regulations promulgated under the National Research Act take into account the subject's right to privacy in research involving passive observation. The regulations generally exempt passive observation from coverage. Researchers lose the exemption, however, if (1) the researchers keep records which identify the subject, (2) publication of the records would expose the subject to legal liability or financial loss, and (3) the research concerns sensitive aspects of the subject's behavior. 45 C.F.R. § 46.101(b)(4).

2. Surveys and Manipulation Studies Without Overt Deception

A second type of behavioral research involves some manipulation of the subject's environment, but without any significant deception of the subject. One famous experiment by Meritz and Fowler (1944) involved the use of a "lost letter" technique to test the honesty of persons in various cities. Two different kinds of addressed envelopes were distributed, one containing a letter and the other containing a coin-shaped slug. The difference in the percentage of returns between the two kinds of letters was expected to indicate the honesty of the general population. The experiment would have been impossible to perform if informed consent had been required. The researchers, however, had no duty to inform because participation posed no risk to the subjects greater than that encountered in ordinary life.

Similarly, survey interviews normally create little risk of harm to the subject. But if the subject's responses concern sensitive or personal matters, the researcher has a legal duty to insure the anonymity of the subject. If the subject must be identified in the researcher's records, the researcher may need to take special precautions to insure that the subject's responses remain confidential. Again, HHS regulations exempt interviews and surveys, provided that the researcher maintain the subject's anonymity, the subject's responses do not place the subject at risk of legal liability, and the responses do not pertain to sensitive aspects of the subject's behavior. 45 C.F.R. § 46.101(b)(3).

3. Studies Involving Deception

A third type of behavioral research combines manipulation of the subject's environment with some form of deception. One study found that as much as 44% of recent research in social psychology involved deception of the subjects. Diener & Crandall, Ethics in Social and Behavioral Research, 74 (1978). Some social scientists have expressed concern that the use of deceit lessens public respect for the social sciences and may, because of participants' suspicions that researchers employ deception, become valueless as a research tool. Id. at 80.

Nevertheless, deceit is a necessity in some types of behavioral research. The research subject's knowledge of the manipulation would in many situations compromise the validity of the research outcome. Imposing traditional standards of informed consent on researchers would obviously preclude the conduct of research involving deception. Behavioral studies frequently entail manipulation of some external variables under controlled conditions. The HHS regulations recognize this problem by allowing an IRB to completely waive the informed consent requirement where the research poses no more than minimal risk to the subject. 45 C.F.R. § 46.117(c).

The nature and degree of risk of psychological harm varies with the type of deception employed by the researcher. Psychological harm might arise from the subject's misapprehension, intended by the researcher, of what appears to be an emergency situation. For example, in an experiment conducted by the United States Army, military recruits were placed in an aircraft and flown to an altitude of 5,000 feet. The researcher then instructed the pilot to turn off the plane's propellers. The subjects were allowed to overhear communications designed to convince them that the pilot would be forced to crash land the plane. The behavior of the subjects under these artificial stress conditions was monitored by researchers who were also aboard the aircraft.

The threat of psychological harm also might arise from a deception that causes subjects to misapprehend the nature of their own personalities. In a study by Bergin (1965) on dissonance theory, researchers falsely told male subjects that personality tests had revealed that the subjects had latent homosexual tendencies. Eventually, researchers "dehoaxed" the subjects, but not before many of the subjects suffered a blow to their self-esteem.

Either of these experiments could have exposed the researchers to liability for failure to obtain informed consent or for the tort of intentional infliction of emotional distress. To demonstrate intentional infliction of emotional distress, the plaintiff subject would have to show that the plaintiff's action amounted to conduct "so outrageous in character, and so extreme in degree, as to go beyond all possible bounds of decency." Restatement (Second) of Torts, § 46 comment *d* (1965). Some states have the added requirement that the emotional distress cause some physical manifestation of illness or injury. Thus, under current standards except, in those states which do require a physical manifestation of the injury, the subjects in both the Army and Bergin studies could conceivably prevail in an action for intentional infliction of mental distress.

Questions and Comments

1. *Behavioral research and the requirement of informed consent.* It has been contended by some commentators that the low risk of injury from participation in behavioral research brings into question the necessity of applying the HHS regulations to behavioral research situations. See Pattullo, "Who Risks What in Social Research," 2 IRB: A Review of Human Subject

Research 1, 3 (1980). Cumbersome IRB procedures have undoubtedly discouraged some researchers from engaging in valuable scientific inquiry. See, Hunt, "Research Through Deception," N.Y. Times, Sept. 12, 1982, § 6 (Magazine) at 143. At the same time, the overwhelming consensus both within and outside the social sciences profession is that some regulation and institutional control of the actions of individual researchers is necessary.

2. *Debriefing.* Researchers employing deception have developed several safeguards to decrease the risks that subjects will become emotionally upset as a result of the deception. Most researchers as a matter of course debrief their subjects at the experiment's conclusion. In debriefing sessions, researchers meet with subjects and fully disclose the hoax. Disturbed subjects are comforted and reassured. To what extent does such debriefing protect against any psychological trauma which may have accompanied the experiment?

3. *Incomplete disclosure.* Behavioral and biomedical researchers have also developed several forms of "consent" that fall short of giving the subject all the information required to satisfy legal standards of informed consent. Some researchers have asked their subjects to consent to not being informed of the real purposes of the experiment. Levine, "Consent to Incomplete Disclosure as an Alternative to Deception," 4 IRB: A Review of Human Subject Research 10 (1982). Another technique consists of asking subjects to waive their right to disclosure without any forewarning to the subject that the research involves deception. Still another technique, heretofore used primarily in biomedical research, is to inform an incompetent subject's proxy of the experiment, but withhold the option of denying consent from the proxy. Within a specific period after the beginning of the experiment, however, the researcher must obtain the proxy's consent. The theory behind this technique, called "deferred consent," is that by delaying the consent decision, the subject's proxy will have more time to consider the matter and come to a "correct" decision. The HHS regulations under the National Research Act appear to authorize such techniques, but only if the research poses no more than minimal risk to the subject. 45 C.F.R. § 46.116(d). See, Fost & Robertson, "Deferring Consent with Incompetent Patients in an Intensive Care Unit," 2 IRB: A Review of Human Subject Research 5 (1980). *Cf.,* Beauchamp, "The Ambiguities of 'Deferred Consent,'" 2 IRB: A Review of Human Subject Research 6 (1980) (article critical of deferred consent technique).

Should the use of any of these techniques constitute a defense in an action based on a failure to obtain informed consent (assume that the plaintiff is able to prove damages)?

Chapter Five

CONFIDENTIALITY AND ACCESS TO RECORDS

I. PROTECTION OF PRIVACY AND CONFIDENTIALITY

A. MEDICAL/PSYCHOTHERAPY PRIVACY LAW DEVELOPMENT

The right of individuals to control the disclosure and distribution of information contained in their medical records is closely tied to the concept of personal privacy that first gained recognition as a legal concept close to the end of the nineteenth century. As initially conceived by Mr. Justice Brandeis the right of privacy as he stated it, is "[t]he right to be left alone".[1] While personal privacy as an interest deserving of constitutional protection has not crystallized as a stand alone right, numerous Supreme Court decisions have over time given constitutional protection to privacy interests in the adjudication of claims under both the First Amendment and the search and seizure clause of the Fourth Amendment. The protection of privacy interests has also been the bedrock or various decisions under the due process clause of the Fourteenth Amendment recognizing freedom of choice in a variety of personal activities including procreation and sexual expression.[2]

The protection of personal privacy from private actor intrusion gained increasing recognition particularly in the last half of the Twentieth Century. However, this development, which was the product of either state legislation or common law development, was very uneven with the degree of protection given to particular privacy interests vary-

1. Brandeis and Warren, 'The Right of Privacy', 4 Harv. L. Rev.193 (1890).

2. As noted by the Supreme Court in *Paul v. Davis*, 424 U.S. 693, 96 S.Ct. 1155, 47 L.Ed.2d 405 (1976), this penumbra of [privacy] rights has to do only with "matters relating to marriage, procreation, conception, family relationship, and child rearing and education." Whether medical records are entitled to constitutional protection was an issue before the Supreme Court in *Whalen v. Roe*, 429 U.S. 589, 97 S.Ct. 869, 51 L.Ed.2d 64 (1977). The *Whalen* court was presented with the question "Whether the state of New York may record in a centralized computer file, the names and addresses of all persons who have obtained, pursuant to a doctor's prescription, certain drugs for which there is both a lawful and an unlawful market." While the court in an opinion by Mr. Justice Stevens upheld the statute, the court announced that "in some circumstances," [the State may be under a constitutional duty to avoid] "unwarranted disclosures". These words have led one commentator to conclude that the *Whalen* decision "created a framework by which future courts would develop the right to privacy in medical records." J. Grover & E. Toll, 'The Right to Privacy and Medical Records,' 2002 Denver University Law Review 540 (2002).

ing from state to state. For instance, the tort of public disclosure of a private fact was an actionable tort in some states but not others. The same is true of medical privacy, which was protected to varying degrees in some states but not others.[3] In some the physician's duty to not disclose information obtained in the course of treatment was embedded in a specific statute. In others, a physician's duty to preserve the confidentially of patient records was either inferred from cognate statutory provisions such as laws giving patients the right to exclude their doctor's testimony in civil litigation or derived from medical licensing statutes or professional codes of conduct.[4]

While medical privacy laws covered psychiatrists who are by definition licensed physicians, they did not cover psychologists or other non-physician professionals involved in mental health treatment. At the same time there was a growing recognition that the privacy interest of patients being treated for mental disorders is as compelling if not more so than where the treatment involved general medical conditions. The very nature of psychotherapy[5] requires the full and frank disclosure of private facts. As noted by the Supreme Court,

> "a psychiatrist's ability to help [a patient] 'is completely dependent upon [the patients'] willingness and ability to talk freely. This makes it difficult if not impossible for [a psychiatrist] to function without being able to assure ... patients of confidentiality and, indeed, privileged communication. Where there may be exceptions to this general rule, there is wide agreement that confidentiality is *sine qua non* for successful psychiatric treatment.'"[6]

The critical role of confidentiality in mental health treatment, led various states over the past fifty years to enact special psychotherapy statutes that barred the disclosure of records and communications between the patient and the therapist. Significantly, these laws generally applied not only to psychiatrists but also to all classes of mental health professionals including psychologists and clinical social workers. Even where a state had not enacted legislation protecting the confidentiality of mental health treatment records or failed to provide remedies for private litigants, courts were able in some instances to adapt established doctrines of general application such as defamation or intentional infliction of mental distress to provide redress for patients whose privacy had been compromised. The different doctrinal approaches that courts used to provide a remedy for plaintiffs whose privacy had been compromised is detailed in section 3.b. *infra* (Remedies Arising from Breach of the Patient–Therapist Relationship).

3. *Biddle v. Warren General Hospital*, 86 Ohio St.3d 395, 715 N.E.2d 518 (1999).

4. *Humphers v. First Interstate Bank of Oregon*, 298 Or. 706, 696 P.2d 527 (1985).

5. As used in this chapter, "psychotherapy" includes both biological therapies and

the range on non-biological treatments described in Chapter 1.

6. *Jaffee v. Redmond*, 518 U.S. 1, 116 S.Ct. 1923, 135 L.Ed.2d 337 (1996). The *Redmond* case is set out in full at pp. 363–69.

B. FEDERAL PROTECTION OF HEALTH CARE PRIVACY

1. *Overview of HIPAA Legislation*

Federal protection of health care privacy derives from Congress's enactment of the Health Insurance Portability and Accountability Act of 1996 [HIPAA].[7] The legislation's primary purpose was to enable persons covered by group health plans to transfer their coverage when changing employers. The health benefit portability provisions are set out in what is known as Title I.

Primarily, in support of the benefits portability provisions, Title II of the Act establishes a regulatory regime for what are termed "administrative simplification provisions" designed to promote the replacement of paper-based transactions with more efficient electronic communications. Included within Title II are three major components: (1) transactions and code sets, (2) privacy, and (3) security and electronic signatures. In brief, the transactions code set provisions require that certain transactions pertaining to health care when conducted electronically follow standards prescribed by the Secretary of the Department of Health and Human Services (DHHS).

The privacy provisions that are discussed in greater detail in subsection C *infra* established rules for the use of disclosure of personal health information in the hands of (1) health care providers (both individuals and institutions), (2) health plan sponsors (e.g. employer sponsored group health plans, Medicare, etc.), and (3) health maintenance organizations (HMOs) and Health Care Clearinghouses. These three categories are termed "covered entities", which under the terms of the Act, are under duty to prevent unwarranted disclosure, destruction or corruption of personal health information. Title II also authorizes the Department of Health and Human Services (hereinafter DHHS) to issue regulations establishing enforcement mechanisms to ensure compliance with the mandated terms of the Act.

In enacting Title II, Congress charged the DHHS with the task of filling in the gaps, which given the generalized nature of the statutory mandates, means that it is the DHHS that has established ground rules governing the protection of privacy. Given the multiplicity of issues and the complexity and fragmentation of the health care industry, this has proved to be a massive undertaking. The results of this several year effort are the rules implementing the privacy provisions that take up 367 pages in the federal register.[8] DHHS issued final standards for privacy of individual identifiable health information ("privacy rule") on December 28, 2000.[9] While the privacy rule became effective April 14, 2001, the compliance date was delayed to April 14, 2003.[10]

---

7. Prior to HIPAA, federal law only protected medical information for specific groups, including medicare participants and individuals with AIDS. See Butera, "Preemption Implications for Covered Entities Under State Law, 2002," Tort & Insurance L.J., Summer, 3 (2002).

8. 45 CFR pts. 160; 164.

9. 65 FR 82462.

10. 67 FR 53182–02. The privacy rules are supplemented by the Security Rule, which was issued in final form on February 20, 2003, but will not become effective for

2. *Rationale for Federal Regulation of Health Care Privacy*

DEPARTMENT OF HEALTH AND HUMAN SERVICES

Office of the Secretary.
65 FR 82462. 45 CFR Parts 160 and 164. Thursday, December 28, 2000.

In enacting HIPAA, Congress recognized the fact that administrative simplification cannot succeed if we do not also protect the privacy and confidentiality of personal health information. The provision of high-quality health care requires the exchange of personal, often-sensitive information between an individual and a skilled practitioner. Vital to that interaction is the patient's ability to trust that the information shared will be protected and kept confidential. Yet many patients are concerned that their information is not protected. Among the factors adding to this concern are the growth of the number of organizations involved in the provision of care and the processing of claims, the growing use of electronic information technology, increased efforts to market health care and other products to consumers, and the increasing ability to collect highly sensitive information about a person's current and future health status as a result of advances in scientific research.

* * *

INCREASING USE OF INTERCONNECTED ELECTRONIC INFORMATION SYSTEMS

Until recently, health information was recorded and maintained on paper and stored in the offices of community-based physicians, nurses, hospitals, and other health care professionals and institutions. In some ways, this imperfect system of record keeping created a false sense of privacy among patients, providers, and others. Patients' health information has never remained completely confidential. Until recently, however, a breach of confidentiality involved a physical exchange of paper records or a verbal exchange of information. Today, however, more and more health care providers, plans, and others are utilizing electronic means of storing and transmitting health information. In 1996, the health care industry invested an estimated $10 billion to $15 billion on information technology. See National Research Council, Computer Science and Telecommunications Board, "For the Record: Protecting Electronic Health Information," (1997). The electronic information revolution is transforming the recording of health information so that the disclosure of information may require only a push of a button. In a matter of seconds, a person's most profoundly private information can be shared with hundreds, thousands, even millions of individuals and organizations at a time. While the majority of medical records still are in paper form, information from those records is often copied and transmitted through electronic means.

enforcement purposes until April 2005. Marks, et al., 'Analysis and Comments on HHS's just Released HIPAA Security Rules,' Davis Wright Tremaine, LLP Memorandum, February 17, 2003.

This ease of information collection, organization, retention, and exchange made possible by the advances in computer and other electronic technology affords many benefits to individuals and to the health care industry. Use of electronic information has helped to speed the delivery of effective care and the processing of billions of dollars worth of health care claims. Greater use of electronic data has also increased our ability to identify and treat those who are at risk for disease, conduct vital research, detect fraud and abuse, and measure and improve the quality of care delivered in the U.S.

At the same time, these advances have reduced or eliminated many of the financial and logistical obstacles that previously served to protect the confidentiality of health information and the privacy interests of individuals. And they have made our information available to many more people. The shift from paper to electronic records, with the accompanying greater flows of sensitive health information, thus strengthens the arguments for giving legal protection to the right to privacy in health information. In an earlier period where it was far more expensive to access and use medical records, the risk of harm to individuals was relatively low. In the potential near future, when technology makes it almost free to send lifetime medical records over the Internet, the risks may grow rapidly. It may become cost-effective,for instance, for companies to offer services that allow purchasers to obtain details of a person's physical and mental treatments. In addition to legitimate possible uses for such services, malicious or inquisitive persons may download medical records for purposes ranging from identity theft to embarrassment to prurient interest in the life of a celebrity or neighbor.

* * *

Moreover, electronic health data is becoming increasingly "national"; as more information becomes available in electronic form, it can have value far beyond the immediate community where the patient resides. Neither private action nor state laws provide a sufficiently comprehensive and rigorous legal structure to allay public concerns, protect the right to privacy, and correct the market failures caused by the absence of privacy protections. Hence, a national policy with consistent rules is necessary to encourage the increased and proper use of electronic information while also protecting the very real needs of patients to safeguard their privacy.

* * *

THE CHANGING HEALTH CARE SYSTEM

The number of entities who are maintaining and transmitting individually identifiable health information has increased significantly over the last 10 years. In addition, the rapid growth of integrated health care delivery systems requires greater use of integrated health information systems. The health care industry has been transformed from one that relied primarily on one-on-one interactions between patients and clinicians to a system of integrated health care delivery networks and managed care providers. Such a system requires the processing and collection of information about patients and plan enrollees (for example, in claims files or enrollment records), resulting in the creation of databases that can be easily transmitted. This dramatic change in the practice of medicine brings with it important prospects for the improvement of the quality of care and reducing the cost of that care. It also, however, means that increasing numbers of people have access to health information. And, as health plan functions are increasingly outsourced, a growing number of organizations not affiliated with our physicians or health plans also have access to health information.

According to the American Health Information Management Association

(AHIMA), an average of 150 people "from nursing staff to x-ray technicians, to billing clerks" have access to a patient's medical records during the course of a typical hospitalization. While many of these individuals have a legitimate need to see all or part of a patient's records, no laws govern who those people are, what information they are able to see, and what they are and are not allowed to do with that information once they have access to it. According to the National Research Council, individually identifiable health information frequently is shared with:

Consulting physicians;

Managed care organizations;

Health insurance companies;

Life insurance companies;

Self-insured employers;

Pharmacies;

Pharmacy benefit managers;

Clinical laboratories;

Accrediting organizations;

State and Federal statistical agencies; and

Medical information bureaus.

Much of this sharing of information is done without the knowledge of the patient involved. While many of these functions are important for smooth functioning of the health care system, there are no rules governing how that information is used by secondary and tertiary users. For example, a pharmacy benefit manager could receive information to determine whether an insurance plan or HMO should cover a prescription, but then use the information to market other products to the same patient. Similarly, many of us obtain health insurance coverage though our employer and, in some instances, the employer itself acts as the insurer. In these cases, the employer will obtain identifiable health information about its employees as part of the legitimate health insurance functions such as claims processing, quality improvement, and fraud detection activities. At the same time, there is no comprehensive protection prohibiting the employer from using that information to make decisions about promotions or job retention.

* * *

Congress recognized the importance of protecting the privacy of health information by enacting the Health Insurance Portability and Accountability Act of 1996. The Act called on Congress to enact a medical privacy statute and asked the Secretary of Health and Human Services to provide Congress with recommendations for protecting then confidentiality of health care information. The Congress further recognized the importance of such standards by providing the Secretary with authority to promulgate regulations on health care privacy in the event that lawmakers were unable to act within the allotted three years.

3. *Regulatory Implementation of HIPAA Privacy Provisions*

The recently promulgated HIPAA privacy rules for the first time establish national standards governing patient privacy rights in all health treatment situations, including mental health. The length and complexity of the privacy regulations preclude detailed examinations of the Privacy Regulations that came into effect April 2001. Nevertheless, given their impact, an examination of at least the key provisions of the regulations is necessary. For one thing, the key features of the regulations set out below will serve as a backdrop for a consideration of many of the issues treated in this chapter, which in some instances, will now be controlled by the new rules established by HIPAA.

HIPAA's privacy protection rules extend to not only health care providers but also to other participants in the health care industry such as health plans and health care clearinghouses. While the privacy rules are basically the same for the different classes, some provisions apply only to one of the above because of its distinct functions within the health care system. Given the focus of this and prior chapters on the treatment function of mental health professionals, the materials which follow will only consider the HIPAA privacy protection rules as they pertain to health providers.

a. *Covered Health Providers*

HIPAA regulations apply only to "covered entities" [hereinafter CE]. An entity or person is deemed to be covered if it is (1) a "health plan";[11] (2) a "health care clearinghouse";[12] or (3) "a health care provid-

11. "Health plan" has been interpreted to mean "a program that provides or pays the cost of health care services. Types of health plans include employer-sponsored group health insurance, self-funded employer-sponsored health plans, and health insurance sold to individuals, Medicare, Medicaid, and other public protection pro-

grams." 2002 HIPAA Desk Reference—A Physician's Guide to Understanding the Administration Simplification Provisions, at 3, Ingenix (2001)

12. "Health care clearinghouse" has been interpreted to mean "A public or private entity that does one of the following

er [and] who transmits any health information in electronic form in connection with a transaction covered [by HIPAA regulations]".[13] Thus, only providers of health care that transmit health information in electronic form are subject to HIPAA's privacy protection regime.

A health care *provider* is defined to include any" provider of medical or health services . . . and any other person or organization who furnishes, bills or is paid for health care in the normal course of business".[14] The other operative term "health care" is broadly defined to include:

> (1) Preventive, diagnostic, therapeutic, rehabilitative, maintenance, or palliative care, and counseling, service, assessment, or procedure with respect to the physical or mental condition, or functional status, of an individual or that affects the structure or function of the body; and

> (2) Sale or dispensing of a drug, device, equipment, or other item in accordance with a prescription.

45 C.F.R. § 160.103

The breadth of the definition of "provider" means that in addition to medical personnel, other professions who furnish or are paid for mental health treatment services such as psychologists and clinical social workers are included.

Since only health care providers that use electronic means to transmit health information[15] are subject to HIPAA's privacy provisions, the definition of both "electronic means" and "health information" becomes relevant for purposes of determining coverage. While the term "electronic" is not defined by the regulations, the DHHS has taken the position that the term includes any hard wire or wireless electronic communications of health information including in particular e-mail.[16] However, in general, voice telephone and paper-to-paper FAX transmissions are not covered.[17] Also, coverage is triggered even if the electronic communication pertaining to health information is only internal. Moreover, as noted by one commentator, "[d]espite a less-than-transparent statutory mandate, however, HHS decided that once an organization constitutes a CE under HIPAA, [having once used an electronic communication] all [fu-

---

two things: (1) processes or facilitates the processing of information that is received in a nonstandard format, or that contains nonstandard data content, into standard data elements or a standard transaction; and (2) receives a standard transaction and processes or facilitates the processing of information into nonstandard format or nonstandard data content for a receiving entity. Health care clearinghouses may include billing services, repricing companies, community health information systems, 'value-added' networks and switches—among other things." *Id.* at 3.

13.   45 C.F.R. § 160.102.

14.   45 C.F.R. § 160.103.

15.   See "Protected Health Information" in subsection b. which follows for the definition of "health information."

16.   As a result, "a nursing home that transmits health plan participants' information electronically to an auditor triggers HIPAA, whereas one that submits only paper copies does not." Butera, 'Preemption Implications for Covered Entities Under State Law, 2002', Tort & Insurance Law Journal, 3 (2002) [hereinafter Butera].

17.   "Experts Report", 8 Electronic Commerce & Law 485 (May 21, 2000) BNA; "Analysis & Comment on HHS's Just Released HIPPA Security Rule", Davis Wrights & Tremaine, Feb. 17, 2003.

ture] individually identifiable health information maintained or transmitted in any medium—electronic, paper, or oral—are protected."[18]

The result of this somewhat catch-all definition of electronic means
that any provider that seeks reimbursement for services from Medicare
or a defined health plan automatically becomes a covered entity since
HIPAA mandates that applications for reimbursement under these programs must be submitted by the use of standardized claims forms sent
electronically.[19]

b. Protected Health Information

The fundamental purpose of the privacy rule "is to enable the
individual who receives health care treatment to control the manner in
which the information is used and to whom it is disclosed".[20] Accordingly, HIPPA establishes rules governing both disclosures to third parties
and internal use of "protected health information" [hereinafter PHI].
The key term "information" is broadly defined to include:

> "[A]ny information, whether oral or recorded in any form or medi-
> um, that:
>
> (1) Is created or received by a health care provider, health plan,
> public health authority, employer, life insurer, school or university,
> or health care clearinghouse; and
>
> (2) Relates to the past, present, or future physical or mental
> health or condition of an individual; the provision of health care to
> an individual; or the past, present, or future payment for the
> provision of health care to an individual."

45 C.F.R. § 160.103

As a result, the prohibition on unauthorized disclosure covers virtually any information pertaining to past, current or future health care,
including the payment for such care. Also, coverage extends to information in any form including electronic, written or oral.[21] However, since
the definition of health care is restricted to information that can be used
to identify an individual, information that is "de-identified"[22] renders
the information free of restrictions. This makes it possible for treatment

---

18. Butera at 3.

19. 'Health Insurance Reform: Standards for Electronic Transactions,' 63 Fed.
Reg. 25272 (1998), 45 C.F.R. Pt. 142 (1998).
In fact, as of October 16, 2003, it will be a
potential civil and criminal violation to pay
claims that do not satisfy HIPAA's standards as specified in HIPAA's Transition
Rules. Marks, 'Surviving Standard Transactions: A HIPAA Road Map', 8 Electronic
Commerce and Law Report, 563 (2003)
BNA.

20. '2002 HIPAA Desk Reference—A
Physician's Guide to Understanding the Ad-

ministration Simplification Provisions', at
73, Ingenix (2001) [hereinafter 2002 HIPAA
Desk Reference].

21. 45 C.F.R. § 160.103. HIPAA presumably covers oral information to ensure
that information retains protection when
discussed or read aloud from a computer
screen or a written document or when communicated in the course of a treatment
session.

22. The specific identifiers that must be
removed to achieve de-identification are
listed in 45 C.F.R. § 164.514

providers to provide third-party aggregate or statistical data without the consent of the patient so long as it does not identify any individual.[23]

c. *Regulation of Disclosure*

The rules governing disclosure of PHI vary depending on (1) the relationship of the provider to the third person or entity that is to be the recipient of information or (2) the purpose of the disclosure. Where the person or entity to whom disclosure is to be made is involved in providing "indirect treatment" (i.e. providing treatment or diagnosis services at the direction of the primary provider),[24] PHI may be disclosed to the indirect provider without the consent of the patient.

Similarly, disclosure of PHI may be made without the consent of the patient to a "business associate," which includes among others, consultants, lawyers and accountants.[25] Both in the case of indirect health care providers and business associates the regulations require that the disclosure be limited to the "minimum necessary" to accomplish the specific purpose. Moreover, where the third party is a business associate the provider must establish a "business associate contract" as a condition for the disclosure of any PHI ... Such contract must specify (1) "the protected health information to be disclosed and the uses that may be made of the information and, (2) impose security, inspection and reporting requirements on the business associate."[26] However, since under current law, simply being a business associate is not classified under HIPAA as a covered entity, such entities are not directly subject to DHHS regulation.[27]

The rules governing disclosure are also relaxed where the disclosure is to a third party covered entity and the disclosure pertains to: "treatment, payment[28] or health care operations."[29] For these purposes, the provider has the option of disclosing PHI either with or without the consent of the patient. In any event, the disclosure must be the "minimum necessary" to accomplish the intended purpose.[30] This limitation

23. 2002 HIPAA Desk Reference at 73.

24. "An 'indirect treatment' relationship arises where the individual who has a direct relationship with a health case provider is referred by the direct provider to the indirect provider who typically will report the results of the test results of diagnosis to the direct provider." 2002 HIPAA Desk Reference at 45.

25. Business associates may also include third party administrators, data aggregators and processors, etc.

26. 2002 HIPAA Desk Reference at 56.

27. However, if the business associate is either a health plan, health care clearing house or health care provider, they may, on that basis, be a covered entity.

28. **Payment** includes activities undertaken by a health plan or provider to obtain or provide reimbursement or premiums for the provision of health care and other activities, such as determinations of eligibility or coverage (including coordination of benefits), risk adjustments, billing, claims management, collections, medical necessity reviews, and utilization review. 45 C.F.R. § 164.501.

29. **Health care operations** includes, for example, conducting quality assessment, developing clinical guidelines, evaluating provider performance, conducting or arranging for medical review, legal services, and auditing (including detection of fraud and abuse), business planning or development, resolution of internal plan grievances and implementation of HIPAA. 45 C.F.R. § 164.501.

30. 45 C.F.R. § 164.502.

does not apply to disclosures made to a covered entity for the purpose of treatment.[31] While the regulations permit disclosure in connection with treatment, payment or health care operations treatment without the consent or authorization of the patient, the risk of unauthorized use or disclosure by the recipients of the PHI is minimized by the fact that the recipient entity must be a covered entity such as an insurance company or HMO and therefore also subject to HIPAA's privacy rules.[32]

In all other cases except the above, PHI may not be disclosed to a third party except with the express authorization[33] of the patient or where the disclosure is permitted by one of the specific exceptions discussed below. Where the patient is an un-emancipated minor or a person under guardianship, the individual's personal representative is with limited exceptions[34] authorized to act on the patient's behalf in authorizing disclosure of PHI.[35] The designation of a personal representative is determined by "applicable [state] law."[36]

The regulations draw a distinction between "authorization" and "consent." The requirements pertaining to the former are far more stringent and require strict adherence to a set of protocols set out by the regulations. These include detailed information as to the identity of the person(s) to whom PHI is to be disclosed, an expiration date for the proposed disclosure and the right of the patient to revoke the authorization at any time.[37] Consent, on the other hand, has few formal requirements and, in general, can only be used where the disclosure of the PHI is to another covered entity.

While for the most part, mental health treatment is subject to the same privacy protection provisions as apply to other classes of treatment, "psychotherapy notes" constitute a separate class of protected health information.[38] In particular, this class of data is treated as distinct from the rest of the individual's health record and subject to more stringent

31. *Id.*

32. 45 C.F.R. § 164.506.

33. "Consent" and "authorization" are different concepts under HIPAA and the purpose of the proposed disclosure will determine which applies. A provider has the option but is not required to use the *consent* format where the purpose of disclosure of PHI is restricted to treatment, payment, or health care operations. 45 C.F.R. § 164.506. Where the provider chooses to use consent for this purpose, it can be drafted to permit multiple disclosures for this same purpose. For instance patient consent at the outset of treatment will permit a health provider to disclose PHI in connection with future payment requests by an insurance carrier.

An *authorization* on the other hand refers to a specific permission to use or disclose PHI for any purpose other than treatment, payment or health care operations. Moreover, the requirements are more stringent in that an authorization will only be valid if

it provides the patient with detailed information including: the precise PHI to be disclosed, the identity of the person(s) to whom it is to be disclosed, an expiration date for the proposed disclosure and the right of the patient to revoke the authorization at any time. 45 C.F.R. § 164.508

34. These exceptions pertain to health care that under state law an un-emancipated minor is permitted to obtain without their parent's of guardian's consent.

35. 45 C.F.R. § 164.500(g)(2)

36. 45 C.F.R. § 164.500(g)(2). Since death of a patient does not terminate the protection afforded by HIPAA, a personal representative is authorized by the regulations to have the power to consent to disclosure a decedent's PHI. The "personal representative" is designated in accordance with state law. 45 C.F.R. § 164.502.

37. 45 C.F.R. § 164.508.

38. 45 C.F.R. § 164.501.

rules.[39] For instance, a health provider may not use the consent format to disclose psychotherapy noted information, but can only do so upon authorization by the patient except in very limited circumstances discussed *infra* in *Exceptions to Authorization Requirement*. Moreover, authorization can only be sought by a provider where the psychiatric note information is in connection with "treatment, payment or health operations" and employed for one of the following purposes:

(A) Use by the originator of the psychotherapy notes for treatment;

(B) Use or disclosure by the covered entity for its own training programs in which students, trainees, or practitioners in mental health learn under supervision to practice or improve their skills in group, joint, family, or individual counseling; or

(C) Use or disclosure by the covered entity to defend itself in a legal action or other proceeding brought by the individual.

45 C.F.R. § 164.508

The above restrictions applicable to psychotherapy notes do not, however, prevent disclosure of other information pertaining to mental health treatment of an individual. For instance, providers may disclose to covered entities PHI pertaining to medication prescription and monitoring, counseling sessions and start and stop times.[40]

d. *Exceptions to Authorization Requirement*

The Regulations authorize the disclosure of PHI to specified persons and entities without the patient's consent in a variety of special circum-

39. Psychotherapy notes, in contrast to general health information, are subject to special restrictions. These restrictions include the following: (1) except for the special circumstances listed below they may only be disclosed to a third party when specifically authorized by the patient (45 CFR § 164.508); (2) a patient has a right to inspect and make copies of all his or her health information though this right does not extend to psychotherapy notes 45 CFR § 164.524. While the patient does not have a right to the notes, the provider may at its discretion disclose the psychotherapy notes to the patient.

The regulations set out a list of special circumstance under which the provider may disclose the psychotherapy notes without the patient's authorization. These include:

(1) use by the originator of the note for treatment, payment of health care operations (since treatment, payment or health care operations can only involve covered entities any disclosure for these purposes would be limited to covered entities). 45 CFR 164.508(a)(2)(i)(A);

(2) use by the covered entity for training programs to improve skills in group,

joint, family or individual counseling. 45 CFR 164.508(a)(2)(i)(B);

(3) by the covered entity to defend itself in a legal action brought by the patient. 45 CFR 164.508(a)(2);

(4) when disclosure is required by law and the use or disclosure complies with the relevant requirements of the law. 45 CFR 164.508(a)(2); 164.512 (a)(1)

(5) To a coroner or medical examiner for the purpose of identification of the patient or determine the cause of death. 164.508(a)(2), 164.512(G)(1).

(6) Where necessary to prevent or lessen a serious and imminent threat to the health of safety of a person or the public. 45 CFR 164,508, 164.512(J)(1)(i)

40. 45 C.F.R. § 164.501 "Psychotherapy notes excludes medication prescription and monitoring, counseling session start and stop times, the modalities and frequencies of treatment furnished, results of clinical tests, and any summary of the following items: Diagnosis, functional status, the treatment plan, symptoms, prognosis, and progress to data."

stances.[41] Among the various special circumstances permitting disclosure are the following: (1) to public health authorities for the purpose of controlling or preventing disease; (2) where authorized by state law to report child abuse or neglect, or domestic violence; (3)where needed for various law enforcement purposes including the apprehension of an individual who has admitted participating in a violent crime;[42] (4) where necessary to prevent or lessen an immediate threat to the health and safety of the person or the public;[43] (5) in any judicial or administrative proceeding in response to an express order or subpoena or to a subpoena discovery request.[44] A number of these exceptions only apply where the disclosure is specifically authorized by state law. The interplay of the HIPAA exception and state law authorization is taken up.

e. Miscellaneous Requirements

The regulations impose various patient privacy notification requirements including in particular the posting and/or distribution to all present of prospective patients a notice that spells out the provider's privacy policies. Such notice must include: (1) the provider's policies and procedures concerning the use and disclosure of PHI; (2) the individual's rights under HIPAA; and (3) the covered entity's legal obligation under HIPAA with respect to PHI.[45]

Under the regulations, a covered entity must undertake to train all of its workforce who have access to PHI in privacy policies and procedures. As used in the regulations, "workforce" is not limited to employees, but includes independent contractors, volunteers, trainees and other persons under the direct control of the covered entity. Further, all levels and stages of training must be documented in a training log.

The privacy rules also provide that: "[a] covered entity must have in place appropriate administrative, technical and physical safeguards to protect the privacy of protected health information."[46]

These provisions that are commonly referred to as the "mini-security rules" are embedded in HIPPA's privacy regulations. At the same time, a separate set of regulations that expand on these provisions is contained in the security rules that were announced in the Federal Register on February 20, 2003 and will become effective for enforcement purposes in April 2005.[47] These security rules that contain a 244–page preamble and 45 typed pages of rules are less a series of check lists and more a description of principles to be used by covered entities and their business associates to evaluate and apply specific security protections

41. 45 C.F.R. § 160.512.

42. 45 C.F.R. § 164.512 (j)(1)(ii)(A).

43. 45 C.F.R. § 164.512 (j)(1)(i)(A).

44. The conditions governing disclosure in response to a subpoena or discovery motion are discussed *infra* at Section II.D, Judicial Proceedings and the Testimonial Privilege *infra*.

45. 45 C.F.R. § 164.520.

46. 45 C.F.R. § 154.530.

47. The security rules are contained in a new Subpart C in Part 164, Volume 45 of the Code of Federal Regulations ("CFR"). They may be downloaded from the CMS website at www.cms.gov.

based on an entity's particular situation. Among its mandates is the adoption of intensive management of processes that will enable the covered entity to detect intrusions in its data systems and to respond with appropriate counter measures.[48]

Finally, HIPAA grants patients a qualified right of access to their health information and a right to seek amendment of the health information. The scope of the right of access is discussed more fully in Section III(b), Patient Access to Records, at pp. 417–21.

f. Enforcement

Butera, "HIPAA Preemption Implications for Covered Entities Under State Law", 2002, Tort and Insurance Law Journal, Summer (2002)

... HIPAA authorizes the Secretary of HHS to conduct general compliance reviews. CEs must cooperate with any compliance investigation, which includes providing broad access to administrative records. This means that CEs must properly record all activities to implement, manage, and monitor HIPAA compliance.

HIPAA contains a host of civil and criminal penalties. For example, any CE (including employees) that unintentionally violates the privacy provisions without exercising reasonable diligence may be liable for up to $100 for each violation, not to exceed $25,000 per year. A civil penalty will not be imposed, however, if a person did not know or, by exercising reasonable diligence, would not have known that his or her action constituted a violation. Criminal penalties are considerably more severe. Any person who knowingly obtains or discloses individually identifiable health information in violation of HIPAA may be fined up to $50,000 and/or imprisoned for no more than one year. If the disclosure is done under "false pretenses," the fine increases to $100,000 and imprisonment of up to five years. The severest punishment applies to offenses done with intent to "sell, transfer, or use" individually identifiable health information for commercial advantage, personal gain, or malicious harm. This violation demands a fine not to exceed $250,000 and/or imprisonment of not more than ten years.

Neither HIPAA nor the Privacy Rule explicitly grants a private cause of action, including qui tam actions. Still, CEs and business associates fear that the plaintiff's bar, in state and federal tort actions, will use a Privacy Rule violation as evidence that the duty of care was ignored. Moreover, CEs have increased exposure to civil and criminal actions because they may be liable for the privacy breaches of their business associates. For purposes of OCR compliance, CEs are not expected to guarantee the privacy of PHI, as HHS noted in its first

---

48. See 'Analysis & Comment on HHS's Just Released HIPAA Security Rule', Davis Wright Tremaine LLP, Feb. 17, 2003.

clarification; however, CEs must take "reasonable" steps to protect the confidentiality of the PHI subject to business associate use.

g.   *Relationship to State Laws*

HIPAA's privacy provisions are intertwined with state law in two ways. At one level there is a preemption aspect that displaces state laws that conflict with the national standards established by HIPAA. At the same time, HIPAA defers to state law to the extent that state law more restrictively limits disclosure of PHI without the patient's consent. For instance, as discussed previously, HIPAA privacy regulations authorize disclosure of PHI without the patient's consent in a variety of circumstances such as disclosures in connection with litigation or disclosures pertaining to the dangerousness of a patient only when permitted or required by state law. Thus, state law can in certain instances, serve to define HIIPA's disclosure rules. [A number of the exceptions that permit disclosure of PHI without the patient's consent when authorized by state law are considered in section II, Exceptions to the Duty of Confidentiality at pp. 350–415.]

HIPAA's preemption aspects are express but selective. The excerpt below summarizes the scope and operation of the preemption provisions:

> "Congress adopted a general rule that any HIPAA medical privacy statute, standard or implementation specification 'shall supercede any contrary provision of State law, including a provision of state law that requires medical or health plan records ... to be maintained in written rather than electronic form.'[49] However, conflict between state and federal law is not presumed, and whenever possible, state and federal provisions should be construed in a manner that makes them compatible. In practice, HIPAA preemption does not represent a wholesale federal preemption of the field of privacy law, but rather a national floor of medical privacy protection.

> Congress created three protected areas of state law, or statutory carve-outs, where federal HIPAA does not trump or override state law by preemption. Certain portions of state public health law are protected, with Congress stating that "[n]othing in this part shall be construed to invalidate or limit" the authority, power or procedures established under any law providing for the reporting of disease, injury, child abuse, birth or death; public health surveillance; public health investigation; and (public health) intervention.

> Certain, other, mandatory state regulatory reporting and state licensure investigatory activities are also expressly saved by statute from federal preemption. These include requiring a health plan to report or provide access to information for management audits, financial audits, program monitoring and evaluation, facility licensure or certification, or individual licensure or certification. Thus,

---

49. 42 USC § 1320d–7(a)(1).

the statute gives state health departments and licensing boards broad access for the uninterrupted conducting of traditional state public health licensure and programmatic financial review activities. The HIPAA statute contains another savings provision which was designed to go into effect only if HIPAA privacy was promulgated by Department of Health and Human Services (DHHS) rulemaking, rather than by Congressional passage. Since Congress itself did not pass comprehensive medical privacy law, but instead, by inaction, delegated it to DHHS, an uncodified statutory provision states that the federal regulations "shall not supersede a contrary provision of State law, if the provision of State law imposes requirements, standards, or implementation specifications that are 'more stringent'[50] than" the comparable federal DHHS standard.

By definition, DHHS has clarified several aspects of this savings clause. First, DHHS sets the bar quite high when it finds a conflict, defining "contrary" to mean either, 1) that an entity would find it impossible to comply with both the state and federal provisions ("impossibility test"), or 2) that the provision of the state law stands as an obstacle to the full purposes and objectives of HIPAA ("obstacle test"). Similarly, the term "more stringent" means that the state law restricts a disclosure permitted under HIPAA, grants greater access to a person's own health information, more severely restricts the scope or duration of authorized access by another, requires greater record-keeping or generally provides greater privacy protection to the individual who is the subject of the record."

Ryland, "Federal Health Privacy Comes to Maryland: What's the Big Deal?" 2003, Maryland Bar Journal, Jan./Feb. (2003).

Questions and Comments

1. *Non-covered health providers.* Mental health professionals who treat patients are not necessarily covered by HIPAA. All mental health professionals, including psychiatrist, would be exempt from coverage if they do not use electronic modes of communication to transmit health information in their practice, including for instance, billing for services. Thus, a therapist who only has patients who themselves pay for their treatment and who are billed by mail would not be subject to HIPAA. However, a therapist who bills a third party private insurer or under a public insurance plan such as Medicare or Medicaid must by law submit the billing electronically with the result that such health provider would therefore be a covered entity and subject to HIPAA privacy regulations.

2. *Professions covered by HIPAA.* Are marriage counselors and other "helping" professions covered by HIPAA? As indicated in the review of

50. "More stringent" has been interpreted to include any of the following: (1) imposes greater restrictions on disclosure; (2) permits greater access to individuals who are the subject of the PHI; (3) provides a greater amount of health information to individuals who are subjects of the PHI; (4) narrows the scope or duration of a consent or authorization; (5) reduces the coercive effect of the circumstances surrounding authorization and consent; (6) requires record retention of greater duration or more detailed information.

HIPAA provisions *supra*, a person or entity involved in providing health care and uses electronic means of communication to transmit health information. Health care, in turn, is sufficiently broadly defined that marriage counselors and similar professions would be covered persons if they billed for their services electronically or used electronic communications for other purposes related to the provisioning of health services.

3. *Disclosures authorized by state law.* Numerous states also authorize a physician or mental health professional to disclose any confidential information when the patient's condition makes it necessary to set in motion commitment proceedings. For instance, in Illinois records and communications may be disclosed where it is "necessary to the provision of emergency medical care to a recipient" or in "commitment proceedings." Ill.—S.H.A. ch. 9 1/2, ¶ 8–11 (Mental Health and Development Disability Confidentiality Act, 1979). HIPAA does not expressly authorize disclosure in connection with civil commitment, but does permit disclosure when "necessary to prevent or lessen a serious imminent threat to the safety of the individual [patient] ..." 45 C.F.R. § 164.512. Presumably, the imminent threat of suicide by a patient would thus meet the HIPAA test.

4. *Continuing importance of state confidentiality laws.* In spite of HIPAA, state confidentiality laws that do not conflict with HIPAA retain their vitality. Such laws may provide protections exceeding those called for by HIPAA and moreover, may provide private rights of action to patients whose privacy rights have been compromised in contrast to HIPAA, which only provides for remedies and enforcement by the Department of Health and Human Services. See *Smith v. American Home Products Corp. Wyeth–Ayerst Pharmaceutical*, 372 N.J. Super. 105, 855 A.2d 608 (2003) (holding that New Jersey law that offered broader protection of health records than HIPAA controlled]

5. *Hypothetical.* Rick Rocker, a famous rock star, had come to Metro City for a rock concert in which he was the featured performer. In the early morning hours of January 1, 2005, friends of Rick's called 9–1–1 to report that Rick, who was in a hotel penthouse suite, was unconscious and turning blue. The 9–1–1 operator immediately relayed the call to the Metro City Emergency Response Office, which in turn dispatched an ambulance owned and operated by the hospital. By coincidence, Brenda Star, ace reporter with the Metro Sentinel, a local newspaper, happened to be interviewing a doctor at the Metro City Emergency Response Office when the call came in. Having overhead the call on a speakerphone, Brenda thought that this might make an interesting story and decided to follow the ambulance in her own vehicle to Rocker's hotel. A short time later, two ambulance paramedics emerged from the hotel wheeling Rocker out on a stretcher. Just as the ambulance was ready to leave for the hospital, Brenda asked one of the paramedics what had caused Rocker's collapse and "Will he be okay?" In response, the paramedic replied, "It looks like he overdid the partying bit—we gave him a shot of Narcan to help bring him out of it". Knowing that Narcan is used to neutralize opiates, Brenda concluded that Rocker's condition was the result of an overdose of percocet or another opiate.

Ten days later, Rocker recovers and upon being released from Metro City Hospital is told by his manager that the press report on his overdose will probably hurt his career and that he has already been dropped by one TV sponsor, who was planning to use a video he had previously made. Unhappy at this turn of events, Rick asked his legal representative to file a complaint with the DHHS Office of Civil Rights (OCR) based on a violation on his HIPAA privacy rights. Is there any basis for the OCR to bring charges against any of the parties involved in this case, and if so, which party?

6. *Review of HIPAA constitutionality.* Challenges to HIPAA regulations governing privacy have withstood constitutional challenges asserting a violation of the non-delegation of legislative power doctrine. See *South Carolina Medical Association v. Thompson*, 327 F.3d 346 (4th Circuit 2003), cert den. 540 U.S. 981, 124 S.Ct. 464, 157 L.Ed.2d 371 (2003).

7. *Application to state facilities.* While the HIPAA legislation does not expressly purport to cover public sector entities, it has been assumed that the regulations concerning privacy protection are not limited to the private sector. Apparently states agencies and institutions are complying with the HIPAA rules. However, at some point, some provisions of HIPAA could be challenged by a state on the basis that HIPAA may not constitutionally be applied to the states because of the Eleventh Amendment. The doctrinal basis for a challenge to the application of HIPAA to the states and the relevant cases that have addressed this issue are discussed in Chapter 12 at pp. 1280–82.

C. PROTECTION OF EDUCATIONAL RECORDS UNDER FER-PA

The Family Educational Rights and Privacy Act of 1974 (FERPA) protects the confidentiality of school records maintained by any educational institution that accepts federal funding (which, as a practical matter, includes virtually all institutions of higher learning as well as public elementary and secondary schools). In general, FERPA bars disclosure to any external person or agency personal or identifiable information contained in educational records without the written consent of the parent if the student is under 18, and the student if he or she is 18 years or older. Under FERPA, the term "educational records" is defined as "[t]hose records, files, documents and other materials which (i) contain information directly related to a student; and (ii) are maintained by an educational agency or institution or by a person acting for such agency or institution." 20 U.S.C. § 1232g(a)(4)(A); 34 CFR § 99.3. However, FERPA excludes from the definition of educational records:

> records of a student who is eighteen years of age or older, or is attending an institution of postsecondary education, which are made or maintained by a physician, psychiatrist, psychologist, or other recognized professional or paraprofessional acting in his professional or paraprofessional capacity, or assisting in that capacity, and which are made, maintained, or used only in connection with the provision of treatment to the student . . .

20 U.S.C. § 1232 (a)(4)(B)(iv); 34 CFR § 99.3.

It is not clear whether HIPAA covers the latter records. Compare 45 CFR § 160.103 and Memorandum, Sharing Information about Potentially Dangerous Students, Office of the General Counsel, University of Texas System, July 10, 2007 with U.S. Department of Education Guidance Letter of Nov. 29, 2004 to M. Baise, Associated University Counsel, University of New Mexico. In any event, even if HIPAA applies, HIPAA regulations permit disclosure when "necessary to prevent or lessen a serious and imminent threat to the health and safety of a person of the public, . . . to a person or persons reasonably able to prevent or lessen the threat, including the target of the threat." 45 C.F.R. § 164.512(j). New FERPA regulations use virtually identical language. See pp. 357–59. As a practical matter, the generality in which the FERPA and HIPAA exceptions are phrased makes it likely that a university would have wide discretion to disclose information drawn from treatment records where a university believes in good faith that a student presents a serious danger to themselves or third persons.

Aside from the possibility that health treatment records maintained by a university may be covered by FERPA or HIPPA Privacy Rules, state law could come into play in determining whether non-consensual disclosure may be made in a particular circumstance. The exceptions for non-consensual disclosure under both HIPPA and FERPA do not displace state laws that are more protective of health record privacy. Thus, even where disclosure is authorized by one of the HIPPA or FERPA exceptions, state law could prevent disclosure or at least limit disclosure to specific persons and entities.

Questions and Comments

1. *Contrasting scope of HIPAA and FERPA.* Differences in the scope of HIPAA's and HIPAA's privacy rules are summarized in the report of the Virginia Tech Review Panel:

> . . . FERPA was drafted to apply to educational records, not medical records [and therefore does not enumerate the different types of disclosures that are authorized]. . . FERPA also has a different scope than HIPAA. Medical privacy laws such as HIPAA apply to all information— written or oral—gained in the course of treatment. FERPA applies only to information in student *records.* Personal observations and conversations with a student fall outside FERPA. Thus, for example, teachers or administrators who witness students acting strangely are not restricted by FERPA from telling anyone–school officials, law enforcement, parents or any other person or organization."

Review Panel Report, at 66.

2. *Transfer of health information from medical unit to university administration.* While the treatment records of a university health facility are not subject to FERPA, a record that originates as a university medical record but is shared with another university official for a legitimate educational purpose becomes an education record subject to FERPA. For example, if a medical record is provided at a student's request to a faculty member or the dean of students in support of the student's request to be granted a medical leave of absence, that record would become part of the student's education record and would be subject to FERPA.

D. LEGAL REMEDIES FOR BREACH OF CONFIDENTIALITY UNDER STATE LAW

State remedies for breach of confidentiality in the mental health treatment context retain their vitality notwithstanding the enactment of HIPAA and the promulgation of the privacy regulations. HIPAA does not provide patients whose privacy interests have been compromised with a private cause of action. As noted, HIPAA authorizes enforcement action only by the Department of Health and Human Services Office of Civil Rights. Thus, patients whose privacy rights have been violated would need to seek redress against an offending health provider under state laws. At the same time, it is likely that HIPAA's privacy protection standards will influence the development and application of state remedial laws. This is likely to happen where state laws are drafted in general terms with HIPAA standards being incorporated by courts in the application of state law.

1. *General Remedies*

a. *Actions Based on Breach of Privacy*

Essentially four distinct types of privacy actions have been identified. In one, the privacy refers to a physical intrusion into a person's private affairs, such as wiretapping his telephone. In the second aspect of the doctrine the phrase refers to appropriation, *i.e.,* the use of another person's photograph or likeness for advertising without permission. A third form entails publication of incomplete or misleading information, which places another person in a "false light" in the public eye. For instance, use of a person's photograph to illustrate a story about drug addicts, when that person is neither a drug addict nor has any relationship to the story, may violate his privacy rights. A fourth and final aspect of the right to privacy and the one that most concerns therapists is the revelation of confidential information about the plaintiff. The action is founded on the premise that if information that the patient could reasonably expect to remain private is disclosed, a cause of action may arise based on that disclosure. This branch of privacy is most often referred to as the public disclosure of private facts and covers the disclosure of those matters that would be embarrassing to the average individual. The following case which arose from the efforts of a noted producer of documentary films to expose abuses in a state psychiatric facility illustrates the application of this doctrine.

COMMONWEALTH v. WISEMAN

Supreme Judicial Court of Massachusetts, 1969.
356 Mass. 251, 249 N.E.2d 610.

CUTTER, JUSTICE.

This bill seeks, among other relief, to enjoin all showings of a film entitled "Titicut Follies," containing scenes at Massachusetts Correctional Institution at Bridgewater (Bridgewater), to which insane persons charged with crime and defective delinquents may be committed. The film was made between April 22, and June 29, 1966. Mr. Wiseman and Bridgewater Film Company, Inc. (BFC) appeal from an interlocutory decree, an order for a decree, and the final decree which enjoins showing the film "to any audience" and requires Mr. Wiseman and BFC to deliver up to the Attorney General for destruction specified films, negatives, and sound tapes. The plaintiffs appeal from the final decree because it did not order sums realized by various defendants from showing the film to be held for distribution as the court might direct.

The trial judge made a report of material facts. The evidence (2,556 pages of proceedings on eighteen trial days and sixty-four exhibits) is reported. The facts, except as otherwise indicated, are stated on the basis of the trial judge's findings and certain exhibits. The film has been shown to the Justices participating in this decision.

In 1965, Mr. Wiseman first requested permission from the Superintendent and from the Commissioner to make an educational documentary film concerning Bridgewater. His first request was denied. On January 28, 1966, permission was granted, subject to the receipt of a favorable opinion from the Attorney General (that the officials could grant permission) and to the conditions (a) that "the rights of the inmates and patients * * * [would be] fully protected," (b) that there would be used only "photographs of inmates and patients * * * legally competent to sign releases," (c) that a written release would be obtained "from each patient whose photograph is used in the film," and (d) that the film would not be released "without first having been * * * approved by the Commissioner and Superintendent." The existence of the final condition was the subject of conflicting evidence but there was oral testimony upon which the trial judge could reasonably conclude that it had been imposed.

* * *

In April, 1966, Mr. Wiseman and his film crew started work at Bridgewater. They were given free access to all departments except the treatment center for the sexually dangerous, whose director made "strong objections" in writing to any photography there without compliance with explicit written conditions. In three months, 80,000 feet of film were exposed. Pictures were made "of mentally incompetent patients * * * in the nude * * * [and] in the most personal and private situations."

In approaching the Commissioner and the Superintendent, Mr. Wiseman had indicated that he planned a documentary film about three people: an adult inmate, a youthful offender, and a correctional officer. It was to be an effort "to illustrate the various services performed— custodial, punitive, rehabilitative, and medical." The judge concluded (a) that the "plain import of [Mr.] Wiseman's representations was that his film was to be * * * non-commercial and non-sensational," whereas, in the judge's opinion, it was "crass * * * commercialism"; (b) that, in fact, the film "constitutes a most flagrant abuse[a] of the privilege * * * [Mr. Wiseman] was given"; and (c) that, instead of "a public service project," the film, as made, is "to be shown to the general public in movie houses."

* * *

In September, 1967, Mr. Wiseman made an agreement with Grove for distribution of the film for "showing to the general public * * * throughout the United States and Canada," with Mr. Wiseman to receive "50% of the theatrical gross receipts, and 75% from any television sale." Grove, for promotion of the film, was to have "complete control of the manner and means of distribution." The film was shown privately, and to the public for profit, in New York City in the autumn of 1967.

The trial judge ruled, inter alia, (a) that such "releases as may have been obtained [from inmates] are a nullity"; (b) "that the film is an unwarranted * * * intrusion * * * into the * * * right to privacy of each inmate" pictured, degrading "these persons in a manner clearly not warranted by any legitimate public concern"; (c) that the "right of the public to know" does not justify the unauthorized use of pictures showing identifiable persons "in such a manner as to * * * cause * * * humiliation"; (d) that "it is the responsibility of the State to protect" the inmates "against any such * * * exploitation"; and (e) that the Commonwealth is under "obligation * * * to protect the right of privacy of those * * * committed to its * * * custody."

Reactions to the film set out in the record vary from the adversely critical conclusions of the trial judge to those expressed by witnesses who regarded it as fine journalistic reporting, as education, and as art.[b] The Attorney General (Mr. Richardson) testified that the film "was impressive in many ways * * * powerful in impact." He, however, expressed concern about the problem of obtaining valid releases, even from those "conceivably competent," since the releases would have been given

a. [Authors Note: Up to this point of Chapter 5, footnotes have been numbered sequentially. In order to avoid confusion and clearly identify original case footnotes, all case numerical designations have been converted to an alphabetical format]. Among the findings are the following: The film "is a hodge-podge of sequences * * * depicting mentally ill patients engaged in repetitive, incoherent, and obscene rantings * * *. The film is excessively preoccupied with nudity. * * * [N]aked inmates are shown desperately attempting to hide * * * their privates with their hands. * * * There is a scene of * * * [a priest] administering the last rites of the church to a dying patient [and] the preparation of corpse for burial. * * * A * * * patient, grossly deformed by * * * congenital brain damage, is paraded before the camera."

b. For example the Life review said, in part, "The Bridgewater atmosphere is one of aimless hopelessness. * * * A psychiatrist turns an interview with an inmate into a sadistic baiting, or, with malicious cheerfulness, forcefeeds a dying old man, while we wonder whether the ash from the doctor's carelessly dangling cigarette is really going to fall into the glop being funneled into the convulsively shuddering throat. A society's treatment of the least of its citizens * * * is perhaps the best measure of its civilization. The repulsive reality * * * forces us to contemplate our capacity for callousness. No one seeing this film can but believe that reform of the conditions it reports is urgent business. * * * "

before the inmates "could have any idea how they would be depicted." There was testimony from experts about the value of the film for instruction of medical and law students, and "exposture [sic] of conditions in a public institution."

* * *

1. [As an initial matter, the Court held that since the film constituted documentary evidence the appellate court could undertake its appraisal without regard to the findings of the trial court.]

2. The Commissioner and the Superintendent would have acted wisely if they had reduced any agreement to writing rather than to have risked the misunderstandings possible in oral discussions. They also might have avoided dispute if they had supervised the filming itself much more closely.

* * *

Early in the negotiations, Mr. Wiseman represented in writing that only pictures of inmates "legally competent to sign releases" would be used and that the "question of competency would * * * be determined by the Superintendent and his staff." In the 1966 request for the Attorney General's opinion, Mr. Wiseman was quoted as giving assurance that a written release would be obtained "from each * * * patient whose photograph is used." The latter assurance was quoted in the opinion (March 21, 1966) stating that the Superintendent had power to permit the film to be made. In the circumstances, the judge reasonably could conclude that these representations were a part of the arrangement.

The judge was also clearly justified in deciding on the basis of expert testimony, that some of sixty-two inmates identified as shown in the film were incompetent to understand a release and, on the basis of a stipulation, that releases were obtained only from eleven or twelve of the numerous inmates depicted. There was ample basis for concluding that Mr. Wiseman had not fulfilled important undertakings clearly designed to assure that the film would show only those consenting in writing to their appearance in the film and competent to understand and to give such consent.

3. The film shows many inmates in situations which would be degrading to a person of normal mentality and sensitivity. Although to a casual observer most of the inmates portrayed make little or no specific individual impression, others are shown in close-up pictures. These inmates are sufficiently clearly exhibited (in some instances naked) to enable acquaintances to identify them. Many display distressing mental symptoms. There is a collective, indecent intrusion into the most private aspects of the lives of these unfortunate persons in the Commonwealth's custody.

We need not discuss to what extent in Massachusetts violation of privacy will give rise to tort liability *to individuals*. [Emphasis added]

We think, in any event, that Mr. Wiseman's massive, unrestrained invasion of the intimate lives of these State patients may be prevented by properly framed injunctive relief. The Commonwealth has standing and a duty to protect reasonably, and in a manner consistent with other public interests, the inmates from any invasions of their privacy substantially greater than those inevitably arising from the very fact of confinement.

There is a "general power of the Legislature, in its capacity as parens patriae, to make suitable provision for incompetent persons." A "comprehensive system for their care and custody" is contained in [Massachusetts statutory provisions]. The Legislature has exercised that power with specific reference to Bridgewater, among other institutions. These general provisions import all reasonable power, and the duty, to exercise proper controls over the persons confined and the conditions of their custody and to afford the inmates protection and kindness consistent with the terms and rehabilitative purposes of their commitments.

The Commissioner and Superintendent, under reasonable standards of custodial conduct, could hardly permit merely curious members of the public access to Bridgewater to view directly many activities of the type shown in the film. We think it equally inconsistent with their custodial duties to permit the general public (as opposed to members of groups with a legitimate, significant, interest) to view films showing inmates naked or exhibiting painful aspects of mental disease.

These considerations, taken with the failure of Mr. Wiseman to comply with the contractual condition that he obtain valid releases from all persons portrayed in the film, amply justify granting injunctive relief to the Commonwealth. The impracticability of affording relief to the inmates individually also supports granting this collective relief to the Commonwealth as parens patriae, in the interest of all the affected inmates. We give no weight to any direct interest of the Commonwealth itself in suppressing the film.

4. The defendants contend that no asserted interest of privacy may be protected from the publication of this film because the conditions at Bridgewater are matters of continuing public concern, as this court has recognized.

Indeed, it was concern over conditions at Bridgewater which led various public officials in 1965 and 1966 to consider a documentary film, in the hope that, if suitable, it might arouse public interest and lead to improvement.

Even an adequate presentation to the public of conditions at Bridgewater, however, would not necessitate the inclusion of some episodes shown in the film, nor would it justify the depiction of identifiable inmates, who had not given valid written consents and releases, naked or in other embarrassing situations. We agree with the trial judge that Mr. Wiseman's wide ranging photography amounted to "abuse of the privilege he was given to make a film" and a serious failure to comply with conditions reasonably imposed upon him. Mr. Wiseman could hardly have fairly believed that officials, solicitous about obtaining consent and releases from all inmates portrayed, could have been expected to approve this type of film for general distribution.

The record does not indicate to us that any inmate shown in the film, by reason of past conduct, had any special news interest as an individual. Each inmate's importance to the film was that he was an inmate of Bridgewater, that he suffered from some form of mental disease, and that he was undergoing in the Bridgewater facilities particular types of custody and treatment. Recognizable pictures of individuals, although perhaps resulting in more effective photography, were not essential. In the circumstances, there will be no unreasonable interference with any publication of matters of public concern if showing the film to the general public is prevented (a) to protect interests of the inmates in privacy, and (b) because Mr. Wiseman went unreasonably beyond the scope of the conditional permission to enter, and take pictures upon, State owned premises properly not generally open for public inspection and photography.

The case is distinguishable from decisions which have permitted publication of newsworthy events where the public interest in reasonable dissemination of news has been treated as more significant than the private interests in privacy. We need not now consider to what extent Mr. Wiseman could have been wholly excluded from making a film at Bridgewater. In this aspect of the case, we hold merely that he violated the permission given to him, reasonably interpreted, and did not comply with valid conditions that he obtain written releases.

* * *

5. That injunctive relief may be granted against showing the film to the general public on a commercial basis does not mean that all showings of the film must be prevented. As already indicated the film gives a striking picture of life at Bridgewater and of the problems affecting treatment at that or any similar institution. It is a film which would be instructive to legislators, judges, lawyers, sociologists, social workers, doctors, psychiatrists, students in these or related fields, and organizations dealing with the social problems of custodial care and mental infirmity. The public interest in having such persons informed about Bridgewater, in our opinion, outweighs any countervailing interests of the inmates and of the Commonwealth (as parens patriae) in anonymity and privacy.

The effect upon inmates of showing the film to persons with a serious interest in rehabilitation, and with potential capacity to be helpful, is likely to be very different from the effect of its exhibition merely to satisfy general public curiosity. There is possibility that showings to specialized audiences may be of benefit to the public interest, to the inmates themselves, and to the conduct of an important State institution. Because of the character of such audiences, the likelihood of humiliation, even of identifiable inmates, is greatly reduced. In any event the likelihood of harm seems to us less than the probability of benefits.

* * * The decree is to be modified to permit (according to standards to be defined in the decree) the showing of the film to audiences of the specialized or professional character already mentioned.

* * *

[The Court held that individual inmates who had been filmed were not entitled to damages.]

Questions and Comments

1. *Impact of HIPAA.* What would have been the impact of HIPAA had law been in effect at the time that Mr. Wiseman filmed the documentary? HIPAA privacy rules apply to any psychiatric hospital that is "a covered entity" (possible challenges on Eleventh Amendment grounds to the application of HIPAA to state institutions are discussed at p. 324). If the Bridgewater correctional institution were a covered entity, would it be in violation of HIPAA for Bridgewater to allow a documentary filmmaker to film the inmates? Would HIPAA limitations also cover the documentary filmmaker?

2. *"Titicut Follies" revisited.* As indicated by the following news report, the film "Titicut Follies" continued to be the subject of judicial proceedings twenty years after the court rendered the above decision.

> BOSTON, Sept. 29—A judge has said that a 22–year–old ban on the public showing of a film that depicts brutality in a state prison hospital for the mentally ill may be lifted if the faces of many of the inmates are blurred.
>
> But the filmmaker, Frederick Wiseman, says that blurring faces is not technically feasible. Even if it were, he said, such an action would violate his right to free speech as a journalist and the public's right to know how state-supported institutions are run.
>
> "The film would lose its meaning," said Mr. Wiseman, an award-winning director known for his unflinchingly realistic portrayal of the police, schools, hospitals and other institutions that bring people in contact with the state. "The whole point is that these are not faceless people. Their faces reflect the lives they've lived and how they've been treated."

N.Y. Times, Sept. 30, 1989, at 8 col. 6.

3. *Basis for standing to bring action.* The action, brought by the state of Massachusetts to enjoin the showing of the film, relied on the *parens patriae* power of the state to protect persons unable to care for themselves. The dimensions of this power will be explored in greater detail in Chapter Nine.

4. *Capacity to consent.* Some inmates were so afflicted with mental illness as to lack capacity to consent to the filming. Could state authorities acting under the *parens patriae* power consent on behalf of these patients? If

not, under what circumstances, if any, could they be filmed? Issues relating to this question are also taken up in Chapter Nine.

5. *Privacy vs. the public's interest to know.* In some circumstances, the general public may have a legitimate interest in the proper conduct of incompetency or involuntary commitment hearings. As the court noted in *Commonwealth v. Wiseman,* a public interest in the treatment of the mentally ill may sufficiently outweigh the patient's countervailing interest in privacy. To what extent should public concerns override privacy rights? Should disclosure be limited to cases where it is hoped that public attention will lead to improved conditions for patients, as in *Commonwealth v. Wiseman?*

Consider *In re New York News, Inc.,* 67 N.Y.2d 472, 503 N.Y.S.2d 714, 494 N.E.2d 1379 (1986). The New York Court of Appeals described the facts as follows:

> During the evening rush hour on October 22, 1985, at the Times Square subway station in Manhattan, appellant Mary Ventura, in what the police termed "an unprovoked assault", pushed a young woman into the path of an oncoming train, causing serious injury. * * *

> In the ensuing days, the newspapers reported that in July 1985 Ventura had been a psychiatric patient in Kings County Hospital, and that she had been released on September 27, 1985—only weeks before the assault—following a judicial proceeding under the Mental Hygiene Law. Her name and photograph, the details of the incident, her hospitalization and her background were widely publicized. Ventura's mother and her neighbors made public statements about her hospitalization, her release and her past erratic, even violent behavior. Within two days of the incident, a spokesman for appellant Health and Hospitals Corporation (HHC) announced that the Judge who had presided at Ventura's retention hearing ordered release over the objection of psychiatrists, and the Judge and his law clerk responded that the psychiatric recommendation had been followed. Controversy immediately erupted over whether procedures for the release of mental patients, designed for the protection of both the patients and the public, were being properly applied—and if not where the fault lay.

After HHC's disclosure, New York News, Inc. petitioned for release of the retention hearing transcript, redacted to include only counsel's arguments, the psychiatrist's recommendation, and the court's determination. Although New York law limited disclosure to a party or to "someone properly interested," the paper argued that the press was "properly interested" because of the surrounding controversy. In holding that release was justified, the court noted that Ventura's assault and statements made by her mother and neighbors focused attention on her identity and condition; public apprehension concerning the proceeding which resulted in her release naturally resulted. The court concluded that blindly maintaining secrecy "even where a patient's identity is known * * * sacrifices a legitimate public interest in information regarding procedures for the release of mental patients." 494 N.E.2d at 1381.

b. Defamation

Defamation is the tort of making a statement to a third person which tends to injure the reputation of another, that is, which tends to diminish the person's esteem and respect in the eyes of the community or to excite adverse or unpleasant opinions about him. When the statement is oral, the tort is called slander; when it is written, the tort is called libel. Sometimes courts require that the statement be made with malice or ill will toward the plaintiff. Even when the speaker made the statement without actual malice, however, he may be held liable for the injury to the plaintiff. In such cases the malice is said to be implied.

Generally, two defenses are available in an action for defamation. One is truth; the second is privilege. The privilege in the law of defamation is not coextensive with the testimonial privilege to be discussed later. Privilege here means that certain statements which might otherwise be considered defamatory are immune from attack given the context in which they were spoken. For example, statements made by a therapist during the course of judicial or quasi-judicial proceedings are absolutely immune from legal challenge. This would apply to a therapist's testimony in commitment or malpractice trials.

It is also a general rule that defamatory statements, if made in good faith to discharge a legitimate duty with which the speaker is charged, or to advance a valid and important interest of the speaker, are privileged if the statements are made to another person having a corresponding interest or responsibility. This interest need not necessarily be of a legal nature, but may arise from a moral or social imperative.

While a detailed analysis of the law of defamation is beyond the scope of these materials, it may be useful to consider a case which illustrates its application in the context of treatment.

HUGHLEY v. McDERMOTT

Court of Special Appeals of Maryland, 1987.
72 Md.App. 391, 530 A.2d 13.

KARWACKI, JUDGE.

David E. Hughley appeals from a summary judgment rendered against him by the Circuit Court of Prince George's County in the defamation action he filed against Michael T. McDermott, the appellee. We disagree with the hearing judge's conclusion that the pleadings, depositions, answers to interrogatories, admissions and affidavits filed in the proceeding showed that there was no genuine dispute between the parties as to any material fact and that the appellee was entitled to judgment as a matter of law. Consequently, under Rule 2–501, summary judgment was not appropriate, and we shall vacate that judgment and remand the case for trial.

We restate the questions presented by the parties as follows:

1. Did the appellee enjoy an absolute privilege in publishing the allegedly defamatory matter because of appellant's actual or implied consent to its publication?

2. Was the content of the publications actionable as defamation?

3. Did the appellee abuse the qualified privilege he enjoyed to publish the defamatory matter concerning the appellant?

* * *

The record before the hearing judge discloses the following "facts."

The appellant applied to the Maryland–National Capital Park and Planning Commission (MNCPPC) for the position of a Park Police Officer in October of 1981. He was accepted as a Park Police candidate on August 9, 1982. At that time he was advised that he would have to complete candidate training school, as well as a 12 month probationary period before final acceptance as a Park Police Officer. He worked as a police dispatcher through November of 1982 and then entered the Police Academy in Prince George's County. After completing his training at the Academy in April of 1983, he began field patrol training. When the appellant learned that he might be transferred to the horse mounted training unit, he wrote to Captain George Klotz, who was the commanding officer of that unit. He advised Captain Klotz that he had "no love of horses," and would be uncomfortable in mounted training. Captain Klotz met with the appellant, and the appellant explained his reservations about working with horses, relating his limited personal experiences with horses which included vivid childhood recollections of falling off a pony and of a disfiguring injury suffered by his uncle who was kicked in the face by a horse. Nevertheless, Captain Klotz informed the appellant that he was a "natural" for mounted training because he "was bow-legged and skinny," and convinced the appellant to "try" the mounted unit. He began training with the mounted unit on August 15, 1983.

The appellant's first contact with horses precipitated the onset of nausea which plagued the appellant whenever he rode a horse or was in a stall with one. His symptoms progressed from "mild stomach problems" to vomiting. At first the appellant was determined to overcome his fear which he felt produced the physical discomfort he experienced. At the conclusion of the first week of training the appellant informed Captain Klotz that he was "uncomfortable." On the morning of Monday, August 22, 1983, the appellant had stomach cramps and diarrhea, and called in sick. On the following Tuesday and Wednesday he participated in the program but advised his supervisors of his condition. The appellant was absent from work from August 25 until September 6 because he was experiencing leg, back and hip pain from riding horses. The appellant sought medical treatment from Dr. Gary Jones at his group health association for this problem.

When he returned to work on September 6, 1983, the appellant again spoke with Captain Klotz who insisted that the appellant complete mounted training, notwithstanding appellant's pleas that his illnesses were related to contact with horses. Later that day the appellant went to see Dr. Ann L.B. Williams, another physician at his group health association. On September 7, 1983, Dr. Williams, after consulting a psychiatrist, wrote a letter to MNCPPC on the appellant's behalf which recommended that the appellant be excused from mounted training because of his "extreme anxiety with associated physical symptoms" when around horses.

On September 12, 1983, appellant was summoned to appear before Lieutenant Robert Fox of the mounted unit. After they discussed the problems which appellant had experienced with horse mounted training, Lieutenant Fox told appellant that he would have to see the appellee [a psychologist]. Two days later appellant received a telephone call from Lieutenant Fox advising him to report for an appointment with appellee that evening.

The appellee, a psychologist, had contracted with MNCPPC to act as its consultant and to provide counseling and referral services for its employees who needed help in resolving emotional problems which affected their work. The appellee met with the appellant for approximately 30 minutes on September 14, 1983.

At that meeting the appellant described his above mentioned unhappy childhood experiences with horses, and his observations as a Park Police candidate that several mounted officers had injured their knees as a result of horseback riding accidents. He chronicled his physical reactions to horseback riding and to being in a stall with a horse. He told the appellee that Captain Klotz insisted that he ride, and that other officers referred to the captain's methods of training as "Gestapo tactics." [During the interview, according to the plaintiff's complaint, the appellee stated:] "They told me you had an authority problem but I don't think you have one, I don't think you are abnormal." Finally, the appellee agreed to provide a copy of his diagnosis to the appellant.

On September 29, 1983, the appellant was ordered to appear before Major Richard Belt of MNCPPC, Larry Brownlee of the Fraternal Order of Police, and the appellee. The appellee opened the meeting by stating that he had advised Major Belt that appellant's phobia of horses was real. Appellee next stated that he and appellant had agreed that appellant would submit to hypnosis to treat his phobia. At that point appellant interrupted and advised those present that he had not agreed to hypnosis. That contradiction precipitated an argument between appellant and appellee, and the meeting deteriorated. The appellee told the appellant to sign a "release" for his lawyers before leaving the meeting. The appellant complied. That document, preprinted with blanks which were completed in handwriting, is entitled "Consent for Release of Confidential Information." As completed and signed on September 29, 1983, it provided:

> I do hereby authorize Michael T. McDermott, Ph.D. to disclose to Major Belt the following information: Diagnosis and Recommendations for the purpose of suitability for mounted training.

* * * On October 4, 1983, the appellee wrote to Major Belt:

At the request of Lt. Fox, I conducted an evaluation of POC David Hughley on September 22, 1983.[a] As an outcome of this evaluation, a meeting was scheduled with you and Mr. Hughley on September 29, 1983. The purpose of these meetings was to determine if POC Hughley suffers a phobic reaction to horses which prevents him from receiving training in the Mounted Unit.

It is my opinion based on the session with Officer Hughley and conversation with other officers that no such phobic reaction exists and the symptoms of anxiety (stomach cramps) are presentations of false and grossly exaggerated symptoms. The symptoms appear to be produced to avoid working in the Mounted Unit and specifically to avoid working under the command of Captain Klotz. In a word, this is termed "malingering." Most notable in the process of arriving at this diagnosis was POC Hughley's lack of cooperation with the evaluation and prescribed treatment regimen.

I will supply you with a full detailed explanation of these findings in the near future. If I can be of further assistance in this matter, please feel free to call me.

As he had promised, the appellee supplemented that correspondence on October 22, 1983. On that date he related to Major Belt:

This report will elaborate on my letter of October 4, 1983 regarding POC Hughley in which I reported my findings that he was "malingering" in regard to work on the Mounted Unit.

* * *

[After detailing appellant's rejection of appellee's hypnotherapy recommendation, the appellee's report concluded:]

Based on his irascible mood, refusal to cooperate in any way to alleviate this situation at the Mounted Unit other than to be removed, the symptomatology occurring only when given an order, and his stated dislike of the Unit commander, I was forced to conclude that this was not a bona fide phobia but a manipulation to get out of a work assignment he did not like.

Beyond the issues in this incident, one must speculate on the viability of such an officer to be relied upon in the future to follow orders and deal with your organization in a forthright and honest manner. I would also question his ability to deal with authority in an orderly way and become a contributing member of the force. To date his actions have been a severe drain on all involved from supervisory personnel to fellow officers. The manipulations he demonstrated indicate there may be more pathological character issues involved here than just contempt for superiors. Other than with criminal elements, I have not seen an individual lie so boldly or so vehemently when to cooperate or to be truthful would only be in his

a. Both the appellant and the appellee in their deposition testimony stated that the date of this interview was September 14, 1983.

best interest. In sum, one must wonder about his ability to be a police officer and carry out that task responsibly and honestly.

In summary I find that POC Hughley does not suffer from a phobia to horses which prevents his working in the Mounted Unit. I did find that he was trying to avoid working in the Unit and specifically avoiding the command of Capt. Klotz. His exaggerated symptoms are false presentations aimed at reassignment.

If I can be more detailed or of further assistance in this matter, please call me.

The appellant was notified on October 18, 1983 of MNCPPC's intention to fire him, and he was officially terminated on December 2, 1983.

I.

Appellee contends that his publication of any defamatory matter in his letters of October 4 and 22, 1983, was absolutely privileged because the appellant consented to such publication. He posits that the record before the hearing judge indisputably showed that, (1) the appellant, at the time of his appointment with the appellee on September 14, 1983, was aware of the fact that the appellee would be reporting his diagnosis and recommendations with regard to the appellant's suspected phobia to the officials at MNCPPC, (2) the appellant implicitly consented to a lack of confidentiality in connection with that meeting by participating in the interview, and (3) the appellant expressly consented to the contents of appellee's reports to his employer by requesting a copy of the appellee's reports and by execution of the "Consent for Release of Confidential Information" on September 29, 1983. The hearing judge rejected the appellee's defense based upon absolute privilege as do we.

* * *

Appellant did not volunteer to see the appellee; he was ordered to that interview by one of his supervisors, Lieutenant Fox. Moreover, at the conclusion of the interview, appellant was advised by appellee that his phobia to horses was real and that the appellee would recommend to MNCPPC that appellant be transferred from the mounted unit. Finally, at the beginning of the meeting on September 29, 1983, appellee reported to those present that appellant's phobia was not feigned. Given these "facts," appellant could not reasonably be charged with knowledge either of the language of appellee's reports, or that appellee's reports would be defamatory when he consented to their publication.

II.

Appellee argues that the summary judgment of the court should be affirmed because his letters of October 4 and 22, 1983 contained only expressions of his opinions following his professional evaluation of the appellant. We are not persuaded.

Accepting, as we must, appellant's version of what occurred on September 14, 1983, the appellee diagnosed the appellant's condition as a genuine phobia to horses and advised him that he would recommend his transfer from the mounted unit. Appellee repeated his diagnosis at the commencement of the meeting on September 29, 1983. After appellant contradicted appellee's report at the meeting that appellant was willing to undergo hypnosis as a treatment for his phobia, they argued, and the meeting abruptly ended. Appellee in his letters which followed that disagreement knowingly falsified his earlier diagnosis. That knowing falsehood is the basis of the appellant's cause of action. * * * In the case *sub judice* the record before the hearing judge would support a finding by the trier of fact that the statements of the appellee, although couched as expressions of opinion, were calculated untruths which adversely affected the appellant's employment and were therefore defamatory.

* * *

III.

In granting the appellee's motion for summary judgment the hearing judge rested his decision on the ground that appellee enjoyed a qualified privilege for the defamatory statements he made in his letters of October 4 and 22, 1983 and that there was no evidence of an abuse of that privilege. We hold that he erred in his second conclusion.

The appellee, as a consultant retained by the appellant's employer to examine the appellant, enjoyed a qualified privilege to communicate defamatory information derived from that examination to the employer.

* * *

It is well settled, however, that the qualified privilege accorded to a defamatory communication published within the employer-employee relationship is defeasible where the publication is made with knowledge of its falsity or with reckless disregard for its truth. * * * Furthermore, where there is any evidence of such knowing falsity or reckless disregard for truth, the issue of whether the qualified privilege has been lost by its abuse must be resolved by the trier of fact and not as a matter of law by the court. * * * Since there was disputed evidence before the hearing judge in the instant case as to whether the appellee defamed the appellant in his letters of October 4 and 22, 1983, with knowledge that the information contained in those communications was false, the issue of appellee's forfeiture of his privilege by abuse was not one which could be resolved by summary judgment.

Judgment vacated; case remanded to the Circuit Court for further proceedings consistent with this Opinion.

Questions

Psychologists are frequently retained by employers to evaluate job applicants and employees. What are the risks that a psychologist who provides a negative evaluation will be sued for defamation? Is the test for potential liability whether the therapist/defendant had *knowledge* of the falsity of the conclusions contained in the evaluation? If knowledge is a requirement, what was the plaintiff's offer of proof in this regard in the *Hughley v. McDermott* case?

2. Remedies Arising From Breach of the Patient–Therapist Relationship

DOE v. ROE

Supreme Court, New York County, 1977.
93 Misc.2d 201, 400 N.Y.S.2d 668.

MARTIN B. STECHER, JUSTICE:

This action for an injunction and for damages for breach of privacy is a matter of first impression in this State, and so far as I am able to ascertain, a matter of first impression in the United States. It arises out of the publication, verbatim, by a psychiatrist of a patient's disclosures during the course of a lengthy psychoanalysis. I have made and filed detailed findings of fact which are briefly summarized here.

Dr. Joan Roe is a physician who has practiced psychiatry for more than fifty years. Her husband, Peter Poe, has been a psychologist for some 25 years. The plaintiff and her late, former husband were each patients of Dr. Roe for many years. The defendants, eight years after the termination of treatment, published a book which reported verbatim and extensively the patients' thoughts, feelings, and emotions, their sexual and other fantasies and biographies, their most intimate personal relationships and the disintegration of their marriage. Interspersed among the footnotes are Roe's diagnoses of what purport to be the illnesses suffered by the patients and one of their children.

The defendants allege that the plaintiff consented to this publication. This defense is without substance. Consent was sought while the plaintiff was in therapy. It was never obtained in writing. In Dr. Roe's own words consent "was there one day and not there another day. That was the nature of the illness I was treating, unreliable." I need not deal with the value of an oral waiver of confidentiality given by a patient to a psychiatrist during the course of treatment. It is sufficient to conclude that not only did the defendants fail to obtain the plaintiff's consent to publication, they were well aware that they had none.

[The plaintiff contended that in the absence of a statutory provision expressly recognizing a cause of action against a therapist who wrongfully discloses confidential information, an action is impliedly authorized by various state laws including sections of the New York Civil Practice Law and Rules (Sec. 4504(a)) and provisions of the New York Licensing and Disciplinary Statutes (Ed.L. 6509 et seq.). Following a review of the text and history of these statutory provisions the court concluded that these sections standing by themselves did not authorize a private cause of action. The court next addressed the plaintiff's contention that other theories including the right to privacy and rights flowing from the contract between the therapist and patient grant a cause of action for wrongful disclosure.]

* * *

As hereafter indicated there are theories on which liability may be predicated other than violation of the CPLR [4504(a)], the licensing and disciplinary statutes [Ed.L. 6509 et seq.] and what I perceive as this State's public policy. In two of the very few cases which have come to grips with the issue of wrongful disclosure by physicians of patients' secrets the courts predicated their holdings on the numerous sources of obligation which arise out of the physician-patient relationship.

* * *

I too find that a physician, who enters into an agreement with a patient to provide medical attention, impliedly covenants to keep in confidence all disclosures made by the patient concerning the patient's physical or mental condition as well as all matters discovered by the physician in the course of examination or treatment. This is particularly and necessarily true of the psychiatric relationship, for in the dynamics of psychotherapy "(t)he patient is called upon to discuss in a candid and frank manner personal material of the most intimate and disturbing nature * * * He is expected to bring up all manner of socially unacceptable instincts and urges, immature wishes, perverse sexual thoughts—in short the unspeakable, the unthinkable, the repressed. To speak of such things to another human being requires an atmosphere of unusual trust, confidence and tolerance. * * * "

There can be little doubt that under the law of the State of New York and in a proper case, the contract of private parties to retain in confidence matter which should be kept in confidence will be enforced by injunction and compensated in damages.

The contract between the plaintiff and Dr. Roe is such a contract.

* * *

Every patient, and particularly every patient undergoing psychoanalysis, has such a right of privacy [emanating from the plaintiff's contract right to confidentiality and other state laws including the licensing and disciplinary statute and the New York civil practice law]. Under what circumstances can a person be expected to reveal sexual fantasies, infantile memories, passions of hate and love, one's most intimate relationship with one's spouse and others except upon the inferential agreement that such confessions will be forever entombed in the psychiatrist's memory, never to be revealed during the psychiatrist's lifetime or thereafter? The very needs of the profession itself require that confidentiality exist *and be enforced.* As pointed out in *Matter of Lifschutz,* 2 Cal.3d 415, 85 Cal.Rptr. 829, 467 P.2d 557 [1970] "a large segment of the psychiatric profession concurs in Dr. Lifschutz's strongly held belief that an absolute privilege of confidentiality is essential to the effective practice of psychotherapy" [*cf.* Annotation, 20 A.L.R.3d, 1109, 1112].

Despite the fact that in no New York case has such a wrong been remedied due, most likely, to the fact that so few physicians violate this fundamental obligation, it is time that the obligation not only be recognized but that the right of redress be recognized as well.

What label we affix to this wrong is unimportant [although the category of wrong could, under certain circumstances—such as determining the applicable statute of limitations—be significant]. It is generally accepted that "There is no necessity whatever that a tort must have a name. New and nameless torts are being recognized constantly". [Prosser, Torts (2d ed.), p. 3]. What is important is that there must be the infliction of intentional harm, resulting in damage, without legal excuses or justification.

* * *

The defendants contend that the physician's obligation of confidentiality is not absolute and must give way to the general public interest. The interest, as they see it in this case, is the scientific value of the publication.

It is not disputed that under our public policy the right of confidentiality is less than absolute. * * *

Despite the duty of confidentiality courts have recognized the duty of a psychiatrist to give warning where a patient clearly presents a danger to others to disclose the existence of a contagious disease, to report the use of "controlled substances" in certain situations and to report gunshot and other wounds.

In no case, however, has the curiosity or education of the medical profession superseded the duty of confidentiality. I do not reach the question of a psychiatrist's right to publish case histories where the identities are fully concealed for that is not our problem here, nor do I find it necessary to reach the issue of whether or not an important scientific discovery would take precedence over a patient's privilege of non-disclosure. I do not consider myself qualified to determine the contribution which this book may have made to the science or art of psychiatry. I do conclude, however, that if such contribution was the defendants' defense they have utterly failed in their proof that this volume represented a major contribution to scientific knowledge. The evidence is to the contrary and this defense must necessarily fail.

Nor is the argument available that by enjoining the further distribution of this book the court will be engaging in a "prior restraint" on publication.

* * *

There is no prior restraint in the case at bar. The book has been published and it does offend against the plaintiff's right of privacy, contractual and otherwise, not to have her innermost thoughts offered to all for the price of this book. There is no prior restraint and, therefore, no censorship within constitutional meaning.

* * *

The liability of Dr. Roe to respond in damages is clear, and Mr. Poe's liability is equally clear. True, he and the plaintiff were not involved in a physician-patient relationship and he certainly had no contractual relationship to her. But, the conclusion is unassailable that Poe, like anyone else with access to the book, knew that its source was the patient's production in psychoanalysis. He knew as well as, and perhaps better than Roe, of the absence of consent, of the failure to disguise. If anyone was the actor in seeing to it that the work was written, that it was manufactured, advertised and circulated, it was Poe. He is a co-author and a willing, indeed avid, co-violator of the patient's rights and is therefore equally liable.

The plaintiff seeks punitive damages and suggests that a proper measure of those damages, in addition to compensatory damage, is approximately $50,000, the sum plaintiff has thus far expended on and incurred for attorneys' fees.

* * *

In order to warrant an award of punitive damages, it must have been affirmatively demonstrated that the wrong committed was willful and malicious, that the act complained of was "morally culpable or * * * actuated by evil and reprehensible motives, not only to punish the defendant but to deter him, as well as others * * * "

Where the act complained of is willful, malicious and wanton, punitive damages are sometimes available to "express indignation at the defendants' wrong rather than a value set on plaintiff's loss." Certainly, the acts of the defendants here are such as to warrant an expression of indignation and punishment for the purpose of deterring similar acts by these defendants or others. The difficulty, however, is that the defendants' acts were not willful, malicious or wanton—they were merely stupid. I have no doubt that the defendants were of the opinion that they had sufficiently concealed the identity of the plaintiff and her family. I have no doubt that in addition to the commercial success they hoped to have, they believed that they were rendering a public service in publishing what they considered an in-depth description of the plaintiff's family. But there was no motive to harm. Under these circumstances, punitive damages are not available.

* * *

The plaintiff has suffered damage as a consequence of this publication. She suffered acute embarrassment on learning the extent to which friends, colleagues, employer, students and others, had read or read of the book. Her livelihood, as indicated in the findings, was threatened; but fortunately, the actual cash loss was only some $1,500. Medical attention, principally treatment with Dr. Lowenfeld, cost an additional

$1,400. But beyond these sums the plaintiff suffered in health. She had insomnia and nightmares. She became reclusive as a consequence of the shame and humiliation induced by the book's publication and her well-being and emotional health were significantly impaired for three years. In my opinion the fair and reasonable value of the injury she sustained—to the extent it can be compensated in damages—is $20,000.

Damages, of course, do not provide an adequate remedy; for should the book circulate further, beyond the 220 copies already sold, the damage must accrue anew. The plaintiff is entitled to a judgment permanently enjoining the defendants, their heirs, successors and assigns from further violating the plaintiff's right to privacy whether by circulating this book or by otherwise disclosing any of the matters revealed by the plaintiff to Dr. Roe in the course of psychotherapy.

Questions and Comments

1. *Health evaluations at the request of third parties.* Insurance companies frequently require an applicant to supply their medical background and, in that connection, may request that applicants undergo a physical or other health examination. Similarly, employers may sometimes require a current or prospective employee to undergo a medical or mental status evaluation. Frequently, these evaluations are arranged and paid for by the third party. Under the laws of some states, a health provider's duty of confidentiality does not arise were the treatment was at the request of a third party. However, under HIPAA, patients retain their privacy rights even where the evaluation was performed at the request of a third party. However, a third party such as an employer or insurer may gain access to the evaluation, or PHI in general, by obtaining the individual's authorization prior to the referral for diagnosis.

2. *HIPAA and disclosure of PHI in research context.* A researcher or research institution is only subject to HIPAA privacy rules if she or it is a covered entity. However, if the research facility is also involved in treatment and meets HIPAA's covered entity criteria it must comply with the privacy rules. This means that it can transfer personal health information (PHI) to another covered entity without the patient's authorization. On the other hand, transfer of PHI to a non-covered entity requires the research subject's authorization. However, as a practical matter such authorization will generally have been obtained before an individual is admitted into the research program. Such pre-admission authorization is permitted by HIPAA privacy rules. 45 CFR § 164.508(b)(4)(i).

3. *Confidentiality rights following the death of the patient.* May a therapist disclose confidential information following the death of the patient? This issue has arisen in the context of several celebrated cases where the therapist, following the death of the patient, either wrote a book concerning the patient or made public disclosures on television or to other media of information obtained from the patient in the course of providing treatment.

Anne Sexton, a noted poet who committed suicide in 1974, had been treated for a number of years by Dr. Martin T. Orne, a psychiatrist. In 1991, Dr. Orne, with co-author Diane Wood Middlebrook, published a biography of Anne Sexton. That book relied in part on material taken from Ms. Sexton's private therapy sessions and covered her revelations which chronicled "harrowing detail [of] Sexton's madness, alcoholism and sexual abuse of her daughter, along with her many extramarital affairs, including one with a woman and another with the second of her many therapists". N.Y. Times, Jul. 15, 1991, at 1.

More recently, following the 1994 murder of Nicole Simpson, the ex-wife of O.J. Simpson, Susan Forward (a licensed clinical social worker) disclosed to the media in various interviews that she had counseled Nicole Simpson on two occasions and that Ms. Simpson told her that she had been battered and threatened by O.J. Simpson. L.A. Times, June 16, 1994, at A13.

What are the legal rights, if any, of the next of kin or heirs of a deceased patient to prevent disclosure of information obtained by a therapist in the course of treatment? Leading legal commentators have in the past subscribed to the view that the patient's rights of privacy terminate at death and that the heirs or next of kin do not have any cause of action for unauthorized disclosures. Harper & James, The Law of Torts, § 9.6 at 645 (2d ed. 1986). The Supreme Court, in a different context, held that the attorney-client privilege does not survive the death of the client. *Swidler & Berlin v. United States,* 524 U.S. 399, 118 S.Ct. 2081, 141 L.Ed.2d 379 (1998).

4. Post mortem *privacy of PHI under HIPAA.* Unlike many state health privacy laws, under HIPAA personal Health information (PHI) in the hands of a covered entity retains its protection and disclosure to non covered third parties may not be made without the authorization of the decedents personal representative (see supra note 36). The designation of a personal representative is a matter of state law .. What factors justify protecting health information *post mortem* when other privacy interests are not generally protected under the law of most states? Also, an action for defamation cannot be brought where the alleged defamation occurred after the death of the defamed party. Is there not, in some instances, a public interest in the disclosure of health information of an individual after their death? For instance, does the public have a right to know if a senior government official such as a president was suffering from various disorders and taking heavy doses of medication during his term as president? Presumably health providers would not be permitted to disclose such information after the death of the senior official without the authorization of the individual's personal representative who, if a family member, might well prefer to not have such information disclosed. What public interest might be served in the *post mortem* disclosure of health information of this kind?

MacDONALD v. CLINGER

Supreme Court, Appellate Division, Fourth Department, 1982.
84 A.D.2d 482, 446 N.Y.S.2d 801.

DENMAN, JUSTICE.

We here consider whether a psychiatrist must respond in damages to his former patient for disclosure of personal information learned during the course of treatment and, if he must, on what theory of recovery the action may be maintained. We hold that such wrongful disclosure is a breach of the fiduciary duty of confidentiality and gives rise to a cause of action sounding in tort.

The complaint alleges that during two extended courses of treatment with defendant, a psychiatrist, plaintiff revealed intimate details about himself which defendant later divulged to plaintiff's wife without justification and without consent. As a consequence of such disclosure, plaintiff alleges that his marriage deteriorated, that he lost his job, that he suffered financial difficulty and that he was caused such severe emotional distress that he required further psychiatric treatment. The complaint set forth three causes of action: breach of an implied contract; breach of confidence in violation of public policy; and breach of the right of privacy guaranteed by article 5 of the Civil Rights Law. Defendant moved to dismiss for failure to state a cause of action, asserting that there was in reality only one theory of recovery, that of breach of confidence, and that such action could not be maintained against him because his disclosure to plaintiff's wife was justified. The court dismissed the third cause of action but denied the motion with respect to the first two causes of action and this appeal ensued.

Research reveals few cases in American jurisprudence which treat the doctor-patient privilege in this context. That is undoubtedly due to the fact that the confidentiality of the relationship is a cardinal rule of the medical profession, faithfully adhered to in most instances, and thus has come to be justifiably relied upon by patients seeking advice and treatment. This physician-patient relationship is contractual in nature, whereby the physician, in agreeing to administer to the patient, impliedly covenants that the disclosures necessary to diagnosis and treatment of the patient's mental or physical condition will be kept in confidence.

Examination of cases which have addressed this problem makes it apparent that courts have immediately recognized a legally compensable injury in such wrongful disclosure based on a variety of grounds for recovery: public policy; right to privacy; breach of contract; breach of fiduciary duty. As the Supreme Court of Washington stated in *Smith v. Driscoll,* 94 Wash. 441, 442, 162 P. 572:

> Neither is it necessary to pursue at length the inquiry of whether a cause of action lies in favor of a patient against a physician for wrongfully divulging confidential communications. For the purposes of what we shall say it will be assumed that, for so palpable a wrong, the law provides a remedy.

An excellent and carefully researched opinion exploring the legal ramifications of this confidentiality is *Doe v. Roe,* 93 Misc.2d 201, 400 N.Y.S.2d 668, a decision after a non-jury trial in which plaintiff sought injunctive relief and damages because of the verbatim publication by her former psychiatrist of extremely personal details of her life revealed during years of psychoanalysis. The court considered several proposed theories of recovery, including violation of public policy and breach of privacy rights. We agree with the court's observation that the several statutes and regulations requiring physicians to protect the confidentiality of information gained during treatment are clear evidence of the public policy of New York but that there is a more appropriate theory of recovery than one rooted in public policy.

Neither do we believe that an action for breach of the right of privacy may be maintained despite some current predictions to the contrary.

* * *

* * * I * * * find that a physician, who enters into an agreement with a patient to provide medical attention, impliedly covenants to keep in confidence all disclosures made by the patient concerning the patient's physical or mental condition as well as all matters discovered by the physician in the course of examination or treatment. This is particularly and necessarily true of the psychiatric relationship, for in the dynamics of psychotherapy "[t]he patient is called upon to discuss in a candid and frank manner personal material of the most intimate and disturbing nature * * * He is expected to bring up all manner of socially unacceptable instincts and urges, immature wishes, perverse sexual thoughts—in short, the unspeakable, the unthinkable, the repressed. To speak of such things to another human requires an atmosphere of unusual trust, confidence and tolerance. * * * "

* * *

It is obvious then that this relationship gives rise to an implied covenant which, when breached, is actionable. If plaintiff's recovery were limited to an action for breach of contract, however, he would generally be limited to economic loss flowing directly from the breach and would thus be precluded from recovering for mental distress, loss of his employment and the deterioration of his marriage. We believe that the relationship contemplates an additional duty springing from but extraneous to the contract and that the breach of such duty is actionable as a tort. Indeed, an action in tort for a breach of a duty of confidentiality and trust has long been acknowledged in the courts of this state.

* * * When such duty grows out of relations of trust and confidence, as that of the agent to his principal or the lawyer to his client, the ground of the duty is apparent, and the tort is, in general, easily separable from the mere breach of contract. * * *

* * *

Such duty, however, is not absolute, and its breach is actionable only if it is wrongful, that is to say, without justification or excuse. Although public policy favors the confidentiality described herein, there is a countervailing public interest to which it must yield in appropriate circumstances. Thus where a patient may be a danger to himself or others a physician is required to disclose to the extent necessary to protect a threatened interest.

* * *

Although the disclosure of medical information to a spouse may be justified under some circumstances, a more stringent standard should apply with respect to psychiatric information. One spouse often seeks counseling concerning personal problems that may affect the marital relationship. To permit disclosure to the other spouse in the absence of an overriding concern would deter the one in need from obtaining the help required. Disclosure of confidential information by a psychiatrist to a spouse will be justified whenever there is a danger to the patient, the spouse or another person; otherwise information should not be disclosed without authorization. Justification or excuse will depend upon a showing of circumstances and competing interests which support the need to disclose (cf. *Berry v. Moench,* 8 Utah 2d 191, 331 P.2d 814, *supra*). Because such showing is a matter of affirmative defense, defendant is not entitled to dismissal of the action.

The order should be modified to dismiss the cause of action for breach of contract and as modified should be affirmed.

Order modified on the law and as modified affirmed with costs to defendant.

SIMONS, J.P., concurs in a separate opinion.

Questions and Comments

1. *Question.* If a case involving a similar fact situation were to arise post-HIPAA, would a breach of confidentiality, such as occurred in *MacDonald v. Clinger,* be the basis for administrative sanctions by the Office of Civil Rights under HIPAA? What additional facts would need to be known to answer this question?

2. *Disciplinary proceedings for breach of confidentiality.* Wrongful disclosure can also lead to discipline by a regulatory authority. For instance, in *Mississippi State Board of Psychological Examiners v. Hosford,* 508 So.2d 1049 (Miss.1987), the psychologist had provided family counseling to a husband and wife. Later, during the couple's divorce proceeding, he submitted an authorized affidavit to the court recommending the award of custody to the father. This recommendation was based in part on disclosures made by the wife during counseling. These facts were deemed sufficient to justify disciplinary action against the psychologist for his violation of the ethical principles of psychologists.

3. *Claim under contract theory.* Technically, a violation of a patient's right to confidentiality could be the basis for an action based on breach of a contract involving an implied covenant on the part of the therapist to maintain confidentiality. In fact this theory was the basis of a claim in *Allen v. Smith,* 179 W.Va. 360, 368 S.E.2d 924 (1988). While the court found a breach, it was unwilling to award damages for emotional distress alone.

4. *Defenses.* In a proceeding brought under state law for breach of confidentiality by a therapist, the defendant is generally be entitled to raise certain defenses whose merits can determine the outcome of the case. All of these defenses may best be understood as falling within four possible categories: absolute privilege, qualified privilege, patient consent, or absence of malice.

"Privilege" is a term frequently used in discussions about confidential information. Perhaps the best way to understand the term is to think of privilege as an exemption from liability which would otherwise attach to the actor's disclosure or withholding of information. A privilege may be either "absolute" or "qualified." An absolute privilege attaches whenever disclosure is compelled by law. Examples of compelled disclosure, which are treated in greater detail in section II of this chapter, include reports of child abuse, drug dependency, or illnesses which pose a threat to the public safety, such as persons with venereal disease or other serious contagious diseases. Disclosure may also be compelled by courts or legislative and administrative agencies.

When disclosure of confidential information is not unequivocally mandated by law, a therapist's disclosures may nevertheless be immune under the doctrine of "qualified privilege," which allows disclosure only if certain conditions are met. The first condition is that the therapist's purpose in disclosing the confidential information must be to achieve some societal purpose of importance comparable to the patient's interest in preserving confidentiality. Such interests may include, for example, protection of the safety of another endangered by a violent patient or disclosures made in good faith in proceedings for the civil commitment of a patient. A second condition is that the disclosure be no greater than reasonably necessary to achieve the purpose sought. Third, the disclosure must be by a method which is appropriate under the circumstances to achieve the purpose sought. A therapist usually will not be liable, for example, for entrusting a confidential report to an office secretary for typing. He may incur liability, on the other hand, for submitting the report to the patient's employer, when such action is neither authorized nor necessary to achieve any legitimate purpose outweighing the patient's interest in confidentiality.

It remains to be seen whether in the light of HIPAA, these traditional defenses will continue to be recognized in proceedings applying state law. HIPAA's exceptions to disclosure of PHI may, depending on the state law in question, be narrower. Thus, in a proceeding brought by the DHHS's Office of Civil Rights for violation of HIPAA privacy rules, some of the defenses would not be available to a defendant. However, this would not necessarily bind state courts applying state law in determining an actual breach of confidentiality occurred. Nevertheless, there is the possibility that the HIPAA standards will influence the development of state law with a result that some of the traditional defenses will be curtailed.

5. *The defense of consent or authorization.* If a patient has authorized disclosure of PHI, the therapist cannot be held liable under either HIPAA or proceeding under state law. While HIPAA establishes very clear criteria for the requirements for a valid authorization, state laws frequently do not. Thus, it may not always be clear whether under state law, a patient has consented to disclosure. The patient's consent thus constitutes a third possible defense in an action for wrongful disclosure. The issue of consent is not as simple as it may appear at first. First, it is not always clear whether a patient has consented to disclosure.

Also, even if the patient's express consent is obtained, the scope of disclosure permitted by the consent under state law is not always clear. A patient may consent to allow a therapist to disclose to the patient's prospective employer that he has received therapy. Would such consent authorize disclosure of the nature of the patient's problem? The nature or length of treatment? Specific facts about the patient relating to his suitability for employment?

II. EXCEPTIONS TO THE DUTY OF CONFIDENTIALITY

A. INTRODUCTION

The preceding materials have explored doctrines that protect patients from unauthorized disclosures by professionals with whom they have entered into a patient-therapist relationship. The patient's rights of privacy, however, are not absolute, and in some circumstances a therapist may be under a legal duty to make disclosures to either agencies of the state or private citizens.

There are three principal situations where disclosure of information by the therapist may be *required*. One situation is created by compulsory reporting statutes, which cover such matters as child abuse or narcotics addiction. The second category is the duty of a therapist in some jurisdictions to communicate to endangered parties the known dangerous propensities of the patient.

A third category of compelled disclosure is the duty to give testimony in a judicial proceeding. However, this duty is not applied universally, and in fact the legal system has carved out special exceptions for professionals, including physicians and psychotherapists. These exceptions fall within the ambit of what is known as the testimonial privilege, are fairly technical in nature, and do not apply with equal force in all jurisdictions. While any comprehensive treatment of the testimonial privilege is beyond the purview of these materials, subsection D below seeks to set forth the general legal framework governing the application of the privilege.

Significantly, in all of the situations noted above, HIPAA regulations defer to state law where such law authorizes disclosure without the patient's consent.

B. MANDATORY REPORTING REQUIREMENTS

Nearly all states have enacted laws which require physicians and mental health professionals to disclose to designated authorities certain types of patient information, even if the information would otherwise be confidential. Most states, for instance, require reporting to health authorities the fact that a patient is suffering from certain communicable diseases. *Hammonds v. Aetna Casualty & Surety Co.*, 243 F.Supp. 793 (N.D.Ohio 1965). Nearly all states also impose a duty on physicians or hospital administrators to report to police authorities any case where a patient appears for treatment of gunshot injuries. Jon R. Waltz & Fred E. Inbau, Medical Jurisprudence at 364 (1971). Some states also require attending or consulting physicians to report the name of any person known to be a "habitual user of a narcotic drug." Id. at 365. Finally most states require any physician or mental health professional who has reasonable cause to suspect an incidence of child abuse to report such fact to a designated agency. Id. at 320–322. In some jurisdictions psychiatrists are covered by these provisions whereas other mental health professionals are not. There is an interplay between these reporting statutes and the testimonial privilege. It has been argued that mandatory reporting statutes destroy the privilege of confidentiality granted by testimonial privilege statutes. The case set forth below addresses the question of whether the legislature, by requiring reporting, also intends to abrogate confidentiality rights.

DAYMUDE v. STATE

Court of Appeals of Indiana, First District, 1989.
540 N.E.2d 1263.

BAKER, JUDGE.

STATEMENT OF THE FACTS

The Greene County Division of the Indiana State Department of Public Welfare (Department) filed a petition in the Greene Circuit Court, Juvenile Docket, alleging that Daymude's 13–year–old daughter was a "child in need of services" as defined by IND.CODE 31–6–4–3. As provided by the CHINS statute, the Department, pursuant to court order, provided services to the child and her family. The daughter was admitted as an in-patient at Charter Hospital of Terre Haute (the hospital). In addition, the juvenile court ordered Daymude, the alleged victim, and her mother to undergo family counseling.

The hospital's clinical director referred the daughter's case to James Walker (Walker), a certified clinical mental health counselor working as an independent contractor for the hospital. Walker worked under the supervision of Dr. Mary Anne Johnson, the hospital's chief psychiatrist for the child and adolescent division. Walker developed and scheduled a treatment program in which the alleged victim and her family were to participate in a series of individual and group therapy sessions. During the course of a counseling session, Daymude disclosed information relating to alleged instances of sexual abuse.

On July 8, 1989, the State formally charged Daymude with child molesting and criminal deviate conduct in violation of IND.CODE 35–42–4–2 and 35–42–4–3, and with the offense of incest in violation of IND.CODE 35–26–1–3. Thereafter, the State sought to depose Walker regarding the content of communications between Walker and Daymude disclosed in the course of the family therapy. Daymude objected to the State's inquiry, insofar as it related to privileged and confidential communications between himself and Walker or any other member of the hospital's treatment team. The question was certified to the trial court and on January 31, 1989, the trial court overruled the defendant's objection and ordered Walker to answer such questions as were asked by the State pertaining to his communication with Daymude during the course of counseling. It is from this order that the instant interlocutory appeal is taken.

ISSUE

Whether the trial court erred in finding that Daymude's right to privileged communication with his health care provider was abrogated by IND.CODE 31–6–11–8 when that communication was undertaken subsequent to the State's involvement in allegations of child sexual abuse against Daymude, and when that communication was undertaken in the course of treatment and rehabilitation recommended by the State through its Department of Public Welfare.

DISCUSSION AND DECISION

Communications between a physician and a patient, of a confidential nature, are privileged and may not be disclosed by the physician without a waiver of that privilege by the patient. * * * This physician-patient privilege is codified in IND.CODE 34–1–14–5 which provides, in pertinent part:

The following persons shall not be competent witnesses:

. . .

4th. Physicians, as to matter communicated to them, as such, by patients, in the course of their professional business, or advice given in such cases, except as provided in IND.CODE 9–4–4.5–7.[a]

The privilege applies to those communications undertaken in the course of, and necessary to treatment.

However, in Indiana "*any individual* who has reason to believe that a child is a victim of child abuse or neglect shall make a report" as required by statute (emphasis added). IND.CODE 31–6–11–3. Thus, this language and the physician-patient privilege place conflicting duties upon a physician who learns of child abuse during the course of a physician-patient relationship. Consequently, the Indiana legislature adopted IND.CODE 31–6–11–8 which abrogates the physician-patient privilege when reporting child abuse. The abrogation statute states:

The privileged communication between a husband and wife, between a health care provider and that health care provider's patient, or between a school counselor and a student is not a ground for:

(1) excluding evidence in any judicial proceeding resulting from a report of a child who may be a victim of child abuse or neglect, or relating to the subject matter of such a report; or (2) failing to report as required by this chapter.

---

a. IND.CODE 9–11–4–6, formerly 9–4–4.5–7, provides for the abrogation of the physician-patient privilege in certain cases involving chemical tests for purposes of Title 9, Criminal Investigations.

Id.

Daymude acknowledges that Walker, as a mental health professional had a duty under IND.CODE 31–6–11–3 to report suspected or known instances of child abuse or neglect even though such information is received in the course of confidential communications. *See* IND.CODE 31–6–11–3 (Duty to Report); IND.CODE 34–1–14–5 (Physician–Patient Privilege); IND.CODE 31–6–11–8 (Abrogation of Privilege). However, Daymude argues that the privilege is abrogated only in reporting child abuse, and that the abrogation does not extend to communications made during counseling ordered by the court as a result of CHINS proceedings.

Because of the special circumstances of this case, this appeal presents an issue of first impression for this court. However, we believe that the purpose of the reporting statutes and decisions from courts facing similar issues clearly support Daymude's contentions here.

The purpose of the Indiana reporting statute is:

> [T]o encourage effective reporting of suspected or known incidents of child abuse or neglect, to provide in each county an effective child protection service to quickly investigate reports of child abuse or neglect, to provide protection for such a child from further abuse or neglect, and to provide rehabilitative services for such a child and his parent, guardian, or custodian.

IND.CODE 31–6–11–1. Thus, the reporting statute attempts to promote the reporting of child abuse cases, and thereafter, to provide a mechanism for the investigation of the abuse in order to protect the child and provide rehabilitative services for the child and parents, guardian, or custodian. The abrogation statute as set forth in IND.CODE 31–6–11–8 must be read in light of the purpose of the entire act.

Clearly, confidential communications between a health care provider and his patient are abrogated to the extent that the health care provider must report all suspected or known instances of child abuse. However, to extend the abrogation statute to information disclosed during Daymude's court ordered counseling goes beyond the purpose of the statute. The statute makes no mention of prosecuting alleged abusers, and instead only discusses means to facilitate the identification of the children who need the immediate attention of child welfare professionals.

* * *

In the present case, the reporting of child abuse is not an issue. The alleged abuse was reported long before Daymude made confidential statements to Walker. In fact the confidential communications arose only after the CHINS proceedings during which the court ordered Daymude to attend and participate in individual and family counseling sessions. Thus, because the alleged abuse already had been reported, the reporting statute's purpose had been served and the physician-patient privilege need not be abrogated further.

There is no question that the family therapy sessions are an integral and necessary part of the patient's diagnosis and treatment. If the physician-patient privilege is denied to those family members involved in CHINS counseling, then the alleged child abusers will be discouraged from openly and honestly communicating with their counselors. Without open and honest communications between the physician and the family members, the rehabilitative process will fail. Consequently, the child, whom the statute is designed to help and protect, is denied an opportunity for complete rehabilitation. As the *Andring* court stated:

> Once the abuse is discovered, however, the statute should not be construed, nor can the legislature have intended it to be construed, to permit total elimination of this important privilege. The central purpose of the child abuse reporting statute is the protection of children, not punishment of those who mistreat them.

Id.

* * *

In the present case, the physician-patient privilege arose as a direct result of therapy ordered by the court during a CHINS proceeding. The privileged communications were made long after the report of the child abuse. Since the abuse already had been reported, the purpose of the reporting statute had been fulfilled. To allow the abrogation of the privileged communication under these specific facts goes beyond the purpose of the statute. Thus, because of the specific facts of the present case, we hold that the physician-patient privilege is not abrogated with regard to confidential communications disclosed by a defendant while participating in counseling sessions ordered by a trial court pursuant to a report of child molesting.

For the above reasons, we reverse the trial court's ruling.

Judgment reversed.

RATLIFF, C.J., and ROBERTSON, J., concur.

Comments

1. *Constitutional limits on state disclosure requirements.* Recent cases suggest that there are constitutional limits on the power of legislatures to impose medical reporting requirements. For instance, a majority of the justices of the Supreme Court have found broad state law requirements for notification of the parents of minors seeking an abortion to be constitutionally defective. *Bellotti v. Baird,* 443 U.S. 622, 99 S.Ct. 3035, 61 L.Ed.2d 797 (1979). But see, *H. L. v. Matheson,* 450 U.S. 398, 101 S.Ct. 1164, 67 L.Ed.2d 388 (1981).

In the psychiatric context a California appellate court has held that a state law provision that required institutions to notify a "responsible relative" of the patient prior to the administration of ECT or psychosurgery violated the patient's right to privacy. *Aden v. Younger,* 57 Cal.App.3d 662, 129 Cal.Rptr. 535 (1976).

2. *Rule for covered entities under HIPAA.* HIPAA authorizes disclosure of PHI without the patient's authorization when mandated by state law or regulation when it relates to *child abuse or neglect where the covered entity believes the individual is the victim of domestic violence.* Additionally, disclosure may be made in a number of other situations including the following: (1) where necessary to prevent serious harm to the individual or other potential victims; (2) when requested by a public health authority for the purpose of preventing or controlling disease; and (3) in the case of the death of a patient, reports to a relevant agency to determine the cause of death or whether the death occurred as a result of criminal conduct by a third party; (4) where disclosure is needed for the protective services for the President and other senior government officials; (5) to federal officials in connection with lawful intelligence activities; (6) to military authorities when necessary to ensure proper execution of the military mission; and (7) at the request of law enforcement agencies for the purpose of deterring a crime involving a serious risk of injury to an individual or the public. 45 C.F.R. § 164.512.

3. *Duty to report versus statutory confidentiality rules.* The potential conflict between confidentiality rules and reporting statutes was addressed by the Vermont Supreme Court in *Peck v. Counseling Service of Addison County:*

> Defendant also argues that the therapist could not lawfully have warned the plaintiffs * * * because of the physician-patient privilege against disclosure of confidential information. 12 V.S.A. § 1612(a). * * * Defendant points out that the legislature has specified certain "public policy" exceptions to the physician-patient privilege, see, e.g., 33 V.S.A. §§ 683–684 (Supp.1984) (report of child abuse), 13 V.S.A. § 4012 (disclosure of gunshot wounds), 18 V.S.A. §§ 1152–1153 (report of abuse of the elderly), and that a therapist's duty to disclose the risk of harm posed by his or her patient to a foreseeable victim is not a recognized legislative exception. Given this, defendant argues that this Court is preempted from finding a duty-to-warn exception to the physician-patient privilege. The statutory exceptions to the physician-patient privilege indicate to this Court, however, that the privilege is not sacrosanct and can properly be waived in the interest of public policy under appropriate circumstances. A mental patient's threat of serious harm to an identified victim is an appropriate circumstance under which the physician-patient privilege may be waived.

146 Vt. 61, 499 A.2d 422, 426 (1985).

4. *Disclosure of past crimes.* May a therapist disclose information as to the patient's past commission of a crime? While such disclosure may constitute a breach of confidentiality, the violation cannot be asserted as a defense in a criminal proceeding. *State v. Beatty,* 770 S.W.2d 387 (Mo.App.1989) (holding that a therapist's report that the patient had been involved in a robbery could not be raised as a defense in a criminal proceeding). The court however, suggested that the patient might have a private cause of action against the therapist for a breach of confidentiality. What would be the extent of damages she could obtain? Should the term of imprisonment that resulted from the conviction be compensable?

What is the scope of permitted disclosure of past crimes under HIPAA? Unfortunately, the relevant section, § 164.512 (f)(6)(i), which covers disclosure of crimes, is extraordinarily opaque even by HIPAA standards. The section reads as follows:

> (i) A covered health care provider providing emergency health care in response to a medical emergency, other than such emergency on the premises of the covered health care provider, may disclose protected health information to a law enforcement official if such disclosure appears necessary to alert law enforcement to:

> (A) The commission and nature of a crime;

> (B) The location of such crime or of the victim(s) of such crime; and

> (C) The identity, description and location of the perpetrator of such crime."

See also discussion of the *Menendez v. Superior Court* pp. 414–16.

C. DISCLOSURES OF INFORMATION INDICATIVE OF MENTAL DISORDER AND/OR DANGEROUSNESS

1. *Disclosure by Entities Covered by HIPAA*

As outlined on p. 325, HIPAA regulations permit disclosure "necessary to prevent or lessen a serious and imminent threat to the health or safety of a person or the public ... to a person or persons reasonably able to prevent or lessen the threat, including the target of the threat." 45 C.F.R. § 164.512. HIPAA does not provide any further guidance as to who may qualify as a "person or persons" reasonably able to prevent or lessen the threat. In any event, where there is an imminent threat to the health and safety of the person or the public, HIPAA gives health provider significant leeway to disclose that information to appropriate third parties.

Moreover, in most states, state law provides a similar exception. The primary difference among state laws pertains to the authorized scope of disclosure. In some states, the disclosure of imminent harm may be made not only to other mental health care providers and law enforcement personnel but also to identifiable third persons who are at risk. Such a rule is sometimes the result of judicial interpretation rather than an explicit legislative mandate. For instance, as noted above, in *Peck v. Counseling Service of Addison County*, 146 Vt. 61, 499 A.2d 422, 426 (1985), the Vermont Supreme Court held that even though legislation only authorized disclosure of protected medical information in the case of child abuse or gun shot wounds, public policy requires that where there is a threat of serious harm to an identifiable victim, disclosure may be made to the potential victim. Other states, such as Texas, only authorize the disclosure of the imminent dangerous propensities of a person under treatment to law enforcement personnel or other health providers. Thus, in states that follow the Texas model, disclosure of covered health information cannot be made to persons at risk of imminent harm.

2. Disclosure by Institutions Covered by FERPA (institutions of higher learning)

As noted in Chapter 3 (pp. 232–39), a series of recent incidents involving either student suicides or mass shootings on campuses have focused attention on the responsibility of universities to detect mental problems of students and to take preventive action where a student poses a significant threat to self or others. The capacity of institutions of higher learning to detect student mental illness requires exchange of information between relevant units of the university. Such exchanges might involve faculty, administrators, residence hall advisors, university health center personnel, campus law enforcement units and special university units with responsibility to assess threats. As detailed below, the disclosure of student records or information between university staff are subject to both federal and state law, the most significant of which is the Federal Educational Rights and Privacy Act (FERPA). In some instances, these laws may serve to prevent the aggregation of relevant information that is needed if a university is to have the capacity to identify students with serious mental problems who are potentially dangerous to self or others. As noted in the report on the Virginia Tech shootings, involving the murder of 32 students and staff on campus:

> Information privacy laws governing mental health, law enforcement, and educational records and information revealed widespread lack of understand, conflicting practice and laws that were poorly designed to accomplish their goals. Information privacy laws are intended to strike a balance between protecting privacy and allowing information sharing that is necessary or desirable. Because of this difficult balance, the laws are often complex and hard to understand."

"Mass Shootings at Virginia Tech," Report of the Review Panel (August 2007), at 58, available at http://www.vtreviewpanel.org/report/index. html) [hereinafter Review Panel Report]

Noted earlier in this chapter is the possibility that HIPAA privacy rules exempt from coverage the records of health maintenance entities operated by institutions of higher learning and the fact that FERPA exempts from its coverage "[r]ecords made or maintained by a university mental health care provider in the course of providing a student with medical or psychological care." See p. 324. Thus, the records of a university operated health treatment facility may not be subject to either HIPPA or FERPA privacy rules and their disclosure may only be governed by state law. In some states, mental health treatment records are subject to the same rules as general medical records. In other states, records associated with mental health treatment are subject to special and more restricted disclosure rules. Under Virginia in effect at the time of the Virginia Tech shootings, disclosure of health information held by health providers was only authorized under the following circumstances:

(1) with the consent of the patient; (2) to other health providers where the sharing of information is necessary for treatment; and (3) in selected situations including where a person "presents an imminent threat to the health or safety of individuals and the public." Review Panel Report, at 65. Similar laws have been adopted by other states. Also, there are variations among state laws governing the class of persons to whom information about dangerousness can be communicated. Under Texas law, for instance, disclosures of the imminent danger of an individual under treatment may only be disclosed to law enforcement offices and other health providers and not to university officials. Memorandum "Sharing Information about Potentially Dangerous Students." Office of General Counsel, University of Texas System (July 10, 2007), at.4 [hereinafter Memo, University of Texas General Counsel]

FERPA does govern the disclosure of student "educational records." While these records do not encompass university records maintained by university health units, they do include most other records kept by the university, and also apply to *communications* between and among campus personnel as well as disclosures to persons outside of the community. *Within* the university, student records covered by FERPA may only be disclosed to anyone "who has a legitimate educational interest in these records." 34 CFR § 99.31(a)(1)). Disclosure of student record information to external persons or agencies is in general limited to disclosures that are consented to by the student. However, FERPA permits nonconsensual disclosure in some limited circumstances. A recent analysis of the FERPA exceptions reached the following conclusion:

> If the university determines that individuals outside of the university should be informed about student conduct, other FERPA exceptions permit student education records to be shared with third parties. Notably, disclosure of information in education records is always permitted in connection with a health or safety emergency under certain conditions. FERPA permits disclosure to appropriate parties in connection with an emergency if knowledge of the information is necessary to protect the health or safety of the student or other individuals. This exception allows university officials to act quickly in emergencies to contact outside parties such as law enforcement or health authorities for assistance in arresting or detaining a student without regard to whether the information about the student is contained in the student's education record.

> Release under the health or safety emergency exception must be limited to "appropriate parties." FERPA does not define "appropriate parties," and thus it would be a matter for the university to determine who is an "appropriate party" based on the particular circumstances. So, for example, the emergency exception would permit university officials to share necessary information with local broadcast media as needed to alert the public to a threat posed by a student during an emergency situation, but it would not justify the university's sharing of information from a student's education record with a reporter for a news feature about the incident. In

addition, once the threat of harm has dissipated, the exception is no longer available to the university. Even in the absence of an emergency, FERPA permits an institution to contact its own law enforcement unit to investigate possible violations of and to enforce any local, state, or federal law."

Memo, University of Texas General Counsel, at 3.

Questions and Comments

1. *Scope of FERPA and HIPAA exemptions.* Assume that a university establishes a unit to assess campus safety and security. The unit is not part of a university's mental health treatment center. The unit gathers information from residence dorm advisors and academic units about student behavior that is indicative of mental illness and potential dangerousness either to self or others. Assuming that no student has violated any law, what course of action is open to a university to deal with such findings? For instance, could a university require an at risk student to undergo treatment as a condition for continued enrollment? In the event that a student declines to voluntarily undergo treatment and is suspended, should anyone be contacted or can the university assume that the suspension has removed the threat?

2. *FERPA regulations amendment.* Largely in response to the Virginia Tech shootings, the United States Department of Education issued a proposal to amend the regulations governing federal educational rights and privacy under FERPA. Under the proposed rule where there is "an articulable and significant threat to the health or safety of a student or other individuals" disclosure may be made to "any person whose knowledge of the information is necessary to protect against the threat." 34 CFR Part 99, 73 Fed. Reg.1558 (March 24, 2008). Moreover, "to provide appropriate flexibility and deference [to an institution's decision] the Secretary has determined that if, based on the information available at the time of the determination, there is a rational basis for the determination, the Department will not substitute its judgment for that of the educational agency or institution in evaluating the circumstance and making its determination." Assuming this change in regulations becomes final, would a covered educational institution that makes an appropriate finding as to dangerousness be authorized to notify the parents of a student who is deemed to present a danger to self or others? Would the rule also authorize an institution to also notify a student's dorm mates?

3. *Disclosures by university health care facilities.* Obviously, where a student has received treatment in a university operated health facility, the facility would be a good source of information concerning the mental health and propensities of the student. Yet the law of some states, such as Texas, restricts the disclosure of health information by mental health treatment to law enforcement agencies and other health providers. At the same time, universities can be liable for failing to take appropriate action to avert student suicides. How might the rules governing communications between a university health center and the administration be modified to provide reasonable protection to student privacy while also providing the university with sufficient information to determine whether the student needs to be suspended academically so that he or she may be moved into a different environment?

4. *Disclosing limits of confidentiality to patients.* The normal rules pertaining to confidentiality are, of course, partially waived in those jurisdictions that adhere to *Tarasoff*, since therapists in such jurisdictions have not only a duty but also a legal right to warn third persons of the dangerous propensities of their patients. In those jurisdictions where *Tarasoff* applies, should a therapist have an obligation to inform potential patients that confidentiality might be broken if the therapist later perceives the patient to be a threat to a third person? One commentator has suggested that failing to inform patients of the risk that their confidential communications will be disclosed could constitute a breach of the informed consent doctrine. See Note, "The Doctrine of Informed Consent Applied to Psychotherapy," 72 Geo.L.J. 1637 (1984).

5. *Problem.* Dr. I is a noted psychiatrist and a clinical professor at New York Medical College. He is also President of the Academy of Psychoanalysis and editor of the American Journal of Psychoanalysis. As part of his faculty duties, he acts as a teaching analyst for psychiatric residents who plan to specialize in psychoanalysis (full membership in a psychoanalytic institute, the qualifying emblem of a psychoanalyst, requires a period of specialized training including personal analysis by a training analyst).

Dr. D is a third-year resident in psychiatry at New York Medical College. As part of his psychoanalytic training, he is being analyzed by Dr. I. In the course of an analytic session, he tells Dr. I that he had recently gone to South America to see the night sky in the southern hemisphere. He also confesses that another reason for his trip was to "meet a nice child." Following the disclosure, Dr. I continues his regular bi-weekly analysis of Dr. D. Concluding that Dr. D is both intelligent and very professionally focused and is therefore able to control his impulses, Dr. I does nothing to have him removed from the residency program. He also concludes that his completion of the analysis is likely either to reorient Dr. D's sexual preferences or, at a minimum, to enhance his impulse controls. Four months after his confession during analysis, Dr. D, who at the time was working as a psychiatric resident at Danbury Hospital in Connecticut, is charged with molesting a ten-year-old boy, who was a patient in the hospital. The boy and his family subsequently filed a lawsuit against Dr. I and New York Medical College alleging that he should have taken steps to prevent Dr. D from working with children. (Additional details concerning the case, which was filed in the Federal District Court in Connecticut in the spring of 1998, are reported in Frank Bruni, 'A Child Psychiatrist and Pedophile; His Therapist Knew But Didn't Tell Victim,' N.Y.Times, April 19, 1998 at Sec. 1, 35).

Would HIPAA have permitted the disclosure of the information pertaining to Dr. D's pederast inclinations?

D. JUDICIAL PROCEEDINGS AND THE TESTIMONIAL PRIVILEGE

1. *Introduction*

a. *Perspectives on the Judicial Process*

In many situations society, through an arm of government, needs information known only to a few. In these situations, according to an old maxim, the public has a right to every man's evidence. That is, each person has a duty to disclose information of vital importance to society. The duty to disclose arises when society's need to ascertain the truth outweighs the individual's interest in concealing the information. The public, through the coercive forces of government, may then compel disclosure. The usual contexts in which the need for information arises include civil and criminal trials and hearings and investigations by legislatures and administrative agencies. In each of these contexts, ascertaining the truth is essential to promote an important societal interest.

The potential tension between a governmental interest in truth ascertainment in the legal process and the protection of privacy of health records (PHI) is made evident by the cases that follow where the contours of the testimonial privilege are sometimes defined depending on how the balance is struck. Whatever rule governing the scope of the testimonial privilege emerges as a result of a legislative or judicial decision, its application is not impeded by HIPAA. As noted previously, HIPAA's privacy rules do not protect a patient's health records including those pertaining to mental health treatment when they are obtained in response to an order or subpoena by a either a state or federal court or administrative tribunal.[a] Moreover, in discovery proceedings the PHI must be disclosed to either the court or an opposing party even in the absence of a court issued subpoena so long as the individual about whom health information is being sought is provided with adequate notice and has a reasonable opportunity to challenge the subpoena or discovery request.

* * *

b.   *Role and Function of the Testimonial Privilege*

Governmental authority to compel disclosure is not unlimited. It extends only as far as necessary to achieve the governmental purpose at hand. Thus, no witness may be compelled to testify concerning matters irrelevant to the case before the court or other tribunal.

Governmental authority is also limited when mandatory disclosure conflicts with rights or interests, which are highly valued in a free society. To preserve important rights and interests, courts and other tribunals may recognize a "privilege" on the part of a witness to decline to answer certain questions. For example, no person may be compelled to make statements which might incriminate him. The privilege against self-incrimination is inherent in the American concept of liberty. Long recognized under the English common law, the privilege was incorporated in the Fifth Amendment to the federal Constitution and is made applicable to the states through the Fourteenth Amendment. Similarly, under the First Amendment guarantees of free speech and religion, no person may be compelled to state his political or religious beliefs under

a.   45 C.F.R. § 164.512 (e) (1)(ii). See generally, Singhai, et al., 'Recent Developments in Medicine and Law,' 2002 Insurance Tort Journal 1 (2002).

oath. Of course, a witness may waive the privilege and volunteer this information. The privilege merely protects against compulsory disclosure.

In addition to privileges which arise under the Constitution, legislatures may create testimonial privileges by statutes. In the absence of a statute or constitutional mandate, courts may recognize a privilege because of the importance of the interests thereby protected.

A testimonial privilege may protect certain *topics,* such as the witness' political or religious beliefs or information tending to incriminate the witness. Another form of privilege protects confidential communications in the context of certain relationships which society seeks to foster. When such a privilege is asserted, *neither* party to such a relationship may be compelled to disclose information exchanged in confidence. Relationships which traditionally have given rise to privileges of this sort include those between attorney and client, physician and patient, husband and wife, and priest and penitent. In recent years this privilege for confidential communications has been extended by statute or by courts in various states to such diverse professional groups as journalists, accountants, and psychotherapists.[51]

Traditionally, privilege for confidential communications is justified when four conditions are met. First, the relationship must be one which society seeks to foster. Second, the communications must originate in a confidence that they will not be disclosed. Third, the element of confidentiality must be essential to achieve the purpose of the relationship. Finally, injury to the relationship resulting from compelled disclosure must be greater than the benefit gained in correct disposal of litigation.

The availability and scope of the testimonial privilege depend upon the profession of the psychotherapist and upon the law of the particular jurisdiction. Confidential communications between psychiatrist and patient can be protected by physician-patient privilege statutes, which have been enacted by about two-thirds of the states. In addition, statutes in a few states provide a special psychiatrist-patient privilege. In most states, statutes licensing psychologists provide a privilege for communications between psychologist and client. Finally, some states provide a privilege for other mental health professionals who provide psychotherapy, such as marriage counselors and social workers. Privilege statutes, however, are frequently ambiguous, and the availability and scope of the privilege in various contexts may be difficult to predict. The case which follows establishes the dimensions of the privilege in all federal civil cases where it is being asserted by the defendant in a civil action.

---

51. The reader may recall that the term "privilege" arises in many contexts. Generally, the term privilege refers to an exemption from liability for an action which would ordinarily give rise to liability. See, for example, the discussion of privilege as a defense to defamation this chapter, at pp. 334–40. In the present context, the action which would ordinarily give rise to liability is the withholding of subpoenaed testimony or information. Although the ordinary penalty for withholding subpoenaed information may be a fine or imprisonment, the valid assertion of a recognized testimonial privilege exempts a witness from liability.

JAFFEE v. REDMOND

Supreme Court of the United States, 1996.
518 U.S. 1, 116 S.Ct. 1923, 135 L.Ed.2d 337.

JUSTICE STEVENS delivered the opinion of the Court.

[Plaintiff, the administrator of the estate of Ricky Allen, brought a civil suit against the defendant, Mary Lu Redmond, a police officer who shot and killed Mr. Allen in the line of duty for allegedly violating constitutional rights of the deceased. Following the shooting, the defendant officer received extensive counseling from Karen Beyer, a licensed clinical social worker. Plaintiff petitioned the trial court for access to the records of the counseling session.]

The question we address is whether statements the officer made to her therapist during the counseling sessions are protected from compelled disclosure in a federal civil action brought by the family of the deceased. Stated otherwise, the question is whether it is appropriate for federal courts to recognize a "psychotherapist privilege" under Rule 501 of the Federal Rules of Evidence.

* * *

The Court of Appeals for the Seventh circuit ... concluded that "reason and experience," the touchstones for acceptance of a privilege under Rule 501 of the Federal Rules of Evidence, compelled recognition of a psychotherapist-patient privilege. Reason tells us that psychotherapists and patients share a unique relationship, in which the ability to communicate freely without the fear of public disclosure is the key to successful treatment. As to experience, the court observed that all 50 States have adopted some form of the psychotherapist-patient privilege. The court attached particular significance to the fact that Illinois law expressly extends such a privilege to social workers like Karen Beyer. The court also noted that, with one exception, the federal decisions rejecting the privilege were more than five years old and that the "need and demand for counseling services has skyrocketed during the past several years."

The Court of Appeals qualified its recognition of the privilege by stating that it would not apply if "in the interests of justice, the evidentiary need for the disclosure of the contents of a patient's counseling sessions outweighs that patient's privacy interests." Balancing those conflicting interests the court observed, on the one hand, that the evidentiary need for the contents of the confidential conversations was diminished in this case because there were numerous eyewitnesses to the shooting, and, on the other hand, that Officer Redmond's privacy interests were substantial. Based on this assessment, the court concluded that the trial court had erred by refusing to afford protection to the confidential communications between Redmond and Beyer. The United States courts of appeals do not uniformly agree that the federal courts should recognize a psychotherapist privilege under Rule 501. Because of the conflict among the courts of appeals and the importance of the question, we granted certiorari. We affirm.

* * *

III

Like the spousal and attorney-client privileges, the psychotherapist-patient privilege is "rooted in the imperative need for confidence and trust." Treatment by a physician for physical ailments can often proceed successfully on the basis of a physical examination, objective information supplied by the patient, and the results of diagnostic tests. Effective psychotherapy, by contrast, depends upon an atmosphere of confidence and trust in which the patient is willing to make a frank and complete disclosure of facts, emotions, memories, and fears. Because of the sensitive nature of the problems for which individuals consult psychotherapists, disclosure of confidential communications made during counseling sessions may cause embarrassment or disgrace. For this reason, the mere possibility of disclosure may impede development of the confidential relationship necessary for successful treatment. As the Judicial Conference Advisory Committee observed in 1972 when it recommended that Congress recognize a psychotherapist privilege as part of the Proposed Federal Rules of Evidence, a psychiatrist's ability to help her patients

> "is completely dependent upon [the patients'] willingness and ability to talk freely. This makes it difficult if not impossible for [a psychiatrist] to function without being able to assure ... patients of confidentiality and, indeed, privileged communication. Where there may be exceptions to this general rule, there is wide agreement that confidentiality is a *sine qua non* for successful psychiatric treatment."

By protecting confidential communications between a psychotherapist and her patient from involuntary disclosure, the proposed privilege thus serves important private interests.

Our cases make clear that an asserted privilege must also "serve public ends." *Upjohn Co. v. United States,* 449 U.S. 383, 389, 101 S.Ct. 677, 682, 66 L.Ed.2d 584 (1981). Thus, the purpose of the attorney-client privilege is to "encourage full and frank communication between attorneys and their clients and thereby promote broader public interests in the observance of law and administration of justice." *Ibid.* And the spousal privilege, as modified in *Trammel* [*v. United States,* 445 U.S. 40, 47, 100 S.Ct. 906, 63 L.Ed.2d 186 (1980)], is justified because it "furthers the important public interest in marital harmony." The psychotherapist privilege serves the public interest by facilitating the provision of appropriate treatment for individuals suffering the effects of a mental or emotional problem. The mental health of our citizenry, no less than its physical health, is a public good of transcendent importance.[a]

a. This case amply demonstrates the importance of allowing individuals to re- ceive confidential counseling. Police officers engaged in the dangerous and difficult tasks

In contrast to the significant public and private interests supporting recognition of the privilege, the likely evidentiary benefit that would result from the denial of the privilege is modest. If the privilege were rejected, confidential conversations between psychotherapists and their patients would surely be chilled, particularly when it is obvious that the circumstances that give rise to the need for treatment will probably result in litigation. Without a privilege, much of the desirable evidence to which litigants such as petitioner seek access—for example, admissions against interest by a party—is unlikely to come into being. This unspoken "evidence" will therefore serve no greater truth-seeking function than if it had been spoken and privileged.

* * *

IV

All agree that a psychotherapist privilege covers confidential communications made to licensed psychiatrists and psychologists. We have no hesitation in concluding in this case that the federal privilege should also extend to confidential communications made to licensed social workers in the course of psychotherapy. The reasons for recognizing a privilege for treatment by psychiatrists and psychologists apply with equal force to treatment by a clinical social worker such As Karen Beyer. Today, social workers provide a significant amount of mental health treatment. Their clients often include the poor and those of modest means who could not afford the assistance of a psychiatrist or psychologist, but whose counseling sessions serve the same public goals. Perhaps in recognition of these circumstances, the vast majority of States explicitly extend a testimonial privilege to licensed social workers. We therefore agree with the Court of Appeals that "[d]rawing a distinction between the counseling provided by costly psychotherapists and the counseling provided by more readily accessible social workers serves no discernible public purpose."

We part company with the Court of Appeals on a separate point. We reject the balancing component of the privilege implemented by that court and a small number of States. Making the promise of confidentiality contingent upon a trial judge's later evaluation of the relative importance of the patient's interest in privacy and the evidentiary need for disclosure would eviscerate the effectiveness of the privilege. As we explained in *Upjohn,* if the purpose of the privilege is to be served, the participants in the confidential conversation "must be able to predict with some degree of certainty whether particular discussions will be protected. An uncertain privilege, or one which purports to be certain

associated with protecting the safety of our communities not only confront the risk of physical harm but also face stressful circumstances that may give rise to anxiety, depression, fear, or anger. The entire community may suffer if police officers are not able to receive effective counseling and treatment after traumatic incidents, either because trained officers leave the profession prematurely or because those in need of treatment remain on the job.

but results in widely varying applications by the courts, is little better than no privilege at all."

These considerations are all that is necessary for decision of this case. A rule that authorizes the recognition of new privileges on a case-by-case basis makes it appropriate to define the details of new privileges in a like manner. Because this is the first case in which we have recognized a psychotherapist privilege, it is neither necessary nor feasible to delineate its full contours in a way that would "govern all conceivable future questions in this area."

V

The conversations between Officer Redmond and Karen Beyer and the notes taken during their counseling sessions are protected from compelled disclosure under Rule 501 of the Federal Rules of Evidence. The judgment of the Court of Appeals is affirmed.

It is so ordered.

JUSTICE SCALIA, with whom the CHIEF JUSTICE joins as to Part III, dissenting.

* * *

... Effective psychotherapy undoubtedly is beneficial to individuals with mental problems, and surely serves some larger social interest in maintaining a mentally stable society. But merely mentioning these values does not answer the critical question: are they of such importance, and is the contribution of psychotherapy to them so distinctive, and is the application of normal evidentiary rules so destructive to psychotherapy, as to justify making our federal courts occasional instruments of injustice? On that central question I find the Court's analysis insufficiently convincing to satisfy the high standard we have set for rules that "are in derogation of the search for truth."

When is it, one must wonder, that *the psychotherapist* came to play such an indispensable role in the maintenance of the citizenry's mental health? For most of history, men and women have worked out their difficulties by talking to, *inter alios,* parents, siblings, best friends and bartenders—none of whom was awarded a privilege against testifying in court. Ask the average citizen: Would your mental health be more significantly impaired by preventing you from seeing a psychotherapist, or by preventing you from getting advice from your mom? I have little doubt what the answer would be. Yet there is no mother-child privilege.

How likely is it that a person will be deterred from seeking psychological counseling, or from being completely truthful in the course of such counseling, because of fear of later disclosure in litigation? And even more pertinent to today's decision, to what extent will the evidentiary privilege reduce that deterrent? The Court does not try to answer the first of these questions; and it *cannot possibly have any notion* of what the answer is to the second, since that depends entirely upon the scope of the privilege, which the Court amazingly finds it "neither necessary nor feasible to delineate." If, for example, the psychotherapist can give the patient no more assurance than "A court will not be able to make me disclose what you tell me, unless you tell me about a harmful act," I doubt whether there would be much benefit from the privilege at all. That is not a fanciful example, at least with respect to extension of the psychotherapist privilege to social workers.

Even where it is certain that absence of the psychotherapist privilege will inhibit disclosure of the information, it is not clear to me that that is an unacceptable state of affairs. Let us assume the very worst in the circumstances of the present case: that to be truthful about what was troubling her, the police officer who sought counseling would have to confess that she shot without reason, and wounded an innocent man. If (again to assume the worst) such an act constituted the crime of negligent wounding under Illinois law, the officer would of course have the absolute right not to admit that she shot without reason in criminal court. But I see no reason why she should be enabled *both* not to admit it in criminal court (as a good citizen should), *and* to get the benefits of psychotherapy by admitting it to a therapist who cannot tell anyone else. And even less reason why she should be enabled to *deny* her guilt in the criminal trial—or in a civil trial for negligence—while yet obtaining the benefits of psychotherapy by confessing guilt to a social worker who cannot testify. It seems to me entirely fair to say that if she wishes the benefits of telling the truth she must also accept the adverse consequences. To be sure, in most cases the statements to the psychotherapist will be only marginally relevant, and one of the purposes of the privilege (though not one relied upon by the Court) may be simply to spare patients needless intrusion upon their privacy, and to spare psychotherapists needless expenditure of their time in deposition and trial. But surely this can be achieved by means short of excluding even evidence that is of the most direct and conclusive effect.

The Court confidently asserts that not much truth-finding capacity would be destroyed by the privilege anyway, since "[w]ithout a privilege, much of the desirable evidence to. which litigants such as petitioner seek access ... is unlikely to come into being." If that is so, how come psychotherapy got to be a thriving practice before the "psychotherapist privilege," was invented? Were the patients paying money to lie to their analysts all those years? Of course the evidence-generating effect of the privilege (if any) depends entirely upon its scope, which the Court steadfastly declines to consider. And even if one assumes that scope to be the broadest possible, is it really true that most, or even many, of those who seek psychological counseling have the worry of litigation in the back of their minds? I doubt that, and the Court provides no evidence to support it.

* * *

III

Turning from the general question that was not involved in this case to the specific one that is: The Court's conclusion that a social-worker psychotherapeutic privilege deserves recognition is even less persuasive. In approaching this question, the fact that five of the state legislatures that have seen fit to enact "some form" of psychotherapist privilege have elected not to extend *any form* of privilege to social workers ought to give one pause. The Court, however, has "no hesitation in concluding ... that the federal privilege should also extend" to social workers, and goes on to prove that by polishing off the reasoned analysis with a topic sentence and two sentences of discussion:

"The reasons for recognizing a privilege for treatment by psychiatrists and psychologists apply with equal force to treatment by a clinical social worker such as Karen Beyer. Today, social workers provide a significant amount of mental health treatment. Their clients often include the poor and those of modest means who could not afford the assistance of a psychiatrist or psychologist, but whose counseling sessions serve the same public goals."

So much for the rule that privileges are to be narrowly construed.

Of course this brief analysis—like the earlier, more extensive, discussion of the general psychotherapist privilege—contains no explanation of why the psychotherapy provided by social workers is a public good of such transcendent importance as to be purchased at the price of occasional injustice. Moreover it considers only the respects in which social workers providing therapeutic services are *similar* to licensed psychiatrists and psychologists; not a word about the respects in which they are different. A licensed psychiatrist or psychologist is an expert in psychotherapy—and that may suffice (though I think it not so clear that this Court should make the judgment) to justify the use of extraordinary means to encourage counseling with him as opposed to counseling with one's rabbi, minister, family or friends. One must presume that a social worker does *not* bring this greatly heightened degree of skill to bear, which is alone a reason for not encouraging that consultation as generously. Does a social worker bring to bear at least a significantly heightened degree of skill—more than a minister or rabbi, for example? I have no idea, and neither does the Court. The social worker in the present case, Karen Beyer, was a "licensed clinical social worker" in Illinois, a job title whose training requirements consist of "master's degree in social work from an approved program," and "3,000 hours of satisfactory, supervised clinical professional experience." It is not clear that the degree in social work requires any training in psychotherapy. The "clinical professional experience" apparently will impart some such training, but only of the vaguest sort....

* * *

Another critical distinction between psychiatrists and psychologists, on the one hand, and social workers, on the other, is that the former professionals, in their consultations with patients, *do nothing but psycho-*

therapy. Social workers, on the other hand, interview people for a multitude of reasons. The Illinois definition of "[l]icensed social worker," for example, is as follows:

> 'Licensed social worker' means a person who holds a license authorizing the practice of social work, which includes social services to individuals, groups or communities in any one or more of the fields of social casework, social group work, community organization for social welfare, social work research, social welfare administration or social work education.

Thus, in applying the "social worker" variant of the "psychotherapist" privilege, it will be necessary to determine whether the information provided to the social worker was provided to him *in his capacity as a psychotherapist,* or in his capacity as an administrator of social welfare, a community organizer, etc. Worse still, if the privilege is to have its desired effect (and is not to mislead the client), it will presumably be necessary for the social caseworker to advise, as the conversation with his welfare client proceeds, which portions are privileged and which are not.

Questions and Comments

1. *Validity of* Jaffee *case rationale.* The facts of the *Jaffee* case starkly present the potential conflict between society's interest in truth ascertainment in the judicial process versus the facilitation of mental health treatment. In giving preference to the latter, the majority assumes that without the protection of confidentiality associated with the testimonial privilege, the public would be less likely to seek treatment, or that the treatment provided would be less effective because patients may be hesitant to disclose all to the therapist. Is this conclusion based on empirical fact or, as the dissent suggests, merely speculation? In this connection, consider a 1982 study that concluded that "patients are probably not deterred [by the lack of privilege] from seeking psychiatric help to any significant degree." In surveying a group of lay people, the study found that "93% of those surveyed 'would have sought help for serious emotional problems' without the privilege and 74% 'did not know whether there was a privilege statute or guessed incorrectly that there was (no privilege statute')." Daniel Shuman & Myron S. Weiner, 'The Privilege Study: An Empirical Examination of the Psychotherapist–Patient Privilege,' 60 N.Car. L.Rev. 893, 924–25 (1982).

If patients are in fact not significantly deterred from seeking mental health treatment by the absence of the testimonial privilege, what policy reasons support the majority's rule?

2. *Doctrinal basis underlying* Jaffee. Is the majority decision recognizing the privilege based on a constitutional right of privacy or on more general policy grounds? In *United States v. Glass*, 133 F.3d 1356 (1998), the 10th Circuit found that the privilege in *Jaffee* "is not rooted in any constitutional right of privacy, but in a public good, which overrides the quest for relevant evidence."

Further, Justice Scalia and the Chief Justice dissented in *Jaffee* primarily on public policy grounds. If the majority's approach was also based on public policy, which opinion is the more persuasive, given the interests at stake?

3. *Who is covered by privilege statutes?* It is sometimes difficult to determine whether a specific professional group, particularly in the mental health field, is covered by a particular privilege statute and, if so, the extent of the exemption. States have commonly enacted separate privilege statutes for various professional groups such as physicians, psychologists, marriage counselors, and social workers. Various problems are raised by the existence of multiple privilege statutes. For instance, in the absence of explicit legislative direction, should psychiatrists be entitled to the special privilege for psychologists which is normally broader and more comprehensive than that of physicians? In one jurisdiction the court held that the psychologist privilege did *not* cover psychiatrists. See *Ritt v. Ritt*, 98 N.J.Super. 590, 238 A.2d 196 (1967). In another state the court held that the psychologist privilege did cover psychiatrists. See *Day v. State*, 378 So.2d 1156 (Ala.Cr. App.1979), reversed sub nom. *Ex parte Day*, 378 So.2d 1159 (Ala.1979). As noted by the court in *Jaffee* a number of states have enacted privilege statutes specifically covering clinical social workers. However, the privilege is generally limited to clinical social workers who are registered with the state. See *In re Westland*, 48 Ill.App.3d 172, 6 Ill.Dec. 331, 362 N.E.2d 1153, 1157 (1977).

Similar problems are encountered where the coverage of the privilege for psychologists and marriage counselors differ. For instance, in New Jersey the privilege for marriage counselors is virtually absolute, and confidential communications are not admissible in a divorce proceeding. However, under the Practicing Psychology Licensing Act the privilege would not necessarily bar the admission of confidential information in a divorce proceeding. In *Wichansky v. Wichansky*, 126 N.J.Super. 156, 313 A.2d 222 (1973), the court held that a psychologist who engages in marriage counseling is covered by the broader marriage counselor's privilege, even though he was not a licensed marriage counselor.

4. *Clinical social workers and other counselors.* If the privilege is applied to social workers, should it also apply to communications with other types of counselors (e.g., school counselors, pastoral counselors, marriage counselors)? Rape counselors were held to be covered by the privilege in *United States v. Lowe*, 948 F.Supp. 97 (D.Mass. 1996).

5. *The privilege and plaintiffs.* *Jaffee* describes the privilege as "absolute" but it also recognizes situations where the privilege might not apply. Would Mary Lou Redmond, the defendant in *Jaffee*, have been able to assert the privilege had she been the plaintiff in a lawsuit against the estate of the man she killed (suppose that she had previously been assaulted by the deceased)? The status of the privilege when asserted by the plaintiff is discussed in *In Re Lipschutz* at pp. 379–87 *infra*.

2. *Conditions Giving Rise to the Privilege*

a. *The Course of Treatment Requirement*

STATE v. COLE

Supreme Court of Iowa, 1980.
295 N.W.2d 29.

* * *

LARSON, JUSTICE.

This defendant appeals her conviction, in a jury-waived trial, of first-degree murder in violation of section 690.2, The Code 1977. She challenges the trial court's rulings in regard to psychiatric evidence secured by depositions and in-trial testimony * * * We affirm the trial court.

It is undisputed that on September 15, 1977, the defendant shot and killed Dr. Alan Tyler, her ex-husband, in his office at Wilden Clinic. Immediately after the shooting, she proceeded to the reception area and announced that she had "shot her husband." She then called the police and waited for them at the clinic. She was brought before a magistrate for an initial appearance where she was represented by Lawrence Scalise and Thomas Levis. At that time an order was signed by the magistrate to take the defendant to Iowa Lutheran Hospital "to undergo psychiatric and physical examination and evaluation." It is this order and the related evidence concerning the mental condition of the defendant which give rise to the most troublesome issues.

I. THE PSYCHIATRIC EVIDENCE

A. *Effect of the commitment order.* Pursuant to the court's order, the defendant was first examined by Dr. Michael Taylor, a psychiatrist who had been treating her on a private basis since before the shooting. He ceased his examination of her on September 30, 1977, at which time he was replaced by Dr. Vernon Varner. The defendant filed notice, * * * that she intended to rely upon the defense of diminished capacity. The State then sought to obtain psychiatric evidence through these doctors' depositions and in-trial testimony.

Upon application of the State, and over defendant's objections, pretrial depositions of Doctors Taylor and Varner were ordered by the court. Dr. Varner complied, and his deposition was taken. * * * Again over objection, the trial court permitted Dr. Taylor to testify at trial in the State's case in chief.

Defendant argues the trial court's rulings on the admissibility of the psychiatric evidence was erroneous because they violated her doctor-patient privilege, set out in section 622.10, The Code, as follows:

> No practicing attorney, counselor, physician, surgeon, or the stenographer or confidential clerk of any such person, who obtains such information by reason of his employment, * * * shall be allowed, in giving testimony, to disclose any confidential communication proper-

ly entrusted to him in his professional capacity, and necessary and proper to enable him to discharge the functions of his office according to the usual course of practice or discipline. Such prohibition shall not apply to cases where the person in whose favor the same is made waives the rights conferred. * * *

[N]ot every doctor-patient relationship provides a basis for exclusion of the doctor's testimony. In some cases the privilege never arises; in others it exists but is held to be waived by the patient. The privilege did not exist at common law, and its embodiment by statute has been criticized by at least one writer.

While our cases have evidenced no hostility to the rule itself, they have uniformly required three elements to be established: (1) the relationship of doctor-patient; (2) acquisition of the information or knowledge during this relationship; and (3) the necessity of the information to enable the doctor to treat the patient skillfully.

The order signed by the magistrate was as follows:

ORDER FOR PSYCHIATRIC EVALUATION AND REPORT

Now, on this 15th day of September, 1977, this matter having been brought to the attention of the court, and the court being fully advised of the charges against the defendant in the above captioned cause, and the present condition of the defendant; it is the considered opinion of this court that before further proceedings may be had an evaluation of the above-named defendant's physical and psychological state should be made by competent professionals in the fields of medicine and psychology in order that the court may be more fully advised and that the best interests of the parties and of justice may be realized.

* * *

The effect of [the Court's] order, and of the medical relationship which followed it, are determinative on the issue of whether or not the defendant could assert the doctor-patient privilege. In court-ordered evaluations, the third requirement of the privilege is lacking; the communication is not for the purpose of treatment but to determine the existence of a fact or condition for the benefit of the court. Therefore, "[t]he physician-patient privilege does not arise where on order of the court a defendant is examined to determine his mental or physical condition."

* * * The order clearly provided for evaluation and report to the court and made no provision for diagnosis or treatment.

The defendant, while acknowledging that the order appears to be for evaluation and report, argues it was really only intended to provide for her safekeeping in order to avoid a possible suicide. We do not believe the intentions of the parties can be properly used to countermand the unambiguous provisions of a court order.

* * *

Even if we were to consider the intentions of the parties, as appellant suggests, we do not believe the record supports her contention that "[t]he record unquestionably shows that Kathleen Cole was sent to Lutheran Hospital for the primary, if not the sole purpose, of obtaining diagnosis and treatment." Even under her own evidence, the commitment was for her protection; no one testified she was committed for treatment.

* * *

We find no reversible error; we therefore affirm the trial court.

Affirmed.

All Justices concur except HARRIS, J., who dissents, joined by REES and ALLBEE, JJ.

Questions and Comments

1. *Court ordered examinations.* The *Cole* case affirms the basic rule that under state law, a privilege only attaches where the client's relationship to the psychologist or psychiatrist was in the course of treatment. Problems may arise in the application of this rule when the professional relationship involves both diagnosis undertaken as a result of a court order and treatment which is carried out at the initiative of the examining facility.

2. *Disclosure requirement.* Where the psychiatrist or psychologist examines a person on behalf of the court or an adverse party, is there any obligation on the part of the examiner to inform the person being examined as to the nature of the relationship and that any disclosures that are made will not be privileged? This question has only been addressed in the context of criminal cases where it has generally been held that, unless the person being examined is specifically informed that the purpose of the examination is not for treatment, any disclosures that may be made are not admissible in a subsequent criminal trial. See, *State v. Shaw,* 106 Ariz. 103, 471 P.2d 715 (1970) and *State v. Cole,* 295 N.W.2d 29, 34 (Iowa 1980).

3. *Scope of privilege.* In those jurisdictions where a privilege attaches to information or disclosures communicated in the course of psychotherapy, the scope of such privilege may require judicial interpretation. An issue that has arisen is whether confidential information as used in statutes setting forth a privilege includes observations or any other information the therapist may have learned about the patient from sources other than the verbal communication of the patient himself. Illustratively, in *People v. Doe,* 103 Ill.App.3d 56, 58 Ill.Dec. 664, 430 N.E.2d 696 (1981), the psychiatric therapist was subpoenaed to appear before the grand jury and was presented with a drawing purporting to be a composite sketch of a person suspected of an ax murder. Claiming statutory privilege, the therapist refused to state whether she had seen anyone resembling the drawing even though there was independent evidence indicating that the person depicted by the composite drawing had been admitted to the psychiatric unit where the psychiatrist was working at the time. In finding the psychiatrist-patient privilege inapplicable, the court construed "communications" as used by the privilege statute to include only information obtained from conversations with the patient and not observations. Courts of other jurisdictions, however, have given a

different interpretation to similar language. The American Psychiatric Association's proposed Model Law of Confidentiality of Health and Social Service Records specifically would extend the privilege to all "confidential information" which is defined to include "the fact that a person is or has been a patient/client." See, Sloan & Hall, 'Confidentiality of Psychotherapeutic Records,' 5 J. of Legal Medicine 435, 463 (1984).

4. *Hospital admissions.* In some jurisdictions, the patient-psychotherapist privilege does not protect the existence of the fact of a hospital admission, the dates of hospitalization, or the purpose of the admission, so long as the purpose does not implicate a patient-psychotherapist communication. In *Commonwealth v. Clancy,* 402 Mass. 664, 524 N.E.2d 395 (1988), the court held that defense counsel was allowed this limited access to a witness' record without any showing of need, since this was not privileged information.

5. *Records covered.* When privilege protects confidential communications with a psychotherapist, the privilege extends as well to the patient records the psychotherapist maintains. Generally, such records are protected to the same extent as the communications they describe. When patient records are maintained at a hospital, school, or other public agency, however, the status of privilege is unclear. Similarly, when a patient is committed for treatment at a mental hospital, a variety of personnel may have access to his records. Courts, therefore, may regard the records as non-confidential and hence not privileged. On the other hand, other courts view nurses and ward staff as agents of the patient's psychiatrist and, accordingly, extend any applicable psychiatrist-patient or physician-patient privilege to hospital records.

Records at publicly funded hospitals pose additional problems. A few courts have found no confidential relationship between a resident-patient and psychiatrists employed at a state hospital, and hence no privilege for psychiatric records of state hospital patients. Additionally, courts sometimes treat state hospital records as public documents and therefore not privileged, or privileged under privilege statutes for government documents generally, and hence subject to waiver by the government, without consent of the patient. (See, for example, dissent in *Taylor v. United States,* 222 F.2d 398, 404 (D.C.Cir.1955) and New York cases cited therein.)

6. *Question.* A distraught person telephones a state psychiatric hospital and reaches the hospital's receptionist. He informs the receptionist that he has just "strangled a kid." The receptionist contacts the psychiatrist on duty, who without the knowledge of the caller, asks her to keep the caller on the line so that the sheriff's office can trace the call. The psychiatrist then gets on the line and speaks to the caller for ten to fifteen minutes, "asking him for background information similar to that the psychiatrist usually obtains from a patient in a psychiatric interview." During the conversation with the psychiatrist, the caller makes a number of incriminating statements about his homosexual encounters with the victim and his role in the victim's death.

While the caller is on the line with the psychiatrist, the police, who have in the meantime been notified by the hospital, trace the call and arrest the caller in a hotel room where they also discover the deceased victim's body.

The caller is charged with murder and brought to trial. At the trial, the prosecution seeks to obtain the testimony of both the hospital psychiatrist and receptionist to whom the defendant had made incriminating statements.

Under the law of the state where the case is being tried, a testimonial privilege is available for statements made in the course of examination and treatment. The statutory provisions also extend to "persons *present* [emphasis added] to further the interests of the patient in the consultation, examination, or interview." If the privilege were applicable, it would preclude the testimony of either the psychiatrist or the receptionist. The prosecution asserts that the privilege is inapplicable since the psychiatrist was not diagnosing or treating the defendant, but rather was keeping him on the line to assist police apprehension. Also, the prosecution contends that the privilege does not apply to the receptionist since she was not "present" at the examination or interview. How should the privilege issue be resolved by the court? See *State v. Miller*, 300 Or. 203, 709 P.2d 225 (1985).

b. Scope of the Privilege: Communications Made in the Presence of Others

STATE v. ANDRING

Supreme Court of Minnesota, 1984.
342 N.W.2d 128.

WAHL, JUSTICE.

Defendant David Gerald Andring is charged with three counts of criminal sexual conduct in the second degree in violation of Minn.Stat. § 609.343 (1982). The two complaints setting out these counts allege that defendant had sexual contact with his 10–year–old stepdaughter and his 11–year–old niece. A hearing was held to consider a probable cause challenge to the complaints. Probable cause was found. Defendant was released on bond, pending trial, on condition that he have no contact with the alleged victims.

Defendant voluntarily entered the Crisis Intervention Unit at Bethesda Lutheran Medical Center (crisis unit) after the probable cause hearing but before trial. A social history of defendant was taken by a registered nurse; the admitting diagnosis was acute alcoholism and depression. During his stay, defendant received one-on-one counseling with staff physicians and other medical personnel. He also participated in a daily 2–hour group therapy session with other patients in the crisis unit, sessions which were supervised by physicians and registered nurses. Those present at the group therapy sessions were informed that such sessions were confidential and that only the staff would have access to information disclosed in the sessions. Defendant related his experience of sexual conduct with young girls (1) during one-on-one counseling sessions with registered nurses and a medical student, (2) during the taking of his social history with a registered nurse, and (3) during group therapy sessions.[a]

---

a. The trial court found no reason to believe that any minor children other than defendant's stepdaughter and niece were involved in any of defendant's disclosures to the crisis unit's personnel.

The state, in the course of its investigation of the case, learned of inculpatory disclosures made by defendant at the crisis unit. The state then moved for discovery and disclosure of defendant's medical records and statements made to crisis unit personnel. No request for disclosure from non-staff participants in the group therapy sessions was made. The trial court, after an extensive inquiry into the ramifications of the state's motion, denied the state's motion for discovery of statements made by defendant during the taking of his social history and during one-on-one therapy but granted the motion for discovery of defendant's disclosures made during group therapy sessions.

Considering the issue of confidentiality of group therapy disclosures as both important and doubtful, the trial court certified the following question to this court:

> Whether the scope of the physician-patient and/or registered nurse-patient privilege is to be extended to prevent disclosures of communications concerning Defendant's sexual conduct with minor children during group therapy sessions, a crime for which he has already been charged, where such group therapy sessions are an integral and necessary part of Defendant's diagnosis and treatment and consist of physicians and/or registered nurses and other patients, who participate in said group therapy sessions and are an aid to Defendant's diagnosis and treatment as well as their own, i.e., are such patients to be considered as agents of the physicians and/or registered nurses and/or do such patients come within the meaning of "being reasonably necessary for the accomplishment of the purpose of such a communication" so as to render the relationship confidential?

* * *

We now reach the question as to whether confidential group therapy sessions which are an integral and necessary part of a patient's diagnosis and treatment are to be included within the scope of the medical privilege. The troublesome aspect of this question lies in the fact that third parties, other patients and participants in the therapy, are present at the time the information is disclosed. Does their presence destroy the privilege?

McCormick, in discussing the issue of whether the presence of third parties renders a statement to a physician nonprivileged, argues that the court should analyze the problem in terms of whether the third persons are necessary and customary participants in the consultation or treatment and whether the communications were confidential for the purpose of aiding in diagnosis and treatment. McCormick's Handbook of the Law of Evidence, § 101 (E. Cleary 2d ed. 1972). Under this approach, we conclude that the medical privilege must be construed to encompass statements made in group psychotherapy. The participants in group psychotherapy sessions are not casual third persons who are strangers to the psychiatrist/psychologist/nurse-patient relationship. Rather, every participant has such a relationship with the attending professional, and, in the group therapy setting, the participants actually become part of the diagnostic and therapeutic process for co-participants.

This point is more fully developed in Cross, 'Privileged Communications Between Participants in Group Psychotherapy,' 1970 L. & Soc.Order 191, 196–98, 200–01 (1970):

> [T]he chief characteristic of group therapy that distinguishes it from individual analysis is that each patient becomes the therapeutic agent of the others * * *. Effective social interaction within the group is therefore a crucial prerequisite to group therapy. The type of interaction required can only be achieved, however, when group members respond to each other spontaneously, both in their speech and their actions * * *. No group participant would make himself vulnerable to community scorn and loss of spouse, job, or freedom by placing his most secret thoughts before the group, unless he could be assured of confidentiality. * * * [S]ociety should certainly foster a relationship that has an important prophylactic effect and thus shields both society and the patient from the consequences of antisocial behavior. * * * [A]lthough there may be occasional losses [of relevant important information] such sporadic occurrences are overshadowed by the potential destruction of the therapeutic relationship.

An interpretation which excluded group therapy from the scope of the psychotherapist-patient privilege would seriously limit the effectiveness of group psychotherapy as a therapeutic device. This would be particularly unfortunate because group therapy is a cost-effective method of psychotherapy in that it allows the therapist to treat a number of patients at the same time. It is also more effective with some patients, who, upon hearing other people reveal their innermost thoughts, are less reluctant to reveal their own. Many commentators agree that the psychotherapist-patient privilege should be extended to include group therapy. [Citation] Because the confidentiality of communications made during group therapy is essential in maintaining its effectiveness as a therapeutic tool, we answer the certified question in the affirmative. We hold that the scope of the physician-patient/medical privilege extends to include confidential group psychotherapy sessions where such sessions are an integral and necessary part of a patient's diagnosis and treatment. We reverse the order of the trial court allowing disclosure of defendant's statements made during group therapy.

Certified question answered in the affirmative.

Reversed.

Questions and Comments

1. *Co-joint therapy.* Marriage counselors as well as psychotherapists in general are increasingly resorting to co-joint therapy of both the husband

and wife. As a result, in some therapy sessions both spouses may be present. This practice presents a particular problem in terms of confidentiality, particularly where the parties may later be involved in litigation against each other such as in a divorce proceeding. To what extent, for instance, are decisions made during a therapy session in the presence of a spouse privileged? Under the traditional test no privilege would attach to prevent a spouse from testifying as to the communications made during a therapy session. At least one state (Colorado) has enacted legislation which

> prohibits the questioning of any persons who have participated in group therapy sessions "concerning any knowledge gained during the course of such therapy without the consent of the person to whom the testimony sought relates."

Extension of privilege to support Colo.Rev.Stat.Ann. § 13–90–107 (West 1998).

2. *Casual third party rule.* It is unclear to what extent multiple-person interactions are protected by the rules of privileged communication. If a "casual third party" is present during communications between patient and therapist, then such communications usually are not privileged. There is a presumption that the patient did not intend that the information remain confidential.

* * *

3. *Express or Implied Waiver of the Privilege*

A common element of psychotherapist-patient privilege is that its purpose is to protect the *patient's* interest in confidentiality. It is the patient, not the therapist, who is injured by compulsory public disclosure, for the patient is thereby deterred either from seeking needed treatment or from confiding fully during therapy. Privilege, therefore, belongs to the patient, not to the therapist, and a patient's assertion or waiver of privilege is binding upon the therapist. That is, if a patient asserts privilege, the therapist may not be compelled to testify, nor may he voluntarily testify concerning confidential communications. Similarly, if a patient waives privilege, the therapist may not invoke the privilege to refuse to testify.

A patient must assert or waive privilege when a party to litigation seeks to compel disclosure of confidential information. A litigant may compel testimony from the patient or from the psychotherapist by obtaining a subpoena issued by the court, and he may compel production of a psychotherapist's records by obtaining a subpoena *duces tecum*. The patient need not be a party to the litigation to assert the privilege.

A patient may waive privilege in two ways. First, he may simply fail to assert privilege when confidential information is sought by a party in litigation. That is, the patient may provide the information himself, or he may consent to its acquisition from the therapist. The therapist, however, is under an affirmative duty to assert the privilege for the patient if the patient is not present or is incapable of asserting privilege. Second, a patient may waive privilege by making his mental or emotional condition an element of a claim or defense. This form of waiver is often called the patient-litigant exception to privilege. In some jurisdictions a criminal defendant who raises an insanity defense, for example, may not invoke privilege to bar testimony concerning the results of a psychiatric interview to evaluate his sanity. See, e.g., *People v. Edney* at p. 387 *infra*. Similarly, a patient who initiates a malpractice suit against his therapist may not invoke the privilege to preclude testimony concerning the conduct of therapy. Finally, a patient makes his mental condition an element of a claim, and thereby waives privilege, when he seeks to recover damages for mental or emotional distress allegedly caused by another person's actions.

Generally, courts attempt to limit compulsory disclosures to those elements of the communications which are essential to the issues of a case. The practice reflects recognition of the sensitive nature of the information and accords with a general policy to protect witnesses and litigants from unnecessary harassment.

Privilege persists despite the termination of therapy, even after the patient's death. Although usually only a patient may waive privilege, in some circumstances a patient's personal representative, acting on behalf of the patient, may waive the privilege. Persons who may be granted this authority include the guardian of a mentally incompetent patient and the heirs or persons appointed to manage the estates of a deceased patient. Waiver of privilege after the death of a patient occurs most often in disputes concerning the patient's mental capacity at the time of making a will.

State law rules governing waivers of the privilege are not curtailed by HIPAA. The regulations permit disclosure of PHI without the patient's authorization "in any judicial or administrative proceeding in response to an express order or subpoena or to a subpoena discovery request".

a.   *Civil Proceedings*

IN RE LIFSCHUTZ

Supreme Court of California, 1970.
2 Cal.3d 415, 85 Cal.Rptr. 829, 467 P.2d 557.

TOBRINER, JUSTICE.

Dr. Joseph E. Lifschutz, a psychiatrist practicing in California, seeks a writ of habeas corpus to secure his release from the custody of the Sheriff of the County of San Mateo. Dr. Lifschutz was imprisoned after he was adjudged in contempt of court for refusing to obey an order of the San Mateo County Superior Court instructing him to answer questions and produce records relating to communications with a former patient. Dr. Lifschutz contends that this underlying court order was invalid as unconstitutionally infringing his personal constitutional right of privacy, his right effectively to practice his profession, and the constitutional privacy rights of his patients. He also attacks the order, or more specifically, the statutory provisions which authorize the compulsion of his testimony in these circumstances, as unconstitutionally denying him the equal protection of the laws since, under California law, clergymen could not be compelled to reveal certain confidential communications under these circumstances.

The instant proceeding arose out of a suit instituted by Joseph F. Housek against John Arabian on June 3, 1968, for damages resulting from an alleged assault. Housek's complaint alleged that the assault caused him "physical injuries, pain, suffering and severe mental and emotional distress." Defendant Abrabian [sic] deposed the plaintiff and during the course of that deposition Housek stated that he had received psychiatric treatment from Dr. Lifschutz over a six-month period approximately 10 years earlier. Nothing in the record indicates that the plaintiff revealed the nature or contents of any conversation with or treatment by Dr. Lifschutz.

Arabian then subpoenaed for deposition Dr. Lifschutz and all of his medical records relating to the treatment of Housek. Although Dr. Lifschutz appeared for the deposition, he refused to produce any of his medical records and refused to answer any questions relating to his treatment of patients; the psychiatrist declined even to disclose whether or not Housek had consulted him or had been his patient.

* * *

[Plaintiff] Housek has neither expressly claimed a psychotherapist-patient privilege, statutory or constitutional, nor expressly waived such a privilege.

In response to the psychiatrist's refusal to cooperate, defendant Arabian moved for an order of the superior court compelling the production of the subpenaed records and the answers to questions on deposition.

Relying on the patient-litigant exception of section 1016 of the Evidence Code, the superior court determined that because the plaintiff, in instituting the pending litigation, had tendered as an issue his mental and emotional condition, the statutory psychotherapist-patient (Evid. Code, § 1014) privilege did not apply. On December 20, 1968, the court therefore ordered Dr. Lifschutz to comply with the subpena and to answer questions posed during deposition. On January 15, 1969, defendant attempted to continue with the deposition of Dr. Lifschutz as ordered by the superior court, but petitioner remained resolute in his refusal to respond or produce records.

* * *

* * * Evidence Code, section 912, subdivision (a), provides that: " * * * the right of any person to claim a privilege provided by Section * * * 1014 (psychotherapist-patient privilege) * * * is waived with respect to a communication protected by such privilege if any holder of the

privilege, without coercion, has disclosed a significant part of the communication or has consented to such disclosure made by anyone. Consent to disclosure is manifested by any statement or other conduct of the
holder of the privilege indicating his consent to the disclosure, including
his failure to claim the privilege in any proceeding in which he has the
legal standing and opportunity to claim the privilege.''

Since Housek, the holder of the privilege disclosed at a prior
deposition that he has consulted Dr. Lifschutz for psychiatric treatment,
he has waived whatever privilege he might have had to keep such
information confidential. * * *

Defendant contended in the superior court, however, that *any* communication between the plaintiff and Dr. Lifschutz has lost its privileged
status because the plaintiff has filed a personal injury action in which he
claims recovery for "mental and emotional distress." Defendant relies on
section 1016 of the Evidence Code, the patient-litigant exception to the
psychotherapist-patient privilege, which provides that: "[t]here is no
privilege under this article as to a communication relevant to an issue
concerning the mental or emotional condition of the patient if such issue
has been tendered by: (a) the patient * * *." To avoid the necessity for
further contempt proceedings or delaying appellate review in the instant
case, we have considered whether defendant has accurately identified the
proper reach of the patient-litigant exception.

As we explain more fully below, the patient-litigant exception allows
only a limited inquiry into the confidences of the psychotherapist-patient
relationship, compelling disclosure of only those matters directly relevant to the nature of the specific "emotional or mental" condition which
the patient has voluntarily disclosed and tendered in his pleadings or in
answer to discovery inquiries. Furthermore, even when confidential
information falls within this exception, trial courts, because of the
intimate and potentially embarrassing nature of such communications,
may utilize the protective measures at their disposal to avoid unwarranted intrusions into the confidences of the relationship.

In interpreting this exception we are necessarily mindful of the
justifiable expectations of confidentiality that most individuals seeking
psychotherapeutic treatment harbor. As has been aptly pointed out by
Judge Edgerton in *Taylor v. United States* (1955) 95 U.S.App.D.C. 373,
222 F.2d 398, 401 (quoting from Guttmacher, M., et al., Psychiatry and
the Law (1952) p. 272), " 'The psychiatric patient confides more utterly
than anyone else in the world. He exposes to the therapist not only what
his words directly express; he lays bare his entire self, his dreams, his
fantasies, his sins, and his shame. Most patients who undergo psychotherapy know that this is what will be expected of them, and that they
cannot get help except on that condition. * * * It would be too much to
expect them to do so if they knew that all they say—and all that the
psychiatrist learns from what they say—may be revealed to the whole
world from a witness stand.' "

We believe that a patient's interest in keeping such confidential revelations from public purview, in retaining this substantial privacy, has deeper roots than the California statute and draws sustenance from our constitutional heritage.

* * *

Dr. Lifschutz presents a novel challenge, attempting to raise far-reaching questions of constitutional law. From the affidavits and correspondence included in the record we note that a large segment of the psychiatric profession concurs in Dr. Lifschutz's strongly held belief that an absolute privilege of confidentiality is essential to the effective practice of psychotherapy.

We recognize the growing importance of the psychiatric profession in our modern, ultracomplex society. The swiftness of change—economic, cultural, and moral—produces accelerated tensions in our society, and the potential for relief of such emotional disturbances offered by psychotherapy undoubtedly establishes it as a profession essential to the preservation of societal health and well-being. Furthermore, a growing consensus throughout the country, reflected in a trend of legislative enactments, acknowledges that an environment of confidentiality of treatment is vitally important to the successful operation of psychotherapy. California has embraced this view through the enactment of a broad, protective psychotherapist-patient privilege.

The nature of the actual interests involved in this case can only be properly evaluated against the California statutory background. Although petitioner, in pressing for judicial acceptance of a genuine and deeply held principle, seeks to cast the issue involved in this case in the broadest terms, we must properly address, in reality, a question of more modest dimensions. We do not face the alternatives of enshrouding the patient's communication to the psychotherapist in the black veil of absolute privilege or of exposing it to the white glare of absolute publicity. Our choice lies, rather, in the grey area.

Properly viewed, the broadest issue before our court is whether the Legislature, in attempting to accommodate the conceded need of confidentiality in the psychotherapeutic process with general societal needs of access to information for the ascertainment of truth in litigation, has unconstitutionally weighted its resolution in favor of disclosure by providing that a psychotherapist may be compelled to reveal relevant confidences of treatment when the patient tenders his mental or emotional condition in issue in litigation. For the reasons discussed below, we conclude that, under a properly limited interpretation, the litigant-patient exception to the psychotherapist-patient privilege, at issue in this case, does not unconstitutionally infringe the constitutional rights of privacy of either psychotherapists or psychotherapeutic patients. As we point out, however, because of the potential of invasion of patients' constitutional interests, trial courts should properly and carefully control compelled disclosures in this area in the light of accepted principles.

* * *

The primary contention of Dr. Lifschutz's attack on the judgment of contempt consists of the assertion of a constitutional right of a psychotherapist to absolute confidentiality in his communications with, and treatment of, patients. Although, as we understand it, the alleged right draws its substance primarily from the psychological needs and expectations of patients, Dr. Lifschutz claims that the Constitution grants him an absolute right to refuse to disclose such confidential communications, regardless of the wishes of a patient in a particular case.

[The court held that the privilege is that of the patient and that a psychotherapist has no constitutional right to assert the privilege in his own behalf.]

* * *

The second basis of petitioner's contention raises a more serious problem. Petitioner claims that if the state is authorized to compel disclosure of some psychotherapeutic communications, psychotherapy can no longer be practiced successfully. He asserts that the unique nature of psychotherapeutic treatment, involving a probing of the patient's subconscious thoughts and emotions, requires an environment of total confidentiality and absolute trust. Petitioner claims that unless a psychotherapist can truthfully assure his patient that all revelations will be held in strictest confidence and never disclosed, patients will be inhibited from participating fully in the psychotherapeutic process and proper treatment will be impossible. Petitioner concludes that the patient-litigation exception involved here conflicts with the preservation of an environment of absolute confidentiality and unconstitutionally constricts the field of medical practice.

Petitioner's argument, resting as it does on assertions of medical necessity, exemplifies the type of question to which the judiciary brings little expertise. Although petitioner has submitted affidavits of psychotherapists who concur in his assertion that total confidentiality is essential to the practice of their profession, we cannot blind ourselves to the fact that the practice of psychotherapy has grown, indeed flourished, in an environment of a non-absolute privilege. No state in the country recognizes as broad a privilege as petitioner claims is constitutionally compelled. Whether psychotherapy's development has progressed only because patients are ignorant of the existing legal environment can only be a matter for speculation; psychotherapists certainly have been aware of the limitations of their recognized privilege for some time.

Petitioner's broad assertion, moreover, overlooks the limited nature of the intrusion into psychotherapeutic privacy actually at issue in this case. As we explain more fully in part III infra, the patient-litigant exception of section 1016 of the Evidence Code compels disclosure of only those matters which the patient himself has chosen to reveal by tender-ing them in litigation. We do not know, of course, to what extent patients are deterred from seeking psychotherapeutic treatment by the knowledge that if, at some future date, they choose to place some aspect of their mental condition in issue in litigation, communications relevant to that issue may be revealed. We can only surmise that an understanding of the limits of section 1016, and the realization that the patient retains control over subsequent disclosure, may provide a measure of reassurance to the prospective patient.

* * *

In previous physician-patient privilege cases the exception [to the privilege of confidentiality] has been generally applied only to compel disclosure of medical treatment and communication concerning the very injury or impairment that was the subject matter of the litigation. There is certainly nothing to suggest that in the context of the more liberal psychotherapist-patient privilege this exception should be given a broader reading.

If the provision had as broad an effect as is suggested by petitioner, it might effectively deter many psychotherapeutic patients from instituting any general claim for mental suffering and damage out of fear of opening up all past communications to discovery. This result would clearly be an intolerable and overbroad intrusion into the patient's privacy, not sufficiently limited to the legitimate state interest embodied in the provision and would create opportunities for harassment and blackmail.

In light of these considerations, the "automatic" waiver of privilege contemplated by section 1016 must be construed not as a complete waiver of the privilege but only as a limited waiver concomitant with the purposes of the exception. Under section 1016 disclosure can be compelled only with respect to *those mental conditions* the patient-litigant has "disclose[d] * * * by bringing an action in which *they* are in issue" communications which are not directly relevant to those specific conditions do not fall within the terms of section 1016's exception and therefore remain privileged. Disclosure cannot be compelled with respect to other aspects of the patient-litigant's personality even though they may, in some sense, be "relevant" to the substantive issues of litigation. The patient thus is not obligated to sacrifice all privacy to seek redress for a specific mental or emotional injury; the scope of the inquiry permitted depends upon the nature of the injuries which the patient-litigant himself has brought before the court.

In some situations, the patient's pleadings may clearly demonstrate that his entire mental condition is being placed in issue and that records of past psychotherapy will clearly be relevant.

* * *

In other cases, however, the determination of the specific "mental condition" in issue may present more complex problems. The difficulties involved in analyzing the applicability of the exception in the instant case may be illustrative. The plaintiff's complaint, containing the typical allegations of "mental and emotional distress" arising out of a physical assault, does not specifically identify the nature of the "mental or emotional condition" at issue. In incorporating this allegation in his complaint, plaintiff obviously neither disclosed his entire medical history [of] treatment for mental or emotional conditions nor realistically waived his interest in maintaining the confidentiality of that treatment. The generality of the claim, however, does create the possibility that some feature of plaintiff's psychological history will be directly relevant to the determination of whether his emotional or mental distress can be properly attributed to the alleged assault. Although we doubt that the 10–year–old therapeutic treatment sought to be discovered from Dr. Lifschutz would be sufficiently relevant to a typical claim of "mental distress" to bring it within the exception of section 1016, we cannot determine from the present state of the record whether plaintiff's "mental and emotional" distress is merely the "normal" distress experienced as a result of physical assault or whether it includes unusual or particularly serious elements upon which prior history may be directly relevant.

Because only the patient, and not the party seeking disclosure, knows both the nature of the ailments for which recovery is sought and the general content of the psychotherapeutic communications, the burden rests upon the patient initially to submit some showing that a given confidential communication is not directly related to the issue he has tendered to the court. A patient may have to delimit his claimed "mental or emotional distress" or explain, in general terms, the object of the psychotherapy in order to illustrate that it is not reasonably probable that the psychotherapeutic communications sought are directly relevant to the mental condition that he has placed in issue. In determining whether communications sufficiently relate to the mental condition at issue to require disclosure, the court should heed the basic privacy interests involved in the privilege.

* * *

Inasmuch as plaintiff had already disclosed that he had consulted Dr. Lifschutz for psychotherapeutic treatment, petitioner could not properly have refused to answer at least that question concerning the communications; since neither plaintiff nor the psychotherapist has as yet made any claim that the subpenaed records are not directly relevant to the specific "mental and emotional" injuries for which plaintiff is claiming relief, Dr. Lifschutz had no right to refuse to produce the records. Thus the trial court's order requiring the production of records and the answering of questions was valid; the trial court properly adjudged Dr. Lifschutz in contempt of court for intentionally violating that valid court order.

The order to show cause is discharged and the petition for writ of habeas corpus is denied.

Mosk, Acting C.J., McComb, Peters, Burke, and Sullivan, JJ., and Molinari, J. pro tem., concur.

Questions and Comments

1. *Critique of* Lifschutz *rule.* Lifschutz in effect requires the plaintiff-patient to "disclose at least part of the contents of protected communications to his lawyer and the trial judge as a condition to retaining its confidentiality of the communication." *Caesar v. Mountanos,* 542 F.2d 1064, 1075 (9th Cir.1976). This result has been criticized because it forces a plaintiff who wants to preserve confidentiality to elect either to make partial disclosure or possibly forego recovery for mental distress. Some, like Judge Hufstedler of the Ninth Circuit Court of Appeals, would avoid this problem by restricting compelled disclosures in a personal injury action to "the fact of treatment, the time and length of treatment, the cost of treatment, and the ultimate diagnosis unless the party seeking disclosure establishes in the trial court a compelling need for its production." *Caesar v. Mountanos,* 542 F.2d 1064, 1075 (9th Cir.1976), (Hufstedler, J., concurring and dissenting).

2. *Good cause limitations on waiver of privilege.* The rule that a plaintiff who places his or her mental state in issue potentially waives the privilege is applied in most jurisdictions. At the same time, a defendant seeking the plaintiff's psychiatric records must show good cause in order to obtain them. The good cause showing required varies considerably, even between federal courts. In *Doe v. Oberweis Dairy*, 456 F.3d 704, 718 (7th Cir. 2006), *cert. denied* ___ U.S.___, 127 S.Ct. 1815, 167 L.Ed.2d 317 (2007), Judge Posner's opinion sweepingly stated: "If a plaintiff by seeking damages for emotional distress places his or her psychological state in issue, the defendant is entitled to discover any records of that state." In contrast, *Koch v. Cox*, 489 F.3d 384 (D.C. Cir. 2007), held that such holdings "*sub silento* . . . overrule" *Jaffee*; it instead required that the defendant show the plaintiff "bas[ed] his claim upon the psychotherapist's communications with him" or " 'selectively disclosed part of a privileged communication in order to gain an advantage in litigation.' " Other courts have adopted an intermediate position, holding that the plaintiff waives the privilege if he or she alleges a "specific mental or psychiatric injury or disorder" but not if only a general claim for pain and suffering or emotional distress is made. See *EEOC v. Serramonte*, 237 F.R.D. 220, 224–25 (N.D. Cal. 2006); *Ruhlmann v. Ulster Cty.*, 194 F.R.D. 445, 450 (N.D.N.Y. 2000); *LeFave v. Symbios, Inc.*, 2000 WL 1644154 (D.Colo. 2000).

In announcing the adoption of the psychotherapist privilege in federal court, *Jaffee* emphasized the need to avoid discouraging psychotherapy. If, as is usually the case (but was not the case in *Jaffee*), the psychotherapy at issue in emotional distress cases occurs *before* the allegedly stressful event (e.g., before the alleged tort, sexual harassment or employment discrimination), should the patient-litigant exception be broadly construed, as in *Doe v. Oberweis Diary*? Is it relevant that a broad construction of the exception might deter such suits from being brought in the first instance? Is there a privacy concern, independent of the desire to encourage psychotherapy, that should be considered in developing the good cause standard?

3. *Assertion of privilege by third parties.* As noted in *In re Lifschutz*, the testimonial privilege belongs to the patient. Once the patient has waived the privilege, the psychiatrist or other mental health professional does not have standing to challenge that waiver. However, in some states, parties other than the patient have been given standing to challenge the waiver.

For instance, under New York law anyone having official custody of psychiatric records, such as "a treating hospital, physician or other institution" may request a protective order on the grounds that disclosure of all or part of the record "may be seriously detrimental to the interest of the patient, to uninvolved third parties, or to an important program of the custodian of the record." See *Cynthia B. v. New Rochelle Hosp. Med. Ctr.,* 60 N.Y.2d 452, 470 N.Y.S.2d 122, 458 N.E.2d 363, 365 (1983).

Where the privilege has been waived by the plaintiff, what public policy grounds, if any, support the right of a third party that is not a party to the lawsuit to assert the privilege belonging to the plaintiff-patient in the lawsuit?

b. *The Insanity Defense Context*

PEOPLE v. EDNEY

Court of Appeals of New York, 1976.
39 N.Y.2d 620, 385 N.Y.S.2d 23, 350 N.E.2d 400.

GABRIELLI, JUDGE.

Defendant was charged with kidnapping and the brutal killing of the eight-year-old daughter of his former girlfriend. He interposed the defense of insanity.

The jury found defendant guilty, as charged, of manslaughter, first degree and kidnapping in the first and second degrees. He was sentenced to a term of 25 years to life on the first degree kidnapping charge and to concurrent terms of up to 25 years on the other charges. The Appellate Division unanimously affirmed.

The critical and principal issue is whether the testimony of a psychiatrist, who had examined defendant prior to trial at the request of his attorney, was admissible over objections that the physician-patient and attorney-client privilege acted to bar its admission.

At trial, the prosecution showed that late in the afternoon on July 24, 1968, defendant grabbed Lisa Washington, the victim, off the street where she was playing with friends, and forcibly pushed her into a taxicab. At approximately 8:30 p.m., Lisa's aunt, with whom she was residing, received a call from defendant who stated that "If you don't get 'C' [the nickname of Lisa's mother] on the phone in the next couple of hours, I am going to rape and kill Lisa". A barmaid testified that defendant and a young girl were in the Nu–Way Lounge at about 9:30 p.m. and that she observed defendant leave the tavern with the girl, walk around a corner toward the back of the building, and return a short while later without her. Less than an hour later, police officers, responding to a call by a woman who had reported a disturbance in her backyard which adjoined the rear of the Nu–Way Lounge, found Lisa's lifeless body. She had been stabbed 11 times. The police questioned persons in the bar and learned of defendant's presence in the bar earlier in the evening with a little girl.

Defendant was located at his father's home early the next morning and taken into custody. As he was leaving with the officers, he was asked by his father whether he had "hurt that little child", to which he replied "I'm sorry, I'm sorry". Granules of dirt taken from defendant's trousers confirmed that defendant had been in the area behind the Nu–Way Lounge.

Following his arrest, and after receiving the standard preinterrogation admonitions defendant volunteered to a detective that he had been in the Nu–Way Lounge that evening, that he had been hearing voices which told him that God wanted Lisa, and that he might have killed Lisa but he was not sure. Taking the witness stand in his own defense, defendant testified that on the day in question, he had drunk large quantities of alcohol, had been smoking marijuana cigarettes, and that sometime after 9:00 p.m., he and Lisa had left the Nu–Way Lounge to go to his father's place; that he might have killed Lisa but he was not sure he had done so. He recalled walking to a cab across the street from the bar but could remember no more. He explained that he regained consciousness under a tree near his father's home and that he walked inside and blacked out; the next thing he was able to remember was someone pounding on him to wake up because the police were there.

A psychiatrist called by the defense testified that defendant suffered from paranoid schizophrenia of mild severity and that the condition was of long standing. It was his opinion that defendant was mentally ill to such an extent that he was unaware of the nature and quality of his act and did not know that his act was wrong.

In rebuttal, the prosecution called Dr. Daniel Schwartz, a psychiatrist, who originally examined defendant at the behest of defendant's attorney, who was not present during the examination. The defense unsuccessfully objected to his testifying on the ground that the attorney-client and physician-patient privileges barred his testimony. Dr. Schwartz described defendant as having an alcoholic psychosis, which occasionally manifested itself through hallucinations and delusions; however, he found no evidence of an underlying disease or defect. It was his opinion that at the time of the murder defendant knew and appreciated the nature of his conduct and knew that such conduct was wrong.

Another rebuttal psychiatrist, who had independently examined the defendant for the prosecution, supported the conclusions of Dr. Schwartz that defendant knew and appreciated the nature of his conduct and that such conduct was wrong.

Two other psychiatrists, produced by the defense as surrebuttal witnesses, each testified that he was unable to form an opinion as to whether defendant knew or appreciated the nature of his acts, or whether such acts were wrong, although they did agree that defendant had some form of mental disease.

People v. Al–Kanani, 33 N.Y.2d 260, 351 N.Y.S.2d 969, 307 N.E.2d 43, is dispositive of the physician-patient privilege claim. There we held

> "that where insanity is asserted as a defense and * * * the defendant offers evidence tending to show his insanity in support of this plea, a complete waiver is effected, and the prosecution is then permitted to call psychiatric experts to testify regarding his sanity even though they may have treated the defendant. When the patient first fully discloses the evidence of his affliction, it is he who has given the public the full details of his case, thereby disclosing the secrets which the statute was designed to protect, thus creating a waiver removing it from the operation of the statute and once the privilege is thus waived, there is nothing left to protect against for once the revelation is made by the patient there is nothing further to disclose 'for when a secret is out it is out for all time and cannot be caught again like a bird, and put back in its cage. * * * The legislature did not intend to continue the privilege when there was no reason for its continuance and it would simply be an obstruction to public justice.' * * *."

Our holding in the case now before us comports with this rationale and is but a logical extension of our determination in *Al–Kanani.*

Equally unavailing to defendant is the claim that the attorney-client privilege bars admission of Dr. Schwartz' testimony. Essentially, defendant relies on decisions in other jurisdictions which have excluded such testimony apparently because a psychiatrist would inevitably be required to reveal a defendant's statements to him to justify his opinion and because a contrary rule would deter attorneys from freely seeking sound professional advice as to the soundness of an insanity plea. We do not find the reasoning of these cases compelling and, accordingly, do not follow them. Rather, we think the better rationale underlies the *Al–Kanani* rule that a plea of innocence by reason of insanity constitutes a complete and effective waiver by the defendant of any claim of privilege.

A defendant who seeks to introduce psychiatric testimony in support of his insanity plea may be required to disclose prior to trial the underlying basis of his alleged affliction to a prosecution psychiatrist. Hence, where, as here, a defendant reveals to the prosecution the very facts which would be secreted by the exercise of the privilege, reason does not compel the exclusion of expert testimony based on such facts, or cross-examination concerning the grounds for opinions based thereon. It follows that no harm accrues to the defense from seeking pretrial psychiatric advice where an insanity plea is actually entered, for in such circumstances, the underlying factual basis will be revealed to the prosecution psychiatrist. Conversely, were the defendant not to enter an insanity plea, no physician-patient waiver would occur and any information divulged to the psychiatrist would remain privileged. There is, therefore, no deterrent to seeking expert psychiatric advice for, in one instance, there will be disclosure to the prosecution in any event and, in the other, disclosure will never occur. In short, no reason appears why a criminal defendant who puts his sanity in issue should be permitted to thwart the introduction of testimony from a material witness who may be called at trial by invoking the attorney-client privilege anymore than he should be able to do so by invoking the physician-patient privilege.

This is not to say, however, that an attorney cannot consult a psychiatrist in order to obtain advice concerning the efficacy of an insanity plea or, for that matter, any trial strategy, without fear of later courtroom disclosure. The product of such a consultation is protected, of course, by the work product doctrine (see CPLR 3101). However, that doctrine affords protection only to facts and observations disclosed *by the attorney*. Thus, it is the information and observations of the attorney that are conveyed to the expert which may thus be subject to trial exclusion. The work product doctrine does not operate to insulate other disclosed information from public exposure.

It is significant that the underlying purpose of the attorney-client privilege would not be diminished by the admission of the testimony of Dr. Schwartz. The privilege is grounded in the salutary policy of encouraging "persons needing professional advice to disclose freely the facts in reference to which they seek advice, without fear that such facts will be made public to their disgrace or detriment by their attorney" * * * That policy is not harmed, however, by the admission of evidence which, in any event, in these circumstances would be available to the prosecution. Indeed, with respect to the testimony of Dr. Schwartz, it is readily apparent that the traditional and statutory requirements of an attorney-client relationship were simply not established (CPLR 4503, subd. [a]). We hold, therefore, that the privilege was inapplicable.

We find no merit in defendant's other contentions.

Accordingly, the order of the Appellate Division should be affirmed.

[The dissenting opinion of Judge Fuchsberg is omitted.]

PEOPLE v. KNUCKLES

Supreme Court of Illinois, 1995.
165 Ill.2d 125, 209 Ill.Dec. 1, 650 N.E.2d 974 (1995).

JUSTICE McMORROW delivered the opinion of the court:

The primary issue raised in this appeal is whether Illinois will permit the application of the attorney-client privilege to communications between a defendant who raises an insanity defense and the psychiatrist who examines the accused at the request of defense counsel to aid in preparation of the defense.

Defendant, Pamela J. Knuckles, was charged in the circuit court of Du Page County with the 1984 slaying of her mother, Nancy Knuckles. She pleaded guilty, but that plea was later set aside on grounds of ineffective assistance of counsel. The State reinstated murder charges in

1990, and, in preparation for trial, the State issued two subpoenas to Dr. Kyle Rossiter, a psychiatrist who had examined Knuckles at her counsel's request approximately two weeks after the killing. Defense counsel disclosed other expert witnesses expected to testify for the defendant and indicated that the defense did not plan to call Dr. Rossiter to testify at trial. Knuckles moved to quash the subpoenas served on the psychiatrist and thereby preclude the State from discovering or using the psychiatrist's notes and testimony in its case. The motion to quash was sustained. The State appealed from the trial court's order quashing the subpoenas. The appellate court affirmed, and we granted the State's petition for leave to appeal (145 Ill.2d R. 315).

BACKGROUND

In November 1984, Pamela Knuckles and her brother, sister, and others were charged with killing Nancy Knuckles by strangulation and suffocation. Pamela Knuckles' court-appointed public defender obtained court authorization to retain a psychiatrist to interview her. The psychiatrist, Dr. Kyle Rossiter, met with Knuckles at the Du Page County jail approximately two weeks after the murder. He took notes of her statements but did not prepare a written report, nor did he testify at any proceeding involving her. Knuckles' counsel disclosed to the State in April 1985 that the defense would not be offering evidence of physical or mental examinations or scientific tests. Following plea negotiations, Knuckles pleaded guilty and was sentenced to 33 years in prison.

New attorneys entered an appearance on Knuckles' behalf, and in January 1989, Knuckles filed a post-conviction petition challenging the validity of her guilty plea on grounds of ineffective assistance of counsel. Her petition stated that she had pleaded guilty because her appointed counsel advised her that if she went to trial she faced the death penalty. However, at the time of the killing, Knuckles was 17 years old and would have been exempted from the death penalty under Illinois law. Following an evidentiary hearing, the trial court granted Knuckles' post-conviction petition and allowed her to withdraw her plea of guilty.

Knuckles' attorneys retained several experts to evaluate Knuckles' history of physical and psychological abuse and her mental state at the time of the charged offenses ... [D]efense lawyers notified the prosecution that their client would rely on two defenses at trial: insanity and self-defense. At the same time, the defense disclosed the names of its five expert witnesses, the experts' reports, and test results indicating the possibility that Knuckles suffered from a brain abnormality. Dr. Rossiter was not among the experts whom the defense listed as witnesses for trial.

The State then served two subpoenas on Dr. Rossiter. One sought any written memoranda he had made of his interview with Knuckles and the other sought to compel his testimony at trial. The State also invoked its statutory right to compel Knuckles to submit to a psychiatric examination by an expert retained by the State.

On July 20, 1990, the trial court quashed the two subpoenas that had been issued to Dr. Rossiter. The court held that a psychiatrist hired by defense counsel to examine the client for purposes of trial preparation is an agent of defense counsel and therefore the communications between the defendant and the defense-retained psychiatrist are protected by the attorney-client privilege. The trial court further held that the privilege is not waived by the assertion of the insanity defense.

ANALYSIS

This appeal highlights the tension between two competing policies: one that favors the broad discovery of relevant information and another that guards the narrow discovery exemptions, based on privilege, which are deeply rooted in the common law and the Federal and State Constitutions. The State argues that since Dr. Rossiter is the only psychiatrist who examined Pamela Knuckles near the time her mother was killed, his impressions of Knuckles' mental state are of surpassing importance in this case. If the potential relevance of the information sought were the key to determining whether the attorney-client privilege should yield to the truth-seeking process, the State's argument would be persuasive. However, the policies underlying the privilege exist apart from and run counter to the primary goals of discovery. The *raison d'être* of the privilege is to secure for the client the ability to confide freely and fully in his or her attorney, without fear that confidential information will be disseminated to others.

*I.   Extension of the Attorney–Client Privilege
to Communications Between Defense*

Initially, this court must determine whether the attorney-client privilege should be extended to communications made to or made by an expert witness, here a psychiatrist, whose engagement by the defense is necessary to the preparation of an insanity defense. No Illinois case has decided that precise issue. [The court held that as a matter of common law, the attorney-client privilege extends to communications with and findings by a psychiatrist who has been retained by defendant's counsel to evaluate the client.]

*II.   Waiver of Attorney–Client Privilege
by Assertion of Insanity Defense*

A minority of jurisdictions have held that the attorney-client privilege is automatically waived whenever the accused puts his or her mental state in issue in the form of an insanity defense.

In the case at bar, the State argues that we should follow the reasoning of those cases that employ the automatic waiver rule when a defendant puts his mental state in issue. However, we do not find those cases persuasive. In *Edney,* the New York Court of Appeals held that the attorney-client privilege was waived because State law allowed prosecutors to compel a defendant to submit to an examination by a State-retained psychiatric expert, and therefore the very facts that would be secreted by the privilege necessarily would be disclosed through the compelled examination. (*Edney,* 39 N.Y.2d at 625, 350 N.E.2d at 403, 385 N.Y.S.2d at 26.) We note that the rationale of *Edney* has been questioned. See *Miller,* 737 P.2d at 838 n. 4 ("[*Edney*] represents the clear minority view and has been sharply criticized by the American Bar Association as 'confused' and 'unpersuasive' ").

After carefully considering the cases from other jurisdictions, we find that the better-reasoned decisions hold that the privilege is waived only with respect to the testimony and reports of those experts who are identified by the defense as witnesses who will be called to testify on behalf of the defendant at trial, or whose notes and reports are used by other defense experts who testify. Policy reasons for recognizing the privilege in the mental health context and for limiting the waiver doctrine include the "chilling effect" disclosure of experts would have upon a client's willingness to confide in his or her attorney and consultants; inherent prejudice that occurs if the trier of fact learns that a mental health professional testifying at trial was originally retained by the defense; concern that allowing waiver would, in effect, cause the defense to assist the State in discharging its burden of proof; and recognition that the defense would be inhibited from consulting with mental health professionals for fear of creating prosecution witnesses, and might not consult them even though professional assistance might be crucial to the case.

We hold that the attorney-client privilege in Illinois protects communications between a defendant who raises an insanity defense and a psychiatrist employed by defense counsel to aid in the preparation of the defense, if the psychiatrist will not testify and the psychiatrist's notes and opinions will not be used in the formulation of the other defense experts' trial testimony. Accordingly, we hold that the attorney-client privilege has not been waived in the case at bar with respect to the testimony and notes of Dr. Rossiter.

III. *Public Interest Exception*

The State next argues that if we uphold the privilege and find that it was not waived by defendant's assertion of the insanity defense, we should "make an exception for the unique circumstances of this case." The State urges us to find that the privilege must yield to the public interest in the truth-finding process, because here the State's ability to rebut the insanity defense may be seriously hampered by its inability to discover the notes and opinions of the one doctor who examined defendant near the time of the alleged homicide [six years prior to the retrial following reversal of the guilty plea].

Both sides have retained experts who presumably are prepared to render their opinions as to Knuckles' mental condition at the time of the homicide with which she is charged. Neither side will present the results of Dr. Rossiter's evaluation of Knuckles' sanity shortly after the crime was committed. Although the defense may derive a benefit from the exclusion of Dr. Rossiter's testimony, we have no way of knowing what evidence may have been presented if Knuckles had received competent assistance of counsel and received a trial, instead of entering a plea of guilty on the erroneous advice of counsel. The interests served by the preservation of the attorney-client privilege should not turn on the passage of time alone. Such a rule would be illogical and arbitrary. Although the State argues that its ability to prosecute Knuckles will be severely hampered because the prosecutors will be denied discovery and use of Dr. Rossiter's examination of her, it cites no case in which the mere passage of time and resulting loss of opportunity to discover information have been deemed to nullify the fundamental purpose of the attorney-client privilege. Indeed, to adopt the State's argument would be to eviscerate the privilege with the sword of expediency, disregarding historical policy and reasoned analysis.

For the reasons set out in this opinion, we hold that the attorney-client privilege applies to communications between the defense and nontestifying mental health experts retained by the defense to probe the defendant's mental condition in anticipation of relevant defenses. We further hold that the privilege is not waived merely by the assertion of defenses which place the defendant's mental condition in issue. Finally, we decline to adopt a generalized public interest exception in the case at bar to allow the State's interest in gathering evidence to overcome the attorney-client privilege. Therefore, we affirm the judgment of the appellate court.

Appellate court affirmed.

[The dissenting opinion of Justices Miller and Heiple are omitted.]

Questions and Comments

Effect of waiver on subsequent proceedings. A psychiatrist called upon to examine a criminal defendant on the issue of the defendant's sanity at the time of the offense may have performed the examination at the request of the defendant, the prosecutor, or the court. In the latter case the examiner is treated as an "independent" expert. Particularly complex Fifth and Sixth Amendment issues are raised when the prosecutor seeks to introduce evidence based on a psychiatric interview conducted by a court-appointed expert. The issues raised by such use are treated in the materials beginning in Chapter Six. What effect should the defendants waiver in a criminal proceeding have in a subsequent civil suit? Compare *Novak v. Rathnam,* 106 Ill.2d 478, 88 Ill.Dec. 608, 478 N.E.2d 1334 (1985) with *Simpson v. Braider,* 104 F.R.D. 512 (D.D.C.1985). In *Novak,* the defendant, Rathnam, discharged Endicott from a mental health facility in Illinois. Endicott traveled to Florida where he shot and killed Novak's daughter. At his Florida murder trial Endicott called four psychiatrists, including Rathnam, in successfully asserting insanity as a defense. Thereafter, Novak filed a wrongful death action in Illinois alleging that Rathnam was negligent in approving Endicott's discharge. Rathnam refused to permit Novak to depose him, arguing that any information about his treatment of Endicott was privileged by state statute. The Illinois Supreme Court rejected Rathnam's claim that he could not testify unless Endicott waived the privilege. The court held that "[i]f there is a disclosure of confidential information by the individual for whose benefit the privilege exists, or if he permits such a disclosure, the privilege is waived and cannot be reasserted." 478 N.E.2d at 1337.

In contrast, the district court in *Simpson v. Braider* focused on the context of the defendant's disclosures in the criminal proceeding. "[T]hese revelations [about the defendant's history of mental health treatment] in the Superior Court criminal case, since they were made in defense of criminal charges, cannot be truly considered voluntary. There Justin Braider was an accused, a defendant, and these revelations were made only to protect his interests in that proceeding. These were not revelations undertaken on his own initiative, where he sought advantage such as where a person seeks to use information to obtain an advantage, but then invokes the privilege to preclude the adversary from challenging a claim." The district court concluded that no waiver should be implied from "circumstances indicating there was realistically no voluntary disclosure." 104 F.R.D. at 522–23.

Which is the better view? Does the passage from *People v. Al–Kanani,* quoted in *People v. Edney, supra,* implicitly reject the rationale articulated by the court in *Simpson v. Braider?*

4. *Admissibility of Disclosures During Treatment in Criminal Prosecutions*

a. *Treatment Information Concerning Prosecution Witnesses*

PENNSYLVANIA v. RITCHIE

Supreme Court of the United States, 1987.
480 U.S. 39, 107 S.Ct. 989, 94 L.Ed.2d 40.

JUSTICE POWELL announced the judgment of the Court and delivered the opinion of the Court with respect to Parts I, II, III–B, III–C, and IV, and an opinion with respect to Part III–A in which THE CHIEF JUSTICE, JUSTICE WHITE, and JUSTICE O'CONNOR join.

The question presented in this case is whether and to what extent a State's interest in the confidentiality of its investigative files concerning child abuse must yield to a criminal defendant's Sixth and Fourteenth Amendment right to discover favorable evidence.

I

As part of its efforts to combat child abuse, the Commonwealth of Pennsylvania has established Children and Youth Services (CYS), a protective service agency charged with investigating cases of suspected mistreatment and neglect. In 1979, respondent George Ritchie was charged with rape, involuntary deviate sexual intercourse, incest, and corruption of a minor. The victim of the alleged attacks was his 13–year-old daughter, who claimed that she had been assaulted by Ritchie two or three times per week during the previous four years. The girl reported the incidents to the police, and the matter then was referred to the CYS.

During pretrial discovery, Ritchie served CYS with a subpoena, seeking access to the records concerning the daughter. Ritchie requested disclosure of the file related to the immediate charges, as well as certain records that he claimed were compiled in 1978, when CYS investigated a separate report by an unidentified source that Ritchie's children were being abused. CYS refused to comply with the subpoena, claiming that the records were privileged under Pennsylvania law. The relevant statute provides that all reports and other information obtained in the course of a CYS investigation must be kept confidential, subject to 11 specific exceptions.[a] One of those exceptions is that the Agency may disclose the reports to a "court of competent jurisdiction pursuant to a court order." Pa.Stat.Ann., Title 11, § 2215(a)(5) (Purdon Supp.1986).

Ritchie moved to have CYS sanctioned for failing to honor the subpoena, and the trial court held a hearing on the motion in chambers. Ritchie argued that he was entitled to the information because the file might contain the names of favorable witnesses, as well as other, unspecified exculpatory evidence. He also requested disclosure of a medical report that he believed was compiled during the 1978 CYS investigation. Although the trial judge acknowledged that he had not examined the entire CYS file, he accepted a CYS representative's assertion that there was no medical report in the record.[b] The judge then denied the motion and refused to order CYS to disclose the files.[c]

At trial, the main witness against Ritchie was his daughter. In an attempt to rebut her testimony, defense counsel cross-examined the girl at length, questioning her on all aspects of the alleged attacks, and her reasons for not reporting the incidents sooner. Except for routine evidentiary rulings, the trial judge placed no limitation on the scope of cross-examination. At the close of trial Ritchie was convicted by a jury on all counts, and the judge sentenced him to 3 to 10 years in prison.

On appeal to the Pennsylvania Superior Court, Ritchie claimed, *inter alia,* that the failure to disclose the contents of the CYS file violated the Confrontation Clause of the Sixth Amendment, as applied to the States through the Due Process Clause of the Fourteenth Amendment. The court agreed that there had been a constitutional violation, and

a. The statute provides in part:

"(a) Except as provided in section 14 [Pa. Stat.Ann., Title 11, § 2214 (Purdon Supp.1986)], reports made pursuant to this act including but not limited to report summaries of child abuse * * * and written reports * * * as well as any other information obtained, reports written or photographs or X-rays taken concerning alleged instances of child abuse in the possession of the department, a county children and youth social service agency or a child protective service shall be confidential and shall only be made available to:

* * *

"(5) A court of competent jurisdiction pursuant to a court order." Pa.Stat.Ann., Title 11, § 2215(a) (Purdon Supp.1986).

At the time of trial the statute only provided five exceptions to the general rule of confidentiality, including the exception for court-ordered disclosure. * * *

b. The trial judge stated that he did not read "50 pages or more of an extensive record." The judge had no knowledge of the case before the pretrial hearing.

c. There is no suggestion that the Commonwealth's prosecutor was given access to the file at any point in the proceedings, or that he was aware of its contents.

accordingly vacated the conviction and remanded for further proceedings. * * *.

On appeal by the Commonwealth, the Supreme Court of Pennsylvania agreed that the conviction must be vacated and the case remanded to determine if a new trial is necessary. * * * [I]t concluded that Ritchie, through his lawyer, is entitled to review the entire file to search for any useful evidence. It stated: "When materials gathered become an arrow of inculpation, the person inculpated has a fundamental constitutional right to examine the provenance of the arrow and he who aims it." The Pennsylvania Court concluded that by denying access to the file, the trial court order had violated both the Confrontation Clause and the Compulsory Process Clause. The court was unpersuaded by the Commonwealth's argument that the trial judge already had examined the file and determined that it contained no relevant information. It ruled that the constitutional infirmity in this trial court's order was that Ritchie was unlawfully denied the opportunity to have the records reviewed by "the eyes and the perspective of an advocate," who may see relevance in places that a neutral judge would not.

In light of the substantial and conflicting interests held by the Commonwealth and Ritchie, we granted certiorari. 476 U.S. 1139, 106 S.Ct. 2244, 90 L.Ed.2d 690 (1986). We now affirm in part, reverse in part, and remand for proceedings not inconsistent with this opinion.

II

[The plurality opinion rejects the defendant's contention that the Court lacked jurisdiction on the grounds that the decision below was not final.]

III

The Pennsylvania Supreme Court held that Ritchie, through his lawyer, has the right to examine the full contents of the CYS records. The court found that this right of access is required by both the Confrontation Clause and the Compulsory Process Clause. We discuss these constitutional provisions in turn.

A

The Confrontation Clause provides two types of protections for a criminal defendant: the right physically to face those who testify against him, and the right to conduct cross-examination. *Delaware v. Fensterer,* 474 U.S. 15, 19, 106 S.Ct. 292, 294, 88 L.Ed.2d 15 (1985) *(per curiam).* Ritchie does not allege a violation of the former right. * * * Instead Ritchie claims that by denying him access to the information necessary to prepare his defense, the trial court interfered with his right of cross-examination.

Ritchie argues that he could not effectively question his daughter because, without the CYS material, he did not know which types of questions would best expose the weaknesses in her testimony. Had the files been disclosed, Ritchie argues that he might have been able to show that the daughter made statements to the CYS counselor that were inconsistent with her trial statements, or perhaps to reveal that the girl acted with an improper motive. * * *

The Pennsylvania Supreme Court accepted this argument, relying in part on our decision in *Davis v. Alaska,* [415 U.S. 308, 94 S.Ct. 1105, 39 L.Ed.2d 347 (1974)]. In *Davis* the trial judge prohibited defense counsel from questioning a witness about the latter's juvenile criminal record, because a state statute made this information presumptively confidential. We found that this restriction on cross-examination violated the Confrontation Clause, despite Alaska's legitimate interest in protecting the identity of juvenile offenders. The Pennsylvania Supreme Court apparently interpreted our decision in *Davis* to mean that a statutory privilege cannot be maintained when a defendant asserts a need, prior to trial, for the protected information that might be used at trial to impeach or otherwise undermine a witness' testimony.

If we were to accept this broad interpretation of *Davis,* the effect would be to transform the Confrontation Clause into a constitutionally-compelled rule of pretrial discovery. Nothing in the case law supports such a view. The opinions of this Court show that the right of confrontation is a *trial* right, designed to prevent improper restrictions on the types of questions that defense counsel may ask during cross-examination. The ability to question adverse witnesses, however, does not include the power to require the pretrial disclosure of any and all information that might be useful in contradicting unfavorable testimony.[d] Normally the right to confront one's accusers is satisfied if defense counsel receives wide latitude at trial to question witnesses. *Delaware v. Fensterer, supra,* 474 U.S., at 21, 106 S.Ct., at 295. In short, the Confrontation Clause only guarantees "an *opportunity* for effective cross-examination, not cross-examination that is effective in whatever way, and to whatever extent, the defense might wish." *Id.,* at 20, 106 S.Ct., at 294 (emphasis in original).

* * *

The lower court's reliance on *Davis v. Alaska* therefore is misplaced. There the state court had prohibited defense counsel from questioning the witness about his criminal record, even though that evidence might have affected the witness' credibility. The constitutional error in that case was *not* that Alaska made this information confidential; it was that the defendant was denied the right "to expose to the jury the facts from which jurors * * * could appropriately draw inferences relating to the reliability of the witness." 415 U.S., at 318, 94 S.Ct., at 1111. Similarly, in this case the Confrontation Clause was not violated by the withholding of the CYS file; it only would have been impermissible for the judge

---

d. This is not to suggest, of course, that there are no protections for pretrial discovery in criminal cases. See discussion in Part III(B), *infra.* We simply hold that with respect to this issue, the Confrontation Clause only protects a defendant's trial rights, and does not compel the pretrial production of information that might be useful in preparing for trial. * * *

to have prevented Ritchie's lawyer from cross-examining the daughter. Because defense counsel was able to cross-examine all of the trial witnesses fully, we find that the Pennsylvania Supreme Court erred in holding that the failure to disclose the CYS file violated the Confrontation Clause.

B

The Pennsylvania Supreme Court also suggested that the failure to disclose the CYS file violated the Sixth Amendment's guarantee of compulsory process. Ritchie asserts that the trial court's ruling prevented him from learning the names of the "witnesses in his favor," as well as other evidence that might be contained in the file. Although the basis for the Pennsylvania Supreme Court's ruling on this point is unclear, it apparently concluded that the right of compulsory process includes the right to have the State's assistance in uncovering arguably useful information, without regard to the existence of a state-created restriction— here, the confidentiality of the files.

1

This Court has had little occasion to discuss the contours of the Compulsory Process Clause. * * *

* * * Instead, the Court traditionally has evaluated claims such as those raised by Ritchie under the broader protections of the Due Process Clause of the Fourteenth Amendment. Because the applicability of the Sixth Amendment to this type of case is unsettled, and because our Fourteenth Amendment precedents addressing the fundamental fairness of trials establish a clear framework for review, we adopt a due process analysis for purposes of this case. Although we conclude that compulsory process provides no *greater* protections in this area than those afforded by due process, we need not decide today whether and how the guarantees of the Compulsory Process Clause differ from those of the Fourteenth Amendment. It is enough to conclude that on these facts, Ritchie's claims more properly are considered by reference to due process.

2

It is well-settled that the Government has the obligation to turn over evidence in its possession that is both favorable to the accused and material to guilt or punishment. Although courts have used different terminologies to define "materiality," a majority of this Court has agreed, "[e]vidence is material only if there is a reasonable probability that, had the evidence been disclosed to the defense, the result of the proceeding would have been different. A 'reasonable probability' is a probability sufficient to undermine confidence in the outcome."

At this stage, of course, it is impossible to say whether any information in the CYS records may be relevant to Ritchie's claim of innocence, because neither the prosecution nor defense counsel has seen the information, and the trial judge acknowledged that he had not reviewed the full file. The Commonwealth, however, argues that no materiality inquiry is required, because a statute renders the contents of the file privileged. Requiring disclosure here, it is argued, would override the Commonwealth's compelling interest in confidentiality on the mere speculation that the file "might" have been useful to the defense.

Although we recognize that the public interest in protecting this type of sensitive information is strong, we do not agree that this interest necessarily prevents disclosure in all circumstances. This is not a case where a state statute grants CYS the absolute authority to shield its files from all eyes. Cf. 42 Pa.Cons.Stat. § 5945.1(b) (unqualified statutory privilege for communications between sexual assault counselors and victims).[e] Rather, the Pennsylvania law provides that the information shall be disclosed in certain circumstances, including when CYS is directed to do so by court order. Given that the Pennsylvania Legislature contemplated *some* use of CYS records in judicial proceedings, we cannot conclude that the statute prevents all disclosure in criminal prosecutions. In the absence of any apparent state policy to the contrary, we therefore have no reason to believe that relevant information would not be disclosed when a court of competent jurisdiction determines that the information is "material" to the defense of the accused.

We therefore affirm the decision of the Pennsylvania Supreme Court to the extent it orders a remand for further proceedings. Ritchie is entitled to have the CYS file reviewed by the trial court to determine whether it contains information that probably would have changed the outcome of his trial. If it does, he must be given a new trial. If the records maintained by CYS contain no such information, or if the nondisclosure was harmless beyond a reasonable doubt, the lower court will be free to reinstate the prior conviction.

C

This ruling does not end our analysis, because the Pennsylvania Supreme Court did more than simply remand. It also held that defense counsel must be allowed to examine all of the confidential information, both relevant and irrelevant, and present arguments in favor of disclosure. The court apparently concluded that whenever a defendant alleges that protected evidence might be material, the appropriate method of assessing this claim is to grant full access to the disputed information, regardless of the State's interest in confidentiality. We cannot agree.

A defendant's right to discover exculpatory evidence does not include the unsupervised authority to search through the Commonwealth's files. Although the eye of an advocate may be helpful to a defendant in ferreting out information, this Court has never held—even in the absence of a statute restricting disclosure—that a defendant alone may make the determination as to the materiality of the information. Settled practice is to the contrary. In the typical case where a defendant makes only a general request for exculpatory material it is the State that decides which information must be disclosed. Unless defense counsel

---

e. We express no opinion on whether the result in this case would have been different if the statute had protected the CYS files from disclosure to *anyone*, including law-enforcement and judicial personnel.

becomes aware that other exculpatory evidence was withheld and brings it to the court's attention, the prosecutor's decision on disclosure is final. Defense counsel has no constitutional right to conduct his own search of the State's files to argue relevance.

We find that Ritchie's interest (as well as that of the Commonwealth) in ensuring a fair trial can be protected fully by requiring that the CYS files be submitted only to the trial court for *in camera* review. Although this rule denies Ritchie the benefits of an "advocate's eye," we note that the trial court's discretion is not unbounded. If a defendant is aware of specific information contained in the file (*e.g.*, the medical report), he is free to request it directly from the court, and argue in favor of its materiality. Moreover, the duty to disclose is ongoing; information that may be deemed immaterial upon original examination may become important as the proceedings progress, and the court would be obligated to release information material to the fairness of the trial.

To allow full disclosure to defense counsel in this type of case would sacrifice unnecessarily the Commonwealth's compelling interest in protecting its child abuse information. If the CYS records were made available to defendants, even through counsel, it could have a seriously adverse effect on Pennsylvania's efforts to uncover and treat abuse. Child abuse is one of the most difficult crimes to detect and prosecute, in large part because there often are no witnesses except the victim. A child's feelings of vulnerability and guilt, and his or her unwillingness to come forward are particularly acute when the abuser is a parent. It therefore is essential that the child have a state-designated person to whom he may turn, and to do so with the assurance of confidentiality. Relatives and neighbors who suspect abuse also will be more willing to come forward if they know that their identities will be protected. Recognizing this, the Commonwealth—like all other States—has made a commendable effort to assure victims and witnesses that they may speak to the CYS counselors without fear of general disclosure. The Commonwealth's purpose would be frustrated if this confidential material had to be disclosed upon demand to a defendant charged with criminal child abuse, simply because a trial court may not recognize exculpatory evidence. Neither precedent nor common sense requires such a result.

IV

We agree that Ritchie is entitled to know whether the CYS file contains information that may have changed the outcome of his trial had it been disclosed. Thus we agree that a remand is necessary. We disagree with the decision of the Pennsylvania Supreme Court to the extent that it allows defense counsel access to the CYS file. An *in camera* review by the trial court will serve Ritchie's interest without destroying the Commonwealth's need to protect the confidentiality of those involved in child-abuse investigations. The decision of the Pennsylvania Supreme Court is affirmed in part, reversed in part, and remanded for further proceedings not inconsistent with this opinion.

It is so ordered.

JUSTICE BLACKMUN, concurring in part and concurring in the judgment.

I join Parts I, II, III–B, III–C, and IV of the Court's opinion. I write separately, however, because I do not accept the plurality's conclusion, as expressed in Part III–A of Justice Powell's opinion, that the Confrontation Clause protects only a defendant's trial rights and has no relevance to pretrial discovery. In this, I am in substantial agreement with much of what Justice Brennan says, *post,* in dissent. In my view, there might well be a confrontation violation if, as here, a defendant is denied pretrial access to information that would make possible effective cross-examination of a crucial prosecution witness.

* * *

Despite my disagreement with the plurality's reading of the Confrontation Clause, I am able to concur in the Court's judgment because, in my view, the procedure the Court has set out for the lower court to follow on remand is adequate to address any confrontation problem. Here I part company with Justice Brennan. Under the Court's prescribed procedure, the trial judge is directed to review the CYS file for "material" information. This information would certainly include such evidence as statements of the witness that might have been used to impeach her testimony by demonstrating any bias towards respondent or by revealing inconsistencies in her prior statements. * * *

JUSTICE BRENNAN, with whom JUSTICE MARSHALL joins, dissenting.

I join Justice Stevens' dissenting opinion regarding the lack of finality in this case. I write separately to challenge the Court's narrow reading of the Confrontation Clause as applicable only to events that occur at trial. That interpretation ignores the fact that the right of cross-examination also may be significantly infringed by events occurring outside the trial itself, such as the wholesale denial of access to material that would serve as the basis for a significant line of inquiry at trial. In this case, the trial court properly viewed Ritchie's vague speculations that the agency file might contain something useful as an insufficient basis for permitting general access to the file. However, in denying access to the prior statements of the victim the court deprived Ritchie of material crucial to any effort to impeach the victim at trial. I view this deprivation as a violation of the Confrontation Clause.

* * *

The right of a defendant to confront an accuser is intended fundamentally to provide an opportunity to subject *accusations* to critical scrutiny. Essential to testing a witness' account of events is the ability to compare that version with other versions the witness has earlier recounted. Denial of access to a witness' prior statements thus imposes a handicap that strikes at the heart of cross-examination.

* * *

The Court today adopts an interpretation of the Confrontation Clause unwarranted by previous case law and inconsistent with the underlying values of that constitutional provision. I therefore dissent.

JUSTICE STEVENS, with whom JUSTICE BRENNAN, JUSTICE MARSHALL, and JUSTICE SCALIA join, dissenting.

[Justice Stevens dissented on the grounds that the Court did not have jurisdiction to consider the case because in its present posture it lacked finality.]

Questions and Comments

1. *Constitutional basis for decision.* The plurality's opinion holds that the defendant has a constitutional right in appropriate circumstances to have the CYS's files, including communications with the counselor, subject to *in camera* review by the trial judge. Does the plurality's opinion indicate the specific provision of the Constitution this right is based on?

2. *Effect of absolute privilege.* As noted by Justice Powell in footnote 14 of *Ritchie*, the plurality opinion does not purport to decide whether the same result would be reached where there is an absolute privilege under state law. For instance, Pennsylvania statute, 42 Pa.Cons.Stat. Ann. § 5945.1, in contrast to the records of the Children and Youth Services Agency, provides that a sexual assault counselor has "a privilege not to be examined as a witness in any civil or criminal proceedings without the prior written consent of the victim being counseled by the counselor as to any confidential communication." The affect of absolute privilege laws on a defendant's rights to access data has not been conclusively adjudicated by the Supreme Court. However, state courts have divided on the right of access where state law provides an absolute privilege. Compare *Commonwealth v. Two Juveniles*, 397 Mass. 261, 266, 491 N.E.2d 234, 238 (1986) with *Commonwealth v. Kyle*, 367 Pa.Super. 484, 533 A.2d 120 (1987).

3. *Pre-trial discovery of privileged records.* Left open by *Ritchie* is whether the right to have privileged records reviewed *in camera* by a trial judge extends to the pre-trial discovery phase. A number of courts have drawn a distinction between a defendant's right to *in camera* review at the pre-trial stage and during the trial. For instance, in *People v. Hammon*, 15 Cal.4th 1117, 65 Cal.Rptr.2d 1, 938 P.2d 986 (1997), the court, in refusing to extend the defendant's right to an *in camera* review at the pre-trial stage, noted "[I]t is not at all clear 'whether and to what extent the confrontation or compulsory process clause of the sixth amendment grant pre-trial discovery rights to the accused ... For the reasons stated, therefore, we decline to extend the defendant's Sixth Amendment rights of confrontation and cross-examination to authorize *pretrial* [emphasis added] disclosure of privileged information.' "

4. *A proposal.* In answering the questions posed in the foregoing notes, consider this analysis, from Clifford S. Fishman, "Defense Access to a Prosecution Witness's Psychotherapy or Counseling Records," 86 Or. L. Rev. 1, 62–63 (2007):

> Whether a defense attorney should have access to a prosecution witness's psychotherapy or counseling records presents a conflict between

three highly held values: a prosecutor's right and duty to bring a suspect to trial, the witness's right to privacy and to avoid exposure that might interfere with his or her recovery, and a defendant's right to obtain exculpatory evidence. A procedure has developed that requires the trial judge to conduct an in camera inspection of such records to determine whether they contain exculpatory information, but only if the defendant first makes an adequate preliminary showing that such information will be found. The law governing this procedure, however, is ridden with vagueness and uncertainties. [T]hese uncertainties are best resolved as follows:

(1) Just as a defendant has a right pursuant to the Due Process Clause of the Sixth Amendment to seek such in camera review when records are in possession of the State, so too a defendant must be allowed to seek in camera review of records that are possessed by a private entity, pursuant to the Compulsory Process Clause of the Sixth Amendment.

(2) In camera review of such records must be available whether the privilege on its face is conditional or absolute.

(3) A judge must conduct an in camera inspection of such records if, but only if defense counsel can offer specific evidence that establishes probable cause to believe that the records in question contain information that casts serious doubts on the truthfulness or accuracy of the witness's testimony, and such information is not available from less intrusive sources. As a rule, the judge should not conduct such an inspection until the witness has testified at trial but may conduct the inspection prior to trial where it appears that postponing the review until after the witness testifies may require a lengthy adjournment.

(4) The judge must release portions of the records to defense counsel only if they contain information that raises a significant question about the credibility of a witness or the accuracy of testimony that is important to resolving important issues in the case.

The solution I propose has its costs. The possibility that a judge might review a witness's therapy or counseling records may undermine the witness's ability to cope with whatever experiences or difficulties led the witness to therapy or counseling in the first place. The far-more-upsetting possibility is that the fear that such information will be provided to the defense may diminish the witness's willingness to engage in therapy or counseling at all. Each of these results is lamentable. The alternative, however, is to increase the risk that an innocent person will be convicted of a serious crime and deprived of his or her liberty or, in an extreme case, his or her life. I believe the latter is the greater evil, and a more liberal approach toward judicial in camera review of such records, coupled with the flexible disclosure standard for evidence that may raise a serious question about the truthfulness or accuracy of the witness's testimony regarding important issues of the case, strikes the best balance.

5. *Scope of* Ritchie *as applied to information held by third parties.* Another issue left open by *Ritchie* is the defendant's rights under *Ritchie* to require *in-camera* examination of data that is not in the hands of the prosecutor: As noted by the authors of a leading criminal procedure treatise:

"Another related issue left open in Ritchie was the proper scope of the due process right of access when the material sought by defense subpoena was privileged under state law such that, unlike the records in Ritchie, the information was never available to court or prosecutor. FN129 Some courts have rejected claims by defendants that the Constitution entitled them to even in camera review in these circumstances, reasoning that the due process holding in Ritchie applies only to information possessed by the government." [4 LaFave, Israel & King, Criminal Procedure § 24.3(f) (2d ed. 1999)]

b.   Defendant Disclosures During Treatment

UNITED STATES v. HAYES

United States Court of Appeals, Sixth Circuit, 2000.
227 F.3d 578.

RYAN, Circuit Judge.

In this appeal, we are required to decide whether there is a "dangerous patient" exception to the federal psychotherapist/patient testimonial privilege under Fed.R.Evid. 501. We hold there is not.

The United States seeks to prosecute the defendant Roy Lee Hayes under 18 U.S.C. § 115 for making threats, during several psychotherapy sessions, to murder his supervisor at the United States Postal Service. Shortly after being indicted, Hayes filed a motion to suppress medical records prepared by his psychotherapists, and to exclude his therapist's expected testimony, on the ground that the medical records and testimony were privileged. The district court granted Hayes's motion to suppress and, soon thereafter, dismissed the indictment. We will affirm.

Aside from a period of military service, Hayes has worked for the United States Postal Service his entire adult life. In July 1996, Veda Odle assumed the position of postmaster in Marion, Virginia, and, consequently, interacted regularly with Hayes, who was the union steward for that post office branch.

Beginning in 1997, Hayes began to behave erratically at work, at times becoming inconsolably depressed and unable to function. On February 9, 1998, after several episodes of irregular behavior, Hayes sought professional help at the Veterans Administration Mountain Home Hospital (MHH), Johnson City, Tennessee. The admitting diagnosis for Hayes was major depression accompanied by severe psychotic features. During treatment, Hayes informed Dr. Dianne Hansen of a desire to kill Odle, a desire Hayes claimed he could resist only because he "recognized" that such action could jeopardize his continued employment. Dr. Hansen released Hayes on February 18, instructing him to contact a local health care provider and to return to work on February 23. Although records at MHH indicate plans to warn Odle of the potential threat Hayes posed, it is undisputed that Odle never received any warning from the staff at MHH.

On February 22, Hayes returned to MHH, admitting himself as an in-patient for several days. During this stay, Hayes reiterated his homicidal inclinations, but MHH doctors concluded that he was capable of controlling himself and understanding the consequences of his actions. Consequently, on February 26, MHH again released Hayes with a prescription for various psychotropic drugs ...

On March 24, 1998, because Hayes was experiencing certain undesirable side effects from the drugs he was taking, Dr. Hansen discontinued Hayes's prescriptions. Soon thereafter, apparently due to the termination of his prescriptions, the death of his uncle, and sleep deprivation prior to undergoing an EEG on March 31, Hayes began to experience increased anxiety and some unraveling of his previous self restraint.

On the evening of March 31, Hayes attended a session with Van Dyke at the Veterans Center. At that time, Hayes outlined in great detail his plan to kill Odle, describing the layout of Odle's home and explaining that he knew when she would be home alone. According to Van Dyke, during this visit, he again advised Hayes that his serious threats toward Odle could not be kept confidential. When the session concluded, however, Van Dyke allowed Hayes to leave for a therapy appointment at MHH. Van Dyke took no further action that evening.

The next day, Van Dyke spoke with a supervisor about Hayes's statements and the supervisor advised contacting the Veterans Center's legal counsel for advice on how to handle this potentially dangerous situation. Counsel for the Veterans Center informed Van Dyke that he had a legal obligation to warn Odle of the threat that Hayes posed, and a short time later Van Dyke did so.

Upon receipt of Van Dyke's warning, Odle understandably became frightened and immediately contacted Postal Inspector Terrance Vlug, who requested all of Hayes's medical records from Van Dyke. Van Dyke provided the records which disclosed Hayes's repeated homicidal statements. Vlug then filed a criminal complaint on April 3, 1998, charging Hayes with threatening to murder a federal official in violation of *18 U.S.C. § 115.*

A grand jury issued a three-count indictment against Hayes, charging that, on three occasions, Hayes's murderous remarks to psychotherapists constituted criminal wrongdoing under 18 U.S.C. § 115(a)(1), which provides, in pertinent part:

> Whoever ... threatens to assault, kidnap, or murder, a United States official ... with intent to impede, intimidate, or interfere with such official ... while engaged in the performance of official duties, or with intent to retaliate against such official ... on account of the performance of official duties, shall be punished[.]

After a judicial determination that Hayes was competent to stand trial and discussion on various preliminary motions, Hayes filed a motion to dismiss the indictment and to suppress his medical records and any testimony from his psychotherapists, asserting the psychotherapist/patient privilege . . .

The district court ordered suppression of any testimony by Van Dyke. Citing *United States v. Glass*, 133 F.3d 1356 (10th Cir.1998*)*, the district court held that a psychotherapist may testify as to otherwise privileged statements of threats allegedly made by a patient only where such "disclosure was the only means of averting harm to the [federal official] when the disclosure was made." The district court held that any communications made to psychotherapists at MHH remained privileged because those doctors had never disclosed to third parties the substance of their therapy sessions with Hayes. Based on Van Dyke's admissions that he considered no option other than disclosure to protect Odle and, in fact, disclosed Hayes's statements only because of an order from a supervisor, the district court held that Van Dyke could not testify since his disclosure was not "the only means of averting harm." Accordingly, the court granted Hayes's motion to exclude the testimony of his psychotherapists whose information formed the basis of the indictment. Soon thereafter, the district court dismissed the case, an order which the government timely appealed.

II.

The Federal Rules of Evidence leave the establishment of testimonial privileges to the federal courts . . .

* * *

A psychotherapist/patient evidentiary privilege has been well-established in the Sixth Circuit for some time. The Supreme Court recently recognized the privilege in *Jaffee,* holding that "confidential communications between a licensed psychotherapist and her patients in the course of diagnosis or treatment are protected from compelled disclosure under Rule 501 of the Federal Rules of Evidence." *Jaffee v. Redmond*, 518 U.S. 1, 15 (1996*)*. The Court observed that recognizing as privileged psychotherapist/patient discussions in the course of therapy would likely facilitate "an atmosphere of confidence and trust" conducive to meaningful treatment. *Id.* at 10. The Court also reasoned that a federal psychotherapist/patient privilege would "serv[e] public ends" as "[t]he mental health of [the American citizen] . . . is a public good of transcendent importance." *Id.* at 11. The Court observed that all 50 States and the District of Columbia had "enacted into law some form of psychotherapist privilege." *Id.* at 12. The Court rejected a "balancing component . . . [m]aking the promise of confidentiality contingent upon a trial judge's later evaluation of the relative importance of the patient's interest in privacy and the evidentiary need for disclosure." *Id.* at 17. The Court wisely declined to identify all situations where the privilege would and would not apply, but observed in a footnote: "[W]e do not doubt that there are situations in which the privilege must give way, *for example,* if a serious threat of harm to the patient or to others can be averted only by means of a disclosure by the therapist." *Id.* at 18 n. 19 (emphasis added).

Among the courts of appeals, only the Tenth Circuit has decided whether there exists a "dangerous patient" exception to the federal psychotherapist/patient privilege. In *Glass,* the defendant told his psychotherapist that he intended to kill the President. *See Glass,* 133 F.3d at 1357.[52] Although, initially, the defendant's threats were not taken seriously, after the defendant could not be located for 10 days, a nurse reported the threat to local law enforcement. *Id.* Eventually, the Secret Service became involved and the defendant's psychotherapist revealed the defendant's threatening statements. *Id.* After the government charged the defendant under 18 U.S.C. § 871, the defendant moved to exclude his psychotherapist's testimony as privileged. The district court denied the motion. *Id.*

On appeal, the Tenth Circuit reversed and held that the alleged "exception" to the *Jaffee* privilege, described in footnote 19, is applicable only where the threat was serious *when made* and disclosure was literally the only means of averting harm. *See id.* at 1359. The court concluded that, given that the psychotherapist had initially released the defendant, his threat could not be classified as serious. *Id.* Moreover, the court ruled, the government failed to show that disclosure was the only means of protecting the President from harm and, therefore, the privilege applied to the psychotherapist's testimony. *Id.*

Before *Jaffee* was handed down, this court decided *United States v. Snelenberger,* 24 F.3d 799 (6th Cir.1994*),* in which Snelenberger, attempting to establish an entitlement to social security benefits, informed his psychotherapist that he intended to kill an administrative law judge who had ruled against him on a previous claim to benefits. *Id.* at 801. After hearing this and other similarly disturbing statements, the psychotherapist decided that involuntary hospitalization was appropriate and directed Snelenberger to the hospital staff for transportation to an institution. *Id.* While in the custody of the hospital staff, Snelenberger repeated several times his plan to kill the ALJ. *Id.* Eventually, Snelenberger was indicted on three counts of threatening to murder an ALJ, in violation of 18 U.S.C. § 115(a)(1)(B). Id. Over Snelenberger's objection, the psychotherapist testified against him at his trial. This court ruled that such testimony was proper because the Michigan legislature had enacted a statute requiring a psychotherapist to take steps to protect those "seriously threatened." *Id.* at 802. In the alternative, this court ruled that Snelenberger had waived the privilege by disclosing his intentions toward the ALJ to various parties after speaking with the psychotherapist. *Id.*

The government argues that the purported exception to the psychotherapist/patient privilege, set forth in the *Jaffee* footnote, applies here and that Van Dyke's testimony is admissible, an argument which relies heavily on *Snelenberger,* and is structured as follows: (1) Tennessee law placed an affirmative obligation on Van Dyke to protect Odle after he learned of the serious threat Hayes posed, Tenn.Code Ann. § 33–10–

---

52. [author's note] United States v. Glass is discussed at in Note 9, at p. 369.

302(a); (2) Van Dyke complied with this duty; and (3) after Van Dyke made this disclosure, the psychotherapist/patient privilege became inapplicable for all future court proceedings. Moreover, the government contends, once Hayes's statements to Van Dyke ceased to be privileged, Hayes could no longer claim that statements made during therapy sessions with psychotherapists other than Van Dyke were privileged.

* * *

III.

Before turning to the question whether it is advisable to graft a "dangerous patient" exception for criminal proceedings onto the federal psychotherapist/patient privilege, we will first clarify a misperception held by Hayes, the government, and, to some extent, the Tenth Circuit that the standard of care exercised by a treating psychotherapist prior to complying with (or, for that matter, failing to comply with) a state's "duty to protect" requirement is somehow pertinent to the applicability of the psychotherapist/patient privilege in criminal proceedings. We think there is little correlation between those two inquiries.

The "duty to protect" now imposed on psychotherapists throughout the country began with *Tarasoff v. Regents of the University of California*, 17 Cal.3d 425, 131 Cal.Rptr. 14, 551 P.2d 334 (Cal.1976). In that case, the California Supreme Court held that "once a therapist does in fact determine, or under applicable professional standards reasonably should have determined, that a patient poses a serious danger of violence to others, he bears a duty to exercise reasonable care to protect the foreseeable victim of that danger." *Id.* at 345. The obvious rationale behind this rule is that the preservation and protection of the health and safety of innocent third parties outweighs the good achieved by maintaining the confidentiality of life-threatening communications. After that decision, Tennessee, like most other states, codified the psychotherapist's "duty to protect" third parties from serious threats. *See, e.g.,* Tenn.Code Ann. § 33–10–302.

We see only a marginal connection, if any at all, between a psychotherapist's action in notifying a third party (for his own safety) of a patient's threat to kill or injure him and a court's refusal to permit the therapist to testify about such threat (in the interest of protecting the psychotherapist/patient relationship) in a later prosecution of the patient for making it. State law requirements that psychotherapists take action to prevent serious and credible threats from being carried out serve a far more immediate function than the proposed "dangerous patient" exception. Unlike the situation presented in *Tarasoff,* the threat articulated by a defendant such as Hayes is rather unlikely to be carried out once court proceedings have begun against him.

Moreover, we think that conditioning the applicability of the proposed "dangerous patient" exception on the standard of care exercised by a treating psychotherapist is unsound in theory and in practice. Were we to adopt the analytical methodology proposed by Hayes and the government, future cases of this sort will devolve into a battle of experts testifying whether a psychotherapist behaved "reasonably" before disclosing what was believed to be a serious threat. Such an inquiry would, at a minimum, be highly speculative and very likely lead to erratic results. More fundamentally, we think it would be rather perverse and unjust to condition the freedom of individuals on the competency of a treating psychotherapist. Moreover, it cannot be the case that the scope of a federal testimonial privilege should vary depending upon state determinations of what constitutes "reasonable" professional conduct. Thus, we reject the purported relevance of the degree of care exercised by Van Dyke or the psychotherapists at MHH on the issue of Hayes's right to assert the psychotherapist/patient privilege. Given that the "dangerous patient" exception crafted by the Tenth Circuit in *Glass* is linked to the standard of care exercised by the psychotherapist, we respectfully decline to follow that court's treatment of the privilege.

IV.

At the threshold, we note the paradoxical nature of this case. On the one hand, Hayes should be applauded for seeking professional help for the mental and emotional difficulties he was suffering. Yet, because the psychotic delusions for which he sought treatment took the form of homicidal intentions toward an employee of the federal government, Hayes now finds himself facing a felony conviction and incarceration because his professional care givers are prepared to testify against him.

* * *

. . . [R]ecognition of a "dangerous patient" exception surely would have a deleterious effect on the "atmosphere of confidence and trust" in the psychotherapist/patient relationship. While early advice to the patient that, in the event of the disclosure of a serious threat of harm to an identifiable victim, the therapist will have a duty to protect the intended victim, may have a marginal effect on a patient's candor in therapy sessions, an additional warning that the patient's statements may be used against him in a subsequent criminal prosecution would certainly chill and very likely terminate open dialogue. Thus, if our Nation's mental health is indeed as valuable as the Supreme Court has indicated, and we think it is, the chilling effect that would result from the recognition of a "dangerous patient" exception and its logical consequences is the first reason to reject it.

Second, we think that allowing a psychotherapist to testify against his or her patient in a criminal prosecution about statements made to the therapist by the patient for the purposes of treatment arguably "serv[es] [a] public end," but it is an end that does not justify the means. The *Jaffee* footnote recognizes that in cases such as this, there are at least two interests at stake: the improvement of our citizens' mental health achieved, in part, by open dialogue in psychotherapy, on the one hand, and the protection of innocent third parties, on the other. Both are "public ends" which the federal common law should foster . . . [P]sychotherapists will sometimes need to testify in court proceedings, such as those for the involuntary commitment of a patient, to comply with their "duty to protect" the patient or identifiable third parties. After involuntary hospitalization, for example, the patient would no longer pose a "serious threat of harm" to anyone and, hopefully, the psychotherapist/patient relationship can continue during the patient's hospitalization. While that patient, by definition, will initially reject the prospect of hospitalization, it may ultimately improve his mental state and should not leave a stigma after the stay concludes. In such a case, therefore, both "public ends" will likely be served.

On the other hand, a psychotherapist's testimony used to prosecute and incarcerate a patient who came to him or her for professional help cannot be similarly justified. Once in prison, even partly as a consequence of the testimony of a therapist to whom the patient came for help, the probability of the patient's mental health improving diminishes significantly and a stigma certainly attaches after the patient's sentence is served. While, as with involuntary hospitalization, incarceration would serve the "public end" of neutralizing the threat posed by a patient, the price paid in achieving that neutralization may often be that many patients will not seek the professional help they need to regain their mental and emotional health. Thus, we conclude that the proposed "dangerous patient" exception is unnecessary to allow a psychotherapist to comply with his or her professional responsibilities and would seriously disserve the "public end" of improving the mental health of our Nation's citizens.

Third, we are persuaded that adoption of a "dangerous patient" exception as part of the federal common law is ill-advised. The majority of states have no such exception as part of their evidence jurisprudence; California, alone, has enacted a "dangerous patient" exception as part of its evidence code which would arguably apply in a criminal case. West's Ann. CAL. EVID. CODE § 1024. We note, too, that the Proposed Rules of Evidence on the subject of privileges submitted by the Supreme Court in 1972 recognized a psychotherapist patient privilege with three exceptions, none of which approximated what is proposed here. *See* Rules of Evidence for United States Courts and Magistrates, 56 F.R.D. 183, 241 (1972). To conclude, "reason and experience" teach us that a "dangerous patient" exception which would allow a psychotherapist to testify against a patient in criminal proceedings should not become part of the federal common law.

We hold, therefore, that the federal psychotherapist/patient privilege does not impede a psychotherapist's compliance with his professional and ethical duty to protect innocent third parties, a duty which may require, among other things, disclosure to third parties or testimony at an involuntary hospitalization proceeding. Conversely, compliance with the professional duty to protect does not imply a duty to testify against a patient in criminal proceedings or in civil proceedings other than directly related to the patient's involuntary hospitalization, and such testimony is privileged and inadmissable if a patient properly asserts the psychotherapist/patient privilege.

Finally, our holding today and the Supreme Court's discussion of the psychotherapist/patient privilege in *Jaffee* require a revisitation of *Snelenberger,* a case which preceded *Jaffee.* We conclude that, to the extent that this court held that once the Michigan "duty to protect" attached, the federal psychotherapist/patient privilege ceased to apply in any further court proceedings, *Jaffee* requires the conclusion that *Snelenberger* is no longer good law. *See* Snelenberger, 24 F.3d at 802.

* * *

For the foregoing reasons, the district court orders suppressing the testimony of Hayes's psychotherapists and dismissing the indictment against Hayes are AFFIRMED.

BOGGS, CIRCUIT JUDGE, dissenting.

The court's opinion quite properly distinguishes the questions of whether a mental health professional (apparently including, in this case, a social worker) can inform the intended victim of a threat, from the question of whether that person can testify in court. I agree with the court's analysis of the former question. With respect to the latter question, I believe that when the social worker has specifically informed the patient that the social worker will not keep the communications confidential, there is no barrier to that person testifying, and I therefore respectfully dissent from the court's holding to the contrary.

* * *

In my opinion, the court's view of this case may be somewhat muddled by the fact that the "crime" at issue here is what some would consider the purely victimless one of making a threat that is not made to the subject of the threat. It is true that, on one view, simply making a threat that is not intended to be conveyed to the potential victim is not a traditional *malum in se* crime. However, it is important to recognize that, if the proffered evidence is believed, what occurred here was a crime, no different in nature than making similar threats against Odle to fellow drinkers at a bar, or to a policeman in casual conversation, or to one's lawyer. In addition, the court's rule would apparently be the same even if the victim of the threat ended up dead, in a fashion exactly paralleling the material revealed to the mental health professional, after a warning of non-confidentiality. I simply do not see that such tender concern for criminal evidence is required by the common law, or by reason and experience, when the patient has been put on notice ...

Dr. Radford told Hayes in February, as Hayes himself testified, that his threats to kill Odle would have to be reported. Van Dyke warned Hayes twice that his threats would not and could not be kept in confidence ... This constituted more than ample notice that such discussion was outside the bounds of any promised or assumed confidentiality.

* * *

All of the court's concerns in support of encouraging persons to confide in mental health professionals would be satisfied by a more limited rule that such recipients of information could not testify about anything said up to the point at which notice is given that the actual or threatened criminal conduct being discussed is no longer covered by confidentiality. Otherwise, we have the odd spectacle that a criminal can perpetrate his crimes (the threats) simply by either purchasing, or being provided at public expense, a particular type of listener, with no opportunity for the listener to avoid facilitating the crime.

If the real problem is that we don't think that this type of threat, alone, is a very serious matter, then that is for Congress. I object to creating a barrier that prevents competent testimony as to the commission of a crime by a fully warned patient from coming into court, and I therefore DISSENT.

Questions and Comments

1. *Alternative approach to the dangerous patient situation.* Hayes held that, under the Federal Rules of Evidence, there is no "dangerous patient" exception to the testimonial privilege. State courts may confront similar issues in the interpretation of their privilege statutes. In *Guerrier v. State,* 811 So.2d 852 (Fla.App.5 Dist.2002), the defendant was arrested for stalking his girl friend; while being evaluated by the prison psychiatrist he stated that upon his release he intended to kill her. Following the threat, a nurse who was working with the psychiatrist called and warned the potential victim. The defendant was subsequently charged with aggravated stalking. The prosecution sought to introduce the testimony of the psychiatrist and nurse concerning the death threat made by the defendant. The Florida Evidence Code recognized a psychotherapist-patient privilege similar to that of the Federal Rules of Evidence. However, Florida law authorizes psychotherapists to disclose to a potential victim threats posed by a patient. In the view of the court, by enacting a law that permits psychotherapists to warn foreseeable victims, the legislature made clear that the protection of potential victims is of paramount importance. Barring the admission of the same information in a later prosecution would, according to the court, "thwart the intent of the Legislature".

2. *Impact of evidentiary privilege on willingness of patients to seek counseling.* The *Hayes* opinion places emphasis on the deterrent effect that the admission of the incriminating statements by a patient would have on the "atmosphere of confidence and trust" and the willingness of persons suffering from mental disorders to seek treatment. However, as noted earlier, various studies suggest that the existence of the psychotherapist-patient evidentiary privilege was not a factor in encouraging individuals to seek counseling; people seek counseling in order to get well and it matters little to them that a court may later use or exclude their conversations with a doctor. See Daniel W. Shuman & Myron S. Weiner, "The Privilege Study: An Empirical Examination of the Psychotherapist–Patient Privilege," 60 N.C. L. Rev. 893, 925–26 (1982). See also Edward Imwinkelried review of studies conducted in the 1980s, which concluded:

It is certainly dangerous to extrapolate from the available data, because there have been only a few handfuls of studies. However, the findings in the studies are relatively uniform. The researchers have fairly consistently found that: Even absent a privilege, only a small minority of lay persons would be deterred from consulting the professional; without a privilege, perhaps a significant minority of the layp-persons would be somewhat more guarded in their communications, particularly written communications, with the confidant; but the vast majority of laypersons would still consult and communicate with their confidants to roughly the same extent. On reflection, these findings should not come as a surprise. As Professor Paschal pointed out in the Senate hearings on the proposed Federal Rules of Evidence, most laypersons communicating with confidants are engaged in primary, pre-litigation activities. Typically, at the time of the communication they have little or no concern about subsequent litigation. Moreover, they often have strong, even impelling, reasons to communicate."

Edward Imwinkelried, "The Historical Cycle in the Law of Evidentiary Privileges: Will Instrumentalism Come into Conflict with the Modern Humanistic Theories?," 55 Ark L. Rev. 251, 255–56 (2002).

3. *Disclosure of confessions of past crimes.* A case widely reported by the media, *Menendez v. Superior Court,* raised the question whether confessions made to a treating clinical psychotherapist by two brothers accused of murdering their parents could be introduced in a later homicide prosecution.The prosecution in *Menendez* sought to introduce certain notes and three audiotape cassettes in the custody of Dr. Jerome Oziel, a clinical psychotherapist who had counseled the Menendez brothers following the death of their parents. The notes and audiotapes included confessions by the Menendez brothers that they had carried out the homicides. Dr. Oziel and the defendants contested the introduction of the notes and tapes. The trial court admitted some of the notes and tapes based on a provision of the California Evidence Code, which creates an exception to the usual rule of confidential communications between patient and psychotherapist (Cal. Evid. Code § 1014). In admitting the evidence, the court relied primarily on § 1024 of the Evidence Code which provides:

> There is no privilege . . . if the psychotherapist has reasonable cause to believe that the patient is in such mental or emotional condition as to be dangerous to himself or to the person or property of another and that disclosure of the communication is necessary to prevent the threatened danger.

In its effort to have the incriminating evidence introduced, the prosecution was able to show that Dr. Oziel had disclosed the confession of the Menendez brothers and their threats to harm him to his wife, Laurel Oziel, and his lover, Judalyn Smyth. The recordings and notes made by Dr. Oziel, as well as the disclosures to his wife and confidant concerning the Menendez brothers' threats, were intended to deter them Menendez from harming him. According to the testimony introduced at the hearing on the admission of the evidence "he told the brothers the audiotape recordings would be revealed if 'something happened to him', i.e. he was killed or disappeared mysteriously." *Menendez v. Superior Court*, 3 Cal.4th 435, 445 n. 12, 11 Cal.Rptr.2d 92, 834 P.2d 786 (1992).

The Menendez brothers brought an interlocutory appeal challenging the admission of the evidence. In the interim, while the admissibility of the notes and tapes was being adjudicated in separate proceedings, the criminal trial was suspended. The case challenging the admissibility of the evidence ultimately reached the California Supreme Court, which found the key notes and audiotapes admissible based on the exception under § 1024 of the Evidence Code. 3 Cal.4th 435, 456, 11 Cal.Rptr.2d 92, 834 P.2d 786 (1992). In finding certain of the evidence admissible, the Court construed the § 1024 exception as including threats to the therapist, rather than only third persons. Id. at 451. Under this rationale, the privilege was immediately lost when the Menendez brothers threatened the therapist. The notes and recordings pertaining to the threats, coupled with the admissions of culpability for the parents' deaths, then became admissible.

The subsequent criminal trial against the brothers ended in a hung jury. However, in 1996, at a second trial at which the therapist, Dr. Oziel, did not testify, the brothers were convicted of the homicide of their parents.

4. *Application of HIPAA to Menendez case facts.* Would disclosure by the therapist of the Menendez confessions cited in note 3 *supra* be authorized under HIPAA? In answering this question, assume that the therapist is a covered person under HIPAA. Under HIPAA, a health provider may disclose past crimes by a patient where:

(i) A covered health care provider providing emergency health care in response to a medical emergency, other than such emergency on the premises of the covered health care provider, may disclose protected health information to a law enforcement official if such disclosure appears necessary to alert law enforcement to:

(A) The commission and nature of a crime;

(B) The location of such crime or of the victim(s) of such crime; and

(C) The identity, description and location of the perpetrator of such crime.

Aside from this provision, a psychotherapist is authorized to make a disclosure of PHI "in any judicial or administrative proceeding in response to an express order or subpoena or to a subpoena discovery request." However, the disclosure to authorities that might trigger a court order requiring testimony would not necessarily be privileged under HIPAA unless it meets the specific disclosure requirements of HIPAA, including the exception noted above.

5. *Testimonial privilege in civil commitment proceedings.* In most jurisdictions, the testimonial privilege cannot be invoked by a patient in a civil commitment proceeding where the patient's disclosures to the therapist are introduced to support civil commitment. Presumably, state laws governing the disclosure of personal health information (PHI) in commitment proceedings would not be impacted by HIPAA since the regulations permit disclosure of PHI "in any judicial or administrative proceeding in response to an express order or subpoena or to a subpoena discovery request".

III. INSURANCE MANDATED DISCLOSURES AND PATIENT ACCESS ISSUES

A. COMMUNICATIONS INVOLVING INSURERS AND MANAGED CARE ENTITIES

The public's access to the mental health system has been substantially expanded in recent years. In part, this trend reflects increases in the number of employees covered by insurance, coupled with the expansion of mental health care benefits (e.g. The Mental Health Parity Act of 1996, which mandates equivalency in mental health benefits).

At the same time, employer-sponsored health insurance programs are relying increasingly on managed care systems to administer the programs. In fact, an estimated 70 percent of workers insured through their work are enrolled in some form of managed care. T. Lewin, "Questions of Privacy Roil Arena of Psychotherapy," N.Y. Times, May 22, 1998, at 1 [hereinafter "Privacy," N.Y. Times, May 22, 1996].

By all accounts, the increased reliance on managed care programs has had a very substantial impact on patient privacy interests. Typically, managed companies require patients, as a condition to coverage, to sign broad releases authorizing therapists to submit to the insurer or manage care contractor extensive data pertaining to any proposed or completed treatment. Such data will generally include the therapist's diagnosis together with presenting symptoms, a treatment plan, and an itemization of the treatment contemplated or provided (including dates and treatment modalities). In some instances, particularly where the employer is self-insured, the managed care organization which manages the employer plan may at some point transmit the treatment data to the human resources department of the employer.

From the standpoint of insurers and their managed care contractors, the availability of such patient data is essential to effective utilization review which will normally include a determination of whether the particular disorder is one that is covered under the terms of the policy (for instance, preconditions are sometimes excluded) and whether the proposed treatment is "medically necessary." Clearly, one purpose of managed care is the standardization of care by the use of "protocols outlining what treatment will be allowed for what conditions." "Privacy," N.Y. Times, May 22, 1996.

From the standpoint of the mental health professionals and patient advocacy groups, managed care is an unnecessary intrusion on the professional prerogatives of therapists and the privacy interests of patients. Overall, much of the therapeutic community takes the position that the therapist is better equipped than a managed care organization to determine the health needs of a patient. In response to this claim, the insurance industry notes that there is very little consensus concerning the most effective mode of treatment for many emotional problems and that the therapist has a financial stake in opting for the most time-consuming method of dealing with disorders.

The breach of confidentiality that results from the submission of treatment data to insurers and managed care contractors is seen as an especially onerous consequence of managed care. This is particularly the case where the managed care organization transmits the data to the patient's employer, which is a possibility when the employer is self-insured. Here, the patient may fear that knowledge by the employer of his/her disorder and treatment will have an adverse effect on retention and promotion. As a consequence, employees may choose to forego treatment altogether or pursue treatment and absorb the cost rather than seeking reimbursement under the insurance program. The extent to which confidentiality concerns actually deter the utilization of mental health services is difficult to gauge. However, there is evidence that some patients, in order to avoid disclosure of treatment information to insurers and managed care contractors, opt to pay for the service themselves. See "Psychotherapy Patients Pay a Price for Privacy," The Wall St. J., Jan. 22, 1998, at B2.

Many of the risks associated with the maintenance of records by managed care entities have been substantially reduced by the enactment of HIPAA. While health care providers may still disclose protected health care information (PHI) to the patient's insurer or HMO, the amount of information that can be provided is severely restricted (see Regulatory Implementation of HIPAA Privacy Provisions at pp. 313–25). Moreover, HIPAA regulations mandate that any information received by the covered entity not be disclosed to any non-covered entity and further, that any information maintained by the insurer or HMO be retained in a secure manner.

B. PATIENT ACCESS TO RECORDS

There was no common law right of patients to their medical records. Recipients of health care were not conceived as having a property interest in the medical records nor in having an implied contractual right. However, in the post World War II era, various states enacted legislation giving patients limited access rights to their health information and in some instances, the right to amend such information. Whatever considerations justify patients access to health records for general medical treatment, they are more compelling where the treatment involved a mental disorder. A patient without access confronting either civil commitment or the imposition of involuntary treatment would have difficulty challenging the basis for the proposed action. Paradoxically, a patient who allegedly was a subject of malpractice, either because the treatment was inappropriate or hospitalization was not legally justified, was sometimes stymied in pursuing a legal action against the health provider because of a lack of access by the patient to treatment records. For instance, in *Gotkin v. Miller*, 514 F.2d 125 (2d Cir.1975), the Court of Appeals for the Second Circuit held that a patient who was suing for wrongful commitment did not have a legal right to his/her psychiatric records that had been the basis for the involuntary hospitalization. Cases such as *Miller* brought to the surface the paradox of imposing involuntary treatment while denying plaintiffs the opportunity to challenge in a subsequent lawsuit the correctness of the diagnosis and the appropriateness of the treatment selected by the provider. Partially as result of cases of this kind, a number of states enacted special legislation giving patients who had undergone mental health treatment the right of access to their health records. A typical statute enacted by Illinois provided that any recipient of mental health and developmental disabilities services "shall be entitled, upon request, to inspect and copy [his/her] record or any part thereof." Ill.—S.H.A. ch. 91 1/2, ¶ 804. Significantly, the Illinois statute, like that of other states with similar legislation, distinguished between the "patient's record" and the therapist's "personal notes." Other states, such as California, granted patients access to his or her records unless in the view of the physician or administrative officer in question, release of such records to the patient would not "serve his best interest." West's Ann.Cal.Code § 5328.9. Statutes such as those enacted by Illinois and California became wide spread by the end of the 20th Century and, as a result, most states currently have legislation providing the recipients of mental health services special access rights. However, these state laws tend to vary in terms of the scope of access and the limitations that may be imposed by the health provider.

Existing state laws are now supplemented by HIPAA, which grants an individual a qualified right of access to one's health information.[53] Under HIPAA, individuals have the right to inspect and obtain copies of their personal Health information (PHI) in the hands of covered entities. Also they have the right to amend information that is not "accurate and complete."[54] The right of access is not absolute, however, and various exceptions are set out in the regulations that enable a provider to deny access.[55] For instance a provider may deny access to psychotherapy notes.[56]

Other exceptions include the right to deny access where (1) a licensed health care professional "has determined in the exercise of professional judgment, that the access requested is reasonably likely to endanger the life or physical safety of the individual or another person" or (2) "the protected health information makes reference to another person (unless such other person is a health provider) and a licensed health care professional has determined in the exercise of professional judgment that the access requested is reasonably likely to cause substantial harm to the individual or another person."[57]

---

53. Significantly, the access rights under HIPAA do not include psychotherapy notes. See supra note 39.

54. 45 C.F.R. § 164.526.

55. 45 C.F.R. § 164.524.

56. Psychotherapy notes are discussed supra at note 39.

57. *Id.* Access may also be denied on a number of other grounds including (1) PHI held by correctional institution where release of the information would jeopardize the health safety or security of the individual or other inmates; (2) the PHI was obtained in the course of research which had a treatment component and the patient had agreed to the condition of non-access when

Questions and Comments

1. *Justification for patient access.* What policy reasons support the recipient's access to the records of his mental health services? Are statutes that provide access merely protecting an abstract interest in the patient's right to know, or are there more practical reasons why the patient should have access to his/her records?

2. *Negative consequences of access.* Are there any negative consequences in the right of a patient to gain access to their psychiatric records? For instance, if the treating psychiatrist or psychologist were to enter a tentative diagnosis of "borderline schizophrenia," might the disclosure of the tentative diagnosis to the patient unduly alarm the patient and perhaps interfere with the treatment regimen? In this connection, recall that HIPAA gives the patient the right to access their PHI, though this right does not extend to psychotherapy notes. At the same time, HIPAA does not preclude state laws that provide greater access rights. Thus, state law could authorize access to psychotherapy notes, though this degree of disclosure could, as noted above, possibly interfere with treatment and generally be detrimental to the interest of the patient.

consenting to participate in the program; (3) the PHI information was obtained from a third party under a promise of confidentiality and the access would reveal the source.

*

Part II

DEPRIVATIONS OF LIBERTY
AND PROPERTY

Chapter Six

MENTAL HEALTH PROFESSIONALS AND EXPERTISE

Table of Sections

I.   INTRODUCTION

The government acts to deprive its citizens of liberty or property in a number of contexts. These interventions may be subdivided into three types. Under a *punishment* system, the goal of the government is punishment for past acts. The principal example of this type of intervention is the criminal justice process, which penalizes through incarceration or fines those who violate certain norms. Under a *prevention* system, the government deprives individuals of their liberty for the purpose of preventing future harm to others or themselves. The post-sentence detention of so-called "sexual predators" and the civil commitment process (at least that aspect of it which results in involuntary hospitalization of the "dangerous mentally ill") are exemplars of this model. Finally, under a *protection* system, the government acts to prevent "incompetent" choices and ensure that individuals capably exercise rights and privileges. One illustration of this type of intervention is the involuntary hospitalization of those found incompetent to stand trial for the purpose of restoring them to competency. Another is the coerced relinquishment of control over property or person that may occur pursuant to guardianship proceedings.

Under current law, mental disability assumes a significant role in the application of all three intervention models. For instance, under the punishment model as applied in this country, the law has been unwilling to punish those who are considered "insane." With a few exceptions, application of the prevention model is predicated on a finding of mental disorder. Similarly, a finding of incompetency usually requires evidence of diagnosable mental disability.

Part II of this book—composed of Chapters Six through Ten—examines the impact of these three models of state intervention on people who have a mental disability. The punishment model is explored in Chapter Seven, the prevention model in Chapter Eight and the protection model in Chapter Nine. Chapter Ten looks at legal issues connected with post-intervention treatment and habilitation, issues that concern all three models. Finally, this chapter–Chapter Six–deals with an important preliminary matter that also cuts across the three models: our ability to identify who, if anyone, is "mentally disabled" and our ability to assess what the consequences of such disability are. Can we distinguish people with mental illness from those who are not mentally ill, the sane from the insane, the dangerous from the nondangerous, and the incompetent from the competent? The extent to which we can answer such questions may determine the extent to which we ask them, and obviously has practical consequences for the operation of the different models.

Traditionally, laypersons provided the evidence necessary to decide whether a person was insane, committable, or incompetent. But with the growth and acceptance of the mental health professions in the past century and a half (detailed in Chapter One), psychiatrists, and to a lesser extent psychologists and social workers, have all but taken over the evidence-production role and have even assumed the judicial role in some contexts. Such a development is not surprising, since these individuals were, and are, thought to know more about mental disorder and its effects than other groups.

More recently, however, several writers have questioned the wisdom of this development. Relying on an impressive array of research, these commentators have suggested that opinions reached by behavioral scientists lack sufficient reliability for legal purposes. Many conclude that the role of mental health professionals in their evidence-production role should be substantially circumscribed or even eliminated altogether.[a]

a. See, e.g., Margaret Hagen, Whores of the Court: The Fraud of Psychiatric Testimony and the Rape of American Justice (1997); David Faust & Jay Ziskin, "The Expert Witness in Psychology and Psychiatry," 241 Science 31 (1988).

The first section of this chapter focuses on the debate about the appropriate scope of this role.[b] It looks at the core issue of when, if ever, testimony by mental health professionals should be prohibited or substantially limited. On the assumption that mental health professionals should be permitted to testify as experts in some or all of these contexts, the second section examines the types of professionals who should qualify as experts, the proper bases for expert opinions, and the form that those opinions should take.

II. ADMISSIBILITY OF CLINICAL OPINION TESTIMONY

To evaluate the admissibility issue, further knowledge of the topics the law requires mental health professionals to address is necessary. Also essential is some understanding of the law's framework for deciding when evidence is admissible.

Legally Relevant Behavior. As noted in the introduction, one can think of government-sponsored deprivations of liberty under three rubrics: the punishment model, the prevention model, and the protection model. The differences between these models are developed in detail in following chapters. Here only enough will be said to make clear the types of issues that need to be addressed under each system when people with mental disability are involved.

The punishment model, epitomized by the criminal justice system, is primarily concerned with gauging one's culpability. Only if a person is considered sufficiently culpable will he or she be sanctioned. Mental disorder is usually considered relevant under this model because it is thought to diminish or eliminate one's culpability. An individual's responsibility for his or her acts is reduced, it is believed, to the extent mental disorder blunts perception and awareness or makes it difficult to control behavior.

A prevention system, exemplified by commitment, is not interested in culpability for past acts but in preventing future ones. Intervention is authorized if it is predicted that harm may occur. Mental disorder is considered relevant here because it may be related to a propensity toward harmful behavior directed at others or oneself. Its presence also allows the law to hypothesize that a person's dangerousness can be "treated," a hypothesis which, again, can only be proven by making a prediction (as to the person's responsiveness to treatment).

The protection model focuses on neither culpability for one's acts or one's propensities but on one's ability to perform certain functions at the present time. Mental disorder is relevant here because it may make someone dysfunctional in legally relevant ways. It is thought to render a person unable to exercise his or her prerogatives in a capable manner.

b. The extent to which clinicians should be allowed to function as legal decision-makers is an issue left for later chapters.

In short, laws which contemplate depriving the people with mental disorder of liberty pose four issues: (1) the mental disorder predicate; and whether mental disorder is connected with (2) one's responsibility for one's past actions (as with the insanity defense); or (3) one's future behavior (as with civil commitment); or (4) one's ability to function (as with competency to stand trial). Put functionally, the questions posed by the legal system focus on a person's: (1) normality; (2) responsibility; (3) propensity; and (4) competency.

Evidence Law: The Framework of Analysis. All four of these issues are difficult ones. Crucial to determining how they should be addressed is the law of evidence, since it regulates the types of information courts may consider. In this chapter, we will rely on the federal rules of evidence as the guiding source of evidence law, since they reflect the consensus view on the issues we are examining. A brief foray into these rules is necessary as an introduction.

All evidence, whether lay or expert, must clear what could be called "the relevance/prejudice hurdle." Under the federal rules of evidence, evidence is relevant if it has "any tendency to make the existence of any fact that is of consequence to the determination of the action more probable or less probable than it would be without the evidence." Fed.R.Evid. 401. If evidence is found to be relevant, then it is generally admissible unless "its probative value is substantially outweighed by the danger of unfair prejudice, confusion of the issues, or misleading the jury, or by considerations of undue delay, waste of time, or needless presentation of cumulative evidence." Fed.R.Evid. 403. In short, the admissibility of testimony depends initially upon how one balances its probative value against its potential for misleading or confusing the factfinder.

When a witness wishes to go beyond a description of "facts" which he or she has observed or has knowledge of, and instead wants to offer an "opinion" about those facts, additional considerations come into play. Generally, only if the witness is qualified as an "expert" is opinion testimony permissible. Of course, any testimony is inferential to some extent. According to federal rule 701, even the lay witness may recite "opinions or inferences which are rationally based on the perception of the witness and helpful to a clear understanding of his testimony or the determination of a fact in issue." This rule recognizes that the difference between "facts" and "inferences" is difficult to discern at best, but that the lay witness generally must avoid conclusory language unless common everyday usage requires it to make the testimony understandable and helpful. On the other hand, the expert witness is not so limited. According to Rule 702, "[i]f scientific, technical, or other specialized knowledge will assist the trier of fact to understand the evidence or to determine a fact in issue, a witness qualified as an expert by knowledge, skill, experience, training, or education, may testify thereto in the form of an opinion or otherwise, if (1) the testimony is based upon sufficient facts or data, (2) the testimony is the product of reliable principles and methods, and (3) the witness has applied the principles and methods reliably to the facts of the case." Put another way, a witness with the appropriate qualifications may offer testimony in the form of an opinion when it is based on sufficient facts, relies on reliable, specialized knowledge and will add to what the factfinder could discern for itself. Of course, the factual basis for the opinion can be and usually is brought out on direct or cross-examination.

Whereas lay witnesses providing evidence on normality, responsibility, propensity, or competency will normally be confined to giving descriptions of actions and speech that they observed and that are relevant to the issue at hand, mental health professionals are usually asked to offer an interpretation of such behavior. Thus, assuming appropriate education and training on the part of the proffered clinician witness (a topic discussed in section III of this chapter), determining the admissibility of his or her testimony must involve three related inquiries: (1) whether its probative value outweighs its potential prejudicial impact; (2) whether it is based on reliable scientific, technical or other specialized knowledge; and (3) whether it will add to what the factfinder can determine for itself. In practice, these three issues can often be lumped together under the query: will the testimony assist the factfinder? But keeping them distinct may be helpful in the following discussion, which looks at the admissibility issue with respect to each of the topics identified above: normality, responsibility, propensity, and competency.

A. NORMALITY

Traditionally, the principal way mental health professionals have provided information about whether someone is mentally disordered (i.e., abnormal or "crazy") is by indicating whether the person has a diagnosis and what that diagnosis is. For example, in insanity cases, testimony as to whether the defendant was suffering from a "mental disease or defect" which rendered him or her insane at the time of the offense is usually framed in terms of diagnostic categories. The following excerpt from the trial of John Hinckley, who shot President Ronald Reagan and three others, captures the flavor of this type of testimony. The selections that follow argue that this type of testimony should be prohibited.

TESTIMONY IN THE HINCKLEY CASE

John Hinckley's attempted assassination of President Reagan took place on March 30, 1981 in the District of Columbia as the president and his entourage were entering the Washington Hilton. Apparently one reason Hinckley shot the president was to impress the actress Jodie Foster. His actions on the day of the offense were allegedly meant to mimic the actions of a character who tried to shoot the president in the film Taxi Driver, in which Foster played a major role. Hinckley's lawyers indicated that he would plead insanity; under the District of Columbia's test for insanity—the American Law Institute, or ALI test—the jury would thus have to decide whether, at the time of the offense, Hinckley was "substantially unable to appreciate the wrongfulness of his act or conform his behavior to the requirements of the law" as a result of "mental disease or defect." Over the seven month period between the assassination attempt and the trial, various mental health professionals for the defense and the prosecution interviewed Hinckley and collected information about his life in an effort to answer this question. The testimony of two of these clinicians on the preliminary issue of whether Hinckley had a "mental disease or defect"—the normality issue—is set out below. William Carpenter was one of the defense's psychiatrists and Park Dietz was one of the prosecution's psychiatrists.

a.) Direct Examination of William T. Carpenter, M.D.

Q. Doctor, yesterday, before we started the chronological development of your exhaustive interview process, I asked you whether you had an opinion as to whether Mr. Hinckley had suffered from a mental disease on March 30, 1981. Do you recall that question?

A. Yes.

Q. And your answer was?

A. Yes, that I had formed an opinion.

Q. Now, would you tell us how you diagnose the defendant's mental illness, mental disease?

A. Yes.

* * *

THE WITNESS: * * * I concluded then that on March 30th, and before, that he did have the following manifestations of mental illness, that he had blunted affect or restricted affect.

This process where he has an incapacity to have an ordinary emotional arousal that should be associated with events in life. Blunt affect is of critical importance because from the beginning of the descriptions of the major psychotic or major psychiatric illnesses the blunted affect has been one of the prime distinctions of the process of one of the psychotic illnesses, so that I concluded that he did have blunted affect and as a symptomatic expression of an illness process.

He also had what technically we would call an "autistic retreat from reality." The autistic refers to the process of pulling into your own inner mind and away from the outer realty * * *.

The third major symptom status that he had is the depression and the associated features, including the suicidal features that were present in Mr. Hinckley.

And the fourth—* * * [t]here was important illness derived manifestations of dysfunction and his ability to work and his ability to establish social bonds. And these were of a severe magnitude and help measure the impact of illness.

The diagnostic labels that I want to mention, as you say in psychiatry, in approaching diagnoses, there are two somewhat overlapping approaches and it may be important to mention both to you.

The American Psychiatric Association has recently accepted a revision in its diagnostic manual and this is called the Diagnostic and Statistical Manual. It is the third volume.

But it has the listing of the different categories of illness and the descriptions and criteria that go with these different categories and there are many different categories of illness.

This manual notices the fact that we cannot draw emphatically clear distinctions between different types of illnesses, that the manifestations of illnesses may overlap so we don't know exactly where to draw the dividing line.

We are better at drawing the dividing line as to whether illness is present or absent than precisely how to define each illness category. For that reason in this diagnostic manual that is used now in this psychiatrists are encouraged to make multiple diagnoses; that is, if a person meets criteria for a number of diagnoses.

So that Mr. Hinckley does meet either full or partial criteria for a large number of diagnoses listed in that manual. It is only useful to—for me to present in my diagnostic findings the way he fits into a couple of major categories.

The first category that I want to mention, it draws from a concept of schizophrenia, which is one of the major psychotic illnesses which was identified at the turn of the century and has usually lifetime implications in terms of the pattern of illness and the outcome of illness.

And conceptually linked to this are personality dysfunctions, that the term "schizotypal and schizoid personality" mean. To define these labels, "schizoid" refers to someone who is withdrawn from social contacts, aloof from them, a sense of the kind of tender feelings that are associated with tender feelings, usually implying a life-long pattern and may be used for a pattern of socialization and alienation.

The schizotypal personality is a very similar personality formation with the difference being that the person has either something eccentric or bizarre or their use of language gets—but some more severe symptoms than otherwise are similar.

And psychiatrists are directed if schizotypal features are there, to use that instead of the diagnosis of schizoid personality.

Mr. Hinckley did meet criteria for both schizotypal and schizoid. He also met criteria for schizophrenia. This is generally thought of as a more severe form of illness, but that has many of the same kinds of personality features, the development of illness is shown through the personality function that schizotypal and schizoid have.

And I would make, using the criteria of the Diagnostic and Statistical Manual, then from the American Psychiatric Association, a diagnosis of Mr. Hinckley of schizophrenia and would not use the label schizotypal and schizoid, because it is the same symptoms. If they are explained by schizophrenia, you would not resort to those.

Mr. Hinckley at this—to some extent on the point of view he had illness manifestation symptoms that meet the criteria for what is called a major affective disorder. For many years the two major severe psychiatric disorders were the schizophrenia and relating conditions and the manic depressive and related conditions.

Mr. Hinckley in his depression reached the criteria for major depressive disorder and, using DSM–III as a guide, one would make—I would make that diagnosis. The only reason to argue against making that diagnosis is if the presence of schizophrenia can potentially explain the disorder mood that he had, the depression that he had, one could account for the depressive components within the single diagnostic framework.

Those are the diagnoses that I would use in terms of DSM–III.

A more broadly used concept in the world for schizophrenia involves a concept which is called "process schizophrenia" and this term is the primary term that I have used in diagnosing Mr. Hinckley. This term is important because it implies a certain form of development of the illness, an illness that usually begins during adolescence or early adulthood. It has usually a slow development so that the first years in the illness will be the illness manifestation, begin with fairly subtle disorders and social functioning and in personality functioning, and it progresses to a more severe psychiatric disorder and psychotic disorder, and that is where the presence of the delusion and ideas of reference, this type of symptom comes in.

And in this concept people who have developed this disorder, in most instances they are persevering impairments in their health. It runs chronic on long-standing courses. So it is typically slow and gradual in development and once reaching the psychotic state, as the person continues to have continued dysfunction and a broad range of social and psychological measures.

Process schizophrenia, which is the diagnostic conclusion I have reached, is related both in concept and related in a genetic basis to the schizotypal and schizophrenic reference as well as overlapping with schizophrenia as defined in DSM–III so that the clinical diagnosis—that I concluded that the illness Mr. Hinckley had on and before March 30th is process schizophrenia.

[Excerpted from page 3295 through page 3304 of the trial transcript.]

* * *

b.) Cross–Examination

Q. Now you testified Friday Mr. Hinckley had been suffering from what you called "process schizophrenia" from 1976, all the way back to 1976.

A. Well, expressing all the difficulties and pinpointing a beginning date for an illness, it began slowly and developed over time.

Q. But as best you can recall that is when he began to have—

A. I refer to '76 as when it began to reach the proportions that one could begin to consider schizophrenic illness present.

Q. In other words, you would have diagnosed him as process schizophrenic if you had seen him in 1976, from your testimony?

A. I don't know. That I would have if I had seen him. I don't know what I would have found out if I had seen him in 1976. Putting the development of the illness into a picture, you are always helped by subsequent developments. That is part of the very nature.

Q. All right.

A. And so when you find out that when symptoms have reached their greatest intensity in any illness, it helps you to interpret things that would be compatible with that illness as they developed earlier. It is like you went back to the earliest stages now that you know somebody had tuberculosis, if you had seen him when he had the first cough, you would have diagnosed it.

* * *

Q. Friday * * * [you testified that] * * * "his process schizophrenia did not become psychotic until 1976, right?" And you answered: "I think that would be the case." You still stick to that now?

A. Yes.

Q. And * * * your answer on the previous page to the same point, [was] "I don't think it was until about then," 1976, "that it developed to an intensity that it reached psychotic proportions." Right?

A. Right.

Q. Are you aware that Mr. Hinckley in the period of 1976 through 1980, was a student at Texas Tech University from time to time?

A. From time to time.

Q. Were you aware, then, as it comes to your attention, that during that period, '76 to '79, when he was there in certain courses he received As; did you learn that?

A. Yes.

Q. And he got some Bs.

A. Yes.

Q. And generally he kept a pretty good grade point average, right?

A. He had a lot of academic difficulty. He dropped a lot of courses because he was having difficulty with them. He had success in some courses.

Q. Well, Doctor, he got an A in writing, didn't he?

A. Yes.

Q. And he got this A in writing during this period you said he was suffering from process schizophrenia; right?

A. Yes.

Q. And you are aware, are you not, that in early 1977, he held a job at a place called Taylor's Supper Club in the Lakewood, Colorado area?

A. Yes, for about five months.

Q. Five months. And I take it you learned that he worked everyday at a busboy job there; right?

A. He didn't come to work quite everyday, but he did work fairly regularly during that period of time. Some absences.

Q. Right. And this is during a period of time when you say he suffered from process schizophrenia; right?

A. Yes.

Q. And you are also aware that in 1976, Mr. Hinckley traveled all by himself to California for several months; right?

A. Yes.

Q. And while he was there, he went trying to sell his songs; right?

A. Yes.

* * *

Q. And this is during a period of time when you say that Mr. Hinckley was a process schizophrenic; right?

A. Well, this is a time when I think it is beginning to develop its magnitude and it is this information from this very period of time that I would fit into that picture, yes.

Q. And then Mr. Hinckley got back from California all by himself in 1976; are you aware of that?

A. Oh, yes.

Q. I mean his parents didn't have to come out and bring him home in their car, did they?

A. Oh, certainly no.

Q. And this is during the time you said he was suffering from process schizophrenia; right?

A. Yes.

Q. You are aware in 1977, he spent a few weeks in California as well; right?

A. Yes.

Q. And again, he went out there by himself, did he not?

* * *

A. Yes.

Q. He didn't have any trouble getting out there. He didn't get lost in Arizona or run into the Grand Canyon, did he?

A. No.

Q. And while he was there he functioned pretty well, did he not?

A. Oh, no. He had impairments—you see, you may want to define "functioning" for me.

Q. He didn't get arrested by the police, he wasn't found walking around with no clothes on or anything of that sort while he was in California to 1977?

A. That's right and he never walked around without clothes.

[Excerpted from page 3517 through page 3524 of the trial transcript.]

c.) Prosecution Rebuttal Testimony (Park Elliott Dietz, M.D.)

Q. All right. Now, let me ask you formally, if you determined whether at the time of the criminal conduct on March 30, 1981 the defendant Hinckley, as a result of mental disease or defect, lacked substantial capacity to conform his conduct to the requirements of the law?

A. I did make such a determination.

Q. What determination did you make?

A. That on March 30, 1981, as a result of mental disease or defect, Mr. Hinckley did not lack substantial capacity to conform his conduct to the requirements of the law.

* * *

Q. All right. Now, I take it you have some reasons for those conclusions?

A. Yes, I do.

Q. . . . [Y]ou have announced diagnosis of four mental disorders in Mr. Hinckley as of March 30, 1981. And you gave them certain labels, did you not?

A. Yes.

Q. Where did those labels come from?

A. Well, like other labels in medicine, these are derived from Greek and Latin words. These specific labels of mental disorder come from the official diagnostic system, the DSM–III.

Q. In each of the four instances that you mentioned were the diagnoses you announced from DSM–III?

A. Yes.

Q. All right. Now, in connection with DSM–III, can you tell us whether this book is designed for medical purposes or for legal purposes?

A. For medical purposes.

Q. And what do you mean by that?

A. I mean that this volume DSM–III is designed to allow physicians to make reliable diagnoses, to exchange information and know what they are talking about with one another, to be able to speak a common language. But that the diagnoses there do not automatically translate into anything legal and certain not into determination of criminal responsibility.

Q. And criminal responsibility to repeat has how many parts?

A. Depending on how one counts it, it would.

Q. As we have counted it, how many does it have?

A. Two [(1) mental disease or defect which causes (2) substantial inability to appreciate the wrongfulness of actions or to control behavior].

Q. DSM–III deals with how many of those two parts?

A. One.

Q. Now, can you tell us, Doctor, with respect to the matter of mental disorders whether there is a range of mental disorders in DSM–III?

A. Yes, there is.

Q. Can you explain the range of mental disorders to the jury?

A. Well, DSM–III covers every conceivable sort of mental disorder from extremely serious to quite minor ones.

The types of disorders within the volume included such things as organic brain syndromes with psychosis, serious depressions with psychosis. Other serious disturbances of mood with psychosis.

It includes neuroses or what are now called anxiety disorders. It includes sorts of personality disorders that I've mentioned and will be talking more about. And it includes what we call situational stress disorders, when in a certain situation a person develops symptoms. For example, after a serious stressful incident.

It includes addictions of various kinds. It even includes tobacco dependence disorder. It ranges from minor to serious. From long-standing to brief. It includes a whole host of conditions.

Q. Can you compare that range in some way to the range that we all might be familiar with in functional medicine?

A. Well, for just about any system of the body there is a range of disorders that can occur. People may, for example, have the sniffles or a cold which is an infection of the respiratory system. They may have more serious infection of the respiratory system like pneumonia and can have life threatening disorders of the respiratory system like pneumonia in a very old person or lung cancer or serious injuries to the lungs.

Q.   Does that same range exist in mental disorders?

A.   A similar range does.

Q.   A similar range. Now, you have already mentioned, actually, certain psychotic disorders, correct?

A.   Yes.

Q.   And can you briefly describe those in terms of the range of mental disorders?

A.   Well, the psychotic disorders, I think, all would agree, are the most serious of the mental disorders. There are many different ways to look at seriousness. I think it is fair to say that the disorders associated with psychoses at least while an individual is psychotic are the most serious.

Q.   Going down the range, if you will, can you tell us the next general category of disorders?

A.   Well, again, it depends on how one classifies it but there is a group of nonpsychotic mental disorders and, generally speaking, the nonpsychotic disorders are considerably less serious than psychotic. Nonpsychotic disorders that are less serious, for example, include the anxiety disorders and the personality disorders. There are other examples.

Q.   All right. You mentioned personality disorders. Where do they fit on this spectrum?

A.   On the nonpsychotic, less serious side.

Q.   And further down or further along are there any other set of disorders that you would care to comment on?

A.   Farther down.

Q.   Along the range, along the spectrum?

A.   Well, the organic mental disorders one associates with psychoses are further up toward the serious end.

Q.   All right.

A.   Many of the anxiety disorders are toward the less serious end.

Q.   In Mr. Hinckley's case, did you find and determine that he had a psychotic disorder?

A.   No.

Q.   Did you find and determine that Mr. Hinckley had any organic disorder?

A.   No.

Q.   Now, where in the range do the disorders that you found in Mr. Hinckley, that is to say, the dysthymic disorder, the narcissistic and the schizoid disorder and mixed personality disorders, fall?

A. These are all within them, the dysthymic is an affective disorder and this is on the less serious side.

* * *

Q. Before I go any further, you are aware of a category in DSM–III called Schizophrenia; is that right?

A. Yes.

Q. Is Schizoid Personality the same as Schizophrenia?

A. No, it is not.

Q. All right, and briefly at this point could you explain your answer?

A. Schizophrenia is a serious mental disorder in which a patient will at least sometimes and frequently for long times be psychotic.

Schizoid Personality Disorder is a personality disorder. It is not a functional psychotic disorder, as we refer to Schizophrenia.

An individual whose problem is Schizoid Personality Disorder does not become psychotic as a result of it, and does not develop some of the symptoms so characteristic of Schizophrenia such as delusions and hallucinations.

Q. Dr. Dietz, in DSM–III, are Schizoid Personality and Schizophrenia in the same categories or in different categories?

A. They are in different chapters altogether.

Q. Now could you tell us a little bit about the nature of the Schizoid Personality Disorder?

A. Yes, I can. As I have mentioned, this, this is the lonely personality disorder. As a consequence of that, people who have the features of Schizoid Personality Disorder tend to do loner sorts of things. Many of these people, for example, will engage in occupations that don't require much interaction with other people.

For example, cowboys frequently don't have to interact much with others and that's the kind of thing that can appeal to someone who is Schizoid.

Computer operators may not have to interact too much with other people. Even librarians, forest rangers. Now, this is not to say that there is any problem with people who engage in these occupations. It's to say that these are occupations that one can do without having to interact much with others. And people perform beautifully at those kinds of professions if, even if they have this disorder. It's a way to, to be able to function well without having to run into the problem that individuals with these disorders run into when they try to interact with others.

Q. Would people with this Schizoid Personality Disorder function in everyday life without any difficulty?

A. I wouldn't say without any difficulty, but I would say they certainly function in everyday life in many ways. The one way that they are not likely to function, and this is part of the definition, is that they don't have friends.

Q. Can they hold jobs?

A. Yes.

Q. Can they go to school?

A. Yes.

Q. Can they travel?

A. Yes.

Q. Now Schizoid Personality, does that mean a person is out of contact with reality or psychotic?

A. No, it does not.

Q. Could you explain to the jury what you saw in Mr. Hinckley on March 30th, 1981, to indicate that he suffered from a Schizoid Personality Disorder on that day?

A. Well, I think there are really only two features that are known to have been present on that date in Mr. Hinckley, and the first of those is what we describe as emotional coldness and aloofness. That is, being, being cruel and unemotional, not becoming involved emotionally with other people.

Q. Does that mean a person is out of contact with reality?

A. No, no, but it may mean that they have trouble making friends.

Q. All right. What are the other characteristics?

A. Well, another one that I think was observable that day was indifference to the feelings of others. There are, one of the things we use to diagnose many of these mental disorders is to, to say that if there is, there are certain things that must not be present, if it's present, then we can't make this diagnosis, and one of those in Mr. Hinckley's case that was not present on March 30, and which we have to make sure wasn't present was no eccentricities of speech, behavior or thought, and there was nothing eccentric about his speech, behavior or his thought that day, and there were many observers I have interviewed to determine that.

* * *

[Excerpted from page 6388 through page 6411 of the trial transcript.]

d.) Cross–Examination

Q. Before we get into the substance of your testimony, I would like to extract an agreement I think we can reach, and that is that you share the view of other defense psychiatrists that Mr. Hinckley on March 30, 1981 was suffering from a mental disease? You do agree with that statement, do you not?

A. No, I do not.

Q. All right. Was it not your testimony on direct examination that Mr. Hinckley suffered a mental disease of dysthymic mental disorder?

A. No. I testified that Mr. Hinckley suffered in the past and indeed on March 30 from a mental disorder.

Q. Are you distinguishing between a mental disease and mental disorder?

A. Yes.

Q. I see.

Would you agree that on March 30, 1981 Mr. Hinckley had a mental illness in a broad sense?

A. I testified about a mental disorder, and I would have some difficulty agreeing with your statement that he suffered from a mental illness.

Q. All right, taking your term as a mental disorder, how do you distinguish that, sir, from a mental disease?

A. Well, a mental disorder is any of the diagnostic categories listed in DSM–III, the guide book for mental disorders, and for the diagnosis of mental disorders. When one switches to the term mental disease or mental illness, one is suggesting that this is a sickness, that it has some kind of biological basis.

That is quite a difference.

Q. So it is your testimony that all of the descriptions of mental conditions in DSM–III constitute mental disorders as compared or contrasted to mental diseases?

A. Yes, sir.

Q. Accepting your qualification, then, you will agree that on March 30, 1981 Mr. Hinckley suffered from a mental disorder?

A. Yes.

Q. And that the question before this Court and this jury would become as to the question of the severity of that disorder?

A. No, sir. The question before the jury is about his criminal responsibility.

* * *

[Excerpted from page 6388 through page 6411 of the trial transcript.]

* * *

Questions and Comments

1. *Use of DSM–III.* The witness' heavy reliance on the diagnostic categories found in the American Psychiatric Association's Diagnostic and Statistical Manual (now in its fourth edition) is typical. You may want to check the criteria for each diagnosis used by the experts by referring to

Appendix A (pp. 1339–1349). Consider also the following commentary on the Hinckley trial from Professor Alan Stone, past president of the APA:

> The discrepancies in the psychiatric testimony [at the Hinckley trial] would be much easier to understand if the defense and prosecution had agreed that there was a thought disorder but disagreed about its extent—for example, whether it was sufficient to be diagnosed psychosis, and whether it was sufficient to negate criminal responsibility. Such agreement would have placed Hinckley in the problem area of psychiatry's familiar nosological disputes. Thus, if both sides had agreed that he was a schizotypal personality or a paranoid personality and the defense said he had gone over into psychosis while the prosecution insisted he had not, every clinician would have understood the problem. How much thought disorder makes a psychosis? But here the prosecution specifically rejected the diagnoses of schizotypal personality and paranoid personality, the character disorders which suggest a thought disorder. This makes the discrepancies harder to understand and harder to explain to the cynics who believe psychiatrists can be hired to say anything.

A Suggested Diagnosis for John Hinckley

> Based on my own reading of the testimony of all the psychiatrists, I believe that before DSM–III, I would have diagnosed John Hinckley as a case of erotomania, and Freud's classic paper written in 1911 would have helped me to clarify Hinckley's psychopathology. Most clinicians have seen patients with delusions of love—a condition that is not that uncommon. There is even a French name for such delusions—Clerambault's syndrome. * * * But erotomania per se no longer appears in DSM–III, and one could debate whether it is or is not a psychosis. It is my own clinical and theoretical opinion that a delusion of love may protect the person against ego decompensation into florid psychosis, and this may have been the case with Hinckley. His pathological attachment to Jodie Foster is in my view crucial not only to his diagnosis but also to his prognosis. It is interesting, however, that delusions of love seem to have disappeared from DSM–III. Such delusions do not make up a separate diagnosis and are not listed as a specific symptom in any of the diagnostic categories of the paranoid spectrum. Perhaps the Hinckley case may also lead us to reconsider this gap in DSM–III.[c]

Evaluating the Psychiatric Diagnoses

> The defense psychiatrists themselves had trouble finding a place for Hinckley in DSM–III. Whether they were oriented psychoanalytically or biologically, their theoretical understanding of the underlying disorder caused them to fight the theoretical diagnostic categories of DSM–III. The defense's experts all had a more powerful commitment to their theory (biological, psychodynamic, or biopsychosocial) of Hinckley's psychiatric condition than they did to the diagnostic nomenclature in DSM–III. If they had been forbidden to use diagnoses (* * * some favor legislation that forbids diagnoses), they would have been released from a constraint against which they struggled. On the other hand, the prose-

c. The revised version of DSM–IV does include such a diagnosis. See "Delusional Disorders", p. 1343 of this book. [footnote by eds.]

cution witnesses seemed to have no theory about Hinckley's disorder and no real explanation of his actions except that he was a bad narcissistic person. Rather, they carefully and conscientiously applied DSM–III.

In evaluating these conclusions about the psychiatric testimony, several things should be kept in mind. First, the preparation and the quality of the psychiatric testimony in the Hinckley case was far superior to what one usually finds. Second, these experts appear to have genuinely and honestly come to their various conclusions. The Hinckley testimony is not an example of what happens when lawyers buy psychiatric experts for a price. The testimony may have been rehearsed, the experts may have been carefully sorted and selected by the lawyers, but these experts believed what they said. If Hinckley did not fall readily into any DSM–III category, if his disorder is in the gray area between psychosis and personality disorder, then we can see that there was room for honest disagreement. Third, * * * [i]f there was something flawed about the psychiatric testimony, it is in the sense one gets of the psychiatrists getting caught up in and succumbing to the adversarial process. There is a kind of overstatement in their testimony as though they had taken on the responsibility of convincing the jury and outwitting the opposition. Clinical working hypotheses became scientific truths. Clinical possibilities became certainties. And as these truths and certainties from one side meet contradictory truths and certainties from the other side, one has the feeling that psychiatry's credibility hangs in the balance.

Alan Stone, Law, Psychiatry and Morality 92–93 (1984).

2. *The purpose of diagnosis in an insanity trial.* The witnesses obviously agree that Hinckley had *some* diagnosable mental disorder. But, given the wide array of behavior that can be called disordered and that is found in DSM, that finding alone is insufficient as a predicate for the insanity defense. The mental disorder must be a "serious" one. Why did Dietz insist on the term "mental disorder" as opposed to "mental disease"? Using the language of the Federal Rules of Evidence, is the diagnostic testimony "relevant" to deciding whether Hinckley's mental disorder was serious? Reliable? Does it "assist" the factfinder? Consider the following excerpt.

STEPHEN MORSE, CRAZY BEHAVIOR, MORALS & SCIENCE: AN ANALYSIS OF MENTAL HEALTH LAW

51 S.Cal.L.Rev. 527, 604–613.
(1978).

* * *

The crucial question for the law is not, or at least should not be, whether the actor allegedly fits one of the mental health diagnostic categories, but whether the actor behaves crazily enough to warrant special legal treatment on moral and social grounds. The law must therefore decide on legal grounds and for legal purposes which cases fit this criterion of sufficient craziness. These decisions should not and cannot be totally dependent on scientific categories that may serve other purposes, and experts should not testify about whether an actor suffers from a mental disorder or even about whether the actor is normal. Conclusions about mental disorder or psychiatric normality are not particularly and precisely relevant to *legal* decisions about normality. Rather, for various reasons, experts should be limited to describing behavior to the factfinder that laypersons may not notice but that may be relevant to legal decisionmaking.

The first reason for limiting experts to descriptions of behavior is that their conclusions are based, in part, on mental health diagnostic categories that are generally overinclusive. These categories are much broader than the crazy behaviors that seem to compel special legal treatment. The various disorder categories delineated by both the present and proposed diagnostic manuals of the American Psychiatric Association may be ranged along a quantitative and qualitative continuum of craziness. Some categories seem to describe behavior that would be considered quite crazy, at least in its extreme forms, by anyone. Others describe behavior that would not be considered crazy and, at worst, would be considered normally quirky.

Thus, present definitions of mental disorder cover such a wide range of behavior that vast percentages of the population may be considered disordered, including most persons whom the legal system would not consider crazy or different enough to warrant special treatment. A large proportion of the diagnostic categories simply do not describe behavior that seems very crazy and the inexorable product of a deranged mind. If no conclusions about diagnosis, illness, disease, or abnormality are drawn by experts, the law will avoid the confusion engendered by the metaphysical complexities of the mental health debate about which behaviors ought to be labeled and considered illnesses. Further, whether behavior is considered disordered for clinical or research purposes should not be dispositive of legal decision-making where narrower moral and social definitions of craziness are appropriate.

The second reason for limiting experts to descriptions of behavior is that particular diagnoses do not *accurately* convey legally relevant information concerning the person's behavior. A diagnosis will not inform the law whether, how, or to what degree an actor behaves crazily. The major related reasons for this fact are that present psychiatric diagnoses are not highly reliable or descriptively precise.

In behavioral science, reliability is a complex construct, but for the purposes of legal decisionmaking about abnormality it can be defined as the accuracy of a diagnosis. The preeminent "measuring tool" used to make diagnoses is a human observer applying the present diagnostic categories to behavior. Unlike much physical disorder that often can be verified by various tests that measure pathology (whether or not the cause of the symptom, syndrome, or condition is known), there is no objective, empirical referent of *mental* disorder other than crazy behavior itself. Indeed, the only possible verification of the presence of mental disorder is by a consensus of those who have observed the actor's behavior. There is no postmortem pathological examination or other diagnostic procedure to verify conclusively whether or not a person suffered from a particular disorder or any disorder at all. Even if objectively verifiable referents other than behavior itself are present, an actor is not considered mentally disordered unless he behaves crazily.

In a sense, there is no such thing as an independently "correct" or "incorrect" mental health diagnosis; there are only agreed on and disagreed on diagnoses. The crucial issue, then, is the extent of agreement achieved by professional diagnosticians when they apply their categories of disorder to behavior itself. The best evidence of the reliability of present diagnostic categories indicates that if two professionals independently diagnose a person on the basis of the same or similar data, it is rare for them to agree on the diagnosis in more than half the cases. The large amount of disagreement is not narrowed appreciably by limiting the possible diagnoses to broad diagnostic categories. Thus, mental health diagnoses are not terribly reliable; people who do not have mental disorder or a specific disorder will be diagnosed as having it, and vice versa. Of course, in clear cases everyone will agree the actor is crazy, but such cases are few.

* * *

The major cause of diagnostic unreliability—criterion variance—further explains why particular diagnoses do not convey legally relevant information. Criterion variance is both a general cause of unreliability and a bar in specific cases to the ability of a diagnosis to convey precise information, even when observers agree on the diagnosis. The diagnostic categories of mental disorders are descriptions of allegedly recurring clusters of behaviors, that is, of recurring patterns of thoughts, feelings, and actions. It is hypothesized that each category describes a more or less distinguishable disorder. The present and proposed diagnostic categories, however, are vague and overlap; each includes a quite heterogeneous range of behavior. Some persons who receive the most severe diagnoses that seem to map legal craziness, such as "schizophrenia," may not be crazy enough to warrant special legal treatment. Vastly different behavior, ranging from only mildly to wildly crazy, may properly fit into the same and most serious diagnostic categories. Thus, even if two psychiatrists do agree on a diagnosis, it is impossible to know whether social and moral purposes will be served by special legal treatment unless the behavior itself is described to the factfinder.

* * *

* * * There is still a role, however, for expert assistance and expert testimony in deciding whether an actor is crazy.

Because experts interact with all types of crazy persons far more often than laypersons, they may be especially sensitive to or inquire about behavior that would go unnoticed by laypersons. Laypersons may not know to ask, for example, if a person hears voices, entertains crazy beliefs, or has trouble sleeping or staying awake. Because the expert is attuned to crazy behavior, he may help the factfinder attend to a fuller range of the actor's behavior. Nonetheless, the expert need not and should not report conclusions about mental disorder, abnormality, or even craziness; these are legal determinations for the judge or jury. It is far more precise and useful to the judge or jury if the expert simply describes his observations of behavior. For the legal question of normality, then, the relevant expertise of mental health professionals is not their ability to draw inferences from data or to form opinions. Rather, their special skill is observational—to perceive behaviors that nonexperts may fail to notice. The expert should describe, in as much precise but commonsense detail as possible, his observations of how the person thinks, feels, and acts. The test of relevance for the testimony of experts and laypersons alike should be whether their observations of the actor's behavior shed light on the question of whether the actor is crazy.

For example, experts should not testify that an actor is "hallucinatory and probably schizophrenic." Instead, the expert should testify that the actor told the expert that on some (specified) occasions, the actor heard or hears voices despite the fact that no one was or is talking to him and the voices told or tell him the following (specified) things. For another example, experts should not testify that an actor "suffers from loose associations when questioned on an ego-threatening topic and is therefore probably schizophrenic." Rather, the expert should testify that when the expert asked the actor certain (specified) questions about topics that seem to mean a lot to the actor, the actor responded in the following way (specified by examples). Of course, if laypersons such as family, friends, coworkers, or neighbors are aware of such behavior, they too can testify about it.

Using lay as well as expert testimony about the actor's behavior, the decisionmaker can then decide if the person is sufficiently crazy to be an appropriate candidate for the application of mental health laws. If the factfinder's response to the behavioral data it hears is "so what," then the actor probably does not meet the legal criterion of mental disorder; if the response is "that's crazy" or "he's crazy," then the criterion of mental abnormality may be met.

* * *

Questions and Comments

1. *The nature of Morse's argument about diagnoses.* Is Morse arguing that diagnostic testimony is irrelevant (i.e., has no tendency to make the fact at issue—craziness—more or less probable)? That it is relevant, but unduly misleading or confusing? Or that it is not based on reliable specialized knowledge that adds to what the factfinder can determine for itself?

Note that present practice usually requires witnesses to give the basis of their opinions. Federal Rule 705 states that "[t]he expert may testify in terms of opinion or inference and give his reasons therefore without prior disclosure of the underlying facts or data, unless the judge requires otherwise." But the Rule also states "[t]he expert may in any event be required to disclose the underlying facts or data on cross-examination." Thus, in part of the Hinckley trial testimony that is not included in the previous excerpt, the factual basis for the diagnoses given by the witnesses were brought out on direct and cross-examination. For instance, to bolster his diagnosis of process schizophrenia, Dr. Carpenter described Hinckley's beliefs that a "union with Jodie Foster was in some sense ordained," that they "could become an extraordinary couple," and that by killing President Reagan he would gain Foster's "respect and love;" Carpenter labeled these beliefs "delusions"— often defined as "fixed false beliefs," or incorrect beliefs that are unshakable. He also described Hinckley's feeling that, as Reagan went into the Hilton and waved at the crowd, the President's attention was aimed at him in particular, a phenomenon Carpenter termed an "idea of reference," or a tendency to "interpret in a highly personal and idiosyncratic way—that is, a personal and unusual way—what may be common-place events." Dr. Dietz, on the other hand, testified that Hinckley was not delusional about Jodie Foster, but "recognized throughout that the relationship was one-sided;" at most he had "unrealistic hopes" that a relationship would materialize and that his assassination of Reagan would "impress upon her who he is and cause her to remember him." He also testified that, with respect to Reagan's waving at the crowd, Hinckley himself stated only that Reagan had looked "right at me, and I waved back. I was kind of startled but maybe it was just my imagination." According to Dietz, at most Hinckley thought that "the President couldn't see anybody else [because most of the people had cameras] and didn't intend to communicate anything other than 'hello.'"

If this and other descriptive data are provided, are diagnoses helpful or, as Morse argues, merely superfluous? In *Washington v. United States*, 390 F.2d 444 (D.C.Cir.1967), Judge Bazelon, one of the country's most influential judges on mental health law matters, wrote that a trial judge should limit "use of medical labels [like] schizophrenia" and require experts to explain them, but should not bar them altogether, because "they sometimes provide a convenient and meaningful method of communication." Consider also the expert testimony in *Clark v. Arizona*, 548 U.S. 735, 126 S.Ct. 2709, 165 L.Ed.2d 842 (2006), reprinted in full at pp. 587–601. There the defendant killed a police officer who came to his car to tell him to turn down his radio; the prosecution argued that Clark had intentionally played his radio loudly to lure the officer to the car. The defendant asserted an insanity defense, based on a diagnosis of schizophrenia; he claimed he thought the officer was a space alien. The expert testified that people with schizophrenia often use loud music to drown out their hallucinatory voices and also often perceive people to be aliens. Is this testimony helpful within the meaning of the rules of evidence?

2. *The reliability of diagnoses.* Morse notes that, because diagnoses are constructs rather than "facts," there is no independent method of determining whether a diagnosis is correct or not correct (or "valid" or "invalid," to use behavioral science terminology). Rather validity can only be indirectly determined through an assessment of the extent to which different raters agree that a given diagnosis is correct (i.e., a "reliability" assessment). As Morse states, the reliability of most diagnoses is far from perfect. But field tests of the new diagnostic scheme introduced by DSM–III, conducted in two

phases between 1977 and 1980, indicated that inter-rater agreement may be better than the one out of two ratio Morse, who relied on earlier data, reported in the above excerpt. The tests showed that for some major diagnostic categories the inter-rater agreement was quite high: organic disorders (79% in the first phase, 76% in the second phase); schizophrenia (81% in both phases), paranoid disorders (66% and 75%); mood disorders (69% and 83%); impulse disorders (28% and 80%); personality disorders (56% and 65%). This improved diagnostic reliability presumably resulted from the more precise diagnostic criteria found in DSM–III. In other words, the results of the field tests suggest that DSM–III has reduced the criterion variance of which Morse writes.

However, some have questioned the methodology of the DSM–III field tests, Herb Kutchins & Stuart A. Kirk, "The Reliability of DSM–III: A Critical Review," 1986 Social Work Res. & Abstr. 3 (1986), and others have had difficulty replicating their results, at least in the emergency context. Ahmed Aboraya et al., "The Reliability of Psychiatric Diagnosis Revisited: The Clinician's Guide to Improve the Reliability of Psychiatric Diagnosis," 3(1) Psychiatry 41 (2006) (reliability is poor in clinical settings unless evaluators have two to three hours to devote to diagnosis); Samuel Fennig et al., "Comparison of Facility and Research Diagnoses in First–Admission Psychotic Patients," 151 Am. J. Psychiat. 1423, 1426 (1994)(57.1% agreement on schizophrenia); Paul Lieberman & Frances Baker, "The Reliability of Psychiatric Diagnosis in the Emergency Room," 36 Hosp. & Comm. Psychiat. 291 (1985) (41% agreement on schizophrenia, 50% agreement on mood disorders; 37% on organic disorder). Moreover, for sub-categories of the major diagnostic classifications (e.g., subtypes of schizophrenia, schizoid personality disorder), the agreement in the field trials was often much lower. See also, Graham Mellsop, et al. "The Reliability of Axis II of DSM–III," 139 Am J. Psychiat. 1360 (1982) (reliability of personality disorder diagnoses in everyday clinical setting ranged from 49% for antisocial personality to 1% for schizoid personality). See generally, David Faust & Jay Ziskin, "The Expert Witness in Psychology and Psychiatry," 241 Science 31 (1988)("A number of . . . studies show[] that rate of disagreement of specific diagnostic categories often equals or exceeds rate of agreement").

3. *Other causes of unreliability.* Although, as Morse indicates, criterion variance is the major cause of diagnostic unreliability, there are other causes as well, which are worth noting not only because they may infect diagnostic assessments but also because they can influence assessments of responsibility, propensity, and competency as well.

BRUCE ENNIS & THOMAS LITWACK
PSYCHIATRY AND THE PRESUMPTION OF EXPERTISE:
FLIPPING COINS IN THE COURTROOM
62 Cal.L.Rev. 693, 719–729.
(1974).

* * *

REASONS WHY PSYCHIATRIC JUDGMENTS ARE UNRELIABLE AND INVALID

* * *

A. *Orientation and Training*

It has been suggested that psychiatrists are prone to diagnose mental illness and to perceive symptoms in ambiguous behavior because they are trained in medical school that it is safer to suspect illness and be wrong, than to reject illness and be wrong. In other words, "being a mental health professional may constitute a set to perceive mental illness...."[90]

In addition, each school of psychiatry has a different view of what mental illness is, how it is caused, and how it should be treated. Substantial evidence suggests that psychiatric judgments are strongly influenced by these different schools of thought and training. Pasamanick, Dinitz, and Lefton, for example, inferred from their findings that:

> ... despite their protestations that their point of view is always the individual patient, clinicians in fact may be so committed to a particular school of psychiatric thought that the patient's diagnosis and treatment is largely predetermined. Clinicians ... may be selectively perceiving only those characteristics and attributes of their patients which are relevant to their own pre-conceived system of thought. As a consequence, they may be overlooking other patient characteristics which would be considered crucial by colleagues who are otherwise committed....

B. *Context*

* * *

[T]he effect of "suggestion" or "set" was examined in a study in which an actor portrayed a healthy man while talking about himself in a diagnostic interview with a clinician. The interview was recorded and played to groups of a) graduate students in clinical psychology, b) psychiatrists, c) law students, and d) undergraduates. Before playing the tape, however, a prestige figure—a different person for each group—told the groups that the interview was interesting because the subject "looked neurotic but actually is quite psychotic." As a control four comparable groups heard the taped interview but were given no prestige suggestion for "psychosis." After hearing the tape, the groups were asked to assign the interviewee to one of 30 specified diagnostic categories. None of the control groups diagnosed the subject as psychotic, and the majority diagnosed him as healthy. By contrast, 60 percent of the psychiatrists, 30 percent of the undergraduates, 28 percent of the psy-

90. In one study two groups of graduate students in clinical psychology viewed a taped interview and were asked to evaluate the interviewee. One group represented the behaviorist and the other the psychoanalytic orientation. Behaviorists are trained to describe carefully the behavior an individual manifests but to refrain from making any judgments or inferences about that individual or his behavior; analysts are more willing to make such speculations. Half the clinicians were told the interviewee in the film was a "job applicant," and half were told he was a "patient." It was found that the behaviorists rated the subject approximately the same (on an adjustment rating scale) regardless of the "set;" the analysts, on the other hand, agreed with the behaviorists on the adjustment of the "job applicant" but saw the "patient" as a much more disturbed person.

chologists, 17 percent of the law students, and 11 percent of the graduate psychology students diagnosed psychosis. The authors conclude that prestige suggestion influences diagnosis, and that an initial diagnosis "may have a profound effect" upon a subsequent diagnosis by influencing "interpersonal perception, whether or not the [initial] diagnostic label refers to a disease which actually exists." In other words, clinicians often perceive what they expect to perceive and the impact of suggestion on clinical perception may be profound.

In a study of pseudo-patients, eight sane individuals feigning one symptom of schizophrenia were admitted to various mental hospitals with that diagnosis. Rosenhan found that even though immediately after admission the pseudo-patients ceased displaying that symptom and behaved normally,

> once a person is designated abnormal, all of his other behaviors and characteristics are colored by that label. Indeed, that label is so powerful that many of the pseudo-patient's normal behaviors were overlooked entirely or profoundly misinterpreted.

For example, when several of the pseudo-patients took notes of their experiences, that activity was noted in three of their records as "an aspect of their pathological behavior." The purpose of Rosenhan's study was to determine whether "the salient characteristics that lead to diagnoses reside in the patients themselves or in the environment and contexts in which observers find them." Although the pseudo-patients related absolutely normal life histories, Rosenhan found that "diagnoses were in no way affected by the relative health of the circumstances of a pseudo-patient's life. Rather, the reverse occurred: the perception of his circumstances was shaped entirely by the diagnosis."

C. Time

Since even "normal" people speak and behave differently from one day to the next, it is no less natural for an allegedly mentally ill individual to appear agitated one day and composed the next. Consequently, the timing of a prospective patient's examination may substantially influence the diagnosis he or she is given. In his 1967 review of studies, Zubin found that the consistency over time of specific diagnoses of nonorganic conditions is quite low, and that even the "broad diagnostic categories appear to display a low order of consistency [about 50 percent] over time." In a related study Edelman found that diagnostic impressions change by a fourth interview-therapy session about 25 percent of the time. He also noted that:

> The typical procedure for establishing a diagnosis is a single unstandardized interview, the results of which may be augmented by psychological testing. An implicit assumption of this procedure is that interviewee behavior has been adequately sampled in the allotted time span and that the interviewee is sufficiently motivated to reveal all pertinent information. Yet, there are numerous studies which indicate that interviewee behavior is mediated by complex

process variables suggesting that such assumptions may not always be justified.

In other words, even if a patient's behavior is consistent over time, different aspects of that behavior may be observed at different times.

D. Class and Culture

There is considerable evidence that psychiatric judgments are strongly influenced by the socio-economic backgrounds of the clinician and patient. Philips and Draguns reviewed the literature from 1966 to 1969 and concluded:

> ... The influence of the client's socio-economic class in facilitating the attribution of some, and impeding the application of other, nosological designations is particularly well documented ... [T]he findings converge in suggesting social distance as the mediating variable. Across socio-economic or other subcultural lines, the middle class diagnostician is prone to assign categories of severe psychopathology. . . .

In a controlled experiment, Lee and Temerlin found that the diagnoses of psychiatric residents were highly influenced by the imagined socio-economic history of the patient (and by the perceived diagnoses of other, prestigious psychiatrists) independent of the clinical picture presented. A lower socio-economic history biased diagnosis toward greater illness and poorer prognosis. Similarly, according to studies conducted by Ordway, clinicians may be influenced to conclude that lower socio-economic class individuals are dangerous because such individuals are presumed to be impulsive and therefore more prone to violence.

* * *

E. Personal Bias

The factor which may most influence diagnosis is the clinician's own personality, value system, self-image, personal preferences, and attitudes.

Grosz and Grossman present evidence suggesting that the clinicians' varying personal biases may account for the significant differences in their evaluation of ambiguous and emotionally charged case history data. They summarize their findings, as follows:

> ... The more complex, ill-defined, ambiguous, unfamiliar and uninformative the data, the more strongly do the observer's set, focused attention, expectation, bias and other intra-observer conditions come into play and influence his perception, judgment, and decision. . . . The possibility exists that such judgments are less informative about the patient whom they are meant to describe than about the clinician who makes them. They may reveal the clinician's concepts of norms or his toleration of deviations compared to those of his peers, his clinical orientation and attitudes toward certain aspects of

the patient's history, his clinical experience and interests, and perhaps even his own background and personality.

Their conclusions are borne out by others. For instance, Dickes, Simons, and Weisfogel demonstrate that the unconscious conflicts of clinicians often cause distortions in perception, and misapprehension of the patient's true condition. And in the context of sanity hearings Pugh found that the ultimate determinations are strongly influenced by the personal idiosyncracies of the examining psychiatrist.

Strupp found that therapists' perceptions of a patient presented in a film interview varied according to the therapist's experience and his attitude toward the patient. As an illustration of the latter factor, if for some reason the therapist disliked the patient the result was often a poor prognostic evaluation. Braginsky and Braginsky suggest a possible context in which a psychiatrist might develop a dislike for a patient. Their study showed that mental health professionals view patients who express radical political views as more disturbed than patients who voice the same psychiatric complaints, but whose political views are more conventional. They also discovered that voicing criticism of the mental health profession, whether from a radical or conservative perspective, may substantially increase a patient's psychopathology in the eyes of mental health professionals, while flattering the profession tends to decrease a patient's otherwise perceived symptomatology. Numerous other studies confirm that the clinician's personal values and attitudes strongly influence diagnosis and judgment.

* * *

Questions and Comments

1. *Rosenhan Study: Labelling and normality.* Ennis and Litwak refer to the Rosenhan study, probably the most controversial of all the research addressing the problem of diagnostic reliability. In that study, as Ennis and Litwak report, eight "normal" individuals showed up at various mental hospitals with feigned symptoms (specifically, they all reported having an auditory hallucination). Otherwise they acted normally. All but one were diagnosed with schizophrenia and all were admitted to the hospital. Their behavior after admission was normal; they never again reported hearing unusual sounds or voices. Although all were eventually discharged (with a diagnosis of schizophrenia in remission), they spent an average of 19 days in the hospital, with the range from 7 to 52 days.

Some have argued that it would have been much more disturbing if the pseudopatients had *not* been admitted for further investigation, since auditory hallucinations are considered indicative of schizophrenia. Kety commented: "If I were to drink a quart of blood and, concealing what I had done, come to the emergency room of any hospital vomiting blood, the behavior of the staff would be quite predictable. If they labeled and treated me as having a bleeding ulcer, I doubt that I could argue convincingly that medical science does not know how to diagnose that condition." Seymour Kety, "From Rationalization to Reason," 131 Am.J.Psychiat. 957 (1974). Does Kety's response explain all of the phenomena observed by Rosenhan's pseudopatients? Spitzer has suggested that, to some extent at least, the study reflects staffing and resource problems rather than deficiencies in psychiatric judgment. Robert Spitzer, "More on Pseudoscience in Science and the Case for Psychiatric Diagnosis," 33 Arch.Gen.Psychiat. 459 (1976).

2. *Implications of variance.* Ways of trying to minimize the effect of the distorting influences described by Ennis and Litwack and Rosenhan are for the most part self-evident, although not always successful. For example multiple interviews by independent interviewers might alleviate the effects of training, context, time and bias. Probably the best minimization technique, already alluded to, is to improve the criteria for decision-making. For instance, if diagnostic criteria are made more precise the possibility that observer bias would affect the ultimate diagnosis should be reduced. Thus, to the extent DSM–IV and its successors reduce criterion variance, the potential for other factors to cause variance should be reduced as well.

Nonetheless, it is probable that diagnostic and other criteria will always carry some ambiguity; greater precision is unlikely to remove entirely the effects of the influences described by Ennis and Litwack. Does this fact make all or most psychiatric judgments so suspect that they should be barred in legal proceedings? Does replacing diagnoses with "descriptive" information solve the problem? Or are "descriptions of facts" just as susceptible to the influences described above?

3. *The admissibility of other types of expert testimony.* Other types of expert testimony have significant validity and reliability problems as well. For instance, one study found that police crime labs misidentify paint samples 51 percent of the time, drug samples 18 percent of the time, blood samples 71 percent of the time, and firearms 28 percent of the time. Joseph Peterson et al., Crime Laboratory Proficiency Testing Research Program: Final Report (1978). Error rates in identifying handwriting and voices may also be over 50% under certain circumstances. David L. Faigman et al., 4 Science in the Law: Forensic Science Issues 346 (2005) (studies in 1980s indicate that handwriting experts correct only 57% of time); 538 (talker identification accuracy ranges from 40 to 80%). Yet courts often allow experts to testify about these matters. Id. 231–38; 298–304; 504–05.

The testimony of economists in antitrust cases is another interesting example of expertise in action. Battles of the experts in such cases are much more common than in insanity cases. As Younger noted:

> Unlike any other country, we submit many issues to the courts that don't turn on factual determinations at all. Should I.B.M. be broken up? Is it good for America to break up A.T. & T.? We pretend those are factual questions and call economists to testify, but they're simply a matter of opinion. And in virtually every case in this country in which experts end up on the witness stand there are vast possibilities for honest differences of opinion. In a case where opinions can reasonably differ on a question, each lawyer simply scouts around until he finds an expert who has an opinion that comports with his client's interest. Experts can testify in good faith and still be testifying to opposites.

Reported in John Jenkins, "Expert's Day in Court," New York Times Magazine, Dec. 11, 1983, p. 98, col. 4. Despite the lack of precision in economic science, courts have allowed experts to offer opinions about market conditions, the opportunities for collusion, market behavior and whether industries conspired to form a cartel. See, e.g., *In re Japanese Electronic Products Antitrust Litigation*, 723 F.2d 238, 280 (3d Cir.1983); reversed on other grounds, 475 U.S. 574, 106 S.Ct. 1348, 89 L.Ed.2d 538 (1986).

Do these examples from other legal arenas support retaining diagnostic and other psychiatric opinion testimony? A revamping of *all* expert testimony? Or are they different from psychiatric testimony in significant ways? Consider these questions again after reviewing the materials on responsibility assessments.

B. RESPONSIBILITY

The relationship between mental disorder and responsibility is most obviously raised by the insanity defense, but is also implicated by a number of criminal law doctrines. Generally, the criminal law assumes that the effect of mental disorder is either "cognitive" or "volitional." In the first instance, the focus is on one's awareness and perceptions about one's actions at the time of the offense; in the second, the emphasis is on one's ability to control one's behavior at the time of the offense. The following case deals with the mental health profession's expertise on the latter issue.

UNITED STATES v. LEWELLYN

United States Court of Appeals, Eighth Circuit, 1983.
723 F.2d 615.

FAGG, CIRCUIT JUDGE.

[Gary Lewellyn, a Des Moines stockbroker, was indicted on fifteen counts of embezzlement, making false statements, and mail fraud for converting over $17 million in money and securities from two Iowa banks. In response to the government's pretrial motion, the district court ruled that Lewellyn could not rely on a defense of insanity "by reason of pathological gambling" and excluded evidence related to that defense. Lewellyn was convicted on all counts. On appeal, he contended that the district court erred in precluding his insanity defense. The test for insanity was the ALI test, which recognizes a defense, *inter alia*, when "mental disease or defect" causes a person to lack "substantial capacity ... to conform his conduct to the requirements of the law."]

We have recognized that in order to raise the issue of insanity a defendant must make a minimum showing. A defendant is presumed sane, but the introduction of evidence of insanity dispels the presumption and subjects the prosecution to the burden of proving sanity beyond a reasonable doubt. *United States v. Dresser*, 542 F.2d 737, 742 (8th Cir.1976), citing *Davis v. United States*, 160 U.S. 469, 486–88, 16 S.Ct. 353, 357–58, 40 L.Ed. 499 (1895). In *Dresser* we referred to this threshold showing as a "prima facie case of insanity." 542 F.2d at 742 n. 7.

[I]n the present case we need not decide whether pathological gambling may never be grounds for an insanity defense. In the particular circumstances of this case we are concerned with the connection between pathological gambling and collateral criminal activity. To make the required minimum showing of insanity Lewellyn had to show that at least some pathological gamblers lack substantial capacity to conform their conduct to the requirements of laws prohibiting criminal activities like embezzlement. We now turn to the record to determine whether Lewellyn made a showing which would have allowed him to rely on an insanity defense at trial.

DSM–III [i.e., Diagnostic and Statistical Manual of Mental Disorders (3d ed.1980)] contains the following description of pathological gambling:

> The essential features are a chronic and progressive failure to resist impulses to gamble and gambling behavior that compromises, disrupts, or damages personal, family, or vocational pursuits. The gambling preoccupation, urge, and activity increase during periods of stress. Problems that arise as a result of the gambling lead to an intensification of the gambling behavior. Characteristic problems include loss of work due to absences in order to gamble, defaulting on debts and other financial responsibilities, disrupted family relationships, borrowing money from illegal sources, forgery, fraud, embezzlement, and income tax evasion.

> Commonly these individuals have the attitude that money causes and is also the solution to all their problems. As the gambling increases, the individual is usually forced to lie in order to obtain money and to continue gambling, but hides the extent of the gambling. There is no serious attempt to budget or save money. When borrowing resources are strained, antisocial behavior in order to obtain money for more gambling is likely. Any criminal behavior—e.g., forgery, embezzlement, or fraud—is typically nonviolent. There is a conscious intent to return or repay the money.

Id. at 291. The diagnostic criteria for pathological gambling included in DSM–III are:

> A.   The individual is chronically and progressively unable to resist impulses to gamble.

> B.   Gambling compromises, disrupts, or damages family, personal, and vocational pursuits, as indicated by at least three of the following:

>> (1) arrest for forgery, fraud, embezzlement, or income tax evasion due to attempts to obtain money for gambling

* * *

> C.   The gambling is not due to Antisocial Personality Disorder.

Id. at 292–93.

The language of DSM–III does not establish that pathological gamblers may lack substantial capacity to refrain from engaging in embezzlement and similar criminal activities. Portions of DSM–III no doubt indicate that criminal activity is often associated with pathological gambling. DSM–III does not state, however, that pathological gamblers who engage in criminal conduct do so because they lack substantial capacity to conform their conduct to the requirements of law, nor does it state anything of equivalent meaning. It is not remarkable, though, that the language of DSM–III does not conform to the legal principles embodied in the ALI insanity rule.

> The purpose of DSM–III is to provide clear descriptions of diagnostic categories in order to enable clinicians and investigators to diagnose, communicate about, study, and treat various mental disorders. The use of this manual for nonclinical purposes, such as determination of legal responsibility, competency or insanity * * * must be critically examined in each instance within the appropriate institutional context.

Id. at 12. When we examine DSM–III carefully within the context of the criminal law we conclude that its language does not establish a relationship between pathological gambling and criminal activity sufficient to constitute insanity under the ALI standard. As a consequence, DSM–III does not alone supply the minimum showing Lewellyn was required to make before he could rely on an insanity defense.

Expert testimony adduced by Lewellyn, couched in terms more like those of the ALI insanity rule, does suggest the requisite connection between pathological gambling and criminal activity because it supports the proposition that some pathological gamblers lack substantial capacity to resist engaging in embezzlement and similar offenses. Dr. Julian Taber, a psychologist, testified that in some instances pathological gamblers are incapable of conforming their conduct to the requirements of law, and are unable to avoid behavior such as forgery, fraud, and embezzlement. Dr. Robert Custer, a psychiatrist, testified that in the late stage of pathological gambling individuals are unable to resist activities like embezzlement or fraud because they have to gamble and they have to obtain money in order to gamble.

Lewellyn is dependent on this scientific expert testimony to sustain his burden of making the required minimum showing that would permit him to rely on an insanity defense at trial. The expert testimony is essential because it supports a proposition not established in DSM–III: that some pathological gamblers lack substantial capacity to refrain from committing embezzlement and similar offenses. We note, however, that established principles control admissibility of scientific evidence. "[W]hile courts will go a long way in admitting expert testimony deduced from a well-recognized scientific principle or discovery, the thing from which the deduction is made must be sufficiently established to have gained general acceptance in the particular field in which it belongs." *Frye v. United States*, 293 F. 1013, 1014 (D.C.Cir.1923). In deciding whether a scientific principle meets the *Frye* standard we have recognized reliability as "one of the most important factors" that should be considered. United States v. Alexander, 526 F.2d 161, 163 (8th Cir.1975). Because our analysis of the *Frye* rule would govern the admission at trial of expert testimony similar to that given at the pretrial hearing, this analysis is equally applicable in determining whether expert testimony adduced by Lewellyn is sufficient to constitute the required minimum showing of insanity.

Pathological gambling has received relatively little scientific attention. Dr. Custer testified that pathological gambling has only recently been recognized as a disease. Both Dr. Taber and Dr. Custer cited the inclusion of pathological gambling in DSM–III, published in 1980, as evidence that the condition is generally accepted as a mental disease by mental health professionals. Pathological gambling was not listed, however, in DSM–II, published in 1968.

From the testimony at the pretrial hearing it is apparent that few psychologists or psychiatrists have had much experience dealing with pathological gamblers. Dr. Taber estimated that there may be perhaps 20 psychologists with some in-depth experience working with pathological gamblers, but he said that to his knowledge he was the only psychologist devoted full-time to their treatment. Dr. Taber knew of no psychiatrist who would work full-time with pathological gamblers. Dr. Custer stated that probably not more than 20 or 25 doctors have had experience with pathological gambling.

There is accordingly little knowledge about pathological gambling within the community of mental health professionals. Dr. Taber testified that in talking with physicians, social workers, and psychologists, he had "found very prevalent ignorance or just lack of concern with the problem." Dr. Custer indicated that it is necessary to spend a significant amount of time working with pathological gamblers in order to understand the problem "because it is so new and there is so very little that has been known about it." Dr. Custer said he does not think many doctors know about pathological gambling, and that as a result they do not recognize it as a disease.

In order to make the necessary minimum showing of insanity Lewellyn was required to demonstrate that there is general acceptance in the fields of psychiatry and psychology of the principle that some pathological gamblers lack substantial capacity to conform their conduct to the requirements of laws prohibiting embezzlement and similar offenses. There is no evidence in the record, however, either in DSM–III or the expert testimony, that this principle is generally accepted in the mental health professions. Indeed, the record shows that the pathological gambling disorder itself has only recently been recognized in DSM–III, and that there is scant experience and limited knowledge concerning this problem. In our view, Lewellyn has failed to show that the opinions espoused by his expert witnesses possess the requisite indicia of scientific reliability.

Because we find that Lewellyn did not make the required minimum showing of insanity, we affirm the district court's exclusion of evidence pertaining to a defense of insanity by reason of pathological gambling.

Questions and Comments

1. *Presumptions and expert testimony.* The court in *Lewellyn* decided that the evidence presented by the defendant did not overcome the presumption of sanity and thus upheld its exclusion by the trial court. In most jurisdictions, the presumption of sanity functions only as a requirement that the defendant produce *some* evidence of insanity in order to get the issue to the jury; as one commentator summarized it, the usual approach is to hold that a "scintilla" of evidence satisfactorily rebuts the presumption. Abraham Goldstein, The Insanity Defense 113 (1967). However, the *Lewellyn* court, relying on precedent, stated that the presumption can be overcome only if a *prima facie* case of insanity is made out by the defendant, thus raising the threshold for admission. Put another way, in most jurisdictions, the defendant overcomes the presumption of sanity if relevant rebuttal evidence (i.e., evidence having any tendency to prove insanity) is presented. But here the court requires the defendant to "establish" insanity to the satisfaction of the court before the jury may hear the evidence.

Relying on the prima facie test for overcoming the presumption of sanity, the *Lewellyn* court found that the language in DSM–III about pathological gambling, by itself, was insufficient. Do you agree? If the court were to adopt the more typical "scintilla" or relevance rule in determining whether the presumption is met, would a diagnosis of pathological gambling be enough? Should a diagnosis, if believed, ever be sufficient by itself to overcome the presumption?

2. *Screening tests*: Frye, *the relevancy rule, and* Daubert. The defendant in *Lewellyn* also relied on the testimony of Drs. Custer and Taber in support of his insanity defense. The court implies that had this testimony been admissible, the defendant would have overcome the presumption of sanity and could have asserted an insanity defense at trial. But it found the testimony inadmissible, relying on a second evidentiary doctrine, announced in *Frye v. United States,* 293 Fed. 1013 (App.D.C.1923). As the court states, the "*Frye* rule" holds that "the thing" from which scientific evidence is deduced "must be sufficiently established to have gained general acceptance in the particular field in which it belongs." Some have criticized the *Frye* rule on the ground that the "general acceptance" standard is confusing and difficult to apply consistently. One commentator has noted that, under the rule, "courts must decide *who* must find the procedure acceptable, they must define exactly *what* must be accepted, and they must determine what methods will be used to establish general acceptance." Paul Gianelli, "The Admissibility of Novel Scientific Evidence: Frye v. United States, A Half–Century Later," 80 Colum.L.Rev. 1197, 1208 (1980). Did the *Lewellyn* court properly address these issues?

A separate criticism of the *Frye* test has to do with its conceptual underpinning. Many commentators reject the *Frye* rule as a means of determining the admissibility of scientific testimony because they feel that the traditional relevance/prejudice inquiry is a more sensitive tool for this purpose. See, e.g., Charles McCormick, Handbook of the Law of Evidence § 203 (6th ed. 2006). Implicit in the relevance inquiry is an accuracy assessment: evidence that is inaccurate has no tendency to make a proposition more or less probable. But if it is not known whether evidence in a particular case is inaccurate, as is often the case with scientific evidence, then exclusion should only occur if the jury is likely to accept it unquestioningly. If, on the other hand, problems with the evidence can be made clear to the jury, it should be admitted and the jury allowed to make up its mind. In other words, questions about the inaccuracy of expert testimony should go to the weight of the evidence and not its admissibility. *Frye* held the opposite. In response to this criticism, it could be argued that the *Frye* rule is merely an application of the relevance/prejudice inquiry in the scientific evidence context. That is, the courts that apply it have decided that scientific evidence is, by its nature, so likely to persuade a jury that it must be "screened" for accuracy before it is admitted. Does this reasoning apply to psychiatric testimony? See Neil J. Vidmar & Regina A. Schuller, "Juries and Expert Evidence: Social Framework Testimony," 1989 Law & Contemp. Probs. 133, 173 (reporting research indicating that jurors do not treat expert behavioral science testimony offered by the defense with an unwarranted aura of accuracy).

The *Frye* and "relevancy" doctrines were the two most prominent screening tests for expert testimony until 1993. In that year, the U.S. Supreme Court decided *Daubert v. Merrell Dow Pharmaceuticals*, 509 U.S. 579, 113 S.Ct. 2786, 125 L.Ed.2d 469 (1993), which held that, in federal courts, neither the relevancy test or the *Frye* test pose the proper question. At first glance, the holding in *Daubert* seemed to call for a relaxed version of *Frye*. That test, according to the Court, was superseded by the adoption of the federal rules of evidence, particularly Rule 702. At the time, the latter rule stated that "if scientific, technical, or other specialized knowledge will assist the trier of fact to understand the evidence or to determine a fact in issue, a witness qualified as an expert . . . may testify thereto in the form of an opinion or otherwise." Justice Blackmun's opinion concluded that "a rigid 'general acceptance' requirement would be at odds with the 'liberal thrust' of the Federal rules." Rather the test for admitting scientific evidence should be a "flexible" one and can rely on a number of factors other than general acceptance, including the "falsifiability" of the underlying theory, the extent to which it has been subject to peer review, and its known or potential "error rates."

The *Daubert* opinion also stated, however, that even under Rule 702 the basis of scientific testimony "must be derived by the scientific method," meaning that the underlying hypothesis "can be (and has been) tested." Further, in *Kumho Tire Co. v. Carmichael*, 526 U.S. 137, 119 S.Ct. 1167, 143 L.Ed.2d 238 (1999), the Court made clear that *Daubert* applies not just to "scientific" expertise, but also to "technical" and "specialized knowledge" (the other two types of expertise mentioned in Rule 702).[d] One year later Congress ratified this relatively rigorous approach to expertise by amending Rule 702 to state that scientific, technical or specialized knowledge is admissible only if "(1) the testimony is based upon sufficient facts or data, (2) the testimony is the product of reliable principles and methods, and (3) the witness has applied the principles and methods reliably to the facts of

d. A third Supreme Court decision, *General Electric Co. v. Joiner*, 522 U.S. 136, 118 S.Ct. 512, 139 L.Ed.2d 508 (1997), stressed that the trial judge is to play a "gatekeep-er" role in determining admissibility of expert testimony, and that the trial judge's decision, whether to exclude or admit, is to be given great deference on appeal.

the case." Thus, in federal courts and in those twenty-five to thirty states that follow *Daubert* (see 90 A.L.R.5th 453 (2001) for a survey of state law), psychiatric expertise must be based on facts, theory and methodology that are "reliable" (i.e., valid or accurate), not simply "generally accepted."

One commentator, noting the relatively unscientific nature of most behavioral science expertise, has stated that *Daubert*, "read literally would dictate the end of the receipt of psychiatric and psychological testimony in federal courts." Michael J. Gottesman, "Admissibility of Expert Testimony After *Daubert*: The "Prestige" Factor," 43 Emory L.J. 867, 875–76 (1994). Another stated that "the testability or falsifiability and potential error rate factors for appraising [social science evidence] will rarely be sufficiently present to meet the *Daubert* standard." Michael H. Graham, *"Daubert v. Merrell Dow Pharmaceuticals, Inc.*: No *Frye*, Now What?," 30 Crim. L. Bull. 153, 162 (1994). In practice, however, these dire predictions have not come to pass. One study of the caselaw addressing the admissibility of psychological "syndrome" evidence between 1993, when *Daubert* was handed down, and 1998 found that "[c]ourts are not generally engaging in scientific reviews of the proffered syndrome[; m]ost typically, the focus is on general acceptance and the qualifications of the expert, and even then the judicial review tends to be cursory." Shirley Dobbin & James Richardson, "A Case Law Survey of Social and Behavioral Science Evidence After *Daubert*," unpublished manuscript presented at 1998 American–Psychology Law Association Annual Meeting. According to one commentator, as of 2001, there had been "no reported *Daubert* challenges to retrospective psychiatric assessments of criminal responsibility." Daniel W. Shuman, "Expertise in Law, Medicine and Health Care," 26 J. Health Policy & L. 267, 282 (2001). The few exclusions of psychiatric testimony that occur in such cases appear to be on the ground the testimony is irrelevant, rather than unreliable. See Henry F. Fradella et al., "The Impact of *Daubert* on the Admissibility of Behavioral Science Testimony," 30 Pepperdine L. Rev. 403, 421–23, 431–34 (2003). Can you think of any reason why lawyers and courts are handling psychiatric testimony regarding responsibility issues with kid gloves?

How, if at all, would a *Daubert* analysis have affected the analysis in *Lewellyn*? Consider also whether the outcome in the following cases would differ depending upon whether *Frye*, relevancy, or *Daubert* is the applicable test:

A. Dr. Dietz' testimony in the Hinckley case that Hinckley had a schizoid personality disorder (see pp. 434–35). Recall that the DSM field tests showed that inter-rater agreement on diagnoses of personality disorders was between 56 and 65% and that one study found that inter-rater reliability of schizoid personality disorder in everyday clinical settings was 1% (see p. 444). Does *Daubert* prohibit testimony associated with high error rates? Does *Frye*? Should testimony be admissible as long as the associated error rates, however high, are known?

B. "Rape trauma syndrome" testimony, offered by the prosecution in a case in which the defendant admits intercourse with the alleged victim but claims it was consensual. The testimony asserts that women who have been raped are "consistently more likely" than women who have not been raped to experience discomfort or fear of men, an inability to sleep, nightmares about rape, and constant anxiety, all of which the alleged victim experiences. The studies on which the testimony is based found that rape victims are more likely than those who have not been raped to experience such symptoms, to a statistically significant degree, but also found that victims' reactions to rape vary from individual to individual, that the symptoms experienced by victims of rape are no different from those experienced by victims of other traumatic events (such as war), and that there is little distinction between the reactions of a victim of rape and the reactions of the victim of any other sort of stressful sexual event. The syndrome is not found in DSM, although the fourth edition of DSM does recognize for the first time that post-traumatic stress disorder (PTSD) can result not only from wartime and "major catastrophes" but also from traumatic events involving "a threat to the physical integrity of self" that "involved intense fear, helpless, or horror." It also states that PTSD is associated with nightmares, anxiety, and attempts to avoid situations associated with the trauma. Assuming the alleged victim in the case suffers from these types of symptoms, should the expert testimony about "rape trauma syndrome" be admissible? Should admissibility analysis under *Daubert* or *Frye* vary depending on whether the prosecution or defense is the initial proponent of psychiatric testimony?

C. Testimony offered by the defense from a psychoanalyst, trained in Freudian theory, that a person's criminal activity was caused by an unconscious desire to be punished. Cf. Ralph Underwager & Hollida Wakefield, "A Paradigm Shift for Expert Witnesses, 5 Issues in Child Sex Abuse Accusations" 158–59 (1993)(stating that one of the "best examples" of unfalsifiable theories is Freudian thought, because unconscious desires are, by definition, difficult to pinpoint and because definitively linking them to particular actions is virtually impossible).

3. *Novel defenses and substantive law.* The pathological gambling defense was of recent vintage at the time it was raised in *Lewellyn*. To the extent they should be relied upon at all, use of the *Frye* rule, *Daubert* and other screening devices is most easily justified in just such a situation, when novel and relatively untested scientific evidence is at issue. But in some cases involving novel defense arguments, reliance on these devices may serve another goal, one that is substantive rather than evidentiary. That is, they might be used to exclude evidence not because of its inaccuracy but because of its effect on accepted legal doctrine. Is it possible that the real concern of the *Lewellyn* court was not that the testimony would be inaccurate or misleading, but that it might lead to an improper expansion of the insanity defense? See Richard Bonnie, "Compulsive Gambling and the Insanity Defense," 9 Newsletter of the Amer.Acad.Psychiat. & Law 6, 7 (1984).

In any event, as noted above, the types of evidentiary issues raised in *Lewellyn* are seldom raised in more "routine" insanity cases, even post-*Daubert* and *Kumho Tire*. The next excerpt takes exception to this practice.

STEPHEN MORSE
CRAZY BEHAVIOR, MORALS & SCIENCE:
AN ANALYSIS OF MENTAL HEALTH LAW

51 S.Cal.L.Rev. 527, 582–88, 618–19.
(1978).

[I]

[T]he law is concerned with specific cases where an actor may be clearly crazy and where the craziness is clearly related to legally relevant behavior.... In terms of responsibility, ... [i]ndividual cases of clear relationship may be separated into two types: *crazy urges* and *crazy reasons*. In each case, this section considers the particular factors that help one decide whether the actor could have behaved otherwise. Even assuming that the craziness was a causal variable, the critical question remains: Was the crazy urge uncontrollable or was the crazy reason and the legally relevant behavior based on it the inexorable result of a disturbed mind?

a. *Crazy urges:* The case of crazy urges refers to what is usually termed an "irresistible impulse." The actor may be perfectly rational cognitively, but he *feels* as if he must carry out a particular behavior and that he cannot prevent himself from doing so. He may be quite aware that the action he feels compelled to perform is weird, deviant, immoral, maladaptive, or the like. Still, he feels incapable of behaving otherwise. If the behavior felt to be compelled is weird, deviant, or immoral, we are inclined to believe that the urge is crazy, because no one would desire to behave in those ways when he comprehends how those behaviors were assessed. The prototypical case of a crazy urge is the sexual deviant, *e.g.,* a child molester, who knows that his actions are viewed as sick or evil (or both) by most persons, and yet who feels an overwhelming desire to molest children.

Is the child molester's behavior the irresistible effect of his crazy urge? To analyze this question we must first ask the threshold question of whether the actor's crazy urge is related to mental illness. This case is a clear example of the situation where craziness is diagnosed because the legally relevant behavior seems crazy itself and where no other significant evidence of mental disorder may exist. We assume that there must be some underlying abnormality because no rational person would choose to molest children unless he was "forced to" by circumstances beyond his control. [T]here is no evidence of underlying abnormality in such cases, but let us accept arguments that it is reasonable to call this person crazy because he experiences a perhaps inexplicable and crazy urge.

Is the urge irresistible? For at least two reasons, most persons would assume that the urge must be very strong. First, the molester reports that the urge is overwhelming. Second, it seems intuitively obvious that most persons would not "give in" to such an urge unless it was overpowering. Let us assume that, indeed, the urge is powerful and perhaps even tormenting to our molester. But could it have been resisted, albeit at the cost of frustration and discomfort? Do all persons who feel such urges give in to them, or are there some who resist?

Although there exists little systematic epidemiological study of such questions, it is clear from clinical practice that many persons report extremely strong "deviant" urges that are often a source of misery to them. Yet most persons do not engage in the urged behavior; indeed, many seek assistance from clergymen, doctors, counselors, and psychotherapists in order to defeat the urge. Holding that the urge is not overwhelming in such cases, but that it is overwhelming in the cases of those who give in, is tautological reasoning: the urge must be overwhelming because the person gave in. In terms more familiar to lawyers, we are faced with the difficulty of distinguishing between the irresistible impulse and the impulse not resisted.

There is no scientific measure of the strength of urges. Nor is there evidence of what percentage of people who experience various urges of various strengths act on those urges. Even if such measures and data were available, as they may be someday, the measured strength of the urge would not answer the question of whether the urge was irresistible. Such data may help us to identify how predisposing, in a statistical sense, the urge might be, but they would not answer the question of moral and legal responsibility. Where to draw the cutting point would clearly be a moral and legal determination. In the future, behavioral science may provide more precise information to help draw the line, but science alone cannot draw the line of legal responsibility.

At present, then, the determination of the irresistibility of crazy urges must rest on commonsense assessments of the craziness and strength of the urge. The data to be evaluated would be first, the report of the urged actor, and second, the craziness of the urged action. Whether certain urges are crazy is not a scientific question that needs expert answers. And whether the urge is sufficiently strong or crazy is a question that is answered by assessing the reported feelings of the actor and the sincerity of his report. There is simply no test for knowing when an urge is irresistible, and indeed, there is no reason to believe that there is any urge that is not, to some degree, resistible. Deciding whether an urge is irresistible is not a scientific decision.

b. *Crazy reasons:* It may also be believed that an actor had no free choice about whether to engage in certain behavior if the actor reports crazy reasons for his behavior. If an actor kills someone because he sincerely believes the victim was a hostile agent, we believe that the killing not only is related to the crazy belief as was seen above, but that it is the compelled result of the crazy belief. After all, no one would hold and act on such beliefs unless there were something uncontrollably wrong with him that caused him to have those beliefs.

Before we can determine whether an actor had control over his crazy reasons and consequent actions, we must first analyze the nature of a crazy reason. Following from our definition of craziness itself, we may define a crazy reason as one that is irrational and inexplicable. Of course, the degree of craziness of a reason varies along a lengthy continuum.

* * *

It may be very hard for a person to think straight; in some cases, crazy beliefs may powerfully compel the crazy person to act on them. But there is no certainty that an actor cannot control his crazy beliefs or, at least, control actions based on them. Indeed, even the craziest persons seem to behave quite normally or rationally a great deal of the time, especially if there is good reason to do so. On at least some occasions, including some instances when they are behaving crazily, crazy persons are clearly capable of playing by the usual rules. Nor do they always act on the basis of their crazy reasons. Moreover, the defects and disordered thinking that supposedly distinguish crazy persons from normal ones are very prevalent in the general population. * * * Even if it is found that the person typically seems out of touch with reality, reasons crazily, and gives mostly crazy reasons for his behavior, scientific evidence cannot demonstrate that such behavior is the result of mental disorder and that related legally relevant behavior is sufficiently unfree to ascribe nonresponsibility to the actor. At most it can be urged that a person who typically does not think "straight" is more or less predisposed to give crazy reasons and to act on them.

* * *

[II]

Whether an actor could have behaved otherwise and is legally and morally responsible for his legally relevant behavior cannot be determined scientifically. No diagnosis gives the answer to these questions, and there are no scientific tests to measure the strength of crazy urges or the strength of the actor's self-control. Nor are there tests to distinguish the person who *cannot* think straight or control himself from the person who *will not* think straight or control himself. Whether a person cannot or will not think straight or control himself is a moral and commonsense judgment that should be made by the legal decisionmaker.

Let us take an example to examine how experts might help or hinder legal decisions about responsibility. In a famous homicide case,[194] clinicians testified that the defendant killed the victim in order to avoid psychic disintegration and insanity. If this formulation is correct, the defendant was faced with a very hard choice indeed—kill or psychically disintegrate—and the defendant would hardly seem as responsible as most criminal homicide defendants, or perhaps, responsible at all. Some clarifying questions, however, should be asked: (1) Are there hard data behind the theorizing that the killing was the inexorable or nearly inexorable result of threatened ego-disintegration?; and (2) What per-

194. People v. Gorshen, 51 Cal.2d 716, 336 P.2d 492 (1959).

centage of persons with such fears kill? The answer to question (1) is "no," and the answer to question (2) is that the data are unavailable although the actual percentage is probably quite low. Such fears are not a proven necessary or sufficient cause of homicidal behavior. In this case, as in all cases, the expert's assertion that the person could not have acted otherwise is really a moral guess and not a scientific fact. Justice would be better served if the expert drew no conclusions and simply described in ordinary language the cognitive and affective state of the defendant without intruding terms and theories of unproven accuracy and usefulness.[195]

* * *

RICHARD BONNIE & CHRISTOPHER SLOBOGIN
THE ROLE OF MENTAL HEALTH PROFESSIONALS
IN THE CRIMINAL PROCESS: THE CASE FOR
INFORMED SPECULATION

66 Va.L.Rev. 427, 461–64, 486–93.
(1980).

* * *

We concede that the central etiological theories and conceptual categories of the clinical behavioral disciplines have not been scientifically validated, and that few clinical opinions can be stated with a high degree of certainty. At best, opinions about psychological processes—beyond merely descriptive observations—are clinical probability judgments rooted in theoretical constructs that are more or less widely shared among mental health professionals.

According to the weight of authority, however, the fact that opinion testimony is uncertain does not by itself justify exclusion, as long as the evidence rises above mere conjecture or speculation. If it has any tendency to prove a fact, and is otherwise qualified as expert opinion, the evidence is admissible unless some overriding reason requires exclusion. The rationale for this position is that many observations, both scientific and lay, can be expressed only in terms of "probabilities" or "possibilities"; to deny the factfinder such evidence on this ground alone might deplete seriously the amount of information available.

Although Professor Morse acknowledges this general evidentiary principle, he asserts that "an exception should be made for mental health professionals, primarily because their expertise is limited on most issues and their unrestricted testimony tends to obscure the moral and

---

195. Of course, an expert who tries to describe the person's past mental state faces grave difficulties. This probably cannot be done with substantial accuracy unless the expert had occasion to know or examine the actor at the past time in question. Thus, experts probably should never testify about an actor's mental state at a time when the expert had no direct knowledge of it. Still, descriptions of a present mental state may help a factfinder draw inferences about a past mental state provided that the time in question is not too remote and that there is some direct evidence of the actor's behavior at the past time.

social nature of the questions being asked." We do not think the case for an exception can be made. Particularly when the defendant determines whether expert testimony by mental health professionals will be introduced—typically the case in the reconstructive inquiries of the criminal law—the opinions of qualified witnesses within their sphere of specialized knowledge should be freely admitted.

A defendant's past psychological functioning cannot be reconstructed with scientific precision. The truth will remain very much in the shadows whether or not mental health professionals are permitted to offer their opinions. In formulating an evidentiary test, then, we should begin by comparing the knowledge of mental health professionals not with the knowledge of physicists about the laws of motion, but with that of laymen about psychological aberration and criminal behavior. We should ask whether the observations, intuitions, and hypotheses of clinicians offer a useful and acceptable supplement to those of Everyman.

Morse insists that inferences concerning the nature, extent, and consequences of mental dysfunction are within the range of lay experience and common sense. To some extent this is correct; the factfinder is competent to draw such inferences in the absence of expert testimony, and need not yield to such testimony even when undisputed.[118] Moreover, lay witnesses sometimes may express opinions on a defendant's mental condition. Nevertheless, we stress the incremental nature of the modern test: we must ask whether "specialized knowledge will assist the trier of fact," not whether the fact finder can manage when left to his own devices.

* * *

[In the responsibility assessment] setting the "factual" inquiry concerns the relationship, if any, between a defendant's aberrational psychological functioning and his behavior. We agree that categorizing the strength of that relationship, and evaluating it according to some externally derived moral gradient, is the responsibility of the judge or jury and not an appropriate subject for expert opinion. Professor Morse's exclusionary approach to expert testimony, however, also would preclude an expert from expressing any opinion regarding why a relationship may or may not exist between the defendant's psychological functioning and his criminal behavior. We think this would unnecessarily deprive the factfinder of helpful insights and would unfairly hamper the defendant's effort to present a case-in-exculpation or-mitigation.

118. It is generally accepted that an opinion of an expert, even if uncontradicted, need not be accepted by the jury as long as there is some evidence to support a contrary conclusion. This same concept has also been expressed as a requirement that a "jury may not arbitrarily disregard expert testimony. . . ." Of course, in jurisdictions where the government bears the burden of proving the defendant's "sanity" beyond a reasonable doubt, a jury cannot find the defendant sane, even if they find the defendant's expert unbelievable, unless the government has presented some evidence from which sanity can be inferred.

Morse refers to the famous *Gorshen* case to illustrate his rationale. Gorshen shot his supervisor after a fight at work. A psychiatric witness testified that Gorshen was a chronic paranoid schizophrenic who for twenty years had experienced trances accompanied by auditory and visual hallucinations. He claimed to see and hear devils in disguise committing abnormal sexual acts, sometimes upon Gorshen himself. These experiences had intensified during the months before the crime.

On the day of the shooting, Gorshen had been drinking at work. His supervisor told him to go home, and a fight ensued. He then went home, obtained a pistol, returned, and shot the victim. According to the psychiatrist, Gorshen said, "All I was thinking about all of this time is to shoot O'Leary. I forgot about my family, I forgot about God's laws and human's laws and everything else. The only thing was to get that guy, get that guy, get that guy, like a hammer in the head."

The expert witness explained that during the period of the offense Gorshen was driven by an obsessive murderous rage aroused by the stress of the beating and by what he perceived as challenges to his manhood. Psychologically, this rage reflected a desperate attempt to ward off imminent and total disintegration of his personality:

> The strength of the obsession is proportioned not to the reality of danger but to the danger of the insanity.... [F]or this man to go insane means to be permanently in the world of these visions and under the influence of the devil.... [A]n individual in this state of crisis will do anything to avoid the threatened insanity....

Professor Morse questions the highly speculative quality of this formulation, pointing out that no "hard data" support the hypothesis "that the killing was the inexorable or nearly inexorable result of threatened ego-disintegration," and that probably very few persons with such fears kill, although there are no data available. Of course, both of these points could have been made very effectively by skillful cross-examination. Skillful redirect examination in response might have brought out the psychodynamic concepts from which this formulation was derived, perhaps with descriptions from the clinical literature of the characteristics of violent behavior committed by individuals with comparable paranoid thought patterns.

Morse characterizes the *Gorshen* expert's testimony as "really a moral guess and not a scientific fact." Although explanatory clinical formulations by careful forensic specialists are hardly "scientific facts," they do represent something more than idiosyncratic "guesses." Such witnesses offer "informed speculation," essentially in the following form:

> I cannot assure you that this is what happened, and I cannot measure for you the impact that these intrapsychic variables had on the defendant's behavior under the circumstances which existed at the time of the offense. Nonetheless, based on our operating theories of psychology, which we employ in our everyday clinical practice, and on my own study of the relevant literature concerning this type

of psychological functioning and this type of criminal behavior, I think the following explanation(s) are possible (or probable).

These explanatory formulations can assist the factfinder, who must speculate in any event, by identifying "clinically reasonable" possibilities that otherwise may not occur to him. Appropriately instructed, the jury will know that these explanations are only possibilities and will not be misled.[192]

* * *

[Indeed] in the context of the reconstructive inquiries of the criminal law, the risk that a jury will give undue weight to such an expert opinion, notwithstanding any cautionary instructions, has been grossly exaggerated. If only the defense has offered psychiatric testimony, the natural skepticism of the jurors, and the corrective value of cross-examination, virtually eliminate the risk that the jury will abdicate its factfinding function to the experts. If each side has its own witness, expert "dominance" is not the problem, and the risk of confusion can be minimized by adequate preparation by counsel and by ordinary judicial supervision. In short, we see little disadvantage in admitting appropriately restricted opinion testimony by qualified mental health professionals.

Most important, the wholesale exclusion of such testimony would unduly restrict the defendant's opportunity to present relevant evidence in his defense, and would enhance the natural advantage enjoyed by the prosecution on reconstructive issues. In particular, a defendant's opportunity to carry his de facto burden of proving that he did not perceive, believe, expect, or intend what a normal person would have under the same circumstances—and that he therefore lacked the mens rea required for the offense—is undermined by rules which altogether exclude qualified opinion testimony or which allow such testimony only if the expert finds that the defendant's abnormal functioning was attributable to a mental disease or defect. Similarly, a defendant's opportunity to offer a plausible explanation for his behavior—and thereby to establish a meaningful case in exculpation or mitigation under the applicable responsibility doctrines—would be restricted severely and unjustifiably by rules that exclude explanatory formulations by qualified mental health professionals.

* * *

Questions and Comments

1. *Levels of inference.* To make clearer the nature of the debate between Morse on the one hand and Bonnie & Slobogin on the other it might be helpful to conceptualize expert testimony as consisting of ascending

---

192. The *Gorshen* trial judge stated that "up till the time that [the defense expert] testified in this case, there was no explanation of why this crime was committed.... [He is] the first person that has any reasonable explanation. Whether it's correct or not, I don't know."

levels of inference. For instance, in an insanity case, the progressive levels of inference might be as follows:

1.　Application of meaning (perception) to a behavioral image (e.g., "He was wringing his hands.")

2.　Perception of general mental state (e.g., "He appeared anxious.")

3.　"Formulation" of the perception of general mental state to fit into theoretical constructs or the research literature and/or to synthesize observations (e.g., "His anxiety during the interview was consistent with a general obsession with pleasing others.")

4.　Diagnosis (e.g., "His behavior on interview and reported history are consistent with a generalized anxiety disorder.")

5.　Relationship of formulation or diagnosis to legally relevant behavior (e.g., "At the time of the offense, his anxiety was so overwhelming that he failed to consider the consequences of his behavior.")

6.　Elements of the ultimate legal issue (e.g., "Although he was too anxious at the time of the offense to *reflect* upon the consequences of his behavior, he *knew* the nature and consequences of his acts and *knew* that what he did was wrong.")

7.　Ultimate legal issue (e.g., "He was sane at the time of the offense.")[e]

At what level of testimony would Morse permit mental health professionals to testify? Bonnie & Slobogin? If you were a judge deciding the admissibility of clinical testimony on the responsibility issue in the *Gorshen* case, up to which level would you allow? If you instead relied on one of the screening rules discussed previously?

2.　*Objective v. suppositional science.* The Morse/Bonnie & Slobogin debate has been carried on by Professors Faigman and Taslitz. Faigman distinguishes between "objective science"—i.e., data or opinion the validity of which has been demonstrated through the scientific method of hypothesis testing—and "suppositional" science, which is based on "social science findings advanced without pretense of having survived scientific test and social science findings advanced as having undergone scientific test but which have not actually been tested adequately." David Faigman, "To Have and Have Not: Assessing the Value of Social Science to the Law as Science and Policy," 38 Emory L.J. 1005, 1013 (1989). He argues that suppositional science–which he analogizes to the type of story-telling engaged in by fiction writers such as Fyodor Dostoevsky in his novel *Crime and Punishment*–should generally be excluded:

> [T]he validity of suppositional science is indefinite, because it has not been subjected to adequate testing. An expert's suppositions may be accurate, or they may not be, and no way exists for the juror to discern which is the case. Presented with conflicting suppositions, the so-called battle of the experts, jurors have no well-founded basis on which to choose between them. Such battles are likely to be won by the more persuasive witness, rather than the more persuasive facts or opinion.

e.　This example is adapted from Gary M. Melton et al., Psychological Evaluations　for the Courts 16–17 (Guilford Press, 3d ed.2007).

Undoubtedly, cases arise in which a suppositional expert's testimony will offer insights or suggest ways of viewing the evidence that can "assist" the fact-finder's task. The difficulty comes from recognizing these cases when they arise. Without knowing the accuracy of their opinions, neither the judge nor the jury can estimate the value of their testimony. [A] Dostoevskean psychologist could sometimes provide assistance to fact-finders, perhaps as much assistance as a Freudian psychologist, but in a battle between the Dostoevskean and Freudian experts, nothing in their training or methods would necessarily enable jurors to say which expert had the more valid opinion or could provide greater assistance.

In addition to the *potential* insights into factual questions that suppositional experts might provide juries, the only remaining potential significance of suppositional science lies in the value preferences it reflects. Perhaps, if the normative basis for nonscientific expert testimony was recognized, its discretionary allowance could be viewed as a function of legal policy formation. Thus, rather than incorporate into legal rules the factual insights and values reflected by suppositional science, suppositional experts could be allowed to testify generally, leaving to juries the task of choosing among competing suppositions. Professor Herbert Hovenkamp, for example, argues that in antitrust litigation juries should be exposed to competing economic theories and be allowed to choose between them the way they choose among conflicting facts. Professor Hovenkamp well recognizes the political component of most economic theories, but asserts that greater stability will be achieved in the long run by leaving theory-finding to juries.

But assigning the responsibility of theory-finding to juries invests vast power in expert witnesses to define the value choices resolved by the judicial process. Because judges cannot admit all experts claiming scientific expertise, if judges do not assess the validity of proffered opinions themselves, they must defer to the professional guilds to decide what scientific evidence to admit. Admissibility of scientific evidence thus becomes a guild issue resolved not by legal principles, nor on the basis of the accuracy of the evidence, but instead by the internal dynamics of professional organizations. Hence, the Dostoevskean psychologist, for example, is barred from the courthouse not because we doubt the validity of her opinion, at least no more so than the Freudian psychologist, but because she is not represented politically in one of the two APAs.

Id. at 1085–87.

Taslitz, on the other hand, believes that there is much to be said for "art" as well as science when it comes to making determinations of criminal responsibility.

[R]ationalist critiques like that of Professor Faigman ... seek to impose the standards of science in the courtroom. Despite its pretensions to the contrary, law is not a science but rather deals with the need for relatively quick, practical decision making in individual cases because judgments cannot be postponed while awaiting scientific confirmation. These decisions are made in a value-laden world of uncertainty. Thus, verdicts, being a practical project, do not and should not seek solely "truth," in some absolute, scientific sense of that term, but rather acceptability and stability, given the constraints and varying goals facing the decisionmaker.

Therefore, while science is not irrelevant—and, indeed, can do much to inform the legal process when truth is one of the competing goals—sometimes art can do in an acceptable fashion in the individual case what science cannot. This is especially true when there are powerful concerns other than truth, such as the political, moral, and cathartic goals of a criminal trial. We may, therefore, turn to art, in this instance, to clinical judgment with its uncertain scientific support, because the artistry serves cathartic goals or because, in our search for truth, artistry is the best means available. Indeed, the professional psychological literature recognizes both the limitations and advantages of clinical artistry.

Thus, the literature recommends a purely actuarial approach when the outcome to be predicted is objective and specific, and interest in the individual case is minimal. On the other hand, clinical judgement is recommended when (1) information is needed about areas or events for which no adequate tests are available, (2) rare, unusual events of a highly individualized nature are to be predicted or judged, or (3) the clinical judgements involve instances for which no statistical equations have been developed. These are precisely the situations likely to arise in criminal trials.

Andrew Taslitz, "Myself Alone: Individualizing Justice Through Psychological Character Evidence," 52 Maryland L.Rev. 1, 99–100 (1993).

Reinforcing his view that "art" can usefully inform the adjudicative process, Taslitz notes the development of "storytelling theory," which suggests that, to be helpful, the story of case must be told in such a way as to satisfy a jury's need for "narrative coherence" and "narrative fidelity." Narrative coherence concerns whether the story "hangs together" in the face of competing stories and consistently depicts a person's character. Narrative fidelity concerns whether relevant facts have been omitted or distorted, whether the connections of facts to conclusions are reasonable, whether the values implied by the story are confirmed by the jurors' own experiences, and whether the story addresses the "real" issues in the cases. Taslitz argues that "suppositional science" can often provide such a story when "objective science" cannot. Id. at 94–97. How does the expert testimony in *Hinckley, Lewellyn, Gorshen* and the three hypotheticals on pp. 455–56 fare under Faigman's view? Taslitz'?

As to whether there is a meaningful difference between "objective science" and "suppositional science," consider this statement from Michael Seigel, "A Pragmatic Critique of Modern Evidence Scholarship," 88 Nw. L.Rev. 995, 1038 (1994):

Determining whether research results are generalizable between places and over time ... requires the use of reasoning techniques that include analogy, imagination, common sense, experience, and induction. These are the very methods of practical reason. In other words, applied social science, though a positive endeavor, is—at least at some stages—predominately an exercise in practical reason.

3. *The importance of context.* Bonnie & Slobogin refrain from taking a position on the admissibility of clinical opinion testimony outside the "reconstructive" setting assessing mental state at the time of the offense. What are the differences between this setting and other settings in which clinical opinion testimony might be offered? In particular, what are the differences between the reconstructive context and the predictive one, to be discussed below?

C. PROPENSITY

Predictions of behavior are required in many different legal settings. Most relevant to this book are the sentencing and commitment contexts, where predictions relevant to dangerousness and treatability are often called for. The following case addresses admissibility issues in the context where such predictions have their greatest impact: death penalty proceedings.

BAREFOOT v. ESTELLE

Supreme Court of United States, 1983.
463 U.S. 880, 103 S.Ct. 3383, 77 L.Ed.2d 1090.

* * *

JUSTICE WHITE delivered the opinion of the Court.

* * *

On November 14, 1978, petitioner was convicted of the capital murder of a police officer in Bell County, Tex. A separate sentencing hearing before the same jury was then held to determine whether the death penalty should be imposed. Under Tex.Code Crim.Proc.Ann., Art. § 37.071 (Vernon 1981), two special questions were to be submitted to the jury: whether the conduct causing death was "committed deliberately and with reasonable expectation that the death of the deceased or another would result"; and whether "there is a probability that the defendant would commit criminal acts of violence that would constitute a continuing threat to society." The State introduced into evidence petitioner's prior convictions and his reputation for lawlessness. The State also called two psychiatrists, John Holbrook and James Grigson, who, in response to hypothetical questions, testified that petitioner would probably commit further acts of violence and represent a continuing threat to society. The jury answered both of the questions put to them in the affirmative, a result which required the imposition of the death penalty.

On appeal to the Texas Court of Criminal Appeals, petitioner urged, among other submissions, that the use of psychiatrists at the punishment hearing to make predictions about petitioner's future conduct was unconstitutional because psychiatrists, individually and as a class, are not competent to predict future dangerousness. Hence, their predictions are so likely to produce erroneous sentences that their use violated the Eighth and Fourteenth Amendments.

* * *

The suggestion that no psychiatrist's testimony may be presented with respect to a defendant's future dangerousness is somewhat like asking us to disinvent the wheel. In the first place, it is contrary to our cases. If the likelihood of a defendant's committing further crimes is a constitutionally acceptable criterion for imposing the death penalty, which it is, *Jurek v. Texas,* 428 U.S. 262, 96 S.Ct. 2950, 49 L.Ed.2d 929 (1976), and if it is not impossible for even a lay person sensibly to arrive at that conclusion, it makes little sense, if any, to submit that psychiatrists, out of the entire universe of persons who might have an opinion on the issue, would know so little about the subject that they should not be permitted to testify. In *Jurek,* seven Justices rejected the claim that it was impossible to predict future behavior and that dangerousness was therefore an invalid consideration in imposing the death penalty.

* * *

Although there was only lay testimony with respect to dangerousness in *Jurek,* there was no suggestion by the Court that the testimony of doctors would be inadmissible. To the contrary, the joint opinion announcing the judgment said that the jury should be presented with all of the relevant information.

* * *

Acceptance of petitioner's position that expert testimony about future dangerousness is far too unreliable to be admissible would immediately call into question those other contexts in which predictions of future behavior are constantly made. For example, in *O'Connor v. Donaldson,* 422 U.S. 563, 576, 95 S.Ct. 2486, 2494, 45 L.Ed.2d 396 (1975), we held that a nondangerous mental hospital patient could not be held in confinement against his will. Later, speaking about the requirements for civil commitments, we said:

> "There may be factual issues in a commitment proceeding, but the factual aspects represent only the beginning of the inquiry. Whether the individual is mentally ill and dangerous to either himself or others and is in need of confined therapy turns on the *meaning* of the facts which must be interpreted by expert psychiatrists and psychologists." *Addington v. Texas,* 441 U.S. 418, 429, 99 S.Ct. 1804, 1811, 60 L.Ed.2d 323 (1979).

In the second place, the rules of evidence generally extant at the federal and state levels anticipate that relevant, unprivileged evidence should be admitted and its weight left to the factfinder, who would have the benefit of cross-examination and contrary evidence by the opposing party. Psychiatric testimony predicting dangerousness may be countered not only as erroneous in a particular case but also as generally so unreliable that it should be ignored. If the jury may make up its mind about future dangerousness unaided by psychiatric testimony, jurors should not be barred from hearing the views of the State's psychiatrists along with opposing views of the defendant's doctors.[5]

Third, petitioner's view mirrors the position expressed in the *amicus* brief of the American Psychiatric Association (APA)[which argued that psychiatrists are not experts at predicting dangerousness].

* * *

[H]owever, [w]e are [not] convinced ... that the view of the APA should be converted into a constitutional rule barring an entire category of expert testimony. We are not persuaded that such testimony is almost entirely unreliable and that the factfinder and the adversary system will not be competent to uncover, recognize, and take due account of its shortcomings.

The *amicus* does not suggest that there are not other views held by members of the Association or of the profession generally. Indeed, as this case and others indicate, there are those doctors who are quite willing to testify at the sentencing hearing, who think, and will say, that they know what they are talking about, and who expressly disagree with the Association's point of view.[7] Furthermore, their qualifications as experts are regularly accepted by the courts. If they are so obviously wrong and should be discredited, there should be no insuperable problem in doing so by calling members of the Association who are of that view and who confidently assert that opinion in their *amicus* brief. Neither petitioner

5. In this case, no evidence was offered by petitioner at trial to contradict the testimony of Doctors Holbrook and Grigson. Nor is there a contention that, despite petitioner's claim of indigence, the court refused to provide an expert for petitioner. In cases of indigency, Texas law provides for the payment of $500 for "expenses incurred for purposes of investigation and expert testimony." Tex.Code Crim.Proc.Ann., Art. 26.05, § 1(d) (Vernon Supp.1982).

7. At trial, Dr. Holbrook testified without contradiction that a psychiatrist could predict the future dangerousness of an individual, if given enough background information about the individual. Dr. Grigson obviously held a similar view. At the District Court hearing on the habeas petition, the State called two expert witnesses, Dr. George Parker, a psychologist, and Dr. Richard Koons, a psychiatrist. Both of these doctors agreed that accurate predictions of future dangerousness can be made if enough information is provided; furthermore, they both deemed it highly likely that an individual fitting the characteristics of the one in the Barefoot hypothetical would commit future acts of violence.

* * *

We are aware that many mental health professionals have questioned the usefulness of psychiatric predictions of future dangerousness in light of studies indicating that such predictions are often inaccurate.

... Dr. John Monahan, upon whom one of the State's experts relied as "the leading thinker on this issue," concluded that "the 'best' clinical research currently in existence indicates that *psychiatrists and psychologists are accurate in no more than one out of three predictions of violent behavior over a several-year period among institutionalized populations that had both committed violence in the past ... and who were diagnosed as mentally ill.*" J. Monahan, The Clinical Prediction of Violent Behavior 47–49 (1981) (emphasis in original).

* * *

All of these professional doubts about the usefulness of psychiatric predictions can be called to the attention of the jury. Petitioner's entire argument, as well as that of Justice Blackmun's dissent, is founded on the premise that a jury will not be able to separate the wheat from the chaff. We do not share in this low evaluation of the adversary process.

nor the Association suggests that psychiatrists are always wrong with respect to future dangerousness, only most of the time. Yet the submission is that this category of testimony should be excised entirely from all trials. We are unconvinced, however, at least as of now, that the adversary process cannot be trusted to sort out the reliable from the unreliable evidence and opinion about future dangerousness, particularly when the convicted felon has the opportunity to present his own side of the case.

* * *

Justice Blackmun, with whom Justice Brennan and Justice Marshall join as to Parts I–IV, dissenting.... The Court holds that psychiatric testimony about a defendant's future dangerousness is admissible, despite the fact that such testimony is wrong two times out of three. The Court reaches this result—even in a capital case—because, it is said, the testimony is subject to cross-examination and impeachment. In the present state of psychiatric knowledge, this is too much for me. One may accept this in a routine lawsuit for money damages, but when a person's life is at stake—no matter how heinous his offense—a requirement of greater reliability should prevail. In a capital case, the specious testimony of a psychiatrist, colored in the eyes of an impressionable jury by the inevitable untouchability of a medical specialist's words, equates with death itself.

I

At the sentencing hearing, the State established that Barefoot had two prior convictions for drug offenses and two prior convictions for unlawful possession of firearms. None of these convictions involved acts of violence. At the guilt stage of the trial, for the limited purpose of establishing that the crime was committed in order to evade police custody, the State had presented evidence that Barefoot had escaped from jail in New Mexico where he was being held on charges of statutory rape and unlawful restraint of a minor child with intent to commit sexual penetration against the child's will. The prosecution also called several character witnesses at the sentencing hearing, from towns in five States. Without mentioning particular examples of Barefoot's conduct, these witnesses testified that Barefoot's reputation for being a peaceable and lawabiding citizen was bad in their respective communities.

Last, the prosecution called Doctors Holbrook and Grigson, whose testimony extended over more than half the hearing. Neither had examined Barefoot or requested the opportunity to examine him. In the presence of the jury, and over defense counsel's objection, each was qualified as an expert psychiatrist witness. Doctor Holbrook detailed at length his training and experience as a psychiatrist, which included a position as chief of psychiatric services at the Texas Department of Corrections. He explained that he had previously performed many "criminal evaluations," and that he subsequently took the post at the Department of Corrections to observe the subjects of these evaluations so that he could "be certain those opinions that [he] had were accurate at the time of trial and pretrial." He then informed the jury that it was "within [his] *capacity as a doctor of psychiatry* to predict the future dangerousness of an individual within a *reasonable medical certainty,*" (emphasis supplied), and that he could give *"an expert medical opinion* that would be *within reasonable psychiatric certainty* as to whether or not that individual would be dangerous to the degree that there would be a probability that that person would commit criminal acts of violence in the future that would constitute a continuing threat to society," (emphasis supplied).

Doctor Grigson also detailed his training and medical experience, which, he said, included examination of "between thirty and forty thousand individuals," including 8,000 charged with felonies, and at least 300 charged with murder. He testified that with enough information he would be able to "give *a medical opinion within reasonable psychiatric certainty* as to the psychological or psychiatric makeup of an individual," (emphasis supplied), and that this skill was "particular to the field of psychiatry and not to the average layman."

Each psychiatrist then was given an extended hypothetical question asking him to assume as true about Barefoot the four prior convictions for nonviolent offenses, the bad reputation for being law-abiding in various communities, the New Mexico escape, the events surrounding the murder for which he was on trial and, in Doctor Grigson's case, the New Mexico arrest. On the basis of the hypothetical question, Doctor Holbrook diagnosed Barefoot "within a reasonable psychiatr[ic] certainty," as a "criminal sociopath." He testified that he knew of no treatment that could change this condition, and that the condition would not change for the better but "may become accelerated" in the next few years. Finally, Doctor Holbrook testified that, "within reasonable psychiatric certainty," there was "a probability that the Thomas A. Barefoot in that hypothetical will commit criminal acts of violence in the future that would constitute a continuing threat to society," and that his opinion would not change if the "society" at issue was that within Texas prisons rather than society outside prison.

Doctor Grigson then testified that, on the basis of the hypothetical question, he could diagnose Barefoot "within reasonable psychiatric certainty" as an individual with "a fairly classical, typical, sociopathic personality disorder." He placed Barefoot in the "most severe category" of sociopaths (on a scale of one to ten, Barefoot was "above ten"), and stated that there was no known cure for the condition. Finally, Doctor Grigson testified that whether Barefoot was in society at large or in a prison society there was a *"one hundred percent and absolute"* chance that Barefoot would commit future acts of criminal violence that would constitute a continuing threat to society. (emphasis supplied).

On cross-examination, defense counsel questioned the psychiatrists about studies demonstrating that psychiatrists' predictions of future dangerousness are inherently unreliable. Doctor Holbrook indicated his familiarity with many of these studies but stated that he disagreed with their conclusions. Doctor Grigson stated that he was not familiar with most of these studies, and that their conclusions were accepted by only a "small minority group" of psychiatrists—"[i]t's not the American Psychiatric Association that believes that."

After an hour of deliberation, the jury answered "yes" to the two statutory questions, and Thomas Barefoot was sentenced to death.

II

* * *

The American Psychiatric Association (APA), participating in this case as *amicus curiae,* informs us that "[t]he unreliability of psychiatric predictions of long-term future dangerousness is by now an established fact within the profession." The APA's best estimate is that *two out of three* predictions of long-term future violence made by psychiatrists are wrong. The Court does not dispute this proposition, and indeed it could not do so; the evidence is overwhelming.

* * *

Neither the Court nor the State of Texas has cited a single reputable scientific source contradicting the unanimous conclusion of professionals in this field that psychiatric predictions of long-term future violence are wrong more often than they are right.[2]

The APA also concludes, as do researchers that have studied the issue, that psychiatrists simply have no expertise in predicting long-term future dangerousness. A layman with access to relevant statistics can do at least as well and possibly better; psychiatric training is not relevant to the factors that validly can be employed to make such predictions, and psychiatrists consistently err on the side of overpredicting violence. Thus, while Doctors Grigson and Holbrook were presented by the State and by self-proclamation as experts at predicting future dangerousness, the scientific literature makes crystal clear that they had no expertise whatever. Despite their claims that they were able to predict Barefoot's future behavior "within reasonable psychiatric certainty," or to a "one

2. Among the many other studies reaching this conclusion are APA Task Force Report, Clinical Aspects of the Violent Individual 28 (1974) (90% error rate "[u]nfortunately ... is the state of the art") (APA, Clinical Aspects); Steadman & Morrissey, The Statistical Prediction of Violent Behavior, 5 Law & Human Behavior 263, 271–273 (1981); Dix, Expert Prediction Testimony in Capital Sentencing: Evidentiary and Constitutional Considerations, 19 Am.Crim.L.Rev. 1, 16 (1981); Schwitzgebel, Prediction of Dangerousness and Its Implications for Treatment, in W. Curran, A. McGarry, & C. Petty, Modern Legal Medicine, Psychiatry, and Forensic Science 783, 784–786 (1980); Cocozza & Steadman, Prediction in Psychiatry: An Example of Misplaced Confidence in Experts, 25 Soc.Probs. 265, 272–273

(1978); Report of the (American Psychological Association's) Task Force on the Role of Psychology in the Criminal Justice System, 33 Am.Psychologist 1099, 1110 (1978); Steadman & Cocozza, Psychiatry, Dangerousness and the Repetitively Violent Offender, 69 J.Crim.L. & Criminology 226, 227, 230 (1978); Cocozza & Steadman, The Failure of Psychiatric Predictions of Dangerousness: Clear and Convincing Evidence, 29 Rutgers L.Rev. 1084, 1101 (1976); Diamond, The Psychiatric Prediction of Dangerousness, 123 U.Pa.L.Rev. 439, 451–452 (1974); Ennis & Litwack Psychiatry and the Presumption of Expertise: Flipping Coins in the Courtroom, 62 Calif.L.Rev. 693, 711–716 (1974). A relatively early study making this point is Rome, Identification of the Dangerous Offender, 42 F.R.D. 185 (1968).

hundred percent and absolute" certainty, there was in fact no more than a one in three chance that they were correct.

* * *

III

A

Despite its recognition that the testimony at issue was probably wrong and certainly prejudicial, the Court holds this testimony admissible because the Court is "unconvinced ... that the adversary process cannot be trusted to sort out the reliable from the unreliable evidence and opinion about future dangerousness." One can only wonder how juries are to separate valid from invalid expert opinions when the "experts" themselves are so obviously unable to do so. Indeed, the evidence suggests that juries are not effective at assessing the validity of scientific evidence. Giannelli, Scientific Evidence, 80 Colum.L.Rev., [1197], 1239–1240, and n. 319 (1980).

There can be no question that psychiatric predictions of future violence will have an undue effect on the ultimate verdict. Even judges tend to accept psychiatrists' recommendations about a defendant's dangerousness with little regard for cross-examination or other testimony. Cocozza & Steadman, *supra* n. 2, 25 Soc.Probs., at 271 (in making involuntary commitment decisions, psychiatric predictions of future dangerousness accepted in 86.7% of cases). There is every reason to believe that inexperienced jurors will be still less capable of "separat[ing] the wheat from the chaff," despite the Court's blithe assumption to the contrary. The American Bar Association has warned repeatedly that sentencing juries are particularly incapable of dealing with information relating to "the likelihood that the defendant will commit other crimes," and similar predictive judgments. Relying on the ABA's conclusion, the joint opinion announcing the judgment in *Gregg v. Georgia,* 428 U.S., at 192, 96 S.Ct., at 2934, recognized that "[s]ince the members of a jury will have had little, if any, previous experience in sentencing, they are unlikely to be skilled in dealing with the information they are given." But the Court in this case, in its haste to praise the jury's ability to find the truth, apparently forgets this well-known and worrisome shortcoming.

As if to suggest that petitioner's position that unreliable expert testimony should be excluded is unheard of in the law, the Court relies on the proposition that the rules of evidence generally "anticipate that relevant, unprivileged evidence should be admitted and its weight left to the factfinder, who would have the benefit of cross-examination and contrary evidence by the opposing party." But the Court simply ignores hornbook law that, despite the availability of cross-examination and rebuttal witnesses, "opinion evidence is not admissible if the court believes that the state of the pertinent art or scientific knowledge does not permit a reasonable opinion to be asserted." Because it is feared that the jury will overestimate its probative value, polygraph evidence, for example, almost invariably is excluded from trials despite the fact that, at a conservative estimate, an experienced polygraph examiner can detect truth or deception correctly about 80 to 90 percent of the time. Ennis & Litwack, *supra* n. 2, at 736. In no area is purportedly "expert" testimony admitted for the jury's consideration where it cannot be demonstrated that it is correct more often than not. "It is inconceivable that a judgment could be considered an 'expert' judgment when it is less accurate than the flip of a coin." *Id.*, at 737. The risk that a jury will be incapable of separating "scientific" myth from reality is deemed unacceptably high.

B

The Constitution's mandate of reliability, with the stakes at life or death, precludes reliance on cross-examination and the opportunity to present rebuttal witnesses as an antidote for this distortion of the truth-finding process. Cross-examination is unlikely to reveal the fatuousness of psychiatric predictions because such predictions often rest, as was the case here, on psychiatric categories and intuitive clinical judgments not susceptible to cross-examination and rebuttal. Psychiatric categories have little or no demonstrated relationship to violence, and their use often obscures the unimpressive statistical or intuitive bases for prediction. The APA particularly condemns the use of the diagnosis employed by Doctors Grigson and Holbrook in this case, that of sociopathy:

> "In this area confusion reigns. The psychiatrist who is not careful can mislead the judge or jury into believing that a person has a major mental disease simply on the basis of a description of prior criminal behavior. Or a psychiatrist can mislead the court into believing that an individual is devoid of conscience on the basis of a description of criminal acts alone.... The profession of psychiatry has a responsibility to avoid inflicting this confusion upon the courts and to spare the defendant the harm that may result.... Given our uncertainty about the implications of the finding, the diagnosis of sociopathy ... should not be used to justify or to support predictions of future conduct. There is no certainty in this area." Draft Report 30.

It is extremely unlikely that the adversary process will cut through the facade of superior knowledge. The Chief Justice long ago observed:

> "The very nature of the adversary system ... complicates the use of scientific opinion evidence, particularly in the field of psychiatry. This system of partisan contention, of attack and counterattack, at its best is not ideally suited to developing an accurate portrait or profile of the human personality, especially in the area of abnormal behavior. Although under ideal conditions the adversary system can develop for a jury most of the necessary fact material for an adequate decision, such conditions are rarely achieved in the courtrooms in this country. These ideal conditions would include a highly skilled and experienced trial judge and highly skilled lawyers on both sides of the case, all of whom in addition to being well-trained

in the law and in the techniques of advocacy would be sophisticated in matters of medicine, psychiatry, and psychology. It is far too rare that all three of the legal actors in the cast meet these standards." Burger, Psychiatrists, Lawyers, and the Courts, 28 Fed.Prob. 3, 6 (June 1964).

* * *

Nor is the presentation of psychiatric witnesses on behalf of the defense likely to remove the prejudicial taint of misleading testimony by prosecution psychiatrists. No reputable expert would be able to predict with confidence that the defendant will *not* be violent; at best, the witness will be able to give his opinion that all predictions of dangerousness are unreliable. Consequently, the jury will not be presented with the traditional battle of experts with opposing views on the ultimate question. Given a choice between an expert who says that he can predict with certainty that the defendant, whether confined in prison or free in society, will kill again, and an expert who says merely that no such prediction can be made, members of the jury charged by law with making the prediction surely will be tempted to opt for the expert who claims he can help them in performing their duty, and who predicts dire consequences if the defendant is not put to death.[13]

Moreover, even at best, the presentation of defense psychiatrists will convert the death sentence hearing into a battle of experts, with the Eighth Amendment's well-established requirement of individually focused sentencing a certain loser. The jury's attention inevitably will turn from an assessment of the propriety of sentencing to death the defendant before it to resolving a scientific dispute about the capabilities of psychiatrists to predict future violence. In such an atmosphere, there is every reason to believe that the jury may be distracted from its constitutional responsibility to consider "particularized mitigating factors," in passing on the defendant's future dangerousness.

* * *

IV

* * *

---

13. "Although jurors may treat mitigating psychiatric evidence with skepticism, they may credit psychiatric evidence demonstrating aggravation. Especially when jurors' sensibilities are offended by a crime, they may seize upon evidence of dangerousness to justify an enhanced sentence." Dix, *supra* n. 2, at 43, n. 215. Thus, the danger of jury deference to expert opinions is particularly acute in death penalty cases. Expert testimony of this sort may permit juries to avoid the difficult and emotionally draining personal decisions concerning rational and just punishment. *Id.,* at 46. Doctor Grigson himself has noted both the su-

perfluousness and the misleading effect of his testimony:

"'I think you could do away with the psychiatrist in these cases. Just take any man off the street, show him what the guy's done, and most of these things are so clearcut he would say the same things I do. But I think the jurors feel a little better when a psychiatrist says it—somebody that's supposed to know more than they know.'" Bloom, Killers and Shrinks, Texas Monthly 64, 68 (July 1978) (quoting Doctor Grigson).

The Court ... errs in suggesting that the exclusion of psychiatrists' predictions of future dangerousness would be contrary to the logic of *Jurek*. *Jurek* merely upheld Texas' substantive decision to condition the death sentence upon proof of a probability that the defendant will commit criminal acts of violence in the future. Whether the evidence offered by the prosecution to prove that probability is so unreliable as to violate a capital defendant's rights to due process is an entirely different matter, one raising only questions of fair procedure.

* * *

It makes sense to exclude psychiatric predictions of future violence while admitting lay testimony, because psychiatric predictions appear to come from trained mental health professionals, who purport to have special expertise. In view of the total scientific groundlessness of these predictions, psychiatric testimony is fatally misleading. Lay testimony, frankly based on statistical factors with demonstrated correlations to violent behavior, would not raise this substantial threat of unreliable and capricious sentencing decisions, inimical to the constitutional standards established in our cases; and such predictions are as accurate as any a psychiatrist could make.

* * *

Questions and Comments

1. *Evidentiary analysis.* In arriving at their conclusions, both the majority and the dissent in *Barefoot* seem to structure their analysis primarily around the federal rules of evidence. The central arguments are over whether the jury will be able to "separate the wheat from the chaff" and whether psychiatrists can add anything to what the jury could figure out for itself. Dix, on the other hand, suggests applying the *Frye* rule in this context and concludes that, under this analysis, clinical prediction testimony should generally be excluded. George Dix, "Expert Prediction Testimony in Capital Sentencing: Evidentiary and Constitutional Considerations," 19 Am. Crim. L.Rev. 1, 19–21 (1981). Do you agree that prediction testimony is not "generally accepted"? What is the relevant "field" for purposes of determining general acceptance in this context: The APA? Forensic clinicians such as Grigson and Holbrook? What would be the outcome in *Barefoot* if *Daubert/Kumho Tire* were applicable? Interestingly, the Supreme Court did not cite *Barefoot* in *Daubert*. At least one lower court has held that *Daubert* does not require re-analysis of the *Barefoot* holding, calling any objection to clinical prediction testimony "frivolous." *Johnson v. Cockrell*, 306 F.3d 249, 254 (5th Cir.2002).

2. *Prediction testimony in other settings.* Many commentators have argued that clinical prediction testimony should be barred not just from capital sentencing proceedings but from other proceedings as well. See sources cited in note 2 of Blackmun's opinion in *Barefoot*. Even before *Barefoot*, however, the courts had been reticent about adopting such a position in capital cases, much less in other types of cases. See *People v. Murtishaw*, 29 Cal.3d 733, 767–75, 175 Cal.Rptr. 738, 758–63, 631 P.2d 446, 466–71 (1981). One court did prohibit clinical prediction testimony in civil

commitment proceedings. *In re Wilson*, 33 Crim.L.Rep. (BNA) 2115 (D.C.Super.Ct. Apr. 14, 1983). But it stood alone and now, presumably, is nullified by *Barefoot*.

The majority in *Barefoot* states that a different holding "would immediately call into question those other contexts in which predictions of future behavior are constantly made." Does it make sense to say, as Justice Blackmun seems to be saying in his dissent, that clinical prediction testimony is too inaccurate for capital proceedings but is permissible in other proceedings, such as civil commitments? Within a particular setting (e.g., capital sentencing), does it make sense to bar clinical prediction testimony, but allow clinical testimony on normality and responsibility issues (which also are relevant at capital sentencing[f])?

3. *The accuracy of dangerousness assessments.* The Court quotes Professor Monahan to the effect that, at best, clinical predictions of dangerousness are accurate no more than one out of three times. This statement needs to be looked at more closely from at least four different perspectives.

(a) New Research. Much of the literature on predictive capacity focuses on the "false positive" rate, that is, the rate at which a positive finding of dangerousness is falsely or erroneously made. This terminology is used to emphasize the percentage of people who may be wrongfully sentenced to death or confined if decisions are based on dangerousness predictions. Putting Monahan's summary of the research in these terms, the "best" false positive rate obtained by clinical prediction studies has been around 66%. Some studies have found false positive rates as high as 92%. See Ernest Wenk & Robert Emrich, "Assaultive Youth: An Exploratory Study of the Assaultive Experience and Assaultive Potential of California Youth Authority Wards," 9 J. Res. Crime & Delinq. 171 (1972).

However, more recent research, relying on more sophisticated predictive models, has obtained better results, with false positive rates often falling below 50%. John Monahan et al., "An Actuarial Model of Violence Risk Assessment for Persons with Mental Disorders," 56 Psychiatric Serv. 810, 814 (2005) (51%); Charles Lidz et al., "The Accuracy of Predictions of Violence to Others," 269 J.Amer.Med.Ass. 1007 (1993)(47%); Jay Apperson et al., "Short–Term Clinical Prediction of Assaultive Behavior: Artifacts of Research Methods," 150 Am. J. Psychiat. 1374 (1993)(25%); Deidre Klassen & William O'Connor, "A Prospective Study of Predictors of Violence in Adult Male Mental Patients," 12 Law and Human Behavior 143 (1988)(40%); Diana Sepejak et al., "Clinical Predictions of Dangerousness: Two–Year Follow-up of 408 Pre–Trial Forensic Cases," 11 Bull. Am. Acad. Psychiat. & L. 171 (1983)(44%). To be reliable under *Daubert* or generally accepted under *Frye*, should prediction testimony be based on a methodology that avoids high false positive rates? If so, what should the cut-off be: 50%, 25%, 5%? Should the answer to the latter question depend on the standard of proof that must be met (beyond a reasonable doubt, clear and convincing

---

f. For instance, the Model Penal Code's capital sentencing statute specifies as a mitigating circumstance the fact that, at the time of the murder, "the capacity of the defendant to appreciate the criminality [wrongfulness] of his conduct or to conform his conduct to the requirements of law was impaired as a result of mental disease or defect or intoxication." § 210.6(3)(g).

evidence, preponderance of the evidence)? Or should the prediction testimony always be admissible, as long as error rate information is available for the factfinder?

(b) Methodological Problems. To some extent, false positive findings may be attributable to factors other than poor predictive capabilities. Most of the research relies on police or hospital records to determine whether a person predicted to be violent subsequently was so. But such records notoriously underreport the amount of violent acts committed, some suggest by a factor of ten. Paul Meehl, "The Insanity Defense," Minn. Psychol. 11, 15 (Summer, 1983). Thus, a number of the supposed "false positives" may simply be undiscovered "true positives" (i.e., individuals correctly predicted to be dangerous). As Monahan has suggested, it is possible that those who were arrested committed many of the unreported and unsolved crimes; if this is true, then the false positive rates may not be as grossly overstated as Meehl claims. John Monahan, The Clinical Prediction of Violent Behavior 52–56 (NIMH 1981). But one study suggests that even taking this factor into account "more than one-quarter of the 'false positives' may not, in fact, be false positives if self reports are a valid measure of violence." Deidre Klassen & William O'Connor, "Predicting Violence in Mental Patients: Cross–Validation of an Actuarial Scale," paper presented at the Annual Meeting of the American Public Health Association (1987).

A second methodological problem with the research literature on dangerousness results from the fact that, for obvious reasons, most of the studies cannot be based on "natural experiments" involving release of persons designated as dangerous into the community. That is, the *usual* response to a prediction of dangerousness, if one occurs, is to institutionalize, not release, the person thought to be violence-prone. Thus the clinical prediction that someone will be dangerous *in the community* is tested by reference to whether the person considered dangerous is assaultive *in the institution*. Because institutionalization and treatment may seriously curb the individual's assaultive behavior, the false positive rates reported in studies that use institutional violence as a criterion for violence may be significantly exaggerated. See George Dix, "Clinical Evaluation of the "Dangerousness" of "Normal" Criminal Defendants," 66 Va.L.Rev. 523, 544 n. 82 (1980). Even those studies that use violence in the community as the criterion variable are tainted by the fact that, once a prediction of violence is made, institutionalization and/or treatment almost always takes place before the individual returns to the community.

Because of these methodological problems, some have suggested that predictions of violence may meet the "clear and convincing" level of proof, at least when based on either a recent history of repeated violence, a more distant history of violence together with proof that the personality traits and attitudes that led to the past violence still exist, or unequivocal threats of serious intentions to commit violence. Thomas Litwack & Louis Schlesinger, "Assessing and Predicting Violence: Research, Law, and Applications," in Irving Weiner & Allen Hess, eds., Handbook of Forensic Psychology 205, 224 (1987).

(c) Base Rates. It must also be emphasized that even relatively high false positive rates do not mean that overall predictive validity is poor, given

the low "base rate" for violence in most populations. The following excerpt explains why:

> [W]hen, as is usually the case, the truly violent population is quite small compared to the nonviolent population (i.e., when there is a low "base rate" for violence), even prediction methods that are highly valid will generate large numbers of false-positive errors. A brief example illustrates this phenomenon. Assume that in a population of 1,000 subjects, 15% (n = 150) will commit a violent act and 85% (n = 850) will not. Assume also that the clinician can accurately classify 90% of each group. In this example, the clinician will accurately label as violent 135 (150 x .90) truly violent individuals, whereas only 85 cases labeled "violent" (850 x .10) will be persons who on follow-up in fact will not be violent. Thus, the percent-false-positive figure will be a relatively respectable 39% (85/(135 + 85). As the incidence of violence gets smaller, however, this error rate increases. If, for instance, the incidence of violence in the 1,000–person population is only 5%, the same clinician (with the same accuracy rate of 90%) will have a false-positive rate of 68% (95/(45 + 95)).

Gary Melton et al., Psychological Evaluations for the Courts: A Handbook for Mental Health Professionals and Lawyers 302–03 (3d ed.2007).

(d) Coin-flipping and chance. Assuming psychiatric predictions of dangerousness are at best correct only one out of three times, Justice Blackmun claims that such predictions yield results that are less accurate than flipping a coin. The coin flipping analogy, first made by Bruce Ennis and Thomas Litwack in "Psychiatry and the Presumption of Expertise: Flipping Coins in the Courtroom," 62 Calif.L.Rev. 693 (1974), is seriously misleading to the extent it suggests that clinical predictions are no better than "chance." To discover why this is so, one must first determine the "base rate" for violent behavior among the population being evaluated for dangerousness. For instance, say that the base rate for violence in the general population is roughly one out of 300, meaning that only one person out of every 300 in the general population will commit a violent act in their lifetime. If a psychiatrist could predict accurately one-third of the time who was dangerous in the general population, his or her predictions would be much better than chance, specifically *100 times* better than a random selection from amongst the population. The populations involved in the research to which Monahan refers were usually institutionalized patients or criminals and tended to have a much higher base rate for violence than the general population, in the vicinity of one out of nine, rather than one out of 300. But a predictive accuracy ratio of one out of three for such a population would still be three times better than chance. This predictive ratio would be worse than chance only for a population with a base rate for violence higher than one out of three. Thus, the coin-flipping analogy would appear to be inapt. See Christopher Slobogin, "Dangerousness and Expertise," 133 Pa.L.Rev. 97, 110–14 (1984).

More recent research has confirmed that mental health professionals "offer predictions that are more accurate than would occur by chance, suggesting that they have some predictive power or ability," at least when the concept of "dangerousness" is "broadly conceived (i.e., threatening behavior and/or physically assaultive behavior)." Randy Otto, "Prediction of Dangerous Behavior: A Review and Analysis of 'Second–Generation' Research," 5 Forensic Reports 103 (1992); see also, Charles Lidz et al., "The Accuracy of Predictions of Violence to Others," 269 J.Amer.Med.Ass. 1007, 1010 (1993)("Not only did the clinicians pick out a statistically more violent group, but the violence that the predicted group committed was more serious than the acts of the comparison group"); Douglas Mossman, "Assessing Predictions of Violence: Being Accurate About Accuracy," 62(4) J. Consulting & Clinical Psychology 783 (1994) ("This article's re-evaluation of representative data from the past two decades suggests that clinicians are able to distinguish violent from non-violent persons with a modest, better-than-chance level of accuracy."). Do these data mean that dangerousness predictions are "reliable," as that word is used in *Daubert* and the amended version of Rule 702? Are they at least "relevant," which the Federal Rules of Evidence defines as "any tendency to make the existence of any fact that is of consequence to the determination of the action more probable or less probable than it would be without the evidence"? Rule 401. In the death penalty context, does it matter that, as Dr. Otto notes in the above-cited article, the better-than-chance predictions focus on threatening or assaultive behavior, not homicide?

4. *Diagnosis and dangerousness.* Relevant both to predictive accuracy and to whether mental health professionals possess "specialized knowledge" about violence-proneness is the extent to which certain diagnoses can be viewed as indicative of dangerousness. The state's psychiatrists in *Barefoot* diagnosed Barefoot as a "sociopath." This diagnosis, often used interchangeably with "psychopathy," describes people who lack empathy, have shallow emotions, and feel no accountability for their actions. It is analogous to, but not congruent with, the DSM–IV diagnosis of antisocial personality disorder (see Appendix A, p. 1349). Forensic clinicians have often correlated all three of these diagnoses with dangerousness. For instance, Dr. Grigson, who testified for the state of Texas in scores of death penalty sentencing proceedings (and, as a result, was dubbed 'Dr. Death' by the media[g]), usually coupled his prediction that the defendant would be violent with a diagnosis of sociopathy.

There is significant research supporting such a correlation. See, e.g., George Vaillant, "Crime and Mental Illness in a Group of Psychopathic Personalities," 9 Med. Sci & L. 11 (1969) (psychopaths committed 23 times as many offenses as controls); Martin et al., "Female Criminality and the Prediction of Recidivism," 35 Arch. Gen. Psychiat. 207 (1978). Others have suggested that the diagnosis has no predictive power independent of that provided by the number and types of past antisocial acts committed by the individual labeled a sociopath. T.C.N. Gibbens et al., "A Follow-up Study of Criminal Psychopaths," 105 J. Mental Sci. 108 (1969); Dix, supra, at 573. But more recent reports confirm that the psychopathy/sociopathy/antisocial

g. See Time, June 1, 1981, at 64. In 1995, Dr. Grigson was expelled from the American Psychiatric Association and the Texas Society of Psychiatric Physicians for ethics violations relating to his court predictions of "future dangerousness." Jeffrey L. Kirchmeier, "Aggravating and Mitigating Factors: The Paradox of Today's Arbitrary and Mandatory Capital Punishment Scheme," 6 Wm. & Mary Bill Rts. J. 345, 372 (1998).

diagnosis is highly correlated with violence. Robert Hare & Leslie McPherson, "Violent and Aggressive Behavior by Criminal Psychopaths," 7 Int'l J. Law & Psychiat. 35 (1984). There is now a "Psychopathy Checklist" that yields ratings on 20 scales having to do with behavioral traits and historical features; a score of 30 or higher (out of 40) is probably indicative of psychopathy and considered a good indicator of risk. Robert Hare et al., "The Revised Psychopathy Checklist: Reliability and Factor Structure," 2 Psychological Assessment: Journal of Consulting & Clinical Psychology 338 (1990). The primary author of this checklist has argued that "psychopathy is the single most important clinical construct in the criminal justice system, with particularly strong implications for the assessment of risk for recidivism and violence." Robert Hare, "The Hare PCL–R: Some Issues Concerning Its Use and Misuse," 3 Legal & Criminol. Psychol. 99 (1998).

The evidence concerning the usefulness of other diagnoses in determining dangerousness is mixed, although it appears that serious mental illness may be correlated with a somewhat increased risk of violence. More is said about the relationship between violence and serious mental illness in Chapter Eight (see pp. 718–19).

5. *Alternatives to clinical prediction testimony.* In his dissent in *Barefoot,* Justice Blackmun contended that "[l]ay testimony, frankly based on statistical factors with demonstrated correlations to violent behavior" could competently fill the gap created by prohibiting psychiatric testimony on dangerousness. Testimony "based on statistical factors" may have its own set of evidentiary problems, depending upon how it is implemented. Consider the following materials.

UNITED STATES v. BARNETTE

United States Court of Appeals, Fourth Circuit, 2000.
211 F.3d 803.

[Aquilia Barnette was charged with killing Donald Allen and Robin Williams. Three months before the murders, Williams had ended her relationship with Barnette and moved to the apartment of Benjamin Greene because she was scared of being alone. Two months before the murders, Barnette came to Greene's house, smashed the windows of Greene's car with a baseball bat and, when he saw Williams in the window, began breaking the building's windows and threw a firebomb into the apartment. Williams and Greene escaped, although Williams was badly burned. Two months later, having evaded arrest, Barnette approached Allen (whom he apparently did not know) while Allen was in his car, aimed a shotgun at him, ordered him out, and shot him three times in the back. He then drove Allen's car to the home of Williams' mother, where he knew Williams' was staying since leaving Green's apartment. There he stated he was going to kill her and himself. When Williams ran away he shot her twice, killing her. He then escaped, but turned himself in two days later. He confessed to both crimes, was convicted of capital murder and sentenced to death. One of the aggravating factors that was considered by the jury was future dangerousness. To prove that factor, the government relied on Dr. Scott Duncan, who testified that Barnette would be "a future danger in prison" based on three factors: his high score on the Psychopathy Checklist Revised; research on predicting future dangerousness; and an actuarial analysis comparing Barnette to groups of people with characteristics similar to him. Dr. Duncan found that Barnette was likely to be violent in the future. Barnette challenged the admissibility of this testimony.]

Barnette claims as inadmissible Dr. Duncan's testimony relying on the Psychopathy Checklist Revised because it was not evaluated for reliability as required by *Daubert v. Merrell Dow Pharmaceuticals*. Barnette argues that the Psychopathy Checklist Revised is unreliable because it has not been standardized with respect to black inmates, and Dr. Duncan improperly used race, wealth, age, and sex to support his opinion that Barnette was a psychopath.... In *Daubert*, the Supreme Court radically changed the standard for admissibility of scientific testimony. Instead of requiring that the scientific community generally accept scientific evidence before a court could admit it, the Court set out a looser, two-step gatekeeping function that a trial court must perform when evaluating the admissibility of all expert testimony. The trial judge must ensure that the evidence is based on scientific knowledge, or is reliable, and ensure that the evidence will assist the trier of fact, or is relevant. The Court provided four factors that could be used in this evaluation, but stressed its determination that the analysis should be flexible. The Court also noted that "[v]igorous cross examination, presentation of contrary evidence and careful instruction on the burden of proof are traditional and appropriate means of attacking shaky but admissible evidence." The *Daubert* test's gatekeeping requirement is to ensure that the expert witness in question in the courtroom employs the same level of intellectual vigor that characterizes the practice of an expert in the relevant field. *Kumho Tire Co.* When making this determination, the trial judge must have considerable leeway in both his reliability determination and the means he uses to conduct it. We have consistently given the trial judge's decision on whether to admit expert testimony under *Daubert* great deference. However, we must reverse if there is a clear error in judgment on the part of the district court.

While Barnette essentially alleges that the district court made an improper initial determination that the Psychopathy Checklist Revised was reliable scientific evidence, he does not contest its relevancy. When deciding whether to admit the testimony based on the Psychopathy Checklist Revised, the court considered Barnette's objections to the test, that the list had not been standardized as to the black population (Barnette is black) or as to the post middle-age population. Barnette offered two articles written by his own expert, Dr. Cunningham, to support his position, but no other evidence. On this record, the decision to admit the evidence was not a clear error of judgment. Taking into account the discretion afforded the district court's decision, we are of opinion that its examination of the issue was sufficient and that the record does not support a determination that admitting the evidence was an abuse of discretion.... Here, Barnette only proffered two articles written by his expert, Dr. Cunningham, as evidence disputing the scientific validity of the Psychopathy Checklist Revised. He did not, at that time, proffer any other evidence of unreliability. In our opinion, that evidence alone is not sufficient to show unreliability when an expert in the field did rely on that type of testing. Absent evidence indicating more than such a disagreement between professionals, we do not believe the district court needed to go further to evaluate reliability.

Finally, Barnette argues that Dr. Duncan's opinion that Barnette is a psychopath rests on impermissible factors: race, age, and poverty. We find no merit in this argument. Dr. Duncan used 20 characteristics in his evaluation of Barnette under the Psychopathy Checklist Revised, in addition to the 11 characteristics he used in his future dangerousness prediction, three of which were race, age, and poverty. Barnette does not offer sufficient reasons for us to believe that Dr. Duncan's entire opinion was based only on these three factors, and not upon all the other factors combined. Additionally, Dr. Duncan utilized several other bases for his diagnosis of psychopathy and future dangerousness: the Diagnostic and Statistical Manual, Fourth Edition; his observations of Barnette's behavior; the actuarial approach; and the research on predicting future dangerousness. Under these circumstances, we do not find that Dr. Duncan based his opinion on impermissible factors. . . .

Questions and Comments

1. Daubert *analysis and actuarial prediction.* Is the Court correct in stating that *Daubert* established "a looser analysis" than *Frye*? Is it correct in requiring Barnette to prove the unreliability of the PCL–R, rather than requiring the state to demonstrate its reliability?

In terms of determining reliability under *Daubert*, how much weight should be given to Barnette's argument that the PCL–R was not standardized with respect to African Americans or people who are past middle age (both attributes of Barnette)? Should it matter whether the PCL–R has been normed on populations in prison? In fact, among prediction instruments, the PCL–R is one of the most heavily researched, and has demonstrated fairly good generalizability to various populations. But consider this statement about actuarial instruments in general:

> [F]ailure to scientifically cross-validate RAIs [risk assessment instruments] can be fatal because characteristics of offender populations can vary dramatically, and an RAI constructed on one population may not generalize, or cross over, to a different population. . . . The problem presented by population demographics, or cohort characteristics, is vast and potentially insurmountable: Does an RAI derived from a study comprised of a cohort that included convicted rapists generalize to those offenders diagnosed with pedophilia? Is an instrument that excluded from its construction sample noncoercive incest offenders useful in evaluating risk in offenders with a history of noncoercive incest? Elusive as the answers to these questions may be, many scientists and professionals assert that without appropriate, scientifically scrutinized cross-validation, absolute risk predictions based upon RAI scores are meaningless.

Donna Cropp Bechman, "Sex Offender Civil Commitments: Scientists or Psychics?" 16 Crim. J. 24, 29 (2001). The same author makes additional points about the "inter-rater" reliability of risk assessments instruments.

> "[I]nter-rater reliability" is an important part of the development of any testing procedure, including RAIs, yet little is published in peer review literature that establishes whether or not these instruments have been appropriately evaluated for reliability when used by different raters in the field. Although the concept of assigning a weighted score to a risk factor, adding up the numbers, and achieving a quantification provided by mathematical calculation may sound fairly objective in nature, and, therefore, not easily the subject of inconsistencies among raters, nothing could be farther from the truth. Even the very definition of "offense" differs from instrument to instrument. Where one instrument intends by the use of the word "offense" to have the rater take into account offenses charged regardless of conviction, another instrument defines the word "offense" as only that which resulted in conviction. And is a conviction for an attempted sex offense sufficient? What if the conviction is for burglary, but the underlying intent was to commit a rape? If the conviction was later overturned on appeal due to error in the trial court, is it still a conviction? Are all raters in the field answering these questions consistently for each instrument? Are all raters aware that most instruments do not intend to include in their calculations self-reported offenses that never result in a charge or conviction?

Id. In terms of admissibility analysis, should it matter that this type of information on problems with cross-validation and inter-rater reliability may be difficult for juries to understand?[h]

2. *Admissible statistical factors*. The court finds nothing wrong with relying on race, age and poverty in making predictions. Do you agree? Is the use of race to make predictions a violation of the equal protection clause? Even if it is, does the state nonetheless have a compelling interest in using race as a predictor (assume, for instance, that use of race improves the accuracy of prediction by 30%)?

Whatever the outcome with respect to race as a predictor, use of age or poverty clearly does not violate equal protection principles as long as they have some predictive validity. The Violence Risk Appraisal Guide (VRAG) tells evaluators to look at a number of similar factors, including whether the person was separated from his or her parents before 16, and his or her diagnosis (with a personality disorder diagnosis signaling a greater likelihood of recidivism than a diagnosis of schizophrenia), as well as his or her marital status and alcohol abuse history. Are there subconstitutional concerns associated with using factors such as these to make predictions that can result in deprivation of liberty or execution? Some commentators have argued that reliance on "fixed factors over which the individual has no control runs counter to basic traditions of criminal law that stress free will and self-determination" and that "[a] procedure that allows judgements about an individual's blameworthiness to be based on statistical correlations to anony-

h. Monahan and Walker suggest that at least some statistical information could be relayed via jury instructions. John Monahan & Laurens Walker, "Social Frameworks: A New Use of Social Science in Law," 73 Va.L.Rev. 559, 592–98 (1987).

mous prior male-factors is deeply inconsistent with the general principles undergirding our system of law." See Daniel S. Goodman, "Demographic Evidence in Capital Sentencing," 39 Stanford L. Rev. 499, 525–27 (1987); Barbara Underwood, "Law and the Crystal Ball: Predicting Behavior with Statistical Inference and Individualized Judgment," 88 Yale L.J. 1408, 1436– 38 (1979). Are these concerns relevant when the context is commitment, where dangerousness rather than blameworthiness is the central issue? Are they relevant at sentencing, where incapacitation as well as retribution is considered a purpose of punishment? Adopting Goodman's view, Monahan has argued that the only risk factor that one can consider at sentencing (as opposed to civil commitment) is past acts. See John Monahan, "A Jurisprudence of Risk Assessment, Forecasting Harm Among Prisoners, Predators, and Patients," 92 Va. L. Rev. 391, 428 (2006). In practice, this limitation would seriously curtail the accuracy of predictions.

3. *Comparing clinical and statistical evidence.* Many actuarial devices developed to predict dangerousness have no more predictive accuracy than clinical evaluations. See Antonio Convit, et al., "Predicting Assaultiveness in Psychiatric Inpatients: A Pilot Study," 39 Hosp.Comm.Psychiat. 429 (1988)(63% false positive rate using actuarial techniques). But some actuarial instruments purport to be able to identify small groups of individuals who have a very high rate of recidivism. See, e.g., Vernon Quinsey et al., Violent Offenders: Appraising and Managing Risk 148–151 & Fig. 1 (1998) (discussing the VRAG's ability to identify groups of offenders with a 55%, 75% and 95% likelihood of recidivism); John Monahan et al., Rethinking Risk Assessment: The MacArthur Study of Mental Disorder and Violence 127 (2001) (using an "iterative classification tree" actuarial approach, which determines on a "yes/no" basis whether a certain variable is present and then moves to the next branch of the "tree," researchers able to place individuals in five risk categories representing risk levels from 1% to 76%). Furthermore, the *probabilities* obtained by statistical information, as opposed to clinical assessment, are relatively accurate; for example, the probability of violent behavior associated with being a white male opiate user can be fairly reliably ascertained.

Some nonetheless argue that actuarial predictions are inferior to clinical prediction judgments. Consider the following comments:

> As an instrument of judicial decisionmaking, [statistical or demographic] evidence is in a very palpable way substantially less 'relevant' to an individual's circumstances than is clinical psychiatric evidence. Unlike demographic studies, psychiatric evaluations are—at least in some sense—mediated through the individual. Clinical and statistical methods differ because "a clinical decisionmaker is not committed in advance of decision to the factors that will be considered and the rule for combining them. He is free to respond to individual differences whose relevance was not anticipated by any rule." Since the clinical approach recognizes the individuality of each defendant, it permits the psychiatrist or psychologist to alter in a particular case the general judgment of actuarial reckoning.... The fact that all assessments are to some extent relational—that is, implicitly relative or based upon some unstated empirical assumptions—does not obviate the distinction between judicial methods that focus on the individual and those that are avowedly abstract or

generic. And where those generic methods rely on statistics, their potential to mislead the jury outweighs their usefulness.

Goodman, supra, at 525–27.

Goodman asserts that statistical evidence lacks relevance because it is not "individualized," and is prejudicial because it is difficult to rebut and might mislead the factfinder; that is, in attempting to rebut statistical evidence that a white male opiate user with one conviction for violent crime has, say, a one in five chance of committing a violent act within the next five years, such a person might find it very difficult to convince the jury that other personal characteristics he possesses place him in the group of white male opiate users who will not commit another violent act within that time period. How is clinical prediction testimony different? As Goodman admits, mental health professionals often rely on "unstated empirical assumptions" about relationships between certain traits (e.g., race, sex and opiate use) and certain behavior (e.g., violent behavior). If these assumptions are "unstated," how is it easier for the individual to rebut them?[i] Is the point that before arriving at a conclusion the clinician will observe all aspects of the individual and thus arrive at a fairer, less "stereotyped" assessment than would a jury hearing only demographic evidence and any rebuttal information the individual cares to present? To what extent do you think this is the case, given what has been discussed about the reasons for variance in clinical assessments?

Some commentators have argued for an "adjusted actuarial" approach to prediction, where the evaluator "begins with an actuarial prediction, but . . . can then adjust (or not) the actuarial prediction after considering potentially important factors that were not included in the actuarial measure." R. Karl Hanson, "What Do We Know About Sex Offender Risk Assessment?" 4 Psychology, Pub. Pol. & L. 50, 52 (1998). Apparently, this was the type of prediction methodology Dr. Duncan used in *Barnette*. Others, however, have argued that "adjusted" decisions are typically no more accurate and may be less accurate that those made through statistics alone. For instance, one commentary states that "[a]ctuarial methods are too good and clinical judgment too poor to risk contaminating the former with the latter." Quinsey et al., supra, at 171.

Would it be best to prohibit *both* clinical and statistical prediction evidence, permit both, or rely on only one type of evidence? If the latter, which one? Courts have registered decidedly different points of view on the latter issue. Compare *State v. Kienitz*, 221 Wis.2d 275, 585 N.W.2d 609 (App. 1998)(rejecting the argument that only the actuarial method of prediction provides sufficient "precision" to make predictions) with *Massachusetts v. Reese*, 13 Mass. L.Rptr. 195 (2001), rev'd 438 Mass. 519, 781 N.E.2d 1225 (2003)("while a factfinder may have good reason modestly to adjust a statistical probability based on idiosyncratic clinical information unique to the . . . offender, there would need to be a compelling reason to justify a dramatic adjustment to the statistical probability"). Compare also *In re*

---

i. Note that in *Barefoot,* Justice Blackmun concluded that psychiatric prediction testimony is difficult to rebut "because such predictions often rest . . . on psychiat-ric categories and intuitive clinical judgments . . . ; their use often obscures the unimpressive statistical or intuitive bases for prediction."

Valdez, No. 99–000045CI (Fla. 2000)(rejecting actuarial prediction devices such as the VRAG because they are based on scientific principles—i.e., that a prediction can be made solely on the basis of selected items of demographic information, that a scoring system can be devised to capture the relevant information, and that the scoring scheme can apply "to any individual, anywhere, at any time" to yield a prediction—that are not "generally accepted," partly because the only professionals using these devices are the approximately 150 psychologists performing sex offender evaluations), with *State ex rel. Romley v. Fields*, 201 Ariz. 321, 35 P.3d 82 (2001)(holding that actuarial opinion testimony should be not be subject to *Frye* or any other screening test).

4. *Hypothetical questions.* In *Barefoot,* it will be remembered, both Dr. Grigson and Dr. Holbrook (the prosecution's witnesses) testified in answer to "hypothetical" questions. They did not interview Barefoot but rather were given information about his prior record and other aspects of his character and asked to formulate an opinion on that basis. Barefoot argued that use of hypotheticals is unconstitutional, both generally (because they allow testimony not based on personal examination), and in his particular case (because they allowed testimony that was based on controverted facts). The Court rejected these arguments, noting that hypothetical questions have long been in use and that, if the defendant was concerned about the accuracy of their assumptions in his particular case, he could have constructed his own questions using a different version of the facts. 463 U.S. at 903–05, 103 S.Ct. at 3399–3400, 77 L.Ed.2d at 1110–12. How is testimony based on a hypothetical question different from testimony based on statistical evidence? Should the same rule, whether it be admission or exclusion, be adopted for both?

5. *Substantive concerns.* Clearly, predicting future behavior is not easy, no matter which route is taken. Yet, as the majority in *Barefoot* noted, the Court has upheld the use of dangerousness as an aggravating factor in capital cases. *Jurek v. Texas*, 428 U.S. 262, 96 S.Ct. 2950, 49 L.Ed.2d 929 (1976). Should *Jurek* be overturned? Should dangerousness be a criterion in *any* type of legal proceeding? Would it be consistent to jettison dangerousness as a justification for legal intervention, but not abnormality or incompetency? We will revisit these questions in subsequent chapters.

D. COMPETENCY

The "competency paradigm" permeates the law. One must be "competent" to stand trial, plead guilty or make a valid confession. If one is not "competent," a guardian may be appointed to manage one's affairs, treatment may be administered involuntarily, or one's will may be declared void. Mental health professionals are often called upon to help decide competency issues because it is usually assumed that mental disorder "causes" most, if not all, incompetency; indeed, many statutes require a finding that the incompetency results from mental disorder.

The evidentiary question is whether mental health professionals possess specialized knowledge that can assist the factfinder in answering any or all of the different types of questions raised by the competency issue. This subsection will focus on the mental health profession's expertise with respect to competency to stand trial, because of the relatively greater amount of legal and empirical material on the subject. The commonly accepted legal test in this context consists of two prongs: (1) whether the person is able to assist the attorney in his or her defense; and (2) whether the person understands the nature of the charges and the trial process. In reading the sample competency to stand trial report below, taken from an actual case file,[j] consider the extent to which it provides relevant reliable information that helps answer these two questions.

COMPETENCY REPORT

This [27 year old] patient was admitted on eight different occasions to the Broughton Hospital, Morgantown, North Carolina. His first hospitalization was on 28 March 1961 and he was discharged from the last, the eighth hospitalization, on 7 June 1969. His hospital records indicate that during the first few hospitalizations at Broughton it was felt that his main problem was a personality disorder, which was manifested primarily in anti-social behavior and excessive drinking. During the last few hospitalizations at Broughton, however, it has become apparent that this patient is suffering of schizophrenia, he displayed bizarre behavior and ideations and obviously the patient was delusional. The patient received a variety of different psychiatric treatments, his hospital course was rather unpredictable and also he has escaped a number of different occasions.

The personal past history indicates that he was born in 1942 in Shelby, North Carolina. This patient was reared mostly by his grandparents and there is very little known about his birth and early development. It should be noted that his grandmother and two maternal uncles have been in Broughton Hospital as patients. Apparently he developed properly and at the usual age began school. He stopped his education at age 18 and was in the eleventh grade. It is stated that he has stopped his education on account of earning some money. Shortly after his school he entered the United States Air Force and remained in service for approximately six months. The reason for the separation was his emotional inability to adjust to service life. This patient is described while he was in high school as a fairly well adjusted individual who showed considerable interest in reading. From the age of 16 he began to drink, at times excessively. He has shown very little interest in the opposite sex and never married. Following his short service in the United States Air Force in 1960 this patient began to show disinterest in his environment and was reluctant to assume responsibilities. In 1961 he was hospitalized the first time in Broughton. From here on until the present date this patient has been in and out of the hospital and obviously has shown evidence of a mental disturbance.

j. This sample report is presented and analyzed in Ronald Roesch and Stephen Golding, "Competency to Stand Trial" 83–85 (1980).

On admission the patient appeared to be alert but his affect[k] was rather fixed and at times inappropriate. He was well oriented in time, place and person.[l] He became somewhat confused and tense when he was asked about the circumstances under which he entered this Hospital. He freely admitted to paranoid ideations and pedophilia. Obviously the patient was very preoccupied and there was evidence of dissociation[m] of his thoughts. His hospital course was rather uneventful. On the ward the patient has presented no particular difficulties in his management. It is noted, that he is somewhat neglecting in his appearance and shows little interest in his environment. Generally speaking this patient appears to be tense and the psychomotor activity is somewhat increased.

During the consequent [sic] interviews the patient has expressed a great deal of his delusional system. It appears, that this patient firmly believes about his abilities to determine some individuals' future by looking in the sun. With an inappropriate affect the patient stated, that "you wouldn't understand" just what those signs mean, nevertheless he does and therefore he is a different individual from us.

He gave a rather coherent and detailed account of the incidence [sic] leading to his present charges. The patient stated, that he cannot resist to these impulses although he realizes the wrongness of such. During the interview the patient has become several times confused and irrelevant. He appears to be of above average intelligence and from that standpoint he is fully aware of his present legal situation.

The physical examination on admission revealed a well developed and nourished white male with a scar on the left knee, and otherwise the findings were essentially within normal limits. The laboratory findings were within normal, including a nonreactive VDRL.[n] The skull x-ray revealed a little irregularity at the outer side of the left antral sinus and this might possibly be the result of an old fracture. Otherwise the bony structure was normal and all other findings of the skull x-ray were normal. The chest x-ray was normal. The electroencephalogram was normal.

The psychological testing revealed a full-scale I.Q. of 98, which places this patient in the average intellectual functioning level.

Diagnosis: Schizophrenic Reaction, Chronic, Undifferentiated Type. APA Code: 295–90.

Recommendations: The examination and observations reveals that this patient is subject to a mental disturbance constituting insanity. This condition is manifested primarily in delusional thinking and inability to reason or to exercise proper judgment. This patient is fully aware of the wrongness of his alleged act, however, due to his mental disturbance he was unable to adhere to right and because of his disorganized thinking

k. Emotional demeanor [eds.]

l. This is standard psychiatric jargon (oriented times three) suggesting a basic awareness of surroundings. [eds.]

m. Usually means distancing oneself from an idea, situation, or object. Not clear what it means here. [eds.]

n. A test for syphilis. [eds.]

he is unable to assist in his own defense. He should continue hospitalization for a minimum necessary period of time as provided in G.S. 122–91 and 122–65 as being incompetent to stand trial at this time.

Questions and Comments

1. *The setting for competency determinations.* Adversarial hearings on competency to stand trial are rare. In many jurisdictions, the court making the competency determination usually relies entirely on a report or reports submitted by mental health professionals. Studies show that judges abide by the recommendations in such reports over 90% of the time. John Petrila, "The Insanity Defense and Other Mental Health Dispositions in Missouri," 5 Int'l J.L.Psychiat. 81 (1982); Ronald Roesch & Stephen Golding, Competency to Stand Trial 193 (1980) (35% of judges in North Carolina never disagree with hospital recommendations about competency; other 65% rarely or occasionally disagree). Should reports like the one above be admissible under these conditions? Are there sufficient facts about the defendant's mental state to aid the court in making a decision? How much of the report is irrelevant and/or prejudicial? Is the report internally consistent?

2. *Diagnosis and competency.* Like the author of the report, many mental health professionals apparently equate psychosis (e.g., schizophrenia) with incompetency to stand trial. A. Louis McGarry, "Competency for Trial and Due Process Via the State Hospital," 122 Am.J.Psychiat. 623 (1965) (100% correlation between psychosis and incompetency finding). But many courts have held that someone who is mentally ill might well be able to meet the relatively undemanding requirements of the competency standard; that is, they might be able to exhibit an understanding of the legal process and a capacity to recount relevant facts and the names of witnesses despite mental disability. See, e.g., *Swisher v. United States,* 237 F.Supp. 921 (W.D.Mo. 1965). Based on what you can glean from the above report, do you agree? In any event, is the diagnostic information relevant to the competency issue?

3. *Competency protocols.* In an effort to assist the mental health professional in avoiding the pitfalls illustrated by the above report, a number of structured interview formats have been developed. The Competency Assessment Instrument (CAI), for instance, requires the evaluator to assess competency by looking at 13 different functions (e.g., "appraisal of available legal defenses", "capacity to testify relevantly"), and then producing a rating from 1 ("total incapacity") to 5 ("no incapacity"). Laboratory of Community Psychiatry, Competency to Stand Trial and Mental Illness 98–125 (1974). The Interdisciplinary Fitness Interview (IFI) requires the evaluator to rate on a scale of 0 through 2 (with 2 representing "substantial incapacity") the person's capacity with respect to five "legal items" (e.g., "capacity to appreciate the nature of the alleged crime, and to disclose pertinent facts, events and motives"; "quality of relationship with one's current attorney") and eleven "psycho-pathological items" (e.g., "delusional processes", "disturbances of memory/amnesia"); the evaluator must also rate on a 0–2 scale the weight given each particular dimension in the opinion formation process. Stephen Golding et al., "Assessment and Conceptualization of Competency to Stand Trial: Preliminary Data on the Interdisciplinary Fitness Interview," 8 Law & Hum.Behav. 321 (1984). Neither the CAI or the IFI equate a certain numerical score with a finding of competency; the numbers are

merely meant to serve as a guide. In contrast, the Competency Screening Test (CST) consists of 22 sentence stems which the defendant is to complete (e.g., "When I go to court the lawyer will ..."; When they say a man is innocent until proven guilty, I ...) and the evaluator is to grade on a scale of 0–2 (with 2 being a "competent" answer). A score of 19 or below is supposed to indicate that the person requires further, more in-depth evaluation. A score of 20 or above means the person is competent. This device was developed specifically for use by laypeople as a device for screening out those who are clearly competent. Laboratory of Community Psychiatry, supra at 67. Are such devices a good way of improving competency evaluations and reports or is it not possible to reduce the competency construct to a numerical finding?

4. *Assistance to the factfinder.* Several studies have found that interrater agreement on competency to stand trial is quite high, usually over 90%. If mental health professionals are equating psychosis with incompetency, as recounted in note 2, this percentage may merely reflect the ability of clinicians to agree when someone is severely mentally ill. But even when clinicians understand and apply the specific competency criteria, reliability is very high, whether or not a structured interview format is used. Stephen Golding et al., supra, at 188–191 (97% agreement using IFI); Norman Poythress & Harley Stock, "Competency to Stand Trial: A Historical Review and Some New Data," 8 J.Psychiat.L. 131 (1980) (100% agreement between raters using unstructured interview). Thus, competency to stand trial determinations may be much more valid, or accurate, than normality, responsibility or propensity assessments.

Yet, it also appears that laypersons who have received a minimal amount of training can produce reliable conclusions on the competency issue, at least when using a structured interview format. Roesch & Golding, supra, at 188–191 (90% agreement between trained laypersons and hospital evaluators using IFI). Moreover, Roesch & Golding state that "it appears that ward observations, psychological tests, and other data collected during hospitalization have little influence on the [competency to stand trial] determination." Roesch & Golding, supra, at 190. What would be the Morsian argument in the competency to stand trial context? Who should be allowed to write competency reports and testify at competency hearings, and under what limitations?

III. IMPLEMENTATION ISSUES

Despite the arguments for eliminating or limiting expert testimony from mental health professionals, courts continue to permit such testimony on normality, responsibility, propensity and competency issues. This section addresses several topics related to how this testimony should be presented: which types of mental health professionals should be qualified to offer clinical opinions, when the state is required to provide the defendant/subject with such experts, when the state can obtain its own evaluation of the defendant/subject, what types of third party information experts may rely upon in forming their opinions, and the extent to which these opinions may embrace "ultimate" legal issues.

A. WHO IS AN EXPERT?

Federal Rule 702 defines an expert as one who is qualified to speak on a given issue "by knowledge, skill, experience, training or education." Arguably, any mental health professional—whether a psychiatrist, psychologist, social worker or psychiatric nurse—could possess specialized knowledge, skill, experience, training and education related to mental disorder and its consequences. But the courts have been cautious about opening the door to non-psychiatrists, as the following case illustrates.

JENKINS v. UNITED STATES

United States Court of Appeals, District of Columbia Circuit, 1962.
307 F.2d 637.

BAZELON, CIRCUIT JUDGE

[W]e [will now] discuss ... the [trial] court's instruction to the jury to disregard testimony of the three defense psychologists that appellant had a mental disease when he committed the crimes charged.

* * *

The first psychologist, Dr. Tirnauer, administered a battery of tests to appellant, studied his case history, and concluded he had been suffering from schizophrenia when he committed the crimes. In his opinion, the disease and the crimes were "related." The second psychologist, Dr. Margaret Ives, had reviewed Dr. Tirnauer's test results, had seen appellant at a staff conference, and had administered part of a Szondi profile test. She stated that appellant was suffering from schizophrenia and that his crimes were the product of the disease. The third psychologist, Dr. Levy, interpreted test results obtained by members of the District General staff in October 1959, and administered two additional tests shortly before trial. He testified that defendant had been suffering from schizophrenia on June 10, 1959, but could give no opinion concerning the relationship between the illness and the crimes. At the conclusion of the trial the court instructed the jury:

> "A psychologist is not competent to give a medical opinion as to a mental disease or defect. Therefore, you will not consider any evidence to the effect that the defendant was suffering from a mental disease or a mental defect on June 10, 1959, according to the testimony given by the psychologists."

The trial court apparently excluded these opinions because psychologists lack medical training. We agree with the weight of authority, however, that some psychologists are qualified to render expert testimony in the field of mental disorder.

* * *

The test ... is whether the opinion offered will be likely to aid the trier in the search for truth. ...Thus, non-medical witnesses who have had experience in electrical work may testify to the effects of electrical shock upon the human body. Optometrists, whose training includes instruction in the symptoms of certain eye diseases, may testify to the presence of a cataract discovered in the course of fitting glasses, and to the effect of a scar upon vision. A toxicologist has been permitted to testify to the effect of oxalic acid, a poison, upon the human eye. The kinds of witnesses whose opinions courts have received, *even though they lacked medical training and would not be permitted by law to treat the conditions they described,* are legion. The principle to be distilled from the cases is plain: if experience or training enables a proffered expert witness to form an opinion which would aid the jury, in the absence of some countervailing consideration, his testimony will be received.

* * *

[T]he Ph.D. in Clinical Psychology involves some—and often much—training and experience in the diagnosis and treatment of mental disorders. Typically, candidates are trained, *inter alia,* in general psychology, theory of personality and psychodynamics, psychopathology, diagnostic methods, therapeutic techniques, selected aspects of physiology and anatomy, and clinical methods. A one-year internship in a mental hospital is required for this degree. After graduation, many clinical psychologists administer and interpret diagnostic tests which elicit the patient's intellectual level, defenses, personality structure, attitudes, feelings, thought and perceptual processes. In many institutions and clinics their reports, which regularly include opinions concerning the presence or absence of mental disease or defect, are important aids to psychiatrists who customarily have the final responsibility for diagnosis. Some psychologists, moreover, regularly administer psychotherapy and related non-organic therapies in the treatment of certain types of mental disorders.

The determination of a psychologist's competence to render an expert opinion based on his findings as to the presence or absence of mental disease or defect must depend upon the nature and extent of his knowledge. It does not depend upon his claim to the title "psychologist." And that determination, after hearing, must be left in each case to the traditional discretion of the trial court subject to appellate review. Although there are no statutory criteria for licensing psychologists in the District of Columbia to assist trial courts, the American Psychological Association's list of approved graduate training programs provides some guidance. When completion of such training is followed by actual experience in the treatment and diagnosis of disease in association with psychiatrists or neurologists, the opinion of the psychologist may properly be received in evidence. We need not decide whether the three psychologists who testified for the defense at the trial under review were qualified to offer expert opinions since they may not be called to testify at the retrial. We hold only that the lack of a medical degree, and the lesser degree of responsibility for patient care which mental hospitals usually assign to psychologists, are not automatic disqualifications. Where relevant, these matters may be shown to affect the weight of their testimony, even though it be admitted in evidence. The critical factor in respect to admissibility is the actual experience of the witness and the probable probative value of his opinion. The trial judge should make a finding in respect to the individual qualifications of each challenged expert. Qualifications to express an opinion on a given topic are to be decided by the judge alone. The weight to be given any expert opinion admitted in evidence by the judge is exclusively for the jury. They should be so instructed.

* * *

BURGER, CIRCUIT JUDGE (concurring).

I concur in the remand because the court's basic holding that a psychologist is not barred as a matter of law from giving expert testimony about mental diseases makes it essential that we have a comprehensive record before us on the education and training of psychologists in general and clinical psychologists in particular.

* * *

At the outset certain factors should be kept in mind. The issue is not now and never was whether a psychologist's testimony is admissible in litigation where "sanity" is in issue. Such testimony has long been admissible in the form of psychological tests and the analysis and explanation of such tests by a psychologist. No one doubts that such matter is admissible. The real issue in dispute is whether the clinical psychologists in this case, by which we mean persons having degrees of Doctor of Philosophy in Psychology, and also additional training as clinical psychologists, are competent in a scientific sense and hence legally qualified

(1) to make a diagnosis of the existence and character of a mental disease, and

(2) whether there is a causal relationship between a disease and an unlawful act.

The issue can be stated also in terms of whether *medical* opinions and *medical* diagnoses can be made by and be the subject of expert testimony by a Doctor of Philosophy in Psychology with added clinical experience. For convenience I will hereafter refer to such a psychologist as a Clinical Psychologist.

While the issue is new to this court it is not new to medicine and psychiatry. In 1954 a Resolution was adopted by the American Medical Association, the Council of the American Psychiatric Association and the Executive Council of the American Psychoanalytical Association to the effect that psychologists and other related professional groups were autonomous and independent in matters where *medical* questions were *not* involved, but that where *diagnosis* and *treatment* of mental illness was involved the participation of psychologists "must be co-ordinated under medical responsibility." This Resolution, while not controlling on the courts is plainly entitled to great weight.

* * *

The cases cited by the majority concerning the optometrist, the toxicologist and other skilled specialists who are not medical doctors are not in any real sense relevant. Indeed they tend to divert us from the central issue. Of course an optometrist or the toxicologist is permitted to give *some* expert testimony within his competence just as a skilled shoemaker might be qualified to testify from long observation and experience as to the effect of wearing certain kinds of shoes, or a farrier to give expert testimony about the effect of certain types of shoeing on horses.

The heart of our problem is not whether a clinical psychologist is qualified to testify as an expert, for of course he is in some areas, but whether he is qualified to give expert testimony in the form of a diagnosis of a mental disease or illness, and to express an opinion on whether a stated mental disease "caused" the patient to commit a given unlawful act or "produced" that act. More rationally the question ought to be whether mental disease so substantially affected him that he was unable to control his conduct.

I agree with the majority that the scope of the training of the psychologist is of critical importance and that many factors other than academic degrees go to the admissibility and weight of the expert testimony. For example, if a general medical practitioner testified on the subject of mental disease, and gave a diagnosis of presence or absence of mental illness in opposition to a trained psychiatrist it would obviously be proper for the trial judge to tell the jury they could take into account the differences in training and experience in weighing the testimony of the one against the other. In the same way it would be proper, if a clinical psychologist is found qualified to testify as to the presence or absence of a mental disease and does so in opposition to a psychiatrist, to tell the jury they could take into account the difference in the education, training and experience of psychologists and psychiatrists and the absence of medical training in the former.

BASTIAN, CIRCUIT JUDGE, with whom WILBUR K. MILLER, CHIEF JUDGE, joins, dissenting.

* * *

In the first place, we think it must be concluded beyond doubt that the existence of a mental disease or defect is, first and foremost, a *medical* problem. The ascertainment of such a medical illness in a given individual with reference to kind, quality, degree and influence is, except in extreme cases, a highly unverifiable process, judged by any objective standard, even when undertaken by a *medical* doctor with years of special training in the detection of medical disturbances of the mind.

* * *

If the issue is so debatable among conceded professional medical experts, it is sheer folly, in our opinion, to attribute to a lay psychologist, who admittedly is not a doctor of medicine, such presumptive medical knowledge and diagnostic acuity as to entitle him to wear in a criminal courtroom the badge of an expert witness with respect to the existence of that elusive *medical* condition known as mental disease or defect.

* * *

We are not alone in our views on this precise issue. The American Psychiatric Association, an organization "comprised of those twelve thousand qualified Doctors of Medicine who specialize and practice as psychiatrists," in its amicus curiae brief, urges this court not to allow psychologists to qualify as experts to express opinions. We find in the brief this pertinent observation in regard to the proper medical ascertainment of mental disease or defect:

> "The diagnostic synthesis of *all data* collected is properly carried out only by an individual Doctor of Medicine with a broad training, experience, and familiarity with *all* of the areas indicated, and the diagnosis must reflect a comprehensive medical judgment in which the proper weight is given to all of the data available. Further, we know of no mental illness which does not have a biological as well as a psychological component. No facet of the data can be assumed to reflect the total diagnosis until viewed in the context of the total picture. A clinical psychologist, lacking *medical* training and the specialization required of the qualified psychiatrist, is not qualified to make this total *medical* diagnosis or to testify as a *medical* expert thereon." [Emphasis appears in amicus brief.]

The majority of the court ignores the above quoted wise counsel from the only undisputed experts now at work in the area of medical illness of the mind. In doing so, the court, we suggest, is bypassing all objective criteria in reaching the highly questionable and subjective conclusion that lay psychologists, whose opinions are predicated on the basis of test results, may qualify as experts on the medical question of the diagnosis of mental disease or defect, as well as experts concerning the causal relationship between a particular defendant's mental abnormality, as such may be "diagnosed" by these psychologists, and that defendant's criminal activity. In our opinion, the holding of the majority on this issue is wholly untenable. We would affirm the judgment and sentence of the District Court.

Questions and Comments

1. *Current state of the law.* Since *Jenkins* was decided in 1962, most states have provided by statute or case law that doctoral level clinical psychologists may offer opinions on insanity, as well as on other issues concerning people with mental disorder. See "Qualifications of Nonmedical Psychologist to Testify as to Mental Condition or Competency," 72 A.L.R.5th 579 (1999); Ronald Gass, "The Psychologist as Expert Witness: Science in the Courtroom," 38 Md.L.Rev. 539, 544–554 (1979). But some states still

refuse to allow psychologists as free a rein as psychiatrists. For instance, in insanity cases, some courts still limit psychologists to interpretations of psychological tests; testimony by psychologists about degree of cognitive or volitional impairment or causes of mental deficiencies is prohibited or limited. *State v. Bricker*, 321 Md. 86, 581 A.2d 9 (1990); *People v. McDarrah,* 175 Ill.App.3d 284, 124 Ill.Dec. 827, 529 N.E.2d 808 (1988); *Commonwealth v. Williams,* 270 Pa.Super. 27, 410 A.2d 880 (1979). Many civil commitment provisions permit certification or testimony only by "physicians," Vernon's Ann.Tex. Const. art. 1, § 15a; N.Y.—McKinney's Mental Hygiene Law § 9.27, or, if they do allow psychologists to testify, require them to meet higher experiential standards than psychiatrists. West's Ann.Cal.Welf. & Inst.Code § 5251. A survey of guardianship statutes in the 50 states found 85 different provisions which reserved the role of expert exclusively to physicians. Thomas Hafemeister & Bruce Sales, "Responsibilities of Psychologists Under Guardianship and Conservatorship Laws," 13 Prof.Psychol. 354 (1982). Even where doctoral level psychologists may testify, masters level clinical psychologists, and masters and doctoral level social workers are often barred from giving opinion (as opposed to factual) testimony. See, e.g., *White v. Commonwealth*, 44 Va.App. 429, 605 S.E.2d 337, 345 (2004) (insanity defense); *State v. Zola*, 112 N.J. 384, 548 A.2d 1022, 1040 (1988) (diminished capacity defense); *State v. Baucom,* 28 Or.App. 757, 561 P.2d 641 (1977) (insanity defense).

Finally, it has been noted that, even when psychologists are allowed to testify, judges and juries continue to view them (and therefore, presumably, social workers as well) as "second-class" experts. Michael Perlin, "The Legal Status of the Psychologist in the Courtroom," 4 Men.Dis.L.Rptr. 194, 195–6 (1980). See also, Norman Poythress, "Judicial Preference Regarding Expert Testimony," 10 Crim.Just. & Beh. 175 (1983).

2. *Justifications.* The limitations on and perceptions about expert qualifications of the various mental health professions can be interpreted as another illustration of the law's continued preference for the medical model of mental disorder. Such a preference clearly motivates the concurring and dissenting opinions in *Jenkins.* Are there other justifications for the law's current approach?

The psychiatric profession appears to continue to adhere to the position it took in 1954, described in *Jenkins.* In 1980, American Psychiatric Association President Langsley acknowledged that psychologists, social workers, and others can and should be members of the "treatment team," but asserted that "it is [now] more appropriate than ever that the psychiatrist is the member of the team best equipped to perform triage, make differential diagnosis, [and to] plan and render treatment for a variety of psychological and somatic problems." Donald Langsley, "Viewpoint, A Commentary by APA's President," Psychiatric News, Sept. 19, 1980, at 25, col. 1. If, as Langsley asserts, psychiatrists are superior at treatment and diagnosis then, presumably, they are superior at forensic tasks as well. In its opinions that have touched on the clinical testimony issue, the United States Supreme Court has lent considerable credence to this view—whether consciously or unconsciously is hard to say—by its tendency to speak only of psychiatrists, or to mention psychologists and other mental health professions only in passing. See, e.g., *Kansas v. Hendricks,* 521 U.S. 346, 117 S.Ct. 2072, 138

L.Ed.2d 501 (referring to the "psychiatric profession's" definition of mental disorder); *Ake v. Oklahoma,* 470 U.S. 68, 105 S.Ct. 1087, 84 L.Ed.2d 53 (1985)(finding a constitutional right to "psychiatric assistance" in insanity and death penalty cases); *Barefoot v. Estelle,* 463 U.S. 880, 103 S.Ct. 3383, 77 L.Ed.2d 1090 (1983) (speaking of the validity of "psychiatric" predictions of dangerousness); *Addington v. Texas*, 441 U.S. 418, 99 S.Ct. 1804, 60 L.Ed.2d 323 (1979) (the "psychiatric diagnosis [necessary for civil commitment] is to a large extent based on medical 'impressions'"). But see *Clark v. Arizona*, 548 U.S. 735, 126 S.Ct. 2709, 165 L.Ed.2d 842 (2006) (referring continually to psychologists and psychiatrists, in that order).

Research indicates that non-psychiatrists may be just as competent as psychiatrists in addressing many forensic issues. George Dix & Norman Poythress, "Propriety of Medical Dominance of Forensic Mental Health Practice: The Empirical Evidence," 23 Ariz.L.Rev. 961, 971–984 (1981). Of particular interest, one study found that psychologists and social workers tend to do more thorough forensic evaluations and more comprehensive and more relevant forensic reports than their psychiatric colleagues. Russell Petrella & Norman Poythress, "The Quality of Forensic Examinations: An Interdisciplinary Study," 51 J. Consult. & Clinical Psychol. 76 (1983).

Morse has suggested that, under his scheme, described in section II of this chapter, "almost any person with extensive clinical experience with crazy persons should qualify as an expert." Stephen Morse, "Crazy Behavior, Morals and Science: An Analysis of Mental Health Law," 51 S.Cal.L.Rev. 527, 623–624 (1978). On the other hand, "[p]rofessionals without extensive, recent, and relevant mental health *clinical* experience, whatever their formal training, should not be qualified as experts" on these subjects. With respect to statistical evidence, "an expert from any field [e.g., sociology as well as psychiatry] who possesses data relevant to the specific . . . issue is competent to be qualified." Id. Do you agree?

3. *Knowledge of legal issues.* Clinical knowledge and training may not be enough to qualify a mental health professional as an expert witness. Many commentators have suggested that, unless the witness can demonstrate knowledge of the relevant legal test, he or she should remain unqualified regardless of clinical background. See, e.g., Burton Pollack, "Forensic Psychiatry: A Specialty," 2 Bull.Am.Acad.Psychiat. & L. 1 (1974). For instance, as we saw in the previous section, failure on the part of clinicians to understand the legal test for competency to stand trial can lead to virtually useless reports or testimony. In an effort to remedy this situation, both disciplines have established forensic boards designed to provide certification of those members who have exhibited proficiency in forensic matters. See, "The American Board of Forensic Psychiatry, Inc., 1976," 4 Bull.Am.Acad.Psychiat. & L. 95 (1976). In a separate effort, several states have initiated, with some success, training programs for forensic clinicians in an attempt to eliminate excess psychiatric jargon, irrelevant detail and confusion about legal standards. Gary Melton et al., Community Mental Health Centers and the Courts: An Evaluation of Community–Based Forensic Services 56–67 (1985).

B. THE RIGHT TO AN EXPERT EVALUATION

AKE v. OKLAHOMA

Supreme Court of the United States, 1985.
470 U.S. 68, 105 S.Ct. 1087, 84 L.Ed.2d 53.

JUSTICE MARSHALL delivered the opinion of the Court.

The issue in this case is whether the Constitution requires that an indigent defendant have access to the psychiatric examination and assistance necessary to prepare an effective defense based on his mental condition, when his sanity at the time of the offense is seriously in question.

I

Late in 1979, Glen Burton Ake was arrested and charged with murdering a couple and wounding their two children. He was arraigned in the District Court for Canadian County, Okla., in February 1980. His behavior at arraignment, and in other prearraignment incidents at the jail, was so bizarre that the trial judge *sua sponte* ordered him to be examined by a psychiatrist "for the purpose of advising with the Court as to his impressions of whether the Defendant may need an extended period of mental observation." The examining psychiatrist reported: "At times [Ake] appears to be frankly delusional. * * * He claims to be the 'sword of vengeance' of the Lord and that he will sit at the left hand of God in heaven." He diagnosed Ake as a probable paranoid schizophrenic and recommended a prolonged psychiatric evaluation to determine whether Ake was competent to stand trial.

In March, Ake was committed to a state hospital to be examined with respect to his "present sanity," i.e., his competency to stand trial. On April 10, less than six months after the incidents for which Ake was indicted, the chief forensic psychiatrist at the state hospital informed the court that Ake was not competent to stand trial. The court then held a competency hearing, at which a psychiatrist testified:

> "[Ake] is a psychotic * * * his psychiatric diagnosis was that of paranoid schizophrenia—chronic, with exacerbation, that is with current upset, and that in addition * * * he is dangerous. * * * [B]ecause of the severity of his mental illness and because of the intensities of his rage, his poor control, his delusions, he requires a maximum security facility within—I believe—the State Psychiatric Hospital system."

The court found Ake to be a "mentally ill person in need of care and treatment" and incompetent to stand trial, and ordered him committed to the state mental hospital.

Six weeks later, the chief forensic psychiatrist informed the court that Ake had become competent to stand trial. At the time, Ake was receiving 200 milligrams of Thorazine, an antipsychotic drug, three times daily, and the psychiatrist indicated that, if Ake continued to receive that dosage, his condition would remain stable. The State then resumed proceedings against Ake.

At a pretrial conference in June, Ake's attorney informed the court that his client would raise an insanity defense. To enable him to prepare and present such a defense adequately, the attorney stated, a psychiatrist would have to examine Ake with respect to his mental condition at the time of the offense. During Ake's 3–month stay at the state hospital, no inquiry had been made into his sanity at the time of the offense, and, as an indigent, Ake could not afford to pay for a psychiatrist. Counsel asked the court either to arrange to have a psychiatrist perform the examination, or to provide funds to allow the defense to arrange one. The trial judge rejected counsel's argument that the Federal Constitution requires that an indigent defendant receive the assistance of a psychiatrist when that assistance is necessary to the defense, and he denied the motion for a psychiatric evaluation at state expense.…

Ake was tried for two counts of murder in the first degree, a crime punishable by death in Oklahoma, and for two counts of shooting with intent to kill. At the guilt phase of trial, his sole defense was insanity. Although defense counsel called to the stand and questioned each of the psychiatrists who had examined Ake at the state hospital, none testified about his mental state at the time of the offense because none had examined him on that point. The prosecution, in turn, asked each of these psychiatrists whether he had performed or seen the results of any examination diagnosing Ake's mental state at the time of the offense, and each doctor replied that he had not. *As a result, there was no expert testimony for either side on Ake's sanity at the time of the offense.* The jurors were then instructed that Ake could be found not guilty by reason of insanity if he did not have the ability to distinguish right from wrong at the time of the alleged offense. They were further told that Ake was to be presumed sane at the time of the crime unless *he* presented evidence sufficient to raise a reasonable doubt about his sanity at that time. If he raised such a doubt in their minds, the jurors were informed, the burden of proof shifted to the State to prove sanity beyond a reasonable doubt. The jury rejected Ake's insanity defense and returned a verdict of guilty on all counts.

At the sentencing proceeding, the State asked for the death penalty. No new evidence was presented. The prosecutor relied significantly on the testimony of the state psychiatrists who had examined Ake, and who had testified at the guilt phase that Ake was dangerous to society, to establish the likelihood of his future dangerous behavior. Ake had no expert witness to rebut this testimony or to introduce on his behalf evidence in mitigation of his punishment. The jury sentenced Ake to death on each of the two murder counts, and to 500 years' imprisonment on each of the two counts of shooting with intent to kill.

On appeal to the Oklahoma Court of Criminal Appeals, Ake argued that, as an indigent defendant, he should have been provided the services of a court-appointed psychiatrist. The court rejected this argument, observing: "We have held numerous times that, the unique nature of capital cases notwithstanding, the State does not have the responsibility of providing such services to indigents charged with capital crimes." 663 P.2d 1, 6 (1983). Finding no error in Ake's other claims, the court affirmed the convictions and sentences. We granted certiorari. 465 U.S. 1099, 104 S.Ct. 1591, 80 L.Ed.2d 123 (1984).

We hold that when a defendant has made a preliminary showing that his sanity at the time of the offense is likely to be a significant factor at trial, the Constitution requires that a State provide access to a psychiatrist's assistance on this issue, if the defendant cannot otherwise afford one. Accordingly, we reverse.

* * *

III

This Court has long recognized that when a State brings its judicial power to bear on an indigent defendant in a criminal proceeding, it must take steps to assure that the defendant has a fair opportunity to present his defense. This elementary principle, grounded in significant part on the Fourteenth Amendment's due process guarantee of fundamental fairness, derives from the belief that justice cannot be equal where, simply as a result of his poverty, a defendant is denied the opportunity to participate meaningfully in a judicial proceeding in which his liberty is at stake.

* * * We recognized long ago that mere access to the courthouse doors does not by itself assure a proper functioning of the adversary process, and that a criminal trial is fundamentally unfair if the State proceeds against an indigent defendant without making certain that he has access to the raw materials integral to the building of an effective defense. Thus, while the Court has not held that a State must purchase for the indigent defendant all the assistance that his wealthier counterpart might buy, see *Ross v. Moffitt,* 417 U.S. 600, 94 S.Ct. 2437, 41 L.Ed.2d 341 (1974), it has often reaffirmed that fundamental fairness entitles indigent defendants to "an adequate opportunity to present their claims fairly within the adversary system," *id.,* at 612, 94 S.Ct., at 2444. To implement this principle, we have focused on identifying the "basic tools of an adequate defense or appeal," *Britt v. North Carolina,* 404 U.S. 226, 227, 92 S.Ct. 431, 433, 30 L.Ed.2d 400 (1971), and we have required that such tools be provided to those defendants who cannot afford to pay for them.

To say that these basic tools must be provided is, of course, merely to begin our inquiry. In this case we must decide whether, and under what conditions, the participation of a psychiatrist is important enough to preparation of a defense to require the State to provide an indigent defendant with access to competent psychiatric assistance in preparing the defense. Three factors are relevant to this determination. The first is the private interest that will be affected by the action of the State. The second is the governmental interest that will be affected if the safeguard is to be provided. The third is the probable value of the additional or substitute procedural safeguards that are sought, and the risk of an erroneous deprivation of the affected interest if those safeguards are not provided. We turn, then, to apply this standard to the issue before us.

A

The private interest in the accuracy of a criminal proceeding that places an individual's life or liberty at risk is almost uniquely compelling. Indeed, the host of safeguards fashioned by this Court over the years to diminish the risk of erroneous conviction stands as a testament to that concern. The interest of the individual in the outcome of the State's effort to overcome the presumption of innocence is obvious and weighs heavily in our analysis.

We consider, next, the interest of the State. Oklahoma asserts that to provide Ake with psychiatric assistance on the record before us would result in a staggering burden to the State. We are unpersuaded by this assertion. Many States, as well as the Federal Government, currently make psychiatric assistance available to indigent defendants, and they have not found the financial burden so great as to preclude this assistance. This is especially so when the obligation of the State is limited to provision of one competent psychiatrist, as it is in many States, and as we limit the right we recognize today. At the same time, it is difficult to identify any interest of the State, other than that in its economy, that weighs against recognition of this right. The State's interest in prevailing at trial—unlike that of a private litigant—is necessarily tempered by its interest in the fair and accurate adjudication of criminal cases. Thus, also unlike a private litigant, a State may not legitimately assert an interest in maintenance of a strategic advantage over the defense, if the result of that advantage is to cast a pall on the accuracy of the verdict obtained. We therefore conclude that the governmental interest in denying Ake the assistance of a psychiatrist is not substantial, in light of the compelling interest of both the State and the individual in accurate dispositions.

Last, we inquire into the probable value of the psychiatric assistance sought, and the risk of error in the proceeding if such assistance is not offered. We begin by considering the pivotal role that psychiatry has come to play in criminal proceedings. More than 40 States, as well as the Federal Government, have decided either through legislation or judicial decision that indigent defendants are entitled, under certain circumstances, to the assistance of a psychiatrist's expertise. For example, in subsection (e) of the Criminal Justice Act, 18 U.S.C. § 3006A, Congress has provided that indigent defendants shall receive the assistance of all experts "necessary for an adequate defense." Numerous state statutes guarantee reimbursement for expert services under a like standard. And in many States that have not assured access to psychiatrists through the legislative process, state courts have interpreted the State or Federal Constitution to require that psychiatric assistance be provided to indigent defendants when necessary for an adequate defense, or when insanity is at issue.

These statutes and court decisions reflect a reality that we recognize today, namely, that when the State has made the defendant's mental condition relevant to his criminal culpability and to the punishment he might suffer, the assistance of a psychiatrist may well be crucial to the defendant's ability to marshal his defense. In this role, psychiatrists gather facts, both through professional examination, interviews, and elsewhere, that they will share with the judge or jury; they analyze the information gathered and from it draw plausible conclusions about the defendant's mental condition, and about the effects of any disorder on behavior; and they offer opinions about how the defendant's mental condition might have affected his behavior at the time in question. They know the probative questions to ask of the opposing party's psychiatrists and how to interpret their answers. Unlike lay witnesses, who can merely describe symptoms they believe might be relevant to the defendant's mental state, psychiatrists can identify the "elusive and often deceptive" symptoms of insanity, *Solesbee v. Balkcom,* 339 U.S. 9, 12, 70 S.Ct. 457, 458, 94 L.Ed. 604 (1950), and tell the jury why their observations are relevant. Further, where permitted by evidentiary rules, psychiatrists can translate a medical diagnosis into language that will assist the trier of fact, and therefore offer evidence in a form that has meaning for the task at hand. Through this process of investigation, interpretation and testimony, psychiatrists ideally assist lay jurors, who generally have no training in psychiatric matters, to make a sensible and educated determination about the mental condition of the defendant at the time of the offense.

Psychiatry is not, however, an exact science, and psychiatrists disagree widely and frequently on what constitutes mental illness, on the appropriate diagnosis to be attached to given behavior and symptoms, on cure and treatment, and on likelihood of future dangerousness. Perhaps because there often is no single, accurate psychiatric conclusion on legal insanity in a given case, juries remain the primary factfinders on this issue, and they must resolve differences in opinion within the psychiatric profession on the basis of the evidence offered by each party. When jurors make this determination about issues that inevitably are complex and foreign, the testimony of psychiatrists can be crucial and "a virtual necessity if an insanity plea is to have any chance of success." By organizing a defendant's mental history, examination results and behavior, and other information, interpreting it in light of their expertise, and then laying out their investigative and analytic process to the jury, the psychiatrists for each party enable the jury to make its most accurate determination of the truth on the issue before them. It is for this reason that States rely on psychiatrists as examiners, consultants, and witnesses, and that private individuals do as well, when they can afford to do so. In so saying, we neither approve nor disapprove the widespread reliance on psychiatrists but instead recognize the unfairness of a contrary holding in light of the evolving practice.

The foregoing leads inexorably to the conclusion that, without the assistance of a psychiatrist to conduct a professional examination on issues relevant to the defense, to help determine whether the insanity defense is viable, to present testimony, and to assist in preparing the cross-examination of a State's psychiatric witnesses, the risk of an inaccurate resolution of sanity issues is extremely high. With such assistance, the defendant is fairly able to present at least enough information to the jury, in a meaningful manner, as to permit it to make a sensible determination.

A defendant's mental condition is not necessarily at issue in every criminal proceeding, however, and it is unlikely that psychiatric assistance of the kind we have described would be of probable value in cases where it is not. The risk of error from denial of such assistance, as well as its probable value, are most predictably at their height when the defendant's mental condition is seriously in question. When the defendant is able to make an *ex parte* threshold showing to the trial court that his sanity is likely to be a significant factor in his defense, the need for the assistance of a psychiatrist is readily apparent. It is in such cases that a defense may be devastated by the absence of a psychiatric examination and testimony; with such assistance, the defendant might have a reasonable chance of success. In such a circumstance, where the potential accuracy of the jury's determination is so dramatically enhanced, and where the interests of the individual and the State in an accurate proceeding are substantial, the State's interest in its fisc must yield. We therefore hold that when a defendant demonstrates to the trial judge that his sanity at the time of the offense is to be a significant factor at trial, the State must, at a minimum, assure the defendant access to a competent psychiatrist who will conduct an appropriate examination and assist in evaluation, preparation, and presentation of the defense. This is not to say, of course, that the indigent defendant has a constitutional right to choose a psychiatrist of his personal liking or to receive funds to hire his own. Our concern is that the indigent defendant have access to a competent psychiatrist for the purpose we have discussed, and as in the case of the provision of counsel we leave to the State the decision on how to implement this right.

B

Ake also was denied the means of presenting evidence to rebut the State's evidence of his future dangerousness. The foregoing discussion compels a similar conclusion in the context of a capital sentencing proceeding, when the State presents psychiatric evidence of the defendant's future dangerousness. We have repeatedly recognized the defendant's compelling interest in fair adjudication at the sentencing phase of a capital case. The State, too, has a profound interest in assuring that its ultimate sanction is not erroneously imposed, and we do not see why monetary considerations should be more persuasive in this context than at trial. The variable on which we must focus is, therefore, the probable value that the assistance of a psychiatrist will have in this area, and the risk attendant on its absence.

This Court has upheld the practice in many States of placing before the jury psychiatric testimony on the question of future dangerousness, see *Barefoot v. Estelle,* 463 U.S. 880, 896–905, 103 S.Ct. 3383, 3396–3400, 77 L.Ed.2d 1090 (1983), at least where the defendant has had access to an expert of his own, *id.,* n. 5. In so holding, the Court relied, in part, on the assumption that the factfinder would have before it both the views of the prosecutor's psychiatrists and the "opposing views of the defendant's doctors" and would therefore be competent to "uncover, recognize, and take due account of * * * shortcomings" in predictions on this point. Without a psychiatrist's assistance, the defendant cannot offer a well-informed expert's opposing view, and thereby loses a significant opportunity to raise in the jurors' minds questions about the State's proof of an aggravating factor. In such a circumstance, where the consequence of error is so great, the relevance of responsive psychiatric testimony so evident, and the burden on the State so slim, due process requires access to a psychiatric examination on relevant issues, to the testimony of the psychiatrist, and to assistance in preparation at the sentencing phase.

* * *

IV

We turn now to apply these standards to the facts of this case. On the record before us, it is clear that Ake's mental state at the time of the offense was a substantial factor in his defense, and that the trial court was on notice of that fact when the request for a court-appointed psychiatrist was made. For one, Ake's sole defense was that of insanity. Second, Ake's behavior at arraignment, just four months after the offense, was so bizarre as to prompt the trial judge, *sua sponte,* to have him examined for competency. Third, a state psychiatrist shortly thereafter found Ake to be incompetent to stand trial, and suggested that he be committed. Fourth, when he was found to be competent six weeks later, it was only on the condition that he be sedated with large doses of Thorazine three times a day, during trial. Fifth, the psychiatrists who examined Ake for competency described to the trial court the severity of Ake's mental illness less than six months after the offense in question, and suggested that this mental illness might have begun many years earlier. Finally, Oklahoma recognizes a defense of insanity, under which the initial burden of producing evidence falls on the defendant. Taken together, these factors make clear that the question of Ake's sanity was likely to be a significant factor in his defense.

In addition, Ake's future dangerousness was a significant factor at the sentencing phase. The state psychiatrist who treated Ake at the state mental hospital testified at the guilt phase that, because of his mental illness, Ake posed a threat of continuing criminal violence. This testimony raised the issue of Ake's future dangerousness, which is an aggravating factor under Oklahoma's capital sentencing scheme, and on which the prosecutor relied at sentencing. We therefore conclude that Ake also was entitled to the assistance of a psychiatrist on this issue and that the denial of that assistance deprived him of due process.

Accordingly, we reverse and remand for a new trial.

It is so ordered.

CHIEF JUSTICE BURGER, concurring in the judgment.

This is a capital case in which the Court is asked to decide whether a State may refuse an indigent defendant "any opportunity whatsoever" to obtain psychiatric evidence for the preparation and presentation of a claim of insanity by way of defense when the defendant's legal sanity at the time of the offense was "seriously in issue."

The facts of the case and the question presented confine the actual holding of the Court. In capital cases the finality of the sentence imposed warrants protections that may or may not be required in other cases. Nothing in the Court's opinion reaches noncapital cases.

JUSTICE REHNQUIST, dissenting.

The Court holds that "when a defendant has made a preliminary showing that his sanity at the time of the offense is likely to be a significant factor at trial, the Constitution requires that a State provide access to a psychiatrist's assistance on this issue, if the defendant cannot otherwise afford one." I do not think that the facts of this case warrant the establishment of such a principle; and I think that even if the factual predicate of the Court's statement were established, the constitutional rule announced by the Court is far too broad. I would limit the rule to capital cases, and make clear that the entitlement is to an independent psychiatric evaluation, not to a defense consultant.

* * *

[E]ven if I were to agree with the Court that some right to a state-appointed psychiatrist should be recognized here, I would not grant the broad right to "access to a competent psychiatrist who will conduct an appropriate examination *and assist in evaluation, preparation, and presentation of the defense.*" A psychiatrist is not an attorney, whose job it is to advocate. His opinion is sought on a question that the State of Oklahoma treats as a question of *fact.* Since any "unfairness" in these cases would arise from the fact that the only competent witnesses on the question are being hired by the State, all the defendant should be entitled to is one competent opinion—whatever the witness' conclusion— from a psychiatrist who acts independently of the prosecutor's office. Although the independent psychiatrist should be available to answer defense counsel's questions prior to trial, and to testify if called, I see no reason why the defendant should be entitled to an opposing view, or to a "defense" advocate.

For the foregoing reasons, I would affirm the judgment of the Court of Criminal Appeals of Oklahoma.

Questions and Comments

1. *Implications of* Ake. As Justice Marshall points out, almost every state provides indigent defendants the opportunity to obtain, at state expense, an evaluation on sanity. Most states also provide evaluation services on sentencing issues in capital cases. Usually, these evaluations are performed by state hospital employees, although with increasing frequency they are conducted by community mental health professionals who receive payment from the courts for their services. If an indigent defendant receives evaluative assistance from a state employee, are the requirements of *Ake* met? Or can the defendant demand an expert who is not a regular employee of the state? In this regard, consider:

> If the indigent defendant could be guaranteed an 'impartial' evaluation by the state-employed clinician, then he should be satisfied with the opinion that results. But such a guarantee is not possible. Personal and professional predilections heavily influence clinical opinion. While it cannot be assumed that clinicians will find for the state merely because they are paid by it, as a practical matter, they are subject to institutional pressures that make it likely they will be 'prosecution-oriented',[265] at least in borderline cases. The bias inherent in their situation is suggested by the fact that, in most states, the indigent who requests an evaluation is sent to the same expert or experts who would be conducting the examination for the prosecution had the defendant been able to afford a private clinician. The state should not be allowed to force the defendant to accept such an evaluation on the ground that it is 'impartial' anymore than it should be required to concede that the opinion of a private clinician offered by a non-indigent defendant is scientifically objective.

Christopher Slobogin, "*Estelle v. Smith:* The Constitutional Contours of the Forensic Evaluation," 31 Emory L. 71, 132–33 (1981). Most courts hold that appointment of a state employee as the expert does not violate *Ake*. See 84 A.L.R. 19, § 17 (1991).

Once a "competent psychiatrist" is selected, he or she is required, under *Ake,* to "conduct an appropriate examination and assist in evaluation, preparation and presentation of the defense." Does this language merely require, as Justice Rehnquist asserts, that the defendant be able to ask questions of and elicit testimony from "a psychiatrist who acts independently of the prosecutor's office," or does it require something more? What if the expert's conclusion is that the defendant is sane or dangerous—is this expert able to "assist in evaluation, preparation and presentation of the defense?" If not, does the due process clause entitle the defendant to another expert? What if the appointed expert concludes that another expert is needed? Cf. *Vickers v. Arizona*, 497 U.S. 1033, 110 S.Ct. 3298, 111 L.Ed.2d 806 (1990)

---

265. A study involving interviews of former members of the federal prosecutor's office in the District of Columbia and [of] St. Elizabeth's Hospital, the District's forensic unit, found that the doctors frequently contacted the prosecutor's office, but rarely contacted the defense attorney. The study also noted that it was not uncommon "for the hospital doctors to ask the prosecutor if he would oppose a certain diagnosis; if the prosecutor indicates opposition, the questioned diagnosis may never come to light." Chernoff & Schaffer, "Defending the Mentally Ill: Ethical Quicksand," 10 Am.Crim.L.Rev. 505, 510 (1972).

(rehearing denied). In that case both the defense experts and the state expert stated that neuropsychological testing was necessary to confirm the defendant's diagnosis but the trial court denied the motion for such testing, because another psychiatrist had made a contrary diagnosis (based on a review of the defendant's medical records and a brief interview with the defendant).

A number of states allow the defendant to seek an independent evaluation if he or she is dissatisfied with the results of the evaluation. Samuel Brakel et al., The Mentally Disabled and the Law 719 (1985). But in those states that do not, *Ake* has brought no change. Lower court decisions since *Ake* have condoned statutory procedures which permit a state-employed expert to report to the court or to the prosecution for transmittal to the defense, as well as procedures which simply give the defense access to the findings of the state's experts. See Note, "Expert Services and the Indigent Criminal Defendant: The Constitutional Mandate of *Ake v. Oklahoma*," 84 Mich.L.Rev. 1326, 1348–49 nn. 150–52 (1986); see also, *Granviel v. Texas*, 495 U.S. 963, 110 S.Ct. 2577, 109 L.Ed.2d 758 (1990) (1989)(denying certiorari in a case challenging such a procedure, over a dissent by Justice Marshall). Moreover, a number of courts have held that in order to obtain an *Ake* evaluation the defendant must make a "clear showing" that mental state is a "genuine" or "real" issue, a showing that may be difficult without psychiatric assistance. Note, "The Indigent Defendant's Right to Psychiatric Assistance: *Ake v. Oklahoma,* 17 N.Car.Cen.L. 208, 220–22 (1988). See also *Guinan v. Armontrout*, 909 F.2d 1224, 1227 (8th Cir. 1990) (motion noting defendant's history of violence, the brutality of the crime, and counsel's unexplained difficulty in communicating with the defendant insufficient to trigger *Ake* at either trial or capital sentencing proceeding).

2. *Sixth amendment analysis.* Note that *Ake* is based on the due process clause. Some courts have held that the sixth amendment right to effective assistance of counsel entitles the defendant to an "exploratory" evaluation designed to assist the attorney in deciding what claims to make and in preparing for the case. See, e.g., *United States v. Edwards*, 488 F.2d 1154, 1163 (5th Cir.1974) (stressing the "particularly critical interrelation between expert psychiatric assistance and minimally effective representation of counsel"). See also *Wood v. Zahradnick*, 578 F.2d 980 (4th Cir.1978). Does framing the right to expert assistance in sixth amendment terms offer any advantages to the defendant? Perhaps worth noting is the Supreme Court's decision in *Wheat v. United States*, 486 U.S. 153, 108 S.Ct. 1692, 100 L.Ed.2d 140 (1988), which stated that "a defendant may not insist on representation by an attorney he cannot afford." If this is true for the right to counsel, it is likely to be true for the right to expert assistance as well.

3. *Expert assistance in other contexts.* Besides forming the basis for an insanity defense and for rebuttal of the state's case in capital sentencing, expert assistance may be useful in raising or rebutting a number of other claims in criminal cases. Discussed in the next chapter are various other "psychiatric" defenses (e.g., diminished capacity, automatism) which might result in acquittal, and various sentencing provisions which contemplate psychiatric testimony about past mental state and future dangerousness. As noted earlier in this chapter, competency to stand trial is also often viewed as a psychiatric issue. Does anything in Justice Marshall's analysis in *Ake*

foreclose a right to psychiatric assistance in these situations? Should it matter, as Marshall seems to suggest, whether a judge or a jury is the factfinder? Those courts that have considered the issue have found that *Ake* entitles the indigent to psychiatric assistance when psychiatric defenses other than insanity are raised. However, most courts have found that *Ake* does not require the state to provide expert assistance on sentencing issues other than dangerousness. Pam Casey & Ingo Keilitz, "An Evaluation of Mental Health Expert Assistance Provided to Indigent Criminal Defendants: Organization, Administration, and Fiscal Management," 34 N.Y. L.Rev. 19, 51–55 (1989). See also *Goodwin v. Johnson*, 132 F.3d 162 (5th Cir. 1997) (*Ake* does not require appointment of a rehabilitation expert in a capital sentencing proceeding even when the state argues dangerousness).

Expert assistance may also be necessary in noncriminal proceedings, such as civil commitment and guardianship hearings. Does *Ake* have implications for these types of proceedings or is it limited to criminal proceedings? The right to an independent expert in civil commitment is discussed further at pp. 840–41.

4. *State access to results.* As noted above, in many states the results of the indigent's evaluation are immediately made available to both the defense *and* the prosecution (as well as the court). See, e.g., *Buttrum v. Black*, 721 F.Supp. 1268 (N.D. Ga. 1989), aff'd 908 F.2d 695 (11th Cir. 1990)(holding that *Ake* does not provide indigent defendants with a right to confidential evaluation). Assuming this procedure does not compromise the expert's "independence," does state access nonetheless violate *Ake* to the extent it "chills" the exercise of the right to expert assistance by a defendant who is not sure how the evaluation will come out? Even if disclosing the results of the defense's exploratory evaluation to the prosecution does not violate *Ake,* does not state access run afoul of the attorney-client privilege and the associated right to effective assistance of counsel? An increasing number of states provide that the attorney-client privilege protects against disclosure of the results of the indigent's "exploratory" evaluation until the defendant decides to use them. See, e.g., West's Fla.S.A.R.Crim.Proc. 3.216(a).

A derivative issue arises when a *non*indigent defendant retains more than one expert, but decides to use only one or some of the experts at trial. May the prosecution call the unused expert or experts? Two leading cases on the issue, *People v. Edney*, 39 N.Y.2d 620, 385 N.Y.S.2d 23, 350 N.E.2d 400 (1976) and *People v. Knuckles,* 165 Ill.2d 125, 209 Ill.Dec. 1, 650 N.E.2d 974 (1995), are reprinted in Chapter Five at pp. 387–94; here they will only be summarized. *Edney* found that the state should have access to unused defense experts. Otherwise, the defendant would "be permitted to suppress any unfavorable psychiatric witness whom he had retained in the first instance, under the guise of the attorney-client privilege, while he endeavors to shop around for a friendly expert, and take unfriendly experts off the market." *Pratt,* on the other hand, rejected *Edney's* approach on the ground that it would discourage defense attorneys from seeking expert assistance and disturb the rapport between the defendant and the defense-retained expert. Are the concerns evinced by either court realistic? The American Bar Association Criminal Justice Mental Health Standards adopt *Knuckles'* approach, but allow the prosecution access to unused defense experts if it can show a bad faith effort on the part of the defense to "gag" the available experts. Standard 7–3.3(b)(ii).

C. THE BASIS OF CLINICAL OPINION

Although mental health professionals increasingly rely on actuarial data, expert testimony still typically depends on the clinical evaluation process. For both criminal and civil cases, the primary source of information in this process is, of course, the interview of the person whose mental condition is at issue. The good evaluator also attempts to obtain as much third party information as possible to fill in gaps in the subject's story and for corroborative purposes. This section first discusses constitutional issues surrounding use of the defendant-subject as a source of clinical information; it then focuses on subconstitutional, evidentiary concerns which arise primarily in connection with use of third party information.

1. The Defendant as a Source: Constitutional Considerations

The fifth amendment states in part that "no person shall be compelled in any criminal case to be a witness against himself." The values said to underlie this right, summarized in *Murphy v. Waterfront Commission*, 378 U.S. 52, 55, 84 S.Ct. 1594, 1596, 12 L.Ed.2d 678 (1964), are manifold: the prevention of abuse by government officials, the protection of privacy, the fear that coerced statements will be unreliable, "our unwillingness to subject those suspected of crime to the cruel trilemma of self-accusation, perjury or contempt," the "preference for an accusatorial rather than an inquisitorial system of criminal justice," and "our sense of fair play which dictates 'a fair state-individual balance . . . by requiring the government in its contest with the individual to shoulder the entire load . . .'." The primary issue addressed here is whether the traditional attributes of the "accusatorial" system—which prevents the state from forcing the defendant to help it convict him or her—applies to state-requested psychiatric evaluations, or whether, instead, an "inquisitorial" approach—which relies more heavily on statements from the defendant—is permissible when the issue is the defendant's mental condition.

ESTELLE v. SMITH

Supreme Court of the United States, 1981.
451 U.S. 454, 101 S.Ct. 1866, 68 L.Ed.2d 359.

CHIEF JUSTICE BURGER, delivered the opinion of the Court.

We granted certiorari to consider whether the prosecution's use of psychiatric testimony at the sentencing phase of respondent's capital murder trial to establish his future dangerousness violated his constitutional rights.

I

A

On December 28, 1973, respondent Ernest Benjamin Smith was indicted for murder arising from his participation in the armed robbery of a grocery store during which a clerk was fatally shot, not by Smith, but by his accomplice. In accordance with Art. 1257(b)(2) of the Tex.Penal Code Ann. (Vernon 1974) concerning the punishment for murder with malice aforethought, the State of Texas announced its intention to seek the death penalty. Thereafter, a judge of the 195th Judicial District Court of Dallas County, Texas, informally ordered the State's attorney to arrange a psychiatric examination of Smith by Dr. James P. Grigson to determine Smith's competency to stand trial.[1]

Dr. Grigson, who interviewed Smith in jail for approximately 90 minutes, concluded that he was competent to stand trial. In a letter to the trial judge, Dr. Grigson reported his findings: "[I]t is my opinion that Ernest Benjamin Smith, Jr., is aware of the difference between right and wrong and is able to aid an attorney in his defense." This letter was filed with the court's papers in the case. Smith was then tried by a jury and convicted of murder.

In Texas, capital cases require bifurcated proceedings—a guilt phase and a penalty phase. If the defendant is found guilty, a separate proceeding before the same jury is held to fix the punishment. At the penalty phase, if the jury affirmatively answers three questions on which the State has the burden of proof beyond a reasonable doubt, the judge must impose the death sentence. See Tex.Code Crim.Proc.Ann., Arts. 37.071(c) and (e) (Vernon Supp.1980). One of the three critical issues to be resolved by the jury is "whether there is a probability that the defendant would commit criminal acts of violence that would constitute a continuing threat to society." Art. 37.071(b)(2). In other words, the jury must assess the defendant's future dangerousness.

At the commencement of Smith's sentencing hearing, the State rested "[s]ubject to the right to reopen." Defense counsel called three lay witnesses: Smith's stepmother, his aunt, and the man who owned the gun Smith carried during the robbery. Smith's relatives testified as to his good reputation and character. The owner of the pistol testified as to Smith's knowledge that it would not fire because of a mechanical defect. The State then called Dr. Grigson as a witness.

Defense counsel were aware from the trial court's file of the case that Dr. Grigson had submitted a psychiatric report in the form of a

1. This psychiatric evaluation was ordered even though defense counsel had not put into issue Smith's competency to stand trial or his sanity at the time of the offense. The trial judge later explained: "In all cases where the State has sought the death penalty, I have ordered a mental evaluation of the defendant to determine his competency to stand trial. I have done this for my benefit because I do not intend to be a participant in a case where the defendant receives the death penalty and his mental competency remains in doubt." See Tex. Code Crim.Proc.Ann., Art. 46.02 (Vernon 1979). No question as to the appropriateness of the trial judge's order for the examination has been raised by Smith.

letter advising the court that Smith was competent to stand trial. This report termed Smith "a severe sociopath," but it contained no more specific reference to his future dangerousness. Before trial, defense counsel had obtained an order requiring the State to disclose the witnesses it planned to use both at the guilt stage, and, if known, at the penalty stage. Subsequently, the trial court had granted a defense motion to bar the testimony during the State's case in chief of any witness whose name did not appear on that list. Dr. Grigson's name was not on the witness list, and defense counsel objected when he was called to the stand at the penalty phase.

In a hearing outside the presence of the jury, Dr. Grigson stated: (a) that he had not obtained permission from Smith's attorneys to examine him; (b) that he had discussed his conclusions and diagnosis with the State's attorney; and (c) that the prosecutor had requested him to testify and had told him, approximately five days before the sentencing hearing began, that his testimony probably would be needed within the week. The trial judge denied a defense motion to exclude Dr. Grigson's testimony on the ground that his name was not on the State's list of witnesses. Although no continuance was requested, the court then recessed for one hour following an acknowledgment by defense counsel that an hour was "all right."

After detailing his professional qualifications by way of foundation, Dr. Grigson testified before the jury on direct examination: (a) that Smith "is a very severe sociopath"; (b) that "he will continue his previous behavior"; (c) that his sociopathic condition will "only get worse"; (d) that he has no "regard for another human being's property or for their life, regardless of who it may be"; (e) that "[t]here is no treatment, no medicine * * * that in any way at all modifies or changes this behavior"; (f) that he "is going to go ahead and commit other similar or same criminal acts if given the opportunity to do so"; and (g) that he "has no remorse or sorrow for what he has done." Dr. Grigson, whose testimony was based on information derived from his 90–minute "mental status examination" of Smith (*i.e.*, the examination ordered to determine Smith's competency to stand trial), was the State's only witness at the sentencing hearing.

The jury answered the three requisite questions in the affirmative, and, thus, under Texas law the death penalty for Smith was mandatory. The Texas Court of Criminal Appeals affirmed Smith's conviction and death sentence, *Smith v. State,* 540 S.W.2d 693 (Tex.Cr.App.1976), and we denied certiorari, 430 U.S. 922, 97 S.Ct. 1341, 51 L.Ed.2d 601 (1977).

B

After unsuccessfully seeking a writ of habeas corpus in the Texas state courts, Smith petitioned for such relief in the United States District Court for the Northern District of Texas pursuant to 28 U.S.C. § 2254. The District Court vacated Smith's death sentence because it found constitutional error in the admission of Dr. Grigson's testimony at the penalty phase. 445 F.Supp. 647 (1977). The court based its holding on the failure to advise Smith of his right to remain silent at the pretrial psychiatric examination and the failure to notify defense counsel in advance of the penalty phase that Dr. Grigson would testify. The court concluded that the death penalty had been imposed on Smith in violation of his Fifth and Fourteenth Amendment rights to due process and freedom from compelled self-incrimination, his Sixth Amendment right to the effective assistance of counsel, and his Eighth Amendment right to present complete evidence of mitigating circumstances.

The United States Court of Appeals for the Fifth Circuit affirmed. 602 F.2d 694 (1979). The court held that Smith's death sentence could not stand because the State's "surprise" use of Dr. Grigson as a witness, the consequences of which the court described as "devastating," denied Smith due process in that his attorneys were prevented from effectively challenging the psychiatric testimony. The court went on to hold that, under the Fifth and Sixth Amendments, "Texas may not use evidence based on a psychiatric examination of the defendant unless the defendant was warned, before the examination, that he had a right to remain silent; was allowed to terminate the examination when he wished; and was assisted by counsel in deciding whether to submit to the examination." Because Smith was not accorded these rights, his death sentence was set aside. While "leav[ing] to state authorities any questions that arise about the appropriate way to proceed when the state cannot legally execute a defendant whom it has sentenced to death," the court indicated that "the same testimony from Dr. Grigson, based on the same examination of Smith" could not be used against Smith at any future resentencing proceeding.

II

A

Of the several constitutional issues addressed by the District Court and the Court of Appeals, we turn first to whether the admission of Dr. Grigson's testimony at the penalty phase violated respondent's Fifth Amendment privilege against compelled self-incrimination because respondent was not advised before the pretrial psychiatric examination that he had a right to remain silent and that any statement he made could be used against him at a sentencing proceeding. Our initial inquiry must be whether the Fifth Amendment privilege is applicable in the circumstances of this case.

(1)

The State argues that respondent was not entitled to the protection of the Fifth Amendment because Dr. Grigson's testimony was used only to determine punishment after conviction, not to establish guilt. In the State's view, "incrimination is complete once guilt has been adjudicated," and, therefore, the Fifth Amendment privilege has no relevance to the penalty phase of a capital murder trial. We disagree.

The Fifth Amendment, made applicable to the states through the Fourteenth Amendment, commands that "[n]o person * * * shall be compelled in any criminal case to be a witness against himself." The essence of this basic constitutional principle is "the requirement that the State which proposes to convict *and punish* an individual produce the evidence against him by the independent labor of its officers, not by the simple, cruel expedient of forcing it from his own lips."

The Court has held that "the availability of the [Fifth Amendment] privilege does not turn upon the type of proceeding in which its protection is invoked, but upon the nature of the statement or admission and the exposure which it invites." *In re Gault,* 387 U.S. 1, 49, 87 S.Ct. 1428, 1455, 18 L.Ed.2d 527 (1967). In this case, the ultimate penalty of death was a potential consequence of what respondent told the examining psychiatrist. Just as the Fifth Amendment prevents a criminal defendant from being made " 'the deluded instrument of his own conviction,' " it protects him as well from being made the "deluded instrument" of his own execution.

We can discern no basis to distinguish between the guilt and penalty phases of respondent's capital murder trial so far as the protection of the Fifth Amendment privilege is concerned. Given the gravity of the decision to be made at the penalty phase, the State is not relieved of the obligation to observe fundamental constitutional guarantees. Any effort by the State to compel respondent to testify against his will at the sentencing hearing clearly would contravene the Fifth Amendment. Yet the State's attempt to establish respondent's future dangerousness by relying on the unwarned statements he made to Dr. Grigson similarly infringes Fifth Amendment values.

(2)

The State also urges that the Fifth Amendment privilege is inapposite here because respondent's communications to Dr. Grigson were nontestimonial in nature. The State seeks support from our cases holding that the Fifth Amendment is not violated where the evidence given by a defendant is neither related to some communicative act nor used for the testimonial content of what was said.

However, Dr. Grigson's diagnosis, as detailed in his testimony, was not based simply on his observation of respondent. Rather, Dr. Grigson drew his conclusions largely from respondent's account of the crime during their interview, and he placed particular emphasis on what he considered to be respondent's lack of remorse. Dr. Grigson's prognosis as to future dangerousness rested on statements respondent made, and remarks he omitted, in reciting the details of the crime. The Fifth Amendment privilege, therefore, is directly involved here because the State used as evidence against respondent the substance of his disclosures during the pretrial psychiatric examination.

The fact that respondent's statements were uttered in the context of a psychiatric examination does not automatically remove them from the reach of the Fifth Amendment. The state trial judge, *sua sponte,* ordered a psychiatric evaluation of respondent for the limited, neutral purpose of determining his competency to stand trial, but the results of that inquiry were used by the State for a much broader objective that was plainly adverse to respondent. Consequently, the interview with Dr. Grigson cannot be characterized as a routine competency examination restricted to ensuring that respondent understood the charges against him and was capable of assisting in his defense. Indeed, if the application of Dr. Grigson's findings had been confined to serving that function, no Fifth Amendment issue would have arisen.

Nor was the interview analogous to a sanity examination occasioned by a defendant's plea of not guilty by reason of insanity at the time of his offense. When a defendant asserts the insanity defense and introduces supporting psychiatric testimony, his silence may deprive the State of the only effective means it has of controverting his proof on an issue that he interjected into the case. Accordingly, several Courts of Appeals have held that, under such circumstances, a defendant can be required to submit to a sanity examination conducted by the prosecution's psychiatrist.[10]

Respondent, however, introduced no psychiatric evidence, nor had he indicated that he might do so. Instead, the State offered information obtained from the court-ordered competency examination as affirmative evidence to persuade the jury to return a sentence of death. Respondent's future dangerousness was a critical issue at the sentencing hearing, and one on which the State had the burden of proof beyond a reasonable doubt. See Tex.Code Crim.Proc.Ann., Arts. 37.071(b) and (c) (Vernon Supp.1980). To meet its burden, the State used respondent's own statements, unwittingly made without an awareness that he was assisting the State's efforts to obtain the death penalty. In these distinct circumstances, the Court of Appeals correctly concluded that the Fifth Amendment privilege was implicated.

(3)

In *Miranda v. Arizona,* 384 U.S. 436, 467, 86 S.Ct. 1602, 1624, 16 L.Ed.2d 694 (1966), the Court acknowledged that "the Fifth Amendment privilege is available outside of criminal court proceedings and serves to protect persons in all settings in which their freedom of action is curtailed in any significant way from being compelled to incriminate themselves." *Miranda* held that "the prosecution may not use statements, whether exculpatory or inculpatory, stemming from custodial interrogation of the defendant unless it demonstrates the use of procedural safeguards effective to secure the privilege against self-incrimination." Thus, absent other fully effective procedures, a person in custody must receive certain warnings before any official interrogation, including that he has a "right to remain silent" and that "anything said can and will be used against the individual in court." The purpose of these admonitions is to combat what the Court saw as "inherently compelling

---

10. On the same theory, the Court of Appeals here carefully left open "the possibility that a defendant who wishes to use psychiatric evidence in his own behalf [on the issue of future dangerousness] can be precluded from using it unless he is [also] willing to be examined by a psychiatrist nominated by the state." 602 F.2d at 705.

pressures" at work on the person and to provide him with an awareness of the Fifth Amendment privilege and the consequences of forgoing it, which is the prerequisite for "an intelligent decision as to its exercise."

The considerations calling for the accused to be warned prior to custodial interrogation apply with no less force to the pretrial psychiatric examination at issue here. Respondent was in custody at the Dallas County Jail when the examination was ordered and when it was conducted. That respondent was questioned by a psychiatrist designated by the trial court to conduct a neutral competency examination, rather than by a police officer, government informant, or prosecuting attorney, is immaterial. When Dr. Grigson went beyond simply reporting to the court on the issue of competence and testified for the prosecution at the penalty phase on the crucial issue of respondent's future dangerousness, his role changed and became essentially like that of an agent of the State recounting unwarned statements made in a postarrest custodial setting. During the psychiatric evaluation, respondent assuredly was "faced with a phase of the adversary system" and was "not in the presence of [a] perso[n] acting solely in his interest."

Yet he was given no indication that the compulsory examination would be used to gather evidence necessary to decide whether, if convicted, he should be sentenced to death. He was not informed that, accordingly, he had a constitutional right not to answer the questions put to him.

The Fifth Amendment privilege is "as broad as the mischief against which it seeks to guard," *Counselman v. Hitchcock*, 142 U.S. 547, 562, 12 S.Ct. 195, 198, 35 L.Ed. 1110 (1892), and the privilege is fulfilled only when a criminal defendant is guaranteed the right "to remain silent unless he chooses to speak in the unfettered exercise of his own will, and to suffer no penalty * * * for such silence." We agree with the Court of Appeals that respondent's Fifth Amendment rights were violated by the admission of Dr. Grigson's testimony at the penalty phase.

A criminal defendant, who neither initiates a psychiatric evaluation nor attempts to introduce any psychiatric evidence, may not be compelled to respond to a psychiatrist if his statements can be used against him at a capital sentencing proceeding. Because respondent did not voluntarily consent to the pretrial psychiatric examination after being informed of his right to remain silent and the possible use of his statements, the State could not rely on what he said to Dr. Grigson to establish his future dangerousness. If, upon being adequately warned, respondent had indicated that he would not answer Dr. Grigson's questions, the validly ordered competency examination nevertheless could have proceeded upon the condition that the results would be applied solely for that purpose. In such circumstances, the proper conduct and use of competency and sanity examinations are not frustrated, but the State must make its case on future dangerousness in some other way.

"Volunteered statements * * * are not barred by the Fifth Amendment," but under *Miranda v. Arizona, supra,* we must conclude that, when faced while in custody with a court-ordered psychiatric inquiry, respondent's statements to Dr. Grigson were not "given freely and voluntarily without any compelling influences" and, as such, could be used as the State did at the penalty phase only if respondent had been apprised of his rights and had knowingly decided to waive them. These safeguards of the Fifth Amendment privilege were not afforded respondent and, thus, his death sentence cannot stand.

B

When respondent was examined by Dr. Grigson, he already had been indicted and an attorney had been appointed to represent him. The Court of Appeals concluded that he had a Sixth Amendment right to the assistance of counsel before submitting to the pretrial psychiatric interview. We agree.

The Sixth Amendment, made applicable to the states through the Fourteenth Amendment, provides that "[i]n all criminal prosecutions, the accused shall enjoy the right * * * to have the assistance of counsel for his defense." The "vital" need for a lawyer's advice and aid during the pretrial phase was recognized by the Court nearly 50 years ago in *Powell v. Alabama,* 287 U.S. 45, 57, 71, 53 S.Ct. 55, 60, 65, 77 L.Ed. 158 (1932). Since then, we have held that the right to counsel granted by the Sixth Amendment means that a person is entitled to the help of a lawyer "at or after the time that adversary judicial proceedings have been initiated against him * * * whether by way of formal charge, preliminary hearing, indictment, information, or arraignment."

* * *

Here, respondent's Sixth Amendment right to counsel clearly had attached when Dr. Grigson examined him at the Dallas County Jail,[14] and their interview proved to be a "critical stage" of the aggregate proceedings against respondent. Defense counsel, however, were not notified in advance that the psychiatric examination would encompass the issue of their client's future dangerousness, and respondent was denied the assistance of his attorneys in making the significant decision

---

14. Because psychiatric examinations of the type at issue here are conducted after adversary proceedings have been instituted, we are not concerned in this case with the limited right to the appointment and presence of counsel recognized as a Fifth Amendment safeguard in *Miranda v. Arizona,* 384 U.S. 436, 471–473, 86 S.Ct. 1602, 1626–1627, 16 L.Ed.2d 694 (1966). See *Edwards v. Arizona,* 451 U.S. 477, 101 S.Ct. 1880, 68 L.Ed.2d 378. Rather, the issue before us is whether a defendant's Sixth Amendment right to the assistance of counsel is abridged when the defendant is not given prior opportunity to consult with

counsel about his participation in the psychiatric examination.

Respondent does not assert, and the Court of Appeals did not find, any constitutional right to have counsel actually present during the examination. In fact, the Court of Appeals recognized that "an attorney present during the psychiatric interview could contribute little and might seriously disrupt the examination." 602 F.2d at 708. Cf. *Thornton v. Corcoran,* 132 U.S.App.D.C. 232, 242, 248, 407 F.2d 695, 705, 711 (1969) (opinion concurring in part and dissenting in part).

of whether to submit to the examination and to what end the psychiatrist's findings could be employed.

Because "[a] layman may not be aware of the precise scope, the nuances, and the boundaries of his Fifth Amendment privilege," the assertion of that right "often depends upon legal advice from someone who is trained and skilled in the subject matter." As the Court of Appeals observed, the decision to be made regarding the proposed psychiatric evaluation is "literally a life or death matter" and is "difficult * * * even for an attorney" because it requires "a knowledge of what other evidence is available, of the particular psychiatrist's biases and predilections, [and] of possible alternative strategies at the sentencing hearing." It follows logically from our precedents that a defendant should not be forced to resolve such an important issue without "the guiding hand of counsel."

Therefore, in addition to Fifth Amendment considerations, the death penalty was improperly imposed on respondent because the psychiatric examination on which Dr. Grigson testified at the penalty phase proceeded in violation of respondent's Sixth Amendment right to the assistance of counsel.

C

Our holding based on the Fifth and Sixth Amendments will not prevent the State in capital cases from proving the defendant's future dangerousness as required by statute. A defendant may request or consent to a psychiatric examination concerning future dangerousness in the hope of escaping the death penalty. In addition, a different situation arises where a defendant intends to introduce psychiatric evidence at the penalty phase. See n. 10, *supra*.

Moreover, under the Texas capital sentencing procedure, the inquiry necessary for the jury's resolution of the future dangerousness issue is in no sense confined to the province of psychiatric experts.

* * * While in no sense disapproving the use of psychiatric testimony bearing on the issue of future dangerousness, the inquiry mandated by Texas law does not require resort to medical experts.

III

Respondent's Fifth and Sixth Amendment rights were abridged by the State's introduction of Dr. Grigson's testimony at the penalty phase, and, as the Court of Appeals concluded, his death sentence must be vacated. Because respondent's underlying conviction has not been challenged and remains undisturbed, the State is free to conduct further proceedings not inconsistent with this opinion. Accordingly, the judgment of the Court of Appeals is

Affirmed.

[Concurring opinions by BRENNAN, MARSHALL, and STEWART, JJ., are omitted.]

JUSTICE REHNQUIST, concurring in the judgment.

I concur in the judgment because, under *Massiah v. United States,* 377 U.S. 201, 84 S.Ct. 1199, 12 L.Ed.2d 246 (1964), respondent's counsel should have been notified prior to Dr. Grigson's examination of respondent. As the Court notes * * *, respondent had been indicted and an attorney had been appointed to represent him. Counsel was entitled to be made aware of Dr. Grigson's activities involving his client and to advise and prepare his client accordingly. This is by no means to say that respondent had any right to have his counsel present at any examination. In this regard I join the Court's careful delimiting of the Sixth Amendment issue * * *.

Since this is enough to decide the case, I would not go on to consider the Fifth Amendment issues and cannot subscribe to the Court's resolution of them. I am not convinced that any Fifth Amendment rights were implicated by Dr. Grigson's examination of respondent. Although the psychiatrist examined respondent prior to trial, he only testified concerning the examination after respondent stood convicted.

Even if there are Fifth Amendment rights involved in this case, respondent never invoked these rights when confronted with Dr. Grigson's questions. The Fifth Amendment privilege against compulsory self-incrimination is not self-executing. "Although *Miranda's* requirement of specific warnings creates a limited exception to the rule that the privilege must be claimed, the exception does not apply outside the context of the inherently coercive custodial interrogations for which it was designed." *Roberts v. United States,* 445 U.S. 552, 560, 100 S.Ct. 1358, 1364, 63 L.Ed.2d 622 (1980). The *Miranda* requirements were certainly not designed by this Court with psychiatric examinations in mind. Respondent was simply not in the inherently coercive situation considered in *Miranda.* He had already been indicted, and counsel had been appointed to represent him. No claim is raised that respondent's answers to Dr. Grigson's questions were "involuntary" in the normal sense of the word. Unlike the police officers in *Miranda,* Dr. Grigson was not questioning respondent in order to ascertain his guilt or innocence. Particularly since it is not necessary to decide this case, I would not extend the *Miranda* requirements to cover psychiatric examinations such as the one involved here.

Questions and Comments

1. *State access to the defendant; the necessity of warnings. Estelle* appears to hold that had Dr. Grigson given Smith warnings, to the effect that he had the right to remain silent and that anything he said could be used against him at a subsequent capital sentencing proceeding, the prosecution could have relied on the results of the interview at that proceeding. Will the typical defendant being evaluated for competency or sanity understand such warnings? Or is the answer to this latter question irrelevant if, as *Estelle* now requires, the defendant's attorney is notified of the evaluation?

More fundamentally, in the typical state-requested evaluation, will *Miranda*-type warnings be accurate? *Estelle* speaks only of when the defendant "neither initiates a psychiatric evaluation nor attempts to introduce any psychiatric evidence." What if, as is more likely to be the case, the defendant has already obtained or is about to obtain an evaluation (either privately or as authorized by *Ake*) and plans to introduce psychiatric testimony? May such a defendant constitutionally remain silent during a state-requested evaluation? Or may the state sanction non-cooperation? Put another way, does the accusatorial paradigm continue to apply or should it give way to the inquisitorial approach? The answers to these questions depend upon the precise issue about which the state is seeking information.

Sanity Evaluations. Assume that the state is seeking evaluation of the defendant's sanity. One of the first decisions to address the implications of the fifth amendment in this context, *Pope v. United States,* 372 F.2d 710 (8th Cir.1967), held that, once the defendant gives formal notice of an intent to raise an insanity defense, the state may compel an evaluation of the defendant; in other words, there is no right to remain silent during a state-requested evaluation once the defense is formally asserted. The court gave two reasons for this result. First, assertion of an insanity defense waives the fifth amendment privilege:

> [B]y raising the issue of insanity, by submitting to psychiatric and psychologic examination by his own examiners, and by presenting evidence as to mental incompetence from the lips of the defendant and these examiners, the defendant raised the issue for all purposes and ... the government was appropriately granted leave to have the defendant examined by experts of its choice and to present their opinions in evidence.

Second, permitting the defendant to remain silent after asserting the defense would unfairly tip the "state-individual balance" in the defendant's favor:

> It would be a strange situation, indeed, if, first, the government is to be compelled to afford the defense ample psychiatric service and evidence at government expense and, second, if the government is to have the burden of proof, ... and yet it is to be denied the opportunity to have its own corresponding and verifying examination, a step which perhaps is the most trustworthy means of attempting to meet the burden.

Both the waiver and fairness rationales have been attacked. As to the waiver rationale, one court has pointed out: "It is difficult to understand how a waiver could be characterized as either voluntary or intentional if automatically triggered by a defendant's assertion of the defense of insanity." *Commonwealth v. Pomponi,* 447 Pa. 154, 160, 284 A.2d 708, 711 (1971). In response to the fairness argument, it has been argued that the prosecution does not require access to the defendant to meet its evidentiary burden but rather can rely on lay witnesses, cross-examination of the defendant's experts, and hypothetical questions addressed to its own experts. Julia Meister, "*Miranda* on the Couch: An Approach to Problems of Self–Incrimination, Right to Counsel and *Miranda* Warnings in Pre–Trial Psychiatric Examinations of Criminal Defendants," 11 Colum.J.L. & Soc.Probs. 403, 425 (1975). Compare in this regard decisions refusing to permit criminal defendants to compel evaluations of rape complainants with a history of mental problems. *Nobrega v. Commonwealth,* 271 Va. 508, 628 S.E.2d 922 (2006) (emphasizing victim's constitutional right to be treated with dignity and the discretion given trial judges to exclude expert testimony re credibility); *State v. Nelson*, 235 Neb. 15, 453 N.W.2d 454 (1990) (permitting such evaluations only when defendant demonstrates a "compelling need" and holding that conflicting accounts by an allegedly emotionally unstable complainant does not demonstrate a compelling need).

Nonetheless, most courts continue to agree with *Pope,* usually relying on the fairness rationale. The argument that the prosecution does not need its own evaluation of the defendant was forcefully rejected by Justice Scalia in an opinion he wrote while on the District of Columbia Circuit Court of Appeals:

> Appellant and *amici* would have us believe that the mere availability of cross-examination of the defendant's experts is sufficient to provide the necessary balance in the criminal process. That would perhaps be so if psychiatry were as exact a science as physics, so that, assuming the defense psychiatrist precisely described the data (consisting of his interview with the defendant), the error of his analysis could be demonstrated. It is, however, far from that. Ordinarily the only effective rebuttal of psychiatric opinion testimony is contradictory opinion testimony; and for that purpose ... '[t]he basic tool of psychiatric study remains the personal interview, which requires rapport between the interviewer and the subject.'
>
> Our judgment that these practical considerations of fair but effective criminal process affect the interpretation and application of the Fifth Amendment privilege against self-incrimination is supported by the long line of Supreme Court precedent holding that the defendant in a criminal or even civil prosecution may not take the stand in his own behalf and then refuse to consent to cross-examination. The justification for this similarly 'coerced' testimony is precisely that which we apply to the present case. As said in *Brown* [*v. United States,* 356 U.S. 148, 78 S.Ct. 622, 2 L.Ed.2d 589 (1958)], a defendant cannot reasonably claim that the Fifth Amendment gives him not only this choice [whether to testify or not] but, if he elects to testify, an immunity from cross-examination on the matters he has himself put in dispute. It would make of the Fifth Amendment not only a humane safeguard against judicially coerced self-disclosure but a positive invitation to mutilate the truth a party offers to tell.... The interests of the other party and regard for the function of courts of justice to ascertain the truth become relevant, and prevail in the balance of considerations determining the scope and limits of the privilege against self-incrimination.

United States v. Byers, 740 F.2d 1104 (D.C.Cir.1984).

Judge Bazelon, in a dissenting opinion in *Byers,* agreed that the fifth amendment does not necessarily bar the state from obtaining its own post-notice evaluation. But he argued that because the "state psychiatrist's aim is diagnosis, not therapy" and "[h]is primary commitment is to his institution, not to his patient," the state-referred evaluation "poses a threat of coercion similar to that in the interrogation deemed unconstitutional in *Miranda.*" Thus, he contended that the constitution requires that all such interviews be taped. This step "would quiet our concern that psychiatrists might manipulate or intimidate the defendant in an *in camera* interview" and "help inform the court's judgment regarding the voluntariness and reliability of the defendant's statement." Scalia responded that such a requirement is not imposed even on police interrogators and that, in any event, it stemmed from a concern over reliability, not compulsion; only the latter is the proper focus of fifth amendment analysis. How should the debate over the proper scope of the right to remain silent in the post-notice context be resolved? What, if anything, does *Estelle* say about this issue?

The preceding discussion has focused on state evaluations after notice of an insanity defense has been given. In many states, the prosecution may obtain such an evaluation *before* the defendant has given formal notice of an intent to raise an insanity defense. Should this practice be permitted? Why would the prosecution need such an evaluation? The American Bar Association's Criminal Justice Mental Health Standards recommend that, to guarantee the prosecution evaluation results that are "as fresh" as those obtained by the defense, the state should be notified of a defense evaluation within 48 hours and should be able to obtain its own evaluation shortly thereafter. However, the results of this pre-notice evaluation are to be disclosed to the prosecution only if and when the defense gives formal notice of an intent to raise an insanity defense. Standard 7–3.4.

Capital Sentencing Evaluations. Estelle holds that the fifth amendment applies in the capital sentencing context. Does this mean that the evaluation procedures applicable in the insanity context also apply to capital sentencing evaluations? In other words, does *Estelle* hold that the state is barred from compelling evaluation of the defendant on sentencing issues such as dangerousness if the defendant does not intend to use clinical testimony at sentencing? If the defendant *does* present clinical testimony at the sentencing proceeding, but limits it to responsibility issues having to do with culpability at the time of the offense, may the state compel an evaluation of the defendant to determine propensity, i.e., dangerousness, or is its examiner limited to addressing responsibility issues? See n.10 of *Estelle*.

Other Contexts. In a footnote, the Court in *Estelle* cautioned that it was not holding "that the same Fifth Amendment concerns are necessarily presented by all types of interviews and examinations that might be ordered or relied upon to inform a sentencing determination." 451 U.S. at 469 n. 13, 101 S.Ct. at 1876 n. 13. However, in *Mitchell v. United States*, 526 U.S. 314, 119 S.Ct. 1307, 143 L.Ed.2d 424 (1999), the Court noted that "[w]here [a noncapital] sentence has not yet been imposed a defendant may have a legitimate fear of adverse consequences from testimony" and held that the sentencing court may not use a defendant's silence against him to enhance his sentence (except, perhaps, as evidence of lack of remorse or unwillingness to accept responsibility). Thus, the defendant may also be able to refuse to cooperate with a state-requested evaluation in the typical noncapital sentencing context, at least if he or she does not plan to use expert testimony. In contrast, the Court has made clear, in *Allen v. Illinois*, 478 U.S. 364, 106 S.Ct. 2988, 92 L.Ed.2d 296 (1986), that the fifth amendment does not apply to "special" sentencing evaluations and proceedings conducted pursuant to mentally disordered sex offender (MDSO) statutes, because the primary purpose of such statutes is "treatment," not punishment. For the same reason, the fifth amendment does not apply to competency to stand trial or civil commitment evaluations and proceedings. For present purposes,[o] the importance of *Allen* is that the state may compel an evaluation of the defendant in any of these contexts, at least when, as discussed below, the results of the evaluation are used only to adjudicate the issue for which the evaluation is sought.

2. *Sanctions.* In situations where there is no right to remain silent, but the defendant still refuses to cooperate,[p] a sanction is necessary. In insanity cases, the courts have imposed four different types of sanctions. They have: (1) prohibited the defendant from presenting any evidence of insanity; (2) allowed the defendant to make the insanity claim, but prohibited use of expert testimony to support it; (3) allowed the defendant to present clinical testimony but only that which is based on facts that were revealed to the state's expert as well (in those cases where there was partial, but not complete cooperation); and (4) allowed the defendant to present unrestricted clinical testimony but also allowed the prosecution to inform the factfinder about the defendant's refusal to cooperate with the state's expert. See Christopher Slobogin, *"Estelle v. Smith* : The Constitutional Contours of the Forensic Evaluation," 31 Emory L.J. 71, 103–104 (1981). Which option is fairest to both sides? Do any of these sanctions work when the defendant refuses to cooperate at an evaluation of competency to stand trial or on civil commitment issues? What would be an appropriate sanction in such situations?

3. *Use of evaluation results.* An issue separate from determining when the state may compel a defendant to undergo an evaluation is when, and for what purpose, the state may use the results of any evaluations that have taken place. Even when a compelled evaluation is permissible, prosecution use of its results may be limited or barred altogether. For instance, while the prosecution may compel the defendant to undergo a competency to stand trial evaluation, it may not, in most states, use the results of the evaluation for any purpose other than adjudication of competency. See, e.g., West's Fla.R.Crim.Proc. 3.211(e). Is such an approach required under *Estelle?* If not, should it be?

Most states have a similar rule with respect to the use of results from evaluations of mental state at the time of the offense. The federal rule is perhaps the most comprehensive:

> No statement made by the defendant in the course of any [psychiatric] examination ... , whether the examination be with or without the consent of the defendant, no testimony by the expert based upon such statement, and no other fruits of the statement shall be admitted in evidence against the defendant in any criminal proceeding except on an issue respecting mental condition on which the defendant has introduced testimony.

o. *Allen* is reprinted at pp. 842 et seq., where its implications for civil commitment are discussed.

p. Defining "non-cooperation" is a difficult issue. As one court has stated:

> The fact, amply demonstrated over the years, is that a failure of a defendant who pleads insanity ... to cooperate most often reflects an even greater degree of

insanity rather than less. He is not always controllable by his lawyer, and many a psychotic defendant, who may or may not be legally insane, refuses to be represented by a lawyer. In short, non-cooperation may be evidence of insanity.

Lee v. County Ct., 27 N.Y.2d 432, 448–49, 267 N.E.2d 452, 461–62, 318 N.Y.S.2d 705, 718–19 (1971).

Fed.R.Crim.Pro. 12.2. This rule prohibits three things: (1) prosecution use of evaluation results when the defendant has not asserted a clinically-based defense or claim; (2) when such a claim is asserted, prosecution use of evaluation results for purposes other than rebuttal of that claim (e.g., use of an evaluator solely to establish that the defendant committed the criminal act); (3) prosecution use of evidence derived from the results of the evaluation (e.g., introduction of a murder weapon discovered as a result of leads developed solely from the psychiatric evaluation). Is there a reason other than fear of compulsion or manipulation by the expert which underlies this extensive protection?

Even this degree of protection may not satisfy the dictates of the fifth amendment. For instance, if an insanity defense is raised, expert testimony is very likely to recount in detail the defendant's actions at the time of the offense. In cases where the defendant readily admits he or she committed the criminal act, such testimony presumably does not present a problem. But what if the defendant asserts not only an insanity defense, but also a "factual" defense (e.g., self-defense)? In jurisdictions where such dual pleading is permitted, the state's expert may disclose information, highly prejudicial to the factual defense, which was obtained during a compelled evaluation. Courts have resorted to two practices in such a situation. The first is an instruction to the jury cautioning that the expert testimony is to be considered only on the issue of insanity. The second is bifurcation of the trial, with the first stage addressing the factual defense, and the second addressing, if necessary, the insanity defense. The expert testimony would be deferred until the second stage, thus avoiding revelation of disclosures that were compelled from the defendant at a psychiatric evaluation during adjudication of the factual defense.

Should the rules with respect to using evaluation results change if the results come from a *defense*-requested evaluation? In *Buchanan v. Kentucky*, 483 U.S. 402, 107 S.Ct. 2906, 97 L.Ed.2d 336 (1987), the prosecution rebutted the defendant's psychiatric defense with the results of a post-offense evaluation that was conducted to determine whether the defendant required psychiatric hospitalization and was competent to stand trial; the evaluation had been jointly requested by the prosecution and the defense. The Supreme Court found no constitutional violation because, unlike in *Estelle*, the defendant had raised a psychiatric defense and the defendant had joined in the evaluation motion. Is *Buchanan* correctly decided? What are the possible consequences of the decision? In *Penry v. Johnson*, 532 U.S. 782, 121 S.Ct. 1910, 150 L.Ed.2d 9 (2001), the state was allowed to introduce a report from a defense-requested competency evaluation in an earlier case after the defense expert, who had testified that the defendant was suffering from a mental disability and thus should not receive the death penalty, indicated he had reviewed the report in preparing his testimony. The Court strongly suggested that here too the fifth amendment was not violated, despite the absence of any warning that the original competency results might be used at a capital sentencing proceeding, because the defense had commissioned the evaluation in the earlier case, and had used an expert to address mental state in the instant case.

4. *The right to counsel.* According to *Estelle,* the sixth amendment's guarantee of a right to counsel "in all criminal prosecutions" requires that,

after the initiation of formal proceedings against the defendant, any state-requested evaluation of the defendant must be preceded by notice to counsel. Accord, *Satterwhite v. Texas*, 486 U.S. 249, 108 S.Ct. 1792, 100 L.Ed.2d 284 (1988). Presumably, this notice will permit counsel to explain the purpose of the evaluation to the defendant and to advise him or her whether to cooperate with the evaluator. However, the Supreme Court specifically avoided deciding whether there is a right to counsel's *presence* during the evaluation; if anything, it expressed some distaste for the idea. See n. 14.

Determining whether there should be a right to presence of counsel at state-requested evaluations is made difficult by the Court's somewhat muddled approach to the right to counsel generally. Under *United States v. Wade*, 388 U.S. 218, 87 S.Ct. 1926, 18 L.Ed.2d 1149 (1967), cited by *Estelle*, the right to counsel attached at any stage of the criminal prosecution which is deemed "critical"—that is, any stage where "the presence of counsel is necessary to preserve the defendant's basic right to a fair trial as affected by his right meaningfully to cross-examine the witnesses against him and to have effective assistance of counsel at the trial itself." In *Wade*, the Court found a right to counsel at post-indictment lineup identifications because (1) "the trial which might determine the accused's fate may well be not that in the courtroom but at the pretrial confrontation"; (2) "there is a serious difficulty in depicting what transpires at lineups", particularly if "the jury's choice is between the accused's unsupported version and that of the police officers present"; and (3) the "vagaries of eyewitness identification are well-known." If counsel is not present to observe, and thus enabled to reconstruct at trial, any irregularities in the identification process, these three factors create "a grave risk of erroneous conviction."

Wade's critical stage analysis was significantly modified, however, by *United States v. Ash*, 413 U.S. 300, 93 S.Ct. 2568, 37 L.Ed.2d 619 (1973), in which the Court found no right to counsel when the police show a witness photo displays for purposes of identification. Rejecting *Wade's* emphasis on whether the procedure in question might prejudice the defendant and whether counsel could alleviate the prejudice, the Court concluded that instead the key inquiry should be whether the procedure involves a "trial-like confrontation"—that is, whether it confronts the accused with the "intricacies of the law and the advocacy of the public prosecutor." *Wade's* approach, the Court stated, would give the right to counsel too broad a scope; as an example, the Court mentioned that critical stage analysis would improperly entitle the defendant to counsel at prosecutorial interviews of the victim and other witnesses.

Whether they apply the critical stage test or the trial-like confrontation test, most courts have held there is no right to have counsel present during state-requested clinical evaluations. Comment, "The Right to Counsel During Court–Ordered Psychiatric Examinations of Criminal Defendants," 26 Vill.L.Rev. 135 (1980). *United States v. Byers*, supra, is again illustrative. Then–Judge Scalia, relying on *Ash*, concluded for the majority that there is no right to counsel at a post-notice insanity evaluation. The defendant who has been advised of his or her rights by counsel prior to the evaluation "ha[s] no decisions in the nature of legal strategy or tactics to make" during the evaluation. Moreover, the "examining psychiatrist is not an adversary" or "expert in 'the intricacies of substantive and procedural criminal law.' "

Scalia also registered practical objections to having counsel present during the evaluation:

> The "procedural system" of the law, which is one justification for the presence of counsel and which, by the same token, the presence of counsel brings in its train, is evidently antithetical to psychiatric examination, a process informal and unstructured by design. Even if counsel were uncharacteristically to sit silent and interpose no procedural objections or suggestions, one can scarcely imagine a successful psychiatric examination in which the subject's eyes move back and forth between the doctor and his attorney. Nor would it help if the attorney were listening from outside the room, for the subject's attention would still wander where his eyes could not. And the attorney's presence in such a purely observational capacity, without ability to advise, suggest or object, would have no relationship to the Sixth Amendment's 'Assistance of Counsel.'

The latter observation also led Scalia to find, as he already had with respect to the fifth amendment, that the sixth amendment does not require taping of state-requested evaluations. He concluded: "It is enough, as far as the constitutional minima of the criminal process are concerned, that the defendant has the opportunity to contest the accuracy of witnesses' testimony by cross-examining them at trial, and introducing his own witnesses in rebuttal."

If *Wade* were applicable, how would you evaluate the result in *Byers*? Accepting *Ash* as the governing precedent, is Scalia's characterization of the psychiatrist as a non-adversary realistic? Is it consistent with *Estelle's* characterization of Dr. Grigson?

5. *Summary problems on evaluation issues.* How would you rule in the following scenarios and why? What are the counterarguments to your conclusions?

A. Assume Jones, charged with second degree murder, hires three mental health professionals to evaluate his sanity at the time of the offense. He then notifies the court and the prosecution that he intends to raise an insanity defense and that he intends to use the first two experts to support the defense. The prosecution wants to subpoena the third expert. Jones objects.

B. Same facts as A. The prosecution also wants to compel an evaluation of Jones' sanity at the time of the offense. Jones objects.

C. The court grants the prosecution's motion in B. Jones's attorney requests to be present during the evaluation. The state objects.

D. At the state-requested evaluation, Jones will not talk about the day of the offense, claiming the state's expert is a CIA agent intent on "stealing my mind." The prosecution asks the court to sanction Jones.

E. Smith, who is indigent, is charged with capital murder. He has no documented history of mental disorder, but his attorney claims that Smith is suffering from severe depression and that the depression affects his ability to communicate at the present time and affected his behavior at the time of the offense. The attorney moves for a state-paid evaluation of Smith's competency to stand trial, his sanity, and issues related to capital sentencing, including whether he was under emotional stress at the time of the offense and his treatability. He specifically requests Dr. Black as the evaluator. Dr. Black is a private psychiatrist whose rates are very high. The state argues that Smith is not entitled to an evaluation of any sort and that, even if he is, an evaluation at the state hospital would be sufficient.

F. The court orders that Smith be evaluated at the state hospital on the competency, sanity and sentencing issues. Smith moves that the results of this evaluation be sent only to him. The state objects, arguing that it is entitled to the results as well.

G. The motion in F is granted. Smith indicates he will use expert testimony only at sentencing. The state moves for an evaluation on the competency and sanity issues. In support of its motion, the state points to the defense attorney's representations in E. Smith objects.

H. The court grants the state's motion in G. Smith is found competent to stand trial, tried and convicted of capital murder. At his capital sentencing proceeding he plans to present expert testimony to the effect that he was under extreme emotional distress at the time of the offense as a result of severe depression and that, with proper care, the prognosis for his condition is good. The state wants to introduce expert testimony, based on the results of the competency evaluation it obtained, that Smith is dangerous; dangerousness is an aggravating circumstance under the state's capital punishment statute. Smith objects, noting that no warnings were given him prior to the state's evaluation and that, in any event, he "opened the door" only on mitigation issues.

2. *Hearsay and Other Evidentiary Considerations*

Rarely will the testifying mental health professional have observed directly all of the behavioral or biological evidence upon which he or she relies. For instance, in evaluating a criminal accused who has asserted an insanity defense, the mental health professional will not only interview the defendant, but interview, or obtain statements made by, family, friends and witnesses of the alleged offense. Various types of records— medical, psychological, criminal, educational, and occupational—will be acquired. Clinical reports from other mental health professionals (e.g., psychological test results, social histories) are also usually obtained.

Unless the individuals who possess or created this information are produced at trial, the evidence is "hearsay"—that is, statements from declarants who are not in court. Hearsay is generally considered inadmissible because the declarant cannot be subjected to cross-examination. Federal Rule of Evidence, Rule 802. Of course, there are several exceptions to this rule. For instance, pre-trial statements by the person who is the subject of legal proceedings are admissible, even if the person does not take the witness stand and undergo cross-examination, under the party admissions exception.[q] Documentary information may also be admissible under the so-called "business records" exception to the hearsay rule, if the custodian of the record or "other qualified witness"

---

q. Under the federal rules, if the party admission is offered *against* the party, then it is not hearsay to begin with. Rule 801(d)(2).

can attest to the fact that the document was kept as a regular practice of the business or profession.[r] But much of the third party information which mental health professionals rely upon is hearsay for which there is not a traditionally accepted exception. The following case addresses this problem.

UNITED STATES v. SIMS

United States Court of Appeals, Ninth Circuit, 1975.
514 F.2d 147.

* * *

The substance of this appeal ... involves the opinion expressed by a psychiatrist who testified for [the Government]. His opening testimony revealed that he based his opinion regarding appellant's mental state on his own examination of appellant, other psychiatric reports, and information derived from conversations with Government attorneys and IRS agents. The Government psychiatrist concluded that there was no evidence to support the contention that appellant lacked the capacity to appreciate the wrongfulness of his acts or to conform his conduct to the law. He added that appellant's "excessive amount of religiosity" was not "delusional thinking."

During cross-examination, appellant's counsel questioned the psychiatrist concerning the basis for his opinion, specifically in regard to appellant's pre–1971 conduct, which counsel contended to be free from aberration. "[I]s it a fact ... that at least from the facts we know, that Mr. Sims had been practicing as a tax preparer, according to information you have, for at least ten years before he had any difficulty with the law[?]" asked appellant's counsel. The psychiatrist then revealed that he had learned from IRS agents that appellant had been investigated for "alleged irregularities" prior to 1971. He added that this information was taken into account in reaching his opinion on appellant's sanity. The information came solely from out-of-court sources.[1]

---

r. Rule 803(6) creates an exception to the hearsay rule for records of regularly conducted activity, i.e.: "[a] memorandum, report, record, or data compilation, in any form, of acts, events, conditions, opinions, or diagnoses, made at or near the time by, or from information transmitted by, a person with knowledge, if kept in the course of a regularly conducted business activity, and if it was the regular practice of that business activity to make the memorandum, report, record, or data compilation, all as shown by the testimony of the custodian or other qualified witness, ... unless the source of information or the method or circumstances of preparation indicate lack of trustworthiness. The term 'business' as used in this paragraph includes business, institution, association, profession, occupation, and calling of every kind, whether or not conducted for profit." Rule 803(8) creates a similar exception for "public records," except that, in light of Confrontation Clause concerns, such records are inadmissible if introduced by the government against a criminal defendant.

1. The hardcore of the testimony here under challenge is as follows:

"Q. Did some investigating agent tell you that Mr. Sims may have been in some difficulty before 1971 with the law?

* * *

"A. Yes.

* * *

"Q. This was in the private interview with these agents—

The court thereupon *sua sponte* admonished the jury to consider the hearsay evidence only "... with reference to the basis for the doctor's opinion ..." and not "... in any way in a determination as to whether the defendant did or did not commit the offenses that are charged...."

Appellant moved that the Government psychiatrist's entire testimony be stricken because it was based on hearsay evidence unavailable to appellant prior to trial. The motion was denied, as was appellant's motion for a mistrial, thus forming the basis of this appeal.

* * *

The traditional rule is that an expert opinion is inadmissible if it is based upon information obtained out of court from third parties. The rationale behind this rule is that the trier of fact should not be presented with evidence grounded on otherwise inadmissible hearsay statements not subject to cross-examination and other forms of verification.

However, recent decisions, especially in the Federal courts, indicate there is a strong emerging trend in favor of admissibility. The new rule has been endorsed as the better reasoned and preferable approach in McCormick, Evidence § 15 (1972). *See also* 3 Wigmore, Evidence § 688 (1970).

The rationale in favor of the admissibility of expert testimony based on hearsay is that the expert is fully capable of judging for himself what is, or is not, a reliable basis for his opinion. This relates directly to one of the functions of the expert witness, namely to lend his special expertise to the issue before him. In so doing, various experts customarily rely on evidence not independently admissible in the courtroom. [T]he opinion "... is regarded as evidence in its own right and not as hearsay in disguise." In a sense, the expert synthesizes the primary source material—be it hearsay or not—into properly admissible evidence in opinion form. The trier of fact is then capable of judging the credibility of the witness as it would that of anyone else giving expert testimony. This rule respects the functions and abilities of both the expert witness and the trier of fact, while assuring that the requirement of witness confrontation is fulfilled.

Fully consistent with this view, though not yet controlling, is Rule 703 of the Federal Rules of Evidence for the United States Courts and Magistrates, effective July 1, 1975, which reads:

> "The facts or data in the particular case upon which an expert bases an opinion or inference may be those perceived by or made known to him at or before the hearing. If of a type reasonably relied upon by experts in the particular field in forming opinions or inferences upon the subject, the facts or data need not be admissible in evidence." 65 F.R.D. 139, 152.

"A. Yes.

"Q.—that you had, and these private interviews and this private information is one of the reasons you reached this opinion?

"A. It was taken into account in reaching an opinion, yes."

The rule merely codifies the law recently stated in the above-cited authorities.

It seems logical that an expert, such as a psychiatrist in formulating an opinion in a case such as this, should be permitted to interview the agents who made the investigation leading up to the indictment and secure from them relevant facts developed during the investigation. Because of his professional background, knowledge, and experience, we should, in circumstances such as these, leave to the expert the assessment of the reliability of the statements on which he bases his expert opinion. He should not be precluded, in forming an opinion, from interviewing those who for one reason or another have had occasion to investigate and study the defendant's background. Years of experience teach the expert to separate the wheat from the chaff and to use only those sources and kinds of information which are of a type reasonably relied upon by similar experts in arriving at sound opinions on the subject.

We do not open the gates to a wholesale use of all types of hearsay in formulating expert opinions. We only approve the use of that type of information upon which experts may reasonably rely. This follows the spirit of the Federal Rules of Evidence, *supra*. Upon admission of such evidence, it then, of course, becomes necessary for the court to instruct the jury that the hearsay evidence is to be considered solely as a basis for the expert opinion and not as substantive evidence. This the district court here did *sua sponte*.

CONCLUSION

After thorough consideration of all relevant factors, we conclude that no error was committed in admitting the expert's opinion. Finding no error, we affirm the district court's conviction of appellant.

Affirmed.

Questions and Comments

1. *Rule 703.* As the *Sims* court notes, Rule 703 significantly modifies the traditional rule. The Advisory Committee's Note on the new rule justified this change with the following words:

> [The] rule is designed . . . to bring the judicial practice into line with the practice of the experts themselves when not in court. Thus a physician in his own practice bases his diagnosis on information from numerous sources and of considerable variety, including statements by patients and relatives, reports and opinions from nurses, technicians and other doctors, hospital records, and X rays. Most of them are admissible in evidence, but only with the expenditure of substantial time in producing and examining various authenticating witnesses. The physician makes life-and-death decisions in reliance upon them. His validation, expertly performed and subject to cross-examination, ought to suffice for judicial purposes.

56 F.R.D. 183, 283.

Are the Committee's rationale and the *Sims* court's reasoning persuasive when the expert testimony at issue is from mental health professionals? See Note, "Hearsay Bases of Psychiatric Opinion Testimony: A Critique of Federal Rule of Evidence 703," 51 S.Cal.L.Rev. 129 (1977). What if, for instance, the hearsay is an account of the defendant's early childhood from the defendant's parents? A description of apparently illegal conduct committed by the defendant, related to the clinician by the victim (or, as in *Sims,* by an IRS agent)? A diagnosis given the defendant ten years ago by a psychiatrist?

2. *The Confrontation Clause and hearsay as a basis for expert testimony.* The Confrontation Clause states that a criminal accused shall have the right "to be confronted with the witnesses against him." In *Crawford v. Washington*, 541 U.S. 36, 124 S.Ct. 1354, 158 L.Ed.2d 177 (2004), the Supreme Court held that this language prohibits the government from introducing in a criminal trial out-of-court statements that are "testimonial," unless the maker of the statements is unavailable (i.e., dead, not accessible through subpoena, or claiming the fifth amendment) and the defendant had a prior opportunity to cross-examine the declarant. Testimonial statements include those made to a government agent "for the purpose of establishing or providing some fact." Are the statements alluded to by the expert witness in *Sims* testimonial? If so, what are the implications? One court has held that, after *Crawford*, third-party statements solicited by a mental health professional during a forensic evaluation and relied on at trial by the state are testimonial. *People v. Goldstein*, 6 N.Y.3d 119, 843 N.E.2d 727 (2005). Thus, presumably, they may not be admitted either through the expert or independently unless: (1) the declarant testifies; (2) the declarant is unavailable and the defendant had an opportunity to cross-examine him or her at some earlier proceeding, or (3) there is a waiver or forfeiture of confrontation rights, which is most likely to occur if the defendant killed the declarant with the purpose of preventing the declarant's testimony (*Giles v. California*, ___ U.S. ___, 128 S.Ct. 2678, 171 L.Ed.2d 488 (2008)).

3. *Other bases for testimony.* Information that forms the basis of a clinical opinion may be inadmissible for reasons other than the hearsay rule. For instance, mental health professionals sometimes administer sodium amytal (a disinhibiting drug) or use hypnosis during their interview process. Although such techniques are not viewed as "truth determinants" by experienced clinicians, they may provide valuable information that the subject has "repressed" or "suppressed." Ira Packer, "The Use of Hypnotic Techniques in the Evaluation of Criminal Defendants," 9 J. Psychiatry & Law 313, 319–20 (1981). The statements of a person who is under the influence of hypnosis or amytal are usually barred, not on hearsay grounds (because the statements are usually party admissions), but because of the unreliability of the technique used. See, e.g., *State v. Pierce*, 263 S.C. 23, 207 S.E.2d 414 (1974); *State v. Chase*, 206 Kan. 352, 480 P.2d 62 (1971). The courts that reach this result generally rely on some version of the *Frye* rule, discussed at pp. 454–55.

Evidence may also be excluded for constitutional reasons. For instance, soon after the attempted assassination of President Reagan, John Hinckley's hotel room in Washington, D.C. was searched and a diary, containing a wealth of information relevant to his mental state, was discovered. The trial court held that since the police did not have a warrant or probable cause at the time of the search, the diary was inadmissible.

4. *Explaining the opinion.* Suppose a clinician offers an opinion based in whole or in part on hearsay, the results of an amytal or hypnosis interview, or illegally seized evidence. Suppose further that the court finds that the evidence is not independently admissible, but that it is of the type reasonably relied upon by mental health professionals. Should the court allow the opinion but exclude the factual evidence? See *Greenfield v. Commonwealth*, 214 Va. 710, 204 S.E.2d 414 (1974). Or should it, like the court in *Sims*, allow both the opinion and the evidence, with an instruction telling the jury that the problems with the latter should be considered only in evaluating the strength of the opinion? See Robert Spector & Teree Foster, "Admissibility of Hypnotic Statements: Is the Law of Evidence Susceptible?" 38 Ohio St.L.J. 568, 597–601 (1977). Under the first approach, how is the clinician to explain the opinion? Under the second (assuming it is permitted after *Crawford*), can the jury be trusted to follow the instruction?

5. *Judicial monitoring of evaluation process.* A final issue which could arise under Rule 703 is whether a clinical opinion is admissible when the facts undergirding it, although "reasonably relied upon," are so minimal that most clinicians would consider them an insufficient basis for an opinion. For instance, one study of the civil commitment process in a midwestern city found that clinicians often perform only cursory evaluations and seem to assume the person is ill. Thomas Scheff, "The Societal Reaction to Deviance: Ascriptive Elements in the Psychiatric Screening of Mental Patients in a Midwestern State," 11 Social Probs. 401 (1964). As another example, the evaluation procedures of Dr. Grigson, the psychiatrist who testified in *Estelle v. Smith* and *Barefoot v. Estelle*, appear to fall far short of the ideal. In *Estelle,* he conducted a 90–minute interview on the basis of which he purported to be able to deliver opinions about not only the subject's dangerousness but also his competency to stand trial and sanity. *Estelle v. Smith,* 451 U.S. 454, 457, 459–60, 101 S.Ct. 1866, 1870, 1871, 68 L.Ed.2d 359 (1981). In *Barefoot,* he based his opinion about the defendant's dangerousness on a brief hypothetical question. Yet, according to Monahan, a comprehensive evaluation of dangerousness would include a personal interview, as well as data collection designed to investigate the person's history, future environment, reactions to stress, and base rate for violence based on actuarial factors. John Monahan, The Clinical Prediction of Violent Behavior 101–23 (NIMH, 1981).

6. *Differing contexts.* It should be noted that in some settings the hearsay rule and other exclusionary evidence rules may not apply with the same force as they do in criminal cases. For instance, some courts have held that hearsay is admissible in civil commitment proceedings. This position might have an impact on Rule 703 analysis. But see *In re Melton*, 597 A.2d 892 (D.C.1991) (holding in civil commitment context that hearsay is "reasonably relied upon" only if "the judge concludes that the information . . . is of a type for which the underlying reliability of the data can be sufficiently explored through cross-examination of the testifying expert"). The admissibility of hearsay in commitment hearings is discussed in more detail in Chapter Eight, pp. 830–31.

D. THE ULTIMATE ISSUE ISSUE

One final limitation on expert testimony may exist, even if one assumes that clinical opinion testimony is generally admissible, and even if it is offered by a qualified mental health professional who has relied solely on permissible sources of information. Traditionally, a witness, whether expert or lay, was barred from addressing the "ultimate" legal issue (e.g., in this context, sanity, competency, or committability). Usually, the reason given for this rule was that such an opinion usurped the function of the factfinder. As originally promulgated, Federal Rule 704 specifically did away with the ultimate issue limitation on testimony. It stated: "Testimony in the form of an opinion or inference otherwise admissible is not objectionable because it embraces an ultimate issue to be decided by the trier of fact." The Advisory Committee justified this change for two reasons. First, it contended that the rule was impossible to enforce, because witnesses would merely paraphrase their testimony in an effort to avoid the ultimate issue language. Second, it noted that the old rule tended to deprive the factfinder of helpful testimony. "Thus . . . in cases of medical causation, witnesses were sometimes required to couch their opinions in cautious phrases of 'might or could,' rather than 'did,' though the result was to deprive many opinions of the positiveness to which they were entitled, accompanied by the hazard of a ruling of insufficiency to support a verdict." The Committee also pointed out that opinion testimony must still be helpful to the trier of fact under Rules 701 and 702, which should "afford ample assurances against the admission of opinions which would merely tell the jury what result to reach . . . [or which are] phrased in terms of inadequately explored legal criteria." 56 F.R.D. 183, 284.

However, in 1984, largely in response to the outcome of John Hinckley's trial, Congress added paragraph (b) to Rule 704. It reads: "No expert witness testifying with respect to the mental state or condition of a defendant in a criminal case may state an opinion or inference as to whether the defendant did or did not have the mental state or condition constituting an element of the crime charged or of a defense thereto. Such ultimate issues are matters for the trier of fact alone." The purpose of this amendment to Rule 704, according to the Report of the House Committee on the Judiciary, "is to eliminate the confusing spectacle of competing expert witnesses testifying to directly contradictory conclusions as to the ultimate legal issue to be found by the trier of fact." H.R.Report 98–1030, 98th cong., 2d Sess., p. 230.

In reading the following case, think about whether it makes sense for Congress to have singled out clinical testimony in this way.

UNITED STATES v. EDWARDS

United States Court of Appeals, Eleventh Circuit, 1987.
819 F.2d 262.

Vance, Circuit Judge:

Roland Edwards was charged with unarmed bank robbery under 18 U.S.C. § 2113(a). He pleaded not guilty by reason of insanity. After a two day trial, a jury returned a verdict of guilty. Edwards appeals, claiming that the district court allowed improper psychiatric testimony. He argues that the district court erred in permitting a government witness to give opinion testimony in violation of Fed.R.Evid. 704(b). We affirm.

* * *

At trial Edwards did not contest his role in the bank robbery, but argued that he was insane at the time that he committed the offense. Edwards' ex-wife and an old friend testified that they believed Edwards to be incapable of criminal activity. The crux of the defense case, however, was the testimony of Doctor Adolfo Vilasuso, a board-certified psychiatrist. Doctor Vilasuso examined Edwards approximately six times during October, 1985 and continued seeing Edwards once or twice a week up to the date of trial in February, 1986. Doctor Vilasuso noted that Edwards had endured a difficult past and stated that he thought Edwards was "off the wall." Doctor Vilasuso testified that he had a "very, very strong suspicion" that Edwards suffered from "manic-depressive" illness during April, 1984. The government countered with the rebuttal testimony of Doctor Albert Jaslow, another psychiatrist. Doctor Jaslow concluded from Edwards' description of events that Edwards was not in "an active manic state" at the time of the robbery because Edwards' actions were reasonably well controlled and goal directed.

The testimony at issue concerns Doctor Jaslow's analysis of Edwards' frustration with his financial problems at the time of the robbery:

Q: [by Prosecutor]:

What sort of things were going on that would have depressed him?

A: [by Doctor Jaslow]:

His inability to come to grips with his financial problems; inability to handle the relationship with the I.R.S., who were after him and who were not permitting him to, according to him, of course, to settle down sufficiently so he could gain enough monies to take care of the financial problems and so on. These were bothering him tremendously, of course.

Q: Were these feelings understandable, in your opinion?

Defense Counsel: Objection. It's improper. That's not a proper question for a doctor.

The Court: Overruled.

A: Under the circumstances of the responsibilities, the problems that he had, it was quite understandable. He would be disturbed; it was quite understandable he would be upset. It's quite understandable he would be frantically trying to find ways to modify his situation so he could get on with his life.

Edwards contends that the trial court erred in allowing this testimony because it contained a psychiatrist's opinion concerning his sanity, the ultimate issue at trial. We disagree. "In resolving the complex issue of criminal responsibility, it is of critical importance that the defendant's entire relevant symptomatology be brought before the jury and explained." It has long been the position of our court that this is the only way a jury may become sufficiently informed so as to make a determination of a defendant's legal sanity. This was also the attitude of Congress when it passed Rule 704(b):

> Psychiatrists, of course, must be permitted to testify fully about the defendant's diagnosis, mental state and motivation (in clinical and commonsense terms) at the time of the alleged act so as to permit the jury or judge to reach the ultimate conclusion about which they and only they are expert.

Congress did not enact Rule 704(b) so as to limit the flow of diagnostic and clinical information. Every actual fact concerning the defendant's mental condition is still as admissible after the enactment of Rule 704(b) as it was before. Rather, the Rule "changes the style of question and answer that can be used to establish both the offense and the defense thereto." The prohibition is directed at a narrowly and precisely defined evil:

> When, however, "ultimate issue" questions are formulated by the law and put to the expert witness who must then say "yea" or "nay," then the expert witness is required to make a leap in logic. He no longer addresses himself to medical concepts but instead must infer or intuit what is in fact unspeakable, namely, the probable relationship between medical concepts and legal or moral constructs such as free will. These impermissible leaps in logic made by expert witnesses confuse the jury.

S.Rep. No. 225, 98th Cong., 1st Sess. 231 (quoting APA Statement on the Insanity Defense, Dec. 1982, at 18), *reprinted in* 1984 U.S.Code Cong. & Admin.News 3182, 3412–18. Accordingly, Rule 704(b) forbids only "conclusions as to the ultimate legal issue to be found by the trier of fact." *Id.* at 3412. See, e.g., *United States v. Hillsberg,* 812 F.2d 328, 331 (7th Cir.1987) (expert cannot state opinion as to whether defendant had the capacity to conform his conduct to the law); *United States v. Buchbinder,* 796 F.2d 910, 917 (7th Cir.1986) (expert could not testify as to whether defendant had the requisite mental state to defraud, but could testify as to the extent of defendant's depression over son's death).

The ultimate legal issue at Edwards' trial was whether Edwards "lack[ed] substantial capacity either to appreciate the wrongfulness of his conduct or to conform his conduct to the requirements of law." In fact, the challenged statements offer no conclusions at all about Edwards. Doctor Jaslow was simply observing that people who are not insane can nevertheless become frantic over a financial crisis.

The prosecution placed Doctor Jaslow on the stand to dispute Doctor Vilasuso's diagnosis. Using a common sense generalization, Doctor Jaslow explained why the defendant's behavior—his frantic efforts to pay bills, his manifestations of energy, his lack of sleep, and his feelings of depression—did not necessarily indicate an active manic state. We think that the doctor played exactly the kind of role which Congress contemplated for the expert witness:

> [I]t is clear that the psychiatrist's first obligation and expertise in the courtroom is to "do psychiatry," i.e., to present medical information and opinion about the defendant's mental state and motivation and to explain in detail the reason for his medical-psychiatric conclusions.

S.Rep. No. 225 supra, at 3413. We conclude that the district court committed no error in permitting this testimony.

AFFIRMED.

Questions and Comments

1. *Justification for the ultimate issue ban.* The *Edwards* court quotes the American Psychiatric Association to the effect that testimony on the ultimate issue involves the expert in a "leap of logic" from medical concepts to legal or moral ones. If Dr. Jaslow had testified that Edwards could appreciate the wrongfulness of the robbery or control his behavior at that time, would his testimony have intruded more into moral considerations than his actual testimony? How does one draw the line between "medical" or "clinical" concepts on the one hand, and moral concepts on the other? Does the language of Rule 704(b) help? Is Rule 704(b) necessary, given the existence of Rule 702 (requiring expert testimony to be based on specialized knowledge, skill, education, etc.)?

In answering these questions, compare *United States v. Manley*, 893 F.2d 1221 (11th Cir.1990)(defense counsel not permitted to ask expert whether a person with manic-depressive psychosis would "be able to appreciate the nature and quality or the wrongfulness of their actions") to *United States v. Salamanca*, 990 F.2d 629 (D.C.Cir. 1993)(permitting an expert to testify that "someone who had drunk as much [as the defendant] would have a diminished capacity to seek and plan"); *United States v. Davis*, 835 F.2d 274, 276 (11th Cir.1988)(approving a prosecutor's question as to whether a person diagnosed with multiple personalities was capable of understanding what he or she was doing); and *United States v. Kristiansen*, 901 F.2d 1463 (8th Cir. 1990) (permitting defense counsel to ask whether the mental disease of the type the defendant allegedly had "would affect a person's ability to appreciate their actions"). Does the following excerpt from *Kristiansen* make sense?

> [T]he defense clearly could ask whether Kristiansen was suffering from a mental disease or defect at the time of the offense. Just as clearly, the defense could not ask whether Kristiansen was unable to appreciate the nature and quality of his actions. . . . The more difficult question is whether the court erred in not permitting the defense to ask whether the mental disease or defect of the type that Kristiansen allegedly had would affect a person's ability to appreciate their actions. . . . We conclude that the defense should have been permitted to ask this question because it relates to the symptoms and qualities of the disease itself and does not call for an answer that describes Kristiansen's culpability at

the time of the crime. Rule 704(b) was not meant to prohibit testimony that describes the qualities of a mental disease. "Under this proposal, expert psychiatric testimony would be limited to presenting and explaining their diagnoses, such as whether the defendant had a severe mental disease or defect and what the characteristics of such a disease or defect, if any, may have been." Comprehensive Crime Control Act of 1984, S.Rep. No. 98–225, 98th Cong., 2d Sess. 230 (1984) (Senate Report), *reprinted in* 1984 U.S.Code Cong. & Admin. News 3182, 3412. The fact that part of the wording of a question may track the legal test by asking if the disease prevents one suffering from the disease from understanding the nature and quality of an act does not violate the rule. The jury is left to ultimately decide whether the disease was so strongly present that the defendant himself suffered the effect of being unable to appreciate the quality of his act.

2. *The ABA position.* Ultimate legal language can usually be subdivided into two types. "Ultimate" conclusions directly address the dispositive legal issue, e.g., whether a person is or is not "incompetent," "insane," "committable" and so on. In contrast, a penultimate conclusion does not reach this level of generalization but only speaks to the relevant legal test: for example, testimony that, under the American Law Institute test for insanity, a person accused of crime does or does not "as a result of mental disease or defect, lack substantial capacity to understand the wrongfulness of his act or to conform his behavior to the requirements of the law." Rule 704(b) is apparently meant to bar both types of testimony in federal court. The American Bar Association, on the other hand, distinguishes between the two. While barring testimony on the ultimate issue, the ABA would permit penultimate testimony, at least in insanity cases, because the language of the legal test (e.g., concerning a person's ability to "appreciate" the wrongfulness of his or her acts) expresses a concept which has clinical content. However, the ABA would forbid use of such language if statutory provisions or appellate decisions have given it particular legal content. American Bar Association, Criminal Justice Mental Health Standards, commentary to standard 7–6.6, at 336–338 (Little, Brown: 1987). Is the ABA claiming that penultimate testimony does not involve a moral issue, or that it combines clinical and moral issues? Whatever the answer to this question, why does further definition of the penultimate language through statute or appellate decision change the situation?

3. *Ultimate language and the adversary process.* As noted, the reason given by Congress for adopting Rule 704(b) is the desire "to eliminate the confusing spectacle of competing expert witnesses testifying to directly contradictory conclusions as to the ultimate legal issue to be found by the trier of fact." Aren't contradictory conclusions the inevitable result of the adversary process? On the other hand, if a proceeding is *not* effectively adversarial (as is often true with competency and commitment determinations, for instance), should the expert be allowed to give *any* opinion (legal or otherwise)? See Christopher Slobogin, "The 'Ultimate Issue' Issue," 7 Behav.Sciences & Law 259 (1989).

It has been suggested that judges rely more heavily on the authority granted them under the federal rules and many state rules to appoint a "neutral" expert who would testify for the court rather than either of the parties. Stephen Golding, "Mental Health Professionals and the Courts: The Ethics of Expertise," 13 Int'l J.L. & Psychiat. 281 (1990). Federal rule 706 provides:

> [T]he court may on its own motion or on the motion of any party enter an order to show cause why expert witnesses should not be appointed, and may request the parties to submit nominations. The court may appoint any expert witnesses agreed upon by the parties, and may appoint expert witnesses of its own selection.... A witness so appointed shall advise the parties of the witness' findings, if any; the witness' deposition may be taken by any party; and the witness may be called to testify by the court or any party. The witness shall be subject to cross-examination by each party, including a party calling the witness.

Will witnesses "appointed by the court" rather than retained by the parties be less likely to act in an "adversarial" manner? If so, would this be a good thing?

4. *Education of the legal profession.* To some extent, poor communication in court is the fault of mental health professionals who are ignorant of, or unwilling to call attention to, the limits of their expertise. But ultimately the blame has to fall on the legal system. Research indicates that many judges and lawyers *prefer* conclusory testimony. Gary Melton et al., Community Mental Health Centers & the Courts: An Evaluation of Community–Based Forensic Services 94–5, 99 (1985). Lawyers often are unfamiliar with the law, not to mention basic behavioral science concepts. C. Rosenberg & A. Louis McGarry, "Competency for Trial: The Making of an Expert," 128 Am.J.Psychiat. 82 (1972) (only 10 of 28 criminal attorneys knew competency to stand trial standard). And even when they have some understanding of both, they may make little effort to use the tools of their trade in exposing spurious testimony. Norman Poythress, "Psychiatric Expertise in Civil Commitment: Training Attorneys to Cope with Expert Testimony," 2 Law. & Hum.Behav. 1 (1978) (lawyers taught the inadequacies of clinical testimony persisted in avoiding careful cross-examination in commitment proceedings because of paternalistic attitudes). As Bonnie stated:

> The bench and bar are ultimately responsible for improving the administration of justice. If judges and juries are confused or misled by expert testimony, this usually means there has been poor lawyering. If experts give conclusory testimony, encompassing so-called ultimate issues—and fail to explain the bases for their opinions—the fault lies with the bench and bar, not with the experts. If forensic evaluators do not have access to the same information and reach different opinions for this reason, the fault lies with the legal system, not with the experts.

Richard Bonnie, "Morality, Equality, and Expertise: Renegotiating the Relationship Between Psychiatry and the Criminal Law," 12 Bull.Am.Acad.Psychiat. & L. 5, 5–6 (1984).

Chapter Seven

MENTAL DISABILITY AND CRIMINAL LAW

Table of Sections

I. INTRODUCTION

The role of mental disability in determining whether those charged with crime should be punished and, if so, to what extent, is potentially quite broad. To understand why this is so, one must first analyze the purposes of criminal punishment. Most criminal law scholars would agree that criminal punishment has at least five possible purposes: retribution, general deterrence, specific deterrence, incapacitation, and rehabilitation. Under retributive theory, punishment is imposed when a person makes a choice that deserves blame because it offends certain shared moral sensibilities; the person owes society a debt which must be paid. Deterrence theory, on the other hand, views punishment as a means of dissuading persons from committing acts which harm society, whether or not they are "blameworthy." General deterrence refers to the impact of punishment on others, while specific deterrence refers to its impact on the particular offender. Punishment is justified on incapacitative grounds when necessary to prevent an individual from committing crime again. Similarly, punishment is justified on rehabilitation grounds if treatment would prevent a person from engaging in further criminal behavior.

Upon close examination, one can make a good argument that, in deciding *what* to punish, the focus should be on retribution and general deterrence. Only in determining *how much* we want to punish should specific deterrence, incapacitation, and rehabilitation assume great significance. Put another way, the first two purposes logically are the primary considerations in defining the type of behavior that should be subject to criminal sanction, while the latter three are most usefully considered at sentencing in determining the type and scope of sanction once an individual has been identified as an offender. For instance, every jurisdiction makes knowingly killing another without justification or excuse a crime. In describing why, it makes sense to say that this type of conduct deserves punishment (i.e., requires societal vengeance), or that punishing it will serve as a disincentive to others who are contemplating such an act. In contrast, it makes little sense to say that such conduct is criminal because everyone who engages in it is in need of further (specific) deterrence, incapacitation, treatment, or some combination thereof. In fact, there are probably many individuals who commit unjustified and unexcused homicide who are not particularly dangerous or treatable. Only at sentencing, once a person has been found guilty of conduct which is considered blameworthy or in need of deterrence, can considerations of specific deterrence, incapacitation and rehabilitation be meaningfully considered in shaping the precise punishment to be meted out to each individual.

There may be a second, more complicated reason for considering only retributive and general deterrent goals in defining the elements of criminal liability. Our criminal justice system, if not society generally, is founded on the assumption that we are autonomous beings who can justly be punished; although science may suggest that some or all behavior is "determined" by biological or environmental forces, thus rendering us nonresponsible, the law assumes we have "free will" (for lack of a better shorthand term). For purposes of criminal punishment, it has further been assumed that this will is not manifested until the person acts. Thoughts alone are not enough to establish criminal liability. Professor Packer justified this position in part by noting that historically "we have not been sufficiently stirred by the danger presented or sufficiently confident of our ability to discern propensities in the absence of conduct to use the instruments of the criminal law [to punish thoughts alone]." But even if we were, the assumption of free will should stand, according to Packer: "the capacity of the individual human being to live his life in reasonable freedom from socially imposed external constraints (the only kind with which the law is concerned) would be fatally impaired unless the law provided a *locus poenitentiae*, a point of no return beyond which external constraints may be imposed but before

which the individual is free—not free of whatever compulsions determin-
ists tell us he labors under but free of the very specific social compulsions of the law." Herbert Packer, The Limits of the Criminal Sanction
73–75 (1968).

The moral assumptions that persons have free will and can thus be
punished, but only once their will has been manifested through behavior,
are relatively easily implemented through retributive and deterrence
theories. Because they are virtually impossible to control, thoughts and
inclinations, even if criminal, are hard to call "blameworthy"; for most
retributivists, liability can justifiably attach only when the person has
acted on those thoughts or inclinations. For similar reasons, punishing
thoughts and inclinations makes little sense from a deterrence perspective; such punishment would not (because it could not) deter others from
having similar thoughts or inclinations, nor is it likely to deter criminal
actions beyond the disincentive already provided by punishing antisocial
acts.

On the other hand, achieving specific deterrence, incapacitation, and
rehabilitation does not require waiting for the commission of a criminal
act; whether punishment will accomplish these goals rests instead on a
prediction of behavior—in essence, whether the person *will* commit
crime if he or she is not confined and treated. While past behavior may
be useful in making this prediction, it need not be of any particular type
or seriousness. Moreover, in theory at least, proving an act occurred is
not necessary to a determination of whether someone is dangerous or
treatable; thoughts and inclinations may be the most probative information on what will happen in the future.[a] Thus, the specific deterrence,
incapacitation and rehabilitation punishment goals can undermine the
principle that criminal liability be based on acts. However, once a person
is convicted for a (blameworthy, deterrence-worthy) act, allowing predictions to govern the type and duration of punishment is not as repugnant
to this principle. Thus, again, while the three individual prevention goals
should probably not be relied upon in defining the scope of criminal
liability, they are usefully considered at sentencing.

This brief summary of the purposes of criminal punishment and
their importance to the two stages of the criminal justice system,
although highly simplified, helps put in perspective the role of mental
disability in the criminal law. At the guilt adjudication stage, mental
disability is theoretically relevant whenever it renders a person's decision to act less blameworthy or more difficult to deter. For instance, the
oldest criminal law doctrine focusing specifically on people with mental
disability—the insanity defense—is often justified on the ground that the
insane are so irrational in their behavior, or so unable to control
themselves, that they do not deserve to be punished, and are unlikely to

a. See John Monahan, The Clinical Prediction of Violent Behavior 109–112
(1981)(describing how predictions might be
made based on how the person "appraises"
situations (e.g,. as provocative or acciden-
tal) and the type and intensity of the person's emotional reactions to stress (e.g., anger and hatred, or guilt, empathy, anxiety,
and fear)).

understand or pay attention to criminal sanctions. As Professor Gold-stein stated: "It would be widely regarded as incalculably cruel and unjust to incarcerate men who are not personally responsible in order to serve social functions. The notion of 'desert' or culpability is too deeply rooted." Further, "[u]nder the deterrent theory, . . . the insanity defense describes the man who is sufficiently different from the rest of us that he cannot be used as an effective example and who, in quite personal terms, cannot be expected to approach events mindful of the warnings sent to him by the criminal code." Abraham Goldstein, The Insanity Defense 13–14 (1967). For the same reasons, when a person's "actions" are "involuntary" (as when an epileptic seizure results in death of another), criminal punishment may be inappropriate, a notion recognized by the "automatism" defense. Indeed, anyone whose mental state at the time of the offense is "abnormal" might be able to argue that his or her culpability and deterrability was diminished at that time.

The impact of mental disability at sentencing is potentially even greater, because here future deterrence, incapacitative and rehabilitative concerns, as well as retributive and general deterrence considerations, may enter in. Evidence of mental condition could be very useful in finetuning the punishment imposed, either as a "mitigating factor" (e.g., to show diminished responsibility or to suggest amenability to treatment outside the prison setting), or as an "aggravating factor" (e.g., as proof of dangerousness).

Over the past century, the criminal law has, with some significant exceptions, moved toward full realization of the possibilities outlined above. Here these developments will only be outlined, in order to place them in historical perspective. More detailed discussion occurs in the body of this chapter.

Particularly significant has been the increasing relevance of mental disability in determining criminal liability. The tendency toward expansion of the insanity defense is well known. Even more significant are developments with respect to the mental state element (mens rea) of criminal offenses. The common law usually required proof only of "objective," or inferred, intent rather than "subjective," or actual, intent. Thus, the prosecution could often secure conviction if it showed that the accused committed the criminal act under circumstances in which a "reasonable person" would intend such an act; the accused's actual intent was irrelevant. Probably the single most important trend in the substantive criminal law during this century has been the continuing erosion of this position. The highly influential Model Penal Code, officially promulgated in 1962 by the American Law Institute, expresses a strong preference for criminal liability based solely on proof of criminal intent or awareness of the risk of harm. Following logically from this proposition, the Code permits evidence of mental abnormality to be introduced not only on the insanity issue, but also on the issue of whether the accused could form the intent associated with the alleged crime whenever that intent is subjective—sometimes called the "diminished capacity" defense. Additionally, the Model Penal Code's definitions of defensive doctrines such as mistake of fact, duress, self-defense and provocation—doctrines which were traditionally defined in "objective" terms (e.g., would a "reasonable" person be provoked to kill under given circumstances)—permit the defendant to submit evidence about his or her own feelings, desires, urges, and thoughts at the time of the offense. Theoretically, evidence of mental abnormality is relevant under any of these defenses.

The types of evidence an offender can present at sentencing—traditionally limited to pleas for mercy—have also expanded considerably over the past century. In many states, offenders may now submit virtually any mitigating information they can muster, including evidence of mental abnormality. Indeed, in death penalty cases, the Supreme Court has held that offenders have a constitutional right to offer such evidence. At the same time, the state is often permitted to introduce evidence of dangerousness or untreatability at sentencing.

While mental abnormality has thus become increasingly relevant in the determination of whether and what type of punishment should be imposed, there are also signs that courts and legislatures are reconsidering the wisdom of this development. For instance, in the 1980's several jurisdictions, many of them responding to the outcome of John Hinckley's trial on charges of attempting to assassinate President Reagan, significantly reduced the scope of the insanity defense or eliminated it altogether. In a separate effort to curb the impact of the insanity defense, many states have adopted the "guilty but mentally ill" verdict as an intermediate option between insanity and a straight finding of guilt. Moreover, several states have rejected or severely limited the Model Penal Code's recommendation that mental abnormality be considered on the issue of intent, and many courts have demonstrated antipathy toward broadening other defenses.

Similar developments have occurred in the non-capital sentencing setting. Beginning in the 1970's, several states have moved toward "determinate sentencing," or sentencing schemes that provide decision-makers with relatively little leeway in setting punishment. In an effort to remove discretion from decision-makers, the thrust of these reforms has been to base sentence lengths primarily on backward-looking culpability assessments rather than on forward-looking assessments of dangerousness, treatability and so on.

To some extent, these differing views on the role of mental disability in the criminal justice system are a function of varying perceptions about the limits of clinical expertise, a topic discussed in the previous chapter. But at bottom they stem from assumptions about the fundamental purposes of the criminal sanction. The primary aim of this chapter is to examine these assumptions in an effort to provoke thought on the extent to which mental disability ought to be relevant to the doctrines of the substantive criminal law. The first section examines doctrines relevant to mental state at the time of the offense, including the defenses of insanity, "diminished capacity," and "automatism," and the guilty but mentally ill verdict. The second section looks at sentencing. In particular, it will focus on capital sentencing—the area in which sentencing law is most highly developed—and those special sentencing situations in which mental disability plays a significant role.

II. CRIMINAL RESPONSIBILITY

As explained above, the primary justifications for exculpatory and mitigating criminal law doctrines based on mental abnormality flow from retributive and deterrence theory. The criminal law assumes "free will," the capacity to make and act upon choices. But the law is also willing to assume that mental disability reduces this capacity, thus making the person less blameworthy and less able to obey the law's mandates. The assumption that people with mental disability are incapable of being minimally rational or are less deterrable than others has been called more of an "intuitive hunch" than an empirically verified fact. See Stephen Morse, "Treating Crazy People Less Specially," 90 West.Va. L.Rev. 353, 370 (1988). Moreover, as Hart has pointed out, the deterrence rationale for defenses based on mental disability may be logically flawed because, even if some persons are undeterrable as a result of mental disorder, permitting such defenses may *encourage* others to commit crime in the hope that they can escape conviction through feigning mental disability. Henry Hart, Punishment and Responsibility 18–20 (1968). Despite these possible problems, the central question remains the extent to which retributive or deterrence theory requires or suggests that inroads be made on the free will paradigm.

The possible impact of specific deterrence, incapacitation, and rehabilitation concerns should also be mentioned, however. For reasons given earlier, in deciding upon the proper scope of defenses based on mental disability one should generally not engage in the predictive inquiry required by the individual prevention goals of punishment. Nonetheless, these goals probably do influence legislatures and courts in deciding how to frame defenses based on mental disability. For instance, as Goldstein has noted, one view of the insanity defense "sees the defense almost entirely as a path to treatment in a mental hospital.... The tacit assumption is that a paternal state can put [the acquittee] right by psychotherapy or by judicious social planning, if only the 'helping' professions are provided with the resources to do the job." Abraham Goldstein, The Insanity Defense 14 (1967). As another example, consider from the incapacitative perspective the impact of narrowing the insanity defense. In most states, those adjudged insane are confined in a mental hospital for as long as they are considered mentally disordered and dangerous. If the insanity defense were abolished or its scope reduced significantly, individuals considered to be violent who previously might have been found insane and hospitalized indefinitely would be convicted and released from secure confinement at the end of their sentence, perhaps much earlier than they would have been had they been committed as insane. By changing the substantive law, the government would be deprived of a flexible dispositional device. As these examples illustrate, the extent to which policymakers want to implement rehabilitative and incapacitative goals might influence their efforts to define defenses based on mental disability.

These considerations should be kept in mind throughout the following materials.

A. THE INSANITY DEFENSE[b]

1. A Brief History

This section discusses the various formulations of the insanity defense that have been advanced through the years. A later section discusses whether the defense should be abolished, after examining its alternatives. As should become clear, the various tests set out below are the result of many variables, including changes in medical knowledge, the criminal justice system, and attitudes of society toward people with mental disability.

Early Development. The idea of a defense to criminal responsibility based on mental disability goes back as far as the ancient Greek and Hebrew civilizations. English case law, which heavily influenced early American courts, has long recognized the concept. At least as early as 1300, records show that English kings were pardoning murderers because their crimes were committed "while suffering from madness." Over the next several centuries, many different formulations of the defense emerged. Sir Edward Coke, a famous legal scholar of the late 16th and early 17th century, felt that "idiots" and "madmen" who "wholly loseth their memory and understanding" should be found insane. Sir Matthew Hale, Chief Justice of the King's Bench in the 17th century, concluded in his private papers that the "best measure" for determining insanity was whether the accused had "as great understanding as ordinarily a child of fourteen hath." In 1723 Justice Tracy held that in order to be found insane "a man must be totally deprived of his understanding and memory so as not to know what he is doing, no more than an infant, brute or a wild beast." At about the same time, other English courts were excusing those who lacked the capacity to distinguish "good from evil" or "right from wrong."

The M'Naghten Test. It was this latter approach that, in slightly modified form, became the so-called "M'Naghten test" of insanity. In response to controversy surrounding the insanity acquittal of Daniel M'Naghten on a charge of murdering the private secretary of Prime Minister Robert Peel, the House of Lords announced the following rule:

> To establish a defense on the ground of insanity, it must be clearly proved that, at the time of the committing of the act, the party accused was laboring under such a defect of reason, from disease of

b. This and the following descriptions in the text about criminal responsibility doctrines are adapted from Gary Melton et al., Psychological Evaluations for the Courts: A Handbook for Mental Health Professionals and Laywers, Chap. 8 (3d ed. 2007).

the mind, as not to know the nature and quality of the act he was doing; or, if he did know it, that he did not know he was doing what was wrong.

This formulation, announced in 1843, became the accepted rule in both England and the United States.

Criticism of the test was immediate, especially from the medical community. Indeed, five years before the House of Lords' pronouncement, Sir Isaac Ray, a noted American physician, had argued that the "insane mind" is often "perfectly rational, and displays the exercise of a sound and well-balanced mind." Thus, according to Ray, a defense based on mental illness that focuses merely on cognitive impairment is incomplete; the defendant's ability to control his or her acts must also be considered. Although directed at the law as it existed in 1838, Ray's comments applied with equal force to the M'Naghten test, which varied only slightly from its predecessors.

A second criticism of the rule was its rigidity. Even if one accepts the premise that cognitive dysfunction is the only appropriate focus of the insanity defense, the M'Naghten rule, it was claimed, did not fairly pose the question; a literal interpretation of the M'Naghten test would seldom, if ever, lead to exculpation. In the words of one psychiatrist, "[if the test language were taken seriously,] it would excuse only those totally deteriorated, drooling hopeless psychotics of long-standing, and congenital idiots."

The Irresistible Impulse Test. In the United States, the legal response to the first criticism came in the form of a supplementary test for insanity, which eventually came to be called the "irresistible impulse" rule. Although versions of this test appeared in the first half of the nineteenth century, see *State v. Thompson*, Wright's Ohio Rep. 617 (1834); *Commonwealth v. Rogers*, 48 Mass. 500 (1844), the leading decision on the issue was handed down in 1887 and described the test as follows:

> [The defendant is not] legally responsible if the two following conditions concur: (1) If, by reason of the duress of ... mental disease he had so far lost the power to choose between the right and wrong, and to avoid doing the act in question, as that his free agency was at the time destroyed; (2) and if, at the same time, the alleged crime was so connected with such mental disease, in the relation of cause and effect, as to have been the product of it solely.

Parsons v. State, 81 Ala. 577, 596, 2 So. 854, 866 (1887). The adoption of the test was usually justified on the ground that those offenders who could not control their behavior at the time of the offense were not deterrable by criminal sanctions; therefore, no legitimate moral or policy purpose was served by convicting them.

The "irresistible impulse" test met resistance from several fronts. Many in the legal community believed that impulsivity could easily be feigned, and feared that the test would lead to numerous invalid insanity acquittals. From the medical side came the criticism that a separate "control" test furthered the mistaken impression that the human psyche is compartmentalized into cognitive and volitional components. And, like M'Naghten, the test was seen as too rigid, excusing only those who were totally unable to prevent their unlawful behavior.

The Durham Rule. In 1954, partly in response to the latter two contentions and the criticisms of M'Naghten, the federal District of Columbia Court of Appeals adopted the "product test" for insanity—a rule originally devised by Sir Isaac Ray and adopted by the New Hampshire Supreme Court in 1870, but one that had received little notice since that time. As set forth in *Durham v. United States,* 214 F.2d 862 (D.C.Cir.1954), the test stated simply that "an accused is not criminally responsible if his unlawful act was the product of mental disease or defect." Judge Bazelon, the author of the *Durham* opinion, hoped the rule would encourage mental health professionals to explain all aspects of a defendant's personality and functioning by removing legal strictures on such professionals' testimony.

In time, however, this lack of guidance became a problem in itself. The product test asked essentially two questions: (1) Did mental disease or defect exist at the time of the offense? (2) Was the offense the product of this disease or defect? The *Durham* court failed to define either "mental disease" or "product." Trial courts had particular difficulty dealing with the meaning of the former term, since it was no longer modified by functional criteria, as it had been in earlier tests. The problem surfaced dramatically in 1957 when staff members at St. Elizabeth Hospital, which provides the District of Columbia courts with most of their experts on the insanity issue, suddenly voted to incorporate the personality disorders, including the so-called "sociopathic personality," within the definition of "mental disease" for purposes of the insanity defense. Since many criminal offenders have some type of personality disorder, this weekend change in hospital policy had a major impact in the courts.

In *McDonald v. United States,* 312 F.2d 847 (D.C.Cir.1962), the District of Columbia Court of Appeals finally conceded that trial courts required some guidelines in implementing the product test, and declared that henceforth "the jury should be told that a mental disease or defect includes any abnormal condition of the mind which substantially affects mental or emotional processes and substantially impairs behavior controls." With the judicial gloss added by *McDonald,* the difference between the product test and a test combining M'Naghten and the "irresistible impulse" rule was reduced substantially. Even so, definitional problems persisted, and *Durham* was finally overruled in 1972. New Hampshire remains the only state to follow the test.

The American Law Institute Test. In place of the product test, the District of Columbia Court of Appeals adopted still another version of the insanity test, which was first proposed a year after the *Durham* decision. This test, drafted by the American Law Institute (ALI), was an attempt to deal with most of the problems associated with previous tests by avoiding the "all-or-nothing" language of the M'Naghten and "irresistible impulse" formulations, while retaining some specific guidelines for the jury. The rule reads as follows: "A person is not responsible for criminal conduct if at the time of such conduct as a result of mental disease or defect he lacks substantial capacity either to appreciate the criminality [wrongfulness] of his conduct or to conform his conduct to the requirements of the law." This language combines the notions underlying both the M'Naghten and irresistible impulse formulations, but makes it clear that a defendant's cognitive or volitional impairment at the time of the offense need only be "substantial," rather than total, in order to merit an insanity defense.

The ALI's proposal also included a second paragraph, which, according to its drafters, was designed specifically "to exclude from the concept of 'mental disease or defect' the case of so called 'psychopathic personality.'" It states: "As used in this Article, the terms mental disease or defect do not include an abnormality manifested only by repeated criminal or otherwise anti-social conduct." Interestingly, this proposal was published two years before the St. Elizabeth's incident.

The ALI test proved to be a popular one: Over the next two decades, a majority of the country's jurisdictions adopted the first paragraph, and many of these also adopted the second.

Rejection of Medical Model. Nonetheless, the ALI test came under attack as well. One criticism was that the ALI test, as well as all of the tests that preceded it, relied too heavily on the so-called "medical model." Judge Bazelon, the author of the failed *Durham* test, was the most prominent proponent of this point of view. In a concurring opinion in *United States v. Brawner*, 471 F.2d 969 (D.C.Cir.1972), the decision which overturned *Durham*, he argued that a person should be found insane "if at the time of his unlawful conduct his mental or emotional processes or behavior controls were impaired to such an extent that he cannot justly be held responsible for his act." This test does away with the "mental disease or defect" requirement, as well as any specific requirement of functional impairment. It gives the factfinder virtually limitless discretion to decide the types of "impairment" which excuse one for one's behavior. No state has adopted the test.[c]

Several other proposed formulations also eschew the mental disease or defect predicate, but more explicitly require the jury to focus on the accused's mental state. For instance, Moore argued that the inquiry should focus on whether the accused is "so irrational as to be nonresponsible." According to Moore,

> One is a moral agent only if one is a rational agent. Only if we can see another being as one who acts to achieve some rational end in light of some rational beliefs will we understand him in the same fundamental way that we understand ourselves and our fellow

---

c. Rhode Island excuses those who cannot justly be held responsible as a result of mental disease or defect. *State v. Johnson,* 121 R.I. 254, 399 A.2d 469, 476 (1979).

persons in everyday life. We regard as moral agents only those beings we can understand in this way.

In determining whether the accused is rational, Moore explained, one should look at the intelligibility, consistency and coherency of the desires and beliefs that motivate the offense. Michael Moore, Law & Psychiatry: Rethinking the Relationship 244–45, 207 (1985). In a similar vein, Fingarette and Hasse asserted that a "lack of capacity for rational conduct" is the core of insanity. Herbert Fingarette & Ann Hasse, Mental Disabilities and Criminal Responsibility 218 (1979).[d] Although using different language, Morse tried to capture the same idea with his proposal: "A defendant is not guilty by reason of insanity if at the time of the offense the defendant was extremely crazy and the craziness affected the criminal behavior." According to Morse, "this test tracks the moral issues with greater honesty and precision, is more workable, and will not lead to the acquittal of more defendants than present tests or reformed versions of present tests." Stephen Morse, "Excusing the Crazy: The Insanity Defense Reconsidered," 58 S.Cal.L.Rev. 780 (1985). No jurisdiction has adopted any of these tests.

Elimination of Volitional Prong. A more popular (and the most recent) trend in insanity jurisprudence has been to attack the volitional prong of the defense. Soon after the insanity acquittal of John Hinckley, both the American Bar Association and the American Psychiatric Association recommended the elimination of the so-called "control" inquiry, although they continued to support the "appreciation" prong of the ALI's test, thereby indicating an unwillingness to return to the original M'Naghten formulation. The ABA's test reads as follows: "[A] person is not responsible for criminal conduct if, at the time of such conduct, and as a result of mental disease or defect, that person was unable to appreciate the wrongfulness of such conduct." American Bar Association, Criminal Justice Mental Health Standards, Standard 7–6.1 (1987). Echoing past criticism, both the ABA and the APA reasoned that if mistakes do occur in the administration of the insanity defense, they are most likely to result from utilizing a volitional test. The commentary to the ABA's standard stated: "Clinicians can be more precise and arrive at more reliable conclusions about awareness, perceptions, and understanding of an event than about the 'causes' of a person's behavior, especially when the determinants of behavior are felt to be unconscious."

In 1984, the United States Congress adopted an insanity test for the federal courts which essentially tracked the ABA proposal. The legislation, found in Title 18 of the United States Code, states:

d. Sendor also views irrationality as the proper test, but explains its importance somewhat differently:

[R]ationality is not important standing alone, but rather as a condition for engaging in conduct that others can interpret. When a mentally ill person injures legally protected interests through irra-tional conduct, we excuse the individual because we do not interpret his conduct as expressing disrespect for those interests.

Benjamin Sendor, "Crime as Communication: An Interpretive Theory of the Insanity Defense and the Mental Elements of Crime," 74 Geo.L.J. 1371, 1415 (1986).

§ 20. Insanity Defense.

(a) Affirmative Defense.—It is an affirmative defense to a prosecution under any federal statute that, at the time of the commission of acts constituting the offense, the defendant, as a result of severe mental disease or defect, was unable to appreciate the nature and quality or the wrongfulness of his acts. Mental disease or defect does not otherwise constitute a defense.

Several states have followed this lead. Today fewer than 20 states recognize volitional impairment as a basis for an insanity defense and another four do not recognize insanity as a defense (p. 624).

Questions and Comments

1. *Constitutional constraints on the scope of the insanity test.* In *Clark v. Arizona,* 548 U.S. 735, 126 S.Ct. 2709, 165 L.Ed.2d 842 (2006), the Supreme Court was asked to decide whether an insanity formulation that eliminated the first part of the *M'Naghten* test (what the Court called the "cognitive capacity" prong, given its focus on whether the defendant knows the nature and quality of the act) was constitutional under the due process clause. The Court held that the second prong of *M'Naghten* (what the Court called the "moral capacity" prong, given its focus on knowledge of wrongfulness) was constitutionally sufficient. In the course of doing so, it suggested that any of the foregoing formulations would satisfy constitutional requirements:

> History shows no deference to *M'Naghten* that could elevate its formula to the level of fundamental principle, so as to limit the traditional recognition of a State's capacity to define crimes and defenses.... Even a cursory examination of the traditional Anglo–American approaches to insanity reveals significant differences among them, with four traditional strains variously combined to yield a diversity of American standards. The main variants are the cognitive incapacity, the moral incapacity, the volitional incapacity, and the product-of-mental-illness tests. [The Court then noted the number of states that had adopted each test].

> With this varied background, it is clear that no particular formulation has evolved into a baseline for due process, and that the insanity rule, like the conceptualization of criminal offenses, is substantially open to state choice. Indeed, the legitimacy of such choice is the more obvious when one considers the interplay of legal concepts of mental illness or deficiency required for an insanity defense, with the medical concepts of mental abnormality that influence the expert opinion testimony by psychologists and psychiatrists commonly introduced to support or contest insanity claims. For medical definitions devised to justify treatment, like legal ones devised to excuse from conventional criminal responsibility, are subject to flux and disagreement. There being such fodder for reasonable debate about what the cognate legal and medical tests should be, due process imposes no single canonical formulation of legal insanity.

* * *

Nor does Arizona's abbreviation of the *M'Naghten* statement raise a proper claim that some constitutional minimum has been shortchanged. Clark's argument of course assumes that Arizona's former statement of the *M'Naghten* rule, with its express alternative of cognitive incapacity, was constitutionally adequate (as we agree). That being so, the abbreviated rule is no less so, for cognitive incapacity is relevant under that statement, just as it was under the more extended formulation, and evidence going to cognitive incapacity has the same significance under the short form as it had under the long.

Though Clark is correct that the application of the moral incapacity test (telling right from wrong) does not necessarily require evaluation of a defendant's cognitive capacity to appreciate the nature and quality of the acts charged against him, his argument fails to recognize that cognitive incapacity is itself enough to demonstrate moral incapacity. Cognitive incapacity, in other words, is a sufficient condition for establishing a defense of insanity, albeit not a necessary one. As a defendant can therefore make out moral incapacity by demonstrating cognitive incapacity, evidence bearing on whether the defendant knew the nature and quality of his actions is both relevant and admissible. In practical terms, if a defendant did not know what he was doing when he acted, he could not have known that he was performing the wrongful act charged as a crime.[23]

126 S.Ct. at 2719–22.

2. *Effect of the language.* In terms of outcome, does it matter which of the various formulations described above are incorporated into jury instructions? Using a mock case based on the facts of *Durham,* Professor Simon asked ten juries to decide the case under the *M'Naghten* standard and ten juries to decide the case under the *Durham* standard. She found a very small, although statistically significant, chance that jurors were more likely to find the defendant insane under the latter test. Rita Simon, The Jury and the Defense of Insanity 215 (1967). A more recent study used five mock cases and six different instructions: the "wild beast" test, M'Naghten, M'Naghten plus irresistible impulse, *Durham,* the ALI test and the test developed by Fingarette and Hasse. It found no overall significant differences among the six instructions, Norman Finkel et al., "Insanity Defenses: From the Jurors's Perspective," 9 L. & Psychol.Rev. 77 (1985), a finding which has been replicated in later studies. See Norman Finkel, "The Insanity Defense: A Comparison of Verdict Schemas," 15 L. & Hum. Beh. 533 (1991). Professor Goldstein came to a similar conclusion after an extensive survey of the cases. Abraham Goldstein, The Insanity Defense 213–14 (1967).

On the other hand, a review of studies looking at the effect of changes in the insanity standard in five states concluded that differences in acquittal rates can result when the M'Naghten test is replaced by the ALI test. Ingo Kielitz, "Researching and Reforming the Insanity Defense," in Alexander Brooks & Bruce Winick, Current Issues in Mental Disability Law 47, 57–61 (1987). Moreover, as the American Bar Association has pointed out:

---

23. He might, of course, have thought delusively he was doing something just as wrongful as the act charged against him, but this is not the test: he must have understood that he was committing the act charged and that it was wrongful.

the impact of particular language on decisions made *before* a jury retires to deliberate also must be considered—the decisions of experts whether or not to testify and, if so, the formulation of their testimony; the strategic decisions by defense counsel relating to the insanity defense, direct and cross-examination, and summation; and trial court rulings on the legal sufficiency of the evidence to raise a jury question.

ABA, Criminal Justice Mental Health Standards, Commentary to Standard 7–6.1 at 343 (1989). The ABA concluded that the difference in outcome in jurisdictions with a test that included a volitional prong and those that did not might be significant. Finally, even if the language makes no appreciable difference in terms of specific case resolutions, it may have an important effect symbolically and on the public's perception of the criminal justice system.

3. *Burden and standard of proof.* Another aspect of jury instructions in insanity cases concerns the burden and standard of proof that apply when the defense is asserted. By far the majority of the states require the defendant to prove insanity by the preponderance of the evidence standard. About one-third of the states place the burden of disproving insanity on the prosecution beyond a reasonable doubt. Until 1984, federal jurisdictions followed this practice. After the Hinckley case, however, in the same legislation that changed the federal insanity test, the burden was switched dramatically, to require that the *defendant* show insanity by *clear and convincing evidence.* 18 U.S.C. § 20(b). Arizona has also adopted this approach. Ariz. Rev.Stat. § 13–502.

Apparently, none of these approaches is unconstitutional. In *Leland v. Oregon,* 343 U.S. 790, 72 S.Ct. 1002, 96 L.Ed. 1302 (1952) the Supreme Court held that a state rule requiring the defendant to prove insanity beyond a reasonable doubt did not deny a state defendant his federal constitutional right to due process of law. Almost two decades later, the Court held that the prosecution must prove beyond a reasonable doubt "every fact necessary to constitute proof of the crime with which [the defendant] is charged." *In re Winship,* 397 U.S. 358, 90 S.Ct. 1068, 25 L.Ed.2d 368 (1970). *Winship* suggested that *Leland* was no longer good law. But in 1976 the Court dismissed, for want of a substantial federal question, an appeal of a conviction under an instruction placing the burden of proving insanity on the defendant by a preponderance of the evidence. *Rivera v. Delaware,* 429 U.S. 877, 97 S.Ct. 226, 50 L.Ed.2d 160 (1976). Apparently the Court did not consider "sanity" a "fact necessary to constitute proof of the crime." In dissenting to the dismissal in *Rivera,* Justice Brennan wrote:

> In *Mullaney* [*v. Wilbur,* 421 U.S. 684, 95 S.Ct. 1881, 44 L.Ed.2d 508 (1975)], we considered a Maine rule that placed upon a criminal defendant charged with murder the burden of proving by a preponderance of the evidence that he had acted in the heat of passion on sudden impulse in order to reduce the homicide to manslaughter. We concluded that this rule did not comport with the due process requirement, as defined in *In re Winship* ... that the prosecution must prove beyond a reasonable doubt every fact necessary to constitute the crime charged.... Like the state rule invalidated in *Mullaney,* which implied malice unless the accused negated it, the plea of insanity, whether or not the State

chooses to characterize it as an affirmative defense, relates to the accused's state of mind, an essential element of the crime....

429 U.S. at 878–80, 97 S.Ct. at 226–27 (Brennan, dissenting). As Brennan suggests, at least in some cases evidence of insanity is relevant to whether the defendant had the required mental state for the crime charged (such as intent or knowledge). Dix has suggested an argument in support of the Court's position in *Rivera*, however. He notes that because the insanity defense almost always relies on relatively untrustworthy or perplexing expert testimony, telling juries "that they must acquit if this evidence raises a reasonable doubt ... may [create] an unacceptably high risk of unjustified acquittals due to what are actually 'unreasonable' doubts generated simply by confusion." George Dix, "Criminal Responsibility and Mental Impairment in American Criminal Law," in 1 Law and Mental Health: International Perspectives 1, 24 (1984). Does this argument necessarily justify placing the burden on the defendant or does it simply support lowering the standard of proof the prosecution must meet?

It may be that the choice of a particular burden or standard of proof is primarily of symbolic value. The data that exist suggest little or no relationship between a particular burden of proof and outcome. One informal study sampled the acquittal rates of five states, three of which used the ALI test and two of which used M'Naghten. Only one of the five placed the burden on the defendant. That state, which used the ALI test, had the second highest acquittal rate overall and the *highest* acquittal rate of the three states that used the ALI test. Melton, et al., supra note b, at 125, n. 149. However, Steadman and his colleagues found that, in Georgia and New York, switching the burden of proof from the prosecution to the defense significantly reduced both the rate at which the insanity defense was raised and its success rate. Henry Steadman et al., Before and After Hinckley: Evaluating Insanity Defense Reform 84–85 (1993).

4. *Consequences of an insanity acquittal.* A third issue that might be addressed in instructions to the jury is the impact of an insanity acquittal. As noted earlier, most states confine insanity acquittees in mental institutions for as long as they remain mentally ill and dangerous.[e] The precise duration of post-acquittal confinement is therefore unknown at the time of trial and could be either much shorter or much longer than the sentence that would have been imposed had the person been found guilty. In most states, the jury is not informed of these facts, just as, in the typical criminal trial, they are kept in the dark about possible sentences, on the theory that dispositional information may improperly influence its decision. About a third of the states, however, authorize an instruction about the consequences of an insanity acquittal. The American Bar Association, which also adopts this position, supported its view as follows:

> [D]espite instructions cautioning them to consider only the evidence they have heard, jurors who are not informed about dispositional consequences will speculate about the practical results of a nonresponsibility verdict and, in ignorance of reality, will convict persons who are not

e. The criteria and procedures for commitment of insanity acquittees are discussed in detail at pp. 868–83.

criminally responsible in order to protect society. Jurors surely know, without being told, what happens to most convicted offenders, as well as defendants who are acquitted outright; the proposed instruction provides the same level of knowledge with respect to the fate of persons acquitted by reason of insanity.

In *Shannon v. United States*, 512 U.S. 573, 114 S.Ct. 2419, 129 L.Ed.2d 459 (1994), the Supreme Court held that such an instruction need not be given in federal court unless the prosecution suggests to the jury that an acquittal allows the defendant to "go free" or commits a similar error. In addition to pointing out that jurors have traditionally not been given dispositional information, the majority opinion, by Justice Thomas, speculated that, given the publicity attending cases like Hinckley, many jurors are aware of the consequences of an acquittal. In any event, Thomas surmised, an instruction to the effect that acquittal will lead to confinement until the acquittee is no longer dangerous and mentally ill might not have the effect the defendant would want. Thomas went on to state:

> Whether the instruction works to the advantage or disadvantage of a defendant is, of course, somewhat beside the point. Our central concern here is that the inevitable result of such an instruction would be to draw the jury's attention toward the very thing—the possible consequences of its verdict—it should ignore.

Justice Stevens, in a dissent joined by Justice Blackmun, agreed with the ABA position quoted above. To the last point made by the majority, he pointed out that the instruction might help the jury focus on issues of guilt because it would no longer be worried about the practical effect of its verdict. See also, *State v. Shickles*, 760 P.2d 291, 298 (Utah 1988).

Empirical evidence as to jurors' understanding of dispositional consequences is spotty. Simon found that the overwhelming majority of jurors are aware, without being instructed, that dangerous persons are not released upon acquittal by reason of insanity, Rita Simon, The Jury and the Defense of Insanity 38 (1967), but she later admitted that her methodology may have produced inaccurate results. Harold Schwartz, "Should Juries Be Informed of the Consequences of the Insanity Verdict?", 8 J. Psychiat. & L. 167, 173–74 (1980). Morris found that, overall, jurors have inconsistent perceptions about disposition. Grant Morris, "Whither Thou Goest?: An Inquiry into Jurors' Perceptions of the Consequences of a Successful Insanity Defense," 14 San Diego L.Rev. 1058 (1977). If you were a defense attorney, would you want dispositional instructions? A prosecutor? Would you also want instructions on the average duration of hospitalization for insanity acquittees?

5. *The reality of the insanity defense.* The public's position regarding the defense of insanity seems to be heavily influenced by the perception that the defense is frequently raised and widely abused. For instance, a survey taken in Wyoming revealed that the "average" resident in that state believed the defense was raised in 43% of all criminal cases in Wyoming between 1970 and 1972 and that it was successful 38% of the time. In fact, however, only 102 defendants—fewer than half of 1% of those arrested in Wyoming during the period relevant to the survey—raised the plea, and only one person out of these 102 was acquitted. Richard Pasewark et al., "Opinions About the Insanity Plea," 8 J.Forensic Psychiat. 8 (1981). Nationwide,

the insanity defense appears to be raised in less than 1% of all criminal cases and appears to be successful about 25% of the time. Henry Steadman et al., "Factors Associated with a Successful Insanity Defense," 140 Am.J.Psychiat. 401 (1983). It should also be noted that in many states a sizeable proportion (over 70%) of acquittals by reason of insanity result from plea-bargaining or quasi-plea-bargaining with the prosecution; in these cases the prosecution agrees that the defendant should be acquitted, and there is no opportunity to "fool" a judge or jury. Jeffrey Rogers et al., "Insanity Defenses: Contested or Conceded?" 141 Am.J.Psychiat. 885 (1984).

The public also seems to believe that those who successfully assert the insanity defense are released from custody quickly, thus endangering the public. In fact, although as noted above confinement time varies widely, the *average* duration of confinement for persons acquitted by reason of insanity roughly correlates with the time they would have spent in prison had they been convicted of the crime charged. See, e.g., Mark Pantle et al., "Comparing Institutionalization Periods and Subsequent Arrests of Insanity Acquittees and Convicted Felons," 8 J.Psychiat. & L. 305 (1980). See also, Henry Steadman, et al., supra, at 98 ("insanity acquittees in New York were confined as long or longer than those found guilty"). Moreover, current evidence suggests that, as a group, acquittees who are released are no more dangerous than felons who are released on parole or after serving their time. Pantle et al., supra; Stuart B. Silver et al., "Follow-up after Release of Insanity Acquittees, Mentally Disordered Offenders, and Convicted Felons," 17 Bull. Am. Acad. Psychiatry & L. 387 (1989).

6. *The insanity defense and treatment for people with mental illness.* As noted earlier, some see the insanity defense as a means of ensuring that people with mental illness avoid the harshness of prison and receive treatment. Unless its scope is expanded considerably, however, the defense is not likely to be an efficient treatment vehicle for this group. One commentator estimates there are 87,000 people with severe mental disorders currently in prison. T. Howard Stone, "Therapeutic Implications of Incarceration for Persons with Severe Mental Disorders: Searching for Rational Health Policy," 24 Am. J. Crim. L. 283, 285 (1997).

2. *Cognitive Impairment*

THE HEADS CASE

Shortly after midnight on August 22, 1977, Charles Heads shot and killed the husband of his wife's sister in Shreveport, La. Heads, a resident of Houston, had traveled to Shreveport in search of his wife, who had departed from Houston with their three children four days before in an effort to leave him. During those four days, Heads had taken a leave of absence from work and made repeated local and long distance phone calls to locate his family. He also visited his wife's parents home, again in an effort to find his wife and children. Finally he called his wife's sister. The sister's denial of knowledge about his wife's whereabouts aroused his suspicion and he drove to her home, although it was nearing midnight. No one answered his repeated knocks on the doors and windows. Heads then kicked in a door leading from the carport, entered and found his sister-in-law's husband at the end of the bedroom hall, armed with a pistol.

Though the evidence is not clear as to the precise moment when the shooting began, both the victim's wife and Heads' wife testified that Heads began firing his pistol shortly after breaking into the house. The sister-in-law's husband informed the defendant that he, too, was armed and did not want to be forced to shoot him. But Heads continued firing his pistol down the bedroom hallway until he had emptied the pistol of bullets. He then ran to his car, retrieved a rifle from the trunk, and returned, firing several blasts, one of which struck the victim in the eye, killing him.

At his first trial, despite a plea of insanity, Heads was convicted of first degree murder. See *State v. Heads,* 385 So.2d 230 (La.1980). According to Heads' attorney, "the insanity defense at this first trial never got off the ground because neither of the psychiatrists who had examined the defendant had found evidence of any recognized mental disorder." Although Heads had had a difficult tour in Vietnam and "many suspected a Vietnam connection" to the killing, "no one could articulate it. The defendant himself denied any connection in his testimony under oath." Jack Welborn, "The Vietnam Connection: Charles Heads' Verdict," 9 Crim.Def. 7, 8 (1982).

Heads' conviction was overturned on unrelated grounds and his case was set for retrial. Between the two trials, the American Psychiatric Association issued the third edition of its Diagnostic and Statistical Manual, in which it recognized the so-called Post–Traumatic Stress Disorder (PTSD), with the following criteria:

A. Existence of a recognizable stressor that would evoke significant symptoms of distress in almost everyone [such as rape or assault, military combat, earthquakes, torture and car accidents].

B. Reexperiencing of the trauma as evidenced by at least one of the following:

(1) recurrent and intrusive recollections of event;

(2) recurrent dreams of the event;

(3) sudden acting or feeling as if the traumatic were reoccurring, because of an association with an environmental or ideational stimulus;

C. Numbing of responsiveness to or reduced involvement with the external world, beginning some time after the trauma, as shown by at least one of the following:

(1) markedly diminished interest in one or more significant activities;

(2) feeling of detachment or estrangement from others;

(3) constricted affect [emotion];

D. At least two of the following symptoms that were not present before the trauma:

(1) hyperalterness or exaggerated startle response;

(2) sleep disturbance;

(3) guilt about surviving when others have not, or about behavior required for survival;

(4) memory impairment or trouble concentrating;

(5) avoidance of activities that arouse recollection of the traumatic event;

(6) intensification of symptoms by exposure to events that symbolize or resemble the traumatic event.

The Manual notes that, "[i]n rare instances there are dissociative states, lasting from a few seconds to several hours, or even days, during which components of the event are relived, and the person behaves as though experiencing the event at that moment." Under "Associated Features", the Manual states: "Increased irritability may be associated with sporadic and unpredictable explosions of aggressive behavior, upon even minimal or no provocation."

At Heads' second trial, Heads again asserted an insanity defense, this time relying on a PTSD diagnosis. Under Louisiana law: "If the circumstances indicate that because of a mental disease or defect the offender was incapable of distinguishing between right and wrong with reference to the conduct in question, the offender shall be exempt from criminal responsibility." At trial, Heads presented three experts who testified that he had been incapable of distinguishing right from wrong at the time of the killing because of post-traumatic stress. Reliance on the PTSD allowed the defense not only to construct a plausible theory of insanity but to introduce evidence normally not admissible: a film comparing Vietnam and World War II, extensive testimony by Vietnam veterans describing the war, and considerable testimony about Heads' childhood.

There follows a facsimile of the closing arguments for the defense and the prosecution at Heads' second trial, based in part on a description of the trial by Heads' attorney Jack Welborn, see Welborn, supra, and in part on other cases in which a PTSD defense has been raised. See, e.g., *Louisiana v. Sharp,* 418 So.2d 1344 (La.1982).

DEFENSE ARGUMENT

The evidence shows that, while he was in Vietnam, Charles Heads experienced incredible trauma. Usually he was able to deal with the stress created by his horrible sojourn there. But when the anxiety created by Vietnam combined with the stress of his family leaving him, as happened on the night of the killing, Charles was not himself. On that night, he was literally unaware of what he was doing.

Charles has not had an easy life. He grew up in a section of Houston which once called itself "The Murder Capitol of the World." When he was nine years old, his mother was killed by his father, who was sentenced to life imprisonment for this and another murder. Yet Charles managed to finish elementary and high school.

Eight months after graduation, he enlisted in the Marines, where he volunteered for the First Reconnaissance Battalion. As a Reconner, he was part of an "elite within an elite"; his mission was to collect intelligence about enemy activities deep in hostile country, staying out on lightly armed patrols for several days to a week in an attempt to locate the VietCong. By his 20th birthday, Charles had his first confirmed kill. Six more followed, including a woman and an old man. The duties of a Reconner, according to the experts, were "extraordinarily stressful." As Dr. John Yost testified, it was not just the stress of combat, but the stress of waiting for something horrible to happen. No place was secure or safe. Everybody who was not an American was the enemy.

After nine months, Charles' days as a Reconner came to an abrupt end when his sixteen man patrol was ambushed one misty morning by an estimated battalion-sized VC regular unit. Charles was the point man and was hit first, twice in the gut. Eventually, those surviving the patrol were saved by an airstrike and airlifted out. Charles was considered too badly wounded to continue his tour in Vietnam. He can remember very little about his nine months in Vietnam or the ambush, although he did remember being shot in the gut.

Dr. Williams, a psychologist and a Marine Corps company commander in Vietnam, testified here at trial that this memory deficit and Charles' difficulty in talking about his Vietnam experience reflected the "psychological defense mechanism of denial." He stated that Charles had probably "used" this defense mechanism in overcoming the catastrophes of his childhood and it stood him in good stead when he returned to the United States. He became a postal employee, as did his wife. Together, they earned over $30,000 a year and, to outward appearances, Charles seemed to have put Vietnam behind him.

However, as his wife testified, Charles experienced many restless, sleepless nights. He also had many nightmares, in which he relived painful memories about the war. It was one of these nightmares, a particularly severe one, which frightened his wife so much that she took the children and went to Shreveport. Dr. John Wilson testified that Charles was on the "extreme edge of vulnerability in terms of his capacity to cope with stress." Indeed, on one occasion two years before the killing and five years after he left Vietnam, when his wife briefly left him, he vaulted onto the roof of his house with a rifle, assumed the assault position, and fired harmlessly for a few minutes into the tops of the trees in the neighborhood. This was significant evidence that Charles was a victim of the post-traumatic stress syndrome, the diagnosis given

Charles by all three of our experts. Yet there were no vet centers or outreach centers, no rap groups to help him out.

When his wife left with the children shortly before the killing, Charles lost his only support system. When he went unanswered at his sister-in-law's house he felt rejected and bereft. According to the doctors, it was at this point that the post-traumatic stress triggered his violent action. As it turned out, it was shortly after midnight, the ground and foliage were wet with two inches of rain that had fallen that day, the humidity was 100% and ground fog was beginning to form. According to Charles, his attention momentarily centered on the treeline in the small field across the street. This field, according to seven other Vietnam vets who had seen it or a videotape of it, symbolized or resembled Vietnam. To Charles, "It was just like Vietnam, in a way—that last patrol when we were ambushed, the way the mist hung in the trees." Charles said he was "hit" with a "boom", and he turned back toward the house. He says he was "on automatic." From this moment until he killed, his behavior was, according to the testimony of the vets, like that of a trained Marine Reconner surviving by cleaning out a hooch. When asked whether Charles was aware of the wrongness of the killing, Dr. Williams, a vet himself, replied: "Are you kidding? They gave us ice cream for that."

When the police arrived minutes later, they found Charles wandering in a daze inside the house in the midst of frantically scurrying children, his arms hanging at his side, in one hand the barrel of his own weapon, in the other the barrel of the weapon he had secured from his brother-in-law's body. They led him quietly away. The battle was over. Ladies and gentlemen of the jury, do not let this battle be for naught. Charles was not himself on the night of the killing. He thought he was in Vietnam. He did not know that what he was doing was wrong; he thought he was fighting for his country.

PROSECUTION ARGUMENT

Ladies and gentlemen of the jury, there is no doubt that Vietnam was a stressful environment. But Vietnam is not on trial here; Mr. Charles Heads is. He did not kill because he thought he was in Vietnam. He killed because he was upset his wife had left him and because she was unwilling to take him back or respond to his entreaties. In an overreaction to the sight of a gun, he intentionally and deliberately killed a man. If Vietnam is relevant at all here, it is relevant only because it made Mr. Heads better able and more willing to use violence to achieve his ends.

The defense experts testified that Mr. Heads is suffering from something called post-traumatic stress syndrome. Even assuming there is such a thing, and that Mr. Heads meets the criteria, the defense does not explain why most veterans who experienced the same stresses do not act violently. The defense presented witnesses from the same Reconner patrol who have never committed any violent acts since leaving Vietnam. Having bad dreams is one thing; acting them out is another.

But this whole Vietnam fantasy idea—that Mr. Heads thought he was in Vietnam on the night of the killing, and that he thought his relative was an ambushing VietCong—is preposterous in any event. The prosecution's expert provided a much more plausible explanation. Mr. Heads was not crazy on the night of the murder; he was just angry. The prosecution expert testified that the defendant has an "explosive personality disorder." Mr. Heads has stored up alot of anger, starting with his father's murder of his mother. Every once in awhile, when a similar rejection occurs, this anger comes out, like the time his wife left him and he went up on the roof to let off a few rounds. This explosiveness, in fact, was one of the reasons his wife left him the final time, as she admitted.

These tantrums might have been pretty intense. But they were not signs of insanity. And they also were infrequent. Most of the time, Mr. Heads' behavior was entirely normal, even right before the murder. During the four days prior to the killing he made several calls, visited his wife's parents' home, and made personal visits to mutual friends and acquaintances. None of these people reported anything out of the ordinary. He rode his bicycle, listened to music, and studied his Vietnam photo album. This was the kind of normal behavior that he exhibited throughout the entire seven years after he left Vietnam.

So why did he act so violently on the night of the murder? By his own admission, he remembers thinking the day before the murder that he wished he were back in the service where, as he stated, "we were one big family, where you were close, where you could count on each other, where people didn't lie to you." To Mr. Heads, his wife was not acting like family, could not be counted on, and had lied to him. He was angry at her, so angry he made sure he had guns with him when he went to her sister's. When she rejected him by not answering his knocks, he exploded. Again, this is not the reaction of a diseased man. It is the reaction of a man who has alot of pent-up anger and who acts aggressively on those occasions when he can no longer hold it in. Not only did he know it was wrong to kill on the night of the murder, he probably did not feel particularly bad about it, given his experience with killing in Vietnam. It is a sad thing, but combat makes some people less sensitive to the taking of life.

The state is asking that you convict Mr. Heads of first degree murder. The evidence shows that he intentionally brought weapons with him to the house in which he thought his wife was located, intentionally brought a pistol with him when he first entered the house and then, although he had not been fired upon himself, intentionally ran back to his car to get another weapon. He then intentionally shot to kill. He acted with deliberation and without adequate provocation.[f]

Questions and Comments

1. *Mental disease or defect and the cognitive prong.* Every insanity test currently in use requires a threshold finding of mental disease or defect.

f. Heads was acquitted by reason of insanity at his second trial.

Historically, mental disease referred to mental illness and mental defect referred to mental retardation. But further definition was usually imprecise. What role does this concept play in fixing the exculpatory scope of the insanity defense? How should it be defined?

One possible approach is to equate the law's definition of mental disease or defect with the psychiatric definition of mental disorder. In the *Heads* case, for instance, it appears that the "recognition" of the PTSD by the American Psychiatric Association had a significant impact on the legal outcome. Would the aims of the legal system be met by a simple correlation between the law's definition of mental disease or defect and the disorders found in DSM–IV, assuming that the law recognized only those disorders which have received "general acceptance" in the behavioral science community and can be reliably diagnosed?[g]

Professor LaFave, after surveying application of the various insanity tests by the courts, concluded that "any mental abnormality, be it psychosis, neurosis, organic brain disorder, or congenital intellectual deficiency . . . will suffice *if* it has caused the consequences described in the second part of the test." Wayne LaFave, Criminal Law 331 (3d ed. 2000) (emphasis in original). In other words, the mental disease or defect predicate is relatively unimportant; what is important is whether the individual was so cognitively or volitionally impaired at the time of the offense that exculpation is necessary. In a similar vein, the ALI test leaves mental disease or defect undefined except to exclude "abnormality manifested only by repeated or otherwise anti-social conduct." This approach allows an insanity defense based on any diagnosis found in DSM–IV (other than perhaps anti-social personality) that the courts are willing to recognize as sufficiently trustworthy. Presumably, it also allows a defense based on conditions not found in the Manual, as was true of the post-traumatic stress disorder prior to DSM–III. (See also, *Zamora v. Florida*, 361 So.2d 776 (Fla.App.1978), in which the defendant argued he was insane, ultimately unsuccessfully, based on "involuntary subliminal television intoxication" which produced a lessened appreciation of the wrongfulness of killing).

In contrast, other formulations attempt to limit the mental disease or defect predicate by requiring that it be serious. The federal statute, for example, provides that the mental condition must be "severe." According to the House Committee, this word was added "to emphasize that nonpsychotic behavior disorders or neuroses such as an 'inadequate personality,' 'immature personality,' or a pattern of 'antisocial tendencies' do not constitute the defense." H.R.Rep. No. 98–1030, 98th Cong., 2nd Sess. 229 (1984). The American Psychiatric Association would permit an insanity defense based only on "those severely abnormal mental conditions that grossly and demonstrably impair a person's perception or understanding of reality and that are not attributable primarily to the voluntary ingestion of alcohol or other psychoactive substances." APA, Statement on the Insanity Defense 12 (1983).

g. The "general acceptance" or *Frye* test of admissibility is discussed at pp. 454–55.

In defining mental disease or defect, the analysis may differ depending upon whether one is applying a cognitive as opposed to a volitional test. Focusing solely on the cognitive prong of the insanity defense for present purposes, which of the various formulations described above do you prefer? Would Heads have a "mental disease or defect" under your formulation? Note that one study has found that 20 to 30 percent of all Vietnam veterans "would be formally diagnosable" as experiencing a Post–Traumatic Stress Disorder. Arthur Egendorf, "The Postwar Healing of Vietnam Veterans: Recent Research," 33 Hosp. & Comm. Psychiat. 901 (1981). Another study found that, in 1979, 25% of the inmates in state prisons were veterans. Reported in 9 Crim.Def. 18 (1982).

2. *Know v. Appreciate.* Whatever the definition of mental disease or defect, it must cause, under the typical formulations of the cognitive prong, either a failure to "know" (under M'Naghten) or a "substantial inability to appreciate" (under ALI) the wrongness of the act. Although the M'Naghten test seems more rigid, Professor Goldstein's study of evidence presented and instructions given in jurisdictions that use that test indicates that the language is construed liberally, when it is defined at all. Abraham Goldstein, The Insanity Defense 49–53 (1967).

With respect to the difference between the "knowledge" and "appreciation" formulations, consider some of the facts developed in United States v. Hinckley, in which John Hinckley was charged with attempting to assassinate the president of the United States in 1981. Before the attempt, Hinckley had never been charged with a criminal offense. But he seemed very interested in violent action. He read several books on famous assassinations. He joined the Nazi Party and then was expelled in November, 1979, apparently because the party was alarmed over his open advocacy of violence. He subsequently tried to organize on his own a group called The American Front, which was designed to alert white Protestants to the threat posed by minority groups.

According to evidence derived from Hinckley's diaries, his letters to his parents and interviews with Hinckley, the key aspects of his mental state at the time of the offense revolved around his obsession with the actress Jodie Foster. This preoccupation began in 1976, when Hinckley first viewed the film Taxi Driver. The film's main character, Travis Bickle, rescues Iris, a child-prostitute played by Foster, from her pimp. Hinckley identified strongly with Bickle, who, like Hinckley, was a loner and alienated from society. Over the next several years, he bought an army jacket and boots like Bickle's, acquired the same number of weapons that Bickle had possessed, and tried to develop a relationship with Foster. He left cards at her door, spoke with her over the telephone twice and tried to reach her on several other occasions. Rejected by these advances, he did what Bickle had done when rebuffed by women; he began to stalk the president of the United States, at that time Jimmy Carter. On two occasions he was near enough to Carter to attempt an assassination, but he made no move.

After Ronald Reagan became president, Hinckley continued to think about some action against the chief executive as a way of improving his relationship with Foster. He copied a skyjacking note contained in a biography of a skyjacker, intending to use it to force President Reagan to resign and to have Jodie Foster brought to him. A postcard written to Foster in mid-February of 1981 contained a message promising Foster that one day she and Hinckley would occupy the White House together. Shortly before this, on New Year's Eve, 1980, he recorded a monologue. He noted that, as usual, he was alone and afraid. He proclaimed Jodie Foster to be the only thing that mattered in his life and made allusions to a death pact between himself and Foster and to his own suicide. Poetry written during the same period explored similar themes: mental deterioration, suicide, alienation, and an assassination that receives world-wide publicity.

On March 30, the day of the assassination attempt, he was in Washington, D.C. From the newspaper, he read of President Reagan's itinerary for the day. It was at this point that he decided to kill President Reagan. He showered, took some Valium to calm his nerves, and loaded his .22 caliber revolver with six Devastator bullets, ammunition which explodes on impact with the skin. Travis Bickle had achieved a similar effect in Taxi Driver by carving crosses on the tops of bullets. At about 12:45 he sat down to write a letter to Jodie Foster. He described how he had repeatedly tried to gain her attention and affection, but that time was running out. In order to win her respect and love, he was willing to give up his freedom or possibly even his life in the perpetration of what he called a "historic deed." Shortly after finishing the letter, he concealed his weapon in the pocket of his raincoat and took a cab to the Washington Hilton, where Reagan was scheduled to speak. As Reagan came out of the hotel, Hinckley drew his revolver and fired six rounds, wounding four men, including the President.

One of the defense experts testified that on the day of the assassination Hinckley was preoccupied with two things: "the termination of his own existence" and accomplishing a "union with Jodie Foster through death, after life ...". The President and the other victims "were bit players who were there in a way to help him to accomplish the two major roles [which] ... weighed far heavier in his emotional appreciation." The prosecution's expert emphasized the degree of planning involved in carrying out the attempt, the concealment of the weapon, Hinckley's admission that he knew the Secret Service might try to kill an assassin, and his decision to shoot when "[t]he Secret Service and the others in the presidential entourage looked the other way." On these facts, might one reasonably arrive at different conclusions about Hinckley's insanity, depending upon whether the test focused on "knowledge" of wrongfulness rather than on "substantial inability to appreciate" wrongfulness?[h]

Under a flexible definition of appreciation, even hardened criminals might have an insanity defense, given their lack of remorse for their criminal activity. This possibility perhaps explains the second paragraph of the ALI test excluding those whose mental illness is evidenced solely by repeated antisocial acts. The California Supreme Court offered further elaboration for the exception:

h. Hinckley was tried until the ALI test; the burden was on the prosecution to disprove insanity beyond a reasonable doubt. He was acquitted by reason of insanity, although it is unclear whether under the cognitive or volitional prong. Excerpts from the trial testimony in his case are found on pp. 427–37 and in Appendix B, at pp. 1353–72.

[T]he assertion of the insanity defense by recidivists with no apparent sign of mental illness except their penchant for criminal behavior would burden the legal system, bring the insanity defense into disrepute, and imperil the ability of persons with definite mental illness to assert that defense.... To classify persons with "antisocial personality" as insane would put in the mental institutions persons for whom there is currently no suitable treatment, and who would be a constant danger to the staff and other inmates. Mental hospitals are not designed for this kind of person; prisons are.

People v. Fields, 35 Cal.3d 329, 370–72, 197 Cal.Rptr. 803, 830–31, 673 P.2d 680, 707–08 (1983). Consider, in response, this excerpt from *United States v. Currens,* 290 F.2d 751, 774 n. 32 (3d Cir.1961):

Our study has ... revealed two very persuasive reasons why this court should not hold that evidence of psychopathy is insufficient, as a matter of law, to put sanity or mental illness in issue. First, it is clear that as the majority of experts use the term, a psychopath is very distinguishable from one who merely demonstrates recurrent criminal behavior ... [From our survey], it can be seen that in many cases the adjective "psychopathic" will be applied by experts to persons who are very ill indeed.

Our second reason for not holding that psychopaths are "sane" as a matter of law is based on the vagaries of the term itself. In each individual case all the pertinent symptoms of the accused should be put before the court and jury and the accused's criminal responsibility should be developed from the totality of his symptoms.... The criminal law is not concerned with ... classifications but with the fundamental issue of criminal responsibility.

Are *Fields* and *Currens* necessarily inconsistent? The older term for psychopathy was "moral insanity." (The diagnostic criteria for antisocial personality disorder, which is a related, but somewhat broader, mental condition, are found in Appendix A). Should a person who experiences no remorse for his crime or empathy for his victims and who, in Freudian terms has no "superego" or conscience, but who knows that his criminal acts are illegal and wrong in society's eyes, be subject to punishment? Professor Arenella argues that a "threshold conception of moral agency ... must include the following character-based attributes: the capacity to care for the interests of other human beings; the internalization of others' normative expectations, including self-identification as a participant in the community's blaming practices; the ability to engage in moral evaluation of one's character and acts, the capacity to respond to moral norms as a motivation for one's choices; and the power to control those firmly entrenched aspects of character that impair one's ability to act in accordance with one's moral judgments," because "if part of what we are communicating in our criminal culpability judgments is that the criminal deserves our moral blame and that his punishment is justified in part by a showing of his moral desert, then we need to take the concept of moral agency far more seriously than we presently do." Peter Arenella, "Convicting the Morally Blameless: Reassessing the Relationship Between Legal and Moral Accountability," 39 UCLA L. Rev. 1511, 1525, 1622 (1992).

The Louisiana insanity law under which Heads was tried seems closer to the M'Naghten "knowledge" test than to the ALI "appreciation" language. If one accepts the defense theory of the case, is it plausible that Heads not only did not "appreciate" but did not "know" that his act was wrong? If one accepts the *prosecution's* theory of the case, does Heads have a plausible argument under either approach?

3. *Criminality v. wrongfulness.* The final aspect of the cognitive tests has to do with whether "wrongness" is objectively or subjectively defined. The M'Naghten decision permitted an insanity defense only if the accused did not know the act was *legally* wrong. Moreover, in cases where the delusion was "partial"—meaning, apparently, that it affects only the accused's thinking about the offense and not other aspects of his life—then he would not have an insanity defense even if he thought his act was legal, unless the delusion, if true, would justify the act. As the House of Lords stated:

> For example, if, under the influence of his delusion, he supposes another man to be in the act of attempting to take away his life, and he kills that man, as he supposes, in self-defense, he would be exempt from punishment. If his delusion was that the deceased had inflicted a serious injury to his character and fortune, and he killed him in revenge for such supposed injury, he would be liable to punishment.

Subsequently, several American courts rejected this view, at least in part. For instance, in *People v. Schmidt,* 216 N.Y. 324, 110 N.E. 945 (1915), Judge Cardozo stated that if a person has "an insane delusion that God has appeared to [him] and ordained the commission of a crime, we think it cannot be said of the offender that he knows the act to be wrong." This language would appear to permit an insanity acquittal of a person who, though knowing his act was legally wrong, felt "morally justified" in committing it because of mental illness. However, Judge Cardozo also expressed caution about this rule:

> The anarchist is not at liberty to break the law because he reasons that all government is wrong. The devotee of a religious cult that enjoins polygamy or human sacrifice as a duty is not thereby relieved from responsibility before the law.

The drafters of the ALI test did not attempt to resolve this issue. Instead they provided two options, the "legal wrong" approach encapsulated by the word "criminality" and the "moral wrong" approach represented by the word "wrongfulness." The states are divided evenly on the question. Washington takes a hybrid approach. It generally follows the criminality rule. According to the Washington Supreme Court, "[i]f wrong meant moral wrong judged by the individual's own conscience, this would seriously undermine the criminal law, for it would allow one who violated the law to be excused from criminal responsibility solely because, in his own conscience, his act was not morally wrong." *State v. Crenshaw,* 98 Wash.2d 789, 659 P.2d 488 (1983). However, *Crenshaw* also created a "deific decree" exception to the general rule that "wrong" means legal wrong, thus allowing a defense in a case like the one described by Cardozo in *Schmidt.* It then found that the exception did not apply in the case before it, upholding the homicide conviction of a person who claimed he was a member of the Moscovites—

apparently a religious group that believes there is a "duty to assassinate an unfaithful spouse." The defendant had killed his wife because he "knew," despite the absence of objective evidence, that she had been unfaithful. There was also evidence that the defendant had been hospitalized on several occasions with a diagnosis of paranoia. Contrast this decision to *People v. Skinner*, 39 Cal.3d 765, 217 Cal.Rptr. 685, 704 P.2d 752 (1985), where the defendant, suffering from schizophrenia, killed his wife because he delusionally believed that "the marriage vow 'till death do us part' bestows on a marital partner a God-given right to kill the other partner who has violated or was inclined to violate the marital vows, and that because the vows reflected the direct wishes of God, the killing is with complete moral and criminal impunity." The California Supreme Court reversed the defendant's conviction and directed that he be found insane, concluding on these facts that the defendant did not know that the killing was wrongful or criminal (under a version of M'Naghten).

Some commentators have argued that a deific decree defense should not be recognized:

> A "deific decree" commanding the defendant to kill has been characterized, not as a religious belief, but as a delusional belief justifying an insanity verdict. But if a "religiousity" defense is not available to exculpate the hyperreligious from criminal liability for acts they believe are morally right, should the mentally disordered be exculpated for their religiously motivated, though illegal, acts? ... If a mentally disordered person claims that God ordered him or her to kill, are psychiatrists competent to assess whether the defendant acted from a delusional belief, or whether he or she acted from a religious conviction? In our society in which all sincerely held religious beliefs are entitled to equal treatment, can we appropriately declare a defendant's claimed religious belief to be a false belief, the product of a mentally disordered mind?

> To answer these questions, [one must examine] the meaning of delusion, especially as that concept is explained in the psychiatric profession's standard diagnostic manual. Psychiatry specifically excludes religious beliefs from the definition of delusion because a religious belief cannot be declared to be a false belief. Because a person's sincerely held belief that God ordered him or her to kill qualifies as a religious belief, it should not be characterized as a delusion. Thus, the insanity defense should not be available to those who kill at God's command.

Grant H. Morris & Ansar Haroun, " 'God Told Me to Kill': Religion or Delusion?," 39 San Diego L. Rev. 973, 977 (2001). In support of this position, the authors report research suggesting the value-laden nature of distinguishing delusional and non-delusional religious sentiments.

> In a recent study, researchers developed eighteen written vignettes designed to assess clinical judgments of religious authenticity and psychopathology. A core vignette was used for each of six dimensions of religious experience. Three variations of each core vignette were written to reflect conventional, less conventional, and unconventional practices. For example, in one core vignette that focused on the dimension of what is communicated, individuals heard the voice of God telling them to: (1) baptize their newborn child—a conventional religious practice, (2) pre-

pare a worship service—a less conventional religious practice, or (3) sacrifice their child—an unconventional religious practice. The vignettes were tested on sixty-seven mental health practitioners of varying professional backgrounds, experience, and religious affiliation.

The results were not surprising. For every vignette tested, the conventional response was rated significantly more religiously authentic and significantly less pathological than the less conventional response. For every vignette tested, the less conventional response was rated significantly more religiously authentic and significantly less pathological than the unconventional response. According to the researchers: "The essential determining factor in the ratings was not the dimensions of religious experience, but the degree to which religious experience deviated from conventional religious beliefs and practices. The more unconventional the experience, the less religiously authentic and less mentally healthy it was deemed to be." The experience that was rated as least religiously authentic and most pathological of all vignettes was complying with God's request to sacrifice a child. Ironically, this experience, at least when performed by Abraham, is often considered the most religiously authentic by Jews, Christians, and Muslims; it is the supreme test of religious faith.

Id. at 1038–39.

Assuming the other criteria for insanity are met, does Heads have an insanity defense under the criminality approach? The wrongfulness approach? Had Heads sincerely believed he had been ordered by God to kill his wife for her transgressions, should he have a defense?

4. *Alternative formulations.* Most people with mental illness who commit violent acts have some idea that their act is against the law. Only rarely, as in the oft-used but probably unrealistic example of the man who strangles his wife thinking she is a lemon, will they have no idea they are committing a crime. Is the legal wrong approach thus too restrictive? Does the "deific decree" exception, or use of the "appreciation" language, broaden the rule sufficiently? If neither of these solutions is acceptable and the moral wrong approach must be adopted, how does one restrict that approach to avoid acquittal of anyone who has a strongly held belief that he or she is "in the right"? Does the mental disease or defect predicate handle this problem?

Several scholars reject knowledge of wrongness as the proper test for insanity. As noted in the introduction to this section some have suggested that insanity should be equated with "irrationality" or "craziness." Do these tests better capture the moral scope of the insanity defense?

5. *Other cases involving cognitive impairment.* Consider whether the individuals in the following cases should be found insane.

Case A: Jones, a 60 year-old retired military person, shoots at a low-flying cropduster, puncturing the fuselage and causing the plane to crash, which kills the pilot. Jones claims that the plane was sent by the government to spy on him and to bombard his house with electronic particles meant to destroy his house (he can show point to the cracks in the foundation) and kill his animals (one of his dogs had died a few days before). He also believes that the government has bugged his house and arranged for his neighbors to spy on him. There is no objective evidence that the government has ever paid any attention to Jones. Psychiatrists say his diagnosis is delusional paranoia.

Case B: Griffin suffers from paranoid schizophrenia. He is also a very devout Catholic. He becomes convinced that he is one of the principal defenders of Catholicism against a world-wide conspiracy that is out to destroy the church. In his mind, the conspiracy includes those who support abortion and those who work in abortion clinics. He buys automatic weapons and ammunition and proceeds to scout out one of the local abortion clinics. One day he enters the clinic with his gun, shouts "The Church says you must die!" and sprays the waiting room with bullets, killing a doctor, a clerk and two clients waiting for abortions. He is captured nearby trying to dispose of the weapons.

Case C: Andrea Yates drowned all five of her children, one by one, in the bathtub. She began with Paul, age three, then drowned two-year-old Luke, five-year-old John, six-month-old Mary, and finally Noah, age seven. She lined up the bodies of the youngest four on her bed and covered them with a sheet, and left Noah, who had attempted to flee before she was able to overcome him, facedown in the tub. She then called 911 and requested police assistance. When officers arrived they noticed that all the doors had been locked and that the bathmat had been removed from the bath to reduce traction. During her interrogation, she said she killed her children because she had not been a "good mother." She later stated that she believed that, had she not killed her children, they would have suffered eternal damnation and have been "tormented by Satan." These beliefs could be traced back to the period after her third child was born, when Andrea and her husband Rusty began following an itinerant preacher, whose fire and brimstone sermons made her worried that she was not protecting her children from sinful influences. Four months after her fourth child was born (and after the family had moved into a bus purchased from the preacher), Yates attempted suicide and told doctors she had seen at least ten visions over a period of days. Three weeks later she tried again to commit suicide and was admitted to a hospital with a diagnosis of a postpartum depression. She was put on antipsychotic and antidepressant medication. When released after 19 days in the hospital (to a new home, Rusty having moved them out of the bus), she was told that having another child could mean a severe relapse. But Yates stopped taking her medication (despite hearing voices that, she told a friend, told her to do things she was unable to describe), and gave birth to a fifth child. Within a few months she stopped eating, drinking and speaking. She was again prescribed antidepressants and antipsychotic medication, but doctors took her off the latter medication three weeks before the crime. Although her relationship with the children was strained, she was able to make their lunches and carry out other cursory tasks. To give Andrea some independence, Rusty and his mother decided Andrea would have one hour alone with the children between Rusty leaving for work and the mother arriving to help, which was the period during which the children were killed. (At her first trial, Yates was convicted and sentenced to life, failing in her claim that she was insane under a version of M'Naghten. That verdict was overturned because the prosecution's main witness had erroneously testified that Yates, who was a fan of the Law & Order TV show, had patterned her acts after an episode on that show in which a mother had killed her children and then feigned insanity; in fact the episode had never aired. At her second trial, Yates was found not guilty by reason of insanity.).

3. *Volitional Impairment*

United States v. Pollard[i]

Marmion Pollard, in April, 1956, had been for several years a member of the Detroit Police Department. He was an apparently well-adjusted, highly intelligent black officer on the force, of an active nature, pleasing personality, and happy disposition. His rating as a member of the Police Department was excellent, and his intelligence quotient, as appeared from the examination of the Department, was very high. He was married and had four children. He was a good husband and father and had never been in any trouble. He left a Detroit high school, where he was a good student, when he was in the twelfth grade, to enlist in the Navy, earning, after his full service there, an honorable discharge.

In April, 1956, while he was on police duty, his wife and small daughter were brutally murdered in their home by a drunken neighbor. After the murder, Pollard's three other children, all sons, continued to live with him and his mother-in-law, who cared for the children and the home. Gradually, Pollard became the victim of chronic depression or melancholia, appearing generally to be overcome with fatigue, bursting into tears and crying and sobbing for considerable periods, and repeatedly threatening to commit suicide with his police gun. His brother-in-law on one occasion prevented him from deliberately running onto a thruway, where he probably would have been killed by swift-moving cars. On another occasion, his brother-in-law found him lying on the floor in his home, sobbing; his body was so limp he could hardly be lifted to the bed. After many of these incidents, Pollard seemed to recover and would become suddenly cheerful with no memory of what had happened.

His fellow officers in the Police Department noticed various changes about him after the death of his wife. They weren't abrupt changes. Sometimes a week would pass and he would seem all right; but then he would do something out of the ordinary. In the course of his duties as a policeman, on one day he would insist upon enforcing the law and issue loitering tickets for violation of ordinances, and the next day, he would express an opinion that he did not see anything wrong with such conduct. When asked a question by his fellow policemen, while driving with them in a scout car, he would sometimes be silent for about ten minutes, and then answer the question as though he had just been asked. Sometimes when he came to work with a fellow officer, they might talk to each other normally. Other times he would sit for two hours at a time and say nothing. This was a change from his prior

---

i. The "majority" opinion in this book's version of *Pollard* is taken from the district court opinion in the *Pollard* case, 171 F.Supp. 474 (E.D.Mich.1959), and the dissenting opinion is taken from the circuit court of appeals decision reversing the district court, 282 F.2d 450 (6th Cir.1960), mandate clarified, 285 F.2d 81 (6th Cir. 1960).

general demeanor, when he had always been very lively and talkative. Once when he drove the scout car, he constantly beat on the steering wheel with his fist for approximately half an hour. When, on this occasion, he was asked if anything was wrong, he acted as though he didn't know he was doing it, and would continue. It should also be noted, however, that a police lieutenant of the Detroit Police Department testified that the defendant's police work, during the period with which we are now concerned, as evidenced by his efficiency rating and his written duty reports, was, if anything, more effective than his service prior to the death of his wife.

A little more than two years after the murder of his wife and daughter, Pollard remarried, on May 22, 1958. On the day before his remarriage, Pollard attempted to hold up a branch of the Detroit Bank & Trust Company about eleven o'clock in the morning. With a gun, he threatened the teller, ordering her to fill up a paper bag with money. The teller did so and handed the bag to Pollard, who ordered a bank official to accompany him to the exit. As they approached the door, the official suddenly threw his arms around Pollard, who then dropped the bag of money and ran out of the building.

About 4:00 P.M., on the same day, he entered the Chene–Medbury Branch of the Bank of the Commonwealth and walked to a railing behind which a bank employee was sitting. He pointed his gun at the man and told him to sit quietly. The employee, however, did not obey this order but instead raised an alarm, whereupon the defendant ran from the bank and again escaped.

The defendant later admitted to agents of the Federal Bureau of Investigation that after his abortive attempts to rob the two banks, he decided to rob a third bank and actually proceeded on the same day to an unnamed bank he had selected but decided not to make the attempt when he discovered that the bank was "too wide open"—had too much window area so that the possibility of apprehension was enhanced.

On June 3, at about 3:00 P.M., the defendant entered the Woodrow Wilson–Davison Branch of the Bank of the Commonwealth and went directly to an enclosure behind which a male and female employee were sitting at desks facing each other. Defendant held his gun under a jacket which he carried over his right arm. He ordered the woman employee to come out from behind the railing. In doing so, she grasped the edge of her desk. Defendant, in the belief that she may have pushed an alarm button, decided to leave but ordered the woman to accompany him out of the bank. When they reached the street, he told her to walk ahead of him, but not to attract attention. Defendant noticed a police car approaching the bank and waited until it passed him, then ran across an empty lot to his car and again escaped.

On June 11, 1958, he attempted to hold up a grocery market. He was thwarted in the attempt when the proprietor screamed and, becoming frightened, the defendant fled. In so doing, he abandoned his automobile in back of the market where he had parked it during the holdup attempt. Routinely, this car was placed under surveillance and later when the defendant, dressed in his Detroit Police Officer's uniform, attempted to get in it, he was arrested by detectives of the Detroit Police Force.

After his apprehension, the defendant confessed to eleven other robberies, or attempted robberies.

The three psychiatrists who submitted the written reports, all qualified and respected members of their profession, testified that in their opinion the defendant, at the time he committed the criminal acts, knew the difference between right and wrong and knew that the acts he committed were wrong but was suffering from a "traumatic neurosis" or "dissociative reaction", characterized by moods of depression and severe feelings of guilt, induced by the traumatic effect of the death of his wife and child and his belief that he was responsible for their deaths because by his absence from home he left them exposed to the actions of the crazed, drunken neighbor. They further stated that he had an unconscious desire to be punished by society to expiate these guilt feelings and that the governing power of his mind was so destroyed or impaired that he was unable to resist the commission of the criminal acts. In their opinion, however, the defendant was not then, nor is he now, psychotic or committable to a mental institution.

Counsel for defendant contends that since all the medical testimony was to the effect that the defendant was suffering from an irresistible impulse at the time of the commission of the offenses, this Court must accept this uncontroverted expert testimony and find him not guilty by reason of insanity.

* * *

Psychiatry and law approach the problem of human behavior from different philosophical perspectives. Psychiatry purports to be scientific and takes a deterministic position with regard to behavior. "Its view of human nature is expressed in terms of drives and dispositions which, like mechanical forces, operate in accordance with universal laws of causation." Hall, "Psychiatry and Criminal Responsibility", 65 Yale Law Journal 761, 764. For psychiatry, what we do is determined by what we are, and there is little or no room for moral or ethical judgments. In a sense, all criminal behavior, whether it be the acts of the rapist, the forger, the embezzler, the sender of licentious literature through the mails or tax evasion by a reputable businessman, is evidence of mental disease. But the uncritical adoption of this point of view would completely do away with the concept of criminal responsibility. Dangell, Criminal Law, Sec. 128; White, Insanity and the Criminal Law, at page 26; Weihofen, "Crime, Law and Psychiatry," 4 Kansas Law Review 377, 386. Criminal law is "a practical, rational, normative science which, although it draws upon theoretical science, also is concerned to pass judgment on human conduct. Its view of human nature asserts the reality of free choice and rejects the thesis that the conduct of normal adults is a mere expression of imperious psychological necessity. Given the additional purpose to evaluate conduct, some degree of autonomy is a necessary postulate." Hall, supra at page 764.

The psychiatrists, as hereinbefore related, testified that the defendant suffered from severe feelings of depression and guilt; and that in their opinion he had an irresistible impulse to commit criminal acts, an unconscious desire to be apprehended and punished; and that he geared his behavior to the accomplishment of this end. However, his entire pattern of conduct during the period of his criminal activities militates against this conclusion. His conscious desire not to be apprehended and punished was demonstrably greater than his unconscious desire to the contrary. After his apprehension, despite searching interrogation for over five hours by Detroit Police Officers and by agents of the Federal Bureau of Investigation, he denied any participation in criminal conduct of any kind. It was only after he was positively identified by bank personnel that he finally admitted that he did attempt to perpetrate the bank robberies. The trial judge asked one of the psychiatrists to explain this apparent inconsistency. In answer, he stated that although the defendant had an unconscious desire to be apprehended and punished, when the possibility of apprehension became direct and immediate, the more dominating desire for self-preservation asserted itself. This explanation may have merit if applied to individual acts. However, the validity of a theory that attempts to explain the behavior of a person must be determined in light of that person's entire behavioral pattern and not with reference to isolated acts which are extracted from the pattern. The defendant's pattern of behavior of May 21, 1958, discloses that the desire for self-preservation was not fleeting and momentary but continuing, consistent and dominant. What, then, becomes of the theory of irresistible impulse? Looking to the events of that day, we are asked to believe, first, that the defendant, acting pursuant to an irresistible impulse, selected a bank site to rob, entered the bank to accomplish that end, purposely failed in the attempt and when the end he sought, apprehension, was in view, escaped because of the dominance, at the moment of ultimate accomplishment, of the stronger drive for self-preservation. We must then believe that when the defendant knew he was apparently free from detection, his compulsive state reasserted itself and that he again went through the steps of planning, abortive attempt and escape. And if we acquiesce in this theory, what other psychiatric theory explains his subsequent conduct—his plan to rob a third unnamed bank and the rejection of that plan because of his subjective belief that the possibility of apprehension would be too great? If the theory remains the same, then it appears that in the latter case, the fear of apprehension and punishment tipped "the scales enough to make resistible an impulse otherwise irresistible." It is a logical inference that, in reality, the other robbery attempts were made as the result of impulses that the defendant did not choose voluntarily to resist because, to him, the possibility of success outweighed the likelihood of detection which is in essence a motivation for all criminal conduct. The impulse being resistible, the defendant is accountable for his criminal conduct.

Psychiatrists admit that the line between irresistible impulse and acts which are the result of impulses not resisted is not easy to trace. To the extent that the line may be traced, the distinguishing motivation of the action, whether the act is performed to satisfy an intrinsic need or is the result of extrinsic provocation, is a determining factor. Admittedly, motivations may be mixed. However, all the facts have clearly established that defendant's criminal activity was planned to satisfy an extrinsic need by a reasoned but anti-social method. The defendant had financial problems of varying degrees of intensity throughout his life. He had financial difficulties during his first marriage. He was now embarking upon a second marriage. He was about to undertake the responsibility of supporting not only a wife and himself, but also four children, three of them the product of his first marriage. In statements given to agents of the Federal Bureau of Investigation admitting his criminal activity, he stated: "Inasmuch as I was about to marry my second wife, I decided that I would not lead the same type of financially insecure life that I led with my first wife. I needed about $5,000 in order to buy a home. My only purpose in deciding to rob a bank was to obtain $5,000 and if I obtained the money, I did not intend to continue robbing." Defendant's entire pattern of conduct was consistent with this expressed motivation.

Life does not always proceed on an even keel. Periods of depression, feelings of guilt and inadequacy are experienced by many of us. Defendant was a devoted husband and loving father. His feelings of despondency and depression induced by the brutal killing of his wife and infant daughter were not unnatural. How else the defendant should have reacted to his tragic loss we are not told. His conduct throughout this crucial period did not cause any concern among his colleagues. All stated unequivocally that in their opinion he was sane. Significant also is the fact that his present wife married him on May 22, 1958, after a year of courtship. It is a permissible inference that defendant's conduct relative to his mental condition, as related by her, did not suggest to her that the defendant was insane.

We are satisfied beyond a reasonable doubt that the defendant committed the acts for which he is now charged and that when he committed them he was legally sane.

DISSENT

If the mere preponderance of evidence created a reasonable doubt as to whether appellant acted under an irresistible impulse, the government did not prove his guilt. When there has been created, by the evidence, a reasonable doubt as to whether an accused person acted under an irresistible impulse, the burden is upon the prosecution to establish, beyond a reasonable doubt, that he did not act under an irresistible impulse.

In the instant case, the psychiatric witnesses had unanimously agreed that Pollard suffered from severe feelings of depression and guilt; that, in their opinion, he had an irresistible impulse to commit criminal acts; an unconscious desire to be apprehended and punished; and that he geared his behavior to the accomplishment of this end. The court, however, states that his entire pattern of conduct during the period of his criminal activities militated against this conclusion, and that his conscious desire not to be apprehended and punished was demonstrably greater than his unconscious desire to the contrary. Without drawing any conclusions from the foregoing as to whether appellant's conscious or unconscious desires were the stronger, it can be said that acts that appear rational are not to be taken by the factfinder as evidence of sanity, where all of the other evidence in the case is proof of a defendant's mental unsoundness.

It should also be mentioned that in the Report of the Neuropsychiatric Staff Conference of the Medical Center for Federal Prisoners, it was pointed out that the attempted robberies by Pollard were bizarre and ineffectively planned and executed; that when he tried to leave one bank, he ordered a bank official to follow behind him instead of ahead of him, which resulted in his being caught from behind and barely escaping after a struggle, during which he dropped the paper bag of money he had collected; that on the various occasions of his attempted robberies, he would suddenly enter a bank that he had never seen before, without prior knowledge of the arrangement of the premises, or of the personnel. Taken in consideration with all of the other factors, such conduct, on the part of a highly intelligent police officer with a knowledge of how crimes are committed, has about it nothing of sanity.

It is emphasized by the government that Pollard was motivated to attempt the bank robberies because of his need for financial security. The claimed motivation seems pointless. Pollard, during his first marriage, had been receiving the regular salary of a policeman with promotions, of approximately $450 a month. His first wife, at that time, was receiving about $300 a month as a clerk with the Michigan Unemployment Compensation Commission. Their joint income was almost twice what a regular policeman's salary would be. His second wife, at the time of her marriage to him, had money of her own—enough to pay her own bills, and take care of her daughter with the money which was paid for support by her former husband. She had previously held a position for six years with the Michigan Bell Telephone Company. She considered herself to be relatively comfortable financially. Between the time of Pollard's arrest on June 11, 1958, and his trial, she had, herself, paid off about $700 in bills that he had owed. Pollard's financial condition could not be considered a reasonable motivation for his attempted bank robberies. As far as income went, he was much better off than most other policemen and if such a financial condition could be considered a reasonable motivation for Pollard's attempted robberies, every other policeman in the department would have had twice the motivation to commit such crimes as Pollard had.

Certain distinctions have been drawn by courts in applying the rule of irresistible impulse. While anger, greed, and passion are said, in ordinary parlance, to result in acts because of desires that have become irresistible, this is not, in law, the "irresistible impulse" that results from a mental defect or mental disease. Further, it is held that "emotional insanity," which is an unbridled passion lasting just long enough to enable the act complained of to be done, and then subsiding, does not relieve the accused of accountability, even in those jurisdictions where the doctrine of irresistible impulse, arising out of a mental defect, is recognized. Moreover, to like effect, in *Bell v. State,* 120 Ark. 530, 180 S.W. 186, 196 (1915), the court although sustaining the doctrine of irresistible impulse as a defense to crime, distinguished between such impulse and "emotional" insanity, as follows: "But it must be remembered that one who is otherwise sane will not be excused from a crime he has committed while his reason is temporarily dethroned not by disease, but by anger, jealousy, or other passion."

From all of the evidence of the lay and expert witnesses, however, it cannot be affirmatively concluded that Pollard was sane. Obviously, as a result of the murder of his wife and child while he was absent from his home, he was suffering from some grave disorder, and that disorder was, in the opinion of all the psychiatric and medical experts, a disassociative reaction resulting in Pollard's commission of the acts charged because of an irresistible impulse.

Questions and Comments

1. *Volition, causation and compulsion.* The "majority" opinion cites several commentators to the effect that the "deterministic" premise of psychiatry, if given full sway, could "do away with the concept of criminal responsibility." This concern is most often voiced when discussing application of the volitional tests for insanity, because these tests directly pose the question of whether a person could control his or her behavior. If mental health professionals answer this question honestly, the argument goes, they will always say that an individual's acts are caused by various endogenous or exogenous factors over which the individual had little or no control.

In *Pollard,* for instance, the psychiatric testimony suggested that Pollard was not aware of his true reasons for acting, and thus, in some sense, he was not "in control of" his actions. Another common type of case in which "lack-of-control" defenses are raised involves defendants diagnosed as having "impulse disorders" such as kleptomania, pyromania, or pedophilia. Other examples are legion. For example, in *People v. Yukl,* 83 Misc.2d 364, 372 N.Y.S.2d 313 (1975), the defendant raised an insanity defense relying on evidence that individuals with an extra Y (or male) chromosome are particularly aggressive, and thus less able to control their behavior. See Note, "The XYY Chromosomal Abnormality: Use and Misuse in the Legal Process," 9 Harv.J.Legis. 469 (1972). Several cases have involved claims that the type of posttraumatic stress syndrome raised in *Heads* not only made it difficult for the defendant to distinguish right from wrong, but also "compelled" the defendant to act violently. See, e.g., *Louisiana v. Sharp,* 418 So.2d 1344 (La.1982) (defendant had "uncontrollable 'rage reaction'" as a result of PTSD). Unusual plasma androgen levels are said to "overinfluence" sexual offenders. Richard Rada, "Plasma Androgens and the Sex Offender," 8 Bull.Am.Acad.Psychiat. & L. 456 (1980). It has also been asserted that women, just prior to or during early menstruation, may be prone to uncontrollable impulses resulting in violence. See Note, "Premenstrual Syndrome: A Criminal Defense," 59 Notre Dame L.Rev. 253 (1983).

Other defenses have been predicated on pressures that appear to be as much "external" as "internal." In *United States v. Alexander and Murdock,* 471 F.2d 923 (D.C.Cir.1972), for instance, the evidence showed that Murdock grew up in the Watts section of Los Angeles in a large family with little love or attention and no father. He became "greatly preoccupied with the unfair treatment of negroes in this country and believe[d] that racial war is inevitable." Early one morning, Murdock and his companions became involved in an argument with a group of Marines, all of whom were white. Murdock admitted that, during the altercation, which took place in a hamburger shop, he drew his fully loaded gun and emptied it. He killed two of the Marines, even though he had not seen any weapons. As they drove from the scene, he took his companion's gun and continued firing into the restaurant. In explanation, he said that just before he began firing he had heard someone say "Get out, you black bastards." He also claimed he saw Marines advancing toward him, although the surviving Marines denied this allegation. His attorney argued that Murdock was unable to control his conduct because of a "deepseated emotional disorder that was rooted in his 'rotten social background.'" An expert witness testified that "it is probable that when the Marine called him a 'black bastard,' Murdock had an irresistible impulse to shoot." Id. at 957–59.

How should the criminal law respond to these types of claims? In "Responsibility and the Unconscious," 53 So.Cal.L.Rev. 1563 (1980), Professor Michael Moore draws a distinction between "causation" on the one hand and "compulsion" on the other:

> Everyone is undoubtedly caused to act as they do by a myriad of environmental, physiological, or psychological factors. Yet to say that any actions are caused, for example, by an unhappy childhood, a chemical imbalance, or a belief that it is raining, is not to say the actions are compelled. One must point to something other than causation to make out the excuse of compulsion. . . .

Moore then uses the *Pollard* case to illustrate his point.

> Suppose Pollard did unconsciously feel guilty at the death of his first wife and child. He may have felt guilty because he had not been there; alternatively, he may have felt guilty because he had unconsciously wished to kill them himself. In either case, could such unconscious guilt *compel* Pollard to do an act for which he would be punished?

In answering this question, Moore compares Pollard to the kleptomaniac (a person who appears to experience a strong urge to steal). The kleptomaniac, according to Moore, feels compelled to steal and knows he is yielding to the compulsion, "yet he does not know the object of his passionate desire. . . . A few thefts readily tell him it is not the stolen objects themselves." Pollard on the other hand, "had a perfectly intelligible, conscious motive for acting. In such circumstances one is often more reluctant to accept as a factual matter that some unconscious emotion really explains his behavior."

Even accepting Moore's distinction between causation and compulsion, one may have difficulty differentiating between the two in an individual case. Do you agree with Moore that Pollard was probably not "compelled" by his unconscious guilt to commit the robberies and attempted robberies? Consider recent research indicating that over 85% of a large sample of males who have both low levels of MAOA neuro-transmitter (a chemical thought to modulate aggression) and a history of abuse as children engaged in some form of serious antisocial behavior by the time they were 26. Caspi Avshalom et al., "Role of Genotype in the Cycle of Violence in Maltreated Children," 297 Science 851 (2002). Or consider research that shows that individuals with frontal lobe damage exhibit significant deficits in impulse control and ability to adjust behavior to changing circumstances, with one study finding that 73% of inmates with front lobe damage committed violent crimes compared to only 28% of non-injured inmates who did so. E.T. Bryant et al., "Neuropsychological Deficits, Learning Disabilities, and Violent Behavior," 52 J. Consulting & Clin. Psychol. 323 (1984). See generally Richard E. Redding, "The Brain–Disordered Defendant: Neuroscience and Legal Insanity in the Twenty–First Century," 56 Am. U. L. Rev. 51, 57–76 (2006). Can it be said that defendants who meet these type of criteria are "compelled," or should an excuse depend upon whether they had "a perfectly intelligible, conscious motive for acting" (which will normally be the case)? Finally, using Moore's compulsion-causation distinction, how do you evaluate Murdock's claim?

2. *Reform efforts.* The previous note identified two concerns associated with the volitional prong. The first is that it could swallow up the criminal law by providing an excuse for everyone, particularly as the behavioral sciences become more sophisticated. The second is that, even if the volitional prong can theoretically be limited, as Moore has tried to do, difficulties associated with determining who is properly excused under the test could lead to mistake or abuse. Of the reforms advanced to address these problems, three stand out.

Elimination of Volitional Prong. The first, of course, is abolition of the volitional prong, a step the U.S. Congress took in the Insanity Defense Reform Act of 1984. Is this solution justifiable, assuming that there are people who knowingly commit crime but apparently "can't help themselves?" Consider the following comment by Bonnie, an opponent of the volitional tests:

It might be argued, of course, that the risk of mistake should be tolerated if the volitional prong of the defense is morally necessary. The question may be put this way: Are there clinically identifiable cases involving defendants whose behavior controls were so pathologically impaired that they ought to be acquitted although their ability to appreciate the wrongfulness of their actions was unimpaired? I do not think so. The most clinically compelling cases of volitional impairment involve the so-called impulse disorders—pyromania, kleptomania, and the like. These disorders involve severely abnormal compulsions that ought to be taken into account in sentencing, but the exculpation of pyromaniacs would be out of touch with commonly shared moral intuitions.

Richard Bonnie, "The Moral Basis of the Insanity Defense," 69 A.B.A.J. 194, 197 (1983). Do you agree that the conviction of pyromaniacs for arson and kleptomaniacs for theft is in "touch with commonly shared moral intuitions"?[j] Under Bonnie's approach, would Pollard be convicted and the psychiatric testimony relegated to a sentencing hearing? Or is the expert testimony in this case possibly relevant to cognitive impairment as well?

Related to this latter question, as well as the movement toward elimination of the volitional prong, consider the effect of adopting an "irrationality" test for insanity. Would volitional impairment be irrelevant under this test? If Pollard's real reason for committing the robberies was to assuage his guilt by getting caught, was he rational? How would a kleptomaniac fare under such a test? An "XYY" defendant? Consider this excerpt from Herbert Fingarette, The Meaning of Insanity, 160–172 (1972), an advocate of the rationality test:

> We may find it congenial to speak idiomatically of the insane person as one who is driven, or seized, or overwhelmed, or possessed by fear, anxiety, emotions or delusions. Yet there is one literal truth we must never lose sight of: it is the person himself who initiates and carries out the deed, it is his desire, his mood, his passion, his belief which is at issue, and it is he who acts to satisfy this desire, or to express this mood, emotion, or belief of his. Even if his motive is unconscious, it is his motive, and it is he who acts out of this motive.

From this premise, Fingarette argues that "[t]here is a crucial difference between saying a person lacks capacity to conform to law (that is, cannot conform to law) and saying that he does not control his conduct in the way a normal person does." Virtually all nonresponsible insane persons can control their conduct in the latter sense. What distinguishes them from responsible sane people "is the way in which [they come] to adopt one or another course of action"—the fact that they do so irrationally.

Tightening the Definition of Mental Disease. An alternative solution to the dangers of mistake or abuse associated with the volitional prong is to narrow the definition of mental disease or defect for purposes of the insanity defense. The traditional unstructured approach is illustrated by the "dissent" in *Pollard,* which cited several authorities for the proposition that the irresistible impulse must result from a persistent disease, rather than a "temporary," "normal" reaction. Along these lines is *United States v. Lyons,* 731 F.2d 243 (5th Cir.1984), which held that drug addiction is not a mental disease or defect for purposes of the insanity defense unless it causes "actual drug-induced or drug-aggravated psychosis, or physical damage to the brain or nervous system." Other attempts to narrow the mental disease or defect predicate have been described in the previous discussion of the cognitive prong. The most restrictive definitions are found in the federal statute,

---

j. One study in Maryland concluded that manic patients are often severely impaired in their capacity to control behavior, while their cognitive impairment is less striking. As a result, the authors asserted, elimination of the volitional prong could lead to conviction of "a class of psychotic patients whose illness is clearest in symptomatology, most likely biologic in origin, most eminently treatable and potentially most disruptive in penal detention." Governor's Task Force to Review the Defense of Insanity, State of Maryland (reported in Rita Simon & David Aaronson, The Insanity Defense 167 (1988)).

which limits the insanity defense to "severe" diseases, and in the recommendation of the American Psychiatric Association, which would only permit an insanity defense based on proof of "conditions that grossly and demonstrably impair a person's perception or understanding of reality." Neither the federal statute nor the APA recognizes a volitional impairment defense. But if their approach to the mental disease or defect predicate were applied in the volitional context, would persons with impulse disorders (e.g., the kleptomaniac) and personality disorders (e.g., Murdock) have a defense under a control test? Would Pollard? Would the volitional prong have any significance independently of the cognitive prong?

Tightening the Definition of Volitional Impairment. A final reform, more widely espoused when the volitional prong was first adopted than presently, is to require that the impulsive act be truly "irresistible." This concept has been colloquially captured by the "policeman at the elbow" rubric: would the accused have committed the act had a policeman been present at the time? Even kleptomaniacs try to elude detection, and thus would probably not have a defense under a tightened volitional prong. However, determining whether the impulse was irresistible or merely not resisted will still be difficult for some cases. For instance, Hinckley committed his assassination attempt in the midst of several policemen and Secret Service agents. But was his attempt "irresistible"?

Other ways of conceptualizing volitional impairment that might have the effect of limiting its scope have been proposed. Professor Morse has suggested two. At one time, he proposed that a person might be excused for the criminal act if "the desire or craving was so intense that fear of the pain of not satisfying it was the true motive for offending." Stephen Morse, "Excusing the Crazy: The Insanity Defense Reconsidered," 58 S.Cal. L. Rev. 777, 815 (1985). More recently, he borrowed from the law of duress (which excuses those who commit crime because of unbearable *external* pressures), to derive three criteria for determining when internal coercion should excuse:

> *First*, the person is subjected to an unjustifiable threat, that is a set of circumstances that will make the person worse off compared with some baseline if she doesn't perform the wrongful act.

> *Second*, performing the wrongful act and suffering the threatened consequences for failing to perform it are both aversive choices, but doing the wrongful act is an excusable alternative because it is unfair to require the agent to refrain under the circumstances.

> *Third*, the person is not responsible either for placing herself in or for failing to avoid the circumstances that produced the hard choice.

Stephen Morse, "Culpability and Control," 142 U.Pa.L.Rev. 1587, 1613–14 (1994).

Morse also argues, however, that most cases of internal coercion are better analyzed as cases involving lack of rationality (i.e., *cognitive* impairment). For instance, he contends, "the 'policeman at the elbow' test, which is usually understood as a volitional standard, is ... better interpreted as a rationality test. Those who offend in the face of certain capture have either rationally decided for political or other reasons that the offense is worth the punishment, as in cases of civil disobedience, or they are irrational." Stephen Morse, "Causation, Compulsion and Involuntariness," 22 Bull. Am. Acad. Psych & L. 159, 179 (1994). In this regard, see also Robert Schopp, Automatism, Insanity and the Psychology of Criminal Responsibility (1991), who argues that current control tests are "unnecessary and irrelevant or they are vacuous," id. at 174, and that "severe cognitive psychopathology" should be the sole basis for a volitional impairment excuse. Id. at 202–03. These suggestions may have the same effect as the limitations on the mental disease or defect threshold described above.

3.　*Research on the volitional prong.* Empirical evidence suggests that the concern over mistake or abuse that underlies at least some of the foregoing proposals may be unwarranted. Relying on results obtained by trained mental health professionals using a structured interview format, one study found that, while neither determination is likely to lead to highly reliable results, inter-rater agreement on the volitional and cognitive prongs was virtually identical. Richard Rogers, "Empiricism v. Emotionalism," 42 Am.Psychol. 840, 841–42 (1987). Using the same interview format, a second study found that reliance on the volitional prong resulted in 23.5% fewer insanity recommendations from mental health professionals than did use of the cognitive prong. Richard Rogers & Charles Clark, "Diogenes Revisited: Another Search for the Ultimate NGRI Standard," Paper presented at American Academy of Psychiatry and Law meeting, Albuquerque (October, 1985). Assume that research substantiates that psychiatric assessment of volitional impairment is at least as reliable as assessment of cognitive impairment, as well as less likely to result in acquittal. How would these findings affect your attitude toward eliminating the volitional prong or, if that prong is retained, narrowing the definition of mental disease or defect or increasing the level of control required?

4.　*The Supreme Court and the volitional prong.* Although the Supreme Court has made clear that an insanity defense without a volitional prong is constitutional (see discussion of *Clark v. Arizona* on pp. 551–52), in *Robinson v. California*, 370 U.S. 660, 82 S.Ct. 1417, 8 L.Ed.2d 758 (1962) and *Powell v. Texas*, 392 U.S. 514, 88 S.Ct. 2145, 20 L.Ed.2d 1254 (1968), the Court suggested that some aspects of volition must be considered in gauging criminal liability. *Robinson* held that the Eighth Amendment's prohibition against cruel and unusual punishment bars punishing someone merely for being addicted to heroin. In *Powell* five justices interpreted this holding as a ban on convicting a person for an "irresistible urge," at least under certain circumstances. While the majority in *Powell* decided that an alcoholic could constitutionally by convicted for being drunk *in public*, Justice White wrote a concurring opinion in which he stated that, after *Robinson*, "the chronic alcoholic with an irresistible urge to consume alcohol should not be punishable [merely] for drinking or for being drunk", a statement with which the four dissenters agreed. Does this language, if it reflects the position of a majority of the Court, impose any limitations on the extent to which the state may punish someone who is mentally ill?

5.　*Other cases involving volitional impairment.* Consider whether the individuals in the following cases should be found insane.

Case A. Foreman, age 18, is charged with six counts of arson and, in connection with one of the fires, three counts of murder. His earliest childhood memory was watching a neighbor burn trash in the backyard and he was setting fires around his home at the age of eight. He also set fires on four separate occasions at his high school. At 16 he began calling for emergency assistance from the rescue squad by pretending to be suffocating. He felt a great sense of satisfaction from being cared for by the emergency crews on these occasions. Soon he joined the local squad and became especially close to James, an older member of the squad. Foreman had fantasies of being rescued from a fire by James, and reported sexual arousal in seeing fireman, particularly James, in their rubberized firefighting clothes. He soon began setting fires, hoping that James would arrive. An expert testified that Foreman was suffering from pyromania and that his "need to start the fire [that led to the deaths] in order to bring himself and Carson together was so strong that he unconsciously was able to keep from his awareness the possibility that others might be hurt or that extensive property damages might occur."

Case B. Tally, a 22 year-old college student, is charged with several counts of attempted rape. Immediately prior to each of his offenses, he experienced a powerful impulse to have forcible intercourse with a woman. As he put it, "there was a feeling of real power and hate and anger ... I was really excited sexually. You, I just felt ... there is a word, I can't think of it ..." When he was overcome by these strong urges, Tally would become "panicky". He felt he had to have a woman or he would "go crazy." At times he would be able to stifle the urge by shutting himself up in his room and listening to music, thinking about his girlfriend, or masturbating. At other times, usually after drinking or doing drugs, he would succumb. None of his victims were acquaintances. He says he always became "scared" after entering the homes of his victims, but could not force himself to leave. He would be "horrified" at what he was doing but could not do anything about it. "I would watch myself doing this stuff and I couldn't believe it. One part of me was observing and didn't want to go through it, but I couldn't stop." Other than the intercourse itself, he never physically harmed the victims and he never penetrated the victim's vagina (either because he was unable to obtain an erection or he masturbated). Once through he would apologize, and become depressed at what he had done, but his panicky feeling was gone.

Case C. Gorshen, a person who suffered from chronic schizophrenia, killed his employer. For twenty years he had periods where he hallucinated, seeing and hearing devils committing abnormal sexual acts, sometimes upon Gorshen himself. The hallucinations had increased of late. He had been drinking at work, and when his employer sent him home, a fight ensued. Gorshen went home, got a gun, and shot his employer. Expert testimony claimed that Gorshen's rage was a desperate attempt to ward off the imminent and total disintegration of his personality that would occur through regression into a schizophrenic relapse. (Based on *People v. Gorshen*, 51 Cal.2d 716, 336 P.2d 492 (1959), see pp. 463–64).

B.   THE AUTOMATISM DEFENSE

NOTE ON AUTOMATISM

Except for strict liability offenses, which are not relevant to the topic of this chapter, every crime is comprised of at least two elements:

(1) the physical conduct associated with the crime (known as the "actus reus"); and (2) the mental state, or level of intent, associated with the crime (known as the "mens rea"). To convict an individual of a particular crime, the state must prove beyond a reasonable doubt that the defendant committed the actus reus with the requisite mens rea for that crime.

The automatism defense developed out of the law's attempt to define the actus reus concept. The actus reus contemplates a voluntary physical act. For instance, if A pushes B's arm into C, B cannot be convicted of assault even though B's arm committed the actual touching, because B's act was not voluntary. It could also be said that B did not intend to commit the assault, and thus did not have the mens rea for the crime. But a distinction is usually made between an act over which there is no conscious control and a conscious action with unintended consequences. The assault above is an example of the first type of act and has traditionally been analyzed under the voluntariness requirement of the actus reus. An example of the latter situation would be if B, in tapping C, meant only to frighten him but instead killed him; B's act would be voluntary, but he would not have the mens rea for murder.

The automatism (or "unconsciousness") defense recognizes that some criminal acts may be committed "involuntarily," even though no third party (like A in the example above) is involved. The classic example of the "automaton" is the person who commits an offense while sleepwalking; courts have held that such an individual does not have conscious control of his or her physical actions and therefore acts involuntarily. See, e.g., *Fain v. Commonwealth*, 78 Ky. 183 (1879). Other situations in which the defense might be implicated arise when a crime occurs during a state of unconsciousness induced by concussion following a head injury; by shock created by bullet wounds; or by metabolic disorders such as anoxia, hypoglycemia, or the involuntary ingestion of alcohol or drugs. Events caused by epilepsy are probably best placed in this category as well.

Several courts have limited the automatism defense by holding that a person claiming to have been affected by one of the above-named conditions at the time of the offense cannot prevail with the defense if the disability has been experienced on previous occasions and steps reasonably could have been taken to prevent the criminal occurrence. Thus, if a man knows he is subject to epileptic seizures, loses control of a car because of a seizure, and kills someone in the process, he may not be able to take advantage of the defense. See, e.g., *People v. Decina*, 2 N.Y.2d 133, 157 N.Y.S.2d 558, 138 N.E.2d 799 (1956).

Conceptually, the automatism defense differs from the insanity defense in three ways. First, insane persons, unlike "automatons," are generally conscious of their acts but either do not understand the true nature of the acts or cannot stop themselves from performing them. Second, while there is some dispute over whether sanity is an element that must be proven for each offense, the prosecution clearly bears the burden of establishing the actus reus and thus bears the burden of negating an automatism claim beyond a reasonable doubt. Finally, to prevail, a person alleging insanity must be found to have a mental disease or defect; there is no such requirement when automatism is involved.

Questions and Comments

1. *Application.* As indicated above, the automatism defense contemplates a loss of conscious control over one's bodily movements. Does either Heads or Pollard have a viable automatism claim? In *People v. Lisnow,* 88 Cal.App.3d Supp. 21, 26–27, 151 Cal.Rptr. 621, 623 (1978), the court held that a Vietnam veteran who struck a maitre d' in a restaurant for "no apparent reason" and then went into the parking lot and engaged in other "acts of violence" while in a "dreamlike" state was entitled to an instruction on the automatism defense. See also, Donald Apostle, "The Unconsciousness Defense as Applied to Post Traumatic Stress Disorder in a Vietnam Veteran," 8 Bull.Am.Acad.Psychiat. & L. 426 (1980). In a jurisdiction where the volitional prong of the insanity test is eliminated, would the automatism defense take up the slack? Why or why not?

Consider also cases involving multiple personality disorder. According to DSM–IV (which has re-labeled the diagnosis "dissociative identity disorder"), this diagnosis requires "[t]he presence of two or more distinct identities or personality traits (each with its own relatively enduring pattern of perceiving, relating to, and thinking about the environment and self)" and an "[i]nability to recall important personal information that is too extensive to be explained by ordinary forgetfulness." In *United States v. Denny–Shaffer,* 2 F.3d 999 (10th Cir.1993), the defendant kidnapped an infant while impersonating a medical student; she was later found by her former boyfriend with the child in his bed, blood on the sheets, a human placenta in a bag, and claiming to have just given birth to the child. Defense and prosecution experts agreed that she had a "host," or dominant, personality and several different "alter" personalities, that the host did not control the alters, and that none of the personalities were necessarily aware of the others' actions. Both experts also agreed that two alters were in control during the planning of the abduction, the act itself, and the ensuing travel, but they could not agree on what role, if any, the host personality may have played. Neither expert was willing to testify that the alters, by themselves, met the test for insanity. Based on the experts' ambivalence about the latter issue, the trial court held that there was insufficient evidence to support an insanity verdict, but the Tenth Circuit reversed, holding that the issue should have been whether the dominant personality was unaware of the offense, or not in control when it took place.

Consider also *Washington v. Wheaton,* 121 Wash.2d 347, 850 P.2d 507 (1993), where the parties agreed that the defendant, charged with first-degree theft, had multiple personalities, and also agreed that the host personality was "not conscious or in executive control of the physical body and ha[d] no independent knowledge of the acts constituting the offense." The trial court nonetheless rejected the defendant's insanity claim, on the ground that the alter in control at the time of the offense was not insane. On appeal, the Washington Supreme Court admitted that multiple personality disorder was recognized in DSM–III–R, but held that not enough was known about the nature of the disorder to decide whether the insanity assessment should be based on the sanity of the alter or instead on the extent to which the host was aware of the alter's actions; it then affirmed the conviction. In light of the automatism analysis described above, is the insanity defense the proper rubric for analyzing multiple personality cases?

Professor Saks argues that people with multiple personalities should be presumed *non*responsible for crimes they commit, either because they do not know the nature of their act, could not control it, or do not deserve punishment on characterological grounds. However, she would allow the presumption of nonresponsibility to be rebutted in those "rare" situations when: (1) "all of a multiple's alters know about and acquiesce in the crime;" (2) "the host personality commits the crime and the appearance of other alters is so extremely limited that punishing the person/body does not seem problematic;" and (3) a multiple "has a ringleader alter in addition to well-established lines of responsibility for different tasks [such that] each alter has sufficient knowledge and control over the others that group liability makes sense." Elyn Saks, "Multiple Personality Disorder and Criminal Responsibility," 25 U.C. Davis L. Rev. 383, 452–54 (1992). She also argues that knowledge that one is a multiple should *not* lead to rebuttal of the presumption, because, in contrast to the person who knows he or she suffers from epilepsy, the multiple would have to take drastic steps (i.e., commit oneself) in order to avoid possible harm: "we simply cannot penalize people for failing to do what only the most saintly would do." Id. at 454–57.

2. *Incapacitation concerns.* Most commentators agree that an epileptic seizure is best characterized as an involuntary act rather than an "irresistible impulse," because the seizure is not triggered by the individual's conscious, or even unconscious, processes. Yet courts in Britain, where the law of automatism is well developed, have rejected automatism defenses based on epilepsy and instead have permitted only claims of insanity in such cases, on the explicit ground that to do otherwise would result in immediate release of dangerous individuals. See, e.g., *Bratty v. Attorney–General for Northern Ireland,* 3 All E.R. 523 (1961). Why might commitment statutes for insanity acquittees not apply to those acquitted on an automatism defense? Is there any way to avoid distorting the insanity doctrine while at the same time protecting the public in the latter type of case?

C. EXPERT TESTIMONY ON MENS REA (THE DIMINISHED CAPACITY DOCTRINE)

NOTE ON MENS REA

The principal device the law uses to grade culpability of sane individuals is mental state. A person who deliberately plans a crime is more culpable than one who accidentally commits one. Under the common law, courts developed literally scores of "mens rea" terms to describe various levels of culpability. Unfortunately, these terms—"willful and wanton," "with a depraved heart," and so on—were more colorful than descriptive. Over the years, two generic categories were created to help categorize these diverse mental states, although they were only partially successful in doing so. "Specific intent" was meant to designate the mens rea for those crimes that require a further intention beyond that identified with the physical act connected with the offense (e.g., "premeditated" murder, "aggravated" assault, assault "with intent to rape"). "General intent" crimes, on the other hand, were those that merely required proof that the defendant was conscious or should have been conscious of his or her physical actions at the time of the offense (e.g., manslaughter, assault, rape).

Because neither the original mens rea terms nor the concepts of specific and general intent were necessarily self-defining, modern statutory codes have attempted to be more precise on issues relating to mental state. Most influential in this regard has been the ALI's Model Penal Code formulation, which attempts to simplify the mens rea inquiry by specifying a total of four levels of mens rea. In descending order of culpability, they are (1) "purpose," requiring proof that the offender intended the relevant conduct or result; (2) "knowledge," requiring proof that the offender was aware of the conduct or result; (3) "recklessness," requiring proof that the offender consciously disregarded "a substantial and unjustifiable risk" that he or she was engaging in the conduct or causing a result; and (4) "negligence," requiring proof that the offender should have been aware of "a substantial and unjustifiable risk" that he or she was engaging in the conduct or causing a result. The first two mental states clearly focus on subjective mental state, "negligence" is commonly said to be objectively defined, and "recklessness" falls somewhere in between. Although the common-law terms are so amorphous that equating them with Model Penal Code mental states is a somewhat risky venture, it is probably fair to say that "specific intent" most closely coincides with "purpose" and "knowledge," while "general intent" can be analogized to "recklessness" and "negligence."

As will become clear below, distinguishing between subjective mental states (purpose, knowledge, and specific intent) and objectively defined mental states (negligence, general intent) is important in understanding the courts' approach to clinical input on mens rea. It is also important to recognize that the mens rea inquiry described above is quite distinct from the insanity inquiry. While it may be true that persons who meet the M'Naghten test may also be incapable of forming the requisite intent for an offense, it is theoretically and practically possible for insane persons to have the appropriate mens rea. Their *reasons* for committing acts may be so "crazy" that no jury would be willing to hold them criminally responsible, even though their knowledge of what they were doing was relatively unimpaired. To use the *M'Naghten* case as an example, Daniel M'Naghten probably met the mens rea requirements for the crime charged (i.e., knowingly shooting at another with the purpose of killing him), but he was nonetheless found insane.

Out of this distinction has developed the so-called "diminished capacity" concept. In its broadest sense, the diminished capacity doctrine permits the accused to introduce clinical testimony focusing directly on the mens rea for the crime charged, without having to assert an insanity defense.[k] If the testimony negates the mens rea, the defendant is acquitted only of that charge and may still be prosecuted on lesser charges. Thus, a person charged with first degree murder might be able to escape conviction on that charge if clinical testimony shows that he or she did not kill purposely or knowingly (or with specific intent). However, conviction may still occur on a lesser charge requiring a lesser intent (e.g. manslaughter or assault). The following materials evaluate the ramifications of this idea.

CLARK v. ARIZONA

Supreme Court of the United States, 2007.
548 U.S. 735, 126 S.Ct. 2709, 165 L.Ed.2d 842.

JUSTICE SOUTER delivered the opinion of the Court.

* * *

In the early hours of June 21, 2000, Officer Jeffrey Moritz of the Flagstaff Police responded in uniform to complaints that a pickup truck with loud music blaring was circling a residential block. When he located the truck, the officer turned on the emergency lights and siren of his marked patrol car, which prompted petitioner Eric Clark, the truck's driver (then 17), to pull over. Officer Moritz got out of the patrol car and told Clark to stay where he was. Less than a minute later, Clark shot the officer, who died soon after but not before calling the police dispatcher for help. Clark ran away on foot but was arrested later that day with gunpowder residue on his hands; the gun that killed the officer was found nearby, stuffed into a knit cap.

Clark was charged with first-degree murder under Ariz.Rev.Stat. Ann. 13–1105(A)(3) for intentionally or knowingly killing a law enforcement officer in the line of duty.[1] In March 2001, Clark was found incompetent to stand trial and was committed to a state hospital for treatment, but two years later the same trial court found his competence restored and ordered him to be tried. Clark waived his right to a jury, and the case was heard by the court. At trial, Clark did not contest the shooting and death, but relied on his undisputed paranoid schizophrenia at the time of the incident in denying that he had the specific intent to

---

k. As the American Bar Association has pointed out, the phrase "diminished capacity" can be misleading since it implies a "quasi-insanity defense" that the defendant must prove, when in fact the underlying notion is merely a recognition that clinical testimony may be just as relevant to the mens rea inquiry as evidence of mistake or intoxication. See commentary to ABA Criminal Justice Mental Health Standard 7–6.2. This book will nonetheless use the phrase "diminished capacity doctrine" because, as subsequent materials make clear, most jurisdictions have developed special rules with respect to clinical mens rea testimony that go far beyond the simple relevance notion that usually applies to other mens rea testimony. At the same time, in recognition of the fact that the prosecution bears the burden of proving beyond a reasonable doubt that the defendant had the requisite mens rea, this book avoids calling the diminished capacity notion a "defense."

1. Section 13–1105(A)(3) provides that "[a] person commits first degree murder if ... [i]ntending or knowing that the person's conduct will cause death to a law enforcement officer, the person causes the death of a law enforcement officer who is in the line of duty."

shoot a law enforcement officer or knowledge that he was doing so, as required by the statute. Accordingly, the prosecutor offered circumstantial evidence that Clark knew Officer Moritz was a law enforcement officer. The evidence showed that the officer was in uniform at the time, that he caught up with Clark in a marked police car with emergency lights and siren going, and that Clark acknowledged the symbols of police authority and stopped. The testimony for the prosecution indicated that Clark had intentionally lured an officer to the scene to kill him, having told some people a few weeks before the incident that he wanted to shoot police officers. At the close of the State's evidence, the trial court denied Clark's motion for judgment of acquittal for failure to prove intent to kill a law enforcement officer or knowledge that Officer Moritz was a law enforcement officer.

In presenting the defense case, Clark claimed mental illness, which he sought to introduce for two purposes. First, he raised the affirmative defense of insanity, putting the burden on himself to prove by clear and convincing evidence that "at the time of the commission of the criminal act [he] was afflicted with a mental disease or defect of such severity that [he] did not know the criminal act was wrong". Second, he aimed to rebut the prosecution's evidence of the requisite *mens rea,* that he had acted intentionally or knowingly to kill a law enforcement officer.

The trial court ruled that Clark could not rely on evidence bearing on insanity to dispute the *mens rea.* The court cited *State v. Mott,* 187 Ariz. 536, 931 P.2d 1046 (en banc), cert. denied, 520 U.S. 1234 (1997), which "refused to allow psychiatric testimony to negate specific intent," and held that "Arizona does not allow evidence of a defendant's mental disorder short of insanity ... to negate the *mens rea* element of a crime." As to his insanity, then, Clark presented testimony from classmates, school officials, and his family describing his increasingly bizarre behavior over the year before the shooting. Witnesses testified, for example, that paranoid delusions led Clark to rig a fishing line with beads and wind chimes at home to alert him to intrusion by invaders, and to keep a bird in his automobile to warn of airborne poison. There was lay and expert testimony that Clark thought Flagstaff was populated with "aliens" (some impersonating government agents), the "aliens" were trying to kill him, and bullets were the only way to stop them. A psychiatrist testified that Clark was suffering from paranoid schizophrenia with delusions about "aliens" when he killed Officer Moritz, and he concluded that Clark was incapable of luring the officer or understanding right from wrong and that he was thus insane at the time of the killing. In rebuttal, a psychiatrist for the State gave his opinion that Clark's paranoid schizophrenia did not keep him from appreciating the wrongfulness of his conduct, as shown by his actions before and after the shooting (such as circling the residential block with music blaring as if to lure the police to intervene, evading the police after the shooting, and hiding the gun).

At the close of the defense case consisting of this evidence bearing on mental illness, the trial court denied Clark's renewed motion for a directed verdict grounded on failure of the prosecution to show that Clark knew the victim was a police officer. The judge then issued a special verdict of first-degree murder, expressly finding that Clark shot and caused the death of Officer Moritz beyond a reasonable doubt and that Clark had not shown that he was insane at the time. The judge noted that though Clark was indisputably afflicted with paranoid schizophrenia at the time of the shooting, the mental illness "did not . . . distort his perception of reality so severely that he did not know his actions were wrong." For this conclusion, the judge expressly relied on "the facts of the crime, the evaluations of the experts, [Clark's] actions and behavior both before and after the shooting, and the observations of those that knew [Clark]." The sentence was life imprisonment without the possibility of release for 25 years.

Clark moved to vacate the judgment and sentence, arguing, among other things, that Arizona's insanity test and its *Mott* rule each violate due process. . . . The court denied the motion.

The Court of Appeals of Arizona affirmed Clark's conviction, treating the conclusion on sanity as supported by enough evidence to withstand review for abuse of discretion, and holding the State's insanity scheme consistent with due process. . . . Beyond that, the appellate court followed *Mott*, reading it as barring the trial court's consideration of evidence of Clark's mental illness and capacity directly on the element of *mens rea*. The Supreme Court of Arizona denied further review.

We granted certiorari to decide whether due process prohibits Arizona from thus narrowing its insanity test or from excluding evidence of mental illness and incapacity due to mental illness to rebut evidence of the requisite criminal intent. We now affirm.

* * *

[The Court's analysis of why Arizona's insanity test does not violate due process is found on pp. 551–52]

* * *

Clark's second claim of a due process violation challenges the rule adopted by the Supreme Court of Arizona in *State v. Mott*. This case ruled on the admissibility of testimony from a psychologist offered to show that the defendant suffered from battered women's syndrome and therefore lacked the capacity to form the *mens rea* of the crime charged against her. The opinion variously referred to the testimony in issue as "psychological testimony," and "expert testimony,"and implicitly equated it with "expert psychiatric evidence" and "psychiatric testimony". The state court held that testimony of a professional psychologist or psychiatrist about a defendant's mental incapacity owing to mental disease or defect was admissible, and could be considered, only for its bearing on an insanity defense; such evidence could not be considered on the element of *mens rea*, that is, what the State must show about a defendant's mental state (such as intent or understanding) when he performed the act charged against him.

Understanding Clark's claim requires attention to the categories of evidence with a potential bearing on *mens rea*. First, there is "observation evidence" in the everyday sense, testimony from those who observed what Clark did and heard what he said; this category would also include testimony that an expert witness might give about Clark's tendency to think in a certain way and his behavioral characteristics. This evidence may support a professional diagnosis of mental disease and in any event is the kind of evidence that can be relevant to show what in fact was on Clark's mind when he fired the gun. Observation evidence in the record covers Clark's behavior at home and with friends, his expressions of belief around the time of the killing that "aliens" were inhabiting the bodies of local people (including government agents),[27] his driving around the neighborhood before the police arrived, and so on. Contrary to the dissent's characterization, observation evidence can be presented by either lay or expert witnesses.

Second, there is "mental-disease evidence" in the form of opinion testimony that Clark suffered from a mental disease with features described by the witness. As was true here, this evidence characteristically but not always comes from professional psychologists or psychiatrists who testify as expert witnesses and base their opinions in part on examination of a defendant, usually conducted after the events in question. The thrust of this evidence was that, based on factual reports, professional observations, and tests, Clark was psychotic at the time in question, with a condition that fell within the category of schizophrenia.

Third, there is evidence we will refer to as "capacity evidence" about a defendant's capacity for cognition and moral judgment (and ultimately also his capacity to form *mens rea*). This, too, is opinion evidence. Here, as it usually does, this testimony came from the same experts and concentrated on those specific details of the mental condition that make the difference between sanity and insanity under the Arizona definition. In their respective testimony on these details the experts disagreed: the defense expert gave his opinion that the symptoms or effects of the disease in Clark's case included inability to appreciate the nature of his action and to tell that it was wrong, whereas the State's psychiatrist was of the view that Clark was a schizophrenic who was still sufficiently able to appreciate the reality of shooting the officer and to know that it was wrong to do that....

It is clear that *Mott* itself imposed no restriction on considering evidence of the first sort, the observation evidence. We read the *Mott* restriction to apply, rather, to evidence addressing the two issues in testimony that characteristically comes only from psychologists or psy-

27. Clark's parents testified that, in the months before the shooting and even days beforehand, Clark called them "aliens" and thought that "aliens" were out to get him. One night before the shooting, according to Clark's mother, Clark repeatedly viewed a popular film characterized by her as telling a story about "aliens" masquerading as government agents, a story Clark insisted was real despite his mother's protestations to the contrary. And two months after the shooting, Clark purportedly told his parents that his hometown, Flagstaff, was inhabited principally by "aliens," who had to be stopped, and that the only way to stop them was with bullets.

chiatrists qualified to give opinions as expert witnesses: mental-disease evidence (whether at the time of the crime a defendant suffered from a mental disease or defect, such as schizophrenia) and capacity evidence (whether the disease or defect left him incapable of performing or experiencing a mental process defined as necessary for sanity such as appreciating the nature and quality of his act and knowing that it was wrong).

* * *

Clark's argument that the *Mott* rule violates the Fourteenth Amendment guarantee of due process turns on the application of the ... principle that a criminal defendant is entitled to present relevant and favorable evidence on an element of the offense charged against him....[28] As already noted, evidence tending to show that a defendant suffers from mental disease and lacks capacity to form *mens rea* is relevant to rebut evidence that he did in fact form the required *mens rea* at the time in question; this is the reason that Clark claims a right to require the factfinder in this case to consider testimony about his mental illness and his incapacity directly, when weighing the persuasiveness of other evidence tending to show *mens rea,* which the prosecution has the burden to prove.

As Clark recognizes, however, the right to introduce relevant evidence can be curtailed if there is a good reason for doing that. "While the Constitution ... prohibits the exclusion of defense evidence under rules that serve no legitimate purpose or that are disproportionate to the ends that they are asserted to promote, well-established rules of evidence permit trial judges to exclude evidence if its probative value is outweighed by certain other factors such as unfair prejudice, confusion of the issues, or potential to mislead the jury." And if evidence may be kept out entirely, its consideration may be subject to limitation, which Arizona claims the power to impose here. State law says that evidence of mental disease and incapacity may be introduced and considered, and if sufficiently forceful to satisfy the defendant's burden of proof under the insanity rule it will displace the presumption of sanity and excuse from criminal responsibility. But mental-disease and capacity evidence may be considered only for its bearing on the insanity defense, and it will avail a defendant only if it is persuasive enough to satisfy the defendant's burden as defined by the terms of that defense. The mental-disease and capacity evidence is thus being channeled or restricted to one issue and given effect only if the defendant carries the burden to convince the factfinder of insanity; the evidence is not being excluded entirely, and the question is whether reasons for requiring it to be channeled and restricted are good enough to satisfy the standard of fundamental fairness that due process requires. We think they are.

---

28. Clark's argument assumes that Arizona's rule is a rule of evidence, rather than a redefinition of *mens rea,* see *Montana v. Egelhoff,* 518 U.S. 37, 58–59, 116 S.Ct. 2013, 135 L.Ed.2d 361 (1996) (GINSBURG, J., concurring in judgment); *id.,* at 71, 116 S.Ct. 2013 (O'Connor, J., dissenting). We have no reason to view the rule otherwise, and on this assumption, it does not violate due process.

The first reason supporting the *Mott* rule is Arizona's authority to define its presumption of sanity (or capacity or responsibility) by choosing an insanity definition, ... and by placing the burden of persuasion on defendants who claim incapacity as an excuse from customary criminal responsibility. No one, certainly not Clark here, denies that a State may place a burden of persuasion on a defendant claiming insanity. And Clark presses no objection to Arizona's decision to require persuasion to a clear and convincing degree before the presumption of sanity and normal responsibility is overcome.

But if a State is to have this authority in practice as well as in theory, it must be able to deny a defendant the opportunity to displace the presumption of sanity more easily when addressing a different issue in the course of the criminal trial. Yet ... just such an opportunity would be available if expert testimony of mental disease and incapacity could be considered for whatever a factfinder might think it was worth on the issue of *mens rea*. [T]he presumption of sanity would then be only as strong as the evidence a factfinder would accept as enough to raise a reasonable doubt about *mens rea* for the crime charged; once reasonable doubt was found, acquittal would be required, and the standards established for the defense of insanity would go by the boards.

Now, a State is of course free to accept such a possibility in its law. After all, it is free to define the insanity defense by treating the presumption of sanity as a bursting bubble, whose disappearance shifts the burden to the prosecution to prove sanity whenever a defendant presents any credible evidence of mental disease or incapacity. In States with this kind of insanity rule, the legislature may well be willing to allow such evidence to be considered on the *mens rea* element for whatever the factfinder thinks it is worth. What counts for due process, however, is simply that a State that wishes to avoid a second avenue for exploring capacity, less stringent for a defendant, has a good reason for confining the consideration of evidence of mental disease and incapacity to the insanity defense.

It is obvious that Arizona's *Mott* rule reflects such a choice. The State Supreme Court pointed out that the State had declined to adopt a defense of diminished capacity (allowing a jury to decide when to excuse a defendant because of greater than normal difficulty in conforming to the law). The court reasoned that the State's choice would be undercut if evidence of incapacity could be considered for whatever a jury might think sufficient to raise a reasonable doubt about *mens rea*, even if it did not show insanity. In other words, if a jury were free to decide how much evidence of mental disease and incapacity was enough to counter evidence of *mens rea* to the point of creating a reasonable doubt, that would in functional terms be analogous to allowing jurors to decide upon some degree of diminished capacity to obey the law, a degree set by them, that would prevail as a stand-alone defense.[42]

42. It is beyond question that Arizona may preclude such a defense, see *Fisher v.* *United States*, 328 U.S. 463, 466–476, 66 S.Ct. 1318, 90 L.Ed. 1382 (1946), and there

A State's insistence on preserving its chosen standard of legal insanity cannot be the sole reason for a rule like *Mott,* however, for it fails to answer an objection the dissent makes in this case. An insanity rule gives a defendant already found guilty the opportunity to excuse his conduct by showing he was insane when he acted, that is, that he did not have the mental capacity for conventional guilt and criminal responsibility. But, as the dissent argues, if the same evidence that affirmatively shows he was not guilty by reason of insanity (or "guilty except insane" under Arizona law) also shows it was at least doubtful that he could form *mens rea,* then he should not be found guilty in the first place; it thus violates due process when the State impedes him from using mental-disease and capacity evidence directly to rebut the prosecution's evidence that he did form *mens rea.*

Are there, then, characteristics of mental-disease and capacity evidence giving rise to risks that may reasonably be hedged by channeling the consideration of such evidence to the insanity issue on which, in States like Arizona, a defendant has the burden of persuasion? We think there are: in the controversial character of some categories of mental disease, in the potential of mental-disease evidence to mislead, and in the danger of according greater certainty to capacity evidence than experts claim for it.

To begin with, the diagnosis may mask vigorous debate within the profession about the very contours of the mental disease itself. And Members of this Court have previously recognized that the end of such debate is not imminent. Though we certainly do not "condem[n mental-disease evidence] wholesale," the consequence of this professional ferment is a general caution in treating psychological classifications as predicates for excusing otherwise criminal conduct.

Next, there is the potential of mental-disease evidence to mislead jurors (when they are the factfinders) through the power of this kind of evidence to suggest that a defendant suffering from a recognized mental disease lacks cognitive, moral, volitional, or other capacity, when that may not be a sound conclusion at all. Even when a category of mental disease is broadly accepted and the assignment of a defendant's behavior to that category is uncontroversial, the classification may suggest something very significant about a defendant's capacity, when in fact the classification tells us little or nothing about the ability of the defendant to form *mens rea* or to exercise the cognitive, moral, or volitional capacities that define legal sanity. The limits of the utility of a professional disease diagnosis are evident in the dispute between the two

is no doubt that the Arizona Legislature meant to do so, see Ariz.Rev.Stat. Ann. § 13–502(A) (West 2001) ("Mental disease or defect does not include disorders that result from acute voluntary intoxication or withdrawal from alcohol or drugs, character defects, psychosexual disorders or impulse control disorders. Conditions that do not constitute legal insanity include but are not limited to momentary, temporary conditions arising from the pressure of the circumstances, moral decadence, depravity or passion growing out of anger, jealousy, revenge, hatred or other motives in a person who does not suffer from a mental disease or defect or an abnormality that is manifested only by criminal conduct").

testifying experts in this case; they agree that Clark was schizophrenic, but they come to opposite conclusions on whether the mental disease in his particular case left him bereft of cognitive or moral capacity. Evidence of mental disease, then, can easily mislead; it is very easy to slide from evidence that an individual with a professionally recognized mental disease is very different, into doubting that he has the capacity to form *mens rea,* whereas that doubt may not be justified. And of course, in the cases mentioned before, in which the categorization is doubtful or the category of mental disease is itself subject to controversy, the risks are even greater that opinions about mental disease may confuse a jury into thinking the opinions show more than they do. Because allowing mental-disease evidence on *mens rea* can thus easily mislead, it is not unreasonable to address that tendency by confining consideration of this kind of evidence to insanity, on which a defendant may be assigned the burden of persuasion.

There are, finally, particular risks inherent in the opinions of the experts who supplement the mental-disease classifications with opinions on incapacity: on whether the mental disease rendered a particular defendant incapable of the cognition necessary for moral judgment or *mens rea* or otherwise incapable of understanding the wrongfulness of the conduct charged. Unlike observational evidence bearing on *mens rea,* capacity evidence consists of judgment, and judgment fraught with multiple perils: a defendant's state of mind at the crucial moment can be elusive no matter how conscientious the enquiry, and the law's categories that set the terms of the capacity judgment are not the categories of psychology that govern the expert's professional thinking. Although such capacity judgments may be given in the utmost good faith, their potentially tenuous character is indicated by the candor of the defense expert in this very case. Contrary to the State's expert, he testified that Clark lacked the capacity to appreciate the circumstances realistically and to understand the wrongfulness of what he was doing, but he said that "no one knows exactly what was on [his] mind" at the time of the shooting. And even when an expert is confident that his understanding of the mind is reliable, judgment addressing the basic categories of capacity requires a leap from the concepts of psychology, which are devised for thinking about treatment, to the concepts of legal sanity, which are devised for thinking about criminal responsibility. See ... P. Giannelli & E. Imwinkelried, Scientific Evidence § 9–3(B), p. 286 (1986) ("[N]o matter how the test for insanity is phrased, a psychiatrist or psychologist is no more qualified than any other person to give an opinion about whether a particular defendant's mental condition satisfies the legal test for insanity"); cf. R. Slovenko, Psychiatry and Criminal Culpability 55 (1995) ("The scope of the DSM is wide-ranging and includes 'conduct disorders' but 'evil' is not mentioned"). In sum, these empirical and conceptual problems add up to a real risk that an expert's judgment in giving capacity evidence will come with an apparent authority that psychologists and psychiatrists do not claim to have. We think that this risk, like the difficulty in assessing the significance of mental-disease evidence, supports the State's decision to channel such expert testimony to consideration on the insanity defense, on which the party seeking the benefit of this evidence has the burden of persuasion.

It bears repeating that not every State will find it worthwhile to make the judgment Arizona has made, and the choices the States do make about dealing with the risks posed by mental-disease and capacity evidence will reflect their varying assessments about the presumption of sanity as expressed in choices of insanity rules. The point here simply is that Arizona has sensible reasons to assign the risks as it has done by channeling the evidence.[45]

* * *

The judgment of the Court of Appeals of Arizona is, accordingly, affirmed.

It is so ordered.

JUSTICE BREYER, concurring in part and dissenting in part [deleted].

JUSTICE KENNEDY, with whom JUSTICE STEVENS and JUSTICE GINSBURG join, dissenting.

In my submission the Court is incorrect in holding that Arizona may convict petitioner Eric Clark of first-degree murder for the intentional or knowing killing of a police officer when Clark was not permitted to introduce critical and reliable evidence showing he did not have that intent or knowledge. . . .

The Court . . . adopts an evidentiary framework that, in my view, will be unworkable in many cases. The Court classifies Clark's behavior and expressed beliefs as observation evidence but insists that its description by experts must be mental-disease evidence or capacity evidence. These categories break down quickly when it is understood how the testimony would apply to the question of intent and knowledge at issue here. The most common type of schizophrenia, and the one Clark suffered from, is paranoid schizophrenia. The existence of this functional psychosis is beyond dispute, but that does not mean the lay witness understands it or that a disputed issue of fact concerning its effect in a particular instance is not something for the expert to address. Common symptoms of the condition are delusions accompanied by hallucinations, often of the auditory type, which can cause disturbances of perception. Clark's expert testified that people with schizophrenia often play radios

---

45. Arizona's rule is supported by a further practical reason, though not as weighty as those just considered. As mentioned before, if substantial mental-disease and capacity evidence is accepted as rebutting *mens rea* in a given case, the affirmative defense of insanity will probably not be reached or ruled upon; the defendant will simply be acquitted (or perhaps convicted of a lesser included offense). If an acquitted defendant suffers from a mental disease or defect that makes him dangerous, he will neither be confined nor treated psychiatrically unless a judge so orders after some independent commitment proceeding. But if a defendant succeeds in showing himself insane, Arizona law (and presumably that of every other State with an insanity rule) will require commitment and treatment as a consequence of that finding without more. It makes sense, then, to channel capacity evidence to the issue structured to deal with mental incapacity when such a claim is raised successfully. . . .

loudly to drown out the voices in their heads. Clark's attorney argued to the trial court that this, rather than a desire to lure a policeman to the scene, explained Clark's behavior just before the killing. The observation that schizophrenics play radios loudly is a fact regarding behavior, but it is only a relevant fact if Clark has schizophrenia.

Even if this evidence were, to use the Court's term, mental-disease evidence, because it relies on an expert opinion, what would happen if the expert simply were to testify, without mentioning schizophrenia, that people with Clark's symptoms often play the radio loudly? This seems to be factual evidence, as the term is defined by the Court, yet it differs from mental-disease evidence only in forcing the witness to pretend that no one has yet come up with a way to classify the set of symptoms being described. More generally, the opinion that Clark had paranoid schizophrenia-an opinion shared by experts for both the prosecution and defense-bears on efforts to determine, as a factual matter, whether he knew he was killing a police officer. The psychiatrist's explanation of Clark's condition was essential to understanding how he processes sensory data and therefore to deciding what information was in his mind at the time of the shooting. Simply put, knowledge relies on cognition, and cognition can be affected by schizophrenia. The mental-disease evidence at trial was also intertwined with the observation evidence because it lent needed credibility. Clark's parents and friends testified Clark thought the people in his town were aliens trying to kill him. These claims might not be believable without a psychiatrist confirming the story based on his experience with people who have exhibited similar behaviors. It makes little sense to divorce the observation evidence from the explanation that makes it comprehensible.

* * *

The central theory of Clark's defense was that his schizophrenia made him delusional. He lived in a universe where the delusions were so dominant, the theory was, that he had no intent to shoot a police officer or knowledge he was doing so. It is one thing to say he acted with intent or knowledge to pull the trigger. It is quite another to say he pulled the trigger to kill someone he knew to be a human being and a police officer. If the trier of fact were to find Clark's evidence sufficient to discount the case made by the State, which has the burden to prove knowledge or intent as an element of the offense, Clark would not be guilty of first-degree murder under Arizona law.

The Court attempts to diminish Clark's interest by treating mental-illness evidence as concerning only "judgment," rather than fact. This view appears to derive from the Court's characterization of Clark's claim as raising only general incapacity. This is wrong for the reasons already discussed. It fails to recognize, moreover, the meaning of the offense element in question here. The *mens rea* element of intent or knowledge may, at some level, comprise certain moral choices, but it rests in the first instance on a factual determination. That is the fact Clark sought to put in issue. Either Clark knew he was killing a police officer or he did not.

The issue is not, as the Court insists, whether Clark's mental illness acts as an "excuse from customary criminal responsibility," but whether his mental illness, as a factual matter, made him unaware that he was shooting a police officer. If it did, Clark needs no excuse, as then he did not commit the crime as Arizona defines it. For the elements of first-degree murder, where the question is knowledge of particular facts-that one is killing a police officer-the determination depends not on moral responsibility but on empirical fact. Clark's evidence of mental illness had a direct and substantial bearing upon what he knew, or thought he knew, to be the facts when he pulled the trigger; this lay at the heart of the matter.

The trial court's exclusion was all the more severe because it barred from consideration on the issue of *mens rea* all this evidence, from any source, thus preventing Clark from showing he did not commit the crime as defined by Arizona law. Quite apart from due process principles, we have held that a bar of this sort can be inconsistent with the Confrontation Clause. See *Delaware v. Van Arsdall*, 475 U.S. 673, 106 S.Ct. 1431, 89 L.Ed.2d 674 (1986). In *Van Arsdall* the Court held a state court erred in making a ruling that "prohibited *all* inquiry into" an event. At issue was a line of defense questioning designed to show the bias of a prosecution witness. In the instant case the ruling in question bars from consideration all testimony from all witnesses necessary to present the argument that was central to the whole case for the defense: a challenge to the State's own proof on an element of the crime. The Due Process and Compulsory Process Clauses, and not the Confrontation Clause, may be the controlling standard; but the disability imposed on the accused is every bit as substantial and pervasive here as it was in *Van Arsdall*.

Arizona's rule is problematic because it excludes evidence no matter how credible and material it may be in disproving an element of the offense. The Court's cases have noted the potential arbitrariness of *per se* exclusions and, on this rationale, have invalidated various state prohibitions. . . . This is not to suggest all general rules on the exclusion of certain types of evidence are invalid. If the rule does not substantially burden the defense, then it is likely permissible. Where, however, the burden is substantial, the State must present a valid reason for its *per se* evidentiary rule.

In the instant case Arizona's proposed reasons are insufficient to support its categorical exclusion. While the State contends that testimony regarding mental illness may be too incredible or speculative for the jury to consider, this does not explain why the exclusion applies in all cases to all evidence of mental illness. "A State's legitimate interest in barring unreliable evidence does not extend to *per se* exclusions that may be reliable in an individual case." *Rock v. Arkansas*, 483 U.S., at 61, 107 S.Ct. 2704 [striking down statute that categorically prohibited defense use of hypnotically-induced statements]. States have certain discretion to bar unreliable or speculative testimony and to adopt rules to ensure the reliability of expert testimony. Arizona has done so, and there is no reason to believe its rules are insufficient to avoid speculative evidence of mental illness. This is particularly true because Arizona applies its usual case-by-case approach to permit admission of evidence of mental illness for a variety of other purposes. See, *e.g., State v. Lindsey,* 149 Ariz. 472, 474–475, 720 P.2d 73, 74–75 (1986) (en banc) (psychological characteristics of molestation victims); *State v. Hamilton,* 177 Ariz. 403, 408–410, 868 P.2d 986, 991–993 (App.1993) (psychological evidence of child abuse accommodation syndrome); *Horan v. Indus. Comm'n,* 167 Ariz. 322, 325–326, 806 P.2d 911, 914–915 (App.1991) (psychiatric testimony regarding neurological deficits).

The risk of jury confusion also fails to justify the rule. The State defends its rule as a means to avoid the complexities of determining how and to what degree a mental illness affects a person's mental state. The difficulty of resolving a factual issue, though, does not present a sufficient reason to take evidence away from the jury even when it is crucial for the defense. "We have always trusted juries to sort through complex facts in various areas of law." Even were the risk of jury confusion real enough to justify excluding evidence in most cases, this would provide little basis for prohibiting all evidence of mental illness without any inquiry into its likely effect on the jury or its role in deciding the linchpin issue of knowledge and intent. Indeed, Arizona has a rule in place to serve this very purpose.

Even assuming the reliability and jury-confusion justifications were persuasive in some cases, they would not suffice here. It does not overcome the constitutional objection to say that an evidentiary rule that is reasonable on its face can be applied as well to bar significant defense evidence without any rational basis for doing so. In *Van Arsdall,* for example, the Court rejected the application of Delaware Rule of Evidence 403, which allows relevant evidence to be excluded where its probative value is substantially outweighed by the risk of unfair prejudice or other harms to the trial process. While the Rule is well established and designed for a legitimate function, the Constitution prevented an application that deprived the defendant of all inquiry into an important issue. Other cases have applied this same case-specific analysis in deciding the legitimacy of an exclusion. See, *e.g., Rock, supra,* at 62, 107 S.Ct. 2704 (the "circumstances present an argument for admissibility of petitioner's testimony in this particular case, an argument that must be considered by the trial court").

The Court undertakes little analysis of the interests particular to this case. By proceeding in this way it devalues Clark's constitutional rights. The reliability rationale has minimal applicability here. The Court is correct that many mental diseases are difficult to define and the subject of great debate. Schizophrenia, however, is a well-documented mental illness, and no one seriously disputes either its definition or its most prominent clinical manifestations. The State's own expert conceded that Clark had paranoid schizophrenia and was actively psychotic at the time of the killing. The jury-confusion rationale, if it is at all applicable here, is the result of the Court's own insistence on conflating the insanity defense and the question of intent. Considered on its own terms, the issue of intent and knowledge is a straightforward factual question. A trier of fact is quite capable of weighing defense testimony and then determining whether the accused did or did not intend to kill or knowingly kill a human being who was a police officer. True, the issue can be difficult to decide in particular instances, but no more so than many matters juries must confront.

The Court says mental-illness evidence "can easily mislead," and may "tel[l] us little or nothing about the ability of the defendant to form *mens rea.*" These generalities do not, however, show how relevant or misleading the evidence in this case would be (or explain why Arizona Rule of Evidence 403 is insufficient for weighing these factors). As explained above, the evidence of Clark's mental illness bears directly on *mens rea,* for it suggests Clark may not have known he was killing a human being. It is striking that while the Court discusses at length the likelihood of misjudgment from placing too much emphasis on evidence of mental illness, it ignores the risk of misjudging an innocent man guilty from refusing to consider this highly relevant evidence at all. Clark's expert, it is true, said no one could know exactly what was on Clark's mind at the time of the shooting. The expert testified extensively, however, about the effect of Clark's delusions on his perceptions of the world around him, and about whether Clark's behavior around the time of the shooting was consistent with delusional thinking. This testimony was relevant to determining whether Clark knew he was killing a human being. It also bolstered the testimony of lay witnesses, none of which was deemed unreliable or misleading by the state courts.

For the same reasons, the Court errs in seeking support from the American Psychiatric Association's statement that a psychiatrist may be justifiably reluctant to reach legal conclusions regarding the defendant's mental state. In this very case, the American Psychiatric Association made clear that psychiatric evidence plays a crucial role regardless of whether the psychiatrist testifies on the ultimate issue: "Expert evidence of mental disorders, presented by qualified professionals and subject to adversarial testing, is both relevant to the mental-state issues raised by *mens rea* requirements and reliable.... Such evidence could not be condemned wholesale without unsettling the legal system's central reliance on such evidence."

Contrary to the Court's suggestion, the fact that the state and defense experts drew different conclusions about the effect of Clark's mental illness on his mental state only made Clark's evidence contested; it did not make the evidence irrelevant or misleading. The trial court was capable of evaluating the competing conclusions, as factfinders do in countless cases where there is a dispute among witnesses. In fact, the potential to mislead will be far greater under the Court's new evidentiary system, where jurors will receive observation evidence without the necessary explanation from experts.

The fact that mental-illness evidence may be considered in deciding criminal responsibility does not compensate for its exclusion from consideration on the *mens rea* elements of the crime. The evidence addresses different issues in the two instances. Criminal responsibility involves an inquiry into whether the defendant knew right from wrong, not whether he had the *mens rea* elements of the offense. While there may be overlap between the two issues, "the existence or nonexistence of legal insanity bears no necessary relationship to the existence or nonexistence of the required mental elements of the crime." *Mullaney v. Wilbur*, 421 U.S. 684, 706, 95 S.Ct. 1881, 44 L.Ed.2d 508 (1975) (Rehnquist, J., concurring).

Even if the analyses were equivalent, there is a different burden of proof for insanity than there is for *mens rea*. Arizona requires the defendant to prove his insanity by clear and convincing evidence. The prosecution, however, must prove all elements of the offense beyond a reasonable doubt. See *Mullaney, supra,* at 703–704, 95 S.Ct. 1881; *In re Winship*, 397 U.S. 358, 364, 90 S.Ct. 1068, 25 L.Ed.2d 368 (1970). The shift in the burden on the criminal responsibility issue, while permissible under our precedent, cannot be applied to the question of intent or knowledge without relieving the State of its responsibility to establish this element of the offense. While evidentiary rules do not generally shift the burden impermissibly, where there is a right to have evidence considered on an element of the offense, the right is not respected by allowing the evidence to come in only on an issue for which the defendant bears the burden of proof. By viewing the Arizona rule as creating merely a "presumption of sanity (or capacity or responsibility)," rather than a presumption that the *mens rea* elements were not affected by mental illness, the Court fails to appreciate the implications for *Winship*.

The State attempts to sidestep the evidentiary issue entirely by claiming that its mental-illness exclusion simply alters one element of the crime. The evidentiary rule at issue here, however, cannot be considered a valid redefinition of the offense. Under the State's logic, a person would be guilty of first-degree murder if he knowingly or intentionally killed a police officer or committed the killing under circumstances that would show knowledge or intent but for the defendant's mental illness. To begin with, Arizona law does not say this. And if it did, it would be impermissible. States have substantial discretion in defining criminal offenses. In some instances they may provide that the accused has the burden of persuasion with respect to affirmative defenses. See *Patterson v. New York,* 432 U.S. 197, 210, 97 S.Ct. 2319, 53 L.Ed.2d 281 (1977). "But there are obviously constitutional limits beyond which the States may not go in this regard." If it were otherwise, States could label all evidentiary exclusions as redefinitions and so evade constitutional requirements. There is no rational basis, furthermore, for criminally punishing a person who commits a killing without knowledge or intent only if that person has a mental illness. Cf. *Robinson v. California,* 370 U.S. 660, 666, 82 S.Ct. 1417, 8 L.Ed.2d 758 (1962). The

State attempts to bring the instant case within the ambit of *Montana v. Egelhoff*, 518 U.S. 37, 116 S.Ct. 2013, 135 L.Ed.2d 361 (1996); but in *Egelhoff* the excluded evidence concerned voluntary intoxication, for which a person can be held responsible. Viewed either as an evidentiary rule or a redefinition of the offense, it was upheld because it "comports with and implements society's moral perception that one who has voluntarily impaired his own faculties should be responsible for the consequences." An involuntary mental illness does not implicate this justification.

Future dangerousness is not, as the Court appears to conclude, see *ante* n. 45, a rational basis for convicting mentally ill individuals of crimes they did not commit. Civil commitment proceedings can ensure that individuals who present a danger to themselves or others receive proper treatment without unfairly treating them as criminals. The State presents no evidence to the contrary, and the Court ought not to imply otherwise.

* * *

While Arizona's rule is not unique, either historically or in contemporary practice, this fact does not dispose of Clark's constitutional argument. . . . While 13 States still impose significant restrictions on the use of mental-illness evidence to negate *mens rea*, a substantial majority of the States currently allow it. The fact that a reasonable number of States restrict this evidence weighs into the analysis, but applying the rule as a *per se* bar, as Arizona does, is so plainly unreasonable that it cannot be sustained. . . .

These are the reasons for my respectful dissent.

Questions and Comments

1. *Rationales for Clark.* The Court holds that expert testimony that provides "mental disease" or "capacity" evidence, as opposed to "observation" evidence, may constitutionally be excluded. One rationale the Court gives for this holding is that such testimony is too speculative and misleading. Do you agree (consider the materials on admissibility of expert testimony on pp. 437–68 as well as the dissent's points)? In any event, is the speculative nature of psychiatric testimony a justifiable ground for exclusion in *all* mens rea cases, as the majority states? If so, then may the state also exclude such testimony when presented to bolster an insanity defense? If not, why not? Because insanity is a more fundamental issue than mens rea? Because the defense bears the burden of proof on insanity, but the prosecution bears the burden of proof on mens rea? Because the result of a successful insanity defense is usually long-term or at least indeterminate incapacitation, but the result of a successful diminished capacity defense is release or a significantly shortened sentence? See note 45 of the majority opinion.

A second rationale the Court gives for its holding is that allowing the defendant to present expert mental disease and capacity testimony would "undercut" the state's entitlements to the presumption of sanity and to place the burden of proving insanity on the defendant, because it would enable a defendant raising an impaired mental state claim to obtain acquittal simply by creating a reasonable doubt (a far cry from the proof of insanity by clear and convincing demanded under Arizona's insanity statute). Justice Kennedy's dissent dismisses this point on the ground that due process, the Compulsory Process Clause and the Confrontation Clause prevent the state from categorically prohibiting testimony that negates an essential element of the crime. In rebuttal, the majority cites *Fisher v. United States*, 328 U.S. 463, 466–476, 66 S.Ct. 1318, 90 L.Ed. 1382 (1946), which held that states may deny defendants a diminished capacity defense. See note 42. But that case was decided long before the Court decided *In re Winship*, 397 U.S. 358, 90 S.Ct. 1068, 25 L.Ed.2d 368 (1970), which made clear that the prosecution must prove every element of the crime, including mens rea, beyond a reasonable doubt. More relevant is the holding in *Montana v. Egelhoff*, 518 U.S. 37, 116 S.Ct. 2013, 135 L.Ed.2d 361 (1996), mentioned by both the majority, see note 28, and the dissent. There the Court held that elimination of the voluntary intoxication defense does not violate due process. One rationale for this holding, endorsed by the four-member plurality in *Egelhoff*, was that the voluntary intoxication defense was of "recent vintage" and thus not a fundamental aspect of fair process. A second rationale, proffered by Justice Ginsburg in concurrence, was that Montana's intoxication statute had redefined the mens rea for first degree murder to include "intoxication-related automatism" in order to reflect the judgment that such a condition, which is often self-induced, entails sufficient culpability for murder; thus, she argued, Egelhoff's proffer of evidence about intoxication was irrelevant. Does either rationale in *Egelhoff* answer the dissent's concern?

2. *Legal status of diminished capacity doctrine.* As Justice Kennedy's dissent notes, over half the states disagree with the result in *Mott* and permit clinical testimony relevant to mens rea, at least under certain circumstances. Federal courts have also permitted such testimony. See, e.g., *U.S. v. Cohen*, 510 F.3d 1114 (9th Cir. 2007). Some courts have held, in agreement with the dissent in *Clark*, that this position is constitutionally mandated. In *Commonwealth v. Walzack,* 468 Pa. 210, 360 A.2d 914, 920 (1976), for instance, the Pennsylvania Supreme Court held that, under the Pennsylvania constitution, due process requires the admission of psychiatric testimony that is relevant to the mens rea issue. The court stated: "It is inconsistent with fundamental principles of American jurisprudence to preclude an accused from offering relevant and competent evidence to dispute the charge against him." See also, *Hendershott v. People,* 653 P.2d 385, 394 (Colo.1982).

The drafters of the Model Penal Code came to the same conclusion on policy grounds. Section 4.02(1) of the Code provides: "Evidence that the defendant suffered from a mental disease or defect is admissible whenever it is relevant to prove that the defendant did not have a state of mind that is an element of the crime." In support of this provision, the drafters stated: "If states of mind such as deliberation or premeditation are accorded legal significance, psychiatric evidence should be admissible when relevant to prove or disprove their existence to the same extent as any other evidence." Model Penal Code, Comments to § 4.02, 193 (Tent.Draft No. 4, 1955). More recently, the American Bar Association, finding that "logical relevance" so requires, has recommended an identical rule. American Bar Association Criminal Justice Mental Health Standard 7–6.2 (1987).

Similarly, while the federal Insanity Defense Reform Act of 1984 states that, other than in insanity cases, "mental disease or defect does not . . . constitute a defense," most federal courts have found that this language was meant only to bar "affirmative" psychiatric defenses which the defendant seeks to raise (e.g., self-defense), not evidence which negates intent, an element of the crime. See 118 ALR Fed 281–85 (1993).

3. *Diminished capacity v. diminished responsibility.* To be distinguished from the diminished capacity idea, which focuses on the defendant's mens rea, is what is sometimes called the "partial" or "diminished responsibility" defense, which permits the factfinder to consider mitigating evidence of cognitive or volitional impairment that neither constitutes insanity nor negates mens rea. In Great Britain, for instance, a sane defendant for whom the actus reus and mens rea of murder have been proven may nonetheless be convicted only of manslaughter if the defense shows that at the time of the killing the defendant "was suffering from such abnormality of mind . . . as substantially impaired his mental responsibility for acts and omissions in . . . the killing." English Homicide Act, 5 & 6 Eliz. II, ch. 11, § 2. A somewhat less broad formulation of this idea is found in the Model Penal Code, in language followed by many American jurisdictions, which provides that a person who intentionally kills another may nonetheless be convicted only of manslaughter if, at the time of the killing, the person was "under the influence of extreme mental or emotional disturbance for which there is reasonable explanation or excuse" (see p. 613 for more elaborate discussion of this provision). If the diminished responsibility doctrine were recognized and made applicable to *all* crimes (rather than just homicide, as in Great Britain), how would one gauge its mitigating impact? Morse has suggested that, if such a defense were permitted, it should lead to a sentence one-half the length normally received for the crime. Stephen Morse, "Diminished Capacity: A Moral and Legal Conundrum," 2 Int'l J.Psychiat. 271 (1979).

One criticism of the diminished capacity doctrine is that, while it is theoretically distinguishable from diminished responsibility, in practice it will open the door wide to undifferentiated psychiatric testimony similar to that contemplated by the latter doctrine. In perhaps the leading case supporting this position, *Bethea v. United States,* 365 A.2d 64 (D.C.App. 1976), the District of Columbia Court of Appeals stated:

> The concept of mens rea involves what is ultimately the fiction of determining the actual thoughts or mental processes of the accused. It is obvious that a certain resolution of this issue is beyond the ken of scientist and laymen alike. Only by inference can the existence of intent—or the differentiation between its forms, such as general or specific—be determined. The law presumes that all individuals are capable of the mental processes which bear the jurisprudential label "mens rea"; that is, the law presumes sanity . . . The concept of insanity is simply a device the law employs to define the outer limits of that segment of the general population to whom these presumptions concerning the capacity for criminal intent shall not be applied. The line

between the sane and the insane for the purposes of criminal adjudication is not drawn because for one group the actual existence of the necessary mental state (or lack thereof) can be determined with any greater certainty, but rather because those whom the law declares insane are demonstrably so aberrational in their psychiatric characteristics that they are incapable of possessing the specified state of mind. Within the range of individuals who are not "insane", the law does not recognize the readily demonstrable fact that as between individual criminal defendants the nature and development of their mental capabilities may vary greatly.... By contradicting the presumptions inherent in the doctrine of mens rea, the theory of diminished capacity inevitably opens the door to variable or sliding scales of criminal responsibility. We should not lightly undertake such a revolutionary change in our criminal justice system.

Id. at 88–89.

Consider expert evidence presented in the prosecution of Damian Williams on twelve charges, including attempted murder. The charges arose out of an assault on Reginald Denny and seven others during the Los Angeles riots that followed the acquittal of the white police officers who beat Rodney King, an African–American, after stopping him on the highway. The lawyers in the Williams case used a social scientist to support the (successful) argument that the defendant, an African–American, was caught up in the "group contagion" of anger and frustration following the King verdict, so much so that he did not possess the mens rea for attempted murder. See George P. Fletcher, With Justice for Some: Victims' Rights in Criminal Trials 38, 234 (1995). In other words, the testimony was that the defendants were "out of control" at the time of the offense. Is such testimony evidence of diminished capacity, or instead only evidence of diminished responsibility? If the latter, is it admissible?

4. *Limitations on clinical mens rea testimony.* Although many states permit clinical testimony that is relevant to mens rea (as opposed to diminished responsibility), they have done so cautiously. Most have placed limitations on such testimony beyond those constraints that are imposed by the rules of evidence on all expert opinion evidence.[1] The principal limitations are of three types: a requirement that the lack of mens rea be due to a significant mental disorder; a requirement that the testimony only address whether the defendant had the capacity to formulate the requisite mens rea; and a prohibition on mens rea testimony for certain types of crimes.

The Mental Disease or Defect Limitation. The first limitation is a requirement, imposed explicitly in several states and implicitly in any state that adopts the Model Penal Code language, that the diminished capacity be associated with a "mental disease or defect" similar to that required for the insanity defense. See, e.g., *State v. Humanik,* 199 N.J.Super. 283, 489 A.2d 691 (A.D.1985). Is such a requirement justifiable? Are the reasons for the mental disease or defect predicate in the insanity context applicable when

---

1. See Chapter Six, particularly pp. 450–68 for a thorough treatment of the constraints on expert testimony.

the issue is whether the defendant had the requisite mental state at the time of the offense?

In *United States v. Bright,* 517 F.2d 584 (2d Cir.1975), the defendant was charged with three counts of violating a statute which penalizes anyone who knowingly possesses stolen mail. It was undisputed that Bright had had in her possession nine welfare checks that had been stolen from the mail and that she had cashed at least three of them. Her defense was that she had not known they were stolen. She had been given the checks by one Fred Scott, an acquaintance of her boyfriend Leslie; Scott gave Bright the checks to cash for him on the pretense that he had no bank account of his own. She testified that, although the checks were clearly made out to someone other than Scott, she had believed everything Scott had told her about the checks and had not suspected their source. In addition to her own testimony, she proffered the testimony of a psychiatrist, Dr. Weiss, who stated in part:

> [T]hough I do not consider Mrs. Bright to have been suffering mental illness, I believe that her dependent, childlike character structure unconsciously "needed" to believe that these men would never involve her in illegal activities and that Leslie could do no wrong. I believe that at the time of the alleged crime, because of this unconscious 'need', she did not think that the checks had been stolen.... I do not believe that she knew that the checks that she allegedly possessed were stolen as a result of her need to deny the possibility that the men involved would in any way take advantage of her. This passive-dependent personality disorder rendered her incapable of understanding this [see p. 1351 for a description of this diagnosis].

Although the court appeared to be unwilling to foreclose a diminished capacity argument under all circumstances, it upheld the exclusion of the expert testimony, primarily because no mental disease analogous to that required for the insanity defense was found to be present:

> Couched in simpler language [the psychiatrist] was prepared to testify that [Bright] was a gullible person but a person unaffected either by psychosis or neurosis....

> The mind and motivation of an accused who is not on the other side of the line [drawn by the insanity defense] is, by the judgment of experience, left to the jury to probe. The complexity of the fears and long-suppressed traumatic experiences of a lifetime is in the personality of all of us. All humankind is heir to defects of personality.

> To transmute the effect of instability, of undue reliance on another, of unrequited love, of sudden anger, of the host of attitudes and syndromes that are a part of daily living, into opinion evidence to the jury for exculpation or condemnation is to go beyond the boundaries of current knowledge. The shallower the conception the deeper runs the danger that the jury may be misled....

> In short, [Bright] asks us to go beyond the boundaries of conventional psychiatric opinion testimony. We think the testimony offered was not sufficiently grounded in scientific support to make us reach or, indeed, cross the present frontier of admissibility. On the instant appeal

we need decide no more than that [the trial judge] did not abuse her discretion in rejecting the opinion evidence.

Is it true, as suggested by the *Bright* court, that clinical testimony is less reliable if it is not based on a finding of significant mental disorder? Is such testimony any more suspect than the testimony offered in *Heads* or *Pollard* (see pp. 556–61; 570–76)? If it is, why not let the rules of evidence governing the admission of expert testimony take care of the problem rather than resorting to a mental disease limitation? Perhaps the rules of evidence are insufficient protection against testimony on the "outer boundaries?" Or is there another concern—similar to that evinced by the Supreme Court in *Clark*—underlying the court's position?

Because the psychiatric testimony was excluded, the sole basis for Bright's assertion—that she did not know the checks were stolen because she was abnormally willing to believe those upon whom she depended emotionally—was her own testimony. Consider the following comment about the *Bright* case.

> [E]xclusion [of the psychiatric testimony] compromises [Bright's] ability to persuade the factfinder not to draw inferences about her beliefs on the basis of what a normal person would have believed under the circumstances. Because [Bright] carries a de-facto burden of proof on this issue, the exclusion of expert testimony in effect holds her to the standards of a normally suspicious person, selectively redefining the offense to apply objective standards to her and subjective standards to everyone else.

Richard Bonnie & Christopher Slobogin, "The Role of Mental Health Professionals in the Criminal Process: The Case for Informed Speculation," 66 Va.L.Rev. 427, 480–81 (1980). Is this concern, assuming it exists, sufficiently significant to outweigh the concerns identified by the *Bright* court?

The Capacity Limitation; Character Testimony. A second reason given by the *Bright* court for excluding the psychiatric testimony in that case centered on the form in which the testimony was offered. The court noted that the psychiatrist went beyond stating that Bright "did not have the capacity to form a specific intent to commit the crime" and instead directly asserted that Bright did not believe the checks were stolen. The court suggested that diminished capacity testimony should address *only* the capacity of the defendant to harbor the required mental state, not whether the defendant actually had that mental state. Several other courts have explicitly required that psychiatric testimony on mens rea be couched in terms of the defendant's "capacity." See, e.g., *Simpson v. State,* 269 Ind. 495, 381 N.E.2d 1229 (1978); *State v. Craig,* 82 Wash.2d 777, 514 P.2d 151 (1973). Most formulations of the diminished capacity doctrine do not limit clinical testimony in this way. See Model Penal Code § 4.01(1). What is the purpose of the limitation?

For one possible answer to this question, consider *Waine v. State,* 37 Md.App. 222, 377 A.2d 509 (1977). There the defendant was charged with two counts of first degree murder. In his defense, he called a psychiatrist who testified off the record that the defendant was a passive person and that, in his opinion, violence on the part of the defendant would be very unlikely. The psychiatrist also stated, again off the record, that there "is no way in the world I can say he didn't commit these [homicides] but I can say according to his lifestyle, this would be totally out of character." After hearing the proffer of the psychiatrist, the trial court allowed the psychiatrist to testify as to the "psychiatric makeup" of the defendant—to the effect that he was a "passivist"—but did not allow him to testify as to "whether or not this person might possibly be able to commit an act of violence ... , or did in fact commit, possibly or not possibly, an act of violence ... at the time these people were killed." The Maryland Court of Special Appeals upheld this ruling. Apparently, it was willing to allow this and like testimony, short of the "ultimate conclusion" as to whether the defendant committed the murders, because of a perceived analogy to evidentiary rules permitting criminal defendants to present "character evidence."[m]

How similar is the evidence in *Waine* to the evidence in *Bright*? In the former case the defendant's expert testimony aimed at proving the defendant did not have the capacity to commit the criminal act. In the latter case, the defendant admitted the actus reus but used expert testimony to support the argument that mens rea was lacking. The Maryland Supreme Court upheld *Waine* in *Kanaras v. State*, 54 Md.App. 568, 460 A.2d 61, 73 (1983), one year after it held that diminished capacity testimony is *not* admissible. *Johnson v. State*, 292 Md. 405, 439 A.2d 542 (1982). Can *Kanaras* and *Johnson* be reconciled?

On the general issue of whether *any* psychiatric evidence on "character" short of insanity is material to criminal responsibility issues, consider the analysis of Professor Andrew Taslitz, in "Myself Alone: Individualizing Justice Through Psychological Character Evidence," 52 Md. L.Rev. 1, 95–95 (1993). He argues that such evidence is important in a criminal system like ours, which recognizes a need for "individualized justice."

> Individualized justice requires consideration of a defendant's unique traits and circumstances to determine what that individual did or thought, not only what she should have done or thought. Yet our assembly-line justice system and common myths, prejudices, and misconceptions combine to lead to "normalized justice," to the trial of defendants for whom they are assumed to be and what they are assumed, therefore, to have done and thought. Such assumptions are largely based on what most people would do, clearly the opposite of individualized treatment. [P]sychological character evidence [is] a way to move judges and juries back toward an individualized assessment of the particular defendant before them. Psychological character testimony, because it focuses in part on a defendant's history, on special traits and their consequences, and on the interaction between those traits and situational factors, offers the prospect of leading juries to think of defendants as special human beings, rather than as stereotypes.

m. Cf. Fed.R.Evid., Rule 404(a)(1) ("Evidence of a person's character or a trait of character is not admissible for the purpose of proving action in conformity therewith on a particular occasion, except [when it is] evidence of a pertinent trait of character offered by an accused, or by the prosecution to rebut the same."); Fed.R.Evid., Rule 405(a) ("In all cases in which evidence of character or a trait of character of a person is admissible, proof may be made by testimony as to reputation or by testimony in the form of an opinion....")

Id. at 120. In light of the above, Taslitz would allow not only expert testimony about character that tends to negate mens rea (as in the *Bright* case), but also character testimony that suggests the defendant did not commit the criminal act (as in *Waine*).

Should a concern for individualized justice lead to admission of any credible psychiatric evidence on character, as Taslitz proposes? Taslitz admits that "[p]sychological research supports the notion that behavior may often be controlled as much by situational factors as by one's essential 'nature' or one's thoughts and feelings." Id. at 57. He also notes "the well-documented 'fundamental attribution error': the tendency of people to inflate the importance of personality traits while failing to recognize the importance of situational factors in prompting behavior." Id. at 110. Given these observations, one might argue that testimony about a defendant's dependent or passive nature is not of much value in a criminal case (which presumably centers around abnormal "situational factors"), and is also likely to be given too much weight by the factfinder. On the other hand, as noted above, the rules of evidence allow the defendant to present lay evidence of character in criminal cases (and permit the prosecution to present rebuttal evidence as well, once the defendant raises the character issue).

Would you allow expert testimony that a defendant charged with rape, who admittedly had intercourse with the victim, did not have the psychological traits of a rapist and therefore probably could not have forced intercourse on the victim? Cf. *New Jersey v. Cavallo*, 88 N.J. 508, 443 A.2d 1020 (1982)(finding the testimony relevant but not admissible under *Frye*). Testimony by a prosecution expert witness that a rape defendant, who had testified that the intercourse was consensual, *did* fit the profile of an aggressive rapist? Cf. *State v. Hickman*, 337 N.W.2d 512 (Iowa 1983) (permitting the testimony as rebuttal evidence).

Crime Limitation. Finally, most states restrict the admissibility of clinical mens rea evidence to certain types of crimes. This third limitation is itself of two types. One approach permits clinical testimony only in cases where defendants are charged with some type of intentional homicide. For instance, although the Pennsylvania Supreme Court has held that competent evidence of diminished capacity cannot constitutionally be prohibited, *Walzack,* supra, it has nonetheless limited such evidence to murder cases. *Commonwealth v. Garcia,* 505 Pa. 304, 479 A.2d 473, 477 (1984). A second approach admits clinical testimony on mens rea for any crime involving specific intent, but does not admit such evidence for crimes involving general intent. In "Model Penal Code" jurisdictions, an analogous result is achieved by permitting expert evidence for any element requiring purpose or knowledge, but barring such evidence when the mens rea is recklessness or negligence. See *State v. Thompson,* 695 S.W.2d 154, 159 (Mo.App.1985) and cases cited therein.

The murder-only rule plainly violates the premise of the diminished capacity doctrine, since mental abnormality can lead to the absence of mens rea for other crimes as well. Expanding the doctrine's applicability to all specific intent crimes does not necessarily solve this problem. If the mens rea for general intent crimes (or recklessness and negligence) were truly "objectively" defined, then diminished capacity evidence would indeed be irrelevant in such cases. But such is not always the case.

Looking first at the Model Penal Code approach to mens rea, it is clear that even negligence contemplates some degree of investigation into the defendant's actual mental state. Section 2.02(2)d of the Model Penal Code states:

> A person acts negligently with respect to a material element of an offense when he should be aware of a substantial and unjustifiable risk that the material element exists or will result from his conduct. The risk must be of such a nature and degree that the actor's failure to perceive it, *considering the nature and purpose of his conduct and the circumstances known to him*, involves a gross deviation from the standard of care that a reasonable person would observe *in the actor's situation*.

(Emphasis supplied). Under § 213.4 of the Code, the crime of sexual assault is defined as, *inter alia*, "sexual contact with another . . . [when] (6) the other person is less than 16 years old and the actor is at least four years older than the other person." It is a defense to this crime if the victim was between 10 and 16 and the actor had a non-negligent belief that the victim was older than 16. See §§ 213.6; 1.13(16). Suppose a defendant wants to submit expert testimony that, due to mental illness or mental retardation, he thought a person with whom he admittedly had sexual contact was over 16 (even though a "normal" person should have known otherwise). Under the above definition of negligence, could not one make a plausible argument that such testimony should be admissible on diminished capacity grounds? The commentary to the Model Penal Code suggests a negative answer to this question:

> The standard for ultimate judgement [in negligence cases] invites consideration of the "care that a reasonable person would observe in the actor's situation." There is an inevitable ambiguity in "situation." If the actor were blind or if he had just suffered a blow or experienced a heart attack, these would certainly be facts to be considered in a judgement involving criminal liability, as they would be under traditional law. But the heredity, intelligence or temperament of the actor would not be held material in judging negligence, and could not be without depriving the criterion of all its objectivity. The Code is not intended to displace discriminations of this kind, but rather to leave the issue to the courts.

Model Penal Code § 2.02 comment 4, at 242 (1985). Doesn't the language "considering . . . the circumstances known to him" in the MPC's definition of negligence undercut the comment's statement that heredity, intelligence or temperament are not "material"? In any event, the comment ends by saying "discriminations" between physical-external and psychological-internal aspects of one's "situation" should be left to the courts. What would you do?

The same sort of problem occurs under the common law in distinguishing specific and general intent crimes, primarily because the courts are so idiosyncratic in defining these terms. In *State v. McVey*, 376 N.W.2d 585 (Iowa 1985), for instance, the defendant was charged under a statute which makes it theft for a person to "[exercise] control over stolen property, knowing such property to have been stolen, or having reasonable cause to believe that such property has been stolen, unless the person's purpose is to promptly restore it to the owner or to deliver it to an appropriate public officer." West's Ann.Iowa Code 714.1(4). According to prior case law, the Iowa Supreme Court noted, "the mens rea of this offense requires proof that the accused actually believe the property is stolen." But case law had also established that the offense did not require proof of "specific intent." Rather "[t]he offense is a general intent crime because it is complete without intent to do a further act or achieve a further consequence." Id. at 586. The court then upheld the trial court's exclusion of psychiatric evidence proffered to show that the defendant did not know that an automobile in which he was apprehended was stolen. The court noted that, although Iowa courts had long recognized that a diminished capacity defense "is available to any crime in which specific intent is an element," expanding it to general intent crimes would be unsound:

> In practical terms a court's refusal to recognize the relevancy of evidence of mental impairment short of legal insanity results from the court's understanding of the legislative intention concerning the blameworthiness of the defendant's conduct. To the extent evidence of mental impairment that does not meet the legal insanity standard permits an accused to avoid responsibility for otherwise culpable conduct, the policy inherent in the insanity defense is undermined.

If the defendant's evidence proves that he did not know the car was stolen, is he blameworthy? Is this case any different from *Bright?*

Even in cases that clearly involve general intent crimes, psychiatric evidence might be considered relevant. Consider *New York v. Wilcox*, 194 A.D.2d 820, 599 N.Y.S.2d 131 (N.Y.App.Div.1993), in which a New York appeals court reversed a manslaughter conviction because the trial court failed to instruct the jury to consider whether the defendant's diminished mental capacity limited his ability to form the requisite mental state. The psychiatric expert had testified that the defendant had an IQ of 69 and a mental age of 10, and consequently could not perceive any danger to the victim (his 12–week old son) when he threw him on a chair. Presumably, in other words, the expert believed that while the defendant "intended" to throw the child, he did not intend to hurt him, much less kill him. Should the latter fact, if true, matter?

The usual justification given for limiting diminished capacity evidence to certain types of mens rea is not the one advanced by the Iowa Supreme Court in *McVey* but rather stems from a utilitarian rationale: if no such limitation were imposed, some defendants with mental illness (including those who ordinarily would have pleaded insanity and thus been committed) would be able to use clinical evidence to elude confinement completely (cf. note 45 in *Clark v. Arizona*). The public is protected in states limiting clinical testimony on mens rea to murder cases because a defendant who escapes a murder conviction through using diminished capacity evidence can still be convicted of manslaughter. Similarly, in those states that have adopted the specific intent limitation, the defendant who successfully argues diminished capacity can still usually be convicted of a lesser included offense requiring only general intent.

In *People v. Wetmore,* 22 Cal.3d 318, 149 Cal.Rptr. 265, 583 P.2d 1308 (1978), the defendant was charged with burglary after being discovered in another person's apartment wearing that person's clothes and cooking his food. The defendant credibly showed that as a result of mental illness he had come to believe that he owned the apartment. He had lived in the apartment for three days prior to his arrest and been shocked and embarrassed when the police arrived and informed him that the apartment was not his. In overturning his conviction for burglary (for which there was no lesser included offense), the California Supreme Court stated:

> We reject the suggestion that we sustain the trial court by holding that a defense of diminished capacity cannot be raised whenever, owing to the lack of a lesser included offense, it might result in the defendant's acquittal. A defendant who, because of diminished capacity, does not entertain the specific intent required for a particular crime is entitled to be acquitted of that crime. If he cannot be convicted of a lesser offense and cannot safely be released, the state's remedy is to institute civil commitment proceedings, not to convict him of a specific-intent crime which he did not commit.

In California, the relevant civil commitment statute permits confinement of any person who "as a result of mental disorder [is] a danger to others, or to himself, or gravely disabled." Confinement under the first two criteria may last only 90 days unless the person "has threatened, attempted, or actually inflicted physical harm to another during his period of post-certification treatment." Is the court's solution sufficiently protective of the public? Would it be wise to amend the civil commitment statute to permit longer confinement of those acquitted on diminished capacity grounds? Or should we condone conviction of *some* offense, even one for which the defendant did not have the required mental state, as a compromise between retributive and utilitarian notions?

D. OTHER DEFENSES

NOTE ON SELF-DEFENSE, PROVOCATION AND DURESS

In adjudicating guilt, evidence of mental abnormality is most likely to be considered relevant to insanity, automatism or diminished capacity. Increasingly, however, psychiatric and psychological testimony has been proffered in support of other claims. This development is a direct outgrowth of the criminal law's movement toward a subjective definition of culpability. To illustrate this development and its ramifications, this section looks briefly at three criminal law doctrines: self-defense, provocation, and duress.

The traditional approach to self-defense is summarized by Professor LaFave as follows: "One who is not the aggressor in an encounter is justified in using a reasonable amount of force against his adversary when he reasonably believes that he is in immediate danger of unlawful bodily harm from his adversary and that the use of such force is necessary to avoid this danger." Wayne LaFave, Criminal Law, at 491 (2000). In a majority of jurisdictions a person may use deadly force to repel an attack that is reasonably believed to be deadly even if he or she could safely retreat from the attack; however, in a "strong minority" of jurisdictions, one must retreat before using deadly force, if the retreat can be accomplished safely. Even in the minority jurisdictions, one need not retreat if the attack takes place in the defendant's house, on the theory that one is entitled to stand firm in one's home. See id., § 5.7. A valid self-defense claim leads to acquittal on any charge.

The provocation "defense," on the other hand, is available only in homicide cases and, rather than acquittal, leads to reduction of the charge from murder to voluntary manslaughter. In most jurisdictions, this reduction occurs when the defendant can show that (1) the killing was in reaction to provocation that, while insufficient to justify the killing, would cause the "reasonable" person to lose control; (2) this provocation in fact provoked the defendant; (3) a "reasonable" person so provoked would not have cooled off in the interval of time between the provocation and the delivery of the final blow; and (4) the defendant did not in fact cool off. LaFave, supra, at 705. The provocation defense has sometimes been characterized as imperfect self-defense because it recognizes that some types of provocation, although they do not justify the use of deadly force in return, might make a "reasonable" person impulsively kill someone, and thus should be given mitigating (but not exculpatory) effect. The common law identified a number of situations in which such provocation might occur, e.g., serious battery not rising to deadly force, serious assault (i.e., attempted battery), mutual combat not involving deadly force, and discovery of adultery by the offended spouse. See id., § 7.10.

Finally, the defense of duress is recognized when a person's unlawful threat causes the defendant reasonably to believe that the only way to avoid imminent death or serious bodily injury to him or herself or to another is to engage in conduct which violates the criminal law, and the defendant acts on that belief. LaFave, supra, at 467–68. Duress is not normally a defense, however, to intentional homicide, since the rationale for the defense is generally thought to be that acquittal should be permitted only when the defendant, faced with a choice of evils, chooses to do the lesser evil.

It should be clear even from this brief description that, under the common law, "reasonableness" language dominates the definition of these defenses. Use of such language presumably renders mental abnormality irrelevant, since a person who is mentally disordered at the time of the offense never acts "reasonably". The reasonable person is the "normal" person as defined by the judge or members of the jury. Thus, for instance, with respect to provocation, in most jurisdictions "the defendant's special mental qualities ... are not to be considered." LaFave, supra, at 711.

Modern developments in these three areas demonstrate an increasing willingness to consider the personal characteristics of the accused in deciding whether a defense is available. The Model Penal Code is representative. The Code permits "the use of force upon or toward another person ... when the actor believes that such force is immediately necessary for the purpose of protecting himself against the use of unlawful force by such person on the present occasion." Model Penal Code § 3.04. This formulation makes the actor's beliefs relevant to a self-defense claim regardless of how "unreasonable" they are. The provision of the Code that is analogous to the common law provocation doctrine is somewhat more objectively defined but still incorporates subjective elements. It states that a homicide which would otherwise be murder is manslaughter if it "is committed under the influence of extreme mental or emotional disturbance for which there is reasonable explanation or excuse[,] ... the reasonableness of such explanation or excuse [to] be determined *from the viewpoint of a person in the actor's situation under the circumstances as he believes them to be*." Model Penal Code § 210.3 (emphasis added). Similarly, with respect to duress, the Code provides for an affirmative defense when a person commits a crime "because he was coerced to do so by the use of, or a threat to use, unlawful force against his person or the person of another, which a person of reasonable firmness *in his situation* would have been unable to resist." Model Penal Code § 2.09(1)(emphasis added). The commentary to this provision states that its intent "is to give effect to the defense when an actor mistakenly believes that a threat to use unlawful force has been made." Id. § 2.09, comment 3, at 380 (1985). But the defense is not available when the "actor recklessly placed himself in a situation in which it was probable that he would be subjected to duress." Id. § 2.09(2).

According to LaFave, a "few" states have adopted the Model Penal Code's subjectified version of self-defense, a "substantial minority" have adopted its provocation formulation, and "a very distinct majority" have adopted its duress provision. As the following materials make clear, behavioral science testimony is often admitted on these types of issues. That is true even in federal courts, where the Insanity Defense Reform Act limits the admissibility of testimony about mental disease or defect to insanity and lack of mens rea issues. *United States v. Brown*, 891 F.Supp. 1501 (D. Kan. 1995)(duress).

JAHNKE v. STATE

Supreme Court of Wyoming, 1984.
682 P.2d 991.

THOMAS, JUSTICE.

The essential questions presented in this case arise out of a notion that a victim of abuse has some special justification for patricide.

* * *

The appellant's father, Richard Chester Jahnke, died on November 16, 1982, as a result of gunshot wounds. Those gunshot wounds were inflicted by the appellant, and that fact has never been an issue in this case.

* * *

The material facts relating to the death of the appellant's father can be briefly stated. On the night of his death the father took the mother out to dinner, apparently to celebrate the anniversary of their meeting. Earlier the appellant had been involved in a violent altercation with his father, and he had been warned not to be at the home when the father and mother returned. During the absence of his parents the appellant made elaborate preparation for the final confrontation with his father. He changed into dark clothing and prepared a number of weapons which he positioned at various places throughout the family home that he selected to serve as "backup" positions in case he was not successful in his first effort to kill his father. These weapons included two shotguns, three rifles, a .38 caliber pistol and a Marine knife. In addition, he armed his sister, Deborah, with a .30 caliber M–1 carbine which he taught her how to operate so that she could protect herself in the event that he failed in his efforts. The appellant removed the family pets from the garage to the basement to protect them from injury in a potential exchange of gunfire between him and his father, and he closed the garage door. He then waited inside the darkened garage in a position where he could not be seen but which permitted him to view the lighted driveway on the other side of the garage door. Shortly before 6:30 p.m. the parents returned, and the appellant's father got out of the vehicle and came to the garage door. The appellant was armed with a 12–gauge shotgun loaded with slugs, and when he could see the head and shoulders of his father through the spacing of the slats of the shade covering the windows of the garage door, he blew his R.O.T.C. command-sergeant-major's whistle for courage, and he opened fire. All six cartridges in the shotgun were expended, and four of them in one way or another struck the father.

* * *

After the shooting, and while the mother still was screaming in the driveway, the appellant and his sister exited the family home through a window in the mother's bedroom, which was at the far end of the house from the garage. The appellant and his sister then went separate ways, and the appellant was arrested at the home of his girl friend. Prior to the arrival of authorities the appellant told his girl friend's father that he had shot his dad for revenge. Subsequently, after being advised of his constitutional rights, the appellant made a statement in which he explained he had shot his father "for past things."

[Jahnke was convicted of voluntary manslaughter and sentenced to 5 to 15 years. On appeal he argued that the trial court erroneously excluded expert testimony describing him as a victim of the "battered person syndrome" who was in constant fear of serious bodily harm from his father but at the same time unable to leave the site of the battering.]

It is clear that self-defense is circumscribed by circumstances involving a confrontation, usually encompassing some overt act or acts by the deceased, which would induce a reasonable person to fear that his life was in danger or that at least he was threatened with great bodily harm.

* * *

Although many people, and the public media, seem to be prepared to espouse the notion that a victim of abuse is entitled to kill the abuser that special justification defense is antithetical to the mores of modern civilized society. It is difficult enough to justify capital punishment as an appropriate response of society to criminal acts even after the circumstances have been carefully evaluated by a number of people. To permit capital punishment to be imposed upon the subjective conclusion of the individual that prior acts and conduct of the deceased justified the killing would amount to a leap into the abyss of anarchy.

* * *

This record contained no evidence that the appellant was under either actual or threatened assault by his father at the time of the shooting. Reliance upon the justification of self-defense requires a showing of an actual or threatened imminent attack by the deceased.

Absent [such] a showing, the reasonableness of appellant's conduct at the time was not an issue in the case, and the trial court, at the time it made its ruling, properly excluded the hearsay testimony sought to be elicited from the forensic psychiatrist.

* * *

ROSE, JUSTICE, dissenting, with whom CARDINE, JUSTICE, joins

* * *

This case concerns itself with what happens—or can happen—and did happen when a cruel, ill-tempered, insensitive man roams, gun in hand, through his years of family life as a battering bully—a bully who, since his two children were babies, beat both of them and his wife regularly and unmercifully. Particularly, this appeal has to do with a 16–year–old boy who could stand his father's abuse no longer—who could not find solace or friendship in the public services which had been established for the purpose of providing aid, comfort and advice to abused family members—and who had no place to go or friends to help either him or his sister for whose protection he felt responsible and so—in fear and fright, and with fragmented emotion, Richard Jahnke shot and killed his father one night in November of 1982.

* * *

THE REASONABLENESS OF SELF-DEFENSE

* * *

In contemplating the overall problem which brings on my dissent, it is initially necessary to be aware of at least these following facts:

Richard Jahnke, a sensitive boy who had never been in any sort of trouble in his life, had been beaten regularly and unmercifully by his father since he was two years old. On the night of the homicide he had received a severe beating, and when his father and mother left the house to go to dinner that night, his father said:

"I'm disgusted with the shit you turned out to be. I don't want you to be here when I get back."

The father also said:

"I don't care what I have to do, I'm going to get rid of you. I don't know how but I'm going to get rid of you, you bastard."

The boy felt he had to protect his sister who was hysterical when the mother and father left for dinner. He did not believe that there was any place or anyone where or to whom they could go for safety. The mother testified that the elder Jahnke always carried a gun, and Richard believed he had one with him that night. Mrs. Jahnke said that when the father said to Richard, "I'm going to get rid of you"—

"He was trying to frighten him and maybe do something else besides just throwing him out of the house."

When Richard was in the garage after having stationed his father's guns around the house for "backup," he reflected upon past confrontations with his father and he was afraid the father would kill him when he returned and found what Richard had done with the guns. Even as he contemplated these things, the father drove the car into the driveway. Richard said he wanted to go and hug him and tell him he loved him, but he remembered when he had done this before, he had received a beating for his efforts. He knew from past experience that when his father "stomped" after him that he was in for a beating. He testified about how his father approached the garage door that night:

"A. Yes. I remember he was stomping. When he stomped down the hall when he was really mad and really prepared to beat someone up, beat on one of us. I remember being a little kid, just sitting in my room. My dad stomping after me to hit me, that I could never stop him. This time I stopped him."

* * *

[In] the *ordinary* self-defense situation where there are no psychiatric implications and where the jury is permitted to know what the accused knew about the violent character of his victim, there need be no expert testimony touching upon the reasonableness of the defendant's behavior. In normal circumstances, these are things that jurors can fathom for themselves. However, when the beatings of 14 years have—or may have—caused the accused to harbor types of fear, anxiety and apprehension with which the nonbrutalized juror is unfamiliar and which result in the taking of unusual defensive measures which, in the ordinary circumstances, might be thought about as premature, excessive or lacking in escape efforts by those who are uninformed about the fear and anxiety that permeate the world of the brutalized—then expert testimony is necessary to explain the battered-person syndrome and the way these people respond to what they understand to be the imminence of danger and to explain their propensity to employ deadly force in their self-defensive conduct. Given this information, the jury is then qualified to decide the reasonableness of a self-defense defendant's acts at the time and place in question.

THE PROFFERED TESTIMONY OF THE FORENSIC PSYCHIATRIST

Dr. McDonald, a forensic psychiatrist, was offered by the defendant for the purpose of testifying about the behavior of battered children—that Richard was a battered child—all as an aid to the triers of fact with respect to their obligation to decide whether or not this defendant—as a battered person—behaved reasonably on the night of November 16, 1982, but the court would not permit the jury to hear the testimony.

The defendant suggests that his offer of proof represented that Dr. McDonald would testify that:

1.   The doctor had diagnosed Richard Jahnke as a battered child, based on interviews with him and upon other information.

2.   Battered children behave differently from other children, and perceive things differently from other children.

3.   Because he was a battered child, Jahnke reasonably believed himself to be in immediate danger on the night he shot his father, and perceived himself as acting in self-defense.

* * *

The doctor described an extensive background of Richard receiving physical abuse from his father. His earliest memory was of his father beating him, his mother and his sister. Between the ages of four and 12, there was seldom a day without some sort of punishment by his father. The punishment became less frequent between 12 and 15—more like every other day, but there were more beatings when his father used his fists on him. He was beaten with his father's fists every couple of weeks between 15 and 16. He would be beaten for such things as not cleaning the basement the right way—for walking along with his mouth open—for spending too much time polishing his ROTC uniform. At one juncture, the doctor testified that the children were forced to eat with plastic spoons and forks because their father did not like the noise they made while eating with ordinary utensils. Dr. McDonald testified that Richard related that he would be beaten for things like defending his sister. If Richard would react to verbal abuse by changing facial expression, the father would physically abuse him. When Richard and his mother had an argument, she would call him a "bastard" and report him to his father who would beat him.

On May 2, 1982, after a severe beating by his father, he ran out of the house in his bare feet, then put his sneakers on and ran five miles to his ROTC instructor's home. He sat outside the instructor's house, afraid to go in, and was finally discovered there by the instructor. The doctor explained that children who are victims of abuse are often reluctant to report their problems to others. In Richard's case, he believed for many years that child beatings were the normal behavior for a father. He was humiliated by the abuse and even had trouble reporting it to the ROTC instructor with whom he had a close relationship. On this occasion, however, the instructor and Richard went to the sheriff to report the abuse. The family was then interviewed together, and Richard chose to return home rather than go to a foster home, principally because he saw himself as the protector of his mother and sister.

Richard believed the May visit to the sheriff's office was useless even though his father did not beat him for a week or more. When he returned from reporting his beating to the sheriff, he put a chair against his door every night so his father could not get in. A week and a half after the sheriff's incident, the father exclaimed, "That bastard reported me to the Sheriff," and would say things like

> "I'll give him something that he can really complain about, that is if he can talk,"

the implication being that he would be in a condition that would prevent him from talking about anything.

* * *

[T]he doctor took other factors into account to reach his evaluation conclusion. For example, the beatings and verbal abuse had an adverse effect on Richard's psychological development. He testified that the boy does not have the ability to handle stress that other young people of his age have and any ability he does have in this regard has come about as a developed defensive mechanism against the brutality of his father. That was the problem on November 16, 1982—that is, when his mother turned on him, blaming him for all the trouble with her marriage and in the home generally, and when she kept calling him a bastard and throwing things at him it was too much for him to stand. He felt victimized when his mother reported him to his father that night because she reported things that he had never said about her. This series of events and its repercussions, together with his father's beating him that night and the father's threat that he should leave home, was more than Richard Jahnke could handle. In addition, according to Dr. Mc-Donald, he was afraid of another beating when his father and mother returned from dinner. Therefore, taking all of these things into account, he was under unusual and, for him, unbearable pressure on the evening of November 16, 1982.

* * *

THE INSANITY MISCONCEPTION

Both the State and the trial court believed the defendant was urging an insanity or diminished-capacity defense and thus were of the opinion that the proffered testimony was irrelevant.

The theory of Richard Jahnke's defense was misunderstood by the prosecuting attorney, the trial court and now, I submit, this court.

* * *

In these proceedings, the mental state of Richard Jahnke was not offered as a defense as would be the case with an insanity plea. Neither his mental capacity nor his intent to commit the crime was in issue. Rather, the specific defense is self-defense, which requires a showing that Jahnke reasonably believed it was necessary to use deadly force to prevent imminent death or great bodily harm to himself. In this situation, the expert testimony is offered, when the battered defendant pleads self-defense, as an aid to the jury in interpreting the surrounding circumstances as they affected the reasonableness of his belief. The expert testimony offered was secondary to the defense asserted. Given the opportunity, the defendant would not seek to show through the expert testimony that the mental and physical mistreatment which he suffered affected his mental state so that he *could not be responsible* for his actions; rather, the testimony was offered to show that, because he suffered from 14 years of brutalizing, *it was reasonable* for him to have remained in the home—to have prepared to respond to the beating that he had been promised would surely come and to have believed at that time and place that he was in imminent danger.

* * *

It is because a jury would not understand and would not be expected to understand why Richard Jahnke would remain in that environment and believe that he was in imminent danger that the expert testimony is critical to aid and assist them in evaluating these conditions, circumstances and behavior patterns.

* * *

Questions and Comments

1. *Analyzing* Jahnke. Assuming that it otherwise met the criteria for expert testimony,[n] should the psychiatric opinion and associated factual evidence in *Jahnke* have been admitted under the traditional definition of self-defense? Provocation? Under the Model Penal Code's definitions of self-defense and provocation? Is the expert's testimony relevant to mens rea or insanity issues (is there a mental illness)? Or is it irrelevant to criminal liability? Note that one week after the court's decision, the governor commuted Jahnke's sentence to three years.

If, instead of killing his father, the defendant had stolen something in order to prove that he was "tough" rather than "sensitive" and thus avoid further beatings, should he have a duress defense to a charge of theft?

n. In a part of the opinion not reprinted, the majority suggested that the "battered-child syndrome" was not a "generally accepted diagnosis". See discussion of the general acceptance doctrine at pp. 454–55.

2. *The battered woman syndrome.* The issues raised in *Jahnke* were presaged in a number of cases involving women charged with killing their husbands after suffering through years of abuse. According to Dr. Lenore Walker, who is often credited with recognizing the "battered wife syndrome", some women who are subjected to abuse by their husbands develop what has come to be called "learned helplessness". Because of low self-esteem, passivity, an inability to express terror and anger, and inculcation of traditional societal attitudes toward females, these women believe that the batterer is all-powerful, that they are to blame for the battering, and that no one can help them. Emotionally and financially dependent upon the battering husband, and perhaps fearful of being stigmatized as failures, they develop "coping" responses rather than "escape" responses as a method of surviving the relationship. In other words, rather than leaving the batterer, they remain with him and put up with the beatings. The battering cycle usually proceeds through three stages. The first phase—the "tension-building" stage—involves minor battering incidents and verbal abuse, during which the woman tries to placate the man and be as passive as possible to stave off further violence. Phase two is the "acute battering incident", usually precipitated by some event in the man's life outside the relationship, but sometimes triggered by the woman when she can no longer tolerate or control her reaction to the man's phase one actions. Phase three is characterized by contrition and reconciliation on the part of the man; he often promises to seek professional help, stop drinking and refrain from further violence. Sometimes, however, the normal cycle is disrupted during phase one or two. The woman either precipitates an incident or fights back and the husband is killed or badly hurt. See Lenore Walker, The Battered Woman (1979).

A number of researchers have challenged both the notion that domestic violence is cyclical and that women who are battered always or usually experience "learned helplessness." Their conclusion is that there is no "single profile" of the battered woman. See Regina Schuller & Sara Rzepa, "The Scientific Status of Research on Domestic Violence Against Women," in David Faigman et al., Science in the Law: Social and Behavioral Science Issues 206, 237 (2002). Nonetheless, the term "battered woman syndrome" now pervades the literature and court decisions. Evidence of the syndrome is introduced to support a number of legal theories, including insanity and diminished capacity, but it is most often offered to support a self-defense claim. The courts are split as to whether evidence of the syndrome is relevant to such a claim. See Jeffrey Cross, "The Expert as Educator: A Proposed Approach to the Use of Battered Women Syndrome Expert Testimony," 35 Vand.L.Rev. 753 (1982). In *State v. Kelly,* 97 N.J. 178, 478 A.2d 364 (1984), the court permitted evidence about the syndrome in a homicide case:

> At the heart of the claim of self-defense was defendant's story that she had been repeatedly subjected to "beatings" over the course of her marriage.... The crucial issue of fact on which this expert's testimony would bear is why, given such allegedly severe and constant beatings, combined with threats to kill, defendant had not long ago left decedent. Whether raised by the prosecutor as a factual issue or not, our own common knowledge tells us that most of us, including the ordinary

juror, would ask himself or herself just such a question. And our knowledge is bolstered by the experts' knowledge, for the experts point out that one of the common myths, apparently believed by most people, is that battered wives are free to leave. To some, this misconception is followed by the observation that the battered wife is masochistic, proven by her refusal to leave despite the severe beatings; to others, however, the fact that the battered wife stays on unquestionably suggests that the "beatings" could not have been too bad for if they had been, she certainly would have left. The expert could clear up these myths, by explaining that one of the common characteristics of a battered wife is her inability to leave despite such constant beatings; her "learned helplessness"; her lack of anywhere to go; her feeling that if she tried to leave, she would be subjected to even more merciless treatment; her belief in the omnipotence of her battering husband; and sometimes her hope that her husband will change his ways.

Consider whether *Kelly's* rationale supports a self-defense claim on the facts of *State v. Norman*, 89 N.C.App. 384, 366 S.E.2d 586 (1988), rev'd, 324 N.C. 253, 378 S.E.2d 8 (1989). Norman was beaten by her husband for years. He would demand that she bark like a dog, eat dog or cat food, and sleep on the cold concrete floor. If she refused he would hit her with whatever was handy: his fist, a flyswatter, a baseball bat, a shoe, an ashtray, all of which left scars. Two days before the killing, he took her to a truck stop and forced her to prostitute herself, something he had done on numerous other occasions. He also assaulted her, for which he was arrested. Upon returning from jail the next day, he beat her continuously, and Norman, apparently in distress, took an overdose of nerve pills. When emergency personnel arrived to treat her, the husband tried to interfere, stating, "Let the bitch die.... She ain't nothing but a dog. She don't deserve to live." Then next day, the day of the shooting, the husband again beat Norman all day, kicking her in the head, smashing food in her face, and putting a cigarette out on her chest. When he decided to take a nap, Norman took her daughter's baby, whom she had been babysitting, to her mother's house so her husband would not wake up from the crying. At her mother's, Norman picked up a gun, returned home, and killed her husband while he lay sleeping. Norman's self-defense claim failed.

Are claims such as those made in *Kelly* and *Norman* better characterized as claims of insanity or diminished responsibility that focus on inner "disease" states (i.e., an "excuse") rather than on the manner in which the woman's relationship with the batterer makes her actions reasonable (a "justification")? Compare *State v. Necaise*, 466 So.2d 660 (La.Ct.App. 1985)(concluding that syndrome testimony is meant to support a "partial responsibility" defense, and rejecting it as such) with *People v. Torres*, 128 Misc.2d 129, 488 N.Y.S.2d 358, 361–62 (Sup.Ct. 1985)(observing that the syndrome is not "intended to establish ... a mental disease or defense relieving defendant of criminal responsibility" but rather "is best understood as being descriptive of an identifiable group of symptoms that characterize the behavior and state of mind of abused women rather than being disease-like in character"). Some writers have resisted the excuse characterization as demeaning to women. Elizabeth M. Schneider, "Describing and

Changing Women's Self–Defense Work and the Problem of Expert Testimony," 9 Women's Rights Law Reporter 195 (1986).

3. *Other cases that might raise "other defense" issues.* Consider what defenses, if any, should be available in the following cases:

Case A. According to Parisie, charged with murder, on the night of the crime he was walking on 5th Street in Springfield when the decedent pulled up next to him in his car and offered him a lift. Parisie accepted, and they drove out of Springfield, turned down a gravel road and parked. After turning off the lights and sliding back the seat, the decedent made a homosexual advance, smiled and said if the defendant refused he would have to walk. Parisie just 'blew up, went crazy,' and vaguely remembered struggling with the decedent and hearing a noise that he assumed to be gunshots. The next thing he remembered clearly was being in the deceased's car in a Springfield parking lot. At trial, Parisie called a clinical psychologist who testified that Parisie suffered from paranoid schizophrenia, was a loner with a basic distrust of people, and was a highly latent homosexual with strong feelings of inferiority. Parisie then called a psychiatrist who testified that "homosexual panic" is a severe panic or fear reaction that is provoked by extreme anxiety connected with admitting homosexual tendencies or experiences, and that this panic often takes the form of a state of amnesia, in which the person sets aside or forgets unconsciously something that his conscious mind cannot tolerate. The psychiatrist also stated that a person suffering from this type of reaction, although not mentally ill, could act purely instinctively. See *People v. Parisie*, 5 Ill.App.3d 1009, 287 N.E.2d 310 (1972)(finding evidence insufficient for insanity, but not addressing other defensive issues).

Case B. "The defendant, charged with assaulting a jail guard, had been raped a year earlier in a small motel room by a man who had torn off her clothing. When she was arrested a year later on a charge of domestic violence, she was placed in a small holding room and approached by one of the guards, who forced her to stand up by grabbing her sweatpants in a way that resembled the actions of the rapist. She reacted by hitting the guard with a food tray. A psychologist testified that a post-traumatic stress disorder [stemming from the rape] caused her to be more fearful in that situation than a normal person would have been under the same circumstances." See Brett C. Trowbridge, "Self Defense as a Mental Defense," 19 Am. J. Forensic Psychology 63, 67 (2001).

4. *The outer boundary of exculpation.* In contrast to the court in *Kelly*, the majority in *Jahnke* asserts that allowing self-defense in such abuse cases would be "antithetical to the mores of modern civilized society." Consider, in support of this position, the arguments of Justice Oliver Wendell Holmes in The Common Law (1881) to the effect that the deterrent purpose of the criminal law must take precedence over the retributive goal. Holmes began by asserting that "prevention" of criminal conduct is "the chief and only universal purpose of punishment." To accomplish the prevention goal, the criminal law must inflict pain on individuals who commit crime, thus using them as a "tools" to ensure the general welfare. Furthermore, the primacy

of the prevention goal means that the purpose of the criminal law is only to induce "external conformity to rule;" the precise reasons why people obey the law are not important. Because the law uses people as tools to achieve this "external" result, "the actual degree of personal guilt involved in any particular transgression cannot be the only element ... in the liability incurred."

To Holmes this conclusion did not mean that blameworthiness is irrelevant to criminal liability. But it did mean that blameworthiness should be defined in terms of the "average member of the community." He continued:

> [W]hen we are dealing with that part of the law which aims more directly than any other at establishing standards of conduct, we should expect there more than elsewhere to find that the tests of liability are external, and independent of the degree of evil in the particular person's motives or intentions. The conclusion follows directly from the nature of the standards to which conformity is required. These are not only external, as was shown above, but they are of general application. They do not merely require that every man should get as near as he can to the best conduct possible for him. They require him at his own peril to come up to a certain height. They take no account of incapacities, unless the weakness is so marked as to fall into well-known exceptions, such as infancy or madness. They assume that every man is as able as every other to behave as they command. If they fall on any one class harder than on another, it is on the weakest. For it is precisely to those who are most likely to err by temperament, ignorance, or folly, that the threats of the law are the most dangerous.

> The reconciliation of the doctrine that liability is founded on blameworthiness with the existence of liability where the party is not to blame ... is founded in the conception of the average man, the man of ordinary intelligence and reasonable prudence. Liability is said to arise out of such conduct as would be blameworthy in him. But he is an ideal being, represented by the jury when they are appealed to, and his conduct is an external or objective standard when applied to any given individual. That individual may be morally without stain, because he has less than ordinary intelligence or prudence. But he is required to have those qualities at his peril. If he has them, he will not, as a general rule, incur liability without blameworthiness.

How does Holmes' "average man" focus apply in Jahnke's case? The other cases described above? Should the test be adjusted in the relevant cases to focus on the "average child" or the "average woman"? The "average battered child or woman" or the average "latent homosexual"? On what grounds?

E. ABOLITION OF THE INSANITY DEFENSE

This topic has been reserved until now because proposals to abolish the insanity defense cannot properly be evaluated until one has some grasp of the framework of the criminal law. For instance, one could conclude that eliminating the insanity defense would change little if the automatism, diminished capacity, self-defense, and duress doctrines were given their full potential scope. See Christopher Slobogin, "An End to

Insanity: Recasting the Role of Mental Disability in Criminal Cases," 86 Va. L. Rev. 1199 (2000)(making this argument).

A more draconian way of limiting the exculpatory scope of the insanity defense has been termed the "mens rea" alternative. Although most jurisdictions retain the insanity defense, at least four states (Kansas, Idaho, Montana, and Utah) have adopted this alternative, which replaces the defense with a provision allowing acquittal if the accused, as a result of mental disability, lacked the mens rea for the crime charged. In Montana, for instance, the defendant is to be acquitted if the jury finds that "due to a mental disease or defect he could not have had a particular state of mind that is an essential element of the offense charged." Other evidence of cognitive or volitional impairment due to mental disability is admissible only at sentencing; if the sentencing court finds that the offender "was suffering from a mental disease or defect which rendered him unable to appreciate the criminality of his conduct or to conform his conduct to the requirements of law," it may "sentence him to be committed to the custody of the director of the department of institutions to be placed in an appropriate institution for custody, care, and treatment for a definite time not to exceed the maximum term of imprisonment that could be imposed." Mont.Code Ann. 46–14–201(2), 46–14–311, 46–14–312. The provisions relating to the disposition of those who are acquitted by reason of mental disease or defect are similar to typical commitment statutes for insanity acquittees. Id.

The American Medical Association, in a report released shortly after the Hinckley verdict, supported this approach. See "Insanity Defense in Criminal Trials and Limitations of Psychiatric Testimony: Report of the Board of Trustees," 251 J.Am.Medical Ass. 2967 (1984). The Association's report stated in part:

> The essential goal of an exculpatory test for insanity is to identify the point at which a defendant's mental condition has become so impaired that society may confidently conclude that he has lost his free will. Psychiatric concepts of mental illness are ill-suited to this task. . . . Because free will is an article of faith, rather than a concept that can be explained in medical terms, it is impossible for psychiatrists to determine whether a mental impairment has affected the defendant's capacity for voluntary choice, or caused him to commit the particular act in question.

* * *

> Even under a truncated test of insanity limited to cognitive impairments, the inscrutable cause-and-effect relationship between mental illness and free will remains the central question. . . . Meaningful reform can be achieved only if the focus of the inquiry is shifted away from the elusive notion of free will, and its relationship to mental disease, and back to the relatively objective standards of *mens rea* where it fell traditionally.

The AMA also asserted that several practical problems associated with the insanity defense would be solved by its approach.

> Most significantly, perhaps, abandonment of the moral pretense of the insanity defense in favor of a *mens rea* concept may lead to a more realistic appreciation of the relationship between mental impairment and criminal behavior. Some observers of the criminal justice system maintain that this relationship extends far beyond its manifestations in the case of those few offenders acquitted on claims of insanity; recognition of a special defense applicable to these few detracts from the legitimate treatment needs of the many. *Mens rea* proposals seek to correct this myopic focus of the insanity defense by emphasizing considerations of mercy and appropriate treatment for all mentally disordered offenders.

Additionally, according to the AMA, the mens rea approach would make expert testimony on volitional impairment irrelevant, and "diminish the scope and importance of psychiatric testimony relating to cognitive impairment in the vast majority of cases." Thus, for example, "psychiatric testimony would not be permitted to establish that a defendant's conscious premeditation or deliberation was the consequence of a mental disorder or that his intent to kill was motivated by unconscious aberrational influences."

Questions and Comments

1. *Constitutional status of the insanity defense.* In *State v. Korell*, 213 Mont. 316, 690 P.2d 992 (1984), the Montana Supreme Court upheld the constitutionality of the statute described above. Abolishing the insanity defense, the court concluded, does not violate the federal constitution as long as mental impairment is taken into account at sentencing. In modern times, most courts have followed *Korell's* lead.[o] In contrast, in 1910 the Washington Supreme Court declared unconstitutional a scheme that reserved the insanity issue until the sentencing stage. It stated that preventing the accused from offering evidence tending to prove that "he was insane at the time to the extent that he could not comprehend the nature and quality of the act— in other words, if he had no will to control the physical act of his physical body— . . . is in our opinion as much a violation of his constitutional right to trial by jury as to take from him the right to offer evidence before the jury tending to show that he did not physically commit the act or physically set in motion a train of events resulting in the act." *State v. Strasburg*, 60 Wash. 106, 110 P. 1020 (1910). See also, *State v. Lange*, 168 La. 958, 123 So. 639 (1929); *Sinclair v. State*, 161 Miss. 142, 132 So. 581 (1931).

The Supreme Court's position on the issue is unclear. In *Clark v. Arizona*, 548 U.S. 735, 126 S.Ct. 2709, 165 L.Ed.2d 842 (2006), it held that virtually any insanity formulation is permissible (see pp. 551–52), but did not directly address the predicate issue of whether an insanity defense is constitutionally mandated. Possibly relevant is the Supreme Court's decision

---

o. See *State v. Searcy*, 118 Idaho 632, 798 P.2d 914 (Idaho 1990); *State v. Herrera*, 895 P.2d 359 (Utah 1995); *State v. Bethel*, 275 Kan. 456, 66 P.3d 840 (2003). But see *Finger v. State*, 117 Nev. 548, 27 P.3d 66 (2001), discussed below.

in *Montana v. Egelhoff*, 518 U.S. 37, 116 S.Ct. 2013, 135 L.Ed.2d 361 (1996). There, as recounted in the materials on diminished capacity, the Court held that Montana's statute eliminating the "voluntary intoxication defense" does not violate the Due Process Clause. The Montana Supreme Court had found that, since evidence of intoxication was "clearly relevant" to whether the defendant had the mens rea for murder ("purposely or knowingly" causing another's death), the statute was unconstitutional. But a four-member plurality of the Supreme Court held that the voluntary intoxication defense is not a "fundamental principle of justice." Their primary justification for this view was the fact that voluntary intoxication had not been an excuse in colonial times and that, although the defense had gained considerable acceptance since the nineteenth century, it was "of too recent vintage, and has not received sufficiently uniform and permanent allegiance to qualify as fundamental." In *Finger v. State*, 117 Nev. 548, 27 P.3d 66 (2001), the Nevada Supreme Court relied on *Strasburg*, *Sinclair* and *Egelhoff* in holding that a state statute abolishing the insanity defense violated due process under both the state and federal constitutions.

Even if there are no constitutional problems with eliminating the insanity defense, the mens rea alternative may run afoul of the due process clause if it is meant to bar the automatism defense as well. Like mens rea, the actus reus is a fundamental element of each offense. Thus, analogous to those cases finding that the admission of diminished capacity evidence is constitutionally mandated, the due process clause might prohibit exclusion of evidence relevant to the "involuntariness" of the accused's act.

2. *Evaluating the theory behind the mens rea alternative.* Constitutional concerns aside, does limiting evidence concerning mental disease or defect to the mens rea issue capture the universe of mental disabled people who should have their disability accorded exculpatory effect? The American Bar Association rejected the mens rea alternative, noting that it would permit conviction of any defendants who "knew what they were doing at the time of an offense and possessed the intent to commit it." According to the ABA:

> The issue of criminal blameworthiness merits deeper inquiry because it implies a certain *quality* of knowledge and intent transcending a minimal awareness and purposefulness. Otherwise, for example, a defendant who knowingly and intentionally killed his son under the psychotic delusion that he was the biblical Abraham, and his son the biblical Isaac, could be held criminally responsible.

In response, consider this argument from Morris, a vigorous advocate of the mens rea approach:

> It too often is overlooked that one group's exculpation from criminal responsibility confirms the inculpation of other groups. Why not permit the defense of dwelling in a Negro ghetto? Such a defense would not be morally indefensible. Adverse social and subcultural background is statistically more criminogenic than is psychosis; like insanity, it also severely circumscribes the freedom of choice which a non-deterministic criminal law ... attributes to accused persons. True, a defense of social adversity would politically be intolerable; but that does not vitiate the analogy for my purposes. [Some might argue] that insanity destroys, undermines, diminishes man's capacity to reject what is wrong and to

adhere to what is right. So does the ghetto—more so. But surely, [it will be replied,] I would not have us punish the sick. Indeed I would, if [one insists] on punishing the grossly deprived. To the extent that criminal sanctions serve punitive purposes, I fail to see the difference between these two defenses. To the extent that they serve rehabilitative, treatment, and curative purposes I fail to see the need for the difference.

... It seems clear that there are different degrees of moral turpitude in criminal conduct and that the mental health or illness of an actor is relevant to an assessment of that degree—as are many other factors in a crime's social setting and historical antecedents. This does not mean, however, that we are obliged to quantify these pressures for purposes of a moral assessment ... leading to conclusions as to criminal responsibility.

Norval Morris, "Psychiatry and the Dangerous Criminal," 41 S.Cal.L.Rev. 514, 520–21 (1968). Is Morris' equation of poverty and mental illness for purposes of determining criminal responsibility persuasive? See Stephen Morse, "Excusing the Crazy: The Insanity Defense Reconsidered," 58 S.Cal. L.Rev. 779, 788–90, 793–95 (1985). If it is, why isn't it an argument for *expanding* the insanity defense rather than for its abolition?

3. *Evaluating the practical impact of the mens rea alternative.* Is the AMA correct in asserting that the mens rea alternative will reduce psychiatric testimony and acquittals based on mental disability? Professor Dershowitz has argued that it will not:

The clash of experts testifying about the defendant's state of mind will continue, as it has for more than a century. The battlefield may shift from the issue of right versus wrong to the equally troublesome issue of intent, but the jurors will hear testimony not substantially different—or more informative—from what they hear today.

In the last analysis, it is the jury that decides whether an accused is to be convicted or acquitted. No matter how the law reads, it is a deeply entrenched human feeling that those who are grossly disturbed—whether they are called "madmen," "lunatics," "insane," or "mentally ill"— should not be punished like ordinary criminals. This feeling, which is as old as recorded history, is unlikely to be rooted out by new legislation.

Alan Dershowitz, "Abolishing the Insanity Defense," 9 Crim.L.Bull. 434, 438–39 (1973). Current empirical evidence on the impact of the mens rea alternative is inconclusive. In a study of the impact of Montana's legislative changes in 1979 abolishing the insanity defense and limiting the mental disability defense to mens rea, researchers looked at various factors for the three years prior to and the three years after the reform. They found that the proportion of defendants who claimed a defense based on mental disease or defect was virtually unchanged between the pre and post periods. However, of those who claimed a psychiatric defense, 22.7% were successful and 49.3% were found guilty in the pre-reform period, while 2.3% were successful and 60.9% were found guilty in the post-reform period. At the same time, the number of psychiatric cases which were dismissed rose from 17.3% to 29.9% between the two periods, suggesting to the researchers that, after the reform, many of those who would have been found not guilty by reason of insanity were found incompetent to stand trial instead. They also found that, after the reform, a smaller percentage of those who raised a defense were imprisoned (35.4 to 29.1) or hospitalized (30.0 to 16.3) and a greater percentage were put on probation, conditional release or released altogether (25.7 to 46.5). Lisa Callahan, et al., "The Impact of Montana's Insanity Defense Abolition," paper published by Policy Research Associates, Inc. (July, 1988). See also, H. Steadman, et al., Before and After Hinckley: Evaluating Insanity Defense Reform 136 (1994)(in Montana after the reform "if a person's mental status was seen as sufficient to warrant reduced criminal responsibility, they were found [incompetent to stand trial], and committed to the same hospital and the same wards where they would have been confined if they had been found NGRI.").

4. *Bifurcation.* An alternative that is functionally similar to the mens rea approach is to "bifurcate" the trial, adjudicating the issue of "factual guilt" at the first stage and leaving the insanity issue to the second stage. Bifurcation was first proposed as a method of (1) alleviating jury confusion by avoiding complex psychiatric testimony about insanity until after the defendant had been found "guilty" of the crime; (2) eliminating the risk of the jury returning a verdict of insanity out of sympathy for a mentally ill, but guilty, defendant; and (3) conserving judicial resources where the defendant was acquitted at the first stage.[p] The difference between the bifurcation and mens rea approaches is that in the former the insanity issue is still litigated at trial (albeit at the second stage), while in the latter any psychiatric information not relevant to mens rea is considered only at sentencing.

As originally conceived, bifurcation was different from the mens rea alternative in an additional way: psychiatric testimony was to be excluded entirely from the first stage. But, as discussed previously, most courts found this scheme unconstitutional on the ground that such evidence could not be excluded if it was relevant to mens rea. See, e.g., *Sanchez v. State,* 567 P.2d 270 (Wyo.1977); but see, *Steele v. State,* 97 Wis.2d 72, 294 N.W.2d 2 (1980). According to the American Bar Association, once this position is accepted, "mandatory bifurcation loses its allure" because "relevant evidence of mental abnormality must be allowed at the first stage as well as the second, which uselessly duplicates evidence and nullifies many of the supposed advantages of bifurcation." ABA Criminal Justice Mental Health Standards, commentary to Standard 7–6.7, p. 341 (1987). Can the same type of claim be leveled at the mens rea approach? Colorado reverses the bifurcation process, adjudicating the insanity issue before the guilt issue. C.R.S. 16–8–105. Would this approach alleviate the problems discussed above?

5. *Abolition of insanity and mens rea defenses.* A final approach has been most forcefully presented by Lady Wootton in her book Crime and the Criminal Law (1963). She too suggests a bifurcated approach to determining the appropriate punishment, but with a significant difference. The first stage would consider only whether the defendant committed an antisocial act. *No*

p. Bifurcation was also supported by a fourth reason—protecting the fifth amendment right of a defendant who wanted to assert both a not guilty plea and a plea of not guilty by reason of insanity, without having to present possibly damaging psychi-atric testimony during the adjudication of the first plea. Bifurcation allows adjudication of the factual defense at the first stage while adjudication of the second plea, if necessary, is reserved for the second stage. See p. 525.

consideration of mental state, psychiatric or otherwise, would take place at this stage. At the second stage, the appropriate disposition of the defendant would be decided, based on expert opinion if deemed necessary or desirable. Lady Wootton defended her proposal as follows:

> The law, of course, always requires clear-cut distinctions. The responsible and sane stand on one side of the line, the irresponsible or insane on the other: every single defendant must be appropriately classified. Yet natura non facit saltum: in reality we are all strung out along a continuum which reaches from the most responsible to the most hopelessly weak-willed and weak-minded; and in many cases the degree of our responsibility almost certainly varies from time to time in accordance with our circumstances or physiological condition. In short, the "vital distinction between illness and evil" is anything but clear-cut. Indeed the worst feature of all the formulae that have been tried—McNaghten, Durham, British Homicide Act, or what have you—is their insistence on a hard and fast and totally unrealistic line between the sheep and the goats. Anyone who has followed trials in which this issue has been raised will be well aware of the sophisticated forensic subtleties for which it offers opportunity. Is careful planning of a crime consistent with diminished responsibility? Is it possible that a man should be fully responsible when he seizes a stick in the entrance to a house, but only partially so when he uses it to beat an old gentleman in bed upstairs? In these and the many similar examples which can be culled from trials in which the defendant's mens rea is in issue, all contact with reality seems to have been lost.

> Clearly the only way to avoid getting entangled in these niceties and absurdities is to demote the concept of blame from its dominant position in the criminal process. If we could emancipate ourselves from the deep-rooted tradition that the basic function of the criminal law is to identify and punish wickedness, all this farcical hairsplitting about the limits of mental abnormality could be done away with. Questions of the accused's mental condition could be ignored in the actual trial, the purpose of which would be to establish responsibility in a purely physical sense for the actus reus without reference to the presence, or absence, of malicious intent. Mens rea would thus no longer be written into the definition of every crime. Only after the accused's physical responsibility for a forbidden action had been proved would it be permissible to inquire into his mental condition, in order to determine how best he could be dealt with. In other words an offender's state of mind would be regarded as relevant, not to the measure of his guilt, or to the crime of which he should be convicted, but to the choice of the treatment most appropriate to his case.

* * *

Hitherto, of course, strict liability has generally been restricted to such statutory offenses as are generally regarded as of minor importance. In such cases disregard of mens rea is defended on the dual ground, first, that the number of these offenses is so enormous that life is simply not long enough to inquire in every case into the accused's motivation or mental state (imagine what would happen, for example, in a busy city court which disposes of some 300 parking offenses in a morning if proof of mens rea were required in every case!); and, second, that in any case these offenses are not "truly criminal" and do not involve any serious "moral turpitude."

Yet could not an equally compelling argument be made the other way round; i.e., in favor of eliminating the requirement of mens rea from particularly grave offenses such as homicide or rape? Crimes such as these are just as damaging to their victims whether they are the result of calculated wickedness or of insane delusions. Is it not, therefore, proper that anyone who is suspected of having committed such an actus reus should be liable to answer for it in a criminal court, whatever the state of his mind—so long, that is, as he is not too ill to be able to instruct counsel or to understand court proceedings?

* * *

Obviously, if the essential purpose of a criminal court is to punish the blameworthy as they deserve, the compassionworthy must be rescued from its clutches. But, were this obsession with the punitive once dispelled, the courts could be free to deal with every lawbreaker in whatever way, consonant with the moral standards of the community, seemed best calculated to discourage future lawbreaking. Their eyes would be on the future, not on the past. Nor need they be bound by rigid diagnostic categories.

* * *

It follows logically that, once the practice of classifying offenders into the wicked and the weak-minded is abandoned, the similar distinction between prisons and hospitals becomes equally inappropriate. Already hybrid institutions, such as Grendon Underwood in Britain and similar establishments in the United States, are beginning to make their appearance; and suggestions that the courts should simply pass "custodial" sentences without specifying under what conditions, penal or medical, this sentence is to be served are much in the air, and much to be commended. Obviously, in the case of sentences of any considerable duration, the court is in no position to forecast what kind of regime will be best suited to an offender several years ahead. Hence the need for a variety of institutions and for easy transfer from one to another without inhibiting labels, at the discretion of those who are in continuous touch with persons under detention. Nor must this be read as merely a plea for the "soft" treatment of offenders. If the weaker vessels need the protection of a kindly environment, there are others for whom a more demanding regime is certainly indicated; and the response of a single individual to different types of treatment is not necessarily constant throughout his history.

Barbara Wootton, "Book Review of A. Goldstein, The Insanity Defense," 77 Yale L.J. 1019, 1028–1032 (1968).

Is Wootton's proposal coherent? Can it be seen as the logical extension of Holmes' arguments described at pp. 622–23, or does it stray too far from Holmes' premise? Under her proposal, what happens to the person who wants to plead self-defense or duress? To what extent does her proposal undercut what was described in the introduction to this chapter as the central assumption of our criminal justice system—that we have "free will"? Consider the following from Donald Hermann, The Insanity Defense, 91–93 (1983):

> An influential critique of the concept of responsibility has come from behaviorists who maintain that the determination of responsibility, in a moral or traditional legal sense, with elements of culpability and blameworthiness, is meaningless and reflects a fallacious understanding of human behavior. At the same time, it is argued that there should be a reformulation of the utilitarian objectives of the criminal law into one that can be stated succinctly as crime-preventive. Such a view [has been] urged quite eloquently by Lady Wooton....

* * *

> Even assuming the soundness of the determinism of the behaviorist view, there is a fundamental mistake in supposing that law is unrealistic in retaining the concepts of responsibility and punishment. This mistake stems from the assumption that ethics and law have the same point of view with regard to responsibility as does science. Unlike science, the ethical and legal systems are moral enterprises. The ascription of responsibility promotes ethical and legal values. Thus, even if it were true that a person cannot control the determinants of his conduct, and therefore is not free and responsible in some ultimate libertarian sense, the interest of law and ethics in minimizing socially harmful conduct is promoted by fostering feelings of responsibility in society. This need not be regarded as some "noble lie" but, rather, should be viewed in terms of an "as if" constituting an example of a pragmatic sense of truth. Ethical prohibitions and criminal law sanctions can themselves act as a determinant of choices, thereby assuring that actors will avoid condemnation and sanction. The influence of attribution of responsibility has been suggested by one commentator who observed: "[T]he individual who perceives himself as free and responsible behaves very differently than the individual who believes that he lacks choice and responsibility. In general, the direction of this difference is toward a higher level of awareness, initiative, achievement, independence and complexity for those who perceive themselves as freely choosing to behave in certain ways and as responsible for the behavior." Moreover, the criminal sanction with its corollary of blameworthiness strengthens the resolve of persons to obey the law.

> Another significant legal purpose is served by treating persons as responsible and blameworthy when they violate the law. By requiring guilt before criminal sanctions can be applied, the law-abiding person is protected from governmental interference. As one commentator succinctly stated: "The rule of law now guards the innocent, but its protective wall would not survive the dissolution of criminal responsibility." Elimination of the principle of responsibility would result in every attitude, disposition, or accidental movement seen by the state as undesirable, becoming a potential source of coercive intervention in the life of any and every citizen no matter how well intentioned he might be.

6. *Tort liability.* By way of comparison to the foregoing materials, note that traditionally an "insane" person could not escape tort liability by reason of mental disability, at least in a negligence action. See Prosser & Keeton, Torts 1072–1075 (5th ed. 1984). As described by the court in *Jolley v. Powell,* 299 So.2d 647 (Fla.App.1974):

> [L]iability without subjective fault, under some circumstances, is one price men pay for membership in society. The sane and the insane, the awkward and the coordinated are equally liable for their acts or omissions. In such cases, we do not decide fault, rather we determine upon whom our society imposes the burden of redress for a given injury. As Holmes implied in his "awkward man" parable, a principle at least co-equal with that of the fault principle in the law of torts is that the innocent victim should have redress.

> * * *

> We therefore reiterate, when the predicate for a wrongful death action is unintentional tort the standard against which such tort is measured is the objective, "reasonable man standard" and the subjective state of mind of the tortfeasor is irrelevant.

Other reasons that have been given for *Jolley's* approach are that imposing liability on people with mental disability will encourage those responsible for such people to prevent them from doing harm, discourage malingering, and avoid the problems the criminal justice system has confronted in determining insanity. See James Ellis, "Tort Responsibility of the Mentally Disabled," 1981 Am. Bar Found. Res. J. 1079. A small number of courts reject this view. As stated in *Fitzgerald v. Lawhorn,* 29 Conn.Supp. 511, 294 A.2d 338 (Com.Pl.1972):

> If a child too young cannot be held liable in negligence, then an insane person would not be held liable; it is unjust to hold one responsible for a wrong that he is incapable of avoiding; a man who is so devoid of intelligence or reason as to be unable to apprehend danger and do something to avoid it cannot be held negligent. . . .

What are the differences and similarities between Lady Wootton's approach to criminal liability and the tort law's traditional approach to negligence liability? Are the justifications for the two approaches similar? Note that, as *Jolley* implies, mental disability is often considered a defense in intentional tort and punitive damage actions on grounds of lack of intent. See, e.g., *State Farm Fire & Casualty Co. v. James C. Wicka,* 474 N.W.2d 324 (Minn. 1991)(holding that an intentional act exclusion in an insurance policy does not apply to an insured whose act "is the product of a failure of . . . volitional or cognitive capacities" even though it was clear the insured, suffering from schizophrenia, "intended" to kill his victim). What are the implications of that fact for the tort-crime analogy?

F. THE "GUILTY BUT MENTALLY ILL" PLEA

A final reform aims not at abolishing the insanity defense, but at reducing the number of insanity pleas and acquittals by offering an alternative to the insanity verdict. Since 1976, at least 14 states have passed statutes authorizing the factfinder to return a verdict of "guilty but mentally ill" (GBMI). Although there are many different versions of the GBMI concept, most proposals work basically as follows: A defendant who pleads not guilty by reason of insanity may be found not guilty, guilty, insane, or, in the alternative, guilty but mentally ill at the time of the offense. If the jury makes the last mentioned finding, the defendant may be sentenced to any term appropriate for the offense, with the opportunity for treatment in a mental hospital during that period. Thus, jurors in insanity cases are given three sets of instructions with respect to the ultimate verdict they may reach: One explains under what circumstances a defendant may be found guilty of the crime charged; one describes the state's test for insanity; and one informs the jury when a defendant who is guilty beyond a reasonable doubt but not insane may be found GBMI. See, e.g., Mich.Comp.Laws Ann. § 768.36; Ill.—S.H.A. ch. 38, ¶ 115–2(b); Ky.Rev.Stat. 504.120. The definition of mental illness found in the last of these instructions varies from state to state, but usually borrows heavily from the definition of mental illness in the state's civil commitment statute. In Michigan, for instance, the definition is taken directly from the mental health code and states that mental illness is "[a] substantial disorder of thought or mood which significantly impairs judgment, behavior, capacity to recognize reality, or ability to cope with the ordinary demands of life." Mich.Comp.Laws Ann. § 330.1400a.

As the following case illustrates, a person who is found guilty but mentally ill is subject to the same dispositions as a person found guilty.

PEOPLE v. CREWS

Supreme Court of Illinois, 1988.
122 Ill.2d 266, 119 Ill.Dec. 308, 522 N.E.2d 1167.

* * *

JUSTICE MILLER delivered the opinion of the court:

The defendant, William Crews, pleaded guilty but mentally ill to one count each of murder and attempted murder in the circuit court of Randolph County. The trial judge sentenced the defendant to death for the murder conviction and imposed a 30–year prison term for the conviction for attempted murder. The defendant's execution was stayed pending direct review by this court.

The defendant's convictions stem from his attack on two correctional officers at Menard Correctional Center on November 30, 1984. The defendant was an inmate of Menard at the time of the offenses and was serving a 20–to–60–year term for an earlier murder conviction. The attack occurred on the gallery outside the defendant's cell. The defendant stabbed correctional officer Cecil Harbison to death with a shank and wounded another guard, Lamont Gilbert. The defendant then fled from the gallery, and he was captured moments later on the ground floor of the cellhouse.

The defendant initially pleaded not guilty to the charges here, but he later asked to change his plea to guilty but mentally ill (GBMI). As required by statute (see Ill.Rev.Stat.1983, ch. 38, pars. 113–4(d), 115–2(b)), the trial judge ordered the defendant to undergo a psychological examination, and a hearing was held in August 1985 on the defendant's mental condition. At the hearing, defense counsel presented the testimony of three psychiatrists—Drs. Pichardo, Vallabhaneni, and Parwatikar—who had treated the defendant at Menard Correctional Center or Menard Psychiatric Center. Dr. Pichardo first saw the defendant in February 1980 and last saw him in the middle of September 1984, a little more than two months before the defendant's attack on the two guards. Dr. Pichardo believed that the defendant was suffering from a mental illness during that period, but he could not say whether the defendant had a judgment-impairing, substantial disorder of thought, mood, or behavior. According to Dr. Pichardo, the defendant had attempted to commit suicide in April 1980.

Dr. Vallabhaneni saw the defendant several days after his attack on the guards and believed that at the time of the offenses the defendant was suffering from a mental illness and that his judgment was impaired, but he did not have a specific diagnosis for the defendant's condition.

Dr. Parwatikar believed that at the time of the offenses the defendant was mentally ill, in that he had a substantial disorder of mood, thought, or behavior. Dr. Parwatikar saw the defendant on December 2, 1984, two days after the offenses here, and his diagnosis then was of an intermittent explosive disorder.

The State disputed the defendant's contention that he was mentally ill at the time of the offenses. Dr. Daniel Cuneo, a clinical psychologist, testified in the State's behalf at the hearing. Dr. Cuneo had interviewed the defendant on two occasions—in March 1985 and in August 1985—and, based on those examinations, as well as on his review of the defendant's records, Dr. Cuneo concluded that the defendant was malingering and that he had an antisocial personality disorder. Dr. Cuneo believed that the defendant was only feigning mental illness.

The State also introduced into evidence statements the defendant made to authorities concerning the offenses here. In an initial statement given on the night of his attack on the two guards, the defendant said simply that he had gone berserk, and he did not provide a motive for his acts. In a statement given the next day, however, the defendant explained that he attacked the officers because he resented an order Harbison had given him shortly before that. The State also presented testimony from two inmates who spoke with the defendant in the period following his attack on the two guards. They testified that the defendant told them that he was trying to convince psychiatrists that he was crazy. Also, one of the inmates recalled that on the day of the occurrence here the defendant mentioned the name of a friend who had been killed earlier that year and made a comment suggesting that the friend's death should be avenged. Finally, the State presented evidence of the defendant's extensive history of disciplinary violations since 1974, when he began serving the prison sentence for his earlier murder conviction. These disciplinary tickets included 16 violations of rules, 10 assaults, 5 instances of damaging property, 19 instances of disobeying orders, and 11 instances of possession of contraband or dangerous weapons.

The trial judge accepted the defendant's GBMI plea, finding that there was a factual basis that the defendant was mentally ill when he committed the offenses here. The State then requested a death penalty hearing, and the defendant waived his right to a jury for that purpose. The defendant, who was born in 1952 and therefore 18 or older at the time of the offenses, was eligible for the death penalty because the murder victim was a correctional officer.

[Under the Illinois death penalty statute, the sentencing authority is to consider both aggravating and mitigating circumstances in deciding between life imprisonment and death. The prosecution must prove the existence of one aggravating circumstance (such as a significant history of criminal conduct); if it does so, the death penalty may be imposed unless the defense can convince the factfinder that mitigating factors outweigh the aggravating factor or factors. One of the mitigating factors listed in the Illinois statute is proof that the defendant "was under the influence of extreme mental or emotional disturbance" at the time of the offense.]

Dr. Cuneo testified in the State's behalf at the sentencing hearing, and he repeated his earlier diagnosis that the defendant had an antisocial personality disorder. Dr. Cuneo did not believe that the defendant was functioning under an extreme mental or emotional disturbance at the time of the offenses. Dr. Cuneo also said that he was familiar with capital sentencing in Illinois and that he did not know of any case in which a defendant received the death sentence after being found guilty but mentally ill.

* * *

The defendant did not present any testimony at the sentencing hearing. Included in a presentence investigation report, however, was a report dated August 5, 1985, by a psychiatrist, Dr. Moisy Shopper, who had examined the defendant and reviewed his prison file. Dr. Shopper described the defendant's suicide attempt in April 1980 and noted parallels between that event and the defendant's later attack on the two guards. Also, Dr. Shopper described the defendant's condition at the time of the offense as "an acute paranoid psychotic state with marked depressive features."

The trial judge sentenced the defendant to death for the murder conviction. The trial judge did not believe that imposition of the death penalty was precluded by the defendant's GBMI plea. The trial judge found that the defendant had a significant history of criminal conduct, and he did not believe that the defendant was acting under the influence of an extreme mental or emotional disturbance sufficient to preclude imposition of the death penalty.

* * *

The defendant ... argues that the legislature did not intend the death penalty to be available as a possible punishment for GBMI offenders.

* * *

In support of this argument, the defendant relies on section 5–2–6 of the Unified Code of Corrections (Ill.Rev.Stat.1983, ch. 38, par. 1005–2–6). Section 5–2–6 bears the heading "Sentencing and Treatment of Defendant Found Guilty but Mentally Ill," and the defendant contends that certain provisions in the statute signify the legislature's intent to preclude the death penalty as a possible punishment for GBMI offenders.

* * *

Although we agree with the defendant that section 5–2–6 of the Unified Code of Corrections is applicable to GBMI offenders, we do not believe that the statute may be understood as precluding the imposition of the death penalty. To the contrary, the plain language of the statute indicates otherwise. Section 5–2–6(a) provides, "The court may impose any sentence upon the defendant which could be imposed pursuant to law upon a defendant who had been convicted of the same offense without a finding of mental illness." Clearly, that language leaves available for GBMI offenders the full range of sentences—including the death penalty—that may be imposed on persons who are guilty of offenses and who are not mentally ill. This is entirely consistent with the legislature's definition of the term "mental illness" as a condition distinct from insanity. Section 6–2(c) of the Criminal Code of 1961 provides, "A person who, at the time of the commission of a criminal offense, was not insane but was suffering from a mental illness, is not relieved of criminal responsibility for his conduct and may be found guilty but mentally ill." (Ill.Rev.Stat.1983, ch. 38, par. 6–2(c).) Section 6–2(d) of the Criminal Code of 1961 provides, "For purposes of this Section, 'mental illness' or 'mentally ill' means a substantial disorder of thought, mood, or behavior which afflicted a person at the time of the commission of the offense and which impaired that person's judgment, but not to the extent that he is unable to appreciate the wrongfulness of his behavior or is unable to conform his conduct to the requirements of law." (Ill.Rev.Stat.1983, ch. 38, par. 6–2(d).) A GBMI offender is no less guilty than one who is guilty and not mentally ill; unlike insanity, a GBMI finding or plea does not relieve an offender of criminal responsibility for his conduct. By its plain terms, section 5–2–6(a) authorizes imposition on a GBMI offender of any sentence that could be imposed on one convicted of the same offense without the additional finding of mental illness; the death penalty therefore is available as a sentence for

GBMI offenders who have been convicted of murder (see Ill.Rev.Stat. 1983, ch. 38, par. 1005–5–3(c)(1)).

* * *

Opposing that interpretation of section 5–2–6 of the Unified Code of Corrections, the defendant argues that sentencing a GBMI offender to death would be inconsistent with the treatment alternatives prescribed for GBMI offenders in section 5–2–6 of the Unified Code of Corrections. The provisions concerning treatment do not pertain to defendants sentenced to death, however. Rather, they apply to persons sentenced to terms of imprisonment (see Ill.Rev.Stat.1983, ch. 38, pars. 1005–2–6(b), (c), (d)) and to those placed on probation or sentenced to a term of periodic imprisonment or a period of conditional discharge (see Ill.Rev. Stat.1983, ch. 38, par. 1005–2–6(e)). The statute thus does not mandate what is referred to in the dissent as the "meaningless" requirement of treatment for one awaiting execution. Having rejected the defendant's interpretation of section 5–2–6, we conclude that the statute does not preclude imposition of the death penalty on GBMI offenders.

* * *

The defendant also contends that the trial judge's stated reasons for imposing the death penalty in this case were inconsistent with his earlier finding of a factual basis for the defendant's GBMI plea.... The defendant contends that the trial judge's decision to accept the GBMI plea cannot be reconciled with his later statement, made at the sentencing hearing, that the defendant "may not have been under an extreme mental or emotional disturbance."

The defendant's argument assumes that mental illness, as that term is applied to GBMI offenders, is more serious than the mitigating circumstance of extreme mental or emotional disturbance, as that term is used in the death penalty statute.... We have already concluded that the legislature authorized imposition of the death penalty on GBMI offenders, and, consistent with that holding, we do not believe that a finding of mental illness necessarily establishes the mitigating circumstance of extreme mental or emotional disturbance. It is important to note here that the distinction between mental illness and the statutory mitigating circumstance of extreme mental or emotional disturbance does not mean that a GBMI plea or finding is irrelevant in a capital case. Because mitigating circumstances are not limited to those specifically enumerated in section 9–1(c) of the Criminal Code of 1961 (Ill.Rev.Stat. 1983, ch. 38, par. 9–1(c)), evidence of a defendant's mental illness is admissible at a capital sentencing hearing regardless of the relationship between the GBMI provisions and the statutory mitigating circumstance of extreme mental or emotional disturbance. The trial judge's decision here to sentence the defendant to death was not contrary to the findings he made in accepting the defendant's GBMI plea. In accordance with the provisions of section 9–1(h) of the Criminal Code of 1961 (Ill.Rev.Stat. 1983, ch. 38, par. 9–1(h)), the trial judge balanced the conflicting evidence and found that any mental or emotional disturbance of the defendant was not sufficient to preclude imposition of the death penalty.

* * *

JUSTICE SIMON, dissenting.

* * *

A sentence of death is completely inconsistent with the goals of the GBMI statutory provisions—providing treatment for the mentally ill as well as punishing them for the crimes they committed. During a reading of the GBMI bill on the Senate floor, the bill's co-sponsor, Senator Adeline J. Geo–Karis, emphasized this goal of treatment, stating that a "guilty but mentally ill defendant, for example, can be ... sentenced exactly as a healthy defendant charged with the same crime, except that his sentence, either to probation, periodic imprisonment, or to the penitentiary, must include psychiatric and psychological treatment or counseling." The bill as enacted includes this requirement of treatment for the offender's mental illness. The statute also requires the Department of Corrections to make periodic inquiry and examination "concerning the nature, extent, continuance, and treatment of the defendant's mental illness" for those GBMI offenders who are imprisoned. The Department of Corrections is also to provide psychological, psychiatric and other counseling and treatment to the defendant and may transfer the inmate to the Department of Mental Health if necessary. This treatment requirement, however, would be meaningless for someone who is going to be put to death. "In view of the statutory treatment rights that underlie a GBMI verdict, to order death as a GBMI's treatment would not only be contrary to the legislature's objectives, but also would be morally reprehensible." Note, "Disposition of the Mentally Ill Offender in Illinois—'Guilty But Mentally Ill,'" 31 DePaul L.Rev. 869, 889–90 (1982).

* * *

[T]he majority [also] concludes that a finding of mental illness does not necessarily establish the mitigating circumstance of mental or emotional disturbance. On the contrary, a finding of mental illness is a recognition of the likelihood of a more serious disorder than the mental state of an extreme emotional disturbance.

Under Illinois law, a finding of mental illness is a recognition that the defendant's judgment at the time of the offense was seriously impaired, a mental state exceeded only by insanity, a complete defense. The legislature has provided for a special verdict form for GBMI defendants. Thus mental illness is unique among mitigating factors because it is the only one that can be incorporated into the judgment at trial. Finally, in order for a GBMI plea to be accepted, the defendant must be examined by a clinical psychologist or psychiatrist, the judge must examine the psychiatric or psychological report or reports and conduct a hearing on the issue of the defendant's mental health.

A finding of extreme mental or emotional disturbance requires none of the above procedures, indicating that the standard for this mitigating factor is much less stringent than that for mental illness. The failure to require a psychological or psychiatric examination to establish an extreme mental or emotional disturbance indicates that it can be established without a finding of mental illness, thus making it a much broader, less serious condition than mental illness. This is evidenced by cases where an extreme mental or emotional disturbance has been found without a finding that the defendant was mentally ill at the time of the offense. Moreover, a finding of extreme mental or emotional disturbance does not necessitate treatment for the offender, and there is no special verdict form for this type of disturbance.

The conclusion of the trial court and the majority that a finding of mental illness does not necessarily establish the mitigating factor of extreme mental or emotional disturbance is therefore clearly in error. By failing to recognize that mental illness is a more serious condition than extreme mental or emotional disturbance, the sentencing court did not give proper weight to the defendant's illness as a mitigating factor, and, a new sentencing hearing is required.

* * *

Questions and Comments

1. *The GBMI verdict as a finding of diminished responsibility.* The court states that a person who is found guilty but mentally ill "is no less guilty than one who is guilty and not mentally ill." Clearly, as the court points out, the Illinois legislature did not want the verdict to be a finding of diminished responsibility that would reduce the degree of crime for which the defendant is convicted. But a GBMI verdict could still function as a determination of diminished responsibility that is implemented at *sentencing;* under this interpretation, the defendant found guilty but mentally ill would be convicted of the crime charged but would be entitled to greater mitigation at sentencing than someone found merely guilty of the same charge. Such an approach might seem particularly appealing in the capital sentencing context.[q] Does the majority in *Crews* hold that the evidence of mental illness associated with the GBMI verdict is irrelevant to the extreme mental or emotional distress issue, relevant but not dispositive, or dispositive on that issue but not dispositive of the ultimate decision with respect to the death penalty? Of these three positions and the dissent's position that the verdict precludes imposition of the death penalty, which is the correct reading of legislative intent?

If one agrees with the majority's position, is there any point in having a distinct verdict indicating that the defendant is guilty of the offense and was also mentally ill (but not insane) during its commission? Or is it accurate to say, as Slovenko has asserted, that one might as well have a verdict called "guilty but flat feet"? Ralph Slovenko, "The Insanity Defense in the Wake of the Hinckley Trial," 14 Rutgers L.J. 373, 393 (1983). Data from Georgia

q. The role of mental abnormality in capital sentencing proceedings is discussed in greater detail in the next section, where the *Crews* case will be revisited.

suggest that the GBMI verdict may actually be a prelude to *enhancement* of sentence. Steadman and his colleagues found that:

> GBMIs were more likely than [those who pleaded insanity and were found guilty] to go to prison or jail and to receive a life sentence. Further, those [GBMI] not receiving a life sentence were given longer sentences than their guilty counterparts. They were also confined for much longer periods of time than those found NGRI [and those found guilty].

Henry Steadman, et al., Before and After Hinckley: Evaluating Insanity Defense Reform 119 (1993). However, no GBMIs in Georgia received the death penalty. Id. at 117.

2. *The GBMI verdict and treatment.* Some have contended that, whatever the impact of the GBMI verdict in assessing the degree of culpability or punishment, it does afford better *conditions* of punishment. Mickenberg has argued that "although ... GBMI does not reduce the degree of crime for which defendants are responsible, it does provide necessary and acceptable mitigation in the form of psychiatric assistance for the convicts while they serve their sentences." Ira Mickenberg, "A Pleasant Surprise: The Guilty But Mentally Ill Verdict Has Both Succeeded in Its Own Right and Successfully Preserved the Traditional Role of the Insanity Defense," 55 Cinn. L.Rev. 943, 990 (1987). Isn't the holding in *Crews* inconsistent with this position?

Arguably, if the point of the GBMI scheme is to facilitate treatment for offenders with mental illness, it is both inefficient and unnecessary. A finding by a judge or jury that an offender was mentally ill *at the time of the offense* is not likely to be very useful in determining the offender's treatment needs (a fact which is recognized by provisions in most GBMI legislation—like Illinois'—requiring a post-conviction treatment assessment by mental health professionals). Moreover, every state already provides that prisoners with mental illness be treated. In Illinois, for instance, well before passage of the state's guilty but mentally ill statute, the legislature required the Department of Corrections to ascertain whether *any* person committed to it needed psychiatric treatment, and authorized transfer of prisoners requiring such treatment to special facilities within the Department or to mental hospitals. Ill.—S.H.A. ch. 28, ¶ 1003–8–5. Research indicates that although GBMI legislation has focused attention on the paucity of treatment resources available to prisoners generally, it has not meant that those who are found guilty but mentally ill are more likely to receive treatment than those who are simply convicted and sentenced and are subsequently found to need treatment. Gary Smith & James Hall, "Evaluating Michigan's Guilty But Mentally Ill Verdict: An Empirical Study," 16 Mich.J.Law Ref. 77, 104–106 (1982). Nor are most courts, whatever the original intent of the GBMI legislation, willing to redress this situation by according those found guilty but mentally ill special treatment status. See, e.g., *People v. Marshall,* 114 Ill.App.3d 217, 70 Ill.Dec. 91, 102, 448 N.E.2d 969, 980 (1983); *People v. Sharif,* 87 Mich.App. 196, 200–01, 274 N.W.2d 17, 19–20 (1978). Is this stance wrong? If not, how does the verdict provide "mitigation," as that word is used by Mickenberg, that would not ordinarily be available without the verdict?

3. *The GBMI verdict as a device for easing the factfinder's burden.* Questions about its conceptual underpinnings aside, might the GBMI verdict be sanctioned on the ground that it makes the difficult choice about criminal responsibility easier? In her study of jury reaction to the insanity defense, Simon found:

> Many of the jurors felt constrained by the verdict limitations placed upon them by the court. They would like to have a way of easing the choice between acquitting the defendant on grounds of insanity and finding him guilty. The former designation goes further than they want to go in distinguishing the defendant from the ordinary criminal, and the latter allows for no distinction. In many instances, the jury would have liked to declare the defendant guilty, but insane. That kind of verdict would permit the jurors to condemn the defendant's behavior ... [and fulfill] their desire to commit the defendant to an institution that both punished and treated.

Rita Simon, The Jury and the Defense of Insanity 178 (1967).

Presumably, if the verdict were functioning in the way described by Simon, it would occasion a reduction in insanity acquittals. Certainly this was the hope of many who advocated adoption of the GBMI scheme. Yet a study of Michigan's GBMI reform found that the acquittal rate remained the same after passage of the statute. Smith & Hall, supra, at 100–102. In a mammoth multi-state study, the National Center for State Courts provided data from other states that suggested the same conclusion. See Christopher Slobogin, "The Guilty But Mentally Ill Verdict: An Idea Whose Time Should Not Have Come," 53 Geo.Wash.L.Rev. 494, 507–08 (1985). There is some indication that the verdict reduced the acquittal rate marginally in one or two states. In particular, in Georgia a significant decrease in the success rate of insanity pleas for violent crime occurred after introduction of the GBMI verdict in 1982. But since Georgia law also halted automatic commitment of insanity acquittees at about the same time, the success rate may have been affected by a fear that acquittees would be let loose sooner. Steadman, et. al., supra, at 108–11.

To what extent does any reduction in the insanity acquittal rate caused by the verdict result from "improper" conviction of the insane, rather than prevention of "inappropriate" insanity acquittals? Although such things are obviously difficult to measure, it appears that most persons found guilty but mentally ill are more likely to have characteristics normally associated with guilt, rather than with insanity. Smith & Hall, supra, at 95–100; Criss & Racine, "Impact of Change in Legal Standard for Those Adjudicated Not Guilty By Reason of Insanity," 8 Bull.Am.Acad. Psychiat. & L. 261 (1980). But see, *People v. Murphy,* 416 Mich. 453, 331 N.W.2d 152 (1982), in which the Michigan Supreme Court struck down a verdict of guilty but mentally ill and directed an insanity acquittal, noting that even the prosecution's expert agreed that the defendant was out of touch with reality and unable to control his behavior or appreciate the wrongfulness of his acts at the time of the offense. See also, *Michigan v. Fultz,* 111 Mich.App. 587, 314 N.W.2d 702 (1981).

A sophisticated study of the GBMI verdict reported in 1991 found that:

the field and laboratory studies offer substantial evidence that GBMI . . . does not make juries' decisions easier; it does not decrease their attention to extraneous issues (indeed, it serves as a distractor); . . . it does offer a compromise verdict that permits avoidance of hard questions of criminal responsibility. . . . In view of the fact that juries in the GBMI conditions in our studies still focused most of their attention on relevant variables, though, the question of whether the confusion experienced by such juries is sufficient on average to constitute a violation of defendants' rights to due process, a fair trial, and a jury trial remains an open question of law.

Gary Melton, et. al., "The Effects of the Addition of a GBMI Verdict," National Institute of Mental Health, Grant No. RO1MH39243, p. 28 (1991).

III. SENTENCING

Once convicted, an offender is subjected to the sentencing process. Evidence of mental disorder could have a significantly greater impact here than at trial, for at least two reasons. First, many of the concerns that underlie proposals to restrict the role of mental disability in adjudicating guilt—i.e., the diminishment of the free will paradigm implied by broad psychiatric defenses, the threat to public safety if acquittal occurs, the specter of confusing battles of the experts—are likely to lessen appreciably once the accused is convicted and decision-making takes place in the relatively informal sentencing atmosphere. Indeed, as previous material has suggested, one frequently suggested alternative to considering mental abnormality at trial is to shift most or all psychiatric inquiries to the sentencing stage. A second reason mental disorder is likely to play a greater role at sentencing was noted in the introduction to this chapter: once the question shifts from identifying who is to be punished to determining what kind of punishment should be imposed, attention may focus not just on retributive and general deterrence objectives but also on concerns connected with individual prevention, such as dangerousness and rehabilitative potential. Addressing these issues opens up the inquiry beyond the backward-looking culpability assessments required at trial by necessitating predictions about individuals with mental disorder.

This section will look at the role evidence of mental disability plays in two different sentencing contexts: capital sentencing and special track sentencing, in particular sentencing of those identified as "mentally disordered sex offenders." These two settings raise most starkly the tensions created by consideration of mental disability at the sentencing phase.

A. CAPITAL SENTENCING

NOTE ON SUPREME COURT CASES

Because "death is different," the constitutionality of the death penalty and the procedures for imposing it have been subjected to intense judicial scrutiny, primarily under the Eighth Amendment's ban on cruel and unusual punishment and the Fourteenth Amendment's due process clause. As a result, sentencing criteria in death penalty cases are far more developed than in other cases; most pertinent to our purposes, death penalty litigation has provided the most explicit consideration of the relationship between mental disability and criminal punishment. There follows a brief summary of the Supreme Court's pronouncements concerning the death penalty and the state statutes which attempt to implement those decisions, focusing in particular on material which bears on this relationship.

In 1972, the Supreme Court decided *Furman v. Georgia,* 408 U.S. 238, 92 S.Ct. 2726, 33 L.Ed.2d 346 (1972), which overturned the death sentences in four cases, by a vote of 5–4. In addition to a brief per curiam opinion announcing the court's decision, each of the nine justices wrote an opinion. Although there was no clear majority rationale, *Furman* was widely understood, under either an Eighth Amendment or due process rationale, to prohibit death penalty statutes that left the sentencing decision to the unguided discretion of the jury. For instance, in voting to overturn the death sentences, Justice Douglas spoke of the discriminatory impact of the death penalty on poor, black defendants. Justice Stewart asserted that the death penalty was "wantonly and freakishly imposed" and that death sentences were "cruel and unusual in the same way that being struck by lightning is cruel and unusual." Justice White believed that there was "no meaningful basis for distinguishing the few cases in which [the death penalty] is imposed from the many cases in which it is not." In addition to these three justices, two justices, Brennan and Marshall, concluded that the death penalty is unconstitutional under all circumstances.

Thirty-five states rewrote their statutes in response to *Furman.* Roughly half of these states removed jury discretion by making the death penalty mandatory in certain situations. The other half left the jury considerable decisionmaking power but attempted to set clearer guidelines as to how to exercise it, usually by instructing the jury to weigh specified aggravating and mitigating circumstances. In five cases decided together in 1976, the Court found the former type of statute unconstitutional, but upheld the second type of statute.

One of the statutes that withstood constitutional scrutiny was Georgia's. See *Gregg v. Georgia,* 428 U.S. 153, 96 S.Ct. 2909, 49 L.Ed.2d 859 (1976). A later decision of the Court, *Zant v. Stephens,* 462 U.S. 862, 103 S.Ct. 2733, 77 L.Ed.2d 235 (1983), summarized why the statute was upheld:

> [Our] approval of Georgia's capital sentencing procedure in [*Gregg*] rested primarily on two features of the scheme: that the jury was required to find at least one valid statutory aggravating circumstance and to identify it in writing, and that the state supreme court reviewed the record of every death penalty proceeding to determine whether the sentence was arbitrary or disproportionate. These elements, the opinion concluded, adequately protect-

ed against the wanton and freakish imposition of the death penalty. This conclusion rested ... on the fundamental requirement that ... an aggravating circumstance must genuinely narrow the class of persons eligible for the death penalty and must reasonably justify the imposition of a more severe sentence on the defendant compared to others found guilty of murder.

North Carolina's mandatory statute, on the other hand, was found unconstitutional. See *Woodson v. North Carolina*, 428 U.S. 280, 96 S.Ct. 2978, 49 L.Ed.2d 944 (1976). Although the Court gave several reasons for this holding, the following language has assumed the most significance in later cases:

> A third constitutional shortcoming of the North Carolina statute is its failure to allow the particularized consideration of relevant aspects of the character and record of each convicted defendant before the imposition upon him of a sentence of death.... A process that accords no significance to relevant facets of the character and record of the individual offender or the circumstances of the particular offense excludes from consideration in fixing the ultimate punishment of death the possibility of compassionate or mitigating factors stemming from the diverse frailties of humankind....
>
> ... Consideration of both offender and the offense in order to arrive at a just and appropriate sentence has been viewed as a progressive and humanizing development. While the prevailing practice of individualizing sentencing determinations generally reflects simply enlightened policy rather than a constitutional imperative, we believe that in capital cases the fundamental respect for humanity underlying the eighth amendment requires consideration of the character and record of the individual offender and the circumstances of the particular offense as a constitutionally indispensable part of the process of inflicting the penalty of death.
>
> This conclusion rests squarely on the predicate that the penalty of death is qualitatively different from a sentence of imprisonment, however long. Death, in its finality, differs more from life imprisonment than a 100-year prison term differs from one of only a year or two. Because of that qualitative difference, there is a corresponding difference in the need for reliability in the determination that death is the appropriate punishment in a specific case.

The central message of the 1976 cases appeared to be that while the jury may not be given unlimited discretion, neither may it be prevented from considering information relevant to the offender's characteristics. In two subsequent cases, the Supreme Court reinforced the latter notion. In *Lockett v. Ohio*, 438 U.S. 586, 98 S.Ct. 2954, 57 L.Ed.2d 973 (1978), seven members of the Court struck down a death penalty statute which required the judge to impose the death penalty unless the defendant proved one of three mitigating circumstances—that the victim had induced or facilitated the offense; that the defendant was "under duress, coercion or strong provocation"; or that the offense was "primarily the product of psychosis or mental deficiency." In an opinion joined by four justices,[r] the Court stated that this statute improperly prevented individualization of the sentencing decision: "The eighth and 14th amendments require that the sentencer, in all but the rarest kind of capital case, not be precluded from considering, *as a mitigating factor,* any aspect of a defendant's character or record and any of the circumstances of the offense that the defendant proffers as a basis for a sentence less than death." (emphasis in original). In *Eddings v. Oklahoma,* 455 U.S. 104, 102 S.Ct. 869, 71 L.Ed.2d 1 (1982), the Court reversed, 5–4, the death sentence of a 16 year-old because the sentencing judge had failed to consider evidence of the defendant's "turbulent family history, of beatings by a harsh father and of severe emotional disturbance." Again, the Court made clear that relevant mitigating evidence should not be excluded, although the factfinder has discretion to give it little or no weight.

As a result of these developments, modern death penalty schemes provide that before a person convicted of capital murder[s] can be sentenced to death the factfinder must find at least one aggravating circumstance and find further that any mitigating circumstances that exist do not make imposition of the death penalty inappropriate. As the Court stated in *Zant,* to be sufficiently "aggravating" to justify the death penalty, a circumstance "must genuinely narrow the class of persons eligible for the death penalty and must reasonably justify the imposition of a more severe sentence on the defendant compared to others found guilty of murder." Typical aggravating factors found in state statutes (many of them copied from the Model Penal Code's death penalty provisions) include murder which is committed: (1) against certain types of persons (e.g., a police officer, a correctional officer, or a judge); (2) while the person is under sentence of imprisonment; (3) for "pecuniary gain"; (4) in the course of certain felonies, such as rape, robbery, arson and kidnapping; (5) for the purpose of avoiding arrest; and (6) in a particularly heinous, cruel or vile manner. Other aggravating circumstances focus on the person rather than the capital murder itself, e.g., murder committed by (7) someone who has been convicted of prior violent felonies; and (8) someone considered likely to commit violent acts in the future (the "dangerousness" criterion). In most states, the listed factors are exclusive. In some, so long as a statutory predicate for the death penalty has been established, consideration of non-statutory aggravating factors is permissible.

r. Two other members of the Court, Justices Blackmun and White, concurred in the result because the defendant, who had waited in the "getaway car" during the commission of the robbery murder, may not have been sufficiently involved in the crime. Justice Marshall also joined the result, adhering to his opinion in *Furman* that the death penalty is unconstitutional under all circumstances. Justice Brennan, who had indicated in several opinions that he shared this view, did not participate. Only Justice Rehnquist dissented.

s. The Court's cases appear to hold that the death penalty may be imposed only on defendants who "intended that a killing take place or that lethal force be used." *Enmund v. Florida,* 458 U.S. 782, 102 S.Ct. 3368, 73 L.Ed.2d 1140 (1982); see also, *Coker v. Georgia,* 433 U.S. 584, 97 S.Ct. 2861, 53 L.Ed.2d 982 (1977).

In addition to listing aggravating circumstances, which is apparently required under the Court's cases, most state statutes also list mitigating factors that must be considered by the jury. Again borrowing from the Model Penal Code, most states recognize mitigation for any person who (1) was a juvenile at the time of the murder; (2) was only a "minor" participant in the murder; or (3) has no significant prior criminal history. A good number of state statutes also copy verbatim or with slight variation three other mitigation provisions found in the Model Penal Code: (4) "the defendant acted under duress or under the domination of another person;" (5) "the murder was committed while the defendant was under the influence of extreme mental or emotional disturbance;" and (6) "at the time of the murder, the capacity of the defendant to appreciate the criminality [wrongfulness] of his conduct or to conform his conduct to the requirements of the law was impaired as a result of mental disease or defect."[t] Model Penal Code § 210.6(4)(b), (f), (g). A few states also include as mitigating factors: (7) that the defendant believed the murder to be morally justified or committed under extenuating circumstances; and (8) that the defendant is not dangerous. Note that, after *Lockett,* statutory mitigating factors are not to be considered exclusive. They are meant to focus the factfinder's attention on those circumstances most likely to have mitigating impact.

A final question is how aggravating and mitigating circumstances are to be balanced against one another. Under the Model Penal Code's provisions, the factfinder may consider a death sentence only if it finds that "there are no mitigating circumstances sufficiently substantial to call for leniency." Model Penal Code § 210.6(2). Connecticut makes the death penalty even harder to obtain, by prohibiting its imposition if *any* statutory mitigating criterion is found. On the other hand, most state statutes are similar to Alabama's law, which provides that "the trial court shall determine whether the aggravating circumstances it finds to exist outweigh the mitigating circumstances it finds to exist." Ala.Code 1975, § 13A–5–47(e).

Questions and Comments

1. *Mental disability and aggravating circumstances.* The dangerousness criterion, an explicit aggravating factor only in a handful of state statutes but considered a legally relevant consideration in most death penalty states,[u] is the aggravating circumstance most likely to occasion expert testimony on the impact of mental disorder. In *Barefoot v. Estelle,* reprinted at pp. 468–77, the Supreme Court specifically upheld the admissi-

t. Note that, since *Atkins v. Virginia,* see pp. 653–65, people with mental retardation are exempt from the death penalty.

u. At least six states explicitly make dangerousness an aggravating circumstance (Idaho, Oklahoma, South Carolina, Texas, Virginia, and Washington) and 28 of the remaining death penalty states make it a nonstatutory aggravator (which means that once the prosecutor proves a statutory aggravator the jury may consider dangerousness when determining whether to sentence the offender to death). Mitzi Dorland & Daniel Krauss, "The Danger of Dangerousness in Capital Sentencing: Exacerbating the Problem of Arbitrary and Capricious Decision Making," 29 L. & Psychol. Rev. 63, 64 nn.5, 12 (2005).

bility of psychiatric testimony on "future dangerousness." The predicate for *Barefoot* was *Jurek v. Texas,* 428 U.S. 262, 96 S.Ct. 2950, 49 L.Ed.2d 929 (1976), one of the five 1976 death penalty cases. There, the Supreme Court upheld a Texas statute that included as an aggravating factor proof that "there is a probability that the defendant would commit criminal acts of violence that would constitute a continuing threat to society." To the petitioner's argument that it is impossible to predict future behavior and that the statutory language is so vague as to be meaningless, the Court responded:

> It is, of course, not easy to predict future behavior. The fact that such a determination is difficult, however, does not mean that it cannot be made. Indeed, prediction of future criminal conduct is an essential element in many of the decisions rendered throughout our criminal justice system. The decision whether to admit a defendant to bail, for instance, must often turn on a judge's prediction of the defendant's future conduct. And any sentencing authority must predict a convicted person's probable future conduct when it engages in the process of determining what punishment to impose. For those sentenced to prison, these same predictions must be made by parole authorities. The task that a Texas jury must perform in answering the statutory question in issue is thus basically no different from the task performed countless times each day throughout the American system of criminal justice. What is essential is that the jury have before it all possible relevant information about the individual defendant whose fate it must determine. Texas law clearly assures that all such evidence will be adduced.

Although only three justices joined this language, the other opinions in *Jurek* made it clear that, as *Barefoot* later put it, "seven Justices rejected the claim that it was impossible to predict future behavior and that dangerousness was therefore an invalid consideration in imposing the death penalty."

Strong evidence exists that a prediction, whether by mental health professionals or laypersons, that someone will cause harm to others is wrong as often as it is right.[v] Does dangerousness "genuinely narrow the class of persons eligible for the death penalty" as reliably as do other aggravating circumstances? Assuming so, is there any other reason "proof" of dangerousness should be considered insufficient, by itself, to impose the death sentence on a person convicted of capital murder? In answering this question, is it relevant that, in all but one death penalty state, life without parole is the only alternative to a death sentence, or that the assault rate by those on death row and in the life-without-parole population is considerably lower than it is in the general prison population? See Mark Cunningham, "Dangerousness and Death: A Nexus in Search of Science and Reason," American Psychologist 828, 832–33 (Nov. 2006).

2. *Mental disability and mitigating circumstances.* Of the mitigating circumstances typically listed in state death penalty statutes, four focus on the defendant's mental state at the time of the offense. Using the Model Penal Code language, they are: (a) whether the defendant was "under duress or under the domination of another person;" (b) whether the defendant was suffering from "extreme mental or emotional disturbance"; (c) whether "the

v. See pp. 478–79.

capacity of the defendant to appreciate the criminality [wrongfulness] of his conduct or to conform his conduct to the requirements of law was impaired as a result of mental disease or defect or intoxication''; and (d) whether "the murder was committed under circumstances which the defendant believed to provide a moral justification or extenuation for his conduct." All of these mitigating criteria have obvious analogues to defenses which are usually available at trial. The first is similar to the duress defense,[w] the second to the provocation defense, the third to the insanity defense, and the fourth to the self-defense doctrine. How does the language used to define the mitigating factors differ from the usual formulations of the defenses? Some state statutes use even broader language. For instance, with respect to the second mental state factor, some states omit the word "extreme." With respect to the third factor, some states omit the words "mental disease or defect."

Permissible Limitations. The essential preliminary question in determining the proper mitigating circumstances is whether there should be *any* limitation on the type of mental state evidence which can be presented in mitigation at a death penalty proceeding. Arguably, given the gravity of the penalty, the usual concerns about wide-open consideration of a defendant's psychology should be suspended. In *Lockett,* the Court stated that restricting mitigating claims is impermissible because it "creates the risk that the death penalty will be imposed in spite of factors which may call for a less severe penalty." However, in a footnote, it also cautioned that "nothing in this opinion limits the traditional authority of a court to exclude, as irrelevant, evidence not bearing on the defendant's character, prior record, or the circumstances of his offense." Does this footnote limit mental state evidence in any way?

Consider *North Carolina v. Boyd,* 311 N.C. 408, 319 S.E.2d 189 (1984), cert. denied, 471 U.S. 1030, 105 S.Ct. 2052, 85 L.Ed.2d 324 (1985). In that case, Boyd was convicted of murdering a former girlfriend who had recently left him. At his sentencing hearing, he presented the following evidence: (1) his father had been an alcoholic who had abandoned his family when Boyd was young; (2) his grandfather—whom he had come to view as a father—had then died; (3) he had a history of losing jobs and repeated imprisonment; and (4) his life since adolescence had been characterized by drug and alcohol abuse. He also proffered testimony by a sociologist to the effect that his crime and life history conformed to a common pattern that distinguishes those who kill intimates from those who kill others. In particular, according to the sociologist, those who, like Boyd, suffer repeated deep personal losses often develop strong feelings of self-destructiveness that may cause them to kill a loved one as a way of destroying part of themselves. Thus, the sociologist testified, the defendant's crime could be seen "primarily as a depression-caused self-destructive act, closely related to the impulse of suicide, resulting from a life history of an inordinate number of losses beginning with the abandonment by the defendant's father and the death of his grandfather and culminating with the threatened loss of [the victim]." The expert also testified that Boyd told him during an interview that he so feared the end of his relationship with the girlfriend that he had contemplat-

---

w. Note that although the "duress" factor appears to be identical to the duress defense, it provides meaningful mitigation because the duress defense is usually unavailable in homicide cases.

ed suicide shortly before the murder. The defense attorney explained that the testimony was designed to "link together all of the defendant's mitigating evidence into a unified whole which explained the apparent contradiction of killing the person the defendant loved the most." The trial court excluded the sociologist's testimony. In a somewhat ambiguous opinion, the North Carolina Supreme Court upheld this ruling, either on the ground that the testimony was irrelevant or that it was relevant but was of so little weight that its exclusion was not a proper ground for vacating the death sentence. The United States Supreme Court denied certiorari, over a vigorous dissent by Justice Marshall, which Justice Brennan joined. Should the expert testimony have been admitted? Should it make a difference that the North Carolina statute did not include as an aggravating factor the dangerousness criterion?

Applying the Statutory Factors. A separate question is whether particular evidence, assuming it is admissible, meets the relevant statutory mitigating criteria. Because these criteria are not exclusive, one might conclude that the answer to this question doesn't matter; even if a court or jury determines that the defendant's evidence does not meet a particular criterion, the defendant can still argue it has mitigating value. But in a state like Connecticut, where proof of any statutory mitigating factor precludes the death penalty, the definition of a particular factor can assume extreme importance. Even in those states where the aggravating and mitigating circumstances are balanced against one another, the definition may be significant, since proof of statutory mitigating factors are likely to carry more weight than proof of nonstatutory factors.

Many courts have demonstrated a reluctance to define the statutory factors broadly. For instance, in *People v. Crews,* reprinted at pp. 633–39, the Illinois Supreme Court refused to equate a guilty but mentally ill ruling with extreme mental or emotional distress; more significantly, it was unwilling to overturn the trial judge's ruling in the case that the defendant's evidence of mental illness, which was not insignificant, did not meet this or any other statutory factor. Was it right? Assuming so, should it have ruled differently had the Illinois statutory language, as is true with other statutes, not included the word "extreme"?

Consider also the case of *Johnson v. State*, 292 Md. 405, 439 A.2d 542 (1982), where the defendant was convicted of capital murder. The following testimony, introduced to bolster the argument that the killing was not committed willfully and with premeditation, was excluded at trial on the ground that expert testimony on mental state is relevant only on insanity (which the defendant conceded could not be proven). At the capital sentencing proceeding, should the testimony nonetheless be deemed sufficient to support a finding of extreme mental or emotional stress or impairment in ability to appreciate the wrongfulness of the act?

> The patient is a 19–year old youth of medium height and build who presented a neat and clean appearance. He was extremely sullen and hostile, and his cooperation for interview and test was poor. In view of this test results have to be considered tentative.

TEST RESULTS:

On the WAIS he earned a Verbal I.Q. of 78, a Performance I.Q. of 68, and a Full Scale I.Q. of 72 which places him within the borderline range of intelligence. His potential, as gauged by his abstract reasoning, is at least within the low average range. Intellectual efficiency is decreased by a combination of educational deprivation and negativism. There are some signs which point in the direction of bizarre thinking and a tenuous hold on reality. E.G. on Card 22 of the Holtzman he saw "the devil," and on Card 27 he saw "God over water." But these should be interpreted with caution, as they may also be attempts to embarrass and express contempt for the examiner by giving nonsensical answers.

The personality picture is that of an extremely deprived individual who does not expect any affection and emotional support from either parental figure. He perceives the mother figure as domineering, but distant and devoid of warmth and understanding and the father figure as hostile and threatening. Yet he has conjured up the image of an idealized, all wise and all loving father surrogate with whom he will compare any male elder. Since such a person is bound to fall short of his ideal he is apt to equate this person with the real father figure whom he sees in negative terms and reject him. As a result he not only has trouble with authority figures, but perceives the world about him as a cold inhospitable place where he does not have a chance.

CONCLUSION:

The patient functions at the borderline intellectual level (I.Q. 72), but his potential is at least within the low average range. He can be described as a severely deprived individual with a hostile and negative orientation and an [sic.] *severe authority problem.* Contact with reality is difficult to evaluate on account of his poor productivity resulting from extreme negativism.

3. *Mental disability as both an aggravating and a mitigating circumstance.* As the testimony in the *Johnson* case suggests, in many cases evidence of mental disability is relevant both to aggravating and mitigating circumstances. In *Miller v. State,* 373 So.2d 882 (Fla.1979), the facts adduced at trial were as follows. Miller was released from county jail on the morning of the murder, where he had been incarcerated for possession of a concealed weapon (a fishing knife). He wandered around Ft. Myers and bought a fishing knife similar to the one which had been taken from him by the police. An employee in the store where the weapon was purchased stated that Miller was "wild looking" and was mumbling angrily to himself. This employee called the police and followed Miller to two nearby bars. Finally the employee saw Miller leaving in a taxi cab with a woman driver and contacted the taxi company to inform it of the apparent danger. The woman taxi driver was found murdered a short while later, having been stabbed nine times. Miller had apparently raped her when she was dead or dying. When Miller was arrested at the bus station that evening, his pants were still covered with blood. Blood-soaked money, some of which had been taken from the taxi driver, was found in his pockets.

After Miller was charged with this crime, he was found incompetent to stand trial and was committed to a state mental hospital. Two and a half years later, after being heavily medicated, he was found to be competent to stand trial and convicted of capital murder. At the sentencing hearing psychiatric testimony suggested that Miller was suffering from paranoid schizophrenia and hallucinations. He had been committed to mental hospitals on several previous occasions, and had a long history of drug abuse. Testimony also indicated that Miller had a severe hatred of his mother, and had planned to kill her after his release from the Lee County Jail, just prior to this murder. Apparently this hatred arose in part from the fact that his mother, who had been married four times, had refused any contact with her son for several years. On several previous occasions, Miller suffered hallucinations in which he saw his mother in other persons, in a "yellow haze." On at least one previous occasion, he had senselessly assaulted another woman during such hallucinations. Miller testified that at the time of the capital murder, he saw his mother's face on the 56 year-old woman taxi driver, in a "yellow haze," and proceeded to stab her to death.

The jury recommended a death sentence. In Florida, as in most states, the trial judge must decide if this penalty is appropriate. The relevant portions of the Florida Supreme Court's description of the judge's deliberations and its analysis of the judge's conclusions follows:

> The trial court found that the evidence introduced at the sentencing hearing proved beyond a reasonable doubt three statutory aggravating circumstances: (1) the defendant was previously convicted of a felony involving the threat of violence to another person; (2) the murder was committed while the defendant was engaged in the commission of or attempt to commit robbery, and was thus committed for pecuniary gain; and (3) the murder was especially heinous, atrocious, and cruel.

> In addition, the trial court found several mitigating circumstances to exist: (1) the murder was committed while the defendant was under the influence of extreme mental disturbance; (2) the defendant acted under mental duress; (3) due to mental sickness, the defendant's capacity and ability to conform his conduct to the requirements of law were substantially impaired. In addition, the trial court specifically found from the evidence presented at the sentencing hearing that the defendant was suffering from mental illness at the time the murder was committed.

> Based upon these factual findings, the trial judge explained the reasoning which led him to conclude that the death penalty was appropriate:

>> [I]n weighing the aggravating and mitigating factors, I have to conclude that the aggravating factors are such that the reality of Florida law wherein life imprisonment is not, in fact, life imprisonment; and, in fact, the defendant would be subject to be released into society—In other words, it doesn't mean life imprisonment and there is a substantial chance he could be released into society. And the testimony overwhelmingly establishes that the mental sickness or illness that he suffers from is such that he will never recover from it, it will only be repressed by the use of drugs.

>> Thus, in light of that fact, in light of the aggravating factors here, I have to conclude the only certain punishment and the only assurance society can receive that this man never again commits to

another human being what he did to that lady, is that the ultimate sentence of death is imposed.

If the law in Florida were such that life imprisonment meant the ability to live in a prison environment for the entire, remainder of one's life, I would have the conclusion that there would be sufficient mitigating factors to offset the aggravating factors, and allow him to live in prison.

But since that is not the case, the reality is that life imprisonment does not mean that, I conclude in this case that the aggravating factors heavily outweigh the mitigating factors.

The heinousness of the crime, the way in which it was committed speaks for itself. Now I, as the Judge, must therefore impose the sentence of death and do so.

It is clear from the trial judge's sentencing order that he considered as an aggravating factor the defendant's allegedly incurable and dangerous mental illness. The use of this nonstatutory aggravating factor as a controlling circumstance tipping the balance in favor of the death penalty was improper. The aggravating circumstances specified in the statute are exclusive, and no others may be used for that purpose. This court [has] stated: "We must guard against any unauthorized aggravating factor going into the equation which might tip the scales of the weighing process in favor of death."

Strict application of the sentencing statute is necessary because the sentencing authority's discretion must be "guided and channeled" by requiring an examination of specific factors that argue in favor of or against imposition of the death penalty, thus eliminating total arbitrariness and capriciousness in its imposition. The trial judge's use of the defendant's mental illness, and his resulting propensity to commit violent acts, as an aggravating factor favoring the imposition of the death penalty appears contrary to the legislative intent as set forth in the statute. The legislature has not authorized consideration of the probability of recurring violent acts by the defendant if he is released on parole in the distant future. To the contrary, a large number of the statutory mitigating factors reflect a legislative determination to mitigate the death penalty in favor of a life sentence for those persons whose responsibility for their violent actions has been substantially diminished as a result of a mental illness, uncontrolled emotional state of mind, or drug abuse.

If dangerousness *had* been an aggravating circumstance under the Florida death penalty scheme (or if Florida were one of the states in which non-statutory aggravating factors may be considered once at least one statutory factor is proven), would the trial judge's ruling have been appropriate? Consider another Florida case, *Huckaby v. State,* 343 So.2d 29 (Fla. 1977). There the Florida Supreme Court held that, although there was insufficient proof of insanity, the evidence showed Huckaby's mental illness motivated his murder of members of his family. The court reversed the trial court's imposition of the death penalty and held that the mitigating circumstances outweighed the aggravating circumstances. It explained:

Our decision here is based on the causal relationship between the mitigating and aggravating circumstances. The heinous and atrocious manner in which this crime was perpetrated, and the harm to which the members of Huckaby's family were exposed, were the direct consequence of his mental illness, so far as the record reveals.

Note that one of the aggravating factors found by the trial judge in *Miller* was the heinousness of the crime. In light of *Huckaby,* is this finding permissible? How do you think the Florida Supreme Court would answer the question at the beginning of this paragraph?

More generally, in cases such as *Miller* and *Huckaby,* how should one balance the desire to accord mitigating impact to mental disability on the one hand and, on the other, the two goals of incapacitating the very dangerous (who may be mentally ill) and punishing severely those who commit particularly heinous crimes (perhaps because of mental illness)? Should the conclusion as to when the mitigating impact of mental disability "trumps" its aggravating aspects differ depending upon whether the aggravating aspect is dangerousness or vileness of the crime?

Of what relevance is research showing that unsuccessfully raising an insanity defense (a scenario that describes a significant portion of those defendants who use mental illness as a mitigator at the sentencing phase) correlates *positively* with a death sentence, ahead of such variables as prior record and commission of another crime at the time of the homicide? David Baldus et al., Equal Justice and the Death Penalty 644, 645 (1999). See also David Baldus et al., "Racial Discrimination and the Death Penalty in the Post–Furman Era: An Empirical and Legal Overview, with Recent Findings from Philadelphia," 83 Cornell L. Rev. 1638, 1688–89 (1998) (Table 6) (evidence of "extreme mental or emotional disturbance" correlates *positively* with death sentences); Julie Goetz & Gordon P. Waldo, "Why Jurors in Florida Vote for Life or Death: The Florida Component of the Capital Jury Project" 34 (presented at the conference on Life Over Death XV, Ft. Lauderdale, Fl., Sept. 27, 1996)("[a] defendant's odds of receiving a death sentence increased significantly when the defendant had a history of childhood abuse, drug abuse and/or addiction, and mental and/or emotional disturbance"); Phoebe C. Ellsworth et al., "The Death–Qualified Jury and the Defense of Insanity," 8 Law & Hum Behav. 81 (1984)(finding that mock jurors are much more hostile to defendants with schizophrenia than to defendants with mental retardation and other types of defendants). Are death sentences received under such circumstances a violation of due process of law?

ATKINS v. VIRGINIA

Supreme Court of the United States, 2002.
536 U.S. 304, 122 S.Ct. 2242, 153 L.Ed.2d 335.

JUSTICE STEVENS delivered the opinion of the Court.

Those mentally retarded persons who meet the law's requirements for criminal responsibility should be tried and punished when they commit crimes. Because of their disabilities in areas of reasoning, judgment, and control of their impulses, however, they do not act with the level of moral culpability that characterizes the most serious adult criminal conduct. Moreover, their impairments can jeopardize the reliability and fairness of capital proceedings against mentally retarded defendants. Presumably for these reasons, in the 13 years since we decided *Penry v. Lynaugh*, 492 U.S. 302, 109 S.Ct. 2934, 106 L.Ed.2d 256 (1989), the American public, legislators, scholars, and judges have deliberated over the question whether the death penalty should ever be imposed on a mentally retarded criminal. The consensus reflected in those deliberations informs our answer to the question presented by this case: whether such executions are "cruel and unusual punishments" prohibited by the Eighth Amendment to the Federal Constitution.

I

Petitioner, Daryl Renard Atkins, was convicted of abduction, armed robbery, and capital murder, and sentenced to death. At approximately midnight on August 16, 1996, Atkins and William Jones, armed with a semiautomatic handgun, abducted Eric Nesbitt, robbed him of the money on his person, drove him to an automated teller machine in his pickup truck where cameras recorded their withdrawal of additional cash, then took him to an isolated location where he was shot eight times and killed. Jones and Atkins both testified in the guilt phase of Atkins' trial.[1] Each confirmed most of the details in the other's account of the incident, with the important exception that each stated that the other had actually shot and killed Nesbitt. Jones' testimony, which was both more coherent and credible than Atkins', was obviously credited by the jury and was sufficient to establish Atkins' guilt. At the penalty phase of the trial, the State introduced victim impact evidence and proved two aggravating circumstances: future dangerousness and "vileness of the offense." To prove future dangerousness, the State relied on Atkins' prior felony convictions as well as the testimony of four victims of earlier robberies and assaults. To prove the second aggravator, the prosecution relied upon the trial record, including pictures of the deceased's body and the autopsy report.

In the penalty phase, the defense relied on one witness, Dr. Evan Nelson, a forensic psychologist who had evaluated Atkins before trial and concluded that he was "mildly mentally retarded."[3] His conclusion was based on interviews with people who knew Atkins, a review of school and

---

1. Initially, both Jones and Atkins were indicted for capital murder. The prosecution ultimately permitted Jones to plead guilty to first-degree murder in exchange for his testimony against Atkins. As a result of the plea, Jones became ineligible to receive the death penalty.

3. The American Association of Mental Retardation (AAMR) defines mental retardation as follows: "Mental retardation refers to substantial limitations in present functioning. It is characterized by significantly subaverage intellectual functioning, existing concurrently with related limita-

tions in two or more of the following applicable adaptive skill areas: communication, self-care, home living, social skills, community use, self-direction, health and safety, functional academics, leisure, and work. Mental retardation manifests before age 18." Mental Retardation: Definition, Classification, and Systems of Supports 5 (9th ed.1992). The American Psychiatric Association's definition is similar: "The essential feature of Mental Retardation is significantly subaverage general intellectual functioning (Criterion A) that is accompanied by significant limitations in adaptive functioning in at least two of the following skill

court records, and the administration of a standard intelligence test which indicated that Atkins had a full scale IQ of 59.[5]

The jury sentenced Atkins to death, but the Virginia Supreme Court ordered a second sentencing hearing because the trial court had used a misleading verdict form. At the resentencing, Dr. Nelson again testified. The State presented an expert rebuttal witness, Dr. Stanton Samenow, who expressed the opinion that Atkins was not mentally retarded, but rather was of "average intelligence, at least," and diagnosable as having antisocial personality disorder.[6] The jury again sentenced Atkins to death.

The Supreme Court of Virginia affirmed the imposition of the death penalty. . . . Because of the gravity of the concerns expressed by the dissenters [in that decision], and in light of the dramatic shift in the state legislative landscape that has occurred in the past 13 years, we granted certiorari to revisit the issue that we first addressed in the *Penry* case.

II

The Eighth Amendment succinctly prohibits "excessive" sanctions. It provides: "Excessive bail shall not be required, nor excessive fines

areas: communication, self-care, home living, social/interpersonal skills, use of community resources, self-direction, functional academic skills, work, leisure, health, and safety (Criterion B). The onset must occur before age 18 years (Criterion C). Mental Retardation has many different etiologies and may be seen as a final common pathway of various pathological processes that affect the functioning of the central nervous system." American Psychiatric Association, Diagnostic and Statistical Manual of Mental Disorders 41 (4th ed.2000). "Mild" mental retardation is typically used to describe people with an IQ level of 50–55 to approximately 70.

5. Dr. Nelson administered the Wechsler Adult Intelligence Scales test (WAIS–III), the standard instrument in the United States for assessing intellectual functioning. AAMR, Mental Retardation, supra. The WAIS–III is scored by adding together the number of points earned on different subtests, and using a mathematical formula to convert this raw score into a scaled score. The test measures an intelligence range from 45 to 155. The mean score of the test is 100, which means that a person receiving a score of 100 is considered to have an average level of cognitive functioning. A. Kaufman & E. Lichtenberger, Essentials of WAIS–III Assessment 60 (1999). It is estimated that between 1 and 3 percent of the population has an IQ between 70 and 75 or lower, which is typically considered the cut-

off IQ score for the intellectual function prong of the mental retardation definition. 2 B. Sadock & V. Sadock, Comprehensive Textbook of Psychiatry 2952 (7th ed.2000).

At the sentencing phase, Dr. Nelson testified: "[Atkins'] full scale IQ is 59. Compared to the population at large, that means less than one percentile. . . . Mental retardation is a relatively rare thing. It's about one percent of the population." According to Dr. Nelson, Atkins' IQ score "would automatically qualify for Social Security disability income." Dr. Nelson also indicated that of the over 40 capital defendants that he had evaluated, Atkins was only the second individual who met the criteria for mental retardation. He testified that, in his opinion, Atkins' limited intellect had been a consistent feature throughout his life, and that his IQ score of 59 is not an "aberration, malingered result, or invalid test score."

6. Samenow's testimony was based upon two interviews with Atkins, a review of his school records, and interviews with correctional staff. He did not administer an intelligence test, but did ask Atkins questions taken from the 1972 version of the Wechsler Memory Scale. Dr. Samenow attributed Atkins' "academic performance [that was] by and large terrible" to the fact that he "is a person who chose to pay attention sometimes, not to pay attention others, and did poorly because he did not want to do what he was required to do."

imposed, nor cruel and unusual punishments inflicted." In *Weems v. United States*, 217 U.S. 349, 30 S.Ct. 544, 54 L.Ed. 793 (1910), we held that a punishment of 12 years jailed in irons at hard and painful labor for the crime of falsifying records was excessive. We explained "that it is a precept of justice that punishment for crime should be graduated and proportioned to the offense." We have repeatedly applied this proportionality precept in later cases interpreting the Eighth Amendment. Thus, even though "imprisonment for ninety days is not, in the abstract, a punishment which is either cruel or unusual," it may not be imposed as a penalty for "the 'status' of narcotic addiction," *Robinson v. California*, 370 U.S. 660, 666–667, 82 S.Ct. 1417, 8 L.Ed.2d 758 (1962), because such a sanction would be excessive. As Justice Stewart explained in Robinson: "Even one day in prison would be a cruel and unusual punishment for the 'crime' of having a common cold."

A claim that punishment is excessive is judged not by the standards that prevailed in 1685 when Lord Jeffreys presided over the "Bloody Assizes" or when the Bill of Rights was adopted, but rather by those that currently prevail. As Chief Justice Warren explained in his opinion in *Trop v. Dulles*, 356 U.S. 86, 78 S.Ct. 590, 2 L.Ed.2d 630 (1958): "The basic concept underlying the Eighth Amendment is nothing less than the dignity of man. . . . The Amendment must draw its meaning from the evolving standards of decency that mark the progress of a maturing society." Proportionality review under those evolving standards should be informed by " 'objective factors to the maximum possible extent.' " We have pinpointed that the "clearest and most reliable objective evidence of contemporary values is the legislation enacted by the country's legislatures." *Penry.*

Relying in part on such legislative evidence, we have held that death is an impermissibly excessive punishment for the rape of an adult woman, *Coker v. Georgia*, 433 U.S. 584, 593–596, 97 S.Ct. 2861, 53 L.Ed.2d 982 (1977), or for a defendant who neither took life, attempted to take life, nor intended to take life, *Enmund v. Florida*, 458 U.S. 782, 789–793, 102 S.Ct. 3368, 73 L.Ed.2d 1140 (1982). In *Coker*, we focused primarily on the then-recent legislation that had been enacted in response to our decision 10 years earlier in *Furman v. Georgia*, 408 U.S. 238, 92 S.Ct. 2726, 33 L.Ed.2d 346 (1972) (per curiam), to support the conclusion that the "current judgment," though "not wholly unanimous," weighed very heavily on the side of rejecting capital punishment as a "suitable penalty for raping an adult woman." The "current legislative judgment" relevant to our decision in *Enmund* was less clear than in *Coker* but "nevertheless weigh[ed] on the side of rejecting capital punishment for the crime at issue."

We also acknowledged in *Coker* that the objective evidence, though of great importance, did not "wholly determine" the controversy, "for the Constitution contemplates that in the end our own judgment will be brought to bear on the question of the acceptability of the death penalty under the Eighth Amendment." For example, in *Enmund*, we concluded by expressing our own judgment about the issue: "For purposes of imposing the death penalty, Enmund's criminal culpability must be limited to his participation in the robbery, and his punishment must be tailored to his personal responsibility and moral guilt. Putting Enmund to death to avenge two killings that he did not commit and had no intention of committing or causing does not measurably contribute to the retributive end of ensuring that the criminal gets his just deserts. This is the judgment of most of the legislatures that have recently addressed the matter, and *we have no reason to disagree* with that judgment for purposes of construing and applying the Eighth Amendment." (emphasis added). Thus, in cases involving a consensus, our own judgment is "brought to bear," by asking whether there is reason to disagree with the judgment reached by the citizenry and its legislators. Guided by our approach in these cases, we shall first review the judgment of legislatures that have addressed the suitability of imposing the death penalty on the mentally retarded and then consider reasons for agreeing or disagreeing with their judgment.

III

The parties have not called our attention to any state legislative consideration of the suitability of imposing the death penalty on mentally retarded offenders prior to 1986. In that year, the public reaction to the execution of a mentally retarded murderer in Georgia apparently led to the enactment of the first state statute prohibiting such executions. In 1988, when Congress enacted legislation reinstating the federal death penalty, it expressly provided that a "sentence of death shall not be carried out upon a person who is mentally retarded." In 1989, Maryland enacted a similar prohibition. It was in that year that we decided *Penry*, and concluded that those two state enactments, "even when added to the 14 States that have rejected capital punishment completely, do not provide sufficient evidence at present of a national consensus."

Much has changed since then. Responding to the national attention received by the Bowden execution and our decision in *Penry*, state legislatures across the country began to address the issue. In 1990 Kentucky and Tennessee enacted statutes similar to those in Georgia and Maryland, as did New Mexico in 1991, and Arkansas, Colorado, Washington, Indiana, and Kansas in 1993 and 1994. In 1995, when New York reinstated its death penalty, it emulated the Federal Government by expressly exempting the mentally retarded. Nebraska followed suit in 1998. There appear to have been no similar enactments during the next two years, but in 2000 and 2001 six more States—South Dakota, Arizona, Connecticut, Florida, Missouri, and North Carolina—joined the procession. The Texas Legislature unanimously adopted a similar bill, and bills have passed at least one house in other States, including Virginia and Nevada.

. . . Given the well-known fact that anticrime legislation is far more popular than legislation providing protections for persons guilty of violent crime, the large number of States prohibiting the execution of mentally retarded persons (and the complete absence of States passing legislation reinstating the power to conduct such executions) provides powerful evidence that today our society views mentally retarded offenders as categorically less culpable than the average criminal. The evidence carries even greater force when it is noted that the legislatures that have addressed the issue have voted overwhelmingly in favor of the prohibition. Moreover, even in those States that allow the execution of mentally retarded offenders, the practice is uncommon. Some States, for example New Hampshire and New Jersey, continue to authorize executions, but none have been carried out in decades. Thus there is little need to pursue legislation barring the execution of the mentally retarded in those States. And it appears that even among those States that regularly execute offenders and that have no prohibition with regard to the mentally retarded, only five have executed offenders possessing a known IQ less than 70 since we decided *Penry*. The practice, therefore, has become truly unusual, and it is fair to say that a national consensus has developed against it.[21]

To the extent there is serious disagreement about the execution of mentally retarded offenders, it is in determining which offenders are in fact retarded. In this case, for instance, the Commonwealth of Virginia disputes that Atkins suffers from mental retardation. Not all people who claim to be mentally retarded will be so impaired as to fall within the range of mentally retarded offenders about whom there is a national consensus. As was our approach in *Ford v. Wainwright,* with regard to insanity, "we leave to the State[s] the task of developing appropriate ways to enforce the constitutional restriction upon its execution of sentences." 477 U.S. 399, 405, 416–417, 106 S.Ct. 2595, 91 L.Ed.2d 335 (1986).[22]

21. Additional evidence makes it clear that this legislative judgment reflects a much broader social and professional consensus. For example, several organizations with germane expertise have adopted official positions opposing the imposition of the death penalty upon a mentally retarded offender. See Brief for American Psychological Association et al. as Amici Curiae; Brief for AAMR et al. as Amici Curiae. In addition, representatives of widely diverse religious communities in the United States, reflecting Christian, Jewish, Muslim, and Buddhist traditions, have filed an amicus curiae brief explaining that even though their views about the death penalty differ, they all "share a conviction that the execution of persons with mental retardation cannot be morally justified." See Brief for United States Catholic Conference et al. as Amici Curiae in *McCarver v. North Carolina*, O.T.2001, No. 00–8727, p. 2. Moreover, within the world community, the imposition of the death penalty for crimes committed by mentally retarded offenders is overwhelmingly disapproved. Brief for The European Union as Amicus Curiae in *McCarver v. North Carolina*, O.T.2001, No.

00–8727, p. 4. Finally, polling data shows a widespread consensus among Americans, even those who support the death penalty, that executing the mentally retarded is wrong. R. Bonner & S. Rimer, Executing the Mentally Retarded Even as Laws Begin to Shift, N.Y. Times, Aug. 7, 2000, p. A1; App. B to Brief for AAMR as Amicus Curiae in *McCarver v. North Carolina*, O.T.2001, No. 00–8727 (appending approximately 20 state and national polls on the issue). Although these factors are by no means dispositive, their consistency with the legislative evidence lends further support to our conclusion that there is a consensus among those who have addressed the issue. See *Thompson v. Oklahoma*, 487 U.S. 815, 830, 831, n. 31, 108 S.Ct. 2687, 101 L.Ed.2d 702 (1988)(considering the views of "respected professional organizations, by other nations that share our Anglo–American heritage, and by the leading members of the Western European community").

22. The statutory definitions of mental retardation are not identical, but generally conform to the clinical definitions set forth in n. 3, supra.

IV

This consensus unquestionably reflects widespread judgment about the relative culpability of mentally retarded offenders, and the relationship between mental retardation and the penological purposes served by the death penalty. Additionally, it suggests that some characteristics of mental retardation undermine the strength of the procedural protections that our capital jurisprudence steadfastly guards. As discussed above, clinical definitions of mental retardation require not only subaverage intellectual functioning, but also significant limitations in adaptive skills such as communication, self-care, and self-direction that became manifest before age 18. Mentally retarded persons frequently know the difference between right and wrong and are competent to stand trial. Because of their impairments, however, by definition they have diminished capacities to understand and process information, to communicate, to abstract from mistakes and learn from experience, to engage in logical reasoning, to control impulses, and to understand the reactions of others. There is no evidence that they are more likely to engage in criminal conduct than others, but there is abundant evidence that they often act on impulse rather than pursuant to a premeditated plan, and that in group settings they are followers rather than leaders. Their deficiencies do not warrant an exemption from criminal sanctions, but they do diminish their personal culpability.

In light of these deficiencies, our death penalty jurisprudence provides two reasons consistent with the legislative consensus that the mentally retarded should be categorically excluded from execution. First, there is a serious question as to whether either justification that we have recognized as a basis for the death penalty applies to mentally retarded offenders. *Gregg v. Georgia*, 428 U.S. 153, 183, 96 S.Ct. 2909, 49 L.Ed.2d 859 (1976), identified "retribution and deterrence of capital crimes by prospective offenders" as the social purposes served by the death penalty. Unless the imposition of the death penalty on a mentally retarded person "measurably contributes to one or both of these goals, it 'is nothing more than the purposeless and needless imposition of pain and suffering,' and hence an unconstitutional punishment." *Enmund.* With respect to retribution—the interest in seeing that the offender gets his "just deserts"—the severity of the appropriate punishment necessarily depends on the culpability of the offender. Since *Gregg,* our jurisprudence has consistently confined the imposition of the death penalty to a narrow category of the most serious crimes. For example, in *Godfrey v. Georgia*, 446 U.S. 420, 100 S.Ct. 1759, 64 L.Ed.2d 398 (1980), we set aside a death sentence because the petitioner's crimes did not reflect "a consciousness materially more 'depraved' than that of any person guilty of murder."

If the culpability of the average murderer is insufficient to justify the most extreme sanction available to the State, the lesser culpability of the mentally retarded offender surely does not merit that form of retribution. Thus, pursuant to our narrowing jurisprudence, which seeks to ensure that only the most deserving of execution are put to death, an exclusion for the mentally retarded is appropriate. With respect to deterrence—the interest in preventing capital crimes by prospective offenders—"it seems likely that 'capital punishment can serve as a deterrent only when murder is the result of premeditation and deliberation.'" *Enmund*. Exempting the mentally retarded from that punishment will not affect the "cold calculus that precedes the decision" of other potential murderers. *Gregg*. Indeed, that sort of calculus is at the opposite end of the spectrum from behavior of mentally retarded offenders. The theory of deterrence in capital sentencing is predicated upon the notion that the increased severity of the punishment will inhibit criminal actors from carrying out murderous conduct. Yet it is the same cognitive and behavioral impairments that make these defendants less morally culpable—for example, the diminished ability to understand and process information, to learn from experience, to engage in logical reasoning, or to control impulses—that also make it less likely that they can process the information of the possibility of execution as a penalty and, as a result, control their conduct based upon that information. Nor will exempting the mentally retarded from execution lessen the deterrent effect of the death penalty with respect to offenders who are not mentally retarded. Such individuals are unprotected by the exemption and will continue to face the threat of execution. Thus, executing the mentally retarded will not measurably further the goal of deterrence.

The reduced capacity of mentally retarded offenders provides a second justification for a categorical rule making such offenders ineligible for the death penalty. The risk "that the death penalty will be imposed in spite of factors which may call for a less severe penalty," *Lockett v. Ohio*, 438 U.S. 586, 605, 98 S.Ct. 2954, 57 L.Ed.2d 973 (1978), is enhanced, not only by the possibility of false confessions,[25] but also by the lesser ability of mentally retarded defendants to make a persuasive showing of mitigation in the face of prosecutorial evidence of one or more aggravating factors. Mentally retarded defendants may be less able to give meaningful assistance to their counsel and are typically poor witnesses, and their demeanor may create an unwarranted impression of lack of remorse for their crimes. As *Penry* demonstrated, moreover, reliance on mental retardation as a mitigating factor can be a two-edged sword that may enhance the likelihood that the aggravating factor of future dangerousness will be found by the jury. Mentally retarded defendants in the aggregate face a special risk of wrongful execution.

Our independent evaluation of the issue reveals no reason to disagree with the judgment of "the legislatures that have recently addressed the matter" and concluded that death is not a suitable punish-

---

25. Despite the heavy burden that the prosecution must shoulder in capital cases, we cannot ignore the fact that in recent years a disturbing number of inmates on death row have been exonerated. As two recent high-profile cases demonstrate, these exonerations include mentally retarded persons who unwittingly confessed to crimes that they did not commit. See Baker, Death–Row Inmate Gets Clemency; Agreement Ends Days of Suspense, Washington Post, Jan. 15, 1994, p. A1; Holt & McRoberts, Porter Fully Savors First Taste of Freedom; Judge Releases Man Once Set for Execution, Chicago Tribune, Feb. 6, 1999, p. n1.

ment for a mentally retarded criminal. We are not persuaded that the execution of mentally retarded criminals will measurably advance the deterrent or the retributive purpose of the death penalty. Construing and applying the Eighth Amendment in the light of our "evolving standards of decency," we therefore conclude that such punishment is excessive and that the Constitution "places a substantive restriction on the State's power to take the life" of a mentally retarded offender. *Ford*. The judgment of the Virginia Supreme Court is reversed and the case is remanded for further proceedings not inconsistent with this opinion.

It is so ordered.

[The dissenting opinion of CHIEF JUSTICE REHNQUIST, with whom JUSTICE SCALIA and JUSTICE THOMAS join, is deleted.].

JUSTICE SCALIA, with whom THE CHIEF JUSTICE and JUSTICE THOMAS join, dissenting.

. . .

II

. . .

The Court makes no pretense that execution of the mildly mentally retarded would have been considered "cruel and unusual" in 1791. Only the severely or profoundly mentally retarded, commonly known as "idiots," enjoyed any special status under the law at that time.... The Court is left to argue, therefore, that execution of the mildly retarded is inconsistent with the "evolving standards of decency that mark the progress of a maturing society." Before today, our opinions consistently emphasized that Eighth Amendment judgments regarding the existence of social "standards" "should be informed by objective factors to the maximum possible extent" and "should not be, or appear to be, merely the subjective views of individual Justices." "First" among these objective factors are the "statutes passed by society's elected representatives," *Stanford v. Kentucky*; because it "will rarely if ever be the case that the Members of this Court will have a better sense of the evolution in views of the American people than do their elected representatives," *Thompson v. Oklahoma* (SCALIA, J., dissenting).

The Court pays lipservice to these precedents as it miraculously extracts a "national consensus" forbidding execution of the mentally retarded, from the fact that 18 States—less than half (47%) of the 38 States that permit capital punishment (for whom the issue exists)—have very recently enacted legislation barring execution of the mentally retarded.... That bare number of States alone—18—should be enough to convince any reasonable person that no "national consensus" exists. How is it possible that agreement among 47% of the death penalty jurisdictions amounts to "consensus"? Our prior cases have generally required a much higher degree of agreement before finding a punishment cruel and unusual on "evolving standards" grounds. In *Coker*, we proscribed the death penalty for rape of an adult woman after finding that only one jurisdiction, Georgia, authorized such a punishment. In *Enmund*, we invalidated the death penalty for mere participation in a robbery in which an accomplice took a life, a punishment not permitted in 28 of the death penalty States (78%). In *Ford*, we supported the common-law prohibition of execution of the insane with the observation that "[t]his ancestral legacy has not outlived its time," since not a single State authorizes such punishment. In *Solem v. Helm*, 463 U.S. 277, 300, 103 S.Ct. 3001, 77 L.Ed.2d 637 (1983), we invalidated a life sentence without parole under a recidivist statute by which the criminal "was treated more severely than he would have been in any other State." What the Court calls evidence of "consensus" in the present case (a fudged 47%) more closely resembles evidence that we found inadequate to establish consensus in earlier cases. *Tison v. Arizona*, 481 U.S. 137, 154, 158, 107 S.Ct. 1676, 95 L.Ed.2d 127 (1987), upheld a state law authorizing capital punishment for major participation in a felony with reckless indifference to life where only 11 of the 37 death penalty States (30%) prohibited such punishment. *Stanford* upheld a state law permitting execution of defendants who committed a capital crime at age 16 where only 15 of the 36 death penalty States (42%) prohibited death for such offenders.

    . . .

Even less compelling (if possible) is the Court's argument that evidence of "national consensus" is to be found in the infrequency with which retarded persons are executed in States that do not bar their execution. To begin with, what the Court takes as true is in fact quite doubtful. It is not at all clear that execution of the mentally retarded is "uncommon," as even the sources cited by the Court suggest. See also Bonner & Rimer, Executing the Mentally Retarded Even as Laws Begin to Shift, N.Y. Times, Aug. 7, 2000 p. A1 (reporting that 10% of death row inmates are retarded). If, however, execution of the mentally retarded is "uncommon"; and if it is not a sufficient explanation of this that the retarded comprise a tiny fraction of society (1% to 3%), Brief for American Psychological Association et al. as Amici Curiae 7; then surely the explanation is that mental retardation is a constitutionally mandated mitigating factor at sentencing. *Penry*. For that reason, even if there were uniform national sentiment in favor of executing the retarded in appropriate cases, one would still expect execution of the mentally retarded to be "uncommon." To adapt to the present case what the Court itself said in *Stanford*: "[I]t is not only possible, but overwhelmingly probable, that the very considerations which induce [today's majority] to believe that death should never be imposed on [mentally retarded] offenders . . . cause prosecutors and juries to believe that it should rarely be imposed."

But the Prize for the Court's Most Feeble Effort to fabricate "national consensus" must go to its appeal (deservedly relegated to a footnote) to the views of assorted professional and religious organizations, members of the so-called "world community," and respondents to opinion polls. I agree with the Chief Justice that the views of professional and religious organizations and the results of opinion polls are irrelevant. Equally irrelevant are the practices of the "world community," whose notions of justice are (thankfully) not always those of our people. "We must never forget that it is a Constitution for the United States of America that we are expounding. . . . [W]here there is not first a settled consensus among our own people, the views of other nations, however enlightened the Justices of this Court may think them to be, cannot be imposed upon Americans through the Constitution." *Thompson* (SCALIA, J., dissenting).

III

. . .

The genuinely operative portion of the opinion, then, is the Court's statement of the reasons why it agrees with the contrived consensus it has found, that the "diminished capacities" of the mentally retarded render the death penalty excessive. The . . . Court gives two reasons why the death penalty is an excessive punishment for all mentally retarded offenders. First, the "diminished capacities" of the mentally retarded raise a "serious question" whether their execution contributes to the "social purposes" of the death penalty, viz., retribution and deterrence. (The Court conveniently ignores a third "social purpose" of the death penalty—"incapacitation of dangerous criminals and the consequent prevention of crimes that they may otherwise commit in the future," *Gregg* (joint opinion of STEWART, POWELL, STEVENS). But never mind; its discussion of even the other two does not bear analysis.) Retribution is not advanced, the argument goes, because the mentally retarded are no more culpable than the average murderer, whom we have already held lacks sufficient culpability to warrant the death penalty, see *Godfrey v. Georgia* (plurality opinion). Who says so? Is there an established correlation between mental acuity and the ability to conform one's conduct to the law in such a rudimentary matter as murder? Are the mentally retarded really more disposed (and hence more likely) to commit willfully cruel and serious crime than others? In my experience, the opposite is true: being childlike generally suggests innocence rather than brutality.

Assuming, however, that there is a direct connection between diminished intelligence and the inability to refrain from murder, what scientific analysis can possibly show that a mildly retarded individual who commits an exquisite torture-killing is "no more culpable" than the "average" murderer in a holdup-gone-wrong or a domestic dispute? Or a moderately retarded individual who commits a series of 20 exquisite torture-killings? Surely culpability, and deservedness of the most severe retribution, depends not merely (if at all) upon the mental capacity of the criminal (above the level where he is able to distinguish right from wrong) but also upon the depravity of the crime—which is precisely why this sort of question has traditionally been thought answerable not by a categorical rule of the sort the Court today imposes upon all trials, but rather by the sentencer's weighing of the circumstances (both degree of retardation and depravity of crime) in the particular case. The fact that juries continue to sentence mentally retarded offenders to death for extreme crimes shows that society's moral outrage sometimes demands execution of retarded offenders. By what principle of law, science, or logic can the Court pronounce that this is wrong? There is none. Once the Court admits (as it does) that mental retardation does not render the offender morally blameless, there is no basis for saying that the death penalty is never appropriate retribution, no matter how heinous the crime. As long as a mentally retarded offender knows "the difference between right and wrong," only the sentencer can assess whether his retardation reduces his culpability enough to exempt him from the death penalty for the particular murder in question.

As for the other social purpose of the death penalty that the Court discusses, deterrence: That is not advanced, the Court tells us, because the mentally retarded are "less likely" than their non-retarded counterparts to "process the information of the possibility of execution as a penalty and . . . control their conduct based upon that information." Of course this leads to the same conclusion discussed earlier—that the mentally retarded (because they are less deterred) are more likely to kill—which neither I nor the society at large believes. In any event, even the Court does not say that all mentally retarded individuals cannot "process the information of the possibility of execution as a penalty and . . . control their conduct based upon that information"; it merely asserts that they are "less likely" to be able to do so. But surely the deterrent effect of a penalty is adequately vindicated if it successfully deters many, but not all, of the target class. Virginia's death penalty, for example, does not fail of its deterrent effect simply because some criminals are unaware that Virginia has the death penalty. In other words, the supposed fact that some retarded criminals cannot fully appreciate the death penalty has nothing to do with the deterrence rationale, but is simply an echo of the arguments denying a retribution rationale, discussed and rejected above. I am not sure that a murderer is somehow less blameworthy if (though he knew his act was wrong) he did not fully appreciate that he could die for it; but if so, we should treat a mentally retarded murderer the way we treat an offender who may be "less likely" to respond to the death penalty because he was abused as a child. We do not hold him immune from capital punishment, but require his background to be considered by the sentencer as a mitigating factor.

The Court throws one last factor into its grab bag of reasons why execution of the retarded is "excessive" in all cases: Mentally retarded offenders "face a special risk of wrongful execution" because they are less able "to make a persuasive showing of mitigation," "to give meaningful assistance to their counsel," and to be effective witnesses. "Special risk" is pretty flabby language (even flabbier than "less likely")—and I suppose a similar "special risk" could be said to exist for just plain stupid people, inarticulate people, even ugly people. If this unsupported claim has any substance to it (which I doubt) it might support a due process claim in all criminal prosecutions of the mentally retarded; but it is hard to see how it has anything to do with an Eighth Amendment claim that execution of the mentally retarded is cruel and unusual. We have never before held it to be cruel and unusual punishment to impose a sentence in violation of some other constitutional imperative.

IV

... There is something to be said for popular abolition of the death penalty; there is nothing to be said for its incremental abolition by this Court.

. . .

I respectfully dissent.

Questions and Comments

1. *Implementation of* Atkins. *Atkins* left the definition of mental retardation for purposes of administering the death penalty up to the states. Two states (Arkansas and Arizona) define retardation as an IQ below 65 and "significant" impairment in adaptive behavior. Several other states set the minimum IQ at 70, but also require an additional showing of impairment in adaptive functioning. Finally a number of states do not use IQ scores to define retardation, but rather require a showing of "significantly subaverage intelligence" that exists concurrently with deficits in adaptive functioning. Subaverage intelligence is variously defined as "an intelligence quotient more than two stand deviations below the mean for the test" (Connecticut), impairment that is manifested by "limitations in two or more adapative behaviors" (such as communication, self-care, social skills, work)(Missouri), or a condition "which substantially impairs one's capacity to appreciate the criminality of one's conduct or to conform one's conduct to the requirements of law" (Kansas). See Alexis Krulish Dowling, "Post-*Atkins* Problems with Enforcing the Supreme Court's Ban on Executing the Mentally Retarded," 33 Seton Hall L. Rev. 773, 789–93 (2003).

Both IQ and adaptive functioning can be hard to measure precisely. Consider these observations from Professor Mossman, a psychiatrist:

> The availability of IQ test scores suggests that mental health professionals can offer courts objective, precise methods for deciding who is, or is not, impaired enough to receive the death penalty. Yet the numbers that IQ tests generate are far from being perfectly reliable measurements of a person's cognitive ability. Under the best conditions, IQ tests have a "measurement error" of about five points. An individual who scores, say, 68 on one administration has a ninety-five percent chance of scoring between 63 and 73 on subsequent administrations. More than half of those persons whose IQ results fall in the mildly retarded range receive scores of 65 to 70, that is, their scores' margin of error will include 70.

> Another source of uncertainty stems from the fact that, for many items, the test administrator has to decide how many points a subject's response deserves. In normal clinical use, these imperfections do not matter a great deal. When testing a defendant for whom a one- or two-point change in IQ score has life-and-death implications, however, clinicians may have a hard time being dispassionately "objective" about

how they interpret a response. The net result of all these imperfections is that judges, or juries, will often have a hard time deciding on which side of the arbitrary line between mentally retarded and merely "dull" a defendant falls.

If IQ testing generates nettlesome problems with imprecision and measurement error, measuring adaptive functioning-a key feature defining mental retardation—is even trickier. As one leading text on behavioral assessment points out, several features of adaptive behavior make it "difficult to define." Adaptive behavior is really not separable from intelligence; individuals use both cognitive and behavioral abilities to master social problems and function in their environment. What counts as adaptive behavior changes as one grows older: during school years, academic performance is crucial, but in adulthood, living independently and ability to earn a living are paramount. Adaptive behavior is also a function of a person's living situation and the demands of his unique social environment. Some people can function adequately in a close-knit rural town but cannot cope with demands of life in an urban metropolis. Far more than is the case with measuring intelligence, "adaptive behavior represents the interaction of personal, cognitive, social, and situational variables." Finally, the various available instruments for measuring adaptive behavior may give different results. This may be a consequence of differences in the instruments' content, the type of responses the instruments require, the times at which the instruments were created, the types of persons used to develop the instruments, or simply the persons who do the ratings.

Douglas Mossman, "Beyond *Atkins*: A Psychiatric Can of Worms," 33 N.Mex. L. Rev. 255, 269–71 (2003). Consistent with Dr. Mossman's observations is research about the "Flynn Effect," which posits that IQ scores in general rise over time and thus that IQ tests that are not re-normed will overstate an individual's IQ vis-a-vis the rest of the population, by as much as 1/3 of a point per year since the test was normed. See *Walker v. True*, 399 F.3d 315 (4th Cir. 2005) (holding that testimony about the Flynn Effect is admissible to determine whether an offender is mentally retarded under *Atkins*).

Procedural issues left undiscussed in *Atkins* include whether a judge or jury should make the decision about mental retardation, whether the decision should be made before or during the capital sentencing decision, and which party bears the burden of proving or disproving retardation. Cf. *Murphy v. State*, 54 P.3d 556 (Okla.Crim.App. 2002)(holding, post-*Atkins*, that the offender bears the burden of proving mental retardation to the capital sentencing jury by a preponderance of the evidence).

2. *Mental retardation and the purposes of punishment*. As Justice Scalia points out, the majority's evidence of "national consensus" is weaker in *Atkins* that it has been in any other case in which the Court has found the eighth amendment to be violated. The majority's conclusion thus also rests heavily on its assumption that people with mental retardation are relatively less culpable and deterrable than others. With respect to the culpability issue, of what relevance is the fact, cited by Scalia, that perhaps 10% of those on death row are suffering from mental retardation? With respect to the

deterrability issue, of what relevance is the fact that people with mental retardation are not disproportionately likely to commit crime? James Ellis & Ruth Luckasson, "Mentally Retarded Criminal Defendants," 53 Geo. Wash. L.Rev. 414, 426 (1985) ("The best modern evidence suggests that the incidence of criminal behavior among people with mental retardation does not greatly exceed the incidence of criminal behavior among the population as a whole."). Scalia also points out that the majority does not mention incapacitation as a goal of capital punishment. If people with mental retardation are more impulsive, as the majority indicates, doesn't that make them more dangerous? Atkins had 16 prior felony convictions for robbery, attempted robbery, abduction, use of a firearm, and maiming.

Consider also this comment about the relationship between mental retardation and culpability.

> The tests that are typically used to measure "mental retardation" have been used in educational contexts (e.g., to address questions about the student's academic strengths and limitations and what types of special educational services must be provided) and eligibility for services and benefits (e.g., to address whether the individual qualifies for a vocational training or sheltered-living program, or for social security disability benefits). These tests were not developed for the purpose of distinguishing between capital offenders whose deficits in intellectual functioning render them are ineligible for the death penalty from those capital offenders without such deficits.

Lois A. Weithorn, "Conceptual Hurdles in the Application of *Atkins v. Virginia*," 59 Hastings L. J. 1203, 1223 (2008).

3. *Categorical exemptions from the death penalty.* In *Atkins*, Justice Scalia objected to the categorical nature of the majority's exemption, noting that it is antithetical to Supreme Court death penalty jurisprudence which, since *Woodson* and *Lockett*, has called for individualization of punishment, and asking "what scientific analysis can possibly show that a mildly retarded individual who commits an exquisite torture-killing is 'no more culpable' than the 'average' murderer in a holdup-gone-wrong or a domestic dispute?" Disability rights advocates have levied a similar criticism at *Atkins*. Donald Bersoff has argued that *Atkins* mischaracterizes the capacities of people with mental retardation. Noting that people with mental retardation can act with "intent and foresight," he states: "As important as it is to protect those who cannot protect themselves, it is equally important to promote the right of all persons to make their own choices, and, as a corollary, to be accountable for those choices." Donald N. Bersoff, "Some Contrarian Concerns about Law, Psychology, and Public Policy," 26 L. & Hum. Beh. 565, 568–69 (2002). Bersoff also suggests that *Atkins* may lead to a retraction of the rights and privileges that people with disability currently possess. He asserts, "[i]f we accept the concept of blanket incapacity, we relegate people with retardation to second-class citizenship, potentially permitting the State to abrogate the exercise of such fundamental interests as the right to marry, to have and rear one's children, to vote, or such everyday entitlements as entering into contracts or making a will." Id.

Consider as a partial response to these points the following comments:

According to the DSM–IV–TR, even people with "mild" retardation at most can develop academic skills up to the sixth-grade level, amounting to the maturity of a twelve-year-old. By exempting this whole category of people from its purview, *Atkins* constitutionalized the idea that the death penalty may be imposed only on people who are particularly culpable.... More important for present purposes, its holding (as distinguished, perhaps, from some of its language about the average murderer) does not mischaracterize the capacities of people with disability in the way Bersoff suggests. *Atkins* does not say that people with retardation are incapable of committing crime with intent or foresight. Nor, of course, does it say that murderers with serious disability should not be held accountable for their choices, as they still can be given life sentences. All *Atkins* says is that people with retardation, even those who commit a "horrible" murder, can never be as evil as the most evil murderers in our society, and thus that the ultimate punishment may not be imposed on them.

For related reasons, ... Bersoff's claim that *Atkins* will encourage use of categorical disability-based exemptions in the civil rights setting [is overstating the dangers of the decision].... The inquiry in the civil setting is not whether the disabled person is "average," but whether the person meets a minimum level of competence. In other words, even a person whose capacities are "below average" can, under the law, contract, marry, vote, and so on. Thus, neither the holding nor the unnecessarily broad language of *Atkins* sabotages these types of laws.

Christopher Slobogin, Minding Justice: Laws that Deprive People with Disability of Life and Liberty 85–86 (2006).

4. *Mental illness as a bar to the death penalty.* Like people with retardation who kill, people who commit capital murder while experiencing psychosis are, as a class, less blameworthy and less deterrable than the average murderer. Yet they are frequently convicted and sentenced to death. See Dorothy Otnow Lewis et al., "Psychiatric, Neurological, and Psychioeducational Characteristics of 15 Death Row Inmates in the United States," 143 Am. J. Psychiatry 838 (1986)(six of 15 randomly selected death row inmates "had schizophrenia psychosis antedating incarceration and two others were manic-depressive"). Should such death sentences be prohibited in light of *Atkins*? As noted in previous materials, only one state (Connecticut) prohibits execution of a person simply because of mental illness at the time of the offense, and a number of states have upheld death sentences imposed on those found "guilty but mentally ill" (see pp. 633–39). Thus, there is nothing close to the "consensus" that the majority found in *Atkins* against execution of people with retardation, and an eighth amendment argument would presumably be unavailing. But is there an equal protection argument, to the effect that, now that people with mental retardation may not be executed, imposition of the death penalty on capital offenders who were experiencing psychosis at the time of the offense is irrational? In equal protection terms, what are the justifications for continuing to permit, post-*Atkins*, execution of people with severe mental illness at the time of their crime? Are people with mental illness more "at fault" for their condition than those with mental retardation? Do they have greater opportunities or capacities to learn right

from wrong and correct bad behavior? Are they more dangerous than people with mental retardation?

If the answer to these questions is no (consider previous materials), then is there any other rational basis for distinguishing the two groups? Is mental illness more difficult to diagnose than mental retardation? (In this regard, do you think Atkins is "mentally retarded" for purposes of the death penalty bar? Someone with an IQ of 72, like Johnson in *Johnson v. State*, excerpted at pp. 649–50? Someone like Shawn Grell, who scored 72, 67, 69, 70, 57, 65 and 74 on IQ tests administered at various times, as described in *Arizona v. Grell*, 205 Ariz. 57, 66 P.3d 1234 (2003)? See note 1 above and notes 3, 5 & 22 of the majority opinion in *Atkins*). If mental illness is more difficult to diagnose, is that a reason to reject extension of *Atkins* to people with mental illness, or instead merely a reason to require strong proof of mental illness? See Christopher Slobogin, "What *Atkins* Could Mean for People with Mental Illness," 33 N.M. L. Rev. 293 (2003).

In 2007, the American Bar Association, the American Psychiatric Association and the American Psychological Association jointly endorsed a resolution which reads as follows:

> Defendants shall not be executed or sentenced to death if, at the time of the offense, they had a severe mental disorder or disability that significantly impaired their capacity (1) to appreciate the nature, consequences, or wrongfulness of their conduct, (2) to exercise rational judgment in relation to the conduct, or (3) to conform their conduct to the requirements of the law. A disorder manifested primarily by repeated criminal conduct or attributable solely to the acute effects of voluntary use of alcohol or other drugs does not, standing alone, constitute a mental disorder or disability for purposes of this provision.

The ABA's commentary to the Resolution notes that, although this language is similar to the ALI insanity test, most states have more restrictive insanity tests or no insanity defense at all, and thus this language would have an impact at the sentencing stage in most jurisdictions. The Resolution and commentary is available at www.abanet.org/crimjust/policy/am06122a.pdf.

B. NON–CAPITAL SENTENCING

1. *History: Retribution v. Incapacitation/Rehabilitation*

The history of sentencing outside the capital punishment setting reflects the tension between two different models: the retribution/deterrence model and the incapacitation/rehabilitation model. Under the first model, the type and duration of punishment is determined by assessing the offender's blameworthiness (as indicated by the offense committed and perhaps other criminal behavior as well) and the message punishment will send to others. Under the second model, the type and duration of punishment is dependent upon the offender's perceived dangerousness and the extent to which those criminal propensities can be reduced through treatment. Because information about blameworthiness of the offender and the deterrent value of particular punishments is usually known at the time of sentencing, the first model is more likely to result in determinate sentences, or at least sentences with a relatively narrow range. Conversely, the second model is more likely to produce indeterminate sentences with no specific termination point because, at the time of sentencing, it is not known how long a person will have to be incapacitated and treated before he or she is considered nondangerous. It is sometimes suggested that under the first model the effort is to fit the punishment to the crime, while under the second, punishment is designed to fit the criminal. This statement is somewhat misleading, because the blameworthiness assessment called for by the first model may consider individual traits (such as mental state at the time of the offense), while the dangerousness assessment mandated by the second model may in practice focus on the type of crime committed by the offender more than any other single factor. But it is fair to say that, as a general matter, the second model places more emphasis on individualization of punishment than does the first.

In the United States, the retribution/deterrence model dominated sentencing practices until the mid–19th century. Sentences tended to be uniform for each type of crime or at least defined by narrow ranges; an offender's rehabilitative potential was usually ignored. After the Civil War, concurrent with optimism that the causes of crime could be identified and treated, movement toward the incapacitation/rehabilitation approach gained momentum. By 1922, 37 states had enacted indeterminate sentencing statutes, and several others had parole systems functionally similar to the indeterminate sentence. The remaining states set maximum sentences for each crime, but allowed the judge and parole board to determine when within that time limit release would occur. In 1949, the United States Supreme Court seemed to approve of this trend when it described as the "prevalent modern philosophy of penology" the idea that "the punishment should fit the offender and not merely the crime.... Retribution is no longer the dominant objective of the criminal law. Reformation and rehabilitation of offenders have become important goals of criminal jurisprudence." *Williams v. New York*, 337 U.S. 241, 69 S.Ct. 1079, 93 L.Ed. 1337 (1949).

However, in the mid–1970's a countertrend emerged, often labeled the "just deserts" movement. Advocates of this approach believed that "those whose criminal actions are equally reprehensible deserve like amounts of punishment." Andrew VonHirsch & Kathleen Hanrahan, "Determinate Penalty Systems in America: An Overview," 27 Crime & Delinq. 289, 294 (1981). In the next three decades, perhaps twenty jurisdictions, including the federal government, developed "guidelines" imposing "fixed" or "presumptive" sentences, or permitting sentences only within a very narrow range, unless a showing is made that the offender should be treated differently. Under most of these schemes, variance from the legislated sentence is usually permissible only on culpability grounds (such as whether the defendant chose a vulnerable victim, was a leader or follower, accepted responsibility or obstructed justice, and is a career or first-time offender); concerns about dangerousness or rehabilitation are not supposed to influence the sentencing authority or are only secondary considerations. For instance, under the federal Sentencing Reform Act of 1984 the court is generally limited to imposing a sentence within a small range, the maximum of which may not exceed the minimum by more than the greater of 25% or six months. 28 U.S.C. § 994(a). Parole is abolished, 18 U.S.C. § 3624(a)(b), and rehabilitation rejected as a purpose of punishment. 28 U.S.C. § 994(k). While a number of states with guidelines systems emphasize prior record as one of the sentencing factors (which suggests that dangerousness is at least a background consideration), and virtually all guidelines states permit judges to impose probation conditions for certain crimes when an offender is "amenable" to probation, retributive considerations govern the sentence maxima and minima in virtually all of these states. Richard Frase, "State Sentencing Guidelines: Diversity, Consensus and Unresolved Policy Issues," 105 Colum. L. Rev. 1190, 1202–03 (2005). Recent Supreme Court decisions have loosened some of the restrictions imposed on judges in guidelines regimes. See *United States v. Booker*, 543 U.S. 220, 125 S.Ct. 738, 160 L.Ed.2d 621 (2005) (federal sentencing guidelines are not mandatory); *Gall v. United States*, ___ U.S. ___, 128 S.Ct. 586, 169 L.Ed.2d 445 (2007) (sentences that depart from guidelines must be reviewed under a deferential abuse-of-discretion standard). Once departures for cooperation with the government are eliminated, however, the vast majority of sentences in guidelines regimes fall within the guidelines. Guidelines: News from the U.S. Sentencing Commission 7 (May, 2007) (62% of sentences are within guidelines; 24% are government-sponsored downward departures for cooperation with the government; 12% are non-government sponsored downward departures; 2% are upward departures).

These vacillations in sentencing policy reflect several different influences. The just deserts variant of the retribution/deterrence model is founded on the belief that culpability is the touchstone of punishment: while incapacitation and rehabilitation goals may be achieved through punishment indirectly, they should not determine its scope; indeed, even the deterrence objective is deemphasized. The movement also seems to be a product of disenchantment with prison rehabilitation efforts, a belief that neither dangerousness nor treatability predictions are very accurate, and a desire to reduce sentencing disparity and indeterminacy, which are believed to be inequitable and have harmful psychological effects on inmates. See generally, Andrew VonHirsch, Doing Justice (1976).

The incapacitation/rehabilitation model still has many adherents, however. For instance, Halleck argues that because it refuses to consider dangerousness as a punishment variable, the retribution/deterrence model of sentencing is less protective of society; at the same time, because it incarcerates nondangerous, treatable individuals for long periods of time, it is unnecessarily harsh, ignores different people's susceptibility to punishment, and dehumanizes justice and society. Seymour Halleck, The Mentally Disordered Offender 191–93, 198–99 (1987). He asserts that "indeterminate programs have usually released offenders earlier than determinate programs, and they have almost always provided greater numbers of offenders with greater opportunities for freedom." Id. at 199. Compared to the retribution/deterrence model, the incapacitation/rehabilitation approach "is less discriminatory, imposes less pain on offenders as a group, and is especially merciful toward selected offenders who can be released when they are judged to be nondangerous to society." Id. at 202. See also John Clear et al., "Discretion and the Determinate Sentence: Its Distribution, Control, and Effect on Time Served," 24 Crime & Delinq. 428 (1978) (concluding that Indiana's determinate statute has been a failure because it continues to allow prosecutorial and judicial discretion and permits "untenably heavy penalties").

The two models differ significantly in their treatment of evidence concerning psychological makeup. Theoretically, under the incapacitation/rehabilitation approach to sentencing, all aspects of an individual's personality are relevant, including every shade of mental disability. Sentencing under this model

> is premised on the assumption that a sentencing judge, armed with an intimate knowledge of the offender's character and background and aided by scientific and clinical evaluations, can determine an appropriate sentence and treatment program that will rehabilitate the offender. Under this model, the sentencing judge seeks to define the offender's exact personality and social situations, and then prescribes an "individualized" sentence and treatment program.

Alan Dershowitz, "The Role of Psychiatry in the Sentencing Process," 1 Int'l J.L.Psychiat. 63, 66 (1978). In those states that follow this approach or variations on it, sentencing criteria are rarely specified because the information that may be considered by the judge is so wide-ranging.

Under the retributive/deterrence model, on the other hand, only those aspects of mental disability relevant to blameworthiness may be considered and, in most state statutes that reflect the influence of this model, these features are specifically identified as aggravating and mitigating factors. For instance, under the Minnesota sentencing scheme, the judge must normally impose a sentence based on the crime committed and the offender's previous criminal history unless specified aggravating or mitigating circumstances are shown. Included in the statute as mitigating factors are the following:

> (1) the offender played a minor or passive role in the crime or participated under circumstances of coercion or duress.

> (2) the offender, because of physical or mental impairment, lacked substantial capacity for judgment when the offense was committed.

> (3) other substantial grounds exist which tend to excuse or mitigate the offender's culpability, although not amounting to a defense.

See "Research Project: Minnesota Sentencing Guidelines," 5 Hamline L.Rev. 293, 412–15 (1982). In some states, proof of an aggravating or mitigating factor can result in a substantial variance from the presumptive sentence. For instance, in Arizona the judge may increase the sentence by up to 25% if an aggravating factor is shown and reduce the sentence by up to 50% if a mitigating circumstance is proven. Arizona R.S. §§ 13–502, 13–7–1, 13–7–2. See also, *United States v. Chambers*, 885 F.Supp. 12 (D.D.C.1995)(reducing sentence of person with mental retardation from federal guideline minimum of 188 months to 21 months); cf. *United States v. Lewinson*, 988 F.2d 1005 (9th Cir. 1993)(holding that mental disorder need not be "severe" to warrant downward departure, as long as it resulted in "significant impairment" that affects "behavior and decision-making during the offense period").

One review found, however, that downward departures on grounds of mental disability (e.g., depression, manic psychosis, severe emotional stress, psychosis) are usually "summarily rejected" and also noted that in some cases evidence of past insanity acquittals has been viewed as an aggravating circumstance. Michael L. Perlin & Keri K. Gould, "Rashomon and the Criminal Law: Mental Disability and the Federal Sentencing Guidelines," 22 Am. J. Crim. L. 431, 448–49 (1995). For instance, under the Federal Guidelines, a downward departure for diminished capacity should occur only if the individual shows that he had a "significantly impaired ability to (A) understand the wrongfulness of the behavior comprising the offense or to exercise the power to reason; or (B) control behavior that the defendant knows is wrongful." U.S. Sentencing Guidelines Manual § 5K2.13. Further, the downward departure is not permitted if the diminished capacity was the result of voluntary drug use, the offense involved the use of violence or the threat of violence, or the defendant had a dangerous criminal history. Id. Mere mental or emotional "conditions" are "not ... relevant in determining whether a departure is warranted," but "may be relevant in determining the conditions of probation or supervised release." Id. at § 5H1.3. Although the Guidelines are now voluntary, see *Booker*, supra, downward departures on diminished capacity grounds are still relatively rare. Guidelines: News from the U.S. Sentencing Commission 7 (May, 2007) (12% of departures are non-government sponsored downward departures).

To the extent the retribution/deterrence model of sentencing is concerned with mental disability, this book's materials on capital sentencing discuss many of the pertinent issues;[x] little further discussion is warranted. The legal issues connected with the incapacitation/rehabilitation model are worth delving into in more detail. Examples of statutes that adopt this approach are numerous. At the federal level, for instance, they range from the Narcotic Addict Rehabilitation Act, 18 U.S.C. §§ 4251 et seq., which permits the addict with charges pending to elect treatment for a specified period of time, to the Youth Correction Act, 18

---

x. Although they usually do not include predictive criteria such as dangerousness and treatability, determinate sentencing statutes are otherwise similar to capital sentencing statutes in structure; thus, many of the same legal issues may arise (e.g., when is a particular mitigating factor proven, how does the court "count" mental disability which is both mitigating and aggravating).

U.S.C. §§ 5005 et seq., which, before its repeal in 1986, granted the courts authority to sentence persons between 21 and 26 to indeterminate confinement not to exceed four years for "corrective and preventive guidance and training designed to protect the public by correcting the antisocial tendencies of youth offenders." Id. § 5006(f). Probably the purest expression of the incapacitation/rehabilitation model, however, is found in statutes providing for the indeterminate confinement of those found to be "mentally disordered sex offenders." We now turn to an examination of these statutes.

2. Mentally Disordered Sex Offender Statutes[y]

In the early part of the twentieth century, a number of states passed legislation aimed at diverting into special indeterminate treatment programs a category of offenders who came to be known as "defective delinquents." Many of these states had already adopted an indeterminate sentencing system. Thus, apparently, the impetus for these initial special sentencing programs was to remove from the regular prison system particularly disruptive and hard to treat offenders. Although some states still have such statutes, they have rarely been enthusiastically implemented.[z]

Much more popular were statutes aimed at diverting those charged with sex offenses, the first of which was passed by Michigan in 1937. At one time, over 25 states had such statutes, which have come to be called mentally disordered sex offender (MDSO) statutes. Samuel Brakel & Richard Rock, The Mentally Disabled and the Law 341 (1971). Apparently programs singling out sex offenders succeeded where the defective delinquent statutes did not because sex offenders were believed to be particularly likely to recidivate if not treated and at the same time particularly amenable to treatment. Additionally, sex offenders, especially pedophiles, tend to be mistreated by other prisoners and are often segregated from the rest of the prison population in any event.

MDSO statutes vary considerably both substantively and procedurally. A MDSO "commitment proceeding" usually can only be triggered by conviction of a sex offense. However, several states permit such a proceeding upon indictment for a sex offense, and at least one state—Illinois—authorizes initiation of MDSO proceedings after an individual is charged with *any* offense. Commitment as a MDSO usually requires a showing that the person is predisposed to commit sexual offenses as a result of "mental disease or defect." A few statutes also require a separate showing of repeated sexual misconduct (in Illinois, because the

y. Most of this introduction is taken from George Dix, "Special Dispositional Alternatives for Abnormal Offenders," in John Monahan & Henry Steadman, Mentally Disordered Offenders: Perspectives from Law and Social Science 133, 134–145 (1983).

z. An exception was the Maryland Defective Delinquent Act, Art. 31B (1964), which was frequently used to confine defec-tive delinquents indeterminately until 1978, when the duration of confinement was limited to the maximum sentence that would have been received. See Louis Kohlmeyer, "The First Year of Operation Under the New Patuxent Laws," 7 Bull. Amer. Acad. Psychiat. & L. 95 (1979). The Act was repealed in 1989.

proceeding is initiated by indictment, the subject must have "demonstrated propensities towards acts of sexual assault or acts of sexual molestation of children"); a few other states require a showing of treatability. Under most of the original statutes, commitment as a MDSO resulted in indeterminate confinement, with release dependent upon initiation of discharge proceedings by the superintendent of the treating facility and approval by the committing court. Later statutes limited the time of confinement to the maximum term that could have been imposed for the crime committed by the offender, although in some of these states commitment may be renewed if a new commitment proceeding is held at which more stringent criteria are met.

MDSO statutes waned in popularity in the 1970's and 1980's. American Bar Association, Criminal Justice Mental Health Standards 7–424 n. 20. But in the 1990's a new version of these statutes, dubbed "sexual predator" laws, have revived the concept; as of 2007, at least twenty jurisdictions had such laws and over 2700 individuals had been committed under them. Monica Davey & Abby Goodnough, "Doubts Rise as States Hold Sex Offenders After Prison," N.Y. Times, Mar. 4, 2007, § 1, at 1. Sexual predator laws not only permit confinement of those who are charged or convicted but also of those who have completed their sentences for a sex offense. The following U.S. Supreme Court decision upheld one of these laws against several constitutional challenges and, in so doing, raised fundamental questions not just about the scope of MDSO statutes but also about the scope of civil commitment, the subject of the next chapter.

KANSAS v. HENDRICKS

Supreme Court of the United States, 1997.
521 U.S. 346, 117 S.Ct. 2072, 138 L.Ed.2d 501.

J USTICE T HOMAS delivered the opinion of the Court.

In 1994, Kansas enacted the Sexually Violent Predator Act, which established procedures for the civil commitment of persons who, due to a "mental abnormality" or a "personality disorder," are likely to engage in "predatory acts of sexual violence." Kan. Stat. Ann. § 59–29a–1 et seq. (1994). The State invoked the Act for the first time to commit Leroy Hendricks, an inmate who had a long history of sexually molesting children, and who was scheduled for release from prison shortly after the Act became law. Hendricks challenged his commitment on, inter alia, "substantive" due process, double jeopardy, and ex post facto grounds. The Kansas Supreme Court invalidated the Act, holding that its pre-commitment condition of a "mental abnormality" did not satisfy what the court perceived to be the "substantive" due process requirement that involuntary civil commitment must be predicated on a finding of "mental illness." The State of Kansas petitioned for certiorari. Hendricks subsequently filed a cross-petition in which he reasserted his federal double jeopardy and post facto claims. We granted certiorari on both the petition and the cross-petition, and now reverse the judgment below.

I

A

The Kansas Legislature enacted the Sexually Violent Predator Act (Act) in 1994 to grapple with the problem of managing repeat sexual offenders. Although Kansas already had a statute addressing the involuntary commitment of those defined as "mentally ill," the legislature determined that existing civil commitment procedures were inadequate to confront the risks presented by "sexually violent predators." In the Act's preamble, the legislature explained:

> "[A] small but extremely dangerous group of sexually violent predators exist who do not have a mental disease or defect that renders them appropriate for involuntary treatment pursuant to the [general involuntary civil commitment statute].... In contrast to persons appropriate for civil commitment under the [general involuntary civil commitment statute], sexually violent predators generally have anti-social personality features which are unamenable to existing mental illness treatment modalities and those features render them likely to engage in sexually violent behavior. The legislature further finds that sexually violent predators' likelihood of engaging in repeat acts of predatory sexual violence is high. The existing involuntary commitment procedure ... is inadequate to address the risk these sexually violent predators pose society. The legislature further finds that the prognosis for rehabilitating sexually violent predators in a prison setting is poor, the treatment needs of this population are very long term and the treatment modalities for this population are very different than the traditional treatment modalities for people appropriate for commitment under the [general involuntary civil commitment statute]."

As a result, the Legislature found it necessary to establish "a civil commitment procedure for the long-term care and treatment of the sexually violent predator." The Act defined a "sexually violent predator" as:

> "any person who has been convicted of or charged with a sexually violent offense" and who suffers from a mental abnormality or personality disorder which makes the person "likely to engage in the predatory acts of sexual violence."

A "mental abnormality" was defined, in turn, as a "congenital or acquired condition affecting the emotional or volitional capacity which predisposes the person to commit sexually violent offenses in a degree constituting such person a menace to the health and safety of others."

As originally structured, the Act's civil commitment procedures pertained to (1) a presently confined person who, like Hendricks, "has been convicted of a sexually violent offense" and is scheduled for release;

(2) a person who has been "charged with a sexually violent offense" but has been found incompetent to stand trial; (3) a person who has been found "not guilty by reason of insanity of a sexually violent offense"; and (4) a person found "not guilty" of a sexually violent offense because of a mental disease or defect.

The initial version of the Act [which has since been amended in ways irrelevant to the current decision], as applied to a currently confined person such as Hendricks, was designed to initiate a specific series of procedures. The custodial agency was required to notify the local prosecutor 60 days before the anticipated release of a person who might have met the Act's criteria. The prosecutor was then obligated, within 45 days, to decide whether to file a petition in state court seeking the person's involuntary commitment. If such a petition were filed, the court was to determine whether "probable cause" existed to support a finding that the person was a "sexually violent predator" and thus eligible for civil commitment. Upon such a determination, transfer of the individual to a secure facility for professional evaluation would occur. After that evaluation, a trial would be held to determine beyond a reasonable doubt whether the individual was a sexually violent predator. If that determination were made, the person would then be transferred to the custody of the Secretary of Social and Rehabilitation Services (Secretary) for "control, care and treatment until such time as the person's mental abnormality or personality disorder has so changed that the person is safe to be at large."

In addition to placing the burden of proof upon the State, the Act afforded the individual a number of other procedural safeguards. In the case of an indigent person, the State was required to provide, at public expense, the assistance of counsel and an examination by mental health care professionals. The individual also received the right to present and cross-examine witnesses, and the opportunity to review documentary evidence presented by the State.

Once an individual was confined, the Act required that "the involuntary detention or commitment ... shall conform to constitutional requirements for care and treatment." Confined persons were afforded three different avenues of review: First, the committing court was obligated to conduct an annual review to determine whether continued detention was warranted. Second, the Secretary was permitted, at any time, to decide that the confined individual's condition had so changed that release was appropriate, and could then authorize the person to petition for release. Finally, even without the Secretary's permission, the confined person could at any time file a release petition. If the court found that the State could no longer satisfy its burden under the initial commitment standard, the individual would be freed from confinement.

B

In 1984, Hendricks was convicted of taking "indecent liberties" with two 13 year-old boys. After serving nearly 10 years of his sentence, he was slated for release to a halfway house. Shortly before his scheduled release, however, the State filed a petition in state court seeking Hendricks' civil confinement as a sexually violent predator. On August 19, 1994, Hendricks appeared before the court with counsel and moved to dismiss the petition on the grounds that the Act violated various federal constitutional provisions. Although the court reserved ruling on the Act's constitutionality, it concluded that there was probable cause to support a finding that Hendricks was a sexually violent predator, and therefore ordered that he be evaluated at the Larned State Security Hospital.

Hendricks subsequently requested a jury trial to determine whether he qualified as a sexually violent predator. During that trial, Hendricks' own testimony revealed a chilling history of repeated child sexual molestation and abuse, beginning in 1955 when he exposed his genitals to two young girls. At that time, he pleaded guilty to indecent exposure. Then, in 1957, he was convicted of lewdness involving a young girl and received a brief jail sentence. In 1960, he molested two young boys while he worked for a carnival. After serving two years in prison for that offense, he was paroled, only to be rearrested for molesting a 7 year-old girl. Attempts were made to treat him for his sexual deviance, and in 1965 he was considered "safe to be at large," and was discharged from a state psychiatric hospital.

Shortly thereafter, however, Hendricks sexually assaulted another young boy and girl—he performed oral sex on the 8 year-old girl and fondled the 11 year-old boy. He was again imprisoned in 1967, but refused to participate in a sex offender treatment program, and thus remained incarcerated until his parole in 1972. Diagnosed as a pedophile, Hendricks entered into, but then abandoned, a treatment program. He testified that despite having received professional help for his pedophilia, he continued to harbor sexual desires for children. Indeed, soon after his 1972 parole, Hendricks began to abuse his own stepdaughter and stepson. He forced the children to engage in sexual activity with him over a period of approximately four years. Then, as noted above, Hendricks was convicted of "taking indecent liberties" with two adolescent boys after he attempted to fondle them. As a result of that conviction he was once again imprisoned, and was serving that sentence when he reached his conditional release date in September 1994.

Hendricks admitted that he had repeatedly abused children whenever he was not confined. He explained that when he "gets stressed out," he "can't control the urge" to molest children. Although Hendricks recognized that his behavior harms children, and he hoped he would not sexually molest children again, he stated that the only sure way he could keep from sexually abusing children in the future was "to die." Hendricks readily agreed with the state physician's diagnosis that he suffers from pedophilia and that he is not cured of the condition; indeed, he told the physician that "treatment is bull-."[2] The jury unanimously found

---

2. In addition to Hendricks' own testimony, the jury heard from Hendricks' step-   daughter and stepson, who recounted the events surrounding their repeated sexual

beyond a reasonable doubt that Hendricks was a sexually violent predator. The trial court subsequently determined, as a matter of state law, that pedophilia qualifies as a "mental abnormality" as defined by the Act, and thus ordered Hendricks committed to the Secretary's custody.

Hendricks appealed, claiming, among other things, that application of the Act to him violated the Federal Constitution's Due Process, Double Jeopardy, Ex Post Facto Clauses. The Kansas Supreme Court accepted Hendricks' due process claim. The court declared that in order to commit a person involuntarily in a civil proceeding, the State is required by "substantive" due process to prove by clear and convincing evidence that the person is both (1) mentally ill, and (2) a danger to himself or to others. The court then determined that the Act's definition of "mental abnormality" did not satisfy what it perceived to be this Court's "mental illness" requirement in the civil commitment context. As a result, the court held that "the Act violates Hendricks' substantive due process rights."

* * *

II

A

Kansas argues that the Act's definition of "mental abnormality" satisfies "substantive" due process requirements. We agree. Although freedom from physical restraint "has always been at the core of the liberty protected by the Due Process Clause from arbitrary governmental action," *Foucha v. Louisiana* [see pp. 877–80], that liberty interest is not absolute. The Court has recognized that an individual's constitutionally protected interest in avoiding physical restraint may be overridden even in the civil context: "The liberty secured by the Constitution of the United States to every person within its jurisdiction does not import an absolute right in each person to be, at all times and in all circumstances, wholly free from restraint. There are manifold restraints to which every person is necessarily subject for the common good. On any other basis organized society could not exist with safety to its members." *Jacobson v. Massachusetts*. Accordingly, States have in certain narrow circumstances provided for the forcible civil detainment of people who are unable to control their behavior and who thereby pose a danger to the public health and safety. We have consistently upheld such involuntary

abuse at Hendricks' hands. One of the girls to whom Hendricks exposed himself in 1955 testified as well. The State also presented testimony from Lester Lee, a licensed clinical social worker who specialized in treating male sexual offenders, and Dr. Charles Befort, the chief psychologist at Larned State Hospital. Lee testified that Hendricks had a diagnosis of personality trait disturbance, passive-aggressive personality, and pedophilia. Dr. Befort testified that Hendricks suffered from pedophilia and is likely to commit sexual offenses against children in the future if not confined. He further opined that pedophilia qualifies as a "mental abnormality" within the Act's definition of that term. Finally, Hendricks offered testimony from Dr. William S. Logan, a forensic psychiatrist, who stated that it was not possible to predict with any degree of accuracy the future dangerousness of a sex offender.

commitment statutes provided the confinement takes place pursuant to proper procedures and evidentiary standards. *Foucha*; *Addington v. Texas* [see pp. 815–21]. It thus cannot be said that the involuntary civil confinement of a limited subclass of dangerous persons is contrary to our understanding of ordered liberty.

The challenged Act unambiguously requires a finding of dangerousness either to one's self or to others as a prerequisite to involuntary confinement. Commitment proceedings can be initiated only when a person "has been convicted of or charged with a sexually violent offense," and "suffers from a mental abnormality or personality disorder which makes the person likely to engage in the predatory acts of sexual violence." The statute thus requires proof of more than a mere predisposition to violence; rather, it requires evidence of past sexually violent behavior and a present mental condition that creates a likelihood of such conduct in the future if the person is not incapacitated. As we have recognized, "previous instances of violent behavior are an important indicator of future violent tendencies." *Schall v. Martin*, 467 U.S. 253, 104 S.Ct. 2403 (1984) (explaining that "from a legal point of view there is nothing inherently unattainable about a prediction of future criminal conduct"). A finding of dangerousness, standing alone, is ordinarily not a sufficient ground upon which to justify indefinite involuntary commitment. We have sustained civil commitment statutes when they have coupled proof of dangerousness with the proof of some additional factor, such as a "mental illness" or "mental abnormality." See, e.g., *Heller v. Doe* [pp. 896–903] (Kentucky statute permitting commitment of "mentally retarded" or "mentally ill" and dangerous individual); *Allen v. Illinois* [see pp. 842–46]; *Minnesota ex rel. Pearson v. Probate Court*. These added statutory requirements serve to limit involuntary civil confinement to those who suffer from a volitional impairment rendering them dangerous beyond their control. The Kansas Act is plainly of a kind with these other civil commitment statutes: It requires a finding of future dangerousness, and then links that finding to the existence of a "mental abnormality" or "personality disorder" that makes it difficult, if not impossible, for the person to control his dangerous behavior. The precommitment requirement of a "mental abnormality" or "personality disorder" is consistent with the requirements of these other statutes that we have upheld in that it narrows the class of person eligible for confinement to those who are unable to control their dangerousness.

Hendricks nonetheless argues that our earlier cases dictate a finding of "mental illness" as a prerequisite for civil commitment, citing *Foucha* and *Addington*. He then asserts that a "mental abnormality" is not equivalent to a "mental illness" because it is a term coined by the Kansas Legislature, rather than by the psychiatric community. Contrary to Hendricks' assertion, the term "mental illness" is devoid of any talismanic significance. Not only do "psychiatrists disagree widely and frequently on what constitutes mental illness," but the Court itself has used a variety of expressions to describe the mental condition of those properly subject to civil confinement. See, e.g., *Addington*, (using the terms "emotionally disturbed" and "mentally ill"); *Jackson v. Indiana*, 406 U. S., at 732, 737 (using the terms "incompetency" and "insanity"); cf. *Foucha*, 504 U.S., at 88 (O'CONNOR, J., concurring in part and concurring in judgment) (acknowledging State's authority to commit a person when there is "some medical justification for doing so"). Indeed, we have never required State legislatures to adopt any particular nomenclature in drafting civil commitment statutes. Rather, we have traditionally left to legislators the task of defining terms of a medical nature that have legal significance. As a consequence, the States have, over the years, developed numerous specialized terms to define mental health concepts. Often, those definitions do not fit precisely with the definitions employed by the medical community. The legal definitions of "insanity" and "competency," for example, vary substantially from their psychiatric counterparts. Legal definitions, however, which must "take into account such issues as individual responsibility ... and competency," need not mirror those advanced by the medical profession. American Psychiatric Association, Diagnostic and Statistical Manual of Mental Disorders xxiii, xxvii (4th ed. 1994).

To the extent that the civil commitment statutes we have considered set forth criteria relating to an individual's inability to control his dangerousness, the Kansas Act sets forth comparable criteria and Hendricks' condition doubtless satisfies those criteria. The mental health professionals who evaluated Hendricks diagnosed him as suffering from pedophilia, a condition the psychiatric profession itself classifies as a serious mental disorder. See *id.*; American Psychiatric Association, Treatments of Psychiatric Disorders, 617–633 (1989).[3] Hendricks even conceded that, when he becomes "stressed out," he cannot "control the urge" to molest children. This admitted lack of volitional control, coupled with a prediction of future dangerousness, adequately distinguishes Hendricks from other dangerous persons who are perhaps more properly dealt with exclusively through criminal proceedings. Hendricks' diagnosis as a pedophile, which qualifies as a "mental abnormality" under the Act, thus plainly suffices for due process purposes.

B

We granted Hendricks' cross-petition to determine whether the Act violates the Constitution's double jeopardy prohibition or its ban on ex post facto lawmaking. The thrust of Hendricks' argument is that the Act establishes criminal proceedings; hence confinement under it necessarily

---

3. We recognize, of course, that psychiatric professionals are not in complete harmony in casting pedophilia, or paraphilias in general, as "mental illnesses." Compare Brief for American Psychiatric Association as Amicus Curiae 26 with Brief for Menninger Foundation et al. as Amici Curiae 22–25. These disagreements, however, do not tie the State's hands in setting the bounds of its civil commitment laws. In fact, it is precisely where such disagreement exists that legislatures have been afforded the widest latitude in drafting such statutes. Cf. *Jones v. United States* [see pp. 869–74]. As we have explained regarding congressional enactments, when a legislature "undertakes to act in areas fraught with medical and scientific uncertainties, legislative options must be especially broad and courts should be cautious not to rewrite legislation."

constitutes punishment. He contends that where, as here, newly enacted "punishment" is predicated upon past conduct for which he has already been convicted and forced to serve a prison sentence, the Constitution's Double Jeopardy and Ex Post Facto Clauses are violated. We are unpersuaded by Hendricks' argument that Kansas has established criminal proceedings.

The categorization of a particular proceeding as civil or criminal "is first of all a question of statutory construction." *Allen*. We must initially ascertain whether the legislature meant the statute to establish "civil" proceedings. If so, we ordinarily defer to the legislature's stated intent. Here, Kansas' objective to create a civil proceeding is evidenced by its placement of the Sexually Violent Predator Act within the Kansas probate code, instead of the criminal code, as well as its description of the Act as creating a "civil commitment procedure." Nothing on the face of the statute suggests that the legislature sought to create anything other than a civil commitment scheme designed to protect the public from harm. Although we recognize that a "civil label is not always dispositive," *Allen*, we will reject the legislature's manifest intent only where a party challenging the statute provides "the clearest proof" that "the statutory scheme [is] so punitive either in purpose or effect as to negate [the State's] intention" to deem it "civil." In those limited circumstances, we will consider the statute to have established criminal proceedings for constitutional purposes. Hendricks, however, has failed to satisfy this heavy burden.

As a threshold matter, commitment under the Act does not implicate either of the two primary objectives of criminal punishment: retribution or deterrence. The Act's purpose is not retributive because it does not affix culpability for prior criminal conduct. Instead, such conduct is used solely for evidentiary purposes, either to demonstrate that a "mental abnormality" exists or to support a finding of future dangerousness. We have previously concluded that an Illinois statute was nonpunitive even though it was triggered by the commission of a sexual assault, explaining that evidence of the prior criminal conduct was "received not to punish past misdeeds, but primarily to show the accused's mental condition and to predict future behavior." *Allen*. In addition, the Kansas Act does not make a criminal conviction a prerequisite for commitment—persons absolved of criminal responsibility may nonetheless be subject to confinement under the Act. An absence of the necessary criminal responsibility suggest that the State is not seeking retribution for a past misdeed. Thus, the fact that the Act may be "tied to criminal activity" is "insufficient to render the statute punitive." Moreover, unlike a criminal statute, no finding of scienter is required to commit an individual who is found to be a sexually violent predator; instead, the commitment determination is made based on a "mental abnormality" or "personality disorder" rather than on one's criminal intent. The existence of a scienter requirement is customarily an important element in distinguishing criminal from civil statutes. The absence of such a requirement here is evidence that confinement under the statute is not intended to be retributive.

Nor can it be said that the legislature intended the Act to function as a deterrent. Those persons committed under the Act are, by definition, suffering from a "mental abnormality" or a "personality disorder" that prevents them from exercising adequate control over their behavior. Such persons are therefore unlikely to be deterred by the threat of confinement. And the conditions surrounding that confinement do not suggest a punitive purpose on the State's part. The State has represented that an individual confined under the Act is not subject to the more restrictive conditions placed on state prisoners, but instead experiences essentially the same conditions as any involuntarily committed patient in the state mental institution. Because none of the parties argues that people institutionalized under the Kansas general civil commitment statute are subject to punitive conditions, even though they may be involuntarily confined, it is difficult to conclude that persons confined under this Act are being "punished."

Although the civil commitment scheme at issue here does involve an affirmative restraint, "the mere fact that a person is detained does not inexorably lead to the conclusion that the government has imposed punishment." *United States v. Salerno* [upholding pretrial detention of dangerous individuals]. The State may take measures to restrict the freedom of the dangerously mentally ill. This is a legitimate non-punitive governmental objective and has been historically so regarded. The Court has, in fact, cited the confinement of "mentally unstable individuals who present a danger to the public" as one classic example of nonpunitive detention. *Id.* If detention for the purpose of protecting the community from harm necessarily constituted punishment, then all involuntary civil commitments would have to be considered punishment. But we have never so held.

Hendricks focuses on his confinement's potentially indefinite duration as evidence of the State's punitive intent. That focus, however, is misplaced. Far from any punitive objective, the confinement's duration is instead linked to the stated purposes of the commitment, namely, to hold the person until his mental abnormality no longer causes him to be a threat to others. If, at any time, the confined person is adjudged "safe to be at large," he is statutorily entitled to immediate release. Furthermore, commitment under the Act is only potentially indefinite. The maximum amount of time an individual can be incapacitated pursuant to a single judicial proceeding is one year. If Kansas seeks to continue the detention beyond that year, a court must once again determine beyond a reasonable doubt that the detainee satisfies the same standards as required for the initial confinement. This requirement again demonstrates that Kansas does not intend an individual committed pursuant to the Act to remain confined any longer than he suffers from a mental abnormality rendering him unable to control his dangerousness.

Hendricks next contends that the State's use of procedural safeguards traditionally found in criminal trials makes the proceedings here criminal rather than civil. In *Allen*, we confronted a similar argument. There, the petitioner "placed great reliance on the fact that proceedings under the Act are accompanied by procedural safeguards usually found in criminal trials" to argue that the proceedings were civil in name only. We rejected that argument, however, explaining that the State's decision "to provide some of the safeguards applicable in criminal trials cannot itself turn these proceedings into criminal prosecutions." The numerous procedural and evidentiary protections afforded here demonstrate that the Kansas Legislature has taken great care to confine only a narrow class of particularly dangerous individuals, and then only after meeting the strictest procedural standards. That Kansas chose to afford such procedural protections does not transform a civil commitment proceeding into a criminal prosecution.

Finally, Hendricks argues that the Act is necessarily punitive because it fails to offer any legitimate "treatment." Without such treatment, Hendricks asserts, confinement under the Act amounts to little more than disguised punishment. Hendricks' argument assumes that treatment for his condition is available, but that the State has failed (or refused) to provide it. The Kansas Supreme Court, however, apparently rejected this assumption, explaining:

> "It is clear that the overriding concern of the legislature is to continue the segregation of sexually violent offenders from the public. Treatment with the goal of reintegrating them into society is incidental, at best. The record reflects that treatment for sexually violent predators is all but nonexistent. The legislature concedes that sexually violent predators are not amenable to treatment under [the existing Kansas involuntary commitment statute]. If there is nothing to treat under [that statute], then there is no mental illness. In that light, the provisions of the Act for treatment appear somewhat disingenuous."

It is possible to read this passage as a determination that Hendricks' condition was untreatable under the existing Kansas civil commitment statute, and thus the Act's sole purpose was incapacitation. Absent a treatable mental illness, the Kansas court concluded, Hendricks could not be detained against his will.

Accepting the Kansas court's apparent determination that treatment is not possible for this category of individuals does not obligate us to adopt its legal conclusions. We have already observed that, under the appropriate circumstances and when accompanied by proper procedures, incapacitation may be legitimate end of the civil law. *Allen*; *Salerno*. Accordingly, the Kansas court's determination that the Act's "overriding concern" was the continued "segregation of sexually violent offenders" is consistent with our conclusion that the Act establishes civil proceedings, especially when that concern is coupled with the State's ancillary goal of providing treatment to those offenders, if such is possible. While we have upheld state civil commitment statutes that aim both to incapacitate and to treat, see *Allen*, we have never held that the Constitution prevents a State from civilly detaining those for whom no treatment is available, but who nevertheless pose a danger to others. A State could hardly be seen as furthering a "punitive" purpose by involuntarily confining persons afflicted with an untreatable, highly, contagious disease. Accord *Compagnie Francaise de Navigation a Vapeur v. Louisiana Bd. of Health*, 186 U.S. 380 (1902) (permitting involuntary quarantine of persons suffering from communicable diseases). Similarly, it would be of little value to require treatment as a precondition for civil confinement of the dangerously insane when no acceptable treatment existed. To conclude otherwise would obligate a State to release certain confined individuals who were both mentally ill and dangerous simply because they could not be successfully treated for their afflictions.

Alternatively, the Kansas Supreme Court's opinion can be read to conclude that Hendricks' condition is treatable, but that treatment was not the State's "overriding concern," and that no treatment was being provided (at least at the time Hendricks was committed). Even if we accept this determination that the provision of treatment was not the Kansas Legislature's "overriding" or "primary" purpose in passing the Act, this does not rule out the possibility that an ancillary purpose of the Act was to provide treatment, and it does not require us to conclude that the Act is punitive. Indeed, critical language in the Act itself demonstrates that the Secretary of Social and Rehabilitation Services, under whose custody sexually violent predators are committed, has an obligation to provide treatment to individuals like Hendricks. ("If the court or jury determines that the person is a sexually violent predator, the person shall be committed to the custody of the secretary of social and rehabilitation services for control, care and treatment until such time as the person's mental abnormality or personality disorder has so changed that the person is safe to be at large"). Other of the Act's sections echo this obligation to provide treatment for committed persons. Thus, as in *Allen*, "the State has a statutory obligation to provide 'care and treatment for [persons adjudged sexually dangerous] designed to effect recovery,'" and we may therefore conclude that "the State has ... provided for the treatment of those it commits."

Although the treatment program initially offered Hendricks may have seemed somewhat meager, it must be remembered that he was the first person committed under the Act. That the State did not have all of its treatment procedures in place is thus not surprising. What is significant, however, is that Hendricks was placed under the supervision of the Kansas Department of Health and Social and Rehabilitative Services, housed in a unit segregated from the general prison population and operated not by employees of the Department of Corrections, but by other trained individuals. And, before this Court, Kansas declared "absolutely" that persons committed under the Act are now receiving in the neighborhood of "31.5 hours of treatment per week."[5]

Where the State has "disavowed any punitive intent"; limited confinement to small segment of particularly dangerous individuals; provided strict procedural safeguards; directed that confined persons be segregated from the general prison population and afforded the same status as others who have been civilly committed; recommended treatment if such is possible; and permitted immediate release upon a showing that the individual is no longer dangerous or mentally impaired, we cannot say that it acted with punitive intent. We therefore hold that the Act does not establish criminal proceedings and that involuntary confinement pursuant to the Act is not punitive. Our conclusion that the Act is nonpunitive thus removes an essential prerequisite for both Hendricks' double jeopardy and ex post facto claims.

* * *

The concurring opinion of JUSTICE KENNEDY and the dissenting opinion of JUSTICE BREYER, joined by JUSTICES STEVENS, SOUTER and GINSBURG, are deleted.

Questions and Comments

1. *The definition of punishment.* The Kansas Sexually Violent Predator Act permits long-term confinement in a maximum security institution. Why is this confinement not criminal punishment (and thus barred under the double jeopardy clause when imposed on a person who has already served a sentence)? The Court's principal answer to this question is that the confinement "does not implicate either of the two primary objectives of criminal punishment: retribution or deterrence." Do you agree?

Even if the only purposes behind the statute are incapacitation and rehabilitation, does it follow that the confinement it authorizes is not punishment? Recall from the introduction of this chapter that, although retributive and deterrence considerations do control the scope of criminal liability, the individual prevention goals such as incapacitation and rehabilitation can play a significant role at sentencing. Cf. Frank Zimring & Gordon Hawkins, Incapacitation 3 (1995) ("Incapacitation now serves as the principal justification for imprisonment in American criminal justice: offenders are imprisoned in the United States to restrain them from offending again while they are confined. . . ."). Should the state at least have to provide treatment or, as the Court seems to say, is pure incapacitation (without any retributive, deterrent or rehabilitative purpose) also outside the punishment category? The four dissenters in *Hendricks* argued that the statute was punitive in intent because Hendricks' treatment needs had been ignored for the 10 years

5. Indeed, we have been informed that an August 28, 1995, hearing on Hendricks' petition for state habeas corpus relief, the trial court, over admittedly conflicting testimony, ruled that: "The allegation that no treatment is being provided to any of the petitioners or other persons committed to the program designated as a sexual predator treatment program is not true. I find that they are receiving treatment." Thus, to the extent that treatment is available for Hendricks' condition, the State now appears to be providing it. By furnishing such treatment, the Kansas Legislature has indicated that treatment, if possible, is at least an ancillary goal of the Act, which easily satisfies any test for determining that the Act is not punitive.

he was in prison and were likely to be ignored under the new regime as well; "when a State decides offenders can be treated and confines an offender to provide that treatment, but then refuses to provide it, the refusal to treat while a person is fully incapacitated begins to look punitive." 521 U.S. at 381, 117 S.Ct. at 2091–92 (Breyer, J., dissenting).

In *Seling v. Young*, 531 U.S. 250, 121 S.Ct. 727, 148 L.Ed.2d 734 (2001), the Court again rejected the argument that failure to provide treatment to a specific individual committed as a sexual predator can result in punishment of that individual. It concluded that permitting such claims would permit an "end-run" around the determination that sex offender commitment programs are "civil" in nature. However, the Court intimated that committed individuals might be able to bring a due process challenge to confinement conditions. After noting that state law provided that sexual predator commitment is for the purpose of incapacitation and *treatment*, the Court stated that "due process requires that the conditions and duration of confinement under the Act bear some reasonable relation to the purpose for which persons are committed." 531 U.S. at 265, 121 S.Ct. at 736 (see Chapter Ten for further discussion of the right to treatment and remedies for its violation).

2. *The criteria for confinement.* As the introduction to this chapter indicated, because of its retributive and deterrent underpinnings, criminal liability traditionally has been predicated on proof of a criminal act and may not be based on speculation about future criminality. However, if, as the Court held with respect to the Kansas Sexual Predator Act, criminal punishment is not involved, then state deprivation of liberty based on a prediction of behavior may be permissible. Under what circumstances?

Sexually violent predator (SVP) statutes require proof of: (1) the commission of a "sexually violent act;" (2) a propensity to commit sexually violent acts; and (3) some sort of psychological abnormality. The statutes usually define "sexually violent act" as any violent act that is "sexually motivated"; the offense need not be against children, constitute sexual battery or attempted sexual battery, or be recent. See, e.g., Ariz. Stat. § 13–118; Fla. Stat. § 394.912(9)(h). The definition of dangerousness ranges from "more likely than not," Mo.Stat. § 632.480(5), to "substantially probable," Ill. Stat. 207/5(f), to "a propensity to commit acts of sexual violence . . . of such as degree as to pose a menace to the health and safety of others." Kan. § 59–29a02(c). Why require an act if the requisite degree of risk is shown? What degree of risk should have to be shown? Assuming the first two predicates are met, why is the third criterion required?

With respect to the last question, *Hendricks* stated that "[a] finding of dangerousness, standing alone, is ordinarily not a sufficient ground upon which to justify indefinite involuntary commitment"; "some additional factor, such as a 'mental illness' or 'mental abnormality'" is required. If a person is shown by clear evidence to be a threat to the community, why should we require something more? And why should that additional factor be some sort of mental disability?

Consider the following reasoning, which builds on the ideas expressed at the beginning of the chapter:

Assume that we can know, beyond a reasonable doubt, that John will commit a violent act against another person within the next year if he is not confined.... Is there any reason to refrain from confining him? ... The only potentially persuasive ground would seem to be this: that confinement under such circumstances would undermine the tenet of free will which underlies the criminal justice system (and most of Western civilization). When we deprive John of liberty based not on what he has done but rather on a prediction of what he will do, even a prediction that is likely to be accurate, we are treating him like an automaton or an inanimate object. We are in effect asserting that John does not possess the "willpower"—the capacity to choose—necessary to refrain from acting violently. Institutionalizing this decision would violate our notion of what it means to be human....

But, one might respond, cannot a prediction that John will hurt another simply mean we believe he will *choose*, of his own free will, to act in that way? The distinction between acting as if a person can choose to commit a violent act and predicting that he cannot do otherwise is an important one. However, ... when the state intervention consists of prolonged confinement, thus depriving John of any opportunity to exercise his will in the right direction, the effect, if not the intent, is to assert that he cannot choose that course, and thus "to coerce" him "for what [he is]." By way of comparison, prolonged confinement after a conviction for a past act reaffirms the free will paradigm, because it occurs only after a person has chosen to act.

* * *

... [A]ccepting the conclusion that using dangerousness as a legal criterion violates the free will premise does not mean that all state interventions based on that criterion should be prohibited, however. Indeed, it follows from this conclusion that state intervention which does *not* undermine the free will paradigm is justifiable. Two broad sets of circumstances might fall in this latter category: (1) when the state intervention does not significantly denigrate a person's ability to choose [see, e.g., *United States v. Salerno*, upholding short-term pretrial detention]; and (2) when the person does not, in fact, possess an ability to choose [e.g., is suffering from serious mental disability akin to insanity].

Christopher Slobogin, "Dangerousness as a Legal Criterion in the Criminal Process," in Bruce Sales & Daniel Shuman, eds., Law, Mental Health & Mental Disorder 360, 364, 366 (1995). Other commentators have argued that preventive detention of dangerous people with serious mental disability is justified as a "gap-filler." While most dangerous people can be criminally punished, those who are not guilty by reason of insanity cannot be; therefore, society needs some other means of protecting itself from the latter group. Stephen J. Schulhofer, "Two Systems of Social Protection: Comments on the Civil–Criminal Distinction, with Particular Reference to Sexually Violent Predator Laws," 7 J. Contemp. Legal Issues 69, 85 (1996) (" 'civil' deprivation of liberty is permissible only as a gap-filler, to solve problems the criminal process cannot address"). On the other hand, preventive detention of those who are not insane would not be justified by this gap-filling rationale.

The Kansas statute permits commitment of any sex offender "who suffers from a mental abnormality ... which ... predisposes the person to commit sexually violent offenses in a degree constituting such person a menace to the health and safety of others." Does this language adequately define the class of sex offenders who may be committed? Does it require proof of anything other than dangerousness? The *Hendricks* Court construes the Kansas statute to permit confinement only of those "who suffer from a volitional impairment rendering them dangerous beyond their control." Is that construction necessary to save the statute? Sufficient? How is it different from a finding of insanity under the volitional prong (see pp. 570–82)? Put differently, should the state be able to secure a conviction of a sex offender at trial based on the argument that he is sane and then, once he has served his sentence, argue that he should be committed as a sexual predator?

The Supreme Court partially answered these questions in *Kansas v. Crane*, 534 U.S. 407, 122 S.Ct. 867, 151 L.Ed.2d 856 (2002). Consider this excerpt from Justice Breyer's opinion for seven members of the Court:

> ... *Hendricks* set forth no requirement of total or complete lack of control. *Hendricks* referred to the Kansas Act as requiring a "mental abnormality" or "personality disorder" that makes it *"difficult,* if not impossible, for the [dangerous] person to control his dangerous behavior." The word "difficult" indicates that the lack of control to which this Court referred was not absolute. Indeed, as different amici on opposite sides of this case agree, an absolutist approach is unworkable. Brief for Association for the Treatment of Sexual Abusers as Amicus Curiae 3; cf. Brief for American Psychiatric Association et al. as Amici Curiae 10; cf. also American Psychiatric Association, Statement on the Insanity Defense 11 (1982), reprinted in G. Melton, J. Petrila, N. Poythress, & C. Slobogin, Psychological Evaluations for the Courts 200 (2d ed. 1997) (" 'The line between an irresistible impulse and an impulse not resisted is probably no sharper than that between twilight and dusk' "). Moreover, most severely ill people—even those commonly termed "psychopaths"—retain some ability to control their behavior. Insistence upon absolute lack of control would risk barring the civil commitment of highly dangerous persons suffering severe mental abnormalities.
>
> We do not agree with the State, however, insofar as it seeks to claim that the Constitution permits commitment of the type of dangerous sexual offender considered in *Hendricks* without any lack-of-control determination. *Hendricks* underscored the constitutional importance of distinguishing a dangerous sexual offender subject to civil commitment "from other dangerous persons who are perhaps more properly dealt with exclusively through criminal proceedings." That distinction is necessary lest "civil commitment" become a "mechanism for retribution or general deterrence"—functions properly those of criminal law, not civil commitment. Id. (KENNEDY, J., concurring); cf. also Moran, The Epidemiology of Antisocial Personality Disorder, 34 Social Psychiatry & Psychiatric Epidemiology 231, 234 (1999) (noting that 40%–60% of the male prison population is diagnosable with Antisocial Personality Disorder). The presence of what the "psychiatric profession itself classifie[d] ... as a serious mental disorder" helped to make that distinction in *Hendricks*. And a critical distinguishing feature of that "serious ...

disorder" there consisted of a special and serious lack of ability to control behavior.

In recognizing that fact, we did not give to the phrase "lack of control" a particularly narrow or technical meaning. And we recognize that in cases where lack of control is at issue, "inability to control behavior" will not be demonstrable with mathematical precision. It is enough to say that there must be proof of serious difficulty in controlling behavior. And this, when viewed in light of such features of the case as the nature of the psychiatric diagnosis, and the severity of the mental abnormality itself, must be sufficient to distinguish the dangerous sexual offender whose serious mental illness, abnormality, or disorder subjects him to civil commitment from the dangerous but typical recidivist convicted in an ordinary criminal case. *Foucha v. Louisiana*, 504 U.S. 71, 82–83, 112 S.Ct. 1780, 118 L.Ed.2d 437 (1992) (rejecting an approach to civil commitment that would permit the indefinite confinement "of any convicted criminal" after completion of a prison term).

We recognize that *Hendricks* as so read provides a less precise constitutional standard than would those more definite rules for which the parties have argued. But the Constitution's safeguards of human liberty in the area of mental illness and the law are not always best enforced through precise bright-line rules. For one thing, the States retain considerable leeway in defining the mental abnormalities and personality disorders that make an individual eligible for commitment. For another, the science of psychiatry, which informs but does not control ultimate legal determinations, is an ever-advancing science, whose distinctions do not seek precisely to mirror those of the law. Consequently, we have sought to provide constitutional guidance in this area by proceeding deliberately and contextually, elaborating generally stated constitutional standards and objectives as specific circumstances require. *Hendricks* embodied that approach.

. . .

The State also questions how often a volitional problem lies at the heart of a dangerous sexual offender's serious mental abnormality or disorder. It points out that the Kansas Supreme Court characterized its state statute as permitting commitment of dangerous sexual offenders who (1) suffered from a mental abnormality properly characterized by an "emotional" impairment and (2) suffered no "volitional" impairment. It adds that, in the Kansas court's view, *Hendricks* absolutely forbids the commitment of any such person. And the State argues that it was wrong to read *Hendricks* in this way. We agree that *Hendricks* limited its discussion to volitional disabilities. And that fact is not surprising. The case involved an individual suffering from pedophilia—a mental abnormality that critically involves what a lay person might describe as a lack of control. DSM–IV 571–572 (listing as a diagnostic criterion for pedophilia that an individual have acted on, or been affected by, "sexual urges" toward children). Hendricks himself stated that he could not " 'control the urge' " to molest children. In addition, our cases suggest that civil commitment of dangerous sexual offenders will normally involve individuals who find it particularly difficult to control their behavior—in the general sense described above. Cf. *Seling v. Young*; cf. also Abel & Rouleau, Male Sex Offenders, in Handbook of Outpatient Treatment of Adults: Nonpsychotic Mental Disorders 271 (M. Thase, B. Edelstein, & M. Hersen eds.1990) (sex offenders' "compulsive, repetitive, driven behavior ... appears to fit the criteria of an emotional or psychiatric illness"). And it is often appropriate to say of such individuals, in ordinary English, that they are "unable to control their dangerousness." *Hendricks.*

Regardless, *Hendricks* must be read in context. The Court did not draw a clear distinction between the purely "emotional" sexually related mental abnormality and the "volitional." Here, as in other areas of psychiatry, there may be "considerable overlap between a ... defective understanding or appreciation and ... [an] ability to control ... behavior." American Psychiatric Association Statement on the Insanity Defense, 140 Am. J. Psychiatry 681, 685 (1983) (discussing "psychotic" individuals). Nor, when considering civil commitment, have we ordinarily distinguished for constitutional purposes among volitional, emotional, and cognitive impairments. The Court in *Hendricks* had no occasion to consider whether confinement based solely on "emotional" abnormality would be constitutional, and we likewise have no occasion to do so in the present case.

A number of jurisdictions have construed *Crane* to require volitional impairment and a few courts have reversed commitments lacking such proof. See, e.g, *Thomas v. Missouri*, 74 S.W.3d 789 (Mo. 2002), *In re W.Z.*, 173 N.J. 109, 801 A.2d 205 (2002). Yet the last two paragraphs excerpted above suggest that the Court would permit indeterminate long-term commitment of people who are dangerous due to cognitive impairment as well as volitional impairment. Should the former category include only those who are insane under one of the cognitive insanity tests, such as M'Naghten? Or, since the Court is willing to permit commitment of those whose volitional impairments would not amount to insanity under volitional insanity tests, does (should) that category encompass a more broadly defined group? Nationally, only 12% of those committed as sexual predators are diagnosed with a "serious mental illness;" the rest have personality disorders like paraphilia and antisocial personality disorder. W. Lawrence Fitch, Sex Offender Commitment in the United States: Legislative and Policy Concerns (Robert Prentky et al., eds., 2003)(Table I).

3. *Other constitutional challenges to sex offender statutes.* Hendricks raised substantive due process, double jeopardy and ex post facto challenges to the Kansas statute. MDSO statutes have also been challenged on equal protection and eighth amendment grounds. In *State ex rel. Pearson v. Probate Court*, 309 U.S. 270, 60 S.Ct. 523, 84 L.Ed. 744 (1940), briefly mentioned in *Hendricks*, the defendant argued that an indeterminate sentence enhancement scheme that focused solely on sex offenders violates the equal protection guarantee. In rejecting that claim, the Supreme Court stated:

> [T]he legislature is free to recognize degrees of harm, and it may confine its restrictions to those classes of cases where the need is deemed to be clearest. If the law "presumably hits the evil where it is

most felt, it is not to be overthrown because there are other instances to which it might have been applied."

309 U.S. at 275, 60 S.Ct. at 526. Are there not classes of offenders as "dangerous" as sex offenders? Consider, for instance, the fact that people who commit property crime are much more likely to recidivate than sex offenders, and that about three-fifths of all rapes in the home, three-fifths of all home robberies, and about a third of home aggravated and simple assaults are committed by burglars. Bureau of Justice Stats., Home Burglary 1 (Jan. 1985). Of course, another response to such an equal protection challenge is to expand those subject to commitment. California has for some time committed "mentally disordered offenders" after completion of sentence if (1) the original offense used violence or caused serious bodily injury; (2) the offender's mental disorder is severe and not in remission or cannot be kept in remission without treatment; and (3) as a result the person represents a substantial danger of physical harm to others. Cal. Penal Code §§ 2960–2981 (1999). However, offenders committed under this law seem to have more serious disorders than the average sexual predator; further, the average length of commitment is less than two years. Jon Fetterly, Commitment Under California's Mentally Disordered Offender Law (2003).

State v. Little, 199 Neb. 772, 261 N.W.2d 847 (1978), analyzed two eighth amendment challenges to an MDSO statute. The first was based on *Robinson v. California*, 370 U.S. 660, 82 S.Ct. 1417, 8 L.Ed.2d 758 (1962). The *Little* court's description and application of *Robinson* follows:

> In *Robinson*, the defendant had been arrested after a police officer had observed needle marks on his arm. The defendant was convicted under a statute that made it an offense to use or be addicted to narcotics despite the fact that it was never proven the defendant had used drugs while in the jurisdiction. According to the Supreme Court, the effect of the statute was to allow a conviction for the mere status of addiction rather than from the actual use of drugs. It was suggested that punishment for the status of being addicted to drugs is just as repugnant to traditional ideas of fairness and justice as punishment for a physical illness such as leprosy or venereal disease or a mental illness. The Court held that a status offense was one where there is no actus reus present and the imposition of any punishment for such an offense violates the cruel and unusual punishment prohibition of the Eighth Amendment.

> We do not find *Robinson* controlling on the issue of the constitutionality of confinement under Nebraska's Sexual Sociopath Act. [The statute] provides that a proceeding under the act may only be instituted following a criminal conviction. The conviction is the actus reus that was absent in *Robinson* and distinguishes it from that case.

How would the Kansas statute at issue in *Hendricks* fare under a *Robinson*-type challenge? Is the eighth amendment even applicable, given *Hendrick's* holding that the Kansas statute does not involve punishment?

Below is the *Little* court's treatment of the second eighth amendment challenge raised in that case:

> Defendant's major argument that the confinement of untreatable sexual sociopaths dictated by statute constitutes cruel and unusual

punishment rests on the premise that the sentence is disproportionate to the nature of the offense. [Under the statute, a sexual sociopath who is designated "untreatable" is confined to a ward within the Nebraska Penal and Correctional Complex; release from this confinement may be sought at one-year intervals on a motion by or on behalf of the defendant].

We cannot ignore the reality that, even with this procedure for discharge, the indefinite term of confinement may easily become a life sentence. Once the designation of untreatability is made, the statute places the sexual sociopath in legal limbo. The defendant is sent to a segregated portion of the penal complex with no evidence that he is given other than custodial care. By the terms of the statute, he is given no treatment. He is expected to bear the burden of proving he has somehow recovered in the vacuum situation in which the statute places him.... Despite the labeling of the initial commitment as civil, the statute's provision for possible life confinement, without any provisions for treatability or review of treatability, make[s] the statute penal in nature.

* * *

[W]e agree with [the defendant] that treatment is a necessary part of a statutory scheme involving sexual sociopaths. The Nebraska statute has no provision for even review of treatability once the initial determination of untreatability is made. As defendant points out, under the terms of the Sexual Sociopath Act: "For appellant and other untreatable sexual sociopaths, even the milieu of hope and opportunity of a treatment facility is foreclosed." Thus, without more, the untreatable sexual sociopath faces a probable life sentence. As such, the statute is penal in nature and the sentence under it is so disproportionate to the offense committed in this case as to constitute cruel and unusual punishment.

The *Little* court did not strike down the statute, however. Instead, it upheld the statute on condition that "an annual evaluation by qualified professional personnel ... be made of each sexual sociopath housed in the penal complex and an annual review of treatability be made by the District Court from which such individual was originally committed." With that requirement added, commitment under the statute no longer constituted punishment for eighth amendment purposes.

In contrast to the Nebraska law at issue in *Little*, the statute at issue in *Hendricks* requires annual review. Is that enough? Since 1939, Minnesota has had a statute similar to Kansas', including an annual review provision. Based on a review of records beginning in 1975, of 75 individuals committed under the statute, "[n]ot one person committed since 1975 has been discharged from a final sex offender commitment," although one was provisionally discharged and five others were put in state nursing homes. Eric S. Janus, "Preventing Sexual Violence: Setting Principled Constitutional Boundaries on Sex Offender Commitments," 72 Ind. L. J. 157, 206 (1996). Washington, which pioneered sex predator legislation in 1990, had released two individuals committed under that law as of mid–1998. Rael Jean Isaac, "Put Sex Predators Behind Bars, Not on the Couch," Wall St. Journal, May 8, 1998. None of the more than 400 individuals committed under California's law since it was enacted in 1995 had been released by 2002. Grant Morris, "Punishing the Unpunishable—The Abuse of Psychiatry to Confine Those We Love to Hate," 30 J. Am. Acad. Psychiatry & L. 556, 561 (2002).

4. *Treatment considerations.* Perhaps relevant to these constitutional issues is research on the treatability of those who are committed to sex offender programs. Whereas traditional psychotherapy appears to be ineffective with sex offenders, several studies report some success with comprehensive cognitive-behavioral programs, at least among child molesters and exhibitionists (recidivism among rapists is not reduced as significantly). See Marnie Rice & Grant Harris, "The Treatment of Mentally Disordered Offenders," 3 Psychol., Pub. Pol. & L. 126, 154–56 (1997); John Kip Cornwell, "Protection and Treatment: The Permissible Civil Detention of Sexual Predators," 54 Wash. & Lee L. Rev. 1293, 1330 (1996). Such a program might involve a three-tier system: (1) initial placement in a maximum security institution for six months with three hours of daily group therapy and individual therapy for one or two hours, aimed at reducing inappropriate attitudes and addressing issues relating to sexuality, social competence, lifestyle, and relapse prevention; (2) transfer to a minimum security facility where the focus is on developing a relapse prevention plan and continuing to eliminate "inappropriate cognitive processes"; (3) reentry into the community with periodic re-evaluations and outpatient treatment. W.L. Marshall et al., "A Three–Tiered Approach to the Rehabilitation of Incarcerated Sex Offenders," 11 Behav. Sci. & L. 441 (1993).

Dr. Wettstein points out that much of this research, which focuses on treatment of sex offenders generally, may not be applicable to the typical sexual predator, whom he characterizes as the "end of the line" in terms of sex offenders. Because many of those committed as predators will have spent extended periods in incarceration, "the predator program will probably receive the least treatable offenders," who "likely failed to participate or benefit from early attempts at treatment" and "will have persistently and pervasively denied their sexual offending." Furthermore, the delay between the underlying sex offense and treatment will "permit opportunities for significant distortions and defenses by the offender" that will made treatment "relatively more difficult." Robert M. Wettstein, "A Psychiatric Perspective on Washington's Sexually Violent Predators Statute," 15 U. Puget Sound L. Rev. 597, 616–17 (1992). Backing up his claim are results comparing treated and untreated sex offenders showing only small differences in recidivism between the two groups, or higher recidivism rates among the *treated* population. See generally, G.C.N. Hall, "Sexual Offender Recidivism Revisited: A Meta–Analysis of Recent Treatment Studies," 63 J. Consulting & Clinical Psychology 802 (1995)(finding "the net effect" of sexual offender treatment programs to be 8 fewer sex offenders per 100, relative to no treatment). But there is also research showing that recidivism among treated child molesters is half the rate associated with untreated child molesters. See Leroy L. Kondo, "The Tangled Web–Complexities, Fallacies and Misconceptions Regarding the Decision to Release Treated Sexual Offenders from Civil Commitment into Society," 23 N. Ill. L. Rev. 195, 199 n.14 (2003); W.L. Marshall & H.E. Barbaree, "Long Term Evaluation of the Behavioral Treatment Program for Child Molesters," 26 Beh. Res. & Therapy 499, 508 (1988).

Because they act chemically, pharmacologic interventions largely avoid the psychological "distortions and defenses" referred to by Dr. Wettstein. Some of these drugs (in particular, CPA and MPA) have demonstrated effectiveness with some types of sex offenders. However, the offenders view them as one of the least desired therapies because of side effects such as weight gain, fatigue, headaches, reduced body hair, depression, and gastrointestinal problems. Their effectiveness may also be compromised by the fact that the physiological effects are completely (and apparently quickly) reversible upon drug withdrawal. Rice & Harris, supra, at 154. Nonetheless, at least one state permits "chemical castration" with MPA after a first sex offense and *requires* such castration after a second sex offense, if a doctor indicates the defendant is an appropriate candidate for the treatment. Fl. Stat. § 794.0235. The statute also provides that the drug treatment is not to be in lieu of any other punishment provided by statute.

5. *Prediction accuracy.* A final challenge to sex offender statutes is that we lack sufficient predictive power to identify who is a sexual predator. The Supreme Court rejected an identical argument in connection with capital sentencing in *Jurek v. Texas*, described on p. 647, and is likely to do so in this context as well when directly confronted with the issue. Furthermore, courts have not been very demanding with respect to proof of dangerousness. For instance, the California Supreme Court ruled that the language in the state's sexual predator statute requiring that the person be "likely to engage in acts of sexual violence without appropriate treatment and custody" does not require proof that violence is "better than even" but only proof of "substantial danger—that is, a serious and well-founded risk of criminal sexual violence." *People v. Superior Court (Ghilotti)*, 27 Cal.4th 888, 119 Cal.Rptr.2d 1, 44 P.3d 949, 954 (2002).

Nonetheless, it is worth considering how dangerousness is to be proven. Previous materials have looked at the difference between clinical and actuarial prediction methods, including those that might be used in predicting sex offenses (see pp. 482–88). Janus & Meehl believe the actuarial approach is superior, but concede several problems with that approach. For instance, they describe a study finding that 77% of those who scored 5 on a currently available "risk checklist" were reconvicted of a sexual or violent crime during the study period, a success rate they believe approaches the "upper limits of accuracy attainable by the sex offender commitment process." But they note that, even with this relatively accurate instrument, 3% of the nonrecidivists were misidentified (i.e., they scored 5 on the risk checklist), and 85% of the recidivists were misidentified (i.e., they scored 4 or lower). They also noted that the same instrument used on a different population identified only 65.4% of those who were reconvicted (with close to 10% of the nonrecidivists and 80% of the recidivists misidentified). Finally, they note that the sample populations in both studies had a base recidivism rate of 41%, whereas the same instrument used on a group with a base rate for recidivism nearer 20% (which they suggest is close to the average base rate for sex offenders) would only identify somewhat over 50% of those who would be reconvicted. Eric S. Janus & Paul E. Meehl, "Assessing the Legal Standard for Predictions of Dangerousness in Sex Offender Commitment Proceedings," 3 Psychology, Public Policy & L. 33, 49, 58–59 (1997).

In evaluating these numbers, which may well represent the best we can do with current methodologies, consider this assessment of the inaccuracy associated with the criminal justice system:

> Every criminal law professor knows the difficulty of differentiating premeditation from ordinary intent, recklessness from negligence. Even if agreement can be reached as to the precise definition of these concepts, independent judges and juries applying such definitions are bound to arrive at different results on the same facts; for instance, disagreement is highly likely in deciding between first and second degree murder, unprovoked and provoked killing, and voluntary and involuntary manslaughter. These disparities are an inevitable aspect of a system that relies on moral judgments about invisible internal mental states. In social science terms, this high degree of inter-rater inconsistency (or unreliability) cannot help but indicate a high degree of inaccuracy (or invalidity) as well. The assertion that we can know, beyond a reasonable doubt, that a person "deserves" a particular verdict and punishment expresses a hope rather than a reality. And the costs of this inaccuracy are huge—a finding of premeditation can result in the death penalty rather than a 20–year sentence, a conclusion that a defendant's belief was "unreasonable" can mean the difference between conviction and acquittal. If we are willing to countenance a criminal system based on this degree of uncertainty, we may be hard pressed to criticize a preventive detention regime on unreliability grounds.

Christopher Slobogin, "A Jurisprudence of Dangerousness," 98 Nw. L. Rev. 1, 7–8 (2003).

    6. *Political/moral considerations.* Compare these two comments:

> Let us make the reasonable assumption that the risk of a false positive in predicting future sexual violence is approximately 50%. Let us further suppose that we are deciding the disposition of two already convicted sex offenders, now about to be released from prison, one of whom will and one of whom will not commit a violent sexual crime in the future. These two offenders have similar records and psychological profiles. We do not know which of the two will offend if both are not confined.

> We have only two options: to release both or confine both.

* * *

> A mistaken decision to confine, however painful to the offender involved, is, in my view, simply not morally equivalent to a mistaken decision to release. There is a significant difference between the two. One is much less harmful than the other.

> Libertarians who focus exclusively, or heavily, on the injustice being done to a mistakenly confined offender tend to place less significance on the harms caused by the alternative decision, to the extent that they consider them at all. We have been socialized to emphasize injustices to offenders. We have not been sufficiently sensitive to the harm inflicted by sex offenders, especially violent rapists and violent child abusers.

Alexander Brooks, "The Constitutionality and Morality of Civilly Committing Violent Sexual Predators," 15 U. Puget Sound L. Rev. 709,753 (1992).

[Sexual predator laws] permit a legislature to use lifetime preventive detention on any group of offenders who have served their prison terms and have been, or will be, released. All that is required to accomplish such a goal is a statute that labels criminals who have committed a single criminal act as suffering from a "mental abnormality" that makes them "likely to reoffend" and authorizes their lifetime confinement for "treatment." Simply put, the predator commitment law has detached involuntary commitment from the medical model of mental illness and *bona fide* treatment.

Once detached, literally no stopping point exists. The logic of the predator commitment law can be applied to people who drive while under the influence of alcohol, who assault their domestic partners or children, who use crack cocaine, or who commit whatever the new "crime-of-the-month" happens to be. Indeed, if mental abnormality, future recidivism, and the need for treatment can be deduced by the commission of a single past crime, the legislature is totally free to create what Justice Stevens aptly called a "shadow . . . criminal code." Such a code can be invoked, not only as an alternative to crime and punishment, but as a way of extending punishment indefinitely.

John LaFond, "Washington's Sexually Violent Predator Law: A Deliberate Misuse of the Therapeutic State for Social Control," 15 U. Puget Sound L. Rev. 655, 698–99 (1992).

7. *Alternatives to sex predator laws*. As the previous comment suggests, the sexual predator statute could be described as a "hybrid" law that incorporates aspects of both the criminal law and civil commitment. There are at least four alternatives to such laws that are based more firmly on one of these two traditional paradigms: (1) indeterminate sentencing; (2) sentence enhancement; (3) community notification and residential restriction laws; and (4) traditional civil commitment. How are these alternatives different from the sexual predator statute at issue in *Hendricks*? Which approach is preferable in dealing with violent sex offenders?

The typical indeterminate sentencing scheme was described at the beginning of this section (see pp. 669–70). In *Specht v. Patterson*, 386 U.S. 605, 87 S.Ct. 1209, 18 L.Ed.2d 326 (1967), the Supreme Court held that, to the extent an indeterminate sentence imposed on a sex offender is based on a finding of dangerousness, it must be preceded by a formal hearing (with the right to counsel, cross-examine witnesses, etc.). But the Court also appeared to affirm that, if such process is provided, the state may confine a sex offender for as long as he or she remains dangerous (which the Court recognized might amount to lifetime confinement). In what practical sense is a sexual predator statute different?

A sentence enhancement scheme (sometimes called a three-strikes statute or habitual offender law) authorizes an extended sentence after a third (or second) conviction for a particular type of offense. For instance, a person convicted of a third sexual battery (for which the usual sentence is, say, 10 years) could have 30 years added to his sentence for the third offense. This sentence enhancement is not based on the forward-looking incapacitation principle but on backward-looking retributive and deterrent rationales; the theory is that a three-time offender is more blameworthy than those who have offended fewer times, and that maximum deterrence is necessary to forestall those prone to recidivism. The Supreme Court has upheld against eight amendment challenges a number of extremely long sentences. See, e.g., *Ewing v. California*, 538 U.S. 11, 123 S.Ct. 1179, 155 L.Ed.2d 108 (2003)(25 year sentence for a fourth offense involving theft of $1200 of golf equipment); *Rummel v. Estelle*, 445 U.S. 263, 100 S.Ct. 1133, 63 L.Ed.2d 382 (1980)(life sentence for a third minor felony); cf. *Solem v. Helm*, 463 U.S. 277, 103 S.Ct. 3001, 77 L.Ed.2d 637 (1983)(hinting the eighth amendment might be violated on *Rummel*-type facts if there were no right to parole). From a civil libertarian view, which is preferable, the "selective" incapacitation represented by sexual predator statutes, based on dangerousness, or the "general" incapacitation represented by enhancement laws, based on prior offenses?

The third alternative—known as "Megan's Law"—requires released sex offenders to register with the state, which then provides their identity and location to the public. In *Connecticut Dep't of Public Safety v. Doe*, 538 U.S. 1, 123 S.Ct. 1160, 155 L.Ed.2d 98 (2003), the Supreme Court held that sex offenders have no procedural due process right to a pre-registration hearing on whether they are currently dangerous, because the Connecticut law is based solely on the fact of previous conviction, for which adequate process had occurred. In *Smith v. Doe*, 538 U.S. 84, 123 S.Ct. 1140, 155 L.Ed.2d 164 (2003), the Court upheld a notification law against an ex post facto attack, relying heavily on *Hendricks* in concluding that such laws are not punishment. The Court left open whether such laws might be infirm on substantive due process grounds because they infringed a liberty interest. This "alternative" could of course instead serve as a supplement to indeterminate or enhanced sentencing laws, as well as to sexual predator laws. A number of released sex offenders have been killed or assaulted, allegedly by individuals who discovered their identities from Internet sex offender registries. David Crary, "Rethinking Sex Offender Laws a Tough Sell," Associated Press, April 19, 2006 (describing murder of two men listed on Maine's Internet registry and noting "many cases of vigilantism in the past").

Another type of restriction on released sex offenders is a prohibition on living within "buffer zones" around areas in which children congregate. Perhaps 20 states have passed such laws. See Susan Broderick, Innovative Legislative Strategies for Dealing with Sexual Offenders, 18(1) Update 1 (2006), www.ndaa-apri.org/publications/newsletters/update_vol_18_number_10_2006.pdf. For instance, Iowa has enacted a law that prohibits persons convicted of certain sex offenses against minors from living within 2000 feet of a school or a child care facility. As a result, in one county 77% of the residential units were unavailable to sex offenders and cities like Des Moines were virtually off-limits. Nonetheless, citing the two *Doe* cases from the Supreme Court, the Eighth Circuit upheld the statute, finding it did not amount to banishment, and that it was a rational response to the fact that convicted sex offenders are more likely to commit sex offenses against minors than the general population and are tempted to reoffend when around children. *Doe v. Miller*, 405 F.3d 700 (8th Cir. 2005). A subsequent report found that many Iowa towns had further restricted residential options by adding parks, swimming pools, libraries, and bus stops to the locations that sex offenders may not live near. Thus, some sex offenders were sleeping in cars or trucks or clustering in trailer parks, far from potential support networks, and the number who failed to register increased substantially compared to the period before enactment of the laws. Monica Davey, "Iowa's Residency Rules Drive Sex Offenders Underground," N.Y. Times, Mar. 15, 2006. Is this type of restriction different enough from notification laws to require, contrary to the *Miller* holding, a hearing before it is imposed?

The final alternative to the sexual predator law—civil commitment—is the subject of the next chapter. Note the reasons the Kansas legislature gives (described in the beginning of *Hendricks*) in explaining why "general involuntary commitment" was inadequate for its needs. Consider the validity of these reasons as you read the next chapter.

Chapter Eight

CIVIL COMMITMENT

Table of Sections

I. INTRODUCTION

History.[a] Involuntary treatment or care of the mentally disabled, outside the criminal setting, is usually called civil commitment. For many years, the United States did not have a "commitment system" as such. Once a method for committing the mentally disabled did develop, the dominant approach varied considerably over time, tending toward either a purely "libertarian" model—which is aimed at limiting the impact of commitment to those who will otherwise harm society—or a purely "paternalistic" model—which seeks to commit anyone who may benefit from state intervention.

In colonial America, the mentally disabled were the responsibility of their family or friends. For those unfortunate persons who lacked such support, the town sometimes would provide money to a designated individual for their care, but more frequently would banish them; thus they would often end up in bands of "drifters" which roamed the countryside. If a "madd" person became violent, he or she might be punished as a criminal. If not, the person was subjected to restraint and perhaps whipping; no treatment was provided, since none existed. In most locales, it is doubtful any explicit legal authority existed for such non-criminal detention. One exception was Massachusetts which, in 1676, enacted a statute ordering the selectmen of towns which had "dangerously distracted persons" to restrain them "that they do not damify others."

During the last half of the eighteenth century, the community became considerably more involved in dealing with the mentally disabled. In 1752, the Pennsylvania Assembly, in response to a petition drawn by Benjamin Franklin, authorized establishment of the first hospital to receive the sick poor, including the poverty-stricken mentally ill. The first hospital devoted exclusively to the mentally disabled was constructed at Williamsburg, Virginia in 1773. Also during this period, state legislatures began enacting statutes which expressly provided authority for confining the mentally disabled in community institutions. For instance, in 1788, the New York legislature passed a statute which permitted constables, after procuring a warrant from two or more justices, to apprehend and lock up the "furiously madd" or those "so far disordered in their senses that they may be dangerous to be permitted to go abroad." Confinement was permitted for the duration of the individual's dangerous condition, although the statute also provided that it should not be construed to prevent friends or relatives from assuming custody of the individual. Thus, this statute appeared to be aimed primarily at people who were violent and who could not be cared for privately; those disordered individuals who were non-threatening or who

---

a. The following historical account through the 1960's is taken from Samuel Brakel et al., The Mentally Disabled and the Law 12–15 (1986); Albert Deutsch, The Mentally Ill in America: A History of the Their Care and Treatment from Colonial Times (2d ed. 1949).

could be controlled by private citizens were not the principal targets of the law.

By the middle of the nineteenth century, some evidence suggests that detention of these latter two groups of individuals may have become more commonplace. For example, a 1842 New York statute *required* the confinement of *all* "lunatics," not just dangerous ones who were at large. It commissioned "assessors" to search for such people and allowed commitment, upon the authority of two assessors, for a *minimum* of six months. Another example of the loosening standards for commitment is furnished by the case of Josiah Oakes. In 1845, Oakes was detained in a hospital, not because he was violent, but on the ground that he suffered from hallucinations and had incompetently conducted his business affairs, as evidenced by the fact that he became engaged to a young woman of "unsavory" character a few days after the death of his wife. Oakes sought release via a writ of habeas corpus, alleging he had been illegally committed. In rejecting this claim, the Massachusetts Supreme Court stated:

> The right to restrain an insane person of his liberty is found in that great law of humanity, which makes it necessary to confine those whose going at large would be dangerous to themselves or others.... And the necessity which creates the law, creates the limitation of the law. The question must then arise in each particular case, whether a patient's own safety, or that of others, requires that he should be restrained for a certain time, and whether restraint is necessary for his restoration, or will be conducive thereto. The restraint can continue as long as the necessity continues.

Although the court recognized that limitations should be placed on the state's authority, it explicitly permitted indeterminate detention not only for those who demonstrated a proneness to harm others but also for those who might harm themselves.

The reasons for this "expansion"[b] of commitment authority are undoubtedly complex, but two explanations stand out. First, as society became more interdependent and government more pervasive, the traditional view that the family was obligated to take care of its own became outmoded. Second, a perception developed that techniques for caring for the disabled had improved. The American Psychiatric Association was founded in 1844. Many of its members, including Benjamin Rush and Isaac Ray, advocated and tried to develop a scientific approach to the treatment of the mentally disabled. These apparent advances in medicine meant that commitment could be characterized not merely as detention

---

b. Some authors, see, e.g., John Myers, "Involuntary Civil Commitment of the Mentally Ill: A System in Need of Change," 29 Vill.L.Rev. 367, 380 n. 62, 386 n. 102 (1983), have suggested that *Oakes* was merely a restatement of law that had existed for centuries, permitting the state to intervene when a person's mental disability might lead to dissipation of his or her estate. (For a description of this law, see the introduction to guardianship in Chapter Nine). Assuming this is so, *Oakes* still marks one of the first times a court explicitly permitted involuntary *commitment* of a nondangerous person.

but as a means of providing treatment, or "restoration", as the *Oakes* court put it.

Nonetheless, for a time after the Civil War, a movement aimed at curtailing the reach of commitment law flourished, motivated in large part by a former mental hospital patient named Mrs. Packard. Packard was committed in 1860 under the following statute: "Married women and infants, who in the judgment of the medical superintendent are evidently insane or distracted, may be received and detained in the hospital at the request of the husband, ... or [the] guardian of the infants, without the evidence of insanity or distraction required in other cases." Apparently, the primary evidence supporting Packard's commitment under this statute was provided by two doctors, one of whom stated she was rational but was a "religious bigot like Henry Ward Beecher and Horace Greeley," and the second of whom opined that her ideas were "novel." After her release three years later, Packard campaigned against laws and practices which permitted hospitalization solely on the basis of a person's opinions, with no attempt to gauge moral accountability. Her efforts were aided by the publication of "muckraking" books describing pitiful hospital conditions. By the 1890's, many states had adopted statutes which required a jury determination of the commitment issue, authorized the presence of counsel at the hearing, and penalized criminally anyone who knowingly sought the illegal commitment of another.

The movement toward a more legalized commitment process was relatively short-lived, however. From the "Packard era" until the 1970's (with the exception of a period during the 1930s), most changes in civil commitment law aimed at making commitment easier rather than more difficult, again in large part due to medical advances that increased optimism about treatment efficacy. By the early years of the twentieth century, in response to the ceaseless efforts of Dorothea Dix and others, at least 20 states established mental hospitals or enlarged or improved those in existence. Through the middle of the twentieth century, the construction of mental hospitals continued apace, and medical science developed several new treatment modalities, including modern psychotherapy, electro-convulsive therapy, psychosurgery and, probably most importantly, chemical therapy. Concurrent with these developments, many states "medicalized" the procedural requirements associated with commitment. Judges and juries were replaced by physicians or "lunacy commissions" and dangerousness almost disappeared as a criterion for commitment. By 1970, 31 states provided for hospitalization based simply on the certification of one or more physicians that the individual suffered from mental illness and needed treatment.

In the early 1970's, the pendulum swung once again. Influenced by the civil rights movement of the 1960's, by exposés of poor hospital conditions and commitment abuses, and by a growing distrust of psychiatric expertise and the medical model of mental illness upon which it is based, groups of lawyers, mental health professionals and patients successfully exerted pressure for legal reform. The leading statutory indication of the shift was the adoption of the Lanterman–Petris–Short Act in California. Passed in 1969, this statute made dangerousness to self or others the core criteria for commitment, defined these criteria relatively narrowly, and provided extensive procedural protections. It provided a model for many other state statutes. On the judicial front, the most important decision was handed down in 1973 by the federal district court for the Eastern District of Wisconsin. In *Lessard v. Schmidt* (see pp. 726–27), that court found the Wisconsin civil commitment statute unconstitutional "insofar as it . . . permits commitment without proof . . . that the patient is both 'mentally ill' and dangerous." *Lessard* also mandated procedural changes similar to those available in the criminal context. Several other federal and state courts followed *Lessard's* lead.

More recently, there have been signs of retrenchment. In 1979, the United States Supreme Court refused to hold that the criminal reasonable doubt standard is constitutionally required in the civil commitment context. *Addington v. Texas,* infra. The same year, it also found that the right to counsel and a judicial tribunal were not necessary attributes of a system for hospitalizing minors. *Parham v. J.R.* (see pp. 907–18). In 1997, the Court upheld a statute which permitted commitment upon proof of dangerousness and "mental abnormality," suggesting that the (more severe) "mental illness" required by *Lessard* may not be constitutionally necessary under some circumstances. *Kansas v. Hendricks* (see pp. 675–86). With the refinement of the American Psychiatric Association's Diagnostic and Statistical Manual, the advent of new chemical therapies, and the creation of Professional Standards Review Organizations (PSRO), some have claimed—as has been claimed in the past—that psychiatric science has improved substantially and the danger of overcommitment and improper treatment accordingly reduced. See, e.g., Alan Stone, Mental Health and Law: A System in Transition 20–21, 65–76 (1975). Some states have returned to broad commitment criteria. Whether the pendulum will continue to swing back toward a more paternalistic and protectionist model and, if so, how far it will go, remains to be seen.

Modern Commitment Statutes. There are three general diagnostic populations subject to today's civil commitment laws: people with mental illnessl, people with developmental disability (including people with mental retardation), and persons addicted to drugs and alcohol. Many states have separate commitment laws for each. Commitment statutes may also vary depending upon the legal context. For instance, most states distinguish between adults and minors in establishing criteria and procedures for commitment of people with mental disability. Most states also have separate statutes for commitment of those persons acquitted by reason of insanity and prisoners transferred to mental hospitals for treatment. The first four sections of this chapter examine the laws dealing with commitment of the adults with mental illness who have not been processed by the criminal system, because these laws have served as the model for other commitment laws. The final section examines commitment of insanity acquittees, prisoners, people with developmental disability, people who abuse substance, and minors.

Modern statutes governing the commitment of adults with mental illness are relatively uniform. At the present time, virtually no state still adheres to the "mental illness plus need for treatment" standard of commitment; typically a person may not be involuntarily hospitalized unless the government can show that, as a result of mental illness, the person is "dangerous to others or to self." Almost all states also permit commitment of a person who is shown to be, as a result of mental illness, "unable to provide for his or her basic needs," "gravely disabled" or "likely to deteriorate." Even if the proper criteria are met, virtually all statutes prohibit institutionalization if there is a less restrictive alternative available in the community. Every state also provides for a commitment hearing, with notice and counsel, and requires periodic reviews of the legal status of committed persons. Additionally, most states have enacted statutes which provide those who have been hospitalized with various rights, including the right to a treatment plan, the right to a safe, clean environment, and the right to communicate with the outside world. The various issues raised by these statutes will be treated in this and subsequent chapters.

The Context of Civil Commitment Law: Deinstitutionalization, Reinstitutionalization, and Privatization. In evaluating and interpreting civil commitment laws, it is important to have some sense of the context in which they operate—the public mental health system. Providing a full description of this context is not attempted here. But the following remarks should be sufficient to set the stage for an intelligent assessment of civil commitment law.

Probably the most significant historical fact connected with the public mental health system is that the census of public mental hospitals has dropped dramatically since the mid–1950's. In 1956, the number of patients in such institutions on an average day was 551,390. By 1980, one estimate indicated that the average daily population had dropped to 132,000. During the same time period, however, the annual admission rate for public mental hospitals almost doubled, from 185,597 to 390,000. Samuel Brakel et al., The Mentally Disabled and the Law 47 (1986). By 2004, the number of involuntarily committed patients in a given year was down to 57,151 (out of a population of 275 million), but because of the "revolving door" phenomenon as many as 660,000 people were subject to hospitalization each year. Bruce J. Winick, Civil Commitment: A Therapeutic Justice Model 7 (2004).

There are several explanations for this process of "deinstitutionalization," as it has come to be called, and the accompanying surge in admissions rates. It is tempting to ascribe most of these changes to the legal reforms of the 1960's and 70's. Certainly, to some extent, changes in civil commitment laws had an effect. In a number of states, narrowed commitment criteria, the least restrictive alternative doctrine, and additional procedural protections helped reduce the number of people sent to hospitals, at the same time shortened commitment terms made possible recommitments within the same year and thus increased the annual admission rate.[c] However, a number of studies also concluded that the "libertarian" reforms of the 1970's had only a minimal impact on the number or type of people hospitalized, largely because the new statutory language is still broad enough to be flexibly applied.[d] This research suggests that factors other than legal reform were responsible for much of the change in the hospital population and the admission rate.

One important such factor was the advent of psychotropic medication, first introduced as a treatment option in the mid–1950's. Because the various types of medication which fall under this rubric tend to suppress the symptomatology of persons diagnosed as suffering from schizophrenia, manic-depressive psychosis, depression and other major illnesses,[e] they offered, for the first time, an inexpensive, relatively quick treatment which could be made available to a large number of people with mental illness. Hospital beds could be emptied at a faster rate, allowing more admissions but also, in the long run, reducing the overall population.

Working in tandem with the medication revolution was the community treatment movement. In 1963, Congress passed the Community Mental Health Centers Act, which provided funding for the establishment of outpatient treatment centers. The CMHC Act was representative of a widespread effort to move the locus of treatment from isolated hospitals to the patients' communities, where they could be closer to support groups and employment opportunities. It reflected a perception that community treatment is at least as effective as confinement in a hospital, which many patient advocates thought aggravated rather than ameliorated patients' symptomatology. The Act and related federal laws also allowed state legislatures to reduce funding by closing state hospitals and shifting much of the financial burden to federal programs. Indeed, some have argued that the *primary* impetus behind deinstitutionalization actions taken by the states was fiscal. See Carol Warren, The Court of Last Resort: Mental Illness and the Law 21–24 (1982). The community mental health centers and other community treatment programs, both outpatient and inpatient, which came into being as a result of this effort to offer an alternative to the traditional public mental hospital undoubtedly contributed to the reduction in the hospital population. However, the admission rate continues to increase because many communities still have not developed adequate aftercare programs for all

c. See Roger Peters, et al., "The Effects of Statutory Change on the Civil Commitment of the Mentally Ill," 11 Law & Hum. Beh. 73 (1987) for a survey of the research.

d. James Luckey & John Berman, "Effects of a New Commitment Law on Involuntary Admissions and Service Utilization Patterns," 3 Law & Hum.Behav. 149 (1979) (Nebraska); Serena Stier & Kurt Stoebe, "Involuntary Hospitalization of the Mentally Ill in Iowa: The Failure of the 1975 Legislation," 64 Iowa L.Rev. 1284, 1371–90 (1979); Larry Faulkner, et al., "Effects of a

New Involuntary Commitment Law: Expectations and Reality," 10 Bull.Am.Acad. Psychiat. & L. 249 (1982); Sara Cleveland, et al., "Do Dangerousness–Oriented Commitment Laws Restrict Hospitalization of Patients Who Need Treatment? A Test," 40 Hosp. & Comm.Psychiat. 266 (1989) (Pennsylvania).

e. The treatment of choice for manic-depressive psychosis is lithium, which is not technically an anti-psychotic drug. For further discussion of these medications, see pp. 27–28.

types of patients; thus perhaps half of the patients who are discharged from the hospital as "stabilized" return within the year because no one monitors their post-discharge treatment or because post-discharge treatment is inadequate. See generally, "The New Snake Pits," Newsweek, May 15, 1978, at 93.

Other factors that have influenced the public hospital census are the increased use of private and veterans hospitals as a result of improved insurance coverage, and the advent of Medicaid and Medicare funding, which made possible largescale release of chronic patients to community nursing homes. Additionally, hospital population was reduced significantly by the death of elderly patients, a factor which accounted for 20 to 40 percent of all "releases" until the early 1960's, when community placement became available. See Howard Goldman et al., "Deinstitutionalization: The Data Demythologized," 34 Hosp. & Comm.Psych. 129 (1983).

Despite the many forces pushing for deinstitutionalization, a process of "reinstitutionalization" is taking place in some locales. Again, changes in the law may be partially responsible for this trend. See, e.g., Mary Durham & John LaFond, "The Empirical Consequences and Policy Implications of Broadening the Statutory Criteria for Civil Commitment," 3 Yale Law & Policy Rev. 395 (1985). But other factors seem to play a bigger role. For instance, civil commitments increased in New York City in the late 1980's, not because of a change in statutory language, but because the city administration decided to take aggressive action against the growing number of homeless individuals in the streets. See William Fisher et al., "How Flexible Are our Civil Commitment Statutes?," 39 Hosp. & Comm.Psychiat. 711, 712 (1988).

At least some increase in the hospital census, independent of increases in the general population, is predictable. There is a growing realization that treatment in the community is an elaborate and expensive proposition. Only somewhat over half of the projected 2,000 community mental centers have become operational. Moreover, community resources that are available are not always effective, at least for certain classes of people. As described by Scull: "Quite apart from the [community mental health] centers' uneven geographical distribution and their current fiscal problems, 'both their ideology and their most common services are not directed at the needs of those who have traditionally resided in state psychiatric institutions.'" Andrew Scull, "A New Trade in Lunacy: The Recommodification of the Mental Patient," 24 Amer.Behav. Scientist 724, 743–44, 748–49 (1981). See also H. Richard Lamb, "Deinstitutionalization at the Crossroads," 39 Hosp. & Comm.Psychiat. 941 (1988). Given these facts, some degree of reinstitutionalization was probably inevitable.

The relationship of the public mental health system to the criminal system must also be noted. Clearly, some of the individuals who in the past were hospitalized are now being processed through the criminal justice system—often on misdemeanor charges akin to "vagrancy" violations—in an effort to remove them from the community. A debate has raged over whether this development represents the "criminalization of mentally disordered behavior" or whether, instead, deinstitutionalization and commitment law reforms have prevented further "psychiatrization of criminal behavior." See Marc Abramson, "The Criminalization of Mentally Disordered Behavior: Possible Side–Effect of a New Mental Health Law," 23 Hosp. & Comm.Psychiat. 101 (1972) and John Monahan, "The Psychiatrization of Criminal Behavior: A Reply," 24 Hosp. & Commun.Psychiat. 105 (1973). Whatever the outcome of this debate, the key point for present purposes is that changes in one system have usually brought about changes in the other, much like squeezing a balloon and rearranging the air inside. Although the most recent reforms have been of the public mental health system, one would expect that if legislatures were to narrow the misdemeanor jurisdiction of the criminal courts, the population subject to civil commitment would expand.

A final development that is likely to have significant impact on the civil commitment process is the trend toward government contracts with private companies, often associated with managed care regimes, to administer publicly financed human service programs. In many jurisdictions, people who are involuntarily committed are hospitalized in a state hospital only after assessment and treatment in a private or quasi-private setting. In Florida, for instance, the 60,000 or so people subject to commitment each year are assessed and initially treated in a community hospital or similar setting. Whether or not they stay in the community or are instead committed to a state hospital may depend upon whether they are enrolled in a managed care program and whether that program will pay for the community treatment. In such cases the ultimate commitment decision "is influenced by external factors having little to do with the statutory terms of the civil commitment law." John Petrila, "Ethics, Money, and the Problem of Coercion in Managed Behavioral Health Care," 40 St. Louis Univ. L. J. 359, 397 (1996). Another conflict between public and private goals might arise when a managed care company, concerned about costs, disagrees with a commitment court's exercise of "clinical" judgment and refuses to pay for or provide the ordered treatment. Although such an occurrence may seem unlikely, if the company is the payor, as opposed to the provider of the service, it may not be directly subject to a contempt citation from the court; further its liability for any consequences of a failure to treat may be significantly limited by the Employee Retirement Income Security Act (ERISA) (see pp. 229–31). See John Petrila, "Courts as Gatekeepers in Managed Care Settings," Mental Health Care 109, 113–14 (Mar.-Apr. 1998). See also Paul Appelbaum, "A History of Civil Commitment and Related Reforms," 25 Dev. Mental Health L. 13, 20 (2006) (noting that "managed care organizations . . . have adopted a de facto admission standard of dangerous to self or others . . . , whether it be voluntary or involuntary" and that "[w]ith an increasingly smaller number of publicly-funded beds available, if managed care does not sign-off on admission,

admission does not occur, regardless of the existing criteria for civil commitment.'').

In short, while attempting to understand the theoretical underpinnings of commitment and formulate appropriate commitment standards and procedures is important, it should be recognized that commitment law is just one of many variables affecting the numbers and types of individuals who are subject to involuntary commitment. The implementation of the legal doctrines discussed in this chapter is likely to be heavily influenced by factors only tangentially related to the language found in civil commitment statutes.

II. THE BASIS FOR STATE INTERVENTION

A. INTRODUCTION

CASE ILLUSTRATIONS

The following descriptions of twelve individuals who were hospitalized in a psychiatric facility are taken from 45 cases reported in George Dix, "Acute Psychiatric Hospitalization of The Mentally Ill in the Metropolis: An Empirical Study", 1968 Wash.U.L.Q. 485, 504–47. Each of these individuals was admitted to the St. Louis Acute Facility, as either a voluntary or involuntary patient. In about one-fifth of the 45 cases the patient "presented" him or herself. In another fifth the police brought the patient. In the rest of the cases, family members, relatives or members of the community were responsible for bringing the individual to the attention of the facility. Id. at 503.

Illustration 2. The patient was observed by police wandering on the street wearing hospital pajamas and a surgical cap. He did not respond to attempts to elicit information from him. Several hospitals in the vicinity were contacted but reported that they were not missing any patients. The patient was then taken to the Acute Facility.

Illustration 5. The patient believed that he was an F.B.I. agent, and he carried at least one weapon. He had accused his wife of being a "spy" and his mother-in-law of poisoning him. Three weeks before presentation he had been arrested for carrying a concealed weapon. Although it is extremely likely that he was exhibiting these symptoms at that time, he was not presented until several days before his preliminary hearing, when his wife called police and asked that they assist in presentation.

Illustration 6. The patient reportedly drank one pint of whiskey and, becoming irritated at a group of children, shook one of them. Police were called and the child was taken to a hospital where it was determined that she had suffered no significant harm. The officers then took the patient to the Acute Facility and told the resident that if the patient were not admitted he would be released, as there were no charges against him. The patient exhibited no symptoms of present mental illness. When the decision to admit was made, one officer called his superior and reported in a relieved tone, "They'll take him."

Illustration 7. The family reported that for the last two months the patient had been sleeping poorly and his general level of activity had increased. He spent money freely and the family was consequently forced into debt. Recently he had attempted to open several new charge accounts. The family also complained of the patient's argumentativeness and "resentfulness" at home and repeated complaints of his irritability at work.

Illustration 10. The patient had been depressed for a period of time and had considered attempting suicide for two weeks. He had specifically threatened to kill himself, but no attempt was made to present him to the Acute Facility until his wife happened to notice an apparatus apparently designed by the patient to hang himself.

Illustration 15. The patient, a 44 year old woman, was brought to the Acute Facility by her husband who was 85 years old. He reported that she suffered from insomnia and sometimes locked herself in the bathroom. During the interview with the resident, the patient talked to the empty emergency room. Among the factors influencing the decision to admit her on an involuntary basis was the resident's observation that in her neighborhood "people were robbing and raping all the time" and that she would be particularly subject to such attacks.

Illustration 17. The patient had been given a ride by a truck driver who found him hitchhiking along a highway. When the truck driver noticed that the patient had a gun, he took him to the police station. The police brought him to the Acute Facility where he refused to divulge anything other than the pronunciation of his name. He was admitted on a nonvoluntary basis.

Illustration 19. A 26 year old woman had reportedly been "imagining things" since her marriage six months before presentation. She had accused her husband of spying on other men in public washrooms and believed that he had holes in the wall of their home through which he spied on her. She was presented at the facility by her husband and police officers after she called police and reported that her husband, in an attempt to kill her, had filled the apartment with gas. When police arrived they observed no gas and found the husband asleep. When the patient returned to her home, she was taken to the Acute Facility. In explaining her nonvoluntary admission, the resident emphasized her symptoms of psychosis.

Illustration 20. A medical report submitted to the probate court contained the following assertion offered to support the conclusion that the patient's judgment and insight were "poor": "He still sees no harm in the fact that he lived with a sixteen year old girl as husband and wife ... [H]is reasoning at the present time is that his wife was not satisfactory at that time so why not have the girl ..."

Illustration 22. An 18 year old youth was admitted after being in an auto accident while under the influence of a drug. He denied taking amphetamines in addition to the drug which he had taken prior to the accident, but the staff psychiatrist indicated that he would be retained, involuntarily if necessary, for a week, because it was believed that he was in fact taking amphetamines and the psychiatrist expected withdrawal symptoms to develop.

Illustration 24. The patient, a 61 year old woman, lived alone. She had a history of persecutory delusions extending back over fifteen years. On a number of previous occasions, she had screamed at the neighbors; they finally responded by calling the police. On the occasion preceding her presentation, the neighbors specifically demanded that the police secure the patient's hospitalization. When examined at the Acute Facility, the patient indicated that she believed spirits came to her home and attempted to have "spiritual sex" with her. The resident, who admitted her on a nonvoluntary basis, indicated that a major factor in his decision was that he was not certain "how much the neighbors could take."

Illustration 29. The patient, who lived with her sister's family, reportedly threatened the members of the family. On the morning of her presentation to the Acute Facility, she threw a cup of hot coffee on her sister; this stimulated her presentation.

NOTE: GOVERNMENT AND INDIVIDUAL INTERESTS

Whether in its libertarian or paternalistic guise, civil commitment law is usefully contrasted to the criminal law. Theoretically, the primary purpose of the criminal law is to punish; entry into the criminal justice system depends upon whether a person has engaged in behavior that is considered blameworthy enough, and sufficiently costly to society, that harsh sanctions are deserved, as well as necessary to deter others from engaging in similar behavior. The primary purpose of civil commitment, on the other hand, is not to punish for past acts but to control future ones: the impetus for a civil commitment system does not stem from retributive or deterrence concerns but rather is based on a perceived need for incapacitation or treatment, or both. This is not to say that civil commitment has never been used as a sanctioning device, or that the criminal law does not perform a control function. But, in theory at least, punishment is the preserve of the criminal system, while civil commitment is reserved for those who the state cannot, or will not, punish but who nonetheless need to be controlled for their own good or the good of others. As a result, the criminal law focuses on already committed conduct, while the civil commitment system relies on predictions of conduct.

The criminal justice system is justified as an exercise of the state's "police power," the power to act in furtherance of the general welfare and public safety. In *Jacobson v. Massachusetts*, 197 U.S. 11, 25 S.Ct. 358, 49 L.Ed. 643 (1905), the Supreme Court upheld a Massachusetts provision that permitted fines or imprisonment to be imposed on those who refused or neglected to be vaccinated for smallpox. In support of this decision, the Court described as a "fundamental principle" the idea that

> persons and property [can be] subjected to all kinds of restraints and burdens, in order to secure the general comfort, health, and prosper-

ity of the State[.] . . . The possession and enjoyment of all rights are subject to such reasonable conditions as may be deemed by the governing authority of the country essential to the safety, health, peace, good order and morals of the community. Even liberty itself, the greatest of all rights, is not unrestricted license to act according to one's will.

Clearly, when someone has committed a crime the state has the authority to deprive that person of liberty under the police power described in *Jacobson.*

The justification advanced for civil commitment depends upon the reason for commitment. When the government commits a person with mental disability on the ground that he or she is "dangerous to others," the usual justification advanced for this deprivation of liberty is, as with criminal punishment, the police power. Confining a dangerous person is permissible to protect the public. On the other hand, when a person is committed for reasons other than potential harmfulness to others, the government's action is usually justified on a different ground: the parens patriae, or "parental," authority of the state. With respect to this second governmental power, the Supreme Court has stated:

> The concept of *parens patriae* is derived from the English constitutional system. As the system developed from its feudal beginnings, the King retained certain duties and powers, which were referred to as the "royal prerogative." . . . These powers and duties were said to be exercised by the King in his capacity as guardian of persons under legal disabilities to act for themselves. For example, Blackstone refers to the sovereign or his representative as "the general guardian of all infants, idiots and lunatics," and as the superintendent of all "charitable uses in the kingdom." In the United States, the "royal prerogative" and the "parens patriae" function of the King passed to the States.

Hawaii v. Standard Oil, 405 U.S. 251, 92 S.Ct. 885, 31 L.Ed.2d 184 (1972).

Accepting that both the police power and the parens patriae power are inherent attributes of sovereignty does not necessarily justify civil commitment, however. As the Supreme Court has recognized (in dictum), civil commitment results in a "massive deprivation of liberty." *Humphrey v. Cady*, 405 U.S. 504, 509, 92 S.Ct. 1048, 1052, 31 L.Ed.2d 394 (1972). One commentary described the impact of commitment as follows:

> The most basic deprivation caused by civil commitment is the restriction of liberty—the interest of "transcending value"—for a possibly indefinite period. When a patient is hospitalized, not only are his movements restricted to the confines of the institution, but his freedom to move about within the institution itself may also be regulated or completely deprived for safety or disciplinary reasons. Even if the individual is committed to a community mental health center, he will probably be required to report to the center periodi-

cally, a restriction quite similar to that involved in parole from a penal institution.

Equally important, although a physically ill individual is ordinarily permitted to choose whether to seek medical attention and is protected in this right by common law tort doctrines, an involuntarily committed patient may not have the right to refuse treatment [see pp. 963–90]. This refusal to allow a committed individual to decline unwanted medical examination and treatment might, in the absence of a compelling state interest, infringe a constitutional right to bodily privacy which has been adumbrated in various judicial statements. Moreover, hospitalization itself interferes with privacy, since the patient cannot shield himself from constant observation by both his fellow patients and the staff of the institution. Furthermore, patients in hospitals risk brutality at the hands of their fellow residents and even their attendants, and may be subjected to life in an institution which is overcrowded, inadequately staffed, poorly maintained, and unsanitary.

Compounding all of these deprivations is the fact that most persons are currently committed for an indefinite period of time. While statistics reveal that the average length of stay in mental institutions is relatively short, in most states an individual facing civil commitment is potentially exposed to lifelong deprivation of many of his most basic civil rights.

Individuals face further legal and social deprivations as a result of commitment.... Law enforcement officials might view a prior commitment as reason for viewing otherwise innocuous behavior with suspicion, and the entry of the patient's fingerprints and photographs in official records might have an impact similar to that of a criminal record. [Although commitment no longer leads to automatic loss of the right to vote, serve on a jury, have a driver's license, and similar rights and privilege,] a patient whose release from commitment is conditional may be subject to summary recommitment, mandatory psychiatric tests, prior approval of his choice of home or job, and other deprivations of his civil rights.... Along with these official deprivations, a former mental patient may suffer from the social opprobrium which attaches to treatment for mental illness and which may have more severe consequences than do the formally imposed disabilities. Many people have an "irrational fear of the mentally ill." The former mental patient is likely to be treated with distrust and even loathing; he may be socially ostracized and victimized by employment and educational discrimination. Finally, the individual's hospitalization and posthospitalization experience may cause him to lose self-confidence and self-esteem.

Note, "Developments in the Law—Civil Commitment of the Mentally Ill," 87 Harv.L.Rev. 1190, 1193–1201 (1974). Given the consequences of involuntary commitment on a person's liberty, privacy, association and movement interests, it remains a matter of some controversy whether the state should be able to exercise its police and parens patriae powers through civil commitment and, if so, under what limitations.

B. POLICE POWER COMMITMENT

1. *Rationale*

Preventive detention—confinement based on a prediction of antisocial behavior rather than on conviction of crime—has been condemned primarily on two grounds. The first is that predicting behavior is much more difficult than ascertaining whether certain behavior has occurred and therefore should not normally form the basis for state intervention. As John Stuart Mill stated:

> The preventive function of government ... is far more liable to be abused, to the prejudice of liberty, than the punitory function, for there is hardly any part of the legitimate freedom of action of a human being which would not admit of being represented, and fairly too, as increasing the facilities for some form or other of delinquency. [I]f a public authority, or even a private person, sees any one evidently preparing to commit a crime, they are not bound to look on inactive.... Nevertheless, when there is not a certainty, but only a danger of mischief, no one but the person himself can judge of the sufficiency of the motive which may prompt him to incur the risk....

John Stuart Mill, "On Liberty," in The Philosophy of John Stuart Mill 197, 196 (1961).

Even if the requisite certainty of harm to society is present, preventive detention may be repugnant for a second reason. In describing why the criminal law requires proof of an act prior to criminal conviction, Professor Packer wrote:

> It is important, especially in a society that likes to describe itself as "free" and "open," that a government should be empowered to coerce people only for what they do and not for what they are.... Now, this self-denying ordinance can be and often is attacked as being inconsistent with the facts of human nature. People may in fact have little if any greater capacity to control their conduct ... than their emotions or their thoughts. It is therefore unrealistic or hypocritical, so the argument runs, to deal with conduct as willed or to treat it differently from personality and character. This attack is, however, misconceived.... The idea of free will in relation to conduct is not, in the legal system, a statement of fact, but rather a value preference having very little to do with the metaphysics of determinism and free will....

Herbert Packer, The Limits of the Criminal Sanction 74–75 (1968).

For these reasons, it is probable that imposing *criminal liability* based on a prediction of harm (as opposed to a past act) violates the eighth amendment's prohibition against cruel and unusual punishment. In *Robinson v. California,* 370 U.S. 660, 82 S.Ct. 1417, 8 L.Ed.2d 758 (1962), the Supreme Court held that the eighth amendment was violated by a statute which criminalized narcotics addiction, as opposed to possession or sale of narcotics. In *Powell v. Texas,* 392 U.S. 514, 532, 88 S.Ct. 2145, 2154, 20 L.Ed.2d 1254 (1968), four members of the Supreme Court explained this holding in the following words:

> Evidence of propensity can be considered relatively unreliable and more difficult for a defendant to rebut; the requirement of a specific act thus provides some protection against false charges.... Perhaps more fundamental is the difficulty of distinguishing, in the absence of any conduct, between desires of the day-dream variety and fixed intentions that may pose a real threat to society; extending the criminal law to cover both types of desire would be unthinkable, since "[t]here can hardly be anyone who has never thought evil." When a desire is inhibited it may find expression in fantasy; but it would be absurd to condemn this natural psychological mechanism as illegal.

While the Supreme Court has thus signaled that criminal liability may not be based solely on a prediction, it has also held that "regulatory," nonpunitive confinement may be. *United States v. Salerno,* 481 U.S. 739, 107 S.Ct. 2095, 95 L.Ed.2d 697 (1987). In particular, it has made clear that civil commitment of people with mental disability may be predicated on speculation about future behavior. See *Addington v. Texas,* 441 U.S. 418, 99 S.Ct. 1804, 60 L.Ed.2d 323 (1979); *Heller v. Doe,* 509 U.S. 312, 113 S.Ct. 2637, 125 L.Ed.2d 257 (1993); *Kansas v. Hendricks,* 521 U.S. 346, 117 S.Ct. 2072, 138 L.Ed.2d 501 (1997). It has also authorized preventive detention of other populations. See *Salerno* (upholding a pretrial detention statute that authorized incarceration of people charged with serious offenses if necessary to "reasonably assure ... the safety of any other person or the community."); *Pennsylvania ex rel. Sullivan v. Ashe,* 302 U.S. 51, 61, 58 S.Ct. 59, 82 L.Ed. 43 (1937) (recognizing that a sentence *after* conviction for an act can be based in whole or part on a desire to "deter or to reform the offender"). But no group other than those with mental disability may be subject to long-term preventive detention of the type associated with civil commitment. In *Salerno,* for instance, the Court emphasized the fact that pretrial preventive detention is strictly limited in duration (e.g., by speedy trial requirements), and a sentence requires a conviction. In contrast, civil commitment may last many years (albeit usually with periodic reviews every six months or so) and does not require commission of a crime. Why are people with mental disability singled out in this way? Consider the following excerpts.

NOTE, CIVIL COMMITMENT OF THE MENTALLY ILL: DEVELOPMENTS IN THE LAW

87 Harvard Law Rev. 1190, 1230.
(1974).

... One potential justification for the restriction of preventive detention to the mentally ill might be that the mentally ill, solely by reason of their condition, are substantially more dangerous than other groups. Although there is evidence that this belief is commonly held, studies indicate that the mentally ill as a class are at most slightly more dangerous, and quite possibly less dangerous, than their fellow citizens. Society would therefore obtain roughly similar protection against antisocial conduct if involuntary commitment were limited to the mentally healthy or were employed randomly. Since the vast majority of mentally ill individuals will not engage in dangerous behavior if they are permitted to retain their freedom, preventive detention based solely on mental illness would not appear to be even rationally related to the state's police power interest in protecting society. . . .

A second possible rationale for limiting preventive detention of the dangerous to the mentally ill is premised on the ability of society to provide treatment which benefits them. However, to the extent that the state relies on the benefit which the individual will derive from treatment to support his commitment, it confuses the *parens patriae* and police power justifications for commitment. Requiring a competent individual to accept treatment for his own benefit should be viewed as an additional deprivation of liberty rather than as a benefit which justifies confinement for the protection of others.

Nevertheless, the state might argue that only the dangerous mentally ill are preventively detained because the ability to cure their illness enables the state to safeguard society's interests without indefinite deprivation of their liberty. However, since some mental illnesses are presently untreatable and others cannot be readily cured, many of the dangerous mentally ill face indefinite institutionalization as a result of commitment. Moreover, dangerousness, the link between preventive detention and the police power, may be treated through behavior conditioning which is applicable to the mentally ill and nonmentally ill alike.

A final justification for limiting involuntary police power commitments to the mentally ill can be derived from the reasons apparently underlying the decision not to authorize preventive detention of other dangerous individuals. By requiring a conviction before depriving persons who are not mentally ill of their liberty, the criminal law system relies on deterrence to reduce antisocial behavior. A state could argue that this punishment-deterrence approach fosters personal autonomy by allowing its citizens to choose whether to obey the law. The state's interest in employing a deterrence system that recognizes individual autonomy furnishes a rationale for excluding criminally responsible individuals—those able to appreciate the sanctions imposed for criminal activity and capable of conforming their actions to the dictates of the criminal law—from a prediction-prevention approach to harmful conduct. This justification would seem to provide a distinction between equally dangerous groups of mentally healthy and criminally insane individuals sufficient to satisfy the demands of equal protection. The latter group contains individuals whose mental condition excludes them from the operation of the traditional punishment-deterrence system, because they are both unable to make autonomous decisions about their antisocial behavior and unaffected by the prospect of punishment. . . .

STEPHEN MORSE, A PREFERENCE FOR LIBERTY: THE CASE AGAINST INVOLUNTARY COMMITMENT OF THE MENTALLY DISORDERED

70 Cal.L.R. 54, 59–65.
(1982).

The belief that disordered persons particularly lack competence or behavioral control is a strongly ingrained social dogma that underlies the special legal treatment accorded mentally disordered persons.

* * *

But the assertion that the crazy behavior of mentally disordered persons is compelled, in contrast to the freely chosen behavior of normal persons, is a belief that rests on commonsense intuitions and not on scientific evidence. Indeed, the degree of lack of behavioral control necessary to justify involuntary commitment is fundamentally a moral, social, and legal question—not a scientific one. Social and behavioral scientists can only provide information about the pressures affecting an actor's freedom of choice. The law must determine for itself when the actor is no longer to be treated as autonomous.

In fact, empirical evidence bearing on the question of the control capacity of mentally disordered persons would seem to indicate that mentally disordered persons have a great deal of control over their crazy behavior and legally relevant behavior related to it; indeed, often they may have as much control over their behavior as normal persons do.

* * *

For comparison, imagine the case of a habitually hot-tempered person who takes offense at something his doctor says and threatens to harm the doctor. Is this person more in control or rational than the delusional person? Or, consider the case of a severely ill cardiac patient who refuses to modify dietary, exercise, or smoking habits because the person prefers his or her habitually unhealthy lifestyle. The person's behavior can disrupt the well-being of the family, help drive up health care and insurance costs, and, if the result is an untimely death, impoverish the family. Is this person more in control or rational than the delusional person, and if so, in what sense? Of course, we all "understand" the behavior of the hot-tempered person and the cardiac patient, while the behavior of the delusional person makes no sense whatsoever. Still, there is no conclusive means to prove that any of these persons has greater or lesser control than any of the others.

Questions and Comments

1. *Dangerousness and people with mental illness.* Based on research conducted before the mid–1970s, the Developments piece asserts that people with mental illness are no more dangerous as a class than the general population. More recent research is inconclusive on this point. Professor Monahan, summarizing research through the early 1990s, stated:

> The data that have recently become available, fairly read, suggest the one conclusion I did not want to reach: whether the measure is the prevalence of violence among the disordered or the prevalence of disorder among the violent, whether the sample is people who are selected for treatment as inmates or patients in institutions or people randomly chosen from the open community, and no matter how many social and demographic factors are statistically taken into account, there appears to be a relationship between mental disorder and violent behavior. Mental disorder may be a robust and significant risk factor for the occurrence of violence. . . .

John Monahan, "Mental Disorder and Violent Behavior: Perceptions and Evidence," 47 Am.Psychol. 511, 519 (1992).

This conclusion seemed to be undercut, however, by a mammoth study funded by the MacArthur Foundation in the mid–1990s, involving over a thousand patients released into the community and a comparison group of over 500 people living in the neighborhoods in which the patients resided after discharge. Over its year-long followup period, this study found *"no significant differences between the prevalence of violence by patients without symptoms of substance abuse and the prevalence of violence by others living in the same neighborhoods who were also without symptoms of substance abuse."* Henry Steadman, et al., "Violence by People Discharged from Acute Psychiatric Inpatient Facilities and by Others in the Same Neighborhoods," 55 Arch. Gen Psychiatry 15 (1998). In other words, substance abuse symptoms were highly correlated with violence in both discharged patient and community groups, but mental illness symptoms were not.

A more recent summary of the MacArthur study's findings with respect to violence and serious mental illness describes the data somewhat differently:

> The MacArthur data suggest that the presence of delusions does not predict higher rates of violence among recently discharged psychiatric patients. This conclusion remains accurate even when the type of delusions and their content (including violent content) is taken into account. In particular, the much-discussed findings of a relationship between threat/control-override delusions [beliefs that one is being persecuted or that one's thoughts are being controlled] were not confirmed in the MacArthur study. On the other hand, non-delusional suspiciousness—perhaps involving a tendency toward misperception of other's behavior as indicating hostile intent—does appear to be linked with

subsequent violence, and may account for the findings of previous studies. Although command hallucinations [e.g., a belief that God is commanding violence] per se did not elevate violence risk, if the voices commanded violent acts, the likelihood of their occurrence over the subsequent year was significantly increased.

John Monahan, "Violence Risk Assessment," in Comprehensive Handbook of Psychology (Alan Goldstein ed., 2003). Still other studies suggest that threat/control-override symptoms, in particular persecutory delusions (i.e., unfounded fears that others are hostile), *do* increase the risk of violence. Dale E. McNiel, "The Relationship between Aggressive Attributional Style and Violence by Psychiatric Patients," 71 J. Consulting & Clin. Psychology 404, 405 (2003); Sven Bjorkly, "Psychotic Symptoms and Violence Toward Others—A Literature Review of Some Preliminary Findings," 7 Aggression and Violent Behavior 605–631 (2002); Bruce Link et al., "Real in Their Consequences: A Sociological Approach to Understanding the Association between Psychotic Symptoms and Violence," 64 Am. Sociological Rev. 316 (1999). Thus, certain subgroups of individuals with severe mental illness, such as those with acute symptoms of schizophrenia and manic-depressive psychosis, may be more dangerous than the general population.

At the same time, there are many groups that are more dangerous than these subgroups of people with mental illness. As Ennis & Emery point out:

> Probably 50 to 80 percent of all ex-felons will commit crimes after release from prison. But when their sentences expire, we let them go, and do not "civilly commit" them as dangerous. Ghetto residents and teenage males are also much more likely to commit dangerous acts than the "average" citizen, but we do not confine them.

Bruce Ennis & Richard Emery, The Rights of Mental Patients 45 (1978). In contrast, the base rate for violence among people with serious mental illness, even those with acute symptoms, is probably much lower, around 10% if substance abuse and psychopathy are controlled for. Sheilagh Hodgins et al., "The Antecedents of Aggressive Behavior Among Men with Schizophrenia: A Prospective Investigation of Patients in Community Treatment," 21 Beh. Sci. & L. 523, 540 (Table 4)(2003)(finding recidivism rates among people who experience threat/control override symptoms to be between 5.5% and 10.6%).

What implications does this information have for police power civil commitment of people with mental disability? Should it be abolished? Limited to those with severe mental illness? Those with only persecutory delusions (threat/control override symptoms)? Expanded to include those with mental conditions associated with a relatively high recidivism rate? In connection with this latter question, note that certain non-psychotic "mental disorders," in particular antisocial personality disorder, are highly correlated with violence-proneness (see pp. 481–82) and Robert D. Hare, "Diagnosis of Antisocial Personality Disorder in Two Prison Populations," 140 Am. J. Psychiatry 887, 888 (1983)(reporting 39% prevalence of anti-social personality disorder in prison, using criteria more restrictive than those found in DSM–III).

   2. *Treatability and people with mental illness.* The Development authors' assertion that some mental disorders are difficult or impossible to treat also retains validity. However, as noted in the introduction to this

chapter and in Chapter One, many of the psychoses (e.g., schizophrenia, manic-depressive psychosis) and depression are responsive to medication. Thus, a person whose dangerousness stems from one of these mental disorders *may* be more "treatable" (with respect both to efficacy and to necessary duration of confinement) than a person whose dangerousness can only be treated through the behavioral therapy mentioned in the excerpt. Does this possibility justify treating people with mental illness differently?

Conversely, if the person who is dangerous to others is not treatable or no treatment is available should commitment be barred? Consider the following excerpt from *Lynch v. Baxley,* 386 F.Supp. 378, 391–2 (M.D.Ala. 1974):

> An exception to this general requirement of due process [that commitment occur only when treatment is available] is recognized in the case of a presently and seriously dangerous person for whose illness there is no known cure or treatment. In such instances, the state may well have an obligation under the police power to restrain the liberty of the threatening individual, even though his condition is not amenable to any currently available treatment. Since the involuntary commitment of an untreatable person is an exception to the general due process requirement that treatment be available and afforded, the committing court must make a finding, based upon clear and convincing evidence, that confinement even without a proposed treatment program is necessary for the safety and well-being of the community and of the person to be committed. Such orders of commitment, when granted, shall provide that, should treatment for the patient's illness become available at any time during the period of his confinement, such treatment shall be made available to him immediately.

3. *Rational control and people with mental illness.* The Developments article suggests that the best explanation for allowing long-term preventive detention of people with mental illness is that they lack autonomy and therefore cannot be deterred by the dictates of the criminal law. In other words, even if they are no more dangerous or treatable than other identifiable groups, people who are mentally ill can justifiably be singled out for preventive detention because of their relative undeterrability. Assuming people with mental illness are less autonomous, does this rationale make sense? Are there not other groups of individuals (pedophiles, recidivist burglars, terrorists) who are not deterred by the threat of punishment? Is there a way in which their undeterrability is different from the undeterrability of people with mental illness?

As to the assertion made by Morse that people with mental disability "often ... have as much control over their behavior as normal persons do," considerable research supports his conclusion. For instance, several studies show that the hospitalized mentally ill respond to rewards and disincentives in a way that is consistent with rationally controlled behavior. William Fisher, et. al. "Implications for Concepts of Psychopathology of Studies of Economic Principles in Behavior Therapy," 166 J. Nervous & Mental Disease 187, 191–93 (1978). However, none of these studies permit the conclusion that all people with mental illness behave as rationally as others. As Morse stated in another article:

> Again, I do not mean to make an absurd claim. A chronically disabled, hallucinating, and delusional person who wanders the streets in rags speaking gibberish is not "like" normal persons, and the law should probably treat this person specially. Nevertheless, the law should be far more cautious before concluding that large numbers of crazy people are so incapable of responsible behavior that deprivation of liberty is justified.

Stephen Morse, "Treating Crazy People Less Specially," 90 W.Va.L.Rev. 353, 370 (1988).

4. *Ease of prediction and people with mental illness.* A final possible justification for permitting at least certain types of preventive detention of those with mental illness, not mentioned in either excerpt, is that their dangerousness might be easier to predict. As explained in Chapter 6 (pp. 478–79), the commonly accepted wisdom is that a prediction of dangerousness to others is likely to be wrong two out of three times. See John Monahan, The Clinical Prediction of Violent Behavior 60 (1980). Yet perhaps mental health professionals and others are better at predicting violence of those who have severe mental illness than of ex-felons and other categories of individuals. See, e.g., Dianne Sepajak, et al., "Clinical Prediction of Dangerousness: Two–Year Follow-up of 408 Pretrial Forensic Cases," 11 Bull. Am Acad. Psychiatry & L. 171 (1983)(finding a relatively "low" 44% false positive rate when predicting recidivism of persons with mental disability found incompetent to stand trial).

Furthermore, Monahan has suggested that *short-term* predictions—i.e., predictions of future behavior in the immediate future—are likely to be more valid than the long-term predictions studied in most of the research to date, given the "small situational and temporal 'gap' between the behavior used as a predictor and the outcome that is being predicted." John Monahan, The Clinical Prediction of Violent Behavior 59 (1980). See also Dale McNeil & R.L. Binder, "Judgments of Dangerousness in Emergency Civil Commitment," 144 Am.J.Psychiat. 197 (1987) (those committed as dangerous to others much more likely than others to be assaultive in first 24 hours after prediction); Randy Otto, "Prediction of Dangerous Behavior: A Review and Analysis of 'Second–Generation' Research," 5 Forensic Reports 103 (1992)("the second-generation studies indicate that the predictive accuracy of mental health professionals is greatest when short-term predictions are made, with people with a history of dangerous behavior, in settings similar to those in which the subject may ultimately be placed."); Jay Apperson et al., "Short–Term Clinical Prediction of Assaultive Behavior: Artifacts of Research Methods," 150 Am. J. Psychiat. 1374 (1993)(finding a 25% false positive rate for short-term predictions).

Of course, even if predictive accuracy is 50 or 75%, one might object to a process that erroneously subjects 1 out of every 2 or 3 people to the "massive deprivation of liberty" associated with commitment. The following materials flesh out the meaning of dangerousness to others in the civil commitment context.

2. *Implementing the Police Power*

a. *Defining Mental Illness*

DODD v. HUGHES

Supreme Court of Nevada, 1965.
81 Nev. 43, 398 P.2d 540.

THOMPSON, JUSTICE.

By a habeas corpus application addressed to the Second Judicial District Court, Dodd sought his release from the Nevada State Hospital (NRS 433.040). He had been committed to that institution as a mentally ill person by order of the Fourth Judicial District Court. At the habeas hearing, the Superintendent of the Nevada State Hospital gave his opinion that Dodd, though a sociopath, was not psychotic, and therefore not "mentally ill" within the meaning of NRS 433.200. He suggested that Dodd be released from his confinement. Another doctor was of a different view. Though he agreed that Dodd was not psychotic, he believed that a sociopathic personality may be considered "mentally ill" as that term is used in the state. Additionally, he stressed Dodd's high potential for homicidal activity. At the conclusion of the hearing, the court directed the superintendent to apply to the board of the state prison commissioners for that board's consent to confine Dodd at the Nevada State Prison. The superintendent did as directed. The prison commissioners consented, and Dodd was delivered to the Nevada State Prison for confinement until further order of the court (NRS 433.310).[1]

The legislature did not define "mentally ill" when it passed the law governing the Nevada State Hospital (NRS 433.010–433.640). Its failure to do so supplies the basis for Dodd's appeal. It is his position that a person must exhibit one of the psychotic reactions as classified by the American Psychiatric Association before he may be considered mentally ill. Absent a classified psychosis, one may not be committed and confined. A sociopath (defined in the testimony as a disorder of personality affecting the ethical and moral senses) like Dodd, (and all the evidence is in accord that Dodd is, indeed, a sociopath), does not fall within any of the classified psychotic reactions and, therefore, may not be institutionalized. So it is that we are urged to fashion a definition for the words "mentally ill" and thereby fill the void in the statutory hospital law. It is suggested that we confine mental illness to the psychotic reactions as classified by the American Psychiatric Association. We are wholly unable to follow that suggestion. The record before us shows that the psychia-

---

1. NRS 433.310 provides:

"1. Whenever a person legally adjudged to be mentally ill is deemed by the court or the superintendent to be a menace to public safety, and the court is satisfied that the facilities at the hospital are inadequate to keep such mentally ill person safely confined, the court may, upon ap- plication of the superintendent, commit such person to the Nevada state prison. The person shall be confined in the Nevada state prison until the further order of the committing court either transferring him to the hospital or declaring him to be no longer mentally ill."

trists who testified do not agree on the statutory meaning of "mentally ill." Further, the record reflects that psychiatrists in general are at war over the propriety of the classifications of psychosis as specified by the American Psychiatric Association. We seriously doubt that the legislature ever intended medical classifications to be the sole guide for judicial commitment. The judicial inquiry is not to be limited so as to exclude the totality of circumstances involved in the particular case before the court. Recidivism, repeated acts of violence, the failure to respond to conventional penal and rehabilitative measures, and public safety, are additional and relevant considerations for the court in deciding whether a person is mentally ill. The assistance of medical examination and opinion is a necessary concomitant of the court hearing, but the court alone is invested with the power of decision. That power is to be exercised within the permissible limits of judicial discretion.

Here the record demonstrates a combination of things which should, and did, unquestionably, influence the lower court to enter the order it did. Dodd, an 18 year old, was shown, by testing, to have the intelligence quotient of a high grade moron. All agree that he is a sociopath almost devoid of moral sense. He has been proven, at least to date, wholly unresponsive to either penal or rehabilitative measures,[2] nor does he give promise of response to available probation services or psychiatric treatment. He possesses homicidal tendencies, and is dangerous. Finally, one of the testifying psychiatrists stated that Dodd is mentally ill within the intendment of the statute. In these circumstances the lower court did not abuse its discretion in denying habeas relief and ordering that Dodd be transferred to the Nevada State Prison for confinement.

Affirmed.

Questions and Comments

1. *State statutes.* Every state requires proof of mental illness or mental disorder as a predicate for police power commitment. At one time, most commitment statutes, like the Nebraska statute at issue in *Dodd*, did not define mental illness or defined it tautologically. See, e.g., Vernon's Ann. Texas Civ.Stat. § 5547–4(k)(1982)(defining a mentally ill person as "a person whose mental health is substantially impaired"). Some states still do so. See, e.g., Or. Stat. § 426.005(1)(d)("Mentally ill person" means a person who, because of a mental disorder, is one or more of the following: (A) Dangerous to self or others. (B) Unable to provide for basic personal needs and is not receiving such care as is necessary for health or safety."). Most state laws today, however, contain language similar to that found in New Mexico's statute: "Mental disorder means the substantial disorder of the person's emotional processes, thought or cognition which grossly impairs judgment, behavior or capacity to recognize reality." N.M.Stat.Ann. 1978,

2. He experienced trouble with the police when eight years old. He was placed in the Elko Boys School from 1960–1962. While there he fought frequently. He escaped. While loose he hit an elderly man on the head with a crowbar, covered him with kerosene or gas, and set him on fire. He was then sent to Preston, California, a prison for hardcore youth criminals. In 1963 he was committed to the Nevada State Hospital, from which he "eloped" on four separate occasions.

§ 43–1–3(O). Usually this definition applies both to police power and parens patriae commitment.

2. *Antisocial personality disorder.* Probably the most controversial issue connected with the definition of mental illness in police power commitment is that posed in *Dodd*—whether the definition should include sociopathy (a condition that today might be labeled as antisocial personality disorder). What are the implications of the holding in *Dodd*? Why do you think the superintendent of the Nevada State Hospital was arguing that Dodd was *not* mentally ill? Assuming Dodd was mentally ill, should it be permissible to transfer him from the hospital to the state prison, as provided by NRS 433.310?

The Supreme Court of Minnesota has held that an antisocial personality is not within the definition of mental illness unless the individual has "lost the ability to control his actions." *Johnson v. Noot,* 323 N.W.2d 724, 727 (Minn.1982). Arizona's statute excludes from the definition of mental disorder "[c]haracter and personality disorders characterized by lifelong and deeply ingrained anti-social behavior patterns, including sexual behaviors which are abnormal and prohibited by statute unless the behavior results from a mental disorder." Ariz.Rev.Stat. § 36–501(1)(c). Is either of these a better approach than *Dodd's*? Would Dodd be committable under the New Mexico statute quote in Note 1? Look at the definition of antisocial personality disorder in the Appendix (p. 1349) before answering.

3. *The Supreme Court and police power commitment.* In *Foucha v. Louisiana,* 504 U.S. 71, 112 S.Ct. 1780, 118 L.Ed.2d 437 (1992), the defendant sought release from the hospital four years after his acquittal by reason of insanity on charges of aggravated burglary and unlawful discharge of a firearm. At the release hearing, experts stated that Foucha no longer suffered from "mental illness," but further noted that, because of his untreatable "antisocial personality disorder," Foucha might still be a danger to others. On the basis of this testimony, the Louisiana trial judge refused release. In an opinion for five members of the Court, Justice White *assumed* (but did not *hold*) that Foucha was no longer mentally ill, and concluded that, as a result, under the due process clause "the basis for holding Foucha as an insanity acquittee has disappeared, and the State is no longer entitled to hold him on that basis." In a part of the opinion in which only three other members of the Court joined, White also argued that continued confinement of Foucha would violate the equal protection clause:

> The State ... insists on holding [Foucha] indefinitely because he at one time committed a criminal act and does not now prove he is not dangerous. Louisiana law, however, does not provide for similar confinement of other classes of persons who have committed criminal acts and who cannot later prove they would not be dangerous. Criminals who have completed their prison terms, or are about to do so, are an obvious and large category of such persons. Many of them will likely suffer from the same sort of personality disorder that Foucha exhibits. However, state law does not allow for their continuing confinement based merely on dangerousness. Instead, the State controls the behavior of these similarly situated citizens by relying on other means, such as punishment, deterrence, and supervised release. Freedom from physical re-

straint being a fundamental right, the State must have a particularly convincing reason, which it has not put forward, for such discrimination against insanity acquittees who are no longer mentally ill.

Foucha is excerpted more fully in the materials on commitment of insanity acquittees (pp. 877–80).

Compare the above language in *Foucha* to *Kansas v. Hendricks*, 521 U.S. 346, 117 S.Ct. 2072, 138 L.Ed.2d 501 (1997), reprinted at pp. 675–86. *Hendricks*, the Court considered the constitutionality of Kansas' Sexually Violent Predator Act, which authorizes longterm commitment of a prisoner who has completed his sentence for a serious sex offense if the person is found to be dangerous due to a "mental abnormality" or "personality disorder." Hendricks argued that, as a matter of substantive due process, only a finding of "mental illness" may serve as the predicate for civil commitment. The Court, in a 5–4 opinion, rejected this argument:

> Contrary to Hendricks' assertion, the term "mental illness" is devoid of any talismanic significance. "[P]sychiatrists disagree widely and frequently on what constitutes mental illness...." [W]e have never required State legislatures to adopt any particular nomenclature in drafting civil commitment statutes. Rather we have traditionally left to legislators the task of defining terms of a medical nature that have legal significance....

> To the extent that the civil commitment statutes we have considered set forth criteria relating to an individual's inability to control his dangerousness, the Kansas Act sets forth comparable criteria and Hendricks' condition doubtless satisfies those criteria. The mental health professionals who evaluated Hendricks diagnosed him as suffering from pedophilia, a condition the psychiatric profession itself classifies as a serious mental disorder. Hendricks even conceded that, when he becomes "stressed out," he cannot "control the urge" to molest children. This admitted lack of volitional control, coupled with a prediction of future dangerousness, adequately distinguished Hendricks from other dangerous persons who are perhaps more properly dealt with exclusively through criminal proceedings. Hendricks' diagnosis as a pedophile, which qualifies as a "mental abnormality" under the Act, thus plainly suffices for due process purposes.

In *Kansas v. Crane*, 534 U.S. 407, 122 S.Ct. 867, 151 L.Ed.2d 856 (2002), the Court further construed the definition of mental illness for purposes of committing people likely to commit sex offenses, in response to the argument that emotional or cognitive impairment, as well as volitional impairment, can form the predicate for such commitment.

> *Hendricks* must be read in context. The Court did not draw a clear distinction between the purely "emotional" sexually related mental abnormality and the "volitional." Here, as in other areas of psychiatry, there may be "considerable overlap between a ... defective understanding or appreciation and ... [an] ability to control ... behavior." American Psychiatric Association Statement on the Insanity Defense, 140 Am. J. Psychiatry 681, 685 (1983) (discussing "psychotic" individuals). Nor, when considering civil commitment, have we ordinarily distinguished for constitutional purposes among volitional, emotional, and

cognitive impairments. The Court in *Hendricks* had no occasion to consider whether confinement based solely on "emotional" abnormality would be constitutional, and we likewise have no occasion to do so in the present case.

With respect to the mental disorder predicate for civil commitment, what are the implications of the opinions in *Foucha* and the majority opinions in *Hendricks* and *Crane*? May a person who has "only" a personality disorder be committed? If so, does that disorder have to cause a "lack of volitional control" or can a disorder that leads to a lack of "moral sense" (the language used by the court to describe Dodd) also be the basis of commitment? Is there a difference between the two?

4. *Incompetency and police power commitment.* The American Psychiatric Association's Model Law for civil commitment permits commitment of people who are mentally ill and dangerous but only upon a showing that the person lacks "capacity to make an informed decision concerning treatment." Clifford Stromberg & Alan Stone, "A Model State Law on Civil Commitment of the Mentally Ill," 20 Harv.J.Leg. 275, 301 (1982). A few states appear to have adopted such a requirement. See, e.g., Kan. Stat. Ann. § 59–2946(f)(1). Apparently, it was the fact that its general commitment statute only permitted confinement of those who lack "capacity to make an informed decision concerning treatment" that led the state of Kansas to conclude that it could not confine sexual predators under that law and that the special commitment law at issue in *Hendricks* was needed. 521 U.S., at 377, 117 S.Ct. at 2089 (Breyer, J., dissenting). Is this capacity restriction on the effect of mental illness required in the context of police power commitments? Advisable?

5. *Causation.* Most state statutes require proof that the person's dangerousness is "caused by" or is "the result of" mental illness before commitment may occur. Does this requirement follow from the purported rationales of police power commitment? If so, is the Nevada statute under which Dodd was committed invalid on its face? Assuming sociopathy is a mental illness for purposes of civil commitment, was Dodd's dangerousness "caused" by his mental disorder?

b.	*Defining Danger to Others*

LESSARD v. SCHMIDT

United States District Court, E.D. Wisconsin, 1972.
349 F.Supp. 1078.

SPRECHER, CIRCUIT JUDGE.

* * *

Wisconsin defines "mental illness" as "mental disease to such extent that a person so afflicted requires care and treatment for his own welfare, or the welfare of others, or of the community." Wis.Stat.Ann. § 51.75, Art. II(f) (1971 Supp.). Interpreting § 51.02(5) in the light of this provision in Humphrey v. Cady, 405 U.S. 504, 509, 92 S.Ct. 1048, 1052, 31 L.Ed.2d 394 (1972), the Supreme Court noted (in dicta) that implicit in this definition is the requirement that a person's "potential for doing harm, to himself or to others, is great enough to justify such a massive curtailment of liberty." In other words, the statute itself requires a finding of "dangerousness" to self or others in order to deprive an individual of his or her freedom. The Court did not directly address itself to the degree of dangerousness that is constitutionally required before a person may be involuntarily deprived of liberty. However, its approval of a requirement that the potential for doing harm be *"great enough* to justify such a *massive curtailment* of liberty"* implies a balancing test in which the state must bear the burden of proving that there is an extreme likelihood that if the person is not confined he will do immediate harm to himself or others. Although attempts to predict future conduct are always difficult, and confinement based upon such a prediction must always be viewed with suspicion, we believe civil confinement can be justified in some cases if the proper burden of proof is satisfied and dangerousness is based upon a finding of a recent overt act, attempt or threat to do substantial harm to oneself or another.

* * *

ALEXANDER BROOKS, DANGEROUSNESS DEFINED IN LAW PSYCHIATRY & MENTAL HEALTH SYSTEMS 680

(1974).

* * *

Definitions of what is "dangerous" tend to be as diverse as the views of individual judges, courts, and jurisdictions. It may be that persons committed on the basis that they are "dangerous" need not be, and would not be, if the term were more carefully defined and its component elements identified, even if those elements could not be evaluated with a high degree of accuracy or quantification. A more rigorous analysis, if not too cumbersome, might well result in more sophisticated judicial decision-making.

The term "dangerous" can be broken down into at least four component elements: (1) magnitude of harm; (2) probability that the harm will occur; (3) frequency with which the harm will occur; (4) imminence of the harm.

To call a person "dangerous" is to express a judgment in the form of a prediction about his potential behavior. A person can be characterized as "dangerous" or not, depending on a balancing of these four components. For example, a harm which is not likely to occur, but which is very serious, may add up to "dangerousness." By the same token, a relatively trivial harm which is highly likely to occur with great frequency might also add up to dangerousness. On the other hand, a trivial harm, even though it is likely to occur, might not add up to dangerousness.

* * *

MATTER OF GREGOROVICH

Appellate Court of Illinois, First District, 1980.
89 Ill.App.3d 528, 44 Ill.Dec. 615, 411 N.E.2d 981.

LORENZ, JUSTICE:

This is an appeal by respondent from an order entered in the circuit court of Cook County, finding her to be a person subject to involuntary admission under the provisions of the Mental Health and Developmental Disabilities Code. (Ill.Rev.Stat.1979, ch. 91 1/2, pars. 1–100 et seq., 1–119.) * * *

On May 9, 1979, respondent's mother, Celia Gregorovich filed a petition for involuntary judicial admission, alleging that respondent was reasonably expected to inflict serious physical harm upon herself or another in the near future and was unable to provide for her basic physical needs so as to guard herself from serious harm and that she was in need of immediate admission for the prevention of such harm. The petition alleged that respondent had threatened to harm herself and her mother after she had cut all the cords to the electrical lamps and television.

The following pertinent evidence was adduced at the hearing on May 9, 1979.

Celia Gregorovich

Her husband, respondent's father, had been sick for 7 years with Parkinson's Disease and had been hospitalized since January 1979. Respondent, who was 21 years of age, blamed her mother for her father's illness, started talking to herself and would not eat. About a month earlier, when respondent cursed her, she struck respondent with a broom, and respondent then scratched her hand with her nails. The scratch marks took 3 weeks to heal. When she asked respondent to lower the television volume, respondent cut the television wires with scissors. Respondent then held the scissors in her fist, with the point sticking out, and pointed them at her mother, who was about 2 or 3 feet away. When respondent put down the scissors, Mrs. Gregorovich called the police. On cross-examination, she testified she did not have to seek medical attention when respondent scratched her hands, and respondent had never physically harmed her before this or tried to hurt herself. She further indicated respondent took care of herself at home and was very clean and neat about herself.

Gregory Nooney, mental health worker at Northwestern Hospital

Respondent, who was hospitalized at Northwestern, said she would not change her clothes until she went to court because that would prove she was not crazy; she slept in her clothes and had not bathed although she was eating. Respondent told him she knew that mental patients often had symptoms similar to ESP and she wanted to prove that she had ESP and that she was not crazy. On cross-examination, he testified respondent had never attacked any other patient on the hospital unit or caused any physical harm to anyone.

Dr. David Altman, a Board Certified Psychiatrist

He examined respondent on May 4, 1979. Respondent was sitting on the couch, moving her mouth and gesturing toward the television set which was turned on. When he was introduced to her, respondent yelled at him, then turned back toward the television set and continued to gesture toward it. When he attempted to engage her in a conversation, she moved to another part of the room and continued to face the television and gesture toward it. When he saw that respondent was becoming more upset, he told her he would stop, and respondent became calm and laughed in the direction of the television set. This process was repeated during the day on May 4. He also observed respondent in front of the television on other occasions when she would at times be watching the television with other patients, moving her mouth and occasionally making gestures. He spoke to her again the morning of the hearing, May 9, when respondent was again in front of the television set. She told him she did not want to talk to him, and the only information he was able to obtain from the interview was that respondent believed that it was dangerous for her to be in the hospital and that she would gain more ESP power from other patients and this would be dangerous. When he asked her to elaborate, respondent said that she would explain it to the judge.

In his opinion, based on information he received from other members of the staff and based on his contact with respondent, she was suffering from an acute schizophrenic episode, a mental illness involving auditory and visual hallucinations. He believed she was under a delusion, a fixed false belief, since she thought she had the power to control peoples' minds and read other persons' minds. He concluded that respondent would be unable to take care of her basic physical needs and protect herself against physical injury based on the fact that she cut the electrical wires prior to admission, that she was quite hostile, that she refused a physical examination and routine laboratory work upon admission because it would somehow prejudice her case, that she thinks she has extra sensory powers rather than having a mental illness, and that she had not bathed and was "essentially not caring for herself in a manner which she would need to do in order to be released." He recommended that she continue to be hospitalized although she had not inflicted injury on herself or anyone else in the hospital.

* * *

Dr. Sydney Wright, licensed Physician and Psychiatric Resident at Northwestern Memorial Hospital

He examined respondent on May 3, 1979. Respondent told him she felt she was being brought into the hospital against her will. In an effort to demonstrate her dissatisfaction about being brought to the hospital, she kicked a police officer when she was being escorted to Northwestern

Hospital. Respondent told this doctor that she had received ESP powers, but that people doubted that she had these powers. She said she had been involved in a power struggle with another person called Jeffery who had ESP and lived in Philadelphia and who had sent her ESP messages that he loved her; but she subsequently became aware of the fact that he wished to harm her and became involved in an ESP power struggle with him in which he attempted to kill her. She believed her ESP powers may have killed Jeffery since she had not recently heard from him.

Respondent also told him she had cut the television cord because God had told her to do so, and she became convinced that a university was "bugging" her house and was receiving information about her activities which would end if she cut the cord. She also stated that she was going to kill her mother.

In his opinion, respondent was suffering from a mental illness and would be unable to take care of her basic physical needs or protect herself against physical injury. Dr. Wright also noted that respondent showed gross disorganization of her thought processes characterized by concrete thinking, a looseness of association, and a marked pressure of speech. When asked if she might intentionally or unintentionally harm others, he answered, "I believe that is a possibility based on her statements to me." When asked if she was more likely than not to harm herself or others without further treatment, he related another episode which occurred the day following hospitalization. When the nurse assigned to work with respondent approached respondent, she told her she was a whore and would have nothing to do with her.

When he was again asked if it was more likely than not without further treatment that respondent might intentionally or unintentionally harm someone within a reasonable time, Dr. Wright responded: "Well, it is very difficult for me to predict the future. I would say there is a possibility she could harm someone." He recommended that respondent remain in the hospital for continued treatment. This course of action was based on respondent's statements to him that she believed her powers were sufficient to kill another individual, that she wanted to kill her mother and that she had an "aggressive and hostile stance toward specific staff members." He concluded, "I would say there is a possibility she could injure someone."

Respondent, on her own Behalf

She would get out-patient treatment if she were discharged. On cross-examination, when asked why she would not accept out-patient treatment at Northwestern Hospital, respondent explained that she was not told why she was there and that she was taken there forcibly even though she did not do anything violent. When asked if she needed any help from a mental point of view, she answered, "Possible, but I don't think so, I just need someone to talk to." She admitted she had "mental problems" in the past but had "got over it." When asked if there was anything currently wrong, she mentioned her mother saying, "but, if you knew my mother you would understand."

OPINION

Section 1–119 of the Mental Health and Developmental Disabilities Code (Ill.Rev.Stat.1979, ch. 91 1/2, par. 1–119) defines persons subject to involuntary admission as:

"(1) A person who is mentally ill and who because of his illness is reasonably expected to inflict serious physical harm upon himself or another in the near future; or

(2) . . . who because of his illness is unable to provide for his basic physical needs so as to guard himself from serious harm."

The State is required to prove that respondent is a person subject to involuntary admission by clear and convincing evidence. Respondent argues she was not proven to be a person subject to involuntary commitment in that it was not established that she was unable to provide for her basic physical needs so as to guard herself from serious harm. The State does not address this argument in its brief; however, we do not consider the evidence establishes respondent was unable to take care of her basic physical needs so as to guard herself from physical harm.

Respondent also argues there was insufficient evidence that she was reasonably expected in the near future to inflict serious physical harm upon herself or another. For reasons set forth below we conclude that the evidence presented in this case was clear and convincing that respondent was mentally ill and because of this was reasonably expected to inflict serious physical harm upon another person in the near future.[1]

* * *

We first conclude that the uncontradicted expert medical evidence, which was supported by the lay testimony, clearly and convincingly established respondent was "mentally ill." Respondent's assertion that she merely had powers of extra sensory perception, given evidence to the contrary, is unconvincing.

In *People v. Sansone* (1974), 18 Ill.App.3d 315, 326, 309 N.E.2d 733, this court held that the State must prove the person is in need of mental treatment by means of a medical opinion which is clear and convincing and which is based upon facts which are established by clear and convincing evidence. Thus, we held both (1) that the facts upon which the medical opinion was based must be established by clear and convincing evidence, and (2) that the medical opinion, itself, must be clear and convincing. * * *

In this case, we find Dr. Wright's testimony, when considered along with the evidence of previous dangerous conduct, was sufficiently clear and convincing evidence that respondent was reasonably expected to inflict serious physical harm upon another in the near future. Respondent's actions including scratching her mother on the hand during an

---

1. We do not therefore, find it necessary to consider whether the evidence was suffi-   cient to show she was likely to harm herself[.]

altercation and holding a pair of scissors a few feet from her mother on the occasion which led to her emergency hospitalization are supportive of this conclusion. The latter conduct was a serious threat which (apart from the issue of criminal intent), could constitute an aggravated assault.

Obviously, her mother felt threatened, since she immediately called police. Respondent, in cross-examining her mother through her attorney, attempted to show that although respondent at this time had the opportunity to harm her mother, she did not do so, and she repeats this argument here. However, the statute [does] not require the infliction of actual harm before commitment was authorized. Other evidence, including respondent's admissions and her own testimony, established respondent's continuing hostility, particularly toward her mother. Respondent in fact threatened to kill her mother following her hospitalization on an emergency basis, and it is apparent that respondent's hostility toward her mother increased following her hospitalization. Respondent in her testimony blamed her present difficulties on her mother. Respondent had the opportunity, when she testified, to explain the incident with the scissors, but she failed to do so.

* * *

Respondent would have us focus narrowly on Dr. Wright's use of the term "possibly" in evaluating his testimony, to show it was of an equivocal nature. A similar opinion was found not to be a clear and convincing medical opinion of the type required in *Sansone*. *People v. Bradley*. In *Bradley*, the expert witness phrased his opinion in terms of "conceivably," rather than "possibly." However, this requirement has been somewhat relaxed in subsequent cases especially when there is clear evidence of prior dangerous conduct or strong lay evidence. This court has upheld commitment orders under resembling circumstances in which there was no explicit medical opinion regarding the patient's future dangerous conduct, but where there was evidence of actual prior dangerous conduct and other evidence such as lay opinion. After considering the doctor's entire testimony together with the other evidence presented, we conclude that there was sufficient evidence in the present case to show respondent's dangerous propensities.

IN INTEREST OF NYFLOT

Supreme Court of North Dakota, 1983.
340 N.W.2d 178.

GIERKE, JUSTICE.

This is an appeal by the respondent, Cynthia Jewel Nyflot, from an Order for Hospitalization and Treatment Following Treatment Hearing entered in the County Court of Cass County on September 14, 1983. We affirm.

* * *

The respondent's fourth contention is that the facts do not support the conclusion that the respondent is a person requiring treatment because she did not present a serious risk of harm, as defined by § 25–03.1–02(11), N.D.C.C.

The court found as a fact that:

"... on August 29 and September 2, 1983, the respondent started two separate fires in the women's bathroom at the dormitory and that on one of those occasions a great amount of smoke escaped from the bathroom causing personnel to check into the bathroom where the respondent was found by herself in her pajamas; ..."

Respondent contends that because these fires amounted to little property damage, due to the fact that the bathrooms where the fires were started were virtually inflammable, there was no substantial likelihood that significant property damage or bodily harm could have resulted to the respondent or others as a result of the fires. The statute, however, is not concerned with harm which occurred in the past except as it establishes a potential for serious harm by future behavior of the respondent acting in conformity with previous conduct. The respondent testified that she started the fires to gain attention and to dramatize the fact that she did not want to be in the institution. She also testified that it was not her intent to harm anyone, including herself, and that she felt that there was no likelihood of such harm under the circumstances. Her subjective intentions and assessment of the likelihood of harm, however, do not alter the fact that she was willing to start fires to attract attention to herself. Absent compelling evidence to the contrary, it is a mere fortuity that more damage was not done or that the respondent suffered no ill effects from the smoke produced.

Other undisputed facts further support the conclusion that the respondent presented a serious risk of harm. She rolled lit cigarettes under the door of another patient's room. When the attendants attempted to take her cigarette lighter away from her, she concealed it in her vagina. She cut the screen on a window, using wire cutters which had been smuggled into the institution to her by a friend and, when discovered, she hid the wire cutters in her panties. We believe that these facts clearly support the court's determination that the respondent presented a serious risk of harm to herself, to others, and to property.

For the reasons stated in the opinion, the order of the county court is affirmed.

ERICKSTAD, C.J., and PEDERSON, VANDEWALLE and SAND, JJ., concur.

WHALEY v. JANSEN

District Court of Appeal, Fourth District, California, 1962.
208 Cal.App.2d 222, 25 Cal.Rptr. 184.

[Whaley brought a civil action against the city of San Diego, the police of that city, and two psychiatrists, among others, alleging false arrest and false imprisonment. According to the court]:

Plaintiff alleges generally that on May 29, 1959, while he was going from house to house in San Diego "exposing wrong-doers in government," he carried with him a letter entitled, "A MOST APPALLING CONDITION," which letter outlined his grievances and requested the use of the home to call in the neighbors and friends so he could deliver a lecture and obtain voluntary contributions from them to carry on his work; that about noon he was walking on the sidewalk in a residential district when defendant Officer Ludvigson stopped him and questioned him; that plaintiff told Officer Ludvigson what he had been doing and the officer asked him to get into the patrol car and talk and that plaintiff walked away; that the officer told him that if he walked away he would place him under arrest; that plaintiff continued walking away from the officer and the officer stated, "You're under arrest for vagrancy"; that plaintiff was forced into the car and literature was removed from his pocket with such titles as "A MOST APPALLING CONDITION, KIDNAPPED AND RAILROADED TO THE BUG HOUSE," and "Earl Warren a Travesty of Equal Justice Under the Law"; that after reading the articles and talking to plaintiff, Officer Ludvigson transported plaintiff to the police station and plaintiff remained in the car while the officer went to the office; that Officer Ludvigson returned and asked plaintiff if he had a permit to solicit and plaintiff answered that he had none because he was not soliciting money; that the officer then went back and in a few minutes returned with another officer and they took plaintiff to the county psychiatric unit; that plaintiff told them that they had no right to do this and attempted to walk away from them and Officer Drake took him into the psychiatric unit; that he was there interviewed by Dr. Reed and plaintiff demanded of the doctor that he be released; that the doctor replied that he had no authority to do so and that plaintiff's release would have to be effected through defendants Dr. Wiend or Dr. Lengyel; that on June 1, 1959, these two doctors interviewed plaintiff and on June 3, 1959, without being formally charged with a crime or mental illness, he was released.

* * *

Sufficient facts are recited in the complaint to justify the officer's belief that plaintiff was so mentally ill as to be likely to cause injury to himself or others and to require medical care or restraint.

Questions and Comments

1. *Typical state statutes; vagueness doctrine.* Some state statutes, like *Lessard* and the California statute at issue in *Whaley*, still do not identify the type of danger to others that must be manifested in order to justify commitment. For instance, Alabama defines the danger that justifies commitment as a "real and present threat of substantial harm to self and/or others." Ala. Stat. 22–52–10.4(a). California's Lanterman–Petris–Short Act, enacted seven years after the *Whaley* decision, merely requires proof of a "demonstrated danger of inflicting substantial physical harm upon others." Cal.Welf. & Inst.Code § 5300(a). Even the most elaborate statutes provide little more by way of definition. For example, in Massachusetts the relevant

criterion permits commitment upon a showing of "a substantial risk of physical harm to other persons as manifested by evidence of homicidal or other violent behavior or evidence that others are placed in reasonable fear of violent behavior and serious physical harm to them." Mass.St., c. 123, § 1.

Consider this criticism of commitment statutes from Professor Dershowitz:

> Imagine ... a penal code which simply made it an imprisonable crime to cause injury to self or others, without defining injury.... To be sure there are differences between the criminal and the civil commitment processes: the criminal law is supposed to punish people for having committed harmful acts in the past; whereas civil commitment is supposed to prevent people from committing harmful acts in the future. While this difference may have important implications in some contexts, it would seem entirely irrelevant in deciding which acts are sufficiently harmful to justify incarceration either as an after-the-fact punitive sanction or as a before-the-fact preventive sanction. The considerations which require clear definition of such harms in the criminal process would seem to be fully applicable to the civil commitment process.

Alan Dershowitz, "Dangerousness as a Criterion for Confinement," 11 Bull.Amer.Acad.Psychiat. & Law 172 (1974).

Should commitment statutes be more specific, as is usually the case with the criminal law? To answer this question, some understanding of the void-for-vagueness doctrine might be useful. The doctrine developed in the nineteenth century as a means of judicially monitoring the precision of the criminal law. Two rationales are advanced to support it. The first is that ambiguous language fails to give potential violators fair warning of the conduct that is criminal. The second, more important, rationale is that such language allows law enforcement officials, the jury and the courts, rather than duly elected legislators, to decide at their whim the type of conduct that will be defined as criminal.

Although the doctrine is potentially quite broad in its reach, given the imprecision found in many statutes, it has been applied sparingly. Most of the laws that the Supreme Court has found unconstitutional on vagueness grounds impinged upon "fundamental" interests, such as freedom of expression, or were perceived to be vehicles for harassment of minority groups or the poor. See, e.g., *N.A.A.C.P. v. Button*, 371 U.S. 415, 83 S.Ct. 328, 9 L.Ed.2d 405 (1963); *Coates v. City of Cincinnati*, 402 U.S. 611, 91 S.Ct. 1686, 29 L.Ed.2d 214 (1971); *Kolender v. Lawson*, 461 U.S. 352, 103 S.Ct. 1855, 75 L.Ed.2d 903 (1983). In *Papachristou v. City of Jacksonville*, 405 U.S. 156, 92 S.Ct. 839, 31 L.Ed.2d 110 (1972), for instance, the Supreme Court considered a municipal ordinance which classified as "vagrants," among others, "rogues and vagabonds, or dissolute persons who go about begging ... common drunkards, ... lewd, wanton and lascivious persons, ... persons wandering or strolling around from place to place without any lawful purpose or object, habitual loafers, disorderly persons, [and] ... persons able to work but habitually living upon the earnings of their wives or minor children. ..." In striking down this statute on vagueness grounds, and reversing the convictions of two white women and two black men found driving on the main thoroughfare of Jacksonville, the Court stated:

Those generally implicated by the imprecise terms of the ordinance—poor people, non-conformists, dissenters, idlers—may be required to comport themselves according to the lifestyle deemed appropriate by the Jacksonville police and the courts. Where, as here, there are no standards governing the exercise of the discretion granted by the ordinance, the scheme permits and encourages an arbitrary and discriminatory enforcement of the law. ...It results in a regime in which the poor and the unpopular are permitted to "stand on a public sidewalk ... only at the whim of any police officer." ... Under this ordinance, "[I]f some carefree type of fellow is satisfied to work just so much, and no more, as will pay for one square meal, some wine, and a flophouse daily, but a court thinks this kind of living subhuman, the fellow can be forced to raise his sights or go to jail as a vagrant."

... Of course, vagrancy statutes are useful to the police. Of course, they are nets making easy the roundup of so-called undesirables. But the rule of law implies equality and justice in its application. Vagrancy laws of the Jacksonville type teach that the scales of justice are so tipped that even-handed administration of the law is not possible. The rule of law, evenly applied to minorities as well as majorities, to the poor as well as the rich, is the great mucilage that holds society together.

When a statute does not "chill" fundamental rights or create the type of problem described in *Papachristou,* it is less likely to be found vague, even if the language is very ambiguous. See, e.g., *Nash v. United States*, 229 U.S. 373, 33 S.Ct. 780, 57 L.Ed. 1232 (1913) (upholding a provision in the Sherman Antitrust Act which makes illegal "[e]very contract, combination in the form of trust or otherwise, or conspiracy in restraint of trade or commerce," so long as it is interpreted to prohibit only "undue" restraints of trade). Moreover, the Supreme Court has indicated that a statute is less likely to be declared void for vagueness if more precise language would be difficult to produce. *United States v. Petrillo*, 332 U.S. 1, 67 S.Ct. 1538, 91 L.Ed. 1877 (1947).

The following notes explore whether more precision is possible in drafting police power commitment laws. Brooks' four-factor analysis of dangerousness (excerpted above) will be used as an organizing device, beginning with the first factor, magnitude of harm.

2. *Magnitude of harm.* Assuming the validity of police power commitment, homicide or serious bodily injury would presumably be a harm the state may act to prevent. For what other types of predicted harms may the state deprive one of liberty?

Minor physical injury. Should the type of injury suffered by the mother of Gregorovich be sufficient to justify commitment, if we could predict accurately that it would occur again? Note that the assault statutes in most states require "bodily injury" for the result element of that crime. See, e.g., Model Penal Code § 211.1. Under the Model Penal Code, this term is defined as "physical pain, illness, or any impairment of physical condition." Model Penal Code § 210.0(2).

Non-physical danger to others. A few states explicitly permit commitment if the court finds that a person may cause "emotional" or "psychic" harm to others. For instance, Iowa law authorizes commitment of a person with mental illness who is "likely to inflict serious emotional injury on members of his or her family or others who lack reasonable opportunity to avoid contact with the afflicted person if the afflicted person is allowed to remain at liberty without treatment." Iowa Code Ann. § 229.1(16)(b). "Serious emotional injury" is defined as "[i]njury which does not necessarily exhibit any physical characteristics, but which can be recognized and diagnosed by a licensed physician or other qualified mental health professional and which can be causally connected with the act or omission of a person who is, or is alleged to be, mentally ill." § 229.1(15). In *State v. Hungerford,* 84 Wis.2d 236, 267 N.W.2d 258 (1978), the Wisconsin Supreme Court held that, in connection with commitment as a mentally disordered sex offender, a prediction of physical harm is not required and that "moral" harm alone might be sufficient.

The criminal law contains provisions that are analogous. For instance, the Model Penal Code includes a crime called "harassment" which is defined as follows:

> A person commits a petty misdemeanor if, with purpose to harass another, he: (a) makes a telephone call without purpose of legitimate communication; or (b) insults, taunts or challenges another in a manner likely to provoke violent or disorderly response; or (c) makes repeated communications anonymously or at extremely inconvenient hours, or in offensively coarse language; or (d) engages in any other course of harmful conduct serving no legitimate purpose of the actor.

Model Penal Code § 250.4. Professor Feinberg argued that such criminal law provisions are justified based on what he calls the "offense" principle, which he distinguishes from the "harm" principle, the latter being the primary justification for criminalizing behavior. In Feinberg's view, the state may penalize seriously offensive behavior, even though it does not cause physical harm. Borrowing from nuisance theory in tort, he attempts to provide some guidelines for evaluating the offensiveness of behavior:

> The seriousness of the offensiveness would be determined by (1) the intensity and durability of the repugnance produced, and the extent to which repugnance could be anticipated to be the general reaction of strangers to the conduct displayed or represented (conduct offensive only to persons with an abnormal susceptibility to offense would not count as *very* offensive); (2) the ease with which unwilling witnesses can avoid the offensive displays; and (3) whether or not the witnesses have willingly assumed the risk of being offended either through curiosity or the anticipation of pleasure....
>
> These factors would be weighed as a group against the reasonableness of the offending party's conduct as determined by (1) its personal importance to the actors themselves and its social value generally, remembering always the enormous social utility of unhampered expression (in those cases where expression is involved); (2) the availability of alternative times and places where the conduct in question would cause less offense; (3) the extent, if any, to which the offense is caused with spiteful motives.

Joel Feinberg, Offense to Others 26 (1985). Should this type of analysis be applied to the civil commitment context? How would you apply it to *Whaley*? To Case 24 on p. 711?

In answering these questions, should it matter what the alternative to hospitalization is? Consider these comments:

[F]ailure to commit those with grave mental disorders in treatment facilities paradoxically results in involuntary confinement of a different sort. A consequence of this failure is that they are frequently incarcerated for minor crimes. In fact, in the first year following the enactment of the [Lanterman–Petris–Short] Act, the number of mentally ill people in the prisons rose dramatically. Most of these arrests were for misdemeanors and were highly correlated with the offender's mental illness and corresponding behavior. Police often use catch-all charges to sweep mentally ill people off the street. These charges may include petty theft, assault, trespassing, and disorderly conduct. "Mercy-bookings" by policemen are also common as a way to protect people the police feel are easily victimized.

The consequences of this situation are drastic. One article in the Los Angeles Times described the prison system as "the world's largest mental institution." This speculation has been corroborated with statistics. Depending on the study, researchers investigating the records of prison inmates have found that between six to eight percent suffer from a serious psychiatric illness. Research based on inmate interviews shows that the number of prisoners with a psychiatric disorder jumps to ten to fifteen percent. Furthermore, much research indicates that there is a large overlap between the mentally ill who are homeless and those in jail. One study of people living in shelters who had previously been hospitalized for mental illness found that 76% of them had also been arrested. By limiting the numbers to include only schizophrenia, manic-depression, and severe depression, about ten percent of the prison population in the U.S. qualifies, which is approximately 159,000 people.

This incarceration is particularly unfortunate because people who are gravely disabled are not necessarily dangerous to others. Moreover, the incarceration of people who are gravely disabled by mental illness can lead to tragic results. Prison is designed for criminals and operates by rigid rules that the mentally ill might find difficult to follow. The bizarre behavior that mentally ill people display is often met with a lack of understanding and violence by guards and inmates. Suicide is also common for mentally ill inmates, and about half of prison suicides are committed by people who were previously hospitalized for mental illness. Furthermore, incarcerating a mentally ill person is likely to exacerbate their symptoms, often resulting in solitary confinement sometimes without any medical treatment. In 1995, a federal judge wrote an opinion severely criticizing the deplorable conditions facing the mentally ill in the California jails, citing "a rampant pattern of improper or inadequate care that nearly defies belief."

Meredith Karasch, "Where Involuntary Commitment, Civil Liberties, and the Right to Mental Health Care Collide: An Overview of California's Mental Illness System," 54 Hastings L.J. 493, 520–21 (2003).

Danger to property. Some states also include harm to "property" as a commitment criterion. In *Suzuki v. Yuen*, 617 F.2d 173 (9th Cir.1980), the Ninth Circuit Court of Appeals found such a provision in Hawaii's statute unconstitutionally broad. It stated:

> We need not decide whether a state may ever commit one who is dangerous to property. This statute would allow commitment for danger to any property regardless of value or significance.... Under the current Hawaii definition of "danger to property," a person could be committed if he threatened to shoot a trespassing dog. The state's interest in protecting animals must be outweighed by the individual's interest in personal liberty.

Do you agree? How can the state legislature retain danger to property as a criterion for commitment while avoiding the court's prohibition? Could Nyflot be committed under a standard consistent with *Yuen*? Consider also Case 7 on p. 710. Such a person risks certain losses—money, job, friends, embarrassment. But he is not risking serious physical harm to himself or others. Should he therefore not be committable?

3. *Frequency of harm.* No state statute makes explicit a requirement that the factfinder assess the frequency of the anticipated harm, perhaps because, as the excerpt from Feinberg illustrates, frequency is an integral part of the magnitude-of-harm analysis. Consider, however, *Millard v. Harris,* 406 F.2d 964 (D.C.Cir.1968), where the court reversed the recommitment of an exhibitionist, who conceded he was receiving treatment at the government hospital. Writing for the court, Judge Bazelon stated:

> The unanimous testimony of all the expert witnesses that serious psychological harm would result from public exposure only to unusually sensitive adult women and small children leads us to conclude that the future sexual misconduct of the appellant, if any, is not sufficiently likely to cause the sort of harm required by the statute to justify further commitment. The appellant did not, it is true, prove that no such "potential viewers" would view him in the course of any future exhibitionism. But having shown that he was unlikely to commit such acts with great or uncontrollable frequency, and that in the event of such misconduct harm would be produced in only a small proportion of the population, the appellant could fairly demand of the Government that it show that the members of these restricted classes were not merely "potential viewers," but likely viewers. This the Government wholly failed to do. And without the assistance of any evidence adduced on this score, we cannot conclude that supersensitive women and small children are likely to suffer serious harm from isolated instances of exhibitionism. "Very seclusive, withdrawn, shy, sensitive" women are a minority. While the law must and does protect them like other citizens, there are limits on the extent to which the law can sweep the streets clear of all possible sources of occasional distress to such women. Small children present a different problem. But the expert testimony was not that the typical small child would be injured by witnessing an isolated act of exposure on the part of a stranger, but rather that psychological danger to their development was likely from repeated exposure to such abnormal adult sexual behavior. We therefore conclude that the likelihood of

serious injury to a child happening to see the appellant expose himself in public is too remote to justify commitment. As for harm to the appellant's own children, we have already adverted in passing to the questionable nature of the sole evidence that the appellant ever did expose himself in his home before them. Even if we accept this evidence, however, and assume that the appellant might expose himself in his home if released, his children can be protected from the harm which might follow from repeated exposure by other means than his involuntary hospitalization. His wife need not permit the appellant to so abuse his children, and other legal remedies are available to her to insure that he does not inflict such harm on his children.

4. *Probability of harm.* As noted earlier, the Supreme Court has held that, under the due process clause of the federal constitution, the criteria for civil commitment must be proven by clear and convincing evidence, a standard of proof below the criminal reasonable doubt standard and above the preponderance of the evidence standard used in most civil trials. A few states have opted for the higher reasonable doubt standard. See Superintendent of Worcester State Hospital v. Hagberg, 374 Mass. 271, 372 N.E.2d 242 (1978); see also, Hawaii Rev.Stat. § 334–60.5(i); Lausche v. Commissioner of Public Welfare, 302 Minn. 65, 225 N.W.2d 366 (1974), cert. denied 420 U.S. 993, 95 S.Ct. 1430, 43 L.Ed.2d 674 (1975).

Given the research finding, reported earlier, that a prediction that someone will act violently in the future may be wrong as often as 2 out of 3 times, is it possible to prove dangerousness beyond a reasonable doubt, or even by clear and convincing evidence? Litwack and Schlesinger think so. After a meticulous review of the literature, they assert that few if any of the existing studies on risk assessment have tested the accuracy of explicit predictions of dangerousness for people who are subsequently released in the community rather than confined and treated.[f] Thus, they "suggest",

clear and convincing evidence exists whenever any of the following indicia of future violence are evident: (1) a recent history of repeated violence (absent treatment or evidence of significant changes in the circumstances or attitudes that led to violence in the past); (2) a more distant history of violence together with clear and convincing evidence that the complex of attitudes and personality traits (and physical abilities) that led to violence in the past still exist and that there is a likelihood that the circumstances (or like circumstances) that led to violence in the past will recur in the foreseeable future (or, in any event, before the individual's violence-tending attitudes are likely to change); (3) unequivocal threats or other like evidence of serious intentions to commit violence, especially when based on delusional thinking; and (4) other clear and convincing evidence that the individual whose violence is being predicted is on the brink of violence. One example of this latter criterion would be that of a man who sat incessantly at the edge of his bed with a loaded rifle vigilantly waiting, because of his paranoid delusions, for his home to be attacked. Other examples would include individuals with a history of violence who express paniclike fears of

f. See pp. 478–81 for a more detailed treatment of this research.

losing control over violent impulses or who feel driven toward violence (e.g., by command hallucinations).

[W]e note again that while research has yet to establish the predictive power of these indices—and because of the practical and ethical problems involved may never do so—neither (to our knowledge) is there any evidence that refutes the legitimacy of relying on these indices to establish "clear and convincing" evidence of "dangerousness". On the other hand, we question, again, whether "clear and convincing" evidence of dangerousness can be had without any of these or similar indicia.

Thomas Litwack & Louis Schlesinger, "Assessing and Predicting Violence: Research, Law, and Applications," in Handbook of Forensic Psychology (Weiner & Hess, eds.) 205, 224 (1987).

At least one court has required that certain factors be considered before a clear and convincing finding of dangerousness can be made. In *In re Linehan*, 518 N.W.2d 609 (Minn.1994), the Minnesota Supreme Court held that, in determining the likelihood of violent behavior, courts should consider: (1) the person's demographic traits (e.g., age and education); (2) the person's history of violent behavior (paying particular attention to recency, severity, and frequency of violent acts); (3) base rate statistics for violent behavior among individuals of this person's background; (4) the sources of stress in the environment (cognitive and affective factors which indicate that the person may be predisposed to cope with stress in a violent or nonviolent manner); (5) the similarity of the present or future context to those contexts in which the person has used violence in the past; and (6) the person's record with respect to therapy programs. To the extent information exists, how do the factors identified in *Linehan* and by Litwack and Schlesinger apply in *Gregorovich* and *Nyflot*?

For base rate information, consider the materials in Note 1 on pp. 718–19 and the materials on actuarial prediction on pp. 482–88. Consider also the variables listed in the HCR–20, one of the most heavily researched structured clinical prediction devices. The HCR–20 consists of 20 items relating to historical, clinical and risk factors. The historical factors are previous violence; young age at first violent incident; relationship instability; employment problems; substance use problems; major mental illness; psychopathy; early maladjustment; personality disorder; prior supervision failure. The clinical factors are lack of insight; negative attitudes; active symptoms of major mental illness; impulsivity; unresponsiveness to treatment. The risk management factors are: plans lack feasibility; exposure to destabilizers; lack of personal support; noncompliance with remediation attempts; and stress. The evaluator scores the individual on a scale of 0 to 2 for each factor, with a score of 40 indicating a maximum degree of risk. See Christopher D. Webster et al., The HCR–20 Scheme: The Assessment of Dangerousness and Risk (1995).

One study that applied the HCR–20 to released civil commitment patients found that those who scored in the highest range (27 and over) were 17 times as likely to commit criminal violence within 2 years after release as patients who scored below 19. Yet only 35% of those in the 27–plus range were found to have committed criminal violence during the follow-up period, and "criminal violence" included minor physical harm. K. Douglas et al., "Assessing Risk for Violence Among Psychiatric Patients: The HCR–20 Violence Risk Assessment Scheme and the Psychopathy Checklist: Screening Version," 67 J. Consulting & Clinical Psychology 917 (1999). Assume Gregorovich scores a 27 on the HCR–20. What are the implications of this finding?

Monahan and Wexler have contended that the debate over whether dangerousness can be predicted adequately often fails to take into account the typical definition of dangerousness. Many statutes require only that the state prove the person is "likely" or "probable" or "more likely than not" dangerous to others. Quantifying the matter, these statutes could be said to define "dangerousness" as a 51% chance that the person will harm someone in the future. Assuming that proof by clear and convincing evidence correlates with a 75% degree of certainty, these states only require a showing of something like a 38% (75% x 51%) chance that the person will harm others in the future. John Monahan & David Wexler, "A Definite Maybe: Proof and Probability in Civil Commitment," 2 Law & Hum.Beh. 37 (1978). In those jurisdictions that use the "more-likely-than-not" standard, is commitment of a person based on a 38% chance of harmful behavior justifiable?

Consider *In re M.B.K.*, 639 N.W.2d 473 (N.D. 2002), where the state sought to commit, under a sexually violent predator law, a person who had pleaded guilty to a Class B felony sex offense and was nearing the end of his three-year sentence. The Supreme Court of North Dakota held that the state need merely prove that the individual posed "a threat to society" and further held that statistical proof that the individual had (depending on the actuarial device used) a 37 to 45% chance of "reoffending" within ten years was "clear and convincing" proof under this standard. The court justified its definition of dangerousness on two grounds: (1) other states had adopted the same standard, and (2) the standard "prevents a contest over percentage points and the results of other actuarial tools, and allows experts to use the fullness of their education, experience and resources available to them in order to determine if an individual poses a threat to society."

5. *Imminence requirement. Lessard* and the statutes of most states prohibit commitment as dangerous to others unless the danger is "imminent." Should this be a requirement? If so, should it be made more specific (e.g., within the next two weeks, within the next two days) or should its definition depend upon the other factors discussed above?

c. *The Overt Act Requirement*

PEOPLE v. SANSONE
Appellate Court of Illinois, 1974.
18 Ill.App.3d 315, 309 N.E.2d 733.

STAMOS, JUSTICE.

* * *

Initially, respondent argues that to sustain a finding of likelihood of injury to respondent or others, proof of prior dangerous conduct must be adduced, and in the absence of such proof, civil commitment is preventive detention. Respondent asserts that, pursuant to the theory of Robinson v. California, 370 U.S. 660, 82 S.Ct. 1417, 8 L.Ed.2d 758, confinement based upon a prediction of future dangerous conduct is confinement based upon status. Respondent relies upon Cross v. Harris, 135 U.S.App.D.C. 259, 418 F.2d 1095 and Lessard v. Schmidt, 349 F.Supp. 1078 (E.D.Wis.) for the proposition that a prediction of future dangerousness must be based upon documented prior overt acts or threats.

* * *

In the area of mental health law, the State must balance the curtailment of liberty against the danger of harm to the individual or others. The paramount factor is the interest of society which naturally includes the interest of the patient in not being subjected to unjustified confinement. We agree with respondent that the "science" of predicting future dangerous behavior is inexact, and certainly is not infallible. We also agree that the mere establishment of a mental problem is not an adequate basis upon which to confine a person who has never harmed or attempted to harm either himself or another. However, we are of the opinion that a decision to commit based upon a medical opinion which clearly states that a person is reasonably expected to engage in dangerous conduct, and which is based upon the experience and studies of qualified psychiatrists, is a determination which properly can be made by the State.

Moreover, we cannot agree that commitment in the absence of evidence of prior harmful conduct is preventive detention based upon the patient's status as a mentally ill person. Again, we reiterate that a finding must be based upon an explicit medical opinion regarding the patient's future conduct, and cannot be based upon a mere finding of mental illness. Secondly, the purpose of the Mental Health Code is to provide treatment, and in fact, the Code affords every patient the right to treatment. This is a very different situation from that in Robinson v. California, supra, wherein the Court held that a law which imprisons a person afflicted with a disease inflicts cruel and unusual punishment. The Court in *Robinson* distinguished criminal punishment and detention from detention based upon laws which require medical treatment. 370 U.S. 660, 666, 82 S.Ct. 1417, 8 L.Ed.2d 758. Therefore, we hold that a finding of "in need of mental treatment," absent evidence of prior harmful conduct, is not *per se* violative of due process.

* * *

In the instant case, respondent's delusions regarding law enforcement and law enforcement officers were established without contradiction by the testimony of the psychiatrist and the social worker, both of whom interviewed respondent on two different occasions. The medical opinion was that respondent believed that persons were "after him," and that respondent could be dangerous to others. The psychiatrist testified that persons he had known with the same type of delusions had injured or attempted to injure others. Therefore, although the psychiatrist could not give any degree of probability of dangerousness, and although there was no evidence of prior dangerous conduct, the uncontradicted testimony established by clear and convincing evidence that respondent was in need of mental treatment.

IN MATTER OF MENTAL HEALTH OF D.R.S.

Supreme Court of Montana, 1986.
221 Mont. 245, 718 P.2d 335.

[D.R.S. was committed under a statute which required the state to show that he was "suffering from a mental disorder which has resulted in ... injury to others or the imminent threat thereof...." The statute defined injury to mean "physical injury," Mont.Code Ann. 53–21–102(14), and provided that imminent threat of injury to others "shall be evidenced by overt acts, sufficiently recent in time as to be material and relevant as to the respondent's present condition." Mont.Code Ann. 53–21–126(2). The sole overt act proven by the state was an armed robbery for which D.R.S. was not convicted. As described by the Montana Supreme Court, D.R.S. and another person "committed the robbery" on November 5, 1982. In the course of the robbery, they took the store clerk behind a woodpile by the store, taped him up, covered him with wood and left him in the cold. The clerk identified D.R.S. as the person who taped him and stated that the other person threatened to shoot him if he didn't tell them the combination to the safe. The clerk testified that both robbers frightened him and that he feared for his life.

D.R.S. was found incompetent to stand trial on the robbery charge and hospitalized for the purpose of restoration to competency. After almost two years in the hospital, he was found competent, but charges against him were dismissed on speedy trial grounds on January 8, 1985. On February 14, 1985, he was civilly committed. The Montana Supreme Court upheld the commitment against a challenge that the robbery was insufficiently recent. The court justified this decision as follows]:

The circumstances in the case at bar are such that a lapse of time between the overt act and the commitment proceedings do not preclude relying on the overt act [the robbery] as evidence of D.R.S.' mental condition.

Dr. James Deming, the psychologist who treated D.R.S. for the two-year period at Montana State Hospital testified that D.R.S.' condition was essentially unchanged from that in 1982. He testified that:

[D.R.S.] continued to exhibit symptoms of a significant mental illness, continued to be confused, continued to develop neologisms or new words, continued to be convinced of specific bizarre ideations, as an example, [D.R.S.] was convinced that his lawyer was my brother. On the basis of the information that both of us wore mustaches. He continued to have—to exhibit a significant thought disorder which renders him unpredictable, and in my judgment, imminently dangerous.

Dr. Deming relied on several factors in concluding that D.R.S. is dangerous. In addition to the primary element of the charges against D.R.S., Dr. Deming considered his statements of unwillingness to accept supervision in a community setting for his disorder, D.R.S.' stated intent to use alcohol when he leaves the hospital, and the deterioration of his condition while in the county jail. Dr. Deming explained that a small amount of alcohol would render D.R.S. confused and disoriented, resulting in dangerous behavior, and that he had not received medication during his stay in jail. The fact that D.R.S. had not exhibited dangerous or "acting-out" behavior in the hospital was due to the supervised environment and the control of his medication. If taken out of this supervised setting, Dr. Deming said that D.R.S. would become imminently dangerous within two months. Finally, the doctor expressed his opinion that D.R.S. is seriously mentally ill and imminently dangerous to himself and others due to his mental disease of paranoid schizophrenia.

D.R.S.' conduct during the robbery, under the circumstances presented here, is "sufficiently recent in time as to be material and relevant" to his present condition. The time lapse between the overt act and his commitment hearing was due to his serious mental illness. The evidence showed his condition remained as it was at the time of the overt act. In addition, the psychiatric evaluation stated that D.R.S. would be imminently dangerous within two months of leaving the supervised hospital setting. We hold that the District Court had sufficient evidence to find D.R.S. is seriously mentally ill.

Questions and Comments

1. *The necessity for an overt act requirement.* The *Lessard* decision prohibited commitment unless the person is found to be dangerous "based upon a finding of a recent overt act, attempt or threat to do substantial harm." Approximately ten state statutes include a similar provision. See, e.g., Fl.Stat. § 394.467(1)(a)(2)(b); Kan. Stat. § 59–2946(f)(3)(a). A number of other states accomplish the same effect with wording like that found in the Montana statute recited in *D.R.S.* The rest, well over half of the states, do not require proof of an overt act.

What is the argument that the Constitution mandates such a showing? Cf. *Robinson v. California,* supra. Are there other, "pragmatic," reasons for such a requirement? Under California's Lanterman–Petris–Short Act, those considered dangerous to others are potentially subject to three "stages" of commitment: a 72–hour emergency detention, a 14–day short-term detention, and a 180–day commitment. Proof of an overt act is required for the third-stage 180–day commitment, but not for the first and second stages of the commitment process. Cal.Code §§ 5150, 5200, 5250, 5300. Can you think of a rationale for this approach?

2. *The content of the overt act requirement.* If proof of an overt act is required, how should it be defined? Is a threat to harm another enough?

Statements like those in *Sansone* that "people are out to get me?" Purchase of a weapon?

The criminal law has dealt with an analogous issue through definition of the actus reus for attempt crimes. Typically, "mere preparation" for a crime is considered insufficient conduct to impose liability for attempt. Various tests developed to capture this notion. For instance, one such test asked whether the person had committed the "last proximate act" of the offense in question. Thus, if a person fires a gun at the intended victim and misses, he can be found guilty of attempted murder. If he merely lies in wait for the victim but does not fire the gun, he cannot be. A second, less restrictive test, developed by Justice Holmes, focused on whether the person was in "dangerous proximity to success." See generally, Peter Low et al., Criminal Law: Cases and Materials 132–37 (2d ed. 1986). The Model Penal Code, which has heavily influenced many state legislatures, defines the actus reus for attempt as "an act of omission constituting a substantial step in a course of conduct planned to culminate in his commission of the crime." Model Penal Code § 5.01(1)(c). The Code then states:

> Conduct shall not be held to constitute a substantial step ... unless it is strongly corroborative of the actor's criminal purpose. [T]he following, if strongly corroborative of the actor's criminal purpose, shall not be held insufficient as a matter of law:
>
> a) lying in wait, searching for or following the contemplated victim of the crime;
>
> b) enticing or seeking to entice the contemplated victim of the crime to go to the place contemplated for its commission;
>
> c) reconnoitering the place contemplated for the commission of the crime;
>
> d) unlawful entry of a structure, vehicle or enclosure in which it is contemplated that the crime will be committed;
>
> e) possession of materials to be employed in the commission of the crime, which are specially designed for such unlawful use or which can serve no lawful purpose of the actor under the circumstances;
>
> f) possession, collection or fabrication of materials to be employed in the commission of the crime, at or near the place contemplated for its commission, where such possession, collection or fabrication serves no lawful purpose of the actor under the circumstances;
>
> g) soliciting an innocent agent to engage in conduct constituting an element of the crime.

Model Penal Code § 5.02. Should civil commitment statutes include this list or one like it? What effect would an overt act requirement have in Case 5 on p. 709? Case 17 on p. 710?

3. *Recency of the overt act.* The *Lessard* court also requires that the overt act be "recent," as does the Montana statute in *D.R.S.* Other states (e.g., California) do not explicitly include a recency requirement. What is the purpose of this requirement? Does it link with the imminence requirement? Do you agree with the holding in *D.R.S.* on this issue? How do you evaluate the statute below (which at one time was the law in Arizona)?

§ 36–501(3). "Danger to others" means behavior which constitutes a danger of inflicting substantial bodily harm upon another person based upon a history of having inflicted or having attempted to inflict substantial bodily harm upon another person within twelve months preceding the hearing on court ordered treatment, except that:

(a) If the proposed patient has existed under conditions of being restrained by physical or pharmacological means, or of being confined, or of being supervised, which have deterred or tended to deter him from carrying out acts of inflicting or attempting to inflict bodily harm upon another person, the time limit of within twelve months preceding the hearing may be extended to a time longer than twelve months as consideration of the evidence indicates; or,

(b) If the bodily harm inflicted upon or attempted to be inflicted upon another person was grievous or horrendous, the time limit of within twelve months preceding the hearing may be extended to a time longer than twelve months as consideration of the evidence indicates.

4. *Standard of proof.* Although proof of dangerousness need only be by clear and convincing evidence, can an argument be made that proof of the overt act must be beyond a reasonable doubt? Montana's statute, at issue in *D.R.S.*, is unique among the states, in that it requires proof beyond a reasonable doubt of any "physical facts or evidence" and clear and convincing proof "as to all other matters [except that] mental disorders must be proved to a reasonable medical certainty." Mont.Code Ann. § 53–21–126(2). Is the Montana approach coherent? As applied to the criteria necessary to commit D.R.S., is the standard met?

C. PARENS PATRIAE COMMITMENTS

1. *Rationale*

The parens patriae authority is premised on the power of government to act as "parent" toward its citizens. This country has a strong tradition of anti-paternalism, based on strains of individualism dating back to the colonization of the eastern seaboard by dissidents and outcasts. John Stuart Mill provided one of the earliest and most forceful defenses of the anti-paternalism position.

The only purpose for which power can be rightfully exercised over any member of a civilized community against his will, is to prevent harm to others. His own good, either physical or moral, is not a sufficient warrant. He cannot rightfully be compelled to do or forbear because it will be better for him to do so, because it will make him happier, because in the opinion of others to do so would be wise, or even right. These are reasons for remonstrating with him, or reasoning with him, or persuading him, or entreating him, but not for compelling him, or visiting him with any evil in case he do otherwise.

J.S. Mill, On Liberty, in The Philosophy of John Stuart Mill 197 (1961).

Yet, as Professor Shapiro has pointed out, "if antipaternalism is the dominant strain, it has surely not won the day:"

> Defenders of paternalism, or at least of a more neutral stance, have argued forcefully for their position on both descriptive and normative grounds. Paternalist motives, they suggest, help to account for a vast range of present-day legislation and judicial doctrine (not to speak of the actions of individuals toward one another); failure to recognize these motives can only lead to confusion and hypocrisy. Moreover, paternalism has a legitimate place among human motivations—perhaps more legitimate than other, more selfish, reasons for action—since its regard for others is rooted in "empathy or love."

David Shapiro, "Courts, Legislatures, and Paternalism," 74 Va.L.Rev. 519, 519–20 (1988). As Shapiro notes, paternalistic legislation has become an accepted feature of modern life. Laws regulating food quality and the environment, employment conditions (e.g., minimum wage and maximum hour laws), and transportation (e.g., seat-belt and motorcycle helmut statutes) are just a few examples of legislation that might be characterized as paternalistic in motivation.

Civil commitment remains the most dramatic example of state paternalism. Every state permits involuntary, prolonged hospitalization of someone found to be mentally ill and "dangerous to self," "unable to care" for themselves, "gravely disabled" or some combination thereof. The usual justification advanced for these provisions is that people with mental illness lack the capacity to make decisions about treatment and hospitalization; thus, the state has the authority to make those decisions for them. Note, "Civil Commitment of the Mentally Ill: Developments in the Law," 87 Harv.L.Rev. 1190, 1212 (1974). Even Mill recognized an exception to his general rule for those who are "incompetent," including youth and people with mental disability, on the ground that one cannot exercise one's political rights unless one has the capacity to do so. See Mary Ellen Waithe, "Why Mill Was For Paternalism," 6 Int'l J.L. & Psychiat. 101 (1983).

Several arguments against this use of state power can be advanced. The first, analogous to the argument against police power commitment of people with mental illness, is that people with mental illness as a class are no more incompetent than others and therefore should not be singled out for special treatment. Professor Morse makes the argument most directly:

> Are the mentally disordered particularly incompetent? The question is crucial because involuntary commitment substitutes the state's judgment about the necessity for hospitalization (and often for treatment as well) for the judgment of the individual. Although commitment rarely includes a formal finding of legal incompetence at present, it at least implies the judgment that in some cases the person cannot cope or make decisions in his or her own best interest. * * *

There is however, little empirical or theoretical justification for the belief that the mentally disordered as a class are especially incapable of managing their lives or deciding for themselves what is in their own best interests. Available empirical evidence demonstrates that the mentally disordered as a class are probably not more incompetent than normal persons as a class. Indeed, there is no necessary relationship between mental disorder and legal incompetence.

... While some disordered persons are clearly incompetent according to any reasonable criteria, the social goal of reducing the consequences of incompetence is not well served by allowing involuntary hospitalization, guardianship, or treatment of only the mentally disordered.

Stephen Morse, "A Preference for Liberty: The Case Against Involuntary Commitment of the Mentally Disordered," 70 Cal.L.Rev. 54, 63–64 (1982).

Subsequent research appears to undercut this conclusion, however. In a MacArthur Foundation study comparing the competency of large groups of patients with schizophrenia, patients with depression, patients with heart disease, and persons in the community, the patients with schizophrenia were found to be significantly more impaired.

Nearly one half of the schizophrenia group and 76% of the depression group performed in the "adequate" range (according to *ad hoc* definitions of adequacy used in this study) across all decision-making measures, and a significant portion performed at or above the mean for persons without mental illness.... On the other hand, the data confirm that significant differences exist in decision-making abilities between persons with and without mental illness, especially when the comparisons focus on patients with schizophrenia. For any given measure, approximately 25% of the schizophrenic group scored in the "impaired" range, compared with 5–7% of angina patients and only 2% of community controls.... When all measures are combined, 52% of patients with schizophrenia showed impairment on at least one measure, in contrast to 12% of angina patients and 4% of community controls.

Thomas Grisso & Paul Appelbaum, "Abilities of Patients to Consent to Psychiatric and Medical Treatments," 19 L. & Hum. Beh. 149, 171 (1995). It may also be relevant that major psychiatric illness is implicated in no less than 93% of suicides, with the diagnoses most often implicated being major depression (40–60%), chronic alcoholism (20%) and schizophrenia (10%). David Clark & Jan Fawcet, "Review of Empirical Risk Factors for Evaluation of the Suicidal Patient," in Suicide: Guidelines for Assessment, Management and Treatment 18–19 (Bruce Bongar ed. 1992).

The second argument against parens patriae commitment assumes the theoretical validity of committing people with mental illness who are incompetent (at least when incompetency causes serious dysfunction), but questions whether "reasonable criteria" for judging who is incompetent can be developed and applied. Dr. Szasz is particularly vigorous in advancing this view. In one of his later works, for instance, he stated:

> [W]henever one person, A, claims that another person, B, is incompetent, we are confronted with a situation from which we can draw two quite different inferences, one more probable than the other. The less probable inference is that A's assertion is true: in other words, that B is indeed incompetent. The more probable inference is that A's assertion is untrue: in other words, that A wants to paternistically control or coerce B.

Thomas Szasz, Insanity: The Idea and Its Consequences 249–50 (1987). A more detailed investigation of this difficult issue is left until Chapter Nine, which deals with the question of competency generally. For now, the following definition of competency is offered:

> Since the purpose of the incapacity standard is to distinguish persons whose decisions to refuse treatment must be accepted as final from those whose choices may be validly overridden through *parens patriae* commitments, the standard should focus on the ability to engage in a decision-making process rather than the resulting decision.... [C]ommentary accompanying the National Institute of Mental Health's 1952 Draft Act Governing Hospitalization of the Mentally Ill appears to provide a workable definition of incapacity[:] an individual lacks capacity if, as a result of a mental disease or disorder, he has lost the "power to make choices or become so confused ... [that he cannot] make a decision having any relation to the factors bearing on his hospitalization."

Developments, supra at 1217.

Even if one accepts that parens patriae commitment is theoretically justified and that the incompetent mentally ill can be accurately identified, the following question must also be answered: who among the incompetent mentally ill may be involuntarily hospitalized? This section addresses this question.

NOTE, CIVIL COMMITMENT OF THE MENTALLY ILL: DEVELOPMENTS IN THE LAW
87 Harvard L.R. 1190, 1218–19.
(1974).

* * *

Best Interest of the Individual: A Balancing Requirement.—After the threshold requirement of incapacity has been met, the state may act as *parens patriae* for the individual. Although the state ideally should attempt to duplicate the decision which its ward would have made, the need to ascertain each ward's value structure would make such a process highly impractical. Consequently, the state as substitute decision-maker should objectively evaluate alternatives and select the one which best serves the ward's interest. The propriety of a decision to require psychiatric treatment or to compel hospitalization will thus depend on whether either action constitutes the most desirable response to the individual's condition. The advisability of ordering commitment will naturally vary depending on such individual factors as the debilitating effect of the mental disorder, the prognosis with and without treatment, the expected duration of treatment, the need for and length of institutionalization, the institutional conditions, the legal disabilities resulting from commitment, and the disruptive effect on preexisting lifestyle.

Although the "best interest" test entails a flexible balancing of costs and benefits, the serious stigma and the interference with physical freedom produced by even short term commitment to a mental institution suggest that a substantial expected benefit should be required for involuntary commitment. Consequently, a mental disorder which does not pose a danger to the individual's physical health or substantially impair his ability to function in society should rarely result in forced institutional care. State commitment statutes which require that the individual be dangerous to himself or that his condition create a substantial risk of his physical injury can be viewed as expressing a legislative judgment that the likelihood that individuals who do not meet those standards would not benefit sufficiently to justify their confinement outweighs the possibility that commitment would sometimes be appropriate in such cases.

The potential of beneficial treatment is another possible limitation on *parens patriae* commitments derived from the best interest requirement. In *In re Ballay,* the District of Columbia Circuit contended in dictum that "[w]ithout some form of treatment the state justification for acting as *parens patriae* becomes a nullity." However, the court's belief that custodial care is an impermissible use of the *parens patriae* power seems unwarranted. As with other relevant factors, the untreatable patient's potential need for indefinite confinement for his own protection should be considered in balancing the costs and benefits of imposing various types of care. The danger of substantial physical harm created when an untreatable mental disorder impairs the individual's ability to provide for his basic needs might well be sufficient to justify action under the *parens patriae* power, although there are alternative modes of providing protective care which may be preferable to hospitalization of the untreatable. . . .

O'CONNOR v. DONALDSON

Supreme Court of the United States, 1975.
422 U.S. 563, 95 S.Ct. 2486, 45 L.Ed.2d 396.

* * *

MR. JUSTICE STEWART delivered the opinion of the Court.

The respondent, Kenneth Donaldson, was civilly committed to confinement as a mental patient in the Florida State Hospital at Chattahoochee in January 1957. He was kept in custody there against his will for nearly 15 years. The petitioner, Dr. J.B. O'Connor, was the hospital's superintendent during most of this period. Throughout his confinement Donaldson repeatedly, but unsuccessfully, demanded his release, claiming that he was dangerous to no one, that he was not mentally ill, and that, at any rate, the hospital was not providing treatment for his supposed illness. Finally, in February 1971, Donaldson brought this lawsuit under 42 U.S.C. § 1983, in the United States District Court for the Northern District of Florida, alleging that O'Connor, and other members of the hospital staff named as defendants, had intentionally and maliciously deprived him of his constitutional right to liberty. After a four-day trial, the jury returned a verdict assessing both compensatory and punitive damages against O'Connor and a codefendant. The Court of Appeals for the Fifth Circuit affirmed the judgment. We granted O'Connor's petition for certiorari, because of the important constitutional questions seemingly presented.

I

Donaldson's commitment was initiated by his father, who thought that his son was suffering from "delusions." After hearings before a county judge of Pinellas County, Fla., Donaldson was found to be suffering from "paranoid schizophrenia" and was committed for "care, maintenance, and treatment" pursuant to Florida statutory provisions that have since been repealed.[2] The state law was less than clear in specifying the grounds necessary for commitment, and the record is scanty as to Donaldson's condition at the time of the judicial hearing. These matters are, however, irrelevant, for this case involves no challenge to the initial commitment, but is focused, instead, upon the nearly 15 years of confinement that followed.

The evidence at the trial showed that the hospital staff had the power to release a patient, not dangerous to himself or others, even if he remained mentally ill and had been lawfully committed. Despite many requests, O'Connor refused to allow that power to be exercised in Donaldson's case. At the trial, O'Connor indicated that he had believed that Donaldson would have been unable to make a "successful adjust-

2. The judicial commitment proceedings were pursuant to § 394.22(11) of the State Public Health Code, which provided:

"Whenever any person who has been adjudged mentally incompetent requires confinement or restraint to prevent self-injury or violence to others, the said judge shall direct that such person be forthwith delivered to a superintendent of a Florida state hospital, for the mentally ill, after admission has been authorized under regulations approved by the board of commissioners of state institutions, for care, maintenance, and treatment, ..."

* * *

Donaldson had been adjudged "incompetent" several days earlier under § 394.22(1), which provided for such a finding as to any person who was "incompetent by reason of mental illness, sickness, drunkenness, excessive use of drugs, insanity, or other mental or physical condition, so that he is incapable of caring for himself or managing his property, or is likely to dissipate or lose his property or become the victim of designing persons, or inflict harm on himself or others...." Fla.Gen.Laws 1955, c. 29909, § 3, p. 831.

ment outside the institution,'' but could not recall the basis for that conclusion. O'Connor retired as superintendent shortly before this suit was filed. A few months thereafter, and before the trial, Donaldson secured his release and a judicial restoration of competency, with the support of the hospital staff.

The testimony at the trial demonstrated, without contradiction, that Donaldson had posed no danger to others during his long confinement, or indeed at any point in his life. O'Connor himself conceded that he had no personal or secondhand knowledge that Donaldson had ever committed a dangerous act. There was no evidence that Donaldson had ever been suicidal or been thought likely to inflict injury upon himself. One of O'Connor's codefendants acknowledged that Donaldson could have earned his own living outside the hospital. He had done so for some 14 years before his commitment, and immediately upon his release he secured a responsible job in hotel administration.

Furthermore, Donaldson's frequent requests for release had been supported by responsible persons willing to provide him any care he might need on release. In 1963, for example, a representative of Helping Hands, Inc., a halfway house for mental patients, wrote O'Connor asking him to release Donaldson to its care. The request was accompanied by a supporting letter from the Minneapolis Clinic of Psychiatry and Neurology, which a codefendant conceded was a "good clinic." O'Connor rejected the offer, replying that Donaldson could be released only to his parents. That rule was apparently of O'Connor's own making. At the time, Donaldson was 55 years old, and, as O'Connor knew, Donaldson's parents were too elderly and infirm to take responsibility for him. Moreover, in his continuing correspondence with Donaldson's parents, O'Connor never informed them of the Helping Hands offer. In addition, on four separate occasions between 1964 and 1968, John Lembcke, a college classmate of Donaldson's and a longtime family friend, asked O'Connor to release Donaldson to his care. On each occasion O'Connor refused. The record shows that Lembcke was a serious and responsible person, who was willing and able to assume responsibility for Donaldson's welfare.

The evidence showed that Donaldson's confinement was a simple regime of enforced custodial care, not a program designed to alleviate or cure his supposed illness. Numerous witnesses, including one of O'Connor's codefendants, testified that Donaldson had received nothing but custodial care while at the hospital. O'Connor described Donaldson's treatment as "milieu therapy." But witnesses from the hospital staff conceded that, in the context of this case, "milieu therapy" was a euphemism for confinement in the "milieu" of a mental hospital.[4] For substantial periods, Donaldson was simply kept in a large room that housed 60 patients, many of whom were under criminal commitment. Donaldson's requests for ground privileges, occupational training, and an

4. There was some evidence that Donaldson, who is a Christian Scientist, on occasion refused to take medication. The trial judge instructed the jury not to award damages for any period of confinement during which Donaldson had declined treatment.

opportunity to discuss his case with O'Connor or other staff members were repeatedly denied.

At the trial, O'Connor's principal defense was that he had acted in good faith and was therefore immune from any liability for monetary damages. His position, in short, was that state law, which he had believed valid, had authorized indefinite custodial confinement of the "sick," even if they were not given treatment and their release could harm no one.

The trial judge instructed the members of the jury that they should find that O'Connor had violated Donaldson's constitutional right to liberty if they found that he had

> "confined [Donaldson] against his will, knowing that he was not mentally ill or dangerous or knowing that if mentally ill he was not receiving treatment for his alleged mental illness.

* * *

> "Now, the purpose of involuntary hospitalization is treatment and not mere custodial care or punishment if a patient is not a danger to himself or others. Without such treatment there is no justification from a constitutional stand-point for continued confinement unless you should also find that [Donaldson] was dangerous to either himself or others."[6]

The trial judge further instructed the jury that O'Connor was immune from damages if he

> "reasonably believed in good faith that detention of [Donaldson] was proper for the length of time he was so confined....

> "However, mere good intentions which do not give rise to a reasonable belief that detention is lawfully required cannot justify [Donaldson's] confinement in the Florida State Hospital."

The jury returned a verdict for Donaldson against O'Connor and a codefendant, and awarded damages of $38,500, including $10,000 in punitive damages.

The Court of Appeals affirmed the judgment of the District Court in a broad opinion dealing with "the far-reaching question whether the

6. The District Court defined treatment as follows:

> "You are instructed that a person who is involuntarily civilly committed to a mental hospital does have a *constitutional right to receive such treatment as will give him a realistic opportunity to be cured or to improve his mental condition.*" (Emphasis added.) O'Connor argues that this statement suggests that a mental patient has a right to treatment even if confined by reason of dangerousness to himself or others. But this is to take the above paragraph out of context, for it is bracketed

by paragraphs making clear the trial judge's theory that treatment is constitutionally required only if mental illness alone, rather than danger to self or others, is the reason for confinement. If O'Connor had thought the instructions ambiguous on this point, he could have objected to them and requested a clarification. He did not do so. We accordingly have no occasion here to decide whether persons committed on grounds of dangerousness enjoy a "right to treatment."

* * *

Fourteenth Amendment guarantees a right to treatment to persons involuntarily civilly committed to state mental hospitals." The appellate court held that when, as in Donaldson's case, the rationale for confinement is that the patient is in need of treatment, the Constitution requires that minimally adequate treatment in fact be provided. The court further expressed the view that, regardless of the grounds for involuntary civil commitment, a person confined against his will at a state mental institution has "a constitutional right to receive such individual treatment as will give him a reasonable opportunity to be cured or to improve his mental condition." Conversely, the court's opinion implied that it is constitutionally permissible for a State to confine a mentally ill person against his will in order to treat his illness, regardless of whether his illness renders him dangerous to himself or others.

II

We have concluded that the difficult issues of constitutional law dealt with by the Court of Appeals are not presented by this case in its present posture. Specifically, there is no reason now to decide whether mentally ill persons dangerous to themselves or to others have a right to treatment upon compulsory confinement by the State, or whether the State may compulsorily confine a non-dangerous, mentally ill individual for the purpose of treatment. As we view it, this case raises a single, relatively simple, but nonetheless important question concerning every man's constitutional right to liberty.

The jury found that Donaldson was neither dangerous to himself nor dangerous to others, and also found that, if mentally ill, Donaldson had not received treatment. That verdict, based on abundant evidence, makes the issue before the Court a narrow one. We need not decide whether, when, or by what procedures, a mentally ill person may be confined by the State on any of the grounds which, under contemporary statutes, are generally advanced to justify involuntary confinement of such a person—to prevent injury to the public, to ensure his own survival or safety, or to alleviate or cure his illness. For the jury found that none of the above grounds for continued confinement was present in Donaldson's case.[10]

Given the jury's findings, what was left as justification for keeping Donaldson in continued confinement? The fact that state law may have

10. O'Connor argues that, despite the jury's verdict, the Court must assume that Donaldson was receiving treatment sufficient to justify his confinement, because the adequacy of treatment is a "nonjusticiable" question that must be left to the discretion of the psychiatric profession. That argument is unpersuasive. Where "treatment" is the sole asserted ground for depriving a person of liberty, it is plainly unacceptable to suggest that the courts are powerless to determine whether the asserted ground is present. See *Jackson v. Indiana*, 406 U.S. 715, 92 S.Ct. 1845, 32 L.Ed.2d 435. Neither party objected to the jury instruction defining treatment. There is, accordingly, no occasion in this case to decide whether the provision of treatment, standing alone, can ever constitutionally justify involuntary confinement or, if it can, how much or what kind of treatment would suffice for that purpose. In its present posture this case involves not involuntary treatment but simply involuntary custodial confinement.

authorized confinement of the harmless mentally ill does not itself establish a constitutionally adequate purpose for the confinement. Nor is it enough that Donaldson's original confinement was founded upon a constitutionally adequate basis, if in fact it was, because even if his involuntary confinement was initially permissible, it could not constitutionally continue after that basis no longer existed.

A finding of "mental illness" alone cannot justify a State's locking a person up against his will and keeping him indefinitely in simple custodial confinement. Assuming that that term can be given a reasonably precise content and that the "mentally ill" can be identified with reasonable accuracy, there is still no constitutional basis for confining such persons involuntarily if they are dangerous to no one and can live safely in freedom.

May the State confine the mentally ill merely to ensure them a living standard superior to that they enjoy in the private community? That the State has a proper interest in providing care and assistance to the unfortunate goes without saying. But the mere presence of mental illness does not disqualify a person from preferring his home to the comforts of an institution. Moreover, while the State may arguably confine a person to save him from harm, incarceration is rarely if ever a necessary condition for raising the living standards of those capable of surviving safely in freedom, on their own or with the help of family or friends. See *Shelton v. Tucker,* 364 U.S. 479, 488–490, 81 S.Ct. 247, 252–253, 5 L.Ed.2d 231.

May the State fence in the harmless mentally ill solely to save its citizens from exposure to those whose ways are different? One might as well ask if the State, to avoid public unease, could incarcerate all who are physically unattractive or socially eccentric. Mere public intolerance or animosity cannot constitutionally justify the deprivation of a person's physical liberty.

In short, a State cannot constitutionally confine without more a nondangerous individual who is capable of surviving safely in freedom by himself or with the help of willing and responsible family members or friends. Since the jury found, upon ample evidence, that O'Connor, as an agent of the State, knowingly did so confine Donaldson, it properly concluded that O'Connor violated Donaldson's constitutional right to freedom.

Mr. Chief Justice Burger, concurring.

Although I join the Court's opinion and judgment in this case, it seems to me that several factors merit more emphasis than it gives them. I therefore add the following remarks. * * *

There can be no doubt that involuntary commitment to a mental hospital, like involuntary confinement of an individual for any reason, is a deprivation of liberty which the State cannot accomplish without due process of law. Commitment must be justified on the basis of a legitimate state interest, and the reasons for committing a particular individual must be established in an appropriate proceeding. Equally important, confinement must cease when those reasons no longer exist.

The Court of Appeals purported to be applying these principles in developing the first of its theories supporting a constitutional right to treatment. It first identified what it perceived to be the traditional bases for civil commitment—physical dangerousness to oneself or others, or a need for treatment—and stated:

> "[W]here, as in Donaldson's case, the rationale for confinement is the *'parens patriae'* rationale that the patient is in need of treatment, the due process clause requires that minimally adequate treatment be in fact provided.... 'To deprive any citizen of his or her liberty upon the altruistic theory that the confinement is for humane therapeutic reasons and then fail to provide adequate treatment violates the very fundamentals of due process.' "

The Court of Appeals did not explain its conclusion that the rationale for respondent's commitment was that he needed treatment. The Florida statutes in effect during the period of his confinement did not require that a person who had been adjudicated incompetent and ordered committed either be provided with psychiatric treatment or released, and there was no such condition in respondent's order of commitment. More important, the instructions which the Court of Appeals read as establishing an absolute constitutional right to treatment did not require the jury to make any findings regarding the specific reasons for respondent's confinement or to focus upon any rights he may have had under state law. Thus, the premise of the Court of Appeals' first theory must have been that, at least with respect to persons who are not physically dangerous, a State has no power to confine the mentally ill except for the purpose of providing them with treatment.

That proposition is surely not descriptive of the power traditionally exercised by the States in this area. Historically, and for a considerable period of time, subsidized custodial care in private foster homes or boarding houses was the most benign form of care provided incompetent or mentally ill persons for whom the States assumed responsibility. Until well into the 19th century the vast majority of such persons were simply restrained in poorhouses, almshouses, or jails. The few States that established institutions for the mentally ill during this early period were concerned primarily with providing a more humane place of confinement and only secondarily with "curing" the persons sent there.

As the trend toward state care of the mentally ill expanded, eventually leading to the present statutory schemes for protecting such persons, the dual functions of institutionalization continued to be recognized. While one of the goals of this movement was to provide medical treatment to those who could benefit from it, it was acknowledged that this could not be done in all cases and that there was a large range of mental illness for which no known "cure" existed. In time, providing places for the custodial confinement of the so-called "dependent insane" again emerged as the major goal of the States' programs in this area and remained so well into this century.

In short, the idea that States may not confine the mentally ill except for the purpose of providing them with treatment is of very recent origin, and there is no historical basis for imposing such a limitation on state power. Analysis of the sources of the civil commitment power likewise lends no support to that notion. There can be little doubt that in the exercise of its police power a State may confine individuals solely to protect society from the dangers of significant antisocial acts or communicable disease. *Jacobson v. Massachusetts,* 197 U.S. 11, 25–29, 25 S.Ct. 358, 360–362, 49 L.Ed. 643 (1905). Additionally, the States are vested with the historic *parens patriae* power, including the duty to protect "persons under legal disabilities to act for themselves." The classic example of this role is when a State undertakes to act as " 'the general guardian of all infants, idiots, and lunatics.' "

Of course, an inevitable consequence of exercising the *parens patriae* power is that the ward's personal freedom will be substantially restrained, whether a guardian is appointed to control his property, he is placed in the custody of a private third party, or committed to an institution. Thus, however the power is implemented, due process requires that it not be invoked indiscriminately. At a minimum, a particular scheme for protection of the mentally ill must rest upon a legislative determination that it is compatible with the best interests of the affected class and that its members are unable to act for themselves. Moreover, the use of alternative forms of protection may be motivated by different considerations, and the justifications for one may not be invoked to rationalize another.

However, the existence of some due process limitations on the *parens patriae* power does not justify the further conclusion that it may be exercised to confine a mentally ill person only if the purpose of the confinement is treatment. Despite many recent advances in medical knowledge, it remains a stubborn fact that there are many forms of mental illness which are not understood, some which are untreatable in the sense that no effective therapy has yet been discovered for them, and that rates of "cure" are generally low. There can be little responsible debate regarding "the uncertainty of diagnosis in this field and the tentativeness of professional judgment." Similarly, as previously observed, it is universally recognized as fundamental to effective therapy that the patient acknowledge his illness and cooperate with those attempting to give treatment; yet the failure of a large proportion of mentally ill persons to do so is a common phenomenon. It may be that some persons in either of these categories,[6] and there may be others, are

---

6. Indeed, respondent may have shared both of these characteristics. His illness, paranoid schizophrenia, is notoriously unsusceptible to treatment, see Livermore, Malmquist, & Meehl, On the Justifications for Civil Commitment, 117 U.Pa.L.Rev. 75, 93, and n. 52 (1968), and the reports of the Florida State Hospital staff which were introduced into evidence expressed the view that he was unwilling to acknowledge his illness and was generally uncooperative.

unable to function in society and will suffer real harm to themselves unless provided with care in a sheltered environment. At the very least, I am not able to say that a state legislature is powerless to make that kind of judgment.

* * *

STATE EX REL. HAWKS v. LAZARO

Supreme Court of West Virginia, 1974.
157 W.Va. 417, 202 S.E.2d 109.

* * *

There is persuasive evidence that the alleged improvement in treatment in modern state facilities from medieval times to our own is more myth than reality, and that at the current low level of sociological and psychological knowledge, combined with the current parsimonious level of governmental support for state institutions, the state and its officers have a limited therapeutic role and a predominantly custodial role.

In recognition of the conditions which exist at state institutions, numerous courts have recently required the state to demonstrate a reasonable relationship between the alleged harm which a person is likely to do to himself and the treatment designed to ameliorate the illness which may cause that harm. [T]he ancient doctrine of *parens patriae* is in full retreat on all fronts except in those very narrow areas where the state can demonstrate, as a matter of fact, that its care and custody is superior to any available alternative. Therefore, in determining whether there is any justification under the doctrine of *parens patriae* for deviation from established due process standards, it is appropriate for this Court to consider that the State of West Virginia offers to those unfortunates who are incarcerated in mental institutions Dickensian squalor of unconscionable magnitudes.

In 1970 West Virginia spent $7.19 per day per patient in public mental hospitals, thus ranking 49th among the states. * * * The dry facts concerning financial support are hardly as persuasive as the narrative description of the physical conditions reported by members of the West Virginia Legislature in 1972.

> "The Committee was thoroughly disgusted at the deplorable conditions existing at this facility. Dirt and filth and foul odors were everywhere. Daily housekeeping and routine maintenance were not being performed. There was a need for screens, flies were swarming and garbage cans were uncovered and overflowing. While the hospital could undoubtably (sic) use additional housekeeping and maintenance people, the present personnel have become dilatory in their work. . . .

> "Security is a problem at several state hospitals, but is particularly acute at Weston. . . . There were 91 elopements from the hospital in 1971 and 35 during 1972 up to the time of inspection.

"At the time of inspection, the Committee observed patients administering drugs to patients...."

The parsimonious level of financial support is again reflected in the rate of rehabilitation of mental patients. In 1972–73 the average length of stay for involuntarily committed resident patients in West Virginia mental institutions was 15.91 years, and as of June 30, 1973, of 1,873 involuntarily committed patients, 1,119 patients had been institutionalized for over ten years. In West Virginia as of 1969, only 9.8 percent of total rehabilitations achieved in federal-state programs were rehabilitated mental illness clients, which ranked West Virginia 45th among the states in this category. Recent research demonstrates that institutionalization is frequently the worst treatment which can be provided a person suffering from mental problems. All of these statistics and observations give persuasive support to the following observations of Albert Deutsch, which suggest that the hospitalization of the mentally ill under current conditions may inflict positive harm on the patients:

"The enormous disability associated with mental illness is, to a large extent, superimposed, preventable, and treatable.... Disability is superimposed by rejection mechanism stemming from cultural attitudes.... Hospitalization as such is an important cause of disability.... The best treatment-minded state hospitals perform a disabling function.

"We can no longer tolerate the paradox of depriving mental patients of their civil rights in the name of hospital treatment when we know that it is not only unnecessary for security but harmful to potential recovery...."

* * *

For the foregoing reasons, we hold unconstitutional the standard enunciated in Code, 27–5–4(2), as amended, which permits involuntary hospitalization if the individual:

"(2) Is in need of custody, care or treatment in a hospital and, because of his illness or retardation lacks sufficient insight or capacity to make responsible decisions with respect to his hospitalization...."

* * *

Society abounds with persons who should be hospitalized, either for gallbladder surgery, back operations, corrective orthopedic surgery, or other reasons; yet, in these areas society would not contemplate involuntary hospitalization for treatment. As Code, 27–5–4, as amended, permits incarceration, due process as developed with regard to criminal statutes mandates that the grounds for incarceration be stated with specificity. The standard of hospitalization for the benefit of the individual leaves an entirely subjective determination for the committing authority which violates due process because it forecloses a meaningful appeal and places the individual in jeopardy of losing his freedom without providing an objective standard against which the committing authority's determination can be measured.

* * *

Modern welfare programs, community mental health facilities and private social service agencies have eliminated the problems of actual starvation and persecution of the mentally disturbed which were prevalent in the latter half of the Nineteenth Century. Accordingly, it is possible for many nonviolent people, even those who suffer from a mental disease or retardation to such an extent that they are unable to earn a living, to live outside of an institution, and when these people prefer to do so, regardless of the wisdom of their decision, or the strength of their reasoning powers, the constitution guarantees them the right to follow their own desires.

Notwithstanding the invalidity of Code, 27–5–4(2), as amended, we hold that Code, 27–5–4(1), as amended, does establish reasonable and definite criteria for involuntary hospitalization when it permits the State to hospitalize an individual if:

> "(1) Because of his illness or retardation [he] is likely to injure himself or others if allowed to remain at liberty...."

Society is entitled to protect itself against predatory acts on the part of anti-social people, regardless of the cause of their anti-social actions. Therefore, if the State can prove that an individual is likely to injure others if left at liberty, it may hospitalize him. The State is also entitled to prevent a person from injuring himself in the very specific sense of doing physical damage to himself, either actively or passively. Therefore, when it can be demonstrated that an individual has a self-destructive urge and will be violent towards himself, or alternatively that he is so mentally retarded or mentally ill that by sheer inactivity he will permit himself to die either of starvation or lack of care, then the State is entitled to hospitalize him. The State would also be permitted, under the Constitution, to hospitalize a person who suffers from a mental illness or retardation which is likely to produce some form of injury other than direct physical injury, if the type of injury were definitely ascertainable, and if the State had a treatment program which it could be demonstrated offered a reasonable likelihood of ameliorating the illness or condition.

Questions and Comments

1. *The meaning of* Donaldson. As presented to the Supreme Court, *Donaldson* was in part a "right to treatment" case. The Fifth Circuit Court of Appeals had decided that all civilly committed patients are entitled to treatment. Clearly, the Supreme Court avoided deciding this issue; what is not clear is what the Court did establish. The key sentence in *Donaldson* is usually thought to be the following: "In short, a State cannot constitutionally confine without more a nondangerous individual who is capable of surviving safely in freedom by himself or with the help of willing and responsible family members or friends." From the rest of the opinion, are

you able to discern the conditions under which a person might be considered incapable "of surviving safely"? Does the incapacity have to be the result of mental illness, or can it merely result from physical, financial or motivational limitations? Does use of the phrase "surviving *safely*" mean that people who can "survive" outside the hospital may nonetheless be committable under certain circumstances? What circumstances? Even if a person is shown to be nondangerous and capable of surviving safely without hospitalization, the Court apparently would permit confinement if "more" than mere confinement is provided. Is the "more" to which the Court refers treatment or, as Chief Justice Burger's concurring opinion contends, is "custodial care" sufficient under some circumstances? If treatment is required, precisely what must the treatment accomplish?

Do you agree with the answers to these questions provided by the West Virginia Supreme Court's opinion in *Lazaro?* If the hospital conditions described in *Lazaro* were substantially improved (as they have been in many states), should those answers change?

2. *Treatment efficacy.* As the preceding material makes clear, crucial to an assessment of the validity of parens patriae commitment is a showing that commitment will confer some benefit on, or at least not harm, the potential patient. Research and practice suggest that to the extent suicide or self-neglect is caused by psychosis or depression, various types of treatment using drugs, electro-convulsive therapy, and behavioral therapies can, by treating the underlying condition, reduce the potential for self-harm (see pp. 25–27 in Chapter One). Additionally, vocational training, "socialization" programs, and simulation of community environments can help people with mental illness learn survival skills even if they have spent long periods of time dependent upon others. George Farkas et al., "Rehabilitation Outcome of Long–Term Hospital Patients Left Behind by Deinstitutionalization," 38 Hosp. & Comm.Psychiat. 864 (1987).

But findings such as these do not establish that involuntary hospitalization is beneficial for all individuals with mental illness. According to Durham & LaFond, who conducted an extensive review of research on the efficacy of various treatment modalities as of 1988:

> [P]sychotherapy and drugs are the treatment of choice for non-dangerous mentally ill patients committed involuntarily to hospitals for treatment. The best available evidence shows only that, at a very general level, providing these therapies to mentally ill individuals is better than doing nothing at all. However, the vast majority of studies generally focused on patients who were: (1) not seriously ill; (2) not being treated as inpatients in public institutions; (3) seeking treatment voluntarily. Unfortunately, the evidence simply does not establish that these treatment modalities are effective in treating non-dangerous mentally ill patients confined against their will to hospitals. Perhaps as important, outpatient programs have been shown to offer outcomes which are as good or better than hospital-based treatment and at lower cost.

Mary Durham & John LaFond, "A Search for the Missing Premise of Involuntary Therapeutic Commitment: Effective Treatment of the Mentally Ill," 40 Rutgers L.Rev. 303, 356 (1988). With respect to drug therapy, they also point out that the studies have not established when medication will be effective for a *particular* patient, and that "some 40% of all schizophrenics who are discharged from hospitals suffer relapses within two years, even with continued drug treatment (although the number may increase to 80% if drugs are discontinued)." Id. at 347–48. Newer atypical drugs are apparently more effective but not by a substantial margin. See Sheldon Gelman, "Looking Backward: The Twentieth Century Revolutions in Law, Psychiatry and Public Mental Health," 29 Ohio No. U.L. Rev. 531, 541–44 (2003). It should also be noted that people often avoid seeking treatment for fear they will be subjected to involuntary commitment. John Monahan et al., "Mandated Community Treatment: Beyond Outpatient Commitment," Psychiatric Services 1198 (Sept. 2001)(finding that 47% of patients discharged from hospital stated the fear of subsequent commitment caused them to avoid treatment on prior occasions).

The possible harmful effects of involuntary treatment must also be considered. For instance, as developed further at pp. 28–31, virtually all of the drug therapies, including the new atypicals, have side effects, some of them quite potent (seizures, diabetes, permanent brain damage, and even death) and most of them annoying (lethargy, weight gain, tremors, dry mouth, incontinence). Additionally, even assuming the conditions of squalor described in *Lazaro* are eliminated, hospitalization itself may be detrimental. Focusing on suicide prevention, Greenberg makes the following assertions:

> Commitment to a mental institution, especially if involuntary, may create additional problems for the patient without alleviating old ones.... To adopt so drastic a measure as incarceration may be to convey to the prisoner-patient that both "experts" and the court concur in the belief that a suicide is both likely and difficult or impossible to prevent. Precautions taken to prevent a hospitalized patient from killing himself within the institution may further help the patient to construct for himself an identity as someone who is likely to commit suicide. This construction and the sense of hopelessness engendered by commitment proceedings might well increase the suicide rate from what it would have been had a less drastic and dramatic alternative been chosen. Some clinical evidence suggests that this process does take place. One may also plausibly conjecture that the degradation ceremonies attendant on admission to mental institutions, by stripping away the patient's former social identity, denigrating dignity and enhancing or creating feelings of worthlessness in the patient may contribute further to the likelihood of future suicide attempts.

Andrew Greenburg, "Involuntary Psychiatric Commitments to Prevent Suicide," 49 N.Y.U.L.Rev. 227, 257–58 (1974). Cf. Mark Warren et al., "Suicide, Magical Thinking, and Liability," in Decisonmaking in Psychiatry and the Law 189, 193 (Thomas Gutheil et al. eds., 1991)("male psychiatric inpatients are 5 times as likely to kill themselves as men in the general population, while for females the rate is 10 times as high ... One inference that might be drawn from these data is that the ability to kill oneself transcends anyone's ability to prevent it.").

Similarly, as *Lazaro* points out, there is evidence suggesting that hospitalization can accentuate a *non*-suicidal person's difficulties in coping with the demands of living. At least when institutionalization is prolonged, some patients become dependent upon the hospital and lose whatever survival skills they once had. Irving Goffman, Asylum (1961); Mary Durham & John LaFond, "The Empirical Consequences and Policy Implications of Broadening the Statutory Criteria for Civil Commitment," 3 Yale L. & Pol'y Rev. 395, 428–31 (1985).

3. *The harm of no treatment.* Assuming that hospitalization may actually cause some harm to a patient, should it nonetheless be allowed if that harm is less than the harm that would occur if the person were allowed to remain at liberty? Many commentators believe that involuntary treatment, despite its problems, is preferable to no treatment. Dr. Torrey asserts: "A tragic consequence of the efforts of mental health lawyers to make it difficult to hospitalize and treat the mentally ill is that the person's symptoms may irreversibly worsen." E. Fuller Torrey, M.D., Out of the Shadows: Confronting America's Mental Illness Crisis 152 (1997). Stavis states that "[c]ourt attitudes [that are] based on an archaic view of civil commitment as a life long imprisonment ... ignore[] the current reality that government no longer is motivated to hospitalize patients, if at all, for any longer than is absolutely necessary. Indeed, the contemporary problem is obtaining treatment, not refusing its imposition." Paul Stavis, "Foreword: First Annual Symposium on Mental Illness and the Law," 11 Geo. Mason U. Civ. Rts. L. J. 1, 7 (2000). Recall also that people with mental illness who are not hospitalized are often jailed, even when they are not dangerous to others, a process police call "mercy-booking." See pp. 707–09. Finally, consider these comments by Klein, who describes the kind of people who may be neither hospitalized or jailed:

> For example, some depressed people believe they are unworthy of help. There are also paranoids who reject treatment on such grounds as that the psychiatrist 'is a CIA agent who will plant a tape recorder in my head.' And, perhaps most significantly, there are numerous extremely passive people, including many elderly, who simply will not seek treatment on their own. If they are not treated involuntarily—and here I think the concept of "involuntariness" is largely metaphysical—we know by recent experience that many of them will wander aimlessly through our blighted inner cities, subject to a host of dangers.

Joel Klein, "Legal Doctrine at the Crossroads," Mental Health Law Project Summary of Activities 7, 8 (Mar. 1976) (quoted in Hermann, "Barriers to Providing Effective Treatment: A Critique of Revisions in Procedural, Substantive, and Dispositional Criteria in Involuntary Civil Commitment," 39 Vand.L.Rev. 83, 95 n. 63 (1986)).

4. *Predictions of self-harming behavior.* As with police power commitments, parens patriae commitments usually require a prediction of harm—that the person will commit suicide, starve, or otherwise fare poorly without state intervention. Research on our ability to make predictions of suicidal behavior is voluminous; in general the accuracy rate seems to be quite low. See, e.g., Mark Reinecke & Rogina Franklin–Scott, "Assessment of Suicide: Beck's Scales for Assessing Mood and Suicidality," in Assessment, Treatment and Prevention of Suicidal Behavior (Robert Yufit & David Lester eds., 2005) (there is no empirically validated cut-off score on depression measures for predicting suicide, due in large part to the low base rate for suicide and

the dynamic nature of suicide risk); Alex D. Pokorny, "Prediction of Suicide in Psychiatric Patients: A Prospective Study," 40 Arch. Gen. Psychiatry 249, 257 (1983)("we do not possess any item of information or any combination of items that permit us to identify to a useful degree the particular persons who will commit suicide, in spite of the fact that we do have scores of items available, each of which is significantly related to suicide."). However, as with violence-proneness prediction research, studies of predictive validity in this area are usually compromised by the fact that once such a prediction is made, intervention takes place, thereby presumably reducing the potential for harm. Research on the other types of predictions required for parens patriae commitment is not as well developed. See generally, Stephen Morse, "Crazy Behavior, Morals and Science: An Analysis of Mental Health Law," 51 S.Cal.L.Rev. 527, 596 n. 133 (1978).

5. *Revisiting the incapacity-as-threshold requirement.* Assume that the state can establish by clear and convincing evidence that a particular individual is more likely than not unable to survive "safely" outside the hospital and that short-term treatment or custodial care in a hospital would enable him to do so. Should it also have to show—as traditional theory has posited and we have assumed up to now—that the person is "incompetent" to make a decision about the advisability of hospitalization in order to justify involuntary commitment under the parens patriae authority? This type of issue is most starkly raised when the state seeks commitment of a person who has tried to commit suicide for reasons that cannot clearly be labelled "irrational." Consider the following excerpt:

> Obviously, paternalistic measures taken on behalf of a person *with* his or her consent are ordinarily unobjectionable. Furthermore, as the contemporary philosopher Gerald Dworkin has demonstrated in his essay "Paternalism", there are instances where paternalistic interference can be justified by the doctrine of consent even though, at the precise time of the paternalistic intervention, the affected individual might object to the action[.] ... Dworkin ... gives an example:
>
> > [I]t is very difficult for a child to defer gratification for any considerable period of time.... [G]iven the very real and permanent dangers that may befall the child it becomes not only permissible but even a duty of the parent to restrict the child's freedom in various ways. There is however an important moral limitation on the exercise of such parental power which is provided by the notion of the child eventually coming to see the correctness of his parent's interventions. Parental paternalism may be thought of as a wager by the parent on the child's subsequent recognition of the wisdom of the restrictions. There is an emphasis on what could be called future-oriented consent—on what the child will come to welcome, rather than on what he does welcome.
>
> "Future-oriented" consent, while used in the above example to justify interference with a legally incompetent subject, need not necessarily be restricted to instances of incompetency. Persons who attempt suicide are by no means always mentally incompetent at the time of the attempt. Of the competent ones, some may have rationally wanted to die, while others, though perhaps sincere in their desire to die, may have

been 'wrong.' If all persons who attempted suicide were somehow saved by society's suicide prevention efforts, the saved persons would presumably have differing reactions concerning society's paternalistic efforts. The incompetent ones, if and when they regained competency, might well appreciate society's efforts, as might those who were competent but "wrong" about their decision to die. Only those who were competent and arguably rational about their attempted suicide (for instance, terminally ill persons, etc.) might strongly object to society's "benevolent" action in saving them.

If we wanted to be philosophically pure in our paternalistic suicide prevention efforts—and if we were practically equipped to make the necessary subtle distinctions—we might well let the competent but 'correct' persons die, but might save the others in the expectation of receiving their future consent. Surely, if future consent were to be actually given, we would doubtless feel justified in our earlier paternalistic invasions. And because we cannot in practice determine at the critical time of rescue which persons would give future consent to the rescue efforts and which would not, we feel justified in saving them all, presumably on the assumption—and this is an empirical matter—that not an insubstantial number would be belatedly appreciative.

David Wexler, Mental Health Law: Major Issues 45–7 (1981). Cf. Choron, Suicide 50 (1972) (citing several studies from different countries in which 90% to 100% of rescued suicide attempters reported they were glad they had been saved); Robert Rubinstein et al., "On Attempted Suicide," 79 A.M.A. Archives Neurol. & Psychiat. 103, 111 (1958) ("[W]e have come to regard attempted suicide not as an effort to die but rather as a communication to others in an effort to improve one's life.").

Do you agree with Wexler's suggestion that the degree of incompetency is irrelevant when deciding whether to commit potential suicides? Should this reasoning be extended to those who are not suicidal but merely have trouble subsisting? Cf. William Gardner et al., "Patients' Revisions of Their Beliefs About the Need for Hospitalization," 156 Am. J. Psychiatry 1385 (1999)("[m]ore than 50 percent of the reinterviewed patients who had initially said they did not need to be hospitalized said that now, in retrospect, they believed that they did need hospitalization when they were interviewed at follow-up").

Perhaps of relevance is language from the U.S. Supreme Court's decision in *Cruzan v. Director, Missouri Dept. of Health*, 497 U.S. 261, 110 S.Ct. 2841, 111 L.Ed.2d 224 (1990), which held that a state may require "clear and convincing evidence" that a person who is now in a "persistent vegetative state" had previously expressed a wish, while competent, to have life-sustaining treatment withdrawn. In the course of reaching this conclusion, the Court stated:

Missouri relies on its interest in the protection and preservation of human life, and there can be no gainsaying this interest. As a general matter, the States—indeed, all civilized nations—demonstrate their commitment to life by treating homicide as serious crime. Moreover, the majority of States in this country have laws imposing criminal penalties on one who assists another to commit suicide. We do not think a State is required to remain neutral [even] in the face of an informed and voluntary decision by a physically-able adult to starve to death.

See also, *Washington v. Glucksberg*, 521 U.S. 702, 117 S.Ct. 2258, 2269, 2271, 138 L.Ed.2d 772 (1997)(considering "whether the 'liberty' specially protected by the Due Process Clause includes a right to commit suicide which itself includes a right to assistance in doing so," and finding that the latter is not a "fundamental right").

2. *Implementing the Parens Patriae Authority*

MAYOCK v. MARTIN

Supreme Court of Connecticut, 1968.
157 Conn. 56, 245 A.2d 574, cert. denied 393 U.S.
1111, 89 S.Ct. 924, 21 L.Ed.2d 808 (1969).

RYAN, ASSOCIATE JUSTICE. In this application for a writ of habeas corpus, the plaintiff claims that his confinement in the Norwich State Hospital is illegal because his present mental condition does not require, nor does it legally justify, his involuntary confinement or custodial care. From the judgment dismissing the writ, the plaintiff has appealed.

The few corrections to which the plaintiff has shown himself entitled are incorporated in the following statement of facts found by the trial court: The plaintiff was first confined to the Norwich State Hospital in October, 1943, and was released in January, 1944. On July 23, 1944, the plaintiff removed his right eye and was recommitted but was released subsequently for a probationary period. On July 20, 1947, the last day of the probationary period, the plaintiff, after examination by a staff physician, was unconditionally discharged from the hospital. Three days later, on July 23, 1947, the plaintiff removed his right hand. Shortly thereafter, he was again committed to the state hospital, where he is still confined. The plaintiff runs the newsstand in the hospital's administration building, where he sells newspapers and magazines to employees and to patients of the hospital. In this operation, he has been entrusted with the handling of financial matters. He has been placed in charge of a recreation center for parole-privileged patients which is operated by a committee of patients for group-recreational activity on weekends and which also serves coffee and performs other functions for patients. He believes sincerely that he is a prophet or revelator with a divine message. He believes in God and in doing what God wants us to do on earth. He also believes that society is trying to establish world peace by force but that God's way is by a brotherhood which seeks through the commandment of God to make people love one another; that world peace and brotherhood will be established by a certain church of God which the Old Testament refers to as being established by God in the latter days in the Holy Mountain; that, if the world continues in the present direction, many lives will be lost and that he has a responsibility in this matter; that he has a key role to fulfil in establishing world peace through the revelation and disclosure of the divine message; that he was not born into the country without a reason and that he was not born left-handed without a reason; that God has intended that one man shall be called to make a peace offering to God; that it is far better for one man to believe and accept an appropriate message from God to sacrifice an eye or a hand according to the sacred scriptures rather than for the present course of the world to cause even greater loss of human life; that the removal of his eye in July, 1944, was an offer of thanks to God for a revelation which he received and that it was God's command that he remove it; that the removal of his right hand in July, 1947, was an offering to God as a covenant between God and him as the person selected; that in each of these acts he has complied properly with sacred scripture; and that he is the one man called upon by God to make such spiritual sacrifices. The plaintiff has a strong belief in the Bible. Although he does not plan to cut off either of his feet or any other part of his body, he admits that he would cut off his foot either as a freewill offering or in response to a revelation from the Lord. The plaintiff wants to be released from the hospital so that he can better express his divine message to our people and our policy makers.

The court also found as facts the following: When the plaintiff first entered the state hospital on October 2, 1943, his mental condition was diagnosed as dementia praecox, paranoid type, and this continued to be the diagnosis to the time of trial. This condition is manifested by what psychiatrists term the plaintiff's false beliefs regarding his role as a prophet, his divine message and the meaning of sacred scripture. These beliefs and the fact that he acted upon them by the removal of his eye and the amputation of his hand are the only factors which entered into the diagnosis that the plaintiff is mentally ill. Such beliefs were held by the plaintiff not only before these incidents but ever since then. Because of his persistent false beliefs without any observable improvement, it is expected that these beliefs will remain for a foreseeable period of time, and the possibility of a further self-injurious act cannot be ruled out. Although the possibility of suicide is ruled out, there is a possibility that the plaintiff might receive further communications from God and might respond by removing a foot. The mere medical diagnosis of dementia praecox, paranoid type, would not in itself require the plaintiff's confinement in a hospital for the mentally ill. In the opinion of the psychiatrist from the staff of the state hospital, the plaintiff is not dangerous to anyone other than himself. He has not done any self-injurious act in twenty years. The plaintiff's mental condition has remained about the same since 1947, but there is no evidence of gross worsening of this condition. The fact that the plaintiff currently needs further confinement in a hospital for the mentally ill is based on the opinion of the psychiatrist that there is a possibility that the plaintiff might cut off his right foot. The plaintiff's religious beliefs are considered by the psychiatrist as "grandiose" and "grossly false" and represent a fantasy which is one of the primary symptoms of schizophrenic reaction, paranoid type. The plaintiff's removal of his right eye in 1944 and his right hand in 1947 were not the manifestations of a religious belief but indications of a mental illness. The mental illness from which the plaintiff suffered in

1947 still persists, and he is currently in need of further confinement in a hospital for the mentally ill.

* * *

The plaintiff's basic claim is that he is being illegally confined because of his religious beliefs in violation of the first and fourteenth amendments to the United States constitution and of article first, §§ 3 and 20, of the Connecticut constitution. He urges that he is not likely to injure any other person; that, at the very worst, the state is concerned with a mere possibility that he will remove a foot; and that even if he did remove a foot, there is no evidence that the removal would prevent him from leading a useful and productive life. * * * A "mentally ill person" includes "each person afflicted by mental disease to such extent that he requires care and treatment for his own welfare or the welfare of others or of the community." General Statutes § 17–176. The claim of the plaintiff that he is being confined solely because of his religious beliefs is not supported by the finding. It is common knowledge that the mental illness of many persons is associated with apparently fervent religious beliefs. The court found, on the basis of expert psychiatric evaluation, that the incidents wherein the plaintiff removed his eye and his hand were not manifestations of a religious belief but were symptoms of mental illness which continued to exist to the date of trial.

* * *

Although the psychiatrist who examined the plaintiff had never heard of anyone else having a religious belief which caused the believer to do this kind of damage to himself, and the trial court so found, the plaintiff insists that his confinement discriminates against him because of his religious belief. "The First Amendment declares that Congress shall make no law respecting an establishment of religion or prohibiting the free exercise thereof. * * * No one would contest the proposition that a State may not, by statute, wholly deny the right to preach or to disseminate religious views. Plainly such a previous and absolute restraint would violate the terms of the guarantee. It is equally clear that a State may * * * safeguard the peace, good order and comfort of the community, without unconstitutionally invading the liberties protected by the Fourteenth Amendment." Cantwell v. State of Connecticut, 310 U.S. 296, 303, 60 S.Ct. 900, 903, 84 L.Ed. 1213.

The conclusions of the trial court that the continued confinement for treatment of the plaintiff in accordance with statute is not illegal and that there has been no infringement of the rights accorded him by the constitution of the United States and the constitution of Connecticut cannot be disturbed.

There is no error.

SHEA, ACTING JUSTICE (dissenting).

The opinion of the psychiatrist that there is a possibility that the plaintiff might cut off his right foot is the sole basis for the conclusion that further confinement of the plaintiff is needed. The finding states also that "the plaintiff is not dangerous to anyone other than himself, and the latter danger is not a definite thing, in that it is only a possibility in the plaintiff's mind." . . .

To warrant a conclusion under the statute that the welfare of the plaintiff requires continued treatment in a mental institution, the risk of self-inflicted mayhem on his part ought to be substantially greater than for normal citizens engaged in the many hazardous pursuits of modern life. Perhaps the subordinate facts found, relating to acts performed by the plaintiff twenty years ago, would support such an inference, if it had been drawn by the trial court. A court of review, however, is limited to the finding, and here it is explicitly stated that the need for confinement is based solely on the possibility that the plaintiff may harm himself upon release.

As between the possibility that the plaintiff may amputate his foot and the certainty that, under this judgment, he must remain incarcerated against his will indefinitely, I choose the former.[g]

Accordingly, I dissent.

BOGGS v. N.Y. CITY HEALTH & HOSP. CORP.

Supreme Court, Appellate Division, First Department, 1987.
132 A.D.2d 340, 523 N.Y.S.2d 71.

* * *

Ms. Billie Boggs (Ms. Boggs) is a forty year old woman, whose real name is Ms. Joyce Brown. She chooses to use the name Ms. Billie Boggs, since she admires a television personality of that name, and she desires to thwart her family's efforts to locate her. For the past year, Ms. Boggs has lived on the public sidewalk in front of a restaurant, located on 65th Street and Second Avenue, in New York County, and she has used this location as her bedroom, toilet and living room.

Over the course of the subject year, Ms. Boggs has been observed on an almost daily basis by persons affiliated with Project Help, which is an emergency psychiatric service for allegedly mentally ill homeless persons, who live on the streets in New York City. The personnel of this organization are comprised of a clinical team of psychiatrists, nurses and social workers, who travel around New York City, for the purpose of identifying persons, who live in the street, and who appear to be

g. According to Frances, "The Border-line Self–Mutilator: Introduction," 29 Comp.Psychiat. 259 (1987), "of all disturbing patient behaviors, self-mutilation is the most difficult for clinicians to understand and treat.... Many times an otherwise promising treatment reaches a stalemate or ends because of the inability of the patient and the clinician to manage the self-mutilation in a fashion that will reduce or elimi-

nate it." Another article states: "With the possible exception of patients who are severely mentally retarded or who have diseases with an overwhelming biological component, deviant self-mutilation is best thought of as a purposeful, if morbid, act of self-help." Favazza, "Why Patients Mutilate Themselves," 40 Hosp. & Comm.Psychiat. 137, 143 (1989). [Footnote by eds.]

particularly in need of immediate psychiatric hospital treatment, due to the fact that those persons appear to be in danger of doing serious harm to themselves or others.

On October 28, 1987, Dr. Lincoln Robert Asher Hess, who is a psychiatrist with Project Help, determined, after a number of observations of Ms. Boggs, at her location on the pavement, that Ms. Boggs was severely mentally ill, and that she needed *immediate hospitalization,* since she posed a danger of serious harm to herself. Thereafter, Project Help arranged for Ms. Boggs' transportation, against her will, to Bellevue Hospital (Bellevue), pursuant to § 9.39 of the Mental Hygiene Law (MHL). In pertinent part, subdivision (a) of § 9.39 of the MHL authorizes a hospital to receive and retain as a patient, for a period of fifteen days, any person "alleged to have a mental illness for which immediate observation, care, and treatment in a hospital is appropriate and which is likely to result in serious harm to ... [herself] or others ..." [material in brackets added].

* * *

On October 30, 1987, a hearing was conducted, and both the petitioner and respondents presented evidence.

* * *

The respondents presented their case first, in opposition to Ms. Boggs' release.

* * *

On direct examination, Dr. Hess, after his qualification as an expert by the Court, testified, that he works as a psychiatrist with Project Help three days a week; in the course of his duties with Project Help, he first saw Ms. Boggs in the street on July 23, 1987; on that occasion, he approached her, with the knowledge that Ms. Boggs had exhibited hostility to Project Help's staff in the past; he observed that Ms. Boggs was dressed in disheveled clothing; although, it was not raining, Ms. Boggs was twirling an open umbrella to avoid eye contact with him and the persons passing by; at that time, Dr. Hess heard Ms. Boggs speaking in rhymes, and, according to the witness, the content of these rhymes was sexual, and related to Dr. Hess' and Ms. Boggs' genitals; in the witness' professional opinion this type of verbalization is referred to as "Clanging", and is indicative of a thought disorder, in which a person transfers their thinking from one thought to another without any logical sequence.

The second time Dr. Hess observed Ms. Boggs in the street was five days later, on July 28, 1987. Since the first time that he had seen her, Dr. Hess testified, in substance, that Ms. Boggs' clothing had become more disheveled, dirty and torn, and she was barefoot. When Dr. Hess attempted to speak to Ms. Boggs, she cursed him, flipped open her skirt and exposed her nude buttocks, and made references to his genitals. In

Dr. Hess' professional opinion, on July 28th, Ms. Boggs appeared to be flat and disordered, which he testified is characteristic of schizophrenia.

Dr. Hess made his third street observation of Ms. Boggs on September 22, 1987. As before, Dr. Hess found Ms. Boggs at the same location, which was the sidewalk at Second Avenue near 65th Street. In pertinent part, Dr. Hess testified that Ms. Boggs' clothes were even dirtier than before, and torn to the point that large portions of her torso were exposed, and her clothing was inadequate for the weather; her hair was matted; he noticed the smell of urine and feces emanating from her; he saw pieces of United States currency, which had been torn up in neat pieces stuck to the sidewalk near Ms. Boggs, upon which she appeared to have urinated; Ms. Boggs cursed and shouted obscenities at him; nevertheless, Ms. Boggs did accept food from him, after first refusing it, but, after accepting same, she then threw the contents of this lunch at Dr. Hess, and chased him around the corner. On this occasion of September 22nd, Dr. Hess evaluated Ms. Boggs as having angry, threatening, and intensely hostile feelings, and "again there was a sign of throatiness in the sense there was no modulation . . .".

In evaluating Ms. Boggs, Dr. Hess considered his personal observations, her history, and information he received from other Project Help members, such as psychiatrists, nurses and social workers. As a result of this data, Dr. Hess was of the opinion that Ms. Boggs exhibited a deteriorating psychosis and a deteriorating ability to care for herself. For example, he had received information that Ms. Boggs had run out into the traffic to throw away warm clothing that she had received from personnel representing Project Help.

Finally, on October 28th, Dr. Hess observed Ms. Boggs lying at her location with her head resting on a cardboard box. She smelled strongly of feces, and Dr. Hess again saw torn currency stuck to the pavement and stained by urine. The currency was very neatly torn and urinated upon, and Dr. Hess testified that this was a ritualistic tearing, which suggested magical thinking or delusion. She said repeatedly to Dr. Hess, "What is my name?", which is also indicative of a thought disorder.

* * *

Ms. Putnam was a psychiatric social worker, who had been the coordinator of Project Help for five years and she was qualified by the Court as an expert psychiatric social worker. [A]ccording to Ms. Putnam, as Project Help observed Ms. Boggs, over the course of the year, her behavior changed for the worse. In the winter of 1986–87, Ms. Boggs appeared to be passive, but by the Spring, Ms. Boggs became more aggressive.

On May 8th, 1987, Ms. Putnam personally observed an incident, involving Ms. Boggs' hostile reaction to some delivery men, who were across the street from her location. These men were gathered outside a restaurant, apparently making a delivery. Suddenly, according to Ms. Putnam, Ms. Boggs began screaming racial epithets at these men, calling them f . . . . . n . . . . . , b . . . . . s . . . . . "shouting at them to get away from her, and cursing at them. As a result of this incident, Ms. Putnam became concerned that Ms. Boggs might be assaulted, due to her provocative behavior, and Ms. Putnam perceived that Ms. Boggs might have delusions regarding black men, whom she believed treated her as a prostitute. Also, Ms. Putnam reported her May 8th, 1987 observation about Ms. Boggs' reaction to the delivery men, to Project Help psychiatrists."

* * *

The next witness, for the respondents, was Dr. Mahon, who was Ms. Boggs' treating psychiatrist at respondent Bellevue. Before testifying, Dr. Mahon was qualified by the Court as an expert in psychiatry.

* * *

Dr. Mahon, . . . first saw Ms. Boggs on October 29th; at that time, Dr. Mahon did not speak with Ms. Boggs, since Ms. Boggs' was hostile, angry, and used threatening gestures; verbally, Ms. Boggs was obscene and loud. Thereafter, Dr. Mahon, saw Ms. Boggs on October 30th; and, on that date, Ms. Boggs appeared to be less angry and Dr. Mahon spent about 30 minutes with her. [T]he third time Dr. Mahon saw Ms. Boggs was on October 31st. Dr. Mahon noted that on each encounter, Ms. Boggs and Dr. Mahon established more of a relationship.

Finally, on November 2nd, the morning of the Hearing, Dr. Mahon saw Ms. Boggs again, and found her to be bright, verbal and oriented, as to time and place. Furthermore, that morning, Ms. Boggs was more cooperative than ever, even allowing Dr. Mahon to ask her to interpret certain proverbs.

In her diagnosis, Dr. Mahon found Ms. Boggs to be a chronic schizophrenic, axis one, paranoid type. Moreover, Dr. Mahon stated that Ms. Boggs' mental condition had improved during her hospitalization at Bellevue, and that it was very common for a patient like Ms. Boggs to stabilize in a structured setting. Furthermore, Dr. Mahon thought that some of Ms. Boggs' improvement may have been due to a dose of medication, "Heloperidol", which she received when she was first admitted to the hospital.

* * *

[T]he Court asked if Ms. Boggs' mental status could change markedly in three weeks, from the time Ms. Boggs was seen at Metropolitan Hospital, until she was admitted to Bellevue. Dr. Mahon answered that question, in substance, as follows:

"I think Miss Boggs shows remarkable ability, as is not uncommon with some psychiatric patients, to adapt and to regroup and organize herself temporarily in settings such [as] psychiatric emergency rooms, such as the inpatient service here at Bellevue and appear to be very rational and appear not to have any severe psychosis.

"However, as a psychiatrist what I have to do is make sure I evaluate not only what I am seeing now and on a daily basis with Miss Boggs, but look at the history, and running in front of traffic and saying she has a right to endanger her life is suicidal and as a psychiatrist, I have to call that suicidal behavior and I have to treat it as a clinician . . .". [material in brackets added]

* * *

Ms. Boggs, the petitioner, then presented her case.

* * *

One psychiatrist who testified for Ms. Boggs was Dr. Gould, who was a professor of psychiatry at New York Medical College, and an attending psychiatrist at Metropolitan Hospital. Respondents stipulated that he is an expert in psychiatry.

In substance, on direct examination, Dr. Gould testified, as follows: four days after Ms. Boggs was admitted to Bellevue, on November 1st, 1987, he first examined Ms. Boggs, and found her to be "warm and open, spoke without any pressure spontaneously, coherently, logically, without any tangential thinking . . ."; he had never seen Ms. Boggs on the street; he found no suicidal or homicidal ideation and no delusions or hallucinations concerning Ms. Boggs; and, upon this basis he concluded that Ms. Boggs was not psychotic.

Furthermore, Dr. Gould noted that Ms. Boggs' judgment "was the only thing that was slightly impaired in a sense that she was not aware socially of the kind of troubles ensue from her behavior. [Her] insight was somewhat impaired along the same lines, but by no means nil . . ." In the witness' professional opinion, Ms. Boggs is not schizophrenic; he discussed with Ms. Boggs the incidents reported by other doctors, and, that she explained her reasons for her actions; he indicated that Ms. Boggs has no delusions about money, rather, he explained, that when someone threw paper money at Ms. Boggs and she found it insulting or degrading, she would destroy it; with respect to her urinating and defecating on the street, the witness thought that it was not delusional because Ms. Boggs, according to him, had no alternative; he did not believe Ms. Boggs was either suicidal or dangerous to herself; when Ms. Boggs ran in front of traffic, the witness testified "there was no indication, in my questioning her about this, that she was interested in having herself killed . . ."; he further noted "the fact that she has never been hurt and she's never hurt herself is strong indication that she has very good survival skills"; he believed Ms. Boggs' verbal abuse of others presented no danger, since he explained that Ms. Boggs simply did not wish to be disturbed by some individuals who invaded her privacy and she cursed at them to go away; he stated that Ms. Boggs was congenial to those people she liked, even though he had never observed her in the street; when asked if her verbal response to those she disliked presented a danger, the witness responded "I think that comes under the old cliche of sticks and stones may break my bones, but words can never hurt me.

That is all she's ever done, being verbally abusive ...''; he rejected the testimony of respondents' experts that a paranoid schizophrenic could stabilize within a few days of an involuntary admission to a hospital; in fact, in his opinion, rather than stabilized, he believed that Ms. Boggs would become more angry; he indicated that, in his opinion, the small amount of medication Ms. Boggs had been given could not account for the change in her behavior following her admission to Bellevue; with respect to predictions of future dangerousness, he found them suspect, in view of the fact that to diagnose someone who is suicidal, there must be a history of severe depression and usually suicide attempts; with respect to violent behavior towards others, it would be necessary, in his opinion, to show violence in the past, "that she may have been carrying weapons or using weapons at times ...''; he found no evidence of deterioration in Ms. Boggs mental or physical condition; he believed she provided for herself quite well, by eating every day from a nearby deli; and he found that her only deterioration was in the state of her clothing.

* * *

Ms. Boggs testified in her own behalf. She lives next to a restaurant on Second Avenue, between 65th and 66th Streets and she stays at that location, since there is a hot air vent, although she lived on the streets during the winter of 1986, she indicated that she had never been cold; she panhandles money for food, and, in that fashion, she makes between eight and ten dollars a day; she needs allegedly about seven dollars a day to buy her food; she admitted to urinating and defecating on the street, she denied defecating on herself or in her clothes; ... she admitted ... that she did defecate and urinate in her clothes; she claims she has adequate clothes, and that when she needed more she had "friends" who would supply them to her; she used profanity in order to make the staff of Project Help go away; she claims that her umbrella serves the purpose of protecting her from the sun; she claimed that she had never run in traffic, but, on one occasion, when Project Help tried to offer her a pair of slacks, she stepped between two cars and threw the slacks into the street; she destroys paper money, if it is thrown at her or given to her in an allegedly offensive manner; she has no delusions about black persons giving her money for sex; and, she never hurt anyone on the street or threatened anyone, and no one ever threatened her for using profanity.

Furthermore, Ms. Boggs testified that she would go back to the streets, if released.

* * *

It is well-established in this State that a person may be involuntarily confined for care and treatment, where his or her mental illness manifests itself in neglect or refusal to care for themselves to such an extent that there is presented "serious harm" to their own well-being....

* * *

We find that the Hearing Court erred in placing "great weight on the demeanor, behavior and testimony" of Ms. Boggs, since the Hearing Court does not claim that the demeanor and behavior of Ms. Boggs, when she appeared before it, remotely resembled the demeanor and behavior she exhibited when she lived on the streets, and was involuntarily committed to Bellevue on October 28, 1987.

It is hardly surprising that the Hearing Court stated, "Throughout her testimony, . . . [Ms. Boggs] was rational, logical, coherent. Her use of English, both in syntox (sic) and vocabulary, is very good and bespeaks an educated, intelligent person. She displayed a sense of humor, pride, a fierce independence of spirit, quick mental reflexes . . .", in view of the fact that, when Ms. Boggs was in the courtroom, she had recently been bathed, was dressed in clean clothes, and had just received approximately a week of hospital treatment.

* * *

We reject, as against the weight of the evidence, the Hearing court's conclusion that, in substance, Ms. Boggs' homelessness is not a result of serious mental illness, but, rather, is the result of New York's lack of housing for the poor.

* * *

Accordingly, order, Supreme Court, New York County (Robert D. Lippmann, J.), entered November 12, 1987, which granted the petition of Ms. Billie Boggs, and directed her release from respondent Bellevue Hospital by 6:00 P.M. on November 12, 1987, is reversed, on the law and on the facts, petition is denied and the proceeding is dismissed, without costs.

* * *

MILONAS, JUSTICE (dissenting).

* * *

All of respondents' psychiatrists specifically deny that Brown has suicidal ideation. She has certainly never physically harmed herself, and respondents do not really advance the proposition that she is apt to do so in the future. The record does not show a single instance in which petitioner has ever hurt herself.

* * *

In the end, respondents' effort to institutionalize petitioner can be narrowed down to one claim: she is dangerous to herself because, as a result of her abusive and obscene speech and generally obnoxious behavior, she is likely to provoke others to do injury to her. Respondents contend that Brown has been living on the streets for some time, cursing and shouting and engaging in various bizarre behavior. Yet no one has assaulted her.

* * *

Petitioner's conduct on the street is understandable if we appreciate her obvious pride in her independence and in her ability to survive on her own. She derives a unique sense of success and accomplishment in her street life. In petitioner's words, when poignantly describing her ability to endure on the streets, she has called herself a "professional". Now in the face of petitioner's assessment of herself, and in her own view, Project HELP has been endeavoring to compel her to accept assistance and be dependent. Moreover, on at least five occasions, Project HELP forced her, while handcuffed, to be transported to Metropolitan Hospital, where various physicians always refused to admit her since she was deemed to be not dangerous. In fact, she was taken to Metropolitan Hospital under restraint shortly after both incidents considered significant by respondents—her running into the street and her shouting at the delivery men. Both times she was observed by different doctors while she was at her worst and still determined not to be dangerous to herself or others. Petitioner's explanation for her street conduct is that she has learned that by employing her "profanity" and assorted bag of obnoxious tricks, she was always able to induce Project HELP to retreat.

* * *

It is a tragedy that in our wealthy society so many people have been driven to homelessness, and those of us who are more fortunate must helplessly witness and feel their misery on a daily basis. Regrettably, our affluent, sophisticated and medically advanced society has not developed a more rational, effective and humane way of dealing with the mentally disturbed homeless than in a manner other than what appears to be revolving door mental health—that is, forcibly institutionalize, forcibly medicate, stabilize, discharge back into the same environment, and then repeat the cycle. These ill and unfortunate citizens especially deserve our sympathy since they are not only homeless, but hopeless. Yet, they have shown extraordinary courage, strength and resourcefulness in their ability to survive in conditions where the "normal" person would be unable to endure.

Questions and Comments

1. *Mental illness and parens patriae commitment.* Although incapacity to make treatment decisions has traditionally been thought to be the necessary predicate for parens patriae commitment, only a few states specifically require such a finding; most merely require proof that "mental illness" is causing the self-harming condition. As suggested in the previous materials, there may be theoretical justification for the latter approach. In light of *Mayock* and *Boggs,* do you think an incapacity requirement would make a difference in practice?

2. *Defining the bases for intervention.* A perusal of judicial decisions reveals several separate grounds for intervention under the parens patriae authority. They might be classified generally under two categories: direct physical harm to self and self-neglecting behavior. Under the first category would fall (1) suicide; (2) "self-mayhem", as illustrated by *Mayock;* and (3) harm to self caused by provocation of others (as argued by the state in

Boggs). Self-neglect might be subdivided into (4) an inability to provide for one's survival needs; (5) a present ability to survive, but an inattention to deteriorating mental and physical health; or, most broadly, (6) a need for treatment.

Most state statutes do not explicitly differentiate between these various bases for commitment. For instance, in several states, the only parens patriae ground for commitment is "danger to self." This language clearly encompasses suicidal behavior but is also, as *Boggs* illustrates, often meant to cover other self-harming conduct as well, including at least some versions of self-neglectful behavior. Cf. *Lazaro,* supra. Most other statutes divide parens patriae commitment into two categories: danger to self and inability to care for self. The latter standard is framed in a number of different ways. Many states just use the inability to care language. California permits commitment when a person is "gravely disabled," which is defined to mean "[a] condition in which a person, as a result of a mental disorder, is unable to provide for his basic personal needs for food, clothing, or shelter." Cal.Code § 5008(h)(1). Michigan's statute is more specific, requiring proof that the person "is unable to attend to those of his basic physical needs such as food, clothing, or shelter that must be attended to in order for him to avoid serious harm in the near future, and who has demonstrated that inability by failing to attend to those basic physical needs." Mich.Comp.Laws Ann. § 330.1401(1)(b).

A few states explicitly permit commitment on "potential-for-deterioration" grounds (number (5) above), a standard which has been forcefully recommended by the American Psychiatric Association. The APA's Model Act would permit commitment when the person "will if not treated suffer or continue to suffer severe and abnormal mental, emotional, or physical distress, and this distress is associated with significant impairment of judgement, reason or behavior causing a substantial deterioration of his previous ability to function on his own." Clifford Stromberg & Alan Stone, "A Model State Law on Civil Commitment of the Mentally Ill," 20 Harv.J.Legis. 275, 330 (1983). The APA states that this provision is meant to permit commitment "of severely mentally ill individuals who are moving toward sudden collapse," id. at 305, and that it applies to a group of people "commonly excluded from the mental health system by current legal standards [such as grave disability]." Id. at 304, 335.

Research seems to bear this latter assertion out. In 1979, Washington amended its definition of grave disability to include not only a person with mental illness who "is in danger of harm resulting from a failure to provide for essential human needs of health or safety," but also one who "manifests severe deterioration in routine functioning evidenced by repeated and escalating loss of cognitive or volitional control over his or her actions and [who] is not receiving such care as is essential for his or her health or safety." West's Rev.Code Wash.Ann. 71.05.020(1). A study comparing commitment records for the two years prior to passage of this amendment to the two years after passage found that the amendment had a significant impact on the hospital population. Among its findings were the following:

2) the number of patients committed involuntarily increased significantly, and many patients who had had no previous contact with state

hospitals were committed to psychiatric facilities; 3) these new patients stayed in hospitals longer than other patients and became chronic users of the state mental hospitals; 4) the major state mental hospital became extremely overcrowded and tried unsuccessfully to put a limit on new admissions; 5) voluntary patients were virtually excluded from state hospitals . . .

Mary Durham & John LaFond, "The Empirical Consequences and Policy Implications of Broadening the Statutory Criteria for Civil Commitment, 3 Yale Law & Policy Review, 395, 401 (1985); see also, Tad Hasebe & John McRae," "A Ten–Year Study of Civil Commitments in Washington State," 38 Hosp. & Comm.Psychiat. 983 (1987).

Whether the prevention-of-deterioration standard vastly increases the number hospitalized is open to some dispute, however. Professor Miller's study of eight states, each of which adopted the prevention-of-deterioration standard or in some other way broadened their commitment criteria, found a *decrease* in admissions in at least five of the states after the change. Robert Miller, " 'Need-for-Treatment' Criteria for Involuntary Civil Commitment: Impact in Practice," 149 Am. J.Psych. 1380 (1992). Miller does not conclude, of course, that the broadening of criteria caused the decrease in admissions but rather notes that "[c]hanges in admission and census rates are multidetermined and cannot be simplistically attributed to a single cause, such as changes in commitment criteria." Id. at 1383. The prevention-of-deterioration standard is used most often in connection with *outpatient* commitment, and is discussed in more detail in the materials relating to that issue (see pp. 790–94).

The final variation of parens patriae commitment (number (6) above) is simply a standard which permits involuntary hospitalization if a person needs treatment as a result of mental illness. Although prior to 1970 many statutes used this language, today only one or two do so. See, e.g., N.Y. Men. Hyg. Laws § 9.27(a)(authorizing commitment of a person who is "mentally ill and in need of involuntary care and treatment"). Some commentators, particularly those with a psychiatric background, advocate rejuvenation of this standard. Darold A. Treffert, "The Obviously Ill Patient in Need of Treatment: A Fourth Standard for Civil Commitment," 36 Hosp. and Community Psychiatry 259 (1985).

Under which of these formulations, if any, would Mayock or Brown be committable? The persons described in Cases 2, 19 and 22, on pp. 709–11? Relevant to *Boggs*, consider research which found that the vast majority of the homeless people studied in Los Angeles "would rather live in filth and be subjected to beatings and violence than to be institutionalized, even in our finest mental hospitals." Robert Farr, "A Mental Health Treatment Program for the Mentally Ill in the Los Angeles Skid Row Area," in B. E. Jones, Treating the Homeless 64, 71 (1986).

3. *Vagueness doctrine.* Some courts have held that particular language implementing the parens patriae authority is so vague that it violates the due process clause of the United States Constitution.[h] *Lazaro*, supra, is one

h. Statutory language authorizing state intervention on dangerousness to others grounds has also been challenged on vagueness grounds, see, e.g., Jurek v. Texas, 428

example. Another is *Commonwealth ex rel. Finken v. Roop*, 234 Pa.Super. 155, 339 A.2d 764 (1975), in which the court struck down a Pennsylvania statute which permitted commitment of any person who "is believed to be mentally disabled and in need of care or treatment of such mental disability." The court stated: " 'In need of care' is so broad as to be virtually meaningless. Furthermore, once a finding of mental illness is made, it would be impossible not to find that the individual is in need of care." Is the vagueness doctrine the appropriate vehicle for such a decision? See pp. 734–35. If so, might it not also be used to strike down statutes which permit commitment of those who are "dangerous to self"?

4. *Parens patriae and guardianship.* In several states, procedures exist for appointing a guardian for individuals who are committed for self-neglecting behavior. For instance, in California, a "conservator" may be appointed to make decisions about treatment and other personal matters for anyone who is found to be gravely disabled (but not for those who are committed as suicidal). Cal.Code § 5350. In many jurisdictions, the process may be reversed; that is, a person may be adjudicated incompetent to handle his or her affairs and thus in need of a guardian, who might then seek court authorized institutionalization. Guardianship will be discussed in more detail in Chapter Nine. For present purposes, the following questions about guardianship and its relationship to commitment can be posed. If commitment is under the parens patriae authority, is there some value in having a guardian make the ultimate decisions about treatment or care, rather than the patient or the treatment staff? If so, should a guardian be appointed for every person committed under the parens patriae authority? Or, as is true in California, should a guardian be appointed only for those who fall under certain categories of parens patriae commitment?

5. *Comparing parens patriae and police power commitment.* Setting aside the obvious differences concerning the harms focused upon, provisions implementing the parens patriae and police power authority tend to be consistent. For instance, as already noted, the same definition of mental illness is used in both contexts. Yet arguably the type of mental illness contemplated by each type of commitment is significantly different. Other aspects of the parens patriae and police power perspectives worth comparing are considered below.

The Overt Act and Imminence Requirements. Typically, a state statute which requires a recent overt act and a prediction of imminent danger when defining the police power also does so when defining danger to self; likewise, if these requirements are not present in the definition of danger to others, they are absent when defining danger to self as well. Are the theoretical and practical justifications for the overt act and imminence requirements in police power commitment present when committing someone thought to be suicidal? In this regard, consider that only "one quarter to one half of all completed suicides have a history of prior suicide attempts" and that "the majority of patients who attempt suicide do not go on to commit suicide."

U.S. 262, 96 S.Ct. 2950, 49 L.Ed.2d 929 (1976), but most, if not all, *successful* vagueness challenges of civil commitment statutes have focused on parens patriae provisions.

Robert Hirschfeld & Lucy Davidson, "Clinical Risk Factors for Suicide," 18 Psychiatric Annals 628, 632 (1988).

In connection with the inability to care criterion, most state statutes do not require an overt act in so many words but, as the examples given above illustrate, they do require a showing that the person is unable to provide for basic needs, which may be equivalent. On the other hand, some versions of the deterioration standard (see language from APA Act, supra) do not seem to contemplate any explicit overt act requirement. Professor Wexler argued that this extension of the commitment criterion might actually be countertherapeutic. He noted that "the very process of gathering evidence of a person's committability under a [law which requires specific indicia of inability to care] may operate therapeutically to render commitment unnecessary." In contrast, laws which do not require such indicia may encourage a failure to assert oneself and test one's abilities, thus ultimately creating a dependence upon state institutions. David Wexler, "Grave Disability and Family Therapy: the Therapeutic Potential of Civil Libertarian Commitment Codes," 9 Int'l. J.L. & Psychiat. 39, 54 (1986).

Parens patriae provisions often do not include an imminence requirement either. Is this appropriate? Consider this example from Darold Treffert, "The Practical Limits of Patients' Rights," 5 Psychiat. Annals 4 (1975).

> A 49 year-old woman with anorexia nervosa, admitted to a medical unit in a general hospital because of profound weight loss, steadfastly refused to eat. She presented a life-threatening situation, albeit not an imminent one. This was her response to a family struggle in which she was deeply enmeshed, but she was in good general contact with reality and was not flagrantly psychotic. She refused voluntary psychiatric intervention and, in spite of her frail and deteriorating condition, insisted on leaving the hospital. Her family and physician petitioned the court for psychiatric observation of the patient. The judge believed, however, that the situation lacked dangerousness in an *immediate or imminent sense,* and the patient therefore failed to qualify for involuntary commitment. She was sent home, as she desired, and three weeks later she died from inanition.

[Emphasis in original].

Durational Limitations. Most states also do not differentiate between the length of commitment authorized for police power and parens patriae commitment. California's statute, on the other hand, provides several different durational limits. All patients are subject to an initial 72–hour emergency detention period and a 14 day "intensive treatment" period. But if further commitment is necessary the statute distinguishes between categories. It limits confinement of suicidal individuals to 14 additional days, while authorizing confinement of those considered dangerous to others for up to 180 days (with additional 180–day extensions, if an overt act occurs during confinement). For those who are found to be gravely disabled, after a 30 day investigation period commitment is authorized for up to one year (with continuous one-year extensions permitted). Cal.Code §§ 5260, 5300, 5361.

Overlap. Ultimately, how meaningful is the distinction between the two grounds for intervention when applied to individual cases? Cannot an argument be made that both Mayock and Brown are dangerous to others, at least under the broader definitions of that term? Cannot one say that Nyflot, Sansone and D.R.S. acted in "self-harming" ways? Is there a reason for avoiding such characterizations (perhaps by saying we're only interested in the behavior that is "proximately caused" by mental illness), or should we be willing to classify individuals under both categories if we can possibly do so?

III. THE LEAST RESTRICTIVE ALTERNATIVE DOCTRINE

Whether the basis of state intervention is the police power or parens patriae, almost all state statutes require the committing authority to consider dispositions other than hospitalization in a mental institution. This requirement has come to be known as the least restrictive alternative doctrine. Least restrictive alternative analysis has also played a significant role in two other contexts associated with mental disability law. First, it has been used as a device for regulating treatment imposed on persons *after* they have been committed or otherwise subjected to state intervention. Second, it has been relied upon in asserting that the government has an *obligation to create* community-based services. These second and third variants of the doctrine are considered in Chapter Ten. Here the focus will be on how the least restrictive alternative doctrine regulates the "front-end" dispositional decision made by the committing authority.

LAKE v. CAMERON

United States Court of Appeals, District of Columbia Circuit, 1966.
364 F.2d 657.

BAZELON, CHIEF JUDGE:

Appellant is confined in Saint Elizabeths Hospital as an insane person and appeals from denial of release in habeas corpus. On September 29, 1962, when she was sixty years old, a policeman found her wandering about and took her to the D.C. General Hospital. On October 11, 1962, she filed in the District Court a petition for a writ of habeas corpus. The court transferred her to St. Elizabeths Hospital for observation in connection with pending commitment proceedings, allowed her to amend her petition by naming the Superintendent of Saint Elizabeths as defendant, and on November 2, 1962, dismissed her petition without holding a hearing or requiring a return.

After she filed her appeal from denial of habeas corpus, she was adjudged "of unsound mind" and committed to Saint Elizabeths. At the commitment hearing two psychiatrists testified that she was mentally ill and one of them that she was suffering from a "chronic brain syndrome" associated with aging and "demonstrated very frequently difficulty with her memory * * *. Occasionally, she was unable to tell me where she was or what the date was." Both psychiatrists testified to the effect that she could not care for herself adequately. She did not take a timely appeal from the commitment order. We heard her appeal from the summary dismissal of her petition for habeas corpus and remanded the case to the District Court with directions to require a return and hold a hearing.

At the hearing on remand, the sole psychiatric witness testified that appellant was suffering from a senile brain disease, "chronic brain syndrome, with arteriosclerosis with reaction." The psychiatrist said she was not dangerous to others and would not intentionally harm herself, but was prone to "wandering away and being out exposed at night or any time that she is out." This witness also related that on one occasion she wandered away from the Hospital, was missing for about thirty-two hours, and was brought back after midnight by a police officer who found her wandering in the streets. She had suffered a minor injury which she attributed to being chased by boys. She thought she had been away only a few hours and could not tell where she had been. The psychiatrist also testified that she was "confused and agitated" when first admitted to the Hospital but became "comfortable" after "treatment and medication."

At both the commitment hearing and the habeas corpus hearing on remand, appellant testified that she felt able to be at liberty. At the habeas corpus hearing her husband, who had recently reappeared after a long absence, and her sister said they were eager for her release and would try to provide a home for her. The District Court found that she "is suffering from a mental illness with the diagnosis of chronic brain syndrome associated with cerebral arteriosclerosis"; that she "is in need of care and supervision, and that there is no member of the family able to give the petitioner the necessary care and supervision; and that the family is without sufficient funds to employ a competent person to do so"; that she "is a danger to herself in that she has a tendency to wander about the streets, and is not competent to care for herself." The District Court again denied relief in habeas corpus, but noted appellant's right "to make further application in the event that the patient is in a position to show that there would be some facilities available for her provision." The court thus recognized that she might be entitled to release from Saint Elizabeths if other facilities were available, but required her to carry the burden of showing their availability.

Appellant contends in written and oral argument that remand to the District Court is required for a consideration of suitable alternatives to confinement in Saint Elizabeths Hospital in light of the new District of Columbia Hospitalization of the Mentally Ill Act, which came into effect after the hearing in the District Court. Indeed, her counsel appointed by this court, who had interviewed appellant, made clear in answer to a question from the bench on oral argument that although appellant's formal pro se pleading requests outright release, her real complaint is total confinement in a mental institution; that she would rather be in another institution or hospital, if available, or at home, even though under some form of restraint.

* * *

We are not called upon to consider what action we would have taken in the absence of the new Act, because we think the interest of justice and furtherance of the congressional objective require the application to the pending proceeding of the principles adopted in that Act. It provides that if the court or jury finds that a "person is mentally ill and, because of that illness, is likely to injure himself or other persons if allowed to remain at liberty, the court may order his hospitalization for an indeterminate period, or order any other alternative course of treatment which the court believes will be in the best interests of the person or of the public." D.C.Code § 21–545(b) (Supp. V, 1966). This confirms the view of the Department of Health, Education and Welfare that "the entire spectrum of services should be made available, including outpatient treatment, foster care, halfway houses, day hospitals, nursing homes, etc." The alternative course of treatment or care should be fashioned as the interests of the person and of the public require in the particular case. Deprivations of liberty solely because of dangers to the ill persons themselves should not go beyond what is necessary for their protection.

The court's duty to explore alternatives in such a case as this is related also to the obligation of the state to bear the burden of exploration of possible alternatives an indigent cannot bear. This appellant, as appears from the record, would not be confined in Saint Elizabeths if her family were able to care for her or pay for the care she needs. Though she cannot be given such care as only the wealthy can afford, an earnest effort should be made to review and exhaust available resources of the community in order to provide care reasonably suited to her needs.

At the habeas corpus hearing, the psychiatrist testified that appellant did not need "constant medical supervision," but only "attention"; that the psychiatrist would have no objection if appellant "were in a nursing home, or a place where there would be supervision." At the commitment hearing one psychiatrist testified that "Mrs. Lake needs care, whether it be in the hospital or out of the hospital," and did not specify what, if any, *psychiatric* care she needs. The second psychiatrist testified that she "needs close watching. She could wander off. She could get hurt and she certainly needs someone to see that her body is adequately cared for * * *. [She] needs care and kindness * * *." It does not appear from this testimony that appellant's illness required the complete deprivation of liberty that results from commitment to Saint Elizabeths as a person of "unsound mind."

* * *

We remand the case to the District Court for an inquiry into "other alternative courses of treatment." The court may consider, *e.g.,* whether the appellant and the public would be sufficiently protected if she were required to carry an identification card on her person so that the police or others could take her home if she should wander, or whether she should be required to accept public health nursing care, community mental health and day care services, foster care, home health aide services, or whether available welfare payments might finance adequate private care. Every effort should be made to find a course of treatment which appellant might be willing to accept.

* * *

We express no opinion on questions that would arise if on remand the court should find no available alternative to confinement in Saint Elizabeths.

* * *

Remanded for further proceedings in accordance with this opinion.

[The concurring opinion of J. Skelly Wright is omitted.]

BURGER, CIRCUIT JUDGE, with whom DANAHER and TAMM, CIRCUIT JUDGES, join (dissenting).

We disagree with remanding the case to require the District Court to carry out an investigation of alternatives for which Appellant has never indicated any desire. The only issue before us is the legality of Mrs. Lake's confinement in Saint Elizabeths Hospital and the only relief she herself has requested is immediate unconditional release. The majority does not intimate that Appellant's present confinement as a patient at Saint Elizabeths Hospital is illegal, or that there is anything wrong with it except that she does not like it and wishes to get out of any confinement. Nevertheless, this Court now orders the District Court to perform functions normally reserved to social agencies by commanding search for a judicially approved course of treatment or custodial care for this mentally ill person who is plainly unable to care for herself. Neither this Court nor the District Court is equipped to carry out the broad geriatric inquiry proposed or to resolve the social and economic issues involved.

* * *

If Appellant were to receive precisely the same care she is presently receiving in the geriatrics ward of St. Elizabeths at an institution elsewhere with a name like Columbia Rest Haven, it does not appear that there would be much disagreement over the propriety of her confinement. However, a person's freedom is no less arrested, nor is the effect on him significantly different, if he is confined in a rest home with a euphemistic name rather than at St. Elizabeths Hospital.

* * *

We can all agree in principle that a series of graded institutions with various kinds of homes for the aged and infirm would be a happier solution to the problem than confining harmless senile ladies in St. Elizabeths Hospital with approximately 8000 patients, maintained at a great public expense. But it would be a piece of unmitigated folly to turn this appellant loose on the streets with or without an identity tag; and I am sure for my part that no District Judge will order such a solution. This city is hardly a safe place for able-bodied men, to say nothing of an infirm, senile, and disoriented woman to wander about with no protection except an identity tag advising police where to take her. The record shows that in her past wanderings she has been molested, and should she be allowed to wander again all of her problems might well be rendered moot either by natural causes or violence. . . .

Questions and Comments

1. *The constitutional status of the least restrictive alternative doctrine.* The court in *Lake* based its holding on an interpretation of the District of Columbia's commitment statute. Still unresolved, at least by the United States Supreme Court, is whether the least restrictive alternative doctrine has constitutional status. As a theoretical matter, limiting state intervention to that necessary to achieve the government's objective might seem an important goal; indeed, the Supreme Court has applied this idea in a number of individual cases, most notably those involving the first amendment. In *Shelton v. Tucker*, 364 U.S. 479, 81 S.Ct. 247, 5 L.Ed.2d 231 (1960), the most widely cited case of this type, the Court stated:

> In a series of decisions this Court has held that, even though the governmental purpose be legitimate and substantial, that purpose cannot be pursued by means that broadly stifle fundamental personal liberties when the end can be more narrowly achieved. The breadth of legislative abridgement must be viewed in light of less drastic means for achieving the same basic purpose.

Id. at 488, 81 S.Ct. at 252. But the Court has been unwilling to adopt the "least drastic means" principle as a mandatory aspect of judicial review in any area of the law. See generally, David Chambers, "Alternatives to Civil Commitment of the Mentally Ill: Practical Guides and Constitutional Imperatives," 70 Mich.L.Rev. 1107, 1146–1151 (1972).

This ambivalence toward less drastic means analysis has carried over into civil commitment. In *Sanchez v. New Mexico,* 396 U.S. 276, 90 S.Ct. 588, 24 L.Ed.2d 469 (1970), the Supreme Court dismissed "for want of a substantial federal question" a New Mexico supreme court decision rejecting the argument that *Shelton* and other cases required the committing authority to consider alternatives to hospitalization. However, in *O'Connor v. Donaldson,* supra, the Court cited *Shelton* in support of the following statement: "[W]hile the State may arguably confine a person to save him from harm, incarceration is rarely if ever a necessary condition for raising the living standards of those capable of surviving safely in freedom, on their own or with the help of family or friends." In a more recent case, *Youngberg v. Romeo,* 457 U.S. 307, 321, 102 S.Ct. 2452, 2461, 73 L.Ed.2d 28 (1982), the Supreme Court had occasion to consider the minimal conditions that the due process clause requires the state to provide to hospitalized mental patients. There it expressly adopted the following statement made by a judge in the lower court:

> [T]he Constitution only requires that the courts make certain that professional judgment in fact was exercised. It is not appropriate for the courts to specify which of several professionally acceptable choices should have been made.

While *Youngberg,* which is discussed in detail in Chapter Ten, did not directly address the constitutionality of the least restrictive alternative doctrine, some courts have relied on this language in questioning whether the doctrine is constitutionally required. Other lower courts, however, have held that *Youngberg* does not foreclose such a finding. See generally, Jan Costello & James Preis, "Beyond Least Restrictive Alternative: A Constitutional Right to Treatment for Disabled Persons in the Community," 20 Loyola L.A.L.Rev. 1527, 1545–52 (1987). Finally, in *Heller v. Doe*, 509 U.S. 312, 330, 113 S.Ct. 2637, 2648, 125 L.Ed.2d 257 (1993), the Court held, in connection with commitment *procedures*, that "as long as [the state] 'rationally advances a reasonable and identifiable governmental objective, we must disregard' the existence of alternative methods of furthering the objectives 'that we, as individuals, might have preferred.' "

For the purpose at issue here—that is, evaluating the impact of the doctrine on the dispositional decision made by the committing authority— the constitutional status of the doctrine may not be an important issue. At least forty-seven states require that involuntary patients be committed to treatment in the least restrictive setting. Ingo Keilitz et al., "Least Restrictive Treatment of Involuntary Patients: Translating Concepts Into Practice," 29 St. Louis Univ.L.Rev. 691, 708 (1985).

2. *The meaning of the doctrine.* As Hoffman and Foust point out, in Browning Hoffman & Lawrence Foust, "Least Restrictive Treatment of the Mentally Ill: A Doctrine in Search of Its Senses," 14 San Diego L.Rev. 1100, 1139–43 (1977), neither the purpose of the least restrictive alternative doctrine nor the manner in which it is supposed to operate are clear.

> The [least restrictive alternative] doctrine's current conceptualization and application to the involuntary treatment of the mentally ill . . . raises serious questions about its implementation, definition and fundamental purpose. As applied at the outset of the commitment process, for example, the least restrictive alternative concept makes little practical sense. Virtually all jurisdictions relying upon mandatory application of the doctrine prior to court-ordered hospitalization foresee this application as an additional safeguard to prevent unnecessarily coercive treatment. It is as if no one prior to the commitment hearing had examined or even entertained the possibility of alternatives to hospitalization. But in the majority of cases this is patently absurd. Civil commitment proceedings more often *follow* trials of less restrictive alternatives than trigger them. The competent clinician treating a patient as an outpatient, for example, tries to avoid hospitalization until virtually no other alternative offers sufficient therapeutic promise or safety for the patient and others. Family members and friends of the patient also seek alternatives to involuntary hospitalization even if for no other reason than to avoid the personal discomfort and stigma of formal commitment proceedings. The unworkability of less restrictive alternatives, and not the failure to consider them, ultimately leads to most commitment proceedings. It is little wonder, therefore, that many judges . . . believe the requirement to find less restrictive alternatives inappropriate before ordering involuntary hospitalization to be a mere formality.

> Even assuming a serious judicial interest in less restrictive alternatives, current statutory construction of the doctrine does not designate who will search for or assess the relative merits of less restrictive

treatment alternatives. Moreover, the judiciary's attempts to assign these responsibilities to itself, the state, the clinician, or the patient have failed to achieve meaningful results because these parties have been incapable or unwilling to assume the tasks....

The confusion apparent in the administration of the doctrine is compounded by current legislative and judicial constructions which rely upon simple definitions of its critical elements.... [T]he doctrine's exclusive reliance upon physical restrictiveness is untenable on its face. The psychic intrusiveness of chemical or biological treatments, for instance, which are administered in a variety of therapies may be no less important than the physical aspects of the treatment facility. In addition to the nature of treatment and the setting in which it occurs, the duration of coerced treatment may be relevant to considerations of its restrictiveness.

However slippery its definition of restrictiveness, the doctrine's conceptualization of effectiveness seems even more elusive. Presumably the doctrine contemplates a consensus—medical, legal, and preferably both—about how treatment effectiveness will be measured, and what should be the minimum goals attained by the patient before the state's interest in coerced treatment will no longer prevail. Yet historically, the absence of consensus about the goals of treatment has characterized the endless debates over involuntary treatment of the mentally ill. [Moreover], the clinician is often unable to predict the outcome of a treatment alternative without an adequate trial of that therapeutic option and an empirical assessment of its results.

If there can be no immediate agreement about the goals of treatment, or even about the threshold below which the state will not coerce treatment, perhaps the doctrine would at least presume some relationship between the variables of restrictiveness and treatment effectiveness. Of course, there may be no relationship between these variables, but restrictiveness might vary inversely with effectiveness so that least restrictive treatment provides the least effective care. Finally, a third relationship might exist in which the variables are directly related, rather than inversely, and the most effective treatment is unfortunately also the most restrictive....

This problem arises frequently in decisions to commit patients to the hospital for acute and intensive care in lieu of providing treatment within the community. The acutely psychotic patient, for example, who is out of touch with reality, suffers generally from severe environmental over-stimulation.[118] Literally flooded with confusing sensations and thoughts, these patients frequently benefit from and even request physical isolation or seclusion from other persons to better organize their thoughts and perceptions.[119] Indeed, for these patients, institutions

118. So desperate may be the need of such patients for less, rather than more stimulation, that some authors question whether the normal hospital environment is sufficiently tranquil. See Van Putten, "Milieu Therapy: Contraindications?" 130 Arch. Gen. Psych. 52 (1973).

119. Not only do certain patients seek isolation from others, but they improve with such "treatment." See Goldberg & Rubin, "Recovery of Patients During Periods of Supposed Neglect," 37 Brit. J. Med. Psychiat. 265 (1964).

during the pre-phenothiazine era functioned as true "asylums" for the insane. In the alternative, certain adolescent patients locked in destructive conflicts with their parents or other authorities may consciously or unconsciously seek restrictions on their behavior. A consistent, fair, and even restrictive parent (or parent-substitute) may provide the adolescent with an essential model of human behavior to emulate in later years. To the extent that such goals are thought to be desirable, appropriate treatment may be more restrictive. . . .

Obviously, when effective treatment is also the most restrictive, a balance must be struck between the interests of liberty on the one hand and therapy on the other. Moreover, the balance will be different for individual patients according to their idiosyncrasies. Yet even as a normative statement, the doctrine does not establish a sufficiently precise theoretical basis for making these difficult clinical judgments. Instead, all too often it finds expression in inarticulate statutory construction and simple judicial notions of "need for treatment," and "restrictiveness." . . .

Hoffman and Foust suggest that, at the initial commitment proceeding, the most effective treatment should be sought; the physical restrictiveness of the therapy should be a secondary concern. Only after "the maximum benefits of care have already accrued, or the patient has not responded to the institution and is untreatable in that setting" should "the importance of patient treatability diminish . . . [and] that of treatment restrictiveness emerge. . . ." Id. at 1146. Is the approach suggested by Hoffman and Foust consistent with the premise of the least restrictive alternative doctrine? Does their approach mean that Lake should be institutionalized? How would it apply to Brown in the *Boggs* case (pp. 770–77)?

3. *Effectiveness of community treatment.* As Hoffman and Foust note, whether or not it is the primary consideration, treatment efficacy should presumably at least be considered in deciding between hospitalization and some community alternative, such as a nursing home, a halfway house, or outpatient treatment. Probably the best survey of studies comparing hospital and community treatment is found in Charles Kiesler & Amy Sibulkin, Mental Hospitalization 152–180 (1987). After looking at all the available studies involving random assignment of patients to either hospital or alternative care, these authors concluded that "the most general conclusion one can draw . . . is that alternative care is more effective and less costly than mental hospitalization." Id. at 179. In another summary of basically the same data, Kiesler stated:

It seems quite clear from these studies that for the vast majority of patients now being assigned to inpatient units in mental institutions, care of at least equal impact could be otherwise provided. There is not an instance in this array of studies in which hospitalization had any positive impact on the average patient care investigated in this study. In almost every case, alternative care had more positive outcomes. There were significant and powerful effects on such life-related variables as employment, school attendance, and the like. There were significant and important effects on the probability of subsequent readmission. Not only did the patients in the alternative care not undergo the initial hospitalization but they were less likely to undergo hospitalization later, as well.

Charles Kiesler, "Mental Hospitals and Alternative Care: Noninstitutionalization as Potential Public Policy for Mental Patients," 37 Am.Psychol. 349, 350 (1982).

Other research which looks at the efficacy of community treatment in isolation (that is, without a hospital control group) indirectly confirms these findings, even with those groups, such as the "chronically" mentally ill, which were formerly thought to require constant inpatient care. One review of this second type of research found, for instance, that if a full range of comprehensive community services is provided to such people:

> [h]ospitalization can be virtually eliminated for all but 15% to 25% of these [chronically mentally ill] individuals. Psychotic symptomatology can be dramatically reduced. Client satisfaction with life can be somewhat increased, social functioning can be maintained or restored to pre-morbid levels and in some cases improved. While many of these persons will be unable to sustain normal work and social roles, most will be able to participate in employment and social activities if ongoing supportive or some semi-sheltered environments in these areas are provided.

Mary Ann Test, "Effective Treatment of the Chronically Mentally Ill: What is Necessary", 37 J. Social Issues 71, 82 (1981).

However, as Kiesler and Sibulkin admit, the research consensus that alternative care is more effective than hospital treatment may not apply to *all* potential patients. While they note that most of the studies involved treatment of the severely disabled, they also state that their generalization about the superior quality of community care "may not be true for all disorders, age groups, etc. Insufficient detail is provided in these studies to assess such questions even preliminarily." Id. at 177. Indeed, none of the studies reviewed by Kiesler and Sibulkin appear to involve patients considered imminently dangerous to self or others. Given current perceptions about people with mental disability, it would be difficult, if not impossible, to arrange a study randomly assigning, as all of Kiesler's studies did, half the subjects to community treatment, if the subject population were composed of people who were thought to be on the verge of harming themselves or others.

Assuming that alternative care would be more effective for a particular patient, a second problem with generalizing the research is that many communities lack the types of innovative programs reported in the reviews mentioned above; instead, they offer only mediocre inpatient care in a local facility. This phenomenon, which has been dubbed "*trans*institutionalization," may result in care that is neither more efficacious nor less physically restrictive than care in the hospital. See Leona Bachrach, "Is the Least Restrictive Environment Always the Best? Sociological and Termantic Implications," 31 Hosp.Com.Psychiat. 97 (1980). If the dispositional choice is between a hospital and one of these community inpatient units, is there still an argument to be made in favor of choosing the latter?

4. *Outpatient commitment.* One method of implementing the least restrictive alternative doctrine might be provision for commitment on an

outpatient basis. A typical outpatient commitment might require the patient to report to a community clinic on a weekly basis for medication, therapy or both. In theory, outpatient commitment might also curtail the "revolving door" situation, in which patients are discharged into the community, go off medication, and are recommitted.

Statutes that explicitly authorize outpatient commitment differ significantly, but three general models can be posited. The first—conditional release—permits outpatient commitment only after some form of inpatient commitment, either in a hospital or in the community. Under this model, which is authorized in virtually every state, outpatient commitment functions somewhat like parole; the patient is permitted to leave the hospital so long as he or she continues to follow a certain treatment regimen on an outpatient basis. This approach might be especially useful for those patients who tend to go off their medication. This type of outpatient commitment is discussed more fully at pp. 854–57 in connection with release procedures.

The second model of outpatient commitment, more relevant to the present discussion, authorizes outpatient commitment to a community facility at the "front end" of the commitment process if the traditional commitment criteria are met, without any preliminary requirement of inpatient treatment. Presumably this model is an explicit statutory effort to implement the least restrictive alternative doctrine. At least thirty-seven states have enacted statutes authorizing this type of commitment. Amy Allbright et al., "Outpatient Civil Commitment Laws: An Overview," 26 Men. & Phys. Dis. L. Rep. 179 (2002).

The third model—sometimes called preventive commitment—also permits outpatient commitment at the front end, but under commitment standards which are significantly different from typical "libertarian" commitment standards: they require only a showing that the individual will *soon meet* the traditional standards for institutionalization (and thus are very similar if not identical to the "deterioration" standard described in the previous section, p. 778). Apparently this type of outpatient commitment is a response to a number of factors, including "concerns about . . . a growing number of mentally disordered people in shelters and on the streets, resistant to treatment and in various stages of decompensation, who cannot be hospitalized under the strict commitment criteria; a backlash among psychiatrists and mental health professionals to what is perceived as over-legalization of the mental health system; and advocacy by increasingly vocal parents' groups, particularly the National Alliance for the Mentally Ill, who are demanding treatment for their family members and increasingly allying themselves with mental health professionals to press for the easing of commitment standards." Susan Stefan, "Preventive Commitment: The Concept and Its Pitfalls," 11 Men.Dis.L.Rep. 288 (1987). Perhaps ten states have enacted preventive outpatient commitment statutes. Mark Moran, "Coercion or Caring?," Am Med. News (Apr. 17, 2000).

The implementation of any of these models can present significant obstacles. Professors Schwartz and Costanzo state:

> While outpatient commitment has been an available option in most jurisdictions for many years, several factors have precluded states from relying extensively on what is arguably a more desirable alternative.

These operational barriers include: (1) the lack of appropriate community mental health programs; (2) the difficulty of compelling committed individuals to comply with treatment plans; (3) the probability that few persons would comply with court-ordered treatment and yet be unwilling to voluntarily participate in a community program; (4) the reluctance of mental health providers to treat their clients involuntarily and subject themselves to judicial supervision; (5) the absence of judicial mechanisms and personnel to adequately supervise outpatient care; (6) the resistance of neighbors and public officials to accept committed persons in their community; (7) the fears of professionals concerning liability for inadequate treatment or foreseeable harm; and (8) the potential creation of a governmental obligation to fund a comprehensive system of community services for individuals subject to outpatient commitment.

Steven Schwartz & Cathy Costanzo, "Compelling Treatment in the Community: Distorted Doctrines and Violated Values," 20 Loyola L.A.L.Rev. 1329, 1377 (1987). Consistent with Schwartz and Costanzo's premise that outpatient commitment is rarely used, one survey found that "[t]he available research strongly suggests that the number of individuals likely to be subject to [involuntary outpatient commitment] is relatively small," perhaps 5–10% of those for whom involuntary commitment is considered. Ingo Keilitz, "Empirical Studies of Involuntary Outpatient Civil Commitment: Is It Working?" 14 Men. & Phys. Dis. L. Rep. 368, 370 (1990). Also consistent with their assertions are findings that approximately 50% of those patients who are treated on an outpatient basis stop taking their medication against medical advice. Gerald Kelly, et al., "Utility of the Health Model in Examining Medication Compliance Among Psychiatric Outpatients," 25 Soc. Sci. Med. 1205 (1987); Allen Frances & Peter Weiden, "Promoting Compliance With Outpatient Drug Treatment," 38 Hosp. & Comm. Psych. 1158, 1159 (1987); Stephen Kane, "Prevention and Treatment of Neuroleptic Noncompliance," 16 Psych. Annals 576 (1986).

However, a number of studies also suggest that *intense* outpatient commitment approaches can reduce hospital readmission rates and lengths of stay. The best study of outpatient commitment to date found that, for psychotic individuals, if outpatient commitment is prolonged (180 days or more) and if the level of outpatient services is "high" (with more than 7 encounters a month), readmission rates can be affected significantly. Marvin Swartz et al., "Can Involuntary Outpatient Commitment Reduce Hospital Recidivism?: Findings from a Randomized Trial with Severely Mentally Ill Individuals," 156 Am. J. Psychiatry 1968 (1999). Extended outpatient commitment has also been found to reduce criminal victimization and arrest. Marvin Swartz et al., "Randomized Controlled Trial of Outpatient Commitment in North Carolina," 52 Psychiatric Services 325 (2001). Less clear is whether involuntary outpatient commitment is *needed* to treat the people it targets. See Virginia A. Hiday, "Outpatient Commitment: The State of Empirical Research on Outcomes," 9 Psychol. Pub. Pol'y & L. 8, 23 (2003)("Opponents of outpatient commitment argue that some programs that are designed to be aggressive, comprehensive, and intensive, such as Assertive Community Treatment (ACT) expend mental health resources in manner that works with resistant, severely mentally ill persons and can produce the same positive outcomes without a court order as those seen under outpatient commitment.'').

The legal issues associated with outpatient commitment center around the fact that the patient most likely to be subjected to it is one "who can be maintained in remission with medication but who does not take it voluntarily or consistently." Robert Miller and Paul Fiddleman, "Outpatient Commitment: Treatment in the Least Restrictive Environment?" 35 Hosp. & Comm. Psychiat. 147, 149 (1984). At the time such a person is committed as an outpatient, he or she is not imminently dangerous; the commitment is based on the prediction that the person will deteriorate into dangerousness if medication is not maintained. Under these circumstances, is the second model of outpatient commitment workable? And given the lack of imminent danger (and the likely absence of an overt act) in such situations, is commitment on prevention-of-deterioration grounds (the third model) constitutional? Is a less stringent commitment standard justifiable when the "deprivation of liberty" that occurs is less significant than occurs with full hospitalization? What is the relevance of the finding described above that outpatient commitment generally only "works" if it lasts for more than 180 days and involves multiple contacts? Cf. W. Wood & D. Swanson, "Use of Outpatient Treatment during Civil Commitment: Law and Practice in Nebraska," 41 J. Clinical Psychology 723 (1985)(finding that outpatient commitment in Nebraska lasted an *average* of three years).

In answering these questions, consider *In re Commitment of Dennis H.*, 255 Wis.2d 359, 647 N.W.2d 851 (2002), where the Wisconsin Supreme Court confronted a commitment standard that permitted outpatient *and* inpatient commitment if the state can show that the person is incompetent to make treatment decisions, refuses treatment, and "evidences a substantial probability, as demonstrated by both the individual's treatment history and his or her recent acts or omissions, [of a need for] care or treatment to prevent further disability or deterioration and a substantial probability that he or she will, if left untreated, lack services necessary for his or her health or safety and suffer severe mental, emotional or physical harm that will result in the loss of the individual's ability to function independently in the community or the loss of cognitive or volitional control over his or her thoughts or actions." In upholding this standard, the court declared:

> By permitting intervention before a mentally ill person's condition becomes critical, the legislature has enabled the mental health treatment community to break the cycle associated with incapacity to choose medication or treatment, restore the person to a relatively even keel, prevent serious and potentially catastrophic harm, and ultimately reduce the amount of time spent in an institutional setting. This type of "prophylactic intervention" does not violate substantive due process.

It has also been argued that individuals can be committed on an outpatient basis on a lesser showing than is required for inpatient treatment because, given the fact they will be on the streets rather than in a hospital, those committed on an outpatient basis pose a "higher risk." Rachel A. Scherer, "Toward a Twenty–First Century Civil Commitment Statute: A Legal, Medical, and Policy Analysis of Preventive Outpatient Treatment," 4 Ind. Health L. Rev. 361, 405 (2007). Consider the applicability of outpatient commitment, both preventive and traditional, to Lake, Gregorovich (pp. 728–32) and Brown (pp. 770–77).

5. *Kendra's law and assisted outpatient treatment.* In 1999, Andrew Goldstein, a person suffering from schizophrenia, pushed Ms. Kendra Webdale in front of a subway, killing her. Partly in response to this event, the New York legislature passed "Kendra's Law," which appears to extend the scope of outpatient commitment further than the laws described above. The law authorizes "assisted outpatient treatment" (AOT), a program designed to keep people with mental illness who are in the community in contact with treatment and support services through a comprehensive "case management" system that operates on an indeterminate basis. The law permits intervention for up to six months if, *inter alia*, the person 18 years-old or older (1) "is in need of assisted outpatient treatment in order to prevent a relapse or deterioration which would be likely to result in serious harm to the patient or others" and (2) has a "history" of non-compliance with treatment, as a result of which hospitalization has occurred twice within the last 36 months or violence has occurred within the last 48 months. N.Y. Men. Hyg. Laws § 9.60(c). In contrast to previously described statutes, failure to accept treatment may lead to 72 hours of hospitalization (although further hospitalization requires that the traditional commitment criteria be met). Id. at § 9.60(n).

In *In re K.L.,*1 N.Y.3d 362, 774 N.Y.S.2d 472, 806 N.E.2d 480 (2004), the New York Supreme Court upheld the constitutionality of the law against substantive and procedural due process challenges. Among other findings it rejected the argument that the law's failure to require proof that the patient lacked capacity to make treatment decisions (which the Wisconsin law described in note 4 above requires) made it unconstitutional:

> Since Mental Hygiene Law § 9.60 does not permit forced medical treatment, a showing of incapacity is not required. . . . The restriction on a patient's freedom effected by a court order authorizing assisted outpatient treatment is minimal, inasmuch as the coercive force of the order lies solely in the compulsion generally felt by law-abiding citizens to comply with court directives. For although the Legislature has determined that the existence of such an order and its attendant supervision increases the likelihood of voluntary compliance with necessary treatment, a violation of the order, standing alone, ultimately carries no sanction. Rather, the violation, when coupled with a failure of efforts to solicit the assisted outpatient's compliance, simply triggers heightened scrutiny on the part of the physician, who must then determine whether the patient may be in need of involuntary hospitalization.

> Of course, whenever a physician determines that a patient is in need of involuntary commitment—whether such a determination came to be made after an assisted outpatient failed to comply with treatment or was reached in the absence of any AOT order at all—the patient may be hospitalized only if the standards for such commitment contained in the Mental Hygiene Law are satisfied. These standards themselves satisfy due process. If, however, the noncompliant patient is not found to be in need of hospitalization, the inquiry will be at an end and the patient will

> suffer no adverse consequence. For as the statute explicitly provides, "Failure to comply with an order of assisted outpatient treatment shall not be grounds for involuntary civil commitment or a finding of contempt of court". Moreover, any restriction on an assisted outpatient's liberty interest felt as a result of the legal obligation to comply with an AOT order is far less onerous than the complete deprivation of freedom that might have been necessary if the patient were to be or remain involuntarily committed in lieu of being released on condition of compliance with treatment.

Id. at 484–86. For different views on AOT laws, which now exist in several states, compare Scherer, supra, to Erin O'Connor, "Is Kendra's Law a Keeper? How Kendra's Law Erodes Fundamental Rights of the Mentally Ill," 11 J. Law & Policy 321, 361–62 (2002).

Considerable data have been collected on the operation of Kendra's law. Between 1999 and 2008, 13,260 individuals were referred for evaluation under the law, but only 6,666 AOT orders were issued. Roughly one-third of the individuals under such orders were treated for six months, while the rest had their orders renewed beyond six months and 13% were treated for over 30 months, so that the average treatment period for those individuals released from the program was well over one year. At the six-month mark, medication adherence had increased by 41% statewide, participation in case management services and individual or group therapy had increased by 15%, and among those committed there was a 59% reduction in the incidence of harmful behaviors, a 75% reduction in incarceration rates, a 59% reduction in hospitalization rates, and a 56% reduction in the incidence of homelessness. N.Y. State Office of Mental Health, Kendra's Law: Final Report on the Status of Assisted Outpatient Treatment (2005), available at www.bi.omh. state.ny.us/aot/index/about-aot. Information about post-AOT behavior was not reported.

Interestingly, because Kendra's law focuses on people who are non-compliant, it probably would not have applied to Mr. Goldstein, who had sought treatment for some time prior to the subway incident. In 2001, another person with mental illness pushed an individual in front of a New York City subway; this person too claimed he was "desperate" for treatment, and in any event had not been identified for AOT. In 2002 Peter Troy, suffering from paranoid schizophrenia, shot and killed a priest and a parishioner in the middle of mass on Long Island. His case had been referred for AOT but was never investigated; officials admitted he had "fallen through the cracks." Id. at 365–66.

6. *The Virginia Tech incident.* Another well-known case to consider in this context is that of Sueng–Hui Cho, who killed 32 people and wounded many more at Virginia Tech in April, 2007 in the deadliest school shooting in U.S. history. As recounted in chapter 3 (see pp. 233–40), Cho had been diagnosed with and was treated for a severe anxiety disorder in middle school, and he continued receiving therapy and special education support until his junior year of high school. However, his records were not transferred to Virginia Tech. While in college in 2005, Cho had been accused of stalking two female students and occasionally expressed a desire to kill himself. After a complaint from a female student that Cho had stabbed a

carpet with a knife during a party, Cho was subjected to a screening process by a local Community Services Board (CSB) facility. A social worker found him dangerous to *self* and suffering from a "mood disorder," but an attending physician, who interviewed him for 15 minutes, did not think he was imminently dangerous. Nonetheless, at a hearing a Virginia special justice found him mentally ill and an "imminent danger to self" and ordered unspecified outpatient treatment. After the hearing, the CSB contacted Virginia Tech's counseling service to set up treatment for Cho, but because that service only treats voluntary patients it was up to Cho to decide whether to show up for treatment sessions, which he did not do. Virginia Tech's service did not report Cho's failure to the court or the CSB, perhaps because of the Family Educational Rights and Privacy Act, 20 U.S.C. § 1232g (see pp. 357–60), which only permits disclosure of health records held by an educational institution when there is a specific court order (which arguably did not exist in this case, given the ambiguity of the outpatient commitment order). In the ensuing two years, at least one professor asked Cho to seek counseling and several professors and students noted his reclusiveness and expressions of anger. However, nothing suggested that Cho was incompetent to make treatment decisions, and he had never been hospitalized prior to the shootings. Report on the Virginia Tech Incident to the Governor, Chap IV (Mental Health History of Sueng Hui–Cho) 31–52 (2007).

At the time of the Virginia Tech incident, federal law banned sale of guns to people who had been institutionalized in mental hospitals or declared "mentally defective" (defined as people who have been found mentally ill and dangerous to self or others or incompetent), but the record of Cho's commitment had never been communicated to federal authorities. As a result of Cho's rampage, Congress provided funding to the states for the purpose of ensuring that all people who are the subject of the federal ban are entered into the National Instant Criminal Background Check System. However, federal law still does not require background checks for people buying guns at gun shows. John Cochran, "New Gun Law is Killer's Legacy," ABCNews.com, Jan. 12, 2008. Would Cho have been committable under an AOT law? Can AOT laws or gun laws be reformed to try to prevent these types of occurrences consistent with due process, equal protection, and second amendment principles? Cf. *District of Columbia v. Heller*, ___ U.S. ___, 128 S.Ct. 2783, 2817, 171 L.Ed.2d 637 (2008) (holding that the second amendment guarantees citizens as well as militia a right to bear arms but "should not be taken to cast doubt on longstanding prohibitions on the possession of firearms by felons and the mentally ill.").

IV. PROCEDURES

A. GENERAL CONSIDERATIONS

As recounted at the beginning of this chapter, until the 1970's the civil commitment proceedings of many states were extremely informal. Because they were perceived to be medical rather than legal, commitment decisions were often made by mental health professionals, with little or no input by lawyers and few procedural rules. Today, however, every state requires more legalistic procedures. The model for these reforms has been the criminal justice system, which grants the accused a number of rights, including the right to a public trial in front of a judge and jury, the right to notice of the charges, the rights to an opportunity to confront accusers and subpoena witnesses, the right to the assistance of counsel and the right to remain silent in response to government questions. This section examines the extent to which the criminal process model is an appropriate one for civil commitment; it begins with the first decision to so hold.

LESSARD v. SCHMIDT

United States District Court, E.D.Wisconsin, 1972.
349 F.Supp. 1078.

* * *

[T]he lifting of procedural safeguards in [civil commitment proceedings] appears to rest in part on the realities of better treatment for the person subjected to incarceration in a civil proceeding. In Kent v. United States, the Supreme Court, discussing the issue in the context of juvenile courts, observed:

> "The objectives are to provide measures of guidance and rehabilitation for the child and protection for society, not to fix criminal responsibility, guilt and punishment. The State is *parens patriae* rather than prosecuting attorney and judge. But the admonition to function in a 'parental' relationship is not an invitation to procedural arbitrariness.

> "2. Because the State is supposed to proceed in respect of the child as *parens patriae* and not as adversary, courts have relied on the premise that the proceedings are 'civil' in nature and not criminal, and have asserted that the child cannot complain of the deprivation of important rights available in criminal cases. It has been asserted that he can claim only the fundamental due process right to fair treatment. . . .

> "While there can be no doubt of the original laudable purpose of juvenile courts, studies and critiques in recent years raise serious questions as to *whether actual performance measures well enough against theoretical purpose to make tolerable the immunity of the process from the reach of constitutional guaranties applicable to adults.* There is much evidence that some juvenile courts, . . . lack the personnel, facilities and techniques to perform adequately as representatives of the State in a *parens patriae* capacity, at least with respect to children charged with law violation. There is evidence, in fact, that there may be grounds for concern that the child receives the worst of both worlds: that he gets neither the protections accorded to adults nor the solicitous care and regenerative treatment postulated for children."

(Emphasis added). Few persons familiar with the mental health field will question the applicability of much of the above to persons subjected to involuntary commitment in state institutions.

In any event, the argument in favor of relaxed procedures on the basis of a subsequent right to treatment ignores the fact that unless constitutionally prescribed procedural due process requirements for involuntary commitment are met, no person should be subjected to "treatment" against his will. The argument also ignores the fact that many mental illnesses are untreatable, and the substantial evidence that any lengthy hospitalization, particularly where it is involuntary, may greatly increase the symptoms of mental illness and make adjustment to society more difficult.

* * *

A second justification for less stringent safeguards in civil commitment proceedings is simply that the proceedings are "civil" and not "criminal." That argument should have been laid to rest following the Supreme Court's decision in In re Gault, in which the Court found the distinction unpersuasive as an excuse for providing lesser safeguards for juveniles in delinquency proceedings than were given adults charged with violations of the criminal law.

* * *

Even a brief examination of the effects of civil commitment upon those adjudged mentally ill shows the importance of strict adherence to stringent procedural requirements and the necessity for narrow, precise standards.

An individual committed to a mental institution loses numerous civil rights. In Wisconsin, hospitalization for mental illness, whether by voluntary admission or involuntary commitment, raises a rebuttable presumption of incompetency. The presumption continues as long as the patient is under the jurisdiction of hospital authorities. An individual adjudged mentally ill in Wisconsin also faces restrictions on making contracts and limitations on the right to sue and be sued. Restrictions on licenses required to engage in certain professions also accompany an adjudication of mental illness in Wisconsin. Wis.Stat.Ann. § 441.07 (1972 Supp.) (registered and practical nurses), § 447.07(7) (1972 Supp.) (dentists and dental hygienists), § 256.286 (attorneys). Persons found mentally ill in Wisconsin are, like felons, unable to vote. The mentally ill are also prohibited from driving a car and serving on juries. No person found to be "insane, imbecile, or feeble-minded" may participate in a marriage contract.

It is obvious that the commitment adjudication carries with it an enormous and devastating effect on an individual's civil rights. In some respects, such as the limitation on holding a driver's license, the civil deprivations which follow civil commitment are more serious than the deprivations which accompany a criminal conviction.

In addition to the statutory disabilities associated with an adjudication of mental illness, and just as serious, are the difficulties that the committed individual will face in attempting to adjust to life outside the institution following release. Evidence is plentiful that a former mental patient will encounter serious obstacles in attempting to find a job, sign a lease or buy a house. One commentator, noting that "former mental patients do not get jobs," has insisted that, "[i]n the job market, it is better to be an ex-felon than ex-patient."

In summary, an adjudication of mental illness in Wisconsin carries with it loss of basic civil rights and loss of future opportunities. The damage done is not confined to a small number among the population. * * * It would thus appear that the interests in avoiding civil commitment are at least as high as those of persons accused of criminal offenses. The resulting burden on the state to justify civil commitment must be correspondingly high.

Questions and Comments

1. *Procedural due process analysis.* Two years after *Lessard* the United States Supreme Court formulated what has become the standard analysis for determining how much process is due when a particular government action is contemplated. In *Mathews v. Eldridge,* 424 U.S. 319, 335, 96 S.Ct. 893, 903, 47 L.Ed.2d 18 (1976), involving the administration of social security benefits, the Court outlined three basic factors that must be considered: (1) the private interest that will be affected by the official action; (2) the risk of an erroneous deprivation of such interest through the procedures used, and the probable value, if any, of additional or substitute procedural safeguards; and (3) the government's interest, including the function involved and the fiscal and administrative burdens that the additional or substitute requirements would entail. *Mathews* is usually cited by courts considering the process due in civil commitment cases.

2. *Changes since* Lessard. Although true at the time of *Lessard,* few states today link involuntary hospitalization with incompetency. Most jurisdictions abide by the holding in *Wyatt v. Stickney,* 344 F.Supp. 373 (M.D.Ala. 1972), that "[n]o person shall be deemed incompetent to manage his affairs, to contract, to hold professional or occupational or vehicle operator's licenses, to marry and obtain a divorce, to register and vote, or to make a will *solely* by reason of his admission or commitment to the hospital." Id. at 379. (Emphasis in original). Thus, until the person is adjudicated incompetent and has a guardian appointed, these privileges are not forfeited.[i] In many states, however, the hospitalized person in effect loses the right to refuse treatment; control over personal funds may also be circumscribed to some extent. Samuel Brakel et al., The Mentally Disabled and the Law 258–59 (1985). How do these developments affect the analysis in *Lessard?*

3. *Juvenile justice analogy.* As *Lessard* indicates, presaging the reform of the civil commitment process was an analogous movement in the juvenile justice system. Prior to the mid–1960's, hearings to determine whether a child was "delinquent" (i.e., had committed an act which would be a crime if the child had been an adult) were very informal, often presided over by "judges" who were not legally trained; lawyers were either not present or acted perfunctorily. As with civil commitment, the premise of this system was paternalistic. Intervention by the state was for the purpose of setting

---

i. These issues are addressed further in Chapter Nine.

the child on the right track, not to punish. According to proponents of the system, therefore, delinquency hearings did not need the trappings and procedural rigidity of the adult criminal system.

In a series of decisions between 1966 and 1975, the Supreme Court seriously undermined this position. It revamped procedures for transferring children to adult court in *Kent v. United States,* 383 U.S. 541, 86 S.Ct. 1045, 16 L.Ed.2d 84 (1966), mandated that notice, counsel, confrontation rights and the right to remain silent be provided children alleged to be delinquent in *In re Gault,* 387 U.S. 1, 87 S.Ct. 1428, 18 L.Ed.2d 527 (1967) and, in *In re Winship,* 397 U.S. 358, 90 S.Ct. 1068, 25 L.Ed.2d 368 (1970), held that the reasonable doubt standard of proof applied in such proceedings. The essential rationale of these decisions was the minimal difference between criminal proceedings against adults and delinquency proceedings against children. By 1975, Chief Justice Burger was able to state, in the course of holding that the double jeopardy clause applies to delinquency proceedings, that "it is simply too late in the day to conclude ... that a juvenile is not put in jeopardy at a proceeding whose object is to determine whether he has committed acts that violate a criminal law and whose potential consequences include both the stigma inherent in such a determination and the deprivation of liberty for many years." *Breed v. Jones,* 421 U.S. 519, 95 S.Ct. 1779, 44 L.Ed.2d 346 (1975).

As *Lessard* illustrates, these cases were viewed as precedent for reform-minded courts deliberating on the proper procedures for civil commitment. In particular, note the court's use of *Kent* and *Gault* to rebut the two arguments usually advanced for relaxing procedures in the civil commitment context: the therapeutic goals of civil commitment and its "civil" label. But the comparison between the juvenile system and civil commitment is not necessarily as compelling as *Lessard* suggests. While rehabilitation remains an important goal of juvenile justice, the clear recent trend, triggered in part by the Court's decisions, has been to recognize that dispositions in juvenile delinquency cases have a significant punitive element. See Walter Wadlington et al., Children in the Legal System 198–99 (1983). One consequence of this recognition is that many states have moved away from indeterminate sentences—designed to provide flexibility for juvenile treatment authorities—toward strictly limited dispositions based on culpability. See e.g., the Uniform Juvenile Court Act § 36 (limiting disposition to two years). The explicit punishment orientation of the "new" juvenile court obviously distinguishes it from civil commitment. Should this difference make a difference in terms of procedures used in the two systems? Might the answer to this question depend upon whether the basis for commitment is the police power or parens patriae?

A second point worth considering in trying to draw analogies between the two types of proceedings is that, despite the new punishment orientation of the juvenile system, many policymakers remain ambivalent about imposing adult procedures in their entirety. This ambivalence was evident in the Supreme Court's decision in *McKeiver v. Pennsylvania,* 403 U.S. 528, 91 S.Ct. 1976, 29 L.Ed.2d 647 (1971), which refused to apply the right to jury trial in the juvenile delinquency context. In justifying this decision, the Court stated that applying the right to jury trial would "remake the juvenile proceeding into a fully adversary process and ... put an effective end to what has been the idealistic prospect of an intimate, informal protective proceeding." The jury trial right would not necessarily lead to more accurate factfinding, while it "would tend once again to place the juvenile squarely in the routine of the criminal process" with the attendant "traditional delay, the formality, and the clamor of the adversary system." Imposing the right would also forbid the states "to experiment further and to seek in new and different ways the elusive answers to the problems of the young." The notions suggested by this language in *McKeiver* are worth noting because they resurface in some of the Court's later civil commitment cases.

4. *The impact of reform.* Do criminal-type procedural rules have any effect on outcome? Empirical research on the issue is ambiguous. Some studies show that reforms of both the substantive criteria and procedural rules have reduced hospital admissions. But a number of studies indicate little change in outcome. See e.g., Michael R. Bagby & Leslie Atkinson, "The Effects of Legislative Reform on Civil Commitment Admission Rates: A Critical Analysis," 6 Behav. Sci. & L. 45 (1988)(decline in admissions resulting from reform is short-lived; admission rates reach pre-reform level within a two-year period). Most importantly for purposes of the topic at hand, the research indicates that commitment hearings are usually adversarial in name only even in the most legalistic states.[j]

Representative are the findings of Serena Stier & Kurt Stoebe, in "Involuntary Hospitalization of the Mentally Ill in Iowa: The Failure of the 1975 Legislation," 64 Iowa L.Rev. 1284 (1979). They concluded that, despite being highly "legalized" on paper, the Iowa commitment process was in fact very informal. They found that three-fourths of the referees (judges) and clerks of court admitted that commitment hearings were usually not conducted in an adversary manner. Defense attorneys requested an independent mental health evaluation (available by right under the statute) in fewer than 1% of cases, and they rarely called more than two witnesses (often none). The majority of attorneys failed to put the respondents on the stand. One attorney even reasoned that to do so would risk the respondents persuading the referee that they were not mentally ill. Consistent with their lack of active participation in the hearings, the attorneys uniformly spent less than two hours in preparation of these cases.

For their part, the referees encouraged passivity on the part of defense attorneys. Some referees expressly discouraged cross-examination of witnesses; if questions were to be asked, the referees themselves would ask them. The result was that commitment hearings were little more than a stamp of approval for the attending physician's opinion. In fact, a change in treatment plan from that which the hospital physician had recommended was observed in fewer than 1% of cases. Referees and attorneys generally agreed that clinicians should decide whether the elements of the standard for civil commitment had been met, and, if so, what the conditions of treatment should be.

j. See articles cited in footnotes c and d of this chapter. See also, Virgina Hiday, "Reformed Commitment Procedures: An Empirical Study in the Courtroom," 11 Law Soc'y Rev. 651 (1977); Elliot Andalman & David Chambers, "Effective Counsel for Persons Facing Civil Commitment: A Survey, a Polemic, and a Proposal," 45 Miss. L.J. 43 (1974).

Finally, with respect to the meaningfulness of reform, consider the following excerpt from Samuel Brakel et al., The Mentally Disabled and the Law 27–28 (1985):

The erection of ... legal safeguards [in civil commitment] is based on at least two basic assumptions about "involuntary" commitment: (1) that without the safeguards people who do not belong in mental institutions will be railroaded there and (2) that involuntary commitment is a real contest between parties with opposite interests—the party who applies for institutionalization (the state, the institution, or the family) versus the individual who does not want to be institutionalized. It is the wholesale unreality of these assumptions that threatens to make their implements, the procedural safeguards, inapposite or worse. And once the procedures are enacted, their effects are difficult to avoid: the prospect of being able to apply them with proper selectivity only to those relatively few cases in which they are useful is dim, and the price of such selectivity, as mentioned, is high.

The real nature of the commitment process has been more accurately described by scholars such as Ralph Slovenko, who reports that "[a]pproximately two-thirds of [involuntarily] committed patients are passive, stuporous, or uncommunicative, or in perfect agreement with the physician's recommendation. The others protest initially, but after a few days of hospitalization they have a change of mind."[40] The real problem with institutionalization, according to Slovenko, is not the railroading of unwilling individuals but almost the opposite. In 1971, for example, although around four million Americans received treatment for mental illness in state hospitals, general hospitals, outpatient clinics, and private offices, another two million were turned away because of the lack of treatment personnel to handle them. From this perspective, the legalization and criminalization of civil commitment are an exercise in irrelevance at best. The procedure is dysfunctional—overprotective and overly technical when observed, a block to achieving generally desired results in some cases, mere wasteful and empty ritual in others. But most often, of course, it is simply not followed. Slovenko notes that commitment statutes are ignored for essentially two reasons: "they are overly complicated, and they are for the most part unnecessary."

Psychiatrists have bemoaned their plight of being part of "belegaled" profession. They have a case, and they are not alone in our belegaled society. Slovenko has written derisively of the "junk pile theory" of law: among all the legal garbage that exists to address mental health problems there must be something of use or value. The same intricate legal structure surrounding commitment that is hailed by legal reformers as crowning testimony to the law's concern for the unprotect-

40. There are also patients, however, who come willingly (i.e., voluntarily) to the hospital first but then after a week or two when the worst of their anxiety has passed (though they may still be "ill" and in need of treatment) decide they want out. In a recent medical journal, such patients were described as an identifiable group of "re-volving door type" patients who have slipped into a form of sociopathy that makes them unable to deal either with the freedom of life outside the hospital or with the dependency within it. Geller, The "Revolving Door": A Trap or A Life Style? 33 Hosp. & Community Psychiatry 388 (1982).

ed appears to the psychiatric practitioner and others as an unwieldy, obstructionist mass of procedural "junk" that only inhibits the effort to protect.[k]

5. *The therapeutic effect of adversarial procedures.* A common argument against adversarial procedures, alluded to in the foregoing passage, is that, if they *are* effectively implemented, they will be antitherapeutic. Consider the following summary of such arguments:

[The] belief in the antitherapeutic effect of the civil commitment hearing appears to be almost as old as the institutions into which such involuntary confinement can be made. Reasons suggested in support of this belief include the following.

1. time being lost in the courtroom which can be used to better advantage in treating the prospective patient;

2. revelation in a public setting of embarrassing material, such as hostility toward parents or homosexuality;

3. revelation to the prospective patient of the physician's opinion of a serious diagnosis or poor prognosis;

4. creation of overly optimistic hopes of cure in the patient;

5. confirmation of delusions of persecution, particularly in paranoid types;

6. impairment of the psychiatrist's ability to work due to the impact of directives given by the courts;

7. trauma and exasperation resulting from the length of the hearing;

8. revelation by the therapist of statements made by the patient in sessions, the true significance of which may not yet be apparent;

9. revelation to the prospective patient of opinions of close family members;

10. disclosure of material which the patient justifiably believed was revealed in confidence;

11. rejection of any further attempts at treatment by a patient who refuses to accept suggestion that he is mentally ill;

12. traumatic effect on family members upon hearing testimony concerning their relative.

John Ensminger & Thomas Liguori, in "The Therapeutic Significance of the Civil Commitment Hearing: An Unexplored Potential," 6 J. Psychiat. & L. 5 (1978).

Ensminger and Liguori contest these assertions, arguing on the basis of empirical research and their own experiences in a mental health advocacy

---

k. Actually, a review of psychiatrists' attitudes toward issues related to involuntary civil commitment concluded that a substantial majority of psychiatrists favor the adoption of legal procedures such as a right to notice, counsel, confrontation, and independent experts. Lynn Kahle, et al. "On Unicorns Blocking Commitment Law Reform," 6 J. Psychiat. & L. 89 (1978). [Footnote by eds.]

unit that "the civil commitment process has considerable potential for therapeutic effect." First, they note that the hearing, if properly conducted, represents an open acknowledgement that the patient's hospitalization is involuntary. Without such acknowledgement, they assert, a double message may be conveyed by professionals who act as if they care only about the patient's well-being but nonetheless refuse to let the patient leave and restrict behavior in other ways as well. This conflicting message may be countertherapeutic to the extent the patient feels deceived—his or her response may even be "schizophrenic" if the patient feels unable to comment on the feeling of deception.

Relatedly, the authors assert that the hearing can improve the treatment of the patient and his or her relationship with the treatment staff. They contend that "the introduction of commitment hearings leads to better documentation and earlier staffing for involuntarily committed patients" and that this improvement in preparation "has led to a greater tendency to release patients, when the hospital physicians have that authority, in cases where the case for committability appears to be marginal." They also believe that "the commitment hearing should provide an opportunity for the therapist to clarify his role" and that the therapist's testimony at the hearing "can operate as something close to a reinforcement mechanism." Additionally:

> The members of the hospital staff could analyze the hearing as a group process of considerable significance for the patient.... For instance, the "therapeutic community" concept suggests that crisis resolution should involve (1) a face-to-face confrontation involving all major participants in the crisis situation; (2) occurring as soon as possible after the crisis arises; (3) under skilled neutral leadership; (4) allowing for open communication without fear of reprisal; and (5) with an appropriate level of feeling, neither too little nor too much. The analogies to the commitment process are evident.

Finally, the authors note that the hearing can improve the patient's relationship with the family and assist in understanding that relationship.

> Several of the arguments for the deleterious effect of commitment hearings involve notions of their effect on family relationships—that the patient will be harmed by learning what his relatives think or that they will be disturbed learning about the patient's condition. Neither of these arguments can receive much scientific support. When the patient does not know of the true feelings of his relatives, it will frequently be because they have expressed something else to him. If the hearing exposes this duplicity, it can serve the function of eliminating yet another "double bind" situation. If there is a possibility of embarrassing material being revealed, another reason suggested earlier as to why hearings are harmful, the general public can be excluded to protect the patient and the family members.
>
> Certain trends in psychological research and practice are beginning to view taking into account the family system as vital to the effective treatment of some cases. Indeed, the patient may just be the individual manifesting the most bizarre behavior of a maladaptation of the whole family unit. It is our opinion that the increased acceptance of this

approach must involve radical restructuring of present notions of rights and duties in mental health law, if not also criminal law and jurisprudence generally.

* * *

In some states, notice of the hearing must be given to family members. It has been noted that some judges send patients out of the room while they interrogate the relatives. Aside from the infringement of the defendant's right of confrontation, it is our opinion that this deprives the therapist (who, it is asserted, should not be excluded for such testimony) of an exceptional opportunity to view the family dynamics in action. The hearing may, in fact, provide a mechanism for educating the family as to the needs of a particular member caught in the commitment process. The judge, even though he may not be able to extend his authority to other members of the family, may be able to impress upon them, in a way that doctors cannot, their responsibilities in the matter.

Also relevant to the extent to which procedures are "therapeutic" is research on "procedural justice" which compares two procedural paradigms: the adversarial model (i.e., evidence presentation by openly biased parties) and the inquisitorial model (i.e., evidence investigation by an expert decisionmaker). The classic research on this issue was conducted by John Thibaut and Laurens Walker, reported in Procedural Justice: A Psychological Analysis (1975). Although this research and its progeny have been ambiguous as to which procedural approach produces the most accurate outcomes, it has consistently found that subjects express a preference for adversarial procedures over inquisitorial ones and that the adversarial process is perceived as more fair than the inquisitorial process. Apparently, this is because "the disputants feel they have more control over the outcome of the dispute and because giving them 'voice' in the process accords them status as full-fledged members of society." Joseph Schumacher, et. al. "Procedural Justice Judgments of Alternative Procedures for Resolving Medical Malpractice Claims," paper presented at American Psychological Association Annual Meeting (1991). As a result, disputants in the adversarial mode have greater satisfaction with the outcome and more acceptance of the verdict, even if they lose. Fred Cohen, "Procedural Justice and Participation," 38 Hum.Relations 643, 645 (1985).

Research on the related concept of "coercion" in the civil commitment context has arrived at somewhat more nuanced results. First, whether a person feels coerced is not necessarily linked to the type of procedure (adversarial or inquisitorial) but may depend primarily on the behavior of the participants in the process. As summarized in John Monahan et al., "Coercion in the Provision of Mental Health Services: The MacArthur Studies," 10 Research in Community & Mental Health 13, 26–27 (1999):

> [T]he amount of coercion experienced [by people subjected to civil commitment] is strongly related to a patient's belief about the justice of the process by which he or she was admitted. That is, a patient's beliefs that others acted out of genuine concern, treated the patient respectfully and in good faith, and afforded the patient a chance to tell his or her side of the story, are associated with low levels of experienced coercion.

> This is true for both voluntary and involuntary patients. Patients report that the hospital admission process was characterized by less of this "procedural justice" than their family members or admitting clinicians report.

Second, patients who perceived their admission to be coercive are significantly more likely to react to the admission with sadness, confusion, fright and, in particular, anger, and significantly less likely to respond with pleasure or relief. Henry Steadman et al., "Violence by People Discharged from Acute Psychiatric Inpatient Facilities and by Others in the Same Neighborhoods," 55 Arch. Gen Psych. 1 (1998).

6. *Procedure as surrogate.* In thinking about how much procedure is due in civil commitment proceedings, the following questions, paraphrased from Robert Cover et al., Procedure 133–134 (1988), might be usefully kept in mind. Are your views on the proper level of procedural formality "outcome-driven?" In other words, are you an advocate for more procedural formality because you hope that, under such a regime, fewer people will be committed? Or an opponent because you believe that too many will not be? At a more general level, are you concerned about restraining government power because you have concerns about the likelihood it will be abused? In what sense other than these general outcome measures might increased procedural formality improve the commitment decision? Do you believe it will improve the "accuracy" of the results reached in commitment hearings? Or, believing "accuracy" to be a loaded term, are you more influenced by the degree of participation or "sense of fairness" that various types of procedures produce?

B. EMERGENCY DETENTION AND SCREENING MECHANISMS

The focus of most litigation concerning the process of commitment has been on the procedural accoutrements of the "adjudicatory" commitment hearing, at which a determination is made about long-term commitment. These procedures are examined in the next section. Perhaps more important, however, are the procedures connected with emergency admission, which is the mechanism by which most individuals become enmeshed in the civil commitment system. According to the National Center for State Courts in "Guidelines for Involuntary Civil Commitment," 10 Men.Dis. Law Rep. 409, 427 (1986):

> The greatest activity in involuntary civil commitment proceedings occurs not in the court hearing—inaccurately considered by many to be the centerpiece of involuntary civil commitment—but rather during events before any formal judicial involvement. A person initially may become subject to involuntary civil commitment by one of several ways: by being apprehended by police; by being brought to a hospital by relatives or friends; by being converted from a voluntary patient to an involuntary patient when, after entering a mental health facility voluntarily, the person attempts to leave against the advice of the facility staff; or, finally, by being taken into custody as

a result of a legal petition submitted to and validated by a court.[1] ...
For the most part, [these] persons become involuntary patients by
means of "emergency" commitments resulting from apprehension
by police or by simply appearing on the doorstep of a mental health
facility [not as a result of formal involuntary commitment proceed-
ings].

All states permit, under appropriate circumstances, the emergency
admission of an individual without any prior formal legal hearing. In
California, for instance, either a police officer or a clinician may authorize emergency admission. Cal.Code § 5150. In New York, the decision is
made by a clinician at the admitting facility or by the county director of
mental health. N.Y. Men. Hyg. Law §§ 9.37, 9.39. In Virginia a judge or
magistrate makes the emergency detention decision, but he or she need
not actually see the patient and in fact may make the decision based on
information received over the phone. Va.Code § 37.1–67.1. The standard
of proof to be applied by these decisionmakers is either not stated or
minimal. Neither New York nor Virginia require any particular standard
of proof; California requires that the decisionmaker find that "probable
cause" exists to believe that the person is mentally disordered and, as a
result, gravely disabled or a danger to self or others. Cal.Code § 5150.

The lack of process associated with the initial emergency admission
has rarely been challenged, since most agree that a more formal process
would be counterproductive.[m] A more difficult question has been whether a subsequent "detention" hearing, separate and apart from the
ultimate "adjudicatory" hearing at which committability is decided,
should be held to determine whether the initial admission was appropriate and, if so, how soon and with what procedural requirements. As the
next case indicates, such a preliminary hearing is required in the
criminal process under certain circumstances.

GERSTEIN v. PUGH

Supreme Court of the United States, 1975.
420 U.S. 103, 95 S.Ct. 854, 43 L.Ed.2d 54.

* * *

II

As framed by the proceedings below, this case presents two issues:
whether a person arrested and held for trial on an information is
entitled to a judicial determination of probable cause for detention, and

---

l. This last method of initiating the
commitment process, analogous to an arrest
warrant, is apparently rarely used in any
jurisdiction. [Eds.]

m. One corollary issue which has been
raised has to do with police authority to
arrest people with mental disorder. Under
the common law, the traditional rule was
that a police officer could not, absent a
warrant, arrest someone for a misdemeanor
(as opposed to a felony) unless the officer
witnessed the misdemeanor occurring.
However, at least one court has held that, if
the consequence of the arrest is commitment, this rule need not be followed.
McKinney v. George, 556 F.Supp. 645
(N.D.Ill.1983).

if so, whether the adversary hearing ordered by the District Court and approved by the Court of Appeals is required by the Constitution.

A

Both the standards and procedures for arrest and detention have been derived from the Fourth Amendment and its common-law antecedents. . . . The standard for arrest is probable cause, defined in terms of facts and circumstances "sufficient to warrant a prudent man in believing that the [suspect] had committed or was committing an offense." Beck v. Ohio, 379 U.S. 89, 91, 85 S.Ct. 223, 225, 13 L.Ed.2d 142 (1964). . . . This standard, like those for searches and seizures, represents a necessary accommodation between the individual's right to liberty and the State's duty to control crime. . . .

To implement the Fourth Amendment's protection against unfounded invasions of liberty and privacy, the Court has required that the existence of probable cause be decided by a neutral and detached magistrate whenever possible. The classic statement of this principle appears in Johnson v. United States, 333 U.S. 10, 13–14, 68 S.Ct. 367, 369, 92 L.Ed. 436 (1948):

> "The point of the Fourth Amendment, which often is not grasped by zealous officers, is not that it denies law enforcement the support of the usual inferences which reasonable men draw from evidence. Its protection consists in requiring that those inferences be drawn by a neutral and detached magistrate instead of being judged by the officer engaged in the often competitive enterprise of ferreting out crime."

* * *

Maximum protection of individual rights could be assured by requiring a magistrate's review of the factual justification prior to any arrest, but such a requirement would constitute an intolerable handicap for legitimate law enforcement. Thus, while the Court has expressed a preference for the use of arrest warrants when feasible, . . . it has never invalidated an arrest supported by probable cause solely because the officers failed to secure a warrant. . . .

Under this practical compromise, a policeman's on-the-scene assessment of probable cause provides legal justification for arresting a person suspected of crime, and for a brief period of detention to take the administrative steps incident to arrest. Once the suspect is in custody, however, the reasons that justify dispensing with the magistrate's neutral judgment evaporate. There no longer is any danger that the suspect will escape or commit further crimes while the police submit their evidence to a magistrate. And, while the State's reasons for taking summary action subside, the suspect's need for a neutral determination of probable cause increases significantly. The consequences of prolonged detention may be more serious than the interference occasioned by arrest. Pretrial confinement may imperil the suspect's job, interrupt his source of income, and impair his family relationships.... Even pretrial release may be accompanied by burdensome conditions that effect a significant restraint of liberty. See, e.g., 18 U.S.C. §§ 3146(a)(2), (5). When the stakes are this high, the detached judgment of a neutral magistrate is essential if the Fourth Amendment is to furnish meaningful protection from unfounded interference with liberty. Accordingly, we hold that the Fourth Amendment requires a judicial determination of probable cause as a prerequisite to extended restraint of liberty following arrest.

* * *

B

Under the Florida procedures challenged here, a person arrested without a warrant and charged by information may be jailed or subjected to other restraints pending trial without any opportunity for a probable cause determination. Petitioner defends this practice on the ground that the prosecutor's decision to file an information is itself a determination of probable cause that furnishes sufficient reason to detain a defendant pending trial. Although a conscientious decision that the evidence warrants prosecution affords a measure of protection against unfounded detention, we do not think prosecutorial judgment standing alone meets the requirements of the Fourth Amendment.

* * *

III

Both the District Court and the Court of Appeals held that the determination of probable cause must be accompanied by the full panoply of adversary safeguards—counsel, confrontation, cross-examination, and compulsory process for witnesses.

These adversary safeguards are not essential for the probable cause determination required by the Fourth Amendment. The sole issue is whether there is probable cause for detaining the arrested person pending further proceedings. This issue can be determined reliably without an adversary hearing. The standard is the same as that for arrest. That standard—probable cause to believe the suspect has committed a crime—traditionally has been decided by a magistrate in a nonadversary proceeding on hearsay and written testimony, and the Court has approved these informal modes of proof.

The use of an informal procedure is justified not only by the lesser consequences of a probable cause determination but also by the nature of the determination itself. It does not require the fine resolution of conflicting evidence that a reasonable-doubt or even a preponderance standard demands, and credibility determinations are seldom crucial in deciding whether the evidence supports a reasonable belief in guilt.... This is not to say that confrontation and cross-examination might not enhance the reliability of probable cause determinations in some cases. In most cases, however, their value would be too slight to justify holding, as a matter of constitutional principle, that these formalities and safe-guards designed for trial must also be employed in making the Fourth Amendment determination of probable cause.

* * *

Although we conclude that the Constitution does not require an adversary determination of probable cause, we recognize that state systems of criminal procedure vary widely. ...Whatever procedure a State may adopt, it must provide a fair and reliable determination of probable cause as a condition for any significant pretrial restraint of liberty,[1] and this determination must be made by a judicial officer either before or promptly after arrest.

* * *

Questions and Comments

1. *Applicability of* Gerstein *to commitment.* What implications, if any, does *Gerstein* have for the emergency admission process? Is emergency admission a "seizure" as that word is used in the Fourth Amendment? Should there be a hearing, presided over by a judicial officer, to check the emergency admission decision? Should a showing of probable cause be required? How formal should such a proceeding be in other respects? Should there be a right to be present? The right to an attorney?

Most states require some kind of post-admission check after emergency admission of a person thought to be mentally disabled, but the procedures vary widely. In Virginia, for instance, a hearing presided over by a judge, with the respondent and an attorney for the respondent present, must take place within 48 hours of admission (usually the full-fledged adjudicatory hearing takes place at this time as well). Va.Code § 37.2–814. In California, "certification" must take place within 72 hours, but requires only that two professionals, one of them a physician, sign a notice of certification finding that the person meets the commitment criteria. Once certified, a person may be detained for up to 14 days before a full judicial hearing. Moreover, the patient may be detained for a further 14 days without such a hearing if two professionals find that the patient "threatened or attempted to take his own life or ... was detained for evaluation and treatment because he threatened or attempted to take his own life and ... continues to present an imminent threat of taking his own life." Cal.Code §§ 5250, 5251, 5260, 5261. In New York, the individual may be detained up to 15 days if a mental health professional other than the admitting clinician has examined the person within 48 hours of admission and finds that the individual is mentally ill and dangerous to self or others. N.Y. Men. Hyg. Law § 9.39(a). Confinement for a further *60* days is permitted if two physicians certify that the individual meets the commitment standards and a third physician, at the admitting

---

1. Because the probable cause determination is not a constitutional prerequisite to the charging decision, it is required only for those suspects who suffer restraints on liberty other than the condition that they appear for trial. There are many kinds of pretrial release and many degrees of conditional liberty.... We cannot define specifically those that would require a prior probable cause determination, but the key factor is significant restraint on liberty.

institution, agrees after examining the patient and considering alternatives. N.Y. Men. Hyg. Law §§ 9.33(a). In all states, judicial review (via habeas corpus) is available during the initial detention period, but only upon the patient's request and usually only after some delay (in New York, for instance, review need not take place until five days from the request date). Additionally, in New York, the Mental Hygiene Legal Service, a legal advocacy organization, is located on the grounds of most facilities and monitors the patients who are admitted. N.Y.Men. Hyg. Law § 9.39(a).

2. *Procedural timeframes. Gerstein* does not set any time limits for the criminal probable cause hearing, merely stating that it should be soon after arrest and prior to subjecting the accused to release conditions such as bail. In *Riverside County v. McLaughlin*, 500 U.S. 44, 111 S.Ct. 1661, 114 L.Ed.2d 49 (1991), however, the Supreme Court held that the *"Gerstein* hearing" should normally take place within 48 hours of a warrantless arrest. The time period between the *Gerstein* hearing and trial can vary immensely, limited only by statutory speedy trial provisions (rarely requiring trial less than 100 days from arrest) and the guarantee of a speedy trial in the Sixth Amendment.

In civil commitment, as the foregoing statutory illustrations indicate, the analogous time periods between detention and the detention hearing (if there is one), and between the latter hearing and the adjudicatory hearing also vary significantly, although the latter hearing always occurs much earlier, relatively speaking, than the typical criminal trial. What considerations should govern the duration of these timeframes? In *Lynch v. Baxley*, 386 F.Supp. 378, 388 (M.D.Ala.1974), the court stated:

> Just as emergency detention is justified only until a probable cause hearing can be conducted, temporary detention following a finding of probable cause to believe that confinement is necessary can be justified only for the length of time required to arrange a full hearing on the need for commitment. Due process requires that such hearing be held within a reasonable time following initial detention, but in no event sooner than will permit adequate preparation of the case by counsel or later than thirty (30) days from the date of the initial detention.

The United States Supreme Court is perhaps willing to stretch the pre-hearing periods considerably further. In the 1970's, it summarily affirmed[n] both *French v. Blackburn*, 428 F.Supp. 1351 (M.D.N.C.1977), affirmed 443 U.S. 901, 99 S.Ct. 3091, 61 L.Ed.2d 869 (1979), and *Logan v. Arafeh*, 346 F.Supp. 1265 (D.Conn.1972), affirmed sub nom., *Briggs v. Arafeh*, 411 U.S. 911, 93 S.Ct. 1556, 36 L.Ed.2d 304 (1973). The three-judge district court in *Blackburn* had found a statute permitting a ten-day period between detention and the "probable cause" hearing constitutional. In *Arafeh*, a three-judge court had upheld a statute under which a hearing could be delayed for up to 45 days, so long as a physician certified that the person met the commitment criteria and a "complaint" was filed within fifteen days. Al-

n. A summary affirmance is considered binding precedent. *Hicks v. Miranda*, 422 U.S. 332, 95 S.Ct. 2281, 45 L.Ed.2d 223 (1975). However, "finding the precise limits of a summary affirmance has proven to be no easy task." *Hardwick v. Bowers*, 760 F.2d 1202, 1207 (11th Cir.1985). Without analyzing the ultimate precedential significance of *Blackburn* and *Arafeh,* it is important to note that their weight as precedent is somewhat suspect.

though the Supreme Court did not issue an opinion in connection with its affirmance of these decisions, both lower court opinions relied on the same two grounds, which are concisely summarized by this language from *Blackburn:* "During [the pre-hearing] period the respondent is receiving treatment which may not only aid his health, but which also may be necessary to an adequate and informed hearing on the necessity of his commitment." 428 F.Supp. at 1355. See also, *Arafeh,* 346 F.Supp. at 1268–69.

Are the courts' assumptions accurate about how much time is needed for lawyers and clinicians to develop information relevant to commitment issues? Good clinical practice dictates that decisions about treatment be predicated on careful observation and a trial of treatment. According to a basic psychiatric text, for instance:

> When there is no acute problem (such as severe agitation or life-threatening behavior) that requires use of medication, it is helpful to observe the patient in a drug-free state for several days (or even several weeks) to see how symptoms change over time. This is particularly useful if there is some question about whether medication is likely to be helpful, or when there is confusion about the diagnosis. For example, a patient admitted to the hospital with a psychotic episode might not reveal to you that he has abused drugs. If you immediately administer an antipsychotic, you may erroneously believe that the medication alleviated a psychosis that would have abated of its own accord when the abused substance was cleared from the patient's body. Or an outpatient's depressive symptoms might improve dramatically after one or two meetings with a concerned therapist. If this patient had been given antidepressants immediately, the effect would have been attributed to the medication, and the patient's anxiety might be maintained on the drug unnecessarily. Another patient's anxiety might mask an underlying psychosis. Such a patient could easily be medicated incorrectly with an antianxiety agent before the disordered thinking became apparent.

American Psychiatric Press, Psychiatry for Medical Students (1984). The same source suggests that, before medication is administered, the psychiatrist take a careful history, and perform a routine physical examination and routine laboratory tests to rule out organic causes. Once a patient is on a particular drug, further time is necessary to gauge the patient's response, possible side effects, and the appropriate dosage, a process which can take up to six weeks. Herbert Y. Meltzer & S. Hossein Fatemi, "Treatment of Schizophrenia," in Essentials of Clinical Pharmacology 399, 406 (Alan F. Schatzberg & Charles B. Nemeroff eds., 2001)("Most patients show a near maximal response by 6 weeks of treatment").

3. *Justice Brennan's* Parham *dissent.* In *Parham v. J.R. et al.,* 442 U.S. 584, 99 S.Ct. 2493, 61 L.Ed.2d 101 (1979), the Supreme Court deliberated upon the proper procedural protections for the commitment of juveniles. This decision, reprinted at pp. 907–19, has several possible implications for adult commitment procedures as well, all of which will be explored in this section. Of concern here is Justice Brennan's opinion in *Parham,* concurring in part and dissenting in part, because it suggests still other considerations in deciding whether and when to hold a formal legal hearing. The majority in *Parham* held that juveniles could be admitted initially to a mental

institution based on the authority of their parents and the treating professionals, without benefit of legal counsel; it did not directly address whether the Constitution requires, at some later point in time, more formal procedures to determine whether continuing commitment is justified (although it suggested strongly that it did not). Brennan argued that procedures akin to those provided adults should be required before long-term detention. However, he also stated the following:

> ... While as a general rule due process requires that commitment hearings precede involuntary hospitalization, when parents seek to hospitalize their children special considerations militate in favor of postponement of formal commitment proceedings and against mandatory adversarial preconfinement commitment hearings.
>
> First, the prospect of an adversarial hearing prior to admission might deter parents from seeking needed medical attention for their children. Second, the hearings themselves might delay treatment of children whose home life has become impossible and who require some form of immediate state care. Furthermore, because adversarial hearings at this juncture would necessarily involve direct challenges to parental authority, judgment or veracity, preadmission hearings may well result in pitting the child and his advocate against the parents. This, in turn, might traumatize both parent and child and make the child's eventual return to his family more difficult.
>
> Because of these special considerations I believe that States may legitimately postpone formal commitment proceedings when parents seek in-patient psychiatric treatment for their children. Such children may be admitted, for a limited period, without prior hearing, so long as the admitting psychiatrist first interviews parent and child and concludes that short term in-patient treatment would be appropriate.

442 U.S. at 632–633, 99 S.Ct. at 2519–2520. To what extent is this passage applicable to adult commitment?

4. *Pre-hearing screening.* Beginning in the 1980's, a number of states established, by statute, "screening" organizations at the community level that are charged with referring people with mental disability to the most effective treatment program available. National Center for State Courts, "Guidelines for Involuntary Civil Commitment," 10 Men.Dis.Law Rep. 409, 429–433 (1986). A number of other jurisdictions have set up equivalent systems through local custom. Id. at 429.

In jurisdictions that have institutionalized such programs, the number of people subjected to the involuntary commitment process—including the emergency detention hearing—may be reduced considerably. According to one report, in these localities, "the great majority of persons entering the mental health-judicial system never see the inside of a courthouse, and many persons are screened and diverted to more suitable alternatives, many elect to enter mental health treatment and care programs voluntarily, and some are discharged shortly after arrival at a mental health facility." Id. at 427. For instance, Arizona requires that screening agencies—usually the local community mental health center—complete a "pre-petition screening" within forty-eight hours of initial contact with an individual alleged to be disordered, designed to determine the best possible disposition. Ariz.Stat.

§ 36–529. Although "emergency" cases are specifically exempted from this procedure, it nonetheless appears to have enabled a significant number of individuals who would have been "emergency admissions" under the old system to avoid the involuntary commitment process altogether. In Tucson, about three times as many individuals are diverted through screening—to voluntary care, to halfway houses, and to other social agencies—than proceed through the involuntary petition process. Institute on Mental Disability and the Law, National Center for State Courts, "A Model for the Application of the Least Restrictive Alternative Doctrine in Involuntary Civil Commitment" 291–323 (1984).

Many commentators argue that such pre-hearing diversion is highly beneficial and should be encouraged. For instance, the National Task Force on Guidelines for Involuntary Civil Commitment asserted the following:

> Screening should begin as early as possible in the involuntary civil commitment process in order to avoid unnecessary infringement of liberty, to ensure that persons are guided quickly and effectively toward the placement and treatment indicated by their presenting problems, and to minimize needless waste of limited resources. Initial processing decisions are based not merely on whether the legal criteria for involuntary civil commitment are met. The threshold question may be whether the person who is considered a candidate for involuntary civil commitment is indeed mentally disordered. If so, are there alternative forms of treatment and care, other than involuntary civil commitment? Even if the person is not considered to be mentally disordered, he or she may require social services of some type. Is mandatory hospitalization necessary? Will the person consider seeking mental health treatment voluntarily? Answers to these questions require intervention and decisions long before a candidate for involuntary civil commitment has a judicial hearing.

> Such early intervention may entail no more than a mental health worker answering a telephone call from a distraught individual who is seeking help for a family member. Referral to a community mental health center or a family support group may divert a person who may otherwise become subject to formal involuntary civil commitment proceedings. These early interventions should be based on knowledge of the mental health services delivery in the area and should take into account such factors as the range of treatment and services available, the criteria for admission to various facilities, the security of particular mental health facilities, and the conditions within facilities. Good initial processing decisions also require an understanding of the linkages between the agencies.

Id. at 428.

As this excerpt suggests, in a sense the pre-hearing screening programs function as the procedural facet of the least restrictive alternative doctrine. One possible problem with such programs is that they encourage "voluntary" dispositions which are in fact not voluntary at all. This issue is addressed in detail in the materials on voluntary treatment, at pp. 857–68.

5. *Police use of excessive force.* As noted above, police are often involved in bringing people with mental illness to the attention of the mental health

system. A number of lawsuits have been filed against the police for injuring such people in the course of taking them into custody. For instance, in *Drummond v. City of Anaheim*, 343 F.3d 1052 (9th Cir. 2003), cert. denied, 542 U.S. 918, 124 S.Ct. 2871, 159 L.Ed.2d 775 (2004), police responded to calls on two separate days that a man with a history of mental illness had run out of medication and was hallucinating and paranoid. On the first day they concluded he was not a danger to himself or others, but on the second they decided to take him into custody "for his own safety." When he became agitated, they forced him on the ground, handcuffed him and then placed their knees on his back and neck, even though he told the officers he could not breath. After 20 minutes he lost consciousness, sustained brain damage, and is now in a permanent vegetative state. In *Champion v. Dickhaus*, 380 F.3d 893 (6th Cir. 2004), cert. denied, 544 U.S. 975, 125 S.Ct. 1837, 161 L.Ed.2d 725 (2005), a 32 year-old man with autism brought to a store by his caregiver began to hit himself in the face and bite his hand. The police officer who responded to a 911 call was told he was mentally ill but was not told the man was nonverbal and nonresponsive. When the officer asked the man's name he began hitting and biting himself and approached the officer. When he grabbed her shirt, she sprayed pepper spray to his face. Two other newly arrived officers, both of whom were told the man was mentally ill, then wrestled him to the ground, applied handcuffs and a hobble device that bound his ankles together, then applied pressure to his back and continued to use pepper spray. After several minutes on the ground, the man began to vomit, went into cardiac arrest, and subsequently died. In both cases claims of excessive force were upheld.

C. ADJUDICATORY HEARING PROCEDURES

1. *Standard of Proof*

ADDINGTON v. TEXAS

Supreme Court of the United States, 1979.
441 U.S. 418, 99 S.Ct. 1804, 60 L.Ed.2d 323.

MR. CHIEF JUSTICE BURGER delivered the opinion of the Court.

The question in this case is what standard of proof is required by the Fourteenth Amendment to the Constitution in a civil proceeding brought under state law to commit an individual involuntarily for an indefinite period to a state mental hospital.

* * *

II

The function of a standard of proof, as that concept is embodied in the Due Process Clause and in the realm of factfinding, is to "instruct the factfinder concerning the degree of confidence our society thinks he should have in the correctness of factual conclusions for a particular type of adjudication." The standard serves to allocate the risk of error between the litigants and to indicate the relative importance attached to the ultimate decision.

Generally speaking, the evolution of this area of the law has produced across a continuum three standards or levels of proof for different types of cases. At one end of the spectrum is the typical civil case involving a monetary dispute between private parties. Since society has a minimal concern with the outcome of such private suits, plaintiff's burden of proof is a mere preponderance of the evidence. The litigants thus share the risk of error in roughly equal fashion.

In a criminal case, on the other hand, the interests of the defendant are of such magnitude that historically and without any explicit constitutional requirement they have been protected by standards of proof designed to exclude as nearly as possible the likelihood of an erroneous judgment. In the administration of criminal justice, our society imposes almost the entire risk of error upon itself. This is accomplished by requiring under the Due Process Clause that the state prove the guilt of an accused beyond a reasonable doubt.

The intermediate standard, which usually employs some combination of the words "clear," "cogent," "unequivocal," and "convincing," is less commonly used, but nonetheless "is no stranger to the civil law." One typical use of the standard is in civil cases involving allegations of fraud or some other quasi-criminal wrongdoing by the defendant. The interests at stake in those cases are deemed to be more substantial than mere loss of money and some jurisdictions accordingly reduce the risk to the defendant of having his reputation tarnished erroneously by increasing the plaintiff's burden of proof. Similarly, this Court has used the "clear, unequivocal and convincing" standard of proof to protect particularly important individual interests in various civil cases [*i.e.*, deportation and denaturalization].

Candor suggests that, to a degree, efforts to analyze what lay jurors understand concerning the differences among these three tests on the nuances of a judge's instructions on the law may well be largely an academic exercise; there are no directly relevant empirical studies. Indeed, the ultimate truth as to how the standards of proof affect decisionmaking may well be unknowable, given that factfinding is a process shared by countless thousands of individuals throughout the country. We probably can assume no more than that the difference between a preponderance of the evidence and proof beyond a reasonable doubt probably is better understood than either of them in relation to the intermediate standard of clear and convincing evidence. Nonetheless, even if the particular standard-of-proof catchwords do not always make a great difference in a particular case, adopting a "standard of proof is more than an empty semantic exercise."

III

In considering what standard should govern in a civil commitment proceeding, we must assess both the extent of the individual's interest in not being involuntarily confined indefinitely and the state's interest in committing the emotionally disturbed under a particular standard of proof. Moreover, we must be mindful that the function of legal process is to minimize the risk of erroneous decisions.

A

This Court repeatedly has recognized that civil commitment for any purpose constitutes a significant deprivation of liberty that requires due process protection. Moreover, it is indisputable that involuntary commitment to a mental hospital after a finding of probable dangerousness to self or others can engender adverse social consequences to the individual. Whether we label this phenomena "stigma" or choose to call it something else is less important than that we recognize that it can occur and that it can have a very significant impact on the individual.

The state has a legitimate interest under its *parens patriae* powers in providing care to its citizens who are unable because of emotional disorders to care for themselves; the state also has authority under its police power to protect the community from the dangerous tendencies of some who are mentally ill. Under the Texas Mental Health Code, however, the State has no interest in confining individuals involuntarily if they are not mentally ill or if they do not pose some danger to themselves or others. Since the preponderance standard creates the risk of increasing the number of individuals erroneously committed, it is at least unclear to what extent, if any, the state's interests are furthered by using a preponderance standard in such commitment proceedings.

The expanding concern of society with problems of mental disorders is reflected in the fact that in recent years many states have enacted statutes designed to protect the rights of the mentally ill. However, only one state by statute permits involuntary commitment by a mere preponderance of the evidence, Miss.Code Ann. § 41–21–75 (1978 Supp.), and Texas is the only state where a court has concluded that the preponderance-of-the-evidence standard satisfies due process. We attribute this not to any lack of concern in those states, but rather to a belief that the varying standards tend to produce comparable results. As we noted earlier, however, standards of proof are important for their symbolic meaning as well as for their practical effect.

At one time or another every person exhibits some abnormal behavior which might be perceived by some as symptomatic of a mental or emotional disorder, but which is in fact within a range of conduct that is generally acceptable. Obviously, such behavior is no basis for compelled treatment and surely none for confinement. However, there is the possible risk that a factfinder might decide to commit an individual based solely on a few isolated instances of unusual conduct. Loss of liberty calls for a showing that the individual suffers from something more serious than is demonstrated by idiosyncratic behavior. Increasing the burden of proof is one way to impress the factfinder with the importance of the decision and thereby perhaps to reduce the chances that inappropriate commitments will be ordered.

The individual should not be asked to share equally with society the risk of error when the possible injury to the individual is significantly greater than any possible harm to the state. We conclude that the individual's interest in the outcome of a civil commitment proceeding is of such weight and gravity that due process requires the state to justify confinement by proof more substantial than a mere preponderance of the evidence.

B

Appellant urges the Court to hold that due process requires use of the criminal law's standard of proof—"beyond a reasonable doubt."

* * *

There are significant reasons why different standards of proof are called for in civil commitment proceedings as opposed to criminal prosecutions. In a civil commitment state power is not exercised in a punitive sense. Unlike the delinquency proceeding in *Winship,* a civil commitment proceeding can in no sense be equated to a criminal prosecution.

In addition, the "beyond a reasonable doubt" standard historically has been reserved for criminal cases. This unique standard of proof, not prescribed or defined in the Constitution, is regarded as a critical part of the "moral force of the criminal law," and we should hesitate to apply it too broadly or casually in noncriminal cases.

The heavy standard applied in criminal cases manifests our concern that the risk of error to the individual must be minimized even at the risk that some who are guilty might go free. The full force of that idea does not apply to a civil commitment. It may be true that an erroneous commitment is sometimes as undesirable as an erroneous conviction * * *. However, even though an erroneous confinement should be avoided in the first instance, the layers of professional review and observation of the patient's condition, and the concern of family and friends generally will provide continuous opportunities for an erroneous commitment to be corrected. Moreover, it is not true that the release of a genuinely mentally ill person is no worse for the individual than the failure to convict the guilty. One who is suffering from a debilitating mental illness and in need of treatment is neither wholly at liberty nor free of stigma. It cannot be said, therefore, that it is much better for a mentally ill person to "go free" than for a mentally normal person to be committed.

Finally, the initial inquiry in a civil commitment proceeding is very different from the central issue in either a delinquency proceeding or a criminal prosecution. In the latter cases the basic issue is a straightforward factual question—did the accused commit the act alleged? There may be factual issues to resolve in a commitment proceeding, but the factual aspects represent only the beginning of the inquiry. Whether the individual is mentally ill and dangerous to either himself or others and is in need of confined therapy turns on the *meaning* of the facts which must be interpreted by expert psychiatrists and psychologists. Given the lack of certainty and the fallibility of psychiatric diagnosis, there is a serious question as to whether a state could ever prove beyond a reasonable doubt that an individual is both mentally ill and likely to be dangerous.

The subtleties and nuances of psychiatric diagnosis render certainties virtually beyond reach in most situations. The reasonable-doubt standard of criminal law functions in its realm because there the standard is addressed to specific, knowable facts. Psychiatric diagnosis, in contrast, is to a large extent based on medical "impressions" drawn from subjective analysis and filtered through the experience of the diagnostician. This process often makes it very difficult for the expert physician to offer definite conclusions about any particular patient. Within the medical discipline, the traditional standard for "factfinding" is a "reasonable medical certainty." If a trained psychiatrist has difficulty with the categorical "beyond a reasonable doubt" standard, the untrained lay juror—or indeed even a trained judge—who is required to rely upon expert opinion could be forced by the criminal law standard of proof to reject commitment for many patients desperately in need of institutionalized psychiatric care. Such "freedom" for a mentally ill person would be purchased at a high price.

* * *

That some states have chosen—either legislatively or judicially—to adopt the criminal law standard gives no assurance that the more stringent standard of proof is needed or is even adaptable to the needs of all states. The essence of federalism is that states must be free to develop a variety of solutions to problems and not be forced into a common, uniform mold. As the substantive standards for civil commitment may vary from state to state, procedures must be allowed to vary so long as they meet the constitutional minimum. We conclude that it is unnecessary to require states to apply the strict, criminal standard.

C

Having concluded that the preponderance standard falls short of meeting the demands of due process and that the reasonable-doubt standard is not required, we turn to a middle level of burden of proof that strikes a fair balance between the rights of the individual and the legitimate concerns of the state. We note that 20 states, most by statute, employ the standard of "clear and convincing" evidence; 3 states use "clear, *cogent,* and convincing" evidence; and 2 states require "clear, *unequivocal* and convincing" evidence.

We have concluded that the reasonable-doubt standard is inappropriate in civil commitment proceedings because, given the uncertainties of psychiatric diagnosis, it may impose a burden the state cannot meet and thereby erect an unreasonable barrier to needed medical treatment. Similarly, we conclude that use of the term "unequivocal" is not constitutionally required, although the states are free to use that standard. To meet due process demands, the standard has to inform the factfinder that the proof must be greater than the preponderance-of-the-evidence standard applicable to other categories of civil cases. * * *

Vacated and remanded.

Mr. Justice Powell took no part in the consideration or decision of this case.

Questions and Comments

1. *Implications of* Addington. The selection of the proper standard of proof is really a "substantive" issue, not a "procedural" one. See John Jeffries & Paul Stephan, "Defenses, Presumptions, and Burden of Proof in the Criminal Law," 88 Yale L.J. 1325 (1979). In civil commitment, as previous sections made clear, whether someone is committed should depend upon whether the state can establish by a given *probability,* designated by the standard of proof, that he or she will commit a harmful act or that he or she is gravely disabled.[o] But *Addington* is usefully considered in a discussion of procedural issues as well because of the insight it gives into the Court's general perception of the competing interests involved in civil commitment. In this regard, several aspects of the Court's justification for adopting the clear and convincing standard rather than the reasonable doubt standard are worth noting: (1) the Court's insistence that the decisions made at a civil commitment hearing are primarily "medical" in nature; (2) its implicit conclusion that civil commitment is unlike juvenile delinquency proceedings, as evidenced by its refusal to follow *Winship,* the decision which imposed the reasonable doubt standard in such proceedings; and (3) its statement that "[i]t cannot be said . . . that it is much better for a mentally ill person to 'go free' than for a mentally normal person to be committed." Do you agree with these perceptions?

2. *The basis of intervention.* Should the Court have considered whether the standard of proof should vary depending upon whether the basis for intervention is the police power or the parens patriae authority?

2. The Decisionmaker

In criminal proceedings, the accused is guaranteed a right to a jury trial by the Sixth Amendment. This right may be waived, in which case the trial is presided over by a judge. At the adjudicatory hearing stage of civil commitment, at least four different types of ultimate decisionmakers have been authorized by state statutes: (1) a judicial officer (very often a "special judge" or a probate judge); (2) a jury (usually six strong); (3) an administrative board which does not include a judicial officer; and (4) a psychiatric board. Today almost every state relies upon a legally trained judicial officer to make the long-term commitment decision. However, several provide the respondent with the right to jury trial, if a jury is requested. A small number permit commitment based on the decision of an administrative board. See, e.g., Neb.Rev.Stat. § 71–

o. It should be remembered that the standard of proof may interact with the statutory definition of the criteria to produce a lower burden of proof overall. Thus, if the state defines "danger to others" as a likelihood that a person will harm others, and this likelihood is to be proven by clear and convincing evidence, the state need only show something like a 38% chance of harm to others. See discussion on p. 742.

915 (establishing a "mental health board" consisting of a lawyer, a mental health professional and a third person who is either a mental health professional or a layperson). None currently authorizes the fourth option, although it was the dominant method of decisionmaking prior to 1970. The closest any state comes to a psychiatric board is New York, which permits involuntary hospitalization for up to 60 days based on the authority of three mental health professionals, after which time a judicial hearing must take place. N.Y.Code §§ 9.31, 9.33.

Questions and Comments

1. *Jury trial.* As noted earlier, the United States Supreme Court held in *McKeiver v. Pennsylvania,* 403 U.S. 528, 91 S.Ct. 1976, 29 L.Ed.2d 647 (1971), that there is no right to jury trial in juvenile delinquency proceedings, citing in particular the need to maintain the "intimacy" of the proceeding and to avoid the "clamor" of the adversary process. Most courts have relied on *McKeiver* in deciding that the right is not required at commitment proceedings either. See, e.g., *Lynch v. Baxley,* 386 F.Supp. 378 (M.D.Ala.1974); *Markey v. Wachtel,* 164 W.Va. 45, 264 S.E.2d 437 (1979). In the latter case the court stated:

> The heart of the adversarial issue is the mental condition of the individual which, as *Addington* recognizes, is a technically complex question based on the testimony of experts which a lay jury has difficulty understanding. We are unwilling to hold as a constitutional principle that the resolution of this issue can only be accomplished by a jury. Neither historical precedent nor the requisite due process procedural balance mandates such a conclusion.

Id. at 443.

Duncan v. Louisiana, 391 U.S. 145, 88 S.Ct. 1444, 20 L.Ed.2d 491 (1968), is the Supreme Court decision which held that the right to jury trial is a fundamental right guaranteed to state criminal defendants through the fourteenth amendment. *Duncan* stressed that the jury trial tradition resulted from "a reluctance to entrust plenary powers over the life and liberty of the citizen to one judge or a group of judges" and that the jury "in serious criminal cases is a defense against arbitrary law enforcement." It also pointed to the role of the jury as a means of providing decisionmaking by representatives of the community and promoting a sense of citizen participation. The Court rejected the argument that juries cannot be trusted to reach accurate conclusions. It stated that if juries occasionally reach a different decision than a judge in a particular case, "it is usually because they are serving some of the very purposes for which they were created and for which they are now employed."

Are these same points as valid when applied to civil commitment? To what extent does the jury's traditional role as a group of "peers" affect its usefulness in civil commitment? To what extent, independent of its "accuracy" as a decisionmaker, would the presence of a jury as the decisionmaker affect the "image" of civil commitment? How would it affect the mental state of the respondent? Note that the Supreme Court later limited the jury trial right in criminal proceedings to those cases involving a crime carrying a sentence of more than six months, on the ground that the "disadvantages, onerous though they may be," of imprisonment for six months or less are "outweighed by the benefits that result from speedy and inexpensive nonjury adjudication." Baldwin v. New York, 399 U.S. 66, 90 S.Ct. 1886, 26 L.Ed.2d 437 (1970). Consider also these comments from C. Peter Erlinder, "Of Rights Lost and Rights Found: The Coming Restoration of the Right to a Jury Trial in Minnesota Civil Commitment Proceedings," 29 Wm. Mitchell L. Rev. 1269, 1284 (2003):

> While there is no certainty that juries will reach different conclusions than probate court judges on the same facts, it is clear that the decision to bring a petition seeking indefinite, long-term civil commitment will have much different consequences for county attorneys, defense counsel, and the trial court. Jury trials in both the criminal and civil context usually require commitment of greater resources for all parties than those generally associated with bench trials. The decision to seek indefinite commitment will be far more costly and complicated for all parties concerned. In addition, the impaneling of a jury adds an element of unpredictability into the decision-making process that gives defense counsel a means to encourage opposing counsel to resolve contested matters to avoid an unexpected jury verdict. Perhaps most importantly, all parties will likely benefit from a more careful preparation and presentation of the evidence and judicial rulings in the conduct of the proceedings and opportunities to exercise unreviewable discretion will be reduced. It is also likely that post-commitment procedures, which require additional jury findings to continue indefinite confinement, will result in post-confinement jury procedures far more exacting than those currently in place.

2. *Administrative boards.* In *Doremus v. Farrell,* 407 F.Supp. 509, 516 (D.Neb.1975), the court held that the Nebraska administrative board (at that time composed of a lawyer, a psychiatrist and the clerk of the court) did not violate the constitution:

> Although a judicial determination would be desirable, since courts can more effectively preserve procedural due process and constitutional rights, as well as rule more proficiently on evidentiary questions, we do not believe that due process or equal protection mandates a judicial hearing. The Supreme Court has recognized the power of administrative boards to revoke parole and probation. Gagnon v. Scarpelli, 411 U.S. 778, 93 S.Ct. 1756, 36 L.Ed.2d 656 (1973); Morrissey v. Brewer, 408 U.S. 471, 92 S.Ct. 2593, 33 L.Ed.2d 484 (1972). The deportation of aliens has long been considered a proper function for executive commissions. The procedural safeguards guaranteed by due process, the standards for commitment and the availability of prompt de novo review by the district court after the finding of mental illness by the county board, convinces the Court that an administrative determination is not constitutionally objectionable.

Whether the court would have arrived at the same conclusion had there been no provision for de novo review by a court is unclear. The court also found that using the board did violate the constitution if—as was apparently quite frequently the case in Nebraska—the psychiatrist who examined the respondent for purposes of the commitment proceeding also sat on the board. The court stated that "combin[ing] the investigative, prosecutorial and adjudicative functions in one authority . . . denies the subject due process of law." Id. at 516.

While the Supreme Court has not directly addressed the decisionmaker issue, at least two of its opinions are relevant. The first is *Vitek v. Jones,* 445 U.S. 480, 100 S.Ct. 1254, 63 L.Ed.2d 552 (1980), in which the Court considered the proper procedures for transferring prisoners alleged to need psychiatric care from correctional facilities to psychiatric facilities. Despite the fact that such prisoners are already confined at the time of transfer, the Court found that some process is due prior to such transfers because they occasion "adverse social consequences," including the stigma of being labelled mentally ill, and may involve exposure to mandatory behavior modification. But the Court was unwilling to require that a judicial officer preside over such hearings; rather it mandated only that an "independent decisionmaker" fulfill this role. Moreover, the independent decisionmaker need not come from outside the prison or hospital administration; to hold otherwise would cause "unnecessary intrusion into either medical or correctional judgments."

The second relevant Supreme Court decision is *Parham v. J.R.,* 442 U.S. 584, 99 S.Ct. 2493, 61 L.Ed.2d 101 (1979), in which the Court held that the decision to admit a child to a mental facility may be made by a mental health professional, even, apparently, if that professional is the evaluating clinician. In justifying this decision, the Court stated:

> Due process has never been thought to require that the neutral and detached trier of fact be law-trained or a judicial or administrative officer. Surely, this is the case as to medical decisions for "neither judges nor administrative hearing officers are better qualified than psychiatrists to render psychiatric judgments." Thus, a staff physician will suffice, so long as he or she is free to evaluate independently the child's mental and emotional condition and need for treatment.

> * * *

> What process is constitutionally due cannot be divorced from the nature of the ultimate decision that is being made. . . . Here, the questions are essentially medical in character: whether the child is mentally or emotionally ill and whether he can benefit from the treatment that is provided by the state. While facts are plainly necessary for a proper resolution of those questions, they are only a first step in the process. In an opinion for a unanimous Court, we recently stated in *Addington v. Texas* that the determination of 'whether [a person] is mentally ill turns on the *meaning* of the facts which must be interpreted by expert psychiatrists and psychologists.'

> Although we acknowledge the fallibility of medical and psychiatric diagnosis, we do not accept the notion that the shortcomings of specialists can always be avoided by shifting the decision from a trained specialist using the traditional tools of medical science to an untrained judge or administrative hearing officer after a judicial-type hearing. Even after a hearing, the nonspecialist decisionmaker must make a medical-psychiatric decision. Common human experience and scholarly

opinions suggest that the supposed protections of an adversary proceeding to determine the appropriateness of medical decisions for the commitment and treatment of mental and emotional illness may well be more illusory than real. [Here the Court cited studies showing the informality of supposedly "legalized" proceedings].

Id. at 606–09, 99 S.Ct. at 2506–07. The primary state interests the Court identified in support of this decision were "a significant interest in not imposing unnecessary procedural obstacles that may discourage the mentally ill or their families from seeking needed psychiatric assistance" and a "genuine interest in allocating priority to the diagnosis and treatment of patients as soon as they are admitted to a hospital rather than to time-consuming procedural minuets before the admission." Id. at 605, 99 S.Ct. at 2505. Although, as noted earlier, the Court's decision focused on the process for reviewing the initial admission decision rather than on periodic review procedures, it also stated, in dictum, that the "child's continuing need for commitment" need only be reviewed "by a similarly independent procedure." Id. at 607, 99 S.Ct. at 2506.

Do you think the Court would uphold Nebraska's administrative board as a decisionmaking body for civil commitment of adults? A psychiatric board? Should it? With respect to the last question, consider the following excerpt from David Bazelon, "Institutionalization, Deinstitutionalization and the Adversary Process," 75 Colum.L.Rev. 897, 910–911 (1975).

There is a central but limited role for courts in [the system for involuntarily hospitalizing disturbed or disturbing individuals]—that role is to guide professional decisionmaking, and may be best described by the familiar model of judicial review of administrative decisionmaking. Courts must determine whether there has been a full exploration of all relevant facts, opposing views and possible alternatives, whether the results of the exploration relate rationally to the ultimate decision, and whether constitutional and statutory procedural safeguards have been faithfully observed. Our function is thus not to determine whether the decisions taken by those charged with handling disturbed or disturbing individuals are correct or wise—but whether they are rational in the manner I have just described.

There are some who still say that we should leave these delicate questions of state intervention to the behavioral experts. But I would remind those who suggest this—both outside and within the legal profession—that state intervention involves a serious compromise of individual rights and hence a difficult balancing of power between the state and the individual, where the stakes are highest for human and personal rights. Courts have traditionally been the protector of individual rights against state power, and there is no reason why the particularly difficult problems in the area of state intervention are any different. We cannot delegate this responsibility to the medical professions. Those disciplines are, naturally enough, oriented toward helping people by treating them. Their value system assumes that disturbed and disturbing individuals need treatment, that medical disciplines can provide it, and that attempts to resist it are misguided or delusionary. The medical disciplines can no more judge the legitimacy of state intervention into the lives of disturbed or disturbing individuals than a prosecutor can judge the guilt of a person he has accused.

Finally, it is interesting to note that some research indicates that judges are more likely than psychiatrists to believe that commitment is required. Robert Simon & William Cockerham, "Civil Commitment, Burden of Proof, and Dangerous Acts: A Comparison of the Perspectives of Judges and Psychiatrists," 5 J. Psychiat. & L. 571, 590 (1977).

3.   *The Adversary Process: Notice, Public Trial and Confrontation Rights*

The notion of an "adversary process" is relatively easy to visualize: the relevant parties confront each other with their version of the facts, after which an impartial decisionmaker decides who wins. The specific means by which this process is implemented in criminal trials in the United States derive primarily from the Sixth Amendment, which states in pertinent part:

> In all criminal prosecutions, the accused shall enjoy the right to a . . . public trial . . . and to be informed of the nature and cause of the accusation; to be confronted with the witnesses against him; to have compulsory process for obtaining witnesses in his favor, and to have the Assistance of Counsel for his defence.

The right to notice of one's charges is essential as a means of initiating the adversary process. As Justice Frankfurter stated in *Joint Anti–Fascist Refugee Committee v. McGrath,* 341 U.S. 123, 171–72, 71 S.Ct. 624, 648–49, 95 L.Ed. 817 (1951), "No better instrument has been devised for arriving at truth than to give a person in jeopardy of serious loss notice of the case against him and opportunity to meet it." Notice is considered so important that, as a matter of due process, it has been required prior to virtually all proceedings in which the government is a party, not just prior to the "criminal prosecutions" to which the Sixth Amendment refers. See, e.g., *Vitek v. Jones,* 445 U.S. 480, 100 S.Ct. 1254, 63 L.Ed.2d 552 (1980); *In re Gault,* 387 U.S. 1, 87 S.Ct. 1428, 18 L.Ed.2d 527 (1967).

Although perhaps not theoretically necessary to a well-functioning adversary process, ensuring that the public can observe that process at work has always been considered a second important attribute of the system. The Sixth Amendment's public trial provision was meant to deter the government from engaging in "Star Chamber" proceedings which ignore or merely mimic procedural formality; it thus encourages proceedings which are truly adversarial. In *In re Oliver,* 333 U.S. 257, 68 S.Ct. 499, 92 L.Ed. 682 (1948), the Supreme Court stated that the right "has always been recognized as a safeguard against any attempt to employ our courts as instruments of persecution. The knowledge that every criminal trial is subject to contemporaneous review in the forum of public opinion is an effective restraint on possible abuse of judicial power." Id. at 270. The Court explained further that "the presence of interested spectators may keep [the accused's] triers keenly alive to a

sense of their responsibility and to the importance of their functions."
Id. at 270 n. 25.

The third and most obviously "adversarial" attribute of the adversary process is the right to confront one's accusers and the associated right to subpoena witnesses to rebut one's accusers (the right to "compulsory process"). For reasons that should be apparent, the right to confrontation incorporates the right to be present at trial and the right to cross-examine one's accusers. The Supreme Court has termed the right to be present "one of the most basic of the rights guaranteed by the Confrontation Clause ..." *Illinois v. Allen,* 397 U.S. 337, 90 S.Ct. 1057, 25 L.Ed.2d 353 (1970). And in *Pointer v. Texas,* 380 U.S. 400, 85 S.Ct. 1065, 13 L.Ed.2d 923 (1965), the decision which applied the confrontation clause to the states, the Court stated "probably no one, certainly no one with experience in the trial of lawsuits, would deny the value of cross-examination in exposing falsehood and bringing out the truth in the trial of a criminal case."

The following notes discuss application of these rights to civil commitment. Discussion of the right to counsel, probably the most important method of ensuring a truly adversary process, is deferred until the next subsection.

Questions and Comments

1. *Notice.* The most fundamental issue connected with the right to notice in civil commitment is whether the state can forego such notice to protect the putative patient or a third party (such as the person who brought the petition). This topic is closely connected with the right to be present, discussed below. For now, it should be noted that some states provide for special methods of giving notice to individuals who are allegedly mentally disabled. For instance, Vermont's statute states: "If the court has reason to believe that notice to the proposed patient will be likely to cause injury to the proposed patient or others, it shall direct the proposed patient's counsel to give the proposed patient oral notice prior to written notice under circumstances most likely to reduce likelihood of injury." Vt.Stat.Ann. tit. 18, § 7613(c).

A second issue raised by the cases has to do with the type of information that must be included in the notice. The Supreme Court has held that constitutional requirements are satisfied if the notice "is reasonably calculated to inform the person to whom it is directed of the nature of the proceeding." *Mullane v. Central Hanover Bank & Trust Co.,* 339 U.S. 306, 70 S.Ct. 652, 94 L.Ed. 865 (1950). In *Doremus v. Farrell,* 407 F.Supp. 509 (D.Neb.1975), the court explained that this rule, when applied to civil commitment, meant the following:

> The notice prior to the preliminary inquiry for the emergency detention must inform the person of the nature of grounds, reasons and necessity for the emergency detention, in addition to notice of the time and location of the hearing. The notice should also inform the subject of his right to counsel. The notice prior to the formal hearing must include, in addition to notice of the time and location of the hearing, notice to the

individual of the reasons for his detention, the standards for commitment, and the petition itself . . .

In *French v. Blackburn,* 428 F.Supp. 1351 (M.D.N.C.1977), affirmed 443 U.S.
901, 99 S.Ct. 3091, 61 L.Ed.2d 869 (1979), however, the court held that
notice need not include the reasons for detention, the standards for commitment, nor the petition itself. The court found that the statute before it,
which provided for notice of the purpose of the hearing, the right to counsel,
the right to present evidence, and the possible consequences of the hearing,
was sufficient. It further stated:

> At first blush it would appear that it might be better to serve the
> respondent with a copy of the petition or affidavit forming the basis of
> his custody. This would parallel the service of a copy of the complaint in
> a traditional civil action and a copy of the indictment or information in a
> criminal proceeding. However, . . . [a]s was the case here, the petitions
> may have been filed by members of the respondent's family and service
> of such might possibly cause more harm to such a respondent than
> nonservice.

Id. at 1357 n. 10.

A third issue associated with notice is when it should be given. The
general rule is that it be given "sufficiently in advance of the proceeding to
afford one a reasonable opportunity to prepare." *In re Gault,* 387 U.S. 1, 33,
87 S.Ct. 1428, 1446, 18 L.Ed.2d 527 (1967). In *Blackburn,* the court held that
48 hour notice is sufficient. 428 F.Supp. at 1357. In many states, given the
timeframe between initial admission and the detention hearing, this approxi-
mates the maximum time available (though under the statute at issue in
Blackburn the hearing did not take place until ten days after admission). Of
course, if a detention hearing is held, notice of the adjudicatory hearing can
be, and often is, given at that time.

A final issue that may arise is whether notice should be given to anyone
other than the respondent and the attorney. Many states also provide for
notice to the parents, guardian, spouse or next-of-kin of the patient. See, e.g.,
Tenn.Code § 33–3–605. Do these latter parties have a *right* to notice?

2. *Public trial.* Commitment hearings are likely to canvass very intimate, personal information. Thus, even assuming that respondents have a
right to a public hearing, they may often want to waive the right. The state
may also want to exclude the public, to protect "confidential" information
and to expedite the process. Most state statutes that address the issue
express a preference for private proceedings. Some simply close all hearings
to the public, permitting only those who have "a legitimate interest in the
hearing" to attend. N.D. Stat. § 25–03.1–19; Iowa Code § 229.12(2). Ohio is
representative of many states in keeping the hearing closed unless the
patient and counsel request it to be open. § 5122.15–(a)(5). Finally, a
number of states leave the question to the court's discretion. See, e.g.,
Kansas Stat. § 59–2959 ("all persons not necessary for the conduct of the
proceedings may be excluded").

If the general public or the press want to witness a particular proceeding, should the respondent be able to keep it closed? May the *state,* by
statute, keep the public from attending commitment proceedings? These

issues have seldom been raised, probably because most commitment hearings are of little interest to the public and are not widely publicized.

However, there has been considerable litigation over analogous issues in the criminal and juvenile delinquency contexts. While the Supreme Court has made it clear that a criminal defendant can waive his Sixth Amendment right to a public proceeding, *Gannett Co., Inc. v. DePasquale,* 443 U.S. 368, 99 S.Ct. 2898, 61 L.Ed.2d 608 (1979), it has also vigorously upheld, even over the defendant's objection, the *public's* right of access to trial, based on the First Amendment. In *Richmond Newspapers, Inc. v. Virginia,* 448 U.S. 555, 100 S.Ct. 2814, 65 L.Ed.2d 973 (1980), the Court held that the right of the public and the press to attend criminal trials, which it called "implicit in the guarantees of the First Amendment" rights to free speech and press, would normally outweigh any interest the defendant might have in closing the trial. Only if making the trial public creates problems "beyond the realm of the manageable"—by which the Court seemed to mean problems having to do with maintaining court decorum—can the trial be closed. Id. at 581. See also *Press–Enterprise Co. v. Superior Court,* 478 U.S. 1, 106 S.Ct. 2735, 92 L.Ed.2d 1 (1986).

On the other hand, in the juvenile delinquency context, the clear tendency is to allow closure. All 50 states have statutes which protect the confidentiality of such proceedings. See Pattrick McNulty, "First Amendment Versus Sixth Amendment: A Constitutional Battle in the Juvenile Courts," 10 N.M.L.Rev. 311 (1980). In *In re J.S.,* 140 Vt. 458, 438 A.2d 1125 (1981), the Vermont Supreme Court held that *Richmond Newspapers* does not apply to juvenile proceedings. In the course of its opinion, it quoted from Justice Rehnquist's opinion in *Smith v. Daily Mail Publishing Co.,* 443 U.S. 97, 107, 99 S.Ct. 2667, 2673, 61 L.Ed.2d 399 (1979):

> It is a hallmark of our juvenile justice system in the United States that virtually from its inception at the end of the last century its proceedings have been conducted outside of the public's full gaze and the youths brought before our juvenile courts have been shielded from publicity. This insistence on confidentiality is born of a tender concern for the welfare of the child, to hide his youthful errors and "bury them in the graveyard of the forgotten past." The prohibition of publication of a juvenile's name is designed to protect the young person from the stigma of his misconduct and is rooted in the principle that a court concerned with juvenile affairs serves as a rehabilitative and protective agency of the State.

Most courts do, however, permit the delinquency proceeding to be open if the child so requests. In *RLR v. State,* 487 P.2d 27 (Alaska 1971), for instance, the court stated:

> Delinquency proceedings as much as adult criminal prosecutions can be used as instruments of persecution, and may be subject to judicial abuse. The appellate process is not a sufficient check on juvenile courts, for problems of mootness and the cost of prosecuting an appeal screen most of what goes on from appellate court scrutiny. We cannot help but notice that children's cases appealed to this court have often shown much more extensive and fundamental error than is generally found in adult criminal cases, and wonder whether secrecy is not fostering a

judicial attitude of casualness toward the law in children's proceedings.... Therefore, we hold that children are guaranteed the right to a public trial by the Alaska Constitution.

... It is an abuse of discretion for the court to refuse admittance to individuals whose presence is favored by the child, except in special circumstances such as the unavailability of a courtroom sufficiently large to hold all the individuals whose presence is sought. If a child or his guardian ad litem wants the press, friends, or others to be free to attend, then the hearing must be open to them. The area of discretion in the rule, where the court may refuse to open the hearing, involves persons whose presence is not desired by the child.

3. *Presence of respondent.* The right to be present at one's criminal trial can be abridged if the defendant is so disruptive that an orderly proceeding cannot take place. *Illinois v. Allen,* 397 U.S. 337, 90 S.Ct. 1057, 25 L.Ed.2d 353 (1970). The right may also be waived, if the waiver is "knowing and intelligent." *Tacon v. Arizona,* 410 U.S. 351, 93 S.Ct. 998, 35 L.Ed.2d 346 (1973). Otherwise, the accused's right to be present at trial is sacrosanct. In contrast, a large number of state commitment statutes permit the court to exclude the respondent if, in the court's opinion, presence would be harmful to the respondent. See, e.g., Alas.Stat. § 47.30.735(b)(1)(permitting exclusion if the respondent lacks capacity to decide about presence and there is a "substantial likelihood" that presence would be "seriously injurious" to the person's mental health).

In *Stamus v. Leonhardt,* 414 F.Supp. 439 (S.D.Iowa 1976), the court found such a provision in the Iowa commitment statute unconstitutional.

Section 229.4 of the Code accorded the subject the right to be present at hearings unless the hospitalization commission found that the subject's presence would "probably be injurious" to the subject "or attended with no advantage." Pursuant to this provision, Dorothy Stamus was taken before the hospitalization commission during her hearing and questioned. However, as was the general practice in Polk County, she was excluded from the hearing room preceding and after the questioning period. This restriction on the plaintiff's right to be present was an unconstitutional deprivation of her right to due process.

* * *

... The same purposes for requiring the person's presence exist in both the civil and criminal context: to allow the individual to assure that his or her interests are being protected and to give the fact-finder an opportunity to speak with the person and observe his or her demeanor. The results of the hearings, confinement in an institution and a loss of personal liberty, are often the same in the civil commitment and criminal context. Thus, there must be a right for the individual under discussion to be present at all proceedings for civil commitment....

What is the impact of an adversary hearing on the typical person alleged to be mentally disabled? Recall the assertion by Ensminger and Liguori in the introduction to this section that confronting one's family and the treating professionals can often be "therapeutic." Consider also, however, the following passage:

The patient who has his "day in court" may be subjected to anguish, humiliation, suspicion, alienation from family, self-depreciation, and anxiety. Consider patient A, a paranoid person who thinks people are against him; patient B, a manic who has all kinds of funny, grandiose ideas; patient C, a depressed person who feels nobody loves him or wants him. Suppose each of these patients were to insist on his day in court. Patient A would hear neighbors say why he ought to be hospitalized. What would that do to his paranoid ideas? Patient B would provide an uproariously good time for spectators as he made a clown of himself. What would that do to his loved ones? Patient C would hear his nearest and dearest swear that he ought to be hospitalized. What would this do to his self-evaluation?

Henry Davidson, "Mental Hospitals and the Civil Liberties Dilemma," 51 Mental Hygiene 371, 374 (1967).

According to the Supreme Court, the right to be present in criminal proceedings incorporates not only the right to be physically present but the right to be "mentally present," i.e., competent to stand trial. *Pate v. Robinson,* 383 U.S. 375, 86 S.Ct. 836, 15 L.Ed.2d 815 (1966). Defendants must have a minimal understanding of the proceedings against them and be able to assist the attorney in confronting their accusers, or the state may not try them. Should the right to avoid trial while incompetent be extended to civil commitment respondents? Note that in the criminal system, a person found incompetent to stand trial may be involuntarily treated until restored to competency. See pp. 1027–52.

4. *Cross-examination and hearsay.* The principal issue connected with the right to cross-examine accusers at civil commitment proceedings is the extent to which hearsay is admissible. Since hearsay, by definition, involves out-of-court statements by persons who are not present in the courtroom, the Confrontation Clause could be construed to exclude all hearsay, or at least all hearsay statements made to a government official. Cf. *Crawford v. Washington,* 541 U.S. 36, 124 S.Ct. 1354, 158 L.Ed.2d 177 (2004), discussed on p. 532 However, the Confrontation Clause only applies in "criminal prosecutions." In civil cases, there are many exceptions to the hearsay rule. These exceptions include the party admission rule, which would permit description of the respondent's out-of-court statements about his or her mental state or intended actions by the person who heard them, and the "business records" exception, which would admit virtually all observations of the respondent's mental state made by clinicians and recorded as a routine matter in medical and psychiatric records. See Fed.R.Evid. 801(d)(2); 803(6).

An example of testimony that would not fit any well-accepted hearsay exception would be a description of an out-of-court declaration by a third-party about what the respondent did or said on a particular day (so-called "double hearsay" because the person who observed or heard the respondent is not in court). For instance, the hearsay rule would probably bar a mental health professional's testimony that a family member had told him two days before the hearing that the respondent had threatened to hurt the family member.[p] Similarly, the rule would prohibit the respondent's mother from

---

p. Note, however, that under Federal Rule of Evidence 703 and equivalent state rules such testimony, although hearsay, would still be admissible if of the type "reasonably relied upon" by experts in the field. See pp. 531–32.

testifying that the respondent's friend had told her the respondent had attempted suicide on several occasions.

Should such testimony be admissible in any event? Or should the state be required to present the people who heard the respondent's statements first-hand, if they are available? Several courts have held that the rules of evidence, including the hearsay rule, should apply in commitment proceedings. See, e.g., *State ex rel. Hawks v. Lazaro,* 157 W.Va. 417, 202 S.E.2d 109, 125 (W.Va.1974); *Lessard v. Schmidt,* 349 F.Supp. 1078 (E.D.Wis.1972). Some state statutes take this stance as well; many others are simply silent about the issue, and some provide, as Utah does, that the hearing "shall be conducted in as informal a manner as may be consistent with orderly procedure." Utah Stat. § 62A–15–631(9)(d). The American Psychiatric Association's Model Law provides that "[h]earsay evidence may be received, and experts and other witnesses may, consistent with law, testify to any relevant and probative facts at the discretion of the court." Clifford Stromberg & Alan Stone, "A Model State Law on Civil Commitment of the Mentally Ill," 20 Harv.J.Legis. 275, 340 (1983). In support of this position, the commentary states, id. at 340–41:

> [H]earsay evidence may be especially necessary in some civil commitment cases because the facts sought to be established include the elusive datum of mental status, not just physical events as in most criminal trials. Especially where the issues are tried before a judge, who can weigh the probative value of the evidence, such hearsay need not be excluded. It also may be proper to afford a broader ambit to psychiatric opinion evidence. Similarly, the interests that underlie the privilege against spousal testimony in criminal cases may not be served by invoking such a privilege in civil commitment. There may be proper exceptions to other privileges as well, such as the psychotherapist-patient privilege.

5. *Compulsory process.* Of course, if the respondent in a civil commitment proceeding has a wide-open right to subpoena witnesses, then he or she can circumvent any attempt by the state to rely on hearsay by serving process on the relevant out-of-court declarants. Some states statutes explicitly grant the respondent subpoena authority for persons and documents, but whether such a right is constitutionally required and the extent to which it can be exercised as a discovery mechanism is unclear. Perhaps of relevance here is *Vitek v. Jones,* 445 U.S. 480, 100 S.Ct. 1254, 63 L.Ed.2d 552 (1980), the case involving the process due prisoners who are transferred to psychiatric facilities. In *Vitek,* the Supreme Court held that the state must give the prisoner the "opportunity . . . to present testimony of witnesses . . . and to confront and cross-examine witnesses called by the state, *except* upon a finding, not arbitrarily made, of good cause for not permitting such presentation, confrontation or cross-examination." [emphasis added] The Court held that such a limitation was permissible because it recognized "[t]he interests of the State in avoiding disruption." Id. at 495–96.

Another limitation on the respondent's compulsory process right may arise from the by-now familiar concern that the information thereby obtained will harm either the respondent or third parties who have revealed information about the respondent. Although virtually every state allows the patient to see his or her own records, disclosure is not required of certain types of information, such as information from third parties disclosed in confidence, information which would be "injurious" to the patient or the patient's relationships with others, and the therapist's impressions (as opposed to official diagnostic information). See pp. 417–19. Also of possible relevance here is the Supreme Court's decision in *Pennsylvania v. Ritchie,* 480 U.S. 39, 107 S.Ct. 989 94 L.Ed.2d 40 (1987), in which the Court held that even a criminal defendant's "right to discover exculpatory evidence does not include the unsupervised authority to search through the Commonwealth's files." At most, the Court held, the defense may ask the trial court to review the files *in camera* to determine what information, if any, is material to the defendant's case; even this limited right is conditioned upon the defendant "first establishing a basis for his claim that it contains material evidence." Thus, the state may be able to stymie a respondent's attempt, prior to a civil commitment hearing, to subpoena evidence possessed by the state (e.g., in hospital records) by requiring a showing of materiality and a judicial determination that the records should be disclosed.

4. *The Right to Counsel*

The Supreme Court has clearly established a right to counsel at trial—and a concomitant duty on the part of the state to provide counsel to indigents who cannot afford one—for both the criminal accused, *Argersinger v. Hamlin,* 407 U.S. 25, 92 S.Ct. 2006, 32 L.Ed.2d 530 (1972), and juveniles alleged to be delinquent, *In re Gault,* 387 U.S. 1, 87 S.Ct. 1428, 18 L.Ed.2d 527 (1967), at least when imprisonment is imposed. Endorsement of a right to counsel in civil commitment proceedings has been less firm. While virtually every state provides for counsel at commitment and every modern court that has considered the issue has held that the due process clause requires counsel at the commitment hearing, the Supreme Court has not been as clear on the matter. In both *Parham v. J.R.* (dealing with commitment of children) and *Vitek v. Jones* (dealing with the transfer of prisoners to mental health facilities) the Court refused to find a right to legally trained counsel for persons subjected to a proceeding to determine the existence and extent of their mental disability. The language of Justice Powell's concurring opinion in *Vitek,* which controlled the disposition of the right to counsel issue in that case, is worth looking at in full:

VITEK v. JONES

Supreme Court of the United States, 1980.
445 U.S. 480, 100 S.Ct. 1254, 63 L.Ed.2d 552.

MR. JUSTICE POWELL, concurring in part.

* * *

I

In *Gagnon v. Scarpelli,* 411 U.S. 778, 93 S.Ct. 1756, 36 L.Ed.2d 656 (1973), my opinion for the Court held that counsel is not necessarily required at a probation revocation hearing. In reaching this decision the Court recognized both the effects of providing counsel to each probationer and the likely benefits to be derived from the assistance of counsel. "The introduction of counsel into a revocation proceeding [would] alter significantly the nature of the proceeding," because the hearing would inevitably become more adversarial. We noted that probationers would not always need counsel because in most hearings the essential facts are undisputed. In lieu of a *per se* rule we held that the necessity of providing counsel should be determined on a case-by-case basis. In particular, we stressed that factors governing the decision to provide counsel include (i) the existence of factual disputes or issues which are "complex or otherwise difficult to develop or present," and (ii) "whether the probationer appears to be capable of speaking effectively for himself."

Consideration of these factors, and particularly the capability of the inmate, persuades me that the Court is correct that independent assistance must be provided to an inmate before he may be transferred involuntarily to a mental hospital. The essence of the issue in an involuntary commitment proceeding will be the mental health of the inmate. The resolution of factual disputes will be less important than the ability to understand and analyze expert psychiatric testimony that is often expressed in language relatively incomprehensible to laymen. It is unlikely that an inmate threatened with involuntary transfer to mental hospitals will possess the competence or training to protect adequately his own interest in these state-initiated proceedings. And the circumstances of being imprisoned without normal access to others who may assist him places an additional handicap upon an inmate's ability to represent himself. I therefore agree that due process requires the provision of assistance to an inmate threatened with involuntary transfer to a mental hospital.

II

I do not believe, however, that an inmate must always be supplied with a licensed attorney. "[D]ue Process is flexible and calls for such procedural protections as the particular situation demands." *Morrissey v. Brewer,* 408 U.S. 471, 481, 92 S.Ct. 2593, 2600, 33 L.Ed.2d 484 (1972). Our decisions defining the necessary qualifications for an impartial decisionmaker demonstrate that the requirements of due process turn on the nature of the determination which must be made. "Due Process has never been thought to require that the neutral and detached trier of fact be law-trained or a judicial or administrative officer." *Parham v. J.R.,* 442 U.S. 584, 607, 99 S.Ct. 2493, 2506, 61 L.Ed.2d 101 (1979). In that case, we held that due process is satisfied when a staff physician determines whether a child may be voluntarily committed to a state mental institution by his parents. That holding was based upon recognition that the issues of civil commitment "are essentially medical in nature," and that " 'neither judges nor administrative hearing officers are better qualified than psychiatrists to render psychiatric judgments.' ''

In my view, the principle that due process does not always require a law-trained decisionmaker supports the ancillary conclusion that due process may be satisfied by the provision of a qualified and independent advisor who is not a lawyer. As in *Parham v. J.L.*, the issue here is essentially medical. Under state law, a prisoner may be transferred only if he "suffers from a mental disease or defect" and "cannot be given proper treatment" in the prison complex. Neb.Rev.Stat. § 83–180(1). The opinion of the Court allows a non-lawyer to act as the impartial decisionmaker in the transfer proceeding.

The essence of procedural due process is a fair hearing. I do not think that the fairness of an informal hearing designed to determine a medical issue requires participation by lawyers. Due process merely requires that the State provide an inmate with qualified and independent assistance. Such assistance may be provided by a licensed psychiatrist or other mental health professional. Indeed, in view of the nature of the issue involved in the transfer hearing, a person possessing such professional qualifications normally would be preferred. As the Court notes, "[t]he question whether an individual is mentally ill and cannot be treated in prison 'turns on the meaning of the facts which must be interpreted by expert psychiatrists and psychologists.' ''*Ante*, at 1265, quoting *Addington v. Texas*. I would not exclude, however, the possibility that the required assistance may be rendered by competent laymen in some cases. The essential requirements are that the person provided by the State be competent and independent, and that he be free to act solely in the inmate's best interest.

In sum, although the State is free to appoint a licensed attorney to represent an inmate, it is not constitutionally required to do so. Due process will be satisfied so long as an inmate facing involuntary transfer to a mental hospital is provided qualified and independent assistance.

Questions and Comments

1. *Implications of the Court's cases.* What are the implications of *Vitek* and *Parham* for the civil commitment process? Note that Justice Powell relied heavily on *Gagnon v. Scarpelli* and *Morrissey v. Brewer* in reaching his conclusions. Consider this fuller excerpt from *Scarpelli:*

> The introduction of counsel into a revocation proceeding will alter significantly the nature of the proceeding. If counsel is provided for the probationer or parolee, the State in turn will normally provide its own counsel; lawyers, by training and disposition, are advocates and bound by professional duty to present all available evidence and arguments in support of their clients' positions and to contest with vigor all adverse evidence and views. The role of the hearing body itself, aptly described in *Morrissey* as being "predictive and discretionary" as well as fact finding, may become more akin to that of a judge at a trial, and less attuned to the rehabilitative needs of the individual probationer or parolee. In the greater self-consciousness of its quasi-judicial role, the

hearing body may be less tolerant of marginal deviant behavior and feel more pressure to reincarcerate than to continue nonpunitive rehabilitation. Certainly, the decisionmaking process will be prolonged, and the financial cost to the State—for appointed counsel, counsel for the State, a longer record and the possibility of judicial review—will not be insubstantial.

In some cases, these modifications in the nature of the revocation hearing must be endured and the costs borne because, as we have indicated above, the probationer's or parolee's version of a disputed issue can fairly be represented only by a trained advocate. But due process is not so rigid as to require that the significant interests in informality, flexibility, and economy must always be sacrificed.

Is *Scarpelli* authority for or against a right to counsel at civil commitment?

2. *The role of counsel.* Assuming the person subjected to commitment proceedings has an advocate, should the advocate "act like a lawyer"? Or, as suggested by Justice Powell's reasoning in *Scarpelli,* might the nature of the commitment process justify a different, less adversarial approach? At least three possible advocacy roles can be envisioned. The first is the adversarial role traditionally taken by lawyers, in which it is assumed that the client knows best and the advocate makes the most persuasive arguments available in support of the client's wishes. The second role might be called the "guardian ad litem" stance, in which the advocate acts in the "best interests" of the client, after assessing all the circumstances. Although the client's wishes are taken into account, they are not dispositive; thus, under this model, it is assumed that the lawyer, rather than the client, knows best. Finally, there is a cooperative role in which the advocate assumes that the "doctor knows best." Under this model, the advocate may help develop facts for the expert's consideration, but does not dispute the expert's final decision.

The Model Code of Professional Responsibility is not particularly helpful in deciding, from a professional ethics standpoint, which role may or should be followed. Canon 7 of the Code states: "A lawyer should represent a client zealously within the bounds of the law." Consider the following "Ethical Considerations" (EC) designed to flesh out this Canon:

> EC 7–7 In certain areas of legal representation not affecting the merits of the cause or substantially prejudicing the rights of a client, a lawyer is entitled to make decisions on his own. But otherwise the authority to make decisions is exclusively that of the client and, if made within the framework of the law, such decisions are binding on his lawyer. As typical examples in civil cases, it is for the client to decide whether he will accept a settlement offer or whether he will waive his right to plead an affirmative defense. A defense lawyer in a criminal case has the duty to advise his client fully on whether a particular plea to a charge appears to be desirable and as to the prospects of success on appeal, but it is for the client to decide what plea should be entered and whether an appeal should be taken.

* * *

EC 7–12 Any mental or physical condition of a client that renders him incapable of making a considered judgment on his own behalf casts additional responsibilities upon his lawyer. Where an incompetent is acting through a guardian or other legal representative, a lawyer must look to such representative for those decisions which are normally the prerogative of the client to make. If a client under disability has no legal representative, his lawyer may be compelled in court proceedings to make decisions on behalf of the client. If the client is capable of understanding the matter in question or of contributing to the advancement of his interests, regardless of whether he is legally disqualified from performing certain acts, the lawyer should obtain from him all possible aid. If the disability of a client and the lack of a legal representative compel the lawyer to make decisions for his client, the lawyer should consider all circumstances then prevailing and act with care to safeguard and advance the interests of his client. But obviously a lawyer cannot perform any act or make any decision which the law requires his client to perform or make, either acting for himself if competent, or by a duly constituted representative if legally incompetent.

The ABA's Model Rules of Professional Conduct are not much more helpful. Model Rule 1.14 states: "(a) When a client's ability to make adequately considered decisions in connection with the representation is impaired, whether because of minority, mental disability or for some other reason, the lawyer shall, as far as reasonably possible, maintain a normal client-lawyer relationship with the client; (b) A lawyer may seek the appointment of a guardian or take other protective action with respect to a client, only when the lawyer reasonably believes that the client cannot adequately act in the client's own interests." An earlier, rejected draft of subsection (b) stated: "A lawyer shall secure the appointment of a guardian or other legal representative, or seek a protective order with respect to a client, when doing so is necessary *in the client's best interests*" (emphasis added). Compare the Restatement of the Law Governing Lawyers § 35(2), which states: "A lawyer representing [an impaired client] for whom no guardian or other representative is available to act, must, with respect to a matter within the scope of the representation, pursue the lawyer's reasonable view of the client's objectives or interests as the client would define them if able to make adequately considered decisions on the matter, *even if the client expresses no wishes or gives contrary instructions*" (emphasis added).

Assume that you are representing a client who appears to be imminently suicidal and treatable, but who adamantly refuses to consent to any type of treatment or hospitalization because "the hospital is Hell and if I kill myself I'll go to Heaven." Alternatively, assume your client is extremely malnourished and disheveled, murmuring incoherently, smearing feces on the wall, and able only to nod negatively when asked if he is willing to go to the hospital. Under the Model Code, the Model Rules or the Restatement, what options are available to you? Should you follow the clients' direction? Seek appointment of a guardian? Withdraw? Disregard the clients' wishes because you believe that treatment would be in the client's best interests? The last sentence of the Model Code excerpt prohibits attorneys from performing any act or making any decision "which the law requires his client to perform or make." In the hypothesized situations, what does "the law" leave up to the client? Would your approach to these situations be different if, as is true in many states, the government is "represented" solely by a mental health professional because no provision is made for state attorneys to appear in commitment hearings?

Several commentators have emphasized that, whatever role the advocate assumes—adversarial, guardian ad litem, or cooperative—at the least he or she should perform an investigative function. Fred Cohen, "The Function of the Attorney and the Commitment of the Mentally Ill," 44 Tex.L.Rev. 424, 452 (1966), states:

> Prior to the hearing the attorney must make a thorough study of all the records that are available to him through the court, the hospital, and, at times, social agencies. He must always communicate with the proposed patient and, where possible, family and friends. The attorney should work toward an understanding of the events that led up to and contributed to the filing of the petition. Only in this way can he attempt to develop possible alternatives to hospitalization.

Armed with this knowledge, the advocate may be able to bargain for a less restrictive disposition and will be able to conduct more effective questioning of witnesses. The advocate can also make sure the proper procedures are followed at the hearing, both through objections and through appealing various rulings, if appeal is available. See also, "Preparation and Trial of a Civil Commitment Case," 5 Men.Dis.L.Rep. 201, 281 (1981); National Center for State Courts' Guidelines for Involuntary Civil Commitment, 10 Men. & Phys. Dis. L. Rep. 409 (1986).

The role of counsel is made more difficult by the possibility that the client does not express, or perhaps even know, what he or she "really" wants. For instance, Miller and colleagues assert that patients sometimes make complaints to protect themselves "from having to deal with painful intrapsychic conflicts unrelated to the subjects of the actual grievances." They also contend that attorneys reinforce the resistance of these patients to treatment by taking the complaints at face value. As an example of this process and what might be done about it, they provided the following description of a case:

> Mr. A [a 29 year-old state hospital resident with diagnoses of pedophilia, borderline personality and antisocial personality, among others] frequently stated his intent to sue everyone who could not "cure" these various problems ... In individual psychotherapy, he began to focus on intrapsychic problems such as his extremely negative self-image and his difficulty with intimacy and rejection ... [In therapy with two different therapists,] a pattern began to emerge. He would begin to deal with a significant internal conflict, and then would switch to talking almost exclusively about a grievance or lawsuit.... While the litigious behavior served to help him feel in control, and to project his negative feelings onto the staff, it also provided protection against the pain associated with dealing with powerful internal conflicts. As soon as this pattern was discovered, it was interpreted to Mr. A. by both therapists; after each interpretation, he returned to dealing with his deeper conflicts. He accepted the interpretations, and the frequency of complaints decreased significantly ... Most staff came to accept his

changes as genuine; their responses then also reinforced Mr. A.'s behavior.

Mr. A.'s litigious behavior was initially reinforced by responses of some patient advocates and attorneys.... At first, the supervising attorneys in the state patient's rights office, who had no clinical experience and a significant libertarian orientation, did not recognize the hidden agendas behind many of Mr. A's charges, and unwittingly contributed to his therapeutic resistance by supporting his overt grievances. After considerable effort at education by clinical staff about borderline psychodynamics, however, the attorneys realized how they had been furthering their client's resistance (and thus hindering his treatment) by accepting his grievances at face value. Once they understood the nature of his resistance, they often reinforced the therapy through clinically insightful responses to his grievances, while still maintaining their concern for his rights. Their opinions were initially received by Mr. A. differently from clinical staff's opinions, and helped to set effective limits to his acting-out behavior before the clinical staff's reaction to Mr. A. had changed significantly.

Mr. A. was told of the therapists' contacts with the advocates, and offered the opportunity for joint sessions with both clinicians and advocates. While he declined the sessions, he accepted the reasons for the collaboration and offered no objections to its continuing.

Robert Miller, et. al., "Litigiousness as a Resistance to Therapy," in David Wexler, ed., Therapeutic Jurisprudence: The Law as Therapeutic Agent, 332–35 (1991). This example involved representing a person with mental illness who is already in the hospital. Are the ethical issues different when the same type of dynamic occurs at the commitment hearing?

3. *Ineffective assistance of counsel.* Most commitment attorneys apparently do not undertake even the modest tasks described in the previous note. As indicated earlier, numerous studies have documented that attorneys rarely spend more than a few minutes preparing for the hearing, seldom call witnesses, and usually fail to engage in vigorous cross-examination of the experts. To some extent, this state of affairs may be due to their unfamiliarity with psychiatric issues or the low fees provided by the state for defending commitment respondents. But one study suggests that, even when these factors are not present, many attorneys continue to be passive. Poythress found that lawyers who were specifically trained to adopt a more adversarial stance and who were provided with information about the inadequacies of testimony by mental health professionals persisted in avoiding careful cross-examination of expert witnesses, apparently because of a belief that to do so was in the best interests of their clients. Norman Poythress, "Psychiatric Expertise in Civil Commitment: Training Attorneys to Cope with Expert Testimony," 2 Law Hum.Behav. 1 (1978).

One possible remedy for this situation, if a remedy is thought to be worthwhile, is to require legislatively that the attorneys perform certain duties. For instance, Arizona has granted the commitment court the power to hold attorneys in contempt unless they perform several listed tasks prior the hearing. Ariz.Stat. § 36–537(B)(requiring the attorney, *inter alia*, to interview the client, obtain records, and seek a screening evaluation at least

24 hours before hearing, with failure to perform punishable by contempt of court). A second possible approach is to import Sixth Amendment ineffective assistance of counsel analysis into the commitment context. In *Strickland v. Washington*, 466 U.S. 668, 104 S.Ct. 2052, 80 L.Ed.2d 674 (1984), the Supreme Court established a two-prong test for determining whether defense counsel was ineffective under the Sixth Amendment. The defendant must show both that "counsel's performance was deficient" and that "the deficient performance prejudiced the defense." Performance is "deficient" if the attorney fails "to advocate the defendant's cause[,] . . . consult with the defendant on important decisions, [or] . . . keep the defendant informed of important developments." The attorney must also "bring to bear such skill and knowledge as will render the trial a reliable adversarial testing process" and "make reasonable investigations or . . . make a reasonable decision that makes particular investigations unnecessary." Proof of "prejudice" exists if "there is a reasonable probability that, but for counsel's unprofessional errors, the result of the proceeding would have been different." If both prongs are met, the defendant's conviction must be reversed. Would application of *Strickland's* standards to civil commitment (through the due process clause, since the sixth amendment applies only to "criminal prosecutions") provide a realistic remedy for attorney passivity?

In *In the Matter of the Mental Health of K.G.F.*, 306 Mont. 1, 29 P.3d 485 (2001), the Montana Supreme Court stated:

> Although in numerous respects the procedural due process rights of an involuntary commitment patient-respondent are identical to those afforded an accused criminal defendant, we . . . conclude that the standard under *Strickland* simply does not go far enough to protect the liberty interests of individuals such as K.G.F., who may or may not have broken any law, but who, upon the expiration of a 90–day commitment, must indefinitely bear the badge of inferiority of a once "involuntarily committed" person with a proven mental disorder. The *Strickland* decision, for example, provides that a court "must indulge a strong presumption that counsel's conduct falls within the wide range of reasonable professional assistance;" that is, the defendant must overcome the presumption that, under the circumstances, the challenged action might be considered sound trial strategy. Even a cursory review of legal commentary reveals the flawed reasoning of applying the foregoing *Strickland* standard to involuntary civil commitment proceedings. Namely, "reasonable professional assistance" cannot be presumed in a proceeding that routinely accepts—and even requires—an unreasonably low standard of legal assistance and generally disdains zealous, adversarial confrontation. . . . We also agree with Amicus that the *Strickland* burden of proving that counsel's "deficient performance prejudiced the defense so as to deny the defendant a fair trial," is contrary to our prior case law that mandates that unless civil commitment laws are strictly followed, a commitment order must be reversed. . . .

> [B]ecause the fundamental rights attached to decisions within the "provider-patient relationship" may be overridden by the State's *parens patriae* duties and police power authority, the role of counsel is all the more critical where a patient may be involuntarily committed. The threats to individual liberty posed by involuntary commitment . . . arise

at a time "when the individual with a mental illness is least able to defend against them—during a time of crisis, confusion, fatigue." *See also* Bruce J. Winick, *Therapeutic Jurisprudence and the Civil Commitment Hearing,* 10 J. Contemp. Legal Issues 37, 44–45 (1999) (observing that "[p]erhaps nothing can threaten a person's belief that he or she is an equal member of society as much as being subjected to a civil commitment hearing" and when "legal proceedings do not treat people with dignity, they feel devalued as members of society")....

Relying in part on the National Center for State Courts' Guidelines for Involuntary Civil Commitment cited above in note 2, the court then established a number of rules governing attorneys involved in the commitment process regarding investigation, communication with the client, and advocacy of the client's wishes. The court ended with the following language:

> As the Commentary to the *Guidelines* states: "[w]hen an attorney fails to act as an advocate and assumes a paternalistic or passive stance, the balance of the system is upset, the defense attorney usurps the judicial role, and the defendant's position goes unheard." Accordingly, we agree with the *Guidelines* ... that the proper role of the attorney is to "represent the perspective of the respondent and to serve as a vigorous advocate for the respondent's wishes." ... The foregoing guidelines create the presumption that a client wishes to not be involuntarily committed.... *Thus, we conclude that pursuant to the foregoing guidelines, evidence that counsel independently advocated or otherwise acquiesced to an involuntary commitment—in the absence of any evidence of a voluntary and knowing consent by the patient-respondent—will establish the presumption that counsel was ineffective....* Upon a substantial showing of evidence ... that counsel did not effectively represent the patient-respondent's interests pursuant to the foregoing standards, an order of involuntary commitment should be vacated.

Id. at 500–01 (emphasis added). In the two hypotheticals described in note 2 involving the suicidal and malnourished individuals, should a failure on the part of the attorney to argue vigorously against hospitalization vacate commitment and lead to a finding of ineffective assistance under *K.G.F*?

4. *The right to an independent expert evaluation.* To what extent does the effective assistance of counsel notion require that the advocate seek consultation with a mental health professional? For the wealthy respondent such consultation is easily arranged, but for the indigent (and typical) person subjected to civil commitment, the only expertise available in most jurisdictions is provided by those mental health professionals who testify for the government. Only a few states have authorized the appointment of an independent expert if the defendant so requests. See, e.g., Fl. Stat. § 394.4655(6)(a)2. Some courts have held that the latter type of provision is constitutionally required. In *In re Gannon,* 123 N.J.Super. 104, 301 A.2d 493, 494 (1973), the court stated:

> Commitment to a psychiatric hospital obviously entails a significant loss of liberty which, as in a criminal proceeding, must be under due process of law. It is the opinion of this court that in a commitment proceeding due process of law includes the right to an independent psychiatric examination.

The right of an indigent to have counsel appointed has already been established, but the presence of a lawyer at the commitment hearing is not a sufficient safeguard for the patient's rights. No matter how brilliant the lawyer may be, he is in no position to effectively contest the commitment proceedings because he has no way to rebut the testimony of the psychiatrist from the institution who has already certified to the patient's insanity. . . .

This court has had enough experience to know that psychiatrists differ very definitely in their evaluations and diagnoses of mental illness. In a commitment proceeding where the court is in effect bound by the expertise of the psychiatrist, the right to counsel is of little value without a concurrent right to an independent psychiatric examination.

However, the court limited the right to an independent evaluation in the following manner:

The right to counsel has not been construed to allow an indigent to choose his own lawyer. Similarly, an indigent in a commitment proceeding should not have the right to "shop around" for a psychiatrist who agrees with him. The independent psychiatrist is to assist the court, not the patient; all he need do is render his best judgment and make all relevant information available both to the court and to the defense.

Id. at 494.

Does the court's conclusion follow from its analogy between choosing a lawyer and choosing an expert? Note that in *Ake v. Oklahoma,* 470 U.S. 68, 105 S.Ct. 1087, 84 L.Ed.2d 53 (1985), reprinted at pp. 500–07, the Supreme Court held, using reasoning similar to that used by the *Gannon* court, that the due process clause entitles the indigent criminal defendant to a psychiatric consultant when sanity at the time of the offense is "a significant factor at trial" and, in capital cases, when dangerousness is a factor to be considered at sentencing. More specifically, on the insanity expert issue, the Court held:

We therefore hold that when a defendant demonstrates to the trial judge that his sanity at the time of the offense is to be a significant factor at trial, the State must, at a minimum, assure the defendant access to a competent psychiatrist who will conduct an appropriate examination and assist in evaluation, preparation, and presentation of the defense. This is not to say, of course, that the indigent defendant has a constitutional right to choose a psychiatrist of his personal liking or to receive funds to hire his own. Our concern is that the indigent defendant have access to a competent psychiatrist for the purpose we have discussed, and as in the case of the provision of counsel we leave to the State the decision on how to implement this right.

470 U.S. at 83, 105 S.Ct. at 1096. To what extent does *Ake* support the result in *Gannon*? At least one court has held that an evaluation is "independent" for purposes of civil commitment even when conducted by a state-employed doctor. *In re Barnard*, 247 Ill.App.3d 234, 186 Ill.Dec. 524, 616 N.E.2d 714 (1993).

5. *The Privilege Against Self–Incrimination*

ALLEN v. ILLINOIS

Supreme Court of the United States, 1986.
478 U.S. 364, 106 S.Ct. 2988, 92 L.Ed.2d 296.

JUSTICE REHNQUIST delivered the opinion of the Court.

The question presented by this case is whether the proceedings under the Illinois Sexually Dangerous Persons Act (Act), Ill.Rev.Stat., ch. 38, ¶ 105–1.01 *et seq.* (1985),[q] are "criminal" within the meaning of the Fifth Amendment's guarantee against compulsory self-incrimination.

* * *

The Self–Incrimination Clause of the Fifth Amendment, which applies to the States through the Fourteenth Amendment, *Malloy v. Hogan,* 378 U.S. 1, 84 S.Ct. 1489, 12 L.Ed.2d 653 (1964), provides that no person "shall be compelled in any criminal case to be a witness against himself." This Court has long held that the privilege against self-incrimination "not only permits a person to refuse to testify against himself at a criminal trial in which he is a defendant, but also 'privileges him not to answer official questions put to him in any other proceeding, civil or criminal, formal or informal, where the answers might incriminate him in future criminal proceedings.' "In this case the Illinois Supreme Court ruled that a person whom the State attempts to commit under the Act is protected from use of his compelled answers in any subsequent criminal case in which he is the defendant. What we have here, then, is not a claim that petitioner's statements to the psychiatrists might be used to incriminate him in some future criminal proceeding, but instead his claim that because the sexually dangerous person proceeding is itself "criminal," he was entitled to refuse to answer any questions at all.

The question whether a particular proceeding is criminal for the purposes of the Self–Incrimination Clause is first of all a question of statutory construction. Here, Illinois has expressly provided that proceedings under the Act "shall be civil in nature," ¶ 105–3.01, indicating that when it files a petition against a person under the Act it intends to proceed in a nonpunitive, noncriminal manner, "without regard to the procedural protections and restrictions available in criminal prosecutions." As petitioner correctly points out, however, the civil label is not always dispositive. Where a defendant has provided "the clearest proof" that "the statutory scheme [is] so punitive either in purpose or effect as to negate [the State's] intention" that the proceeding be civil, it must be considered criminal and the privilege against self-incrimination must be applied. We think that petitioner has failed to provide such proof in this case.

q. For a full discussion of sex offender statutes, see pp. 674–98.

The Illinois Supreme Court reviewed the Act and its own case law and concluded that these proceedings, while similar to criminal proceedings in that they are accompanied by strict procedural safeguards, are essentially civil in nature. We are unpersuaded by petitioner's efforts to challenge this conclusion. Under the Act, the State has a statutory obligation to provide "care and treatment for [persons adjudged sexually dangerous] designed to effect recovery," ¶ 105–8, in a facility set aside to provide psychiatric care, *ibid.* And "[i]f the patient is found to be no longer dangerous, the court shall order that he be discharged." ¶ 105–9. While the committed person has the burden of showing that he is no longer dangerous, he may apply for release at any time. *Ibid.* In short, the State has disavowed any interest in punishment, provided for the treatment of those it commits, and established a system under which committed persons may be released after the briefest time in confinement. The Act thus does not appear to promote either of "the traditional aims of punishment—retribution and deterrence." Cf. *Addington v. Texas,* 441 U.S. 418, 428, 99 S.Ct. 1804, 1810, 60 L.Ed.2d 323 (1979) (in Texas "civil commitment state power is not exercised in a punitive sense"); *French v. Blackburn,* 428 F.Supp. 1351, 1358–1359 (M.D.N.C. (1977)), summarily aff'd, 443 U.S. 901, 99 S.Ct. 3091, 61 L.Ed.2d 869 (1979) (state need not accord privilege against self-incrimination in civil commitment proceeding).

Petitioner offers several arguments in support of his claim that despite the apparently nonpunitive purposes of the Act, it should be considered criminal as far as the privilege against self-incrimination is concerned. He first notes that the State cannot file a sexually-dangerous-person petition unless it has already brought criminal charges against the person in question. ¶ 105–3. In addition, the State must prove that the person it seeks to commit perpetrated "at least one act of or attempt at sexual assault or sexual molestation." 107 Ill.2d, at 105, 89 Ill.Dec., at 854, 481 N.E.2d, at 697. To petitioner, these factors serve to distinguish the Act from other civil commitment, which typically is not tied to any criminal charge and which petitioner apparently concedes is not "criminal" under the Self–Incrimination Clause. We disagree. That the State has chosen not to apply the Act to the larger class of mentally ill persons who might be found sexually dangerous does not somehow transform a civil proceeding into a criminal one. And as the State points out, it must prove more than just the commission of a sexual assault: the Illinois Supreme Court, as we noted above, has construed the Act to require proof of the existence of a mental disorder for more than one year and a propensity to commit sexual assaults, in addition to demonstration of that propensity through sexual assault.

The discussion of civil commitment in *Addington, supra,* in which this Court concluded that the Texas involuntary-commitment scheme is not criminal insofar as the requirement of proof beyond a reasonable doubt is concerned, fully supports our conclusion here:

> "[T]he initial inquiry in a civil commitment proceeding is very different from the central issue in either a delinquency proceeding

or a criminal prosecution. In the latter cases the basic issue is a straight-forward factual question—did the accused commit the act alleged? There may be factual issues to resolve in a commitment proceeding, but the factual aspects represent only the beginning of the inquiry. Whether the individual is mentally ill and dangerous to either himself or others and is in need of confined therapy turns on the *meaning* of the facts which must be interpreted by expert psychiatrists and psychologists." 441 U.S., at 429, 99 S.Ct., at 1811 (emphasis in original).

While here the State must prove at least one act of sexual assault, that antecedent conduct is received not to punish past misdeeds, but primarily to show the accused's mental condition and to predict future behavior.

In his attempt to distinguish this case from other civil commitment, petitioner places great reliance on the fact that proceedings under the Act are accompanied by procedural safeguards usually found in criminal trials. In particular, he observes that the Act provides an accused with the right to counsel, ¶ 105–5, the right to demand a jury trial, *ibid.,* and the right to confront and cross-examine witnesses. At the conclusion of the hearing, the trier of fact must determine whether the prosecution has proved the person's sexual dangerousness beyond a reasonable doubt. ¶ 105–3.01. But as we noted above, the State has indicated quite clearly its intent that these commitment proceedings be civil in nature; its decision nevertheless to provide some of the safeguards applicable in criminal trials cannot itself turn these proceedings into criminal prosecutions requiring the full panoply of rights applicable there.

Relying chiefly on *In re Gault,* 387 U.S. 1, 87 S.Ct. 1428, 18 L.Ed.2d 527 (1967), petitioner also urges that the proceedings in question are "criminal" because a person adjudged sexually dangerous under the Act is committed for an indeterminate period to the Menard Psychiatric Center, a maximum security institution that is run by the Illinois Department of Corrections and that houses convicts needing psychiatric care as well as sexually dangerous persons. Whatever its label and whatever the State's alleged purpose, petitioner argues, such commitment is the sort of punishment—total deprivation of liberty in a criminal setting—that *Gault* teaches cannot be imposed absent application of the privilege against self-incrimination. We believe that *Gault* is readily distinguishable.

First, *Gault's* sweeping statement that "our Constitution guarantees that no person shall be 'compelled' to be a witness against himself when he is threatened with deprivation of his liberty" is plainly not good law. Although the fact that incarceration may result is relevant to the question whether the privilege against self-incrimination applies, *Addington* demonstrates that involuntary commitment does not itself trigger the entire range of criminal procedural protections. Indeed, petitioner apparently concedes that traditional civil commitment does not require application of the privilege. * * *

The Court in *Gault* was obviously persuaded that the State intended to *punish* its juvenile offenders, observing that in many States juveniles may be placed in "adult penal institutions" for conduct that if committed by an adult would be a crime. Here, by contrast, the State serves its purpose of *treating* rather than punishing sexually dangerous persons by committing them to an institution expressly designed to provide psychiatric care and treatment. That the Menard Psychiatric Center houses not only sexually dangerous persons but also prisoners from other institutions who are in need of psychiatric treatment does not transform the State's intent to treat into an intent to punish. Nor does the fact that Menard is apparently a maximum security facility affect our analysis:

> "The state has a legitimate interest under its *parens patriae* powers in providing care to its citizens who are unable because of emotional disorders to care for themselves; the state also has authority under its police power to protect the community from the dangerous tendencies of some who are mentally ill." *Addington*, 441 U.S., at 426, 99 S.Ct., at 1809.

Illinois' decision to supplement its *parens patriae* concerns with measures to protect the welfare and safety of other citizens does not render the Act punitive.

Petitioner has not demonstrated, and the record does not suggest, that "sexually dangerous persons" in Illinois are confined under conditions incompatible with the State's asserted interest in treatment. Had petitioner shown, for example, that the confinement of such persons imposes on them a regimen which is essentially identical to that imposed upon felons with no need for psychiatric care, this might well be a different case. But the record here tells us little or nothing about the regimen at the psychiatric center, and it certainly does not show that there are no relevant differences between confinement there and confinement in the other parts of the maximum-security prison complex. Indeed, counsel for the State assures us that under Illinois law sexually dangerous persons must not be treated like ordinary prisoners. We therefore cannot say that the conditions of petitioner's confinement themselves amount to "punishment" and thus render "criminal" the proceedings which led to confinement.

Our conclusion that proceedings under the Act are not "criminal" within the meaning of the Fifth Amendment's guarantee against compulsory self-incrimination does not completely dispose of this case. Petitioner rather obliquely suggests that even if his commitment proceeding was not criminal, the Fourteenth Amendment's guarantee of due process nonetheless required application of the privilege. In particular, petitioner contends that the Illinois Supreme Court "grossly miscalculated" in weighing the interests set out in *Mathews v. Eldridge*, 424 U.S. 319, 96 S.Ct. 893, 47 L.Ed.2d 18 (1976). This Court has never held that the Due Process Clause of its own force requires application of the privilege against self-incrimination in a noncriminal proceeding, where the privilege claimant is protected against his compelled answers in any subsequent criminal case. We decline to do so today.

We think that the parties have in their reliance on *Mathews v. Eldridge* misconceived that decision. *Mathews* dealt with the procedural safeguards required by the Due Process Clause of the Fifth Amendment before a person might be deprived of property, and its focus was on such safeguards as were necessary to guard against the risk of erroneous deprivation. As the Supreme Court of Illinois and the State have both pointed out, it is difficult, if not impossible, to see how requiring the privilege against self-incrimination in these proceedings would in any way advance reliability. Indeed, the State takes the quite plausible view that denying the evaluating psychiatrist the opportunity to question persons alleged to be sexually dangerous would *decrease* the reliability of a finding of sexual dangerousness. As in *Addington,* "to adopt the criminal law standard gives no assurance" that States will reach a "better" result.

The privilege against self-incrimination enjoined by the Fifth Amendment is not designed to enhance the reliability of the fact-finding determination; it stands in the Constitution for entirely independent reasons. Just as in a "criminal case" it would be no argument against a claim of the privilege to say that granting the claim would decrease the reliability of the fact-finding process, the privilege has no place among the procedural safeguards discussed in *Mathews v. Eldridge,* which are designed to enhance the reliability of that process.

For the reasons stated, we conclude that the Illinois proceedings here considered were not "criminal" within the meaning of the Fifth Amendment to the United States Constitution, and that due process does not independently require application of the privilege. * * * The judgment of the Supreme Court of Illinois is therefore

Affirmed.

Questions and Comments

1. *The right to remain silent and civil commitment.* Because it limits application of the right to remain silent to criminal proceedings, *Allen* presumably forecloses a court from finding, under the federal constitution, that the right applies in civil commitment proceedings. See also, *French v. Blackburn,* 428 F.Supp. 1351, 1358–9 (M.D.N.C.1977), affirmed mem. 443 U.S. 901, 99 S.Ct. 3091, 61 L.Ed.2d 869 (1979). In fact, prior to *Allen,* only a few courts had so held. See, e.g., *Lessard v. Schmidt,* 349 F.Supp. 1078 (E.D.Wis.1972). Most decisions, even those which were otherwise sympathetic to constitutional claims in the civil commitment context, presaged *Allen* and found no right to remain silent at any point in the commitment process. See, e.g., *State ex rel. Hawks v. Lazaro,* 157 W.Va. 417, 202 S.E.2d 109, 126 (1974); *Suzuki v. Yuen,* 617 F.2d 173, 177–78 (9th Cir.1980); *Tippett v. Maryland,* 436 F.2d 1153 (4th Cir.1971).

However, some states, including Illinois, require that persons who are the subject of civil commitment proceedings be advised that they may refuse to talk to examining experts. See 405 Ill.Stat. 5/3–208. Moreover, statements that are "compelled" by the state during the commitment process are probably not admissible in a subsequent criminal proceeding; at least, *Allen* strongly implied as much with respect to statements made in the course of sex offender proceedings.

2. *Evaluating* Allen. In deciding that the privilege against self-incrimination does not apply to sex offender proceedings, the Court rejected a "deprivation of liberty" analysis and focused instead on whether the objective of such proceedings is punishment or treatment. Accepting this change in analysis, can it be said that the objective of criminal or civil commitment is *always* treatment?

Perhaps, as its rejection of the petitioner's due process claim suggests, the Court was also concerned about the practical consequences of a contrary decision. Consider the commentary to the American Psychiatric Association's "model" provision recommending that the respondent in civil commitment proceedings not be accorded a right to remain silent:

> Many cases that discuss whether the privilege should apply focus on the metaphysical issue of whether commitment is "essentially" a civil or criminal proceeding. This analysis misses the point. Advising a patient—who may well have an emergency psychiatric condition—at the beginning of an interview about his right to remain silent would be fundamentally inconsistent with the therapeutic purposes of the process. It might bewilder and alarm the patient. It might make it impossible to ascertain the patient's mental state, thereby preventing the assessment both of his need for treatment and his potential dangerousness.
>
> Commitment decisions would be transformed into judgments based solely on overt acts, becoming virtually indistinguishable from decisions made in the criminal process. Granting the Fifth Amendment privilege would establish a bootless procedural right—in some cases forcing the state to instigate criminal proceedings and in many cases depriving seriously mentally ill persons of needed treatment.[226]

Clifford Stromberg & Alan Stone, "A Model State Law on Civil Commitment of the Mentally Ill," 20 Harv.J.Legis. 274, 342–43 (1983).

Would the right to remain silent make it "impossible" to garner evidence about the mental state of a person with mental disability, as the APA commentary suggests might be true in some cases? Note that even in criminal cases, only about 20% of the defendants who are told they have a right to remain silent assert that right. See Richard A. Leo, "Inside the Interrogation Room," 86 J. Crim. L. & Criminol. 266, 276 (1996) (78% waiver rate). Similarly, Miller and his colleagues found that few persons subjected to commitment refuse to talk as a result of warnings. They speculate, based on other studies of the admission process, that this is because "most patients understand and recall little of what they are told on admission," that "many patients tend to perceive clinicians as helpers no matter what the situation," and that "warnings may actually seduce some

---

226. "... It would do a great disservice to individuals to make the procedural requirements so cumbersome that suicidal and maniacal individuals could never be hospitalized until they had injured themselves or others." *State ex rel. Hawks v. Lazaro,* 157 W.Va. 417, 443–44, 202 S.E.2d 109, 126 (1974).

patients into feeling secure enough to reveal more information than they otherwise would have done. . . ." Robert Miller et al., "The Right to Remain Silent During Psychiatric Examination in Civil and Criminal Cases—A National Survey and an Analysis," 9 Int'l J. L. & Psychiat. 77, 91–92 (1986). In any event, how important is it to have access to the subject of the proceeding when the issue is dangerousness or treatability (as compared, for instance, to sanity at the time of the offense)? Would it not be useful, through recognition of the right to remain silent, to encourage the state to develop alternative sources of information?

3. *Consequences of* Allen. If there is no right to remain silent in civil commitment proceedings, then the state may not only compel the respondent to answer questions during a psychiatric examination (as was the case in *Allen*), but may also compel testimony in court. What sanction may be imposed on the person who refuses to speak to the examiner or in court? In the analogous situations in criminal proceedings, the court has several options: (1) a contempt citation; (2) an instruction that the jury may infer guilt from the defendant's silence; and (3) prohibition of the defendant's expert testimony, at least in cases where the defendant has refused to talk to the state's expert. Will any of these sanctions "work" in the civil commitment context? With respect to the first sanction, what "punishment" should be imposed once the respondent is found in contempt? In regard to the second sanction, what inferences can be drawn from the respondent's silence? As to the third sanction, is it fair if the respondent is willing to talk in court?

Another issue associated with the right to remain silent is whether the respondent's attorney may observe the pre-hearing examination process. If the fifth amendment applied, then by analogy to the Supreme Court's opinion in *Miranda v. Arizona*, 384 U.S. 436, 86 S.Ct. 1602, 16 L.Ed.2d 694 (1966), the respondent should be told not only of the right to remain silent but also of the right to have counsel present during the examination. Is this a good idea? Even if there is no fifth amendment right to have counsel present during the evaluation, can one construct a sixth amendment argument in support of that right?

4. *Conditioning treatment on surrendering silence.* The Supreme Court has also held, in *McKune v. Lile*, 536 U.S. 24, 122 S.Ct. 2017, 153 L.Ed.2d 47 (2002), that the state may require sex offenders who want to participate in sex abuse treatment programs to reveal incriminating information about their previous offenses, both charged and uncharged. Under the Kansas program at issue in *Lile*, those offenders who choose not to reveal this information not only are denied access to the treatment program but also have various privileges curtailed, such as visitation from anyone other than lawyers, family or clergy; work opportunities; the ability to send money to family and make canteen expenditures; and access to personal television. Additionally, those who refuse to participate are likely to be transferred to more dangerous maximum security units to make room for those in the program. Five members of the Court found these consequences of refusal too "minimal" to constitute fifth amendment compulsion. Providing the fifth vote for the result was Justice O'Connor, who concluded that none of these consequences was "likely" to compel incrimination. In particular, she noted that prisoners who refused to talk still kept some visitation rights, and did

not require most of the other lost privileges, given the prison's provision of basic needs. With respect to the potential for transfer to a more dangerous prison setting, O'Connor stated that "it may be assumed that the prison is capable of controlling its inmates so that respondent's personal safety is not jeopardized by being placed in maximum security, at least in the absence of proof to the contrary." In light of *Lile*, any program of treatment in the traditional civil commitment setting that is conditioned on surrendering one's right to silence is unlikely to be unconstitutional.

D. RELEASE PROCEDURES

FASULO v. ARAFEH

Supreme Court of Connecticut, 1977.
173 Conn. 473, 378 A.2d 553.

LONGO, ASSOCIATE JUSTICE.

The plaintiffs, Ann Fasulo and Marie Barbieri, alleging that they were illegally confined in the Connecticut Valley Hospital by the defendant superintendent, petitioned the Superior Court for writs of habeas corpus. The court denied the writs and the plaintiffs appealed.

Ann Fasulo was civilly committed to Connecticut Valley Hospital in 1951, as was Marie Barbieri in 1964. * * * They claim that because their commitments are of indefinite duration and there is no procedure for periodic court review of the necessity for their confinement, their confinement is in violation of the due process guarantee of article first, § 8, of the Connecticut constitution.

* * *

As the United States Supreme Court has recognized, "At the least, due process requires that the nature and duration of commitment bear some reasonable relation to the purpose for which an individual is committed." *Jackson v. Indiana,* 406 U.S. 715, 738. Once the purpose of the commitment no longer exists, there is no constitutional basis for the state to continue to deprive the individual of his liberty. To satisfy due process, the procedure for releasing a civilly committed patient must be adequate to assure release of those who may no longer constitutionally be confined.

These plaintiffs have been deprived of their liberty. Their loss is already great, but can be initially justified as a result of the legitimate exercise of the parens patriae power of the state. The plaintiffs, however, have been committed indefinitely and confined for periods of twenty-six and thirteen years respectively, thus requiring us to heed the warning of the United States Supreme Court that the longer the commitment, the greater the safeguards which are required to ensure that no one is deprived of liberty without due process. We must, therefore, review the plaintiffs' claims in light of the important interest at stake—liberty—and the great loss which its extended deprivation constitutes.

Any procedure to allow the release of involuntarily confined civilly committed individuals must take account of the controlled and often isolated environment of the mental hospital from which the confined individuals will seek release. It must calculate the possible incompetence of those confined, their limited knowledge of release procedures, the cost of pursuing review and the amount of effort necessary to pursue review. Further, the procedure must be adapted to the possible effect of drugs or other treatment on the patient's capacity and must be formulated with consideration of institutional pressures to rely on the *medical* judgments of the hospital staff rather than to pursue extrainstitutional *legal* remedies. See note, "Civil Commitment of the Mentally Ill," 87 Harv. L.Rev. 1190, 1398.

At present, Connecticut provides several routes by which a mental patient can challenge his confinement. General Statutes § 17–192 allows for release (1) by order of the Probate Court "upon application and satisfactory proof that such person has been restored to reason," or (2) "[i]f the officers, directors or trustees of a state hospital for mental illness are notified by the superintendent or other person in a managerial capacity of such institution that he has reason to believe that any person committed thereto by order of a probate court is not mentally ill or a suitable subject to be confined in such institution, such officers, directors or trustees may discharge such person." Under the second method the patient runs the risk of having his release prevented by a superintendent whose determination may later be found by a court to have been erroneous. Furthermore, the second procedure disregards the fundamental fact that the state's power legitimately to confine an individual is based on a legal determination under General Statutes § 17–178 "that the person complained of is mentally ill and dangerous to himself or herself or others or gravely disabled" and that the commitment shall only continue "for the period of the duration of such mental illness or until he or she is discharged in due course of law." The state's power to confine terminates when the patient's condition no longer meets the legal standard for commitment. Since the state's power to confine is measured by a legal standard, the expiration of the state's power can only be determined in a judicial proceeding which tests the patient's present mental status against the legal standard for confinement. That adjudication cannot be made by medical personnel unguided by the procedural safeguards which cushion the individual from an overzealous exercise of state power when the individual is first threatened with the deprivation of his liberty.

* * *

We also find the first method of release provided for in General Statutes § 17–192 constitutionally deficient. The method allows release of a patient after he has applied to the Probate Court for discharge and has proved that he has been "restored to reason." We find this procedure inadequate on two grounds. First, it places the burden of initiating review of his status on the patient, a requirement which suffers from conceptual as well as serious practical deficiencies. As we stated previously, since the state's power to confine is premised on the individual's present mental status, the original involuntary commitment proceeding can only establish that the state may confine the individual at the time of the hearing and for the foreseeable period during which that status is unlikely to change. Upon the expiration of that period, the state's power to deprive the patient of his liberty lapses and any further confinement must be justified anew. The state, therefore, must bear the burden of initiating recommitment proceedings.

This same reasoning applies to the burden of proof at the recommitment hearing. The burden should not be placed on the civilly committed patient to justify his right to liberty. Freedom from involuntary confinement for those who have committed no crime is the natural state of individuals in this country. The burden must be placed on the state to prove the necessity of stripping the citizen of one of his most fundamental rights, and the risk of error must rest on the state.

* * *

Furthermore, to require a patient to initiate judicial review of his confinement and to bear the burden of proving the nonexistence of the necessity for that confinement ignores the practical considerations discussed above which are inherent in the mental patient's situation. Briefly, these include the difficulties of overcoming an isolated environment to initiate and coordinate a challenge to one's confinement. For instance, we cannot assume that friends and allies will always be available to secure counsel and marshal evidence on the patient's behalf. Nor can we assume that even if a patient is notified of his right to pursue any of the available remedies, he will be adequately protected. [Merely giving the patient notice] ignores the practical difficulties of requiring a mental patient to overcome the effects of his confinement, his closed environment, his possible incompetence and the debilitating effects of drugs or other treatment on his ability to make a decision which may amount to the waiver of his constitutional right to a review of his status.

* * *

We, therefore, hold that these plaintiffs have been denied their due process rights under the Connecticut constitution by the state's failure to provide them with periodic judicial review of their commitments in the form of state-initiated recommitment hearings replete with the safeguards of the initial commitment hearings at which the state bears the burden of proving the necessity for their continued confinement.

* * *

It is, therefore, ordered that the writs be granted and that the plaintiffs be afforded a hearing at which the state must justify their continued confinement.

There is error, and the case is remanded with direction to grant the writs in accordance with this opinion.

In this opinion SPEZIALE, J., concurs.

BOGDANSKI, ASSOCIATE JUSTICE (concurring).

* * *

[The dissenting opinion of Justice Loiselle in which Chief Justice House concurred is omitted.]

Questions and Comments

1. *Current status of periodic review.* Although at one time commitment in many states was truly indeterminate, virtually every state now requires, in line with the holding in *Fasulo*, that a review hearing be held after a certain period of involuntary treatment. Typically, a hearing similar in kind to the initial adjudicatory hearing must be held within six months of the previous commitment; other fairly common review periods are three months and a year. See Samuel Brakel et al. The Mentally Disabled and the Law 122–126 (1985) (statute chart).

Of course, judicial review through a writ of habeas corpus is always available if the patient requests it. Moreover, most patients are released prior to the first review hearing. The length of hospital stay for the majority of patients was under 90 days even in the 1970's. See Walter Gove & Terry Fain, "A Comparison of Voluntary and Committed Mental Patients," 34 Arch.Gen.Psychiat. 669, 673 (1977) (67% of involuntary patients discharged within 38 days); Carlos Tomelieri et al., "Who are the Committed?" 165 J. Nervous & Mental Dis. 288, 291 (1977) (63% of committed patients discharged within 90 days). Today, with the advent of managed care, the average duration of hospitalization is even shorter in many systems. Frederick Holt et al., "The Length of Psychiatric Hospital Stays and Community Stays," published by Va. Dept. Men. Health & Men. Retardation (2001)(41.7 days is the *average* length of stay in Virginia state psychiatric hospitals). Nonetheless, a substantial number of patients are still *not* voluntarily discharged by the hospital within a short period of time. See W.A. Leginski et al., "Patients Served in State Hospitals: Results from a Longitudinal Data Base," in NIMH, Mental Health United States, DHHS Pub. (ADM) 90–1708 (1990)(reporting a study of eleven state psychiatric hospitals finding that 25% of clients were confined for over four years). And relief via habeas corpus is hampered not only by the requirement that the patient initiate such proceedings but also because the petitioner bears the burden of proving the challenged detention is illegal.

2. *Timing of review. Fasulo* does not indicate when the judicial review it mandates must take place. However, it does quote the Supreme Court's statement in *Jackson v. Indiana*, 406 U.S. 715, 92 S.Ct. 1845, 32 L.Ed.2d 435 (1972), that "due process requires that the nature and duration of commitment bear some reasonable relation to the purpose for which the individual is committed."[r] With this language in mind, of what relevance is research

---

r. *Jackson* held that hospitalization of those found incompetent to stand trial may last only so long as there is a substantial probability that the patient will attain competency in the foreseeable future. See pp. 1027–31.

that shows that the vast majority of civilly committed patients can be treated effectively within 100 days? Gerald Klerman, "National Trends in Hospitalization," 30 Hosp. & Comm. Psychiat. 110 (1979). If this research is substantiated, should a hearing be constitutionally mandated at the end of this period? Alternatively, given the possibility that no further treatment will be effective, should all patients simply be released at the expiration of 100 days? In arguing in favor of such a rule, Stromberg and Stone cite the above-mentioned research and state:

> We believe that after a certain period of treatment and involuntary confinement, society must give patients a chance on their own. We might agree that this should not apply to an imminently suicidal person if it would be predicted that some finite further period of treatment would likely end the person's suicidal impulses. Unfortunately, this is rarely possible.

Clifford Stromberg & Alan Stone, "A Model State Law on Civil Commitment of the Mentally Ill," 20 Harv.J.Leg. 275, 380 (1983). Might agreement with the Stromberg and Stone proposal depend upon whether the commitment is for parens patriae or police power purposes?

3. *Formality of review.* Are there any differences between the initial commitment and the review process that merit additional (or fewer) procedural protections at the latter proceeding? Should the state have to meet a heavier burden if it seeks continued commitment? Might a public jury decision be more useful in the review process than at the initial commitment?

4. *Waiver of review hearing.* The *Fasulo* court suggested that allowing the patient to decide whether a hearing should take place is unconstitutional. Does this mean that the majority would reject a provision allowing a waiver of the right to a hearing? Consider the following, from David Wexler, "The Waivability of Recommitment Hearings," 20 Ariz.L.Rev. 175, 184–86 (1978).

> Clearly, if mechanisms could be devised to eliminate the need for those, and only those, recommitment hearings that are truly unnecessary and truly unwanted by the patients, a host of considerations would favor a rule of waivability. A number of such considerations come quickly to mind.
>
> There is, of course, the sheer economic consideration involving the depletion of judicial, mental health, and related resources. Courts sitting in the vicinity of state hospitals have terribly heavy commitment calendars. They assuredly would wish to be spared the time and expense of conducting unnecessary and unwanted recommitment hearings.
>
> The judicial time-and-cost saving interest would be particularly evident, of course, if an appreciable number of patients wished to waive such hearings. At the moment, the percent of patients desiring waiver is an empirical unknown. It would not be at all surprising, however, for a rather large number of patients to desire waiver. The depressed and suicidal might well constitute one such patient category. So too, many elderly, "gravely disabled" patients might opt for waiver, were it avail-

able, rather than attend hearings only to learn what they already know: that their clinical and family situation is unchanged or has worsened, and that no facilities less restrictive than full-time hospitalization can yet be found for their placement.

Needless to say, physicians, nurses, and ward attendants would also prefer to treat than to testify. To the extent that they are called upon to testify in unnecessary and unwanted hearings, the patients and the public would be best served by those mental health witnesses playing instead a therapeutic role.

* * *

The interests of psychotherapists and of certain patients converge in their concern over the possible traumatic and anti-therapeutic effects of recommitment hearings. Unlike initial hearings, where the possible trauma to the patient is probably outweighed by the feedback to him of the impropriety of his behavior and by the presentation of convincing evidence that commitment is called for, the interests deserve to be balanced differently in the framework of recommitment.

By the time of recommitment, a patient may well be quite aware of what is objectionable about his behavior or of why alternative placement seems unsuitable. Moreover, whether hearing adverse testimony will prove traumatic or anti-therapeutic is no longer a matter of enormous abstract speculation: the patient will have already experienced one commitment hearing and may now be in a fairly good position to assess the relative costs and benefits of contesting recommitment. If recommitment is in any event likely, a number of patients may wish to avoid hearings at which testimony will be given regarding, for example, the persistence of their depressed and suicidal state, or the continuing unwillingness of families or of nursing homes to accept patients who act out conflicts or who are sometimes assaultive.

* * *

... Waivability—consent to recommitment for up to a specified period—should probably be authorized if a lawyer playing an adversary role certifies to the court that he has investigated the case and has consulted with his client, that he has explained to the client the options and the right to consent recommitment, and that he has concluded that the client desires to consent to recommitment.

5. *Conditional release.* One reason for the short hospitalization periods of many patients described in note 1 is the development of conditional release programs. Theoretically, these programs function somewhat like parole. A patient is released on "conditional" or "convalescent" status to a community mental health center, halfway house, or other community service in an effort to ease the transition to normal life, on the condition that the patient adheres to a particular treatment regimen (e.g., periodic medication, attendance at group therapy sessions) and remains stable. Immediate rehospitalization is permissible, however, if the patient is shown to require it. In practice, these programs have been hampered by lack of adequate community resources and poor communication between hospitals and community service providers. See generally, Note, "Constitutional Law: The Summary

Revocation of an Involuntary Mental Patient's Convalescent Leave—Is It Unconstitutional?" 33 Okla.L.Rev. 366, 369 (1980).

A preliminary question with respect to conditional release is whether such programs are permissible exercises of state power. Most statutes imply, if they do not state explicitly, that those patients who are conditionally released no longer meet commitment standards. See *True v. State Department of Health and Welfare*, 103 Idaho 151, 645 P.2d 891, 898 (1982). If so, under what authority may the state continue to maintain *any* control over the patient? Perhaps, as discussed in the materials on the least restrictive alternative doctrine, the justification for such continued interference is that it contemplates a lesser deprivation of liberty and thus is permissible on a lesser showing than that demanded by the commitment standards. There may be other justifications as well. Cf. American Bar Association Criminal Justice Mental Health Standard 7–7.4 (permitting continued confinement of an insanity acquittee who no longer meets the commitment criteria if the state can show that the only reason the criteria are not met is that the patient is undergoing treatment that is likely to end unless commitment continues).

In any event, the most significant litigation with respect to conditional release programs has assumed their constitutionality and focused instead on procedural questions. In particular, courts have been concerned with provisions that permit conditional release to be revoked on the authority of the hospital director, with no requirement of judicial supervision other than, in some states, an ex parte order. Not surprisingly, given the similarity between conditional release and parole, these courts have focused on the Supreme Court's decision in *Morrissey v. Brewer,* 408 U.S. 471, 92 S.Ct. 2593, 33 L.Ed.2d 484 (1972), which held that the "conditional liberty" of paroled criminals entitles them to preliminary and final parole revocation hearings, notice and confrontation rights and, in "complex" revocation proceedings, the right to counsel as well.

In *Dietrich v. Brooks,* 27 Or.App. 821, 558 P.2d 357 (1976), the court found that there are "profound differences of nature, degree and function" between conditional hospital release and parole. Specifically, the court noted three distinctions: (1) the underlying nature of imprisonment and parole is penal, while conditional release is a therapeutic device; (2) the length of the deprivation of liberty differs; and (3) there is a closer relationship between the conditional liberty and the institutional program with conditional release than with parole. Thus, the court held, summary revocation of conditional release is adequate under the due process clause.

Other courts have decided that more process is due patients whose conditional release is revoked. For instance, in *True v. State Department of Health and Welfare,* 103 Idaho 151, 645 P.2d 891 (1982), the court considered the constitutionality of a statute which permitted immediate revocation of conditional release status when (1) the "director of the [mental health] department or his designated representative" believed that the patient had failed to meet the conditions of his release and that "conditions justifying hospitalization continue[d] to exist;" or when (2) the director or his designate had reason to believe that the patient had "relapsed" and was "again in need of hospitalization," based on the report of two persons "who are either licensed physicians, health officers, designated examiners or peace officers, the prosecuting attorney or a judge of a court." The court rejected the state's argument that the patient's ability to appeal any hospitalization decision within 30 days and the additional right to habeas relief adequately protected the patient's due process interests, for the same types of reasons given by the court in *Fasulo* in explaining its requirement of period review. It then required: "(1) prompt written notice to the patient of the reasons for and evidence relied on justifying rehospitalization as well as notice of the right to challenge the allegations and (2) a hearing before a neutral hearing body to be held as soon as is reasonably possible following the patient's rehospitalization, at which time the patient is to be afforded the right to counsel, the right to present evidence and examine witnesses, and upon a decision sustaining the order of rehospitalization, the right to a written statement by the fact-finding body as to the reasons for revocation of the patient's conditional release status." The court did not require an immediate revocation proceeding, distinguishing *Morrissey* on the following grounds:

> [T]iming becomes more critical in the instant case than it is in the parole setting. In the parole situation a delay in the revocation of an individual's parolee status, while highly undesirable in cases where revocation is found to be justified, does not present a serious threat to the degree of rehabilitation achieved prior to the violation. In contrast, in cases where a mental health patient is suspected of remission, the Department's interest in rehospitalization for immediate treatment is paramount, as the progress towards recovery which had been achieved is seriously jeopardized by a remission which is left untreated.

* * *

The great weight we accord the Department's need for immediate rehospitalization of a conditionally released mental health patient suspected of remission is such that the general rule that an individual be given an opportunity for a hearing before he is deprived of a protectible interest is inapplicable. The situation present when a decision is made to revoke the conditional release status of the patient is extraordinary: the patient because of a suspected remission in his mental condition possibly poses a danger to others and/or to himself.

Most statutes are unclear as to whether revocation of conditional release begins an entirely new commitment period or instead only authorizes hospitalization for the remainder of the original commitment. Should this matter? Note that parole revocation, at issue in *Morrissey*, only permits the state to force completion of the sentence already imposed by the sentencing court.

A final issue connected with conditional release that has yet to be extensively litigated concerns the types of limitations the Constitution places on the conditions that may be imposed as part of such a program. For instance, in a jurisdiction that recognizes a right to refuse medication, may release be conditioned upon the patient's agreement to accept medication? In the sentencing context, probationary conditions that are "reasonably related" to the probationer's rehabilitation and protection of the public are virtually always upheld. But conditions which unreasonably trench on first amendment, fourth amendment or foundational privacy rights (e.g., a sterilization requirement) have been declared unconstitutional. H.J. Jaffe, "Probation with a Flair: A Look at Some Out-of-the-Ordinary Conditions," 43 Fed. Probation 25 (1979).

E. VOLUNTARY ADMISSION PROCEDURES

Since the end of the second World War, there has been a growing interest in avoiding involuntary commitment proceedings by encouraging "voluntary" admission of people with mental disorders; today every state but Alabama allows people to admit themselves for psychiatric treatment. Nationally, such admissions probably comprise over 50% of the mental hospital population and about 85% of the population in psychiatric units of general hospitals. Samuel Brakel et al., The Mentally Disabled and the Law 178–79 (1985); Susan C. Reed and Dan A. Lewis, in "The Negotiation of Voluntary Admission in Chicago's State Mental Hospitals," 18 J. Psychiatry & L. 137 (1990)(roughly 75% admitted voluntarily at intake and roughly 80% of those remaining admitted voluntarily within 10 days). One early explanation of why voluntary status has been so favored asserted:

> [Voluntary admission] enjoys the unique position of being favored by all of the groups concerned with influencing legislation in this field. The medical profession endorses this procedure because of its simplicity and the complete lack of any court action. The patient who can recognize his illness and seek hospitalization on his own volition is the one who will actively participate in his treatment, cooperate with his doctor, and benefit the most from the treatment. As a result the voluntary patient will be discharged more rapidly, thereby alleviating the generally crowded conditions that exist in most mental facilities. Those who are concerned with civil liberties of mental patients are reassured, since the dangers of wrongful detention exist only in involuntary hospitalization procedures.

Comment, "Hospitalization of the Mentally Disabled in Pennsylvania: The Mental Health–Mental Retardation Act of 1966," 71 Dick.L.Rev. 307, 308–09 (1967); see also Group for the Advancement of Psychiatry, Forced into Treatment: The Role of Coercion in Clinical Practice (1994). This section examines the procedures associated with hospitalizing a person whom the state is willing to admit as a "voluntary" patient.

JANET SCHMIDT & JOHN GILBOY "VOLUNTARY" HOSPITALIZATION OF THE MENTALLY ILL
66 N.W.L.Rev. 429.
(1971).

Both the medical and legal proponents of voluntary care share a conception of voluntary admission as an individual decision to accept mental treatment, made entirely apart from involuntary commitment procedures, thereby avoiding the therapeutic and legal problems of coercion. We have recently studied the use of voluntary admission procedures in Illinois, a state in which a substantial majority of persons hospitalized in mental institutions are now admitted under voluntary procedures. The results of our study indicate that the foregoing conception is wrong.

In a majority of cases voluntary admission is utilized to hospitalize persons who are already in some form of official custody. Voluntary admission avoids procedural complexity and the need for officials to assume responsibility, both inherent drawbacks to compulsory commitment from the officials' point of view. Individuals are therefore induced to voluntarily commit themselves with the threat of involuntary commitment as the principal means of persuasion, and with little concern for the adequacy of the information on which the individual's decision is based or whether it is "voluntary" at all.

* * *

Although our study was limited to analysis of relevant statistical data and direct personal observation of commitment procedures in Illinois, that state's procedures for commitment of the mentally ill are similar to those of many other states.

Definition of Voluntary Admission

Under Illinois law there are two different procedures for voluntary admission to mental hospitals. Under the first procedure, known as "informal admission," an individual is admitted to a mental hospital without formal application and is free to leave at any time during normal day-shift hours. Under the second procedure, known as "voluntary admission," an individual is admitted to a mental hospital upon formal application and is free to leave "within 5 days, excluding Saturdays, Sundays and holidays, after he gives any professional staff person notice of his desire to leave, ..." However, during that 5–day notice period, the hospital officials may ask a court to hold an involuntary commitment hearing, which must be set within 5 days after such petition. The patient continues to be hospitalized pending a final order of the court at the hearing. Thus, informal admission may be described as an entirely voluntary process. Voluntary admission, in contrast, requires an initial voluntary decision on the part of the patient, but, once that decision is made, the patient is subject to restraint on his right to leave the hospital, and may be required to remain a week or more after he expresses a desire to leave.

A striking preliminary fact which our study disclosed is that informal admission is almost never utilized. In fact, in only about one percent of the cases admitted to mental institutions in Illinois is "informal admission" utilized. In contrast, voluntary admission is used in about 68% of all cases. The reason for the greater use of voluntary admission appears to be the additional restraining power the procedure gives the hospital over the patient. "With 'informal admission' the units just do not feel enough control over the patient," one hospital admissions officer remarked. Another hospital official described informal admission as an "inconvenience" to hospital staff personnel and an unnecessary "allowance" to patients. In one case described to us by an admissions officer, informal admission was used to house overnight an individual admittedly not in need of hospitalization, but for whom no other immediate shelter could be found.

The almost total refusal to use the entirely voluntary informal admission procedure is suggestive at the outset of the general attitude of officials toward voluntary admission procedures. The value of such procedures to officials, as will be more evident below, is not primarily in allowing individuals to remain in control of their own circumstances, but rather in hospitalizing individuals with a minimum of official responsibility and difficulty.

POLICE CUSTODY CASES

The case which proponents of voluntary admission almost always have in mind is that of an individual who arrives at a mental institution by himself, or accompanied by a physician, family, relatives or friends, and asks to be admitted for treatment. We call these "non-custody cases" to denote the absence of any official custody prior to the individual's decision to commit himself.

* * *

Our study disclosed that about 40% of all voluntarily admitted patients are brought to the mental hospital by the police and in about 55% of the cases where individuals are brought to the hospital by the police, voluntary admission results. While some studies of civil commitment have recognized that a significant number of persons are brought to mental institutions by the police, there has been little recognition that such cases often result in voluntary rather than involuntary commitment.

* * *

It is important to understand the difference between these police custody cases and the non-custody cases which proponents of voluntary care have usually assumed. In non-custody cases, the individual is making a choice between voluntarily committing himself or remaining outside the hospital, which is a fairly simple choice. The application form for voluntary admission discloses the restrictions on the right to leave the hospital which that status will impose.

In police custody cases, on the other hand, the alternatives as they appear to the individual are voluntary admission versus involuntary commitment. This is a much more difficult decision. In these cases, to make a reasonable choice, the individual must be informed about the nature of the involuntary commitment process since that is the major alternative before him. [M]ost persons unquestionably have only the vaguest idea, if any at all, about the nature of the involuntary commitment procedure. Indeed, most persons probably have only a vague idea of the substantive legal standard to be applied at such a hearing.

The typical practice in cases, however, is to explain voluntary admission to the patient in a very cursory manner, describing it as a desirable alternative to involuntary commitment. The explanation "If you sign a voluntary admission it will only be between you and the doctor and not the judge," is typical. To regard the uninformed decision to accept hospitalization as "voluntary" is highly artificial.

COURT CASES

Our study disclosed that approximately 10–11% of voluntary admissions to mental hospitals result from decisions made, or announced, in court at the time of an involuntary commitment hearing. Voluntary admission occurs in approximately 35% of the cases which come to court for involuntary commitment hearings. The court hearing may be the result of initial involuntary commitment on the basis of an emergency petition or physician's certificate as described earlier. However, in about 60% of cases the court hearing follows an initial criminal arrest.

* * *

A decision to accept voluntary admission by a defendant at a court hearing raises the same issue of adequate disclosure discussed earlier in connection with voluntary admission of persons brought by the police to the hospital admissions office. It might be expected that the involvement of the public defender and the judge at the time of a court hearing would insure that any decision on admission would be fully informed. However, the judges involved appear to give no consideration to the defendant's awareness of his situation. Any indication that the public defender and state's attorney are agreeable to voluntary admission and that the patient will agree is sufficient to dispose of the case. There is no inquiry to ascertain whether the defendant understands the choices before him and the decision he is making. The public defender, because of the time pressures to which he is subject and the non-adversary conception of his job, does not seek to advise patients of their rights so that they can make an informed judgment. Rather, the public defender makes his own judgment as to whether voluntary admission is appropriate and, if so, then urges the defendant to accept such hospitalization in a manner not unlike that of admissions officers in cases discussed earlier.

Where persons come to civil commitment hearings after having initially been arrested on criminal charges (a majority of the cases in Chicago), a further legal issue is raised. In these cases the individuals are under an added pressure: the threat of criminal prosecution if they should successfully resist civil commitment. If the individual is committed, voluntarily or involuntarily, the criminal charge against him is usually dropped.

* * *

Our study disclosed that in a majority of the cases in which voluntary admission procedures were used, the individuals were already under some form of official custody and were faced with the threat of involuntary commitment proceedings as the principal alternative to voluntary admission.

Questions and Comments

1. *The informed consent model of voluntary admission.* Gilboy and Schmidt suggest that many voluntary admissions in Illinois are not really voluntary because of the implicit and explicit pressures exerted on those who agree to such admissions and because of the failure to explain to them the nature and consequence of such admissions. Would their concerns be addressed by imposing an informed consent requirement on the voluntary admission process? As discussed in Chapter Four, the informed consent doctrine requires that, before treatment is administered, the potential patient must (1) be told of its risks and benefits; (2) be able to competently assess them; and (3) make a voluntary decision to undergo the treatment based on this assessment. The three aspects of the doctrine as they might apply in the voluntary admission context are discussed below.

Disclosure of Information. Gilboy and Schmidt's research indicates that persons who are admitted as voluntary patients rarely have their options fully explained to them and as a result have only vague notions about them. Presumably, all potential patients should be told about the alternatives open to them: the nature and consequences of involuntary commitment (and of the criminal process, if this is a disposition being considered) and the nature and consequences of voluntary commitment. Is this enough?

A study conducted of voluntary admission practices in Chicago conducted almost twenty years after the study reported above found many of the same practices that Gilboy & Schmidt did. Susan Reed & Dan Lewis, "The Negotiation of Voluntary Admission in Chicago State Mental Hospitals," 18 J. Psychiatry & L. 137 (1990). The authors report that in order to get a voluntary admission, hospital staff will often hide the fact that those who are involuntarily committed do not necessarily stay in the hospital any longer than those who are admitted voluntarily. According to one coordinator:

> I tell the person that I will do everything possible to get them out of the hospital as soon as possible, but that if they get committed they'll stay for 60 days. I don't tell them that I would discharge them just as soon whether they sign a voluntary or they go to court. That's true, but you just don't bother to tell them that part of the truth.

Id. at 144. Is this a violation of the disclosure principle?

Competency. As developed in Chapter Nine, determining whether the information which is imparted is competently assessed is problematic, given the difficulty of defining competency. But it is worth noting that every study of the issue has concluded that most voluntary patients have significant difficulty understanding their situation. The best constructed study, which involved interviews of 50 voluntary patients within two days of their admission, found that "a large percentage of the patients who voluntarily entered [the] hospital were not competent to consent to their own admission." Paul Appelbaum et al., "Empirical Assessment of Competency to Consent to Psychiatric Hospitalization," 138 Am.J.Psych. 1170, 1174 (1981). This finding held "whether competency was defined on narrow clinical grounds, with a broader clinically oriented focus, in terms that measure understanding of legal rights, or by means of criteria that combined all of these definitions." Id. Interestingly, the study also found that "50% of the patients did not acknowledge their need to be in a psychiatric hospital; the vast majority of these denied it outright." Id. at 1173.

Another study reported interviews with 100 voluntary patients, each of whom had signed a form setting out their rights, as well as their obligation to remain for three days after giving notice of intent to leave. The interviews, conducted five days after admission, produced the following results:

1.	Patient unable to make relevant answer to questions	13 patients
2.	Patient responsive to questions but had no relevant information	18 patients
3.	Patient responsive but had erroneous information	24 patients
4.	Patient had incomplete information	37 patients
5.	Patient had complete information	8 patients

Ten days after admission 33 of the patients were interviewed again. Fifteen showed a higher level of understanding at the second interview than they had at the first. Grace Olin & Harry Olin, "Informed Consent in Voluntary Mental Hospital Admissions," 132 Am.J.Psychiat. 938 (1975). See also, Lisa Grossman & Frank Summers, "A Study of the Capacity of Schizophrenic Patients to Give Informed Consent," 31 J.Hosp. & Comm.Psychiat. 205 (1980).

Voluntariness. The claim that many voluntary admissions are not truly voluntary, put forth in the Gilboy and Schmidt article, is also made by Reed and Lewis, supra:

> For the treatment coordinator the most desirable resolution of the problem of the patient's legal status is the patient's signature on a voluntary admission form. As soon as the patient signs that form, the treatment coordinator can send it onto the court and avoid any further negotiations with the court and its personnel.... One treatment coordinator said, "I never go to court. I've been here 18 years. If the court depended on me, it would close down."

> * * *

> The most common strategy [to get the signature on the voluntary form], and usually the first, is a combination of *persuasion and coercion.* The treatment coordinator points out to the patient the advantages of voluntary admission over involuntary commitment in order to convince him/her to sign.... Most suggest to patients that they are likely to be involuntarily committed if they refuse to sign a voluntary. For example, one treatment coordinator says, "If they don't sign, I say to them, 'You look committable to me.' They go for that. I tell them to put themselves in the judge's shoes. What would they do? They usually sign."

> * * *

If this combination of persuasion and coercion does not break down the patients' resistance to voluntary admission, the treatment coordinator may try *bartering*. This strategy involves the exchange of hospital privileges for the patient's signature on a voluntary admission form . . . However, patients sometimes complain that the deals they negotiate with their treatment coordinators fall through. As one patient said of his therapist, "He promised me a grounds pass if I signed a voluntary, but he never delivered. I should never should have signed." Staff, of course, have the option of withholding privileges once the form has been signed.

* * *

Stalling can [also] be a strategy. . . . In some few cases emergency certified patients continue to refuse to sign a voluntary admission form despite this massive institutional effort to get them to do so. The hospital staff can solve their legal dilemma by getting additional continuances from the court until the patient is ready for discharge. Only four continuances are allowed per case, but two continuances are usually enough to get a patient ready for discharge. [Lewis and his coauthors] found that continuances kept patients in the hospital an average of just under 10 days.

Id. at 144–152.

Are any of the strategies described by this study impermissible as a legal matter? Consider the law on plea bargaining, the process by which criminal defendants agree to plead guilty in exchange for a reduced charge or sentence. The Supreme Court has made clear that a guilty plea produced by this process may be rendered involuntary by "coercion, terror, inducements, [and] subtle or blatant threats." *Boykin v. Alabama,* 395 U.S. 238, 89 S.Ct. 1709, 23 L.Ed.2d 274 (1969). At the same time, the Court has refused to invalidate guilty pleas simply because the defendant's situation is an unpleasant one. So long as a guilty plea represents a reasoned choice from among alternatives that are legitimately offered by the prosecution, it is not "involuntary." *Bordenkircher v. Hayes,* 434 U.S. 357, 98 S.Ct. 663, 54 L.Ed.2d 604 (1978); *Brady v. United States,* 397 U.S. 742, 90 S.Ct. 1463, 25 L.Ed.2d 747 (1970). Would the decision to be a voluntary patient described above be "involuntary" under these cases? If not, is there still a reason for withholding the voluntary label from such a person?

2. *Alternatives to the informed consent model.* In light of the difficulties with the informed consent model of voluntary admission, particularly with respect to ensuring competent decisionmaking, various alternatives have been proposed. The first alternative is to allow voluntary admission of anyone who is "suitable" for such admission and fails to object to it. Several states appear to permit so-called "non-protesting" admissions. See, e.g., Mass Gen.Laws Ann. ch. 111, § 63(a); D.C.Stat. § 21–513.

Although such [provisions] slight the value of individual autonomy that the informed consent is designed to foster, it would be no worse than the present system and would have the additional virtue of avoiding pretense. This system could, in addition, be augmented with the kind of internal review procedures (e.g. utilization review, staff conferences) that the Supreme Court indicated were adequate to protect the rights of minors admitted by their parents [in *Parham v. J.R.*]. Such a change would maximize therapeutic interests, while relegating more formal, legalistic proceedings to the background.

Appelbaum, supra at 1175. Are provisions which permit admission of non-protesting persons an end-run around the procedural requirements of involuntary commitment? Or are they justified by the "need for a simple, non-traumatic admission process for those individuals who either do not recognize their need for hospitalization or are unwilling to seek admission, but nevertheless do not object when others initiate the admission process?" Note, "District of Columbia Hospitalization of the Mentally Ill Act," 65 Colum.L.Rev. 1062, 1065 (1965). In the past, many of the admissions under such statutes have been of senile persons who make no objection to psychiatric hospitalization. See *Application for Certification of William R,* 9 Misc.2d 1084, 172 N.Y.S.2d 869 (1958).

The second alternative to an informed consent model of voluntary admission is to appoint a guardian for all persons who assent to or do not protest hospitalization. The guardian's function would be to decide whether hospitalization is in the person's best interests, considering all relevant factors, including the person's wishes. This substituted judgment model is widely used as a method of institutionalizing minors and people with developmental disability. Very often the guardian is one of the putative patient's relatives, but it could be a judge or a public guardian. Does this approach provide any better protection against the practices observed by Gilboy and Schmidt?

A third alternative, of course, is to prohibit admission into a public psychiatric facility unless the person meets the criteria for involuntary commitment. Presumably, this would bar some people who want or need treatment from obtaining it. Some commentators argue against *any* procedure which has this effect:

In the vast majority of involuntary *and* voluntary cases, it is the family or relatives who move toward, pressure for, or insist on commitment. If state law enforcement personnel are involved, it is as often as not at the request of the family or relatives. In many instances where it orders commitment, the state's judicial machinery merely formalizes and sanctions a decision arrived at by the family and the family doctor. In admitting a mentally disabled person to one of its institutions, the state often does no more than facilitate the provision of wanted treatment that is difficult or too costly to obtain otherwise. With respect to the commitment process, the patient himself ... may be confused or indifferent, generally agitated, unable to understand its necessity, or simply unable to comprehend. The phenomenon of a freely derived, fully conscious, voluntary decision to enter a mental facility (particularly a public facility) is as rare as knowing, overt resistance to involuntary commitment. In short, the voluntary-involuntary dichotomy of mental institutionalization, the traditional roles that are assigned to the participants in this dichotomized process, and many of the laws and procedures enacted to regulate it suffer from their irrelevance to practical situations.

Brakel et al., supra, at 32.

3. *The Supreme Court and voluntary commitment.* In *Zinermon v. Burch*, 494 U.S. 113, 110 S.Ct. 975, 108 L.Ed.2d 100 (1990), the plaintiff was asked to sign forms giving his consent to admission and treatment, even though staff evaluation showed that, upon his arrival at the evaluating facility, he was "hallucinating, confused, psychotic, and believed he was 'in heaven.'" Within the next three days, he signed voluntary admission forms on two other occasions. He subsequently brought a § 1983 action against the state of Florida, alleging that his due process rights were violated by the staff when they admitted him as a voluntary patient knowing he was incompetent, rather than affording him the procedural protections granted those subjected to involuntary commitment. Although the U.S. Supreme Court did not address the merits, it held that this claim was justiciable in federal court under § 1983. Portions of the Court's opinion may be of interest in deciding between the informed consent model or one of the alternative approaches:

> The Florida statutes, of course, do not allow incompetent persons to be admitted as "voluntary" patients.... A patient who is willing to sign forms but incapable of informed consent certainly cannot be relied on to protest his "voluntary" admission and demand that the involuntary placement procedure be followed. The staff are the only persons in a position to take notice of any misuse of the voluntary admission process, and to ensure that the proper procedure is followed.

> Florida chose to delegate to petitioners a broad power to admit patients to FSH, i.e., to effect what, in the absence of informed consent, is a substantial deprivation of liberty. Because petitioners had state authority to deprive persons of liberty, the Constitution imposed on them the State's concomitant duty to see that no deprivation occurs without adequate procedural protections.

> It may be permissible constitutionally for a State to have a statutory scheme like Florida's, which gives state officials broad power and little guidance in admitting mental patients. But when those officials fail to provide constitutionally required procedural safeguards to a person whom they deprive of liberty, the state officials cannot then escape liability.... It is immaterial whether the due process violation Burch alleges is best described as arising from petitioners' failure to comply with state procedures for admitting involuntary patients, or from the absence of a specific requirement that petitioners determine whether a patient is competent to consent to voluntary admission.

Professor Winick has argued that *Zinermon* is misguided to the extent it suggests that a patient seeking voluntary treatment is required to understand the clinical and legal risks and benefits of hospitalization and its alternatives. He contends that such a rule would "relegate many to the burdens and stigma of involuntary commitment." Instead,

> a low standard of competency is all that should be required. As long as the patient understands that the facility he is seeking admission to is a psychiatric hospital, that he will receive care and treatment there, and that release is not automatic, but can occur if he should change his mind and that in such an event he can obtain help from any staff member to gain his release, he should be deemed competent.

The primary justification for this approach, according to Winick, is the large body of cognitive and social psychology literature (to date not adequately tested in the commitment context) which suggests that people who "feel personally committed" to a goal are more likely to achieve it. The literature also suggests that, "[e]xcept for young children, and sometimes even including them, the more choice we give individuals, the more they will act as mature, self-determining adults." Coercion, on the other hand, "may backfire, producing a negative 'psychological reactance' that sets up failure." Bruce Winick, "Competency to Consent to Voluntary Hospitalization: A Therapeutic Jurisprudence Analysis of Zinermon v. Burch," 14 Int'l J.L. & Psych. 169, 191–98 (1991).

The American Psychiatric Association has essentially endorsed this approach, although its proposal also has elements of the non-protesting admission scheme described earlier. Francine Cournos, et al., "Report on the Task Force on Consent to Voluntary Hospitalization," 21 Bull. Am.Acad.Psychiatry & L. 392 (1993). The APA recommends that voluntary hospitalization should continue even if the capacity of an assenting patient is in doubt, so long as an "independent psychiatrist" confirms that hospitalization is "appropriate and that the patient is continuing to assent to hospitalization." Id. at 304.

4. *Release of voluntary patients.* The procedure for releasing voluntary patients under the Illinois statute described by Gilboy and Schmidt is similar to that found in most states. Typically, a voluntary patient who wants to leave the hospital may not do so immediately but must give notice, ranging from three to ten days, during which time the hospital may initiate commitment proceedings if it feels involuntary commitment is warranted. This restraint on release has been justified by Mannfred Guttmacher and Henry Weihofen, Psychiatry and the Law 306 (1952), as follows:

> With regard to provisions for release, two opposing considerations must be weighed. On the one hand, complete freedom to leave the hospital at any time will almost certainly lead a number of patients to leave a few days after being admitted, for restlessness and dissatisfaction with the restrains of hospitalization are common and natural, especially during the first period of adjustment. This makes the admission a complete waste of time and money. On the other hand, refusal to release a voluntary patient on demand would not only be difficult to justify legally but would be highly undesirable, because resort to voluntary admission will be discouraged unless it is made quite clear that a patient may change his mind and leave. Most voluntary admission statutes meet the problem by providing that a voluntary patient shall be released within a specified number of days after he gives written notice of his desire to leave, unless in the meanwhile the hospital authorities start proceedings to have his status changed to that of involuntary patient.

Some courts have struck down such advance notice provisions. *In Ex parte Romero*, 51 N.M. 201, 181 P.2d 811 (1947), for instance, the patient "was admitted to the sanitarium on his written application ... and the certificate of a doctor of medicine." Four days after admission he verbally requested release but was denied, under authority of a statute which permitted detention of a voluntary patient for ten days after notice of an intent to leave. The court held that the statute violated the due process clause:

> The respondent urges that by the voluntary act of the petitioner in making the request for admission, he contracted with it to there remain and receive treatment until ten days after written notice of his desire or intention to terminate the same was given, unless sooner released. Obviously, it does not require citation of authority that one may not enforce such a contract made with a person he knows to be so disordered in mind as to require treatment in an institution for the treatment of mental diseases.

In contrast to *Romero*, consider *Ortega v. Rasor*, 291 F.Supp. 748 (S.D.Fla.1968). There, pursuant to the Narcotic Rehabilitation Act of 1966, the successor to the statute construed in *Lloyd*, the petitioner "voluntarily requested the Court to order him civilly committed for treatment of a narcotic addiction." As part of standard procedure, he signed a form waiving his right to further hearing if a psychiatrist designated by the Surgeon General found, after a 30–day evaluation period in the hospital, that he was "an addict who is likely to be rehabilitated through treatment." The petitioner also agreed that if such a finding were made, the court could enter a order, in his absence and without further hearing, committing him to the care and custody of the Surgeon General for a treatment period not to exceed six months and such posthospitalization treatment as was authorized by the Act. After the 30–day evaluation period, the examining psychiatrist submitted a report making the requisite findings and the court ordered the petitioner committed.

In holding that the petitioner could not withdraw from the treatment, the district court (the same court that entered the commitment order) stated:

> . . . In the case at bar, the Court is not concerned with a situation of compulsory treatment as such. The petitioner . . . initially instituted the proceeding for his civil commitment with the filing of a petition on his own behalf. . . . The Court, having independently recollected the hearing held pursuant to Mr. Ortega's petition for commitment, which hearing was brought before the Court by the government, and having reviewed the transcript of that hearing, is convinced that the petitioner acted of his own volition in requesting civil commitment and not because he was under the influence of narcotics and did not know what he was doing. The transcript of the hearing as well as the petition for voluntary civil commitment and Waiver of Further Court Appearance, both signed by Mr. Ortega established without a doubt that Mr. Ortega was fully apprised of his responsibilities under the Act and in fact understood those responsibilities. The Court will not permit the petitioner to terminate his treatment simply because the road to recovery is bumpy.

In *Romero* the admission process was non-judicial; in *Ortega,* a court was involved. Should this matter? Is there any other explanation for the difference in the results reached in these decisions? More generally, would invalidating the notice-and-detention provisions found in most state statutes make any practical difference? Couldn't the patient who demands release be discharged and then immediately detained and subjected to involuntary commitment proceedings?

5. *Review of voluntary patients; conversion to voluntary status.* Many patients who are admitted voluntarily never request release, especially those who are admitted under the non-protesting admissions statutes described earlier. Are voluntary patients entitled to periodic review, as is true with involuntary patients? As the next section indicates, there has been considerable litigation on this issue in connection with specific types of "voluntary" patients, i.e., people with developmental disabilities and children. As a general matter, these cases mandate some type of review, although not necessarily judicial.

Some courts have considered the review issue in the context of conversion of involuntary patients to voluntary status. Many states authorize this conversion whenever the hospital staff believes the change is indicated, in the belief that a voluntary relationship enhances therapy. See, e.g., Ark. Stats. § 20–47–224; N.Y.Code § 9.23(a). One court has found that the patient subject to such conversion in status is entitled to a judicial hearing reviewing the change as well as the same sort of periodic review provided involuntary patients. *Matter of Buttonow*, 23 N.Y.2d 385, 297 N.Y.S.2d 97, 244 N.E.2d 677 (1968). The dissenting opinion in *Buttonow* stated, in part: "[T]he salutary effect of voluntary status may be impaired by repeated judicial proceedings, or worse, remove the incentive of the institutions to arrange for conversions of status." Id. at 684 (Breitel, J., dissenting). Perhaps relevant here is literature indicating that voluntary patients are hospitalized twice as long as involuntary patients, and are less frequently considered to have received maximum benefits from their hospitalization. Robert Nicholson, "Characteristics Associated with Change in the Legal Status of Involuntary Psychiatric Patients," 39 Hosp. & Comm. Psychiat. 424 (1988).

V. COMMITMENT OF OTHER POPULATIONS

As noted at the outset of this chapter, most states have enacted separate commitment statutes for certain groups of people with mental disability. The most prominent such groups are insanity acquittees, prison and jail inmates requiring psychiatric treatment, people who abuse psychoactive substances, people who are developmentally disabled, and children with mental disability. This section examines the special considerations involved in commitment of these groups, with frequent comparison to the preceding materials.

A. INSANITY ACQUITTEES

Every state permits immediate commitment of persons who have been found not guilty by reason of insanity. Some states require a hearing before such commitment, but most states allow the acquittee to be committed "automatically" for a short period of time, at which point a hearing is held to determine whether further commitment is proper. Almost all states also provide for later periodic judicial review, although in a few jurisdictions release is left up to the initiation of the hospital or the acquittee. One might argue that because insanity acquittees have by definition eluded conviction, they are similarly situated to persons subject to regular civil commitment and thus should be processed according to the same standards and procedures. But the Supreme Court has indicated that the constitution does not require such an equation.

JONES v. UNITED STATES

Supreme Court of the United States, 1983.
463 U.S. 354, 103 S.Ct. 3043, 77 L.Ed.2d 694.

JUSTICE POWELL delivered the opinion of the Court.

The question presented is whether petitioner, who was committed to a mental hospital upon being acquitted of a criminal offense by reason of insanity, must be released because he has been hospitalized for a period longer than he might have served in prison had he been convicted.

I

In the District of Columbia a criminal defendant may be acquitted by reason of insanity if his insanity is "affirmatively established by a preponderance of the evidence." D.C.Code § 24–301(j) (1981). If he successfully invokes the insanity defense, he is committed to a mental hospital. § 24–301(d)(1). The statute provides several ways of obtaining release. Within 50 days of commitment the acquittee is entitled to a judicial hearing to determine his eligibility for release, at which he has the burden of proving by a preponderance of the evidence that he is no longer mentally ill or dangerous. § 24–301(d)(2).[3] If he fails to meet this burden at the 50–day hearing, the committed acquittee subsequently may be released, with court approval, upon certification of his recovery by the hospital chief of service. § 24–301(e). Alternatively, the acquittee is entitled to a judicial hearing every six months at which he may establish by a preponderance of the evidence that he is entitled to release. § 24–301(k).

Independent of its provision for the commitment of insanity acquittees, the District of Columbia also has adopted a civil-commitment procedure, under which an individual may be committed upon clear and convincing proof by the Government that he is mentally ill and likely to injure himself or others. § 21–545(b). The individual may demand a jury in the civil-commitment proceeding. § 21–544. Once committed, a patient may be released at any time upon certification of recovery by the hospital chief of service. §§ 21–546, 21–548. Alternatively, the patient is entitled after the first 90 days, and subsequently at 6–month intervals, to request a judicial hearing at which he may gain his release by proving

---

3. The statute does not specify the standard for determining release, but the District of Columbia Court of Appeals held in this case that, as in release proceedings under § 24–301(e) and § 21–545(b), the confined person must show that he is either no longer mentally ill or no longer dangerous to himself or others. See 432 A.2d 364, 372, and n. 16 (1981) (en banc).

by a preponderance of the evidence that he is no longer mentally ill or dangerous. §§ 21–546, 21–547.

II

On September 19, 1975, petitioner was arrested for attempting to steal a jacket from a department store. The next day he was arraigned in the District of Columbia Superior Court on a charge of attempted petit larceny, a misdemeanor punishable by a maximum prison sentence of one year. The court ordered petitioner committed to St. Elizabeths, a public hospital for the mentally ill, for a determination of his competency to stand trial. On March 1, 1976, a hospital psychologist submitted a report to the court stating that petitioner was competent to stand trial, that petitioner suffered from "Schizophrenia, paranoid type," and that petitioner's alleged offense was "the product of his mental disease." The court ruled that petitioner was competent to stand trial. Petitioner subsequently decided to plead not guilty by reason of insanity. The Government did not contest the plea, and it entered into a stipulation of facts with petitioner. On March 12, 1976, the Superior Court found petitioner not guilty by reason of insanity and committed him to St. Elizabeths pursuant to § 24–301(d)(1).

On May 25, 1976, the court held the 50–day hearing required by § 24–301(d)(2)(A). A psychologist from St. Elizabeths testified on behalf of the Government that, in the opinion of the staff, petitioner continued to suffer from paranoid schizophrenia and that "because his illness is still quite active, he is still a danger to himself and to others." Petitioner's counsel conducted a brief cross-examination, and presented no evidence.[8] The court then found that "the defendant-patient is mentally ill and as a result of his mental illness, at this time, he constitutes a danger to himself or others." Petitioner was returned to St. Elizabeths. Petitioner obtained new counsel and, following some procedural confusion, a second release hearing was held on February 22, 1977. By that date petitioner had been hospitalized for more than one year, the maximum period he could have spent in prison if he had been convicted. On that basis he demanded that he be released unconditionally or recommitted pursuant to the civil-commitment standards in § 21–545(b), including a jury trial and proof by clear and convincing evidence of his mental illness and dangerousness.

III

It is clear that "commitment for any purpose constitutes a significant deprivation of liberty that requires due process protection." *Addington v. Texas,* 441 U.S. 418, 425, 99 S.Ct. 1804, 1809, 60 L.Ed.2d 323 (1979). Therefore, a State must have "a constitutionally adequate purpose for the confinement." *O'Connor v. Donaldson,* 422 U.S. 563, 574, 95 S.Ct. 2486, 2493, 45 L.Ed.2d 396 (1975). Congress has determined that a criminal defendant found not guilty by reason of insanity in the District

---

8. Petitioner's counsel seemed concerned primarily about obtaining a transfer for petitioner to a less restrictive wing of the hospital. See Tr. 11–12.

of Columbia should be committed indefinitely to a mental institution for treatment and the protection of society. Petitioner does not contest the Government's authority to commit a mentally ill and dangerous person indefinitely to a mental institution, but rather contends that "the petitioner's trial was not a constitutionally adequate hearing to justify an indefinite commitment."

Petitioner's argument rests principally on *Addington v. Texas, supra,* in which the Court held that the Due Process Clause requires the Government in a civil-commitment proceeding to demonstrate by clear and convincing evidence that the individual is mentally ill and dangerous. Petitioner contends that these due process standards were not met in his case because the judgment of not guilty by reason of insanity did not constitute a finding of present mental illness and dangerousness and because it was established only by a preponderance of the evidence. Petitioner then concludes that the Government's only conceivably legitimate justification for automatic commitment is to ensure that insanity acquittees do not escape confinement entirely, and that this interest can justify commitment at most for a period equal to the maximum prison sentence the acquittee could have received if convicted. Because petitioner has been hospitalized for longer than the one year he might have served in prison, he asserts that he should be released unconditionally or recommitted under the District's civil-commitment procedures.

A

We turn first to the question whether the finding of insanity at the criminal trial is sufficiently probative of mental illness and dangerousness to justify commitment. A verdict of not guilty by reason of insanity establishes two facts: (i) the defendant committed an act that constitutes a criminal offense, and (ii) he committed the act because of mental illness. Congress has determined that these findings constitute an adequate basis for hospitalizing the acquittee as a dangerous and mentally ill person. See H.R.Rep. No. 91–907, *supra,* at 74 (expressing fear that "dangerous criminals, particularly psychopaths, [may] win acquittals of serious criminal charges on grounds of insanity" and yet "escape hospital commitment"); S.Rep. No. 1170, 84th Cong., 1st Sess., 13 (1955) ("Where [the] accused has pleaded insanity as a defense to a crime, and the jury has found that the defendant was, in fact, insane at the time the crime was committed, it is just and reasonable in the Committee's opinion that the insanity, once established, should be presumed to continue and that the accused should automatically be confined for treatment until it can be shown that he has recovered"). We cannot say that it was unreasonable and therefore unconstitutional for Congress to make this determination.

The fact that a person has been found, beyond a reasonable doubt, to have committed a criminal act certainly indicates dangerousness. Indeed, this concrete evidence generally may be at least as persuasive as any predictions about dangerousness that might be made in a civil-commitment proceeding.[13] We do not agree with petitioner's suggestion that the requisite dangerousness is not established by proof that a person committed a non-violent crime against property. This Court never has held that "violence," however that term might be defined, is a prerequisite for a constitutional commitment.[14]

Nor can we say that it was unreasonable for Congress to determine that the insanity acquittal supports an inference of continuing mental illness. It comports with common sense to conclude that someone whose mental illness was sufficient to lead him to commit a criminal act is likely to remain ill and in need of treatment. The precise evidentiary force of the insanity acquittal, of course, may vary from case to case, but the Due Process Clause does not require Congress to make classifications that fit every individual with the same degree of relevance. Because a hearing is provided within 50 days of the commitment, there is assurance that every acquittee has prompt opportunity to obtain release if he has recovered.

Petitioner also argues that, whatever the evidentiary value of the insanity acquittal, the Government lacks a legitimate reason for committing insanity acquittees automatically because it can introduce the insanity acquittal as evidence in a subsequent civil proceeding. This argument fails to consider the Government's strong interest in avoiding the need to conduct a *de novo* commitment hearing following every insanity acquittal—a hearing at which a jury trial may be demanded, § 21–544, and at which the Government bears the burden of proof by clear and convincing evidence. Instead of focusing on the critical question whether the acquittee has recovered, the new proceeding likely would have to relitigate much of the criminal trial. These problems accent the Government's important interest in automatic commitment. See *Mathews v. Eldridge,* 424 U.S. 319, 348, 96 S.Ct. 893, 909, 47 L.Ed.2d 18 (1976). We therefore conclude that a finding of not guilty by reason of insanity is a sufficient foundation for commitment of an

13. In attacking the predictive value of the insanity acquittal, petitioner complains that "[w]hen Congress enacted the present statutory scheme, it did not cite any empirical evidence indicating that mentally ill persons who have committed a criminal act are likely to commit additional dangerous acts in the future." He further argues that the available research fails to support the predictive value of prior dangerous acts. We do not agree with the suggestion that Congress' power to legislate in this area depends on the research conducted by the psychiatric community. We have recognized repeatedly the "uncertainty of diagnosis in this field and the tentativeness of professional judgment. The only certain thing that can be said about the present state of knowledge and therapy regarding mental disease is that science has not reached final-

ity of judgment...." The lesson we have drawn is not that government may not act in the face of this uncertainty, but rather that courts should pay particular deference to reasonable legislative judgments.

14. See *Overholser v. O'Beirne,* 112 U.S.App.D.C. 267, 276, 302 F.2d 852, 861 (1961) (Burger, J.) ("'[T]o describe the theft of watches and jewelry as 'non-dangerous' is to confuse danger with violence. Larceny is usually less violent than murder or assault, but in terms of public policy the purpose of the statute is the same as to both") (footnote omitted). It also may be noted that crimes of theft frequently may result in violence from the efforts of the criminal to escape or the victim to protect property or the police to apprehend the fleeing criminal.

insanity acquittee for the purposes of treatment and the protection of society.

B

Petitioner next contends that his indefinite commitment is unconstitutional because the proof of his insanity was based only on a preponderance of the evidence, as compared to *Addington's* civil-commitment requirement of proof by clear and convincing evidence. In equating these situations, petitioner ignores important differences between the class of potential civil-commitment candidates and the class of insanity acquittees that justify differing standards of proof. The *Addington* Court expressed particular concern that members of the public could be confined on the basis of "some abnormal behavior which might be perceived by some as symptomatic of a mental or emotional disorder, but which is in fact within a range of conduct that is generally acceptable." In view of this concern, the Court deemed it inappropriate to ask the individual "to share equally with society the risk of error." But since automatic commitment under § 24–301(d)(1) follows only if the *acquittee himself* advances insanity as a defense and proves that his criminal act was a product of his mental illness, there is good reason for diminished concern as to the risk of error. More important, the proof that he committed a criminal act as a result of mental illness eliminates the risk that he is being committed for mere "idiosyncratic behavior." A criminal act by definition is not "within a range of conduct that is generally acceptable."

We therefore conclude that concerns critical to our decision in *Addington* are diminished or absent in the case of insanity acquittees. Accordingly, there is no reason for adopting the same standard of proof in both cases. "[D]ue process is flexible and calls for such procedural protections as the particular situation demands." The preponderance of the evidence standard comports with due process for commitment of insanity acquittees.[17]

C

The remaining question is whether petitioner nonetheless is entitled to his release because he has been hospitalized for a period longer than he could have been incarcerated if convicted. The Due Process Clause "requires that the nature and duration of commitment bear some reasonable relation to the purpose for which the individual is committed." *Jackson v. Indiana*, 406 U.S. 715, 738, 92 S.Ct. 1845, 1858, 32 L.Ed.2d 435 (1972). The purpose of commitment following an insanity acquittal, like that of civil commitment, is to treat the individual's mental illness and protect him and society from his potential dangerous-

---

17. A defendant could be required to prove his insanity by a higher standard than a preponderance of the evidence. See *Leland v. Oregon*, 343 U.S. 790, 799, 72 S.Ct. 1002, 1007, 96 L.Ed. 1302 (1952). Such an additional requirement hardly would benefit a criminal defendant who wants to raise the insanity defense, yet imposition of a higher standard would be a likely legislative response to a holding that an insanity acquittal could support automatic commitment only if the verdict were supported by clear and convincing evidence.

ness. The committed acquittee is entitled to release when he has recovered his sanity or is no longer dangerous. And because it is impossible to predict how long it will take for any given individual to recover—or indeed whether he ever will recover—Congress has chosen, as it has with respect to civil commitment, to leave the length of commitment indeterminate, subject to periodic review of the patient's suitability for release.

In light of the congressional purposes underlying commitment of insanity acquittees, we think petitioner clearly errs in contending that an acquittee's hypothetical maximum sentence provides the constitutional limit for his commitment. A particular sentence of incarceration is chosen to reflect society's view of the proper response to commission of a particular criminal offense, based on a variety of considerations such as retribution, deterrence, and rehabilitation. The State may punish a person convicted of a crime even if satisfied that he is unlikely to commit further crimes.

Different considerations underlie commitment of an insanity acquittee. As he was not convicted, he may not be punished. His confinement rests on his continuing illness and dangerousness. Thus, under the District of Columbia statute, no matter how serious the act committed by the acquittee, he may be released within 50 days of his acquittal if he has recovered. In contrast, one who committed a less serious act may be confined for a longer period if he remains ill and dangerous. There simply is no necessary correlation between severity of the offense and length of time necessary for recovery. The length of the acquittee's hypothetical criminal sentence therefore is irrelevant to the purposes of his commitment.

IV

We hold that when a criminal defendant establishes by a preponderance of the evidence that he is not guilty of a crime by reason of insanity, the Constitution permits the Government, on the basis of the insanity judgment, to confine him to a mental institution until such time as he has regained his sanity or is no longer a danger to himself or society. This holding accords with the widely and reasonably held view that insanity acquittees constitute a special class that should be treated differently from other candidates for commitment.

* * *

[The dissenting opinion of JUSTICE BRENNAN, with whom JUSTICE MARSHALL and JUSTICE BLACKMUN join, is omitted].

Questions and Comments

1. *"Automatic" commitment.* In parts III(A) and III(B) of its opinion in *Jones,* the Supreme Court focused primarily on the constitutionality of "automatically" committing persons acquitted by reason of insanity. The Court sanctioned confinement without a hearing for at least 50 days when a criminal adjudication establishes beyond a reasonable doubt that the defendant has committed a criminal act and by a preponderance of the evidence

that the defendant was insane at the time of the act. Does the Court's reasoning in Part III(B) of the opinion sanction automatic commitment in jurisdictions which allow an insanity verdict based on a reasonable doubt about sanity?[s] Even if it does not, could resort to automatic commitment in such jurisdictions be supported by analogizing to emergency commitment in the civil commitment context, which is normally permitted on a showing well below the preponderance level?

Of course, even if only minimal proof of mental disability and dangerousness is sufficient for automatic commitment, one might question the Court's conclusion that the evidence adduced at a criminal trial (or, as in *Jones*, pursuant to a plea bargain) meets this standard. At most, all that is proven at such proceedings is that, at some time in the past, the defendant committed an antisocial act while insane. Do you agree with the Court's reasoning in Part III(A) that this finding is sufficient to support an "automatic" finding of present mental illness and dangerousness?

2. *Timing of hearing.* In holding that automatic commitment is permissible, *Jones* stated: "Because a hearing is provided within 50 days of the commitment, there is assurance that every acquittee has prompt opportunity to obtain release if he has recovered." Does the opinion *require* a "prompt" hearing (within 50 days) for the acquittee who has been automatically committed? In *Glatz v. Kort*, 807 F.2d 1514 (10th Cir. 1986), the Court held that hospitalization for 180 days before the "mandatory hearing" was not unconstitutional because (1) the acquittee could petition for earlier release; (2) doctors needed considerable time to treat the acquittee; and (3) acquittees are informed they will be automatically committed until they are eligible for release.

3. *Burden and standard of proof at the commitment hearing.* While *Jones* can be construed to require a hearing at some point after automatic commitment, it probably also sanctions the type of hearing authorized by the District of Columbia, which places the burden of proof on the acquittee by a preponderance of the evidence. See James Ellis, "The Consequences of the Insanity Defense: Proposals to Reform Post–Acquittal Commitment Law," 35 Cath.U.L.Rev. 961, 972 (1986). Whether or not *Jones* so holds, a large number of states, as well as the District of Columbia, continue to place the burden of proof on the acquittee at the commitment hearing; some even require the acquittee to produce *clear and convincing* proof of noncommittability.[t] Of those that place the burden on the state, many require merely a preponderance of the evidence showing. See Samuel Brakel et al., The Mentally Disabled and the Law 786–795 (1985) (chart). Obviously, all of these statutes would be unconstitutional in the civil commitment context, given *Addington*. On what grounds might they be upheld in the post-insanity acquittal context? Several possibilities exist.

Risk of Error Analysis. First, consider again the reasoning in Part III(B) of *Jones* finding that such statutes are constitutional because there is "good

---

s. About 15 states require the state to prove sanity beyond a reasonable doubt. See pp. 553–54.

t. The federal Insanity Defense Reform Act of 1984 requires those acquitted of "vio-

lent" crimes to prove noncommittability by clear and convincing evidence. 18 U.S.C. § 4243(d). This provision was upheld in *United States v. Wattleton*, 296 F.3d 1184, 1198 (11th Cir. 2002).

reason for diminished concern as to the risk of error." By the time of the review hearing, is it still plausible to say that the risk of error on the issue of present mental disability and dangerousness is sufficiently diminished by proof at trial of insanity and a criminal act to differentiate this situation from civil commitment? In *Ernst J. v. Stone*, 452 F.3d 186 (2d Cir. 2006), the court cited *Jones* in holding that, even at a *re*commitment hearing that takes place after the initial hearing, an insanity acquittee may be committed on a preponderance of the evidence "because having concededly once engaged in a criminal conduct as a result of mental illness, the insanity acquittee continues to present a serious risk of recurrence of dangerous behavior derived from mental illness."

The Public Safety Rationale. Most courts justify placing more of an evidentiary burden on insanity acquittees than on others subject to commitment on a different ground—that insanity acquittees, as a class, are more dangerous than other groups. See, e.g., *People v. Chavez,* 629 P.2d 1040, 1047–8 (Colo.1981). There is no doubt that insanity acquittees are more likely to have committed serious antisocial behavior than persons who are subjected to civil commitment. But one study has suggested that this fact does not correlate with a greater likelihood of recidivism. See Note, "Commitment and Release of Persons Found Not Guilty by Reason of Insanity: A Georgia Perspective," 15 Ga.L.Rev. 1065, 1079 (1981). At the least, shouldn't those acquittees charged with "minor" crimes (akin to the type of act which might also trigger civil commitment) be treated the same as those subjected to civil commitment? See American Bar Association Criminal Justice Mental Health Standard 7–7.3(b). Or does the fact that acquittees have been charged with crime, albeit minor, make them different?

More fundamentally, even if one is willing to assume that insanity acquittees are more dangerous than others, is adjustment of the burden and standard of proof the proper response? If the legal system wants to recognize formally the perception that acquittees are a greater threat to public safety, an alternative might be to adopt a presumption to that effect. Such a presumption would require the acquittee to come forward with some evidence of nondangerousness (i.e. carry the burden of production), but leave the ultimate burden of proof (i.e., the burden of persuasion) on the government by whatever standard of proof is considered appropriate (e.g., by clear and convincing evidence or a preponderance of the evidence). The threshold for adopting a presumption is that it must rest on an established probability. In addition, in order to deter any tendency to rely on presumptions for proving *all* probable facts, some other reason for the presumption is usually required, such as the difficulty of proving the issue, a party's superior access to evidence relating to the issue, or the desire to promote a special policy. Charles McCormick, Handbook of the Law of Evidence § 348, at 806–07 (3d. ed. 1982). Would a presumption of dangerousness for insanity acquittees be proper? A presumption of mental illness?

The Lack of Autonomy Rationale. Another argument against applying *Addington* to commitment of insanity acquittees, at least those charged with violent crime, is advanced by Warren Ingber in "Rules for An Exceptional Class: The Commitment and Release of Persons Acquitted of Violent Offenses by Reason on Insanity," 57 N.Y.U.L.Rev. 281, 301–02, 309 (1982). Ingber notes that one reason for limiting exercise of the police power in the civil commitment context is the societal interest in fostering autonomy. But, he contends, the insanity acquittee, unlike the person subjected to civil commitment, has been found deficient as an autonomous human being. Therefore the acquittee charged with a violent crime may be committed under a lower standard of proof.

> In a civil hearing, the state's interest in the safety of its citizens is partly offset by its interest in promoting autonomy; not so in a violent acquittee's commitment hearing. Thus, the state has a greater net interest in favor of a lower standard of proof in the latter hearing. In a word, it has no reason to be concerned about the effects such a standard will have on the autonomy of persons at large in society. The greater net state interest in a lower standard supports a reduction of the standard to a preponderance of the evidence.

Is this reasoning persuasive? Would it support not only reducing the standard of proof but shifting the burden of proof to the defendant?

The Clean-up Doctrine. Finally, consider the strength of what has been called the "clean-up doctrine," see Note, "Commitment Following an Insanity Acquittal," 94 Harv.L.Rev. 605, 617 (1981), as support for placing a heavier burden on insanity acquittees than on those subjected to civil commitment.

> If an insanity acquittee is wrongly committed, so the argument goes, he was probably sane at trial and therefore wrongly acquitted of the crime in the first place. "While the acquittee therefore may be deprived erroneously of his liberty in the *commitment* process, the liberty he loses is likely to be liberty which society mistakenly had permitted him to retain in the *criminal* process."

Id. at 618 (emphasis in original).

4. *Commitment criteria.* A separate question from the burden and standard of proof issue is the extent to which the commitment criteria for insanity acquittees should track civil commitment criteria. This question can be broken down into several subparts.

Is dangerousness alone sufficient ground for commitment? In *Jones*, the Court stated that an acquittee who is found insane by a preponderance of the evidence may be confined to a mental institution "until such time as he has regained his sanity or is no longer a danger to himself or society." This language suggested that, as is true with a civil committee, an acquittee who is no longer mentally disordered must be released. In *Foucha v. Louisiana*, 504 U.S. 71, 112 S.Ct. 1780, 118 L.Ed.2d 437 (1992), the Supreme Court affirmed, as a matter of due process, that once an insanity acquittee is no longer "mentally ill," he or she must be released despite a finding of dangerousness. At a bench trial, Foucha had been acquitted by reason of insanity on charges of aggravated burglary and illegal discharge of a firearm, based on reports from two state-employed medical doctors. Four years later he sought release from the hospital. At the release hearing, the same two doctors who testified about his sanity at the time of the offense testified, in the Court's words, that "upon commitment Foucha probably suffered from a drug induced psychosis but that he had recovered from that temporary condition; that he evidenced no signs of psychosis or neurosis and was in 'good shape' mentally; that he has, however, an antisocial personality, a condition that is not a mental disease and that is untreatable." The doctors also testified that they could "not certify that he would not constitute a menace to himself or others if released." On these facts, the Supreme Court held, 5–4, that Foucha could no longer be confined in the hospital.

According to Justice White, who wrote the majority opinion:

A State, pursuant to its police power, may of course imprison convicted criminals for the purposes of deterrence and retribution. But there are constitutional limitations on the conduct that a State may criminalize. See, e.g., *Robinson v. California*, 370 U.S. 660, 82 S.Ct. 1417, 8 L.Ed.2d 758 (1962). Here, the State has no such punitive interest. As Foucha was not convicted, he may not be punished. *Jones.* Here, Louisiana has by reason of his acquittal exempted Foucha from criminal responsibility as La. Rev. Stat. Ann. § 14:14 (West 1986) requires.

The State may also confine a mentally ill person if it shows "by clear and convincing evidence that the individual is mentally ill and dangerous," *Jones.* Here, the State has not carried that burden; indeed, the State does not claim that Foucha is now mentally ill.

We have also held that in certain narrow circumstances persons who pose a danger to others or to the community may be subject to limited confinement and it is on these cases, particularly *United States v. Salerno* [upholding pretrial detention], that the State relies in this case.

Salerno does not save Louisiana's detention insanity acquittees who are no longer mentally ill. Unlike the sharply focused scheme at issue in *Salerno*, the Louisiana scheme of confinement is not carefully limited.... It was emphasized in *Salerno* that the detention we found constitutionally permissible was strictly limited in duration. Here, in contrast, the State asserts that because Foucha once committed a criminal act and now has an antisocial personality that sometimes leads to aggressive conduct, a disorder for which there is no effective treatment, he may be held indefinitely. This rationale would permit the State to hold indefinitely any other insanity acquittee not mentally ill who could be shown to have a personality disorder that may lead to criminal conduct. The same would be true of any convicted criminal, even though he has completed his prison term. It would also be only a step away from substituting confinements for dangerousness for our present system which, with only narrow exceptions and aside from permissible confinements for mental illness, incarcerates only those who are proved beyond reasonable doubt to have violated a criminal law.

Justice O'Connor, who was the fifth member of the majority for that part of the opinion excerpted above, wrote a concurring opinion suggesting that, because an insanity acquittee in Louisiana has been found, beyond a reasonable doubt, to have committed an offense "with the required level of criminal intent,"

[i]t might therefore be permissible for Louisiana to confine an insanity acquittee who has regained sanity if, unlike the situation in this

case, the nature and duration of detention were tailored to reflect pressing public safety concerns related to the acquittee's continuing dangerousness.

[However,] acquittees could not be confined as mental patients absent some medical justification for doing so; in such a case the necessary connection between the nature and purposes of confinement would be absent. Nor would it be permissible to treat all acquittees alike, without regard for their particular crimes. For example, the strong interest in liberty of a person acquitted by reason of insanity but later found sane might well outweigh the governmental interest in detention where the only evidence of dangerousness is that the acquittee committed a non-violent or relatively minor crime.

The four dissenters argued that Louisiana should be able to confine Foucha. Justice Kennedy, joined by Chief Justice Rehnquist and Justice Scalia, and Justice Thomas, joined by Scalia, concluded that the fact that the state had established Foucha's commission of a criminal act beyond a reasonable doubt to be dispositive, and the Court's neglect of that fact to be an implicit overruling of *Jones*. According to Justice Kennedy:

First, ... the procedural protections afforded in a criminal [trial] surpass those in a civil commitment; indeed, these procedural protections are the most stringent known to our law. Second, proof of criminal conduct in accordance with *In re Winship* eliminates the risk of incarceration "for mere 'idiosyncratic behavior,' [because a] criminal act by definition is not 'within a range of conduct that is generally acceptable.' "*Jones*, quoting *Addington*. The criminal law defines a discrete category of conduct for which society has reserved its greatest opprobrium and strictest sanctions; past or future dangerousness, as ascertained or predicted in civil proceedings, is different in kind. Third, the State presents distinct rationales for these differing forms of commitment: In the civil context, the State acts in large part on the basis of its parens patriae power to protect and provide for an ill individual, while in the criminal context, the State acts to ensure the public safety.

* * *

Although Louisiana has chosen not to punish insanity acquittees, the State has not surrendered its interest in incapacitative incarceration. The Constitution does not require any particular model for criminal confinement, and upon compliance with *In re Winship*, the State may incarcerate on any reasonable basis. Incapacitation for the protection of society is not an unusual ground for incarceration. "[I]solation of the dangerous has always been considered an important function of the criminal law," *Powell v. Texas* (Blackmun, J., concurring), and insanity acquittees are a special class of offenders proved dangerous beyond their own ability to comprehend. The wisdom of incarceration under these circumstances is demonstrated by its high level of acceptance. Every State provides for discretionary or mandatory incarceration of insanity acquittees, and as JUSTICE THOMAS observes in his dissent, provisions like those in Louisiana, predicated on dangerousness alone, have been enforced by the Model Penal Code and adopted by the legislatures of no fewer than 11 other States.

It remains to be seen whether the majority, by questioning the legitimacy of incapacitative incarceration, puts in doubt the confinement of persons other than insanity acquittees. Parole release provisions often place the burden of proof on the prisoner to prove his lack of dangerousness. To use a familiar example, under the federal parole system in place until the enactment of the Sentencing Guidelines, an inmate could not be released on parole unless he established that his "release would not jeopardize the public welfare." This requirement reflected "the incapacitative aspect of the use of imprisonment which has the effect of denying the opportunity for future criminality, at least for a time." U.S. Dept. of Justice, United States Parole Commission Rules and Procedures Manual 69 (July 24, 1989). This purpose is consistent with the parole release provisions of Alabama, Colorado, Hawaii, Massachusetts, Michigan, New York, and the District of Columbia, to name just a few. It is difficult for me to reconcile the rationale of incapacitative incarceration, which underlies these regimes, with the opinion of the majority, which discounts its legitimacy.

Looking first at the majority's reasoning, is the distinction between *Foucha* and *Salerno* persuasive? If so, are there any circumstances under which detention of an insanity acquittee on dangerousness grounds alone would be constitutional? How does Justice O'Connor answer this question? Would due process requirements be met if detention were limited to those acquitted on charges involving violence, the burden of proving dangerousness is placed on the state, review proceedings are frequent, and those found dangerous are not designated as mental patients but housed in prison settings? With respect to Justice Kennedy's dissent, note the reliance on *In re Winship* (which requires the prosecution to prove each essential element of the offense beyond a reasonable doubt). If sanity is not an "essential element" of the offense, then why shouldn't the state be able, as Kennedy suggests, to confine a dangerous person when it otherwise proves its case? If sanity *is* an element of each offense, does his argument make sense? With respect to the "pragmatic" aspect of his dissent, how might one distinguish the parolee and the insanity acquittee?

What is the definition of mental illness? A second issue connected with the commitment criteria for insanity acquittees has to do with the definition of mental illness. As previous materials have made clear,[u] the mental illness predicate for the insanity defense is generally thought to require severe mental disorder. Does the presence of severe mental disorder also have to be shown in order to meet the commitment criteria? In *Jones*, the Court refers to whether the acquittee has "regained sanity" in discussing when an acquittee must be released. In *Foucha*, the Court uses the arguably broader term "mental illness," but assumes that Foucha, who was diagnosed as an antisocial personality disorder "for which there is no effective treatment," was no longer "mentally ill." However, in *Kansas v. Hendricks*, 521 U.S. 346, 117 S.Ct. 2072, 138 L.Ed.2d 501 (1997), dealing with commitment of sexually violent predators, the Court authorized commitment predicated on

u. See pp. 561–62 of the text for a discussion of the mental disease or defect requirement in insanity cases.

"mental abnormality" and on a "personality disorder." For further treatment of this issue, see pp. 675–91; 722–23.

What is the definition of dangerousness? The statutes in both *Jones* and *Foucha* allow continued confinement on danger to self grounds, as well as upon proof of danger to others. Should parens patriae commitment be permissible in this context?

Dangerousness to others may be defined more broadly in this context than in some civil commitment statutes. For instance, in *Jones* the Court asserts that crimes against property should be a legitimate basis for commitment. See n. 14 of the opinion. Lower courts have also held that a showing of imminent danger is not required in order to commit insanity acquittees. See, e.g., *Hill v. State*, 358 So.2d 190 (Fla.App.1978).

5. *Procedures.* The only procedural aspect of the post-acquittal commitment hearing addressed by *Jones* was the right to jury trial. In a footnote, the Court stated:

> The District of Columbia provides for a jury at civil-commitment hearings, … and petitioner contends that equal protection requires that insanity acquittees also be permitted to demand a jury at the 50–day hearing. Because we determine that an acquittee's commitment is based on the judgment of insanity at the criminal trial, rather than solely on the findings at the 50–day hearing, … the relevant equal protection comparison concerns the procedures available at the criminal trial and at a civil-commitment hearing. We therefore agree with the Court of Appeals that the absence of a jury at the 50–day hearing 'is justified by the fact that the acquittee has had a right to a jury determination of his sanity at the time of the offense.'

463 U.S. at 362 n. 10, 103 S.Ct. at 3048 n. 10. Would the Court's analysis justify denying an acquittee counsel or other rights normally associated with civil commitment? Switching from equal protection analysis to a due process perspective, recall that two principal reasons given by the Supreme Court for relaxing procedures in the civil commitment context are the medical nature of the issues involved and the need to avoid procedures which will deter friends and families from seeking treatment. See *Addington,* supra; *Parham v. J.R.* Are these concerns present in the post-insanity acquittal context? What other state interests should be weighed in the balance in deciding how much process is due?

6. *Duration of commitment.* Despite the Supreme Court's holding in *Jones,* several commentators have argued, and several state statutes provide, that commitment of acquittees be limited to the maximum sentence the acquittee would have received had he or she been found responsible for the crime charged. Cf. *Illinois v. Pastewski*, 251 Ill.App.3d 358, 190 Ill.Dec. 659, 622 N.E.2d 69 (1993) (maximum period of commitment of insanity acquittee cannot exceed the maximum sentence for crime with which he was charged, less good conduct credit, with the latter to be determined by the director of the Department of Mental Health). One rationale for such a rule is that commitment of insanity acquittees is, contrary to the Court's assertion, punitive and thus should be limited by the relevant criminal sentence. Three judges of the District of Columbia Court of Appeals panel in the *Jones* case reasoned as follows:

[A]cquittees are not confined to mental institutions for medical reasons alone. They are confined there in part because society is unwilling to allow those who have committed crimes to escape without paying for their crimes. The intent of the statute is partially punitive, and thus the [stricter procedures governing commitment and release of acquittees] reflect this added burden on the defendant. Because of this punitive purpose, the maximum statutory period of confinement becomes relevant, for at that point society no longer has a valid interest in continued confinement on the basis of a shortcut procedure.

Consider also this alternative critique of this aspect of *Jones*, from Ellis, supra at 981–82:

The majority's analysis attempts to answer the wrong question. The issue is not how long Jones could be lawfully committed, but rather how long he could be confined under procedures different from those employed for general commitment patients. The Court is correct in stating that treatment needs should be a determining factor in ascertaining the appropriate length of commitment. But the duration of the applicability of special commitment procedures should be set independently by principles of fairness and equality. Those principles require that special commitment be limited to the period of time during which the individual could have been confined had he been convicted.

* * *

... The state interest occasioned by attempted petit larceny is finite and measured by the maximum sentence; it does not increase when the offender proves to be mentally disabled. Any greater interest in confining the disabled offender must arise from his disability rather than his offense. Confining an acquittee for a longer period than the maximum sentence for his crime can only be justified by his continuing treatment or habilitation needs, and at that point, the fact of his offense becomes irrelevant. Therefore, there is no justification for treating him differently than general commitment patients who have a continuing treatment or habilitation need. Thus general commitment procedures should be the only means of extending such a commitment.

Cf. *Ernst J. v. Stone*, 452 F.3d 186, 201 (2d Cir. 2006) (expressing some doubt as to whether an acquittee subject to recommitment is distinguishable, for equal protection purposes, from a person subject to civil commitment, at least when the recommitment seeks institutionalization of an acquittee who has been released subject to conditions and is alleged to have violated the conditions).

In practice, insanity acquittees tend to spend about the same amount of time in the hospital as do convicted persons charged with similar crimes, although the time periods vary from state to state. Once released, insanity acquittees are no more likely to recidivate than released felons who were charged with similar offenses. Indeed, most research indicates a lower rate of recidivism for insanity acquittees. See, e.g., Richard Pasewark et al., "Detention and Rearrest Rates of People Found Not Guilty by Reason of Insanity," 139 Am.J.Psychiat. 893 (1982).

7. *The Oregon review board.* As with civil commitment, perhaps more important than the various standards and procedures accompanying post-acquittal commitment are the systemic measures established for handling insanity acquittees who are determined to be mentally ill and dangerous. In 1977, the Oregon legislature enacted legislation setting up an innovative approach toward this problem. Or.Rev.Stat. §§ 161.327 to 161.336. Its most significant innovation was to shift responsibility for committed acquittees from the trial court to a Psychiatric Security Review Board (PSRB), on the theory that courts lack the staff, expertise and motivation to assure adequate treatment and monitoring of acquittees. The PSRB consists of five members, usually a psychiatrist, a psychologist, a person with expertise in parole and probation matters, a criminal trial lawyer, and a member of the general public. It has jurisdiction over all committed acquittees for the term of the maximum sentence they would have received had there been a conviction. It has authority to arrange treatment in many different types of programs, and leans heavily on conditional release arrangements. Any acquittee dissatisfied with the Board's disposition of his or her case may appeal to the courts. During the first five years of its operation, 6% of the 295 people conditionally released under the PSRB's authority were arrested for felony charges. Jeffrey Rogers et al., "After Oregon's Insanity Defense: A Comparison of Conditional Release and Hospitalization," 5 Int'l J.L. & Psychiat. 391, 398 (1982).

B. PRISON AND JAIL INMATES

Of those individuals with mental disorder who are processed through the criminal justice system, far fewer than one percent are acquitted by reason of insanity. Only a slightly larger proportion are sentenced under the types of special sentencing provisions discussed in Chapter Seven, such as those which establish indeterminate sentences and separate treatment facilities for persons found to be "mentally disordered sex offenders" or "sexually violent predators." The vast majority of persons with mental disorder who are charged with crime and not diverted out of the system prior to adjudication are convicted and sentenced to jail or prison. A large percentage of these individuals suffer from some type of mental disorder. T. Howard Stone, "Therapeutic Implications of Incarceration for Persons with Severe Mental Disorders: Searching for Rational Health Policy," 24 Am. J. Crim. L. 283, 285 (1997)(estimating 87,000 people with severe mental disorders in prison); President's New Freedom Commission on Mental Health 32 (May, 2002)("about 7% of all incarcerated people have a serious mental illness; the proportion with a less serious mental illness is substantially higher"). At some point during their sentence, many of these people need treatment that cannot be provided in jail or prison. Until 1980, in most states these people could be transferred to a mental health facility (either within the correctional system or within the mental health system) on the say-so of a mental health professional. That has now changed.

VITEK v. JONES

Supreme Court of the United States, 1980.
445 U.S. 480, 100 S.Ct. 1254, 63 L.Ed.2d 552.

MR. JUSTICE WHITE delivered the opinion of the Court, except as to Part IV–B.

The question in this case is whether the Due Process Clause of the Fourteenth Amendment entitles a prisoner convicted and incarcerated in the State of Nebraska to certain procedural protections, including notice, an adversary hearing, and provision of counsel, before he is transferred involuntarily to a state mental hospital for treatment of a mental disease or defect.

I

Nebraska Rev.Stat. § 83–176(2) (1976) authorizes the Director of Correctional Services to designate any available, suitable, and appropriate residence facility or institution as a place of confinement for any state prisoner and to transfer a prisoner from one place of confinement to another. Section 83–180(1), however, provides that when a designated physician or psychologist finds that a prisoner "suffers from a mental disease or defect" and "cannot be given proper treatment in that facility," the director may transfer him for examination, study, and treatment to another institution within or without the Department of Correctional Services. Any prisoner so transferred to a mental hospital is to be returned to the Department if, prior to the expiration of his sentence, treatment is no longer necessary. Upon expiration of sentence, if the State desires to retain the prisoner in a mental hospital, civil commitment proceedings must be promptly commenced. § 83–180(3).

On May 31, 1974, Jones was convicted of robbery and sentenced to a term of three to nine years in state prison. He was transferred to the penitentiary hospital in January 1975. Two days later he was placed in solitary confinement, where he set his mattress on fire, burning himself severely. He was treated in the burn unit of a private hospital. Upon his release and based on findings required by § 83–180 that he was suffering from a mental illness or defect and could not receive proper treatment in the penal complex, he was transferred to the security unit of the Lincoln Regional Center, a state mental hospital under the jurisdiction of the Department of Public Institutions.

Jones challeng[es] on procedural due process grounds the adequacy of the procedures by which the Nebraska statutes permit transfers from the prison complex to a mental hospital.

* * *

III

On the merits, the threshold question in this case is whether the involuntary transfer of a Nebraska state prisoner to a mental hospital implicates a liberty interest that is protected by the Due Process Clause.

* * *

Undoubtedly, a valid criminal conviction and prison sentence extinguish a defendant's right to freedom from confinement. Such a conviction and sentence sufficiently extinguish a defendant's liberty "to empower the State to confine him in any of its prisons." *Meachum v. Fano,* 427 U.S., at 224, 96 S.Ct., at 2538 (emphasis deleted). It is also true that changes in the conditions of confinement having a substantial adverse impact on the prisoner are not alone sufficient to invoke the protections of the Due Process Clause "[a]s long as the conditions or degree of confinement to which the prisoner is subjected is within the sentence imposed upon him."

Appellants maintain that the transfer of a prisoner to a mental hospital is within the range of confinement justified by imposition of a prison sentence, at least after certification by a qualified person that a prisoner suffers from a mental disease or defect. We cannot agree. None of our decisions holds that conviction for a crime entitles a State not only to confine the convicted person but also to determine that he has a mental illness and to subject him involuntarily to institutional care in a mental hospital. Such consequences visited on the prisoner are qualitatively different from the punishment characteristically suffered by a person convicted of crime. Our cases recognize as much and reflect an understanding that involuntary commitment to a mental hospital is not within the range of conditions of confinement to which a prison sentence subjects an individual. *Baxstrom v. Herold,* 383 U.S. 107, 86 S.Ct. 760, 15 L.Ed.2d 620 (1966); *Specht v. Patterson,* 386 U.S. 605, 87 S.Ct. 1209, 18 L.Ed.2d 326 (1967); *Humphrey v. Cady,* 405 U.S. 504, 92 S.Ct. 1048, 31 L.Ed.2d 394 (1972); *Jackson v. Indiana,* 406 U.S. 715, 724, 725, 92 S.Ct. 1845, 1851, 32 L.Ed.2d 435 (1972). A criminal conviction and sentence of imprisonment extinguish an individual's right to freedom from confinement for the term of his sentence, but they do not authorize the State to classify him as mentally ill and to subject him to involuntary psychiatric treatment without affording him additional due process protections.

In light of the findings made by the District Court, Jones' involuntary transfer to the Lincoln Regional Center pursuant to § 83–180, for the purpose of psychiatric treatment, implicated a liberty interest protected by the Due Process Clause. Many of the restrictions on the prisoner's freedom of action at the Lincoln Regional Center by themselves might not constitute the deprivation of a liberty interest retained by a prisoner. But here, the stigmatizing consequences of a transfer to a mental hospital for involuntary psychiatric treatment, coupled with the subjection of the prisoner to mandatory behavior modification as a treatment for mental illness, constitute the kind of deprivations of liberty that requires procedural protections.

IV

The District Court held that to afford sufficient protection to the liberty interest it had identified, the State was required to observe the following minimum procedures before transferring a prisoner to a mental hospital:

"A. Written notice to the prisoner that a transfer to a mental hospital is being considered;

"B. A hearing, sufficiently after the notice to permit the prisoner to prepare, at which disclosure to the prisoner is made of the evidence being relied upon for the transfer and at which an opportunity to be heard in person and to present documentary evidence is given;

"C. An opportunity at the hearing to present testimony of witnesses by the defense and to confront and cross-examine witnesses called by the state, except upon a finding, not arbitrarily made, of good cause for not permitting such presentation, confrontation, or cross-examination;

"D. An independent decisionmaker;

"E. A written statement by the fact-finder as to the evidence relied on and the reasons for transferring the inmate;

"F. Availability of legal counsel, furnished by the state, if the inmate is financially unable to furnish his own; and

"G. Effective and timely notice of all the foregoing rights."

A

We think the District Court properly identified and weighed the relevant factors in arriving at its judgment. Concededly the interest of the State in segregating and treating mentally ill patients is strong. The interest of the prisoner in not being arbitrarily classified as mentally ill and subjected to unwelcome treatment is also powerful, however; and as the District Court found, the risk of error in making the determinations required by § 83-180 is substantial enough to warrant appropriate procedural safeguards against error.

We recognize that the inquiry involved in determining whether or not to transfer an inmate to a mental hospital for treatment involves a question that is essentially medical. The question whether an individual is mentally ill and cannot be treated in prison "turns on the meaning of the facts which must be interpreted by expert psychiatrists and psychologists." *Addington v. Texas,* 441 U.S., at 429, 99 S.Ct., at 1811. The medical nature of the inquiry, however, does not justify dispensing with due process requirements. It is precisely "[t]he subtleties and nuances of psychiatric diagnoses" that justify the requirement of adversary hearings.

Because prisoners facing involuntary transfer to a mental hospital are threatened with immediate deprivation of liberty interests they are currently enjoying and because of the inherent risk of a mistaken transfer, the District Court properly determined that procedures similar to those required by the Court in *Morrissey v. Brewer,* 408 U.S. 471, 92

S.Ct. 2593, 33 L.Ed.2d 484 (1972), were appropriate in the circumstances present here.

The notice requirement imposed by the District Court no more than recognizes that notice is essential to afford the prisoner an opportunity to challenge the contemplated action and to understand the nature of what is happening to him. Furthermore, in view of the nature of the determinations that must accompany the transfer to a mental hospital, we think each of the elements of the hearing specified by the District Court was appropriate. The interests of the State in avoiding disruption was recognized by limiting in appropriate circumstances the prisoner's right to call witnesses, to confront and cross examine. The District Court also avoided unnecessary intrusion into either medical or correctional judgments by providing that the independent decisionmaker conducting the transfer hearing need not come from outside the prison or hospital administration.

B

The District Court did go beyond the requirements imposed by prior cases by holding that counsel must be made available to inmates facing transfer hearings if they are financially unable to furnish their own. We have not required the automatic appointment of counsel for indigent prisoners facing other deprivations of liberty, *Gagnon v. Scarpelli,* 411 U.S., at 790, 93 S.Ct., at 1763; but we have recognized that prisoners who are illiterate and uneducated have a greater need for assistance in exercising their rights. *Gagnon v. Scarpelli, supra,* at 786–787, 93 S.Ct., at 1761–1762. A prisoner thought to be suffering from a mental disease or defect requiring involuntary treatment probably has an even greater need for legal assistance, for such a prisoner is more likely to be unable to understand or exercise his rights. In these circumstances, it is appropriate that counsel be provided to indigent prisoners whom the State seeks to treat as mentally ill.

V

Because Mr. Justice Powell, while believing that Jones was entitled to competent help at the hearing, would not require the State to furnish a licensed attorney to aid him, the judgment below is affirmed as modified to conform with the separate opinion filed by Mr. Justice Powell.

So ordered.

[On the right to counsel issue, Mr. Justice Powell's concurring opinion, reprinted at pp. 832–34, found that due process requires only "a qualified and independent advisor" who "may be ... a licensed psychiatrist or other mental health professional." The remaining four members of the Court dissented on the ground that the case was moot.]

Questions and Comments

1. *Comparison to civil commitment.* Although *Vitek* clearly held that something more than a diagnosis from a mental health professional is

necessary before a prison-to-hospital transfer may take place, it just as clearly does not require as much process as most states provide those subject to civil commitment.[v] Prior to *Vitek* some lower courts held that the equal protection clause required civil commitment procedures prior to such transfers. In *United States ex rel. Schuster v. Herold,* 410 F.2d 1071 (2d Cir.), cert. denied 396 U.S. 847, 90 S.Ct. 81, 24 L.Ed.2d 96 (1969), for instance, the court held that the prison inmate subjected to a transfer should be accorded "substantially the same procedures ... as are granted to civilians when they are involuntarily committed to a mental hospital." Id. at 1084. Accord, *Matthews v. Hardy,* 420 F.2d 607 (D.C.Cir.1969), cert. denied 397 U.S. 1010, 90 S.Ct. 1231, 25 L.Ed 2d 423 (1970). The *Schuster* court based its decision primarily on the Supreme Court's decision in *Baxstrom v. Herold,* 383 U.S. 107, 86 S.Ct. 760, 15 L.Ed.2d 620 (1966). *Baxstrom* held unconstitutional, under the equal protection clause, a New York law providing a relatively informal commitment process for prisoners who were on the verge of completing their prison term; the Court reasoned that prisoners who have served their terms are similarly situated to persons subjected to civil commitment and therefore may only be committed pursuant to normal civil commitment procedures. If raised by the petitioner in *Vitek,* should *Baxstrom* and equal protection analysis have governed the decision, as *Schuster* suggests?

Instead of equal protection analysis, the Court relied on *Morrissey v. Brewer* and *Gagnon v. Scarpelli,* which dealt with the procedures necessary to revoke probation and parole under the due process clause. Recall that traditional due process analysis, under *Mathews v. Eldridge,* 424 U.S. 319, 96 S.Ct. 893, 47 L.Ed.2d 18 (1976), requires balancing (1) the significance of the private interest to be adjudicated under the procedures at issue; (2) the risk of an erroneous deprivation under the procedures; and (3) the government's interest in maintaining them. In *Vitek,* the Court identified two private interests affected by transfer: the stigma associated with being labelled mentally disordered and the possibility of compelled treatment. There are at least two other possible drawbacks to transfer: the "strong likelihood that an inmate transferred to a mental health facility will be paroled later than a like inmate who remained in the correctional facility" (given "that most parole authorities would be wary of releasing a person from a mental health facility directly to the community"), and the possibility that transferees will be denied good-time credits for the time they are in the hospital. Michael Churgin, "The Transfer of Inmates to Mental Health Facilities," in John Monahan & Henry Steadman, eds., Mentally Disordered Offenders 220 (1983). Are these factors enough to make prison-to-hospital transfers equivalent to the deprivation of liberty associated with civil commitment? Are there any relevant differences between transfers and commitment with respect to the second and third prongs of the *Mathews v. Eldridge* analysis?

2. *Pre-trial detainees.* A separate transfer issue arises in the context of pretrial detention. Of the millions of individuals who pass through the jails each year, a substantial percentage are seriously mentally ill. E. Fuller

---

v. Note that the Supreme Court has yet to indicate whether civil commitment requires anything more in the way of procedural formality than it provides prisoners subject to hospital transfers.

Torrey, "Criminalizing the Seriously Mentally Ill: The Abuse of Jails as Mental Hospitals" 13 (1992)(national survey of over 1,300 jails finding that 7.2% of the jail population suffer from a serious mental illness). Although some of these people have been convicted and sentenced to serve time in jail, most are there because they have been unable to make bail and thus are confined pending trial or some other proceeding. Of this latter group, many will eventually be evaluated for and found incompetent to stand trial, a procedure explored in Chapter Nine. But a large number are not found incompetent, yet need treatment that cannot be provided in jail. See Henry Steadman et al., The Mentally Ill in Jail: Planning for Essential Services (1989). Should *Vitek* apply to these people? Or is civil commitment the proper route? If the latter, should commitment *criteria* as well as procedures be applicable?

    3. *Hospital-to-prison transfers.* Usually a person transferred to a mental health facility will eventually be returned to the prison.[w] Sometimes, this retransfer may be premature (if, for example, the hospital believes the person is a "troublemaker"). Is such a person entitled to a hearing to review the hospital's decision? At least two courts have considered this issue; they reached opposite results. *Burchett v. Bower,* 355 F.Supp. 1278 (D.Ariz.1973) (yes); *Cruz v. Ward,* 558 F.2d 658 (2d Cir.1977) (no).

    If such a hearing is held, what criteria should apply? Perhaps of relevance here is *Bowring v. Godwin,* 551 F.2d 44 (4th Cir.1977), which found a right to psychiatric treatment for prisoners, but only when that treatment is a "medical necessity":

> [A prisoner] is entitled to psychological or psychiatric treatment if a physician or other health care provider, exercising ordinary skill and care at the time of observation, concludes with reasonable medical certainty (1) that the prisoner's symptoms evidence a serious disease or injury; (2) that such disease or injury is curable or may be substantially alleviated; and (3) that the potential for harm to the prisoner by reason of delay or the denial of care would be substantial.

Cf. *Estelle v. Gamble,* 429 U.S. 97, 97 S.Ct. 285, 50 L.Ed.2d 251 (1976) (holding that the eighth amendment obligates the government to provide medical care for prisoners, but only to the extent necessary to avoid "deliberate indifference to serious medical needs of prisoners.")

    4. *Mental health courts.* In large part a reaction to failures in the mental health system that have lead to thousands of untreated disordered people in jails and prisons, at least 25 jurisdictions have established "mental health courts" since the late 1990's, and in 2001 Congress allocated $4 million to the U.S. Department of Justice to set up a pilot mental health courts program. Rather than conviction and imprisonment, the goal of these courts is to ensure that people with mental illness who become enmeshed in the criminal system obtain mental health treatment. In most programs, jurisdiction is limited to those who have committed minor offenses, and requires consent of the defendant. Roughly 95% of those given the choice between mental health court and regular criminal court choose the former.

---

w. No court has yet addressed whether transferees are entitled to periodic review.   Presumably, at the least, hospitalization is limited by the length of the sentence.

John Petrila et al., "Preliminary Observations from an Evaluation of the Broward County Florida Mental Health Court," 37 Court Review 14 (2001).

Such a choice may not always be a wise one. According to the Bazelon Center for Mental Health Law, roughly half of the 20 mental health courts surveyed require a guilty plea in order to trigger jurisdiction, and those that instead permit dismissal of charges after "completion of treatment" do not define the term clearly. In at least 40% of the jurisdictions surveyed, length of court supervision significantly exceeds possible length of incarceration and probation for the offense; in most, "treatment" can involve indeterminate supervision, and often requires anti-psychotic medication. In 64% of the courts, the sanction for noncompliance is jail time (with the rest relying primarily on adjustment of services and increased judicial persuasion). Over half the jurisdictions surveyed do not allow the offender to withdraw from mental health court and seek traditional criminal court adjudication. These various aspects of the court's process are not necessarily explained to those who are deciding between mental health court and regular criminal court. Bazelon Center for Mental Health, "The Role of Mental Health Courts in System Reform," available at http://www.bazelon.org/.

While cautiously supportive of the concept if various modifications are made, the Bazelon Center also expressed concern that mental health courts will divert resources from reform of mental health services generally, and tempt government officials and others to use the criminal system as a means of seeking help for those with mental illness, resulting in the criminalization of mental illness. Accordingly, it recommends, contrary to the mandate of most mental health court systems, that mental health courts focus on offenders who commit serious crimes and allow those charged with misdemeanors to be handled through pre-existing, non-judicial diversion programs of the type described on pp. 813–14. It also argues against requiring a guilty plea, which it asserts will "hinder reintegration [by leading] to denial of housing and employment." Id.

Other research looks at the efficacy of mental health courts (MHC) from a number of different perspectives. According to one summary, "[a]cross several studies, there is consistent, if not robust, evidence that MHC participants are better off than comparable non-MHC participants," in terms of booking rates, treatment referral, and overall functioning (although re-arrest rates within a 12–month period can still be as high as 47%). Allison D. Redlich, "Voluntary, But Knowing and Intelligent?: Comprehension in Mental Health Courts," 4 Psychol., Pul. Po'y & L. 605, 613 (2005). At the same time, a substantial percentage of MHC participants may not fully understand their options, with upward of 25% not meeting competency to stand trial standards. Id. at 614–16.

Is the mental health court a good idea? Should it be "voluntary," or mandated for those with serious mental disorder? Should it be limited to people charged with misdemeanors, to those charged with felonies, or should it handle both groups? Why shouldn't the court have jurisdiction over *all* offenders with mental disorder, even those who are not seriously mentally ill? At least one mental health court does not require proof that the person has a mental disorder. Id. at n.11.

C. CHEMICALLY DEPENDENT PERSONS

According to the U.S. Dep't of Health and Human Services' National Household Survey on Drug Abuse, in 2001 an estimated 16.6 million Americans aged 12 or older, comprising 7.3% of the population, were dependent on or abused alcohol or illicit drugs (2.4 million abused both alcohol and illicit drugs, 3.2 million abused only drugs, and 11 million only alcohol). Among the 5.6 million Americans classified with dependence on or abuse of illicit drugs, most were dependent on or abused marijuana (3.5 million), followed by cocaine (1 million), pain relievers (1 million), and heroin (.02 million). According to the Substance Abuse and Mental Health Services Administration, only about 1 million of these individuals were treated for substance abuse problems, roughly 65% of them in facilities focused on substance abuse treatment, 20% in facilities focused on substance abuse and mental health, and the rest in facilities focused on mental health or general health care. Only about 20% of those treated were treated in government institutions, with the rest treated in private for-profit or non-profit facilities or outpatient programs. SAMHSA, Office of Applied Studies (October 1, 2000)(Tables 4.2 & 4.3), available at http://wwwdasis.samhsa.gov/00nssats/chapter_4_nssats_2000.htm.

Most states have special statutes for the commitment of people perceived to be addicted to alcohol or drugs and who are dangerous to self or others as a result. Those states that do not usually permit commitment of these individuals under general commitment statutes. See, e.g., Ind. Code § 12–7–2–130(1); Me. Rev. Stat. Tit. 34–B, § 3801(5). Many of the special commitment statutes define the predicate for commitment as the use of alcohol or drugs that causes a "habitual lack of self-control," unconsciousness, or an inability to make "a rational decision with respect to . . . need for treatment [or] basic personal needs or safety." See, e.g., Colo. §§ 25–1–302(1)(9); 25–1–1101(11). Others are more behaviorally oriented. See, e.g., Fla. Stat. § 397.311(13)(defining an "habitual user" as someone "brought to the attention of law enforcement for being substance impaired . . . and who has been taken into custody for such impairment three or more times during the preceding 12 months"). Finally, some laws are more conclusory. See, e.g., Tex. Health & Safety Code § 461.002(1)(defining "chemical dependency" as "abuse of alcohol or a controlled substance, psychological or physical dependence on alcohol or a controlled substance or addiction to alcohol or a controlled substance"). Many states require that the commitment take place at specialized facilities, but many do not, and some permit commitment to jail if special facilities are not available. See, e.g., Mass. St. ch.123 § 35. In a number of states, commitment periods for those who abuse substances are shorter than for general commitment. See, e.g., N.D. Cent Code § 25–03.1–17 (14 days); Colo. Stat. § 25–1–311(5)(30 days); Haw. Rev. Stat. § 334–60.5(i)(90 days).

Questions and Comments

1. *The definition of disorder.* Should addiction be grounds for commitment? Professor Fingarette has argued that there is no empirical support for

the view that alcoholism is a disease. Herbert Fingarette, Heavy Drinking: The Myth of Alcoholism as a Disease (1988). He asserts that most substance abusers never develop serious dependency problems. He also asserts that, in contrast to those with mental illness, many who suffer addiction rehabilitate themselves (noting, for instance, that many veterans returning from Vietnam abandoned their heroin addictions upon return to civilian life). Nonetheless, the American Psychiatric Association's Diagnostic and Statistical Manual includes a category for substance abuse disorder, which it defines as "recurrent substance use" that (1) results "in a failure to fulfill major role obligations at work, school, or home (e.g., repeated absences or poor work performance due to substance use; substance-related absences, suspensions, or expulsions form school; neglect of children or household);" (2) occurs "in situations in which it is physically hazardous (e.g., driving an automobile or operating a machine when impaired by substance use);" (3) results in "legal problems (e.g., arrests for substance-related disorderly conduct);" or (4) occurs "despite having persistent or recurrent social or interpersonal problems caused or exacerbated by the effects of the substance (e.g., arguments with spouse about consequences of intoxication, physical fights)." DSM–IV–TR, at 197. Is this a sufficient predicate for commitment, assuming the requisite danger is also shown? If not, are the Colorado, Florida or Texas definitions given above any better?

2. *Police power commitment.* In *Robinson v. California*, 370 U.S. 660, 82 S.Ct. 1417, 8 L.Ed.2d 758 (1962), the Supreme Court held that drug and alcohol addiction per se may not be punished criminally because, among other things, addiction is not a voluntary act. But in *Powell v. Texas*, 392 U.S. 514, 88 S.Ct. 2145, 20 L.Ed.2d 1254 (1968), it made clear that if an addict commits any type of crime, even if it is being drunk in public, then he or she may be punished. Thus criminal sanctions continue to be society's primary response to addicted individuals who commit antisocial acts.

Nonetheless, as the foregoing material indicates, most states also authorize commitment of people with addictions who engage in antisocial behavior. Professor Wexler has argued that such commitment is inappropriate, at least as applied to those addicted to narcotics (in particular heroin). He first contends that drug addicts are much less likely to commit *violent* crime than the general population, given the sense of well being that accompanies drug taking. Second, he argues that the fact that some addicts are relatively more likely to commit *property* offenses in order to finance their habits should not authorize their commitment on police power grounds:

> In addition to the offensiveness of committing people partially because they are poor (we would not be willing to commit nonaddict poor people simply on a showing that they were likely to steal), we are faced with the argument that
>
>> the virtual certainty that addicts will break the law is in a direct sense the state's own fault. An addict's need for narcotics is by definition beyond his control. By denying him legal access to narcotics, the state makes him *ipso facto* an habitual criminal. By obliging him to obtain his drugs at exorbitant black market prices, the same legislative policy also drives poor addicts inexorably to theft. It

flouts fundamental fairness for the state to force a man to commit crimes and at the same time to punish or confine him on grounds of his resultant criminality.

Fundamental fairness or not, current law and practice permits the state *both* to punish and to commit because of the resultant criminality....

One response to this problem, Wexler notes, is to establish drug maintenance programs (such as methadone treatments). If such programs were properly implemented, then neither the criminal law or preventive detention would be necessary, since addicts would not need to steal. However, if maintenance programs are not thought feasible or wise, the state should still be forced to rely on the criminal law rather than commitment for handling addicts. He explains: "Only if we had a sure-fire cure for addiction by brief confinement or by some miracle drug might we, by analogy to a quarantine, preventively detain to avoid rather minor offenses such as property crimes." Wexler then recommends a hybrid sanction-control approach to the problem:

Instead of preventive detention ... we could devise an acceptable alternative: the criminal law process could be used to detect those addicts who commit or attempt property offenses and, by enabling them to elect treatment in lieu of punishment, could be used to encourage them to seek treatment for their addiction.... Proper completion of treatment should result in vitiating the criminal proceedings, but an uncooperative attitude toward therapy could result in a transfer to the criminal system, with, however, credit toward the criminal sentence for all time spent in the therapeutic process. Interestingly and perhaps significantly for this peno-therapeutic paradigm, a study of the federal Narcotic Addict Rehabilitation Act, which has provision both for pure civil commitment and for the election of treatment while criminal charges remain pending, found the success rate under the latter provision to exceed the success rate under the former, which, according to the authors of the study, suggests that external legal pressure to comply with the program is a factor in success.

David Wexler, Mental Health Law 37–39 (1981).

Do you agree with Wexler's analysis? Recall that the standard justifications for police power commitment of people with mental illness are that they are either more dangerous, more treatable or less deterrable than the general population. Do addicts fit into any of these categories? If property theft by poverty-stricken addicts is the state's "fault," should either civil commitment *or* criminal sanction be permissible? Finally, does any of this apply to people who are alcoholics?

3. *Drug courts.* In line with Wexler's suggestion, many jurisdictions permit commitment of drug addicts who are charged with crime as an alternative to criminal sentence. One of the first efforts in this regard was the National Addict Rehabilitation Act of 1966, 42 U.S.C. 3401 et seq., mentioned by Wexler and still in force today.[x] Another federal initiative is a court diversion program known as Treatment Alternatives to Street Crime

---

x. The Narcotic Addict Rehabilitation Act of 1966 was also discussed at pp. 866– 68 in the context of "voluntary" commitment [footnote by eds].

(TASC), which operated in over thirty states as recently as 1991. Beth Weinman, "A Coordinated Approach for Drug–Abusing Offenders," in Drug Abuse Treatment in Prisons and Jails 234 (Carel G. Leukefeld & Frank M. Tims eds., 1992). The newest development in this regard is the concept of "drug courts." Analogous to the mental health courts discussed in the previous section, they differ from earlier court diversion programs in that

> the court rather than a treatment center is the focal point of the treatment process ... The judge engages the clients directly, asks personal questions, and encourages them in the treatment process. Judges interact with clients in a manner more like proactive therapists than dispassionate judicial officers. The role of attorneys is also substantially different in the drug court than in a traditional court. Not only is the relationship between public defender and prosecutor no longer adversarial, but lawyers generally play a less prominent role. In many drug courts the lawyers do not even show up for the regular drug court sessions, and even when they do, it is often difficult to determine just which persons in the courtroom are the attorneys.... As Judge Jeff Rosnik of the Miami drug court put it, in drug court "the players' roles are altered, modified, inextricably changed.... Legal Justice becomes therapeutic jurisprudence. And crime and punishment becomes holistic justice."

James L. Nolan, Reinventing Justice: The American Drug Court Movement 40, 42 (2001). The heavy involvement of judges in treatment supervision is thought to enhance treatment compliance. The de-emphasis of traditional lawyering stems from the courts' focus on treatment rather than adjudication of guilt and punishment. How similar are drug courts to traditional civil commitment? Are they a model worth emulating throughout the criminal justice system?

4. *Parens patriae commitment.* Professor Wexler also has doubts about the propriety of committing narcotics addicts under the parens patriae power.

> Drug addicts ... are seldom classified as psychotic, and they ordinarily retain contact with reality. If addicts are to be considered incompetent, then, it must be because their overpowering compulsion to consume drugs prevents them from reaching a rational decision regarding treatment ... But it is true, of course, that some addicts *do* decide to enter treatment, and that cuts against a blanket notion equating addiction with incompetence. One commentator has argued rather persuasively that addiction should not in itself establish incompetency.

> > But if addicts have lost their powers of self-control, so have all chain smokers and compulsive gamblers. They have all lost control over a partial and clearly limited area of conduct, but not over conduct or decision-making capacity generally. They are unable to decide not to smoke or gamble, but they are as competent to decide to attempt a cure of their habit as to decide whether to undergo an operation or to come in out of the rain. Addiction, as a shorthand expression for compulsive psychological dependence, makes no man a ward of the state unless his weakness has some additional effects on his mental processes generally.

Wexler points out that the benefit the addict receives from commitment is also unclear. First, the addict may prefer his addicted state to confinement and indefinite supervision or even to his or her previous life prior to addiction. Second, there is "virtually no empirical data to support the claim that institutionalization in a drug-free environment followed by an intensive aftercare supervision offers even a fair chance of cure for the average narcotic addict."[y] Thus, "so long as the addict may be physically committed and subjected to the traditional abstinence approaches, the validity of the paternalistic intervention will remain questionable ..." However, Wexler suggests, a court might be able to order *outpatient* commitment, perhaps to a maintenance program, "if the conceptual and empirical questions regarding the competency of addicts were resolved in the negative." Id. at 42–44.

How do you respond to this analysis? Does it have relevance for those addicted to alcohol?

D. PEOPLE WITH DEVELOPMENTAL DISABILITIES

The term "developmental disability" was not widely used until the 1970's. It is meant to designate a large group of individuals with mental disorder who are distinguished from both persons with mental illness and persons addicted to alcohol and drugs. Under the federal Developmentally Disabled Assistance and Bill of Rights Act, 42 U.S.C. §§ 6000, 6001(7), the term is defined to include:

> a severe, chronic disability of a person which (A) is attributable to a mental or physical impairment or combination of mental and physical impairments; (B) is manifested before the person attains age twenty-two; (C) is likely to continue indefinitely; (D) results in substantial functional limitations in three or more of the following areas of major life activity: (i) self-care, (ii) receptive and expressive language, (iii) learning, (iv) mobility, (v) capacity for independent living, and (vi) economic self-sufficiency; and (E) reflects the person's need for a combination and sequence of special, interdisciplinary, or generic care, treatment or other services which are of lifelong or extended duration and are individually planned and coordinated.

The group of individuals most commonly categorized as developmentally disabled are people with mental retardation. But also included are people who suffer from learning disabilities, epilepsy, cerebral palsy and autism.

Almost every state has a special commitment statute for people with developmental disability; many use this term specifically, while the rest focus on people with mental retardation. In many of these states, the

---

y. This is a quote from the 1967 Task Force Report on Narcotics and Drug Abuse issued by the President's Commission on Law Enforcement and the Administration of Justice. More recent programs report much better results, using methadone maintenance, residential therapeutic communities, and out-patient programs. See Robert Hubbard, et al., "Drug Abuse Treatment: A National Study of Effectiveness" 125 (1989)(less than 20% of participants in any treatment modality were regular users of opiates or heroin three to five years after entering treatment). See generally, Lawrence Gostin, "An Alternative Public Health Vision for a National Drug Strategy: 'Treatment Works,' "28 Hous.L.Rev. 285, 300–303 (1991).

differences between this statute and the commitment statute for people with mental illness are insignificant. In a number of states, however, the commitment criteria for people with developmental disability are both broader and more narrow: they permit commitment based on a finding of a need for treatment or inability to care, at the same time dangerousness is removed as a criterion. Ark. Stat. § 20–48–404(1); Del.Code tit. 16, § 5504; Mont.Stat. § 53–20–125. Several statutes also appear to contemplate only "voluntary" admissions, initiated either by the person or the person's relatives of guardian. Ga.Stat. § 37–4–40. As the following case makes clear, in some states there are other differences as well.

HELLER v. DOE

Supreme Court of the United States, 1993.
509 U.S. 312, 113 S.Ct. 2637, 125 L.Ed.2d 257.

JUSTICE KENNEDY delivered the opinion of the Court.

In the Commonwealth of Kentucky, involuntary civil commitments of those alleged to be mentally retarded and of those alleged to be mentally ill are governed by separate statutory procedures. Two differences between these commitment proceedings are at issue in this case. First, at a final commitment hearing, the applicable burden of proof for involuntary commitment based on mental retardation is clear and convincing evidence, while the standard for involuntary commitment based on mental illness is beyond a reasonable doubt. Second, in commitment proceedings for mental retardation, unlike for mental illness, "[g]uardians and immediate family members" of the subject of the proceedings "may participate ... as if a party to the proceedings," with all attendant rights, including the right to present evidence and to appeal. Respondents are a class of mentally retarded persons committed involuntarily to Kentucky institutions. They argue that these distinctions are irrational and violate the Equal Protection Clause of the Fourteenth Amendment.... We reject these contentions and hold the Kentucky statutes constitutional.

* * *

II

Respondents contend that, in evaluating the constitutionality of the distinctions drawn by Kentucky's statutes, we should apply not rational-basis review, but some form of heightened scrutiny. This claim is not properly presented. Respondents argued before the District Court and the Court of Appeals only that Kentucky's statutory scheme was subject to rational-basis review, and the courts below ruled on that ground.... We therefore decide this case as it has been presented to the courts whose judgments are being reviewed.

III

We many times have said, and but weeks ago repeated, that rational-basis review in equal protection analysis "is not a license for courts to judge the wisdom, fairness, or logic of legislative choices." Nor does it authorize "the judiciary [to] sit as a superlegislature to judge the wisdom or desirability of legislative policy determinations made in areas that neither affect fundamental rights nor proceed along suspect lines." For these reasons, a classification neither involving fundamental rights nor proceeding along suspect lines is accorded a strong presumption of validity.... A State, moreover, has no obligation to produce evidence to sustain the rationality of a statutory classification. "[A] legislative choice is not subject to courtroom factfinding and may be based on rational speculation unsupported by evidence or empirical data." A statute is presumed constitutional, and "[t]he burden is on the one attacking the legislative arrangement to negative every conceivable basis which might support it," whether or not the basis has a foundation in the record. Finally, courts are compelled under rational-basis review to accept a legislature's generalizations even when there is an imperfect fit between means and ends. A classification does not fail rational-basis review because it "is not made with mathematical nicety or because in practice it results in some inequality." ... We have applied rational-basis review in previous cases involving the mentally retarded and the mentally ill. See *Cleburne v. Cleburne Living Center, Inc.*, 473 U.S. 432, 105 S.Ct. 3249, 87 L.Ed.2d 313 (1985); *Schweiker v. Wilson*, 450 U.S. 221, 101 S.Ct. 1074, 67 L.Ed.2d 186 (1981). In neither case did we purport to apply a different standard of rational-basis review from that just described. True, even the standard of rationality as we so often have defined it must find some footing in the realities of the subject addressed by the legislation. That requirement is satisfied here. Kentucky has proffered more than adequate justifications for the differences in treatment between the mentally retarded and the mentally ill.

A

Kentucky argues that a lower standard of proof in commitments for mental retardation follows from the fact that mental retardation is easier to diagnose than is mental illness. That general proposition should cause little surprise, for mental retardation is a developmental disability that becomes apparent before adulthood. See American Psychiatric Assn., Diagnostic and Statistical Manual of Mental Disorders 29 (3d rev. ed. 1987) (hereinafter Manual of Mental Disorders); American Assn. on Mental Retardation, Mental Retardation: Definition, Classification, and Systems of Support 5, 16–18 (9th ed. 1992) (hereinafter Mental Retardation). By the time the person reaches 18 years of age the documentation and other evidence of the condition have been accumulated for years. Mental illness, on the other hand, may be sudden and may not occur, or at least manifest itself, until adulthood. See, *e.g.*, Manual of Mental Disorders 190 (onset of schizophrenia may occur any time during adulthood); *id.*, at 220, 229 (onset of depression usually is during adulthood). Furthermore, as we recognized in an earlier case, diagnosis of mental illness is difficult. See *Addington v. Texas*. Kentucky's basic premise that mental retardation is easier to diagnose than is mental illness has a sufficient basis in fact.

This difference between the two conditions justifies Kentucky's decision to assign a lower standard of proof in commitment proceedings involving the mentally retarded. In assigning the burden of proof, Kentucky was determining the "risk of error" faced by the subject of the proceedings. *Addington.* If diagnosis is more difficult in cases of mental illness than in instances of mental retardation, a higher burden of proof for the former tends to equalize the risks of an erroneous determination that the subject of a commitment proceeding has the condition in question. From the diagnostic standpoint alone, Kentucky's differential burdens of proof (as well as the other statutory distinction at issue), are rational.

There is, moreover, a "reasonably conceivable state of facts" from which Kentucky could conclude that the second prerequisite to commitment—that "[t]he person presents a danger or a threat of danger to self, family, or others," Ky. Rev.Stat.Ann. § 202B.040 (Michie 1991)—is established more easily, as a general rule, in the case of the mentally retarded. Previous instances of violent behavior are an important indicator of future violent tendencies. Mental retardation is a permanent, relatively static condition, so a determination of dangerousness may be made with some accuracy based on previous behavior. We deal here with adults only, so almost by definition in the case of the retarded there is an 18–year record upon which to rely.

This is not so with the mentally ill. Manifestations of mental illness may be sudden, and past behavior may not be an adequate predictor of future actions. Prediction of future behavior is complicated as well by the difficulties inherent in diagnosis of mental illness. It is thus no surprise that many psychiatric predictions of future violent behavior by the mentally ill are inaccurate. For these reasons, it would have been plausible for Kentucky to conclude that the dangerousness determination was more accurate as to the mentally retarded than the mentally ill.

A statutory classification fails rational-basis review only when it " 'rests on grounds wholly irrelevant to the achievement of the State's objective.' "Because ease of diagnosis is relevant to two of the four inquiries, it is not "wholly irrelevant" to the achievement of Kentucky's objective, and thus the statutory difference in the applicable burden of proof survives rational-basis review. In any event, it is plausible for Kentucky to have found that, for purposes of determining the acceptable risk of error, diagnosis and dangerousness are the most critical factors in the commitment decision, so the appropriate burden of proof should be tied to them.

There is a further, more far-reaching rationale justifying the different burdens of proof: The prevailing methods of treatment for the mentally retarded, as a general rule, are much less invasive than are those given the mentally ill. The mentally ill are subjected to medical and psychiatric treatment which may involve intrusive inquiries into the patient's innermost thoughts, and use of psychotropic drugs. By contrast, the mentally retarded in general are not subjected to these medical treatments. Rather, " 'because mental retardation is ... a learning disability and training impairment rather than an illness,' the mentally retarded are provided "habilitation," which consists of education and training aimed at improving self-care and self-sufficiency skills. It is true that the loss of liberty following commitment for mental illness and mental retardation may be similar in many respects; but the different treatment to which a committed individual is subjected provides a rational basis for Kentucky to decide that a greater burden of proof is needed before a person may be committed for mental illness.... It may also be true that some persons committed for mental retardation are subjected to more intrusive treatments while confined. Nonetheless, it would have been plausible for the Kentucky Legislature to believe that most mentally retarded individuals who are committed receive treatment that is different from, and less invasive than, that to which the mentally ill are subjected. "States are not required to convince the courts of the correctness of their legislative judgments." Thus, since " 'the question is at least debatable,' " rational-basis review permits a legislature to use just this sort of generalization.

... Kentucky's burden of proof scheme, then, can be explained by differences in the ease of diagnosis and the accuracy of the prediction of future dangerousness and by the nature of the treatment received after commitment. Each of these rationales, standing on its own, would suffice to establish a rational basis for the distinction in question.

B

There is a rational basis also for the other distinction challenged by respondents: that Kentucky allows close relatives and guardians to participate as parties in proceedings to commit the mentally retarded but not the mentally ill. As we have noted, by definition, mental retardation has its onset during a person's developmental period. Mental retardation, furthermore, results in "deficits or impairments in adaptive functioning," that is to say, "the person's effectiveness in areas such as social skills, communication, and daily living skills, and how well the person meets the standards of personal independence and social responsibility expected of his or her age by his or her cultural group." Manual of Mental Disorders 28–29. See also Mental Retardation 5–6, 15–16, 38–41. Based on these facts, Kentucky may have concluded that close relatives and guardians, both of whom likely have intimate knowledge of a mentally retarded person's abilities and experiences, have valuable insights that should be considered during the involuntary commitment process.

Mental illness, by contrast, may arise or manifest itself with suddenness only after minority, when the afflicted person's immediate family members have no knowledge of the medical condition and have long ceased to provide care and support. Further, determining the proper course of treatment may be far less dependent upon observations made in a household setting. Indeed, we have noted the severe difficulties inherent in psychiatric diagnosis conducted by experts in the field. *Addington*. In addition, adults previously of sound mental health who are diagnosed as mentally ill may have a need for privacy that justifies the State in confining a commitment proceeding to the smallest group compatible with due process. Based on these facts, Kentucky may have concluded that participation as parties by relatives and guardians of the mentally ill would not in most cases have been of sufficient help to the trier of fact to justify the additional burden and complications of granting party status. To be sure, Kentucky could have provided relatives and guardians of the mentally retarded some participation in commitment proceedings by methods short of providing them status as parties. That, however, is irrelevant in rational-basis review. We do not require Kentucky to have chosen the least restrictive means of achieving its legislative end. As long as Kentucky "rationally advances a reasonable and identifiable governmental objective, we must disregard" the existence of alternative methods of furthering the objective "that we, as individuals, perhaps would have preferred." *Schweiker*.

* * *

JUSTICE SOUTER, with whom JUSTICE BLACKMUN and Justice STEVENS join, and with whom Justice O'CONNOR joins as to Part II, dissenting.

* * *

II

Obviously there are differences between mental retardation and mental illness. They are distinct conditions, they have different manifestations, they require different forms of care or treatment, and the course of each differs. It is without doubt permissible for the State to treat those who are mentally retarded differently in some respects from those who are mentally ill. The question here, however, is whether some difference between the two conditions rationally can justify the particular disparate treatment accorded under this Kentucky statute.

The first distinction wrought by the statute is the imposition of a lesser standard of proof for involuntary institutionalization where the alleged basis of a need for confinement is mental retardation rather than mental illness. . . . In upholding this disparate treatment, the Court relies first on the State's assertion that mental retardation is easier to diagnose than mental illness. . . . [But] the question whether a lower burden of proof is rationally justified . . . turns not only on whether ease of diagnosis and proof of dangerousness differ as between cases of illness and retardation, but also on whether there are differences in the respective interests of the public and the subjects of the commitment proceedings, such that the two groups subject to commitment can rationally be treated differently by imposing a lower standard of proof for commitment of the retarded. The answer is clearly that they can not. While difficulty of proof, and of interpretation of evidence, could legitimately counsel against setting the standard so high that the State may be unable to satisfy it (thereby effectively thwarting efforts to satisfy legitimate interests in protection, care, and treatment), that would at most justify a lower standard in the allegedly more difficult cases of illness, not in the easier cases of retardation. We do not lower burdens of proof merely because it is easy to prove the proposition at issue, nor do we raise them merely because it is difficult.[5] Nor do any other reasonably conceivable facts cut in favor of the distinction in treatment drawn by the Kentucky statute. Both the ill and the retarded may be dangerous, each may require care, and the State's interest is seemingly of equal strength in each category of cases. No one has or would argue that the value of liberty varies somehow depending on whether one is alleged to be ill or retarded, and a mentally retarded person has as much to lose by civil commitment to an institution as a mentally ill counterpart, including loss of liberty to "choos[e] his own friends and companions, selec[t] daily activities, decid[e] what to eat, and retai[n] a level of personal privacy," among other things. . . .

The Court also rests its conclusion on the view that "it would have been plausible for the Kentucky Legislature to believe that most mentally retarded individuals who are committed receive treatment that is . . . less invasive tha[n] that to which the mentally ill are subjected." Nothing cited by the Court, however, demonstrates that such a belief would have been plausible for the Kentucky Legislature, nor does the Court's discussion render it plausible now. One example of the invasiveness to which the Court refers is the use of (and the results of the administration of) psychotropic drugs. [A]ny apparent plausibility in the Court's suggestion that "the mentally retarded in general are not subjected to th[is] medical treatmen[t]," dissipates the moment we examine readily available material on the subject, including studies of institutional practices affecting the retarded comparable to those studies concerning the treatment of mental illness cited by the Court. One recent examination of institutions for the mentally retarded in Kentucky's neighboring State of Missouri, for example, found that 76% of the institutionalized retarded receive some type of psychoactive drug and that fully 54% receive psychotropic drugs.

. . . The Court also suggests that medical treatment for the mentally retarded is less invasive than in the case of the mentally ill because the mentally ill are subjected to psychiatric treatment that may involve intrusive enquiries into the patient's innermost thoughts. Again, I do not disagree that the mentally ill are often subject to intrusive psychiatric therapy. But the mentally retarded too are subject to intrusive therapy, as the available material on the medical treatment of the mentally

5. And indeed, to the extent *Addington v. Texas* does discuss the difficulty of diagnosing mental illness, it supports use only of a *lesser* standard of proof because of the practical problems created by a supposed "serious question as to whether a state could ever prove beyond a reasonable doubt that an individual is both mentally ill and likely to be dangerous." Of course, in this case Kentucky has determined that the liberty of those alleged to be mentally ill is sufficiently precious that the State should assume the risk inherent in use of that higher standard.

retarded demonstrates. The mentally retarded are often subjected to behavior modification therapy to correct, among other things, anxiety disorders, phobias, hyperactivity, and antisocial behavior, therapy that may include aversive conditioning as well as forced exposure to objects that trigger severe anxiety reactions. . . .

III

With respect to the involvement of family members and guardians in the commitment proceeding, the Court holds it to be justified by the fact that mental retardation "has its onset during a person's developmental period," while mental illness "may arise or manifest itself with suddenness only after minority." [A]lthough these differences might justify a scheme in which immediate relatives and guardians were automatically called as witnesses in cases seeking institutionalization on the basis of mental retardation, they are completely unrelated to those aspects of the statute to which Doe objects: permitting these immediate relatives and guardians to be involved "as parties" so as to give them, among other things, the right to appeal as "adverse" a decision not to institutionalize the individual who is subject to the proceedings. Where the third party supports commitment, someone who is alleged to be retarded is faced not only with a second advocate for institutionalization, but with a second prosecutor with the capacity to call and cross-examine witnesses, to obtain expert testimony and to raise an appeal that might not otherwise be taken, whereas a person said to require commitment on the basis of mental illness is not. This is no mere theoretical difference, and my suggestion that relatives or guardians may support curtailment of liberty finds support in the record in this case. It indicates that of the 431 commitments to Kentucky's state-run institutions for the mentally retarded during a period between 1982 and the middle of 1985, all but one were achieved through the application or consent of family members or guardians.

. . .

Without plausible justification, Kentucky is being allowed to draw a distinction that is difficult to see as resting on anything other than the stereotypical assumption that the retarded are "perpetual children," an assumption that has historically been taken to justify the disrespect and "grotesque mistreatment" to which the retarded have been subjected. As we said in *Cleburne*, the mentally retarded are not "all cut from the same pattern: . . . they range from those whose disability is not immediately evident to those who must be constantly cared for." In recent times, at least when imposing the responsibilities of citizenship, our jurisprudence has seemed to reject the analogy between mentally retarded adults and nondisabled children. See, e.g., *Penry v. Lynaugh*, 492 U.S. 302, 338, 109 S.Ct. 2934, 2957, 106 L.Ed.2d 256 (1989)(controlling opinion of O'CONNOR, J.) (not "all mentally retarded people . . . —by virtue of their mental retardation alone, and apart from any individualized consideration of their personal responsibility—inevitably lack the cognitive, volitional, and moral capacity to act with the degree of culpability associated with the death penalty"); see also id. at 340 ("reliance on mental age to measure the capabilities of a retarded person for purposes of the Eighth Amendment could have a disempowering effect if applied in other areas of the law"). When the State of Kentucky sets up respective schemes for institutionalization on the basis of mental illness and mental retardation, it too is obliged to reject that analogy, and to rest any difference in standards for involuntary commitment as between the ill and the retarded on some plausible reason.

Questions and Comments

1. *Equal protection and people with development disability.* The majority opinion emphasizes that Kentucky needed only a "rational basis," as opposed to a substantial or compelling reason, for its differential treatment of people with mental illness and people with retardation. Thus, the Court suggested, without directly holding, that mental disability is not a "suspect class" for equal protection purposes. Eight years earlier, the Court had supposedly explicitly held that mental disability is not a suspect class in *Cleburne v. Cleburne Living Center, Inc.*, 473 U.S. 432, 105 S.Ct. 3249, 87 L.Ed.2d 313 (1985), a decision briefly mentioned by both the majority and dissenting opinions in *Heller*. Yet, contrary to the usual outcome in a rational-basis review case, in *Cleburne* the government lost; the Supreme Court struck down a zoning ordinance that required group homes for people with retardation to obtain permits that medical hospitals, nursing homes, apartment houses, and fraternities and sororities did not need to obtain. That fact led some commentators to suggest that *Cleburne* actually applied a heightened "rational-basis-with-bite" test to cases involving mental disability. See, e.g., Gayle Lynn Pettinga, *Rational Basis with Bite: Intermediate Scrutiny by Any Other Name*, 62 Ind. L.J. 779, 793–99 (1987). *Heller* did not entirely settle this issue, given its curiously indirect manner of deciding that rational basis review was the appropriate analysis in that case. The implications of *Cleburne*, *Heller* and other cases addressing equal protection for people with mental disability are discussed further on pp. 1312–20.

2. *Analysis of* Heller. Assuming rational-basis review is the correct analysis, is there a rational basis for Kentucky's commitment law? Couldn't the differing burdens of proof be seen as an attempt to provide extra protection for people with mental illness rather than as discrimination against people with mental retardation (who, after all, are still accorded the constitutionally required clear-and-convincing standard of proof)? Is that type of question irrelevant if, as Justice Souter suggests, both groups are subjected to the same degree of liberty deprivation? On the latter score, note that, although Justice Souter's data suggest that the practice is different, in theory only people with mental illness or people who are dually diagnosed (i.e., who are suffering from both mental retardation *and* mental illness) should receive psychotropic medication. On the other hand, as detailed below, people with retardation usually end up hospitalized for much longer periods of time than people with mental illness, and in many states are not accorded as much periodic review. As to the provision making relatives and guardians parties to the case, is it accurate to characterize these individuals as "prosecutors," as Justice Souter does? If, as the notes below suggest, the

main issue in such commitment hearings is placement, might it not make sense to make relatives parties with greater say as to where their loved ones go? As a counter, consider the trial court's findings in *Secretary of Public Welfare of Penn. v. Institutionalized Juveniles,* 442 U.S. 640, 99 S.Ct. 2523, 61 L.Ed.2d 142 (1979), that parents' decision to hospitalize a child with mental retardation may be the result of community pressure, emotional difficulties in dealing with the child, or financial problems connected with providing necessary care. Finally, does *Atkins v. Virginia,* the case which prohibited execution of people with mental retardation (see pp. 653–65), support the majority or the dissent?

3. *Voluntary admission and periodic review.* As mentioned at the beginning of this section, one frequent difference between commitment statutes for people with retardation and people with mental illness is that the former are often admitted by their relatives or guardians as "voluntary" patients.[z] See James W. Ellis, "Decisions by and for People with Mental Retardation: Balancing Considerations of Autonomy and Protection," 37 Villanova L. Rev. 1779, 1809 (1992)("a majority of persons with mental retardation who are confined to large residential institutions are there as 'voluntary patients,' [y]et ... [i]t is certain that a large percentage of these individuals have not validly 'consented' to their placement by any process that will bear inspection."). That practice probably results from the fact that many mildly and moderately retarded persons are not considered capable of communicating their desires. In *In re Hop,* 29 Cal.3d 82, 171 Cal.Rptr. 721, 623 P.2d 282 (1981), the California Supreme Court found that such "voluntary" admissions violated the equal protection clause. Stated the court, "No other class of adults similarly situated and in need of protective custody may lawfully be placed in a state hospital without a knowing and intelligent waiver of rights, or a request, or a judicial determination that placement is appropriate." It thus required a judicial hearing to determine whether a person with developmental disability is gravely disabled or a danger to self or others, and whether placement in a state hospital is warranted. Would the Supreme Court agree with this analysis?

The *Hop* court did not directly address whether and when periodic review should take place once a person with developmental disability is committed. In *Matter of Harhut,* 385 N.W.2d 305 (Minn.1986), the court was confronted with a statutory scheme for commitment of people with retardation which, unlike the statute at issue in *Hop,* required an initial judicial determination of committability but, like that statute, did not establish periodic judicial review procedures. Lawyers for the petitioner, a 35–year–old man who was blind, mildly mentally retarded, and autistic "at times," argued there was no rational or compelling basis for requiring individuals with mental retardation (or their relatives or guardians) to request judicial review when the state mandated such review for people with mental illness and for chemically dependent persons. Citing *Cleburne,* the court rejected this argument:

---

z. See discussion of non-protesting admissions of people with mental illness, pp. 863–64.

[T]he distinction between the commitment periods ... is based on a legislative judgment that mental retardation is, unlike chemical dependency or mental illness, a condition not usually susceptible of great or rapid improvement. The legislature decided that indeterminate commitment subject to judicial review on the motion of the patient was the more effective and efficient way to deal with the state's responsibility to treat retarded persons. This is a legitimate public purpose, and it is not clear beyond a reasonable doubt that indeterminate commitment is an unreasonable means of assuring the state's interest.

Although the court found no equal protection violation, it did find that, under the due process clause, every person with mental retardation who is committed to an institution is entitled to have counsel receive the results of staff medical reviews; according to the statute, these reviews were to occur "as frequently as necessary but not less than annually." It further held that some type of judicial review—not necessarily rising to the level of a hearing—must occur once every three years (the review period for people with mental illness and people deemed chemically dependent was one year).

Is their relative incapacity to communicate their desires a "rational basis" for permitting "non-protesting admission" of people with retardation when it is prohibited for others? Is their relative stability a "rational basis" for relying on patient-initiated review for people with developmental disabilities in those jurisdictions that require periodic review for people with mental illness? If they are unable to communicate their desires, how can they initiate review?

4. *Commitment criteria.* As noted in the introduction to this subsection, many statutes governing commitment of people with developmentally disability allow confinement based merely on a finding of disability and a "need for treatment"—or, to use more modern terminology, "habilitation" or "training in survival skills." At least one court has found such statutes unconstitutional. See, e.g., *Kinner v. State*, 382 So.2d 756 (Fla.App.1980) (the statute must include "criteria limiting persons who may be involuntarily committed to those who lack the capacity to weigh for themselves the risks of freedom and the benefits of hospitalization and/or to those who are dangerous to themselves or others."). See also, *People v. Reliford*, 65 Ill.App.3d 177, 21 Ill.Dec. 778, 382 N.E.2d 72 (1978). In contrast, one court has upheld against a vagueness challenge a statute that permitted commitment if the court certifies simply that the person is "mentally deficient." *Matter of Vandenberg*, 48 Or.App. 609, 617 P.2d 675 (1980). The court found that, unlike the criteria for commitment of people with mental illness, "the standard for commitment [under this statute] is set by scientific tests monitoring levels of intellectual functioning and adaptive behavior." The statute and accompanying regulations permitted court certification only if the examining institution found (a) that the person met the definition of mental retardation found in the Manual of the American Association of Mental Deficiency and (b) that "admission to a state institution for the mentally retarded [is] the optimal available plan and is in the best interest of the person and the community." The definition of mental retardation in the

Manual did not require consideration of the person's ability to understand or consent to treatment.

Is there a rational basis for establishing broader commitment criteria for people with developmental disabilities? How do you think the Supreme Court would answer this question?

5. *Alternatives to institutionalization.* Given the obvious disabilities of many people with developmental disabilities, the major problem connected with their commitment is not that it frequently coerces people who do not want or need state-provided habilitation but that it usually means long-term institutionalization in mega-facilities that are inadequate at providing training and even tend to accentuate dependency and deterioration. See David Ferleger, "Anti–Institutionalization: The Promise of the *Pennhurst* Case," 31 Stanford L.Rev. 717, 720–724 (1979). The least restrictive alternative doctrine has particular applicability here. Dybwad and Herr have suggested that, once it is determined that a person with developmental disability is incapable of giving meaningful consent and requires close supervision due to a lack of survival skills, the relevant placement criteria should be "whether any in-home supportive services or respite care services could be provided as an alternative to removal from home surroundings; factually-grounded expectations of effective treatment in other settings; and a realistic assessment of whether the benefits to the resident of removal from community surroundings outweigh the harms." Gunnar Dybwad & Stanley Herr, "Unnecessary Coercion: An End to Involuntary Civil Commitment of Retarded Persons," 31 Stanford L.Rev. 753, 764 (1979). Unfortunately, many localities are lacking in either home or community services for people with developmental disability. Indeed, most of the litigation that attempts to force states to create alternatives to institutions has been brought on behalf of this group. These efforts, and the legislation they have spawned, are discussed in Chapters Ten, Eleven and Twelve.

E. CHILDREN

Until the 1950's, the procedures for committing children were usually similar, if not identical, to those governing commitment of adults. But since that time, in conjunction with the general trend toward voluntary hospitalization, most states have enacted special statutes allowing "voluntary" admission of children on the petition of their parents or guardians. By the mid–1970's, three-quarters of the states had special statutory provisions allowing parents to commit their children to mental institutions without a court hearing or any lesser form of judicial oversight and leaving release up to the hospital and the parents. Toward the end of the 1970's, motivated by the reforms of adult commitment, some of these states had revised their statutes to require adult-type hearings, at least when the child objected to commitment or requested release. S. Brakel, J. Parry & B. Weiner, The Mentally Disabled and the Law 43–44 (1985). It was in this context that the Supreme Court decided *Parham v. J.R.*

PARHAM v. J.R. ET AL.

Supreme Court of the United States, 1979.
442 U.S. 584, 99 S.Ct. 2493, 61 L.Ed.2d 101.

[The plaintiffs in this class action were two minors who had been institutionalized in a psychiatric facility operated by the state of Georgia at the initiation of their guardians. One of the plaintiffs, J.L., was initially admitted into Central State Hospital at the age of six. At the time of his admission he had been expelled from school for "uncontrollable behavior" and had manifested "extremely aggressive" behavior at home. For a period of time J.L. was permitted to go home, but his behavior during these visits was "erratic," and the parents asked for discontinuance of the home visits. Two years later a new program was implemented that permitted J.L. to live at home and attend school in the hospital. However, when the parents found they were unable to control J.L.'s behavior, they requested his readmission into Central State Hospital.

The second plaintiff, J.R., was declared a neglected child and removed from his natural parents when he was three months old. He lived in a succession of foster homes until he reached the age of seven, when his disruptive and "incorrigible" behavior both at home and school led his seventh set of foster parents to request his removal. J.R. was thereafter institutionalized in Central State Hospital at the initiative of the Georgia Department of Family and Student Services. At the time of his admission, he was diagnosed as "borderline retarded" and suffering from "unsocialized aggressive reaction."]

MR. CHIEF JUSTICE BURGER delivered the opinion of the Court.

The question presented in this appeal is what process is constitutionally due a minor child whose parents or guardian seek state administered institutional mental health care for the child and specifically whether an adversary proceeding is required prior to or after the commitment.

* * *

A three-judge District Court was convened pursuant to 28 U.S.C. §§ 2281 and 2284. After considering expert and lay testimony and extensive exhibits and after visiting two of the State's regional mental health hospitals, the District Court held that Georgia's statutory scheme was unconstitutional because it failed to protect adequately the appellees' due process rights.

To remedy this violation the court enjoined future commitments based on the procedures in the Georgia statute. It also commanded Georgia to appropriate and expend whatever amount was "reasonably necessary" to provide nonhospital facilities deemed by the appellant state officials to be the most appropriate for the treatment of those members of plaintiffs' class, who could be treated in a less drastic, nonhospital environment.

Appellants challenged all aspects of the District Court's judgment.

* * *

Georgia Code, § 88–503.1 provides for the voluntary admission to a state regional hospital of children such as J.L. and J.R. Under that provision admission begins with an application for hospitalization signed by a "parent or guardian." Upon application the superintendent of each hospital is given the power to admit temporarily any child for "observation and diagnosis." If, after observation, the superintendent finds "evidence of mental illness" and that the child is "suitable for treatment" in the hospital, then the child may be admitted "for such period and under such conditions as may be authorized by law."

Georgia's mental health statute also provides for the discharge of voluntary patients. Any child who has been hospitalized for more than five days may be discharged at the request of a parent or guardian. Even without a request for discharge, however, the superintendent of each regional hospital has an affirmative duty to release any child "who has recovered from his mental illness or who has sufficiently improved that the superintendent determines that hospitalization of the patient is no longer desirable."

Georgia's Mental Health Director has not published any statewide regulations defining what specific procedures each superintendent must employ when admitting a child under 18. Instead, each regional hospital's superintendent is responsible for the procedures in his or her facility. There is substantial variation among the institutions with regard to their admission procedures and their procedures for review of patients after they have been admitted.

* * *

[At Southwestern Hospital, after] a child is admitted, the hospital has weekly reviews of his condition performed by its internal medical and professional staff. There also are monthly reviews of each child by a group composed of hospital staff not involved in the weekly reviews and by community clinic staff people. The average stay for each child who was being treated at Southwestern in 1975 was 100 days.

* * *

[At Atlanta Regional Hospital, after] admission the staff reviews the condition of each child every week. In addition, there are monthly utilization reviews by nonstaff mental health professionals; this review considers a random sample of children's cases. The average length of each child's stay in 1975 was 161 days.

* * *

[The Court described similar procedures at three other facilities].

* * *

III

* * *

The parties agree that our prior holdings have set out a general approach for testing challenged state procedures under a due process claim. Assuming the existence of a protectible property or liberty interest, the Court has required a balancing of a number of factors:

> "First, the private interest that will be affected by the official action; second, the risk of an erroneous deprivation of such interest through the procedures used, and the probable value, if any, of additional or substitute procedural safeguards; and finally, the Government's interest, including the function involved and the fiscal and administrative burdens that the additional or substitute procedural requirement would entail."

Mathews v. Eldridge, 424 U.S. 319, 335, 96 S.Ct. 893, 903, 47 L.Ed.2d 18 (1976).

In applying these criteria, we must consider first the child's interest in not being committed. Normally, however, since this interest is inextricably linked with the parents' interest in and obligation for the welfare and health of the child, the private interest at stake is a combination of the child's and parents' concerns. Next we must examine the State's interest in the procedures it has adopted for commitment and treatment of children. Finally, we must consider how well Georgia's procedures protect against arbitrariness in the decision to commit a child to a state mental hospital.

(a) It is not disputed that a child, in common with adults, has a substantial liberty interest in not being confined unnecessarily for medical treatment and that the State's involvement in the commitment decision constitutes state action under the Fourteenth Amendment.

We also recognize that commitment sometimes produces adverse social consequences for the child because of the reaction of some to the discovery that the child has received psychiatric care. This reaction, however, need not be equated with the community response resulting from being labeled by the state as delinquent, criminal, or mentally ill and possibly dangerous. The state through its voluntary commitment procedures does not "label" the child; it provides a diagnosis and treatment that medical specialists conclude the child requires. In terms of public reaction, the child who exhibits abnormal behavior may be seriously injured by an erroneous decision not to commit. Appellees overlook a significant source of the public reaction to the mentally ill, for what is truly "stigmatizing" is the symptomatology of a mental or emotional illness. The pattern of untreated, abnormal behavior—even if nondangerous—arouses at least as much negative reaction as treatment that becomes public knowledge. A person needing, but not receiving, appropriate medical care may well face even greater social ostracism resulting from the observable symptoms of an untreated disorder.

However, we need not decide what effect these factors might have in a different case. For purposes of this decision, we assume that a child has a protectible interest not only in being free of unnecessary bodily restraints but also in not being labeled erroneously by some because of an improper decision by the state hospital superintendent.

(b) We next deal with the interests of the parents who have decided, on the basis of their observations and independent professional recommendations, that their child needs institutional care. Appellees argue that the constitutional rights of the child are of such magnitude and the likelihood of parental abuse is so great that the parents' traditional interests in and responsibility for the upbringing of their child must be subordinated at least to the extent of providing a formal adversary hearing prior to a voluntary commitment.

Our jurisprudence historically has reflected Western Civilization concepts of the family as a unit with broad parental authority over minor children. Our cases have consistently followed that course; our constitutional system long ago rejected any notion that a child is "the mere creature of the State" and, on the contrary, asserted that parents generally "have the right, coupled with the high duty, to recognize and prepare [their children] for additional obligations."

Surely, this includes a "high duty" to recognize symptoms of illness and to seek and follow medical advice. The law's concept of the family rests on a presumption that parents possess what a child lacks in maturity, experience, and capacity for judgment required for making life's difficult decisions. More important, historically it has recognized that natural bonds of affection lead parents to act in the best interests of their children.

As with so many other legal presumptions, experience and reality may rebut what the law accepts as a starting point; the incidence of child neglect and abuse cases attests to this. That some parents "may at times be acting against the interests of their child" creates a basis for caution, but is hardly a reason to discard wholesale those pages of human experience that teach that parents generally do act in the child's best interests. The statist notion that governmental power should supersede parental authority in *all* cases because *some* parents abuse and neglect children is repugnant to American tradition.

Nonetheless, we have recognized that a state is not without constitutional control over parental discretion in dealing with children when their physical or mental health is jeopardized. Moreover, the Court recently declared unconstitutional a state statute that granted parents an absolute veto over a minor child's decision to have an abortion. *Planned Parenthood of Missouri v. Danforth*, 428 U.S. 52, 96 S.Ct. 2831, 49 L.Ed.2d 788 (1976). Appellees urge that these precedents limiting the traditional rights of parents, if viewed in the context of the liberty interest of the child and the likelihood of parental abuse, require us to hold that the parents' decision to have a child admitted to a mental hospital must be subjected to an exacting constitutional scrutiny, including a formal, adversary preadmission hearing.

Appellees' argument, however, sweeps too broadly. Simply because the decision of a parent is not agreeable to a child or because it involves risks does not automatically transfer the power to make that decision from the parents to some agency or officer of the state. The same characterizations can be made for a tonsillectomy, appendectomy or other medical procedure. Most children, even in adolescence, simply are not able to make sound judgments concerning many decisions, including their need for medical care or treatment. Parents can and must make those judgments. * * * The fact that a child may balk at hospitalization or complain about a parental refusal to provide cosmetic surgery does not diminish the parents' authority to decide what is best for the child.

* * *

Appellees place particular reliance on *Planned Parenthood,* arguing that its holding indicates how little deference to parents is appropriate when the child is exercising a constitutional right. The basic situation in that case, however, was very different; *Planned Parenthood* involved an absolute parental veto over the child's ability to obtain an abortion. Parents in Georgia in no sense have an absolute right to commit their children to state mental hospitals; the statute requires the superintendent of each regional hospital to exercise independent judgment as to the child's need for confinement.

In defining the respective rights and prerogatives of the child and parent in the voluntary commitment setting, we conclude that our precedents permit the parents to retain a substantial, if not the dominant, role in the decision, absent a finding of neglect or abuse, and that the traditional presumption that the parents act in the best interests of their child should apply. We also conclude, however, that the child's rights and the nature of the commitment decision are such that parents cannot always have absolute and unreviewable discretion to decide whether to have a child institutionalized. They, of course, retain plenary authority to seek such care for their children, subject to a physician's independent examination and medical judgment.

(c) The State obviously has a significant interest in confining the use of its costly mental health facilities to cases of genuine need. The Georgia program seeks first to determine whether the patient seeking admission has an illness that calls for in-patient treatment. To accomplish this purpose, the State has charged the superintendents of each regional hospital with the responsibility for determining, before authorizing an admission, whether a prospective patient is mentally ill and whether the patient will likely benefit from hospital care. In addition, the State has imposed a continuing duty on hospital superintendents to release any patient who has recovered to the point where hospitalization is no longer needed.

* * *

The State also has a genuine interest in allocating priority to the diagnosis and treatment of patients as soon as they are admitted to a hospital rather than to time-consuming procedural minuets before the admission. One factor that must be considered is the utilization of the time of psychiatrists, psychologists and other behavioral specialists in preparing for and participating in hearings rather than performing the task for which their special training has fitted them. Behavioral experts in courtrooms and hearings are of little help to patients.

The *amicus* brief of the American Psychiatric Association points out at page 20 that the average staff psychiatrist in a hospital presently is able to devote only 47% of his time to direct patient care. One consequence of increasing the procedures the state must provide prior to a child's voluntary admission will be that mental health professionals will be diverted even more from the treatment of patients in order to travel to and participate in—and wait for—what could be hundreds—or even thousands—of hearings each year. Obviously the cost of these procedures would come from the public monies the legislature intended for mental health care.

(d) We now turn to consideration of what process protects adequately the child's constitutional rights by reducing risks of error without unduly trenching on traditional parental authority and without undercutting "efforts to further the legitimate interests of both the state and the patient that are served by" voluntary commitments. We conclude that the risk of error inherent in the parental decision to have a child institutionalized for mental health care is sufficiently great that some kind of inquiry should be made by a "neutral factfinder" to determine whether the statutory requirements for admission are satisfied. That inquiry must carefully probe the child's background using all available sources, including, but not limited to, parents, schools and other social agencies. Of course, the review must also include an interview with the child. It is necessary that the decisionmaker have the authority to refuse to admit any child who does not satisfy the medical standards for admission. Finally, it is necessary that the child's continuing need for commitment be reviewed periodically by a similarly independent procedure.[15]

We are satisfied that such procedures will protect the child from an erroneous admission decision in a way that neither unduly burdens the states nor inhibits parental decisions to seek state help.

Due process has never been thought to require that the neutral and detached trier of fact be law-trained or a judicial or administrative officer. Surely, this is the case as to medical decisions for "neither judges nor administrative hearing officers are better qualified than psychiatrists to render psychiatric judgments." Thus, a staff physician will suffice, so

15. As we discuss more fully later, the District Court did not decide and we therefore have no reason to consider at this time what procedures for review are independently necessary to justify continuing a child's confinement. We merely hold that a subsequent, independent review of the patient's condition provides a necessary check against possible arbitrariness in the *initial* admission decision.

long as he or she is free to evaluate independently the child's mental and emotional condition and need for treatment.

It is not necessary that the deciding physician conduct a formal or quasi-formal hearing. A state is free to require such a hearing, but due process is not violated by use of informal traditional medical investigative techniques. Since well-established medical procedures already exist, we do not undertake to outline with specificity precisely what this investigation must involve. The mode and procedure of medical diagnostic procedures is not the business of judges. What is best for a child is an individual medical decision that must be left to the judgment of physicians in each case. We do no more than emphasize that the decision should represent an independent judgment of what the child requires and that all sources of information that are traditionally relied on by physicians and behavioral specialists should be consulted. * * * [One of the] problem(s) with requiring a formalized, factfinding hearing lies in the danger it poses for significant intrusion into the parent-child relationship. Pitting the parents and child as adversaries often will be at odds with the presumption that parents act in the best interests of their child. It is one thing to require a neutral physician to make a careful review of the parents' decision in order to make sure it is proper from a medical standpoint; it is a wholly different matter to employ an adversary contest to ascertain whether the parents' motivation is consistent with the child's interests.

Moreover, it is appropriate to inquire into how such a hearing would contribute to the long range successful treatment of the patient. Surely, there is a risk that it would exacerbate whatever tensions already existed between the child and the parents. Since the parents can and usually do play a significant role in the treatment while the child is hospitalized and even more so after release, there is a serious risk that an adversary confrontation will adversely affect the ability of the parents to assist the child while in the hospital. Moreover, it will make his subsequent return home more difficult. These unfortunate results are especially critical with an emotionally disturbed child; they seem likely to occur in the context of an adversary hearing in which the parents testify. A confrontation over such intimate family relationships would distress the normal adult parents and the impact on a disturbed child almost certainly would be significantly greater.

* * *

By expressing some confidence in the medical decisionmaking process, we are by no means suggesting it is error free. On occasion parents may initially mislead an admitting physician or a physician may erroneously diagnose the child as needing institutional care either because of negligence or an overabundance of caution. That there may be risks of error in the process affords no rational predicate for holding unconstitutional an entire statutory and administrative scheme that is generally followed in more than 30 states. "[P]rocedural due process rules are shaped by the risk of error inherent in the truthfinding process as applied to the generality of cases, not the rare exceptions." In general, we are satisfied that an independent medical decisionmaking process, which includes the thorough psychiatric investigation described earlier followed by additional periodic review of a child's condition, will protect children who should not be admitted; we do not believe the risks of error in that process would be significantly reduced by a more formal, judicial-type hearing.

* * *

IV

(a) Our discussion in Part III was directed at the situation where a child's natural parents request his admission to a state mental hospital. Some members of appellees' class, including J.R., were wards of the State of Georgia at the time of their admission. Obviously their situation differs from those members of the class who have natural parents. While the determination of what process is due varies somewhat when the state, rather than a natural parent, makes the request for commitment, we conclude that the differences in the two situations do not justify requiring different procedures at the time of the child's initial admission to the hospital.

For a ward of the State, there may well be no adult who knows him thoroughly and who cares for him deeply. * * * Contrary to the suggestion of the dissent, however, we cannot assume that when the State of Georgia has custody of a child it acts so differently from a natural parent in seeking medical assistance for the child. [T]here is no evidence that the State, acting as guardian, attempted to admit any child for reasons unrelated to the child's need for treatment. Indeed, neither the District Court nor the appellees have suggested that wards of the State should receive any constitutional treatment different from children with natural parents.

* * *

Once we accept that the State's application of a child for admission to a hospital is made in good faith, then the question is whether the medical decisionmaking approach of the admitting physician is adequate to satisfy due process. We have already recognized that an independent medical judgment made from the perspective of the best interests of the child after a careful investigation is an acceptable means of justifying a voluntary commitment. We do not believe that the soundness of this decisionmaking is any the less reasonable in this setting.

Indeed, if anything, the decision with regard to wards of the State may well be even more reasonable in light of the extensive written records that are compiled about each child while in the State's custody.

* * *

Since the state agency having custody and control of the child *in loco parentis* has a duty to consider the best interests of the child with respect to a decision on commitment to a mental hospital, the State may constitutionally allow that custodial agency to speak for the child, subject, of course, to the restrictions governing natural parents.

* * *

(b) It is possible that the procedures required in reviewing a ward's need for continuing care should be different from those used to review a child with natural parents. As we have suggested earlier, the issue of what process is due to justify continuing a voluntary commitment must be considered by the District Court on remand. In making that inquiry the District Court might well consider whether wards of the State should be treated with respect to continuing therapy differently from children with natural parents.

The absence of an adult who cares deeply for a child has little effect on the reliability of the initial admission decision, but it may have some effect on how long a child will remain in the hospital. We noted in *Addington v. Texas, supra,* "the concern of family and friends generally will provide continuous opportunities for an erroneous commitment to be corrected." For a child without natural parents, we must acknowledge the risk of being "lost in the shuffle."

* * *

Whether wards of the State generally have received less protection than children with natural parents, and, if so, what should be done about it, however, are matters that must be decided in the first instance by the District Court on remand, if the Court concludes the issue is still alive. * * * [W]e are satisfied that Georgia's medical factfinding processes are reasonable and consistent with constitutional guarantees. Accordingly, it was error to hold unconstitutional the State's procedures for admitting a child for treatment to a state mental hospital. The judgment is therefore reversed and the case is remanded to the District Court for further proceedings consistent with this opinion.

Reversed and remanded.

* * *

MR. JUSTICE BRENNAN, with whom MR. JUSTICE MARSHALL and MR. JUSTICE STEVENS join, concurring in part and dissenting in part.

* * *

I

RIGHTS OF CHILDREN COMMITTED TO MENTAL INSTITUTIONS

It may well be argued that children are entitled to more protection than are adults. The consequences of an erroneous commitment decision are more tragic where children are involved. Children, on the average, are confined for longer periods than are adults. Moreover, childhood is a particularly vulnerable time of life and children erroneously institutionalized during their formative years may bear the scars for the rest of their lives. Furthermore, the provision of satisfactory institutionalized mental care for children generally requires a substantial financial commitment that too often has not been forthcoming.

* * *

In addition, the chances of an erroneous commitment decision are particularly great where children are involved. Even under the best of circumstances psychiatric diagnosis and therapy decisions are fraught with uncertainties. These uncertainties are aggravated when, as under the Georgia practice, the psychiatrist interviews the child during a period of abnormal stress in connection with the commitment, and without adequate time or opportunity to become acquainted with the patient. These uncertainties may be further aggravated when economic and social class separate doctor and child, thereby frustrating the accurate diagnosis of pathology.

These compounded uncertainties often lead to erroneous commitments since psychiatrists tend to err on the side of medical caution and therefore hospitalize patients for whom other dispositions would be more beneficial. The National Institute of Mental Health recently found that only 36% of patients below age 20 who were confined at St. Elizabeths Hospital actually required such hospitalization. Of particular relevance to this case, a Georgia study Commission on Mental Health Services for Children and Youth concluded that more than half of the State's institutionalized children were not in need of confinement if other forms of care were made available or used.

* * *

II

RIGHTS OF CHILDREN COMMITTED BY THEIR PARENTS

* * *

I believe that States may legitimately postpone formal commitment proceedings when parents seek in-patient psychiatric treatment for their children. Such children may be admitted, for a limited period, without prior hearing, so long as the admitting psychiatrist first interviews parent and child and concludes that short term in-patient treatment would be appropriate.

I do not believe, however, that the present Georgia juvenile commitment scheme is constitutional in its entirety. Although Georgia may postpone formal commitment hearings, when parents seek to commit their children, the State cannot dispense with such hearings altogether.

* * *

The informal postadmission procedures that Georgia now follows are simply not enough to qualify as hearings—let alone reasonably prompt hearings. The procedures lack all the traditional due process safeguards. Commitment decisions are made *ex parte*. Georgia's institutionalized juveniles are not informed of the reasons for their commitment; nor do they enjoy the right to be present at the commitment determination, nor the right to representation, the right to be heard, the right to be confronted with adverse witnesses, the right to cross-examine, or the right to offer evidence of their own. By any standard of due process, these procedures are deficient.

The special considerations that militate against preadmission commitment hearings when parents seek to hospitalize their children do not militate against reasonably prompt postadmission commitment hearings. In the first place, postadmission hearings would not delay the commencement of needed treatment. Children could be cared for by the State pending the disposition decision.

Second, the interest in avoiding family discord would be less significant at this stage since the family autonomy already will have been fractured by the institutionalization of the child. In any event, postadmission hearings are unlikely to disrupt family relationships. At later hearings the case for and against commitment would be based upon the observations of the hospital staff and the judgments of the staff psychiatrists, rather than upon parental observations and recommendations. The doctors urging commitment, and not the parents, would stand as the child's adversaries. As a consequence, postadmission commitment hearings are unlikely to involve direct challenges to parental authority, judgment or veracity. To defend the child, the child's advocate need not dispute the parents' original decision to seek medical treatment for their child, or even, for that matter, their observations concerning the child's behavior. The advocate need only argue, for example, that the child had sufficiently improved during his hospital stay to warrant out-patient treatment or outright discharge. Conflict between doctor and advocate on this question is unlikely to lead to family discord.

As a consequence, the prospect of a postadmission hearing is unlikely to deter parents from seeking medical attention for their children and the hearing itself is unlikely to so traumatize parent and child as to make the child's eventual return to the family impracticable.

* * *

III

RIGHTS OF CHILDREN COMMITTED BY THEIR STATE GUARDIANS

Georgia does not accord prior hearings to juvenile wards of the State of Georgia committed by state social workers acting *in loco parentis*. The Court dismisses a challenge to this practice on the grounds that state social workers are obliged by statute to act in the children's best interest.

* * *

To my mind, there is no justification for denying children committed by their social workers the prior hearings that the Constitution typically requires. * * * [First, the] rule that parents speak for their children, even if it were applicable in the commitment context, cannot be transmuted into a rule that state social workers speak for their minor clients. The rule in favor of deference to parental authority is designed to shield parental control of childrearing from state interference. * * * The social worker-child relationship is not deserving of the special protection and deference accorded to the parent-child relationship and state officials acting *in loco parentis* cannot be equated with parents.

Second, the special considerations that justify postponement of formal commitment proceedings whenever parents seek to hospitalize their children are absent when the children are wards of the State and are being committed upon the recommendations of their social workers. The prospect of preadmission hearings is not likely to deter state social workers from discharging their duties and securing psychiatric attention for their disturbed clients. Moreover, since the children will already be in some form of state custody as wards of the State, prehospitalization hearings will not prevent needy children from receiving state care during the pendency of the commitment proceedings. Finally, hearings in which the decisions of state social workers are reviewed by other state officials are not likely to traumatize the children or to hinder their eventual recovery.

For these reasons I believe that, in the absence of exigent circumstances, juveniles committed upon the recommendation of their social workers are entitled to preadmission commitment hearings. As a consequence, I would hold Georgia's present practice of denying these juveniles prior hearings unconstitutional.

Questions and Comments

1. Institutionalized Juveniles. In a companion case to *Parham*, *Secretary of Public Welfare of Penn. v. Institutionalized Juveniles*, 442 U.S. 640, 99 S.Ct. 2523, 61 L.Ed.2d 142 (1979), the Court upheld Pennsylvania's system for committing children with mental illness and mental retardation on the petition of their parents or guardian. As it had in *Parham*, the Court stressed the thoroughness of the preadmission procedure.

> No child is admitted without at least one and often more psychiatric examinations by an independent team of mental health professionals whose sole concern under the statute is whether the child needs and can benefit from institutional care. The treatment team not only interviews the child and parents but also compiles a full background history from all available sources. If the treatment team concludes that institutional care is not in the child's best interest, it must refuse the child's admission. Finally, every child's condition is reviewed at least every 30 days.

Also as in *Parham*, the Court declined to decide what, if any, judicial postadmission procedures are required.

2. *Children's competence.* The majority opinion in *Parham* states that "[m]ost children, even in adolescence, simply are not able to make sound judgments concerning many decisions, including their need for medical care

or treatment." Studies available at the time of *Parham* indicated, to the contrary, that by age 14 minors are typically as competent as adults in making treatment decisions and that some children under that age are equally competent. See, e.g., Lois Weithorn & Susan Campbell, "The Competency of Children and Adolescents to Make Informed Treatment Decisions," 53 Child Dev. 1589 (1982). Most of this research involved "nonclinical" (i.e., non-mentally ill) populations, however. Further, more recent research suggests there might be significant differences between adolescents 17 and older and those who are younger in terms of "maturity" of judgment (as defined by degree of self-reliance, clarity of identity, and ability to limit impulsivity, avoid extremes, evaluate situations, and acknowledge the complexity of situations). See Laurence Steinberg & Elizabeth Cauffman, "Maturity of Judgment in Adolescence: Psychosocial Factors in Adolescent Decision Making," 20 L. & Hum. Beh. 249 (1996). What impact, if any, should these findings have on the due process analysis of commitment of minors?

3. *Parental and governmental good faith.* In holding that children subject to commitment are not entitled to the procedural protections afforded adults, the Court's decisions in *Parham* and *Institutionalized Juveniles* rely in part on the assumption that most parents seeking such commitment act in the "best interest" of their children. There is significant research disputing this assumption. For instance, one review concluded: "[O]ne thing that is clear from a variety of statistical data is that both the decision to place a child in an institution and the selection of the type of institution for him are dependent to a great extent on factors other than the needs of the child." Donell Pappenfort, ed., Child Caring, Social Policy and the Institution 112 (1973). Rather than the child, it may be the parents who are disturbed. One study of Philadelphia admissions indicated that, in 25 percent of the cases in which complainants alleged someone was mentally ill, it was the complainant, not the prospective patient, who was mentally ill. Thomas Scheff, Being Mentally Ill: A Sociological Theory 171 (1966). Others have noted that a child may be made the scapegoat for conflicts, disabilities or emotional deficiencies of the parents or siblings. Ezra Vogel & Norman Bell, "The Emotionally Disturbed Child as the Family Scapegoat," in A Modern Introduction to the Family 412 (N. Bell & E. Vogel rev. ed. 1968).

Even if the parents are relatively "normal," they may decide to hospitalize their child for reasons that may not be in their "best interests." Recall that the district court in *Institutionalized Juveniles* found, based on extensive expert testimony, that the parents' decision to hospitalize a child with mental retardation may be the result of community pressure, emotional difficulties in dealing with the child, or financial problems connected with providing necessary care. This tendency may be exacerbated by the deinstitutionalization of the juvenile justice system (in particular, its divestment of status offenses such as "children in need of supervision" jurisdiction) and "the proliferation of investor-owned, for-profit psychiatric hospitals [that are] often affordable due to insurance policies which fully reimburse for inpatient treatment but which restrict coverage for outpatient services." See Dennis E. Cichon, "Developing a Mental Health Code For Minors," 13 Thomas M. Cooley L. Rev. 529, 530 (1996).* A GAO Report found that, in

* Financially strapped parents of children with mental and physical handicaps have received a significant boost with the Individuals with Disabilities Education Chil-

2001, parents "were forced to place more than 12,700 children in the child welfare or juvenile justice systems as a last resort for those children who needed mental health care treatment." President's New Freedom Commission on Mental Health 33–34 (May, 2003)(also noting that five of the largest states did not submit data for the report).

On the other hand, the social worker in charge of a child who is a ward of the state is presumably not affected by such considerations when making placement decisions. Are there other reasons for suspecting the sincerity of a social worker's decision to seek institutionalization of such a child? Note that the guardianship statutes of several states bar state social service officials from serving as guardians out of a fear of conflict of interest. Legal Counsel for the Elderly, Decisionmaking, Incapacity and the Elderly 75 (1987).

4. *The independent decisionmaker.* The *Parham* Court placed considerable faith in the psychiatric interview as a means of ferreting out inappropriate petitions, whether they are brought by parents or state guardians. James Ellis, in "Volunteering Children: Parental Commitment of Minors to Mental Institutions," 62 Cal.L.Rev. 840, 864 (1974) has questioned the efficacy of this type of review:

> Experience shows that in the most blatant cases of parental error psychiatrists do screen out admissions which are not warranted by apparent pathology in the child. In less obvious cases, however, psychiatrists may fail to perform an effective screening function. There are three reasons for this failure: (1) The performance of psychiatrists in precommitment interviews and examinations is often perfunctory and tends toward overdiagnosis; (2) Psychiatrists may be insensitive to legally important commitment issues; (3) The effectiveness of the psychiatrist in the admitting process is weakened by uncertainty over whose agent he or she is in such circumstances—the parent's or the child's.

On the latter point, Ellis notes: "While the goal of the psychiatrist will be expressed—and perceived—as the best welfare of the child-patient, it is the parent who has come to seek help, whose situation seems most desperate, who seems the most reliable source of information about what is wrong, who is closest to the psychiatrist in age and social outlook, and who is paying the psychiatrist's fee." Id. at 866.

There is little information bearing on the number of "inappropriate" admissions of children under procedures like those in use in Georgia. The figures provided by Justice Brennan in dissent suggesting that a large number of children are improperly hospitalized are probably as much a reflection on the unavailability of community resources as an indication of the accuracy of decisions made by admitting clinicians. However, it is worth noting that the amicus brief submitted by the American Psychiatric Association, upon which the majority heavily relies, questioned the wisdom of leaving the hospitalization decision to a psychiatrist in all circumstances.

dren Act, 20 U.S.C. §§ 1400–1461, which provides federal and state funding for "mainstreaming" handicapped children in the public school system. This Act, which is discussed in detail in Chapter Eleven, may have taken some pressure off the commitment system.

While Amici agree with appellant that psychiatric diagnosis—i.e., identi-fication of specific mental illnesses—are medically reliable, we recognize that this fact is not dispositive of the issue of when a hearing is constitutionally required. Even if a child is properly diagnosed, it does not follow that hospitalization is necessary or desirable. Rather, Amici believe that in appropriate circumstances a due process hearing may provide a reasonable forum for deciding what care should be provided to a properly diagnosed child.

Amicus Brief for the American Psychiatric Association, et. al., at 24. Specifi-cally, the APA advocated following the Georgia procedure only when (a) parents in an intact family wish to admit (b) a preadolescent child (c) to an accredited institution (d) for a short-term period (e.g., less than 45 days). In all other circumstances, concluded the APA, the danger of inappropriate placement merits affording the child more formal due process protections.

5. *Postadmission review.* In *Parham* the Court required some sort of "independent review of the patient's condition" but then remanded to the district court for a determination as to the precise postadmission procedure mandated by the constitution. Several states provide for automatic judicial review procedures akin to those provided in adult commitment. Many, however, provide such review only at the child's request. In other states, because they are "voluntary" patients, children are not entitled to either periodic review or habeas review. At the same time, because they are children, they cannot give notice of an intention to leave, as can adult voluntary patients, unless they obtain approval of their parents or guardian. Ellis, supra at 847.

Although the postadmission issue is at least as important as the issues addressed by the Court, the only guidance the Court provided on remand was to indicate that children confined pursuant to a petition by the state may be entitled to more procedural oversight than children whose confine-ment was sought by their parents. This was because parents are more likely to make sure their children do not get "lost in the shuffle." Are parents any more likely to seek release of their children than the state is of its wards? Consider Allen Shoenberger, " 'Voluntary' Commitment of Mentally Ill or Retarded Children: Child Abuse by the Supreme Court," 7 U.Dayton L.Rev. 1, 30 (1981):

> Once a family decides to institutionalize a mentally retarded child ... reopening that emotionally charged decision is very difficult, even in the context of available supportive social services for in-home care that, if previously available, might have prevented institutionalization. Indeed, every time a family member visits the retarded individual, "all the old guilt feelings and indecisiveness surge up about whether or not they made the right decision."

6. *Criteria.* Do the differences between adults and children permit different *standards* of commitment as well as different procedures? As with some of the statutes governing commitment of people with developmental disabilities, the Georgia statute at issue in *Parham* permits admission of the child solely upon a finding by the admitting psychiatrist that the child is mentally disordered and suitable for treatment. Had the Supreme Court been asked to address the constitutionality of these criteria, how should it

have held? Would a decision upholding the statute be consistent with *O'Connor v. Donaldson?*

7. *Implications of* Parham *for adults.* Should the reasoning found in *Parham* be extended to *adult* civil commitment, thus permitting commitment of adults under a need for treatment criterion as interpreted by a "neutral physician?" How much of the Court's rationale for its decision in *Parham* is dependent upon some special characteristic of children and their situation? At the least, could *Parham's* reasoning be applied to commitment of the adults who are developmentally disabled, given the fact that they are often wards of their relatives or the state?

Chapter Nine

COMPETENCY DETERMINATIONS

Table of Sections

I. INTRODUCTION

The issue of competency—the capacity to decide or to perform certain functions—permeates both the criminal and civil justice systems, although the precise decisions to be made and functions to be carried out vary from context to context. In civil cases, for instance, competency may refer to a capacity to understand and approve the terms of a contract or a will, manage financial affairs, or make treatment decisions. In criminal cases, it may designate the capacity to comprehend legal proceedings and communicate with an attorney, or to understand and waive certain rights, such as the right to remain silent.

In all of these situations, the state may intervene to ensure that a person is capable of performing the required tasks. More significantly, if the state determines the person is incompetent, it may deprive him or her of liberty, property or the option to act. In the illustrative civil situations noted above, the incompetent person may be prohibited from making a contract or will or unable to have it implemented, required to surrender control of financial or personal affairs to a guardian, or subjected to civil commitment. In the noted criminal-law situations, the person found incompetent may be forcibly treated, in a hospital or elsewhere, for the purpose of "restoring" competency to undergo legal proceedings and make waiver decisions; in the meantime he or she will be prevented from obtaining adjudication of the pending charges.

The primary justification for these types of interventions stems from this society's preference for autonomy—the freedom to make and act upon one's decisions. We value autonomy because we assume people are ordinarily the best judges of their own interests and because, even if they are not, taking away their opportunity to decide would show insufficient respect for the person. Because of this preference for autonomy, we generally allow individuals considerable latitude when engaging in behavior that is not directly harmful to others. But when a person appears to lack autonomy, either because of externally imposed coercion or— more relevant to this book—"internal" causes, we are less likely to respect his or her choices, even if they affect no one else. Because these people are not deemed to be able to function or to make decisions in their own best interests, we are more willing to override their decisions even if doing so will make them feel degraded or minimized. At the least, many would argue, the state's parens patriae power—its power to act as parent for disabled citizens—authorizes interfering with an incompetent person when harm to self would otherwise result and the intervention will not itself cause harm.[a] Beyond this, there may even be an affirmative *duty* to intervene under such circumstances.

To take an extreme example, suppose a man is unable to control his bodily movements and is unable to speak. When asked a question, his head might nod "yes" or "no" completely randomly. Most would agree that taking some important action—say, giving or withholding experimental but potentially life-saving treatment—based on such a nod would be improper. There is no necessary correlation between the nod and the person's "true" desires. Indeed, the nod is not really a "choice" in any sense of the word; acting on it could be viewed as an insult to him. Therefore, consistent with the autonomy preference, the state is justified in attempting to enable him to respond in a meaningful fashion and, if that fails, in making the decision for him if a decision is necessary.

A second possible justification for refusing to honor the man's "decision" and allowing government intervention under these circumstances is more general in nature. Not only would acting on a random nod be insulting to the individual; it would also make a mockery of the concept of autonomy itself. It would suggest that society sanctions random decisionmaking. Thus, ensuring competency of the individual protects not only his or her interests but those of society at large.

---

a. See discussion of the parens patriae power in Chapter Eight pp. 747–82.

The central issue addressed in this chapter is the extent to which the state may intervene to further these interests when a person who is allegedly mentally disabled wants to, is asked to, or is required to perform a particular task. Although it will allude to a number of such tasks, this chapter will focus on management of essential survival chores, making treatment decisions, assisting counsel at trial, and waiving constitutional rights. Before looking at these issues, we will look more closely at the competency notion.

II.   GENERAL CONSIDERATIONS

TEST CASES

In the following four cases, the subjects were found incompetent. Reflect on whether you agree as you read the following materials.

Case 1. Mr. B, a 43 year-old man, has long-standing glaucoma in both eyes. In one eye, vision remains only for motion. In the other eye, vision is better, though poorly controlled by medication. Mr. B's ophthalmologist has proposed a drainage procedure for the second eye which has a high chance of improving his vision for several months (at which time it could be undertaken again) and a negligible chance of damaging the eye. Although Mr. B expresses concern about the pressure in his eye and is fearful of going blind, he refuses the drainage procedure, explaining that his "voices" would be "angry with him" if he underwent the procedure. When his reasons for refusal are explored further, he notes that his mother had a similar drainage procedure which had not been helpful. He then discusses his attachment to his mother, stating that he feels that whatever happened to his mother will also happen to him.[b]

Case 2. Ms. N. is 72 years old and is presently in the intensive care unit of General Hospital in Nashville, Tenn., because of gangrenous condition in her two feet. Doctors estimate that the probability of her surviving without amputation of the feet is 5 to 10% and the probability of survival after amputation is about 50%, with possible severe psychotic results. Ms. N. refuses to consent to the amputation or consider the possibility that it is necessary to save her life. She feels very strongly that her physical condition is improving and that she will recover without the necessity of surgery. When asked if she would prefer to die rather than lose her feet, she answered "possibly." The flesh on her feet is black, shriveled, rotting, and stinking; she believes their appearance is a result of soot or dirt.[c]

b. This case is adapted from Paul Appelbaum & Loren Roth, "Clinical Issues in the Assessment of Competency," 138 Am.J.Psychiat. 1462, 1464 (1981). The authors conclude that the patient was "apparently incompetent", thus permitting doctors to override the refusal.

c. These facts are taken from State Dept. of Human Services v. Northern, 563 S.W.2d 197 (Tenn.App.1978), where the court authorized amputation of Ms. Northern's foot if her condition "has developed to such a critical stage as to demand immediate amputation to save her life." Ms. Northern died in 1978 as a result of a clot from

Case 3. Ms. K. dies, leaving only $1.00 of a sizeable estate to her only child, Ms. R., with the rest going to a church. Testimony at a will contest proceeding reveals that, when asked why she wanted to distribute her estate in this way, Ms. K. stated that she had not gotten along well with R., that while living with the R.s she had been required to do things which she did not want to do, that Mr. R. had made a derogatory remark concerning Germans (K. was of German descent), that the R.s were lacking in religious spirit, and that Ms. R. had tried to kill her by putting glass in her pudding. She also stated that she (Ms. K.) had failed to contribute enough in support of the church. Independent evidence disclosed that the daughter had prepared the pudding with the glass in it but that the glass was there accidentally. Furthermore, Ms. K. had been assured by many people that such was the case, but she persisted in believing that her daughter had wanted to harm her.[d]

Case 4. Mr. F., diagnosed as suffering from manic-depressive psychosis, began to emerge from the depressed phase in August. Previously frugal and cautious, he began driving at high speeds, to be sexually more active with his wife and to discuss the purchase of land for development. In September, against the advice of his lawyer, he contracted for land in the Catskills and talked about erecting a 400 room hotel with a marina and golf course. On September 23, he signed another contract—after his lawyer counseled against it and withdrew from negotiations—to buy more property, on which he planned to erect a drug store and merchandise mart. Under this contract, title was not to change hands until October 20. Within two weeks of signing the contract, he arranged for a title search, giving correct details concerning the property and price, and asked that the search be completed within a week. He also persuaded a former employee to join in the enterprise, promising him a salary and a Lincoln Continental when the project was complete, had a sign erected on the premises stating that F. Drug Company and merchandise mart were coming soon, hired an architect, initiated a mortgage application, hired laborers to begin digging, filed plans with city officials, and went to Albany to obtain the necessary approval for building. He also went to a psychiatrist to get help for his wife, who he stated was trying to stop his activities. This psychiatrist saw him on three subsequent occasions. On October 8th Mr. F. was hospitalized after purchasing a hunting gun, with all doctors agreeing on a diagnosis of manic-depressive psychosis.[e]

gangrenous tissue; the surgery was never performed because of complications rendering it more dangerous.

d. The case is based on In re Klein's Estate, 28 Wash.2d 456, 183 P.2d 518 (1947), in which the court declared Ms. Klein's will void.

e. This case is based on Faber v. Sweet Style Mfg. Corp., 40 Misc.2d 212, 242 N.Y.S.2d 763 (1963), in which the court voided Faber's second contract on the ground of incompetency.

PAUL APPELBAUM & LOREN ROTH, COMPETENCY
TO CONSENT TO RESEARCH: A PSYCHIATRIC
OVERVIEW

39 Arch.Gen.Psychiat. 951, 952–56.
(1982).

* * *

EVIDENCING A CHOICE

The least rigorous standard for competency ... is the subject's actual communication of a decision as to his participation in the proposed project. This requirement has been phrased as demanding that the subject "manifest his consent" or "express a positive interest in taking part".

To the uninitiated, operationalizing the requirement that the subject evidence a choice may seem a trivial exercise; in most instances one need only ask the subject whether or not he desires to participate. There are occasions, however, in which the communication from the subject will be so ambiguous as to raise serious questions about whether or not consent has occurred. These include cases in which the subject's verbal and behavioral responses diverge (for example, when a subject declines to participate in a study requiring venipuncture, then rolls up his sleeve and holds out his arm to the experimenter).

* * *

FACTUAL UNDERSTANDING OF THE ISSUES

The subject's understanding of the issues relevant to participation is the single factor that has been most widely accepted as a standard for competency. A typical formulation requires that the subject have "the cognitive capacity to consider the relevant issues". Those areas that have been considered to be crucial for the subject to understand include "the nature of the procedure, its risks, and other relevant information," "the nature and likelihood of success of the proposed treatment and ... of its risks and side-effects," "the available options, their advantages and disadvantages," "the knowledge that he has a choice to make," "who he is, where he is, what he is reading and what he is doing in signing the paper," and "the consequences of participation or non-participation."

* * *

The rigor of the requirement of understanding obviously increases with the amount and complexity of material that is required to be understood. Some writers make understanding the sine qua non of their standard of competency, and it has long been the primary element of legal tests of contractual and testamentary capacity.

"Factual understanding" actually encompasses two different standards: one can require, as many writers do, that the subject have the "ability to understand," or more strictly, one can insist that the subject manifest "actual understanding" of the material.

* * *

Means of demonstrating a subject's actual understanding of issues related to his decision include, in increasing order of difficulty, asking him to repeat the information provided, asking him to paraphrase it in his own words, and requiring that he display an ability to put some or all of the information to practical use. One difficulty in testing understanding of the consequences of a decision (often conceptualized as the risks and benefits) is the possibility of divergence between what the investigator perceives as a benefit or a risk and the subject's view of the matter. Consequences of participation, such as prolonged hospitalization, which are often thought of as a disadvantage, might seem quite desirable to a socially isolated or otherwise impoverished subject.

RATIONAL MANIPULATION OF INFORMATION

One step beyond measuring factual understanding is determining how the information that the subject assimilates is utilized in the decision-making process. The rubrics by which this standard is discussed include judgment, rationality, rational weighing of risks and benefits, reality testing, and decision-making capacity. Legal rules concerning contractual and testimonial capacity traditionally have recognized at least one defect of rationality, the presence of "insane delusions," as grounds for invalidating a person's acts.

* * *

The subjective nature of any assessment of rationality frequently has been pointed to as a major obstacle to the successful use of such a test. But an even greater problem may lie in the consensus of most experts today that an impairment of rationality does not necessarily affect global decision-making ability, that is, that the impact of delusions, for example, may be limited to a discrete area of mental functioning. Although this belief awaits definitive empirical verification, it indicates the possible utility of a test of rationality directed to the specific decision at hand rather than to the person's general functioning.

* * *

APPRECIATION OF THE NATURE OF THE SITUATION

The strictest standard for competency requires that, once understanding has been attained, the rational manipulation of information take place in the context of the subject's appreciation of the nature of his situation.

Appreciation is distinct from factual understanding in that it requires the subject to consider the relevance to his immediate situation of those facts he has understood previously in the abstract. It differs from the rational manipulation of information by requiring that the subject take certain crucial data into consideration, rather than merely asking him to manipulate rationally whatever information is already at hand. This has been phrased in a variety of ways, asking that the subject "appreciate the consequences of giving or withholding consent," have "a sense of who he is and why he is agreeing," recognize, "in a mature fashion, the implications of alternative courses of action and appreciate both cognitively and affectively the nature of the thing to be decided," or "appreciate what is relevant to forming a judgment of the issue in question—i.e., . . . consider relevant evidence."

* * *

Whether the extent of the subject's appreciation needs to coincide precisely with the investigator's is a controversial topic. Some commentators have suggested that, in a therapeutic setting, the patient need only "understand the nature of the mental condition which the psychiatrist believes him to have," without necessarily agreeing with that judgment. Such a standard, however, more closely resembles a factual-understanding test than a genuine test of appreciation. Although some people may be uncomfortable with such a criterion, of necessity the subject's views (e.g., on the presence or absence of illness or the results of accepting or refusing participation) ultimately must be measured by their correspondence with the consensus of knowledgeable (usually professional) opinion on those issues.

Choosing the Standard

Despite wide variation in the wording of many attempts to define the standards for competency, they appear, as was just shown, to be classifiable into four general categories. Rather than deriving a single standard for competency from this discussion of the relevant mental functions and the psychopathologic states that may impair them, one is left with a range of testable functions that, depending on where the line is drawn, can yield multiple standards for competency of varying stringency. Furthermore, it is clear from this approach that any of the four resulting standards, or some combination of them, are "legitimate" as long as they can be justified from some reasonable policy perspective.

DUNCAN KENNEDY, DISTRIBUTIVE AND PATERNALISTIC MOTIVES IN CONTRACT AND TORT LAW, WITH SPECIAL REFERENCE TO COMPULSORY TERMS AND UNEQUAL BARGAINING POWER

41 Md.L.Rev., 563, 642–646.
(1982).

The principled anti-paternalist admits readily that one sometimes has to overrule another's choice in his best interest, but argues that those cases are explained by incapacity, or perhaps by another similar principled exception to the general idea that people are autonomous. (Likewise, the principled paternalist will argue that there are some cases in which people should be allowed to choose on their own—the two positions are indistinguishable for the purposes of my argument here.) . . .

The idea of incapacity will *sometimes* help in explaining the actor's decision to intervene. Sometimes one feels that the other has really and truly lost selfhood, become a walking automaton or disintegrated, so that someone has simply to take care of them, make decisions for them, control their lives. As the actor, you have to worry that you will make bad custodial decisions, but not that you will be criticized for intervening at all. But those are extreme cases, and the difficulties with paternalism arise in situations where you have occasion to act without being able to appeal to any such blanket permission as is afforded by the other being just crazy.

* * *

The problem with the notion of capacity in [the more typical] setting is not that it's positively wrong—just that it doesn't help. The strategy is to divide the decision into two parts, hoping that will make it easier than if the question whether to act is treated as a single whole. First, we try to decide whether the other possesses a trait or quality called "ability to determine her own best interests." If she does, we accede to her wishes even if in that particular case we are convinced that her action is not in her best interests. If it were truly easier to decide the presence or absence of the quality of capacity than to decide on balance whether we should intervene, treating that question all together, then capacity would be useful. But the question of capacity is hopelessly intertwined with the question of what the other wants to do in this particular case.

First, there is no such "thing" as capacity, and there can be no such thing as its "absence" either. We ask the question of capacity already oriented to the further question whether we will have to let the person do something injurious to herself. There is no other reason to ask the question. Now if you ask me to *answer* the question without knowing what the potentially injurious thing is, it seems to me I should refuse. I don't believe that capacity exists except as capacity-to-make-this-decision. But as soon as I am deciding the issue of capacity-to-make-this-decision, I find myself considering all the factors, testing my intuition of the other's false consciousness, the severity of the consequences, the possibility that I want to render the other dependent through paternalism, just as I would if I frankly admitted at the beginning that it's just a big mess, with no principled way to find your way through.

I come back to ad hoc paternalism, by which I mean that in fear and trembling you approach each case determined to act if that's the best thing to do, recognizing that influencing another's choice—another's life—in the wrong direction, or so as to reinforce their condition of dependence, is a crime against them. Of course, I haven't proved the impossibility of a principled anti-paternalist stance. I think I've undermined the idea that we can decide when to act and when not to act through a notion like: "Do not overrule the choice of a person who has the capacity to choose on their own"....

* * *

... Principled anti-paternalism is a defense mechanism. One way to deal with the pain and fear of having to make an ad hoc paternalist decision—one way to deny the pain and fear—is to claim that you "had" to do what you did because principle (say, the principle of incapacity) required it. That the principle doesn't really work is less important than that it anesthetizes....

BRUCE WINICK

THE SIDE EFFECTS OF INCOMPETENCY
LABELING AND THE IMPLICATIONS
FOR MENTAL HEALTH LAW

1 Psychology, Public Policy & Law 6, 41.
(1995).

Incompetency labeling can produce serious adverse consequences for those labeled. They are stigmatized in the eyes of the community in a manner that influences the way others perceive and treat them. Moreover, they may come to view themselves in ways that can reinforce and even worsen their impairment. Labeling them incompetent may cause them to inhibit performance or to avoid it altogether in the area in which they previously have performed poorly. Their motivation to attempt future behavior in the area in question may be altered in ways that prevent future success, and they may experience serious depression and a damaged sense of psychological well-being. Their sense of self-esteem and self-efficacy may be impaired in ways that are debilitating. They may experience learned helplessness, becoming withdrawn, unresponsive, passive, submissive, helpless, and hopeless. In summary, incompetency labeling may itself be psychologically damaging and even disabling. It may set up a self-fulfilling prophecy that serves to increase and perpetuate the individual's social and mental health problems.

An understanding of the serious adverse consequences of incompetency labeling should sensitize legal decision makers to redesign legal standards, procedures, and the roles of counsel, judges, and other legal actors in ways that are calculated to avoid or minimize these damaging effects. The law should rely less on compulsion and paternalism. Instead, it should encourage voluntariness, providing incentives for individuals to act in desired ways rather than requiring them to do so. In some cases it may be preferable to allow individuals to make their own choices, even if unwise.

Incompetency should be narrowly defined, and competency should be presumed. An inquiry into competency should be required only when specific behavior calls an individual's behavior into question. Mental illness alone should not justify such an inquiry, and when a determination of competency is required, the burden of proof should be on the party asserting that individuals are incompetent.

Questions and Comments

1. *Levels of competency.* Appelbaum and Roth appear to rank the four categories of competency tests, from the least demanding to the most demanding, in the following order: evidencing a choice, understanding material information, rational manipulation and appreciation. In more recent work, Appelbaum and Grisso suggest that these categories are best thought of as different *types* of capacities, rather than as a hierarchy. For instance, they state that "[e]ven in the presence of good understanding and appreciation, decision making still might be impaired if patients fail to process information logically. Conversely, the rational manipulation standard might be met even by patients who have impaired understanding or defective appreciation if the reasoning processes are intact." Paul Appelbaum & Thomas Grisso, "Mental Illness and Competence to Consent to Treatment," 19 Law & Hum. Beh. 105, 110 (1995). Nonetheless, the hierarchy they present is a useful starting point.

A fifth competency standard, which will often be more demanding than any of the four identified by Appelbaum and Roth, is the "reasonable outcome" standard suggested by Kennedy's excerpt. This standard looks not at the reasoning process of the individual, but rather at the reasonableness of the decision according to some "objective" observer. A sixth and final competency standard, one that seems to be more stringent than the understanding standard but not as demanding as the rational manipulation, appreciation and reasonable outcome tests, has been called the "understanding and belief" test. See Elyn Saks, "Competency to Refuse Treatment," 69 N.C. L. Rev. 945 (1991). This standard requires understanding of material information, but does not require an ability to rationally manipulate or fully appreciate it. Rather it merely requires that the individual have no "patently false beliefs" about the information (e.g., a belief that medication will make one's head explode). Saks believes that this standard makes the most sense as a normative matter:

> A competency standard [should] designate a reasonably small class of individuals as incompetent in the face of the pervasive influence of the irrational and the unconscious. Indeed, if any person whose decision-making showed irrationality were deemed incompetent, then there would be virtually NO competent decisionmakers to be found; psychiatrists and psychologists have convincingly demonstrated the everpresent influence of primitive hopes, wishes, and fears on the mental lives of us all.... An apparently intact reasoner, for example, may choose a treatment because of fantasies of merger with the doctor/patient, or, less fancifully perhaps, because he overvalues a vivid memory.

Id. at 950. Thus, Saks argues, only a person who does not understand the relevant facts, or who understands them but holds a belief about them for which there is no evidence, is incompetent.

2. *Varying competency with the choice to be made.* Many commentators have argued that differing levels of competency should be required depending upon the decision being made. For instance, Appelbaum and Roth, at the

end of the above excerpt, state that "any of the four categories of [standards], or some combination of them, are 'legitimate' as long as they can be justified from some reasonable policy perspective." This idea is expanded upon in Loren Roth et al., "Tests of Competency to Consent to Treatment," 134 Am.J. Psychiat. 279, 283 (1977):

> When there is a favorable risk/benefit ratio to the proposed treatment in the opinion of the person determining competency and the patient consents to the treatment, there does not seem to be any reason to stand in the way of administering treatment. To accomplish this, a test employing a low threshold of competency may be applied to find even a marginal patient competent so that his or her decision may be honored. This is what happens daily when uncomprehending patients are permitted to sign themselves into the hospital. Similarly, when the risk/benefit ratio is favorable and the patient refuses treatment, a test employing a higher threshold of competency may be applied. Under such a test even a somewhat knowledgeable patient may be found incompetent so that consent may be sought from a substitute decision maker and treatment administered despite the patient's refusal. An example would be the patient withdrawing from alcohol who, although intermittently resistive, is nevertheless administered sedative medication. In both of these cases, in which the risk/benefit ratio is favorable, the bias of physicians, other health professionals, and judges is usually skewed toward providing treatment. Therefore, a test of competency is applied that will permit the treatment to be administered irrespective of the patient's actual or potential understanding.

> However, there is a growing reluctance on the part of our society to permit patients to undergo treatments that are extremely risky or for which the benefits are highly speculative. Thus if the risk/benefit ratio is unfavorable or questionable and the patient refuses treatment, a test employing a low threshold of competency may be selected so that the patient will be found competent and his or her refusal honored. This is what happens in the area of sterilization of mentally retarded people, in which at least from the perspective of the retarded individual, the risk/benefit ratio is questionable. On the other hand, when the risk/benefit ratio is unfavorable or questionable and the patient consents to treatment, a test using a higher threshold of competency may be applied preventing even some fairly knowledgeable patients from undergoing treatment. The judicial opinion in the well-known Kaimowitz psychosurgery case delineated a high test of competency to be employed in that experimental setting.

While these comments pertain to competency to make treatment decisions, similar contentions have been made about other contexts. For instance, it is often said that the level of competency necessary to enter into a contract is greater than the level needed to make a will, see, e.g., *McPheters v. Hapke*, 94 Idaho 744, 497 P.2d 1045 (1972), and that pleading guilty requires more capacity than does going to trial. See, e.g., *Sieling v. Eyman*, 478 F.2d 211 (9th Cir.1973). These statements could be interpreted to mean merely that making a contract or pleading guilty requires understanding more facts, or facts that are more complicated, than does making a will or going to trial (where most decisions will be made by a lawyer). But in context the courts that make these statements appear to be recognizing different *levels* of competency for different types of decisions. Thus, if one followed the courts' suggestion, factual understanding might be sufficient to be competent to stand trial or write a valid will, while full "appreciation" of the situation might be required to plead guilty or make a contract.

Professor Saks disagrees with the "different levels" thesis. She argues that one standard—the understanding and belief standard—should apply to all situations.

> All competency areas encompass decisions ranging from very important to trivial, so that ranking competency areas as generally more or less consequential is extremely difficult. For example, a medical decision may prevent the immediate death of a young, otherwise healthy person, or it may provide relief from a minor headache. A will may dispose of the vast estate of a person whose family is in dire need, or the small estate of a person who has one wealthy, remote relative. And a trial decision may lead to either the death penalty or a day in jail. Because of this, to say that will-making as an area is less important than other competency areas—in particular, than the area of treatment choice—is impermissible, even though will-making involves interests of people other than the testator (he may care for them more than for himself, as it were), and even though it involves only property. The plain fact is that we cannot decide whether liberty, health, or property is more important without knowing how much of each, and with what further consequences: an abstract ranking is simply not possible.

* * *

> Indeed, if varying the level of competency based on the importance of decisions made sense, a competency theorist might urge us to *lower* the level of competency for potentially consequential decisions. Because people care more about more consequential decisions, we should arguably permit them to choose what they will have to live with. Moreover, taking away consequential decisions may entail a greater assault on individual dignity. For example, telling a person that he can decide what kind of ice cream to have, but not where to live, may more seriously injure his self-esteem. Such a theory, indeed, seems already to inform some areas of the law. For example, some states permit minors to accept or to reject psychiatric treatment without regard to their competency, presumably because the decision is so important. In short, if varying levels of competency is acceptable at all, *lowering* the level of competency for crucial decisions would be most in the spirit of competency doctrine.

Id. at 992–998.

With whom do you agree? Under Saks' approach, could we allow voluntary admissions of non-protesting persons (discussed at pp. 863–64)? Should a person be able to consent to extremely experimental and life-threatening treatment if he or she is only able to meet Saks' understanding and belief test? Under the approach advocated by Roth, Meisel and Lidz, who should make the decision as to whether a treatment is "favorable," "questionable" or "dangerous"? Once that decision is made, should the competency level for a "dangerous" treatment be higher or lower than the competency level for a favorable or questionable treatment? Should the answer to that question depend upon whether the person is refusing or consenting to the treatment, as Roth, Meisel and Lidz suggest?

3. *Other possible competency tests.* All of the tests discussed above are essentially cognitive in orientation. Traditionally, competency has been conceptualized as a matter of awareness, understanding, and reasoning ability. But competency can be viewed from other perspectives as well. Two other approaches are worth mentioning.

Volitional Test. Analogous to some versions of the insanity defense, one could require not only a minimal level of cognitive functioning but also a demonstration that the choice being made is "voluntary." Although assessing whether a choice is or is not an exercise of "free will" is problematic conceptually,[f] the rationale for requiring a volitional inquiry is straightforward: a person is not acting autonomously if his or her choices are "compelled." For instance, a severely depressed, suicidal person confronted with various treatment options may understand all of them but find it very difficult to resist choosing the most dangerous treatment, even though the remaining treatments are just as effective. Roth, Meisel and Lidz report the following case: "A 49 year-old woman whose understanding of treatment was otherwise intact, when informed that there was a 1 in 3,000 chance of dying from ECT, replied, 'I hope I am the one.'" Roth, Meisel & Lidz, supra at 282. Should such a person be considered competent to make this treatment decision?

Professor Garrison has expanded on the idea of incompetency as a lack of volition, through a focus on "the coercive influence of depression and disordered insight." Marsha Garrison, "The Empire of Illness: Competence and Coercion in Health–Care Decision Making," 49 Wm. & Mary L. Rev. 781 (2007). People with depression and people with disordered insight can usually understand relevant information about a decision. But Professor Garrison argues that people with these conditions should nonetheless often be found incompetent. With respect to depression, she points to research which indicates that, "for some patients [depression's effects] appear to overcome the desire for life and health and to coerce decisions against the patient's medical interests." Thus, she concludes, "untreated major depression poses a very high risk of unduly influencing treatment preferences and rendering them inauthentic." Id. at 834. Similarly, with respect to disordered insight, she states that "there are six million individuals with serious mental illnesses, half of whom do not believe they are ill ..." As an example, she quotes a patient who was able to understand the supposed benefits of treatment but would always eventually be non-compliant because "[d]elusions and hallucinations support you in the belief that you are very special, and that powerful forces know you are very special, and even on medication individuals will be very reluctant to give that up." Accordingly, "if the patient has been medically assessed and found to be afflicted with severely disordered insight, then it is reasonable to assume that it is the coercive

f. See pp. 576–77 for a discussion of this issue in the context of the insanity defense.

influence of illness, and not the patients authentic goals and values, that lead the patient to favor continuation of her disease over her life and health." Id. at 823. In short, she argues, knowledge of risks and benefits alone is insufficient to make one competent; one must also be free of "undue influence" stemming from mental disability. Does this formulation add anything to the competency tests already discussed?

Different Person Test. A second approach is described and critiqued by Saks, supra.

> The "different person" theory rationalizes our intuition that mentally ill choices are incompetent by focusing on the change in personality that mental illness brings about, and the effects of that change on decisional capacity. The theory holds that a person is incompetent, not if what appear to be her values and beliefs are unacceptable according to some external standard, but rather if they are not *her* values and beliefs, because she has been transformed by mental illness into a "different person." The idea is that the person has lost touch with her own values and ways of looking at the world: she is simply not *herself.* The testamentary capacity cases, with their symbolic notion of testation as representative of the testator's psychic will, at times use language suggestive of this theory, as when they say that a will is not truly the "testator's." The "different person" theory deftly sidesteps the "irrationality" and "unconventionality" criteria; the decisionmaker's irrationality is irrelevant, and her thinking and feeling are not forced into a conventional mold. All that the "different person" theory requires is that the decisionmaker be true to herself. . . .

> Mental illness is often described in a way that lends itself to the "different person" theory. For example, a mentally ill person is said to suffer "ego alien" impulses and thoughts, and, on recovery, to return to his "premorbid personality." Sometimes he does not even remember his experiences and, when he does, he may not recognize himself in them: he *feels* as if he was then a different person. The "different person" theory predicts that the recovered psychiatric patient will repudiate the choices and actions of his mentally ill self, and will thank the treatment provider for overriding his refusal and requiring treatment.

> On examination, however, this theory is not as compelling as it seems. The problem is that the classic model does not fit all, or even most, mental illness—still less the choices made by its sufferers. Most obviously, some patients never return to their "premorbid" personalities, and so their mentally ill choices *become* authentic. Yet even when their illness is temporary, recovered patients may well not repudiate their past choices and thank their caregivers. Of course, all such patients might be unduly grudging. But it seems far more plausible to suppose that many of their choices are *misidentified* as "mentally ill" choices, or—even though truly "mentally ill"—are not experienced as the choices of a different person.

> The essential problem is that determining reliably which choices are "mentally ill" and will later be repudiated is very difficult. . . .

See also, Ruth Faden & Tom Beauchamp, A History of Informed Consent 262–269 (1986).

4. *The* Katz *Case.* A case that might help flesh out some of the concepts discussed above is *Katz v. Superior Court,* 73 Cal.App.3d 952, 141 Cal.Rptr. 234 (1977), which involved a guardianship proceeding. The proposed wards were young adults (over the age of majority) who had become members of the Unification Church, headed by Reverend Moon. The parents of these individuals claimed that psychological pressure exerted by the church had impaired the physical and mental health of their children; specifically, it was alleged that the children had experienced "abrupt personality changes," and were the victims "of mind control through hypnosis, mesmerism, and/or brainwashing." 141 Cal.Rptr. at 239 n. 7. The father of one of the children testified that while his daughter was in the church "she became somewhat child-like in her belief and acceptance of this unitary system of beliefs, and her interests were almost totally devoted to that system of beliefs, to the exclusion of virtually all else." He noted that her voice had changed from being hoarse to high-pitched. He also believed she was being "imposed upon" because she received no compensation outside of minimal food and a place to sleep for her constant work for the church. On cross-examination, he acknowledged that she had looked healthy. Id. at 246.

One of the experts for the parents testified as follows:

It is my opinion that all five of these well-meaning, well-intentioned young people—Jan Kaplan, Leslie Brown, John Hovard, Jacqueline Katz and Barbara Underwood—have several symptoms which are not present in the average individual of their ages and background.

During my interviews with them, it was as though these individuals responded to a pre-set (i.e., there was an effort made to answer all questions out of a limited set of answers). This limited set of answers appeared to be alien or inconsistent with those of their non-cult peers.

They all suffered from gross lack of information regarding current events; they all seemed to be preoccupied with a concern about their selfishness, but all reported that they worked as much as twenty hours a day.

They all showed a moderate degree of memory impairment, especially about their childhoods; their functional vocabulary in terms of the words that they used during the interview was limited and constricted.

Their affects were blunted, emotionality frozen in a child-like inappropriate smile to all input, whether it be hostile or otherwise.

They were all wide-eyed, had short attention spans and a decreased ability towards abstractions; they were full of inconsistencies, contradictions and confabulations when pressured.

They uniformly held that the Unification Church was not responsible for anything unless it was positive.

They had very little concern for previous and future personal goals; they were paranoid about previous relationships, and had defensive attitudes toward id urges.

Their inner sense of authority was lost, and all responded as if they were influenced by an outside authority.

They all showed various degrees of regression and child-like attitudes, especially when stressed.

In general, they did not respond as one would expect from their background and personality types.

The expert did not diagnose any of them psychotic nor did he give them any other standard psychiatric diagnosis, but he did predict that staying in the church environment for the next six months would not be in the best interests of their health. Id. at 248–49.

The children testified at trial, and described their beliefs. They stated that their mode of living was one they had chosen to follow. They denied any coercive persuasion and pointed out that there was no physical restraint involved. One member of the group had left the church, but returned after four days of reflection. They "insisted on their competency." Id. at 250. They also introduced expert testimony which asserted that "the experiences relied upon by the parents' experts were no more than usually accompany devotion to a religious belief." Id. at 250.

Assume the issue is whether the children's decision to stay with the Unification Church was a competent one.[g] What if Saks' "understanding and belief" test were applied to the *Katz* facts? The different person theory? A competency test that recognized a volitional component? One of the standards described by Roth, et al.? Should the fact that religious preferences are involved raise the level of incompetency required before state intervention may take place? Should the fact that the parents only wanted the children to go through a "deprogramming" session after which they would be free to return to the church lower the level of incompetency required for intervention? How do the observations of Professors Kennedy and Winick affect your analysis?

III. GUARDIANSHIP

A. HISTORY AND DEVELOPMENT

GARY MELTON, JOHN PETRILA, NORMAN POYTHRESS & CHRISTOPHER SLOBOGIN PSYCHOLOGICAL EVALUATIONS FOR THE COURTS: A HANDBOOK FOR MENTAL HEALTH PROFESSIONALS AND LAWYERS

(New York: Guilford Press, 3d. ed., 2007).
pp. 370–371.

Guardianship is the legal mechanism by which the state delegates authority over an individual's person or estate to another party. It is

g. The court did not frame the issue this way, but rather held that guardianship could be imposed only if the children were "gravely disabled," as defined by California's commitment law. Since there was "no real showing . . . that the [proposed wards] are physically unhealthy, or actually deprived of, or unable to secure food, clothing and shelter," the court denied the petition for guardianship. The standards for guardianship are discussed further in the next section of this chapter.

probably the most ancient aspect of mental health law. In both Roman and English common law, the sovereign possessed the power and duty to "guard" the estate of incompetent persons. This power, which emanated from the state's interest in the preservation of its wealth, is the historic basis of the *parens patriae* authority, which has since been applied broadly—and perhaps illogically—to the regulation by the state of many other aspects of decisionmaking by children and people with mental disability. In any event, it was this power that the state delegated to third parties (usually family members or members of the government) through the guardianship process.

Today guardianship comes in many forms. In some jurisdictions, there are separate provisions for appointment of a guardian of one's person (e.g., with authority over health care decisions) and a guardian of one's estate (e.g., with authority over contracts to sell one's property). The latter type of guardian is often called a "conservator" or "committee," although this nomenclature is not consistent across jurisdictions (with some, like California, using the former term to cover both person and property). In addition to, or instead of this distinction, some jurisdictions also distinguish between "general" ("plenary") and "specific" guardianship. As the name implies, in the latter form of guardianship, the guardian's powers are restricted to particular types of decisions. Thus, with respect to guardianship of the person, the guardian may have authority only to make a specific treatment decision (e.g., consent to a specific course of treatment that has been proposed) or "nonroutine" treatment decisions (e.g., consent to any major surgery); the ward would remain free to make other health care decisions. Similarly, a person with mental disorder under limited guardianship of the estate might be able to make decisions about the property, except with respect to a particular complicated business deal that has been proposed, or any purchase over $100. On the other hand, under general guardianship, the guardian has total control of the individual's person, estate, or both.

* * *

Beyond these distinctions about the *scope* of guardianship, it is also important to recognize disparate *bases* of guardianship. In most instances, individuals are found, on the basis of particularized evidence, to lack specific or general capacities. They are actually (or *de facto*) incompetent and in need of a guardian to make decisions for them. On the other hand, some people are *presumed* to require a guardian. Regardless of their *de facto* level of competency, they are incompetent in law (*de jure*).

For example, even though older minors are often as competent as adults to make decisions of various types, they are *de jure* incompetent for most purposes and, as a result, lack legal authority to act on their own behalf. Even in those instances in which the law permits some minors to make decisions independently, they generally are presumed incompetent until they are able to rebut this presumption. Because there is such a strong legal presumption of minors' incompetency, there usually is no need to adjudicate their need for guardianship.... In most cases, there also is no need to determine who the guardian will be. Children are generally subject to the wishes of their "natural" guardians—their parents—who are presumed, in the absence of strong evidence to the contrary, to act in their best interests.

Civilly committed adults may also find themselves presumed incompetent to make many decisions. At one time, civil commitment often carried with it collateral loss of rights to marry, possess a driver's license, refuse intrusive treatments, manage one's property, and so forth. Although most states now provide that commitment does not automatically render a person incompetent to perform such functions, vestiges of these practices remain, especially with respect to treatment refusal and management of one's property. In such instances, there often is no need to appoint a guardian, in that state statutes provide authority to particular individuals (often state officials) to make decisions on behalf of the committed person. . . .

B. THE BASIS FOR INTERVENTION

ESTATE OF GALVIN v. GALVIN

Appellate Court of Illinois, First District, First Division, 1983.
112 Ill.App.3d 677, 68 Ill.Dec. 370, 445 N.E.2d 1223.

GOLDBERG, JUSTICE:

After a hearing, the trial court denied the petition of Mildred Tobias (petitioner) to be appointed guardian of the estate and person of Harold Galvin (respondent). Petitioner appeals.

Petitioner called Dr. William Reotutar, a qualified physician, to testify. The doctor testified he first treated respondent in October of 1980, after respondent had been admitted to St. Anne's Hospital. Respondent was suffering from "advanced multiple arthritis." Also, the respondent had a "cerebral vascular accident" or stroke.

* * *

Respondent was readmitted to the hospital in the fall of 1981 for treatment of his heart, cerebral, and arthritic conditions. The witness diagnosed another stroke and noted that respondent was "a little bit confused at times and was a little bit agitated at times." A psychiatric consultant observed that respondent experienced "some delusions" and "hallucinations." Dr. Reotutar diagnosed the respondent as having "organic brain syndrome" which describes "behavioral disorder due to some degeneration or atrophy of the brain cells." Respondent remained in the hospital for about two months. Respondent is currently under medication for his heart condition. Failure to take the medication as prescribed could endanger his life. While his heart condition is currently stable, the condition is irreversible. Similarly organic brain syndrome is irreversible and progressive. Although the doctor did not know how respondent handled his financial affairs, he believed respondent was disabled and unable to manage his affairs. On cross-examination the doctor testified that the respondent had made some recent improvement. He stated the respondent was "more oriented and more realistic."

Under questioning by the trial judge, respondent testified he owns the three-flat building in which he lives. He occupies the basement apartment with two men, John and Mike. They do not pay rent but respondent does collect rent from the other two apartments. Respondent handles his own financial affairs and has a checking account which currently has a balance of $350. Respondent receives social security of about $550 per month. Respondent did not believe he had a heart condition but he continues to take the medication prescribed by the doctor.

Under adverse examination by counsel for petitioner, the respondent testified he never had a checking account, he invented the snowmobile, at one time he had a pet black widow spider, and he could produce fire by pointing his finger. He also testified that John and Mike sometimes prepare his meals but he can and sometimes does prepare his own meals. He stated he could shop by himself and go to the laundromat with use of his walker and pulling a shopping cart. He testified he was able to take care of himself and did not want a guardian.

During the examination of respondent, the trial judge interrupted the proceedings and stated, "There is no way in God's world that I am going to adjudicate him a disabled person. He is physically suffering from some disability. . . . He is eccentric . . . but there is no way I am going to adjudicate him in need of a guardian. . . . He lives a bizarre, strange life. I might not want to do it, but unless you can make an offer of proof that is going to show me that he does not understand the things he's doing—. He understands."

Thereafter, counsel for petitioner made an oral offer of proof that John and Mike would testify respondent had no concept of time relationship, believed he had been a co-worker with the Shah of Iran, and the men plan to move out of respondent's apartment so that respondent would be left alone. In addition, petitioner's attorney offered to call Lorraine Polinski, cousin of the respondent, for examination. . . . The attorney stated this witness would testify that she had hired an attorney and that "She insisted a will be drawn, naming her as executor of this estate." The witness has recommended to respondent that he go to Oak Forest [Hospital]. Also, the respondent is "constantly" at petitioner's home where she and her mother "take care of" the respondent. In addition . . . the respondent [went] outside without shoes or stockings and wearing only slippers during sub-zero weather. Also, "another neighbor" would testify that when respondent went to the hospital his shopping and other needs were provided by the petitioner. The trial judge refused the offer of proof and denied the petition.

In this court, petitioner contends the decision of the trial court was against the manifest weight of the evidence and petitioner was denied due process because the trial judge abused his discretion and did not allow her to a full opportunity to present her case. We disagree.

A trial court is mandated to adjudicate a person incompetent and appoint a guardian only when the alleged incompetent is "not fully able to manage his person or estate. . . ." (Ill.Rev.Stat.1981, ch. 110½, pars. 11a–2, 11a–3.) The pertinent statute applicable to the case before us was amended effective as of September 16, 1979.

* * *

" 'Disabled person' defined. 'Disabled person' means a person 18 years or older who (a) because of mental deterioration or physical incapacity is not fully able to manage his person or estate, or (b) is mentally ill or developmentally disabled and who because of his mental illness or developmental disability is not fully able to manage his person or estate, or (c) because of gambling, idleness, debauchery or excessive use of intoxicants or drugs, so spends or wastes his estate as to expose himself or his family to want or suffering.

"Adjudication of disability—Power to appoint guardian. (a) Upon the filing of a petition by a reputable person or by the alleged disabled person himself or on its own motion, the court may adjudge a person to be a disabled person and may appoint (1) a guardian of his person, if because of his disability he lacks sufficient understanding or capacity to make or communicate responsible decisions concerning the care of his person, or (2) a guardian of his estate, if because of his disability he is unable to manage his estate or financial affairs or (3) a guardian of his person and of his estate.

"Guardianship shall be utilized only as is necessary to promote the well-being of the disabled person, to protect him from neglect, exploitation, or abuse, and to encourage development of his maximum self-reliance and independence. Guardianship shall be ordered only to the extent necessitated by the individual's actual mental, physical and adaptive limitations."

In commenting specifically upon these portions of the pertinent statute, this court stated that the legislature made these amendments "an express part of the statutory scheme for appointed guardians for disabled adults."

* * *

"Under the new sections, the legislature has made it clear that although a person may be a disabled person, in the statutory sense of not being fully able to manage his person, a guardian is not therefore permissible or appropriate, if that person is capable of making and communicating responsible decisions concerning the care of his person. Thus, a person who was physically unable to care for himself, but who could direct others in such activity, would not necessarily need a guardian over his person. Similarly, a person might be a 'disabled person' but nevertheless not be in need of a guardian over his estate, because with help from others he is able to direct and manage his affairs and estate."

* * *

In the case at bar, it is clear the respondent suffers from some physical disability and has some mental peculiarities. Nevertheless, with particular reference to the above citation, we cannot say the determination of the trial judge that respondent was not unable to manage his person and estate is contrary to the manifest weight of the evidence.

IN THE MATTER OF THE GUARDIANSHIP OF MARY LOU RENZ, AN INCAPACITATED PERSON

Supreme Court of North Dakota, 1993.
507 N.W.2d 76.

LEVINE, JUSTICE.

Mary Lou Renz appeals from an order denying her petition to terminate her guardianship and granting her guardian and conservator's petition for authority to sell Renz's home and automobile. As we are satisfied with the trial court's prudent approach to guardianship in this case and we find no clear error in the trial court's findings on guardianship or abuse of discretion in its order authorizing the sale of Renz's home and automobile, we affirm.

Renz has a long history of alcohol abuse and is an admitted alcoholic. She began drinking following the death of her husband in 1973 and since that time, she has undergone inpatient treatment for alcoholism at the North Dakota State Hospital fourteen times and at the Heartview Foundation seven times. Following each course of treatment, she eventually returned to her home. After a particularly serious incident of alcohol abuse in December 1991, the Heartview Foundation refused to admit Renz again unless a guardian was appointed for her.

Subsequently, in late 1991, William Chaussee, the Burleigh County Public Administrator, petitioned the trial court for guardianship. In February 1992, the trial court, finding that Renz was unable to provide for her personal care or perform necessary daily activities due to chronic alcoholism, granted limited guardianship over Renz's legal and financial affairs and full guardianship over her living arrangements.

The next month, after Renz was admitted to the North Dakota State Hospital following another incident of alcohol abuse, Chaussee petitioned the court for modification of the guardianship. The trial court then issued an amended order granting Chaussee authority to place Renz in a structured care facility as recommended by the State Hospital and control over Renz's assets to pay for such care (the court required its approval prior to the sale of Renz's home or automobile).

In June 1992, the court again modified Chaussee's guardianship to include conservatorship and full authority over Renz's place of residence, financial matters, and medical treatment, and limited authority over Renz's legal matters, vocation, and education. Renz did not appeal this order or any of the court's prior orders.

In September 1992, Chaussee petitioned the trial court for authority to sell Renz's home and automobile. Renz then petitioned the court for termination of the guardianship, based on her recent sobriety. The trial court denied Renz's petition for termination and granted Chaussee's petition for authority to sell. Renz appealed.

Renz first argues that although she is an alcoholic with a long history of unsuccessful treatment for alcoholism, she presently is sober and thus, no longer is an incapacitated person. Therefore, she argues, the trial court "abused its discretion" by finding her incapacitated. Renz misstates the appropriate standard of review. We examine the trial court's findings on guardianship under a clearly erroneous standard. NDRCivP 52(a); In re Braaten, 502 N.W.2d 512 (N.D.1993). A finding of fact is clearly erroneous "if it is induced by an erroneous view of the law, if there is no evidence to support it, or if, although there is some evidence to support it, the reviewing court, on the entire evidence, is left with a definite and firm conviction that a mistake has been made." Swanston v. Swanston, 502 N.W.2d 506, 508 (N.D.1993). Renz's argument is twofold: that she presently is capable and that a court may not base a finding of incapacity on the perceived likelihood of a future relapse. We examine each aspect in turn.

The trial court found that Renz is "a chronic, relapse-prone, alcoholic" and "requires a great deal of support and structure to maintain sobriety[, which] will continue to be a struggle for her." The court found that since she has lived at the Chateau, a structured care facility, Renz has remained sober and regularly attends Alcoholics Anonymous meetings. We agree with the trial court that the fact that Renz has maintained sobriety while in a structured setting does not in itself imply that she no longer is an incapacitated person. Renz's argument makes an unfounded leap from the fact that she may be sober while she is in a structured facility and under a guardian's care to the assertion that she is capable of maintaining her sobriety without the structure and support furnished under a guardianship. We conclude that the trial court's finding that Renz remains incapacitated is supported by the evidence, and we are not convinced that the court made a mistake in its finding.

Renz also argues that the trial court incorrectly based its finding of incapacity on the likelihood that Renz would relapse into alcohol abuse. Renz cites several cases in support of this contention, only two of which we find arguably applicable to the case at hand. In Estate of Murphy, 134 Cal.App.3d 15, 184 Cal.Rptr. 363 (1982), the court held that a trial court may not find an alcoholic residing in a care facility and currently able to manage his own affairs "gravely disabled" based only on the likelihood that, were the court to terminate the conservatorship, he would begin drinking again. *Murphy* is distinguishable from the case at hand in two respects. First, as discussed above, we do not believe Renz presently is capable. Second, there is no indication in *Murphy*, as there is here, that the conservatee's sobriety was dependent on his placement in a care facility. In In re Benevenuto, 180 Cal.App.3d 1030, 226 Cal.Rptr. 33 (1986), the court applied *Murphy* to hold that a schizophrenic was not gravely disabled where he currently was able to manage his own affairs, despite evidence that if released from the mental health facility where he resided, he would stop taking his medication and become gravely disabled. Again, *Benevenuto* is distinguishable because Renz presently remains incapacitated. In addition, we note that the California courts may be moving away from *Benevenuto* and *Murphy*. See In re Walker, 206 Cal.App.3d 1572, 254 Cal.Rptr. 552 (1989) [affirming trial court's finding that delusional conservatee presently was gravely disabled based not on future likelihood that conservatee would stop taking medication but on conservatee's present incomprehension of his mental illness]. We also note that none of the cases cited by Renz involves a ward with an extensive history of unsuccessful alcoholism treatment, as does the case before us. Finally, we consider prognostic evidence in other proceedings which bear on an individual's rights. See, e.g., Steckler v. Steckler, 492 N.W.2d 76, 81 (N.D.1992) [stating in a termination of parental rights case that where "there exists a history of visitation violations and allegations of abuse, the court may consider what happened [in the past] as relevant evidence of what might occur in the future. It need not await a more tragic event to take action"]. Accordingly, we pay no heed to the California precedents because they pay no heed to either historical or prognostic evidence. We conclude that the trial court's findings on Renz's proclivity for alcoholism and her need for structure and support are not mistaken.

Renz's second argument is that the trial court "abused its discretion" in finding that no less restrictive form of intervention or alternative resource plan was available to allow Renz to return to her home. Implicit in this argument is that the trial court abused its discretion in authorizing the sale of Renz's home and automobile. Again, we examine the trial court's findings on guardianship under a clearly erroneous standard. In Braaten, supra at 517, we discussed North Dakota's "legislative mandate to maximize the autonomy of an incapacitated person by the least restrictive appointment of limited guardians." We believe the trial court's initial order of a limited guardianship and later orders incrementally broadening the guardian's authority as proved necessary conform to the circumspect approach required by North Dakota law. Here, the trial court found that "[i]t is not reasonable to assume that Mary Lou Renz will be able to live independently again" and that "there is no combination of services available to her [in her home] which would provide the required level of structure for her." The evidence shows that Renz was unable to care for her personal cleanliness or that of her home, even with support services, when she lived independently. Several witnesses testified as to the unsanitary condition of Renz's home and her failure to attend to her incontinence. We believe the court's findings are supported by the record and we are not left with a definite and firm conviction that a mistake has been made. Therefore, we conclude that the findings are not clearly erroneous.

* * *

The portion of the trial court's order denying Renz's petition for termination of the guardianship is not clearly erroneous and the portion authorizing the sale of Renz's home and automobile is not an abuse of discretion. Accordingly, we affirm.

Questions and Comments

1. *Typical criteria for guardianship.* Commentators have identified three approaches to determining whether a person should be subjected to guardianship. See Phillip Tor, "Finding Incompetency in Guardianship: Standardizing the Process," 35 Ariz. L. Rev. 739, 743–44 (1993). The first approach, which has parallels to the reasonable outcome competency test discussed at p. 932, focuses on whether the person is capable of taking "proper" care of self or property. Statutes in this vein also often add inquiries into whether the person can "provide for his family", avoid the "dissipation of his property" or resist "artful and designing persons."

The second approach, widely followed today, is reflected in the Uniform Probate Code, which defines an incapacitated person as "any person who is impaired by reason of mental illness, mental deficiency, physical illness or disability, advanced age . . . or other cause (except minority) to the extent that he lacks sufficient understanding or capacity to make or communicate responsible decisions concerning his person." National Conference of Commissioners on Uniform State Law, Uniform Probate Code § 5 (4th ed. 1975). Consistent with the rational manipulation standard discussed at p. 855, this approach reflects a movement toward "criteria that minimize the importance of the results of an individual's decision and instead examine the ability of the individual to go through the cognitive process of making rational decisions." Samuel Brakel et al., The Mentally Disabled and the Law 371 (1985).

The third approach, sometimes called the "functional" approach, permits guardianship only if specific dysfunctions exist. For instance, under New Hampshire's statute the term "incapacity"

> means a legal, not a medical, disability and shall be measured by functional limitations. It shall be construed to mean or refer to any person who has suffered, is suffering or is likely to suffer substantial harm due to an inability to provide for his personal needs for food, clothing, shelter, health care or safety or an inability to manage his or her property or financial affairs. Inability to provide for personal needs or to manage property shall be evidenced by acts or occurrences, or statements which strongly indicate imminent acts or occurrences. All evidence of inability must have occurred within 6 months prior to the filing of the petition and at least one incidence of such behavior must have occurred within 20 days of the filing of the petition for guardianship.

N.H. § 464 A:2. The functional approach grew out of concern that the Uniform Probate Code's approach was insufficiently objective and therefore subject to abuse. Illustrative of this concern is *In re Boyer,* 636 P.2d 1085 (Utah 1981), where the Utah Supreme Court construed a statute patterned on the Uniform Probate Code. The law was challenged on the ground that the words "capacity to make or communicate responsible decisions concerning his person" would allow appointment of a guardian for a person "who makes decisions regarded by some as irresponsible, even though he has sufficient capacity to make personal management decisions which allow him to function in a manner acceptable to himself and without any threat of injury to himself." The court agreed, but avoided declaring the statute unconstitutionally vague by construing it to require an impairment which renders the person "unable to care for his or her personal safety or attend to or provide for such necessities as food, shelter, clothing, and medical care, without which physical injury or illness may occur."

Recall that the Uniform Probate Code provision was meant to focus the inquiry more on the quality of the person's thought process—"the ability of the individual to go through the cognitive process of making rational decisions"—than on the "results of the individual's decision." Don't *Boyer* and the functional approach return the law of guardianship to a consideration of the results of the individual's decision, albeit one associated with more precise standards? Is there any way out of this circle? Consider the material in section II of this chapter. For instance, if Saks' understanding-and-belief competency standard were adopted, the question would not be whether the person was unable to provide for basic necessities, nor would it be whether the person's thought process was "rational" or "responsible." Rather it would be whether the person understood the consequences of his or her decisions and had no patently false beliefs about the material aspects of his or her situation. Is this a better standard for deciding whether a guardian should be appointed?

Which of these various standards is reflected in the Illinois statute at issue in *Galvin*? How do they apply to Galvin? Is he able to care for himself? Does he make "responsible" decisions? Are any of his delusions patently false beliefs about his situation?

In contrast to Galvin, Renz appears to have had no significant mental problems at the time of the guardianship proceeding. Instead the court seems to be basing its decision on a "potential for deterioration" standard of the type that some states have adopted in the outpatient civil commitment context. See pp. 778–79 Should the state be able to force a guardian on a competent person because it predicts the person will be incompetent sometime in the future? Is the court's analogy to civil commitment, which is explicitly based on prediction of future behavior, appropriate? Conversely, should the state have to wait until Renz decompensates before it can sell the house and car? Is it relevant that a committed patient can be forced to reimburse the state for its treatment expenses (see pp. 1163–64)? Isn't it possible Renz will ultimately cost the state more money if the house is sold?

2. *Guardianship and civil commitment.* The preceding discussion makes clear that the standards for guardianship bear a close relationship to the standards for *parens patriae* commitment. Until the 1970's, most states equated the two, a correlation which was symbolized by the practice in many states of delegating commitment authority to probate courts. In these states,

institutionalized persons were presumed incompetent at least until release and perhaps until a court "restored" them to competency. Thus, as the Melton et al. excerpt noted, these people not only lost the authority to make their own treatment decisions but also were automatically deprived, with no further judicial proceeding necessary, of the right to vote, possess a driver's license, manage property or marry. Today most states specifically eliminate the presumption of incompetency for institutionalized persons and require a separate incompetency adjudication. No state allows the mere fact of commitment to substitute for a general incompetency determination. Brakel et al., supra, at 509.

If their standards are the same, why *shouldn't* guardianship and commitment be dealt with in the same proceeding? In California, for instance, a person who is found to be gravely disabled has a "conservator" appointed who then decides whether or not to commit the ward. Cal.Code § 5350. In thinking about this issue, consider the materials in the following note.

3. *Guardianship and the least restrictive alternative.* As noted previously, while guardians traditionally exerted complete power over the ward, in more recent times a distinction has developed between guardianships of the estate and guardianships of the person. In practice, does this distinction make sense? Both *Galvin* and *Renz* appear to involve both a guardian of the estate and of the person. Should they have?

Also noted in the introductory materials is the movement away from "general" guardianship toward "specific" or "limited" guardianship, whether the guardianship is of the person or of the estate. Ideally, perhaps, general guardianships should be rare. That is, the court should be careful to give control to the guardian only in those areas where the ward has demonstrated incompetence. Thus, a court should gauge a person's ability to vote, handle varying levels of financial transactions, make decisions about food and shelter, choose from among various types of treatment and so on, and shape the guardianship accordingly. A number of states attempt to implement this idea statutorily. See, e.g., Idaho Code § 15–5–420 (authorizing limited conservatorships); Me.Rev.Stat.Ann., tit. 18–A, § 5–304(a)(court shall "make appointive and other orders only to the extent necessitated by the incapacitated person's actual mental and adaptive limitations or other conditions warranting the procedure"); Fla. Stat. § 744.344(1)(2) (authorizing limited guardianships and stating that the order "must be the least restrictive appropriate alternative, and must reserve to the incapacitated person the right to make decisions in all matters commensurate with the person's ability to do so."). Yet research has consistently shown that the limited guardianship option is rarely used. See, e.g., Pat M. Keith & Robbyn R. Wacker, Older Wards and Their Guardians 177, 180 (1994)(after reforms, requests for limited guardianship increased from zero to one percent, with most denied); Lawrence Friedman & Mark Savage, "Taking Care: The Law of Conservatorship in California," 61 S. Cal. L. Rev. 278, 283 (1988). Accordingly, at least one commentator has called for abolition of general guardianship, in order to encourage narrower grants of power to the guardian. Lawrence A. Frolik, "Plenary Guardianship: An Analysis, A Critique and a Proposal for Reform," 23 Ariz.L.Rev. 599, 653 (1981). Is there any downside to the limited guardianship idea? Might it encourage overuse of guardianship, in the same way outpatient commitment might encourage overuse of commitment?[h] Should it have been used in *Galvin*? Was its use in *Renz* appropriate?

There may be circumstances where even a clear finding of incompetency does not merit imposition of either a guardianship or commitment. A number of other "less restrictive" protective arrangements are available. These include "protective services" (in which case workers are appointed to supervise the person and ensure that he or she receives community services, voluntarily or involuntarily), powers of attorney, "living wills" (by which a person authorizes certain actions contingent upon certain conditions developing), court authorizations of single transactions (e.g., kidney transplants), representative payee arrangements (used for receipt of welfare entitlements), trusts, joint tenancies, and transfers of property. See Windsor Schmidt & Roger Peters, "Legal Incompetents' Need for Guardians in Florida," 15 Bull.Am.Acad.Psychiat. & L. 69, 82 (1987). Would any of these alternatives have been useful in *Galvin* or *Renz*?

4. *Procedures.* Every state provides for a hearing to determine the need for guardianship. Concerns connected with notice, the right to be present, the right to a public jury trial, application of the rules of evidence and most other aspects of the hearing are similar to those that arise in the civil commitment context, discussed in Chapter Eight. As a result, the procedures tend to be similar in many jurisdictions. Below is a description of the process afforded people subjected to guardianship.

[A study of practices in ten states] revealed that of 566 cases, twenty-five percent lasted less than five minutes, and fifty-eight percent lasted less than fifteen minutes. Despite a statutory requirement that the respondent attend absent a specific finding by the court, seventy-five percent of guardian ad litem reports specified that the proposed ward should not be required to attend. At least sixty-six percent of respondents were in fact absent, regardless of the statutory language. Despite the reform emphasis on professional testimony, the record clearly indicated that a physician was present at only eight percent of hearings. Further, many physician reports lack detailed information about the respondent's decision-making capacities. A 2001 task force in Illinois found that courts often are not provided with sufficient detailed information about respondents' decision-making capacities, instead receiving information about physical or other impairments.

Most states do not require the court to appoint counsel for the respondent. Perhaps more significant, where counsel was required, a review of the record showed that respondent's counsel might not speak at all at the hearing, which suggests an unusually passive role. All guardian reports in one county were fully missing from half of the case files reviewed; the inventory of assets by the guardian after appointment was absent in thirty percent of reviewed case files.

Alison Barnes, "The Liberty and Property of Elders: Guardianship and Will Contests as the Same Claim," 11 Elder L. J. 1 (2003); see also, Associated Press Special Report, "Guardians of the Elderly: An Ailing System," L.A. Times, Sept. 27, 1987, at 2, 20, 28.

h. See pp. 790–97.

Some courts have upheld these practices. For instance, in *Rud v. Dahl,* 578 F.2d 674, 679 (7th Cir.1978), the court held that counsel for the prospective ward is not "an essential element of due process" at guardianship proceedings:

> First of all, the nature of the intrusion on liberty interests from an adjudication of incompetency is far less than the intrusion resulting from other types of proceedings in which the presence of counsel has been mandated. Involuntary incarceration, for example, does not result from an incompetency proceeding. Moreover, the technical skills of an attorney are less important, as the procedural and evidentiary rules of an incompetency proceeding are considerably less strict than those applicable in other types of civil and criminal proceedings. Finally, the costs associated with the mandatory appointment of counsel will undermine one of the essential purposes of the proceeding itself—protection of the limited resources of the incompetent's estate from dissipation—for few alleged incompetents will be able to effect a 'knowing and intelligent' waiver of undesired counsel.

In many jurisdictions, representation of the ward is required but only by a guardian ad litem, who functions not as an advocate for the client's views but rather acts according to what he or she feels is in the best interests of the proposed ward. Kris Bulcroft et al., "Elderly Wards and Their Legal Guardians: Analysis of County Probate Records in Ohio and Washington," 31 Gerontologist 156, 157 (1991).

For similar reasons, many courts have upheld application of the preponderance of the evidence standard at guardianship proceedings despite the Supreme Court's ruling in *Addington v. Texas,* 441 U.S. 418, 99 S.Ct. 1804, 60 L.Ed.2d 323 (1979), requiring the clear and convincing standard at civil commitment proceedings. As explained by one court:

> We do not feel that more harm will befall an individual who is erroneously subjected to guardianship than to an individual who is in need of a guardian but is erroneously denied one. If an individual is erroneously subjected to a guardianship, then [state law] allows such a ward to file a petition for the removal of his guardian.

Guardianship of Roe, 383 Mass. 415, 421 N.E.2d 40 (1981).

6. *Who may serve as guardian.* The filing of a petition for guardianship is generally considered "jurisdictional"; that is, the court may appoint anyone guardian, not just the petitioner. See *Brown v. Storz,* 710 S.W.2d 402 (Mo.App.1986). Most state statutes establish priorities for deciding who should be guardian, with family members and relatives occupying the foremost positions. See, e.g., Uniform Guardian and Protective Proceeding Act §§ 2–205, 2–309. However, nonfamily members have been appointed in lieu of available and willing family members when "(1) the family member has an adverse interest to that of the ward; (2) there is dissension within the family; (3) the family member lacks business ability; or (4) some other substantial reason for disqualification exists." Legal Counsel for the Elderly, Decisionmaking, Incapacity and the Elderly 75 (1987). An increasing number of states are also requiring that guardians meet certain qualifications and even undergo training programs. See, e.g., Fla.Stat.Ann. § 744.3145 (requiring 8 hours of instruction on the duties of the guardian, the rights of the

ward, the availability of local resources, and the preparation of treatment plans and reports, in a course approved by the court within one year of appointment as guardian).

At least 29 states provide for public guardians, like the one appointed in *Renz*. Legal Counsel for the Elderly, supra, at 76, n. 90. Intended primarily for those with no relatives or relatives who are unsuitable as guardians, the public guardian device appears to fill a significant need. A study of institutionalized individuals in Florida found that over 11,000 people were probably legally incompetent and in need of either a guardianship of the person, guardianship of the estate, or both. Schmidt & Peters, supra, at 78. The identity of the public guardian varies widely among jurisdictions. For instance, some states specifically authorize departments of mental health or social services to serve as public guardians. Others specifically prohibit these entities from serving, because they often provide the treatment or services about which the guardian must decide, thus creating a possible conflict of interest. Legal Counsel for the Elderly, supra, at 76. What are the potential conflicts in *Renz*?

Other studies of public guardianship have found that, even if the conflict of interest problem is solved, the responsible agencies are often overburdened and impersonal in nature, thus resulting in a tendency to institutionalize their wards. Frolik, supra at 648. In one study of 200 wards with public guardians, competency was restored to only four, "possibly because the files for these cases were the few with up-to-date status reports." Phillip B. Tor & Bruce D. Sales, "A Social Science Perspective on the Law of Guardianship: Directions for Improving the Process and Practice", 18 Psychol. & L. Rev. 1, 25 (1994). At the same time, in theory at least, public guardians should offer greater sophistication and expertise and should be more in tune with available services than are private guardians. One possible method of reducing the negative and accentuating the positive aspects of public guardianship is to create a nonprofit corporation using concerned citizens as guardians, as New York has done with the Association for Retarded Citizens. Frolik, supra, at 648–49. Based on the available information, who would have been the best guardian in *Galvin* and *Renz*?

7. *Restoration of competency.* The general practice with respect to terminating a guardianship is described by Brakel et al., supra at 392–93:

> Restoration is a legal determination that individuals who have been adjudged incompetent are now able to manage their business and personal affairs adequately. The law presumes that persons who are adjudicated incompetent remain so. In order for wards to regain their competent status they normally must vindicate themselves in a separate judicial proceeding or, in a few states, be discharged from a mental institution. This second method is a holdover from the time when it was common to merge commitment and competency hearings. It avoids the need to prevail in a hearing that may be even more difficult than challenging an assertion of incompetency in the first instance.

Should the fact that Renz was applying for termination of a guardianship rather than trying to avoid imposition of one in the first instance make a difference in her case, given the presumption of incompetency described by Brakel, et al.?

A few states, including California, provide for automatic restoration of competency after a year period unless the conservator applies for reappointment. In virtually every state, the ward can initiate restoration proceedings, as can a "next friend," and most also have a periodic review process. Are those states which do not provide such review constitutional, in light of the Supreme Court's decision in *Parham v. J.R.,* discussed at pp. 907–22?

C. POWERS AND DUTIES OF THE GUARDIAN

Within the scope of whatever kind of guardianship is established (i.e. of the person or of the estate, general or limited), the guardian has authority to make decisions concerning the ward. However, there are two further types of limitations on this authority. First, the guardian is supposed to take only those actions which will be in the "best interests" of the ward; that is, the guardian is in a fiduciary relationship with the ward. In some jurisdictions, the best interest test has been modified to require the guardian to make the decision that the ward would have made had he or she been competent. Both the best interest and substituted judgment standards are discussed further below.

The second type of limitation on the guardian's authority bars unmonitored surrogate decisions in certain instances. For instance, a guardian of the estate, even one with general powers, is often prohibited by statute from executing a will for the ward, and usually must obtain a court order before selling real property or revoking certain types of trusts. Similarly, a guardian of the person, although authorized to make most medical decisions for the ward, must usually seek court approval before consenting to certain types of procedures viewed as "extraordinary", such as abortion, psychosurgery, organ transplants, or sterilization. The following materials focus on sterilization as paradigmatic of the situations in which guardians must make difficult choices, although several other situations are discussed as well.

MATTER OF GUARDIANSHIP OF HAYES

Supreme Court of Washington, 1980.
93 Wash.2d 228, 608 P.2d 635.

* * *

HOROWITZ, JUSTICE.

* * *

Petitioner Sharon Hayes is the mother of Edith Melissa Maria Hayes, who was born severely mentally retarded on December 17, 1963. She petitioned the Superior Court for an order appointing her as the guardian of Edith's person and specifically authorizing a sterilization procedure on Edith. The court dismissed the petition on a motion for summary judgment on the ground it had no authority to issue an order for sterilization of a retarded person.

* * *

Edith Hayes is severely mentally retarded as a result of a birth defect. Now 16 years old, she functions at the level of a four to five year old. Her physical development, though, has been commensurate with her age. She is thus capable of conceiving and bearing children, while being unable at present to understand her own reproductive functions or exercise independent judgment in her relationship with males. Her mother and doctors believe she is sexually active and quite likely to become pregnant. Her parents are understandably concerned that Edith is engaging in these sexual activities. Furthermore, her parents and doctors feel the long term effects of conventional birth control methods are potentially harmful, and that sterilization is the most desirable method to ensure that Edith does not conceive an unwanted child.

Edith's parents are sensitive to her special needs and concerned about her physical and emotional health, both now and in the future. They have sought appropriate medical care and education for her, and provided her with responsible and adequate supervision. During the year or so that Edith has been capable of becoming pregnant, though, they have become frustrated, depressed and emotionally drained by the stress of seeking an effective and safe method of contraception. They believe it is impossible to supervise her activities closely enough to prevent her from becoming involved in sexual relations. Thus, with the consent of Edith's father, Sharon Hayes petitioned for an order appointing her guardian and authorizing a sterilization procedure for Edith.

I

JURISDICTION

Edith's court appointed guardian ad litem contended below, and now maintains on appeal, that a superior court has no power to authorize a sterilization absent specific statutory authority. He cites in support of that view cases from other jurisdictions in which courts have concurred that specific statutory authority is required.

* * *

The courts of this state have long recognized the inherent power of the superior court "to hear *and determine* all matters legal and equitable in all proceedings known to the common law." Original jurisdiction is granted to superior courts over all cases and proceedings in which jurisdiction is not vested exclusively in some other court by Washington Const. art. 4, § 6.

* * *

We therefore hold that Washington Const. art. 4, § 6 gives the superior courts of this state the jurisdiction to entertain and act upon a request for an order authorizing sterilization of a mentally incompetent person.

II

STANDARDS FOR STERILIZATION

Our conclusion that superior courts have the power to grant a petition for sterilization does not mean that power must be exercised. Sterilization touches upon the individual's right of privacy and the fundamental right to procreate. It is an unalterable procedure with serious effects on the lives of the mentally retarded person and those upon whom he or she may depend. Therefore, it should be undertaken only after careful consideration of all relevant factors. We conclude this opinion with a set of guidelines setting out of the questions which must be asked and answered before an order authorizing sterilization of a mentally incompetent person could be issued. First, however, the consideration which are important to this determination can be best illuminated by discussing briefly the historical context from which they arise.

Sterilization of the mentally ill, mentally retarded, criminals, and sufferers from certain debilitating diseases became popular in this country in the early 20th century. The theory of "eugenic sterilization" was that the above-named traits and diseases, widely believed at that time to be hereditary, could be eliminated to the benefit of all society by simply preventing procreation.

More than 20 states passed statutes authorizing eugenic sterilizations. Washington passed a punitive sterilization law aimed at habitual criminals and certain sex offenders in 1909. The law exists today as RCW 9.92.100. Another statute, also enacted early in the century, denied certain persons, including the mentally retarded, the right to marry unless it is established that procreation by the couple is impossible. RCW 26.04.030, repealed by Laws of 1979, 1st Ex.Sess., ch. 128, § 4. While this statute did not authorize sterilizations, it was clearly based on eugenic principles.

In 1921 the Washington legislature enacted a law providing for sterilization of certain mentally retarded, mentally ill and habitually criminal persons restrained in a state institution. Laws of 1921, ch. 53, p. 162. This statute was held unconstitutional because of its failure to provide adequate procedural safeguards in *In re Hendrickson,* 12 Wash.2d 600, 123 P.2d 322 (1942).

The United States Supreme Court upheld the constitutionality of a eugenic sterilization law which provided adequate procedural safeguards, however, in *Buck v. Bell,* 274 U.S. 200, 47 S.Ct. 584, 71 L.Ed. 1000 (1927). Since that time it has generally been believed that eugenic sterilization statutes are constitutional although, as noted above, more recent Supreme Court decisions suggest the importance of respecting the individual's constitutional rights of privacy and procreation.

More recently scientific evidence has demonstrated little or no relationship between genetic inheritance and such conditions as mental retardation, criminal behavior, and diseases such as epilepsy. Geneticists have discovered, for example, that some forms of mental retardation appear to have no hereditary component at all, while in some others the element of heredity is only one of a number of factors which may contribute to the condition. In short the theoretical foundation for eugenic sterilization as a method of improving society has been disproved.

At the same time other previously unchallenged assumptions about mentally retarded persons have been shown to be unreliable. It has been found, for example, that far from being an insignificant event for the retarded person, sterilization can have longlasting detrimental emotional effects. Furthermore, while retarded persons, especially children, are often highly suggestible, there is evidence they are also capable of learning and adhering to strict rules of social behavior. Many retarded persons are capable of having normal children and being good parents.

Of great significance for the problem faced here is the fact that, unlike the situation of a normal and necessary medical procedure, in the question of sterilization the interests of the parents of a retarded person cannot be presumed to be identical to those of the child. The problem of parental consent to sterilization is of great concern to professionals in the field of mental health, and the overwhelming weight of opinion of those who have studied the problem appears to be that consent of a parent or guardian is a questionable or inadequate basis for sterilization. It is thus clear that in any proceedings to determine whether an order for sterilization should issue, the retarded person must be represented, as here, by a disinterested guardian ad litem.

Despite all that has been said thus far, in the rare case sterilization may indeed be in the best interests of the retarded person. However, the court must exercise care to protect the individual's right of privacy, and thereby not unnecessarily invade that right. Substantial medical evidence must be adduced, and the burden on the proponent of sterilization will be to show by clear, cogent and convincing evidence that such a procedure is in the best interest of the retarded person.

Among the factors to be considered are the age and educability of the individual. For example, a child in her early teens may be incapable at present of understanding the consequences of sexual activity, or exercising judgment in relations with the opposite sex, but may also have the potential to develop the required understanding and judgment through continued education and developmental programs.

A related consideration is the potential of the individual as a parent. As noted above, many retarded persons are capable of becoming good parents, and in only a fraction of cases is it likely that offspring would inherit a genetic form of mental retardation that would make parenting more difficult.

Another group of relevant factors involve the degree to which sterilization is medically indicated as the last and best resort for the individual. Can it be shown by clear, cogent and convincing evidence, for example, that other methods of birth control are inapplicable or unworkable?

In considering these factors, several courts have developed sterilization guidelines. With the assistance of the brief of Amicus Mental Health Law Project, a careful review of these considerations allows us to provide the superior court with standards to be followed in exercising its jurisdiction to issue an order authorizing sterilization of a mentally incompetent individual.

The decision can only be made in a superior court proceeding in which (1) the incompetent individual is represented by a disinterested guardian ad litem, (2) the court has received independent advice based upon a comprehensive medical, psychological, and social evaluation of the individual, and (3) to the greatest extent possible, the court has elicited and taken into account the view of the incompetent individual.

Within this framework, the judge must first find by clear, cogent and convincing evidence that the individual is (1) incapable of making his or her own decision about sterilization, and (2) unlikely to develop sufficiently to make an informed judgment about sterilization in the foreseeable future.

Next, it must be proved by clear, cogent and convincing evidence that there is a need for contraception. The judge must find that the individual is (1) physically capable of procreation, and (2) likely to engage in sexual activity at the present or in the near future under circumstances likely to result in pregnancy, and must find in addition that (3) the nature and extent of the individual's disability, as determined by empirical evidence and not solely on the basis of standardized tests, renders him or her permanently incapable of caring for a child, even with reasonable assistance.

Finally, there must be no alternatives to sterilization. The judge must find that by clear, cogent and convincing evidence (1) all less drastic contraceptive methods, including supervision, education and training, have been proved unworkable or inapplicable, and (2) the proposed method of sterilization entails the least invasion of the body of the individual. In addition, it must be shown by clear, cogent and convincing evidence that (3) the current state of scientific and medical knowledge does not suggest either (a) that a reversible sterilization procedure or other less drastic contraceptive method will shortly be available, or (b) that science is on the threshold of an advance in the treatment of the individual's disability.

There is a heavy presumption against sterilization of an individual incapable of informed consent that must be overcome by the person or entity requesting sterilization. This burden will be even harder to overcome in the case of a minor incompetent, whose youth may make it difficult or impossible to prove by clear, cogent and convincing evidence that he or she will never be capable of making an informed judgment about sterilization or of caring for a child.

Review of the facts in this case in light of these standards make it clear that the burden has not yet been met. It cannot be said that Edith Hayes will be unable to understand sexual activity or control her

behavior in the future. The medical testimony and report of the mental
health board are not detailed enough to provide clear, cogent and
convincing evidence in this regard. Edith's youth is of particular concern,
since she has many years of education before her. Furthermore, although
there is evidence that some methods of birth control have already been
tried, there is insufficient proof that no conventional form of contraception is a reasonable and medically acceptable alternative to sterilization.
Nor is there any evidence such a procedure would not have detrimental
effects on Edith's future emotional or physical health. Finally, there is
no evidence that a pregnancy would be physically or emotionally hazardous to Edith, and insufficient evidence that she would never be capable
of being a good parent.

Additional factfinding at the trial level will help the superior court
judge answer the questions set out in this opinion. Therefore, the case is
reversed and remanded for further proceedings consistent with this
opinion.

* * *

Questions and Comments

1. *The competency standard for sterilization.* Assuming there is the
requisite statutory or judicial authority, when may a court authorize or
undertake a surrogate decision concerning sterilization? The formulation
found in *Hayes* is widely followed. Looking closely at the guidelines of that
case, it would appear that if a person is competent to understand the
sterilization process and its consequences and refuses the procedure, the
state may take no further action. Conversely, if the person is incapable of
understanding the procedure and its consequences, *Hayes* appears to hold
that he or she is incompetent for purposes of making the sterilization
decision and that a surrogate decision (taking into account such factors as
the likelihood of sexual activity and the person's parenting ability) is
permitted.

Is this the correct competency test? Or should the test instead be
whether the person is "competent" to be a parent? Consider this excerpt
from Elizabeth Scott, "Sterilization of Mentally Retarded Persons: Reproductive Rights and Family Privacy," 1986 Duke L.J. 806, 837–38 (1986):

> [C]ompetency to make a meaningful choice to procreate rests on the
> individual's ability to fulfill the basic responsibilities of parenthood. A
> mildly impaired person may have this ability regardless of whether she
> is legally competent to make medical decisions regarding sterilization.
> Her interest in making her own reproductive decisions should be legally
> protected. On the other hand, a severely disabled person's childlike wish
> for a baby does not signify a meaningful choice. A decision to have a
> child is, most importantly, a decision to become a parent—to assume a
> role that requires a minimal level of competency. If the individual lacks
> this capability and the state would predictably intervene to remove any
> child produced in order to protect it, then the choice to have a child is
> not a legally protectable exercise in personal autonomy. Thus, the
> interest in autonomy is derivative of the underlying interest in having

children. If the retarded individual lacks the ability to exercise the substantive interest, she lacks the interest in making the choice.

Under Scott's approach, what should be the competency standard for decisionmaking about abortion?

2. *Best interests analysis.* Assuming a person is found incompetent to make the sterilization decision under the appropriate standard, what factors will justify making a surrogate decision in favor of the procedure? In other words, when is sterilization in an incompetent person's best interests? *Hayes* lists several factors. Note that the court seems to consider sterilization the option of last resort, by requiring a showing that there are no "less drastic" contraceptives that "have been proved unworkable." Other courts are even more restrictive. For instance, one court allowed sterilization of an incompetent person only upon a finding that the procedure is medically essential "to preserve the life or physical or mental health of the incompetent person." In the *Matter of A.W.,* 637 P.2d 366, 375 (Colo.1981).

Are these types of "least restrictive alternative" rules sensible? If the person is not competent to make a decision about having children, why should we prefer a nonpermanent procedure such as contraceptive pills or an intrauterine device? If sterilization is not performed, but because of the increased risks of pregnancy and increased burden on the family, the person is eventually institutionalized, has the "least drastic" method been pursued?

3. *The substituted judgment standard.* Some courts eschew best interests analysis in favor of a substituted judgment test. This approach was described in *Matter of Moe,* 385 Mass. 555, 432 N.E.2d 712 (1982), which also involved a sterilization decision:

> In utilizing the doctrine of substituted judgment, this court seeks to maintain the integrity of the incompetent person by giving the individual a forum in which his or her rights may be exercised. The court dons 'the mental mantle of the incompetent' and substitutes itself as nearly as possible for the individual in the decision making process. In utilizing the doctrine the court does not decide what is necessarily the best decision but rather what decision would be made by the incompetent person if he or she were competent.

The factors the court then listed as considerations in making the substituted judgment decision are virtually identical to those listed in *Hayes,* except that the court added that the individual's religious beliefs, if any, must be ascertained. Would a substituted judgment analysis be any different than a best interests analysis on the *Hayes* facts? Does application of the substituted judgment test make sense in such a situation?

4. *Relevance of the ward's desires; advanced directives.* Under both the best interest and substituted judgment tests, at least as described by *Hayes* and *Moe,* the decisionmaker is to inquire into and take into account the ward's desires. Does this requirement make sense when the individual has been found incompetent?

Should any weight be given to a previous statement made while the person is *competent*? Suppose, for instance, that a woman of 20 suffers an incapacitating head injury which leaves her sexually active but at the mental age of 5, unable either to understand the sterilization procedure or to make a decision concerning having a child. One year before the accident, she had indicated that she would never want to be sterilized or otherwise give up her capacity to have children. Should this fact bar a court under either test from authorizing sterilization? Would it make any difference if the reason given for not wanting sterilization was based on religious preferences? In the alternative, what if, a year before the accident, she had indicated she never wanted to have children?

Consider *Cruzan v. Director, Missouri Dept. of Health*, 497 U.S. 261, 110 S.Ct. 2841, 111 L.Ed.2d 224 (1990). There, the parents and co-guardians of Nancy Cruzan requested the termination of procedures which were sustaining the life of their daughter, a twenty-six year old woman who as a result of an automobile accident was in a permanent vegetative state, but not legally dead under state law. The trial court found that, before the accident, Nancy had been a "vivacious, active, outgoing, independent person who preferred to do for herself." It also found that about a year prior to her accident, she had "discussions with her then housemate, friend and co-worker," during which "she expressed the feeling that she would not wish to continue living if she couldn't be at least halfway normal." The court characterized these conversations as "somewhat serious." The finding that Nancy's "lifestyle and other statements to family and friends suggest that she would not wish to continue her present existence without hope as it is," heavily influenced the trial court in ordering the state of Missouri to honor the co-guardians' request.

The Missouri Supreme Court reversed, calling the evidence about Nancy's wishes "inherently unreliable and thus insufficient to support the co-guardians' claim to exercise substituted judgment on Nancy's behalf." *Cruzan by Cruzan v. Harmon*, 760 S.W.2d 408, 426 (Mo.1988) The court concluded: "The State's interest is in preservation of life, not only Nancy's life, but also the lives of persons similarly situated yet without the support of a loving family. This interest outweighs any rights invoked on Nancy's behalf to terminate treatment in the face of the uncertainty of Nancy's wishes and her own right to life." Id. The U.S. Supreme Court affirmed the Missouri Supreme Court's decision. Specifically, it held that the state may require a "clear and convincing" showing that Cruzan expressed a desire to withdraw life-sustaining treatment prior to her accident before withdrawal is permitted. At least when the treatment refusal will result in death, the Court strongly suggested that only a formal written statement of intent, or so-called "living will," would suffice for constitutional purposes, given the state's interest in preserving life. In support of this decision, the Court stated:

> An erroneous decision not to terminate results in a maintenance of the status quo; the possibility of subsequent developments such as advancements in medical science, the discovery of new evidence regarding the patient's intent, changes in the law, or simply the unexpected death of the patient despite the administration of life-sustaining treatment, at least create the potential that a wrong decision will eventually be corrected or its impact mitigated. An erroneous decision to withdraw life-sustaining treatment, however, is not susceptible of correction.

The *Cruzan* Court also rejected the parents' argument that they should be authorized to terminate life-sustaining treatment because of the Court's decision in *Parham v. J.R.* (reprinted at pp. 907–21), which permitted parents to make the hospitalization decision for their children. The Court stated that "petitioners would seek to turn a decision which allowed a State to rely on family decisionmaking into a constitutional requirement that the State recognize such decisionmaking." It continued:

> [W]e do not think the Due Process Clause requires the State to repose judgment on these matters with anyone but the patient herself. Close family members may have a strong feeling—a feeling not at all ignoble or unworthy, but not entirely disinterested, either—that they do not wish to witness the continuation of the life of a loved one which they regard as hopeless, meaningless, and even degrading. But there is no automatic assurance that the view of close family members will necessarily be the same as the patient's would have been had she been confronted with the prospect of her situation while competent.

Cruzan hastened the development of statutory authorization for "advanced directives" in a number of states. An advanced directive is an instruction from a competent individual that directs or authorizes certain action in the event the individual becomes unable to make a decision about the action. Such directives, if valid, are binding on the guardian; indeed, they are usually meant to eliminate the need for a court-appointed guardian in the specified situation. In Florida, for example, a person (the "principal") can designate a "health care surrogate" through a simple, one-page advanced directive document. The document must be witnessed by two persons, neither of whom is the designated surrogate. Subsequently if two doctors certify that the principal has become incapacitated (meaning "physically or mentally unable to communicate a willful and knowing health care decision"), the surrogate is to make the necessary health care decision in accordance with the principal's instructions in the advanced directive. Although these decisions may be challenged judicially by the attending physicians, the health care facility, the patient's family, or "any other interested person," they are presumptively valid. Fl.Stat.§ 765.101 et. seq. More will be said about advanced directives in connection with mental health care in Part IV of this chapter at pp. 983–84.

5. *Intervention for the benefit of third parties.* Many courts which have sanctioned surrogate decisionmaking in the sterilization context have emphasized that the decision should take into account only the interests of the ward. For instance, in *Moe* supra, the court stated: "No sterilization is to be compelled on the basis of any State or parental interest." 432 N.E.2d at 721. Does the *Hayes* court take a position on this issue? *Should* third party interests be taken into account?

In answering this last question, it might be useful to consider a case involving a decision other than sterilization. *In re Guardianship of Pescinski*, 67 Wis.2d 4, 226 N.W.2d 180 (1975) addressed whether a court may order an operation to remove the kidney of an incompetent person in order to save the life of a relative. Tests showed that Richard Pescinski, who suffered from schizophrenia and had a mental capacity consistent with age twelve, was a suitable kidney donor for his sister, who would die without a transplant. While removal of a kidney is not a particularly risky operation, it causes some discomfort and of course leaves the donor with no backup kidney; for this reason, Richard and Elaine's parents, age 70 and 67, Elaine's six minor children, their older sister (who had diabetes) and their older brother (who had nine minor children, a special diet and a rupture on his left side), either were not suitable donors or refused to donate. Applying the best interest test, the court upheld the guardian's decision not to order the kidney removal from Richard: "In the absence of real consent on his part, and in a situation where no benefit to him has been established, we fail to find any authority for the county court, or this court, to approve this operation."

In his dissent, Justice Day argued in favor of the substituted judgment test:

> I think the court as a court of equity does have authority to permit the kidney transplant operation requested in the petition of the guardian of Richard Pescinski. I agree with the reasoning of the Court of Appeals of the state of Kentucky in Strunk v. Strunk, 445 S.W.2d 145 (Ky.1969). That case involved the authorization of a transplant from a 27–year–old incompetent to his 28–year–old brother. The court in that case did find, based on the testimony of a psychiatrist, that while the incompetent had the mental age of six, it would be of benefit to him to keep his brother alive so that his brother could visit him on occasion[.] ... In the case before us, if the incompetent brother should happily recover from his mental illness, he would undoubtedly be happy to learn that the transplant of one of his kidneys to his sister saved her life. This at least would be a normal response and hence the transplant is not without benefit to him.
>
> The majority opinion would forever condemn the incompetent to be always a receiver, a taker, but never a giver. For in holding that only those things which financially or physically benefit the incompetent may be done by the court, he is forever excluded from doing the decent thing, the charitable thing. The [substituted judgement] approach gives the incompetent the benefit of the doubt, endows him with the finest qualities of his humanity, assumes the goodness of his nature instead of assuming the opposite.

6. *Procedure.* *Hayes* is typical in its requirement that a court be involved in the sterilization decision. For instance, in *Moe,* 432 N.E.2d at 716–17, the court stated:

> Since sterilization is an extraordinary and highly intrusive form of medical treatment that irreversibly extinguishes the ward's fundamental right of procreative choice, we conclude that a guardian must obtain a proper judicial order for the procedure before he or she can validly consent to it. Guardians and parents, therefore, absent statutory or judicial authorization, cannot consent to the sterilization of a ward in their care or custody.

What makes sterilization "extraordinary" and "intrusive," compared for instance to a decision regarding financial affairs? In another Massachusetts case, the court identified several factors to be considered in determining whether there must be a court order before medical intervention may take place:

[T]he extent of impairment of the patient's mental faculties, whether the patient is in custody of a State institution, the prognosis without the proposed treatment, the prognosis with the proposed treatment, the complexity, risk and novelty of the proposed treatment, its possible side effects, the patient's level of understanding and probable reaction, the urgency of decision, the consent of the patient, spouse or guardian, the good faith of those who participate in the decision, the clarity of professional opinion as to what is good medical practice, the interests of third persons, and the administrative requirements of any institution involved.

Matter of Spring, 380 Mass. 629, 405 N.E.2d 115 (1980).

Scott, supra at 859–863, disagrees with the requirement that a judicial hearing be held in all sterilization cases, relying in part on *Parham v. J.R.* (*Parham* permitted parents to commit their children if an independent assessment by a mental health professional concurs.) Scott argues that in some cases a *Parham*-type arrangement is sufficient to authorize the sterilization decision, at least when the ward's parents are the surrogate decision-makers:

> [If a "reliable clinical evaluation" finds that] the child is not potentially capable of reproductive choice, she is less at risk than the child for whom hospitalization is sought. Parents seeking sterilization are not trying to "dump" their retarded child. Their initiative may well be an effort to facilitate her continued care at home. Thus, potential conflicts of interest would seem less probable in this situation than when psychiatric hospitalization is proposed.

* * *

> If the disability is less severe, the possibility of underestimating the interest in reproductive choice becomes greater, and the costs of procedural protection become more acceptable. Thus, if the findings of the expert raise any ambiguity about the individual's potential interest in reproductive choice, judicial review is warranted.

7. *Hospitalizing the ward.* Similar issues arise in the context of making decisions about psychiatric treatment. Is a decision to hospitalize the ward in a mental institution "extraordinary," so that hospitalization may not take place unless procedures for involuntary commitment are followed? Or may a guardian avoid court disposition by admitting the ward as a "voluntary" patient? In most states today, a guardian may not follow the latter course, at least if the ward objects to hospitalization. In the words of one court:

> If we were not to require at least substantial compliance with the [involuntary commitment] law to fully protect the rights of incompetents it would be possible for an unscrupulous person to have himself appointed guardian and then lock his ward in a mental institution and proceed to waste the ward's estate. If a state and the judiciary are not vigilant in the protection of the rights of incompetents it is likely to lead to the abuse of the person and estate of such incompetents. The mentally ill are unable to think and care for themselves in a normal manner and of necessity depend upon the state and the courts for

protection.... We ... must hold in this case that the ward was not afforded either procedural or substantive due process....

Von Luce v. Rankin, 267 Ark. 34, 588 S.W.2d 445 (1979). In *Von Luce* the ward protested the hospitalization. Should involuntary proceedings be required if the ward does not protest? To what extent does *Parham* undercut *Von Luce* and permit a guardian to "voluntary in" his or her ward if a mental health professional employed by the hospital sanctions the decision?

An even more controversial issue has been the guardian's authority to consent to various types of psychiatric treatments, ranging from drug therapy to psychosurgery. That issue is addressed in the next section, as part of a discussion on the larger issue of when persons with mental disability have the right to refuse or consent to psychiatric treatment.

IV. THE RIGHT TO REFUSE AND CONSENT TO PSYCHIATRIC TREATMENT

In Chapter Four, we discussed the informed consent doctrine, which is normally thought to require professionals who are engaged in treating patients to honor an informed, voluntary decision by a competent individual. This common law doctrine regulates the relationship between doctor and patient by imposing liability on doctors who do not obtain informed consent for nonemergency treatment. However, when the treatment at issue is psychiatric in nature and the patient is thought to be seriously mentally ill (as opposed to anguished or neurotic), the informed consent doctrine has not found uniform acceptance. For instance, until the 1970's people who were civilly committed or hospitalized as incompetent to stand trial or criminally insane could be forcibly medicated regardless of their competency to make treatment decisions. Apparently, the assumption was that since these people were subject to involuntary institutionalization, they were not competent to veto a particular treatment decision. At the same time, they were not competent to insist on certain types of treatment. Similarly, uninstitutionalized persons who were supervised by guardians (of the person) had little or no control over their treatment.

These practices continue today in a number of jurisdictions. However, virtually every court that has considered the matter now recognizes a "right to refuse" psychotropic medication for institutionalized populations, in the process constitutionalizing a version of the informed consent doctrine in that context. The precise scope of this right is still being fleshed out, at least at the Supreme Court level; its application to other types of treatment is also unclear. This section first examines the right to refuse antipsychotic medication. It then addresses consent and refusal with respect to three other psychiatric treatment techniques: electroconvulsive therapy, psychosurgery, and behavior modification. Before reading the following materials, review the materials in Chapter One on the efficacy and side effects of medication and the other treatments discussed below (pp. 25–32, 44).

A. PSYCHOTROPIC MEDICATION

WASHINGTON v. HARPER

Supreme Court of the United States, 1990.
494 U.S. 210, 110 S.Ct. 1028, 108 L.Ed.2d 178.

JUSTICE KENNEDY delivered the opinion of the Court.

The central question before us is whether a judicial hearing is required before the State may treat a mentally ill prisoner with antipsychotic drugs against his will. Resolution of the case requires us to discuss the protections afforded the prisoner under the Due Process Clause of the Fourteenth Amendment.

I

Respondent Walter Harper was sentenced to prison in 1976 for robbery. From 1976 to 1980, he was incarcerated at the Washington State Penitentiary. Most of that time, respondent was housed in the prison's mental health unit, where he consented to the administration of antipsychotic drugs. Antipsychotic drugs, sometimes called "neuroleptic" or "psychotropic drugs," are medications commonly used in treating mental disorders such as schizophrenia. As found by the trial court, the effect of these and similar drugs is to alter the chemical balance in the brain, the desired result being that the medication will assist the patient in organizing his or her thought processes and regaining a rational state of mind.

Respondent was paroled in 1980 on the condition that he participate in psychiatric treatment. While on parole, he continued to receive treatment at the psychiatric ward at Harborview Medical Center in Seattle, and was later sent to Western State hospital pursuant to a civil commitment order. In December 1981, the State revoked respondent's parole after he assaulted two nurses at a hospital in Seattle.

Upon his return to prison, respondent was sent to the Special Offender Center (SOC or Center), a 144–bed correctional institute established by the Washington Department of Corrections to diagnose and treat convicted felons with serious mental disorders. At the Center, psychiatrists first diagnosed respondent as suffering from a manic-depressive disorder. At first, respondent gave voluntary consent to treatment, including the administration of antipsychotic medications. In November 1982, he refused to continue taking the prescribed medications. The treating physician then sought to medicate respondent over his objections, pursuant to SOC Policy 600.30.

Policy 600.30 was developed in partial response to this Court's decision in *Vitek v. Jones*, 445 U.S. 480, 100 S.Ct. 1254, 63 L.Ed.2d 552 (1980).[9] The Policy has several substantive and procedural components. First, if a psychiatrist determines that an inmate should be treated with

---

9. *Vitek* is reprinted at pp. 883–87.

antipsychotic drugs but the inmate does not consent, the inmate may be subjected to involuntary treatment with the drugs only if he (1) suffers from a "mental disorder" and (2) is "gravely disabled" or poses a "likelihood of serious harm" to himself, others, or their property.[3] Only a psychiatrist may order or approve the medication. Second, an inmate who refuses to take the medication voluntarily is entitled to a hearing before a special committee consisting of a psychiatrist, psychologist, and the Associate Superintendent of the Center, none of whom may be, at the time of the hearing, involved in the inmate's treatment or diagnosis. If the committee determines by a majority vote that the inmate suffers from a mental disorder and is gravely disabled or dangerous, the inmate may be medicated against his will, provided the psychiatrist is in the majority.

Third, the inmate has certain procedural rights before, during, and after the hearing. He must be given at least 24 hours' notice of the Center's intent to convene an involuntary medication hearing, during which time he may not be medicated. In addition, he must receive notice of the tentative diagnosis, the factual basis for the diagnosis, and why the staff believes medication is necessary. At the hearing, the inmate has the right to attend; to present evidence, including witnesses; to cross-examine staff witnesses; and to the assistance of a lay advisor who has not been involved in his case and who understands the psychiatric issues involved. Minutes of the hearing must be kept, and a copy provided to the inmate. The inmate has the right to appeal the committee's decision to the Superintendent of the Center within 24 hours, and the Superintendent must decide the appeal within 24 hours after its receipt. The inmate may seek judicial review of a committee decision in state court by means of a personal restraint petition or extraordinary writ.

Fourth, after the initial hearing, involuntary medication can continue only with periodic review. When respondent first refused medication, a committee, again composed of a non-treating psychiatrist, a psychologist, and the Center's Associate Superintendent was required to review an inmate's case after the first seven days of treatment. If the committee

---

3. The Policy's definitions of the terms "mental disorder," "gravely disabled," and "likelihood of serious harm" are identical to the definitions of the terms as they are used in the state involuntary commitment statute. "Mental disorder" means "any organic, mental, or emotional impairment which has substantial adverse effects on an individual's cognitive or volitional functions." Wash.Rev.Code § 71.05.020(2) (1987). "Gravely disabled" means "a condition in which a person, as a result of a mental disorder: (a) [i]s in danger of serious physical harm resulting from a failure to provide for his essential human needs of health or safety, or (b) manifests severe deterioration in routine functioning evidenced by repeated and escalating loss of cognitive or volitional control over his or her actions and is not receiving such care as is essential for his or her health or safety." § 71.05.020(1). "Likelihood of serious harm" means "either: (a) [a] substantial risk that physical harm will be inflicted by an individual upon his own person, as evidenced by threats or attempts to commit suicide or inflict physical harm on one's self, (b) a substantial risk that physical harm will be inflicted by an individual upon another, as evidenced by behavior which has caused such harm or which places another person or persons in reasonable fear of sustaining such harm, or (c) a substantial risk that physical harm will be inflicted by an individual upon the property of others, as evidenced by behavior which has caused substantial loss or damage to the property of others." § 71.05.020(3).

reapproved the treatment, the treating psychiatrist was required to review the case and prepare a report for the Department of Corrections medical director every 14 days while treatment continued.

In this case, respondent was absent when members of the Center staff met with the committee before the hearing. The committee then conducted the hearing in accordance with the Policy, with respondent being present and assisted by a nurse practitioner from another institution. The committee found that respondent was a danger to others as a result of a mental disease or disorder, and approved the involuntary administration of antipsychotic drugs. On appeal, the Superintendent upheld the committee's findings. Beginning on November 23, 1982, respondent was involuntarily medicated for about one year. Periodic review occurred in accordance with the Policy.

In November 1983, respondent was transferred from the Center to the Washington State Reformatory. While there, he took no medication, and as a result, his condition deteriorated. He was retransferred to the Center after only one month. Respondent was the subject of another committee hearing in accordance with Policy 600.30, and the committee again approved medication against his will. Respondent continued to receive antipsychotic drugs, subject to the required periodic reviews, until he was transferred to the Washington State Penitentiary in June 1986.

In February 1985, respondent filed suit in state court under 42 U.S.C. § 1983 against various individual defendants and the State, claiming that the failure to provide a judicial hearing before the involuntary administration of antipsychotic medication violated the Due Process, Equal Protection, and Free Speech clauses of both the federal and state constitutions, as well as state tort law. He sought both damages and declaratory and injunctive relief. After a bench trial in March 1987, the court held that, although respondent had a liberty interest in not being subjected to the involuntary administration of antipsychotic medication, the procedures contained in the Policy met the requirements of due process as stated in *Vitek*.

On appeal, the Washington Supreme Court reversed and remanded the case to the trial court. Agreeing with the trial court that respondent had a liberty interest in refusing antipsychotic medications, the Court concluded that the "highly intrusive nature" of treatment with antipsychotic medications warranted greater procedural protections than those necessary to protect the liberty interest at stake in *Vitek*. It held that, under the Due Process Clause, the State could administer antipsychotic medication to a competent, nonconsenting inmate only if, in a judicial hearing at which the inmate had the full panoply of adversarial procedural protections, the State proved by "clear, cogent, and convincing" evidence that the administration of antipsychotic medication was both necessary and effective for furthering a compelling state interest.

We granted certiorari, and we reverse.

* * *

III

* * *

Restated in the terms of this case, the substantive issue is what factual circumstances must exist before the State may administer antipsychotic drugs to the prisoner against his will; the procedural issue is whether the State's nonjudicial mechanisms used to determine the facts in a particular case are sufficient. The Washington Supreme Court in effect ruled upon the substance of the inmate's right, as well as the procedural guarantees, and both are encompassed by our grant of certiorari. We address these questions beginning with the substantive one.

* * *

We have no doubt that respondent possesses a significant liberty interest in avoiding the unwanted administration of antipsychotic drugs under the Due Process Clause of the Fourteenth Amendment. *Vitek*. Upon full consideration of the state administrative scheme, however, we find that the Due Process Clause confers upon respondent no greater right than that recognized under state law.

Respondent contends that the State, under the mandate of the Due Process Clause, may not override his choice to refuse antipsychotic drugs unless he has been found to be incompetent, and then only if the factfinder makes a substituted judgment that he, if competent, would consent to drug treatment. We disagree. The extent of a prisoner's right under the Clause to avoid the unwanted administration of antipsychotic drugs must be defined in the context of the inmate's confinement. The Policy under review requires the State to establish, by a medical finding, that a mental disorder exists which is likely to cause harm if not treated. Moreover, the fact that the medication must first be prescribed by a psychiatrist, and then approved by a reviewing psychiatrist, ensures that the treatment in question will be ordered only if it is in the prisoner's medical interests, given the legitimate needs of his institutional confinement.[8] These standards, which recognize both the prisoner's medical

---

8. The dissent contends that the SOC Policy permits respondent's doctors to treat him with antipsychotic medications against his will without reference to whether the treatment is medically appropriate. For various reasons, we disagree. That an inmate is mentally ill and dangerous is a necessary condition to medication, but not a sufficient condition; before the hearing committee determines whether these requirements are met, the inmate's treating physician must first make the decision that medication is appropriate. The SOC is a facility whose purpose is not to warehouse the mentally ill, but to diagnose and treat convicted felons, with the desired goal being that they will recover to the point where they can function in a normal prison environment. In keeping with this purpose, an SOC psychiatrist must first prescribe the antipsychotic medication for the inmate, and the inmate must refuse it, before the Policy is invoked. Unlike the dissent, we will not assume that physicians will prescribe these drugs for reasons unrelated to the medical needs of the patients; indeed, the ethics of

interests and the State's interests, meet the demands of the Due Process Clause.

* * *

There can be little doubt as to both the legitimacy and the importance of the governmental interest presented here. There are few cases in which the State's interest in combating the danger posed by a person to both himself and others is greater than in a prison environment, which, "by definition," is made up of persons with "a demonstrated proclivity for antisocial criminal, and often violent, conduct." We confront here the State's obligations, not just its interests. The State has undertaken the obligation to provide prisoners with medical treatment consistent not only with their own medical interests, but also with the needs of the institution. Prison administrators have not only an interest in ensuring the safety of prison staffs and administrative personnel, but the duty to take reasonable measures for the prisoners' own safety. These concerns have added weight when a penal institution, like the Special Offender Center, is restricted to inmates with mental illnesses. Where an inmate's mental disability is the root cause of the threat he poses to the inmate population, the State's interest in decreasing the danger to others necessarily encompasses an interest in providing him with medical treatment for his illness.

Special Offender Center Policy 600.30 is a rational means of furthering the State's legitimate objectives. Its exclusive application is to inmates who are mentally ill and who, as a result of their illness, are gravely disabled or represent a significant danger to themselves or others. The drugs may be administered for no purpose other than treatment, and only under the direction of a licensed psychiatrist. There is considerable debate over the potential side effects of antipsychotic medications, but there is little dispute in the psychiatric profession that proper use of the drugs is one of the most effective means of treating and controlling a mental illness likely to cause violent behavior.

The alternative means proffered by respondent for accommodating his interest in rejecting the forced administration of antipsychotic drugs do not demonstrate the invalidity of the State's policy. Respondent's main contention is that, as a precondition to antipsychotic drug treatment, the State must find him incompetent, and then obtain court approval of the treatment using a "substituted judgment" standard. The suggested rule takes no account of the legitimate governmental interest in treating him where medically appropriate for the purpose of reducing the danger he poses. A rule that is in no way responsive to the State's legitimate interests is not a proper accommodation, and can be rejected out of hand. Nor are physical restraints or seclusion "alternative[s] that fully accommodat[e] the prisoner's rights at de minimis cost to valid

the medical profession are to the contrary. See Hippocratic Oath; American Psychiatric Association, Principles of Medical Ethics With Annotations Especially Applicable to Psychiatry, in Codes of Professional Responsibility 129–135 (R. Gorlin ed. 1986)....

penological interests." Physical restraints are effective only in the short term, and can have serious physical side effects when used on a resisting inmate, as well as leaving the staff at risk of injury while putting the restraints on or tending to the inmate who is in them. Furthermore, respondent has failed to demonstrate that physical restraints or seclusion are acceptable substitutes for antipsychotic drugs, in terms of either their medical effectiveness or their toll on limited prison resources.

We hold that, given the requirements of the prison environment, the Due Process Clause permits the State to treat a prison inmate who has a serious mental illness with antipsychotic drugs against his will, if the inmate is dangerous to himself or others and the treatment is in the inmate's medical interest. Policy 600.30 comports with these requirements; we therefore reject respondent's contention that its substantive standards are deficient under the Constitution.

IV

Having determined that state law recognizes a liberty interest ... protected by the Due Process Clause, which permits refusal of antipsychotic drugs unless certain preconditions are met, we address next what procedural protections are necessary to ensure that the decision to medicate an inmate against his will is neither arbitrary nor erroneous under the standards we have discussed above. The Washington Supreme Court held that a full judicial hearing, with the inmate being represented by counsel, was required by the Due Process Clause before the State could administer antipsychotic drugs to him against his will. In addition, the court held that the State must justify the authorization of involuntary administration of antipsychotic drugs by "clear, cogent, and convincing" evidence. We hold that the administrative hearing procedures set by the SOC Policy do comport with procedural due process, and conclude that the Washington Supreme Court erred in requiring a judicial hearing as a prerequisite for the involuntary treatment of prison inmates.

A

The primary point of disagreement between the parties is whether due process requires a judicial decisionmaker. As written, the Policy requires that the decision whether to medicate an inmate against his will be made by a hearing committee composed of a psychiatrist, psychologist, and the Center's Associate Superintendent. None of the committee members may be involved, at the time of the hearing, in the inmate's treatment or diagnosis; members are not disqualified from sitting on the committee, however, if they have treated or diagnosed the inmate in the past. The committee's decision is subject to review by the Superintendent; if the inmate so desires, he may seek judicial review of the decision in a state court. Respondent contends that only a court should make the decision to medicate an inmate against his will.

Respondent's interest in avoiding the unwarranted administration of antipsychotic drugs is not insubstantial. The forcible injection of medication into a nonconsenting person's body represents a substantial interference with that person's liberty. The purpose of the drugs is to alter the chemical balance in a patient's brain, leading to changes, intended to be beneficial, in his or her cognitive processes. While the therapeutic benefits of antipsychotic drugs are well documented, it is also true that the drugs can have serious, even fatal, side effects. One such side effect identified by the trial court is acute dystonia, a severe involuntary spasm of the upper body, tongue, throat, or eyes. The trial court found that it may be treated and reversed within a few minutes through use of the medication Cogentin. Other side effects include akathesia (motor restlessness, often characterized by an inability to sit still); neuroleptic malignant syndrome (a relatively rare condition which can lead to death from cardiac dysfunction); and tardive dyskinesia, perhaps the most discussed side effect of antipsychotic drugs. Tardive dyskinesia is a neurological disorder, irreversible in some cases, that is characterized by involuntary, uncontrollable movements of various muscles, especially around the face. The State, respondent, and amici sharply disagree about the frequency with which tardive dyskinesia occurs, its severity, and the medical profession's ability to treat, arrest, or reverse the condition. A fair reading of the evidence, however, suggests that the proportion of patients treated with antipsychotic drugs who exhibit the symptoms of tardive dyskinesia ranges from 10% to 25%. According to the American Psychiatric Association, studies of the condition indicate that 60% of tardive dyskinesia is mild or minimal in effect, and about 10% may be characterized as severe.

Notwithstanding the risks that are involved, we conclude that an inmate's interests are adequately protected, and perhaps better served, by allowing the decision to medicate to be made by medical professionals rather than a judge. The Due Process Clause "has never been thought to require that the neutral and detached trier of fact be law trained or a judicial or administrative officer." *Parham v. J.R.* Though it cannot be doubted that the decision to medicate has societal and legal implications, the Constitution does not prohibit the State from permitting medical personnel to make the decision under fair procedural mechanisms. Particularly where the patient is mentally disturbed, his own intentions will be difficult to assess, and will be changeable in any event. Respondent's own history of accepting and then refusing drug treatment illustrates the point. We cannot make the facile assumption that the patient's intentions, or a substituted judgment approximating those intentions, can be determined in a single judicial hearing apart from the realities of frequent and ongoing clinical observation by medical professionals. Our holding in *Parham* that a judicial hearing was not required prior to the voluntary commitment of a child to a mental hospital was based on similar observations:

"... [D]ue process is not violated by use of informal, traditional medical investigative techniques.... The mode and procedure of medical diagnostic procedures is not the business of judges.... Although we acknowledge the fallibility of medical and psychiatric diagnosis, we do not accept the notion that the shortcomings of specialists can always be avoided by shifting the decision from a trained specialist using the traditional tools of medical science to an untrained judge or administrative hearing officer after a judicial-type hearing. Even after a hearing, the nonspecialist decisionmaker must make a medical-psychiatric decision. Common human experience and scholarly opinions suggest that the supposed protections of an adversary proceeding to determine the appropriateness of medical decisions for the commitment and treatment of mental and emotional illness may well be more illusory than real."

Nor can we ignore the fact that requiring judicial hearings will divert scarce prison resources, both money and the staff's time, from the care and treatment of mentally ill inmates.

*   *   *

[A]dequate procedures exist here. In particular, independence of the decisionmaker is addressed to our satisfaction by these procedures. None of the hearing committee members may be involved in the inmate's current treatment or diagnosis. . . . In the absence of record evidence to the contrary, we are not willing to presume that members of the staff lack the necessary independence to provide an inmate with a full and fair hearing in accordance with the Policy. In previous cases involving medical decisions implicating similar liberty interests, we have approved use of similar internal decisionmakers. See *Vitek*; *Parham*.[13] As we

13. In an attempt to prove that internal decisionmakers lack the independence necessary to render impartial decisions, respondent and various amici refer us to other cases in which it is alleged that antipsychotic drugs were prescribed not for medical purposes, but to control or discipline mentally ill patients. We rejected a similar claim in *Parham*, and do so again here, using much the same reasoning. "That such a practice may take place in some institutions in some places affords no basis for a finding as to [Washington's] program," *Parham*, particularly in light of the trial court's finding here that the administration of antipsychotic drugs to respondent was consistent with good medical practice. Moreover, the practical effect of mandating an outside decisionmaker such as an "independent psychiatrist" or judge in these circumstances may be chimerical. Review of the literature indicates that outside decisionmakers concur with the treating physician's decision to treat a patient involuntarily in most, if not all, cases. See Bloom, Faulkner, Holm, & Rawlinson, "An Empirical View of Patients Exercising Their Right to Refuse Treatment", 7 Int'l J. Law & Psychiatry 315, 325 (1984) (independent examining physician used in Oregon psychiatric hospital concurred in deci-

sion to involuntarily medicate patients in 95% of cases); Hickman, Resnick, & Olson, "Right to Refuse Psychotropic Medication: An Interdisciplinary Proposal", 6 Mental Disability Law Reporter 122, 130 (1982) (independent reviewing psychiatrist used in Ohio affirmed the recommendation of internal reviewer in 100% of cases). Review by judges of decisions to override a patient's objections to medication yields similar results. Appelbaum, "The Right to Refuse Treatment With Antipsychotic Medications: Retrospect and Prospect", 145 Am. J. Psychiatry 413, 417–418 (1988). In comparison, other studies reveal that review by internal decisionmakers is hardly as lackluster as the dissent suggests. See Hickman, Resnick, & Olson, supra, at 130 (internal reviewer approved of involuntary treatment in 75% of cases); Zito, Lentz, Routt, & Olson, "The Treatment Review Panel: A Solution to Treatment Refusal?", 12 Bull.Am.Acad.Psychiatry Law 349 (1984) (internal review panel used in Minnesota mental hospital approved of involuntary medication in 67% of cases). See generally Appelbaum & Hoge, "The Right to Refuse Treatment: What the Research Reveals", 4 Behavioral Sciences & the Law 279, 288–290 (1986) (summarizing results of studies on how

reasoned in *Vitek*, it is only by permitting persons connected with the institution to make these decisions that courts are able to avoid "unnecessary intrusion into either medical or correctional judgments." *Vitek*.

B

The procedures established by the Center are sufficient to meet the requirements of due process in all other respects, and we reject respondent's arguments to the contrary. The Policy provides for notice, the right to be present at an adversary hearing, and the right to present and cross-examine witnesses. See *Vitek*. The procedural protections are not vitiated by meetings between the committee members and staff before the hearing. Absent evidence of resulting bias, or evidence that the actual decision is made before the hearing, allowing respondent to contest the staff's position at the hearing satisfies the requirement that the opportunity to be heard "must be granted at a meaningful time and in a meaningful manner." We reject also respondent's contention that the hearing must be conducted in accordance with the rules of evidence or that a "clear, cogent, and convincing" standard of proof is necessary. This standard is neither required nor helpful when medical personnel are making the judgment required by the regulations here. See *Vitek*. Finally, we note that under state law an inmate may obtain judicial review of the hearing committee's decision by way of a personal restraint petition or petition for an extraordinary writ, and that the trial court found that the record compiled under the Policy was adequate to allow such review.

Respondent contends that the Policy is nonetheless deficient because it does not allow him to be represented by counsel. We disagree. "[I]t is less than crystal clear why lawyers must be available to identify possible errors in medical judgment." Given the nature of the decision to be made, we conclude that the provision of an independent lay advisor who understands the psychiatric issues involved is sufficient protection. See *Vitek* (Powell, J., concurring).

V

In sum, we hold that the regulation before us is permissible under the Constitution. It is an accommodation between an inmate's liberty interest in avoiding the forced administration of antipsychotic drugs and the State's interests in providing appropriate medical treatment to reduce the danger that an inmate suffering from a serious mental disorder represents to himself or others. The Due Process Clause does require certain essential procedural protections, all of which are provided by the regulation before us. The judgment of the Washington Supreme Court is reversed and the case remanded for further proceedings.

It is so ordered.

various institutions review patients' decisions to refuse antipsychotic medications and noting "the infrequency with which refusals are allowed, regardless of the system or the decisionmaker").

JUSTICE STEVENS, with whom JUSTICE BRENNAN and JUSTICE MARSHALL join, concurring in part and dissenting in part.

* * *

I

The Court acknowledges that under the Fourteenth Amendment "respondent possesses a significant liberty interest in avoiding the unwanted administration of antipsychotic drugs," but then virtually ignores the several dimensions of that liberty. They are both physical and intellectual. Every violation of a person's bodily integrity is an invasion of his or her liberty. The invasion is particularly intrusive if it creates a substantial risk of permanent injury and premature death. Moreover, any such action is degrading if it overrides a competent person's choice to reject a specific form of medical treatment. And when the purpose or effect of forced drugging is to alter the will and the mind of the subject, it constitutes a deprivation of liberty in the most literal and fundamental sense.

> "The makers of our Constitution undertook to secure conditions favorable to the pursuit of happiness. They recognized the significance of man's spiritual nature, of his feelings and of his intellect. They knew that only a part of the pain, pleasure and satisfactions of life are to be found in material things. They sought to protect Americans in their beliefs, their thoughts, their emotions and their sensations. They conferred, as against the Government, the right to be let alone—the most comprehensive of rights and the right most valued by civilized men." Olmstead v. United States, 277 U.S. 438, 478, 48 S.Ct. 564, 572, 72 L.Ed. 944 (1928) (Brandeis, J., dissenting).

The liberty of citizens to resist the administration of mind altering drugs arises from our Nation's most basic values.

The record of one of Walter Harper's involuntary medication hearings at the Special Offense Center (SOC) notes: "Inmate Harper stated he would rather die th[a]n take medication." That Harper would be so opposed to taking psychotropic drugs is not surprising: as the Court acknowledges, these drugs both "alter the chemical balance in a patient's brain" and can cause irreversible and fatal side effects.[5] The

---

5. The Court relies heavily on the brief filed by the American Psychiatric Association and the Washington State Psychiatric Association as Amici Curiae (Psychiatrists' Brief), to discount the severity of these drugs. However, medical findings discussed in other briefs support the conclusions of the Washington Supreme Court and challenge the reliability of the Psychiatrists' Brief. For example, the Brief for American Psychological Association as Amicus Curiae (Psychologists' Brief) points out that the observation of tardive dyskinesia has been increasing "at an alarming rate" since the 1950–1970 data relied on by the Psychiatrists' Brief, and that "the chance of suffering this potentially devastating disorder is greater than one in four." See also Brief for Coalition for the Fundamental Rights and Equality of Ex–Patients as Amicus Curiae 16–18 (court findings and recent literature on side effects); Brief for National Association of Protection and Advocacy Systems et al. Amici Curiae 7–16 (same). Psychiatrists also may not be entirely disinterested experts. The psychologists charge: "As a psychiatrist has written, '[l]itigation from patients suffering from

prolixin injections that Harper was receiving at the time of his statement exemplify the intrusiveness of psychotropic drugs on a person's body and mind. Prolixin acts "at all levels of the central nervous system as well as on multiple organ systems." It can induce catatonic-like states, alter electroencephalographic tracings, and cause swelling of the brain. Adverse reactions include drowsiness, excitement, restlessness, bizarre dreams, hypertension, nausea, vomiting, loss of appetite, salivation, dry mouth, perspiration, headache, constipation, blurred vision, impotency, eczema, jaundice, tremors, and muscle spasms. As with all psychotropic drugs, prolixin may cause tardive dyskinesia, an often irreversible syndrome of uncontrollable movements that can prevent a person from exercising basic functions such as driving an automobile, and neuroleptic malignant syndrome, which is 30% fatal for those who suffer from it. The risk of side effects increases over time.

The Washington Supreme Court properly equated the intrusiveness of this mind altering drug treatment with electroconvulsive therapy or psychosurgery. It agreed with the Supreme Judicial Court of Massachusetts' determination that the drugs have a " 'profound effect' " on a person's " 'thought processes' " and a " 'well-established likelihood of severe and irreversible adverse side effects,' " and that they therefore should be treated " 'in the same manner we would treat psychosurgery or electroconvulsive therapy.' " There is no doubt, as the State Supreme Court and other courts that have analyzed the issue have concluded, that a competent individual's right to refuse such medication is a fundamental liberty interest deserving the highest order of protection.

II

Arguably, any of three quite different state interests might be advanced to justify a deprivation of this liberty interest. The State might seek to compel Harper to submit to a mind altering drug treatment program as punishment for the crime he committed in 1976, as a "cure" for his mental illness, or as a mechanism to maintain order in the prison. The Court today recognizes Harper's liberty interest only as against the first justification.

Forced administration of antipsychotic medication may not be used as a form of punishment. This conclusion follows inexorably from our holding in *Vitek v. Jones* that the Constitution provides convicted felon the protection of due process against an involuntary transfer from the prison population to a mental hospital for psychiatric treatment.

* * *

The Court does not suggest that psychotropic drugs, any more than transfer for medical treatment, may be forced on prisoners as a necessary condition of their incarceration or as a disciplinary measure. Rather, it holds:

TD [tardive dyskinesia] is expected to explode within the next five years. Some psychiatrists and other physicians continue to minimize the seriousness of TD ... [despite] continual warnings.' "

"[G]iven the requirements of the prison environment, the Due Process Clause permits the State to treat a prison inmate who has a serious mental illness with antipsychotic drugs against his will, if the inmate is dangerous to himself or others and the treatment is in the inmate's medical interest. Policy 600.30 comports with these requirements; we therefore reject respondent's contention that its substantive standards are deficient under the Constitution."

Crucial to the Court's exposition of this substantive due process standard is the condition that these drugs "may be administered for no purpose other than treatment," and that "the treatment in question will be ordered only if it is in the prisoner's medical interests, given the legitimate needs of his institutional confinement." Thus, although the Court does not find, as Harper urges, an absolute liberty interest of a competent person to refuse psychotropic drugs, it does recognize that the substantive protections of the Due Process Clause limit the forced administration of psychotropic drugs to all but those inmates whose medical interests would be advanced by such treatment.

[W]hether or not the State's alleged interest in providing medically beneficial treatment to those in its custody who are mentally ill may alone override the refusal of psychotropic drugs by a presumptively competent person, a plain reading of Policy 600.30 reveals that it does not meet the substantive standard set forth by the Court. Even on the Court's terms, the Policy is constitutionally insufficient.

Policy 600.30 permits forced administration of psychotropic drugs on a mentally ill inmate based purely on the impact that his disorder has on the security of the prison environment. The provisions of the Policy make no reference to any expected benefit to the inmate's medical condition.... Although any application of Policy 600.30 requires a medical judgment as to a prisoner's mental condition and the cause of his behavior, the Policy does not require a determination that forced medication would advance his medical interest. Use of psychotropic drugs, the State readily admits, serves to ease the institutional and administrative burdens of maintaining prison security and provides a means of managing an unruly prison population and preventing property damage. By focusing on the risk that the inmate's mental condition poses to other people and property, the Policy allows the State to exercise either parens patriae authority or police authority to override a prisoner's liberty interest in refusing psychotropic drugs. Thus, most unfortunately, there is simply no basis for the Court's assertion that medication under the Policy must be to advance the prisoner's medical interest.

* * *

The State advances security concerns as a justification for forced medication in two distinct circumstances. A SOC Policy provision not at issue in this case permits 72 hours of involuntary medication on an emergency basis when "an inmate is suffering from a mental disorder and as a result of that disorder presents an imminent likelihood of serious harm to himself or others.'' In contrast to the imminent danger of injury that triggers the emergency medication provisions, a general risk of illness-induced injury or property damage—evidenced by no more than past behavior—allows long-term, involuntary medication of an inmate with psychotropic drugs under Policy 600.30. This ongoing interest in security and management is a penological concern of a constitutionally distinct magnitude from the necessity of responding to emergencies. It is difficult to imagine what, if any, limits would restrain such a general concern of prison administrators who believe that prison environments are, '' 'by definition,' ... made up of persons with 'a demonstrated proclivity for antisocial criminal, and often violent, conduct.' '' A rule that allows prison administrators to address potential security risks by forcing psychotropic drugs on mentally ill inmates for prolonged periods is unquestionably an "exaggerated response" to that concern.

[T]he record before us does not establish that a more narrowly drawn policy withdrawing psychotropics from only those inmates who actually refuse consent[15] and who do not pose an imminent threat of serious harm[16] would increase the marginal costs of SOC administration. Harper's own record reveals that administrative segregation and standard disciplinary sanctions were frequently imposed on him over and above forced medication and thus would add no new costs. Similarly,

15. There is no evidence that more than a small fraction of inmates would refuse drugs under a voluntary policy. Harper himself voluntarily took psychotropics for six years, and intermittently consented to them after 1982. See e.g., *Rogers v. Okin*, 478 F.Supp. 1342, 1369 (D.Mass.1979) (only 12 of 1,000 institutionalized patients refused psychotropic drugs for prolonged periods during the two years that judicial restraining order was in effect), modified, 634 F.2d 650 (C.A.1 1980), vacated and remanded, sub nom. *Mills v. Rogers*, 457 U.S. 291, 102 S.Ct. 2442, 73 L.Ed.2d 16 (1982). The efficacy of forced drugging is also marginal; involuntary patients have a poorer prognosis than cooperative patients. See Rogers & Webster, "Assessing Treatability in Mentally Disordered Offenders", 13 Law and Human Behavior 19, 20–21 (1989).

16. As the Court notes, properly used, these drugs are "one of the most effective means of treating and controlling" certain incurable mental illnesses, but they are not a panacea for long-term care of all patients.

"[T]he maintenance treatment literature ... shows that many patients (approximately 30%) relapse despite receiving neuroleptic medication, while neuroleptics can be withdrawn from other patients for many months and in some cases for years without relapse. Standard maintenance medication treatment strategies, though they are indis-

putably effective in group comparisons, may be quite inefficient in addressing the treatment requirements of the individual patient." Lieberman et al., "Reply to Ethics of Drug Discontinuation Studies in Schizophrenia," 46 Archives of General Psychiatry 387, 387 (1989) (footnotes omitted).

Indeed, the drugs appear to have produced at most minor "savings" in Harper's case. Dr. Petrich reported that "medications are not satisfactory in containing the worst excesses of his labile and irritable behavior. He is uncooperative when on medication." [A] therapy supervisor reported before Harper's involuntary medication began: "during the time in which he assaulted the nurse at Cabrini he was on neuroleptic medication yet there is indication that he was psychotic. However, during his stay at SOC he has been off of all neuroleptic medications and at times has shown some preoccupation and appearance of psychosis but has not become assaultive. His problems on medication, such as the paradoxical effect from the neuroleptic medications, may be precipitated by increased doses of neuroleptic medications and may cause an exacerbation of his psychosis. Though Mr. Harper is focused on psychosomatic problems from neuroleptic medications as per the side effects, the real problem may be that the psychosis is exacerbated by neuroleptic medications."

intramuscular injections of psychotropics, such as those frequently forced on Harper, entail no greater risk than administration of less dangerous drugs such as tranquilizers. Use of psychotropic drugs simply to suppress an inmate's potential violence, rather than to achieve therapeutic results, may also undermine the efficacy of other available treatment programs that would better address his illness.

[T]he flaw in Washington's Policy 600.30—and the basic error in the Court's opinion today—is the failure to divorce from each other the two justifications for forced medication [i.e., security and rehabilitation] and to consider the extent to which the Policy is reasonably related to either interest. The State, and arguably the Court, allows the SOC to blend the state interests in responding to emergencies and in convenient prison administration with the individual's interest in receiving beneficial medical treatment. The result is a muddled rationale that allows the "exaggerated response" of forced psychotropic medication on the basis of purely institutional concerns. So serving institutional convenience eviscerates the inmate's substantive liberty interest in the integrity of his body and mind.

III

The procedures of Policy 600.30 are also constitutionally deficient. Whether or not the State ever may order involuntary administration of psychotropic drugs to a mentally ill person who has been committed to its custody but has not been declared incompetent, it is at least clear that any decision approving such drugs must be made by an impartial professional concerned not with institutional interests, but only with the individual's best interests. The critical defect in Policy 600.30 is the failure to have the treatment decision made or reviewed by an impartial person or tribunal.[20]

* * *

The decisionmakers [under Policy 600.30] have two disqualifying conflicts of interest. First, the panel members must review the work of treating physicians who are their colleagues and who, in turn, regularly review their decisions. Such an in-house system pits the interests of an inmate who objects to forced medication against the judgment not only of his doctor, but often his doctor's colleagues.[22] Furthermore, the

---

20. It is not necessary to reach the question whether the decision to force psychotropic drugs on a competent person against his will must be approved by a judge, or by an administrative tribunal of professionals who are not members of the prison staff, in order to conclude that the mechanism of Policy 600.30 violates procedural due process. The choice is not between medical experts on the one hand and judges on the other; the choice is between decisionmakers who are biased and those who are not.

22. As regular SOC staff, 600.30 committee members are: "susceptible to implicit or explicit pressure for cooperation ('If you support my orders, I'll support yours'). It is instructive that month after month, year after year, this 'review' panel always voted for more medication—despite the scientific literature showing that periodic respites from drugs are advisable and that prolonged use of antipsychotic drugs is proper only when the medical need is clear and compelling." Psychologists' Brief 26–27 (footnote omitted).

Court's conclusion that "[n]one of the hearing committee members may be involved in the inmate's current treatment or diagnosis" overlooks the fact that Policy 600.30 allows a treating psychiatrist to participate in all but the initial seven-day medication approval. This revolving door operated in Harper's case. Dr. Petrich treated Harper through 1982 and recommended involuntary medication on October 27, 1982. Dr. Loeken, staff psychologist Giles, and Assistant Superintendent Stark authorized medication for seven days after a 600.30 hearing on November 23, 1982. Dr. Petrich then replaced Dr. Loeken on the committee, and with Giles and Stark approved long-term involuntary medication on December 8, 1982. Solely under this authority, Dr. Petrich prescribed more psychotropic medication for Harper on December 8, 1982 and throughout the following year.

Second, the panel members, as regular staff of the Center, must be concerned not only with the inmate's best medical interests, but also with the most convenient means of controlling the mentally disturbed inmate. The mere fact that a decision is made by a doctor does not make it "certain that professional judgment in fact was exercised." The structure of the SOC committee virtually insures that it will not be. While the initial inquiry into the mental bases for an inmate's behavior is medical, the ultimate medication decision under Policy 600.30 turns on an assessment of the risk that an inmate's condition imposes on the institution. The prescribing physician and each member of the review committee must therefore wear two hats. This hybrid function disables the independent exercise of each decisionmaker's professional judgment. The structure of the review committee further confuses the objective of the inquiry; two of the committee members are not trained or licensed to prescribe psychotropic drugs, and one has no medical expertise at all. The trump by institutional interests is dramatized by the fact that appeals of committee decisions under the Policy are made solely to the SOC Superintendent.

* * *

The institutional bias that is inherent in the identity of the decisionmakers is unchecked by other aspects of Policy 600.30. The committee need not consider whether less intrusive procedures would be effective, or even if the prescribed medication would be beneficial to the prisoner, before approving involuntary medication. Findings regarding the severity or the probability of potential side effects of drugs and dosages are not required. And, although the Policy does not prescribe a standard of proof necessary for any factual determination upon which a medication deci-

Rates of approval by different review bodies are of limited value, of course, because institutions will presumably adjust their medication practices over time to obtain approval under different standards or by different reviewing bodies. However, New Jersey's review of involuntary psychotropic medication in mental institutions is instructive. In 1980 external review by an "independent psychiatrist" who was not otherwise employed by the Department of Human Services resulted in discontinuation or reduction of 59% of dosages. After the Department moved to an internal peer review system, that percentage dropped to 2.5% of cases. Brief for New Jersey Department of Public Advocate as Amicus Curiae 38–54.

sion rests, the Court gratuitously advises that the "clear, cogent, and convincing" standard adopted by the State Supreme Court would be unnecessary.

Nor is the 600.30 hearing likely to raise these issues fairly and completely. An inmate recommended for involuntary medication is no more capable of " 'speaking effectively for himself' " on these "issues which are 'complex or otherwise difficult to develop or present' " than an inmate recommended for transfer to a mental hospital. *Vitek* (Powell, J., concurring in part). Although single doses of some psychotropic drugs are designed to be effective for a full month, the inmate may not refuse the very medication he is contesting until 24 hours before his hearing. Policy 600.30 also does not allow the inmate to be represented by counsel at hearings, but only to have present an advisor, who is appointed by the SOC. These advisors, of questionable loyalties and efficacy, cannot provide the "independent assistance" required for an inmate fairly to understand and participate in the hearing process.[30] In addition, although the Policy gives the inmate a "limitable right to present testimony through his own witnesses and to confront and cross-examine witnesses," in the next paragraph it takes that right away for reasons that "include, but are not limited to such things as irrelevance, lack of necessity, redundancy, possible reprisals, or other reasons relating to institutional interests of security, order, and rehabilitation." Finally, because Policy 600.30 provides a hearing only for the seven-day committee, and just a paper record for the long-term committee, the inmate has no opportunity at all to present his objections to the more crucial decision to medicate him on a long-term basis.

In sum, it is difficult to imagine how a committee convened under Policy 600.30 could conceivably discover, much less be persuaded to overrule, an erroneous or arbitrary decision to medicate or to maintain a specific dosage or type of drug. Institutional control infects the decision-makers and the entire procedure....

I continue to believe that "even the inmate retains an unalienable interest in liberty—at the very minimum the right to be treated with dignity—which the Constitution may never ignore." A competent individual's right to refuse psychotropic medication is an aspect of liberty requiring the highest order of protection under the Fourteenth Amendment. Accordingly, ... I respectfully dissent from the Court's opinion and judgment.

Questions and Comments

1. *The rationale for a right to refuse.* The majority opinion in *Harper* relies on the due process clause in holding that a prisoner has a "right" to

---

30. The prisoner is introduced to, and may consult with, his appointed advisor at the commencement of the hearing. Harper's advisor on November 23, 1982, a nurse practitioner from Washington State Reformatory, asked Harper three questions in the hearing. The other five advisors appointed for Harper never spoke in the hearings. All five were apparently staff at the SOC: SOC Psychiatric Social Worker Hyden (who sat for the SOC Assistant Superintendent on the next 180–day committee that reapproved Harper's medication), a prison chaplain, two registered nurses, and a correctional officer.

refuse unwanted antipsychotic drugs. Other possible bases for a right to refuse which have been advanced by various courts and commentators include: (1) the first amendment's protection of thought and expression; (2) the eighth amendment's prohibition against cruel and unusual punishment; (3) the equal protection clause's requirement that like classes be treated alike (here the comparable class is the non-mentally ill, who are protected by the informed consent doctrine); and (4) the "penumbral" right to privacy's protection of bodily integrity. See 2 Men.Dis.L.Rep. 43, 46 (1977) (discussing these and other bases for the right). Among the lower court decisions that have found a constitutional right to refuse medication, most have relied on the latter theory. See, e.g., *United States v. Charters*, 863 F.2d 302 (4th Cir.1988) (dealing with patients found incompetent to stand trial); *Rogers v. Okin*, 634 F.2d 650 (1st Cir.1980) (civilly committed patients); *Rennie v. Klein*, 653 F.2d 836 (3d Cir.1981) (civilly committed patients). Is the right to privacy approach significantly different from the Supreme Court's approach in *Harper*? Of the various approaches, which is the most persuasive? How would the choice of a particular constitutional basis affect the scope of the right?

2. *The substantive scope of the right.* Focusing solely on the scope of the right, rather than the procedures for implementing it, what are the implications of *Harper* for persons who are civilly committed? For those who are committed after acquittal by reason of insanity? If prison confinement is indistinguishable from commitment in this regard, does *any* involuntarily committed person have a federal constitutional right to refuse medication after *Harper*? See *Hightower by Dahler v. Olmstead*, 959 F.Supp. 1549 (N.D. Ga. 1996)(holding that the state's interest in cases involving refusal by civilly committed patients are "similar" to the interests of prisoners and upholding a policy allowing forcible medication when forgoing medication would be "unsafe to patient or others").

In *Riggins v. Nevada*, 504 U.S. 127, 112 S.Ct. 1810, 118 L.Ed.2d 479 (1992), the Supreme Court dealt with forcible medication of a person during his trial on capital charges. In the course of deciding to remand the case for further deliberations the Court stated:

> Nevada certainly would have satisfied due process if the prosecution had demonstrated and the District Court had found that treatment with antipsychotic medications was medically appropriate and, considering less intrusive alternatives, essential for the sake of Riggins' own safety or the safety of others. Similarly, the State might have been able to justify medically appropriate, involuntary treatment with the drug by establishing that it could not obtain an adjudication of Riggins' guilt or innocence by using less intrusive means.

Riggins is described in more detail in the materials concerning forcible medication of those found incompetent to stand trial (see pp. 1033–34). For present purposes, does the above language broaden the scope of the right to refuse medication announced in *Harper*, at least for populations other than convicted prisoners?

Some state court decisions focusing on the civil commitment context have arrived at standards that appear to establish a stronger right to refuse than the policy upheld in *Harper*. In *Rogers v. Commissioner*, 390 Mass. 489,

458 N.E.2d 308 (1983), the Supreme Judicial Court of Massachusetts developed standards under Massachusetts law that can be summarized as follows:

(1) Administration of antipsychotic medication over a competent patient's objection is permissible if the patient "poses an imminent threat of harm to himself or others, and ... if there is no less intrusive alternative to antipsychotic drugs." Id. at 321.

(2) Otherwise, forcible medication is permissible only if the patient is incompetent to made a treatment decision. A *doctor's* determination of incompetency will justify forcible medication only if the medication is necessary "to prevent the 'immediate, substantial, and irreversible deterioration of a serious mental illness,' in cases in which 'even the smallest of avoidable delays would be intolerable.'" Id. at 322.

(3) If medication is necessary beyond this emergency period, and in all other circumstances, incompetence must be determined by a judge, at a hearing with notice and a guardian ad litem appointed to assist the court in the treatment decision. Id. at 322–23.

(4) If the judge finds the patient incompetent, he or she must make a substituted judgment decision and approve a treatment plan. Either the judge or a court-appointed guardian must monitor the subsequent treatment process. Id. at 318.

Similar state court holdings came in *Rivers v. Katz*, 67 N.Y.2d 485, 495 N.E.2d 337, 504 N.Y.S.2d 74 (1986) and *Riese v. St. Mary's Hospital and Medical Center*, 209 Cal.App.3d 1303, 271 Cal.Rptr. 199 (1st Dist. 1988).

In contrast is *Rennie v. Klein*, 653 F.2d 836 (3d Cir.1981). There, as in *Rogers*, the Third Circuit permitted forcible medication of those who are imminently dangerous to self or others, and of those for whom "there is a significant possibility" of harm to self, provided medication is the least intrusive means of accomplishing the state's goals of treatment and security. But *Rennie* also denied a right to refuse to competent, nondangerous patients, if the medication "would probably improve the patient's condition within a significantly shorter time period" than alternative treatment plans. Id. at 852. Other courts have reduced the right even further, holding that the patient's competency "is properly treated as simply another factor in the ultimate medical decision to administer the medication involuntarily." *United States v. Charters*, 863 F.2d 302 (4th Cir.1988). See also *In re Commitment of G.M.*, 743 N.E.2d 1148, 1152–53 (Ind.Ct.App. 2001).

3. *Defining incompetency.* Under any of these formulations, dangerousness and incompetency diminish or eliminate the right to refuse medication. Dangerousness has already been explored fully in Chapter Eight. How should incompetency be defined in this context? Assume in the following hypotheticals that the person understands the risks and benefits of the medication in the abstract. Is the reason for refusing the medication a "competent" one?

    a. "I've had treatment for so many years and nothing has changed."

    b. "I don't really need the medication. Many people get better without it."

c.   "How could the medication help if nothing else in my life changes?"

d.   "It's in the hands of God. Who knows?"

e.   "The only thing that will work is if you just convince yourself that you are going to get better."

f.   "Those medications just make you feel worse."

g.   "I just think it won't help."

h.   "That medication is poison."

i.   "That medication will harm my baby" (the person is not pregnant).

j.   "Large dosages of that medication hurt my stomach, so I'm not taking small dosages."

k.   "I don't want the medication because you doctors are psychotic."

l.   "You doctors are practicing witchcraft."

m.   "I'm not mentally ill."

n.   "I'm not hearing voices; they're really there."

See Christopher Slobogin, " 'Appreciation' as a Measure of Competency: Some Thoughts about the MacArthur Group's Approach," 2 Psychol. Pub. Pol'y & L. 18, 25–27 (1996)(arguing that reasons a through g do not demonstrate incompetence under Saks' understanding-and-belief test); Grant Morris, "Judging Judgment: Assessing the Competence of Mental Patients to Refuse Treatment," 22 San Diego L. Rev. 343, 408–22 (1995)(describing cases in which reasons h through l were found to demonstrate incompetence).

Some research suggests that a large number of people with schizophrenia suffer from "anosognosia"—an organic condition associated with the right hemisphere of the brain that renders individuals unable to recognize their symptoms–and that such people are much less likely to comply with treatment recommendations. For instance, one study found that 63% of psychiatric patients with anosognosia were noncompliant with medications compared to a 24% noncompliance rate for patients who were aware of their illness. H. Rittmannsberger et al., "Medication Adherence among Psychotic Patients before Admission to Inpatient Treatment," 55 Psychiat. Serv. 174 (2004). For a review of other studies, see Jonathan P. Lacro et al., "Prevalence of and Risk Factors for Medication Nonadherence in Patients with Schizophrenia: A Comprehensive Review of Recent Literature," 63 J. Clin. Psychiat. 892 (2002). People with severe anosognosia are completely unaware that they are having delusions or hallucinations or that they are experiencing abnormal bodily movements, such as those associated with tardive dyskinesia, and are usually unconcerned about their situation. Should such people be considered incompetent to make treatment decisions? Or, as some have claimed, is the notion of anosognosia, which has yet to be correlated with a specific neurological deficit, simply a "Catch–22" for patients: either they admit they are mentally ill or they are labeled mentally ill because of their failure to admit it? Cf. Stephen Morse, "Steel Traps and

Unattainable Aspirations: A Comment on Kress," 24 Beh. Sci. & L. 599, 606 (2006) ("In many cases, I suggest, it will be difficult to distinguish lack of insight from disagreement with the doctor.").

4. *Substituted judgment and advanced directives.* A finding of incompetency does not mean treatment is automatic. As discussed in the previous section, surrogate decisionmaking can be based on a "best interest" or a "substituted judgment" test. To the extent courts have considered the matter in the medication context, they have usually adopted the best interest approach, which means in effect that the doctor's recommendation—imposition of medication—is followed. In contrast, *Rogers*, described in note 2, requires a "substitute judgment decision," which makes dispositive what the incompetent person would have wanted, regardless of its benefit. In *Cruzan v. Director, Missouri Dep't of Health*, 497 U.S. 261, 110 S.Ct. 2841, 111 L.Ed.2d 224 (1990), the Supreme Court appeared to subscribe to this approach, at least when the incompetent person is in a vegetative coma.

Does *Cruzan* require the substituted judgment test in all situations? Consider *In re Jeffers*, 239 Ill.App.3d 29, 179 Ill.Dec. 895, 606 N.E.2d 727 (1992), in which a patient argued that her forcible medication upon her guardian's consent was inappropriate under *Cruzan* because the trial court did not determine whether the guardian's decision "would reflect respondent's decision if she were competent." The appeals court refused to apply *Cruzan's* standard in this context (and opted for the best interest test instead) for three reasons: (1) "the incompetency of an incompetent person in a vegetative state does not lead him to pose a danger to himself or others while the incompetency of the mental health incompetent does," thus permitting the state to ignore what the patient would have wanted if competent; (2) "the choices involved in the present case hold far less drastic consequences than the choices of a guardian on behalf of a person in a vegetative state"; (3) "a person who suffers from mental incompetency might *never* have had the competency to make a reasoned decision regarding medication, as opposed to a person who lives in a vegetative coma."

If the incompetent person *has* previously been competent and, while in that state, clearly indicates a desire to avoid medication in the future, should that desire be honored? In other words, should we recognize the force of advanced directives (see pp. 958–60 in this context)? Professor Winick thinks we should, at least in *parens patriae* cases (when the person is dangerous to others, he believes the state's interest trumps the individual's desires). Bruce Winick, "Advanced Directive Instruments for Those with Mental Illness," 51 U. Miami L. Rev. 57 (1996). Winick argues that this approach is not only more respectful of autonomy, but it also has a beneficial therapeutic effect because "the ability to be self-determining—to plan for the future, to envision future contingencies and bring about those that are desired and avoid those that are undesired, to set goals and see them achieved—is an important aspect of mental health and self-esteem." Id. at 84.

Should we respect an advanced directive that explicitly prohibits medication "even if I become suicidal or homeless and jobless"? Should the answer to this question depend upon whether the person has been suicidal or homeless in the past? What if the advanced directive prohibits medication but circumstances change (e.g., a new drug with fewer side effects—see note 7—is developed)? What if the person's advanced directive *opts* for medication but then, as the person begins to decompensate but before he or she becomes completely incompetent, refusal occurs?

In the changed circumstances scenario, Winick suggests an analogy to the *cy pres* doctrine in probate law. That doctrine allows a court to modify a will provision that, in light of unanticipated circumstances, seems inconsistent with the testator's intentions (e.g., a bequest to the League of Nations will be changed to a bequest to the United Nations). Winick concludes, "[a]pplying a form of the *cy pres* doctrine, courts and administrative bodies can modify advance directive health-care instruments in a similar way." Id. at 91. In the change-of-mind scenario, Winick argues that a person of uncertain competency should be able to change an advanced directive only if the decision comports with medical advice; if, on the other hand, the person's refuses medication against medical advice, the advanced directive stands. Id. at 91–92. Compare this proposal to Roth et al.'s on pp. 932–33.

5. *Procedures.* What are the procedural implications of *Harper* for civilly committed patients? The majority relies heavily not only on *Vitek v. Jones*, which involved the due process rights of prisoners transferred to mental hospitals, but also on *Parham v. J.R.*, which involved the civil commitment of children. Given the liberty interests at stake in those cases, are the citations to either *Vitek* or *Parham* apposite in deciding upon the proper procedures for implementing the right to refuse in the civil commitment context?

Consider the following methods of implementing the right in non-emergency situations: (1) judicial determination and monitoring (see *Rogers*, described in note 2); (2) judicial appointment of a guardian who makes all treatment decisions (an option permitted by *Rogers* after the initial judicial intervention, see note 2); (3) review by professionals from outside the institution (required by the trial court in *Rennie v. Klein*, 462 F.Supp. 1131, 1147 (D.N.J.1978)); (4) review by professionals from the same institution (as permitted in *Harper*); (5) a judicial determination at the commitment hearing, with no further review (see Clifford Stromberg & Alan Stone, "A Model State Law on Civil Commitment of the Mentally Ill," 20 Harv.J.Legis. 265, 356–57 (1983)); (6) no review of the professional's decision (see e.g., *Dautremont v. Broadlawns Hosp.*, 827 F.2d 291 (8th Cir.1987)). In light of the realities described in *Harper*, which option do you prefer? If some type of hearing is appropriate, what standard of proof should apply? Should the patient be entitled to an advocate?

6. *Benefits and costs of the right to refuse.* Some research on the impact of the right to refuse litigation is reported in the following excerpt from Alexander Brooks, "The Right to Refuse Antipsychotic Medication: Law and Policy," 39 Rutgers L.Rev. 339, 367–374 (1987).

Benefits

* * *

Decreasing the amount of medication used was an objective of refusal litigation.... Studies show that there has been a substantial lowering of individual dosages in a number of hospitals....

Another aspect of "too much drugs" is "too many different drugs." The practice of polypharmacy, though widely disapproved, was widespread in pre-litigation years. Current data from Napa State indicate that polypharmacy has been virtually eliminated. In 1974 a mean of 2.3 drugs were used for a single patient in the first eight weeks of confinement, with a range up to five different drugs. In 1983 [after a consent decree required review of refusals by outside psychiatrists] the mean during the same period of time was only 1.1....

A third benefit would result from changing types of medications to see whether patients respond less dysphorically and with fewer side effects to a medication different from one originally prescribed. There is no hard data on this important change, so we can only speculate about it, but there is anecdotal data that this now occurs more frequently than before.

A fourth benefit would be reducing the incidence of inappropriate delegation by physicians to other staff prescribing medication. This was once a major problem.... In *Davis v. Hubbard,* the court found that, at Lima State Hospital in Ohio, PRN orders were being written that permitted attendants to decide when medication should be administered. These PRN orders often had no termination or review date. It was further reported that attendants could obtain medication from the pharmacy by submitting appropriate forms "without a physician's signature." In Ohio hospitals such PRN orders have been eliminated. Inappropriate delegations have been terminated.

A fifth benefit has been the encouragement of processes of negotiation and participation by patients in their own treatment programs, a process that is initiated when a patient refuses medication.... The process of negotiation is not only responsive to patient needs, but also encourages patient autonomy and enhances patient dignity. [Moreover], research has indicated that negative reaction to medication is a powerful predictor of noncompliance and poor outcome.

* * *

Patient Costs

What are the costs to the patient? One is delay in treatment. In states like Massachusetts, the procedure requires a judicial hearing to determine whether the patient is competent to refuse. Veliz and James show that there are long delays between the refusal, the petition to compel medication, and the hearing, on average four and one-half months, and ranging from two to seven months. But ... [i]t is not obvious that patients actually suffer from such delays, nor do Veliz and James present any data to that effect. Put otherwise, there is no evidence that the delays cause patients to "rot."

It has been argued that a significant cost to refusing patients would be longer stays in the hospital. Do refusers, in fact, spend more time in the hospital than consenters? Evidence suggests that refusers are discharged at approximately the same rate as consenters. Refusal seems not to prolong hospitalization.

Do refusers deteriorate, remain the same, or improve? . . . Hargreaves and associates studied forty-seven cases (out of 2,700 reviews) in which refusals were upheld. Deterioration occurred in twenty-five patients of whom twenty were remedicated. No adverse consequences were seen in eight patients. The outcome was "unclear" for the rest. There was thus no harm to the patient in approximately 50 percent of these refusals, and presumably little harm to the twenty who were remedicated.

Have a larger number of antisocial incidents occurred because refusing patients went untreated? Psychiatrists had predicted outbreaks of violence and disruption by non-medicated refusers. Have there been transfers to locked wards, self-injurious behaviors, property destruction, suicide attempts, verbal threats, assaults, AWOLs, escapes, or displays of non-cooperation? Were seclusion and restraint used more extensively? A Minnesota study shows no statistical difference in these areas between refusers and consenters.

Costs to Staff and State

* * *

It is to be expected that many staff members, though not all, would find refusals a burden. . . . Hargreaves and associates asked doctors and nurses for their views about refusal at Napa State. Eighty-five percent of the doctors thought the refusal consent decree made their work more difficult. Nurses were more negative than doctors, saying that the decree went "too far." Twenty-five percent of nurses thought that the consent decree was "absurd." Ninety percent of nurses said that the consent decree made their jobs more difficult. Many felt that the decree was a waste of money, that it impaired treatment quality and made their work more dangerous. . . . It is difficult to evaluate such reactions since they are subjective and unsupported by specific illustrations of ways in which work has been made "more difficult." Some increases in difficulty surely result from an increase in the complexity of the caring task in response to legitimate patient needs. But are there inappropriate burdens unrelated to providing care? . . . A crucial aspect of the problem is that there is a long history of neglect of public sector patients. Any legal requirement that strikes at this neglect increases a burden. It is not clear how this particular "cost" should be weighed as against the benefits described.

Finally, we reach a twofold cost to the state. The first is the cost of hearings, which requires paying outside reviewers, lawyers, and others. The second is the cost involved in diverting personnel from other functions to the job of preparing for and appearing at hearings.

Hargreaves and associates have calculated that salary costs for outside psychiatric reviewers, patient advocates, hospital support staff, departmental staff, and the like, came to over $300,000 in the first year of the consent decree at Napa State Hospital. A "hidden" cost included the diversion of clinicians from other duties to the preparation of paper work for reviews. Since there were 2,800 reviews, each single review cost approximately $100. Hargreaves estimates that at this rate it would cost approximately $1–$1.5 million per year for reviews in all five major mental hospitals in California.

* * *

[I]s the cost too high because relatively few patients refuse and even fewer refusals are upheld? . . . The first data available from the Boston State Hospital, involved in the *Rogers* case, showed an incidence of about 9 percent refusals for 1,400 patients. Later data shows a proportion of refusals in a variety of hospitals ranging from 2.4 and 5 percent to 15 percent.

The data on refusal overrides shows proportions ranging from 100 percent of overrides in a study of nine patients to only 67 percent of overrides in a study of 19 Minnesota patients. In other words, in Minnesota, one-third of refusals were upheld, a much larger proportion than anywhere else. It has been suggested that the greater deference in Minnesota to refusals is a result of the fact that only one member of the five-member Anoka Treatment Review Panel was a physician.

It has been argued that the significance to the patient of a right to refuse has been exaggerated and should be abandoned. It has also been argued that even such a small incidence as 5% refusals interferes with the treatment of more than 15,000 patients a year, assuming an annual commitment rate of 300,000.

What would happen if people with psychosis were not treated, but simply institutionalized? Consider this excerpt from Douglas Mossman, "Unbuckling the 'Chemical Straitjacket': The Legal Significance of Recent Advances in the Pharmacological Treatment of Psychosis," 39 San Diego L. Rev. 1033, 1063–64 (2002):

> Because appellate court decisions and other legal publications often emphasize the adverse effects of older antipsychotic drugs, it is worth pausing to consider what life for psychotic patients was like before the advent of chlorpromazine and other antipsychotic drugs. "Before the introduction of chlorpromazine in 1953, most individuals with schizophrenia were destined to spend their entire adult lives within large, often remote psychiatric hospitals." By 1955, U.S. state mental hospitals housed more than one-half million persons, many of whom suffered from psychotic disorders; patients often spent years and decades living in horrifying, wretched conditions. Writes Ann Braden Johnson:
>
> > If you have ever spent time with a floridly psychotic person who is expressing himself in behavior that was supposed to have been extinguished in childhood, you will never forget how terrifying it is to see someone so utterly out of control. But now imagine yourself in a huge, old building that is visibly falling apart, in charge of sixty to eighty adults, all acting like one-, two-, and three-year-olds in mid-tantrum—such were the patients that the state hospitals, alone and unaided, kept in their wards for over a hundred years [from the

mid–19th to the mid–20th centuries]. A doctor from that era described a women's ward at New York's Pilgrim State Hospital before the introduction of phenothiazines:

> [They were] so wild I couldn't keep them decent. They'd soil themselves, tear their clothes off, smash the windows, and gouge the plaster out of the walls. One of them would even rip radiators right off he wall. We'd sometimes have to surround them with mattresses in order to give them sedative injections, and these would help for a while, but then they'd get addicted to the sedative and we'd have to take them off it.

> [T]he new drugs made the wholesale removal of patients from hospitals imaginable and then possible, which in the end became one of the most effective selling points of the new medications.

7. *Uninstitutionalized persons' right to refuse.* The case law described above concerns the right of institutionalized persons to refuse medication. In contrast to the narrowed right accorded this population, the non-mentally ill individual, as noted at the beginning of this section, is normally entitled to the protections of the informed consent doctrine, which provides a relatively robust right to refuse. What is the scope of the right for the non-institutionalized person who is mentally ill?

In re Guardianship of Roe, 383 Mass. 415, 421 N.E.2d 40 (1981), involved the right of a 21 year-old ward to refuse medication after his release from the hospital. The Massachusetts Supreme Court held that the ward's guardian, his father, could not unilaterally make the treatment decision for the ward unless there was an "emergency." Otherwise, a court must make the treatment decision. Further the court could authorize forcible medication only if one of two circumstances were met:

> (1) where a judicial substituted judgment determination indicates that the incompetent individual would, if competent, accept antipsychotic drugs, or (2) where there exists a State interest of sufficient magnitude to override the individual's right to refuse. If the asserted State interest is the prevention of violent conduct by non-institutionalized mentally ill individuals, then, upon a showing equivalent to that necessary to commit an individual against his will, the State is entitled to force the individual to choose, by way of substituted judgment, either involuntary commitment or medication with antipsychotic drugs.

Id. at 61.

Three issues are raised by *Roe*. The first has to do with the role of the court vis-a-vis the role of the guardian. Do you agree with *Roe's* requirement that a court order be obtained prior to forcibly medicating a ward whose validly appointed guardian has consented to the treatment?[j] The second issue concerns the consequences of a refusal by an uninstitutionalized person. As indicated above, under *Roe*, if a dangerous person chooses hospitalization over medication, then the state must acquiesce in that choice. May the person continue to refuse medication once in the hospital? In a footnote, the *Roe* court stated: "We do not address the question of whether

---

j. The answer to this question may depend upon whether one views antipsychotic medication as an "extraordinary treatment" (see pp. 961–62).

and to what extent the State interest in *institutional* order and safety may be capable of overwhelming the right of an involuntarily committed individual to refuse medical treatment...." Id. at 61 n. 23 (emphasis in original).

Finally, *Roe* seems to hold that if a person does *not* meet the criteria for involuntary hospitalization, forcible medication is impermissible. Doesn't that position make impossible forcible medication in the outpatient setting when outpatient commitment is based on the predicted deterioration standard (see pp. 778–79). See generally, John Kip Cornwell & Raymond Deeney, "Exposing the Myths Surrounding Preventive Outpatient Commitment for Individuals with Chronic Mental Illness," 9 Psychol. Pub. Pol'y & L. 209, 224 (2003)("Were psychiatric medication to be administered forcibly in a state with a lower threshold for outpatient commitment [than for inpatient commitment], its constitutionality would be more open to question; however, because the [preventive commitment] standards typically require a documented history of violence or prior inpatient hospitalization to justify commitment, the practice would likely satisfy substantive due process.").

8. *New and better drugs.* As described in Chapter One, a number of new anti-psychotic medications, known as "atypicals," appear to be more effective and cause fewer side effects than the older neuroleptic drugs at issue in *Harper* and the others cases described above, at least for a sizeable number of people suffering from schizophrenia. How, if at all, should the advent of these new drugs change the right to refuse debate? Consider this excerpt from Douglas Mossman (a psychiatrist), in "Unbuckling the 'Chemical Straightjacket': The Legal Significance of Recent Advances in the Pharmacological Treatment of Psychosis," 39 San Diego L. Rev. 1033, 1048–49 (2002):

> For several reasons, it seems very unlikely that courts will undo the cautions and procedural protections embodied in litigation that addressed involuntary treatment with older, more noxious antipsychotic drugs. First, the newer drugs, though much more tolerable, still carry some risk of the neurological side effects that alarmed courts in the 1970s and 1980s. Second, the newer drugs appear to place patients at more risk than neuroleptics of developing troublesome metabolic conditions, including obesity, alterations in lipid metabolism, and diabetes mellitus. Though these conditions are not as uncomfortable as the acute neurological side effects induced by neuroleptics, they are sources of concern for doctors and patients and should receive courts' consideration as well. Third, when the new drugs serve their intended purpose, they lead to changes in the way patients think. Almost any reasonable observer would characterize quelling psychosis as a desirable outcome of medical treatment. Yet this means that novel antipsychotic drugs are indeed "mind altering," and their unwanted administration therefore should raise legally significant questions about intrusions into a person's privacy. Finally, current legal rules and procedures concerning involuntary drug therapy may, and probably should, be preserved because they serve a valuable ethical purpose beyond protecting patients from side effects. Even if legal barriers to automatic administration of unwanted medication were initially justified in consequentialist terms, these protections also serve the nonconsequentialist purpose of respecting the personhood of patients. This is especially true in those states that

require a judicial finding of incompetence before authorization of involuntary medication.

Though courts can be expected to preserve currently existing legal barriers against automatic treatment of drug refusing psychotic patients, [some recent] decisions may show us how future courts will evaluate and make decisions about involuntary administration of antipsychotic drugs. In these cases ... the flaws of antipsychotic medications are often noted, but so are their benefits. Gone are extensive judicial diatribes about horrible side effects that all but ignore the benefits of medication and the horror of being psychotic. In some cases, courts have even endorsed the values of antipsychotic therapy, and because such treatment can be delivered with less risk to a patient's nervous system, judges have seemed more willing to approve of its involuntary administration.

Professor Mossman notes the "changes" that can result from the new drugs. Assuming the people described in the following excerpt pose no danger to others but require medication of some type to provide for their basic necessities, consider whether they should be allowed to refuse the new drugs for the reasons suggested in their accounts.

We interviewed 15 long-term outpatients with schizophrenia or schizoaffective disorder who were living in the community and who had shown significant clinical improvement on these new compounds.... We found that, because of the extent and longevity of their psychotic symptoms, many awakened patients have experienced a process of psychological redefinition and have confronted developmental tasks that were dormant prior to their improvement.

One 32 year-old man who was diagnosed with schizoaffective disorder 15 years ago told us ... "My brain was preoccupied with discovering whether this is real or this is not real. What clozapine has done is break up this pattern of thought process. I had certain behaviors that I had adopted in dealing with being an inpatient. With clozapine it as ... sort of like waking up. In a lot of ways, the psychosis acted as my defense and was my way of relating to the world for so long. It was a relief initially not to be crazy. But it is also painful ... like being crazy kept me innocent in a way. Sometimes I can't bear the weight of my own grief."

... [A] young woman who repeatedly starts and stops her atypical antipsychotic treatment explains that the weight gain she experiences on clozapine is sufficiently unpleasant to her that she takes breaks from it. Her mental state is strikingly different on clozapine, and she is able to avoid using drugs when she takes it. "It seems I can only have a mind or a body," she reports.

... A 52 year-old man with paranoid schizophrenia, who had been hospitalized more than 20 times, had been living a profoundly isolated life while conventional antipsychotics poorly controlled his positive and negative symptoms. He lived marginally in his own apartment and refused offers of group living or day programs. Following a 14–month trial on olanzapine his grooming improved, as did his ability to describe his affective experiences, and he became romantically involved with a woman at a day treatment center. After living 20 years without an intimate relationship, he felt overwhelmed with the newfound stresses of this connection. He discussed the pressures of being in this relationship and twice switched back between his old medication and the newer medications.

Kenneth Duckworth, "Awakenings with the New Antipsychotics," Psychiatric Times, May, 1998. It is also worth noting that over the long-term people on most of the newer atypical medications are just as likely to discontinue the treatment as those on the older drugs. See Jeffrey A. Lieberman et al., "Effectiveness of Antipsychotic Drugs in Patients with Chronic Schizophrenia," 353 N.Eng. J. Med. 1209 (2005) (finding that a "majority of patients" in each medication group—consisting of three groups on atypicals and one group on an older agent—discontinued the drug within 6 months "owing to inefficacy or intolerable side effects or for other reasons," except for the group taking the atypical drug olanzapine, which discontinued at an average of a little over 9 months).

B. ELECTRO–CONVULSIVE THERAPY AND PSYCHOSURGERY

ADEN v. YOUNGER

Court of Appeal, Fourth District, Division 1, 1976.
57 Cal.App.3d 662, 129 Cal.Rptr. 535.

GERALD BROWN, PRESIDING JUSTICE.

Petitioners Jane Doe and Betty Roe are mentally ill. Doe has had electro-convulsive therapy (ECT) and may need further voluntary treatments. Roe wants a surgical "Multiple target procedure," or psychosurgery. . . .

* * *

The Attorney General, the Director of Health, and the Board of Medical Examiners are respondents.

The law involved in this petition is part of the Lanterman–Petris–Short Act (Welf. & Inst.Code §§ 5000–5404.1). The law changes conditions under which psychosurgery and shock treatment can be performed. The changes applicable to persons involuntarily detained and persons voluntarily admitted to state hospitals, private mental institutions, county psychiatric hospitals and certain mentally retarded persons, are:

Psychosurgery: (§§ 5325, 5326, 5326.3.)

Patients have the right to refuse psychosurgery and the professional person in charge of the facility may not deny them that right. If a patient refuses consent, it must be entered on the record.

If a patient wants psychosurgery, then the conditions for performing such surgery include:

(a) The patient must give written informed consent, dated, witnessed and entered in his record. The consent may be withdrawn at any time. An oral explanation by the doctor is necessary.

(b) The patient must have capacity to consent.

(c) An oral explanation must be given to a responsible relative, guardian or conservator.

(d) The reasons for surgery must be in the patient's treatment record, other treatments must be exhausted and surgery must be critically needed.

(e) Three appointed physicians (two board-certified psychiatrists or neurosurgeons), must examine the patient and unanimously agree with the treating physician's determinations and that the patient has capacity to consent. There must be a 72–hour wait after the patient's written consent before surgery.

Shock Treatment: (§ 5326.4.)

If the treating physician feels shock treatments are necessary, he must give an extensive oral explanation to the patient and his relative, guardian, or conservator.

Shock treatments shall be performed only after:

(a) The patient gives written informed consent.

(b) The patient has capacity to consent.

(c) A relative, guardian or conservator has been given a thorough oral explanation.

(d) "Adequate documentation" has been entered in the patient's record. All other treatments have been exhausted and the treatment is critically needed.

(e) There has been a review by three appointed physicians (two board-certified) who agree with the treating physician that the patient has capacity to consent.

If the patient does not have the capacity to consent, shock treatments can be given if conditions (c), (d) and (e) are met.

No shock treatments may be given if the patient is able to give informed consent and refuses.

* * *

The petitioners, and amici curiae in support of the petition for writ of mandate, rest their attack on the amended and added Welfare & Institutions Code sections on several asserted constitutional infirmities:

* * *

A. EQUAL PROTECTION

Petitioners' equal protection arguments [i.e., that they should be able to obtain psychosurgery or ECT treatment as easily as non-mental patients] are without merit.

* * *

Mental patients are distinct from other ill patients in two special circumstances. First, their competence to accede to treatment is more questionable than that of other patients. Mental patients' incompetence may not be presumed solely by their hospitalization (§ 5331), but it is common knowledge mentally-ill persons are more likely to lack the ability to understand the nature of a medical procedure and appreciate its risks. Second, their ability to voluntarily accept treatment is questionable. The impossibility of an involuntarily detained person voluntarily giving informed consent to these medical procedures is fully treated in *Kaimowitz v. Department of Mental Health for the State of Michigan.* "Voluntary" patients, newly included within the protection of the "Patients' Bill of Rights" (§ 5325) are susceptible to many of the pressures placed on involuntary patients. The Legislature's inclusion of these "voluntary" patients recognizes the fact the "voluntary" label is a creation of the Legislature, and often only means the patient did not formally protest hospitalization. These circumstances make the separate treatment of mental patients clearly rationally related to the objective of insuring their rights to refuse treatment. The special regulation of psychosurgery and ECT is also a reasonable classification because these procedures, associated with *mental* illness, present a great danger of violating the patient's rights.

B. VAGUENESS

[The court found that the provisions in both the psychosurgery and ECT statute requiring that the treatment be "critically needed" were unconstitutionally vague because they provided "no guide to the degree of need required".]

* * *

A patient with acute depression and suicidal tendencies would come within the standard if the form of treatment were essential to protect his life. But what of the patient who does not have self-destructive tendencies and is completely dysfunctional psychologically? Does an inability to remain employed or married qualify as a "critical" condition? Must there be a danger of deterioration, or is a stable condition of severe psychosis critical? If all other forms of appropriate therapies have been attempted, has a "critical" need for ECT or psychosurgery been established?

It seems probable the legislative intent was to require a compelling need for these forms of treatment beyond the mere existence of a behavioral or mental disorder. There seems to be a tacit assumption by the Legislature the cure is sometimes more harmful than the disease, and only the most dangerous and harmful conditions should be so treated. Some persons of "common intelligence" may agree an assessment of impending injury, absent prompt treatment, gives rise to a critical need. Others of like intelligence may demand considerably more, or somewhat less. We conclude on its face the "critically needed" criterion is impermissibly vague.

C. Due Process

The regulation of ECT and psychosurgery is a legitimate exercise of the state's inherent police power. The state has an interest in seeing that these procedures, like other medical procedures, are performed under circumstances insuring maximum safety for the patient. Arrayed against these legitimate state interests are equally valid considerations of rights of privacy, freedom of speech and thought, and the right to medical treatment.

[The court found that the first two rights—the right to privacy and the right to freedom of speech and thought—could be treated together as aspects of the right to "privacy of the mind" or "freedom of thought".]

* * *

Freedom of thought is intimately touched upon by any regulation of procedures affecting thought and feelings. In an effort to protect freedom of thought, the state has put procedural and substantive obstacles in the path of those who both need and desire certain forms of treatment, and in that way their freedom of thought remains impaired because they cannot get treatment. Psychosurgery and ECT are viewed, rightly or wrongly, as drastic, radical forms of treatment compared to psychotherapy or drug therapy, and indicative of more severe illness. Public exposure, or even disclosure to limited numbers of government representatives, may have a chilling effect on patients' efforts to undergo these treatments, thereby restricting their freedom of thought. Some patients will be denied treatment as a natural and intended result of this legislation. Although the reasons for such denials may be the patients' own best interests, such regulation must be justified by a compelling state interest.

* * *

[T]he state's interests, as expressed in the challenged law, may be summarized as the protection of the right to refuse treatment and the prevention of unnecessary administration of hazardous and intrusive treatments. The test of the constitutionality of these provisions will be whether each of them furthers a compelling state interest and is necessary to accomplish the purpose.

* * *

[A]n analysis of the review procedures involved in each form of treatment will be considered separately.

Consent to psychosurgery is regulated and applied differently to three groups of patients: incompetent, involuntary, and all others. The state's interest in protecting patients from unconsented-to and unnecessary administrations of psychosurgery clearly justifies a review procedure which insures the competence of the patient and the truly voluntary nature of his consent. The incompetent patient is incapable of consenting to such a procedure, and the state's interest in protecting him from such procedures fully justifies the attendant invasion of privacy. Although there are substantial problems of procedural due process involved, a review of a patient's competence by a review committee is constitutional where, as here, there is reason to suspect incompetence.

The involuntary patient presents the dilemma of either prohibiting the administration of psychosurgery to such patients (see *Kaimowitz v. Department of Mental Health for the State of Michigan, supra,* 2 Prison L.Rptr. 433), or providing for a substitute decision-making process. Because the voluntariness of such a patient's consent can never be adequately confirmed, the establishment of a review committee to make the treatment decision for the patient is justified by the state's compelling interest in preventing involuntary administration of psychosurgery.

The substantive review of proposed treatments for competent and voluntary patients is a different problem. Once the competency of the patient and voluntariness of the consent is confirmed, what interest of the state can justify the substitution of the review committee's decision for that of the patient and his physician?

The hazardous, experimental nature of psychosurgery is a legitimate reason for the state to regulate its use as a treatment of last resort. Requiring unanimity by the review committee insures each approved treatment is an appropriate use of an experimental procedure. The importance of assuring that consents to psychosurgery be voluntarily given by informed, competent mental patients, plus the need to regulate an experimental procedure, justify the Legislature's decision to remove these considerations from the sole discretion of the treating physician. There are sound reasons why the treating physician's assessment of his patient's competency and voluntariness may not always be objective, and he may not necessarily be the best or most objective judge of how appropriate an experimental procedure would be. Because the consequences to the patient of such a procedure are so serious, and the effects he may suffer are so intrusive and irreversible, tort damages are totally inadequate. The need for some form of restraint is a sufficiently compelling state interest to justify the attendant invasion of the patient's right to privacy. That right to privacy is not absolute and must give way to appropriate regulation.

The new regulatory scheme as it applies to "shock treatment" is almost identical to the regulatory system for psychosurgery. The review procedures of section 5326.3, as applied to involuntary or incompetent patients, function the same as those under section 5326.4, and the review is also constitutional. These procedures for involuntary patients provide for a substitute decision-making process because of the difficulty of acquiring a truly voluntary consent to such a procedure. In the case of incompetent patients, the substitute decision-making process permits the use of this form of treatment for patients who cannot consent for themselves. These applications of section 5326.4 are constitutional for the reasons previously discussed.

The thorny question in section 5326.4 concerns the application of the review system to voluntary competent patients. As already noted, the state has a compelling interest in assuring the competency and voluntariness of patients who undergo this form of treatment. To this end, the review system is compatible with due process. However, once the competency of a voluntary patient has been confirmed, and the truly voluntary nature of his consent is determined, the state has little excuse to invoke the substitute decision-making process. "Shock treatment," or more precisely ECT, is not an experimental procedure, nor are its hazards as serious as those of psychosurgery.... Where informed consent is adequately insured, there is no justification for infringing upon the patient's right to privacy in selecting and consenting to the treatment. The state has varied interests which are served by the regulation of ECT, but these interests are not served where the patient and his physician are the best judges of the patient's health, safety and welfare.

Therefore, insofar as section 5326.4 applies to competent and voluntary patients who have given competent, voluntary and informed consent, it is unconstitutional. Substantive review is proper for involuntary or incompetent patients because there is a need for a substitute decision-maker. Any possible need which exists for the voluntary and competent patient cannot prevail in the face of the serious infringement to the patient's right to privacy as guaranteed by *Roe v. Wade*, 410 U.S. 113, 93 S.Ct. 705, 35 L.Ed.2d 147.

* * *

Relying upon *Jacobson v. Massachusetts*, 197 U.S. 11, 25 S.Ct. 358, 49 L.Ed. 643, petitioners also assert a constitutional right to care for one's own health is unconstitutionally invaded by the new procedure. We reject the notion the case recognizes any such fundamental right. The court deciding *Jacobson* held the vaccination of citizens against smallpox is a valid exercise of the state's police power. Petitioners also unmeritoriously assert a constitutional right to medical treatment. Where this right is concerned, due process requires only that the state, once it has institutionalized a person for the purpose of treatment, provide reasonable treatment or release the person. In the present case, any denial of treatment is tantamount to a finding that that particular form of treatment is not reasonable. It is not a denial of any or all treatment.

Questions and Comments

1. *Consent to treatment. Aden* represents a case in which patients sought treatment rather than refused it. The extent to which persons with mental disability have a right to *some* type of therapy is addressed in subsequent chapters. Here the issue is not whether there is a general entitlement to psychiatric treatment but whether a person who wants a particular treatment (or at least does not refuse it) may be forced to undergo scrutiny and jump procedural hurdles that are not ordinarily required when treatment is sought.

Assume that a person (1) wants psychosurgery or ECT; (2) asserts he or she is competent to consent to such treatment; and (3) is considered competent by the treating physician. May the state require this person to show that the treatment is "critically needed" (as defined in *Aden*) and to convince a review board that he or she is competent before the treatment may occur? *Aden* holds that if the patient is "voluntary" and wants ECT, the answer to this question is no. But if the patient wants psychosurgery, or is an involuntary patient and wants ECT, the answer is yes. Is *Aden's* differentiation between ECT and psychosurgery, involuntary and voluntary patients defensible? How should persons who are not hospitalized and who want psychosurgery or ECT be handled? Do improvements in these two treatment modalities (see pp. 26–27; 32) change the calculus?

2. *Kaimowitz.* Another court has also stressed differences between hospitalized patients and other patients in determining the scope of the "right to consent" to intrusive psychiatric treatment. *Aden* relies on *Kaimowitz v. Department of Mental Health,* No. 73–19434–AW (Cir.Ct. of Wayne Cty., Mich., July 10, 1973), *abstracted* in 13 Crim.L.Rep. 2452 (1974), the best-known case addressing the implications of allowing institutionalized individuals to consent to psychosurgery. The case arose when one "John Doe," who was in a state hospital after being committed under Michigan's sex psychopath statute, signed an "informed consent" form and obtained signatures from his parents authorizing doctors to implant depth electrodes in him. The treatment was part of an experimental program designed to determine whether psychosurgery would reduce aggression. Attorney Kaimowitz became aware of the planned operation and petitioned the court for a restraining order. The court granted relief, concluding that, when the person who consents is involuntarily detained by the state, "the three basic elements of informed consent—competency, knowledge, and voluntariness—cannot be ascertained with a degree of reliability warranting resort to use of such an invasive procedure."

With respect to competency, the court found that

> [i]nstitutionalization tends to strip the individual of the support which permits him to maintain his sense of self-worth and the value of his own physical and mental integrity. An involuntarily confined mental patient clearly has diminished capacity for making a decision about irreversible experimental psychosurgery.

On the knowledge prong, the court held that, from the record developed in the case, "the facts surrounding experimental brain surgery are profoundly uncertain, and the lack of knowledge on the subject makes a knowledgeable consent to psychosurgery literally impossible." Finally, concerning the voluntariness issue, the court stated:

> Involuntarily confined mental patients live in an inherently coercive institutional environment. Indirect and subtle psychological coercion has profound effect upon the patient population. Involuntarily confined patients cannot reason as equals with the doctors and administrators over whether they should undergo psychosurgery. They are not able to

voluntarily give informed consent because of the inherent inequality in their position.[23]

What are the implications of the court's reasoning for involuntarily committed patients who consent to *other* types of treatment? For nonhospitalized persons who want to consent to psychosurgery? At the end of its opinion, the court stated: "When the state of medical knowledge develops to the extent that the type of psychosurgical intervention proposed here becomes an accepted neurosurgical procedure and is no longer experimental, it is possible, with appropriate review mechanisms, that involuntarily detained mental patients could consent to such an operation." Doesn't this language undercut the reasoning in the rest of the opinion?

3. *Ranking treatments.* Assuming the state may make it more difficult procedurally to consent to certain types of treatment, how does one decide which treatments to put in this category? This question is of course related to the previous discussion concerning when a guardian's or clinician's decision about treatment for a refusing or nonprotesting patient must be subject to further monitoring, judicial or otherwise. But the issues are not necessarily identical. In addition to reviewing the previous materials on the subject, consider Professor Michael Shapiro's attempt, in "Legislating the Control of Behavior Control: Autonomy and the Coercive Use of Organic Therapies," 47 S.Cal.L.Rev. 237, 256 n. 51 (1974), to identify factors relevant to determining when judicial or administrative oversight of a treatment decision might be most useful:

(1) the extent to which the effects of the therapy upon mentation are reversible;

(2) the extent to which the resulting psychic state is "foreign," "abnormal," or "unnatural" for the person in question, rather than simply a restoration of his prior psychic state (this is closely related to the "magnitude" or "intensity" of the change);

(3) the rapidity with which the effects occur;

(4) the scope of the change in the total "ecology" of the mind's functions;

(5) the extent to which one can resist acting in ways impelled by the psychic effects of the therapy; and

(6) the duration of the change.

23. It should be emphasized that once John Doe was released in this case and returned to the community he withdrew all consent to the performance of the proposed experiment. His withdrawal of consent under these circumstances should be compared with his response ... to questions placed to him [while he was] waiting the implantation of depth electrodes. The significant questions and answers are as follows:

"1. Would you seek psychosurgery if you were not confined to an institution?

A. Yes, if after testing this showed it would be of help.

2. Do you believe that psychosurgery is a way to obtain your release from the institution?

A. No, but it would be a step in obtaining my release. It is like any other therapy or program to help persons to function again.

3. Would you seek psychosurgery if there were other ways to obtain your release?

A. Yes. If psychosurgery were the only means of helping my physical problem after a period of testing."

Is this list comprehensive enough? Should the extent to which the treatment is considered "experimental" be added as a criterion?

It may also be useful at this point to revisit an issue alluded to at the beginning of this chapter. If a treatment is considered so extraordinary that special procedural precautions are mandated before a consenting person is permitted to undergo the treatment, should we, for the same reason, raise the level of competency required to make the decision (perhaps requiring "full appreciation" of the treatment and its consequences)? Should we also make it particularly easy to refuse the treatment (perhaps by honoring any indication of refusal, regardless of the person's mental capacity)? Conversely, if a treatment is not extraordinary, should we facilitate consent (perhaps by allowing it upon mere assent of the patient) and make refusal more difficult?

C. BEHAVIOR MODIFICATION TECHNIQUES

KNECHT v. GILLMAN

United States Court of Appeals, Eighth Circuit, 1973.
488 F.2d 1136.

ROSS, CIRCUIT JUDGE.

This is an action by Gary Knecht and Ronald Stevenson, both in the custody of the State of Iowa, against officials of that state, under 42 U.S.C. § 1983. Their complaint alleged that they had been subjected to injections of the drug apomorphine at the Iowa Security Medical Facility (ISMF) without their consent and that the use of said drug by the defendants constituted cruel and unusual punishment in violation of the eighth amendment. The trial court dismissed their complaint for injunctive relief. We reverse with directions to enjoin the defendants from further use of the drug except pursuant to specific guidelines hereinafter set forth.

* * * [T]he evidence contained in the report of the magistrate showed that apomorphine had been administered at ISMF for some time prior to the hearing as "aversive stimuli" in the treatment of inmates with behavior problems. The drug was administered by intra-muscular injection by a nurse after an inmate had violated the behavior protocol established for him by the staff. Dr. Loeffelholz testified that the drug could be injected for such pieces of behavior as not getting up, for giving cigarettes against orders, for talking, for swearing, or for lying. Other inmates or members of the staff would report on these violations of the protocol and the injection would be given by the nurse without the nurse or any doctor having personally observed the violation and without specific authorization of the doctor.

When it was determined to administer the drug, the inmate was taken to a room near the nurses' station which contained only a water closet and there given the injection. He was then exercised and within about fifteen minutes he began vomiting. The vomiting lasted from fifteen minutes to an hour. There is also a temporary cardiovascular effect which involves some change in blood pressure and "in the heart." This aversion type "therapy" is based on "Pavlovian conditioning."

The record is not clear as to whether or not the drug was always used with the initial consent of the inmate. It has apparently been administered in a few instances in the past without obtaining written consent of the inmate and once the consent is given, withdrawal thereof was not permitted. Apparently, at the time of trial apomorphine was not being used unless the inmate signed an initial consent, but there is no indication that the authorities now permit an inmate to withdraw his consent once it is given. Neither is there any indication in the record that the procedure has been changed to require the prior approval of a physician each time the drug is administered. Likewise there is no indication that there has been any change in the procedure which permits the administration of the drug upon reports of fellow inmates despite a recommendation by the magistrate that this practice should be avoided.

The testimony relating to the medical acceptability of this treatment is not conclusive. Dr. Steven Fox of the University of Iowa testified that behavior modification by aversive stimuli is a "highly questionable technique" and that only a 20% to 50% success is claimed. He stated that it is not being used elsewhere to his knowledge and that its use is really punishment worse than a controlled beating since the one administering the drug can't control it after it is administered.

On the other hand, Dr. Loeffelholz of the ISMF staff testified that there had been a 50% to 60% effect in modifying behavior by the use of apomorphine at ISMF. There is no evidence that the drug is used at any other inmate medical facility in any other state.

The Iowa Security Medical Facility is established by Section 223.1, Code of Iowa, 1973. It is an institution for persons displaying evidence of mental illness or psychological disorders and requiring diagnostic services and treatment in a security setting.

* * *

* * * [T]he purpose of confinement at ISMF is not penal in nature, but rather one of examination, diagnosis and treatment. Naturally, examination and diagnosis, by their very definition, do not encompass the administration of drugs. Thus, when that course of conduct is taken with respect to any particular patient, he is the recipient of treatment.

The use of apomorphine, then, can be justified only if it can be said to be treatment. Based upon the testimony adduced at the hearing and the findings made by the magistrate and adopted by the trial court, it is not possible to say that the use of apomorphine is a recognized and acceptable medical practice in institutions such as ISMF. Neither can we say, however, that its use on inmates who knowingly and intelligently consent to the treatment, should be prohibited on a medical or a legal basis. The authorities who testified at the evidentiary hearing indicate that some form of consent is now obtained prior to this treatment. The only question then is whether, under the eighth amendment, its use should be prohibited absent such consent; and if so what procedure must be followed to prevent abuses in the treatment procedures and to make certain the consent is knowingly and intelligently made.

At the outset we note that the mere characterization of an act as "treatment" does not insulate it from eighth amendment scrutiny.

* * *

Here we have a situation in which an inmate may be subjected to a morphine base drug which induces vomiting for an extended period of time. Whether it is called "aversive stimuli" or punishment, the act of forcing someone to vomit for a fifteen minute period for committing some minor breach of the rules can only be regarded as cruel and unusual unless the treatment is being administered to a patient who knowingly and intelligently has consented to it. To hold otherwise would be to ignore what each of us has learned from sad experience—that vomiting (especially in the presence of others) is a painful and debilitating experience. The use of this unproven drug for this purpose on an involuntary basis, is, in our opinion, cruel and unusual punishment prohibited by the eighth amendment.

We turn then to the question of how best to prevent abuse in the treatment procedures of consenting participants and how to make certain that the consent is knowingly and intelligently given.

* * *

In this case the trial court should enjoin the use of apomorphine in the treatment of inmates at the ISMF except when the following conditions are complied with:

1. A written consent must be obtained from the inmate specifying the nature of the treatment, a written description of the purpose, risks and effects of treatment, and advising the inmate of his right to terminate the consent at any time. This consent must include a certification by a physician that the patient has read and understands all of the terms of the consent and that the inmate is mentally competent to understand fully all of the provisions thereof and give his consent thereto.

2. The consent may be revoked at any time after it is given and if an inmate orally expresses an intention to revoke it to any member of the staff, a revocation form shall be provided for his signature at once.

3. Each apomorphine injection shall be individually authorized by a doctor and be administered by a doctor, or by a nurse. It shall be authorized in each instance only upon information based on the personal observation of a member of the professional staff. Information from inmates or inmate aides of the observation of behavior in violation of an inmate's protocol shall not be sufficient to warrant such authorization.

The judgment of the district court is reversed with directions to grant the injunction under the terms hereinbefore set forth.

* * *

Questions and Comments

1. *The definition of punishment.* Although the regimen followed in *Knecht* may seem particularly prone to abuse, conceivably any psychiatric treatment—ranging from psychotherapy to psychosurgery—could be used as punishment, depending upon how that concept is defined. Eighth amendment cases hold that the prohibition against cruel and unusual punishment "must draw its meaning from the evolving standards of decency that mark the progress of a maturing society." *Trop v. Dulles*, 356 U.S. 86, 101, 78 S.Ct. 590, 598, 2 L.Ed.2d 630 (1958). Prisoners have successfully used the clause to obtain court censure of corporal punishment, inadequate medical care, solitary confinement, assaults by guards, and generally abysmal conditions. But in reaching these results, the courts have usually required demonstration of "barbarous" conditions that "shock the conscience." See Paul Friedman, "Legal Regulation of Applied Behavior Analysis in Mental Institutions and Prisons," 17 Ariz.L.Rev. 39, 61–62 (1975). The Supreme Court has also been called upon to define punishment in *due process* cases alleging that certain conditions imposed on pretrial detainees constitute punishment prior to a determination of guilt. In *Bell v. Wolfish*, 441 U.S. 520, 99 S.Ct. 1861, 60 L.Ed.2d 447 (1979), the Court stated:

> If a particular condition or restriction of pretrial detention is reasonably related to a legitimate governmental objective, it does not, without more, amount to "punishment." Conversely, if a restriction or condition is not reasonably related to a legitimate goal—if it is arbitrary or purpose-less—a court permissibly may infer that the purpose of the governmental action is punishment that may not constitutionally be inflicted upon detainees qua detainees.

The Court went on to permit a number of practices—such as limits on mail privileges, unannounced searches of detainees' living areas, and visual body cavity inspections—that it felt were related to legitimate security needs.

There are a number of other factors that might be relevant to determining whether a particular treatment is punishment. Consider this excerpt from Friedman, supra at 70–71 n. 159:

> . . . The intent of the person applying the procedure is certainly one factor [in determining whether the procedure is punishment], though probably not a sufficient factor. Physical offensiveness or deprivation of things desired would probably be a second criterion. Even a combination of an actual intent to punish and an offensive procedure, however, would not necessarily define the procedure as punishment. Consider, for example, a normal appendectomy performed in the case of acute appendicitis by a sadistic surgeon who actually intends to punish his patient. In this case, the law would probably deem the procedure treatment rather than punishment despite the painful impact of the procedures and the surgeon's punitive intent. Thus the recognized therapeutic nature of a procedure would be another criterion. On the other hand,

where a hazardous or intrusive procedure of recognized therapeutic value is utilized against a patient's will, it might be deemed punishment, despite its recognized therapeutic value, depending on the surgeon's punitive intent. Thus, the lack of consent of the patient to a procedure would be another criterion of punishment.

The upshot of this discussion is that for a procedure to be considered punishment for eighth amendment purposes, it must first be physically offensive or depriving of things desired and imposed with an intent to punish. In addition, it must be either without recognized therapeutic value or with recognized therapeutic value but imposed without the patient's consent. In this latter instance, the patient's consent would remove the procedure from the category of punishment, making it unnecessary to say that he has waived his protection against cruel and unusual punishment. In the former instance, consent would not be permitted for the same reason one would not be permitted to consent to mayhem; consent would not serve any legitimate interest of either the subject or society.

What procedures should be considered "physically offensive" or "depriving of things desired"? Should antipsychotic medication be included in the first category? Freedom to leave the hospital ward in the second? With respect to the therapeutic value of a procedure, could not any procedure be characterized as "therapeutic" in the abstract? For instance, in *Knecht* cannot one make a reasonable argument for the therapeutic value of apomorphine? Perhaps therapeutic value also should depend upon the type of symptom or event which is meant to be extinguished by use of the procedure? (Consider, for instance, the reasons clinicians gave for using apomorphine in *Knecht*.)

2. *The role of consent.* Finally, what role should the patient's consent play in deciding whether a procedure is punishment? In *Knecht* Dr. Fox testified that the use of apomorphine was "punishment worse than a controlled beating." Would an inmate's consent to a beating make it treatment? Do the considerations discussed in the materials on consent to psychosurgery apply to the *Knecht* facts as well?

3. *Operant conditioning.* Unlike the aversive conditioning at issue in *Knecht,* a number of "behavior modification" programs rely on positive reinforcement. Such operant conditioning procedures may rely upon "withholding approval" when unwanted behavior occurs. More frequently, at least in hospital settings, things such as private lockers or beds, visits with the ward psychiatrist, personal chairs, writing materials, movies, television programs, or grounds privileges are used as reinforcers. See David Wexler, Mental Health Law 215–16 (1981). Is it possible to characterize these "token economy" programs as punishment? If so, would the patient's informed consent convert the program into treatment?

Assuming consent of the patient is required before a token economy program may be instituted, should such consent be revocable, as *Knecht* holds? Can "behavior modification" techniques work if consent is revocable?

V. COMPETENCY IN THE CRIMINAL PROCESS

At several points in the criminal process, the law requires that the criminal accused be "competent." For instance, the Supreme Court has held that, under the fifth amendment, a person may not be subjected to custodial interrogation unless he or she understands and voluntarily waives the right to remain silent and the right to have an attorney present during interrogation. *Miranda v. Arizona,* 384 U.S. 436, 86 S.Ct. 1602, 16 L.Ed.2d 694 (1966). It has also held, under the due process clause, that a guilty plea is not valid unless the accused understands the nature and consequences of the plea and enters the plea voluntarily. *Boykin v. Alabama,* 395 U.S. 238, 89 S.Ct. 1709, 23 L.Ed.2d 274 (1969). Similarly, an accused may not undergo trial unless he or she understands the trial process and can communicate with the attorney. *Drope v. Missouri,* 420 U.S. 162, 95 S.Ct. 896, 43 L.Ed.2d 103 (1975). After conviction, most states require that the defendant be competent to participate in the sentencing proceeding, a rule the Court is likely to constitutionalize when given the opportunity to do so. Cf. *Green v. United States,* 365 U.S. 301, 304, 81 S.Ct. 653, 655, 5 L.Ed.2d 670 (1961) ("The most persuasive counsel may not be able to speak for a defendant [at sentencing] as the defendant might, with halting eloquence, speak for himself."). Finally, the Court has held that persons convicted of capital murder and sentenced to death may not be executed unless competent to understand what is happening to them. *Ford v. Wainwright,* 477 U.S. 399, 106 S.Ct. 2595, 91 L.Ed.2d 335 (1986).

Thus, a finding of incompetency could stall the criminal process at a number of different points. One can imagine a quite different system. Analogous to the plenary power given a guardian of the person, the lawyer for a criminal defendant found incompetent could be empowered to act and make decisions for the defendant. But, in contrast to most areas of the civil law, the criminal law has made incompetency an absolute bar to action under a wide variety of circumstances. The wisdom of this distinction should be considered throughout this section.

The first topic discussed is "competency to proceed" with a given proceeding, which includes competency to stand trial and competency to be sentenced. Then "decisional competency" is examined, in particular competency to plead guilty, waive counsel, waive the insanity defense, and waive rights associated with interrogation. As developed below, these competencies differ from the first type in that they require the defendant to make a particular decision. Finally, the chapter closes with materials concerning competency to be executed, which fits neither of the first two categories. Indeed, this last subject has only a minimal connection to the autonomy interests that underlie the competency notion.

A. COMPETENCY TO PROCEED

1. *Criteria*

GARY MELTON, JOHN PETRILA, NORMAN POYTHRESS AND CHRISTOPHER SLOBOGIN, PSYCHOLOGICAL EVALUATIONS FOR THE COURTS

(New York: Guilford Press) 126–127.
(3d ed. 2007).

(A) Historic Antecedents

The rule that an individual must be competent in order to undergo the criminal process originated in the common law and has been traced at least to the 17th century. In those days, as is true today, the defendant was required to plead to the charge prior to trial. Some commentators believe that the concept of competency first arose as a reaction by the English courts to defendants who, rather than making the required plea, stood mute. In such a case, the court would then seek to ascertain whether the defendant was "mute of malice" or "mute by visitation of God." If the individual fell into the first category, the court sought to force a plea by ordering increasingly heavier weights to be placed upon the individual's chest. If the individual fell into the latter category, he or she was spared this ordeal. The category "mute by visitation from God" initially included the literally deaf and mute, but over time was expanded to include the "lunatic."

Although the requirement that the defendant be competent may have developed as a practical response to a practical problem, it also seems to have its roots in a more general concern that subjecting certain types of individuals to trial was simply unfair. Thus, in the 18th century Blackstone observed that a defendant who "becomes mad ... ought not to be arraigned for it; because he is not able to plead ... with that advice and caution that he ought. And if, after he has pleaded, the prisoner becomes mad, he shall not be tried: for how can he make his defense?" This idea was also reflected in early English court decisions. For example, in *Frith's Case,* the court found that trial must be postponed until the defendant "by collecting together his intellects, and having them entire, he shall be able so to model his defense and to ward off the punishment of the law."

Early American courts, which relied heavily upon English common law, also recognized the incompetency plea. In 1835, for instance, the man who attempted to assassinate President Andrew Jackson was declared unfit to stand trial. In 1899, a federal court of appeals gave the doctrine constitutional status; the court held it to be "fundamental that an insane person can neither plead to an arraignment, be subjected to a trial, or, after trial, receive judgment, or, after judgment, undergo punishment; to the same effect are all the common-law authorities.... It is not 'due process of law' to subject an insane person to trial upon an indictment involving liberty or life." Since that time, the United States

Supreme Court has on several occasions stated that the right of an incompetent defendant to avoid trial is "fundamental to an adversary system of justice." [See, e.g., *Drope v. Missouri*, 420 U.S. 162, 172, 95 S.Ct. 896, 43 L.Ed.2d 103 (1975)].

These holdings have been based on the due process clause but are probably best thought of as attempts to implement the Sixth Amendment, which guarantees criminal defendants the rights to effective counsel, confront one's accusers, and present evidence. Exercise of these rights requires more than physical presence; defendants who are not present mentally cannot help their attorneys rebut the state's case or discover helpful evidence. Put another way, in an ideal world the criminal process should provide a trial between evenly matched adversaries. This process posits defendants able to participate in their own defense. Without the competency doctrine, the rights afforded by the Sixth Amendment would be empty for many individuals.

A second rationale for the competency requirement focuses not on the individual's rights but on society's interests. The defendant must be competent not only to ensure fair results but also to guarantee a dignified criminal process. As one commentator has observed, "The adversary form of the criminal proceeding necessarily rests on the assumption that defendant will be a conscious and intelligent participant; the trial of a defendant who cannot fulfill this expectation appears inappropriate and irrational". Even a proceeding that produces an accurate guilty verdict would be repugnant to our moral sense if the convicted individual were unaware of what was happening or why. [T]his latter rationale for the competency requirement is important, as it seems to underlie many of the substantive and procedural aspects of competency doctrine.

(B) THE COMPETENCY TEST

In *Dusky v. United States* [362 U.S. 402, 80 S.Ct. 788, 4 L.Ed.2d 824 (1960)], the United States Supreme Court set forth a definition of competency to stand trial that has since come to be the standard in federal court and most state jurisdictions. The Court stated that "the test must be whether he [the defendant] has sufficient present ability to consult with his attorney with a reasonable degree of rational understanding and a rational as well as factual understanding of proceedings against him." Although actually only a repetition of a test put forth by the Solicitor General in the case, this formulation is now viewed as having constitutional status, with the result that many state statutes and courts follow it verbatim and most others track its basic components.

These components are several in number. First, the Court's test delineates *two prongs* to the competency test: the defendant's capacity to understand the criminal process, including the role of the participants in that process, and the defendant's ability to function in that process, primarily through consulting with counsel in the preparation of a defense. Legal efforts to define competency further have consistently focused on these two prongs.

Second, *Dusky* makes clear competency focuses on the defendant's *present* ability to consult with counsel and to understand the proceedings. It therefore differs fundamentally from the test for criminal responsibility, which is a retrospective inquiry focusing on the defendant's state of mind at the time of the offense. It also differs from the predictive inquiry required for civil commitment although, as will be noted below, a degree of prediction may be necessary to determine competency in some instances.

Third, the test emphasizes the defendant's *capacity*, as opposed to willingness, to relate to counsel and understand the proceedings. The defendant who refuses to talk to the attorney even though capable of doing so is making a rational choice knowing the consequences. Unless the lack of motivation is based on irrational factors, thereby calling into question one's capacity to assist in one's defense, it is not ground for an incompetency finding. Similarly when a suspect's inability to state the precise charge or describe the role of the judge results from failure to be apprised of the relevant information rather than a cognitive deficiency, a finding of incompetency is unwarranted.

Fourth, the requirement that the defendant possess a *reasonable* degree of understanding suggests that the test as applied to a particular case is a flexible one. "Perfect" or complete understanding on the part of the defendant will not be required—in fact, most observers agree that the threshold for a finding of competency is not particularly high. At the same time, that threshold may vary according to context. With respect to the first prong of the competency test, for instance, a level of capacity sufficient to understand simple charges (e.g., driving without a license) may be grossly insufficient when a complicated offense is involved. Similarly, the defendant's capacity to communicate with counsel may depend as much on the attorney's personality and the facts of the case as one any aspect of the defendant's mental condition. Relevant in the latter regard, however, is the Supreme Court's decision in Morris v. Slappy [461 U.S. 1, 103 S.Ct. 1610, 75 L.Ed.2d 610 (1983)], which held that the Constitution does not guarantee a "meaningful relationship" between a defendant and his or her attorney (primarily because, according to the Court, such a guarantee is impossible). Although this decision was in the context of claims that counsel's assistance was ineffective, it suggests that the Court will not require a particularly high-quality attorney-client relationship in the competency context.

A fifth and final component of the *Dusky* standard is its emphasis on the presence or absence of "rational" and "factual" understanding, which suggests an emphasis on cognitive *functioning*. As many courts have held, the mere fact that a defendant has psychotic symptoms or has a particular IQ does not mean that the defendant is incompetent to stand trial. Neither mental illness nor the defendant's need for treatment is sufficient for an incompetency finding. The presence of mental illness is relevant only insofar as that illness affects one's "rational understanding" as one consults with counsel and undergoes criminal trial. At the same time, note that understanding must be factual and rational; factual understanding alone is not enough. A defendant who understands that a particular prison term is associated with his charges but believes for irrational reasons that he will never serve any time in prison may be incompetent. . . .

There have been a number of efforts by legislators, courts, and clinicians to add content to the rather sparsely worded standard enunciated by the Supreme Court. For example, the Florida Rules of Criminal Procedure provide that "the following factors and any others deemed relevant" should be assessed during a competency evaluation:

The defendant's capacity to:

1.   Appreciate the charges or allegations against him;

2.   Appreciate the range and nature of possible penalties, if applicable, which may be imposed in the proceedings against him;

3.   Understand the adversary nature of the legal process;

4.   Disclose to his attorney facts pertinent to the proceedings at issue;

5.   Manifest appropriate courtroom behavior;

6.   Testify relevantly.

These criteria operationalize both prongs of *Dusky*. The first three criteria relate to the defendant's ability to understand the legal process. Defendants who cannot grasp the charges or possible penalties, or who cannot understand that trial involves an attempt by the prosecutor to obtain a conviction from a jury or judge, are unlikely to be able to confront their accusers or have the motivation to defend themselves. The last three criteria concern defendants' ability to function in the process. The fourth criterion focuses on the ability to communicate facts about the alleged crime to the attorney, obviously an important aspect of confronting accusers and assuring a fair trial. . . . The fifth and sixth criteria relate to the defendant's ability to function in the courtroom.

Note further that the latter two criteria call for predictions as to how the defendant will fare in the courtroom. Competency to stand trial assessments focus primarily on present mental status. These factors are nonetheless important because a defendant who will disrupt and distract the factfinding process may prejudice the factfinder and make defense counsel's job difficult, and a defendant who is incapable of testifying, even though able to talk to the attorney in private, may be deprived of a fair trial.

Questions and Comments

1.   *Competency to proceed.* Competency to stand trial is not the only "competency to proceed" issue that might arise. For instance, cases have dealt with a defendant's capacity to understand and assist counsel with

sentencing and probation revocation proceedings. See, e.g., Saddler v. United States, 531 F.2d 83 (2d Cir.1976).

2. *The first prong: understanding*. Under any competency to proceed standard, the criminal defendant must have some understanding of the proceedings to which he or she will be subjected. Typically, as the above material suggests, it is thought the defendant should grasp the roles of the judge, prosecutor and defense attorney and the general nature of the adversary process. One issue that has arisen in this regard is the extent to which cynical, but perhaps plausible, views of the process suggest incompetency. For instance, one competency interview "protocol" gives a high score (meaning a score suggesting competency) to a statement that the judge is "fair," and a low score to a statement that the judge is "unjust," "too harsh," or "wrong." The same protocol gives low scores for the statement that a defendant's biggest concern with his lawyer is "tardiness" and for a statement that, in disagreeing with his attorney, the defendant might feel there is "no sense arguing." See description of the Competency Screening Test, in Ronald Roesch & Stephen Golding, Competency to Stand Trial 60–61 (1980). Are these ratings "fair"?

The defendant should also be able to understand the *specific* case against him or her. As the above material suggests, this is generally thought to include the charges or issues to be resolved, the consequences of an adverse decision, and the crucial arguments for and against the defense.

3. *The second prong: providing information*. Whether seen as a due process or effective assistance of counsel concern, a key reason underlying the competency to proceed requirement is the belief that defendants must be able to provide the defense attorney with an account of their side of the story. Thus, it is important that the defendant be able to recall and describe the time period surrounding the alleged offense.

Unfortunately, many defendants have or claim to have amnesia for this time period. Such amnesia could be "organic" (i.e., caused by a blow to the head suffered at the time of the offense, or by excessive ingestion of intoxicants prior to the offense), "psychogenic" (the result of a psychological defense mechanism such as "repression," which allows a person to "forget" a traumatic event), or an aspect of malingering. When, if ever, should amnesia require a finding of incompetency?

Most courts hold that amnesia per se is not a bar to a finding of competency. Probably the leading case in this area is *Wilson v. United States*, 391 F.2d 460 (D.C.Cir.1968). There the court held that a defendant who could not remember the time period of the armed robbery with which he was charged because he suffered a fractured skull during the car chase leading to his arrest was competent to stand trial because he understood the charges against him and could otherwise communicate with his attorney. However, the D.C. Circuit also cautioned that the trial court on remand should, before imposing sentence, evaluate the effects of the amnesia on the trial, including:

(1) The extent to which the amnesia affected the defendant's ability to consult with and assist his lawyer.

(2) The extent to which the amnesia affected the defendant's ability to testify in his own behalf.

(3) The extent to which the evidence in suit could be extrinsically reconstructed in view of the defendant's amnesia. Such evidence would include evidence relating to the crime itself as well as any reasonably possible alibi.

(4) The extent to which the Government assisted the defendant and his counsel in that reconstruction.

(5) The strength of the prosecution's case. Most important here will be whether the Government's case is such as to negate all reasonable hypothesis of innocence. If there is any substantial possibility that the accused could, but for his amnesia, establish an alibi or other defense, it should be presumed that he would have been able to do so.

(6) Any other facts and circumstances which would indicate whether or not the defendant had a fair trial.

The court then stated, "After finding all the facts relevant to the fairness of the trial, considering the amnesia, the court will then make a judgment whether, under applicable principles of due process, the conviction should stand.[4]"

Judge Fahy argued in dissent that the indictment against the defendant should have been dismissed:

Appellant by reason of physical brain injury has not simply been completely and permanently deprived of all knowledge of the robbery itself but of all knowledge of anything covering the entire period surrounding it. To try him for crimes which occurred during this period is thus to try him for something about which he is mentally absent altogether, and this for a cause not attributable to his voluntary conduct. The effect is very much as though he were tried in absentia notwithstanding his physical presence at the time of trial.

* * *

The remand proceedings required by the court cannot solve the problem presented by this case. Appellant will no more be able to assist his counsel, and his counsel will no more be able effectively to assist him, at the remand hearing than at the trial itself. The terms of the remand in substance required a hearing on the issue of prejudice. To try separately this issue would leave us where we are now, with the added difficulty

---

4. It would of course be desirable that defendants not only be competent to stand trial, but also have present awareness of their whereabouts and activities at the time of the crime of which they are accused. But courts have not considered such awareness as an essential ingredient of competence itself. As Judge Leventhal [in concurrence] points out, the man accused of committing a crime while drunk may have no recollection concerning the alleged events. And in the so-called "delayed arrest" narcotics cases, while the guilty man may remember his crime, the innocent accused may remember nothing at all about his activities at the critical time. Yet this court, while acknowledging that a delayed arrest may entail loss of memory, has never considered such lack of memory as going directly to competence to stand trial. Instead, it has required that where there has been substantial delay in arrest there can be a conviction only if the Government's case has strong corroboration. This approach . . . makes the probability of prejudice, not lack of memory per se, controlling.

that at the remand hearing it appears appellant would be required to testify whether or not he wished to do so, raising another Fifth Amendment problem. If the case is to turn on the issue of prejudice we should determine now that prejudice is inherent in the situation. . . .

Is the majority's approach fair? Wilson and another man (who died in the crash) were believed to have robbed a pharmacy of money and Desputal, as well as stolen a car; Wilson was found in the stolen car, as was some money, a gun and Desputal, and the pharmacy clerk positively identified him as one of the robbers. What possible defenses might Wilson have been able to raise based on memory of the time period surrounding the alleged offense? Are the intoxication and delayed arrest cases referred to by the majority good precedent? Under Judge Fahy's approach, would it matter whether the amnesia was organic, psychogenic or feigned? In terms of providing assistance to counsel, isn't the result the same, regardless of the reason for the amnesia?

What if instead of claiming amnesia, Wilson had described the offense as an attempt to deprive aliens of material needed to make a bomb to blow up the world (and he honestly believed his story)? Should that fact alone lead to a finding of incompetency?

Competency Problem I

Decide whether the individual interviewed below, whose psychological tests indicate an intelligence quotient of 52, is competent to proceed on a charge of attempted rape. The interview is transcribed verbatim to give the flavor of a typical competency examination.

Q: Hello. This is Dr. Smith and I'm Dr. Falkin. Are you Phil Jones?

A: Yeah.

Q: We would like to talk to you briefly about the criminal case against you. Do you know where you are?

A: Some hospital.

Q: Do you know the name of the hospital?

A: Uh-uh [meaning no].

Q: Do you know what time it is?

A: I really don't know. I can't tell time too good.

Q: Do you have a watch?

A: Uh-uh.

Q: You talked to someone here last week didn't you?

A: Yes sir.

Q: Do you remember the name of that person?

A: I think her name was Sally [real name was Shelley].

Q: Sally?

A: Yeah.

Q: Do you remember what she told you about what was going to happen today?

A: No.

Q: Do you have any idea what is happening today? What we're here for? Why we're asking you questions?

A: Uh-uh.

Q: Can you guess?

A: Something 'bout going to court.

Q: Can you go any further than that?

A: That's all I know.

Q: Did your lawyer talk to you about this at all?

A: Uh-uh.

Q: He didn't say anything about it?

A: He didn't say nothing.

Q: Okay. Can you tell me your attorney's name? Your lawyer's name?

A: I don't know his name neither.

Q: Do you get along with your attorney?

A: He don't care about the case.

Q: How do you know?

A: I just know.

Q: Can you talk to him?

A: He don't talk much.

Q: How many times have you seen him?

A: One time [this turns out to be true].

Q: Just one?

A: Uh-huh [meaning yes].

Q: Do you ever talk to him on the phone?

A: No.

Q: Do you know what he looks like?

A: He's tall and uh, uh, tall and skinny [this is accurate].

Q: The one time you saw him where did you see him?

A: Uh—the courthouse. And he's supposed to let me know when I'm supposed to go back to court, but I ain't heard nothing yet.

Q: Why were you at the courthouse?

A: Uh—something about, something about a girl.

Q: Did you see a judge there?

A: Yeah—the only thing he told me, to stay out of trouble and don't go over there where she's at and he told me to stay out of Greenbrier [the area where the alleged incident occurred].

Q: Did he say anything else?

A: That's all.

Q: You're sure?

A: Yeah, that's all he said.

Q: Did he say anything about why you were in court?

A: Yeah, uh, he asked me that and he said something like—uh you know it's a—uh bad charge against me.

Q: A what?

A: That it's a bad charge against me.

Q: What was it?

A: 'Tempted rape, that's all. The only thing I done—I didn't try to rape her or nothing like that—the only thing I done was pushed her down in the bushes and that's all I did. I don't 'member doing anything else.

Q: The police report says you waited for her and tried to take off her clothes. Is that right?

A: I don't know 'bout that.

Q: After you pushed her in the bushes what happened?

A: She said she was taking medicine, so I jumped on my bike and went to the Seven–Day Junior [a convenience store next to his brother's gas station].

Q: You don't remember anything else?

A: Nope. [The victim claimed that Jones had pushed her and tried to take off her belt. When she screamed, he got on his bike and left. She mentioned nothing about medicine.]

Q: Do you know what an insanity defense is?

A: No.

Q: An insanity defense is—your lawyer might tell the judge or the jury that you were having emotional or mental problems when you pushed the girl.

A: I didn't do nothing wrong.

Q: Would you let your lawyer argue that—the insanity defense?

A: All I done was pushed her in the bushes.

Q: So you are saying you would not be willing to plead guilty to your charges? You would not want to tell the judge that you did something bad?

A: I never done nothing bad.

Q: Let's assume that you had done something bad. Would you be willing to tell the judge that if you could get a good deal?

A: I never done nothing bad.

* * *

Q: What is it—what does the word attempt mean to you?

A: Umm—taking something that belongs to somebody else.

Q: Attempt means that?

A: Yeah.

Q: Do you know the difference between rape and attempted rape?

A: No.

Q: Will you try to think about it and tell me? The difference between rape and attempted rape?

A: (Long pause). That's all I know.

Q: Do you think you're going to go to court?

A: Huh?

Q: Is this, are you going to—are you going to have a trial?

A: Yeah, I hope so.

Q: You hope so. What happens in a trial in a courtroom?

A: I really don't know.

Q: What's your idea of what happens in a trial?

A: Sometimes they throw it out of court.

Q: Throw it out of court. Throw what out of court?

A: Uh, if you, if you, if ah, if ah, if you done it or didn't do it.

Q: And what happens if you throw it out of court—which way does it go?

A: (Pause). I don't know which way it goes.

Q: If you go to court will you see a prosecutor?

A: The prosecutor, yeah.

Q: What does he do?

A: He's . . . ah, I don't know.

Q: He brings the case against you for the state. He tries to convict you.

A: Yeah, he's wants to, uh, get me (laughs).

Q: What could he do to you if he got you?

A: Uh, he'd send me to the state farm [apparently referring to a mental hospital, where Mr. Jones had been briefly confined once before ten years earlier].

Q: The state farm?

A: Yeah, I'd have to stay at the state farm for a long time.

Q: What if the judge said you had to go to jail instead of the state farm?

A: Jail.

Q: Do you understand what a jail is?

A: It's got bars.

Q: If you had to choose between jail and the state farm, where would you like to go?

A: I don't know.

Q: Can you think about it and tell me?

A: Uh ... The people at the state farm make fun.

Q: They make fun of you?

A: Yeah.

* * *

Q: What temperature do you think it is outside?

A: (Pause). Four o'clock.

Q: No, temperature.

A: (Pause). I don't know.

Q: Do you know what temperature means?

A: No.

Q: How hot or cold do you think it is?

A: I don't know.

Q: Weren't you outside today?

A: Yeah. I never did get cold much.

Q: You were outside today, right?

A: Uh-huh.

Q: I thought it was pretty cold, I thought it was really cold, I thought it was almost freezing. It was like almost about to snow [in fact the day was quite warm].

A: Felt like it.

Q: Do you know the month and the day and the year?

A: I don't know the date.

Q: Do you have any idea what month it is?

A: Um ... no.

Q: What season of the year is it?

A: I don't know that either.

Q: You don't?

A: No.

Q: How about the year. Do you keep up with the years at all?

A: No.

Q: Okay, if I'd say it's either March or November or August, which month seems most right [it was November]?

A: August.

Q: Seems like August to you?

A: Yeah.

Q: What is August like? When we talk about the month of August what do you think about? Or what makes right now seem like August?

A: Cold weather.

Q: Cold weather?

A: Cold weather.

Q: Okay, what months make you think about warm weather? Can you name some months?

A: I don't know the months. I ain't gone through school.

Q: Do you know how many months there are in a year?

A: (Pause). Seven.

Q: Seven? Can you count to seven?

A: No.

Q: How far can you count?

A: Um, not too far.

* * *

Q: You say you got a divorce. What happens when you get a divorce and what is a divorce?

A: Just me and her just separated. She got her divorce and I got mine.

Q: If you found a stamped letter laying on the walk somewhere and you were walking along and it was just laying there like somebody just dropped it, what would you do with it?

A: Um, turn it into the postman.

Q: You'd turn it into the postman? Can you count money?

A: Um, not too good.

Q: If I gave you a ten dollar bill and asked for half of it back how much of it would you give me back?

A: (Pause). Five.

Q: Okay. Then you gave me the five dollars back and I said you can have half of that back, I'll give half of it back to you. Then how much would I be giving you back?

A: (Long pause). Four.

Q: Four? If your little girl would start crying what would you think would be wrong with her, what would be the—just crying—what would be some of the things that that could mean?

A: She be crying for something.

Q: Like what maybe?

A: Um, like uh, candy bar or something.

Q: Could there be other reasons?

A: Sometimes she cries and she gets a high fever and she gets sick sometimes.

Q: So she cries sometimes when she's sick? And any other things that you can think about that would make a little child that age cry?

A: Uh uh.

Q: A couple more questions and then we're going to stop I think. But I'm gonna list several things and you try to pick out the thing in the list of three or four things that I say that might be different. Okay? Orange, apple, a pear, baby rattle.

A: Um, baby rattle.

Q: Baby rattle. You picked that out because of what?

A: I don't know why I picked it out, it was a baby rattle.

Q: Okay, let's try it again. Hammer, saw, a square, and an ice cream cone.

A: (Pause). Ice cream cone.

Q: Okay, why did you say an ice cream cone?

A: You can eat an ice cream cone.

Mr. Jones chopped wood for a living. In order to make the competency to proceed decision, what additional information would you want?[1] If you think that the defendant is not at present competent to proceed, do you think he is "restorable" to competency? If so, should he be hospitalized for this purpose? Or can steps short of that be taken?

Competency Problem II

A 42 year-old male defendant is charged with stalking a famous movie actor. He tells the forensic examiner that he will plead "not guilty" as he was acting in "self defense". The defendant completely understands the nature of the criminal proceedings. Regarding his

---

1. When shown the videotape from which this interview was transcribed, approximately half of a group of state court judges stated they would have found the defendant competent to stand trial; the other half found him incompetent. Before his case was resolved, Mr. Jones died from exposure.

defensive strategy, he explains that the actor implanted microchips into his brain and was controlling his behavior through these microchips by administering painful electric shocks to him each time the defendant behaved in a way that the actor did not like. Apart from the alleged stalking, the defendant's behavior and speech was and remains normal.

Competency Problem III

A 23 year-old female defendant is charged with murdering her husband after learning that he was having an affair with her sister. Upon being arrested, she became belligerent with the sheriff, leading to her being "hog tied". Once in jail, she was "pepper sprayed" by the jail staff after she refused to comply with directions. The jail psychiatrist diagnoses the defendant with impulse control disorder not otherwise specified (NOS) and offers her medication, which she refuses. In court, she screams profanities at the judge, spits at the bailiff, and turns over the defense table. She is selectively mute with the forensic examiner but knows why she is in jail and argues: "the dirty bum deserved what he got."

The final two competency problems are taken from Grant H. Morris, Ansar M. Haroun & David Naimark, "Competency to Stand Trial on Trial," 4 Houston J. Health L. & Pol'y 193, 213 (2004). Of 196 psychiatrists and psychologists presented with Competency Problem II, 44.4% found the defendant competent to proceed and 55.6% found the defendant incompetent. Out of 185 psychiatrists and psychologists presented with Competency Problem III, 70.3% found the defendant competent and 29.7% found her incompetent. Id. at 214.

2. *Procedures for Assessing Competency to Proceed*

In *Pate v. Robinson*, 383 U.S. 375, 86 S.Ct. 836, 15 L.Ed.2d 815 (1966), the Supreme Court held that the due process clause requires the trial court to order an inquiry into competency to stand trial any time there is a "bona fide doubt" on the issue. The one case in which it has applied the standard was *Drope v. Missouri,* 420 U.S. 162, 95 S.Ct. 896, 43 L.Ed.2d 103 (1975), in which Drope was charged, along with two others, with the forcible rape of his wife. At the time of trial, Drope had been found competent, based largely on a report submitted by a psychiatrist. The report stated that the defendant had no "delusions, illusions, hallucinations," was "well-oriented in all spheres," and "was able, without trouble to answer questions testing judgement." The report also noted, however, that the defendant "had difficulty in participating well," "had a difficult time relating," and was "markedly circumstantial and irrelevant in his speech." Furthermore, the defendant's wife testified at trial that the defendant was sick, that he would roll down the stairs when he did not "get his way or [was] worried about something," and that he had choked her the Sunday evening before trial (an event which removed her initial reluctance about pursuing the prosecution). On the second day of trial, the defendant shot himself, apparently in a suicide attempt. The Missouri Court of Appeals found that neither the psychiatric report nor the suicide attempt created a reasonable doubt as to the defendant's competence. The Supreme Court reversed. While the Court noted that neither the report nor the defense attorney's motion for a continuance after the suicide attempt provided facts "bearing specifically on the issue of petitioner's competence to stand trial," it found that "the record reveals a failure to give proper weight to the information suggesting incompetence which came to light during trial." Thus, a competency evaluation should have been ordered on the second day of the trial. In the course of its opinion, the Court stated:

> [E]vidence of defendant's irrational behavior, his demeanor at trial, and any prior medical opinion on competence to stand trial are all relevant in determining whether further inquiry is required, but even one of these factors standing alone may, in some circumstances, be sufficient. There are, of course, no fixed or immutable signs which invariably indicate the need for further inquiry to determine fitness to proceed; the question is often a difficult one in which a wide range of manifestations and subtle nuances are implicated. That they are difficult to evaluate is suggested by the varying opinions trained psychiatrists can entertain on the same facts.

Id. at 180, 95 S.Ct. at 908.

In most jurisdictions, any party—the defense attorney, the prosecutor, or the trial judge sua sponte—may raise the competency issue. If the court finds that a bona fide doubt about competency exists, and if the incompetency appears related to mental disability (which is usually the case), the court orders one or more mental health professionals to perform an evaluation. For many years, this assessment was performed in a hospital, where the defendant was "evaluated" for several weeks or even months. Since the 1970's many states shortened the duration of hospital evaluations; many have also moved toward providing outpatient evaluations either in the jail or, if the defendant has obtained pretrial release, in a local clinic. Samuel Brakel et al., The Mentally Disabled and the Law 697 (1985).

Very often, the report that results from the evaluation is the only information available to the court. Twenty-four states explicitly allow the competency decision to be based solely on the expert's report, unless one of the parties disagrees with its conclusions. Id. at 703. In North Carolina, a survey of 55 North Carolina judges disclosed that 59% of them virtually never hold a formal hearing to assess evidence of the defendant's competency. Ronald Roesch & Stephen Golding, Competency to Stand Trial 193 (1980). If a hearing does take place, it is usually informal and perfunctory. In the survey noted above, 35% of the judges said they never disagreed with the clinical report and the remaining 65% stated that disagreement was rare. Id. See also, Patricia A. Zapf, "Have the Courts Abdicated Their Responsibility for Determination of Competency to Stand Trial to Clinicians?," 4 J. Forensic Psychol. Prac. 27, 34 (2004) (finding that courts agreed with the forensic evaluator's judgment in 327 out of 328 cases, or 99.7% of the time); James H. Reich & Linda

Tookey, "Disagreement Between Court and Psychiatrist on Competency to Stand Trial," 47 J. Clinical Psychiatry 29 (1987)(reporting disagreement in six out of 390 cases—1.7%); Henry Steadman, "Beating a Rap?: Defendants Found Incompetent to Stand Trial"54 (1979) (roughly 90% agreement between report and judicial decision). States vary as to which party bears the burden of proof, with the tendency being to put the burden on the party alleging incompetency. Most also adopt the preponderance of the evidence standard of proof. Wayne LaFave, Substantive Criminal Law 8.1(a)(2d ed. 2003).

If the defendant is found competent to stand proceed, then, of course, the proceedings resume. If the defendant is found incompetent, he or she is almost always required to undergo treatment for the purpose of restoring competency. This treatment usually takes place in a hospital, although again there has been some movement toward outpatient treatment. In *Jackson v. Indiana,* 406 U.S. 715, 92 S.Ct. 1845, 32 L.Ed.2d 435 (1972), the Supreme Court imposed limitations on the duration of treatment to restore competency:

> A person charged by a State with a criminal offense who is committed solely on account of his incapacity to proceed to trial cannot be held more than a reasonable period of time necessary to determine whether there is a substantial probability that he will attain the capacity in the foreseeable future. If it is determined that this is not the case, then the State must either institute the customary civil commitment proceedings that would be required to commit indefinitely another citizen or release the defendant.

Id. at 737–38, 92 S.Ct. at 1858. *Jackson* is discussed in more detail after the following notes on procedural issues.

Questions and Comments

1. *The bona fide doubt standard.* In *Drope* the Supreme Court listed three factors—evidence of defendant's irrational behavior, his demeanor at trial and any prior medical opinion on competence to stand trial—and then stated that "even one of these factors standing alone may, in some circumstances, be sufficient." Is this standard too low? In a review of ten studies of the competency evaluation process, Roesch and Golding found that the percentage of defendants referred for evaluation who were subsequently found incompetent varied from 1.2% to 77%, with the proportion of defendants found incompetent across the studies averaging 30%. Ronald Roesch & Stephen Golding, Competency to Stand Trial 47–49 (1980). Moreover, this latter figure probably overstates the number of defendants who were actually incompetent, since mental health professionals tend to err on the side of an incompetency finding, id. at 49, yet, as noted above, judges usually rubberstamp their conclusions. Thus, it is probable that a significant number of those referred for evaluation should not have been.

Why are there so many incompetency referrals? Consider the following possible abuses of the competency system, described in Melton, et al., supra, at 127–128: (1) referral for a competency examination when the real purpose is to obtain evaluations about criminal responsibility or disposition, the procedures for which are more cumbersome; (2) incompetency referrals "used as a ruse to force treatment of persons who do not meet dangerousness requirements for civil commitment and who may be acting bizarrely;" given the low threshold of the bona fide doubt standard, "a defendant [who] acts bizarrely or presents management problems in jail ... is most readily placed in the mental health system through such a referral than through a commitment petition requiring a full hearing with counsel," particularly since the court itself or the prosecution may raise the question; (3) finally,

> [C]ompetency referrals may be for purely strategic reasons unrelated to any concern with defendants' mental status. Perhaps foremost among these purposes is simply delay. In a case where the alleged offense has created public uproar, defense counsel may succeed in bringing about the defendant's removal from the community until public emotions have calmed by having him or her hospitalized for a competency evaluation. Similarly, if the evidence is weak but the public sentiment for prosecution is strong, prosecutors may have the defendant "put away" for a period through a competency evaluation. The result may be pretrial detention without the opportunity for bail.

In a survey of North Carolina judges, Roesch and Golding found that judges suspect abuses of the competency referral process, especially by defense attorneys who misunderstand the concept or who merely seek delay. Nonetheless, the majority of judges reported that they routinely grant motions for competency evaluations without requiring evidence that there is cause to raise the issue. Id. at 192.

2. *Community evaluations.* An indirect way to discourage abuse of the competency system is the development of a community evaluation system. If an order authorizing a competency evaluation results only in a brief evaluation either in jail or in the local clinic, attorneys who seek a competency evaluation to delay trial or remove the defendant from the community will have nothing to gain from an illegitimate referral. Roesch and Golding have demonstrated that a relatively brief interview in the community can arrive at results on the competency issue that are at least as reliable as those reached by hospital clinicians after prolonged observation of the defendant in the hospital. Roesch & Golding, supra at 188–191. Given this finding, one could argue that outpatient evaluations are required under least restrictive alternative analysis. The right to pretrial release and the right to speedy trial may also be infringed by prolonged pretrial hospitalization.[m]

In light of these considerations, should hospitalization for the purpose of evaluating the competency of an individual be prohibited? Alternatively, in addition to a showing that there is a bona fide doubt about competency, should there be a showing that the criteria for civil commitment are met? If the latter route is appropriate, and the defense attorney is the one who raises the competency issue, what role should he or she play at the commitment hearing, if any? Might a conflict of interest arise in this situation? At

m. Note, however, that the state may deny pretrial release for a legitimate "regulatory" reason, *United States v. Salerno,* 481 U.S. 739, 107 S.Ct. 2095, 95 L.Ed.2d 697 (1987), and that statutes which implement the speedy trial right usually exempt time spent performing a competency evaluation or undergoing treatment to restore competency from the time period relevant to determining whether the right is violated. See, e.g., 18 U.S.C. § 3161(h)(4).

the time of his evaluation, Jones, the subject of the Problem, was in jail in the community. Was there potential for the types of abuses described above in his case? If so, what can be done to prevent them?

3. *Parties who may raise the issue.* Another means of limiting abuse of the competency evaluation process is to prohibit the judge or the prosecution, or both, from raising the issue. See, e.g., Stuart Eizenstat, "Mental Competency to Stand Trial," 4 Harv.Civ.Rts. Civ.Lib.L.Rev. 379, 384–85 (1969). Is such a prohibition justifiable?

Given the possibly adverse consequences of a competency evaluation, should the *defense attorney* be barred from raising the issue if the client does not want it raised? The American Bar Association Criminal Justice Mental Health Standards require the defense attorney to move for an evaluation of competency whenever he or she "has a good faith doubt as to the defendant's competence," even over the client's objection. Standard 7–4.2. The commentary to the standard justifies this approach as follows:

> Because the trial of an incompetent defendant necessarily is invalid as a violation of due process, a defense lawyer's duty to maintain the integrity of judicial proceedings requires that the trial court be advised of the defendant's possible incompetence.[16] Ultimately, this requirement provides protections for criminal defendants. In addition, to permit defense counsel to proceed to trial with incompetent clients deprives defendants of their personal right to participate in and to control the thrust of their defense. It further assumes that defense attorneys properly determine the best interests of their clients. Criminal defendants, even though represented by trial counsel, have the exclusive right to make certain critical decisions, e.g., to waive or demand jury trial, to decide whether or not to testify in personal defense, and to decide the plea to be entered. Obviously, incompetent defendants cannot make these decisions and they may not be made by their attorneys.

> Standard 7–4.2(c) recommends a clear requirement that defense counsel raise the issue of a defendant's present mental incompetence whenever counsel has a good faith doubt about competence. It resolves the difficult conflict of concerns inherent in such circumstances ... in favor of counsel's obligation to the court. The conflict, if it exists, arises from a perceived pragmatic failure of the criminal justice system to live up to its promise, in that the deficiencies in the system of incompetence evaluation and treatment implicitly threaten excessive or inappropriate sanctions against defendants. The standard takes the position that, if such problems exist, the thrust should be to correct the problems, not to permit a pragmatic but philosophically unsound mechanism to avoid them. If elements of unfairness are eliminated from the system, defendants will have little reason to prefer a pragmatic avoidance of the competence issue in favor of trial on the merits.

Rodney Uphoff, in "The Role of the Criminal Defense Lawyer in Representing the Mentally Impaired Defendant: Zealous Advocate or Officer of the Court?", 1988 Wisc.L.Rev. 65, 89–96, criticizes the ABA approach:

---

16. See Model Rules of Professional Conduct 3.3(a)(1) ("A lawyer shall not knowingly ... make a false statement of material fact or law to a tribunal").

Although truth, and efficient, fair results are important systemic goals, the lawyer's role in the adversary system generally permits her to represent her client zealously even at the expense of these systemic goals. It is not enough to state in conclusory fashion that requiring defense counsel to assume an officer-of-the-court role serves these systemic goals. Rather, if defense counsel for a mentally impaired defendant is to play a different, lesser role than zealous advocate, it should be incumbent on those who wish to change counsel's role to provide the authority or to explain the policy warranting such a change.

The commentary to ABA Standard 7–4.2, however, offers little authority for its restricted view of defense counsel's role. It suggests that defense counsel's failure to disclose a doubt about her client's competency constitutes a false statement of material fact. Certainly counsel, as an officer of the court, has a duty to avoid perpetrating a fraud on the court. Yet, the ethics codes, acclaiming the virtues of the adversary system and the principle of zealous partisanship, generally permit a criminal defense lawyer to withhold information or even create a misleading impression. The controversy surrounding the lawyer's duty to divulge a client's perjury reflects the limited scope of the criminal defense lawyer's obligation to disclose a client's fraud and the importance of the value of confidentiality. While the Model Rules now require disclosure of a client's intention to commit perjury, it is a major leap to equate nondisclosure of defense counsel's doubts about a client's competence with fraud....

. . . A number of courts have held that a lawyer can be compelled to testify regarding counsel's opinion of a client's competency even though the lawyer's observations would involve privileged client communications, but the better reasoned position is that a lawyer's opinion about a client's competence or state of mind is inextricably mixed with the client's private communications. Accordingly, the lawyer should not be forced to raise competency and thereby disclose privileged matters unless that disclosure is consistent with the client's interests or wishes.

* * *

. . . If a lawyer does not adequately investigate the [competency] issue or fails to raise competency without a legitimate reason, that lawyer's representation should be deemed inadequate. Yet it is neither unduly burdensome nor difficult to scrutinize trial counsel's reasons for not acting.

Appellate review of the limited instances in which counsel decides for strategic reasons not to raise competency is less costly overall to the criminal justice system than obligating defense counsel to act whenever she has a reasonable doubt. If defense lawyers strictly adhere to this duty, they will be raising competency in many cases in which the client ultimately will be found competent. This will mean additional court hearings, unnecessary hospitalization, and increased costs for all of the major participants in the criminal justice system.

Moreover, even if counsel raises competency, the defendant still has a right to challenge the doctor's opinion. At this hearing, the defense lawyer, whose request triggered the evaluation in the first place, will be representing the defendant. The defendant may be understandably reluctant to trust defense counsel in view of counsel's previous actions. Furthermore, defense counsel's role at this hearing will be impossibly complicated. She cannot act as an advocate while at the same time offering testimony, based in part on confidential communications, that is adverse to her client.

* * *

. . . If the prosecutor or the trial court feels that the judicial process is being demeaned by proceeding against an incompetent defendant, either can raise competency. Similarly, either can raise the issue if defense counsel appears to be inadequately protecting a mentally ill client.

Which stance is more persuasive? If you were the attorney for Jones would you press for a competency evaluation if he insisted he did not want to go to the "state farm" (hospital) again?

4. *Hearing procedures.* A final method of discouraging abuse of the system is to formalize the competency determination process. If the parties know that the results of an evaluation (and thus its necessity) will be closely scrutinized by a court, they may be less willing to initiate the process in the first place. Independent of this practical concern is whether the constitution *requires* more formal proceedings than presently occur. In particular: (1) is the present tendency to allow the competency decision to be made by stipulation of the parties proper? (2) when a hearing does take place, is the preponderance of the evidence standard high enough and who should bear the burden of proof? In the Jones case, as the defense attorney would you rather have the burden of proving incompetency or would you rather have the prosecution bear the burden?

On the latter issue, the U.S. Supreme Court has handed down two decisions. In *Medina v. California*, 505 U.S. 437, 112 S.Ct. 2572, 120 L.Ed.2d 353 (1992), it upheld against a due process challenge a state statute which: (1) put the burden of proving incompetency on the party asserting it; and (2) established a presumption of competency. In *Cooper v. Oklahoma*, 517 U.S. 348, 116 S.Ct. 1373, 134 L.Ed.2d 498 (1996), it held unconstitutional a statute which placed the burden on the defendant to show incompetency by clear and convincing evidence (a standard of proof more onerous than the preponderance standard).

Medina is worth looking at in somewhat more detail. Medina, charged with capital murder, was found competent by a jury during a pretrial hearing; he was subsequently tried, convicted, and sentenced to death. After finding that there is "no historical basis for concluding that the allocation of the burden of proving competence to the defendant violates due process," Justice Kennedy's majority opinion turned "to consider whether [California's] rule transgresses any recognized principle of 'fundamental fairness' in operation."

Petitioner relies upon federal and state-court decisions which have said that the allocation of the burden of proof to the defendant in these circumstances is inconsistent with the rule of *Pate v. Robinson*, where we held that a defendant whose competence is in doubt cannot be deemed to have waived his right to a competency hearing. Because " 'it is contradictory to argue that a defendant may be incompetent, and yet knowingly or intelligently "waive" his right to have the court determine his capacity to stand trial,' " it has been said that it is also "contradictory to argue that a defendant who may be incompetent should be presumed to possess sufficient intelligence that he will be able to adduce evidence of his incompetency which might otherwise be within his grasp."

In our view, the question whether a defendant whose competence is in doubt may waive his right to a competency hearing is quite different from the question whether the burden of proof may be placed on the defendant once a hearing is held. The rule announced in *Pate* was driven by our concern that it is impossible to say whether a defendant whose competence is in doubt has made a knowing and intelligent waiver of his right to a competency hearing. Once a competency hearing is held, however, the defendant is entitled to the assistance of counsel, e.g., *Estelle v. Smith*, and psychiatric evidence is brought to bear on the question of the defendant's mental condition. Although an impaired defendant might be limited in his ability to assist counsel in demonstrating incompetence, the defendant's inability to assist counsel can, in and of itself, constitute probative evidence of incompetence, and defense counsel will often have the best-informed view of the defendant's ability to participate in his defense. While reasonable minds may differ as to the wisdom of placing the burden of proof on the defendant in these circumstances, we believe that a State may take such factors into account in making judgments as to the allocation of the burden of proof, and we see no basis for concluding that placing the burden on the defendant violates the principle approved in *Pate*.

In dissent, Justice Blackmun, joined by Justice Stevens, stated in part:

The Court suggests that "defense counsel will often have the best-informed view of the defendant's ability to participate in his defense." There are at least three good reasons, however, to doubt the Court's confidence. First, while the defendant is in custody, the State itself obviously has the most direct, unfettered access to him and is in the best position to observe his behavior. In the present case, Medina was held before trial in the Orange county jail system for more than a year and a half prior to his competency hearing. During the months immediately preceding the competency hearing, he was placed several times for extended periods in a padded cell for treatment and observation by prison psychiatric personnel. While Medina was in the padded cell, prison personnel observed his behavior every 15 minutes.

Second, a competency determination is primarily a medical and psychiatric determination. Competency determinations by and large turn on the testimony of psychiatric experts, not lawyers. "Although competency is a legal issue ultimately determined by the courts, recommendations by mental health professionals exert tremendous influence on judicial determinations, with rates of agreement typically exceeding 90%." Nicholson & Johnson, Prediction of Competency to Stand Trial:

Contribution of Demographics, Type of Offense, Clinical Characteristics, and Psycholegal Ability, 14 Int'l J. Law and Psych. 287, 287 (1991). While the testimony of psychiatric experts may be far from infallible, it is the experts and not the lawyers who are credited as the "best-informed," and most able to gauge a defendant's ability to understand and participate in the legal proceedings affecting him.

Third, even assuming that defense counsel has the "best-informed view" of the defendant's competency, the lawyer's view will likely have no outlet in, or effect on, the competency determination. Unlike the testimony of medical specialists or lay witnesses, the testimony of defense counsel is far more likely to be discounted by the factfinder as self-interested and biased. Defense counsel may also be discouraged in the first place from testifying for fear of abrogating an ethical responsibility or the attorney-client privilege. By way of example from the case at hand, it should come as little surprise that neither of Medina's two attorneys was among the dozens of persons testifying during the six days of competency proceedings in this case.

* * *

The allocation of the burden of proof reflects a societal judgment about how the risk of error should be distributed between litigants. This Court has said it well before: "The individual should not be asked to share equally with society the risk of error when the possible injury to the individual is significantly greater than any possible harm to the state." *Addington v. Texas.*

Professor Winick questions the majority's reasoning in *Medina*, but applauds its conclusion that the defendant be presumed competent. Recognizing that this rule might lead to trial of "marginally incompetent" defendants, he nonetheless defends it on three grounds: (1) it can reduce the "burdens and costs imposed by the incompetency doctrine" by helping to "minimize the inappropriate use of the incompetency doctrine for defendants who are not ... severely impaired;" (2) it will also speed the disposition of criminal charges for these defendants, who in minor cases might otherwise spend a longer time confined (in the hospital) than they would have had they been tried immediately and convicted; (3) it will have a therapeutic effect on the marginally competent, especially when the prosecution rather than the defendant alleges incompetence, because it will tend to avoid both stigmatizing them with the incompetency label and creating an incentive to resist treatment. Bruce Winick, Presumptions and Burdens of Proof in Determining Competency to Stand Trial: An Analysis of *Medina v. California* and the Supreme Court's New Due Process Methodology in Criminal Cases, 47 Miami L. Rev. 817, 849–58 (1993). Do any of these reasons apply in *Medina*?

Note that California is in a distinct minority in affording a jury trial on the competency issue to any defendant who requests one. Indeed, one court has held that a jury trial is not required in competency proceedings even when it is required in civil commitment proceedings, because the consequences of the former are "temporary" rather than "permanent." *State ex rel. Matalik v. Schubert*, 57 Wis.2d 315, 204 N.W.2d 13 (1973). Might the Supreme Court's opinion in *Medina* been influenced by a similar perception about the consequences of an incompetency finding? Consider the materials below.

3. *Disposition*

JACKSON v. INDIANA

Supreme Court of the United States, 1972.
406 U.S. 715, 92 S.Ct. 1845, 32 L.Ed.2d 435.

Mr. Justice Blackmun delivered the opinion of the Court.

We are here concerned with the constitutionality of certain aspects of Indiana's system for pretrial commitment of one accused of crime.

Petitioner, Theon Jackson, is a mentally defective deaf mute with a mental level of a pre-school child. He cannot read, write, or otherwise communicate except through limited sign language. In May 1968, at age 27, he was charged in the Criminal Court of Marion County, Indiana, with separate robberies of two women. The offenses were alleged to have occurred the preceding July. The first involved property (a purse and its contents) of the value of four dollars. The second concerned five dollars in money. The record sheds no light on these charges since, upon receipt of not-guilty pleas from Jackson, the trial court set in motion the Indiana procedures for determining his competency to stand trial. Ind. Ann.Stat. § 9–1706a (Supp.1971), now Ind.Code 35–5–3–2 (1971).

As the statute requires, the court appointed two psychiatrists to examine Jackson. A competency hearing was subsequently held at which petitioner was represented by counsel. The court received the examining doctors' joint written report and oral testimony from them and from a deaf-school interpreter through whom they had attempted to communicate with petitioner. The report concluded that Jackson's almost non-existent communication skill, together with his lack of hearing and his mental deficiency, left him unable to understand the nature of the charges against him or to participate in his defense. One doctor testified that it was extremely unlikely that petitioner could ever learn to read or write and questioned whether petitioner even had the ability to develop any proficiency in sign language. He believed that the interpreter had not been able to communicate with petitioner to any great extent and testified that petitioner's "prognosis appears rather dim." The other doctor testified that even if Jackson were not a deaf mute, he would be incompetent to stand trial, and doubted whether petitioner had sufficient intelligence ever to develop the necessary communication skills. The interpreter testified that Indiana had no facilities that could help someone as badly off as Jackson to learn minimal communication skills.

On this evidence, the trial court found that Jackson "lack[ed] comprehension sufficient to make his defense," § 9–1706a, and ordered him committed to the Indiana Department of Mental Health until such time as that Department should certify to the court that "the defendant is sane."

* * *

For the reasons set forth below, we conclude that, on the record before us, Indiana cannot constitutionally commit the petitioner for an indefinite period simply on account of his incompetency to stand trial on the charges filed against him. Accordingly, we reverse.

* * *

EQUAL PROTECTION

Because the evidence established little likelihood of improvement in petitioner's condition, he argues that commitment under § 9–1706a in his case amounted to a commitment for life. This deprived him of equal protection, he contends, because, absent the criminal charges pending against him, the State would have had to proceed under other statutes generally applicable to all other citizens: either the commitment procedures for feeble-minded persons, or those for mentally ill persons. He argues that under these other statutes (1) the decision whether to commit would have been made according to a different standard, (2) if commitment were warranted, applicable standards for release would have been more lenient, (3) . . . he could have been assigned to a special institution affording appropriate care, and (4) he would then have been entitled to certain privileges not now available to him.

In *Baxstrom v. Herold*, 383 U.S. 107, 86 S.Ct. 760, 15 L.Ed.2d 620 (1966), the Court held that a state prisoner civilly committed at the end of his prison sentence on the finding of a surrogate was denied equal protection when he was deprived of a jury trial that the State made generally available to all other persons civilly committed. Rejecting the State's argument that Baxstrom's conviction and sentence constituted adequate justification for the difference in procedures, the Court said that "there is no conceivable basis for distinguishing the commitment of a person who is nearing the end of a penal term from all other civil commitments." . . . The Court also held that Baxstrom was denied equal protection by commitment to an institution maintained by the state corrections department for "dangerously mentally ill" persons, without a judicial determination of his "dangerous propensities" afforded all others so committed.

If criminal conviction and imposition of sentence are insufficient to justify less procedural and substantive protection against indefinite commitment than that generally available to all others, the mere filing of criminal charges surely cannot suffice. . . .

* * *

Consequently, we hold that by subjecting Jackson to a more lenient commitment standard and to a more stringent standard of release than those generally applicable to all others not charged with offenses, and by thus condemning him in effect to permanent institutionalization without the showing required for commitment or the opportunity for release afforded by [the commitment statutes for those with mental illness and those with mental retardation], Indiana deprived petitioner of equal protection of the laws under the Fourteenth Amendment.

DUE PROCESS

For reasons closely related to those discussed in Part II above, we also hold that Indiana's indefinite commitment of a criminal defendant solely on account of his incompetency to stand trial does not square with the Fourteenth Amendment's guarantee of due process.

* * *

The States have traditionally exercised broad power to commit persons found to be mentally ill. The substantive limitations on the exercise of this power and the procedures for invoking it vary drastically among the States. The particular fashion in which the power is exercised—for instance, through various forms of civil commitment, defective delinquency laws, sexual psychopath laws, commitment of persons acquitted by reason of insanity—reflects different combinations of distinct bases for commitment sought to be vindicated. The bases that have been articulated include dangerousness to self, dangerousness to others, and the need for care or treatment or training. Considering the number of persons affected, it is perhaps remarkable that the substantive constitutional limitations on this power have not been more frequently litigated.

We need not address these broad questions here. It is clear that Jackson's commitment rests on proceedings that did not purport to bring into play, indeed did not even consider relevant, *any* of the articulated bases for exercise of Indiana's power of indefinite commitment. The state statutes contain at least two alternative methods for invoking this power. But Jackson was not afforded any "formal commitment proceedings addressed to [his] ability to function in society," or to society's interest in his restraint, or to the State's ability to aid him in attaining competency through custodial care or compulsory treatment, the ostensible purpose of the commitment. At the least, due process requires that the nature and duration of commitment bear some reasonable relation to the purpose for which the individual is committed.

We hold, consequently, that a person charged by a State with a criminal offense who is committed solely on account of his incapacity to proceed to trial cannot be held more than the reasonable period of time necessary to determine whether there is a substantial probability that he will attain that capacity in the foreseeable future. If it is determined that this is not the case, then the State must either institute the customary civil commitment proceeding that would be required to commit indefinitely any other citizen, or release the defendant. Furthermore, even if it is determined that the defendant probably soon will be able to stand trial, his continued commitment must be justified by progress toward that goal. In light of differing state facilities and procedures and a lack of evidence in this record, we do not think it appropriate for us to attempt to prescribe arbitrary time limits. We note, however, that petitioner Jackson has now been confined for three and one-half years on a record that sufficiently establishes the lack of a substantial probability that he will ever be able to participate fully in a trial.

* * *

IV

DISPOSITION OF THE CHARGES

Petitioner also urges that fundamental fairness requires that the charges against him now be dismissed. The thrust of his argument is that the record amply establishes his lack of criminal responsibility at the time the crimes are alleged to have been committed. . . .

Both courts and commentators have noted the desirability of permitting some proceedings to go forward despite the defendant's incompetency. For instance, § 4.06(3) of the Model Penal Code would permit an incompetent accused's attorney to contest any issue "susceptible of fair determination prior to trial and without the personal participation of the defendant." An alternative draft of § 4.06(4) of the Model Penal Code would also permit an evidentiary hearing at which certain defenses, not including lack of criminal responsibility, could be raised by defense counsel on the basis of which the court might quash the indictment. Some States have statutory provisions permitting pretrial motions to be made or even allowing the incompetent defendant a trial at which to establish his innocence, without permitting a conviction. We do not read this Court's previous decisions to preclude the States from allowing, at a minimum, an incompetent defendant to raise certain defenses such as insufficiency of the indictment, or make certain pretrial motions through counsel. Of course, if the Indiana courts conclude that Jackson was almost certainly not capable of criminal responsibility when the offenses were committed, dismissal of the charges might be warranted. But even if this is not the case, Jackson may have other good defenses that could sustain dismissal or acquittal and that might now be asserted. We do not know if Indiana would approve procedures such as those mentioned here, but these possibilities will be open on remand.

Reversed and remanded.

Questions and Comments

1. *Analyzing* Jackson. With respect to the equal protection basis for *Jackson,* is the Court correct when it concludes that those found incompetent to stand trial are similarly situated to civil committees or to prisoners who have served their sentences? Is the Court's finding in this regard consistent with its decision in *Jones v. United States,* reprinted at pp. 869–74, which held that those acquitted by reason of insanity are not similarly situated to civil committees? With respect to the due process basis of *Jackson,* would the Court's holding authorize hospitalization of an incompetent individual beyond the maximum sentence permitted for the alleged crime?

2. *State implementation of* Jackson. Reaction to *Jackson* has been diverse. As of 1993, four states require immediate civil commitment or

release. Eighteen states limit hospitalization of those found incompetent to stand trial to 18 months or less (with the most common period set at 6 months), at which time they must either be released or civilly committed. Ten states and the District of Columbia set the limit with reference to the maximum potential sentence for the crime charged. Most of these jurisdictions provide that the limit shall be the lesser of the length of the potential sentence (or some proportion thereof) and a given period of time (ranging from 15 months to 10 years). Most of the remaining states either explicitly place no limits on commitment of defendants found incompetent or rely upon the courts to rule in individual cases. See Grant H. Morris & J. Reid Meloy, "Out of Mind? Out of Sight: The Uncivil Commitment of Permanently Incompetent Criminal Defendants," 27 U. C. Davis L.Rev. 1, 77–78 (1993) (as of 1993, a majority of jurisdictions ignore or circumvent *Jackson*).

A separate but analogous concern is when the charge against an incompetent defendant must be dismissed. The Supreme Court in *Jackson* avoided deciding this issue. As a result, even if the state is required to release or civilly commit an incompetent person under *Jackson,* it is not required to dismiss the charge. Many states link dismissal with the end of the "*Jackson* treatment period," others do not provide for dismissal until after release from civil commitment, and several make no explicit provision for dismissal or dismiss "without prejudice" to the state's ability to recharge. Morris & Meloy, supra, at 22 n.106. For instance, Florida requires dismissal of charges against an incompetent defendant after 5 years, but the dismissal may be without prejudice. Fla.Stat. § 916.145.

3. *The clinical perspective.* How sensible are the various approaches adopted by the states in response to *Jackson?* According to Stone, in Mental Health and Law: A System in Transition 212–13 (1975), six months should be the outer limit for hospitalization of defendants found incompetent in most cases:

> Six months is a period much longer than that shown to be necessary to treat most civilly committed patients, particularly since the advent of drug therapy. It is my belief that after 6 months, the vast majority of the alleged incompetents will be in one of two categories: those who are competent to stand trial, and those who are suffering from mental disabilities, such as mental retardation, brain damage, or chronic deteriorated states such that restoration to competency, ever, is unlikely. The first group should be brought to trial, and charges against the second group should be dropped. A small residual category of persons not clearly in either group could, under carefully reviewed procedures, be confined for another 6 months and then disposed of as previously indicated. In the case of those charged with minor offenses, the time should be even shorter and the reviewing court should promptly consider alternatives to prolonged incarceration such as probation, outpatient care, or dismissal of the charges. Courts should, of course, be attentive to any tendency to subvert the previously discussed limits by periodic recommitments on dubious minor charges.

Relevant here is the ruling of several courts that a *mandatory* period of hospitalization, of up to six months, is permissible for *anyone* found incompetent to stand trial. See, e.g., *United States v. Ferro*, 321 F.3d 756 (8th Cir.

2003), cert. denied, 540 U.S. 878, 124 S.Ct. 296, 157 L.Ed.2d 142 (2003) (upholding an automatic four-month detention even when evaluators conclude there is no possibility of restoration, because that period allowed a more careful and accurate diagnosis and was limited in length, and because "the miracles of science suggest that few conditions are truly without the possibility of improvement.").

4. *Reform proposals. Jackson's* ruling that a person charged with a criminal offense who is not restorable to competency must either be released or civilly committed has been attacked from two directions. From the state's point of view, *Jackson* is problematic because it results in release (or relatively insecure civil confinement) of dangerous, mentally unstable individuals. From the defendant's perspective, *Jackson* as implemented results in prolonged confinement of those who have not been found guilty of any crime; indeed, as noted above, many states still permit periods of hospitalization ranging well beyond six months. These two strains of thought have coalesced into a suggestion that, after reasonable attempts at restoration have been made, defendants who remain incompetent should be tried.

The proposal that unrestorably incompetent defendants be tried comes in several forms: (1) At the end of trial but before a verdict is reached, the court determines—along the lines suggested by *Wilson* when dealing with amnesic defendants (see pp. 1009–10)—whether the defendant's participation was necessary and lacking. If so, no verdict is reached; if not, the factfinder reaches a verdict and it stands; (2) The defendant is tried through to verdict at an "innocent only" trial, which results in release of the defendant if there is acquittal, and a vacation of the verdict and a "*Jackson* disposition" if there is conviction. Donal Paull, "S.B. 133: The Near Resolution of a Major Problem: Fitness in the Criminal Law," 56 Chi–Kent L.Rev. 1107, 1118–19 (1980); (3) The defendant is tried through to verdict at a "super-fair" trial (at which a particularly high burden is placed on the prosecution and restrictions on discovery are loosened) whose verdict— whether acquittal or conviction—is final. See Robert Burt & Norval Morris, "A Proposal for the Abolition of the Incompetency Plea" 40 U.Chi.L.Rev. 66, 77 (1972). Combining various aspects of these proposals, the American Bar Association has recommended still another approach for handling those it calls the "permanently incompetent" (i.e., those who are still incompetent after 12 to 18 months of treatment). Under the ABA proposal, permanently incompetent individuals who are charged with minor crimes are released or civilly committed. Those charged with serious felonies are tried; however, if conviction results the defendant is *committed* under the procedures and criteria applicable to those found not guilty by reason of insanity. ABA Criminal Justice Mental Health Standards, Standard 7–4.13 (1989).

Which of these procedures, if any, is constitutional under current law? Does the last paragraph of *Jackson* sanction any of these approaches? Several commentators have argued that language in *Pate* to the effect that convicting an incompetent person violates due process is dictum, since that case (as well as *Drope*) focused on the procedural issue of when a hearing to determine competency must be held, rather than on the substantive issue of when if ever a person may be tried despite incompetency. See, e.g., Burt & Morris, supra at 75–76. Moreover, in *Drope* the Court stated that deferring the competency hearing until after trial "may have advantages." 420 U.S. at

182, 95 S.Ct. at 909. If all of these options are constitutional, are any preferable to *Jackson's* approach?

5. *Incompetent defendants' right to refuse.* As in the civil commitment context, the predominant treatment of those found incompetent is antipsychotic medication. At one time, a number of courts adhered to an "automatic bar" rule, prohibiting trial of those defendants who were restored to competency solely through medication. Bruce Winick, "Psychotropic Medication and Competence to Stand Trial," 3 Am.Bar Found. Research J. 769, 775 (1968). The automatic bar rule prohibited trial of medicated defendants whether or not they refused the medication. The result was a revolving door effect: defendants who were rendered competent through medication and sent back for trial were returned to the hospital untried because the trial judge ordered them taken off medication, thus allowing deterioration into incompetency. Id. at 773.

Partly because of this problem, by 1990 most jurisdictions permitted forcible medication of criminal defendants found incompetent to stand trial. See *United States v. Charters*, 863 F.2d 302 (4th Cir.1988). Three U.S. Supreme Court decisions, however, have changed the legal landscape in this area. In *Washington v. Harper*, 494 U.S. 210, 110 S.Ct. 1028, 108 L.Ed.2d 178 (1990), the Court upheld a prison treatment policy that permitted forcible medication for prisoners who were dangerous to self or others (see pp. 964–82). Although this decision did not change the lower courts' approach to medication in incompetency cases when the defendant was dangerous to self or others, it did lead to a more cautious attitude in some courts when the incompetent defendant was *not* dangerous but rather needed medication solely to restore him to competency. See Dora W. Klein, "Trial Rights and Psychotropic Drugs: The Case Against Administering Involuntary Medications to a Defendant During Trial," 55 Vanderbilt L. Rev. 165, 180–84 (2002).

The second case was *Riggins v. Nevada*, 504 U.S. 127, 112 S.Ct. 1810, 118 L.Ed.2d 479 (1992), in which the Supreme Court focused on the effect of *over*medication on a defendant's ability to assist at trial. During his trial on capital charges, Riggins had been involuntarily medicated with 800 milligrams of Mellaril a day, an extremely high dosage. Although he had previously agreed to take the drug, as trial approached he asked for permission to discontinue its use, arguing that it would infringe on his freedom, affect his demeanor and mental state during trial, and deny him the right to show the jury his true mental state when he offered his insanity defense. The trial court, after hearing testimony from four doctors (at least two of whom concluded that the defendant would remain competent if taken off Mellaril) denied Riggins permission to go off the medication, without stating a rationale. Riggins presented his insanity defense and testified, and was permitted to offer expert testimony describing his demeanor while unmedicated. He was convicted and sentenced to death.

Justice O'Connor, writing for the seven member majority, stated the Court was only deciding whether the medication prevented "a full and fair trial." She began by noting that, under *Washington v. Harper*, forcible medication "is impermissible absent a finding of overriding justification and a determination of medical appropriateness." Whereas in *Harper* the state had shown that medication was necessary to curtail dangerous behavior, the record in *Riggins* reflected no equivalent showing that "treatment with antipsychotic medication was medically appropriate and, considering less intrusive alternatives, essential for the sake of Riggins' own safety or the safety of others." Nor had it shown that it "could not obtain an adjudication of Riggins' guilt or innocence by using less intrusive means." Rather, the majority found, the record suggested that the medication may have diminished the fairness of the defendant's trial: "We ... are persuaded that allowing Riggins to present expert testimony about the effect of Mellaril on his demeanor did nothing to cure the possibility that the substance of his own testimony, his interaction with counsel, or his comprehension at trial were compromised by forced administration of Mellaril." Because the trial court had not developed the effect of the medicine in these respects, the Court remanded the case for a determination of whether Riggins suffered actual prejudice.

Justice Kennedy, in a concurring opinion not joined by any member of the Court, contended that "[i]f the State cannot render the defendant competent without involuntary medication, then it must resort to civil commitment, if appropriate;" prosecution of an involuntarily medicated defendant should be permitted only upon an "extraordinary showing." But the majority made clear that, at most, it was deciding that a competent person cannot be medicated to the extent it impairs the ability to assist counsel. The Court emphasized that "[t]he question whether a competent criminal defendant may refuse antipsychotic medication if cessation of medication would render him incompetent at trial is not before us." In the following case, it finally did confront that issue.

SELL v. UNITED STATES

Supreme Court of the United States, 2003.
539 U.S. 166, 123 S.Ct. 2174, 156 L.Ed.2d 197.

BREYER, J., delivered the opinion of the Court, in which RENHQUIST C.J., and STEVENS, KENNEDY, SOUTERS, and GINSBURG, JJ., joined.

The question presented is whether the Constitution permits the Government to administer antipsychotic drugs involuntarily to a mentally ill criminal defendant—in order to render that defendant competent to stand trial for serious, but nonviolent, crimes. We conclude that the Constitution allows the Government to administer those drugs, even against the defendant's will, in limited circumstances, i.e., upon satisfaction of conditions that we shall describe. Because the Court of Appeals did not find that the requisite circumstances existed in this case, we vacate its judgment.

I

A

Petitioner Charles Sell, once a practicing dentist, has a long and unfortunate history of mental illness. In September 1982, after telling doctors that the gold he used for fillings had been contaminated by communists, Sell was hospitalized, treated with antipsychotic medication, and subsequently discharged. In June 1984, Sell called the police to say that a leopard was outside his office boarding a bus, and he then asked the police to shoot him. Sell was again hospitalized and subsequently released. On various occasions, he complained that public officials, for example, a State Governor and a police chief, were trying to kill him. In April 1997, he told law enforcement personnel that he "spoke to God last night," and that "God told me every [Federal Bureau of Investigation] person I kill, a soul will be saved."

In May 1997, the Government charged Sell with submitting fictitious insurance claims for payment. A Federal Magistrate Judge (Magistrate), after ordering a psychiatric examination, found Sell "currently competent," but noted that Sell might experience "a psychotic episode" in the future. The judge released Sell on bail. A grand jury later produced a superseding indictment charging Sell and his wife with 56 counts of mail fraud, 6 counts of Medicaid fraud, and 1 count of money laundering.

In early 1998, the Government claimed that Sell had sought to intimidate a witness. The Magistrate held a bail revocation hearing. Sell's behavior at his initial appearance was, in the judge's words, " 'totally out of control,' " involving "screaming and shouting," the use of "personal insults" and "racial epithets," and spitting "in the judge's face." A psychiatrist reported that Sell could not sleep because he expected the FBI to " 'come busting through the door,' " and concluded that Sell's condition had worsened. After considering that report and other testimony, the Magistrate revoked Sell's bail.

In April 1998, the grand jury issued a new indictment charging Sell with attempting to murder the FBI agent who had arrested him and a former employee who planned to testify against him in the fraud case. The attempted murder and fraud cases were joined for trial.

In early 1999, Sell asked the Magistrate to reconsider his competence to stand trial. The Magistrate sent Sell to the United States Medical Center for Federal Prisoners at Springfield, Missouri, for examination. Subsequently the Magistrate found that Sell was "mentally incompetent to stand trial." He ordered Sell to "be hospitalized for treatment" at the Medical Center for up to four months, "to determine whether there was a substantial probability that [Sell] would attain the capacity to allow his trial to proceed."

Two months later, Medical Center staff recommended that Sell take antipsychotic medication. Sell refused to do so. The staff sought permission to administer the medication against Sell's will. That effort is the subject of the present proceedings.

B

We here review the last of five hierarchically ordered lower court and Medical Center determinations. First, in June 1999, Medical Center staff sought permission from institutional authorities to administer antipsychotic drugs to Sell involuntarily. A reviewing psychiatrist held a hearing and considered Sell's prior history; Sell's current persecutional beliefs (for example, that Government officials were trying to suppress his knowledge about events in Waco, Texas, and had sent him to Alaska to silence him); staff medical opinions (for example, that "Sell's symptoms point to a diagnosis of Delusional Disorder but ... there well may be an underlying Schizophrenic Process"); staff medical concerns (for example, about "the persistence of Dr. Sell's belief that the Courts, FBI, and federal government in general are against him"); an outside medical expert's opinion (that Sell suffered only from delusional disorder, which, in that expert's view, "medication rarely helps"); and Sell's own views, as well as those of other laypersons who know him (to the effect that he did not suffer from a serious mental illness).

The reviewing psychiatrist then authorized involuntary administration of the drugs, both (1) because Sell was "mentally ill and dangerous, and medication is necessary to treat the mental illness," and (2) so that Sell would "become competent for trial." The reviewing psychiatrist added that he considered Sell "dangerous based on threats and delusions if outside, but not necessarily in[side] prison" and that Sell was "[a]ble to function" in prison in the "open population."

Second, the Medical Center administratively reviewed the determination of its reviewing psychiatrist. A Bureau of Prisons official considered the evidence that had been presented at the initial hearing, referred to Sell's delusions, noted differences of professional opinion as to proper classification and treatment, and concluded that antipsychotic medication represents the medical intervention "most likely" to "ameliorate" Sell's symptoms; that other "less restrictive interventions" are "unlikely" to work; and that Sell's "pervasive belief" that he was "being targeted for nefarious actions by various governmental ... parties," along with the "current charges of conspiracy to commit murder," made Sell "a potential risk to the safety of one or more others in the community." The reviewing official "upheld" the "hearing officer's decision that [Sell] would benefit from the utilization of anti-psychotic medication."

Third, in July 1999, Sell filed a court motion contesting the Medical Center's right involuntarily to administer antipsychotic drugs. In September 1999, the Federal Magistrate who had ordered Sell sent to the Medical Center held a hearing. The evidence introduced at the hearing for the most part replicated the evidence introduced at the administrative hearing, with two exceptions. First, the witnesses explored the question of the medication's effectiveness more thoroughly. Second, Medical Center doctors testified about an incident that took place at the Medical Center *after* the administrative proceedings were completed. In July 1999, Sell had approached one of the Medical Center's nurses, suggested that he was in love with her, criticized her for having nothing to do with him, and, when told that his behavior was inappropriate, added " 'I can't help it.' " He subsequently made remarks or acted in ways indicating that this kind of conduct would continue. The Medical

Center doctors testified that, given Sell's prior behavior, diagnosis, and current beliefs, boundary-breaching incidents of this sort were not harmless and, when coupled with Sell's inability or unwillingness to desist, indicated that he was a safety risk even within the institution. They added that he had been moved to a locked cell.

In August 2000, the Magistrate found that "the government has made a substantial and very strong showing that Dr. Sell is a danger to himself and others at the institution in which he is currently incarcerated"; that "the government has shown that anti-psychotic medication is the only way to render him less dangerous"; that newer drugs and/or changing drugs will "ameliorat[e]" any "serious side effects"; that "the benefits to Dr. Sell . . . far outweigh any risks"; and that "there is a substantial probability that" the drugs will "retur[n]" Sell "to competency." The Magistrate concluded that "the government has shown in as strong a manner as possible, that anti-psychotic medications are the only way to render the defendant not dangerous and competent to stand trial." The Magistrate issued an order authorizing the involuntary administration of antipsychotic drugs to Sell, but stayed that order to allow Sell to appeal the matter to the Federal District Court.

Fourth, the District Court reviewed the record and, in April 2001, issued an opinion. The court addressed the Magistrate's finding "that defendant presents a danger to himself or others sufficient" to warrant involuntary administration of antipsychotic drugs. After noting that Sell subsequently had "been returned to an open ward," the District Court held the Magistrate's "dangerousness" finding "clearly erroneous." The court limited its determination to Sell's "dangerousness *at this time* to himself and to those around him *in his institutional context*" (emphasis added).

Nonetheless, the District Court affirmed the Magistrate's order permitting Sell's involuntary medication. The court wrote that "antipsychotic drugs are medically appropriate," that "they represent the only viable hope of rendering defendant competent to stand trial," and that "administration of such drugs appears necessary to serve the government's compelling interest in obtaining an adjudication of defendant's guilt or innocence of numerous and serious charges" (including fraud and attempted murder). The court added that it was "premature" to consider whether "the effects of medication might prejudice [Sell's] defense at trial." The Government and Sell both appealed.

Fifth, in March 2002, a divided panel of the Court of Appeals affirmed the District Court's judgment. The majority affirmed the District Court's determination that Sell was not dangerous. The majority noted that, according to the District Court, Sell's behavior at the Medical Center "amounted at most to an 'inappropriate familiarity and even infatuation' with a nurse." The Court of Appeals agreed, "[u]pon review," that "the evidence does not support a finding that Sell posed a danger to himself or others at the Medical Center."

The Court of Appeals also affirmed the District Court's order requiring medication in order to render Sell competent to stand trial. Focusing solely on the serious fraud charges, the panel majority concluded that the "government has an essential interest in bringing a defendant to trial." It added that the District Court "correctly concluded that there were no less intrusive means." After reviewing the conflicting views of the experts, the panel majority found antipsychotic drug treatment "medically appropriate" for Sell. It added that the "medical evidence presented indicated a reasonable probability that Sell will fairly be able to participate in his trial." One member of the panel dissented primarily on the ground that the fraud and money laundering charges were "not serious enough to warrant the forced medication of the defendant."

We granted certiorari to determine whether the Eighth Circuit "erred in rejecting" Sell's argument that "allowing the government to administer antipsychotic medication against his will solely to render him competent to stand trial for non-violent offenses," violated the Constitution—in effect by improperly depriving Sell of an important "liberty" that the Constitution guarantees.

* * *

III

We turn now to the basic question presented: Does forced administration of antipsychotic drugs to render Sell competent to stand trial unconstitutionally deprive him of his "liberty" to reject medical treatment? Two prior precedents, *Harper* and *Riggins*, set forth the framework for determining the legal answer.... These two cases ... indicate that the Constitution permits the Government involuntarily to administer antipsychotic drugs to a mentally ill defendant facing serious criminal charges in order to render that defendant competent to stand trial, but only if the treatment is medically appropriate, is substantially unlikely to have side effects that may undermine the fairness of the trial, and, taking account of less intrusive alternatives, is necessary significantly to further important governmental trial-related interests.

This standard will permit involuntary administration of drugs solely for trial competence purposes in certain instances. But those instances may be rare. That is because the standard says or fairly implies the following:

First, a court must find that *important* governmental interests are at stake. The Government's interest in bringing to trial an individual accused of a serious crime is important. That is so whether the offense is a serious crime against the person or a serious crime against property. In both instances the Government seeks to protect through application of the criminal law the basic human need for security. See *Riggins* ("'[P]ower to bring an accused to trial is fundamental to a scheme of "ordered liberty" and prerequisite to social justice and peace' ").

Courts, however, must consider the facts of the individual case in evaluating the Government's interest in prosecution. Special circumstances may lessen the importance of that interest. The defendant's failure to take drugs voluntarily, for example, may mean lengthy confinement in an institution for the mentally ill—and that would diminish the risks that ordinarily attach to freeing without punishment one who has committed a serious crime. We do not mean to suggest that civil commitment is a substitute for a criminal trial. The Government has a substantial interest in timely prosecution. And it may be difficult or impossible to try a defendant who regains competence after years of commitment during which memories may fade and evidence may be lost. The potential for future confinement affects, but does not totally undermine, the strength of the need for prosecution. The same is true of the possibility that the defendant has already been confined for a significant amount of time (for which he would receive credit toward any sentence ultimately imposed, see 18 U.S.C. § 3585(b)). Moreover, the Government has a concomitant, constitutionally essential interest in assuring that the defendant's trial is a fair one.

Second, the court must conclude that involuntary medication will *significantly further* those concomitant state interests. It must find that administration of the drugs is substantially likely to render the defendant competent to stand trial. At the same time, it must find that administration of the drugs is substantially unlikely to have side effects that will interfere significantly with the defendant's ability to assist counsel in conducting a trial defense, thereby rendering the trial unfair. See *Riggins* (KENNEDY, J., concurring in judgment).

Third, the court must conclude that involuntary medication is *necessary* to further those interests. The court must find that any alternative, less intrusive treatments are unlikely to achieve substantially the same results. Cf. Brief for American Psychological Association as Amicus Curiae 10–14 (nondrug therapies may be effective in restoring psychotic defendants to competence); but cf. Brief for American Psychiatric Association et al. as Amici Curiae 13–22 (alternative treatments for psychosis commonly not as effective as medication). And the court must consider less intrusive means for administering the drugs, e.g., a court order to the defendant backed by the contempt power, before considering more intrusive methods.

Fourth, as we have said, the court must conclude that administration of the drugs is *medically appropriate*, i.e., in the patient's best medical interest in light of his medical condition. The specific kinds of drugs at issue may matter here as elsewhere. Different kinds of antipsychotic drugs may produce different side effects and enjoy different levels of success.

We emphasize that the court applying these standards is seeking to determine whether involuntary administration of drugs is necessary significantly to further a particular governmental interest, namely, the interest in rendering the defendant *competent to stand trial*. A court need not consider whether to allow forced medication for that kind of purpose, if forced medication is warranted for a *different* purpose, such as the purposes set out in *Harper* related to the individual's dangerousness, or purposes related to the individual's own interests where refusal to take drugs puts his health gravely at risk. There are often strong reasons for a court to determine whether forced administration of drugs can be justified on these alternative grounds *before* turning to the trial competence question.

For one thing, the inquiry into whether medication is permissible, say, to render an individual nondangerous is usually more "objective and manageable" than the inquiry into whether medication is permissible to render a defendant competent. *Riggins* (KENNEDY, J., concurring in judgment). The medical experts may find it easier to provide an informed opinion about whether, given the risk of side effects, particular drugs are medically appropriate and necessary to control a patient's potentially dangerous behavior (or to avoid serious harm to the patient himself) than to try to balance harms and benefits related to the more quintessentially legal questions of trial fairness and competence.

For another thing, courts typically address involuntary medical treatment as a civil matter, and justify it on these alternative, *Harper*-type grounds. Every State provides avenues through which, for example, a doctor or institution can seek appointment of a guardian with the power to make a decision authorizing medication—when in the best interests of a patient who lacks the mental competence to make such a decision. And courts, in civil proceedings, may authorize involuntary medication where the patient's failure to accept treatment threatens injury to the patient or others.

If a court authorizes medication on these alternative grounds, the need to consider authorization on trial competence grounds will likely disappear. Even if a court decides medication cannot be authorized on the alternative grounds, the findings underlying such a decision will help to inform expert opinion and judicial decisionmaking in respect to a request to administer drugs for trial competence purposes. At the least, they will facilitate direct medical and legal focus upon such questions as: Why is it medically appropriate forcibly to administer antipsychotic drugs to an individual who (1) is *not* dangerous *and* (2) *is* competent to make up his own mind about treatment? Can bringing such an individual to trial *alone* justify in whole (or at least in significant part) administration of a drug that may have adverse side effects, including side effects that may to some extent impair a defense at trial? We consequently believe that a court, asked to approve forced administration of drugs for purposes of rendering a defendant competent to stand trial, should ordinarily determine whether the Government seeks, or has first sought, permission for forced administration of drugs on these other *Harper*-type grounds; and, if not, why not.

When a court must nonetheless reach the trial competence question, the factors discussed above should help it make the ultimate constitutionally required judgment. Has the Government, in light of the efficacy, the side effects, the possible alternatives, and the medical appropriateness of a particular course of antipsychotic drug treatment, shown a need for that treatment sufficiently important to overcome the individual's protected interest in refusing it?

IV

The Medical Center and the Magistrate in this case, applying standards roughly comparable to those set forth here and in *Harper*, approved forced medication substantially, if not primarily, upon grounds of Sell's dangerousness to others. But the District Court and the Eighth Circuit took a different approach. The District Court found "clearly erroneous" the Magistrate's conclusion regarding dangerousness, and the Court of Appeals agreed. Both courts approved forced medication solely in order to render Sell competent to stand trial.

We shall assume that the Court of Appeals' conclusion about Sell's dangerousness was correct. But we make that assumption *only* because the Government did not contest, and the parties have not argued, that particular matter. If anything, the record before us, described in Part I, suggests the contrary.

The Court of Appeals apparently agreed with the District Court that "Sell's inappropriate behavior ... amounted at most to an 'inappropriate familiarity and even infatuation' with a nurse." That being so, it also agreed that "the evidence does not support a finding that Sell posed a danger to himself or others at the Medical Center." The Court of Appeals, however, did not discuss the potential differences (described by a psychiatrist testifying before the Magistrate) between ordinary "overfamiliarity" and the same conduct engaged in persistently by a patient with Sell's behavioral history and mental illness. Nor did it explain why those differences should be minimized in light of the fact that the testifying psychiatrists concluded that Sell was dangerous, while Sell's own expert denied, not Sell's dangerousness, but the efficacy of the drugs proposed for treatment.

The District Court's opinion, while more thorough, places weight upon the Medical Center's decision, taken after the Magistrate's hearing, to return Sell to the general prison population. It does not explain whether that return reflected an improvement in Sell's condition or whether the Medical Center saw it as permanent rather than temporary. Cf. *Harper* (indicating that physical restraints and seclusion often not acceptable substitutes for medication).

Regardless, as we have said, we must assume that Sell was not dangerous. And on that hypothetical assumption, we find that the Court of Appeals was wrong to approve forced medication solely to render Sell competent to stand trial. For one thing, the Magistrate's opinion makes clear that he did not find forced medication legally justified on trial competence grounds alone. Rather, the Magistrate concluded that Sell was dangerous, and he wrote that forced medication was "the only way to render the defendant *not dangerous and* competent to stand trial'' (emphasis added).

Moreover, the record of the hearing before the Magistrate shows that the experts themselves focused mainly upon the dangerousness issue. Consequently the experts did not pose important questions—questions, for example, about trial-related side effects and risks—the answers to which could have helped determine whether forced medication was warranted on trial competence grounds alone. Rather, the Medical Center's experts conceded that their proposed medications had "significant" side effects and that "there has to be a cost benefit analysis." And in making their "cost-benefit" judgments, they primarily took into account Sell's dangerousness, not the need to bring him to trial.

The failure to focus upon trial competence could well have mattered. Whether a particular drug will tend to sedate a defendant, interfere with communication with counsel, prevent rapid reaction to trial developments, or diminish the ability to express emotions are matters important in determining the permissibility of medication to restore competence, *Riggins* (KENNEDY, J., concurring in judgment), but not necessarily relevant when dangerousness is primarily at issue. We cannot tell whether the side effects of antipsychotic medication were likely to undermine the fairness of a trial in Sell's case.

Finally, the lower courts did not consider that Sell has already been confined at the Medical Center for a long period of time, and that his refusal to take antipsychotic drugs might result in further lengthy confinement. Those factors, the first because a defendant ordinarily receives credit toward a sentence for time served, 18 U.S.C. § 3585(b), and the second because it reduces the likelihood of the defendant's committing future crimes, moderate—though they do not eliminate—the importance of the governmental interest in prosecution.

V

For these reasons, we believe that the present orders authorizing forced administration of antipsychotic drugs cannot stand. The Government may pursue its request for forced medication on the grounds discussed in this opinion, including grounds related to the danger Sell poses to himself or others. Since Sell's medical condition may have changed over time, the Government should do so on the basis of current circumstances. The judgment of the Eighth Circuit is vacated, and the case is remanded for further proceedings consistent with this opinion. It is so ordered.

Questions and Comments

1. *Alternative grounds for forcible medication. Sell* states that forcible medication "solely for trial competency purposes . . . may be rare." But it also indicates that forcible medication that restores competency may be justifiable on alternative grounds, such as dangerousness to self or others,

assuming it is "medically appropriate" (as per *Harper*) and would not affect trial rights (as per *Riggins*). Was Sell dangerous? What was the Supreme Court's view on this issue?

Some caselaw suggests that dangerousness is defined somewhat differently in this setting than in other settings. Consider *United States v. Weston*, 255 F.3d 873 (D.C.Cir.2001), decided before *Sell*. On July 24, 1998 Russell Weston, apparently believing that an evil machine was housed inside the United States Capitol building, allegedly forced his way past security checkpoints at the Capitol, shooting and killing two officers of the Capitol Police and seriously wounding a third officer. He was found incompetent to stand trial due to schizophrenia, but refused antipsychotic medication. A panel of the D.C. Circuit had concluded that antipsychotic medication was not needed to contain his dangerousness. As later described by the full court, the panel held that:

> Weston's situation in confinement—total seclusion and constant observation—obviated any significant danger he might pose to himself or others. There appears no basis to believe that Weston's worsening condition renders him more dangerous given his near-total incapacitation. Weston remains in seclusion under constant observation. Absent a showing that Weston's condition now exceeds the institution's ability to contain it through his present state of confinement, the prior decision appears to preclude a finding of dangerousness.... Accordingly, to medicate Weston, the government must prove that restoring his competence to stand trial is necessary to accomplish an essential state policy.

For a similar holding, post-*Sell*, see *United States v. Grape*, 509 F.Supp.2d 484, 494 (W.D. Pa. 2007) (defendant not a danger in confinement).

Are there other alternative justifications for forcibly medicating a defendant found incompetent to stand trial? What if the person is not only incompetent to stand trial but also incompetent to make treatment decisions? If the latter type of incompetency permits forcible medication (see pp. 980–82), doesn't *Sell* become virtually moot? See Robert Schopp, "Involuntary Treatment and Competence to Proceed in the Criminal Process," 24 Beh. Sci. & L. 495, 502–10 (2006) (arguing that virtually every person who is incompetent to stand trial is incompetent to make treatment decisions and thus should not have a right to refuse). Does Justice Breyer recognize this point, reject it, or ignore it? Look at the penultimate paragraph in Part III of the *Sell* opinion.

2.   *Important government interest.* Assuming an alternative justification is not available, *Sell* permits forcible medication for the sole purpose of restoring a defendant to competency only if: (1) an important government interest is at stake; (2) the medication is substantially likely to achieve restoration and substantially unlikely to have side effects that will infringe trial rights; (3) the medication is the least intrusive means of achieving the government's aim; and (4) the medication is medically appropriate. The following notes address these four issues.

The first criterion–the importance of the government interest—itself involves consideration of two issues: which types of prosecutions are so serious that they presumptively trump a medication refusal and when is that presumption overcome because the government interest in protecting society can be met without forcibly medicating a defendant? In analyzing offense seriousness, some federal courts have looked at the relevant statutory maximum, while others have looked at the (usually much lower) federal guidelines maximum (see pp. 670–73 for a discussion of sentencing under guidelines systems). Compare *United States v. Evans*, 404 F.3d 227, 237–38 (4th Cir. 2005) (holding that the statutory maximum is the appropriate benchmark because it determines the right to jury trial and because guidelines sentences cannot be predicted pre-trial) with *United States v. Hernandez–Vasquez*, (9th Cir.2007) (noting that while the guidelines "no longer are mandatory, they are the best available predictor of the length of a defendant's incarceration [and] any difficulty in estimating the likely guideline range exactly is an insufficient reason to ignore *Sell's* direction that courts should consider the specific circumstances of individual defendants in determining the seriousness of a crime."). Courts have also been influenced by other factors in determining the importance of the government's prosecution. See, e.g., *Hernandez-Vasquez*, supra (92–115 month potential guidelines sentence, together with prior convictions for molesting child under 15 and assaulting a corrections officer, is sufficiently serious); *United States v. Dumeny*, 295 F.Supp.2d 131, 132 (D. Me. 2004) (maximum 10–year sentence for possession of firearm by person previously committed to a mental health institute not sufficiently serious); *United States v. Valenzuela–Puentes*, 479 F.3d 1220, 1225 (10th Cir. 2007) (6–to–8–year maximum guidelines sentence for illegally entering the United States sufficiently serious, given defendant's long criminal history); *United States v. Lindauer*, 448 F.Supp.2d 558, 562 (S.D.N.Y. 2006) (10–year maximum sentence for failing to register as an Iraqi agent and engaging in financial transactions with Iraqi agents was insufficiently serious where defendant was alleged only to have met with Iraqi agents and to have delivered a letter pleading Iraq's case to the home of a government official). What are the possible problems with considering the defendant's prior record or alleged actions at the time of the crime in determining offense seriousness?

More complicated still is calibrating the impact of pre-trial and post-release detention on the determination of whether the government's interest in forcible medication is "important" under *Sell*. In *United States v. Evans*, supra, the court held that pre-trial confinement of two years did not outweigh the fact that the defendant still faced eight years in prison if convicted (at least under the statutory maximum; the guidelines sentence in this case was 14–20 months). In *Grape*, supra, the court was willing to consider the likelihood that, if released, Grape would be civilly committed and thus society protected, but ultimately decided that the seriousness of Grape's charges (which upon conviction would bring minimum sentences of 10 and 15 years) outweighed this consideration. In *United States v. Rodman*, 446 F.Supp.2d 487, 496–97 (D.S.C. 2006), the court noted that Rodman had already been held for almost the entire duration of time he'd have been imprisoned if convicted, and also noted that, if tried, Rodman would probably be found not guilty by reason of insanity; thus, the court held, rather than forcibly medicate Rodman and trying him, the state should simply commit him.

Should pre-trial and potential future confinement be relevant in determining the importance of the government's interest under *Sell*? Consider this statement in *Weston*:

> We ... do not believe that the "governmental interest in medicating a defendant in order to try him is diminished ... by the option of civil commitment." The civil commitment argument assumes that the government's essential penological interests lie only in incapacitating dangerous offenders. It ignores the retributive, deterrent, communicative, and investigative functions of the criminal justice system, which serve to ensure that offenders receive their just deserts, to make clear that offenses entail consequences, and to discover what happened through the public mechanism of trial. Civil commitment addresses none of these interests.

More fundamentally, is the Court in *Sell* correct when it states that "[t]he defendant's failure to take drugs voluntarily ... may mean lengthy confinement in an institution for the mentally ill ...". On what ground could such commitment take place? If the defendant is dangerous, then forcible medication is permissible under *Harper*. If the defendant is not dangerous, is the Court stating that, nonetheless, he or she may continue to be confined, albeit "in an institution for the mentally ill"? What are the arguments that such a detention would be unconstitutional?

If detention is permissible and occurs, should the defendant have a right to refuse medication while committed (see pp. 980–81)? If the committed defendant does not have a right to refuse, and the medication works, can the defendant then be tried? If the committed defendant continues to have a right to refuse and exercises that right, then, analogous to disposition under *Jackson v. Indiana* (see pp. 1027–31), should charges be dismissed? Alternatively, should proposals to permit trial of incompetent defendants, described in note 4 on pp. 1032–33, be adapted to permit trial of defendants who are unrestorably incompetent simply because they refuse medication?

3. *Effects of medication.* A good example of a court struggling with the second *Sell* criterion–which involves gauging the likelihood medication will restore competency without infringing trial rights–is found in *Weston*, supra :

> [Weston] claims that the fit between involuntary medication and the government's interest is not sufficiently tight in two respects. First, he argues that the medication will not restore his competence to stand trial because he is not likely to respond to it. Second, he contends that the medication's mind-altering properties and likely side effects will prejudice his right to a fair trial such that the government could not lawfully try him even if his competence were restored. Either way, the argument goes, there is an insufficient probability that forcible medication will satisfy the government's interest.
>
> That antipsychotic medication must be necessary to restore Weston's competence to stand trial does not mean there must be a 100% probability that it will produce this result.... As the Court has recognized, "necessity" may mean "absolute physical necessity or inevitability" or "that which is only convenient, useful, appropriate, suitable, proper, or conducive to the end sought." Even narrow tailoring in strict

scrutiny analysis does not contemplate a perfect correspondence between the means chosen to accomplish a compelling governmental interest. The government has established a sufficient likelihood that antipsychotic medication will restore Weston's competence while preserving his right to a fair trial. The district court acknowledged that "it is not certain that the medication will restore Weston's competency," but "credit[ed] the . . . testimony of the mental health experts that this outcome is likely." The government presented evidence that antipsychotic medication mitigated symptoms for at least 70 percent of patients. Dr. Johnson testified that the response rate is probably higher with the atypicals. The government also provided reason to believe that the probability of restoring competence might be higher in Weston's case because of Weston's "relatively little exposure to antipsychotic medication" and his generally positive response to the limited medication he received in 1996.

. . .

Weston points out that there is also a possibility that antipsychotic medication could prejudice his right to a fair trial by, for instance, altering his courtroom demeanor, interfering with his recollection and ability to testify, and obstructing his right to present an insanity defense. We agree with the district court that "[t]here is no reason to conclude, at this time, that involuntary medication would preclude Weston from receiving a fair trial." The general right to a fair trial includes several specific rights such as the right to be tried only while competent, that is, while able to understand the proceedings, consult with counsel, and assist in the defense. As we determined, there is a sufficiently high probability that antipsychotic medication will restore Weston's competence to stand trial. The district court found and the evidence indicates that "a strong likelihood exists that medication will *enhance* some of Weston's trial rights, particularly his right to consult with counsel and to assist in his defense."[6]

Another aspect of the right to a fair trial is Weston's right to testify and "to present his own version of events in his own words." The defense is concerned that the medication might affect Weston's memory and his capacity to relate his delusions and other aspects of his mental state at the time of the crime, which in turn "may impair his ability to mount an effective insanity defense." But the record contains no basis to suppose that antipsychotic drugs will prevent Weston from testifying in a meaningful way. Rather, it indicates that medication will more likely improve Weston's ability to relate his belief system to the jury.

6. See also Tr. at 8 (Dr. Johnson's testimony that "I would really expect him, from a mental status standpoint, to be functioning in a much enhanced manner over his current psychotic state to the point where I believe his competence could be restored"); id. at 9 (Dr. Johnson stating that "I actually firmly believe that treatment with the medication will enhance his ability to follow the issues at the trial"); Tr. at 24 (Dr. Johnson's testimony that "successful treatment would result in a decrease in his delusional thinking, hopefully a resolution of that, an increase in his attention, ability to concentrate, and a change in his affect, or the way his mood appears to someone who is looking onto the situation. His preoccupation with his delusional system has led me to believe at various points that he has also experienced some hallucinatory phenomena, and I would expect that to resolve.").

The benefits of antipsychotic medication in terms of Weston's ability to understand the proceedings and communicate with his attorneys presumably will also translate into an improved capacity to communicate from the witness stand. And although memory loss is a potential side effect, Dr. Johnson testified that she thought "he'd be able to remember his belief system." Tr. at 50 (also stating that "I don't think the treatment would impact his memory"); see also Tr. at 4–5 (Dr. Johnson's testimony that "I don't expect him to lose the memory of his delusional beliefs as a result of treatment").

There is a possibility that the medication could affect Weston's behavior and demeanor on the witness stand such that the jury might regard his "synthetically sane" testimony as inconsistent with a claim of insanity. As Justice Kennedy put it in *Riggins*, "[i]f the defendant takes the stand . . . his demeanor can have a great bearing on his credibility and persuasiveness, and on the degree to which he evokes sympathy." We recognize this small risk, but we see little basis to suppose that the jury will take Weston's testimony (if he decides to testify) as an indication that he must have been sane at the time of the crime, or that he is making it up, or that he deserves no sympathy. There is ample evidence of Weston's history of mental illness and bizarre behavior; the jury's overall impression of Weston will depend as much on this evidence as his testimony.

The district court also correctly held that a defendant does not have an absolute right to replicate on the witness stand his mental state at the time of the crime. A defendant asserting a heat-of-passion defense to a charge of first degree murder does not have the right to whip up a frenzy in court to show his capacity for rage, nor does a defendant claiming intoxication have the right to testify under the influence. There is little meaningful distinction between these cases and medication-induced competence to stand trial. Either way, the defendant's mental state on the stand is different from the mental state he claims to have operated under at the time of the crime. The tolerable level of difference no doubt increases in a case like this where there is substantial evidence of mental state other than the defendant's present appearance.

Weston will not have to rely solely on his own testimony to show his state of mind on July 24, 1998. Involuntary medication therefore stands little chance of impairing his right to present an insanity defense. There is extensive documentation and testimony concerning Weston's delusional system, his history of mental illness, and his "behavior, appearance, speech, actions, and extraordinary or bizarre acts . . . over a significant period." Multiple experts have examined Weston and presumably may testify. Many of these examinations no doubt related to his trial competence, but "[t]he tapes and psychiatric reports . . . document Weston's delusional state over several years." There is also a taped interview in which Weston discussed his delusional beliefs with the Central Intelligence Agency. Given the wealth of expert and lay testimony and other documentation the district court described, Weston's insanity defense does not stand or fall on his testimony alone.

A third trial right that could be implicated by antipsychotic medication is Weston's right to be present at trial in a state that does not prejudice the factfinder against him. To the extent the medication alters Weston's demeanor, courtroom behavior, or reactions to events in the courtroom, it may cause the jury to see Weston in a state that might seem inconsistent with a claim of insanity. It could also produce a flattened emotional affect that could convey to the jury a lack of remorse, a critical consideration if this case proceeded to sentencing.

Here again the record indicates that medication will likely enhance rather than impair Weston's right to a fair trial. Dr. Johnson stated that medication "will alter [Weston's demeanor] to the extent that it will be more a return to his baseline non-psychotic state. I would anticipate he would have less blunting or flattening of his affect. He would be able to respond more appropriately from an emotional standpoint with his facial expression than he is now." See also Tr. at 22–24 (Dr. Johnson agreeing with the proposition that, with medication, Weston's "expressions potentially could be more appropriate to the context of what's occurring in the courtroom"; also, her testimony that "[i]t is the patient who is overmedicated or whose side effects are not managed who would demonstrate an increased lack of responsiveness").

The possibility of side effects from antipsychotic medication is undeniable, but the ability of Weston's treating physicians and the district court to respond to them substantially reduces the risk they pose to trial fairness. The district court found that Weston's doctors can manage side effects in a number of ways: "the Court credits the testimony of the government experts and Dr. Daniel, the independent expert, that the side effects of medication are manageable through adjustments in the timing and amount of the doses, and through supplementary medications." See also Tr. at 125 (Dr. Daniel's testimony that antipsychotic medications have side effects but "[g]enerally they can be treated or an adjustment made in the medication, or the medication replaced with a different one. There's generally a way to deal with the side effects."); 4 Joint Appendix 102 (Statement in Dr. Daniel's report to the district court that "the side effects can most often be managed or an alternative course of treatment provided to the benefit of the patient. General experience with antipsychotics, particularly the newer medications, indicates that given their benefits they are reasonably safe and well-tolerated."). As the Court wrote in *Harper*, the "risks associated with antipsychotic drugs are for the most part medical ones, best assessed by medical professionals."[7]

---

7. Antipsychotic drugs have progressed since Justice Kennedy discussed their side effects in *Riggins*. There is a new generation of medications having better side effect profiles. See Paul A. Nidich & Jacqueline Collins, Involuntary Administration of Psychotropic Medication: A Federal Court Update, 11 No. 4 Health Lawyer 12, 13 (May 1999) ("[I]n light of the progress made in the development of new antipsychotic medications since the Supreme Court's Riggins decision in 1992, the courts should revisit this issue with an open mind. . . . [Because of new atypicals,] the fear of side effects should not weigh heavily in the decision whether to treat pretrial detainees or civilly committed persons with antipsychotic medication against their will when that treatment is medically appropriate."). Although the government presently plans to medicate Weston with the older generation of typicals, it could switch to the newer atypicals if side effects from the typicals threaten to

The district court also has measures at its disposal: "If Weston is medicated and his competency is restored, the Court is willing to take whatever reasonable measures are necessary to ensure that his rights are protected. This may include informing the jurors that Weston is being administered mind-altering medication, that his behavior in their presence is conditioned on drugs being administered to him at the request of the government, and allowing experts and others to testify regarding Weston's unmedicated condition, the effects of the medication on Weston, and the necessity of medication to render Weston competent to stand trial." Weston is free to propose other options.

255 F.3d at 882–86.

The *Weston* court emphasizes several times that medication will improve Weston's ability to exercise his trial rights (see in particular note 6). Should that be the standard for determining whether medication can be imposed to restore competency? Whatever the standard for competency, is a 70% chance that medication will restore competency sufficient? Cf. *United States v. Rivera–Morales*, 160 Fed. Appx. 648 (9th Cir. 2005) ("although the court declines to determine the exact percentage of success that equates with a substantial likelihood that a defendant's competency is restored, it is clear that a chance of success that is simply more than a 50% chance of success does not suffice to meet this standard"); *Grape*, supra, at 489 (citing a study of federal defendants showing that 23.7% of those who were involuntarily medicated could not be restored).

If Weston were medicated for trial, how is the court to discover whether the medication is negatively affecting his demeanor, memory, ability to testify, or ability to consult with counsel? Should the court hold a hearing, with defense counsel as a witness? Is another evaluation necessary? If the side effects are considered serious, should the court then postpone trial while the medication is more carefully titrated (a process that could take several days or weeks)? In the alternative, should the court seek certification from defense counsel that the side effects are not serious *before* trial begins?

Finally, how is the court to analyze the effects of the medication on the defendant's ability to present an effective defense? Will expert and documentary descriptions of Weston come close to giving the jury as accurate an idea of Weston's mental problems as viewing Weston in an unmedicated state would? On this score, how can the defense desire to show the jury the defendant's unmedicated state be reconciled with the prohibition against trying incompetent defendants? One solution was proposed by the New Hampshire Supreme Court in *State v. Hayes*, 118 N.H. 458, 389 A.2d 1379 (1978). *Hayes* permits the state to compel medication of an incompetent defendant initially, but

> [i]f the defendant by his own voluntary choice, made while competent, becomes incompetent to stand trial because he withdraws from the medication, he may be deemed to have waived his right to be tried while

impair his right to a fair trial. The district court analyzed the side effects of both. Dr. Johnson testified that Weston cannot be treated with atypicals unless he agrees to take them orally. The parties dispute whether Weston would so agree. When Weston originally withheld consent to antipsychotic medication, he indicated that he would comply with court-ordered medication.

competent. The trial court should however carefully examine the defendant on the record, while competent, to establish the following: that the defendant understands that if he is taken off the psychotropic medication he may become legally incompetent to stand trial; that he understands that he has a constitutional right not to be tried while legally incompetent; that the defendant voluntarily gives up this right by requesting that he be taken off the psychotropic medication; and that he understands that the trial will continue whatever his condition may be.

The court also held that, in the event an effective waiver is made, the defendant may still be kept on medication until the point prior to trial when withdrawing medication would reproduce most nearly the defendant's mental state at the time of the offense. Thus, for instance, if a defendant had previously been on medication, but stopped taking it two weeks prior to the offense, the state should be able to forcibly medicate until two weeks prior to trial. *Hayes* in essence proposes an advanced directive approach in the competency to stand trial context. Does it make sense to try to replicate past mental states in this manner? Is it medically ethical to do so? Can a defendant "waive" the right to be tried while competent (an issue discussed further on pp. 1022–24, 1068)?

4. *Least intrusive means.* The evidence adduced in *Grape,* supra, on this third *Sell* criterion and the court's analysis of it is typical:

> Both doctors agreed that treatment other than medication may be helpful but only if such treatment was administered after, or in conjunction with, the administration of antipsychotic medication. Given Mr. Grape's unwillingness to cooperate with virtually everyone and his refusal to believe that he is suffering from any problems, an Order from this Court directing him to take his medications would be futile. If he disobeyed such an Order, which all parties expect that he would, we do not have any practical punishment option to coerce him to obey an Order, as he is already confined in a single cell in a lock down unit at a medical prison. In addition, Mr. Grape's counsel conceded that less intrusive means of treating Mr. Grape are not available. We therefore find that less intrusive means are not available to the Court. We expect that the medical staff will continue to try to persuade Mr. Grape to take his medications. As noted, Dr. Sarrazin's plan clearly contemplates as one of its goals the voluntary participation of Mr. Grape with any medication treatment.

509 F.Supp.2d at 499.

5. *Medically appropriate.* Since *Sell* reiterated *Riggins'* requirements, a number of courts have become quite strict in monitoring this fourth *Sell* criterion. For instance, in *United States v. Hernandez–Vasquez,* 506 F.3d 811, 819 (9th Cir. 2007), the court held that:

> *Sell* does not identify a requisite degree of specificity concerning the drugs to be used for involuntary medication. However, it does imply that a court should consider these issues at a detailed level: "The specific kinds of drugs at issue may matter here as elsewhere. Different kinds of

antipsychotic drugs may produce different side effects and enjoy different levels of success." . . . Accordingly, we hold that a *Sell* order must provide some limitations on the specific medications that may be administered and the maximum dosages and duration of treatment. At a minimum, to pass muster under Sell, the district court's order must identify: (1) the specific medication or range of medications that the treating physicians are permitted to use in their treatment of the defendant, (2) the maximum dosages that may be administered, and (3) the duration of time that involuntary treatment of the defendant may continue before the treating physicians must report back to the court on the defendant's mental condition and progress. By setting such parameters within which physicians must operate, district courts will leave physicians enough discretion to act quickly to respond to changes in the defendant's condition. Moreover, the Government or the defendant may move to alter the court's order as the circumstances change and more becomes known about the defendant's response to the medication.

Some courts have also required use of atypical medications as opposed to older medications, as a means of minimizing side effects. See, e.g., *United States v. Gomes*, 387 F.3d 157, 162 (2d Cir. 2004).

6. *The impact of* Sell. It has been estimated that up to 75% of criminal defendants who are found incompetent to stand trial refuse medication. Robert Miller et al., "The Right to Refuse Treatment in a Forensic Patient Population: Six–Month Review," 17 Bull. Amer.Acad. Psychiatry & L. 107 (1989). If the right to refuse in this context depended primarily on the nature of the crime charged and were relegated to misdemeanor cases, then *Sell* might have the salutary effect of promoting diversion of mentally ill people charged with minor crimes out of the criminal justice system, because prosecutors are likely to dismiss these types of charges when medication refusal creates an obstacle to prosecution. But consider also this description of *Sell's* possible systemic impact:

> Now that the circumstances under which forcible medication solely for the purpose of competency restoration "may be rare," defense lawyers and defendants are more likely to claim incompetency, and defendants are more likely to refuse treatment. In response, courts, prosecutors, and forensic clinicians are more likely to take advantage of the *Harper/Riggins* exception to the right to refuse and find that "dangerousness" exists in a greater number of cases, and prosecutors are more likely to bring the highest possible charge to ensure it is considered "serious." In short, all parties are more likely to act pretextually, with no deserved gain for anyone, since refusing defendants either will still be detained (illegitimately) or will be released without adjudication merely because they have refused treatment.

Christopher Slobogin, "The Supreme Court's Recent Criminal Mental Health Cases: Rulings of Questionable Competence," ABA Crim. Just. Mag. 8, 10 (Fall, 2007).

B. DECISIONAL COMPETENCY

GODINEZ v. MORAN

Supreme Court of the United States, 1993.
509 U.S. 389, 113 S.Ct. 2680, 125 L.Ed.2d 321.

JUSTICE THOMAS delivered the opinion of the Court.

This case presents the question whether the competency standard for pleading guilty or waiving the right to counsel is higher than the competency standard for standing trial. We hold that it is not.

I

On August 2, 1984, in the early hours of the morning, respondent entered the Red Pearl Saloon in Carson City, Nevada, and shot the bartender and a patron four times each with an automatic pistol. He then walked behind the bar and removed the cash register. Nine days later, respondent arrived at the apartment of his former wife and opened fire on her; five of his seven shots hit their target. Respondent then shot himself in the abdomen and attempted, without success, to slit his wrists. Of the four victims of respondent's gunshots, only respondent himself survived. On August 13, respondent summoned police to his hospital bed and confessed to the killings.

After respondent pleaded not guilty to three counts of first-degree murder, the trial court ordered that he be examined by a pair of psychiatrists, both of whom concluded that he was competent to stand trial.[1] The State thereafter announced its intention to seek the death penalty. On November 28, 1984, two and a half months after the psychiatric evaluations, respondent again appeared before the trial court. At this time respondent informed the court that he wished to discharge his attorneys and change his pleas to guilty. The reason for the request, according to respondent, was to prevent the presentation of mitigating evidence at his sentencing.

On the basis of the psychiatric reports, the trial court found that respondent

"is competent in that he knew the nature and quality of his acts, had the capacity to determine right from wrong; that he understands the nature of the criminal charges against him and is able to assist in his defense of such charges, or against the pronouncement of the judgment thereafter; that he knows the consequences of entering a plea of guilty to the charges; and that he can intelligently

---

1. One of the psychiatrists stated that there was "not the slightest doubt" that respondent was "in full control of his faculties" insofar as he had the "ability to aid counsel, assist in his own defense, recall evidence and ... give testimony if called upon to do so." The other psychiatrist believed that respondent was "knowledgeable of the charges being made against him"; that he had the ability to "assist this attorney, in his own defense, if he so desire[d]"; and that he was "fully cognizant of the penalties if convicted."

and knowingly waive his constitutional right to assistance of an attorney."

The court advised respondent that he had a right both to counsel and to self-representation, warned him of the "dangers and disadvantages" of self-representation, inquired into his understanding and his awareness of his rights, and asked why he had chosen to represent himself. It then accepted respondent's waiver of counsel. The court also accepted respondent's guilty pleas, but not before it had determined that respondent was not pleading guilty in response to threats or promises, that he understood the nature of the charges against him and the consequences of pleading guilty, that he was aware of his rights he was giving up, and that there was a factual basis for the pleas. The trial court explicitly found that respondent was "knowingly and intelligently" waiving his right to the assistance of counsel, and that his guilty pleas were "freely and voluntarily" given.

On January 21, 1985, a three-judge court sentenced respondent to death for each of the murders. The Supreme Court of Nevada affirmed respondent's sentences for the Pearl Saloon murders, but reversed his sentence for the murder of his ex-wife and remanded for imposition of a life sentence without the possibility of parole.

On July 30, 1987, respondent filed a petition for post-conviction relief in state court. Following an evidentiary hearing, the trial court rejected respondent's claim that he was "mentally incompetent to represent himself," concluding that "the record clearly shows that he was examined by two psychiatrists both of whom declared [him] competent." The Supreme Court of Nevada dismissed respondent's appeal, and we denied certiorari.

Respondent then filed a habeas petition in the United States District Court for the District of Nevada. The District Court denied the petition, but the Ninth Circuit reversed. The Court of Appeals concluded that the "record in this case" should have led the trial court to "entertai[n] a good faith doubt about [respondent's] competency to make a voluntary, knowing, and intelligent waiver of constitutional rights," and that the Due Process Clause therefore "required the court to hold a hearing to evaluate and determine [respondent's] competency . . . before it accepted his decision to discharge counsel and change his pleas." [Further], the Court of Appeals held that "the state court's post-conviction ruling was premised on the wrong legal standard of competency." "Competency to waive constitutional rights," according to the Court of Appeals, "requires a higher level of mental functioning than that required to stand trial"; while a defendant is competent to stand trial if he has "a rational and factual understanding of the proceedings and is capable of assisting his counsel," a defendant is competent to waive counsel or plead guilty only if he has "the capacity for 'reasoned choice' among the alternatives available to him." The Court of Appeals determined that the trial court had "erroneously applied the standard for evaluating competency to stand trial, instead of the correct 'reasoned choice' standard," and further concluded that when examined "in light of the correct legal standard," the record did not support a finding that respondent was "mentally capable of the reasoned choice required for a valid waiver of constitutional rights."[4] The Court of Appeals accordingly instructed the District Court to issue the writ of habeas corpus within 60 days, "unless the state court allows [respondent] to withdraw his guilty pleas, enter new pleas, and proceed to trial with the assistance of counsel."

Whether the competency standard for pleading guilty or waiving the right to counsel is higher than the competency standard for standing trial is a question that has divided the federal courts of appeals[5] and state courts of last resort. We granted certiorari to resolve the conflict.

II

A criminal defendant may not be tried unless he is competent, Pate v. Robinson, and he may not waive his right to counsel or plead guilty unless he does so "competently and intelligently," Johnson v. Zerbst, 304 U.S. 458, 468 (1938). In Dusky v. United States, we held that the standard for competence to stand trial is whether the defendant has "sufficient present ability to consult with his lawyer with a reasonable degree of rational understanding" and has "a rational as well as factual understanding of the proceedings against him." While we have described the standard for competence to stand trial, however, we have never expressly articulated a standard for competence to plead guilty or to waive the right to the assistance of counsel.

Relying in large part upon our decision in Westbrook v. Arizona, 384 U.S. 150 (1966)(per curiam), the Ninth Circuit adheres to the view that the competency standard for pleading guilty or waiving the right to counsel is higher than the competency standard for standing trial. See Sieling v. Eyman, 478 F. 2d 211 (9th Cir.1973). In *Westbrook*, a two-paragraph per curiam opinion, we vacated the lower court's judgment affirming the petitioner's conviction, because there had been "a hearing on the issue of [the petitioner's] competence to stand trial," but "no hearing or inquiry into the issue of his competence to waive his constitutional right to the assistance of counsel." The Ninth Circuit has reasoned that the "clear implication" of *Westbrook* is that the *Dusky* formulation is not "a high enough standard" for determining whether a defendant is competent to waive a constitutional right. We think the Ninth Circuit has read too much into *Westbrook*, and we think it errs in applying two different competency standards.

4. In holding that respondent was not competent to waive his constitutional rights, the court placed heavy emphasis on the fact that respondent was on medication at the time he sought to discharge his attorneys and plead guilty.

5. While the Ninth Circuit and the District of Columbia Circuit, see United States v. Masthers, 176 U.S.App.D.C. 242, 247, 539 F. 2d 721, 726(1976), have employed the "reasoned choice" standard for guilty pleas, every other circuit that has considered the issue has determined that the competency standard for pleading guilty is identical to the competency standard for standing trial. . . .

A

The standard adopted by the Ninth Circuit is whether a defendant who seeks to plead guilty or waive counsel has the capacity for "reasoned choice" among the alternatives available to him. How this standard is different from (much less higher than) the *Dusky* standard—whether the defendant has a "rational understanding" of the proceedings—is not readily apparent to us. In fact respondent himself opposed certiorari on the ground that the difference between the two standards is merely one of "terminology," and he devotes little space in his brief on the merits to a defense of the Ninth Circuit's standard. But even assuming that there is some meaningful distinction between the "capacity for reasoned choice" and a "rational understanding" of the proceedings, we reject the notion that competence to plead guilty or to waive the right to counsel must be measured by a standard that is higher than (or even different from) the *Dusky* standard.

We begin with the guilty plea. A defendant who stands trial is likely to be presented with choices that entail relinquishment of the same rights that are relinquished by a defendant who pleads guilty: He will ordinarily have to decide whether to waive his "privilege against compulsory self-incrimination," Boykin v. Alabama, 395 U.S. 238, 243 (1969), by taking the witness stand; if the option is available, he may have to decide whether to waive his "right to trial by jury," and, in consultation with counsel, he may have to decide whether to waive his "right to confront [his] accusers," by declining to cross-examine witnesses for the prosecution. A defendant who pleads not guilty, moreover, faces still other strategic choices: In consultation with his attorney, he may be called upon to decide, among other things, whether (and how) to put on a defense and whether to raise one or more affirmative defenses. In sum, criminal defendants—not merely those who plead guilty—may be required to make important decisions once criminal proceedings have been initiated. And while the decision to plead guilty is undeniably a profound one, it is no more complicated than the sum total of decisions that a defendant may be called upon to make during the course of a trial. (The decision to plead guilty is also made over a shorter period of time, without the distraction and burden of a trial.) This being so, we can conceive of no basis for demanding a higher level of competence for those defendants who choose to plead guilty. If the *Dusky* standard is adequate for defendants who plead not guilty, it is necessarily adequate for those who plead guilty.

Nor do we think that a defendant who waives his right to the assistance of counsel must be more competent than a defendant who does not, since there is no reason to believe that the decision to waive counsel requires an appreciably higher level of mental functioning than the decision to waive other constitutional rights. Respondent suggests that a higher competency standard is necessary because a defendant who represents himself " 'must have greater powers of comprehension, judgment, and reason than would be necessary to stand trial with the aid of an attorney.' " But this has a flawed premise; the competence that is required of a defendant seeking to waive his right to counsel is the competence to waive the right, not the competence to represent himself. In Faretta v. California, 422 U.S. 806 (1975), we held that a defendant choosing self-representation must do so "competently and intelligently," but we made it clear that the defendant's "technical legal knowledge" is "not relevant" to the determination whether he is competent waive his right to counsel, and we emphasized that although the defendant "may conduct his own defense ultimately to his own detriment, his choice must be honored." Thus, while "[i]t is undeniable that in most criminal prosecutions defendants could better defend with counsel's guidance than by their own unskilled efforts," a criminal defendant's ability to represent himself has no bearing upon his competence to *choose* self-representation.

B

A finding that a defendant is competent to stand trial, however, is not all that is necessary before he may be permitted to plead guilty or waive his right to counsel. In addition to determining that a defendant who seeks to plead guilty or waive counsel is competent, a trial court must satisfy itself that the waiver of his constitutional rights is knowing and voluntary. In this sense there is a "heightened" standard for pleading guilty and for waiving the right to counsel, but it is not a heightened standard of competence.[12]

This two-part inquiry is what we had in mind in *Westbrook*. When we distinguished between "competence to stand trial" and "competence to waive [the] constitutional right to the assistance of counsel," we were using "competence to waive" as a shorthand for the "intelligent and competent waiver" requirement of Johnson v. Zerbst. This much is clear from the fact that we quoted that very language from *Zerbst* immediately after noting that the trial court had not determined whether the petitioner was competent to waive his right to counsel. (" 'This protecting duty imposes the serious and weighty responsibility upon the trial judge of determining whether there is an intelligent and competent waiver by the accused' "). Thus, *Westbrook* stands only for the unremarkable proposition that when a defendant seeks to waive his right to counsel, a determination that he is competent to stand trial is not enough; the waiver must also be intelligent and voluntary before it can be accepted.

III

Requiring that a criminal defendant be competent has a modest aim: It seeks to ensure that he has the capacity to understand the proceedings

---

12. The focus of a competency inquiry is the defendant's mental capacity; the question is whether he has the ability to understand the proceedings. The purpose of the "knowing and voluntary" inquiry, by contrast, is to determine whether the defendant actually does understand the significance and consequences of a particular decision and whether the decision is uncoerced.

See *Faretta*, supra (defendant waiving counsel must be "made aware of the dangers and disadvantages of self-representation, so that the record will establish that 'he knows what he is doing and his choice is made with eyes open' "); *Boykin*, supra (defendant pleading guilty must have "a full understanding of what the plea connotes and of its consequence").

and to assist counsel. While psychiatrists and scholars may find it useful to classify the various kinds and degrees of competence, and while States are free to adopt competency standards that are more elaborate than the *Dusky* formulation, the Due Process Clause does not impose these additional requirements. The judgment of the Court of Appeals is reversed, and the case is remanded for further proceedings consistent with this opinion.

So ordered.

The opinion of JUSTICE KENNEDY, with whom JUSTICE SCALIA joins, concurring in part and concurring in the judgment, is deleted.

JUSTICE BLACKMUN, with whom JUSTICE STEVENS joins, dissenting.

I

* * *

In August 1984, after killing three people and wounding himself in an attempt to commit suicide, Moran was charged in a Nevada state court with three counts of capital murder. He pleaded not guilty to all charges, and the trial court ordered a psychiatric evaluation. At this stage, Moran's competence to represent himself was not at issue.

The two psychiatrists who examined him therefore focused solely upon his capacity to stand trial with the assistance of counsel. Dr. Jack A. Jurasky found Moran to be "in full control of his faculties insofar as his ability to aid counsel, assist in his own defense, recall evidence and to give testimony if called upon to do so." Dr. Jurasky, however, did express some reservations, observing: "Psychologically, and perhaps legally speaking, this man, because he is expressing and feeling considerable remorse and guilt, may be inclined to exert less effort towards his own defense." Nevertheless, under the circumstances, Dr. Jurasky felt that Moran's depressed state of mind was not "necessarily a major consideration." Dr. William D. O'Gorman also characterized Moran as "very depressed," remarking that he "showed much tearing in talking about the episodes that led up to his present incarceration, particularly in talking about his exwife." But Dr. O'Gorman ultimately concluded that Moran "is knowledgeable of the charges being made against him" and "can assist his attorney, in his own defense, if he so desires."

In November 1984, just three months after his suicide attempt, Moran appeared in court seeking to discharge his public defender, waive his right to counsel, and plead guilty to all three charges of capital murder. When asked to explain the dramatic change in his chosen course of action, Moran responded that he wished to represent himself because he opposed all efforts to mount a defense. His purpose, specifically, was to prevent the presentation of any mitigating evidence on his behalf at the sentencing phase of the proceeding. The trial judge inquired whether Moran was "presently under the influence of any drug or alcohol," and Moran replied: "Just what they give me in, you know, medications." Despite Moran's affirmative answer, the trial judge failed to question him further regarding the type, dosage, or effect of the "medications" to which he referred. Had the trial judge done so, he would have discovered that Moran was being administered simultaneously four different prescription drugs—phenobarbital, dilantin, inderal, and vistaril. Moran later testified to the numbing effect of these drugs, stating: "I guess I really didn't care about anything. I wasn't very concerned about anything that was going on far as the proceedings and everything were going."[1]

Disregarding the mounting evidence of Moran's disturbed mental state, the trial judge accepted Moran's waiver of counsel and guilty pleas after posing a series of routine questions regarding his understanding of his legal rights and the offenses, to which Moran gave largely monosyllabic answers. In a string of affirmative responses, Moran purported to acknowledge that he knew the import of waiving his constitutional rights, that he understood the charges against him, and that he was, in fact, guilty of those charges. One part of this exchange, however, highlights the mechanical character of Moran's answers to the questions. When the trial judge asked him whether he killed his ex-wife "deliberately, with premeditation and malice aforethought," Moran unexpectedly responded: "No. I didn't do it—I mean, I wasn't looking to kill her, but she ended up dead." Instead of probing further, the trial judge simply repeated the question, inquiring again whether Moran had acted deliberately. Once again, Moran replied: "I don't know. I mean, I don't know what you mean by deliberately. I mean, I pulled the trigger on purpose, but I didn't plan on doing it; you know what I mean?" Ignoring the ambiguity of Moran's responses, the trial judge reframed the question to elicit an affirmative answer, stating: "Well, I've previously explained to you what is meant by deliberation and premeditation. Deliberate means that you arrived at or determined as a result of careful thought and weighing the consideration for and against the proposed action. Did you do that?" This time, Moran responded: "Yes."

It was only after prodding Moran through the plea colloquy in this manner that the trial judge concluded that he was competent to stand trial and that he voluntarily and intelligently had waived his right to counsel. Accordingly, Moran was allowed to plead guilty and appear without counsel at his sentencing hearing. Moran presented no defense, called no witness, and offered no mitigating evidence on his own behalf. Not surprisingly, he was sentenced to death.

II

[A] finding that a defendant is competent to stand trial establishes only that he is capable of aiding his attorney in making critical decisions

---

1. Moran's medical records, read in conjunction with the Physician's Desk Reference (46th ed. 1992), corroborate his testimony concerning the medications he received and their impact upon him. The records show that Moran was administered dilantin, an anti-epileptic medication that may cause confusion; inderal, a beta-blocker anti-arrhythmic that may cause lightheadedness, mental depression, hallucinations, disorientation, and short-term memory loss; and vistaril, a depressant that may cause drowsiness, tremors, and convulsions.

required at trial or in plea negotiations. The reliability or even relevance of such a finding vanishes when its basic premise—that counsel will be present—ceases to exist. The question is no longer whether the defendant can proceed with an attorney, but whether he can proceed alone and uncounselled. I do not believe we place an excessive burden upon a trial court by requiring it to conduct a specific inquiry into that question at the juncture when a defendant whose competency already has been questioned seeks to waive counsel and represent himself.

The majority concludes that there is no need for such a hearing because a defendant who is found competent to stand trial with the assistance of counsel is, *ipso facto*, competent to discharge counsel and represent himself. But the majority cannot isolate the term "competent" and apply it in a vacuum, divorced from its specific context. A person who is "competent" to play basketball is not thereby "competent" to play the violin. The majority's monolithic approach to competency is true to neither life nor the law. Competency for one purpose does not necessarily translate to competency for another purpose. See Bonnie, The Competence of Criminal Defendants: A Theoretical Reformulation, 10 Behav. Sci. & L. 291, 299 (1992); R. Roesch & S. Golding, Competency to Stand Trial 10–13 (1980). [I]n Westbrook v. Arizona, 384 U. S. 150 (1966), the Court reiterated the requirement that the determination of a defendant's competency be tailored to the particular capacity in question, observing: "Although petitioner received a hearing on the issue of his competence to stand trial, there appears to have been no hearing or inquiry into the issue of his competence to waive his constitutional right to the assistance of counsel and to proceed, as he did, to conduct his own defense."

* * *

The majority asserts that "the competence that is required of a defendant seeking to waive his right to counsel is the competence to waive the right, not the competence to represent himself." But this assertion is simply incorrect. The majority's attempt to extricate the competence to waive the right to counsel from the competence to represent oneself is unavailing, because the former decision necessarily entails the latter. It is obvious that a defendant who waives counsel must represent himself. Even Moran, who pleaded guilty, was required to defend himself during the penalty phase of the proceedings. And a defendant who is utterly incapable of conducting his own defense cannot be considered "competent" to make such a decision, any more than a person who chooses to leap out of a window in the belief that he can fly can be considered "competent" to make such a choice.

The record in this case gives rise to grave doubts regarding respondent Moran's ability to discharge counsel and represent himself. Just a few months after he attempted to commit suicide, Moran essentially volunteered himself for execution: he sought to waive the right to counsel, to plead guilty to capital murder, and to prevent the presentation of any mitigating evidence on his behalf. The psychiatrists' reports supplied one explanation for Moran's self-destructive behavior: his deep depression. And Moran's own testimony suggested another: the fact that he was being administered simultaneously four different prescription medications. It has been recognized that such drugs often possess side effects that may "compromise the right of a medicated criminal defendant to receive a fair trial ... by rendering him unable or unwilling to assist counsel." Moran's plea colloquy only augments the manifold causes for concern by suggesting that his waivers and his assent to the charges against him were not rendered in a truly voluntary and intelligent fashion. Upon this evidence, there can be no doubt that the trial judge should have conducted another competency evaluation to determine Moran's capacity to waive the right to counsel and represent himself, instead of relying upon the psychiatrists' reports that he was able to stand trial with the assistance of counsel.

Questions and Comments

1. *Competency to plead guilty.* Roughly 90% of all criminal cases are resolved through pleas of guilty. Thus it would seem—contrary to the impression one gets from case law and commentary—that a criminal defendant's competency to plead guilty and participate in plea negotiations, rather than his or her competency to stand trial, should be the primary focus of the parties in most cases (as it was in earlier times—see pp. 1005–06). Many authorities suggest that, in practical terms, this oversight is of little import. For instance, the American Bar Association has stated: "Ordinarily, absent additional information bearing on defendant's competence, a finding made that the defendant is competent to stand trial should be sufficient to establish the defendant's competence to plead guilty." Criminal Justice Mental Health Standard 7–5.1(a)(i). As the majority in *Godinez* points out, most federal courts have found that *Dusky's* language suffices in this context.

However, some differences between the two situations are worth noting. On the one hand, the person pleading guilty will not have to undergo the stress of trial. On the other, unlike the person going to trial, the person who pleads guilty necessarily waives the rights to jury trial and trial counsel, the right to confront one's accusers, and the privilege against self-incrimination. Moreover, the defendant's suggestibility (i.e., likelihood of going along unthinkingly with the suggestions of others) may be more relevant in the latter context, since the Supreme Court has held that a guilty plea must not only be "intelligent" and "knowing" but also "voluntary." In short, the person pleading guilty must make several choices, while the person who is going to trial may not have to make any (although, as *Godinez* points out, a defendant at trial could have to make some decisions which are similar). This difference may explain why the Ninth Circuit rejected *Dusky's* "rational understanding" language in favor of a "rational choice" standard for determining competency to plead guilty.

In practice, would requiring "more" competency to plead guilty than to stand trial be likely to "create a class of semi-competent defendants who are not protected from prosecution because they have been found competent to stand trial, but who are denied the leniency of the plea bargaining process because they are not competent to plead guilty?" Note, "Competence to Plead Guilty: A New Standard," 1974 Duke Law Journal 149, 170. On the other hand, does equation of the standards lead to inappropriate guilty pleas? Assume, for instance, that Jones, subject of the Problem on pp. 1011–17, is competent to stand trial, but cannot meet the Ninth Circuit's reasoned choice test. Should be barred from pleading guilty?

2. *Distinguishing adjudicative competency and decisional competency.* Professor Bonnie has suggested a different way of looking at these issues that may help explain why most courts have not followed the Ninth Circuit. Richard Bonnie, "The Competence of Criminal Defendants: A Theoretical Reformulation," 10 Behav. Sci. & L. 291 (1992). He first makes the distinction, alluded to above, between adjudicative competency and decisional competency. The adjudicative competencies, like competency to stand trial and other competency to proceed standards, focus on generalized capacities—a capacity to understand the proceedings and an ability to relate to one's attorney—and are required to protect the reliability and dignity of the criminal process. Decisional competencies, like competency to plead guilty or competency to waive an attorney, differ from adjudicative competencies because they assess the capacity to make a specified decision and are required as a means of protecting autonomy. Bonnie then analogizes pleading guilty to treatment decisionmaking, which also involves making a specific decision. This analogy enables him to make use of the notion, developed by those who have analyzed treatment decisionmaking, that the level of competency required to consent to a recommended treatment should be lower than the level of competency required for a refusal of a recommended treatment (an idea discussed at pp. 932–35). Applied to guilty pleas, this framework would require greater competency to make a plea that is inconsistent with advice of counsel.

In a later article developing his thesis, Professor Bonnie differentiated between the "basic understanding" test, the "basic rationality" test, the "appreciation" test, and the "reasoned choice" test (which correspond to the understanding, understanding-and-belief, appreciation, and rational manipulation tests described earlier in this chapter at pp. 927–29). Richard Bonnie, "The Competence of Criminal Defendants: Beyond Dusky and Drope," 47 U. Miami L. Rev. 539 (1993). According to Bonnie, a waiver of rights consistent with counsel's advice should require only basic understanding (for waiver of most rights) or basic rationality (for pleading guilty). In contrast, a waiver *against* the advice of counsel should normally be considered valid only if the person can pass the appreciation test (for most rights) or the reasoned choice test (for pleading guilty). Id. at 577–580. Can you see how this analysis might explain why, in cases where client and attorney agree about the plea, courts are willing to equate competency to stand trial and competency to plead guilty? How would Bonnie analyze Moran's competency to plead guilty?

Consider now the following facts, taken from *United States v. Timmins*, 301 F.3d 974 (9th Cir.2002):

> The defendant, indicted on five counts of bank robbery and one count of using and carrying a firearm during a crime of violence, was offered a plea bargain of 12 ½ years. Though faced with overwhelming

evidence against him and a possible 30–year sentence if he was convicted, he refused the plea, rejecting his counsel's strong recommendation to accept it. Because of this disagreement and further disagreement about his mental condition, Timmins requested new counsel. The new attorney stated that, although he also recommended that the defendant accept the plea agreement, the defendant would be able to aid and assist in his defense at a trial, and specifically noted that Timmins was able to discuss the strengths and weaknesses of the case and possible witnesses and strategy. He also noted that the defendant understood that his defenses were "somewhat uphill." At a hearing to determine his competency, one expert likewise concluded Timmins was able to aid and assist his attorney, while the second expert disagreed with this assessment, in large part because Timmins described his charges as "trivial." Both experts agreed, however, that Timmins was delusional and paranoid. Specifically, they noted that he had a fixed delusional belief that he was being harassed by the police and "the system" because of envy and resentment about his athletic ability and his intellect. One expert reported that Timmins was convinced he would be acquitted and the other noted that he would likely "make ineffectual arguments against the apparently strong evidence that exists against him [which] would seem to be the same as allowing any 'obviously' guilty party to proceed to trial with no defense except a denial of guilt." The judge permitted trial to proceed and the defendant was convicted. [The Ninth Circuit reversed the conviction on the ground Timmins was incompetent].

How would the Supreme Court analyze this case? Bonnie? If Timmins had instead agreed to the plea, should that fact alone change the analysis of whether he is competent, as Bonnie implies? Compare *Timmins* to *United States v. Damon*, 191 F.3d 561 (4th Cir. 1999), where the defendant pleaded guilty to capital charges with the *concurrence* of his attorneys. As the dissenting opinion described the facts:

> [T]he district court, after learning that Damon had taken medication during his stay at the hospital, asked Damon whether he understood (1) the charges against him, (2) the constitutional rights he was waiving by pleading guilty, (3) the terms of his Plea Agreement, and (4) the consequences of his guilty plea. Damon answered each question in the affirmative and in a coherent fashion. Damon also told the district court that he was satisfied with his attorneys and that he was in fact guilty of the offense to which he pled guilty. The district court also asked Damon's lawyers whether they had any reason to question Damon's competence to plead guilty. Although aware that Damon had taken some medication earlier, his lawyers, both of whom were highly experienced due to the fact that Damon was subject to the death penalty, answered no.

Id. at 567 (Williams, J., dissenting). Nonetheless the majority held that Damon's guilty plea must be overturned because the district court failed to inquire further into the effects of the anti-depressant medication Damon was taking. Id. at 565. Is this result consistent with *Godinez*?

3. *Competency to waive an attorney. Godinez* also equated competency to waive one's attorney with competency to stand trial. Would Bonnie agree

with the Court's analysis on this point? Does the Court's requirement that waivers of counsel be "voluntary and intelligent" in effect demand a higher level of competency, or is this requirement aimed merely at ensuring the defendant "understands" the consequences of proceeding *pro se*, i.e., the fact that the defendant will be responsible for tactical, evidentiary and procedural decisions? See note 12 of the majority opinion. Should Moran have been permitted to waive his attorney? Note that even if a defendant is permitted to proceed *pro se*, the court may appoint "standby counsel" who may give the defendant legal advice so long as the defendant retains actual control over the case presented to the jury and the jury retains the perception that the defendant represents him or herself. *McKaskle v. Wiggins*, 465 U.S. 168, 104 S.Ct. 944, 79 L.Ed.2d 122 (1984).

In *Indiana v. Edwards*, ___ U.S. ___, 128 S.Ct. 2379, 171 L.Ed. 345 (2008), the Court revisited the waiver-of-counsel issue and concluded that a state may force counsel on a defendant who is competent to stand trial if the trial judge does not believe the defendant is "mentally competent" to represent him or herself. Justice Breyer wrote the majority opinion. He began by distinguishing *Edwards* from *Godinez*:

> We . . . conclude that *Godinez* does not answer the question before us now. . . . [T]he *Godinez* defendant sought only to change his pleas to guilty, he did not seek to conduct trial proceedings, and his ability to conduct a defense at trial was expressly not at issue. Thus we emphasized in *Godinez* that we needed to consider only the defendant's "competence to *waive the right*." And we further emphasized that we need *not* consider the defendant's "technical legal knowledge" about how to proceed at trial. [Further], *Godinez* involved a State that sought to *permit* a gray-area defendant to represent himself. *Godinez*'s constitutional holding is that a State may do so. But that holding simply does not tell a State whether it may *deny* a gray-area defendant the right to represent himself—the matter at issue here. One might argue that *Godinez*'s grant (to a State) of permission to allow a gray-area defendant self-representation must implicitly include permission to deny self-representation. Cf. 509 U.S., at 402 ("States are free to adopt competency standards that are more elaborate than the *Dusky* formulation"). Yet one could more forcefully argue that *Godinez* simply did not consider whether the Constitution *requires* self-representation by gray-area defendants even in circumstances where the State seeks to disallow it (the question here). The upshot is that, in our view, the question before us is an open one.

Are you convinced that *Godinez* did not settle the question in *Edwards*? In any event, Breyer went on to explain why a person who is competent to stand trial under *Dusky*'s standard might nonetheless be denied the right to self-representation.

> [F]irst, . . . the Court's "mental competency" cases set forth a standard that focuses directly upon a defendant's "present ability to consult with his lawyer" [*Dusky*; *Drope*]. These standards assume representation by counsel and emphasize the importance of counsel. They thus suggest (though do not hold) that an instance in which a defendant who would

choose to forgo counsel at trial presents a very different set of circumstances, which in our view, calls for a different standard.

. . .

Second, the nature of the problem before us cautions against the use of a single mental competency standard for deciding both (1) whether a defendant who is represented by counsel can proceed to trial and (2) whether a defendant who goes to trial must be permitted to represent himself. Mental illness itself is not a unitary concept. It varies in degree. It can vary over time. It interferes with an individual's functioning at different times in different ways. . . . In certain instances an individual may well be able to satisfy *Dusky*'s mental competence standard, for he will be able to work with counsel at trial, yet at the same time he may be unable to carry out the basic tasks needed to present his own defense without the help of counsel. The American Psychiatric Association (APA) tells us (without dispute) in its *amicus* brief filed in support of neither party that "[d]isorganized thinking, deficits in sustaining attention and concentration, impaired expressive abilities, anxiety, and other common symptoms of severe mental illnesses can impair the defendant's ability to play the significantly expanded role required for self-representation even if he can play the lesser role of represented defendant." . . .

Third, in our view, a right of self-representation at trial will not "affirm the dignity" of a defendant who lacks the mental capacity to conduct his defense without the assistance of counsel. To the contrary, given that defendant's uncertain mental state, the spectacle that could well result from his self-representation at trial is at least as likely to prove humiliating as ennobling. Moreover, insofar as a defendant's lack of capacity threatens an improper conviction or sentence, self-representation in that exceptional context undercuts the most basic of the Constitution's criminal law objectives, providing a fair trial. As Justice Brennan put it, "[t]he Constitution would protect none of us if it prevented the courts from acting to preserve the very processes that the Constitution itself prescribes."

Further, proceedings must not only be fair, they must "appear fair to all who observe them." An *amicus* brief reports one psychiatrist's reaction to having observed a patient (a patient who had satisfied *Dusky*) try to conduct his own defense: "[H]ow in the world can our legal system allow an insane man to defend himself?" The application of *Dusky*'s basic mental competence standard can help in part to avoid this result. But given the different capacities needed to proceed to trial without counsel, there is little reason to believe that *Dusky* alone is sufficient. At the same time, the trial judge, particularly one such as the trial judge in this case, who presided over one of Edwards' competency hearings and his two trials, will often prove best able to make more fine-tuned mental capacity decisions, tailored to the individualized circumstances of a particular defendant.

We consequently conclude that the Constitution permits judges to take realistic account of the particular defendant's mental capacities by asking whether a defendant who seeks to conduct his own defense at trial is mentally competent to do so. That is to say, the Constitution permits States to insist upon representation by counsel for those competent enough to stand trial under *Dusky* but who still suffer from severe mental illness to the point where they are not competent to conduct trial proceedings by themselves.

Indiana has also asked us to adopt, as a measure of a defendant's ability to conduct a trial, a more specific standard that would "deny a criminal defendant the right to represent himself at trial where the defendant cannot communicate coherently with the court or a jury." We are sufficiently uncertain, however, as to how that particular standard would work in practice to refrain from endorsing it as a federal constitutional standard here. We need not now, and we do not, adopt it.

Indiana has also asked us to overrule *Faretta*. We decline to do so. We recognize that judges have sometimes expressed concern that *Faretta,* contrary to its intent, has led to trials that are unfair. But recent empirical research suggests that such instances are not common. See, *e.g.*, Hashimoto, Defending the Right of Self–Representation: An Empirical Look at the Pro Se Felony Defendant, 85 N. C. L. Rev. 423, 427, 447, 428 (2007) (noting that of the small number of defendants who chose to proceed *pro se*—"roughly 0.3% to 0.5%" of the total, state felony defendants in particular "appear to have achieved higher felony acquittal rates than their represented counterparts in that they were less likely to have been convicted of felonies"). At the same time, instances in which the trial's fairness is in doubt may well be concentrated in the 20 percent or so of self-representation cases where the mental competence of the defendant is also at issue. See *id.*, at 428 (about 20 percent of federal *pro se* felony defendants ordered to undergo competency evaluations). If so, today's opinion, assuring trial judges the authority to deal appropriately with cases in the latter category, may well alleviate those fair trial concerns.

Justice Scalia, joined by Justice Thomas, author of *Godinez*, dissented:

[U]ntil today, the right of self-representation has been accorded the same respect as other constitutional guarantees. The only circumstance in which we have permitted the State to deprive a defendant of this trial right is the one under which we have allowed the State to deny *other* such rights: when it is necessary to enable the trial to proceed in an orderly fashion. That overriding necessity, we have said, justifies forfeiture of even the Sixth Amendment right to be present at trial—if, after being threatened with removal, a defendant "insists on conducting himself in a manner so disorderly, disruptive, and disrespectful of the court that his trial cannot be carried on with him in the courtroom." *Illinois* v. *Allen,* 397 U.S. 337, 343 (1970). A *pro se* defendant may not "abuse the dignity of the courtroom," nor may he fail to "comply with relevant rules of procedural and substantive law," and a court may "terminate" the self-representation of a defendant who "deliberately engages in serious and obstructionist misconduct." This ground for terminating self-representation is unavailable here, however, because Edwards was not even allowed to begin to represent himself, and because he was respectful and compliant and did not provide a basis to conclude a trial could not have gone forward had he been allowed to press his own claims.

Beyond this circumstance, we have never constrained the ability of a defendant to retain "actual control over the case he chooses to present to the jury"—what we have termed "the core of the *Faretta* right." Thus, while *Faretta* recognized that the right of self-representation does not bar the court from appointing standby counsel, we explained in *Wiggins* that "[t]he *pro se* defendant must be allowed to control the organization and content of his own defense, to make motions, to argue points of law, to participate in *voir dire*, to question witnesses, and to address the court and the jury at appropriate points in the trial." Furthermore, because "multiple voices 'for the defense'" could "confuse the message the defendant wishes to convey," a standby attorney's participation would be barred when it would "destroy the jury's perception that the defendant is representing himself."

. . . I would not adopt an approach to the right of self-representation that we have squarely rejected for other rights—allowing courts to disregard the right when doing so serves the purposes for which the right was intended. But if I were to adopt such an approach, I would remain in dissent, because I believe the Court's assessment of the purposes of the right of self-representation is inaccurate to boot. While there is little doubt that preserving individual " 'dignity' " (to which the Court refers), is paramount among those purposes, there is equally little doubt that the loss of "dignity" the right is designed to prevent is *not* the defendant's making a fool of himself by presenting an amateurish or even incoherent defense. Rather, the dignity at issue is the supreme human dignity of being master of one's fate rather than a ward of the State—the dignity of individual choice. *Faretta* explained that the Sixth Amendment's counsel clause should not be invoked to impair " 'the exercise of [the defendant's] free choice' " to dispense with the right, for "whatever else may be said of those who wrote the Bill of Rights, surely there can be no doubt that they understood the inestimable worth of free choice." Nine years later, when we wrote in *Wiggins* that the self-representation right served the "dignity and autonomy of the accused," we explained in no uncertain terms that this meant according every defendant the right to his say in court. In particular, we said that individual dignity and autonomy barred standby counsel from participating in a manner that would to "destroy the jury's perception that the defendant is representing himself," and meant that "the *pro se* defendant is entitled to preserve actual control over the case he chooses to present to the jury." In sum, if the Court is to honor the particular conception of "dignity" that underlies the self-representation right, it should respect the autonomy of the individual by honoring his choices knowingly and voluntarily made.

A further purpose that the Court finds is advanced by denial of the right of self-representation is the purpose of assuring that trials "appear fair to all who observe them." To my knowledge we have never denied a defendant a right simply on the ground that it would make his trial appear less "fair" to outside observers, and I would not inaugurate that principle here. But were I to do so, I would not apply it to deny a defendant the right to represent himself when he knowingly and voluntarily waives counsel. When Edwards stood to say that "I have a defense that I would like to represent or present to the Judge," it seems to me the epitome of both actual and apparent unfairness for the judge to say, I have heard "your desire to proceed by yourself and I've denied your request, so your attorney will speak for you from now on."

. . .

. . . [T]o hold that a defendant may be deprived of the right to make legal arguments for acquittal simply because a state-selected agent has made different arguments on his behalf is, as Justice Frankfurter wrote in *Adams*, to "imprison a man in his privileges and call it the Constitution." In singling out mentally ill defendants for this treatment, the Court's opinion does not even have the questionable virtue of being politically correct. At a time when all society is trying to mainstream the mentally impaired, the Court permits them to be deprived of a basic constitutional right—for their own good.

Today's holding is extraordinarily vague. The Court does not accept Indiana's position that self-representation can be denied " 'where the defendant cannot communicate coherently with the court or a jury.' " It does not even hold that Edwards was properly denied his right to represent himself. It holds only that lack of mental competence can under some circumstances form a basis for denying the right to proceed *pro se*. We will presumably give some meaning to this holding in the future, but the indeterminacy makes a bad holding worse. Once the right of self-representation for the mentally ill is a sometime thing, trial judges will have every incentive to make their lives easier—to avoid the painful necessity of deciphering occasional pleadings of the sort contained in the Appendix to today's opinion—by appointing knowledgeable and literate counsel.

The majority opinion described in detail Edwards' lengthy history of psychiatric hospitalizations and his struggle to maintain competence, as well as the fact that he was still diagnosed with schizophrenia at the time of his second trial. In the appendix referred to by the dissent the majority also included one of his motions, which included sentences such as: "The appointed motion of permissive intervention filed therein the court superior on, 6–26–01 caused a stay of action and apon [sic] it's [sic] expiration or thereafter three years the plan to establish a youth program to and for the coordination of aspects of law enforcement to prevent and reduce crime amoung [sic] young people in Indiana became a diplomatic act as under the Safe Streets Act of 1967, 'A omnibuc [sic] considerate agent: I membered [sic] clients within the public and others that at/production of the courts actions showcased causes.' " However, the trial judge had found Edwards competent based on numerous psychiatric reports, and the dissent noted the following facts:

Edwards made arguments in the courtroom that were more coherent than his written pleadings. In seeking to represent himself at his first trial, Edwards complained in detail that the attorney representing him had not spent adequate time preparing and was not sharing legal materials for use in his defense. The trial judge concluded that Edwards had knowingly and voluntarily waived his right to counsel and proceeded to quiz Edwards about matters of state law. Edwards correctly answered questions about the meaning of *voir dire* and how it operated, and described the basic framework for admitting videotape evidence to trial, though he was unable to answer other questions, including questions about the topics covered by state evidentiary rules that the judge identified only by number. He persisted in his request to represent himself, but the judge denied the request because Edwards acknowledged he would need a continuance. Represented by counsel, he was convicted of criminal recklessness and theft, but the jury deadlocked on charges of attempted murder and battery.

At his second trial, Edwards again asked the judge to be allowed to proceed *pro se*. He explained that he and his attorney disagreed about which defense to present to the attempted murder charge. Edwards' counsel favored lack of intent to kill; Edwards, self-defense. As the defendant put it: "My objection is me and my attorney actually had discussed a defense, I think prosecution had mentioned that, and we are in disagreement with it. He has a defense and I have a defense that I would like to represent or present to the Judge."

128 S.Ct. at 2390. If these were the only reasons Edwards gave for wanting to represent himself (in other words, he did not give other, clearly "crazy" reasons), would you as a trial judge force an attorney on him? What else would you like to know?

4. *Competency to waive the right to tried while competent.* Earlier in this chapter (see pp. 1022–24) the issue of whether counsel should be able to override a client's objection to a competency evaluation was discussed. Reconsider that issue now in light of the present material. What level of competency would Bonnie require of a defendant who wants to proceed to trial despite counsel's concern about competency to stand trial? Is *Edwards* relevant here as well?

5. *Competency to waive an insanity defense.* There are a number of other situations in which "decisional" competency could be implicated. According to the American Bar Association's Model Rules of Professional Conduct, for instance, the client, not the lawyer, should be the ultimate authority for all "fundamental decisions" in the criminal process. In addition to deciding whether or not to plead guilty, the rule lists as "fundamental" the decisions to waive the right to jury trial, testify, and forego an appeal. Proposed Rule 1.2(a) (Final Draft 1982). Left unclear by the ABA Rule is how much control the defendant should have over the legal strategy of the case (outside of the decision to testify).

One issue that arises occasionally in this regard is whether an insanity defense may be raised over the defendant's objection. Several courts have required a separate hearing to determine whether an objecting defendant is voluntarily and intelligently waiving the defense; if so, the defendant's wishes are honored. See, e.g., *Frendak v. United States*, 408 A.2d 364 (D.C.App.1979). In contrast, for some time the District of Columbia Circuit Court of Appeals permitted assertion of the defense over the defendant's objection, even if the defendant was *competent* to make such a decision, on the ground that it would be morally repugnant to convict a person who was insane at the time of the offense. *Whalem v. United States*, 346 F.2d 812 (D.C.Cir.1965). However in *United States v. Marble*, 940 F.2d 1543 (D.C.Cir. 1991), the D.C. Circuit overturned *Whalem*, primarily because Congress had since made clear, via the Insanity Defense Reform Act of 1984, that insanity is an affirmative defense in federal court, thus making its assertion the prerogative of the defense.

Under the *Whalem* approach, the defendant's wishes are to be taken into account but are not dispositive. Is this justifiable? Judge Bazelon, who wrote *Whalem*, undoubtedly would support a competent nondangerous person's right to refuse psychiatric treatment. Cf. David Bazelon, "Implementing the Right to Treatment," 36 Chicago L.Rev. 742 (1969). How, if at all, is compelling the assertion of an insanity defense different from compelling treatment over a competent person's objection?

Under the *Frendak* approach, note that a finding of competency to stand trial does not necessarily mean the person is competent to make a decision about the insanity defense; a separate hearing is required in *all* cases. How does this result comport with *Moran's* analysis? Bonnie's?

Consider in this regard the case of Ted Kaczynski, a.k.a. the Unabomber. Kaczynski was charged with several capital crimes arising from deaths caused by bombs that he sent through the mail. Most mental health professionals who evaluated Kaczynski thought he was suffering from schizophrenia, in large part because of delusions that he was being "maligned and harassed by family members and modern society." See William Glaberson, "Kaczynski's Lawyers Now Say He is Competent," N.Y. Times, Jan. 21, 1998. Yet Kaczynski was adamant that evidence of mental aberration not be presented either at trial, in connection with an insanity or diminished capacity defense, or at sentencing in mitigation. According to his attorneys, he had a "deep and abiding fear" that he would be perceived as mentally ill, a fear he had possessed his entire life. In his famous Manifesto he had suggested that he would rather die than be subjected to the indignity of being called mentally ill. See generally, Stephen J. Dubner, "I Don't Want to Live Long," Time, Oct. 18, 1999, at 44, 46. Either by himself or with the help of lawyers, he apparently planned instead to assert what amounted to a "necessity" defense—an argument that the letter bombs, most of which were sent to people who had some connection with technology, were a necessary way of alerting the world to the deaths and widespread destruction of civilization that technological "progress" will cause. William Glaberson, "Kaczynski Tries Unsuccessfully to Dismiss His Lawyers," N.Y. Times, Jan. 8, 1998. Although the court found Kaczynski competent to stand trial, it never had to decide whether he could forego the insanity defense against his lawyers' wishes because he pleaded guilty to the charges in exchange for four life sentences (a decision he made, he later claimed, because he wanted to avoid his lawyers labeling him paranoid schizophrenic). Dubner, supra.

Was Kaczynski "competent" to waive the insanity defense? How would the Supreme Court analyze this issue? Bonnie? Would it make any difference if the reason Kaczynski gave for wanting to avoid the defense was that testimony bolstering such a defense might reveal that he had wanted a sex-change operation in 1966 and that at one time he had fantasized about mutilating his girl friend (both facts revealed in the psychiatric reports)?

What if his denial that he was mentally ill stemmed from mental illness (the anosognosia condition referred to at p. 982)? Doctor Amador, a psychologist involved in the case, wrote the following:

> In most cases involving people with schizophrenia, severe deficits in illness awareness and the irrational compulsion to prove one's "sanity" despite life threatening consequences, are a consequence of brain dysfunction rather than manipulation or defensiveness. It was anosognosia, a neurological condition that results in the type of unawareness just described, that kept [Kaczynski] from complying with the court order to be examined by experts, as opposed to manipulation or a willful violation of the judge's decree.... The high prevalence of unawareness of illness in schizophrenia has been replicated in several studies.... The International Pilot Study of Schizophrenia, a multinational and cross-cultural study conducted for the World Health Organization, found that eighty-one percent of 811 patients denied that they had an illness. ... In most cases involving patients with schizophrenia, psychological defense played a small role, but accounted for very little of the variation in insight. Neuropsychological deficits, on the other hand, were highly correlated with lower levels of insight.... Research indicates that anosognosia typically does not improve when individuals with schizophrenia are treated with antipsychotic medications. Thus, the patient with anosognosia who is treated successfully, who is less delusional, is still likely to believe he is not ill and feel the compulsion to prove this belief to be true at all costs.... In other words, if [a person like Kaczynski]'s anosognosia persists after treatment with antipsychotic medication and he continues to prohibit his attorneys to mount a mental illness defense, an argument once again can be made that he is incompetent to stand trial.

Xavier F. Amador & Andrew A. Shiva, "Insight into Schizophrenia: Anosognosia, Competency, and Civil Liberties," 11 Geo. Mason Civ. Rts. L. J. 25, 26–39 (2000).

Assume that Kaczynski had not pleaded guilty and had continued to insist that mental state issues not be raised at his trial. What should the lawyers have done? Followed his wishes? Presented the defense over his objection? Withdrawn? (Under the ABA's Model Code of Professional Conduct Rule 1.16(b)(3), the lawyer may withdraw if "a client insists upon pursuing an objective that the lawyer considers repugnant or imprudent.") See generally, Christopher Slobogin & Amy Mashburn, "The Criminal Defense Lawyer's Fiduciary Duty to Clients with Mental Disability," 68 Fordham L. Rev. 1581 (2000)(analyzing the lawyer's ethical duty in Kaczynski case and similar cases).

6. *Competency to waive presentation of mitigating evidence in capital cases.* In *Schriro v. Landrigan*, ___ U.S. ___, 127 S.Ct. 1933, 167 L.Ed.2d 836 (2007), the Supreme Court held that an attorney's failure to fully investigate mitigating evidence in a capital case is not ineffective assistance of counsel when the defendant refuses to permit any mitigating evidence to be presented, even if the defendant's demand may not be good strategy. Presumably, however, the defendant who makes such a decision must be competent to do so, and waiver must be knowing and voluntary, per *Godinez v. Moran* and

Edwards v. Arizona. Recall Professor Garrison's argument, at pp. 935–36, that for some individuals the effects of depression "appear to overcome the desire for life and health and to coerce decisions against the patient's medical interests." If the reason for prohibiting the presentation of mitigating evidence is depression, should the individual be considered competent? Was Moran competent in this respect?

Some commentators and a few courts have taken the position that even if the objecting offender is competent, the state's interest in a reliable outcome under the Eighth Amendment *requires* the attorney, or a substitute attorney, to present mitigating evidence. See Linda E. Carter, "Maintaining Systemic Integrity in Capital Cases: The Use of Court–Appointed Counsel to Present Mitigating Evidence When the Defendant Advocates Death," 55 Tenn. L.Rev. 95, 140–44 (1987); Anthony J. Casey, "Maintaining the Integrity of Death: An Argument for Restricting a Defendant's Right to Volunteer for Execution at Certain Stages in Capital Proceedings," 30 Am. J. Crim. L. 75 (2002). How is presenting psychiatric evidence over a competent defendant's objection at a capital sentencing proceeding different from presenting evidence of insanity at trial over a competent defendant's objection (which, as the previous note indicates, few jurisdictions officially permit today)?

In light of the foregoing material, consider whether the court in *Smith v. State,* 686 N.E.2d 1264 (Ind. 1997), was correct when it affirmed Smith's plea to a capital charge and his refusal to present mitigating evidence. In his testimony at the competency hearing, Smith stated:

> I don't feel I'm incompetent, you know. I don't think my attorneys feel I'm incompetent. You know, I feel [my attorneys actions are] more of a humanitarian act now, you know, and-you know, I'm through pissing around with it. I mean, you know, I come here today to get sentenced, you know. I mean, that's what I want. You know, my attitude has not changed, you know. You probably could hire 50 psychiatrists and have my attorneys pay half of them and the prosecutor pay half of them and they would come up with 50 different evaluations, you know.
>
> . . . .
>
> . . . I know what I'm doing, you know. I'm fully aware, you know. This is one of the tests they gave me here. I want to read it to the court here, some of the questions on here, and this is how they say I'm extremely depressed, you know. I mean, I'm in prison. Everybody in prison is depressed, you know. I mean, if I was happy, I mean, . . . I wouldn't want to die if I was happy where I was at. I mean, it's no secret, you know. Prison isn't a nice place, you know. I've been in prison for the last 13 years, you know. I'm tired of being in prison, you know, and I'm at the point now where life doesn't have a whole lot of meaning for me and-you know, these are some of the questions that they-Question One, ["]I feel downhearted, blue, and sad.["] It says ["]none or little of the time, some of the time, a good part of the time, more or all of the time.["] I mean, how would anybody in prison answer that question? All of the time. I mean, you know, I'm not living at the Hilton Hotel, you know. The second question is, ["]Morning is when I feel the best.["] You know, I don't feel good any of the time, you know. I'm miserable. You know, my life is miserable. It's a miserable existence. I don't blame

anybody for it, you know. I put myself in prison, you know, and I'm dealing with what I've got to do, you know.... Any normal man that's in prison, you know, is, you know, going to feel downhearted, blue, or sad, you know. I mean, I don't see anybody running around the prison smiling and laughing, you know. I mean, it don't happen.... ["]My mind is as clear as it used to be.["] My mind is probably more clear now than its ever been.... ["]I feel hopeful about the future. ["] I don't have a future, you know. I mean, if I don't get the death sentence, I still don't have a future. What I've got is a slow death. I'm asking the court to give me justice, give me-let me die, you know. I mean, I've got a slow death right now, you know. I'm never getting out of prison. You know, I killed somebody. You know, I'm asking the court to give me what I've got coming, you know....

I'm asking the court to get it on. Let's do it and get it over with because you're wasting my time and the court's time, you know. I'm not going to participate in any more psychiatrists or therapists or any of that there, you know. I'm no more incompetent now than I was June 30th when the crime was committed and I will not participate. I mean, if you want to drop the charges on me, go ahead and drop them. If you don't want to drop the charges, then give me what I've got coming and let's get it over with because I'm through pissing around.... I'm not going to sit here and have this guy's family sit in here and look at me.

Id. at 1268. One of Smith's lawyers, who had talked to Smith some time earlier, testified: "If he was out of the [solitary housing unit] and in a different living situation, he has told me point-blank on two occasions that he would probably change his mind about the death penalty." Id. at 1267. In response to this latter testimony, a doctor agreed that solitary confinement could be affecting Smith's decision, but that "[i]f he can make his own decision depending upon those circumstances and [it] varies as a consequence, that would indicate his ability to assess and make judgments about his environment and his future actions on the basis of that environment and that he is not inflexibly, as a consequence of mental disorder or disease, unable to exercise that judgment. That led to my conclusion that he was competent." Id. at 1269.

7. *Waiving the right to remain silent; voluntariness.* Under the constitution, most waiver decisions in the criminal context must not only be "knowing and intelligent" but also "voluntary."" As *Godinez* indicates, for instance, guilty pleas and waivers of counsel must be knowing, intelligent and voluntary. Voluntariness is usually not a significant issue in connection with these latter issues because counsel is intimately involved in the decisionmaking process and can protect against coercion. Consider, however, the Jones case. If you were the judge in that case, would you accept a plea of guilty from the defendant, knowing that his attorney had suggested that he plead guilty?

It is in connection with police interrogation, where counsel is often not present, that the voluntariness concept has received the most attention. The

n. Note the analogy here to the informed consent doctrine, which requires not only a competent decision based on full disclosure of relevant information, but also that the decision be voluntary. See Chapter Four.

law of confessions is governed by two separate constitutional provisions. As with guilty pleas, a confession is invalid under the due process clause if, in the totality of the circumstances, it is involuntarily made. *Brown v. Mississippi,* 297 U.S. 278, 56 S.Ct. 461, 80 L.Ed. 682 (1936). Additionally, a confession may be considered inadmissible by virtue of the fifth amendment's privilege against self-incrimination, as interpreted by *Miranda v. Arizona,* 384 U.S. 436, 86 S.Ct. 1602, 16 L.Ed.2d 694 (1966). *Miranda* requires that, before every "custodial interrogation", the police must inform the defendant of the right to remain silent and the right to an attorney during the interrogation; if these warnings are not given, any admissions obtained during the interrogation are not admissible (even though, in fact, the admissions may not be "coerced"; thus, this part of *Miranda* devised a prophylactic rule designed to provide defendants with information concerning their right to remain silent). If the warnings are given, subsequent admissions may still be inadmissible if the state is unable to show by a preponderance of the evidence that they were given after a knowing, intelligent and voluntary waiver of the right to remain silent. On the other hand, if the admissions are voluntarily made before custodial interrogation begins or are the product of a valid post-warning waiver, then they are admissible. The following materials further explore, in the interrogation context, the problematic "voluntariness" issue.

COLORADO v. CONNELLY

Supreme Court of the United States, 1986.
479 U.S. 157, 107 S.Ct. 515, 93 L.Ed.2d 473.

* * *

CHIEF JUSTICE REHNQUIST delivered the opinion of the Court.

* * *

I

On August 18, 1983, Officer Patrick Anderson of the Denver Police Department was in uniform, working in an off-duty capacity in downtown Denver. Respondent Francis Connelly approached Officer Anderson and, without any prompting, stated that he had murdered someone and wanted to talk about it. Anderson immediately advised respondent that he had the right to remain silent, that anything he said could be used against him in court, and that he had the right to an attorney prior to any police questioning. See *Miranda v. Arizona,* 384 U.S. 436, 86 S.Ct. 1602, 16 L.Ed.2d 694 (1966). Respondent stated that he understood these rights but he still wanted to talk about the murder. Understandably bewildered by this confession, Officer Anderson asked respondent several questions. Connelly denied that he had been drinking, denied that he had been taking any drugs, and stated that, in the past, he had been a patient in several mental hospitals. Officer Anderson again told Connelly that he was under no obligation to say anything. Connelly replied that it was "all right," and that he would talk to Officer Anderson because his conscience had been bothering him. To Officer

Anderson, respondent appeared to understand fully the nature of his acts.

Shortly thereafter, Homicide Detective Stephen Antuna arrived. Respondent was again advised of his rights, and Detective Antuna asked him "what he had on his mind." Respondent answered that he had come all the way from Boston to confess to the murder of Mary Ann Junta, a young girl whom he had killed in Denver sometime during November 1982. Respondent was taken to police headquarters, and a search of police records revealed that the body of an unidentified female had been found in April 1983. Respondent openly detailed his story to Detective Antuna and Sergeant Thomas Haney, and readily agreed to take the officers to the scene of the killing. Under Connelly's sole direction, the two officers and respondent proceeded in a police vehicle to the location of the crime. Respondent pointed out the exact location of the murder. Throughout this episode, Detective Antuna perceived no indication whatsoever that respondent was suffering from any kind of mental illness.

Respondent was held overnight. During an interview with the public defender's office the following morning, he became visibly disoriented. He began giving confused answers to questions, and for the first time, stated that "voices" had told him to come to Denver and that he had followed the directions of these voices in confessing. Respondent was sent to a state hospital for evaluation. He was initially found incompetent to assist in his own defense. By March 1984, however, the doctors evaluating respondent determined that he was competent to proceed to trial.

At a preliminary hearing, respondent moved to suppress all of his statements. Doctor Jeffrey Metzner, a psychiatrist employed by the state hospital, testified that respondent was suffering from chronic schizophrenia and was in a psychotic state at least as of August 17, 1983, the day before he confessed. Metzner's interviews with respondent revealed that respondent was following the "voice of God." This voice instructed respondent to withdraw money from the bank, to buy an airplane ticket, and to fly from Boston to Denver. When respondent arrived from Boston, God's voice became stronger and told respondent either to confess to the killing or to commit suicide. Reluctantly following the command of the voices, respondent approached Officer Anderson and confessed.

Dr. Metzner testified that, in his expert opinion, respondent was experiencing "command hallucinations." This condition interfered with respondent's "volitional abilities; that is, his ability to make free and rational choices." Dr. Metzner further testified that Connelly's illness did not significantly impair his cognitive abilities. Thus, respondent understood the rights he had when Officer Anderson and Detective Antuna advised him that he need not speak. Dr. Metzner admitted that the "voices" could in reality be Connelly's interpretation of his own guilt, but explained that in his opinion, Connelly's psychosis motivated his confession.

On the basis of this evidence the Colorado trial court decided that respondent's statements must be suppressed because they were "involuntary." [T]he court ruled that a confession is admissible only if it is a product of the defendant's rational intellect and "free will." Although the court found that the police had done nothing wrong or coercive in securing respondent's confession, Connelly's illness destroyed his volition and compelled him to confess. The trial court also found that Connelly's mental state vitiated his attempted waiver of the right to counsel and the privilege against compulsory self-incrimination. Accordingly, respondent's initial statements and his custodial confession were suppressed.

The Colorado Supreme Court affirmed. In that court's view, the proper test for admissibility is whether the statements are "the product of a rational intellect and a free will." Indeed, "the absence of police coercion or duress does not foreclose a finding of involuntariness. One's capacity for rational judgment and free choice may be overborne as much by certain forms of severe mental illness as by external pressure." The court found that the very admission of the evidence in a court of law was sufficient state action to implicate the Due Process Clause of the Fourteenth Amendment to the United States Constitution. The evidence fully supported the conclusion that respondent's initial statement was not the product of a rational intellect and a free will. The court then considered respondent's attempted waiver of his constitutional rights and found that respondent's mental condition precluded his ability to make a valid waiver. The Colorado Supreme Court thus affirmed the trial court's decision to suppress all of Connelly's statements.

II

The Due Process Clause of the Fourteenth Amendment provides that no State shall "deprive any person of life, liberty, or property, without due process of law." Just last Term, in *Miller v. Fenton*, we held that by virtue of the Due Process Clause "certain interrogation techniques, either in isolation or as applied to the unique characteristics of a particular suspect, are so offensive to a civilized system of justice that they must be condemned."

Indeed, coercive government misconduct was the catalyst for this Court's seminal confession case, *Brown v. Mississippi*, 297 U.S. 278, 56 S.Ct. 461, 80 L.Ed. 682 (1936). In that case, police officers extracted confessions from the accused through brutal torture. The Court had little difficulty concluding that even though the Fifth Amendment did not at that time apply to the States, the actions of the police were "revolting to the sense of justice." The Court has retained this due process focus, even after holding, in *Malloy v. Hogan,* 378 U.S. 1, 84 S.Ct. 1489, 12 L.Ed.2d 653 (1964), that the Fifth Amendment privilege against compulsory self-incrimination applies to the States.

Thus the cases considered by this Court over the 50 years since *Brown v. Mississippi* have focused upon the crucial element of police overreaching. While each confession case has turned on its own set of factors justifying the conclusion that police conduct was oppressive, all have contained a substantial element of coercive police conduct. Absent police conduct causally related to the confession, there is simply no basis for concluding that any state actor has deprived a criminal defendant of due process of law. Respondent correctly notes that as interrogators have turned to more subtle forms of psychological persuasion, courts have found the mental condition of the defendant a more significant factor in the "voluntariness" calculus. But this fact does not justify a conclusion that a defendant's mental condition, by itself and apart from its relation to official coercion, should ever dispose of the inquiry into constitutional "voluntariness."

Respondent relies on *Blackburn v. Alabama,* 361 U.S. 199, 80 S.Ct. 274, 4 L.Ed.2d 242 (1960), and *Townsend v. Sain,* 372 U.S. 293, 83 S.Ct. 745, 9 L.Ed.2d 770 (1963), for the proposition that the "deficient mental condition of the defendants in those cases was sufficient to render their confessions involuntary." But respondent's reading of *Blackburn* and *Townsend* ignores the integral element of police overreaching present in both cases. In *Blackburn,* the Court found that the petitioner was probably insane at the time of his confession and the police learned during the interrogation that Blackburn had a history of mental problems. The police exploited this weakness with coercive tactics: "The eight-to nine-hour sustained interrogation in a tiny room which was upon occasion literally filled with police officers; the absence of Blackburn's friends, relatives, or legal counsel; [and] the composition of the confession by the Deputy Sheriff rather than by Blackburn." These tactics supported a finding that the confession was involuntary. Indeed, the Court specifically condemned police activity that "wrings a confession out of an accused against his will." *Townsend* presented a similar instance of police wrongdoing. In that case, a police physician had given Townsend a drug with truth-serum properties. The subsequent confession, obtained by officers who knew that Townsend had been given drugs, was held involuntary. These two cases demonstrate that while mental condition is surely relevant to an individual's susceptibility to police coercion, mere examination of the confessant's state of mind can never conclude the due process inquiry.

* * *

"[T]he central purpose of a criminal trial is to decide the factual question of the defendant's guilt or innocence" and while we have previously held that exclusion of evidence may be necessary to protect constitutional guarantees, both the necessity for the collateral inquiry and the exclusion of evidence deflect a criminal trial from its basic purpose. Respondent would now have us require sweeping inquiries into the state of mind of a criminal defendant who has confessed, inquiries quite divorced from any coercion brought to bear on the defendant by the State. We think the Constitution rightly leaves this sort of inquiry to be resolved by state laws governing the admission of evidence and erects no standard of its own in this area. A statement rendered by one in the condition of respondent might be proved to be quite unreliable, but this is a matter to be governed by the evidentiary laws of the forum, see, *e.g.,* Fed.Rule Evid. 601, and not by the Due Process Clause of the Fourteenth Amendment. "The aim of the requirement of due process is not to exclude presumptively false evidence, but to prevent fundamental unfairness in the use of evidence, whether true or false." . . .

We hold that coercive police activity is a necessary predicate to the finding that a confession is not "voluntary" within the meaning of the Due Process Clause of the Fourteenth Amendment. We also conclude that the taking of respondent's statements, and their admission into evidence, constitute no violation of that Clause.

III

* * *

We also think that the Supreme Court of Colorado was mistaken in its analysis of the question of whether respondent had waived his *Miranda* rights in this case.[3] Of course, a waiver must at a minimum be "voluntary" to be effective against an accused. The Supreme Court of Colorado in addressing this question relied on the testimony of the court-appointed psychiatrist to the effect that respondent was not capable of making a "free decision with respect to his constitutional right of silence . . . and his constitutional right to confer with a lawyer before talking to the police."

We think that the Supreme Court of Colorado erred in importing into this area of constitutional law notions of "free will" that have no place there. There is obviously no reason to require more in the way of a "voluntariness" inquiry in the *Miranda* waiver context than in the Fourteenth Amendment confession context. The sole concern of the Fifth Amendment, on which *Miranda* was based, is governmental coercion.

* * *

IV

The judgment of the Supreme Court of Colorado is accordingly reversed, and the cause remanded for further proceedings not inconsistent with this opinion.

* * *

JUSTICE STEVENS, concurring in the judgment in part and dissenting in part.

* * *

---

3. Petitioner conceded at oral argument that when Officer Anderson handcuffed respondent, the custody requirement of *Miranda* was satisfied. For purposes of our decision we accept that concession, and we similarly assume that the police officers "interrogated" respondent within the meaning of *Miranda*.

When the officer whom respondent approached elected to handcuff him and to take him into custody, the police assumed a fundamentally different relationship with him. Prior to that moment, the police had no duty to give respondent *Miranda* warnings and had every right to continue their exploratory conversation with him. Once the custodial relationship was established, however, the questioning assumed a presumptively coercive character. In my opinion the questioning could not thereafter go forward in the absence of a valid waiver of respondent's constitutional rights unless he was provided with counsel. Since it is undisputed that respondent was not then competent to stand trial, I would also conclude that he was not competent to waive his constitutional right to remain silent.

The Court seems to believe that a waiver can be voluntary even if it is not the product of an exercise of the defendant's " 'free will.' " The Court's position is not only incomprehensible to me; it is also foreclosed by the Court's recent pronouncement in *Moran v. Burbine* that "the relinquishment of the right must have been voluntary in the sense that it was the product of a free and deliberate choice ...". Because respondent's waiver was not voluntary in that sense, his custodial interrogation was presumptively coercive. The Colorado Supreme Court was unquestionably correct in concluding that his post-custodial incriminatory statements were inadmissible.

Accordingly, I concur in the judgment insofar as it applies to respondent's precustodial statements but respectfully dissent from the Court's disposition of the question that was not presented by the certiorari petition.

JUSTICE BRENNAN, with whom JUSTICE MARSHALL joins, dissenting.

* * *

I

The respondent's seriously impaired mental condition is clear on the record of this case. At the time of his confession, Mr. Connelly suffered from a "longstanding severe mental disorder," diagnosed as chronic paranoid schizophrenia. He had been hospitalized for psychiatric reasons five times prior to his confession; his longest hospitalization lasted for seven months. Mr. Connelly heard imaginary voices and saw nonexistent objects. He believed that his father was God, and that he was a reincarnation of Jesus.

At the time of his confession, Mr. Connelly's mental problems included "grandiose and delusional thinking." He had a known history of "thought withdrawal and insertion." Although physicians had treated Mr. Connelly "with a wide variety of medications in the past including antipsychotic medications," he had not taken any antipsychotic medications for at least six months prior to his confession. Following his arrest, Mr. Connelly initially was found incompetent to stand trial because the court-appointed psychiatrist, Dr. Metzner, "wasn't very confident that he could consistently relate accurate information." Dr. Metzner testified that Mr. Connelly was unable "to make free and rational choices" due to auditory hallucinations: "[W]hen he was read his *Miranda* rights, he probably had the capacity to know that he was being read his *Miranda* rights [but] he wasn't able to use that information because of the command hallucinations that he had experienced." He achieved competency to stand trial only after six months of hospitalization and treatment with antipsychotic and sedative medications.

* * *

II

* * *

A

* * *

While it is true that police overreaching has been an element of every confession case to date, it is also true that in every case the Court has made clear that ensuring that a confession is a product of free will is an independent concern. The fact that involuntary confessions have always been excluded in part because of police overreaching signifies only that this is a case of first impression. Until today, we have never upheld the admission of a confession that does not reflect the exercise of free will.

* * *

B

Since the Court redefines voluntary confessions to include confessions by mentally ill individuals, the reliability of these confessions becomes a central concern. [W]e have to date not required a finding of reliability for involuntary confessions only because *all* such confessions have been excluded upon a finding of involuntariness, regardless of reliability. The Court's adoption today of a restrictive definition of an "involuntary" confession will require heightened scrutiny of a confession's reliability.

The instant case starkly highlights the danger of admitting a confession by a person with a severe mental illness. The trial court made no findings concerning the reliability of Mr. Connelly's involuntary confession, since it believed that the confession was excludable on the basis of involuntariness. However, the overwhelming evidence in the record points to the unreliability of Mr. Connelly's delusional mind. Mr. Connelly was found incompetent to stand trial because he was unable to relate accurate information, and the court-appointed psychiatrist indicated that Mr. Connelly was actively hallucinating and exhibited delusional thinking at the time of his confession. The Court, in fact, concedes that "[a] statement rendered by one in the condition of respondent might be proved to be quite unreliable...."

Moreover, the record is barren of any corroboration of the mentally ill defendant's confession. No physical evidence links the defendant to the alleged crime. Police did not identify the alleged victim's body as the woman named by the defendant. Mr. Connelly identified the alleged scene of the crime, but it has not been verified that the unidentified body was found there or that a crime actually occurred there. There is not a shred of competent evidence in this record linking the defendant to the charged homicide. There is only Mr. Connelly's confession.

Minimum standards of due process should require that the trial court find substantial indicia of reliability, on the basis of evidence extrinsic to the confession itself, before admitting the confession of a mentally ill person into evidence. I would require the trial court to make such a finding on remand. To hold otherwise allows the State to imprison and possibly to execute a mentally ill defendant based solely upon an inherently unreliable confession.

III

* * *

B

The Court imports its voluntariness analysis, which makes police coercion a requirement for a finding of involuntariness, into its evaluation of the waiver of *Miranda* rights. My reasoning in Part II, applies *a fortiori* to involuntary confessions made in custody involving the waiver of constitutional rights. I will not repeat here what I said there.

I turn then to the second requirement, apart from the voluntariness requirement, that the State must satisfy to establish a waiver of *Miranda* rights. Besides being voluntary, the waiver must be knowing and intelligent. We recently noted that "the waiver must have been made with a full awareness both of the nature of the right being abandoned and the consequences of the decision to abandon it." The two requirements are independent: "Only if the 'totality of the circumstances surrounding the interrogation' reveal *both* an uncoerced choice *and* the requisite level of comprehension may a court properly conclude that the *Miranda* rights have been waived."

* * *

Since the Colorado Supreme Court found that Mr. Connelly was "clearly" unable to make an "intelligent" decision, clearly its judgment should be affirmed. The Court reverses the entire judgment, however, without explaining how a "mistaken view of voluntariness" could "taint" this independent justification for suppressing the custodial confession, but leaving the Supreme Court of Colorado free on remand to reconsider other issues, not inconsistent with the Court's opinion. Such would include, in my view, whether the requirement of a knowing and intelligent waiver was satisfied.

I dissent.

Questions and Comments

1. *Evaluating the voluntariness of confessions.* The majority in *Connelly* holds that "absent police conduct causally related to the confession," a confession is "voluntary" under the due process clause. When is a statement "caused" by police? Consider this comment from Joseph Grano, "Voluntariness, Free Will, and the Law of Confessions," 65 Va.L.Rev. 859, 886–87 (1979):

> Causal language . . . is not helpful in solving concrete cases. Philosophical attempts to explain causation usually focus on the realm of physical impacts and motion, as the example of one billiard ball striking another classically illustrates. When one billiard ball strikes another, it may be appropriate to view the first ball as both a necessary and sufficient cause of the second ball's motion. To say, however, that one individual "caused" another to do something is to use the notion of causation in quite a different sense. With respect to confessions, the conduct of the police, proper or improper, never can be considered a sufficient cause of a resulting confession; the defendant's choice to confess always will be a necessary cause, except in those few cases where hypnosis, a drug, or some other procedure negates the defendant's consciousness. [On the other hand, l]ike the billiard ball, the police conduct can [always] be considered a necessary cause of a resulting confession, except perhaps when a suspect comes to the station desiring to confess. Were admissibility of confessions thus to turn on the sufficiency of the police interrogation process as a cause, few confessions would be suppressed; were it to turn on the necessity of the process as a causal factor, few confessions would be admitted. Neither extreme, of course, describes the law of confessions.

Even if the statements that Connelly made in response to police questions were "caused" by the police, neither a due process or *Miranda* violation necessarily occurred. The majority in *Connelly* requires not only police "causation" but also police "coercion" for there to be a constitutional violation. What are the differences between the majority's and Justice Stevens's definition of "coercion"? More generally, assuming police causation, how much additional pressure by the police is necessary before a confession becomes "coerced" and "involuntary"? Again, an excerpt from Grano, discussing "the extent to which the state may impair the mental freedom of suspects to secure confessions," might be useful:

> A subjective standard of voluntariness, taking into account all the defendant's weakness and infirmities, would make it exceedingly difficult to procure admissible confessions. The vast majority of defendants, weak or strong, initially are disinclined to provide the police self-incriminating statements. The objective of the interrogation session is to overcome this initial unwillingness without creating a risk that an innocent person will falsely confess. To take into account the peculiar weaknesses of each defendant would frustrate this objective, for the permissible level of police pressure would then decrease in direct proportion to the weakness of the suspect, thus leaving room for little more than volunteered statements.

* * *

Nevertheless, we cannot ignore the Court's numerous references to defendants' subjective characteristics. In Haley v. Ohio, for example, a fifteen-year-old boy arrested for murder confessed after continuous interrogation between midnight and five o'clock in the morning. In finding the confession involuntary, the Court reasoned that a fifteen-year-old cannot be judged by the more exacting standards of maturity. Similarly, the Court consistently has held that a defendant's physical or mental condition is a relevant factor [citing, inter alia, *Blackburn*]. The Court thus recently held involuntary a confession obtained from a wounded defendant in a hospital intensive care unit.

Cases such as these reflect society's basic sense of justice. Indeed, it would seem inconceivable to hold a child or a gravely ill person to the same powers of resistance as the normal adult. Thus, the mental freedom test cannot remain true to our fundamental normative judgments unless we incorporate some of the defendant's individual characteristics. . . .

. . . Characteristics that are feigned easily and difficult to verify properly may be excluded, much as they are in everyday discourse and in the substantive criminal law. We generally do not excuse conduct because of social adversity, peculiar personality traits, abnormal temperament, or low intelligence; rather, we expect an individual to overcome these conditions or characteristics. We do, however, morally empathize with the physically or mentally ill, the feeble, the very young, and the very old. These, moreover, are stark characteristics that an interrogating officer can be expected to recognize.

* * *

Thus, the mental freedom component of the due process voluntariness test should ask whether a person of ordinary firmness, innocent or guilty, having the defendant's age, physical condition, and relevant mental abnormalities (but not otherwise having the defendant's personality traits, temperament, intelligence, or social background), and strongly preferring not to confess, would find the interrogation pressures overbearing. Although primarily objective, this test takes sufficient account of the defendant's individual capacities to satisfy our fundamental moral concerns about impairment of mental freedom.

Id. at 900–906. Was Connelly's confession voluntary under this test?

2. *The cognitive aspect of voluntariness.* In addition to considering a person's capacity to withstand police pressure, should we evaluate the person's cognitive capacity when determining voluntariness? Assuming that the police action is insufficient for "coercion," is the resulting confession always "voluntary," even if the confessor does not grasp its significance for the prosecution's case? How does the majority answer this question? Justice Stevens and Justice Brennan? Is it relevant, as both Stevens and Brennan seem to think, that Connelly may have been incompetent to stand trial when he made the statements? Finally, note the majority's holding that, even if the statements were voluntarily obtained, state evidentiary law might bar their admission on remand. How do you evaluate Connelly's chances for success on this score?

3. *Interrogation and people with mental retardation.* People with mental retardation present a special problem in the interrogation context. A number of cases have been documented of people with retardation confessing to crimes they did not commit. See Richard A. Leo & Richard J. Ofshe, "The Consequences of False Confessions: Deprivations of Liberty and Miscarriages of Justice in the Age of Psychological Interrogation," 88 J. Crim. L. & Criminology 429, 452–90 (1998). One possible reason for this result is that people with mental retardation are particularly "suggestible," i.e., they are more likely to answer leading questions affirmatively, and are more easily manipulated. See Solomon M. Fulero & Carolina Everington, "Assessing the Capacity of Persons with Retardation to Waive *Miranda* Rights: A Jurisprudent Therapy Perspective," 28 L. & Psychol. Rev. 53, 56–58 (2004) (describing research indicating that such people usually have "a strong desire to please others, especially those in authority" and often manifest "acquiescence," a tendency to answer "yes" even to absurd questions). Among the reasons for this suggestibility is a desire to appear normal and to hide impairment. Id. at 57.

People with retardation may also have great trouble understanding the interrogation context. Consider these findings about the ability of people with mental retardation to understand the *Miranda* warnings:

> The empirical research conducted in this study shows that contrary to *Miranda*'s core assumption, retarded people simply do not understand their *Miranda* rights. They do not understand the words comprising the warnings. They do not understand the rights themselves. They do not understand the legal context in which the rights arise. *Miranda* fails to protect the rights of mentally retarded people, and it may fail for others as well. The results of our study suggest that people who are not classified as retarded, but who have low IQs, also may not understand the warnings.

> Finally, the empirical results demonstrate that the totality-of-the-circumstances analysis courts typically use to determine whether mentally retarded suspects could understand the *Miranda* warnings also does not work. Factors including the degree of retardation, the mentally retarded suspect's age, education level, experience with the criminal justice system, and history of being *"Mirandized"* fail as indicators of a mentally retarded person's competence to understand the warnings and to execute a valid waiver. The results of the empirical analysis indicate that for this population the factor that matters is the presence of retardation, even mild retardation. If mental retardation is present, the existence of the other factors does not overcome the disabled person's inability to understand the warnings.

> . . .

> Searching for solutions to this problem only accentuates the difficulty of identifying a set of rules or procedures that will protect the rights of these individuals while permitting law enforcers to carry on legitimate investigations. In the end, it may be that this accommodation is not possible. It may be that the only way to ensure the constitutional rights of mentally retarded suspects is to adopt a per se rule excluding their confessions. The cost of this approach is obvious: if the confession

is true, then law enforcers and prosecutors are deprived of probative evidence. The cost of not adopting such a per se rule is just as obvious: confessions pried from the most vulnerable of our people may be false, and those false words may help send them to prison, or even to death row. In the end, we may be forced to decide if we can stomach that cost.

Morgan Cloud et al., "Words Without Meaning: The Constitution, Confessions, and Mentally Retarded Suspects," 69 U. Chi. L. Rev. 495, 590–91 (2002).

Do you agree that confessions from people with retardation should be inadmissible? If so, would this be on the ground of incompetency or some other ground? Should it matter whether the interrogating officer knew the individual had mental retardation?

C. DIGNITARIAN COMPETENCY

FORD v. WAINWRIGHT

Supreme Court of the United States, 1986.
477 U.S. 399, 106 S.Ct. 2595, 91 L.Ed.2d 335.

* * *

JUSTICE MARSHALL announced the judgment of the Court and delivered the opinion of the Court with respect to Parts I and II ...

For centuries no jurisdiction has countenanced the execution of the insane, yet this Court has never decided whether the Constitution forbids the practice. Today we keep faith with our common-law heritage in holding that it does.

I

Alvin Bernard Ford was convicted of murder in 1974 and sentenced to death. There is no suggestion that he was incompetent at the time of his offense, at trial, or at sentencing. In early 1982, however, Ford began to manifest gradual changes in behavior. They began as an occasional peculiar idea or confused perception, but became more serious over time. After reading in the newspaper that the Ku Klux Klan had held a rally in nearby Jacksonville, Florida, Ford developed an obsession focused upon the Klan. His letters to various people reveal endless brooding about his "Klan work," and an increasingly pervasive delusion that he had become the target of a complex conspiracy, involving the Klan and assorted others, designed to force him to commit suicide. He believed that the prison guards, part of the conspiracy, had been killing people and putting the bodies in the concrete enclosures used for beds. Later, he began to believe that his women relatives were being tortured and sexually abused somewhere in the prison. This notion developed into a delusion that the people who were tormenting him at the prison had taken members of Ford's family hostage. The hostage delusion took firm hold and expanded, until Ford was reporting that 135 of his friends and family were being held hostage in the prison, and that only he could help them. By "day 287" of the "hostage crisis," the list of hostages had expanded to include "senators, Senator Kennedy, and many other leaders." In a letter to the Attorney General of Florida, written in 1983, Ford appeared to assume authority for ending the "crisis," claiming to have fired a number of prison officials. He began to refer to himself as "Pope John Paul, III," and reported having appointed nine new justices to the Florida Supreme Court.

Counsel for Ford asked a psychiatrist who had examined Ford earlier, Dr. Jamal Amin, to continue seeing him and to recommend appropriate treatment. On the basis of roughly 14 months of evaluation, taped conversations between Ford and his attorneys, letters written by Ford, interviews with Ford's acquaintances, and various medical records, Dr. Amin concluded in 1983 that Ford suffered from "a severe, uncontrollable, mental disease which closely resembles 'Paranoid Schizophrenia With Suicide Potential' "—a "major mental disorder . . . severe enough to substantially affect Mr. Ford's present ability to assist in the defense of his life."

Ford subsequently refused to see Dr. Amin again, believing him to have joined the conspiracy against him, and Ford's counsel sought assistance from Dr. Harold Kaufman, who interviewed Ford in November 1983. Ford told Dr. Kaufman that "I know there is some sort of death penalty, but I'm free to go whenever I want because it would be illegal and the executioner would be executed." When asked if he would be executed, Ford replied: "I can't be executed because of the landmark case. I won. Ford v. State will prevent executions all over." These statements appeared amidst long streams of seemingly unrelated thoughts in rapid succession. Dr. Kaufman concluded that Ford had no understanding of why he was being executed, made no connection between the homicide of which he had been convicted and the death penalty, and indeed sincerely believed that he would not be executed because he owned the prisons and could control the Governor through mind waves. Dr. Kaufman found that there was "no reasonable possibility that Mr. Ford was dissembling, malingering or otherwise putting on a performance. . . ." The following month, in an interview with his attorneys, Ford regressed further into nearly complete incomprehensibility, speaking only in a code characterized by intermittent use of the word "one," making statements such as "Hands one, face one. Mafia one. God one, father one, Pope one. Pope one. Leader one."

Counsel for Ford invoked the procedures of Florida law governing the determination of competency of a condemned inmate, Fla.Stat. § 922.07 (1985). Following the procedures set forth in the statute, the Governor of Florida appointed a panel of three psychiatrists to evaluate whether, under § 922.07(2), Ford had "the mental capacity to understand the nature of the death penalty and the reasons why it was imposed upon him." At a single meeting, the three psychiatrists together interviewed Ford for approximately 30 minutes. Each doctor then filed a separate two-or three-page report with the Governor, to whom the statute delegates the final decision. One doctor concluded that Ford suffered from "psychosis with paranoia" but had "enough cognitive functioning to understand the nature and the effects of the death penalty, and why it is to be imposed on him." Another found that, although Ford was "psychotic," he did "know fully what can happen to him." The third concluded that Ford had a "severe adaptational disorder," but did "comprehend his total situation including being sentenced to death, and all of the implications of that penalty." He believed that Ford's disorder, "although severe, seem[ed] contrived and recently learned." Thus, the interview produced three different diagnoses, but accord on the question of sanity as defined by state law.

The Governor's decision was announced on April 30, 1984, when, without explanation or statement, he signed a death warrant for Ford's execution.

II

* * *

There is now little room for doubt that the Eighth Amendment's ban on cruel and unusual punishment embraces, at a minimum, those modes or acts of punishment that had been considered cruel and unusual at the time that the Bill of Rights was adopted. "Although the Framers may have intended the Eighth Amendment to go beyond the scope of its English counterpart, their use of the language of the English Bill of Rights is convincing proof that they intended to provide at least the same protection. . . ."

Moreover, the Eighth Amendment's proscriptions are not limited to those practices condemned by the common law in 1789. Not bound by the sparing humanitarian concessions of our forebears, the Amendment also recognizes the "evolving standards of decency that mark the progress of a maturing society." *Trop v. Dulles,* 356 U.S. 86, 101, 78 S.Ct. 590, 598, 2 L.Ed.2d 630 (1958) (plurality opinion). In addition to considering the barbarous methods generally outlawed in the 18th century, therefore, this Court takes into account objective evidence of contemporary values before determining whether a particular punishment comports with the fundamental human dignity that the Amendment protects.

A

We begin, then, with the common law. The bar against executing a prisoner who has lost his sanity bears impressive historical credentials; the practice consistently has been branded "savage and inhuman." 4 W. Blackstone, Commentaries * 24–* 25 (hereinafter Blackstone). Blackstone explained:

> "[I]diots and lunatics are not chargeable for their own acts, if committed when under these incapacities: no, not even for treason itself. Also, if a man in his sound memory commits a capital offence, and before arraignment for it, he becomes mad, he ought not to be arraigned for it: because he is not able to plead to it with that advice and caution that he ought. And if, after he has pleaded, the prisoner

becomes mad, he shall not be tried: for how can he make his defence? If, after he be tried and found guilty, he loses his senses before judgment, judgment shall not be pronounced; and if, after judgment, he becomes of nonsane memory, execution shall be stayed: for peradventure, says the humanity of the English law, had the prisoner been of sound memory, he might have alleged something in stay of judgment or execution." *Ibid.* (footnotes omitted).

Sir Edward Coke had earlier expressed the same view of the common law of England: "[B]y intendment of Law the execution of the offender is for example, . . . but so it is not when a mad man is executed, but should be a miserable spectacle, both against Law, and of extream inhumanity and cruelty, and can be no example to others."

As is often true of common-law principles, the reasons for the rule are less sure and less uniform than the rule itself. One explanation is that the execution of an insane person simply offends humanity, another, that it provides no example to others and thus contributes nothing to whatever deterrence value is intended to be served by capital punishment. Other commentators postulate religious underpinnings: that it is uncharitable to dispatch an offender "into another world, when he is not of a capacity to fit himself for it." It is also said that execution serves no purpose in these cases because madness is its own punishment: *furiosus solo furore punitur.* More recent commentators opine that the community's quest for "retribution"—the need to offset a criminal act by a punishment of equivalent "moral quality"—is not served by execution of an insane person, which has a "lesser value" than that of the crime for which he is to be punished. Unanimity of rationale, therefore, we do not find. "But whatever the reason of the law is, it is plain the law is so." We know of virtually no authority condoning the execution of the insane at English common law.

Further indications suggest that this solid proscription was carried to America, where it was early observed that "the judge is bound" to stay the execution upon insanity of the prisoner. . . .

B

This ancestral legacy has not outlived its time. Today, no State in the Union permits the execution of the insane. It is clear that the ancient and humane limitation upon the State's ability to execute its sentences has a firm a hold upon the jurisprudence of today as it had centuries ago in England. The various reasons put forth in support of the common-law restriction have no less logical, moral, and practical force than they did when first voiced. For today, no less than before, we may seriously question the retributive value of executing a person who has no comprehension of why he has been singled out and stripped of his fundamental right to life. Similarly, the natural abhorrence civilized societies feel at killing one who has no capacity to come to grips with his own conscience or deity is still vivid today. And the intuition that such an execution simply offends humanity is evidently shared across this

Nation. Faced with such widespread evidence of a restriction upon sovereign power, this Court is compelled to conclude that the Eighth Amendment prohibits a State from carrying out a sentence of death upon a prisoner who is insane. Whether its aim be to protect the condemned from fear and pain without comfort of understanding, or to protect the dignity of society itself from the barbarity of exacting mindless vengeance, the restriction finds enforcement in the Eighth Amendment.

* * *

JUSTICE POWELL, concurring in part and concurring in the judgment.

* * *

A

As the Court recognizes, the ancient prohibition on execution of the insane rested on differing theories. . . .

[The contention that prohibiting execution of the insane is justified as a way of preserving the defendant's ability to make arguments on his own behalf] has slight merit today. Modern practice provides far more extensive review of convictions and sentences than did the common law, including not only direct appeal but ordinarily both state and federal collateral review. Throughout this process, the defendant has access to counsel, by constitutional right at trial, and by employment or appointment at other stages of the process whenever the defendant raises substantial claims. Nor does the defendant merely have the right to counsel's assistance; he also has the right to the *effective* assistance of counsel at trial and on appeal. These guarantees are far broader than those enjoyed by criminal defendants at common law. It is thus unlikely indeed that a defendant today could go to his death with knowledge of undiscovered trial error that might set him free.

In addition, in cases tried at common law execution often followed fairly quickly after trial, so that incompetence at the time of execution was linked as a practical matter with incompetence at the trial itself. Our decisions already recognize, however, that a defendant must be competent to stand trial, and thus the notion that a defendant must be able to assist in his defense is largely provided for. . . .

B

The more general concern of the common law—that executions of the insane are simply cruel—retains its vitality. It is as true today as when Coke lived that most men and women value the opportunity to prepare, mentally and spiritually, for their death. Moreover, today as at common law, one of the death penalty's critical justifications, its retributive force, depends on the defendant's awareness of the penalty's existence and purpose. Thus, it remains true that executions of the insane both impose a uniquely cruel penalty and are inconsistent with one of the chief purposes of executions generally. For precisely these reasons,

Florida requires the Governor to stay executions of those who "d[o] not have the mental capacity to understand the nature of the death penalty and why it was imposed" on them. A number of States have more rigorous standards, but none disputes the need to require that those who are executed know the fact of their impending execution and the reason for it.

Such a standard appropriately defines the kind of mental deficiency that should trigger the Eighth Amendment prohibition. If the defendant perceives the connection between his crime and his punishment, the retributive goal of the criminal law is satisfied. And only if the defendant is aware that his death is approaching can he prepare himself for his passing. Accordingly, I would hold that the Eighth Amendment forbids the execution only of those who are unaware of the punishment they are about to suffer and why they are to suffer it.

Petitioner's claim of insanity plainly fits within this standard. According to petitioner's proffered psychiatric examination, petitioner does not know that he is to be executed, but rather believes that the death penalty has been invalidated. If this assessment is correct, petitioner cannot connect his execution to the crime for which he was convicted.

* * *

[The opinion of JUSTICE O'CONNOR, concurring in part and dissenting in part, in which JUSTICE WHITE joined, and the dissenting opinion of JUSTICE REHNQUIST, in which CHIEF JUSTICE BURGER joined, are deleted.]

Questions and Comments

1. *The rationale for the competency requirement in death penalty cases.* The Court in *Ford* notes at least six rationales that might justify its rule that a person be competent prior to execution: (1) an incompetent person might be unable to provide counsel with last minute information leading to vacation of the sentence; (2) madness is punishment enough in itself; (3) an incompetent person cannot make peace with God; (4) execution of an incompetent person has no deterrent effect on the population; (5) such execution "is a miserable spectacle ... of extream inhumanity and cruelty"; (6) the retribution or vengeance meant to be realized by execution cannot be exacted from an incompetent person. Do any of these rationales distinguish the incompetent from the competent sufficiently to justify a prohibition against execution only of the incompetent? Might it not be more "cruel" to execute a fully aware individual than one who is not? Research indicates that, for some individuals, psychosis is a defense mechanism against the horrors of the death penalty. Harvey Bluestone & Carl McGahee, "Reaction to Extreme Stress: Impending Death by Execution," 119 Am.J.Psychiat. 392 (1962).

For a view that, of the rationales advanced by the Court, only the retributive one is supportable, see Barbara Ward, "Competency for Execution: Problems in Law and Psychiatry," 14 Fla.St.U.L.Rev. 35, 49–56 (1986).° As described by Ward:

o. Ward also argues, however, that the rule could be supported on the additional ground that society is ambivalent about the death penalty and thus "the number of death penalties imposed should be decreased in various ways," including the incompetency bar. Id. at 56.

The retributive theory of competency for execution is predicated upon an assumption that every wrong act must be avenged by a punitive act of equal quality. Presumably, killing an insane person does not satisfy the societal interest in reprisal for the previous wrong as well as does killing a sane person. Therefore, imposing the death penalty on incompetent prisoners exacts a punishment less valuable than the crime itself.

Id. at 54. See also, Geoffrey Hazard & David Louisell, "Death, the State, and the Insane: Stay of Execution," 9 UCLA L.Rev. 381 (1962).

In *Panetti v. Quarterman*, ___ U.S. ___, 127 S.Ct. 2842, 168 L.Ed.2d 662 (2007), the Court appeared to agree with this analysis.

[I]t might be said that capital punishment is imposed because it has the potential to make the offender recognize at last the gravity of his crime and to allow the community as a whole, including the surviving family and friends of the victim, to affirm its own judgment that the culpability of the prisoner is so serious that the ultimate penalty must be sought and imposed. The potential for a prisoner's recognition of the severity of the offense and the objective of community vindication are called in question, however, if the prisoner's mental state is so distorted by a mental illness that his awareness of the crime and punishment has little or no relation to the understanding of those concepts shared by the community as a whole.

Id. at 2861.

Professor Bonnie offers a different rationale for the competency requirement—the dignity of the offender:

Whose interests are protected by the bar against executing the incompetent? ... Consider, by way of analogy, the trend toward supposedly more "humane" methods of execution, such as lethal injection. It is conceivable that a prisoner may find death by this method to be offensive to his own sense of dignity because it treats him as an object, like a dog being put to sleep: he may prefer to die by firing squad or on the gallows. When we sterilize the act of execution, do we do it for ourselves or for the prisoner? .. If [the prohibition on executing offenders who are incompetent] has any continuing justification in the contemporary context, I believe it must be found in respect for the dignity of the condemned. The prisoner has a right, even under imminent sentence of death, to be treated as a person worthy of respect, not as an object of the State's effort to carry out its promises. As Justice Powell suggested, a person under the shadow of death should have the opportunity to make the few choices that remain available to him. He should have the opportunity to decide who should be present at his execution, what he will eat for his last meal, what, if anything, he will utter for his last words, and whether he will repent or go defiantly to this grave. A prisoner who does not understand the nature and purpose of the execution is not able to exercise the choices that remain to him.

To execute him in this condition is an affront to his dignity as a person and to the "dignity of man," the core value of the Eighth Amendment.

Richard Bonnie, "*Panetti v. Quarterman*: Mental Illness, the Death Penalty, and Human Dignity," 5 Ohio St. J. Crim. L. 257, 276–77 (2007). How do you answer the question posed by Professor Bonnie at the beginning of this excerpt?

2. *The competency standard.* After *Ford*, most jurisdictions defined competency to be executed using the language suggested by Justice Powell: Offenders must know that they are being executed and why. Applying the retributive rationale, which it said *Ford* adopted, the Supreme Court in *Panetti* rejected a narrow interpretation of this language. Its description of the expert testimony in that case and its analysis of the competency issue follows:

Four expert witnesses testified on petitioner's behalf in the District Court proceedings. One explained that petitioner's mental problems are indicative of "schizo-affective disorder," resulting in a "genuine delusion" involving his understanding of the reason for his execution. According to the expert, this delusion has recast petitioner's execution as "part of spiritual warfare ... between the demons and the forces of the darkness and God and the angels and the forces of light." As a result, the expert explained, although petitioner claims to understand "that the state is saying that [it wishes] to execute him for [his] murder[s]," he believes in earnest that the stated reason is a "sham" and the State in truth wants to execute him "to stop him from preaching." Petitioner's other expert witnesses reached similar conclusions concerning the strength and sincerity of this "fixed delusion."

While the State's expert witnesses resisted the conclusion that petitioner's stated beliefs were necessarily indicative of incompetency, particularly in light of his perceived ability to understand certain concepts and, at times, to be "clear and lucid," they acknowledged evidence of mental problems. Petitioner's rebuttal witness attempted to reconcile the experts' testimony:

"Well, first, you have to understand that when somebody is schizophrenic, it doesn't diminish their cognitive ability.... Instead, you have a situation where-and why we call schizophrenia thought disorder[-]the logical integration and reality connection of their thoughts are disrupted, so the stimulus comes in, and instead of being analyzed and processed in a rational, logical, linear sort of way, it gets scrambled up and it comes out in a tangential, circumstantial, symbolic ... not really relevant kind of way. That's the essence of somebody being schizophrenic.... Now, it may be that if they're dealing with someone who's more familiar ... [in] what may feel like a safer, more enclosed environment ... those sorts of interactions may be reasonably lucid whereas a more extended conversation about more loaded material would reflect the severity of his mental illness."

See also [Record] (suggesting that an unmedicated individual suffering from schizophrenia can "at times" hold an ordinary conversation and that "it depends [whether the discussion concerns the individual's] fixed delusional system''). There is, in short, much in the record to support the conclusion that petitioner suffers from severe delusions.

The Court of Appeals concluded that its standard foreclosed petitioner from establishing incompetency by the means he now seeks to employ: a showing that his mental illness obstructs a rational understanding of the State's reason for his execution. As the court explained, ''[b]ecause we hold that 'awareness,' as that term is used in *Ford*, is not necessarily synonymous with 'rational understanding,' as argued by [petitioner,] we conclude that the district court's findings are sufficient to establish that [petitioner] is competent to be executed.''

In our view the Court of Appeals' standard is too restrictive to afford a prisoner the protections granted by the Eighth Amendment.... The Court of Appeals' standard treats a prisoner's delusional belief system as irrelevant if the prisoner knows that the State has identified his crimes as the reason for his execution. See 401 F.Supp.2d., at 712 (indicating that under Circuit precedent ''a petitioner's delusional beliefs-even those which may result in a fundamental failure to appreciate the connection between the petitioner's crime and his execution-do not bear on the question of whether the petitioner 'knows the reason for his execution' for the purposes of the Eighth Amendment'').Yet the *Ford* opinions nowhere indicate that delusions are irrelevant to ''comprehen[sion]'' or ''aware [ness]'' if they so impair the prisoner's concept of reality that he cannot reach a rational understanding of the reason for the execution. If anything, the *Ford* majority suggests the opposite.

* * *

The principles set forth in *Ford* are put at risk by a rule that deems delusions relevant only with respect to the State's announced reason for a punishment or the fact of an imminent execution, as opposed to the real interests the State seeks to vindicate. We likewise find no support elsewhere in *Ford*, including in its discussions of the common law and the state standards, for the proposition that a prisoner is automatically foreclosed from demonstrating incompetency once a court has found he can identify the stated reason for his execution. A prisoner's awareness of the State's rationale for an execution is not the same as a rational understanding of it. *Ford* does not foreclose inquiry into the latter.

This is not to deny the fact that a concept like rational understanding is difficult to define. And we must not ignore the concern that some prisoners, whose cases are not implicated by this decision, will fail to understand why they are to be punished on account of reasons other than those stemming from a severe mental illness. The mental state requisite for competence to suffer capital punishment neither presumes nor requires a person who would be considered ''normal,'' or even ''rational,'' in a layperson's understanding of those terms. Someone who is condemned to death for an atrocious murder may be so callous as to be unrepentant; so self-centered and devoid of compassion as to lack all sense of guilt; so adept in transferring blame to others as to be considered, at least in the colloquial sense, to be out of touch with reality. Those states of mind, even if extreme compared to the criminal population at large, are not what petitioner contends lie at the threshold of a competence inquiry. The beginning of doubt about competence in a case like petitioner's is not a misanthropic personality or an amoral character. It is a psychotic disorder.

Petitioner's submission is that he suffers from a severe, documented mental illness that is the source of gross delusions preventing him from comprehending the meaning and purpose of the punishment to which he has been sentenced. This argument, we hold, should have been considered.

The flaws of the Court of Appeals' test are pronounced in petitioner's case. Circuit precedent required the District Court to disregard evidence of psychological dysfunction that, in the words of the judge, may have resulted in petitioner's "fundamental failure to appreciate the connection between the petitioner's crime and his execution." To refuse to consider evidence of this nature is to mistake *Ford*'s holding and its logic. Gross delusions stemming from a severe mental disorder may put an awareness of a link between a crime and its punishment in a context so far removed from reality that the punishment can serve no proper purpose. It is therefore error to derive from *Ford*, and the substantive standard for incompetency its opinions broadly identify, a strict test for competency that treats delusional beliefs as irrelevant once the prisoner is aware the State has identified the link between his crime and the punishment to be inflicted.

Id. at 2859–62.

In light of *Panetti*, decide whether the offenders in the following cases, handed down prior to *Panetti*, were competent to be executed. Would the result be different under Professor Bonnie's rationale?

The inmate believed that his dead aunt would protect him from the sedative and toxic effects of the drugs used to execute him. *Garrett v. Collins*, 951 F.2d 57 (5th Cir. 1992) (holding the inmate was competent).

The inmate believed he was God, that his sentence had been overturned, that the State was holding him illegally, and that there was a conspiracy to execute him. He also believed that he had been set free in August 1997. *Singleton v. Norris*, 267 F.3d 859 (8th Cir. 2001) (holding the inmate was incompetent, and granting a permanent stay of execution; but see note 4 in these materials).

The inmate had what doctors called a "delusional hope" that he would not be executed. He was convinced that his death penalty would be overturned and he would be spared execution. *State v. Harris, III*, 114 Wash.2d 419, 789 P.2d 60 (1990) (competent).

The inmate believed he was an angel and that he had received absolution for his crime, which meant the state would not be able to execute him. *Billiot v. State*, 655 So.2d 1 (Miss 1995) (competent).

The inmate believed that death was not real, but only inflicted pleasure and pain. As a result, he was not concerned about his execution. *Calambro v. State*, 114 Nev. 961, 964 P.2d 794 (1998) (competent).

Should a person with psychopathy, who knows he has broken the law but does not believe he has done wrong, be found incompetent to be executed?

3. *Procedures.* The second issue the Court addressed in *Ford* was the proper procedure for determining competency to be executed. As recounted above, Florida allowed the governor to make the final decision on competency, based on reports from three psychiatrists. Three members of the Court joined Justice Marshall in deciding that the due process clause required more: specifically, a hearing on the competency issue, presided over by a judicial officer, at which the prisoner would have the right to be present with counsel and confront the experts. Justice O'Connor, joined by Justice White, also concluded that due process was violated by the Florida procedure, but indicated that all the state was constitutionally required to provide was some procedure for receiving the written submissions of the prisoner. Justice Rehnquist, joined by Chief Justice Burger, voted to uphold the Florida procedure.

As a result of this lineup, Justice Powell's opinion was controlling on the procedural issue. He agreed with Marshall that the Florida procedures were inadequate, but stated: "I would not require the kind of full-scale 'sanity trial' that Justice Marshall appears to find necessary." In explaining this stance, he stated:

> First, the Eighth Amendment claim at issue can arise only after the prisoner has been validly convicted of a capital crime and sentenced to death. Thus, in this case the State has a substantial and legitimate interest in taking petitioner's life as punishment for his crime. That interest is not called into question by petitioner's claim. Rather, the only question raised is not whether, but when, his execution may take place. This question is important, but it is not comparable to the antecedent question whether petitioner should be executed at all. It follows that this Court's decisions imposing heightened procedural requirements on capital trials and sentencing proceedings do not apply in this context.

> Second, petitioner does not make his claim of insanity against a neutral background. On the contrary, in order to have been convicted and sentenced, petitioner must have been judged competent to stand trial, or his competency must have been sufficiently clear as not to raise a serious question for the trial court. The State therefore may properly presume that petitioner remains sane at the time sentence is to be carried out, and may require a substantial threshold showing of insanity merely to trigger the hearing process.

> Finally, the sanity issue in this type of case does not resemble the basic issues at trial or sentencing. Unlike issues of historical fact, the question of petitioner's sanity calls for a basically subjective judgment. And unlike the determination of whether the death penalty is appropriate in a particular case, the competency determination depends substantially on expert analysis in a discipline fraught with "subtleties and nuances." This combination of factors means that ordinary adversarial procedures—complete with live testimony, cross-examination, and oral argument by counsel—are not necessarily the best means of arriving at sound, consistent judgments as to a defendant's sanity. Cf. *Parham v. J.R.*

477 U.S. at 425–26, 106 S.Ct. at 2609–10. In light of this reasoning, Justice Powell concluded that the state needed only to provide an "impartial officer

or board that can receive evidence and argument from the prisoner's counsel, including psychiatric evidence that may differ from the State's own psychiatric examination." Id. at 427, 106 S.Ct. at 2610.

If the rationale for the prohibition on executing incompetent prisoners is retributive (see note 1), does the individual have *any* interest in making sure the conclusion about competency is accurate? Should the individual even have "standing" to raise the issue? In *Panetti*, the Court seemed to answer this latter question in the affirmative, although it refrained from holding that the Constitution requires a hearing, instead merely reiterating that the offender is entitled to respond to the state's evidence with experts of his own. *Panetti*, 127 S.Ct. at 2856–57.

4. *Treating the offender found incompetent.* If a person is found incompetent to be executed, should he or she have the right to refuse treatment that will restore and maintain competency to be executed? Are the reasons given by Justice Powell in justifying minimal procedures at the competency determination relevant here as well? In *Perry v. Louisiana*, 498 U.S. 1075, 111 S.Ct. 804, 112 L.Ed.2d 865 (1991), the Supreme Court granted certiorari in a case involving forcible medication of a person found incompetent to be executed, but then remanded the case in light of its intervening decision in *Washington v. Harper*, reprinted on pp. 964–80. On remand, the Louisiana Supreme Court concluded that forcibly medicating individuals to render them competent to be executed is impermissible. *State v. Perry*, 610 So.2d 746 (La.1992). It distinguished *Harper* by concluding that forcing drugs merely "to facilitate . . . execution does not constitute medical treatment but is antithetical to the basic principles of the healing arts." Id. at 751. It also found, as a matter of state law, that medicating an objecting individual to facilitate execution constitutes cruel and unusual punishment because it "fails to measurably contribute to the social goals of capital punishment," "would add severity and indignity to the prisoner's punishment beyond that required for the mere extinguishment of life," and "is apt to be administered erroneously, arbitrarily or capriciously." Id. at 747–48. In at least one state, an official finding of incompetence requires commutation of the death sentence to a life sentence without parole. Md. Ann. Code art. 27, § 75A(d)(3).

In *Singleton v. Norris*, 319 F.3d 1018 (8th Cir.2003), the Eighth Circuit reached a different conclusion than the Louisiana Supreme Court. There the court relied on *Harper v. Washington*, *Riggins v. Nevada* and its own opinion in *Sell v. United States* (see pp. 1034–42 for discussion of these cases) in holding that a person who is incompetent to be executed may be forcibly medicated under certain circumstances. Specifically,

> the government must (1) "present an essential state interest that outweighs the individual's interest in remaining free from medication," (2) "prove that there is no less intrusive way of fulfilling its essential interest," and (3) "prove by clear and convincing evidence that the medication is medically appropriate." "Medication is medically appropriate if: (1) it is likely to render the patient competent; (2) the likelihood and gravity of side effects do not overwhelm its benefits; and, (3) it is in the best medical interests of the patient."

As to the first requirement, the court stated "[w]e need not decide under what circumstances carrying out a particular sentence is not 'essential.' Society's interest in punishing offenders is at its greatest in the narrow class of capital murder cases in which aggravating factors justify imposition of the death penalty." After finding that medication was necessary to restore Singleton to competency (the second factor), the court addressed the third issue of whether the medication was medically appropriate:

> Central to Singleton's argument is his contention that medication "obviously is not in the prisoner's ultimate best medical interest" where one effect of the medication is rendering the patient competent for execution. Singleton does not dispute that the antipsychotic medication is in his medical interest during the pendency of a stay of execution. He has stated he takes it voluntarily because he does not like the symptoms he experiences without it. He also does not dispute the lack of serious side effects. . . . Singleton's argument regarding his long-term medical interest boils down to an assertion that execution is not in his medical interest. Eligibility for execution is the only unwanted consequence of the medication. The due process interests in life and liberty that Singleton asserts have been foreclosed by the lawfully imposed sentence of execution and the *Harper* procedure. In the circumstances presented in this case, the best medical interests of the prisoner must be determined without regard to whether there is a pending date of execution.

Judge Heaney, who had ordered a permanent stay of execution in Singleton's case two years earlier (see note 2) was joined by three others in dissent.

> Once an execution date was set, I believe that the justification for medicating Singleton under *Harper* evaporated. An inquiry into the State's motivation is unhelpful, for it presupposes a single, directed motivation, which is not the case here. In fact, the evidence suggests two competing interests: the welfare of the prison, and the execution of the prisoner's sentence. At the very least, the setting of an execution date calls into question the State's true motivation for administering the medication in the first instance. The circumstances of Singleton's case changed once the execution date was set, and changed in such a way that *Harper* no longer supports the prison forcing him to take medication.

Singleton was decided by the same court that was reversed by the U.S. Supreme Court in *Sell v. United States*, which significantly limited the government's ability to use medication to restore competency to stand trial over the defendant's objection. Are the state and individual interests stronger or weaker in the competency to be executed context? If Singleton had refused medication because of its side effects should the outcome have been different? In *Sell*, the Supreme Court stated that, while the permissible circumstances under which forcible medication administered solely for the purpose of restoring competency "may be rare," forcible medication will always be permissible to reduce dangerousness (if medically appropriate and necessary to that purpose). Should the same rule apply here? If so, is Judge Heaney's argument in dissent irrelevant? Finally, what is the disposition if a right to refuse is recognized? Commutation of sentence? Singleton argued that he could be executed only if and when he became competent naturally, without psychotropic intervention.

As the Louisiana Supreme Court decision in *Perry* indicates, one problem created by forcible restoration of a person's competence to be executed is ethical rather than legal. It involves the role of the mental health professional in restoring competency. As noted in Note, "Medical Ethics and Competency to be Executed," 96 Yale L.J. 167, 178–79 (1986),

> the express purpose of competency treatment is to guarantee that the patient will be killed. Each treatment strategy to heal the inmate is in fact another strategy to ensure his death. No intervening acts save the minuscule likelihood that, once sane, the inmate will articulate a heretofore unknown reason for a stay of execution, will prevent the execution that the physician has made possible.

In response to this dilemma, the American Medical Association has adopted the following position: "The physician, as a member of a profession dedicated to the preserving of life when there is hope of doing so, should not be a participant in a legally authorized execution." Is this rigid stance ethical in view of the suffering an untreated person might experience? Consider also the fact that many persons on death row decide they would rather be executed than continue living in prison. See Welsh White, "Defendants Who Elect Execution," 48 U.Pitt.L.Rev. 853, 854–55 (1987).

5. *Decisional competency and the death penalty.* In this regard, how competent must a person on death row be before he or she can abort collateral proceedings and demand that the state carry out the death sentence? Cf. *Gilmore v. Utah,* 429 U.S. 1012, 1013, 97 S.Ct. 436, 437, 50 L.Ed.2d 632 (1976) (in which the Supreme Court held that Gilmore could waive further judicial review of his case and proceed to execution because he "made a knowing and intelligent waiver of any and all federal rights he might have asserted …".). Several courts have required a relatively high level of competency in this situation (i.e., higher than what is required for competency to proceed), given the irreversibility of the decision. See e.g., *Franz v. State,* 296 Ark. 181, 188–89, 754 S.W.2d 839, 843 (1988). Is this stance required after *Godinez v. Moran* or *Edwards v. Arizona*?

In 2007, the American Bar Association, the American Psychiatric Association, and the American Psychological Association endorsed a resolution that provides: "If a court finds that a prisoner under sentence of death who wishes to forgo or terminate post-conviction proceedings has a mental disorder or disability that significantly impairs his or her capacity to make a rational decision, the court should permit a next friend acting on the prisoner's behalf to initiate or pursue available remedies to set aside the conviction or death sentence." See ABA Resolution on Mental Disability and the Death Penalty, www.abanet.org/crimjust/policy/am06122a.pdf. When is a decision to waive appeals rational? In particular, if an offender waives appeals because he or she is depressed, is the decision irrational? Note 6 following the materials on *Godinez* discussed when a capital defendant who is suffering from depression may waive the right to present mitigating evidence at the capital sentencing proceeding (see pp. 1070–72). Should the same analysis, whatever it may be, also apply to the decision by a depressed offender to waive collateral proceedings?

Professor John Blume calculates that approximately 13% of all executions have been of "volunteers" (i.e., individuals who have waived their collateral appeals), and that roughly 77% of these individuals were suffering from mental illness at the time of their waiver. John Blume, "Killing the Willing: 'Volunteers,' Suicide and Competency," 103 Mich. L. Rev. 939, 962–63 (2005). Professor Blume concludes: "When a volunteer is both competent to make legal choices and motivated to accept the justness of his punishment, then he should be permitted to waive his further appeals. There are some such defendants, and their decisions should, in fact must, be respected, at least so long as other litigants have the power to override their attorney's recommendations. On the other hand, even if the volunteer is competent, when suicidal desires represent the dominant motivation, courts should not permit waiver." In the latter situation, Professor Blume argues, execution would amount to state-assisted suicide, which is banned in all but a few states (and in the latter states it is permitted only when the person is terminally ill). Id. at 984–85. Do you agree?

If an offender is found incompetent to waive appeals under the appropriate standard and can be restored through medication, is it permissible to medicate the individual over his or her objection? How is this scenario different from forcibly medicating an individual to restore competency to be executed?

Chapter Ten

POST–COMMITMENT ISSUES

Table of Sections

I. INTRODUCTION

The Supreme Court has made clear that "a state is under no constitutional duty to provide substantive services for those within its borders." *Youngberg v. Romeo,* 457 U.S. 307, 316, 102 S.Ct. 2452, 2458, 73 L.Ed.2d 28 (1982). But after the state intervenes in a person's life, it must obey constitutional dictates. This chapter focuses on the states' constitutional obligations toward those it has involuntarily committed through civil or criminal process. It also examines the constitutional prerogatives of various groups of "voluntary" patients (e.g., nonprotesting admittees, children committed by their parents, individuals committed by their guardians). The various *statutory* enactments which may require the state to provide services for certain populations (e.g., the Americans with Disabilities Act and the Individuals with Disabilities Education Act) are touched upon as well, although the primary discussion of these provisions is found in Part III of this book.

The extent to which the state is obligated under the constitution to provide for the needs and demands of those whom it has deprived of liberty is a matter of considerable complexity. For instance, can one justifiably conclude that the state has met its constitutional duty if it provides decent living quarters for those it involuntarily hospitalizes? If it must provide more, is mere prevention of deterioration enough? Or must the state afford committed individuals treatment or habilitation[a]

---

a. Habilitation is the term used to refer to treatment and education of the developmentally disabled.

that will improve their condition? Assuming a duty to provide something more than food and shelter for those it deprives of liberty, is the state also obligated to create community resources when community treatment or habilitation is deemed more effective than traditional hospital treatment? Within an institutional environment (whether or not it is in the "community") to what extent may the state limit access to mail and phone service, contact with the opposite sex, exercise and so on? When, if ever, must the state pay a patient for work performed at the institution?

Additionally, assessing the scope of the constitutional right to treatment and habilitation raises systemic concerns more dramatically than other issues addressed in this book. Do courts have the expertise to assess the effectiveness of treatment? Do they have the authority to force states to create new treatment facilities and programs? If so, how is this authority to be enforced?

These are the primary issues examined in this chapter. To provide a realistic backdrop to this discussion, the following excerpt, describing the experiences of several patients in the Texas mental health system, is offered. Although the excerpt below does not necessarily reflect reality in other states (which vary immensely in their approach to mental health care) and although it is outdated in some respects (especially in terms of the medications provided the patients), it still captures the atmosphere of many mental health systems today, and it also reflects the type of system that courts confronted in much of the litigation described in the rest of this chapter.

JOSEPH NOCERA, THE LONG, LONESOME ROAD

Texas Monthly 43–53.
(1986).

* * *

A real mental health system does not exist in Texas. Instead, a group of independent fiefdoms and power bases all operate under the loose rubric of the Texas Department of Mental Health and Mental Retardation (MHMR). State hospitals are one power base, and local mental health authorities are another. Probate judges try to get mentally ill people into state hospitals, while hospital social workers try just as hard to get them out. There is even a federal judge involved in running the state hospital. As a result of a class-action suit brought a dozen years ago on the behalf of patients, federal district judge Barefoot Sanders is immersed in every aspect of hospital life, and although his intimidating presence has made the hospitals marginally better, the improvements have come at the expense of the local authorities. Part of the reason that everyone seems to be working at cross-purposes is that there is honest disagreement about how best to treat the mentally ill. But the chaos that reigns in the Texas mental health system also results from some of the worst reasons imaginable: bureaucratic infighting and turf battles, and a preference for the status quo over innovation or change.

Fred Thomas is in many ways typical of the people who populate that system. He is black. He is poor. He is unquestionably a tough case, partly because of the severity of his illness, but also because, as I discovered in the five months I spent with him a year ago, he lacks the motivation to try to make something of his life. Though instilling such motivation is perhaps the most fundamental goal of the modern mental health movement, the Texas system has seemed utterly helpless to change Fred. Instead, the system has been content to process him into the state hospital and process him out—always sending him back to his mother's house, where inevitably and tragically he would revert to his old ways. Although Texas' mental health hospitals are no longer hell-holes, they are still little more than benign jails. One former social worker used to tell patients about to be released: "If you can survive in this place, you can survive anything." When I first met Fred Thomas, he had learned to survive in the hospital. The question confronting him was whether he could survive beyond its walls.

* * *

On a bright April day, in a large outdoor area of the Austin State Hospital, Fred Thomas sat down across from me at a picnic table. In hospital jargon, he was in the Harris K patio—the Harris K unit being the drab, one-story, pentagon shaped building that surrounds the patio. The men on Fred's ward were outdoors for an hour of "exercise"—thus satisfying one of Judge Sanders' requirements for structured daily activities. As far as I could see, only two men were actually exercising: a member of the ward staff and a patient were shooting baskets through a worn, bent rim. A few other patients were walking, somewhat frantically, along a cement pathway. The rest were either sitting in chairs or sprawling out under one of the pecan trees, fast asleep. At least half of them were smoking—and constantly fending off requests for a nearly finished cigarette. Almost all the patients wore dirty, ill-fitting clothes. Most of them looked harmless enough, except for one, a black, middle-aged schizophrenic with a Fu Manchu moustache who was standing in the center of the patio screaming about the CIA and the KGB. I would later learn that he was Donald Peterson.

Before coming over to the table, Fred had been among those trying to get someone to give him a cigarette. He was wearing a grimy sweatshirt, slightly tattered green jogging pants, and old-fashioned high-top sneakers without socks. Upon reaching the table, Fred sat down across from me, but at first he ignored me, concentrating instead on the cigarette he had scored. He lighted the cigarette and inhaled with excruciating slowness, savoring each puff as if it might be his last. Before his first admission, Fred had never smoked. But because cigarettes are so integral to life in a state hospital—even to the extent that they are used as carrots in Austin's behavior modification program—he now smoked so much that his fingers had permanent tobacco stains. When his cigarette was finished, he looked up and began talking.

Fred's speech was characterized by what psychiatrists call "loose association" or "tangential thought"—that is, skipping rapidly from one topic to the next, usually with a tenuous thread linking each new thought to the one before it. When I introduced myself, he said, "Joe. Where you gonna go, Joe? Joe Willie Namath." And that led him to a brief discussion of Namath's bad knees, and on to trees and bees, and then to the birds and the bees, and then to honey, which led to girls, and finally to a recently released patient whom he claimed had been his girlfriend.

[T]hat April marked the beginning of Fred's fifth stay at the Austin State Hospital. After his initial admission in 1979, he had managed to stay out of the hospital for four years. But between March 1984 and March 1985, he had been in three times.

* * *

It's 8 a.m. on a Thursday in early May: time for the "morning meds" in Ward B, one of the four male wards in the Harris K unit (there are two female wards). Ward B has been Fred Thomas' home for more than a month.

The heart of an Austin State Hospital ward is the central dayroom, no larger than a bank president's office; it is filled with beat-up chairs, a few card tables, and a television set that is constantly on. Plexiglass windows and locked doors separate the dayroom and a nurse's station, from which the ward staff keeps watch over its charges. There are some 25 men in the Ward B dayroom this morning, at least 7 more than the ward was intended to hold. During the time I spent at Harris K, the dayroom was constantly overcrowded, which greatly increased the level of agitation and even danger. Fred, however, does not seem agitated. He is wearing a clean pair of short pants, a new T-shirt, and his ever-present basketball sneakers, unlaced. He is standing in front of a full-length mirror, mumbling to himself. No one seems to notice.

[T]he two mental health workers sitting in the nurse's station don't notice Fred because, by their lights, he is being good. To such nonprofessionals, who make less than a good grocery clerk, a patient's goodness is measured entirely on the basis of how little trouble he causes. Fred may be incoherent, but at least he's not starting a fight. Besides, they are busy with their morning ration of paperwork, which is voluminous, as usual.

The other patients don't take any special note of Fred because most of them are equally absorbed in their own private worlds. . . . Three or four men are sitting stonily in chairs, grumbling angrily at the walls. Another man erupts into loud, incomprehensible laughter. A new patient tries to flick something off his shoulder, a motion he repeats again and again; there is nothing there. In the bathroom an extremely delusional, muscular man stuffs magazines down a toilet. The man's parents conceived him (so the story goes) while both were patients at Rusk State Hospital. He has been flushing magazines down the toilet every morning for over a week, ever since someone sent dozens of old copies of the New Yorker to Ward B.

Although all the patients were roused out of bed two hours ago, the only things they have been required to do so far are brush their teeth, comb their hair, and make their beds, activities that exhaust no more than five minutes apiece. Thus the rest of their time has been spent doing what they're doing now—milling about. When you're confined to a state hospital ward, you're forced to spend a lot of time with your thoughts, however terrifying they might be. This cruel fact cannot possibly help anyone get better, but that's the way it is. Other than the television, there are very few distractions. Milling about is the basic activity in the ward.

In the middle of the low-level chaos, a nurse holding a carton containing the morning medication walks into the nurse's station. Her name is Sue Dennison. "Okay," she announces in a tone that is both firm and pleasant, "get in line for your morning meds." The two mental health workers go into the dayroom to help the patients form a scraggly line. One by one the patients step up to the nurse's station to receive their medication. The psychotropic drugs they take—with names like Thorazine, Navane, Prolixin, Mellaril, and Haldol—are the primary, indeed, the only, form of real treatment they will receive in the hospital. And while there is no doubt that most of the people in this dayroom need the drugs desperately, there is considerable doubt as to whether some of them might not also benefit from other forms of help—from therapy, for instance. The issue of alternative treatments, which is the subject of a fierce national debate, does not get addressed in Austin. It is drugs that can prop people up the fastest, and get them out the quickest, and soak up the least amount of money. So drugs are what is used.

The first person Sue Dennison sees on this Thursday morning is a short, shy, soft-spoken man who looks about fifty years old. He is a murderer. In June 1980, six weeks after being released from the state hospital, he shot his next-door neighbor. He had heard voices telling him the neighbor was about to shoot him. Every time the doctors think he is well enough to stand trial, he is sent to prison. But as soon as he gets to prison, he regresses and has to be returned to the state hospital.

"How are you feeling today?" Dennison asks him. A few days before, the man had asked a ward staffer if the attendant was going to kill him soon. "Oh, just fine," he says meekly.

Next, a young black man steps up to the window. He has a little goatee and wears a baseball cap turned backward. When he sees Dennison, he puts his chin on the window ledge and stares at her salaciously. "Come on Michael," she says. "I can't give you your medicine if you're doing that." He keeps staring.

Michael is retarded. He was committed by a probate judge in Harris County, thus making him Austin's problem instead of Houston's. Harris County washed its hands of him not long after he arrived by sending a letter to the hospital stating that Michael could not be returned to

Houston because the city lacked an "appropriate placement." But Austin doesn't have any place for him either. He belongs in a state school for the mentally retarded, but he can't get into one; the waiting period is about two years. Judge Sanders' monitors have raised the issue of retarded people languishing in the state hospitals. But what can the staff on Ward B do? All they can do is wait.

[B]ringing up the end of the line is Donald Peterson (not his real name). He is the toughest patient on the ward; he has lived at least half of his adult life in an institution—either a mental hospital or Huntsville State Prison (for armed robbery). The other patients are afraid of him. The staff prefers to keeps its distance too. Peterson, who looks old beyond his 44 years, hasn't shaved or bathed in days. He smells of stale cigarettes and rancid sweat, and the other patients have been complaining about him. Eventually, staff will have to force Peterson to take a shower, but they're not in any hurry. The last time they tried to make Peterson clean up—it happened about a week ago—one of the mental health workers wound up with torn ligaments in his thumb.

Don Peterson seems quite comfortable living in Ward B. And why not? His life on the outside is unrelievedly sad. His elderly father refuses to have anything to do with him. The mental health system barely knows he exists. He sleeps in a sickeningly ramshackle house in a Houston ghetto with a dozen other mentally ill people. For human companionship, he hangs out at the Star of Hope Mission in downtown Houston, where he is prey for thugs.

In the hospital, on the other hand, his living conditions are dramatically improved, he knows the ropes, and he can play the hunter instead of the prey. Soon after [one patient] arrived, for instance, Peterson sidled up to him on a bench with a can of Coke in his hand and asked with a smirk, "Do you think I can kill you with this?" Peterson also, from time to time, initiates sex with other men in the ward. This is not uncommon among the patients; even Fred was once caught trading a sexual act for cigarettes.

... After Sue Dennison gives Peterson his medicine, he quickly walks away—a little too quickly, in Dennison's opinion. She believes Peterson has been "cheeking his meds" lately—that is, only pretending to take his medication until he can get to the bathroom and spit it out. She thinks this because he has begun talking about how John Kennedy and Martin Luther King have deputized him "to be with white women." The mental health workers stop Peterson before he can get to the bathroom. He glares at them for a few seconds, but finally he swallows.

After Fred takes his morning medication and has breakfast in the ward cafeteria, he gets his two-cigarette allotment from the ward's "point store" (patients trade "points" they have earned in return for cigarettes or candy or coffee).

* * *

What happened to Fred in the past month offers a short course in the vagaries of patient care at the state hospital. His commitment began on March 26, when he was admitted to Ward B as an "acute" patient, a status that legally limits his stay to a maximum of ninety days. He told the admissions staff glumly, "This is where I belong."

The doctor for Wards A and B (A is one of the female wards) was a kindly, Egyptian-born psychiatrist whose command of English was tentative at best, and who had a reputation for being cautious—too cautious, in fact, for the bureaucracy, which felt that he was gumming up the works by not releasing patients quickly enough. After about twenty minutes with Fred, the doctor diagnosed his illness as "Schizophrenia undifferentiated chronic"—very much in line with previous diagnoses— and prescribed Prolixin, a safe choice that also reflected Fred's history.

A month later Fred's first doctor left the hospital; he was replaced by a Cuban-born psychiatrist named Heriberto Cabada. Brusque and garrulous, Cabada was almost the complete opposite in temperament from his predecessor, with whom he shares only one apparent trait: heavily accented English. (Like most state hospitals, Austin is full of foreign-born and trained psychiatrists.) A large man with a pronounced girth who favored guayabera shirts and a three-day growth of beard, Cabada was the shortest of the short-timers. In little more than a month he would finish and move to Miami to begin what he hoped to be a lucrative private practice. Wards A and B were about the last place on earth he wanted to be. "This is a first-year resident's rotation," he groused to anyone within earshot. But he knew why he had been brought in.

In his three years at the hospital, Cabada had learned how to play the game, and he had become fairly cynical about it. He knew how to keep his head down whenever there was trouble; he had learned that lesson when one of his patients committed suicide while he was on vacation, and he nearly lost his residency as a result. Although he bridled at the paperwork ("It's a wonder we have time to see any patients at all"), he knew the importance of leaving a paper trail to keep the court and the bureaucracy satisfied. He knew he was there to prescribe drugs and not to administer psychotherapy. "This is a place to stabilize people and to get them out," he said bluntly. And when he got to Wards A and B, he immediately understood what was expected of him. Within a week, Cabada has released enough patients that the census on Ward B had dropped from 24 to 18. "I love that Cabada," said one of the workers on the ward.

And when Cabada saw Fred Thomas for the first time—fifteen minutes on the morning of May 2—he knew what was expected of him there too. Prolixin, which the previous doctor had prescribed, was popular in community outpatient clinics because it was the only drug at the time that could be given by injection with long-lasting (up to two weeks) effect. But the imperative at the state hospital makes Prolixin much less ideal because it is so slow-acting compared with most other psychotropic drugs. As Cabada noted in Fred's chart, the patient "is progressing slowly, although he is not at the point where he should be." To speed things along, Cabada decided to switch Fred to Haldol, a potent, fast-acting ... drug. Haldol is as popular inside the hospital as Prolixin is outside. At an initial dose of thirty milligrams a day, Fred was more drugged, and more sedated, and feeling more side effects than he had in his life.

Late one afternoon, a few days after the change, I got an inkling of how Haldol was affecting Fred. The patients were out on the patio; Fred was sitting in a chair he had pulled out from the ward. He was in a bad way. His lips were tight and trembled slightly, and he constantly touched them. He scratched his legs until they were white with scratch marks, and he was very groggy. Peterson came up to Fred and started screaming at him; Fred barely noticed. Instead he began talking to himself softly; "Rolling bowling green."

* * *

[While Dr. Cabada was on vacation, Fred was seen by a Dr. Kerr. According to Kerr, "When I was in medical school, we were always taught that a psychotic person was schizophrenic until proven otherwise." But after working in state hospitals, Kerr came to believe that many of the delusional patients he saw were not afflicted solely with schizophrenia or solely with manic depression, but rather with some combination of the two. Kerr rediagnosed Fred as suffering from a "schizoaffective disorder" and put him on Tegretol, 200 milligram three times a day, stating "There is nothing empirical about this. All you can do is bring your experience and your training." On this drug, Fred improved to the point where the hospital staff considered releasing him to a community facility].

* * *

No one can doubt that deinstitutionalization has done a lot of good. Many who didn't need to be there were languishing in mental hospitals; their lives have been immeasurably improved. In 1970 alone, the Austin State Hospital's population dropped from 3400 to 1800, and almost all releases were easy cases. But if deinstitutionalization has done some unquestioned good, it has also had its share of unintended consequences. Look around downtown Houston, where as many as 2000 mentally ill people, "freed" from the state hospital, wander the streets like modern-day paupers, and you quickly realize how far the promise of deinstitutionalization is from the reality. The miracle drugs that were going to "cure" the mentally ill have turned out to be not so miraculous after all—helpful, yes, but not miraculous. The extensive network of community programs and halfway houses that were expected to absorb the thousands of mentally ill streaming out of state hospitals never developed—especially not in Texas, where the state hospitals still pull in nearly 80 per cent of all the mental health money even as their populations have been reduced by more than two thirds. A patient's right under the law to be released from a state hospital commitment after ninety days has been largely responsible for the so-called revolving door syndrome, in which patients spend their lives shuttling back and forth from the hospital to the community. The right to live in the least restrictive environment has meant that thousands of mentally ill people, not sick enough to be confined to a hospital ward but still desperately in need of care, live in the least restrictive environment imaginable: the streets.

And yet the pressure on the state hospitals to "get the census down" remains as inexorable as ever. It comes from state and federal law and from a society still unwilling to admit that deinstitutionalization has not worked the way it was supposed to. And it also comes from Judge Sanders. The judge's mental health monitors—the people overseeing the hospital system on his behalf—deny that depopulation is their intent, but they cannot deny the result. Their goal is purely to improve conditions at the state hospital, with little thought given to how the judge's orders will affect the rest of the system. Several years ago, when Judge Sanders, acting on the masters' recommendations, ordered that the staff-to-patient ratio be significantly lowered, his aim was to make each ward a less dangerous place. But since the hospitals didn't have the money to hire the hundreds of staff members needed to comply with the order, they reacted—predictably—not by adding staff but by increasing medication dosages for the patients, to get them out more quickly. The hospitals can say—and do say, all the time—that they are only doing their job while complying with a court order. The judge can say that he is doing his job. (The population in Austin today is around 550.) And meanwhile, a few thousand more mentally ill people are released to the streets, where they find . . . nothing.

Well, not exactly nothing. Houston, for example, does have some outpatient clinics, some apartments for mentally ill people, and one small halfway house to serve the thousands of mentally ill people who live in the city. The halfway house is Tarry Hall, on a residential street in Montrose. It has 27 beds. It is the reality of deinstitutionalization in Houston. . . .

* * *

"Hygiene and room check are now beginning."

It was 9:15 a.m. . . . , and the voice booming over the intercom belonged to Dennis Milam, a bearded, sandaled social worker who is third in command at Tarry Hall. By this time, the residents (as Tarry Hall calls its clientele) had been awake for nearly three hours, and theoretically they should have finished their hygiene and room chores. Instead, most were in the same position as Fred. They hadn't even started.

Tarry Hall is a deceptively large house built in the shape of a square doughnut. Its central feature is an outdoor courtyard surrounded by four wide corridors. In the front of the building is a pool room, and in the back, a den. Because it has a TV and a stereo, the den serves much the same function as the dayroom in Austin; it is where the residents can usually be found when they have nothing else to do. It was where Talvin Paul—a 25–year–old graduate of Grambling who was Fred's caseworker—now found his new charge.

"Have you taken a shower yet, Fred?" asked Talvin.

"Too early for that, man." Fred stared straight ahead while Talvin spoke. "One of the expectations around here is that everybody takes a shower," Talvin said. Still, Fred didn't move. It was 9:25. Over the intercom Dennis said, "Fred Thomas, you are needed in your room." Fred crushed his cigarette butt into the floor—ignoring Talvin's admonition to put it in an ashtray—and shuffled off to his room.

The purpose of the hygiene and room chores is to instill a sense of responsibility in the residents, and those who accomplish their daily tasks are rewarded with access to their money and cigarettes and with the accumulation of free time—time they can spend away from the halfway house. Fred and his new roommate, another recent arrival from Austin, listened impassively as Dennis explained what was expected of them each morning: besides making their beds and putting their clothes away, they were supposed to sweep, mop, and dust their rooms. In addition, each would soon be given a household chore (Fred was eventually assigned a bathroom to keep clean). "Do you understand?" asked Dennis. Fred nodded and began picking up his sheets. But as soon as Dennis left, Fred dropped the sheets, wandered back into the den, and turned on the stereo. It was 9:35.

Fifteen minutes later, Dennis found him. "In the morning," he said, "we don't have the stereo or TV on." He flicked the music off. "Your roommate is sweeping the room right now, so why don't you get the mop?" Annoyed by that, Fred nonetheless got a mop and dragged it behind him toward his bedroom. When he got there he gave the floor a few halfhearted passes. But as soon as the coast was clear, Fred started to walk back to the den. Talvin spotted him. "Fred," he shouted, "you need to be in your room!"

That was more than Fred could bear. He stalked past Talvin into the den and again turned on the stereo. When Talvin caught up with him, Fred glared. "Why are you trying to punish me, man?" he asked. It was 10:15.

Today hygiene and room check took nearly two hours. Up until a few months ago, it had taken a half-hour. Back then, the staff had encouraged residents to look for work, and the residents themselves had run a meeting every Friday to decide how much free time each person had earned. Now the staff was spending its time encouraging residents to comb their hair, and the Friday meeting was run by staff members, who had already decided how much time each resident had earned. Things were different because the residents were different; the mentally ill people whom Tarry Hall once treated had been much less sick than the ones it treated now.

That era had only recently ended, yet it was already viewed nostalgically by the Tarry Hall staff. It had been more fun to work with higher functioning residents: they were more motivated to succeed and easier to reach, and the psychic rewards for the staff were much more immediate. Tarry Hall had enjoyed a great deal of independence in the old days. Stripped of that independence, Tarry Hall was bitter.

For most of its eight-year existence, the halfway house had successfully resisted efforts to make it a port of entry for released state hospital patients. Never mind that Tarry Hall was the only county-funded halfway house in the city and that there were mentally ill people in the streets of Houston who needed the kind of help Tarry Hall could offer. For years Tarry Hall administrators refused to admit that those two facts were connected.

Early in 1985, however, in its never-ending effort to reduce hospital populations, MHMR began dangling money in front of local mental health agencies as an inducement to treat more mentally ill people. Each agency would receive $35.50 per patient per day that the census was reduced in Austin. Gradually, the Harris County mental health authorities began making changes aimed at keeping more people out of the hospital. For instance, they assigned caseworkers to monitor the progress of recently released state hospital patients. They also began scrambling for more placement possibilities: inevitably, they saw Tarry Hall as a luxury they could no longer afford. In late March 1985 Tarry Hall had begun accepting its first handful of residents from Austin.

The change from without imposed on Tarry Hall also brought changes from within. Tarry Hall used to have a library: now the library was being converted to a point store. The former clientele had attended current-events classes; the new clientele took walks in the neighborhood. In general sights were lowered. Among the staff members, who had agreed to the changes only because they had no other choice, morale was very weak.

The question that remained unanswered was whether the new Tarry Hall was equipped to help its new residents. For years the staff had done a good job with the people it chose to work with. Now, though the residents were different, the staff was the same. Could the staff teach residents to comb their hair and take a shower as well as they had once taught current events? Could Tarry Hall motivate the truly unmotivated? As Fred had shown, it would be no easy trick.

* * *

One morning in early July I decided to see how the other half lived—the mentally ill people in Houston who do not have one of the 27 beds in Tarry Hall or access to the other facilities available to the lucky few. I went looking for Don Peterson [who had been released unconditionally at about the same time Fred was released].

I started at the [Reverend] Armstrong house where Peterson lived and talked my way inside for a quick glance around. I didn't find

Peterson, but what I did find left me reeling. Peterson's tiny bedroom, which he shared with two other people, was particularly gruesome. A spoon on his bureau had been there for so long that whatever food it once held had turned moldy and black and so hard that it appeared glued to the surface. I saw a black woman walking around naked. I tried to talk to her, but two young white "attendants" shooed me away. The attendants would be fired a few weeks later when Armstrong found them "misusing one of the girls," as he phrased it, though not sexually, he quickly added. Before I left, one of the tenants told me that Peterson usually hung out at the Star of Hope Mission during the day.

That's where I found Peterson, sitting in a lower downtown parking lot across the street from the mission, a large, two-story building that can accommodate as many as five hundred homeless every night. Next to him was a white teenager, a runaway. Despite the heat, Peterson wore his usual four shirts, a vest, a jacket, and a pair of new tan cowboy boots. Sweat was dripping from the end of his moustache, and a dirty winger coat lay on the sidewalk next to him. He held a Burger King bag that contained a bottle of Thunderbird wine, which he had bought from someone at the mission for 13 cents.

Every day Peterson got up before dawn and took a bus downtown in order to be at the mission in time for breakfast, which began at 5 a.m. He usually stayed through the dinner hour. I thought at first that he came because the food was better, but he quickly disabused me. "Rev's [Reverend Armstrong's] food's about the same." So why did he do it? "Dunno," he said. "Guess it's cause this is where all my friends are." He pointed in the direction of the runaway. I asked him what his friend's name was. He didn't know.

The real reason for Peterson's routine was that the Star of Hope Mission came the closest to approximating life in an institution. He was used to the barter economy of the state hospital; that also existed among the transient population. He was even used to the danger. The runaway told me, somewhat nervously, that in the last week there had been four stabbings outside the mission. From reading the newspaper you can get the impression that mentally ill people commit an inordinate number of violent crimes. At a place like the Star of Hope Mission, you quickly see that the opposite is true: their sickness makes them easy targets.

* * *

You didn't have to spend much time in Houston mental health circles to hear the allegations about the Reverend Alvin Armstrong. They were rampant. There were allegations of sexual abuse at his house, of serious untreated illness, and more. From time to time, someone in the bureaucracy would poke around, but the investigations were always halfhearted at best. The system's dirty little secret is that it needs Armstrong, desperately, to provide his wretched shelter. However many mentally ill people are wandering the streets of Houston, there would be hundreds more without the Alvin Armstrongs of the world. Mentally ill street people shame the society that lets them live as they do. In

Armstrong's house, tucked away in the ghetto, they are out of sight and out of mind.

Everyone in the system knew how bad this house was; everyone felt helpless to do anything. The existence of places like Armstrong's was seen as a fact of life in the mental health business—one of the awful, unintended consequences of deinstitutionalization. A social worker who refers patients to Armstrong told me that she couldn't bring herself to visit the house. "I don't want to see it," she said. "I don't want to know where I'm sending them."

II. THEORETICAL UNDERPINNINGS OF THE RIGHT TO TREATMENT AND HABILITATION

DONALDSON v. O'CONNOR

United States Court of Appeals, Fifth Circuit, 1974.
493 F.2d 507, 519–531.

* * *

The question for decision, whether patients involuntarily civilly committed in state mental hospitals have a constitutional right to treatment, has never been addressed by any of the federal courts of appeals. Four district courts, however, have decided the question within the last three years, three of which held that there is a constitutional right to treatment. The Court of Appeals for the District of Columbia Circuit, in a landmark case decided eight years ago, took note in dictum of the existence and seriousness of the question, although in the same case the court held that the Hospitalization of the Mentally Ill Act of 1964 creates a *statutory* right to treatment on the part of mental patients in the District of Columbia.[11] The idea of a constitutional right to treatment has received an unusual amount of scholarly discussion and support, and there is now an enormous range of precedent relevant to, although not squarely in point with, the issue. The idea has been current at least since 1960, since the publication in the May 1960 issue of the American Bar Association Journal of an article by Dr. Morton Birnbaum, a forensic medical doctor now generally credited with being the father of the idea of a right to treatment. The A.B.A. Journal editorially endorsed the idea shortly after the publication of Dr. Birnbaum's article.

We hold that a person involuntarily civilly committed to a state mental hospital has a constitutional right to receive such individual treatment as will give him a reasonable opportunity to be cured or to improve his mental condition.

In reaching this result, we begin by noting the indisputable fact that civil commitment entails a "massive curtailment of liberty" in the constitutional sense. [B]eyond this, the conclusion that the due process

---

11. Rouse v. Cameron, 1966, 125 U.S.App.D.C. 366, 373 F.2d 451.

clause guarantees a right to treatment rests upon a two-part theory. The first part begins with the fundamental, and all but universally accepted, proposition that "any nontrivial governmental abridgement of [any] freedom [which is part of the 'liberty' the Fourteenth Amendment says shall not be denied without due process of law] must be justified in terms of some 'permissible governmental goal.' " Once this "fairly sweeping concept of substantive due process" is assumed, the next step is to ask precisely what government interests justify the massive abridgement of liberty civil commitment entails.

* * *

The key point of the first part of the theory of a due process right to treatment is that where, as in Donaldson's case, the rationale for confinement is the "*parens patriae*" rationale that the patient is in need of treatment, the due process clause requires that minimally adequate treatment be in fact provided. This in turn requires that, at least for the nondangerous patient, constitutionally minimum standards of treatment be established and enforced. As Judge Johnson expressed it in the *Wyatt* case: "To deprive any citizen of his or her liberty upon the altruistic theory that the confinement is for humane therapeutic reasons and then fail to provide adequate treatment violates the very fundamentals of due process." Wyatt v. Stickney, 325 F.Supp. at 785. This key step in the theory also draws considerable support from, if indeed it is not compelled by, the Supreme Court's recent decision in *Jackson v. Indiana,* 1972, 406 U.S. 715, 92 S.Ct. 1845, 32 L.Ed.2d 435. In *Jackson,* the Supreme Court established the rule that "[a]t the least, due process requires that the nature and duration of commitment bear some reasonable relation to the purposes for which the individual is committed". If the "purpose" of commitment is treatment, and treatment is not provided, then the "nature" of the commitment bears no "reasonable relation" to its "purpose," and the constitutional rule of *Jackson* is violated.

This much represents the first part of the theory of a due process right to treatment; persons committed under what we have termed a *parens patriae* ground for commitment must be given treatment lest the involuntary commitment amount to an arbitrary exercise of government power proscribed by the due process clause. The second part of the theory draws no distinctions between persons committed under "*parens patriae*" rationales and those committed under "police power" rationales. This part begins with the recognition that, under our system of justice, long-term detention is, as a matter of due process, generally permitted only when an individual is (1) proved, in a proceeding subject to the rigorous constitutional limitations of the due process clause of the fourteenth amendment and the Bill of Rights, (2) to have committed a *specific act* defined as an offense against the state. Moreover, detention, under the criminal process, is usually allowed only for a period of time explicitly fixed by the prisoner's sentence. The second part of the theory of a due process right to treatment is based on the principle that when the three central limitations on the government's power to detain—that detention be in retribution for a specific offense; that it be limited to a fixed term; and that it be permitted after a proceeding where fundamental procedural safeguards are observed—are absent, there must be a *quid pro quo* extended by the government to justify confinement.[21] And the *quid pro quo* most commonly recognized is the provision of rehabilitative treatment, or, where rehabilitation is impossible, minimally adequate habilitation and care, beyond the subsistence level custodial care that would be provided in a penitentiary.

* * *

The appellants argue strenuously that a right to constitutionally adequate treatment should not be recognized, because such a right cannot be governed by judicially manageable or ascertainable standards. In making the argument, they rely heavily upon the Northern District of Georgia's decision in *Burnham v. Department of Public Health,* 1972, 349 F.Supp. 1335, 1341–1343. In *Burnham,* the district judge held that a class action seeking declaratory and injunctive relief requiring the Georgia Department of Public Health to provide treatment at Georgia mental hospitals presented a nonjusticiable controversy. He quoted *Baker v. Carr,* 1962, 369 U.S. 186, 198, 82 S.Ct. 691, 700, 7 L.Ed.2d 663, for the proposition that determining whether a suit was justiciable requires determining whether "the duty asserted can be judicially identified and its breach judicially determined, and whether protection for the right asserted can be judicially molded". He then cited the ambiguity of the dictionary definition of treatment, a passage from a law review article noting the fact that there are as many as forty different methods of psychotherapy, and a passage from the Supreme Court's decision in *Greenwood v. United States,* 1956, 350 U.S. 366, 76 S.Ct. 410, 100 L.Ed. 412, concerning the "tentativeness" and "uncertainty" of "professional judgment" in the mental health field. He concluded: "[T]he claimed duty (i.e. to 'adequately' or 'constitutionally treat') defies judicial identity and therefore prohibits its breach from being judicially defined."

The defendants' argument can be answered on two levels. First, we doubt whether, even if we were to concede that courts are incapable of formulating standards of adequate treatment in the abstract, we could or should for that reason alone hold that no right to treatment can be recognized or enforced. There will be cases—and the case at bar is one—where it will be possible to make determination whether a given individual has been denied his right to treatment without formulating in the abstract what constitutes "adequate" treatment.

* * *

21. In *Welsch v. Likins,* 1974, 373 F.Supp. 487, the District of Minnesota described, and rejected, a different *quid pro quo* rationale for a right to treatment. We also reject the rationale described by the *Welsch* court, and the rationale we embrace should be carefully contrasted with it:

One theory is that commitment pursuant to civil statutes generally lacks the proce-

dural safeguards afforded those charged with criminal offense. The constitutional justification for this abridgment of *procedural rights* is that the purpose of commitment is treatment. (Emphasis supplied).

Welsch v. Likins, 373 F.Supp. at 496.

We do not, however, concede that determining what constitutes adequate treatment is beyond the competence of the judiciary. In deciding in individual cases whether treatment is adequate, there are a number of devices open to the courts, as Judge Bazelon noted in discussing the implementation of the statutory right to treatment in the landmark case of Rouse v. Cameron:

> But lack of finality [of professional judgment] cannot relieve the court of its duty to render an informed decision. Counsel for the patient and the government can be helpful in presenting pertinent data concerning standards for mental care, and, particularly when the patient is indigent and cannot present experts of his own, the court may appoint independent experts. Assistance might be obtained from such sources as the American Psychiatric Association, which has published standards and is continually engaged in studying the problems of mental care. The court could also consider inviting the psychiatric and legal communities to establish procedures by which expert assistance can be best provided.

* * *

In summary, we hold that where a nondangerous patient is involuntarily civilly committed to a state mental hospital, the only constitutionally permissible purpose of confinement is to provide treatment, and that such a patient has a constitutional right to such treatment as will help him to be cured or to improve his mental condition. . . .

O'CONNOR v. DONALDSON

Supreme Court of the United States, 1975.
422 U.S. 563, 95 S.Ct. 2486, 45 L.Ed.2d 396.

JUSTICE BURGER, concurring.

A

[The Supreme Court's majority opinion in this case, reprinted at pp. 751–56, avoided the right to treatment issue. However, Chief Justice Burger, in a concurring opinion, directly addressed it, arguing that no such right should be recognized. In the first part of his concurrence, also reprinted at pp. 756–59, he responded to the Fifth Circuit's "first theory" justifying the right to treatment by disputing that court's apparent conclusion that "with respect to persons who are not physically dangerous, a State has no power to confine the mentally ill except for the purpose of providing them with treatment." Burger contended that, historically, parens patriae commitment had been primarily for custodial care, not treatment. Even today, "it remains a stubborn fact that there are many forms of mental illness which are not understood, some of which are untreatable in the sense that no effective therapy has yet been discovered for them, and that rates of 'cure' are generally low." Burger also noted the uncertainty of psychiatric diagnosis and the difficulty of treating mentally ill individuals who are unwilling to recognize they are ill. He concluded: "It may be that some persons in . . . these categories, and there may be others, are unable to function in society and will suffer real harm to themselves unless provided with care in a sheltered environment." Burger then addressed the Fifth Circuit's "second theory" justifying a constitutional right to treatment.]

B

Alternatively, it has been argued that a Fourteenth Amendment right to treatment for involuntarily confined mental patients derives from the fact that many of the safeguards of the criminal process are not present in civil commitment. The Court of Appeals described this theory as follows:

> "[A] due process right to treatment is based on the principle that when the three central limitations on the government's power to detain—that detention be in retribution for a specific offense; that it be limited to a fixed term; and that it be permitted after a proceeding where the fundamental procedural safeguards are observed—are absent, there must be a *quid pro quo* extended by the government to justify confinement. And the *quid pro quo* most commonly recognized is the provision of rehabilitative treatment." 493 F.2d, at 522.

To the extent that this theory may be read to permit a State to confine an individual simply because it is willing to provide treatment, regardless of the subject's ability to function in society, it raises the gravest of constitutional problems, and I have no doubt the Court of Appeals would agree on this score. As a justification for a constitutional right to such treatment, the *quid pro quo* theory suffers from equally serious defects.

It is too well established to require extended discussion that due process is not an inflexible concept. Rather, its requirements are determined in particular instances by identifying and accommodating the interests of the individual and society. Where claims that the State is acting in the best interests of an individual are said to justify reduced procedural and substantive safeguards, this Court's decisions require that they be "candidly appraised." However, in so doing judges are not free to read their private notions of public policy or public health into the Constitution.

The *quid pro quo* theory is a sharp departure from, and cannot coexist with, due process principles. As an initial matter, the theory presupposes that essentially the same interests are involved in every situation where a State seeks to confine an individual; that assumption, however, is incorrect. It is elementary that the justification for the criminal process and the unique deprivation of liberty which it can impose requires that it be invoked only for commission of a specific offense prohibited by legislative enactment.[7] But it would be incongruous, for example, to apply the same limitation when quarantine is

---

7. This is not to imply that I accept all of the Court of Appeals' conclusions regarding the limitations upon the States' power to detain persons who commit crimes. For example, the notion that confinement must be "for a fixed term" is difficult to square with the widespread practice of indeterminate sentencing, at least where the upper limit is a life sentence.

imposed by the State to protect the public from a highly communicable disease.

A more troublesome feature of the *quid pro quo* theory is that it would elevate a concern for essentially procedural safeguards into a new substantive constitutional right. Rather than inquiring whether strict standards of proof or periodic redetermination of a patient's condition are required in civil confinement, the theory accepts the absence of such safeguards but insists that the State provide benefits which, in the view of a court, are adequate "compensation" for confinement. In light of the wide divergence of medical opinion regarding the diagnosis of and proper therapy for mental abnormalities, that prospect is especially troubling in this area and cannot be squared with the principle that "courts may not substitute for the judgments of legislators their own understanding of the public welfare, but must instead concern themselves with the validity under the Constitution of the methods which the legislature has selected." Of course, questions regarding the adequacy of procedure and the power of a State to continue particular confinements are ultimately for the courts, aided by expert opinion to the extent that is found helpful. But I am not persuaded that we should abandon the traditional limitations on the scope of judicial review.

YOUNGBERG v. ROMEO

Supreme Court of the United States, 1982.
457 U.S. 307, 102 S.Ct. 2452, 73 L.Ed.2d 28.

JUSTICE POWELL delivered the opinion of the Court.

The question presented is whether respondent, involuntarily committed to a state institution for the mentally retarded, has substantive rights under the Due Process Clause of the Fourteenth Amendment to (i) safe conditions of confinement; (ii) freedom from bodily restraints; and (iii) training or "habilitation." Respondent sued under 42 U.S.C. § 1983 three administrators of the institution, claiming damages for the alleged breach of his constitutional rights.

I

Respondent Nicholas Romeo is profoundly retarded. Although 33 years old, he has the mental capacity of an 18–month–old child, with an I.Q. between 8 and 10. He cannot talk and lacks the most basic self-care skills. Until he was 26, respondent lived with his parents in Philadelphia. But after the death of his father in May 1974, his mother was unable to care for him. Within two weeks of the father's death, respondent's mother sought his temporary admission to a nearby Pennsylvania hospital.

Shortly thereafter, she asked the Philadelphia County Court of Common Pleas to admit Romeo to a state facility on a permanent basis. Her petition to the court explained that she was unable to care for

Romeo or control his violence.[2] As part of the commitment process, Romeo was examined by a physician and a psychologist. They both certified that respondent was severely retarded and unable to care for himself. On June 11, 1974, the Court of Common Pleas committed respondent to the Pennhurst State School and Hospital, pursuant to the applicable involuntary commitment provision of the Pennsylvania Mental Health and Mental Retardation Act.

At Pennhurst, Romeo was injured on numerous occasions, both by his own violence and by the reactions of other residents to him. Respondent's mother became concerned about these injuries. After objecting to respondent's treatment several times, she filed this complaint on November 4, 1976, in the United States District Court for the Eastern District of Pennsylvania as his next friend. The complaint alleged that "[d]uring the period July, 1974 to the present, plaintiff has suffered injuries on at least sixty-three occasions." The complaint originally sought damages and injunctive relief from Pennhurst's director and two supervisors; it alleged that these officials knew, or should have known, that Romeo was suffering injuries and that they failed to institute appropriate preventive procedures, thus violating his rights under the Eighth and Fourteenth Amendments.

Thereafter, in late 1976, Romeo was transferred from his ward to the hospital for treatment of a broken arm. While in the infirmary, and by order of a doctor, he was physically restrained during portions of each day. These restraints were ordered by Dr. Gabroy, not a defendant here, to protect Romeo and others in the hospital, some of whom were in traction or were being treated intravenously. Although respondent normally would have returned to his ward when his arm healed, the parties to this litigation agreed that he should remain in the hospital due to the pending lawsuit. Nevertheless, in December 1977, a second amended complaint was filed alleging that the defendants were restraining respondent for prolonged periods on a routine basis. The second amended complaint also added a claim for damages to compensate Romeo for the defendants' failure to provide him with appropriate "treatment or programs for his mental retardation." All claims for injunctive relief were dropped prior to trial because respondent is a member of the class seeking such relief in another action.[6]

An 8–day jury trial was held in April 1978. Petitioners introduced evidence that respondent participated in several programs teaching basic self-care skills.[7] A comprehensive behavior-modification program was

---

2. Mrs. Romeo's petition to the Court of Common Pleas stated: "Since my husband's death I am unable to handle him. He becomes violent—kicks, punches, breaks glass; He can't speak—wants to express himself but can't. He is [a] constant 24 hr. care. [W]ithout my husband I am unable to care for him."

6. *Pennhurst State School and Hospital v. Halderman,* 451 U.S. 1, 101 S.Ct. 1531,

67 L.Ed.2d 694 (1981) (remanded for further proceedings).

7. Prior to his transfer to Pennhurst's hospital ward, Romeo participated in programs dealing with feeding, showering, drying, dressing, self-control, and toilet training, as well as a program providing interaction with staff members. Some programs continued while respondent was in

designed by staff members to reduce Romeo's aggressive behavior,[8] but that program was never implemented because of his mother's objections. Respondent introduced evidence of his injuries and of conditions in his unit.

At the close of the trial, the court instructed the jury that "if any or all of the defendants were aware of and failed to take all reasonable steps to prevent repeated attacks upon Nicholas Romeo," such failure deprived him of constitutional rights. The jury also was instructed that if the defendants shackled Romeo or denied him treatment "as a punishment for filing this lawsuit," his constitutional rights were violated under the Eighth Amendment. Finally, the jury was instructed that only if they found the defendants "deliberate[ly] indifferen[t] to the serious medical [and psychological] needs" of Romeo could they find that his Eighth and Fourteenth Amendment rights had been violated. The jury returned a verdict for the defendants, on which judgment was entered.

The Court of Appeals for the Third Circuit, sitting en banc, reversed and remanded for a new trial. The court held that the Eighth Amendment, prohibiting cruel and unusual punishment of those convicted of crimes, was not an appropriate source for determining the rights of the involuntarily committed. Rather, the Fourteenth Amendment and the liberty interest protected by that Amendment provided the proper constitutional basis for these rights. In applying the Fourteenth Amendment, the court found that the involuntarily committed retain liberty interests in freedom of movement and in personal security. These were "fundamental liberties" that can be limited only by an "overriding, non-punitive" state interest. It further found that the involuntarily committed have a liberty interest in habilitation designed to "treat" their mental retardation.

The en banc court did not, however, agree on the relevant standard to be used in determining whether Romeo's rights had been violated. Because physical restraint "raises a presumption of a punitive sanction," the majority of the Court of Appeals concluded that it can be justified only by "compelling necessity." A somewhat different standard was appropriate for the failure to provide for a resident's safety. The majority considered that such a failure must be justified by a showing of "substantial necessity." Finally, the majority held that when treatment has been administered, those responsible are liable only if the treatment is not "acceptable in the light of present medical or other scientific knowledge."[14]

the hospital, and they reduced respondent's aggressive behavior to some extent.

8. The program called for short periods of separation from other residents and for use of "muffs" on plaintiff's hands for short periods of time, i.e., five minutes, to prevent him from harming himself or others.

14. Actually, the court divided the right-to-treatment claim into three categories and adopted three standards, but only the

standard described in text is at issue before this Court. The Court of Appeals also stated that if a jury finds that *no* treatment has been administered, it may hold the institution's administrators liable unless they can provide a compelling explanation for the lack of treatment, but respondent does not discuss this precise standard in his brief and it does not appear to be relevant to the facts of this case. In addition, the court

Chief Judge Seitz, concurring in the judgment, considered the standards articulated by the majority as indistinguishable from those applicable to medical malpractice claims. In Chief Judge Seitz' view, the Constitution "only requires that the courts make certain that professional judgment in fact was exercised." He concluded that the appropriate standard was whether the defendants' conduct was "such a substantial departure from accepted professional judgment, practice, or standards in the care and treatment of this plaintiff as to demonstrate that the defendants did not base their conduct on a professional judgment."

We granted the petition for certiorari because of the importance of the question presented to the administration of state institutions for the mentally retarded.

II

We consider here for the first time the substantive rights of involuntarily committed mentally retarded persons under the Fourteenth Amendment to the Constitution. In this case, respondent has been committed under the laws of Pennsylvania, and he does not challenge the commitment. Rather, he argues that he has a constitutionally protected liberty interest in safety, freedom of movement, and training within the institution; and that petitioners infringed these rights by failing to provide constitutionally required conditions of confinement.

The mere fact that Romeo has been committed under proper procedures does not deprive him of all substantive liberty interests under the Fourteenth Amendment. See, *e.g., Vitek v. Jones,* 445 U.S. 480, 491–494, 100 S.Ct. 1254, 1262–1264, 63 L.Ed.2d 552 (1980). Indeed, the state concedes that respondent has a right to adequate food, shelter, clothing, and medical care. We must decide whether liberty interests also exist in safety, freedom of movement, and training. If such interests do exist, we must further decide whether they have been infringed in this case.

A

Respondent's first two claims involve liberty interests recognized by prior decisions of this Court, interests that involuntary commitment proceedings do not extinguish. The first is a claim to safe conditions. In the past, this Court has noted that the right to personal security constitutes a "historic liberty interest" protected substantively by the Due Process Clause. And that right is not extinguished by lawful confinement, even for penal purposes. If it is cruel and unusual punishment to hold convicted criminals in unsafe conditions, it must be unconstitutional to confine the involuntarily committed—who may not be punished at all—in unsafe conditions.

Next, respondent claims a right to freedom from bodily restraint. In other contexts, the existence of such an interest is clear in the prior decisions of this Court. Indeed, "[l]iberty from bodily restraint always

considered "least intrusive" analysis appropriate to justify severe intrusions on individual dignity such as permanent physical alteration or surgical intervention, but respondent concedes that this issue is not present in this case.

has been recognized as the core of the liberty protected by the Due Process Clause from arbitrary governmental action." This interest survives criminal conviction and incarceration. Similarly, it must also survive involuntary commitment.

B

Respondent's remaining claim is more troubling. In his words, he asserts a "constitutional right to minimally adequate habilitation." This is a substantive due process claim that is said to be grounded in the liberty component of the Due Process Clause of the Fourteenth Amendment.[19] The term "habilitation," used in psychiatry, is not defined precisely or consistently in the opinions below or in the briefs of the parties or the *amici*.[20] [T]he term refers to "training and development of needed skills." Respondent emphasizes that the right he asserts is for "minimal" training, and he would leave the type and extent of training to be determined on a case-by-case basis "in light of present medical or other scientific knowledge."

In addressing the asserted right to training, we start from established principles. As a general matter, a State is under no constitutional duty to provide substantive services for those within its border. See *Harris v. McRae,* 448 U.S. 297, 318, 100 S.Ct. 2671, 2689, 65 L.Ed.2d 784 (1980) (publicly funded abortions); *Maher v. Roe,* 432 U.S. 464, 469, 97 S.Ct. 2376, 2380, 53 L.Ed.2d 484 (1977) (medical treatment). When a person is institutionalized—and wholly dependent on the State—it is conceded by petitioners that a duty to provide certain services and care does exist, although even then a State necessarily has considerable discretion in determining the nature and scope of its responsibilities. Nor must a State "choose between attacking every aspect of a problem or not attacking the problem at all."

Respondent, in light of the severe character of his retardation, concedes that no amount of training will make possible his release. And he does not argue that if he were still at home, the State would have an obligation to provide training at its expense. The record reveals that respondent's primary needs are bodily safety and a minimum of physical restraint, and respondent clearly claims training related to these needs. As we have recognized that there is a constitutionally protected liberty interest in safety and freedom from restraint, training may be necessary to avoid unconstitutional infringement of those rights. On the basis of the record before us, it is quite uncertain whether respondent seeks any

19. Respondent also argues that because he was committed for care and treatment under state law he has a state substantive right to habilitation, which is entitled to substantive, not procedural, protection under the Due Process Clause of the Fourteenth Amendment. But this argument is made for the first time in respondent's brief to this Court. It was not advanced in the courts below, and was not argued to the Court of Appeals as a ground for reversing the trial court. Given the uncertainty of Pennsylvania law and the lack of any guidance on this issue from the lower federal courts, we decline to consider it now.

20. Professionals in the habilitation of the mentally retarded disagree strongly on the question whether effective training of all severely or profoundly retarded individuals is even possible.

"habilitation" or training unrelated to safety and freedom from bodily restraints. In his brief to this Court, Romeo indicates that even the self-care programs he seeks are needed to reduce his aggressive behavior. And in his offer of proof to the trial court, respondent repeatedly indicated that, if allowed to testify, his experts would show that additional training programs, including self-care programs, were needed to reduce his aggressive behavior. If, as seems the case, respondent seeks only training related to safety and freedom from restraints, this case does not present the difficult question whether a mentally retarded person, involuntarily committed to a state institution, has some general constitutional right to training *per se*, even when no type or amount of training would lead to freedom.[23]

Chief Judge Seitz, in language apparently adopted by respondent, observed:

> "I believe that the plaintiff has a constitutional right to minimally adequate care and treatment. The existence of a constitutional right to care and treatment is no longer a novel legal proposition."

Chief Judge Seitz did not identify or otherwise define—beyond the right to reasonable safety and freedom from physical restraint—the "minimally adequate care and treatment" that appropriately may be required for this respondent. In the circumstances presented by this case, and on the basis of the record developed to date, we agree with his view and conclude that respondent's liberty interests require the State to provide minimally adequate or reasonable training to ensure safety and freedom from undue restraint. In view of the kinds of treatment sought by respondent and the evidence of record, we need go no further in this case.

III

A

We have established that Romeo retains liberty interests in safety and freedom from bodily restraint. Yet these interests are not absolute; indeed to some extent they are in conflict. In operating an institution such as Pennhurst, there are occasions in which it is necessary for the State to restrain the movement of residents—for example, to protect them as well as others from violence. Similar restraints may also be appropriate in a training program. And an institution cannot protect its residents from all danger of violence if it is to permit them to have any freedom of movement. The question then is not simply whether a liberty interest has been infringed but whether the extent or nature of the restraint or lack of absolute safety is such as to violate due process.

---

23. In the trial court, respondent asserted that "state officials at a state mental hospital have a duty to provide residents . . . with such treatment as will afford them a reasonable opportunity to acquire and maintain those life skills necessary to cope as effectively as their capacities permit." But this claim to a sweeping *per se* right was dropped thereafter. In his brief to this Court, respondent does not repeat it and, at oral argument, respondent's counsel explicitly disavowed any claim that respondent is constitutionally entitled to such treatment as would enable him "to achieve his maximum potential."

Accordingly, whether respondent's constitutional rights have been violated must be determined by balancing his liberty interests against the relevant state interests. If there is to be any uniformity in protecting these interests, this balancing cannot be left to the unguided discretion of a judge or jury. We therefore turn to consider the proper standard for determining whether a State adequately has protected the rights of the involuntarily committed mentally retarded.

B

We think the standard articulated by Chief Judge Seitz affords the necessary guidance and reflects the proper balance between the legitimate interests of the State and the rights of the involuntarily committed to reasonable conditions of safety and freedom from unreasonable restraints. He would have held that "the Constitution only requires that the courts make certain that professional judgment in fact was exercised. It is not appropriate for the courts to specify which of several professionally acceptable choices should have been made." Persons who have been involuntarily committed are entitled to more considerate treatment and conditions of confinement than criminals whose conditions of confinement are designed to punish. At the same time, this standard is lower than the "compelling" or "substantial" necessity tests the Court of Appeals would require a State to meet to justify use of restraints or conditions of less than absolute safety. We think this requirement would place an undue burden on the administration of institutions such as Pennhurst and also would restrict unnecessarily the exercise of professional judgment as to the needs of residents.

Moreover, we agree that respondent is entitled to minimally adequate training. In this case, the minimally adequate training required by the Constitution is such training as may be reasonable in light of respondent's liberty interests in safety and freedom from unreasonable restraints. In determining what is "reasonable"—in this and in any case presenting a claim for training by a State—we emphasize that courts must show deference to the judgment exercised by a qualified professional. By so limiting judicial review of challenges to conditions in state institutions, interference by the federal judiciary with the internal operations of these institutions should be minimized. Moreover, there certainly is no reason to think judges or juries are better qualified than appropriate professionals in making such decisions. For these reasons, the decision, if made by a professional,[30] is presumptively valid; liability may be imposed only when the decision by the professional is such a substantial departure from accepted professional judgment, practice, or standards as to demonstrate that the person responsible actually did not

---

30. By "professional" decisionmaker, we mean a person competent, whether by education, training or experience, to make the particular decision at issue. Long-term treatment decisions normally should be made by persons with degrees in medicine or nursing, or with appropriate training in areas such as psychology, physical therapy, or the care and training of the retarded. Of course, day-to-day decisions regarding care—including decisions that must be made without delay—necessarily will be made in many instances by employees without formal training but who are subject to the supervision of qualified persons.

base the decision on such a judgment. In an action for damages against a professional in his individual capacity, however, the professional will not be liable if he was unable to satisfy his normal professional standards because of budgetary constraints; in such a situation, good-faith immunity would bar liability.

IV

In deciding this case, we have weighed those postcommitment interests cognizable as liberty interests under the Due Process Clause of the Fourteenth Amendment against legitimate state interests and in light of the constraints under which most state institutions necessarily operate. We repeat that the State concedes a duty to provide adequate food, shelter, clothing, and medical care. These are the essentials of the care that the State must provide. The State also has the unquestioned duty to provide reasonable safety for all residents and personnel within the institution. And it may not restrain residents except when and to the extent professional judgment deems this necessary to assure such safety or to provide needed training. In this case, therefore, the State is under a duty to provide respondent with such training as an appropriate professional would consider reasonable to ensure his safety and to facilitate his ability to function free from bodily restraints. It may well be unreasonable not to provide training when training could significantly reduce the need for restraints or the likelihood of violence.

Respondent thus enjoys constitutionally protected interests in conditions of reasonable care and safety, reasonably nonrestrictive confinement conditions, and such training as may be required by these interests. Such conditions of confinement would comport fully with the purpose of respondent's commitment. Cf. *Jackson v. Indiana*, 406 U.S. 715, 738, 92 S.Ct. 1845, 1858, 32 L.Ed.2d 435 (1972). In determining whether the State has met its obligations in these respects, decisions made by the appropriate professional are entitled to a presumption of correctness. Such a presumption is necessary to enable institutions of this type—often, unfortunately, overcrowded and understaffed—to continue to function. A single professional may have to make decisions with respect to a number of residents with widely varying needs and problems in the course of a normal day. The administrators, and particularly professional personnel, should not be required to make each decision in the shadow of an action for damages.

In this case, we conclude that the jury was erroneously instructed on the assumption that the proper standard of liability was that of the Eighth Amendment. We vacate the decision of the Court of Appeals and remand for further proceedings consistent with this decision.

So ordered.

JUSTICE BLACKMUN, with whom JUSTICE BRENNAN and JUSTICE O'CONNOR join, concurring.

I join the Court's opinion. I write separately, however, to make clear why I believe that opinion properly leaves unresolved two difficult and important issues.

The first is whether the Commonwealth of Pennsylvania could accept respondent for "care and treatment," as it did under the Pennsylvania Mental Health and Mental Retardation Act of 1966, and then constitutionally refuse to provide him any "treatment," as that term is defined by state law. Were that question properly before us, in my view there would be a serious issue whether, as a matter of due process, the State could so refuse. I therefore do not find that issue to be a "frivolous" one, as the Chief Justice does.

In *Jackson v. Indiana,* 406 U.S. 715, 92 S.Ct. 1845, 32 L.Ed.2d 435 (1972), this Court, by a unanimous vote of all participating Justices, suggested a constitutional standard for evaluating the conditions of a civilly committed person's confinement: "At the least, due process requires that the nature and duration of commitment bear some reasonable relation to the purpose for which the individual is committed."

* * *

In respondent's case, the majority and principal concurring opinions in the Court of Appeals agreed that "[b]y basing [respondent's] deprivation of liberty at least partially upon a promise of treatment, the state ineluctably has committed the community's resources to providing minimal treatment." Neither opinion clarified, however, whether respondent in fact had been totally denied "treatment," as that term is defined under Pennsylvania law. To the extent that the majority addressed the question, it found that "the evidence in the record, although somewhat contradictory, suggests not so much a total failure to treat as an inadequacy of treatment."

This Court's reading of the record supports that conclusion. Moreover, the Court today finds that respondent's entitlement to "treatment" under Pennsylvania law was not properly raised below. Given this uncertainty in the record, I am in accord with the Court's decision not to address the constitutionality of a State's total failure to provide "treatment" to an individual committed under state law for "care and treatment."

The second difficult question left open today is whether respondent has an independent constitutional claim, grounded in the Due Process Clause of the Fourteenth Amendment, to that "habilitation" or training necessary to *preserve* those basic self-care skills he possessed when he first entered Pennhurst—for example, the ability to dress himself and care for his personal hygiene. In my view, it would be consistent with the Court's reasoning today to include within the "minimally adequate training required by the Constitution," such training as is reasonably necessary to prevent a person's pre-existing self-care skills from *deteriorating* because of his commitment.

The Court makes clear that even after a person is committed to a state institution, he is entitled to such training as is necessary to prevent unreasonable losses of additional liberty as a result of his confinement—for example, unreasonable bodily restraints or unsafe institutional conditions. If a person could demonstrate that he entered a state institution with minimal self-care skills, but lost those skills after commitment because of the State's unreasonable refusal to provide him training, then, it seems to me, he has alleged a loss of liberty quite distinct from—and as serious as—the loss of safety and freedom from unreasonable restraints. For many mentally retarded people, the difference between the capacity to do things for themselves within an institution and total dependence on the institution for all of their needs is as much liberty as they ever will know.

Although respondent asserts a claim of this kind, I agree with the Court that "[o]n the basis of the record before us, it is quite uncertain whether respondent [in fact] seeks any 'habilitation' or training unrelated to safety and freedom from bodily restraints." Since the Court finds respondent constitutionally entitled at least to "such training as may be reasonable in light of [his] liberty interests in safety and freedom from unreasonable restraints," I accept its decision not to address respondent's additional claim.

If respondent actually seeks habilitation in self-care skills not merely to reduce his aggressive tendencies, but also to maintain those basic self-care skills necessary to his personal autonomy within Pennhurst, I believe he is free on remand to assert that claim.

* * *

The Court finds it premature to resolve this constitutional question on this less than fully developed record. Because I agree with that conclusion, I concur in the Court's opinion.

CHIEF JUSTICE BURGER, concurring in the judgment.

I agree with much of the Court's opinion. However, I would hold flatly that respondent has no constitutional right to training, or "habilitation," *per se*. The parties, and the Court, acknowledge that respondent cannot function outside the state institution, even with the assistance of relatives. Indeed, even now neither respondent nor his family seeks his discharge from state care. Under these circumstances, the State's provision of food, shelter, medical care, and living conditions as safe as the inherent nature of the institutional environment reasonably allows, serves to justify the State's custody of respondent. The State did not seek custody of respondent; his family understandably sought the State's aid to meet a serious need.

I agree with the Court that some amount of self-care instruction may be necessary to avoid unreasonable infringement of a mentally retarded person's interests in safety and freedom from restraint; but it seems clear to me that the Constitution does not otherwise place an affirmative duty on the State to provide any particular kind of training or habilitation—even such as might be encompassed under the essentially standardless rubric "minimally adequate training," to which the Court refers. Since respondent asserts a right to "minimally adequate" habilitation "[q]uite apart from its relationship to decent care," unlike the Court I see no way to avoid the issue.*

I also point out that, under the Court's own standards, it is largely irrelevant whether respondent's experts were of the opinion that "additional training programs, including self-care programs, were needed to reduce [respondent's] aggressive behavior,"—a prescription far easier for "spectators" to give than for an institution to implement. The training program devised for respondent by petitioners and other professionals at Pennhurst was, according to the Court's opinion, "presumptively valid"; and "liability may be imposed only when the decision by the professional is such a substantial departure from accepted professional judgment, practice, or standards as to demonstrate that the person responsible actually did not base the decision on such a judgment." Thus, even if respondent could demonstrate that the training programs at Pennhurst were inconsistent with generally accepted or prevailing professional practice—if indeed there be such—this would not avail him so long as his training regimen was actually prescribed by the institution's professional staff.

Questions and Comments

1. *Choosing a rationale.* Of the various constitutional theories described in the preceding opinions, which is the most convincing? The first rationale advanced by the Fifth Circuit (discussed also by Justice Blackmun in *Youngberg*) is premised on *Jackson v. Indiana's* notion that the nature of confinement must bear a reasonable relationship to its purpose. Does a right to treatment for civilly committed patients necessarily flow from this premise, in light of the points made by Chief Justice Burger in his concurring opinion in *Donaldson?* In *Jackson* itself, the Court required that all persons committed for restoration of competency to stand trial receive treatment to effect that restoration unless they are unrestorable, in which case they should be released *or* civilly committed. See pp. 1027–31. Does not this holding support Burger's assertions about the possible purposes of civil commitment?

In response, consider this excerpt from *Wyatt v. Aderholt,* 503 F.2d 1305, 1313 (5th Cir.1974), in which the Fifth Circuit addressed a contention similar to Burger's:

> [W]e find it impossible to accept the [state's] underlying premise that the "need for care" for the mentally ill—and to relieve their families,

---

* Indeed, in the trial court respondent asserted a broad claim to such "treatment as [would] afford [him] a reasonable opportunity to acquire and maintain those life skills necessary to cope as effectively as [his] capacities permit."

Respondent also maintains that, because state law purportedly creates a right to "care and treatment," he has a *federal substantive* right under the Due Process Clause to enforcement of this state right. This contention is obviously frivolous; were every substantive right created by state law enforceable under the Due Process Clause, the distinction between state and federal law would quickly be obliterated.

friends, or guardians of the burden of doing so—can supply a constitutional justification for civil commitment ... The state interest thus asserted may be, strictly speaking, a "rational" state interest. But we find it so trivial beside the major personal interests against which it is to be weighed that we cannot possibly accept it as a justification for the deprivations of liberty involved.

Note also that a majority of states today recognize by statute a right to treatment (as opposed to "care") for every committed patient, whether committed under parens patriae or police power authority (although some states make the provision of treatment contingent on funding). Samuel Brakel et al., The Mentally Disabled and the Law 337 (1985). Of what significance is this fact in evaluating the importance of *Jackson* in establishing a constitutional right to treatment? In his *Youngberg* concurrence, how does Burger amend his *Donaldson* argument to take into account this modern statutory development (see his footnote)? Does Justice Powell's *Youngberg* opinion foreclose a right to treatment based on the *"Jackson"* rationale?

With respect to the Fifth Circuit's second rationale for a constitutional right to treatment (the "quid pro quo" theory), does not the court's reasoning imply that provision of treatment is the only justification for affording civil committees fewer procedural and substantive protections than criminal defendants? To what extent *are* the differences between civil commitment and the criminal process justified by an assumed treatment orientation of the former (cf. *Addington, Parham, Allen v. Illinois*)?

Turning to the Supreme Court's reasoning in *Youngberg,* note that it avoided reliance on the eighth amendment's cruel and unusual punishment clause. Some lower courts have based a right to treatment on this provision in light of the Supreme Court's opinion in *Robinson v. California,* 370 U.S. 660, 82 S.Ct. 1417, 8 L.Ed.2d 758 (1962), which held that the clause prohibits criminal punishment of a person for the status of being an addict. In *Welsch v. Likins,* 373 F.Supp. 487, 496–7 (D.Minn.1974), for instance, the court held that confining someone who is mentally ill and dangerous without treatment is like punishing someone for being an addict, and thus is a violation of the eighth amendment. One reason for rejecting this approach to the right to treatment is that the cruel and unusual punishment clause has normally been applied only to criminal punishment. See *Bell v. Wolfish,* 441 U.S. 520, 99 S.Ct. 1861, 60 L.Ed.2d 447 (1979) (claims brought by pretrial detainees about conditions imposed on them prior to trial not actionable under the eighth amendment); see also *Kansas v. Hendricks*, 521 U.S. 346, 117 S.Ct. 2072, 138 L.Ed.2d 501 (1997)(holding that incapacitation without treatment under a sexual predator act is not punishment for double jeopardy and ex post facto purposes). Assuming this problem is overcome, is *Robinson* good precedent for establishing a right to treatment?

In *Youngberg,* the Court focused instead on the liberty interests of committed patients under the due process clause. Relying on this clause, the majority clearly established a right to "minimally adequate treatment" which, "in this case," consisted of a right to safe conditions and freedom from bodily restraint. At first glance, this formulation may seem narrow. But consider the following excerpt from Note, "The Supreme Court: 1981 Term," 96 Harv.L.Rev. 77, 82–84 (1982):

> Although the Court [in *Youngberg*] sidestepped a direct affirmation of broad rights to habilitation, Justice Powell's liberty-based rationale for a constitutional right to training may lead to a comparable result by any of three avenues. First, although Justice Powell failed to define the scope of "training related to safety and freedom from restraints," he explicitly included training necessary to prevent the violence of self-destructive behavior that creates both a more dangerous institutional environment and a heightened need for bodily restraint. Moreover, the right must encompass training based upon individualized evaluations of patients; only such training can reasonably ensure effective protection of a given patient's liberty interest. Most significantly, Justice Powell's formulation may itself imply a right to habilitative treatment. Training in basic self-care skills—such as dressing oneself and reading—fits within his formulation, because substantial psychiatric study shows that such training reduces violent and self-destructive behavior.

> Second, if logically extended, Justice Powell's liberty-based rationale would justify even broad constitutional rights to treatment. As Justice Blackmun observed in his concurrence, a constitutional right to "such training as is reasonably necessary to prevent a person's pre-existing self-care skills from deteriorating" is "consistent" with the majority's opinion. The deterioration of basic skills, Justice Blackmun noted, presents 'a loss of liberty quite distinct from—and as serious as—the loss of safety and freedom from unreasonable restraints.'

> Third, the Court's reasoning implies the existence of expansive rights that protect the patient's principal liberty interest—the interest in release from involuntary confinement. Psychiatrists have observed that the absence of the training necessary to improve a person's basic skills can unduly prolong confinement. Thus, the majority's liberty-based rationale suggests that mental patients have a constitutional right to habilitative rather than merely protective treatment.

A variant of this last possible interpretation of *Youngberg* was proposed in Spece, "Preserving the Right to Treatment: A Critical Assessment and Constructive Development of Constitutional Right to Treatment Theories," 20 Ariz.L.Rev. 1, 33–46 (1978). Relying on least restrictive alternative theory, Spece argued that "virtually all patients are entitled to superior, individual treatment ... unless the state can meet the heavy burden of demonstrating either that treatment would neither hasten release nor enhance freedom within the institution or that confinement with treatment would be less effective than confinement simpliciter in achieving the state's commitment goals." Id. at 34–35. According to Spece, this theory "comfortably accommodates the confinement of those who are untreatable but otherwise committable." Id. at 44. At the same time, Spece asserts, it requires the state to provide treatment for virtually every patient who is treatable. To what extent does *Youngberg* endorse this theory? In the majority opinion, look at both the penultimate paragraph and footnote 14.

2. *The professional judgment standard.* Note that whatever the ultimate scope of the right to treatment, the question as to whether that right

has been infringed may well depend upon how courts construe *Youngberg's* professional judgment standard. For instance, even if patients have a right to treatment or habilitation that will enable them to leave the hospital as soon as possible, deciding whether a particular treatment program implements that right may depend solely upon whether "professional judgment was exercised" in deciding upon the program. Note also that *Youngberg* stated that if the reason professional judgment is not exercised or implemented is budgetary, then damages cannot be awarded against an individual professional (the "good faith" defense). However, the Court made no comment on the viability of a "budgetary defense" in an individual or class action suit seeking to enjoin the state to provide treatment.

3. *Aftermath of* Youngberg. Since *Youngberg,* no federal court has subscribed to the Fifth Circuit's version of the right to treatment as the right "to such treatment as will help [the patient] be cured or to improve his mental condition." For instance, one court held that "[w]here the state does not provide treatment designed to improve a mentally retarded individual's condition, it deprives the individual of nothing guaranteed by the Constitution; it simply fails to grant a benefit of optimal treatment that it is under no obligation to grant." *Feagley v. Waddill,* 868 F.2d 1437, 1440 (5th Cir.1989). Another held that because members of the plaintiff class were relatively high functioning mildly or moderately retarded individuals they did not need training "to enhance . . . their right to liberty of movement" and thus were not guaranteed treatment under the constitution. *Phillips v. Thompson,* 715 F.2d 365 (7th Cir.1983). Some courts, however, seem willing to interpret *Youngberg* to mandate something more than just the treatment necessary to ensure safety and the ability to function free of bodily restraints. Representative of this trend is the Second Circuit's decision in *Society for Good Will to Retarded Children, Inc. v. Cuomo,* 737 F.2d 1239 (2d Cir.1984)(hereafter *SGW v. Cuomo*). Although it held that after *Youngberg* the Constitution does not require the state to provide treatment designed to improve the condition of a person with mentral retardation, the Second Circuit endorsed Justice Blackmun's right-to-avoid-deterioration standard. See also, *Frederick L. v. Department of Public Welfare,* 157 F.Supp.2d 509, 524–25 (E.D.Pa.2001); *Salcido v. Woodbury Cty.* 119 F.Supp. 2d 900 (N.D. Iowa 2000); *Assoc. for Retarded Citizens of North Dakota v. Olson,* 561 F.Supp. 473, 487 (D.N.D. 1982), affirmed 713 F.2d 1384 (8th Cir.1983).

Courts have expanded upon *Youngberg* in other ways as well. First, some courts have broadly defined the professional judgment rule. While Chief Justice Burger's concurrence asserted that *Youngberg* would require only that the challenged decision be made by a professional, as of 1993 "[n]one of the courts deciding professional judgment cases has followed Justice Burger's interpretation." Susan Stefan, "What Constitutes Departure from Professional Judgment?", 17 Men. & Phys. Dis. L. Rep. 207, 209 (1993). One court stated in dictum that a psychiatric decision should not be characterized as "professional" where "it is not based on a view as to how best to operate a mental health facility." *Johnson v. Brelje,* 701 F.2d 1201, 1209 n. 9 (7th Cir.1983). Another held that professional judgment is not exercised when "the professional's stated judgment was modified to conform to the *available* treatment, rather than the *appropriate* treatment, for the plaintiff's condition." *Thomas S. v. Morrow,* 601 F.Supp. 1055, 1059

(W.D.N.C.1984) (emphasis in original). Judgments that appear to have been made for administrative or staff convenience or that depart from institutional or state guidelines or regulations have also been found to violate the professional judgment rule. For instance, in a later version of the *Thomas S.* case, the Fourth Circuit held that the state should be liable under *Youngberg* because of "substantial" departures from professional standards involving: confinement of people with retardation in psychiatric hospitals; the use of seclusion and mechanical restraints without employing behavioral treatment programs; the overuse of antispsychotic mediation; and insufficient consideration of treating professionals' recommendations on community placement. *Thomas S. v. Flaherty*, 902 F.2d 250 (4th Cir. 1990). See also *McCartney v. Barg*, 643 F.Supp. 1181, 1188 (N.D. Ohio 1986); *Gary H. v. Hegstrom*, 831 F.2d 1430, 1439 (9th Cir. 1987). On the other hand, mere expert disagreement with the state's experts is very unlikely to rebut the professional judgment presumption. See, e.g., *SGW v. Cuomo*, supra, at 1249.

A second manifestation of judicial resistance to a narrow reading of *Youngberg* is the rejection of the "budgetary defense" in cases seeking injunctions. For instance, in *Clark v. Cohen,* 613 F.Supp. 684, 704 (E.D.Pa. 1985), the court compelled placement of a mildly retarded patient in the community over financially-based objections by the state, emphasizing that professional judgment, to be entitled to judicial deference, "has to be based on medical or psychological criteria and not on exigency, administrative convenience, or other non-medical criteria." See also, *Thomas S. v. Morrow*, 781 F.2d 367, 375 (4th Cir.1986)(*Youngberg* did not apply the budgetary defense to "prospective injunctive relief").

Third, although *Youngberg* obviously involved an involuntarily committed individual, many courts have refused to distinguish between involuntary and voluntary hospital patients in applying its ruling. See, e.g., *SGW v. Cuomo*, supra at 1245–46 ("[O]nce [the state] chose to house ... voluntary patients, thus making them dependent on the state, it was required to do so in a manner that would not deprive them of constitutional rights"). This trend appears to have continued even after the Supreme Court's decision in *DeShaney v. Winnebago County Dept. of Social Servs.*, 489 U.S. 189, 109 S.Ct. 998, 103 L.Ed.2d 249 (1989), which emphasized *Youngberg's* statement that the state has no constitutional duty to ensure an individual's care and safety when it has not affirmatively acted to deprive an individual of liberty. See, e.g., *Torisky v. Schweiker*, 446 F.3d 438, 446–47 (3d Cir. 2006); *Wilson v. Formigoni*, 832 F.Supp. 1152 (N.D.Ill.1993) (despite *DeShaney*, state owes duty of treatment to voluntary patient, at least when patient's request for discharge was refused); *Clark v. Donahue*, 885 F.Supp. 1159 (S.D.Ind.1995); *Conn. Traumatic Brain Injury Ass'n v. Hogan*, 161 F.R.D. 8 (D.Conn.1995).

However, not all courts agree that voluntary patients have a constitutional right to treatment, now that *DeShaney* is law. See, e.g., *Duvall v. Cabinet for Human Resources*, 920 F.Supp. 111, 114 (E.D.Ky.1996). Thus, some understanding of that decision's facts and reasoning may be helpful. The plaintiff in *DeShaney* was the mother of a boy named Joshua who was in a life-threatening coma as a result of a beating by his father, in whose custody Joshua was placed after his parents' divorce. Over one year prior to this beating, the state child protection agency had received complaints suggesting that the father was abusing Joshua; although the state decided there was insufficient evidence to remove custody from the father, it did take several other steps, including enrolling Joshua in a pre-school program, providing the father with counselling services and encouraging the girlfriend to move out of the home; in addition a caseworker made monthly visits. The caseworker noted evidence of abuse during several visits and was told during the two visits previous to the coma-inducing beating that Joshua was too ill to be seen, but no further official action was taken until that beating had occurred. The Supreme Court held that a due process claim against the state would not lie on these facts. Citing *Youngberg*, it stated: "[I]t is the State's affirmative act of restraining the individual's freedom to act on his own behalf—through incarceration, institutionalization, or other similar restraint of personal liberty—which is the 'deprivation of liberty' triggering the protections of the Due Process Clause, not its failure to act to protect his liberty interests against harms inflicted by other means." Id. at 1006. Given what you know about voluntary commitment (see pp. 857–68), after *DeShaney* should there be a constitutional right to treatment for voluntary patients who are institutionalized?

Finally, it should be noted that some state courts have relied on state statutory language rather than the federal constitution in imposing wide-ranging treatment obligations on the government. See, e.g., *Arnold v. Sarn*, No. C–432355 (Ariz.Super.Ct., Maricopa Cty., May 29, 1985). Similarly, a number of federal statutes enacted since *Youngberg* have provided more attractive bases for suit than the holding in *Youngberg* which, despite the above-described interpretations, remains a narrow holding. These statutory-based developments are discussed further in Section IV of this chapter.

III. IMPLEMENTING THE RIGHT: WYATT v. STICKNEY

The following section examines various aspects of one "right to treatment" case, originally styled as *Wyatt v. Stickney*. Although filed over a decade before *Youngberg* and based on a theory of the right to treatment that was not endorsed by that decision, the *Wyatt* litigation is a useful focal point for further study of post-commitment treatment issues for a number of reasons. First, as the first major class action brought to enforce a systemwide right to treatment and habilitation, the case has had a significant impact on judicial and legislative decisions around the country that are still in force today. Second, *Wyatt's* long procedural history provides a particularly good illustration of the vagaries of attempting to implement judicially the right to treatment and habilitation. Third, even assuming *Youngberg* effectively narrows the scope of the right to treatment, *Wyatt* has many lessons to offer future litigators. As the previous notes indicate, *Youngberg* has not deterred courts from using constitutional or state or federal statutory language as a basis for reviewing decisions by state hospital employees and administrators. Moreover, most of these more recent cases are, like *Wyatt* (and unlike *Youngberg*), class action suits that involve requests for injunctive relief. In *Wyatt v. Aderholt*, 503 F.2d 1305, 1316 (5th Cir.1974), the court explained why this kind of suit is likely to be preferred over individual actions:

> . . . In the first place, habeas corpus relief and tort damages are available only after the fact of a failure to provide individual treatment. Here the plaintiffs seek preventive relief, to assure in advance that mental patients will at least have the *chance* to receive adequate treatment by proscribing the maintenance of conditions that foredoom *all* mental patients *inevitably* to inadequate mental treatment. Moreover, there are special reasons why reliance upon individual suits by mental patients would be especially inappropriate. Mental patients are particularly unlikely to be aware of their legal rights. They are likely to have especially limited access to legal assistance. Individual suits may be protracted and expensive, and individual mental patients may therefore be deterred from bringing them. And individual suits may produce distortive therapeutic effects within an institution, since a staff may tend to give especially good—or especially harsh—treatment to patients the staff expects or knows to be litigious.

(Emphasis in original). Given the likelihood of injunctive actions, the tactical lessons derived from the *Wyatt* litigation will continue to be useful, regardless of the theoretical underpinnings of the right to treatment ultimately settled upon.

Ironically, as initially conceived *Wyatt v. Stickney* was not a right to treatment suit. Filed in October, 1970, the original action was brought on behalf of patients at Bryce Hospital in Tuscaloosa, Alabama asking for an injunction prohibiting anticipated layoffs of hospital personnel (which were to occur because a cut in the Alabama cigarette tax reduced the money available to the state hospital system). Although Ricky Wyatt, a patient, was the named plaintiff, in fact "a fairly small number of staff, not a group of indignant patients or their relatives" was the "motivating power behind the suit." Stonewall Stickney, "*Wyatt v. Stickney:* The Right to Treatment," in Bonnie, ed., Psychiatrists and the Legal Process: Diagnosis and Debate 274, 278 (1977). Under the auspices of federal district court judge Frank Johnson, however, the suit triggered a wide-ranging investigation of the deplorable conditions at Bryce and other institutions in Alabama[b] and resulted in substantial changes in the system. In the original *Wyatt* decision, Judge Johnson, relying on a

---

b. The *Wyatt* record is replete with accounts of patients who died or were seriously harmed as a result of inattention by staff, as well descriptions of patient abuse, of filthy conditions, and of general neglect. For instance, the record disclosed that, at one of the institutions involved in the *Wyatt* litigation, four patients had died "due to understaffing, lack of supervision, and brutality."

One of the four died after a garden hose had been inserted into his rectum for five minutes by a working patient who was cleaning him; one died when a fellow patient hosed him with scalding water; another died when soapy water was forced into his mouth; and a fourth died from a self-administered overdose of drugs which had been inadequately secured.

Wyatt v. Aderholt, 503 F.2d 1305, 1311 n. 6. (5th Cir.1974).

"*Jackson*" theory of the right to treatment, held that every civilly committed patient possesses "a constitutional right to receive such individual treatment as will give them a realistic opportunity to be cured or to improve his or her mental condition." 325 F.Supp. 781, 784 (M.D.Ala.1971). The decision set out below is his enforcement decree. Note that it contains standards for virtually every aspect of hospital operation, ranging from the proper temperature of hot water, to the number of social workers and clerk typists per unit, to the types of documents which must be included in each patient's files. The materials following the decision use *Wyatt* and its progeny to provide a flavor of right to treatment litigation and its consequences.

WYATT v. STICKNEY

United States District Court, Middle District Alabama, 1972.
344 F.Supp. 373.

ORDER AND DECREE

JOHNSON, CHIEF JUDGE.

This class action originally was filed on October 23, 1970, in behalf of patients involuntarily confined for mental treatment purposes at Bryce Hospital, Tuscaloosa, Alabama. On March 12, 1971, in a formal opinion and decree, this Court held that these involuntarily committed patients "unquestionably have a constitutional right to receive such individual treatment as will give each of them a realistic opportunity to be cured or to improve his or her mental condition." The Court further held that patients at Bryce were being denied their right to treatment and that defendants, per their request, would be allowed six months in which to raise the level of care at Bryce to the constitutionally required minimum. Wyatt v. Stickney, 325 F.Supp. 781 (M.D.Ala.1971). In this decree, the Court ordered defendants to file reports defining the mission and functions of Bryce Hospital, specifying the objective and subjective standards required to furnish adequate care to the treatable mentally ill and detailing the hospital's progress toward the implementation of minimum constitutional standards. Subsequent to this order, plaintiffs, by motion to amend granted August 12, 1971, enlarged their class to include patients involuntarily confined for mental treatment at Searcy Hospital and at Partlow State School and Hospital for the mentally retarded.

On September 23, 1971, defendants filed their final report, from which this Court concluded on December 10, 1971, that defendants had failed to promulgate and implement a treatment program satisfying minimum medical and constitutional requisites. Generally, the Court found that defendants' treatment program was deficient in three fundamental areas. It failed to provide: (1) a humane psychological and physical environment, (2) qualified staff in numbers sufficient to administer adequate treatment and (3) individualized treatment plans. More specifically, the Court found that many conditions, such as nontherapeutic, uncompensated work assignments, and the absence of any semblance of privacy, constituted dehumanizing factors contributing to the degeneration of the patients' self-esteem. The physical facilities at Bryce were overcrowded and plagued by fire and other emergency hazards. The Court found also that most staff members were poorly trained and that staffing ratios were so inadequate as to render the administration of effective treatment impossible. The Court concluded, therefore, that whatever treatment was provided at Bryce was grossly deficient and failed to satisfy minimum medical and constitutional standards. Based upon this conclusion, the Court ordered that a formal hearing be held at which the parties and amici[3] would have the opportunity to submit proposed standards for constitutionally adequate treatment and to present expert testimony in support of their proposals.

Pursuant to this order, a hearing was held at which the foremost authorities on mental health in the United States appeared and testified as to the minimum medical and constitutional requisites for public institutions, such as Bryce and Searcy, designed to treat the mentally ill. At this hearing, the parties and amici submitted their proposed standards, and now have filed briefs in support of them. Moreover, the parties and amici have stipulated to a broad spectrum of conditions they feel are mandatory for a constitutionally acceptable minimum treatment program. This Court, having considered the evidence in the case, as well as the briefs, proposed standards and stipulations of the parties, has concluded that the standards set out in Appendix A to this decree are medical and constitutional minimums. Consequently, the Court will order their implementation. In so ordering, however, the Court emphasizes that these standards are, indeed, both medical and constitutional minimums and should be viewed as such. The Court urges that once this order is effectuated, defendants not become complacent and self-satisfied. Rather, they should dedicate themselves to providing physical conditions and treatment programs at Alabama's mental institutions that substantially exceed medical and constitutional minimums.

In addition to asking that their proposed standards be effectuated, plaintiffs and amici have requested other relief designed to guarantee the provision of constitutional and humane treatment. Pursuant to one such request for relief, this Court has determined that it is appropriate to order the initiation of human rights committees to function as standing committees of the Bryce and Searcy facilities. The Court will appoint the members of these committees who shall have review of all research proposals and all rehabilitation programs, to ensure that the dignity and the human rights of patients are preserved. The committees also shall advise and assist patients who allege that their legal rights have been infringed or that the Mental Health Board has failed to

3. The amici in this case, including the United States of America, the American Orthopsychiatric Association, the American Psychological Association, the American Civil Liberties Union, and the American Association on Mental Deficiency, have performed exemplary service for which this Court is indeed grateful.

[Note the absence of the American Psychiatric Association, which declined Judge Johnson's offer to participate. Eds.]

comply with judicially ordered guidelines. At their discretion, the committees may consult appropriate, independent specialists who shall be compensated by the defendant Board. Seven members shall comprise the human rights committee for each institution. . . .

This Court will reserve ruling upon other forms of relief advocated by plaintiffs and amici, including their prayer for the appointment of a master and a professional advisory committee to oversee the implementation of the court-ordered minimum constitutional standards.[6] Federal courts are reluctant to assume control of any organization, but especially one operated by a state. This reluctance, combined with defendants' expressed intent that this order will be implemented forthwith and in good faith, causes the Court to withhold its decision on these appointments. Nevertheless, defendants, as well as the other parties and amici in this case, are placed on notice that unless defendants do comply satisfactorily with this order, the Court will be obligated to appoint a master.

Because the availability of financing may bear upon the implementation of this order, the Court is constrained to emphasize at this juncture that a failure by defendants to comply with this decree cannot be justified by a lack of operating funds. As previously established by this Court:

"There can be no legal (or moral) justification for the State of Alabama's failing to afford treatment—and adequate treatment from a medical standpoint—to the several thousand patients who have been civilly committed to Bryce's for treatment purposes. To deprive any citizen of his or her liberty upon the altruistic theory that the confinement is for humane therapeutic reasons and then fail to provide adequate treatment violates the very fundamentals of due process."

From the above, it follows consistently, of course, that the unavailability of neither funds, nor staff and facilities, will justify a default by defendants in the provision of suitable treatment for the mentally ill.

Despite the possibility that defendants will encounter financial difficulties in the implementation of this order, this Court has decided to reserve ruling also upon plaintiffs' motion that defendant Mental Health Board be directed to sell or encumber portions of its land holdings in order to raise funds. Similarly, this Court will reserve ruling on plaintiffs' motion seeking an injunction against the treasurer and the comptroller of the State authorizing expenditures for nonessential State

6. The Court's decision to reserve its ruling on the appointment of a master necessitates the reservation also of the Court's appointing a professional advisory committee to aid the master. Nevertheless, the Court notes that the professional mental health community in the United States has responded with enthusiasm to the proposed initiation of such a committee to as- sist in the upgrading of Alabama's mental health facilities. Consequently, this Court strongly recommends to defendants that they develop a professional advisory committee comprised of amenable professionals from throughout the country who are able to provide the expertise the evidence reflects is important to the successful implementation of this order.

functions, and on other aspects of plaintiffs' requested relief designed to ameliorate the financial problems incident to the implementation of this order. The Court stresses, however, the extreme importance and the grave immediacy of the need for proper funding of the State's public mental health facilities. The responsibility for appropriate funding ultimately must fall, of course, upon the State Legislature and, to a lesser degree, upon the defendant Mental Health Board of Alabama. For the present time, the Court will defer to those bodies in hopes that they will proceed with the realization and understanding that what is involved in this case is not representative of ordinary governmental functions such as paving roads and maintaining buildings. Rather, what is so inextricably intertwined with how the Legislature and Mental Health Board respond to the revelations of this litigation is the very preservation of human life and dignity. Not only are the lives of the patients currently confined at Bryce and Searcy at stake, but also at issue are the well-being and security of every citizen of Alabama. As is true in the case of any disease, no one is immune from the peril of mental illness. The problem, therefore, cannot be overemphasized and a prompt response from the Legislature, the Mental Health Board and other responsible State officials, is imperative.

In the event, though, that the Legislature fails to satisfy its well-defined constitutional obligation, and the Mental Health Board, because of lack of funding or any other legally insufficient reason, fails to implement fully the standards herein ordered, it will be necessary for the Court to take affirmative steps, including appointing a master, to ensure that proper funding is realized[8] and that adequate treatment is available for the mentally ill of Alabama.

This Court now must consider that aspect of plaintiffs' motion of March 15, 1972, seeking an injunction against further commitments to Bryce and Searcy until such time as adequate treatment is supplied in those hospitals. Indisputably, the evidence in this case reflects that no treatment program at the Bryce–Searcy facilities approaches constitutional standards. Nevertheless, because of the alternatives to commitment commonly utilized in Alabama, as well as in other states, the Court is fearful that granting plaintiffs' request at the present time would serve only to punish and further deprive Alabama's mentally ill.

* * *

APPENDIX A

MINIMUM Constitutional STANDARDS for Adequate
Treatment of The Mentally Ill.

I. *Definitions:*

    a. "Hospital"—Bryce and Searcy Hospitals.

---

8. The Court understands and appreciates that the Legislature is not due back in regular session until May, 1973. Nevertheless, special sessions of the Legislature are frequent occurrences in Alabama, and there has never been a time when such a session was more urgently required. If the Legislature does not act promptly to appropriate the necessary funding for mental health, the Court will be compelled to grant plaintiffs' motion to add various State officials and agencies as additional parties to this litigation, and to utilize other avenues of fund raising.

b. "Patients"—all persons who are now confined and all persons who may in the future be confined at Bryce and Searcy Hospitals pursuant to an involuntary civil commitment procedure.

c. "Qualified Mental Health Professional"—

(1) a psychiatrist with three years of residency training in psychiatry;

(2) a psychologist with a doctoral degree from an accredited program;

(3) a social worker with a master's degree from an accredited program and two years of clinical experience under the supervision of a Qualified Mental Health Professional;

(4) a registered nurse with a graduate degree in psychiatric nursing and two years of clinical experience under the supervision of a Qualified Mental Health Professional.

d. "Non–Professional Staff Member"—an employee of the hospital, other than a Qualified Mental Health Professional, whose duties require contact with or supervision of patients.

II. *Humane Psychological and Physical Environment*

1. Patients have a right to privacy and dignity.

2. Patients have a right to the least restrictive conditions necessary to achieve the purposes of commitment.

3. No person shall be deemed incompetent to manage his affairs, to contract, to hold professional or occupational or vehicle operator's licenses, to marry and obtain a divorce, to register and vote, or to make a will *solely* by reason of his admission or commitment to the hospital.

4. Patients shall have the same rights to visitation and telephone communications as patients at other public hospitals, except to the extent that the Qualified Mental Health Professional responsible for formulation of a particular patient's treatment plan writes an order imposing special restrictions. The written order must be renewed after each periodic review of the treatment plan if any restrictions are to be continued. Patients shall have an unrestricted right to visitation with attorneys and with private physicians and other health professionals.

5. Patients shall have an unrestricted right to send sealed mail. Patients shall have an unrestricted right to receive sealed mail from their attorneys, private physicians, and other mental health professionals, from courts, and government officials. Patients shall have a right to receive sealed mail from others, except to the extent that the Qualified Mental Health Professional responsible for formulation of a particular patient's treatment plan writes an order imposing special restrictions on receipt of sealed mail. The written order must be renewed after each

periodic review of the treatment plan if any restrictions are to be continued.

6.   Patients have a right to be free from unnecessary or excessive medication. No medication shall be administered unless at the written order of a physician. The superintendent of the hospital and the attending physician shall be responsible for all medication given or administered to a patient. The use of medication shall not exceed standards of use that are advocated by the United States Food and Drug Administration. Notation of each individual's medication shall be kept in his medical records. At least weekly the attending physician shall review the drug regimen of each patient under his care. All prescriptions shall be written with a termination date, which shall not exceed 30 days. Medication shall not be used as punishment, for the convenience of staff, as a substitute for program, or in quantities that interfere with the patient's treatment program.

7.   Patients have a right to be free from physical restraint and isolation. Except for emergency situations, in which it is likely that patients could harm themselves or others and in which less restrictive means of restraint are not feasible, patients may be physically restrained or placed in isolation only on a Qualified Mental Health Professional's written order which explains the rationale for such action. The written order may be entered only after the Qualified Mental Health Professional has personally seen the patient concerned and evaluated whatever episode or situation is said to call for restraint or isolation. Emergency use of restraints or isolation shall be for no more than one hour, by which time a Qualified Mental Health Professional shall have been consulted and shall have entered an appropriate order in writing. Such written order shall be effective for no more than 24 hours and must be renewed if restraint and isolation are to be continued. While in restraint or isolation the patient must be seen by qualified ward personnel who will chart the patient's physical condition (if it is compromised) and psychiatric condition every hour. The patient must have bathroom privileges every hour and must be bathed every 12 hours.

8.   Patients shall have a right not to be subjected to experimental research without the express and informed consent of the patient, if the patient is able to give such consent, and of his guardian or next of kin, after opportunities for consultation with independent specialists and with legal counsel. Such proposed research shall first have been reviewed and approved by the institution's Human Rights Committee before such consent shall be sought. Prior to such approval the Committee shall determine that such research complies with the principles of the Statement on the Use of Human Subjects for Research of the American Association on Mental Deficiency and with the principles for research involving human subjects required by the United States Department of Health, Education and Welfare for projects supported by that agency.

9.   Patients have a right not to be subjected to treatment procedures such as lobotomy, electro-convulsive treatment, aversive reinforce-

ment conditioning or other unusual or hazardous treatment procedures without their express and informed consent after consultation with counsel or interested party of the patient's choice.

10.   Patients have a right to receive prompt and adequate medical treatment for any physical ailments.

11.   Patients have a right to wear their own clothes and to keep and use their own personal possessions except insofar as such clothes or personal possessions may be determined by a Qualified Mental Health Professional to be dangerous or otherwise inappropriate to the treatment regimen.

12.   The hospital has an obligation to supply an adequate allowance of clothing to any patients who do not have suitable clothing of their own. Patients shall have the opportunity to select from various types of neat, clean, and seasonable clothing. Such clothing shall be considered the patient's throughout his stay in the hospital.

13.   The hospital shall make provision for the laundering of patient clothing.

14.   Patients have a right to regular physical exercise several times a week. Moreover, it shall be the duty of the hospital to provide facilities and equipment for such exercise.

15.   Patients have a right to be outdoors at regular and frequent intervals, in the absence of medical considerations.

16.   The right to religious worship shall be accorded to each patient who desires such opportunities. Provisions for such worship shall be made available to all patients on a nondiscriminatory basis. No individual shall be coerced into engaging in any religious activities.

17.   The institution shall provide, with adequate supervision, suitable opportunities for the patient's interaction with members of the opposite sex.

18.   The following rules shall govern patient labor:

A.   *Hospital Maintenance* No patient shall be required to perform labor which involves the operation and maintenance of the hospital or for which the hospital is under contract with an outside organization. Privileges or release from the hospital shall not be conditioned upon the performance of labor covered by this provision. Patients may voluntarily engage in such labor if the labor is compensated in accordance with the minimum wage laws of the Fair Labor Standards Act, 29 U.S.C. § 206 as amended, 1966.

B.   *Therapeutic Tasks and Therapeutic Labor*

(1) Patients may be required to perform therapeutic tasks which do not involve the operation and maintenance of the hospital, provided the specific task or any change in assignment is:

a.   An integrated part of the patient's treatment plan and approved as a therapeutic activity by a Qualified Mental Health

Professional responsible for supervising the patient's treatment; and

b. Supervised by a staff member to oversee the therapeutic aspects of the activity.

(2) Patients may voluntarily engage in therapeutic labor for which the hospital would otherwise have to pay an employee, provided the specific labor or any change in labor assignment is:

a. An integrated part of the patient's treatment plan and approved as a therapeutic activity by a Qualified Mental Health Professional responsible for supervising the patient's treatment; and

b. Supervised by a staff member to oversee the therapeutic aspects of the activity; and

c. Compensated in accordance with the minimum wage laws of the Fair Labor Standards Act, 29 U.S.C. § 206 as amended, 1966.

C. *Personal Housekeeping* Patients may be required to perform tasks of a personal housekeeping nature such as the making of one's own bed.

D. Payment to patients pursuant to these paragraphs shall not be applied to the costs of hospitalization.

19. *Physical Facilities*

A patient has a right to a humane psychological and physical environment within the hospital facilities. These facilities shall be designed to afford patients with comfort and safety, promote dignity, and ensure privacy. The facilities shall be designed to make a positive contribution to the efficient attainment of the treatment goals of the hospital.

A. *Resident Unit*

The number of patients in a multi-patient room shall not exceed six persons. There shall be allocated a minimum of 80 square feet of floor space per patient in a multi-patient room. Screens or curtains shall be provided to ensure privacy within the resident unit. Single rooms shall have a minimum of 100 square feet of floor space. Each patient will be furnished with a comfortable bed with adequate changes of linen, a closet or locker for his personal belongings, a chair, and a bedside table.

B. *Toilets and Lavatories*

There will be one toilet provided for each eight patients and one lavatory for each six patients. A lavatory will be provided with each toilet facility. The toilets will be installed in separate stalls to ensure privacy, will be clean and free of odor, and will be equipped with appropriate safety devices for the physically handicapped.

C. *Showers*

There will be one tub or shower for each 15 patients. If a central bathing area is provided, each shower area will be divided by curtains to ensure privacy. Showers and tubs will be equipped with adequate safety accessories.

D. *Day Room*

The minimum day room area shall be 40 square feet per patient. Day rooms will be attractive and adequately furnished with reading lamps, tables, chairs, television and other recreational facilities. They will be conveniently located to patients' bedrooms and shall have outside windows. There shall be at least one day room area on each bedroom floor in a multi-story hospital. Areas used for corridor traffic cannot be counted as day room space; nor can a chapel with fixed pews be counted as a day room area.

E. *Dining Facilities*

The minimum dining room area shall be ten square feet per patient. The dining room shall be separate from the kitchen and will be furnished with comfortable chairs and tables with hard, washable surfaces.

F. *Linen Servicing and Handling*

The hospital shall provide adequate facilities and equipment for handling clean and soiled bedding and other linen. There must be frequent changes of bedding and other linen, no less than every seven days to assure patient comfort.

G. *Housekeeping*

Regular housekeeping and maintenance procedures which will ensure that the hospital is maintained in a safe, clean, and attractive condition will be developed and implemented.

H. *Geriatric and Other Nonambulatory Mental Patients*

There must be special facilities for geriatric and other nonambulatory patients to assure their safety and comfort, including special fittings on toilets and wheelchairs. Appropriate provision shall be made to permit nonambulatory patients to communicate their needs to staff.

I. *Physical Plant*

(1) Pursuant to an established routine maintenance and repair program, the physical plant shall be kept in a continuous state of good repair and operation in accordance with the needs of the health, comfort, safety and well-being of the patients.

(2) Adequate heating, air conditioning and ventilation systems and equipment shall be afforded to maintain temperatures and air changes which are required for the comfort of patients at all times and the removal of undesired heat, steam and offensive odors. Such facilities shall ensure that the temperature in the hospital shall not exceed 83° F nor fall below 68° F.

(3) Thermostatically controlled hot water shall be provided in adequate quantities and maintained at the required temperature for patient

or resident use (110° F at the fixture) and for mechanical dishwashing and laundry use (180° F at the equipment).

(4) Adequate refuse facilities will be provided so that solid waste, rubbish and other refuse will be collected and disposed of in a manner which will prohibit transmission of disease and not create a nuisance or fire hazard or provide a breeding place for rodents and insects.

(5) The physical facilities must meet all fire and safety standards established by the state and locality. In addition, the hospital shall meet such provisions of the Life Safety Code of the National Fire Protection Association (21st edition, 1967) as are applicable to hospitals.

19A. The hospital shall meet all standards established by the state for general hospitals, insofar as they are relevant to psychiatric facilities.

20. *Nutritional Standards*

Patients, except for the non-mobile, shall eat or be fed in dining rooms. The diet for patients will provide at a minimum the Recommended Daily Dietary Allowances as developed by the National Academy of Sciences. Menus shall be satisfying and nutritionally adequate to provide the Recommended Daily Dietary Allowances. In developing such menus, the hospital will utilize the Low Cost Food Plan of the Department of Agriculture. The hospital will not spend less per patient for raw food, including the value of donated food, than the most recent per person costs of the Low Cost Food Plan for the Southern Region of the United States, as compiled by the United States Department of Agriculture, for appropriate groupings of patients, discounted for any savings which might result from institutional procurement of such food. Provisions shall be made for special therapeutic diets and for substitutes at the request of the patient, or his guardian or next of kin, in accordance with the religious requirements of any patient's faith. Denial of a nutritionally adequate diet shall not be used as punishment.

III. *Qualified Staff in Numbers Sufficient to Administer Adequate Treatment*

21. Each Qualified Mental Health Professional shall meet all licensing and certification requirements promulgated by the State of Alabama for persons engaged in private practice of the same profession elsewhere in Alabama. Other staff members shall meet the same licensing and certification requirements as persons who engage in private practice of their specialty elsewhere in Alabama.

22. a. All Non–Professional Staff Members who have not had prior clinical experience in a mental institution shall have a substantial orientation training.

    b. Staff members on all levels shall have regularly scheduled in-service training.

23. Each Non–Professional Staff Member shall be under the direct supervision of a Qualified Mental Health Professional.

24. *Staffing Ratios*

The hospital shall have the following minimum numbers of treatment personnel per 250 patients. Qualified Mental Health Professionals trained in particular disciplines may in appropriate situations perform services or functions traditionally performed by members of other disciplines. Changes in staff deployment may be made with prior approval of this Court upon a clear and convincing demonstration that the proposed deviation from this staffing structure will enhance the treatment of the patients.

Classification	Number of Employees
Unit Director	1
Psychiatrist (3 years' residency training in psychiatry)	2
MD (Registered physicians)	4
Nurses (RN)	12
Licensed Practical Nurses	6
Aide III	6
Aide II	16
Aide I	70
Hospital Orderly	10
Clerk Stenographer II	3
Clerk Typist II	3
Unit Administrator	1
Administrative Clerk	1
Psychologist (Ph.D.) (doctoral degree from accredited program)	1
Psychologist (M.A.)	1
Psychologist (B.S.)	2
Social Worker (MSW) (from accredited program)	2
Social Worker (B.A.)	5
Patient Activity Therapist (M.S.)	1
Patient Activity Aide	10
Mental Health Technician	10
Dental Hygienist	1
Chaplain	5
Vocational Rehabilitation Counselor	1
Volunteer Services Worker	1
Mental Health Field Representative	1
Dietitian	1
Food Service Supervisor	1
Cook II	2
Cook I	3
Food Service Worker	15
Vehicle Driver	1
Housekeeper	10
Messenger	1
Maintenance Repairman	2

IV. *Individualized Treatment Plans*

25. Each patient shall have a comprehensive physical and mental examination and review of behavioral status within 48 hours after admission to the hospital.

26. Each patient shall have an individualized treatment plan. This plan shall be developed by appropriate Qualified Mental Health Professionals, including a psychiatrist, and implemented as soon as possible—in any event no later than five days after the patient's admission. Each individualized treatment plan shall contain:

a. a statement of the nature of the specific problems and specific needs of the patient;

b. a statement of the least restrictive treatment conditions necessary to achieve the purposes of commitment;

c. a description of intermediate and long-range treatment goals, with a projected timetable for their attainment;

d. a statement and rationale for the plan of treatment for achieving these intermediate and long-range goals;

e. a specification of staff responsibility and a description of proposed staff involvement with the patient in order to attain these treatment goals;

f. criteria for release to less restrictive treatment conditions, and criteria for discharge;

g. a notation of any therapeutic tasks and labor to be performed by the patient in accordance with Standard 18.

27. As part of his treatment plan, each patient shall have an individualized post-hospitalization plan. This plan shall be developed by a Qualified Mental Health Professional as soon as practicable after the patient's admission to the hospital.

28. In the interests of continuity of care, whenever possible, one Qualified Mental Health Professional (who need not have been involved with the development of the treatment plan) shall be responsible for supervising the implementation of the treatment plan, integrating the various aspects of the treatment program and recording the patient's progress. This Qualified Mental Health Professional shall also be responsible for ensuring that the patient is released, where appropriate, into a less restrictive form of treatment.

29. The treatment plan shall be continuously reviewed by the Qualified Mental Health Professional responsible for supervising the implementation of the plan and shall be modified if necessary. Moreover, at least every 90 days, each patient shall receive a mental examination from, and his treatment plan shall be reviewed by, a Qualified Mental Health Professional other than the professional responsible for supervising the implementation of the plan.

30. In addition to treatment for mental disorders, patients confined at mental health institutions also are entitled to and shall receive appropriate treatment for physical illnesses such as tuberculosis. In providing medical care, the State Board of Mental Health shall take advantage of whatever community-based facilities are appropriate and available and shall coordinate the patient's treatment for mental illness with his medical treatment.

31. Complete patient records shall be kept on the ward in which the patient is placed and shall be available to anyone properly authorized in writing by the patient. These records shall include:

    a. Identification data, including the patient's legal status;

    b. A patient history, including but not limited to:

      (1) family data, educational background, and employment record;

      (2) prior medical history, both physical and mental, including prior hospitalization;

    c. The chief complaints of the patient and the chief complaints of others regarding the patient;

    d. An evaluation which notes the onset of illness, the circumstances leading to admission, attitudes, behavior, estimate of intellectual functioning, memory functioning, orientation, and an inventory of the patient's assets in descriptive, not interpretative, fashion;

    e. A summary of each physical examination which describes the results of the examination;

    f. A copy of the individual treatment plan and any modifications thereto;

    g. A detailed summary of the findings made by the reviewing Qualified Mental Health Professional after each periodic review of the treatment plan which analyzes the successes and failures of the treatment program and directs whatever modifications are necessary;

    h. A copy of the individualized post-hospitalization plan and any modifications thereto, and a summary of the steps that have been taken to implement that plan;

    i. A medication history and status, which includes the signed orders of the prescribing physician. Nurses shall indicate by signature that orders have been carried out;

    j. A detailed summary of each significant contact by a Qualified Mental Health Professional with the patient;

    k. A detailed summary on at least a weekly basis by a Qualified Mental Health Professional involved in the patient's treatment of the patient's progress along the treatment plan;

l. A weekly summary of the extent and nature of the patient's work activities described in Standard 18, *supra,* and the effect of such activity upon the patient's progress along the treatment plan;

m. A signed order by a Qualified Mental Health Professional for any restrictions on visitations and communication, as provided in Standards 4 and 5, *supra*;

n. A signed order by a Qualified Mental Health Professional for any physical restraints and isolation, as provided in Standard 7, *supra*;

o. A detailed summary of any extraordinary incident in the hospital involving the patient to be entered by a staff member noting that he has personal knowledge of the incident or specifying his other source of information, and initialed within 24 hours by a Qualified Mental Health Professional;

p. A summary by the superintendent of the hospital or his appointed agent of his findings after the 15–day review provided for in Standard 33 *infra.*

32. In addition to complying with all the other standards herein, a hospital shall make special provisions for the treatment of patients who are children and young adults. These provisions shall include but are not limited to:

a. Opportunities for publicly supported education suitable to the educational needs of the patient. This program of education must, in the opinion of the attending Qualified Mental Health Professional, be compatible with the patient's mental condition and his treatment program, and otherwise be in the patient's best interest.

b. A treatment plan which considers the chronological, maturational, and developmental level of the patient;

c. Sufficient Qualified Mental Health Professionals, teachers, and staff members with specialized skills in the care and treatment of children and young adults;

d. Recreation and play opportunities in the open air where possible and appropriate residential facilities;

e. Arrangements for contact between the hospital and the family of the patient.

33. No later than 15 days after a patient is committed to the hospital, the superintendent of the hospital or his appointed, professionally qualified agent shall examine the committed patient and shall determine whether the patient continues to require hospitalization and whether a treatment plan complying with Standard 26 has been implemented. If the patient no longer requires hospitalization in accordance with the standards for commitment, or if a treatment plan has not been implemented, he must be released immediately unless he agrees to continue with treatment on a voluntary basis.

34. The Mental Health Board and its agents have an affirmative duty to provide adequate transitional treatment and care for all patients released after a period of involuntary confinement. Transitional care and treatment possibilities include, but are not limited to, psychiatric day care, treatment in the home by a visiting therapist, nursing home or extended care, out-patient treatment, and treatment in the psychiatric ward of a general hospital.

V. *Miscellaneous*

35. Each patient and his family, guardian, or next friend shall promptly upon the patient's admission receive written notice, in language he understands, of all the above standards for adequate treatment. In addition a copy of all the above standards shall be posted in each ward.

Questions and Comments

1. *The Partlow order.* As noted by the court, a second filing in the *Wyatt* case dealt with conditions in Partlow State School and Hospital, an institution for people with mental retardation. Judge Johnson's order concerning Partlow was similar to the order governing Bryce and Searcy, except that it was even more extensive. See *Wyatt v. Stickney*, 344 F.Supp. 387 (M.D.Ala.1972). For instance, in the course of defining the meaning of "adequate habilitation" for residents of Partlow, the order specified the class size, length of school year and minimum length of school day. The guidelines for the first two areas varied depending upon the patient's degree of retardation, while the length of the school day was fixed at 6 hours for all groups. Id. at 397.

2. *Subsequent history and impact of* Wyatt *litigation.* Both of Judge Johnson's orders were substantially affirmed in *Wyatt v. Aderholt*, 503 F.2d 1305 (5th Cir.1974). Between 1970 and 1975, the population at Bryce Hospital was reduced by 61.3%. Although this reduction was due to a number of factors (e.g., the creation of community mental health centers and the initiation of federal welfare programs subsidizing nursing home care), it was,

> in significant part, ... attributable to specific aspects of the *Wyatt* litigation. The ban on nontherapeutic patient labor "made it undesirable to have a large number of productive individuals in the hospital"; pressure to comply with patient-staff ratios "tended to create a climate in which discharge of patients was seen as beneficial;" and the publicity spawned by the suit "probably created more favorable public attitudes toward return of patients to the community than had existed previously."

2 Michael Perlin, Mental Disability Law: Civil and Criminal 52 (1999). Between 1970 and 1975, expenditures of the Alabama Department of Health increased by over 327%. During this time, the state significantly improved its psychologist-patient and social worker-patient ratios. However, it hired only a small number of additional psychiatrists, which meant that the few who were on staff did not have the time to oversee some of the activities the court had ordered them to monitor (such as development and implementa-

tion of individualized treatment and post-hospitalization plans). As a "direct result" of the suit, the state installed air conditioning, shower and toilet partitions and pay phones, and allowed the patients to receive uncensored mail. Patient abuse declined significantly, primarily due to the reduction in patients, the increased number of supervisory personnel and the presence of human rights committees brought about by *Wyatt*. At the same time, staff became fearful of giving patients any "negative feedback" lest it be construed as abuse. Id. at 52–53. Although the overall effect of these changes was probably to improve the quality of care, there is no direct data concerning therapeutic success on an individual basis. L. Ralph Jones & Richard Parlour, *Wyatt v. Stickney:* Retrospect and Prospect xi, xii (1981).

Believing that insufficient progress was made in this regard and in many other areas, in 1977 the plaintiffs asked the court to appoint a receiver who would supervise the functions of the Alabama mental health bureaucracy. Judge Johnson agreed that there had been "substantial noncompliance" in a number of areas. He granted the plaintiffs' motion, giving them three weeks to nominate a receiver. However, because the governor had also asked to be appointed as receiver, the court gave the governor ten weeks to file "specific proposals as to the remedial steps [he] will take if appointed receiver." *Wyatt v. Ireland,* 515 F.Supp. 888 (M.D.Ala.1981). The governor was eventually appointed as the receiver.

Soon thereafter the defendants asked for a modification of the 1972 orders, which they claimed were too rigid. They charged that the court's overall approach "seriously detracted from resident care, treatment and training" because its inordinate recordkeeping requirements, its imposition of "ritualistic and meaningless" procedures, and its failure to stop the "harassment" of the human rights committees demoralized the staff. See Perlin, supra, at 49. The defendants also asked for certain specific relief. They contended, for example, that requiring 6 hours of training per day, as the Partlow order did, was not always in the best interests of the residents, especially those who were profoundly or severely retarded. Continuing a routine training regimen for patients who did not show substantial improvement could be "pejorative and demeaning" and might even constitute "cruel and inhuman treatment." Instead, the defendants argued, residents who failed to improve with extensive education and training should be switched to "a full program of enriching activities, work activities, sheltered employment, physical exercise and therapies, and such other programs that tend to give meaning and dignity to their lives." The court rejected this request, stating that, if granted, it would "threaten [the] constitutional right [of each resident] ... to a habilitation program which will maximize his human abilities and enhance his ability to cope with his environment." Id. at 47–49. How does this holding compare to *Youngberg's*? See footnote 23 of that opinion.

In September, 1986, sixteen years after the initial complaint was filed, the *Wyatt* suit was officially settled. As part of the settlement agreement, the state of Alabama agreed to make "reasonable efforts" to achieve full accreditation by the relevant accrediting authorities. The agreement also required the state to make "substantial progress" toward establishing needed community facilities. Further, the agreement established patient advocacy and quality assurance programs. An advisory committee, which included the plaintiffs' attorney, also informally monitored hospital compliance. Finally, both parties agreed that the original standards set out in *Wyatt v. Stickney* still applied. *Wyatt v. Wallis*, 1986 WL 69194 (M.D.Ala.1986). Thus, the suit seemed to be largely ended at this point.

However, in 1991, when the state moved for a finding that their obligations had been met, the plaintiffs moved for further enforcement of the decree and for further relief. Six years later, the court found that the defendants should be released from the consent decree with respect to 17 of the mental-illness standards and 35 of the mental-retardation standards, but that several standards still needed to be met. *Wyatt v. Rogers*, 985 F.Supp. 1356 (M.D.Ala.1997). In the course of doing so, the court made some interesting comments about the relevance of *Youngberg* to the *Wyatt* ligitation:

> [T]he responsibility of this court is to secure the defendants' swift and full compliance with the 1986 consent decree. Nevertheless, as would be the case with a court seeking to vindicate the liberty interests identified in *Youngberg*, the court is still an interloper, for the ultimate responsibility for the operation of the Alabama Mental Health and Mental Retardation System still lies with the State of Alabama. Therefore, interference by this court "with the internal operations of [the Alabama Department of Mental Health and Mental Retardation] should be minimized," to that necessary to vindicate compliance with the decree. Similarly, because "there certainly is no reason to think [this] judge[] ... [is] better qualified than appropriate professionals in making ... decisions" in the Alabama system calling for professional judgment, a "decision, if made by a professional, [should be] presumptively valid."

> [However,] a decision is entitled to such deference only if it is one that calls for professional judgment. For example, whether a patient should be placed in a community setting would be a decision that would call for professional judgment, and the court should not second guess such a decision as long as it was based on acceptable professional judgment. However, whether the Department of Mental Health and Mental Retardation has met its obligation to create community facilities would not turn exclusively on professional judgment. The bottom line is that, in those instances where professionals have determined that a patient could or should be in a community setting, the decree requires that, within practical administrative and budgetary limits, the department have such settings available, and the court's limited role under the consent decree is to make sure that this is so. The force of the 1986 consent decree is that, if a state professional finds that a patient could or should be in a local community facility, the patient should not he hospitalized far away from home, from family, and from local community simply because an appropriate local community facility is not, within practical limits, available.

> Moreover, it is the court's responsibility to ensure that a judgment is made by a competent professional based on professional standards and practices, appropriate medical and psychological criteria, and not on administrative convenience or nonmedical criteria ... Thus, the court has a responsibility to assess a professional's expert opinion, by assess-

ing the expert's credibility and the reliability of the information on which the expert bases his or her opinion. The court has assessed the credibility of each witness and the weight to be given each witness's testimony. In assessing the credibility of the experts, the court took into account the sources of the expert's opinions. Some of the experts' selection of data was decidedly unprofessional. Where the expert's data were not random, but selected by the party he or she represented, where the expert relied on the representations of the parties instead of making an independent determination, and where the expert deliberately attempted to mislead the court, the court has taken all these into account in its assessment.

Id. at 1386–87.

From 1998 to 2000 the parties worked to resolve disputes with respect to the remaining mental illness and mental retardation standards. They reached a second settlement agreement in 2000, which the court accepted. *Wyatt ex rel. Rawlins v. Sawyer*, 105 F.Supp.2d 1234 (M.D.Ala. 2000). The court found that all facilities under court order had been accredited; that there were at least 26 full-time advocates for the patients in those facilities; that Alabama was committed to reducing the census by 300 patients at Bryce Hospital and related entities and also by 300 at Partlow and related entities; that Alabama would develop a plan for community placement; and that the state would remained committed to meeting the "minimum constitutional standards" set out in the 1986 consent decree. The court retained jurisdiction over the case for the limited purpose of enforcing the settlement agreement until September, 2003. Id. at 1238–39. At the end of 2003, the case was dismissed at the request of both sides. So the *Wyatt* litigation lasted thirty-one years. When it ended, there were 1,500 patients in Alabama state institutions and roughly 100,000 people served through community-based services, compared to 15,000 hospitalized patients and no community-based mental health system when the suit started. Phillip Rawls, The Associated Press, Dec. 6, 2003.

3. *The national impact of* Wyatt. *Wyatt* was very influential at the national level. One commentator concluded that, because of *Wyatt,* thirty-five departments of mental health instituted changes in regulations governing treatment of patients. Harry Schnibbe, "Changes in State Mental Health Service Systems Since *Wyatt,*" in Jones & Parlour, supra at 173, 174. Many states passed "Patients Bill of Rights" legislation which replicated to a greater or lesser extent the *Wyatt* order. "The *Wyatt* Standards: An Influential Force in State and Federal Rules," 28 Hosp. & Comm. Psychiat. 374 (1977). *Wyatt* also influenced the Task Force Panel on Legal and Ethical Issues of the President's Commission on Mental Health, which in turn motivated Congress' passage of the Bill of Rights section of the Mental Health Systems Act. 2 Perlin, supra at 54. This Act, passed in 1983, requested the states to revise their laws taking into account the recommendations of the President's Commission. 42 U.S.C. § 9501.

Finally, *Wyatt* influenced several courts, which issued *Wyatt*-type orders. For instance, Judge Sanders, described in the excerpt at the beginning of this chapter, patterned his monitoring of the Texas mental health system on Judge Johnson's. See also *Welsch v. Likins,* 373 F.Supp. 487 (D.Minn.1974); *Gary W. v. Louisiana,* 437 F.Supp. 1209 (E.D.La.1976). Most of these decisions were narrower in scope than *Wyatt* but, in the areas they dealt with, the relief they granted was at least as extensive as that granted in *Wyatt.* The following notes examine more closely some of the issues addressed by the *Wyatt* litigation and subsequent cases, and the extent to which *Youngberg* has changed the legal landscape. As Professor Perlin notes, although there have been fewer "institutional rights" cases brought since *Youngberg,* "*Youngberg* should emphatically not be read as a bar to further developments in this area." 2 Perlin, supra at 393.

4. *Individualized treatment plans.* A widely copied aspect of the *Wyatt* order is the detailed blueprint it established for preparation of an individualized treatment plan for each patient. See Appendix, paras. 25–29. The individualized plan has become a standard feature of hospital administration in virtually every state. How "individualized" do these plans have to be? If they are not prepared or adhered to, what should the patient's remedy be? See Appendix, para. 33. May the patient force a change in the plan by refusing the treatment indicated?[c] Perhaps most importantly, after *Youngberg,* to what extent is a patient entitled, under the federal constitution, to internal or judicial review of the adequacy of the treatment plan and its implementation? See Appendix, paras. 28, 29, 33. Consider also this excerpt from *United States v. Charters,* 863 F.2d 302, 312–13 (4th Cir.1988), construing *Youngberg's* professional judgment rule.

> Making an acceptable professional judgment [in the treatment context] does not require any internal adversarial hearing. The decision may be based upon accepted medical practices in diagnosis, treatment and prognosis, with the aid of such technical tools and consultative techniques as are appropriate in the profession.... [T]he basis for the decision should be supported by adequate documentation, not only because of normal professional requirements, but as a potential aid to judicial review. One could of course imagine any number of special internal review and consultative practices specifically designed to ensure confidence in the professional basis of specific medical decisions, and medical professionals, aware of the constitutional standard under which they are operating, are of course free to employ any that seem appropriate.

Compare this holding to the thesis of Professor Susan Stefan, in "Leaving Civil Rights to the 'Experts': From Defense to Abdication Under the Professional Judgment Standard," 102 Yale L.J. 639 (1992). Relying on the standard distinction between positive rights (where the claimant is asking the state for a benefit) and negative rights (where the claimant is attempting to avoid state intervention), Stefan concludes the following about *Youngberg's* professional judgment standard:

> The professional judgement standard comes into play at significantly different stages in these two kinds of decisions, with very different effects. In claims for constitutionally adequate government services, the court applies a constitutional analysis to determine whether the plaintiff

---

c. As developed at pp. 964–91, civilly committed patients may not have a right to refuse medication. But if such a right exists, it may be in tension with the right to treatment.

is entitled to state services and the general contours of the services to which she is entitled, and only then relies on professional judgment to determine how, specifically, these services should be provided. This approach defers to professionals in decisions they are competent to make. Such deference is appropriate here because the plaintiff is affirmatively seeking to compel state actors to exercise professional judgment on her behalf.

In negative rights claims, however, the plaintiff seeks protection against the exercise of professional judgment by the state. In this context, professional judgment inappropriately displaces the protection of rights from governmental intrusion. If a court applies the professional judgment standard in negative rights cases, professional judgment as to appropriate services or treatment supersedes any judicial analysis regarding the plaintiff's constitutional rights or liberties. The professional effectively exercises his judgement to choose between a patient's rights to family visitation, speech, or freedom from restraint on the one hand, and treatments that may preclude these on the other, without mediation or review by the court.

This approach thus severely curtails constitutional protection of civil rights.... [V]alues of autonomy, self-determination or freedom from intrusion will probably receive little attention in the medical professional's decision. Indeed, in these cases the very exercise of professional judgment constitutes the alleged abuse of power. This is particularly true in institutional settings, where all aspects of an individual's life are subject to professional oversight: from hygiene to letter writing to marriage. To assert that constitutional rights in these areas are not violated as long as a professional exercises judgment in limiting or eliminating them substitutes professional values for constitutional values and thereby constitutes an abdication by the courts of their critical obligation to protect individual rights. The Due Process Clause, intended to "prevent government 'from abusing [its] power, or employing it as an instrument of oppression'" is virtually erased by such an approach.

Id. at 668–69. Distinguishing between a positive and a negative right can be a difficult task. For instance, suppose Fred, in the excerpt at the beginning of this chapter, demands Zyprexa, a new antipsychotic medication with fewer side effects than the medications the hospital staff is giving him (but one which is much more expensive) (see pp. 30–31). Is this request (and concomitant refusal to take other drugs) an attempt to obtain professional services (i.e., an assertion of a positive right) or an attempt to avoid state intervention (an assertion of a negative right)?

Professor Stefan's analysis focuses on the substantive standard to be applied in treatment cases. Does it have implications for the procedural issue addressed in *Charters*? The issues raised in the following notes?

5. *Treatment in the least restrictive conditions.* Another innovation in *Wyatt* was its application of the least restrictive alternative idea to treatment *within* the institution. See Appendix, para. 2. Although the language in the Bryce order is quite general, the Partlow order provided more detail as to how this aspect of the right to treatment was to be implemented.

[T]he institution shall make every attempt to move residents from (1) more to less structured living; (2) larger to smaller facilities; (3) larger to smaller living units; (4) group to individual residences; (5) segregated from the community to integrated into the community living; (6) dependent to independent living.

344 F.Supp. 373, 386 (M.D.Ala.1972).

Some courts have been even more precise. In *Goodwin v. Shapiro*, 545 F.Supp. 826 (D.N.J.1982), the court created three levels of supervision designed to enforce the "presumption" that "all patients shall be restricted only to the extent which shall be clinically necessary or necessary to the Hospital's internal order and security, but not for administrative convenience." Id. at 847. Supervisory Level A, which allows the patient "maximum institutional flexibility subject only to curfews and the patient's individual responsibility for meeting treatment or obligations" applies to all patients who do not meet Level B or Level C criteria. Level B applies when "[t]here is a reasonable basis to believe that the patient could be a danger to him/herself, or to others, or might cause significant damage to the property of others" or when "[t]here is a reasonable basis to believe that the patient is an elopement risk." This level of restriction allows grounds privileges "for a reasonable period of time every day without supervision" and "additional on-ground activity, off-ground activity, weekend passes and other such unsupervised activities as the treatment team deems appropriate." Level C, which applies to those who are *clearly* dangerous to self, others or property, or who are clearly an elopement risk, contemplates "complete and constant" supervision.

The Third Circuit's decision in *Youngberg* held that the plaintiff had a right to treatment in the least intrusive manner, and devised a three-tier framework for review similar to that set out in *Goodwin*. *Romeo v. Youngberg*, 644 F.2d 147, 164–170 (3d Cir.1980). Although the Supreme Court's decision in *Youngberg* did not explicitly address the least intrusive means issue, in its conclusion it included in the list of rights the plaintiff enjoyed the right to "reasonably nonrestrictive confinement conditions." 457 U.S. at 324. However, the Court also rejected the contention that physical restrictions on liberty should only be imposed in the face of a "compelling" or "substantial necessity;" instead the professional judgment rule applies. Can *Youngberg* be construed to require a system similar to that ordered in *Goodwin?* Is such a system a good idea? Recall Hoffman and Foust's argument that effectiveness of treatment must be taken into account if the least restrictive idea is to make sense (see pp. 787–89).

6. *Restraints and seclusion.* One concrete application of the least restrictive idea arises when hospital staff decide to use physical restraints or seclusion. As indicated in *Youngberg*, restraints are any means of restricting a patient's ability to react physically, usually involving the use of devices such as cuffs, straps, mittens, or braces. "Seclusion . . . involves placing the patient in one of the individual sleeping rooms in the ward, usually furnished with only a bed, and locking the door." *Eckerhart v. Hensley*, 475 F.Supp. 908, 926 (W.D.Mo.1979). Although restraint and seclusion are considered necessary devices for protection of the patient or others and may even be useful treatment mechanisms when the patient is experiencing

"sensory overload," they can also be used to punish problem patients or as a substitute for adequate supervision in an understaffed facility. Robert Schwitzgebel & R. Kirkland Schwitzgebel, Law and Psychological Practice 47 (1980).

Note *Wyatt's* regulation of these two modalities. Appendix, para. 7. A number of states have enacted such provisions legislatively. Some courts provide even more protections. One court, for instance, imposed an absolute prohibition on the use of seclusion for people with mental retardation. *New York State Assoc. for Retarded Children v. Rockefeller,* 357 F.Supp. 752, 768 (E.D.N.Y.1973). In *Davis v. Balson,* 461 F.Supp. 842, 876 (N.D.Ohio 1978), the court required that, before restraints or seclusion can be used, a hearing preceded by 24 hour notice and presided over by an impartial decisionmaker must occur. At the hearing, the patient is to have the opportunity to call witnesses, the assistance of another resident or staff member if the patient is illiterate or the issues complex, and the right to a written statement of the findings of fact and the evidence relied upon. Another court allowed emergency restraint or seclusion without a hearing, but required a physician to write an order if the intervention goes beyond four hours. *Negron v. Ward,* 458 F.Supp. 748 (S.D.N.Y.1978). *Negron* also required that the patient be released every two hours, and barred continued restraint or seclusion after this release unless further overt violent gestures are made. If restraint for more than 48 hours occurs, a qualified psychiatrist not employed by the hospital must examine the patient and make a written report indicating whether continued intervention is justified. How viable are these decisions after *Youngberg?* Recall that the plaintiff in that case was subjected to "soft restraints," allegedly as part of a training regimen.

An analogous issue arises when the state wants to transfer a patient to a more secure unit, usually after the patient is alleged to have committed a crime. In *Jones v. Robinson,* 440 F.2d 249 (D.C.Cir.1971), the court required a procedure akin to that described in *Davis v. Balson,* supra, before transfer of an alleged rapist to a maximum security unit could take place. Is there justification for requiring more procedural formality here than when seclusion or restraints are contemplated?

7. *Privacy and communication.* The *Wyatt* order provided that patients "shall have an unrestricted right to send sealed mail" and conditioned access to the phone. See Appendix, paras. 5, 4. Two years later in *Procunier v. Martinez,* 416 U.S. 396, 94 S.Ct. 1800, 40 L.Ed.2d 224 (1974), the Supreme Court articulated the following test to be applied to regulation of prison inmate correspondence:

> First the regulation or practice in question must further an important or substantial government interest unrelated to the suppression of expression. Prison officials may not censor inmate correspondence simply to eliminate unflattering or unwelcome opinions or factually inaccurate statements. Rather they must show that a regulation authorizing mail censorship furthers one or more of the substantial governmental interests of security, order and habilitation. Second, the limitation on First Amendment freedoms must be no greater than is necessary or essential to the protection of the particular governmental interest involved. Thus a restriction on inmate correspondence that furthers an

important or substantial interest in penal administration will nevertheless be invalid if its sweep is unnecessarily broad.

In *Davis v. Balson,* 461 F.Supp. 842 (N.D.Ohio 1978), the court relied on *Martinez* in holding that interdicting letters from mental patients addressed to the Pope and the Queen of England was not permissible.

In light of this caselaw, consider the examples of actual or contemplated censorship provided in Henry Davidson, "Mental Hospitals and the Civil Liberties Dilemma," 31 Mental Hygiene 371, 374–76 (1967):

> A letter from a patient, addressed to a 12–year–old child, was in an envelope that was bordered by a bizarre design. The child's mother opened it and found a letter containing imaginative sexual proposals, all profusely illustrated by the patient with fine artistic skill. The father called the hospital in understandable indignation.

> A high school team played baseball on the grounds of our hospital. A male patient fell in love with one of the boys—from a distance—and sent him a homosexual love letter.

> A 70–year–old patient, whose 40–year–old daughter had applied for her commitment, sent a letter to her 10–year–old granddaughter, addressing it to her at school. She wrote: "Your mother is a whore. She sent me away to get rid of me so she could entertain men at home. She will do the same to you unless you send her away." The child read this letter, and was brutally shocked. The mother felt that the child was entitled to some protection from communications like this.

* * *

> ... In the last three years we have had to impose restrictions on the outgoing mail of 11 patients. Since we have 3,800 patients, that is not a bad ratio.... The telephone has been a more troublesome instrument and, in three years we have had to put some restrictions on use of the phone by 26 patients, because the recipients of obscene, threatening, or other painful calls made protests to us.

* * *

> Most acutely mental ill patients recover; and they would then be embarrassed by the delusional ideas expressed in their own handwriting. It may sound sanctimonious to say that we are censoring mail for the patient's own good; but, in truth, that *does* happen. I recall a lawyer who came to us in a manic attack. He sent out some very silly letters to his valued clients, overflowing with reckless and grandiose ideas. When he recovered, he found that they would never trust him again. He upbraided us for not stopping those foolish letters.

> Statutes protect the privacy of patients by restricting any general revelation of their identities. Thus, we may not permit "pen pals" to fish for names of patients, no matter how worthy their project may be. Sometimes we get into trouble because a patient has written home identifying another patient as being in the same ward, thus violating that other patient's right of privacy. The only way we could plug that leak would be to censor the first patient's mail—but this is where we came in in the first place. As you see, it is not as simple as it sounds.

How should a hospital handle such situations? Is it permissible to indicate on the outside of the envelope that the sender is a mental patient? Consider also the result in *Martyr v. Mazur–Hart*, 789 F.Supp. 1081 (D.Or. 1992). There the court permitted restrictions on the patient's outgoing mail that were rationally related to treatment—e.g., restrictions on sending letters to general members of the community expressing anger at his commitment that, the court concluded, should have been expressed to treatment staff. But it granted a permanent injunction prohibiting hospital officials from censoring or delaying mail addressed to public officials, advocacy groups, attorneys, or journalists.

Other censorship issues arose in connection with John Hinckley, who was hospitalized after his acquittal by reason of insanity on charges of shooting President Reagan and three others. Hospital officials routinely intercepted his outgoing mail. One letter they found requested aid in killing actress Jodie Foster, the actress about whom Hinckley apparently fantasized in his plotting to assassinate President Reagan. The letter was turned over to the F.B.I. Hinckley was also denied interviews with the media pursuant to the following policy:

> The purpose of this policy is to prohibit personal interviews of patients on the maximum security wards ... by representatives of the media. This policy is being enacted based upon a concern that such interviews and publicity could adversely affect the clinical well-being and treatment progress of such patients. These maximum security patients ... may be unable to understand the implications of their own statements to the media. It is felt that this policy is necessary in order to preserve the integrity of patients' treatment and to prevent a disruption of the therapeutic milieu of these wards.

The policy applied to all personal interviews, face-to-face and over the phone, but not to communication with the media by mail. In a suit brought in federal court, Hinckley alleged the policy violated his first amendment right. The court rejected Hinckley's claim, finding that the policy, as applied to Hinckley "is reasonably related to legitimate therapeutic and institutional interests." *U.S. v. Hinckley,* Criminal No. 81–0306, Nov. 28, 1989.

Note that *Wyatt* allowed restrictions on incoming mail, if a "Qualified Mental Health Professional" so orders (see Appendix, para. 5). Is this permissible under *Martinez?* Why was the *Wyatt* court willing to allow restrictions on incoming but not outgoing mail? If incoming mail is opened by staff, should the patient have the right to be present?

8. *Payment for maintenance labor. Wyatt* included relatively detailed rules concerning patient labor. See Appendix, para. 18. Particularly important are its provisions governing labor involving the operation and maintenance of the hospital or for which the hospital would otherwise have to pay an employee. See Appendix, paras. 18A and 18B(2). These provisions were thought necessary to prevent exploitation of patients. Through the mid–1970's hospitals routinely required patients to perform, without pay, housekeeping in the wards, grounds maintenance, laundry duty, cooking and farming. For instance, in *Weidenfeller v. Kidulis,* 380 F.Supp. 445 (E.D.Wis. 1974) the court described a 44 year-old man with mental retardation who "mowed the grass, cleaned patients' rooms, and washed dishes in the

kitchen," and a 31 year-old male with retardation whose "tasks included such endeavors as unloading various materials, cleaning toilets and sinks, and scrubbing the kitchen floor," neither of whom were paid. In a study of 154 institutions conducted in 1972, approximately 30% of the patient workers (out of a total of 32,180) were not paid at all, and 50% received less than $10.00 a week. Paul Friedman, "The Mentally Handicapped Citizen and Institutional Labor," 87 Harv.L.Rev. 567, 568 (1974). Another study indicated that patient labor saved the state of Pennsylvania roughly $10 million a year. See Samuel Brakel et al., The Mentally Disabled and the Law 280 (1985).

In some hospitals, privileges were denied if a patient refused to perform hospital maintenance work. Moreover, there was some evidence that institutions were reluctant to release people whose work skills had become "valuable" to the institution. Friedman, supra at 361. One commentator even concluded that work programs exacerbated the "institutionalization" process: "formerly skilled persons can become satisfied dishwashers [while] patients on the wards who are not working and who could benefit from learning to wash dishes are denied this opportunity," thus "repeat[ing the patients'] pre-institutional role of failure, this time in the still more destructive role of public charge." John Bartlett, "Institutional Peonage," Atlantic Monthly, July 1964 at 116.

Properly administered, however, hospital work programs have been defended "as a fair and equitable pact mutually beneficial to both parties and as an opportunity for secure work with limited demands not readily found in the society at large." Brakel, Parry & Weiner, supra at 281. Uncompensated maintenance labor has been viewed as "therapeutic" for the patient to the extent it develops "new skills to help economic self-sufficiency . . . [and] a sense of routine." It may also be "a means for the resident to contribute to the costs of his care," thus promoting a feeling of self-worth, and provide "relief from the boredom of doing nothing." Id. Contrary to the suggestion above that work may lead to dependency on the institution, others have argued that a meaningful work role "modifies the tendency for a 'person' to erode into a 'patient';" for the long-term or chronically ill, "it can serve as a pivotal force in rehabilitation." Harold Schwartz, "Expanding a Sheltered Workshop to Replace Nonpaying Patients Jobs," 27 Hosp. & Comm. Psychiat. 98, 99 (1976).

To some extent, Judge Johnson seemed to have been persuaded by the latter arguments. Six months after the *Wyatt* decree was issued, he modified paragraph 18A requiring compensation for institution-maintaining labor, for reasons described in Note, "The *Wyatt* Case: Implementation of a Judicial Decree Ordering Institutional Change," 84 Yale L.J. 1338, 1376 (1975):

> Shortly after the decree was entered, the Partlow Human Rights committee began to note numerous complaints from patients who had been working without compensation before the issuance of the decree but who, after the issuance of the decree, were no longer allowed to work because the administration allegedly lacked the resources to pay them. "These residents are now bored and anxious to be doing something," the PHRC noted. This problem had not been foreseen by the court. It

was eventually corrected by clarifying the decree to allow patients to perform uncompensated labor for therapeutic purposes.

Nonetheless, the courts have generally held that, with the exception of personal chores, maintenance labor must be compensated. Most commonly, these decisions rely on the provisions of the Fair Labor Standards Act. Plaintiffs have also argued, however, that the thirteenth amendment and the right to treatment require the same result. These three legal avenues are examined below.

The Thirteenth Amendment. The thirteenth amendment prohibits "slavery" and "involuntary servitude." Courts have held that a valid thirteenth amendment claim requires proof (1) that the work was done involuntarily and (2) that there is no compelling governmental interest justifying the involuntary labor. *Butler v. Perry,* 240 U.S. 328, 36 S.Ct. 258, 60 L.Ed. 672 (1916). With respect to the involuntariness requirement, the Supreme Court has held, in the context of a criminal action against state officials based on an alleged violation of the thirteenth amendment, that unpaid labor is not involuntary unless it is produced by "the use or threat of physical restraint or physical injury" or "the use or threat of coercion through law or the legal process." *United States v. Kozminski,* 487 U.S. 931, 108 S.Ct. 2751, 101 L.Ed.2d 788 (1988). The Court went on to state:

> Our holding does not imply that evidence of other means of coercion, or of poor working conditions, or of the victim's special vulnerabilities is irrelevant in a prosecution under these statutes. [T]he vulnerabilities of the victim are relevant in determining whether the physical or legal coercion or threat thereof could plausibly have compelled the victim to serve. In addition, a trial court could properly find that evidence of other means of coercion or of extremely poor working conditions is relevant to corroborate disputed evidence regarding the use or threatened use of physical or legal coercion, the defendant's intention in using such means, or the causal effect of such conduct. We hold only that the jury must be instructed that compulsion of services by the use or threatened use of physical or legal coercion is a necessary incident of a condition of involuntary servitude.

One earlier case dealing with the application of the thirteenth amendment to patient labor stated that the "source of coercion" could be "said to be the boredom of institutional life and the belief of patients that it will be advantageous to them to appear to cooperate with the institution." Moreover, "coercion results from deprivation of the right to leave the ward on 'grounds' privileges or being otherwise restricted." *Downs v. Department of Public Welfare,* 368 F.Supp. 454, 458–59 (E.D.Pa.1973). Would any of these "sources of coercion" be found to implicate the thirteenth amendment today? Are there any other sources of coercion?

With respect to the second aspect of thirteenth amendment analysis, all courts agree that the government interest in requiring uncompensated patient labor is "compelling" if the labor can be characterized as "therapeutic." Most courts have placed a "heavy burden" on the plaintiff to demonstrate that a particular task is not therapeutic. *Weidenfuller v. Kidulis,* supra at 451. Thus, one court found that over 6,000 hours of work "at several different jobs, varying from food preparation and service to ...

cleaning and maintenance of the physical plant of the hospital" were "related to a therapeutic program of rehabilitation." *Estate of Buzzelle v. Colorado State Hospital,* 176 Colo. 554, 556, 491 P.2d 1369, 1370–71 (1971). Moreover, many courts have held that, under some circumstances, involuntary work that is admittedly *non*therapeutic fails to implicate the thirteenth amendment. In *Jobson v. Henne,* 355 F.2d 129 (2d Cir.1966), the leading case in this regard, the court held that "the states are not ... foreclosed [by the thirteenth amendment] from requiring that a lawfully committed inmate perform without compensation certain chores designed to reduce the financial burden placed on a state by its program of treatment for people with mental retardation, if the chores are reasonably related to a therapeutic program, or if not directly so related, chores of a normal house keeping type and kind." Id. at 132. In *Krieger v. New York,* 54 Misc.2d 583, 283 N.Y.S.2d 86 (1966), the court found that a resident required to mop floors, clean toilet bowls and other similar work "had no cause of action [under the thirteenth amendment] because the work was 'of a normal housekeeping type and kind.'" Id. at 89.

Fair Labor Standards Act. Until they were significantly limited by the Supreme Court (see below), patient claims for compensation under the Fair Labor Standards Act, 29 U.S.C. §§ 201–219, were much more successful. In 1966, the Act, which establishes minimum wage and maximum hour levels, was amended to apply to state hospitals and institutions for people with mental disability, with provision for payment below the minimum wage to workers unable to work at a normal level because of mental or physical handicap. In *Wyatt,* Judge Johnson ordered that, in those circumstances when payment was due (recall the modification to the order discussed earlier), it had to be in accordance with the FLSA. See Appendix, paras. 18A, 18B(2)(c). Other courts went further. In *Souder v. Brennan,* 367 F.Supp. 808 (D.D.C.1973), the court held that the Act applied to virtually all work performed by patients at state institutions.

> Economic reality is the test of employment and the reality is that many patient-workers perform work for which they are in no way handicapped and from which the institution derives full economic benefit. So long as the institution derives any consequential economic benefit the economic reality test would indicate an employment relationship rather than mere therapeutic exercise. To hold otherwise would make therapy the sole justification for thousands of positions as dishwashers, kitchen helpers, messengers, and the like.

Id. at 813. Obviously, *Souder's* definition of therapeutic work under the FLSA, which was widely followed, is quite different from the typical definition of therapeutic work under the thirteenth amendment. Are there reasons for this distinction? In any event, is it correct to assume, as the *Souder* court seems to, that a particular job's economic benefit to the state is inversely related to its "therapeutic value"? Is there a better way to define the term?

Souder had a dampening effect on patient work programs. Even with the provision for sub-minimum wage compensation for handicapped individuals, most states discontinued such programs because of the financial burden imposed by decisions following the *Souder* rationale. Lebar, "Worker–Patients: Receiving Therapy or Suffering Peonage?" 62 A.B.A.J. 219 (1976).

Furthermore, the basis of *Souder* was eliminated twice, the first time when the Supreme Court invalidated the minimum wage provision of the FLSA under the tenth amendment, *National League of Cities v. Usery*, 426 U.S. 833, 96 S.Ct. 2465, 49 L.Ed.2d 245 (1976), and then, after *Usery* was reversed, when the FLSA was held invalid to the extent it permitted private actions against the states in violation of the eleventh amendment. *Alden v. Maine*, 527 U.S. 706, 119 S.Ct. 2240, 144 L.Ed.2d 636 (1999).

The Right to Treatment. Plaintiffs have also argued that the constitutional right to treatment requires the state to provide paid work programs. Such an argument was made, for instance, in *Schindenwolf v. Klein,* reported in 5 MDLR 60 (N.J.Super.Ct., Mercer Cty.1980); the result was a consent decree in which New Jersey agreed to employ or provide vocational rehabilitation for 25% of the patients in five state facilities. Under the decree, this group of patients would be given institutional work assignments which do "not impede the residents' movement towards discharge" and which are neither "created nor maintained for the sole purpose of providing residents with activity." Id. at 63. The decree required that this work be compensated; personal housekeeping chores required of the patients need not be. See also, *Davis v. Balson*, 461 F.Supp. 842, 852–53 (D.C. Ohio 1978).

Of the arguments that can be advanced in support of the result in *Schindenwolf* the strongest derives from the least restrictive alternative rationale for the right to treatment. As described by Perlin, the plaintiffs' attorney in *Schindenwolf* litigation, the least restrictive alternative doctrine "mandates that infringement of individual interests and liberties go no further than that which is absolutely necessary for the achievement of the state's interest. Since the state's interest in confinement is treatment coupled with security, the right to work, especially in light of the demonstrated viability and success of therapeutic work programs, must be preserved." Michael Perlin, "The Right to Voluntary, Compensated, Therapeutic Work as Part of the Right to Treatment: A New Theory in the Aftermath of *Souder*," 7 Seton Hall L.Rev. 298, 332–33 (1976). Does this argument survive *Youngberg*? If it does, does it also require that work programs be either voluntary or compensated? Consider the conclusion of Pascal Scoles & Eric Fine, in "Aftercare and Rehabilitation in a Community Mental Health Center," Social Work 75, 78 (July, 1971), that "[n]othing appears to be a greater stimulus to engage in activities that reflect health instead of illness than to be paid for the product of those activities."

In light of the foregoing, reread the description of the work required of Fred Thomas by the staff at Tarry Hall (pp. 1107–09). What is your analysis of the work arrangement? Should basic privileges such as access to one's own money be contingent on the performance of routine chores?

9. *Enforcing the right to treatment and habilitation.* In light of *Youngberg's* definition of treatment and its adoption of the professional judgment rule, individual damages actions are not likely to be a useful enforcement mechanism for many of the entitlements dealt with in *Wyatt*. In any event, systemic reform is likely to bring more benefit to more people.

In this regard, *Wyatt* is again instructive. Throughout the *Wyatt* litigation, Judge Johnson attempted to avoid dramatic confrontation with the state. His handling of the state's "budgetary defense" is one example. In

Wyatt v. Stickney, he clearly stated that the state of Alabama would not be able to avoid constitutional dictates through pleading insolvency. As the decision indicates, he even contemplated ordering the state to sell land in order to provide funding for the hospital system. But the order was never issued. The Fifth Circuit was equally circumspect in this regard. In *Wyatt v. Aderholt,* 503 F.2d 1305, 1318 (5th Cir.1974), it stated that "[t]he serious constitutional questions presented by federal judicial action ordering the sale of state land, or altering the state budget, or which may otherwise arise in the problem of financing, in the event the governing authorities fail to move in good faith to ensure what all parties agree are minimal requirements, should not be adjudicated unnecessarily and prematurely." As this passage indicates, the court's caution resulted both from concern over the scope of federal judicial authority over state legislatures and from a perception that the state had been relatively cooperative up to that point.

When the state is *not* cooperative, what options short of the rather dubious step of ordering the state legislature to appropriate money are available to a federal court? One option is to close down the institutions. This approach has been taken in prison cases. See, e.g., *Ramos v. Lamm,* 485 F.Supp. 122, 169–70 (D.Colo.1979). A second option for the court is use of its contempt authority to force the relevant officials to act in accordance with the court order. On one occasion, for instance, the *Wyatt* plaintiffs moved to cite several Bryce staff members for violating paragraph 9 of the order concerning electroshock therapy. Although the citation was not granted, no further violations of this part of the order occurred. See Jack Drake, "Judicial Implementation and *Wyatt v. Stickney,*" 32 Ala.L.Rev. 299, 308 (1981).

Also illustrated by *Wyatt* is the use of masters and receivers. The receiver appointed in *Wyatt v. Ireland* was responsible for overseeing the operation of the Alabama hospitals and reporting to the court. Court-appointed officials can also perform more limited functions. As an example of the latter role, in *Lynch v. Baxley,* 386 F.Supp. 378 (M.D.Ala.1974), the court ordered special judges to preside over discharge hearings at Bryce and Searcy; over 3,100 patients were evaluated, and of that number 1,287 were discharged, 888 were committed, 777 were held pending placement, and 167 were voluntarily committed. Drake, supra at 309. Another potentially powerful enforcement mechanism is economic sanction. The court can assess damages for constitutional violations on a per patient, per day basis. Id. at 309–310.

A final enforcement mechanism, perhaps the most important, is a reliable information-gathering and advocacy system. Judge Johnson appointed human rights committees and monitors who were charged with reporting to the court about compliance with the order. His order also provided that "[p]atients shall have an unrestricted right to visitation with attorneys." Appendix, para. 4. Other approaches are legion. The Developmentally Disabled Assistance and Bill of Rights Act of 1975, 42 U.S.C. § 6012, provided funding for advocates for people with developmental disability. Eleven years later Congress passed the Protection and Advocacy for Mentally Ill Persons Act of 1986, 42 U.S.C. § 10801 et. seq., which is meant "to protect and advocate the rights" of people with mental illness and "investigate incidents of abuse and neglect of individuals with mental illness." Id. These Acts make receipt of federal funding contingent on establishing protection and advocacy systems (P & A's). See *Michigan Protection & Advocacy Serv. v. Miller*, 849 F.Supp. 1202 (W.D.Mich.1994). Many hospitals also have legal aid services, funded by a number of different mechanisms, which provide legal representation on discharge, "institutional" and civil legal issues. See Samuel Brakel, "Legal Aid in Mental Hospitals," 1981 Am.Bar. Found.Res. Journ. 23. One of the best known hospital operations, combining aspects of the advocacy services and legal aid, is the Mental Hygiene Legal Service (formerly the Mental Health Information Service) in New York. Composed of lawyers and mental health professionals, MHLS acts as an intermediary between hospital personnel and patients and between patients and the courts, informs patients of their rights, and investigates patients' claims. See Raj Gupta, "New York's Mental Health Information Service: An Experiment in Due Process," 25 Rutgers L.Rev. 405 (1971).

If a lawyer is involved in monitoring the rights of institutionalized persons, what should his or her role be? At least one commentator has suggested that the traditional adversarial stance is not appropriate in most situations:

> For the in-hospital lawyer to act in [an adversarial] fashion routinely, for him to take seriously and pursue uncompromisingly the bulk of patient complaints and grievances or to generally set himself up as a force hostile to the institution only spells disaster. It bogs the lawyer down in controversies of little merit whose ultimate outcome is often not in the best interests of either the individual patient or the general patient population. It causes him to lose the cooperation of the institutional staff without which—given the knowledge of and control over patients possessed by the staff—it is difficult to do the patients' interests justice. Carried far enough, this approach could also seriously hamper the institution's capacity to work to the benefit of the patients. The achievement of success in institutionally treating mental patients is already difficult enough—the illnesses may not be curable, the staff may be overworked and insufficiently expert, and the prospects upon discharge, even after improvement, may be dismal because the underlying or contributing conditions (problems of family, money, employment) remain unchanged. For a legal project to further reduce the chances of success by creating needless antagonisms between patients and staff and by intimidating medical or supervisory personnel and inhibiting them in carrying out their functions is irresponsible.

Brakel, supra at 90.

10. *The right to treatment in private institutions.* A number of states are now encouraging private operators to establish facilities for treatment and habilitation of people with mental disability. For instance, Illinois is offering private interests long term contracts that provide state reimbursement for services rendered to patients, including institutional treatment. Are such facilities governed by the constitutional rulings described above? In other words, is there "state action" in such situations?

In *Blum v. Yaretsky,* 457 U.S. 991, 102 S.Ct. 2777, 73 L.Ed.2d 534 (1982), the Supreme Court held that residents of a private nursing home had failed to establish that a decision by the home to transfer them to a lower-level facility had a sufficient nexus with the state. Neither the fact that state funds paid for more than 90 percent of the cost of the patients' care nor the fact that the facility was extensively regulated by state agencies was deemed sufficient to establish state action. However, the Court also noted that the home was not performing "a function that has traditionally been the exclusive prerogative of the State."

In *West v. Atkins,* 487 U.S. 42, 108 S.Ct. 2250, 101 L.Ed.2d 40 (1988), the Court indicated that this latter caveat may cover state-retained private caretakers. In *Atkins,* the Court held that Dr. Atkins, a private doctor hired by the state prison to operate two clinics each week at the prison, was a "state official acting under color of state law" for purposes of a civil rights action against the state:

> ... It is the physician's function within the state system, not the precise terms of his employment, that determines whether his actions can fairly be attributed to the State. Whether a physician is on the state payroll or is paid by contract, the dispositive issue concerns the relationship among the State, the physician, and the prisoner. Contracting out prison medical care does not relieve the State of its constitutional duty to provide adequate medical treatment to those in its custody[.] ... The State bore an affirmative obligation to provide adequate medical care to West; the State delegated that function to respondent Atkins; and respondent voluntarily assumed that obligation by contract.

Under the Court's decisions, would a halfway house such as Tarry Hall in Houston, described at pp. 1107–09, be governed by the constitution?

11. *Reimbursement for treatment.* Every state has enacted legislation making voluntary *and* involuntary patients liable for the cost of their treatment. Forty-seven states extend this liability to the patient's relatives, usually including at least the patient's spouse, parents and adult children. Brakel et al., supra, at pp. 169–171 Table 2.17. At least one court has held that since prisoners do not have to pay for the cost of their imprisonment, such statutes are unconstitutional. In *Department of Mental Hygiene v. Kirchner,* 60 Cal.2d 716, 36 Cal.Rptr. 488, 388 P.2d 720 (1964), the California Supreme Court declared:

> Whether the commitment is incidental to an alleged violation of a penal statute ... or is essentially a civil commitment as in the instant case, the purposes of confinement and treatment or care in either case encompass the protection of society from the confined person, and his own protection and possible reclamation as a productive member of the body politic. Hence the cost of maintaining the state institution, including provision of adequate care for its inmates, cannot be arbitrarily charged to one class in the society; such assessment violates the equal protection clause.[d]

Most courts, contrary to *Kirchner,* have upheld state reimbursement statutes against such equal protection challenges. See, e.g., *In re Guardianship of*

d. On remand from the U.S. Supreme Court, the California Supreme Court held that *Kirchner* was based on an interpretation of the equal protection clause in the California constitution. 62 Cal.2d 586, 43 Cal.Rptr. 329, 400 P.2d 321 (1965). *Kirchner's* reach has since been significantly curtailed. See, e.g., *Swoap v. Superior Court,* 10 Cal.3d 490, 111 Cal.Rptr. 136, 516 P.2d 840 (1973).

Nelson, 98 Wis.2d 261, 296 N.W.2d 736 (1980). Is there a rational basis for distinguishing between prisoners and patients in this regard? Might the state have to show *more* than a rational basis?

Consider in this regard *Chill v. Mississippi Hospital Reimbursement Commission,* 429 So.2d 574 (Miss.1983), in which the court held that, given a state statute which prohibited the state from seeking reimbursement "beyond ability to pay," "the legitimate needs and comforts of the patient and his or her dependents or surviving relatives" had an "absolute priority" over state claims. Id. 586–87. In *Nelson,* by contrast, the trial court's order granting the state all but $1,500 of the patient's $27,000 estate was affirmed. Might not the *Nelson* holding deter persons with mental disability and their relatives from seeking treatment?

Assuming the state is entitled to reimbursement from the patient and relatives, how is the amount owed to be computed? Should every patient pay the same per diem amount or are those committed for treatment purposes liable for a greater amount than those committed primarily for incapacitative reasons?

A final question is whether the state may levy on funds the patients earn at the hospital. At the end of its provisions concerning patient labor, the *Wyatt* order states that "[p]ayment to patients pursuant to these paragraphs shall not be applied to the costs of hospitalization." See Appendix, para. 18D. What is the rationale for this rule? Consider the arguments in favor of allowing patient wages to setoff part of the costs of hospitalization in Marshall Kapp, "Residents of State Mental Institutions and Their Money (or, the State Giveth and the State Taketh Away)," 6 J.Psychiat. & Law 287, 304–05 (1979):

> [S]et-offs could provide a fair way to balance the resident's fundamental need to work (and to do so without exploitation), against the legitimate interest of the state mental health official in averting bankruptcy. The resident could be protected by a regulation limiting the percentage of his wages that could be set-off against his institutional charges, so that he would be assured of actually pocketing some of his earnings. Payment of wages, even if immediately recouped by the state, would give the resident knowledge that he or she is earning his or her room and board, and is not a mere ward of the state, knowledge which carries a sense of accomplishment, self-respect, and dignity of considerable therapeutic worth. Finally, permitting a resident to work and earn wages, even if they are subject to a set-off, could potentially provide him or her with certain tangible benefits including social security, state retirement payments, and workmen's compensation.

IV. THE RIGHT TO COMMUNITY SERVICES

In paragraph 34 of the order in *Wyatt v. Stickney,* the court decreed that the Alabama Mental Health Board and its agents "have an affirmative duty to provide adequate transitional treatment and care for all patients released after a period of involuntary confinement." A similar provision appeared in the Partlow order. 344 F.Supp. at 397, 407. Yet subsequently the court substantially undercut these provisions, as described in Note, "The *Wyatt* Case: Implementation of a Judicial Decree Ordering Institutional Change," 84 Yale L.J. 1339, 1374–75 (1975):

> Because some ... members [of the Partlow Human Rights Committee] became concerned that certain former residents had not been properly placed outside the institution but instead were "dumped" into the community, [the Committee] raised the question of whether the decree and the committee's responsibility extended to residents who had been discharged from the institution. In response to a PHRC request for clarification of its responsibility, the district court explicitly restricted the committee to the institution.
>
> Because the PHRC was the only method the court had to supervise the decree, this restriction effectively limited the scope of the decree to the institution's walls. Yet it was clear that problems existed with residents released from the institution. Storekeepers in local communities complained of former residents engaging in such conduct as urinating on the floors, opening up and using packages of make-up, and bouncing on beds in furniture stores. Discharged residents allegedly engaged in improper sexual behavior, leading to complaints and criminal charges. Citizens of one town in Alabama applied for and were granted a state court injunction to close a halfway house for residents discharged from one of the *Wyatt* institutions, alleging that the house was so badly supervised that it constituted a nuisance which devalued local property. The lack of adequate post-institutional placement and followup was also evidenced by complaints received by the Alabama Mental Health Board from local mental health organizations, which stated that Partlow residents had been inappropriately placed under their care in facilities that were not suited to meet those persons' needs.
>
> The district court's decision to limit the PHRC's jurisdiction to the institution was probably founded on well-intentioned beliefs that the problems should be attacked one at a time. However, the court apparently failed to anticipate that the decree itself would create problems outside the institution, through the discharge of residents, and thus did not take sufficient measures to minimize these effects.

* * *

As this passage illustrates, for most patients a right to treatment is not particularly effective unless it also applies outside the institution. The following materials explore the "right" to treatment in the community under the constitution and state and federal statutes.

LELSZ v. KAVANAGH

United States Court of Appeals, Fifth Circuit, 1987.
807 F.2d 1243.

EDITH H. JONES, CIRCUIT JUDGE:

This saga began in 1974 when a class action was filed against officials of the Texas Department of Mental Health and Mental Retardation (MHMR) alleging widespread abuses of mentally retarded patients and advocating their habilitation in the "least restrictive alternative" setting as a minimum standard of care. Simultaneously, a class represented by the same counsel were pursuing the same relief in Pennsylvania. In this appeal, we VACATE the district court's order dated June 5, 1985, which purports to enforce a consent decree between the class and the State by requiring the State to furlough no less than 279 class members from institutional to "community care" centers by September 1, 1986. For reasons elaborated upon below, the district court was without jurisdiction to award such state-law-based relief.

I. Procedural History

The class certified by the district court comprised approximately 2,400 residents of the Austin, Denton and Fort Worth state schools for the mentally retarded, representing approximately 26% of the "clients" of the State's thirteen institutional centers which care for the mentally retarded. In May, 1983, following at least two years of negotiations, a consent decree (the "Resolution and Settlement" or "R & S") was worked out between the parties. After giving appropriate notice and conducting an extensive hearing, the trial court approved the R & S. The court issued a lengthy opinion outlining the background of and legal basis for the consent decree. Order of July 21, 1983. The R & S is 21 pages long, consisting of 45 paragraphs of both specific and general guidelines and directives for the improvement of treatment of the mentally retarded.

The R & S set no timetable for developing community treatment centers, nor did it require the State to do more than exert its "best efforts" to provide such centers. Despite the lack of a timetable, the class representatives determined to press state officials for creation of community care centers by filing a "Motion for Community Placement" in February, 1985, less than two years after the R & S was entered. The motion requested that 779 class members, nearly one-third of those housed in the three state schools, be transferred immediately into the community. According to the class representatives, such a measure was necessary to fulfill the R & S. Further, the class contended that individualized habilitation profiles prepared for the class members by an interdisciplinary team of experts selected pursuant to the R & S reflected that 279 members of the class would be best served by transfer to community facilities. The State responded that it was in good faith complying with the R & S. Specifically, it had developed a comprehensive plan whereby 900 individuals from the thirteen state schools would be placed into community facilities during the 1985–87 biennium.... Obviously, a certain percentage of these statewide placements would be of class members, but the State was unable to estimate the number.

Following a hearing on the plaintiffs' motion, the district court ordered 279 class members to be transferred to community centers on or before September 1, 1986. Order of June 5, 1985. Because the ... State had at the time of the hearing neither so placed those individuals nor guaranteed their transfer, the court found the State in breach of the R & S. The court chastised the State for foot-dragging and delay in implementing community placement, and the court insisted that the "feasible" plan for such furloughs developed by an expert retained in consequence of the class action was more "convincing" than the rationale adduced by the State. In response to the State's argument that it could not discriminatorily favor class members over residents of other institutions when making community placements, the court concluded that "if defendants wish to see in the court's obligation to enforce the Resolution and Settlement as to class members the creation of a 'two-tier' system in Texas, they may so name it...."[4] The court also by its own account "overrode" state law procedures detailing the rights of parents in the determination of community placement, and replaced that law with a complex scheme designed by a court-appointed attorney. The Order of June 5 is the principal subject of this appeal. The State also appeals the denial of its motion to modify the June 5 Order to obtain similar relief.

II. JURISDICTION TO ENTER THE JUNE 5, 1985 ORDER

* * *

[Here the court noted that in *Pennhurst State School & Hosp. v. Halderman*, 465 U.S. 89, 104 S.Ct. 900, 79 L.Ed.2d 67 (1984) (*Pennhurst II*), the Supreme Court had held that the Eleventh Amendment prohibits federal courts from enforcing claims based on state law, unless the state consents to such suits. The court then proceeded to analyze the extent to which the district court's order rested on state law.]

III. THE STATE LAW BASIS FOR PROVISIONS
OF THE RESOLUTION AND SETTLEMENT

Juxtaposing paragraphs 7 and 8 of the Resolution and Settlement, on which the district court rested its Order of June 5, 1985, with applicable state law reflects the congruence between them.

Obligations of Defendants

7. The defendants will provide to each member of the plaintiff class habilitation tailored to the person's individual needs. In meeting the habilitation needs of members of the plaintiff class, the individual's particular circumstances, including age, degree of retardation and handicapping conditions, will be taken into account. Habilitation is that education, training and care required by each plaintiff class member to improve and develop the person's level of social and intellectual functioning, designed to maximize skills and development and to enhance ability to cope with the environment, and

---

4. By its order, the district court reallocated the $12.1 million appropriated by the Texas Legislature to create community placements for the clients of all thirteen state schools. The district court recognized that this sum was allocated to minimize the staff-to-patient ratios within all the state schools and was sufficient to make approximately 300 placements, per year, state wide. One must conclude that the district court knew that its order requiring such reallocation of funds would disadvantage nonclass residents of state schools.

provided in the setting which is least restrictive of the person's liberty. Defendants will provide habilitation services necessary to meet the needs of plaintiff class members until such time as they no longer require services under this Resolution and Settlement.

8. Defendants will provide each member of the plaintiff class with the least restrictive alternative living conditions possible consistent with the person's particular circumstances, including age, degree of retardation and handicapping conditions. Consistent with the person's capacities, each member of the plaintiff class will be taught adequate skills to help the person progress within the environment and to live as independently as possible. Services will be offered with utmost regard for the class member's dignity and personal autonomy.

Tex.Rev.Civ.Stat.Ann. art. 5547–203 § 3.01A (Vernon Supp.1986) provides:

Community centers created pursuant to this Act are intended to be vital components in a continuum of services for the mentally ill and mentally retarded individuals of this state. It is the policy of this state that community centers strive to develop services for the mentally ill and mentally retarded that are effective alternatives to treatment in large residential facilities.

Tex.Rev.Civ.Stat.Ann. art. 5547–300 § 15 (Vernon Supp.1986) provides:

Each client shall have the right to live in the least restrictive habilitation setting appropriate to the individual's needs and be treated and served in the least intrusive manner appropriate to the individual's needs.

Recognizing the decisive impact of the foregoing state law, the July 21, 1983 district court Order approving the Resolution and Settlement states more than once that paragraphs 7 and 8 are governed by state law. The district court observed that "each of these provisions [of the R & S] effectuates rights explicitly protected by Texas law (if not implicitly by federal law), including those provisions concerning individual service plans and 'least restrictive alternative' living arrangements...." The court noted that, "[a]lthough more detailed and far-reaching rights—including the right to habilitation in the least restrictive alternative living arrangement—have been located by district courts in the federal constitution and federal law, in this case it is likely that all such relief could and would have been predicated upon the more explicit Texas statutes. Tex.Rev.Civ.Stat.Ann. art. 5547–300 *et seq.*" As the district court recognized, state law confers on the class members, and on all other residents of state institutions for the mentally retarded, the right to live in the least restrictive setting. Because this is the right recognized in the Resolution and Settlement and enforced in the court's Order of June 5, 1985, that order plainly contravenes *Pennhurst II* unless some constitutional or federal right requires similar relief.

IV. THE CONSTITUTIONAL STANDARD OF CARE FOR THE MENTALLY RETARDED

The district court's uncertainty about the scope of federal support for a least restrictive environment was not misplaced. Appellees suggest, as a threshold matter, that the existence of a generalized "constitutional right" to community services for institutionalized mentally retarded people is not at issue before this Court. On the other hand, they contend that the constitutionally-based rights to enjoy safe conditions and to be free from harm, the right to be free from unnecessary institutionalization, and to have commitment bear some reasonable relation to its purpose are coextensive with the rights conferred in paragraphs 7 and 8 of the Resolution and Settlement. The distinction appellees seek to draw eludes us. Appellees are aware that the Supreme Court cases they cite do not cut such a swath.[8] In fact, the lower court cases on which appellees rely for their due process argument are precisely those which have considered, and uniformly rejected, a constitutionally-founded right to receive treatment in the least restrictive alternative setting.[9]

---

8. The Supreme Court cases relied upon by the appellees do not support the alleged relationship between community placements and the class members' rights to safety, freedom from bodily restraint, and minimally adequate habilitation. For example, the appellees have relied upon the landmark case of *Youngberg v. Romeo*, 457 U.S. 307, 102 S.Ct. 2452, 73 L.Ed.2d 28 (1982) in an attempt to transform the state right of a least restrictive environment into a federal right. The Supreme Court, however, refused to adopt the "least intrusive means" approach which had been relied upon by the Court of Appeals in its opinion in *Youngberg (Romeo v. Youngberg)*, 644 F.2d 147 (3d Cir.1980) (en banc) (*See also Rennie v. Klein*, 720 F.2d 266, 268 (3d Cir.1983)).

Another case, *Parham v. J.R.*, 442 U.S. 584, 99 S.Ct. 2493, 61 L.Ed.2d 101 (1979), is cited by appellees for the proposition that the mentally ill have a right to be free from unnecessary institutionalization. In *Parham* the issue under consideration involved possible *procedural* due process violations resulting from a state's procedures for the commitment of minors. *Parham* had nothing to do with an individual's right to be confined in the least restrictive environment.

* * *

Finally, the appellees look to another Supreme Court case that addresses unacceptable commitment and review procedures for incompetent *criminal defendants*. *Jackson v. Indiana*, 406 U.S. 715, 92 S.Ct. 1845, 32 L.Ed.2d 435 (1972). Again, we find nothing in the case which would sway us toward appellees' view that the case supports a "least intrusive means" analysis. It merely

holds that the nature and duration of a civil commitment must bear some reasonable relationship to the purpose for the confinement.

9. The appellees look to two cases, in particular, to support their argument favoring a constitutionally-founded right to receive treatment in the least restrictive alternative setting. In the first case, *Clark v. Cohen*, 794 F.2d 79 (3d Cir.1986), the Third Circuit entered an order directing the state to develop a program of community services for a mildly retarded individual who had been confined to an institution for 28 years without the benefit of procedural due process. This case differs from the facts now under consideration since the Third Circuit was "dealing with a plaintiff who was committed without notice or hearing as a result of a petition containing an incorrect diagnosis, and who was retained against her will without a hearing for over 28 years." *Id.* at 86.

Clark was an *individual* case where the *only* method to remedy the effects of the unconstitutional confinement was community placement. In other words, community placement was not merely the *best* remedy for the plaintiff but the *only* remedy. The Third Circuit did *not* grant carte blanche, a constitutional right to community placement. Judge Becker in his concurrence noted that the Third Circuit had previously held in *Rennie v. Klein*, 720 F.2d 266 (3d Cir.1983) (en banc) that a right to habilitation did not include the least restrictive alternative theory. *Clark*, 794 F.2d at 93 n. 9 (Becker, J. concurring).

As in *Clark*, *Thomas S. v. Morrow*, 781 F.2d 367 (4th Cir.1986) dealt with an *indi-*

In *Society for Good Will to Retarded Children v. Cuomo,* 737 F.2d 1239 (2d Cir.1984), the court stated, "we may consider only whether there is an entitlement to community placement or a 'least restrictive environment' under the federal Constitution. We hold that there is no such entitlement." The Second Circuit based its decision on the holding of *Youngberg v. Romeo,* 457 U.S. 307, 102 S.Ct. 2452, 73 L.Ed.2d 28 (1982), which confirmed the state's duty under the Fourteenth Amendment to provide adequate food, shelter, clothing, reasonable safety, and such training as "an appropriate professional would consider reasonable to ensure [a person's] safety and to facilitate his ability to function free from bodily restraints." *Youngberg* also held that in determining whether the state has met its obligations in these respects, decisions made by the appropriate professional are entitled to a presumption of correctness. "[L]iability may be imposed only when the decision by the professional is such a substantial departure from accepted professional judgment, practice, or standards as to demonstrate that the person responsible actually did not base the decision on such a judgment." The constitutional minimum standard of habilitation thus relates, not to the qualitative betterment of a retarded person's life, but only to the training necessary to afford him safety and freedom from bodily restraint. Whether that training is adequate must be determined in light of expert testimony; no constitutional violation exists unless the level of training is such a substantial departure from accepted professional judgment or standards as to demonstrate that the person responsible actually did not base the decision on such a judgment.

Reinforcing this view of *Youngberg* is *Society for Good Will, supra,* which further stated that "we may not look to whether the trial testimony established the superiority of a 'least restrictive environment' in general or of community placement in particular. Instead, we may rule only on whether a decision to keep residents at SDC [Suffolk Developmental Center] is a rational decision based on professional judgment." *Society for Good Will,* 737 F.2d at 1249. The court in *Society for Good Will* therefore concluded that while experts disagreed on the appropriateness of institutionalization, retaining residents at the institution did not violate the professional judgment standard enunciated in *Youngberg.*

Appellees would distinguish *Society for Good Will* with the suggestion that the district court there ordered wholesale transfer of patients from an institution to community facilities, irrespective of individualized professional treatment recommendations. This observation is only par-

vidual situation where the plaintiff was found to be on the borderline between average intelligence and mild mental retardation. Thomas S. had the *potential* to live independently of the state's care, but was unable to live independently without *minimal* habilitation which involved a community setting. This community habilitation was not "better" care but the *only* way in which the state could remedy its past transgres-

sions against Thomas S. At one point, he had been lodged in a night care unit operated in conjunction with a drug detoxification center (Thomas S. had no drug problems) which was incompatible with the treatment prescribed for him. At other points, he had been placed in a rest home that housed elderly and emotionally ill adults. Thomas S. was the only young person residing at this rest home.

tially correct. The Second Circuit noted that the number of placements ordered by the district court was virtually irreconcilable with the profound retardation of the majority of the institution's patients. On the other hand, the Second Circuit criticized the district court's willingness to substitute the judgment of plaintiffs' experts for that of the state's experts, in contravention of *Youngberg.* Critically, appellees' focus on the individual optimum habilitation plans misperceives the real issue, which was articulated by *Society for Good Will,* following *Youngberg.* The real issue is whether the existing level of habilitation represents a gross and unwarranted departure from the minimum standard necessary to preserve an individual's safety and freedom from physical restraint. Appellees' evidence in support of community placement in the district court concerned the optimum habilitation of each class member rather than the constitutional minimum standard. There is no evidence in the record concerning whether the State, at the time of the hearing leading to the June 5, 1985 Order, was denying class members the constitutional minimum standard. Moreover, the appellees never requested enforcement of the R & S to correct alleged failures to adequately protect clients from abuse or neglect or to remedy alleged inadequacies in adaptive equipment for physical therapy. The court never ordered any remedial action to improve these areas of care. No effort was made by any party to the Joint Motion for Community Placement, the expert consultant, or the district court to affect a substantive level of care, only its locale.

It is also worthwhile to observe that should the optimum standard of habilitation afforded class members by state law become coextensive with federal constitutional requirements, the emphasis of *Youngberg* on the judgment of the State's professionals will be thoroughly undermined. The constitutional standard in that instance would be determined by the views of expert witnesses, and outside consultants could effectively overrule state programs, contrary to *Youngberg.* While *Youngberg* may eventually have to be squared with the duty of a state to prevent deterioration of skills of the retarded committed to its institutions (*see Youngberg,* 457 U.S. at 327–29, 102 S.Ct. at 2464–65 (Blackmun, J. concurring)) this is by no means the same as requiring the State to provide the best care possible or the optimum location to improve the client's physical, mental and emotional conditions. As the Second Circuit aptly noted in *Society for Good Will,* the due process clause only forbids *deprivations* of liberty without due process of law. "Where the state does not provide treatment designed to improve a mentally retarded individual's condition, it deprives the individual of nothing guaranteed by the Constitution; it simply fails to grant a benefit of optimal treatment that it is under no constitutional obligation to grant."

It is therefore our conclusion that the federal constitution does not confer on these class members a right to habilitation in the least restrictive environment. There being no constitutional scope to paragraphs 7 and 8 of the R & S, the district court's decree purporting to enforce them may not rest on that authority and is unauthorized.

V. ENFORCEMENT OF THE R & S AS A CONSENT DECREE

* * *

[Here the court rejected the appellee's argument that by entering into the consent decree the state waived its Eleventh Amendment protection.]

The judgment of the district court is VACATED and the case REMANDED for further proceedings not inconsistent herewith.

WISDOM, CIRCUIT JUDGE, dissenting:

I agree with the majority's vacating the order of the district court. I would remand the case, however, for a hearing to determine whether the defendants have satisfied the Fourteenth Amendment criteria established in *Youngberg* as the minimum standards for the care of the mentally retarded.

I disagree with the majority's expansive view of the Eleventh Amendment and of *Pennhurst II*. The coexistence of similar federal and state rights and remedies does not deprive a federal court of jurisdiction. The plaintiffs brought the action in the federal court, alleging deprivation of their Fourteenth Amendment rights. As early as its order of May 13, 1983, the district court stated:

> The central focus of this case is the right of plaintiffs to safe conditions and to be free from harm, and the right to be free from unnecessary institutionalization. Also, the nature and duration of commitment must bear some reasonable relation to its purpose. The court recognizes the existence of these rights under the Fourteenth Amendment of the United States Constitution.

Order of May 13, 1983 (filed May 19, 1983), at 2–3. In its order of October 3, 1984, the district court again said:

> *Lelsz v. Kavanagh* was brought under the Fourteenth Amendment to the Constitution, and the court's primary obligation in this case is to enforce the Constitution.

The Eleventh Amendment enjoys no exalted position over the Fourteenth. If the plaintiffs have not had a full and fair hearing on their federal rights, they are entitled to one. The decision of the majority deprives them of a hearing on their federal claim.

Questions and Comments

1. *The nature of community treatment.* Since *Wyatt*, the objective of most right-to-treatment litigation has been obtaining treatment in the community. Sometimes the community treatment sought is outpatient, but often the need is for inpatient treatment or a local living arrangement that affords easy access to treatment, as in *Lelsz*. In many states, financial incentives from the federal government and fiscal pressures provide much more of a push toward this deinstitutionalization process than does litigation (see Chapter One, pp. 59–61).

Whether in response to litigation or something else, many states have made efforts to create community resources. Unfortunately, as the Nocera piece at the beginning of this chapter suggests, they sometimes replicate the problems found in mental hospitals. A particularly problematic type of community service is the "adult home" for people with mental disorder. Created for the purpose of caring for the thousands of patients released from closed or restructured mental hospitals, adult homes are state licensed entities that provide room-and-board, case management, and assistance with medication and personal care. One multi-state congressional survey of these residences concluded they were "a national tragedy." Adena Genn, "For the Mentally Ill, A Long Search for a Bed," N.Y. Times, Jan. 26, 2003, at 1, col. 3 (Long Island). More recently, a series of articles in the New York Times described the horrible conditions in many of the homes in New York. According to the Times, even the well-run homes are plagued by "untrained staff and gaps in supervision." Id. And many of the homes are run-down, filthy, and neglectful. Drug-dealing, prostitution and violence are common. Residents are sometimes beaten, and premature deaths from lack of medical or personal care are frequent. Clifford J. Levy, "For Mentally Ill, Death and Misery," N.Y. Times, April 28, 2002, at 1, col. 3. Treatment at one of the homes, dubbed "The New Warehouse for the Insane" by the state inspection agency, was described as follows:

> The home itself does not provide psychiatric services, but it is expected to ensure that residents obtain them, either from the Kingsboro clinic at the home or from other psychiatrists who periodically visit. But the clinic, staffed by a psychiatrist and a few other trained workers, writes prescriptions that go unfilled. It asks that fragile residents be closely watched, and they are not, according to interviews with clinic workers and their records. The home's administrators, meanwhile, have long accused clinic workers of not doing their jobs.

> At nights and on weekends, the residents are largely on their own. The clinic is closed, and the home has almost no one on duty. "Nobody wanted to take responsibility for patients who went berserk at night," said Louis Rossetti, who worked as a nurse at the clinic from 1980 until 1996 and then as a volunteer. "We would come in the morning and have to go upstairs and calm them down. It just over all got worse and worse."

Clifford J. Levy, "Here, Life is Squalor and Chaos," N.Y. Times, April 29, 2002, at A–1, col. 2.

The cost of New York's adult homes is about $600 million a year. Most of this money comes from federal sources, which mandate that the homes be maintained as residences rather than as hospitals. As a result, treatment must primarily come from off-site services. The typical adult home might cost each patient $3000 a month, while "community residences" (which do not provide as much case management or treatment) cost $2,000 to $2,500 a month, and supported apartments (which do not provide meals) cost around $800 a month. Yet the typical disability check is about $600 a month, meaning that residents without outside assistance must be subsidized or double or triple-up in the rooms. Genn, supra; Clifford J. Levy, "Ingredients of a Failing System: A Lack of State Money, A Group Without a Voice," N.Y. Times, April 28, 2002, at 32, col. 1.

2. *Community treatment for institutionalized patients. Lelsz* represents the predominant judicial response to the claim that the Constitution requires the state to transfer institutionalized patients who can be treated outside the hospital to community facilities and to create such facilities if they don't exist. In line with *Lelsz* and *Society for Good Will,* cited in *Lelsz,* most courts hold that *Youngberg's* professional judgment rule is the dispositive test in this context: so long as such judgment is exercised, the resulting placement, whether it is an institution or a community facility, is constitutional. See e.g., *Rennie v. Klein,* 720 F.2d 266 (3d Cir.1983); *Phillips v. Thompson,* 715 F.2d 365, 368 (7th Cir.1983).

A few courts appear to reject this narrow view of *Youngberg,* however, at least under certain circumstances. In *Association for Retarded Citizens v. Olson,* 561 F.Supp. 473, 486 (D.N.D.1982), affirmed 713 F.2d 1384 (8th Cir.1983), the court construed *Youngberg* to mean "that a constitutional right to the least restrictive method of care or treatment exists ... insofar as professional judgment determines that such alternatives would measurably enhance the resident's enjoyment of basic liberty interests." In *Thomas S. v. Morrow,* 601 F.Supp. 1055 (W.D.N.C.1984), affirmed 781 F.2d 367 (4th Cir.1986), the court applied this reasoning in finding that the plaintiff was entitled to a "a non-institutional specialized adult foster care situation" or "a group home with adults of average intelligence." The state had presented affidavits by state officials contending that the plaintiff's past treatment (which had consisted of placement in over 40 facilities, including mental hospitals) had been "minimally adequate." But the district court rejected this evidence as immaterial "because the professional's stated judgment was modified to conform to the *available* treatment, rather than to the *appropriate* treatment, for the plaintiff's condition." 601 F.Supp. at 1059. Instead the court relied on evidence the plaintiff presented, as well as evidence presented by other state-employed mental health professionals, in finding a "professional consensus" in favor of the ordered placement. Given the existence of the consent decree in *Lelsz,* how would this reasoning affect the outcome in *Lelsz?* See note 9 of the *Lelsz* opinion.

3. *Community treatment for non-institutionalized patients.* Another important aspect of *Thomas S.* was the way in which both the district court and the circuit court of appeals in that case dealt with the fact that, at the time of the district court's final order, the plaintiff had been out of the hospital for about five months and was residing in a "detoxification and night care facility." The defendants argued that under such conditions—not involving commitment to an institution—the state is not infringing any liberty interests, and thus *Youngberg* did not apply. But both the district court and the Fourth Circuit held that the plaintiff's interest in liberty was implicated in this situation. As the Fourth Circuit put it:

> Although during the course of this litigation Thomas's lodging has changed from a state hospital to a night care unit at a detoxification center, his status has not changed. He remains a legally incompetent adult who is a ward of a guardian appointed by the state. He did not choose to live at the detoxification center, and he is neither an alcoholic

nor a drug addict. *Youngberg* does not suggest that an incompetent person sheds the basic liberty interests that the Court identified when state officials and his guardian move him from one facility to another.

See also, *Clark v. Cohen*, 794 F.2d 79 (3d Cir.), cert. denied 479 U.S. 962, 107 S.Ct. 459, 93 L.Ed.2d 404 (1986). Can this analysis be reconciled with *Youngberg's* statement that "a State is under no constitutional duty to provide substantive services for those within its borders"? With the statement in *DeShaney v. Winnebago Cty. Dep't of Social Services*, 489 U.S. 189, 109 S.Ct. 998, 103 L.Ed.2d 249 (1989) (see pp. 1130–31), that "it is the State's affirmative act of restraining the individual's freedom to act on his own behalf—through incarceration, institutionalization, or other similar restraint of personal liberty—which is the 'deprivation of liberty' triggering the protections of the Due Process Clause, not its failure to act to protect his liberty interests against harms inflicted by other means"? What if Thomas had not been a ward of the state?

Consider *Philadelphia Police & Fire Ass'n v. Philadelphia*, 874 F.2d 156 (3d Cir.1989). The state of Pennsylvania, like many states, provides habilitation services for people with mental retardation in a variety of settings, ranging from state institutions to the retarded person's home. The plaintiff class in *Police and Fire Ass'n* received their habilitation at their homes, financed primarily by the city of Philadelphia. When the city cut its funding for these home habilitation programs (as a result of a cutback in state funding), the class sued under *Youngberg*. The members of the class claimed that because they had to be accepted by the habilitation program, which determines their placement, and because without state services they might end up in an institution, the cutbacks were unconstitutional. The Third Circuit disagreed, citing *DeShaney* for the proposition that "the State does not become the permanent guarantor of an individual's safety by having once offered him shelter." Id. at 168. To the argument that people with mental retardation are uniquely dependent on the state, the court noted that, in *DeShaney*, "the state of Wisconsin had acted in such a way as to make Joshua particularly dependent upon it for protection from abuse, but the majority found no substantive due process violation." Id.

Compare this decision to the arguments of Professors Jan Costello and James Preis in "Beyond Least Restrictive Alternative Doctrine: A Constitutional Right to Treatment for Mentally Disabled Persons in the Community," 20 Loyola L.A.L.Rev. 1527 (1987). They conclude that when professional consensus indicates that a particular institutionalized individual or group of institutionalized individuals is "capable of functioning outside an institution with assistance, institutional care *cannot be* 'minimally adequate' treatment." Id. at 1552 (emphasis in original). They go on to argue that this reasoning should apply *whenever* a person or group of people can show that they require community treatment to avoid institutionalization, even if they are not hospitalized at the time they make the claim.

A "minimally adequate" system of community-based programs and services, by increasing mentally disabled persons' ability to function in the community, will reduce the risk of state restriction on their liberty through the criminal justice or the civil mental health systems. Thus, the right to "minimally adequate" treatment in the community may be asserted for mentally disabled persons who are now inappropriately hospitalized, who have been institutionalized and are trapped in the "revolving door," or for those who, although never hospitalized, are dependent upon the state for assistance and thus subject to state restrictions on their liberty.

Id. at 1523. Do you agree? If the courts adopted the stance advocated by Costello and Preis, how would they enforce it?

4. *State law bases for the right to community treatment.* In light of the trend in the cases described above, it is important to consider alternatives to a federal constitution-based right to community services. Like *Lelsz, Dixon v. Weinberger,* 405 F.Supp. 974 (D.D.C.1975), was a class action brought in federal court alleging that hospitalized patients should be transferred to the community. More specifically, it alleged that, due to a deficiency in outpatient facilities, 43 percent of the patients in St. Elizabeths Hospital in Washington, D.C. were improperly institutionalized (based on an assessment by the hospital staff itself). However, the district court in *Dixon,* unlike the district court in *Lelsz,* relied exclusively on *state statutory* grounds in ordering the federal and District of Columbia governments to reallocate funds to create community facilities. The court found that the purpose of the District of Columbia's Hospitalization of the Mentally Ill Act was to return patients to a full and productive life in the community through care and treatment. It held further that patients were entitled to placement in the most appropriate setting, including non-hospital settings, and that the government had the primary responsibility for creating alternative settings.

To implement these findings, the court ordered the defendants to submit a plan for the creation of alternative facilities (including nursing homes, personal care homes, foster homes, and halfway houses). The plan was to specify how many patients qualified and how many would probably qualify for less restrictive treatment; why the remainder did not qualify; standards, procedures and personnel that would be used for care in alternative facilities; a timetable for implementation of the order; and the division of responsibility for implementation between the federal and District governments. The defendants submitted an "outline" of this plan in April, 1976, setting out the problems and tentative solutions. The District also indicated that it planned to construct two 400–bed nursing homes and to divert half of the hospital's budget for community care. The court subsequently ordered the defendants to implement the plan within six months. But the deadline passed, St. Elizabeth's lost its accreditation, and the plaintiff class remained in the hospital. Well into the 1990's many patients who had been identified as treatable in the community remained in the hospital, despite continued pressure by the court-appointed "*Dixon* committee." A 2004 Government Accountability Office report found that while the number of occupied beds at St. Elizabeth's Hospital had declined about 18% between 2000 and 2003, the absence of additional community acute care beds, services and supports limited further reductions, and it predicted that the District would have difficulty meeting the deinstitutionalization criteria set by the court throughout the remainder of the decade. U.S. GAO, District of Columbia: Status of Reforms to the District's Mental Health System (March, 2004).

A federal court ruling finding a right to community treatment based on local law, like the one in *Dixon,* is probably no longer possible, given the Supreme Court's decision in *Pennhurst II* (described in *Lelsz*). Partly as a result, some *state* courts have flexed their muscle in this area. For instance, in *Arnold v. Sarn,* No. C 432455 (Ariz.Super.Ct. Maricopa Cty. Mar. 15, 1985), the court found a right to community-based treatment for persons who are chronically mentally ill based on statutory provisions which required the state mental health director to undertake "unified" mental health programs (including "the functions of state hospital and community mental health"), and to take "appropriate steps to provide health care services to the medically dependent citizens of this state." See Jose Santiago, et al., "Changing a State Mental Health System Through Litigation: The Arizona Experiment," 143 Am.J.Psychiat. 1575 (1986). However, a California court rejected a similar claim, finding that the relevant statutory scheme merely expressed a preference for community-based treatment rather than a right; further, it held that even if such a right existed a court would lack authority to enforce it. *Mental Health Ass'n v. Deukmejian,* 233 Cal.Rptr. 130 (1986). Had *Lelsz* been brought in state court and relied on state law, should the plaintiff class have prevailed?

Another state law source for a right to community-based treatment is the state constitution, which usually contains provisions protecting liberty and privacy rights, as well as a provision guaranteeing due process of law. In some jurisdictions, these provisions have been construed to provide more protection to people with mental disability than analogous provisions in the federal constitution. See Michael Perlin, "State Constitutions and Statutes as Sources of Rights for the Mentally Disabled: The Last Frontier?" 20 Loyola L.A.L.Rev. 1249, 1292–3 (1987). At least one court has relied on the state constitution to mandate state-funded community services. *State ex rel. Cottrill v. Meigs Cty. Bd. of Mental Retardation & Dev. Disabilities,* 86 Ohio App.3d 596, 621 N.E.2d 728 (1993).

5. *Federal statutory grounds for a right to community treatment.* A final possible basis for a right to community-based treatment is federal statutory law. For instance, the Developmentally Disabled Assistance and Bill of Rights Act, 42 U.S.C. §§ 6000–6081, which provides federal funds to those states willing to develop habilitation programs for the developmentally disabled, provides that this group has "a right to appropriate treatment, services, and habilitation" in the "setting that is least restrictive of . . . personal liberty." Id. § 6010. The American with Disabilities Act, 42 U.S.C. §§ 12101 et. seq., which prohibits discrimination "by reason of . . . disability" when "reasonable accommodations" for the disability are possible, might also form the basis for a right to community treatment claim. Finally, the Individuals with Disabilities Education Act, 20 U.S.C. §§ 1411–1420, establishes an entitlement to education in the public school system for disabled children who qualify.

The DD Act is, on its face, potentially the most useful federal statute for those seeking a right to treatment in the community, since it clearly announces a right to treatment in a less restrictive setting, at least for all developmentally disabled individuals. However, in *Pennhurst State School & Hospital v. Halderman,* 451 U.S. 1, 101 S.Ct. 1531, 67 L.Ed.2d 694 (1981) (*Pennhurst I*), the Supreme Court destroyed any hope that this provision could be used to pressure states into creating community facilities. *Pennhurst* was the culmination of lengthy *Wyatt*-like litigation challenging the conditions of confinement at the Pennhurst institution for people with mental retardation in Pennsylvania. The Third Circuit had held that § 6010 of the DD Act created a substantive right in favor of the retarded, and that the conditions at Pennhurst violated those rights. 612 F.2d 84 (3d Cir.1979). The Supreme Court held, however, that § 6010 merely expresses a preference for treatment services in the least restrictive setting. The Court emphasized that courts should be cautious in attributing to Congress an intent to create rights when those rights impose affirmative obligations on the states to fund certain services. According to the Court, unless Congress unambiguously states its intent in such situations, no substantive right exists. The Court found "nothing" in the Act or its legislative history "to suggest that Congress intended to require the States to assume the high cost of providing 'appropriate treatment' in the 'least restrictive environment' to their mentally retarded citizens."

Although its language does not in so many words endorse the least restrictive alternative idea, the Americans with Disabilities Act may turn out to be a much more fruitful source of support for community services than the DD Act, as the following case suggests.

OLMSTEAD v. L.C. EX REL. ZIMRING

Supreme Court of the United States, 1999.
527 U.S. 581, 119 S.Ct. 2176, 144 L.Ed.2d 540.

Justice Ginsburg announced the judgment of the Court and delivered the opinion of the Court with respect to Parts I, II, and III–A, and an opinion with respect to Part III–B, in which Justice O'Connor, Justice Souter, and Justice Breyer join.

This case concerns the proper construction of the anti-discrimination provision contained in the public services portion (Title II) of the Americans with Disabilities Act of 1990 (ADA), 104 Stat. 337, 42 U.S.C. § 12132. Specifically, we confront the question whether the proscription of discrimination may require placement of persons with mental disabilities in community settings rather than in institutions. The answer, we hold, is a qualified yes. Such action is in order when the State's treatment professionals have determined that community placement is appropriate, the transfer from institutional care to a less restrictive setting is not opposed by the affected individual, and the placement can be reasonably accommodated, taking into account the resources available to the State and the needs of others with mental disabilities. In so ruling, we affirm the decision of the Eleventh Circuit in substantial part. We remand the case, however, for further consideration of the appropriate relief, given the range of facilities the State maintains for the care and treatment of persons with diverse mental disabilities, and its obligation to administer services with an even hand.

I

... Mindful that it is a statute we are construing, we set out first the legislative and regulatory prescriptions on which the case turns. In the opening provisions of the ADA, Congress stated findings applicable to the statute in all its parts. Most relevant to this case, Congress determined that "(2) historically, society has tended to isolate and segregate individuals with disabilities, and, despite some improvements, such forms of discrimination against individuals with disabilities continue to be a serious and pervasive social problem; (3) discrimination against individuals with disabilities persists in such critical areas as . . . institutionalization . . . ; . . . (5) individuals with disabilities continually encounter various forms of discrimination, including outright intentional exclusion, . . . failure to make modifications to existing facilities and practices, . . . [and] segregation. . . ." Congress then set forth prohibitions against discrimination in employment (Title I), public services furnished by governmental entities (Title II), and public accommodations provided by private entities (Title III). The statute as a whole is intended "to provide a clear and comprehensive national mandate for the elimination of discrimination against individuals with disabilities."[2] There is no dispute that L.C. and E.W. [the respondents in the case] are disabled within the meaning of the ADA.

This case concerns Title II, the public services portion of the ADA. The provision of Title II centrally at issue reads: "Subject to the provisions of this subchapter, no qualified individual with a disability shall, by reason of such disability, be excluded from participation in or be denied the benefits of the services, programs, or activities of a public entity, or be subjected to discrimination by any such entity." 42 U.S.C. § 12132. Title II's definition section states that "public entity" includes "any State or local government," and "any department, agency, [or] special purpose district." The same section defines "qualified individual with a disability" as "an individual with a disability who, with or without reasonable modifications to rules, policies, or practices, the removal of architectural, communication, or transportation barriers, or the provision of auxiliary aids and services, meets the essential eligibility requirements for the receipt of services or the participation in programs or activities provided by a public entity." . . .

Congress instructed the Attorney General to issue regulations implementing provisions of Title II, including § 12132's discrimination proscription. The Attorney General's regulations, Congress further directed, "shall be consistent with this chapter and with the coordination regulations . . . applicable to recipients of Federal financial assistance under [§ 504 of the Rehabilitation Act]." One of the § 504 regulations requires recipients of federal funds to "administer programs and activities in the most integrated setting appropriate to the needs of qualified handicapped persons."

As Congress instructed, the Attorney General issued Title II regulations, see 28 CFR pt. 35 (1998), including one modeled on the § 504

---

2. The ADA defines "disability," "with respect to an individual," as "(A) a physical or mental impairment that substantially limits one or more of the major life activities of such individual;" (B) a record of such an impairment; or "(C) being regarded as having such an impairment."

regulation just quoted; called the "integration regulation," it reads: "A public entity shall administer services, programs, and activities in the most integrated setting appropriate to the needs of qualified individuals with disabilities." 28 CFR § 35.130(d) (1998). The preamble to the Attorney General's Title II regulations defines "the most integrated setting appropriate to the needs of qualified individuals with disabilities" to mean "a setting that enables individuals with disabilities to interact with non-disabled persons to the fullest extent possible." Another regulation requires public entities to "make reasonable modifications" to avoid "discrimination on the basis of disability," unless those modifications would entail a "fundamenta[l] alter[ation]"; called here the "reasonable-modifications regulation," it provides: "A public entity shall make reasonable modifications in policies, practices, or procedures when the modifications are necessary to avoid discrimination on the basis of disability, unless the public entity can demonstrate that making the modifications would fundamentally alter the nature of the service, program, or activity." 28 CFR § 35.130(b)(7) (1998).

* * *

III

Endeavoring to carry out Congress' instruction to issue regulations implementing Title II, the Attorney General, in the integration and reasonable-modifications regulations made two key determinations. The first concerned the scope of the ADA's discrimination proscription, 42 U.S.C. § 12132; the second concerned the obligation of the States to counter discrimination. As to the first, the Attorney General concluded that unjustified placement or retention of persons in institutions, severely limiting their exposure to the outside community, constitutes a form of discrimination based on disability prohibited by Title II. See 28 CFR § 35.130(d) (1998) ("A public entity shall administer services ... in the most integrated setting appropriate to the needs of qualified individuals with disabilities."). Regarding the States' obligation to avoid unjustified isolation of individuals with disabilities, the Attorney General provided that States could resist modifications that "would fundamentally alter the nature of the service, program, or activity." 28 CFR § 35.130(b)(7) (1998). The Court of Appeals essentially upheld the Attorney General's construction of the ADA. [T]he appeals court ruled that the unjustified institutionalization of persons with mental disabilities violated Title II; the court then remanded with instructions to measure the cost of caring for L.C. and E.W. in a community-based facility against the State's mental health budget.

We affirm the Court of Appeals' decision in substantial part. Unjustified isolation, we hold, is properly regarded as discrimination based on disability. But we recognize, as well, the States' need to maintain a range of facilities for the care and treatment of persons with diverse mental disabilities, and the States' obligation to administer services with an even hand. Accordingly, we further hold that the Court of Appeals' remand instruction was unduly restrictive. In evaluating a State's funda-mental-alteration defense, the District Court must consider, in view of the resources available to the State, not only the cost of providing community-based care to the litigants, but also the range of services the State provides others with mental disabilities, and the State's obligation to mete out those services equitably.

A

We examine first whether, as the Eleventh Circuit held, undue institutionalization qualifies as discrimination "by reason of . . . disabili-ty." The Department of Justice has consistently advocated that it does. Because the Department is the agency directed by Congress to issue regulations implementing Title II, its views warrant respect.... The State argues that L.C. and E.W. encountered no discrimination "by reason of" their disabilities because they were not denied community placement on account of those disabilities. Nor were they subjected to "discrimination," the State contends, because " 'discrimination' neces-sarily requires uneven treatment of similarly situated individuals," and L.C. and E.W. had identified no comparison class, i.e., no similarly situated individuals given preferential treatment. We are satisfied that Congress had a more comprehensive view of the concept of discrimina-tion advanced in the ADA.[10]

The ADA stepped up earlier measures to secure opportunities for people with developmental disabilities to enjoy the benefits of communi-ty living. The Developmentally Disabled Assistance and Bill of Rights Act, a 1975 measure, stated in aspirational terms that "[t]he treatment, services, and habilitation for a person with developmental disabilities . . . should be provided in the setting that is least restrictive of the person's personal liberty." In a related legislative endeavor, the Rehabilitation Act of 1973, Congress used mandatory language to proscribe discrimina-tion against persons with disabilities. Ultimately, in the ADA, enacted in 1990, Congress not only required all public entities to refrain from

---

10. The dissent is driven by the notion that "this Court has never endorsed an interpretation of the term 'discrimination' that encompassed disparate treatment among members of the same protected class" (opinion of THOMAS, J.), that "[o]ur decisions construing various statutory pro-hibitions against 'discrimination' have not wavered from this path," and that "a plain-tiff cannot prove 'discrimination' by demon-strating that one member of a particular protected group has been favored over an-other member of that same group." The dissent is incorrect as a matter of precedent and logic. See O'Connor v. Consolidated Coin Caterers Corp., 517 U.S. 308, 312, 116 S.Ct. 1307, 134 L.Ed.2d 433 (1996) (The Age Discrimination in Employment Act of 1967 "does not ban discrimination against employees because they are aged 40 or old-er; it bans discrimination against employees because of their age, but limits the protect-ed class to those who are 40 or older. The fact that one person in the protected class has lost out to another person in the pro-tected class is thus irrelevant, so long as he has lost out because of his age."); cf. Oncale v. Sundowner Offshore Services, Inc., 523 U.S. 75, 76, 118 S.Ct. 998, 140 L.Ed.2d 201 (1998) ("[W]orkplace harassment can vio-late Title VII's prohibition against 'discri-minat[ion] . . . because of . . . sex' when the harasser and the harassed employee are of the same sex."); Jefferies v. Harris County Community Action Assn., 615 F.2d 1025, 1032 (C.A.5 1980) ("[D]iscrimination against black females can exist even in the absence of discrimination against black men or white women.").

discrimination; additionally, in findings applicable to the entire statute, Congress explicitly identified unjustified "segregation" of persons with disabilities as a "for[m] of discrimination." See § 12101(a)(2) ("historically, society has tended to isolate and segregate individuals with disabilities, and, despite some improvements, such forms of discrimination against individuals with disabilities continue to be a serious and pervasive social problem"); § 12101(a)(5) ("individuals with disabilities continually encounter various forms of discrimination, including ... segregation").

Recognition that unjustified institutional isolation of persons with disabilities is a form of discrimination reflects two evident judgments. First, institutional placement of persons who can handle and benefit from community settings perpetuates unwarranted assumptions that persons so isolated are incapable or unworthy of participating in community life. Second, confinement in an institution severely diminishes the everyday life activities of individuals, including family relations, social contacts, work options, economic independence, educational advancement, and cultural enrichment. Dissimilar treatment correspondingly exists in this key respect: In order to receive needed medical services, persons with mental disabilities must, because of those disabilities, relinquish participation in community life they could enjoy given reasonable accommodations, while persons without mental disabilities can receive the medical services they need without similar sacrifice. The State urges that, whatever Congress may have stated as its findings in the ADA, the Medicaid statute "reflected a congressional policy preference for treatment in the institution over treatment in the community." The State correctly used the past tense. Since 1981, Medicaid has provided funding for state-run home and community-based care through a waiver program. Indeed, the United States points out that the Department of Health and Human Services (HHS) "has a policy of encouraging States to take advantage of the waiver program, and often approves more waiver slots than a State ultimately uses."

We emphasize that nothing in the ADA or its implementing regulations condones termination of institutional settings for persons unable to handle or benefit from community settings. Title II provides only that "qualified individual[s] with a disability" may not "be subjected to discrimination." 42 U.S.C. § 12132. "Qualified individuals," the ADA further explains, are persons with disabilities who, "with or without reasonable modifications to rules, policies, or practices, ... mee[t] the essential eligibility requirements for the receipt of services or the participation in programs or activities provided by a public entity." § 12131(2). Consistent with these provisions, the State generally may rely on the reasonable assessments of its own professionals in determining whether an individual "meets the essential eligibility requirements" for habilitation in a community-based program. Absent such qualification, it would be inappropriate to remove a patient from the more restrictive setting. Nor is there any federal requirement that community-based treatment be imposed on patients who do not desire it. See 28 CFR

§ 35.130(e)(1) (1998) ("Nothing in this part shall be construed to require an individual with a disability to accept an accommodation ... which such individual chooses not to accept."). In this case, however, there is no genuine dispute concerning the status of L.C. and E.W. as individuals "qualified" for noninstitutional care: The State's own professionals determined that community-based treatment would be appropriate for L.C. and E.W., and neither woman opposed such treatment.

B

The State's responsibility, once it provides community-based treatment to qualified persons with disabilities, is not boundless. The reasonable-modifications regulation speaks of "reasonable modifications" to avoid discrimination, and allows States to resist modifications that entail a "fundamenta[l] alter[ation]" of the States' services and programs. 28 CFR § 35.130(b)(7) (1998). The Court of Appeals construed this regulation to permit a cost-based defense "only in the most limited of circumstances," and remanded to the District Court to consider, among other things, "whether the additional expenditures necessary to treat L.C. and E.W. in community-based care would be unreasonable given the demands of the State's mental health budget."

The Court of Appeals' construction of the reasonable-modifications regulation is unacceptable for it would leave the State virtually defenseless once it is shown that the plaintiff is qualified for the service or program she seeks. If the expense entailed in placing one or two people in a community-based treatment program is properly measured for reasonableness against the State's entire mental health budget, it is unlikely that a State, relying on the fundamental-alteration defense, could ever prevail. Sensibly construed, the fundamental-alteration component of the reasonable-modifications regulation would allow the State to show that, in the allocation of available resources, immediate relief for the plaintiffs would be inequitable, given the responsibility the State has undertaken for the care and treatment of a large and diverse population of persons with mental disabilities.

When it granted summary judgment for plaintiffs in this case, the District Court compared the cost of caring for the plaintiffs in a community-based setting with the cost of caring for them in an institution. That simple comparison showed that community placements cost less than institutional confinements. As the United States recognizes, however, a comparison so simple overlooks costs the State cannot avoid; most notably, a "State ... may experience increased overall expenses by funding community placements without being able to take advantage of the savings associated with the closure of institutions."

As already observed, the ADA is not reasonably read to impel States to phase out institutions, placing patients in need of close care at risk. Nor is it the ADA's mission to drive States to move institutionalized patients into an inappropriate setting, such as a homeless shelter, a placement the State proposed, then retracted, for E.W. Some individuals, like L.C. and E.W. in prior years, may need institutional care from time to time "to stabilize acute psychiatric symptoms." For other individuals, no placement outside the institution may ever be appropriate. See Brief for American Psychiatric Association et al. as Amici Curiae 22–23 ("Some individuals, whether mentally retarded or mentally ill, are not prepared at particular times—perhaps in the short run, perhaps in the long run—for the risks and exposure of the less protective environment of community settings"; for these persons, "institutional settings are needed and must remain available."); Brief for Voice of the Retarded et al. as Amici Curiae 11 ("Each disabled person is entitled to treatment in the most integrated setting possible for that person—recognizing that, on a case-by-case basis, that setting may be in an institution.")

To maintain a range of facilities and to administer services with an even hand, the State must have more leeway than the courts below understood the fundamental-alteration defense to allow. If, for example, the State were to demonstrate that it had a comprehensive, effectively working plan for placing qualified persons with mental disabilities in less restrictive settings, and a waiting list that moved at a reasonable pace not controlled by the State's endeavors to keep its institutions fully populated, the reasonable-modifications standard would be met. See Tr. of Oral Arg. 5 (State's attorney urges that, "by asking [a] person to wait a short time until a community bed is available, Georgia does not exclude [that] person by reason of disability, neither does Georgia discriminate against her by reason of disability"); see also id., at 25 ("[I]t is reasonable for the State to ask someone to wait until a community placement is available."). In such circumstances, a court would have no warrant effectively to order displacement of persons at the top of the community-based treatment waiting list by individuals lower down who commenced civil actions.

For the reasons stated, we conclude that, under Title II of the ADA, States are required to provide community-based treatment for persons with mental disabilities when the State's treatment professionals determine that such placement is appropriate, the affected persons do not oppose such treatment, and the placement can be reasonably accommodated, taking into account the resources available to the State and the needs of others with mental disabilities. The judgment of the Eleventh Circuit is therefore affirmed in part and vacated in part, and the case is remanded for further proceedings. It is so ordered.

JUSTICE KENNEDY, concurring in the judgment.

... Putting aside issues of animus or unfair stereotype, I agree with Justice THOMAS [in dissent] that on the ordinary interpretation and meaning of the term, one who alleges discrimination must show that she "received differential treatment vis-à-vis members of a different group on the basis of a statutorily described characteristic." In my view, however, discrimination so defined might be shown here.... [I]f respondents could show that Georgia (i) provides treatment to individuals suffering from medical problems of comparable seriousness, (ii) as a general matter, does so in the most integrated setting appropriate for the treatment of those problems (taking medical and other practical considerations into account), but (iii) without adequate justification, fails to do so for a group of mentally disabled persons (treating them instead in separate, locked institutional facilities), I believe it would demonstrate discrimination on the basis of mental disability. . . .

. . . This inquiry would not be simple. Comparisons of different medical conditions and the corresponding treatment regimens might be difficult, as would be assessments of the degree of integration of various settings in which medical treatment is offered. For example, the evidence might show that, apart from services for the mentally disabled, medical treatment is rarely offered in a community setting but also is rarely offered in facilities comparable to state mental hospitals. Determining the relevance of that type of evidence would require considerable judgment and analysis. However, as petitioners observe, "[i]n this case, no class of similarly situated individuals was even identified, let alone shown to be given preferential treatment." Without additional information regarding the details of state-provided medical services in Georgia, we cannot address the issue in the way the statute demands. As a consequence, the judgment of the courts below, granting partial summary judgment to respondents, ought not to be sustained. . . .

[Justice Kennedy did not join Part IIIB of Justice Ginsburg's opinion because he believed the case should be remanded to determine whether there was a statutory violation of the type described above. Justice STEVENS did not join Part IIIB because he believed the fundamental alteration issue was not ripe].

[The dissenting opinion of JUSTICE THOMAS, joined by CHIEF JUSTICE REHNQUIST and JUSTICE SCALIA, is omitted.]

Questions and Comments

1. *Impact of* Olmstead. Writing soon after *Olmstead*, one commentator wrote that the decision was potentially "the most important civil mental disability law case since the Supreme Court decided *Youngberg v. Romeo* in 1982. . . . [If] taken seriously, it may change the debate on [mental health issues], . . . and perhaps most importantly, on how we feel about persons with [mental] disabilities." Michael L. Perlin, "Institutional Segregation, Community Treatment, the ADA, and the Promise of *Olmstead v. L.C.*," 17 Cooley L. Rev. 53, 56 (2000). In 2001, the White House ordered that *Olmstead* be implemented vigorously, stating "[t]he Federal Government must assist States and localities to implement swiftly the *Olmstead* decision, so as to help ensure that all Americans have the opportunity to live close to their families and friends, to live more independently, to engage in productive employment, and to participate in community life." Exec. Order No. 13217 (1)(e)(June 18, 2001). A number of suits have been brought on *Olmstead* grounds, including one attacking the New York system of adult homes that was described in Note 1 on pp. 1172–73. See Clifford Levy, "Suit Says State is Segregating Mentally Ill," N.Y. Times, July 1, 2003, B1, col. 5.

But several developments, explored in the following notes, may curb *Olmstead's* potential.

2. *Limitations on the ADA.* As recounted in more detail in Chapter Twelve, since *Olmstead* the Supreme Court has significantly limited the remedial potential of the ADA. In *Board of Trustees of Univ. of Alabama v. Garrett*, 531 U.S. 356, 121 S.Ct. 955, 148 L.Ed.2d 866 (2001), the Court held that private damages claims under Title I of the ADA are barred by the Eleventh Amendment, which has been construed to immunize states from damages suits under certain circumstances. *Garrett* did not specifically address the Eleventh Amendment's application to Title II, the section of the ADA at issue in *Olmstead*. See *Hason v. Medical Bd. of Calif.*, 279 F.3d 1167, 1171 (9th Cir.2002)(continuing to permit damages actions under Title II). Moreover, *Garrett* only limited damages claims; injunctive actions under the ADA, of the type brought in *Olmstead*, are probably unaffected by its holding. Id. However, these matters are not completely settled. See, e.g., Erwin Chemerinsky, Federal Jurisdiction 453–462 (4th ed. 2003); *Thompson v. Colorado*, 258 F.3d 1241, 1245–46 n.2 (10th Cir.2001)(holding that Title II cannot be used to sue state officials for damages, and noting the possibility that injunctive relief against individual state officers may not be available either, if the ADA is not a valid exercise of congressional power).

3. *The meaning of discrimination.* Assuming Title II of the ADA is available as a basis for injunctive action against the states, how is its prohibition of "discrimination" against people with mental disability violated by treating people with mental disability in an institution rather than in a community setting? According to Justice Thomas in his *Olmstead* dissent, "the type of claim approved of by the majority does not concern a prohibition against certain conduct (the traditional understanding of discrimination), but rather concerns imposition of a standard of care. As such, the majority can offer no principle limiting this new species of 'discrimination' claim apart from an affirmative defense [of fundamental alteration] because it looks merely to an individual in isolation, without comparing him to otherwise similarly situated persons, and determines that discrimination occurs merely because that individual does not receive the treatment he wishes to receive." 527 U.S. at 623–24, 119 S.Ct. at 2198 (Thomas, J., dissenting). What is Justice Kennedy's answer to this complaint? Consider, as an alternative, this answer:

> The difference between Justice Ginsburg's and Justice Thomas's versions of the ADA is crucial to the goal of integration. The dissenters' view of the ADA adopts a "traditional" view of discrimination law. That "traditional" view is purely and formally equalitarian. It takes current social structures as given and simply mandates precisely equal treatment: no person may be treated differently on the basis of, for example, their race, ethnic group, religion, or gender than a similarly-situated person of another race, ethnic group, religion, or gender except in narrow situations, to remedy past unequal treatment. Viewed from the disability rights perspective, this interpretation of the ADA simply blinks at reality. The lower-caste treatment of people with disabilities is due in part to invidious, irrational treatment at the hands of those who dislike or fear them. But it also derives from the social structures and practices that are designed for the benefit of the able-bodied and that

inhibit people with disabilities from participating fully in society. Correcting inequality requires more than raising the consciousness of bigots. It requires affirmative changes in the social context that render and support the disparate treatment of people with disabilities.

. . . As the *Olmstead* majority recognized, the harm suffered by L.C. and E.W. was traceable directly to their isolation, without any therapeutic justification, in a locked ward in a psychiatric hospital, and not to the disparate treatment vis-á-vis some other group under traditional discrimination law. Failure to recognize this integrationist aspect of the ADA would deprive people with severe psychiatric and cognitive disabilities of any benefit. Disparate treatment is often rational in the strict sense, and is therefore untouched by equalitarian norms. The opportunity for "[l]ife, [l]iberty and the pursuit of [h]appiness" for *Olmstead* plaintiffs depends almost entirely on the integration mandate.

John V. Jacobi, "Federal Power, Segregation, and Mental Disability," 39 Hous. L. Rev. 1231, 1246–48 (2003). Is Professor Jacobi providing a definition of "discrimination" or instead is he defining, in Justice Thomas' words, a "standard of care"? Does it matter, under the ADA and its implementing regulations?

4. *The fundamental alteration defense.* Even if a state is found to have discriminated against institutionalized people with mental disability, relief may be granted under the ADA only if it would not require the state to alter its programs "fundamentally." Does this defense prevent L.C. and E.W. from obtaining relief under the ADA if the state does not already have a program for them in their respective communities? Consider this excerpt from the Eleventh Circuit's opinion in *Olmstead*:

There is evidence in the record that suggests that, because of fixed overhead costs associated with providing institutional care, the State will be able to save money by moving patients from institutionalized care to community-based care only when it shuts down entire hospitals or hospital wings, but not when it moves one or two patients from a hospital into the community. Thus, it may be that requiring the State to treat L.C. and E.W. in a community-based program will require additional expenditure of state funds.

Nonetheless, the ADA may still require the State to expend additional funds in order to provide L.C. and E.W. with integrated services. Unless the State can prove that requiring it to make these additional expenditures would be so unreasonable given the demands of the State's mental health budget that it would fundamentally alter the service it provides, the ADA requires the State to make these additional expenditures . . .[10]

L.C. by Zimring v. Olmstead, 138 F.3d 893, 905 (1998). Consider in contrast this assessment of the fundamental alteration defense:

. . . No bright line has been identified to separate states that can rely on the fundamental-alteration defense from those that cannot. The reluc-

10. We note that this case is not a class action, but a challenge brought on behalf of two individual plaintiffs. Our holding is not meant to resolve the more difficult ques- tions of fundamental alteration that might be present in a class action suit seeking deinstitutionalization of a state hospital.

tance of the courts to trample on executive branch prerogatives has always been the bugaboo of the least restrictive alternative doctrine. Whatever else it may accomplish, the decision in *Olmstead* v. L.C. is unlikely to precipitate the widespread creation of community-based services for persons with mental disabilities.

Paul S. Appelbaum, "Least Restrictive Alternative Revisited: *Olmstead's* Uncertain Mandate for Community–Based Care," 50 Psychiatric Serv. 1271, 1272 (1999).

5. *Community treatment for the non-institutionalized.* Could the reasoning in *Olmstead* be construed to grant an entitlement to treatment under the ADA to those who are *not* institutionalized? Building on the analysis excerpted above, Professor Jacobi answers this question in the affirmative:

> Just as the failure to provide appropriate community placements causes isolation by locking people into unwarranted institutionalization, so too the lack of a sound system of services for the mentally disabled risks the institutionalization of people with mental illness that could be treated in the community. Social supports comprising therapeutic resources, social services, and housing and employment assistance are necessary to enable the mentally disabled not only to avoid unnecessary institutionalization, but also to avoid inpatient care in the first instance. The integrationist focus, then, should be on both the person in an institution who can be returned to the community with proper services, as well as the person in the community who can remain there—avoiding institutional care, with appropriate service support.

Jacobi, supra, at 1251–52.

Of course, even if one agrees with this interpretation of the ADA, the fundamental alteration defense might pose a significant obstacle to its implementation. In contrast, the Individuals with Disabilities Education Act (IDEA), the third federal statute mentioned earlier (see p. 1177), clearly does provide an entitlement to "community treatment" for people (specifically, children) who are not institutionalized, and does not explicitly contain a fundamental alteration defense. The IDEA, as well as the ADA and similar federal statutes, are examined further in Part III of this book.

Part III

BENEFITS ELIGIBILITY AND LEGAL PROTECTION AGAINST DISCRIMINATION

Chapter Eleven

ENTITLEMENTS FOR PEOPLE
WITH MENTAL DISABILITIES

I. SPECIAL EDUCATIONAL BENEFITS

Originally called the Education of All Handicapped Children Act when it was passed in 1975, the Individuals with Disabilities Education Act (IDEA), 20 U.S.C. § 1401 et seq., seeks to provide a "free appropriate public education" in the "least restrictive environment" for all children with disabilities. The 1975 preamble to the IDEA stated that over eight million children in the United States were disabled, that over half of these children were not receiving an appropriate education, and that more than one million of them were excluded from the public school system entirely. 20 U.S.C. § 1400(b). In passing the Act, Congress appeared to be motivated by findings that many children with disabilities were educable, yet were being housed in abominable institutions, often unconnected with the school system or with the community from which they came.

The Act is clearly meant to benefit children with mental as well as physical disabilities. As amended in 2004, the Act covers children with the following mental disabilities if "by reason thereof" the children require "special education and related services:" mental retardation, "serious emotional disturbance," "traumatic brain injury," and "specific learning disabilities". At the same time, learning problems that result from "conduct disorders," family dysfunction, psychosocial stressors, or "lack of appropriate instruction in reading [or] math," or "limited

1190

English proficiency" do not come within the coverage of the Act. 20 U.S.C. § 1414(b)(5).

Despite the latter limitations (which were largely designed to avoid misdiagnosis of disadvantaged children who are not disabled), the potential scope of IDEA is quite broad. Thus, the IDEA could be viewed as a government-subsidized regime for community-based treatment and habilitation of young people who are mentally ill or retarded, to the extent such treatment or habilitation can be categorized as "educational"; as such, it could potentially provide a significant alternative to the mental health system discussed in Part II of this book. Whether it does so depends primarily on how one defines "free appropriate education" for children "with disabilities" and the provision that such education take place in the "least restrictive environment" (the latter a requirement that the Act also refers to as "mainstreaming"). These two topics are examined below.

A.　SCOPE OF GUARANTEED BENEFITS

BOARD OF EDUCATION v. ROWLEY

Supreme Court of the United States, 1982.
458 U.S. 176, 102 S.Ct. 3034, 73 L.Ed.2d 690.

JUSTICE REHNQUIST delivered the opinion of the Court.

This case presents a question of statutory interpretation. Petitioners contend that the Court of Appeals and the District Court misconstrued the requirements imposed by Congress upon States which receive federal funds under the Education of the Handicapped Act. We agree and reverse the judgment of the Court of Appeals.

I

The Education of the Handicapped Act (Act), 84 Stat. 175, as amended, 20 U.S.C. § 1401 *et seq.* (1976 ed. and Supp. IV), provides federal money to assist state and local agencies in educating handicapped children, and conditions such funding upon a State's compliance with extensive goals and procedures. The Act represents an ambitious federal effort to promote the education of handicapped children, and was passed in response to Congress' perception that a majority of handicapped children in the United States "were either totally excluded from schools or [were] sitting idly in regular classrooms awaiting the time when they were old enough to 'drop out.'" H.R.Rep. No. 94–332, p. 2 (1975).

* * *

In order to qualify for federal financial assistance under the Act, a State must demonstrate that it "has in effect a policy that assures all handicapped children the right to a free appropriate public education." 20 U.S.C. § 1412(1). That policy must be reflected in a state plan submitted to and approved by the Secretary of Education, § 1413, which describes in detail the goals, programs, and timetables under which the

State intends to educate handicapped children within its borders. §§ 1412, 1413. States receiving money under the Act must provide education to the handicapped by priority, first "to handicapped children who are not receiving an education" and second "to handicapped children ... with the most severe handicaps who are receiving an inadequate education," § 1412(3), and "to the maximum extent appropriate" must educate handicapped children "with children who are not handicapped." § 1412(5).[1] The Act broadly defines "handicapped children" to include "mentally retarded, hard of hearing, deaf, speech impaired, visually handicapped, seriously emotionally disturbed, orthopedically impaired, [and] other health impaired children, [and] children with specific learning disabilities." § 1401(1).

The "free appropriate public education" required by the Act is tailored to the unique needs of the handicapped child by means of an "individualized educational program" (IEP). § 1401(18). The IEP, which is prepared at a meeting between a qualified representative of the local educational agency, the child's teacher, the child's parents or guardian, and, where appropriate, the child, consists of a written document containing

"(A) a statement of the present levels of educational performance of such child, (B) a statement of annual goals, including short-term instructional objectives, (C) a statement of the specific educational services to be provided to such child, and the extent to which such child will be able to participate in regular educational programs, (D) the projected date for initiation and anticipated duration of such services, and (E) appropriate objective criteria and evaluation procedures and schedules for determining, on at least an annual basis, whether instructional objectives are being achieved." § 1401(19).

Local or regional educational agencies must review, and where appropriate revise, each child's IEP at least annually. § 1414(a)(5). See also § 1413(a)(11).

In addition to the state plan and the IEP already described, the Act imposes extensive procedural requirements upon States receiving federal funds under its provisions. Parents or guardians of handicapped children must be notified of any proposed change in "the identification, evaluation, or educational placement of the child or the provision of a free appropriate public education to such child," and must be permitted to bring a complaint about "any matter relating to" such evaluation and education. §§ 1415(b)(1)(D) and (E).

1. Despite this preference for "mainstreaming" handicapped children—educating them with nonhandicapped children—Congress recognized that regular classrooms simply would not be a suitable setting for the education of many handicapped children. The Act expressly acknowledges that "the nature or severity of the handicap [may be] such that education in regular classes with the use of supplementary aids and services cannot be achieved satisfactorily." § 1412(5). The Act thus provides for the education of some handicapped children in separate classes or institutional settings. See *ibid.;* § 1413(a)(4).

Complaints brought by parents or guardians must be resolved at "an impartial due process hearing," and appeal to the state educational agency must be provided if the initial hearing is held at the local or regional level. §§ 1415(b)(2) and (c). Thereafter, "[a]ny party aggrieved by the findings and decision" of the state administrative hearing has "the right to bring a civil action with respect to the complaint ... in any State court of competent jurisdiction or in a district court of the United States without regard to the amount in controversy." § 1415(e)(2).

Thus, although the Act leaves to the States the primary responsibility for developing and executing educational programs for handicapped children, it imposes significant requirements to be followed in the discharge of that responsibility. Compliance is assured by provisions permitting the withholding of federal funds upon determination that a participating state or local agency has failed to satisfy the requirements of the Act, §§ 1414(b)(2)(A), 1416, and by the provision for judicial review. At present, all States except New Mexico receive federal funds under the portions of the Act at issue today.

II

This case arose in connection with the education of Amy Rowley, a deaf student at the Furnace Woods School in the Hendrick Hudson Central School District, Peekskill, N.Y. Amy has minimal residual hearing and is an excellent lipreader. During the year before she began attending Furnace Woods, a meeting between her parents and school administrators resulted in a decision to place her in a regular kindergarten class in order to determine what supplemental services would be necessary to her education. Several members of the school administration prepared for Amy's arrival by attending a course in sign-language interpretation, and a teletype machine was installed in the principal's office to facilitate communication with her parents who are also deaf. At the end of the trial period it was determined that Amy should remain in the kindergarten class, but that she should be provided with an FM hearing aid which would amplify words spoken into a wireless receiver by the teacher or fellow students during certain classroom activities. Amy successfully completed her kindergarten year.

As required by the Act, an IEP was prepared for Amy during the fall of her first-grade year. The IEP provided that Amy should be educated in a regular classroom at Furnace Woods, should continue to use the FM hearing aid, and should receive instruction from a tutor for the deaf for one hour each day and from a speech therapist for three hours each week. The Rowleys agreed with parts of the IEP, but insisted that Amy also be provided a qualified sign-language interpreter in all her academic classes in lieu of the assistance proposed in other parts of the IEP. Such an interpreter had been placed in Amy's kindergarten class for a 2-week experimental period, but the interpreter had reported that Amy did not need his services at that time. The school administrators likewise concluded that Amy did not need such an interpreter in her first-grade classroom. They reached this conclusion after consulting the school district's Committee on the Handicapped, which had received expert evidence from Amy's parents on the importance of a sign-language interpreter, received testimony from Amy's teacher and other persons familiar with her academic and social progress, and visited a class for the deaf.

When their request for an interpreter was denied, the Rowleys demanded and received a hearing before an independent examiner. After receiving evidence from both sides, the examiner agreed with the administrators' determination that an interpreter was not necessary because "Amy was achieving educationally, academically, and socially" without such assistance. The examiner's decision was affirmed on appeal by the New York Commissioner of Education on the basis of substantial evidence in the record. Pursuant to the Act's provision for judicial review, the Rowleys then brought an action in the United States District Court for the Southern District of New York, claiming that the administrators' denial of the sign-language interpreter constituted a denial of the "free appropriate public education" guaranteed by the Act.

The District Court found that Amy "is a remarkably well-adjusted child" who interacts and communicates well with her classmates and has "developed an extraordinary rapport" with her teachers. It also found that "she performs better than the average child in her class and is advancing easily from grade to grade," but "that she understands considerably less of what goes on in class than she could if she were not deaf" and thus "is not learning as much, or performing as well academically, as she would without her handicap." This disparity between Amy's achievement and her potential led the court to decide that she was not receiving a "free appropriate public education," which the court defined as "an opportunity to achieve [her] full potential commensurate with the opportunity provided to other children." According to the District Court, such a standard "requires that the potential of the handicapped child be measured and compared to his or her performance, and that the resulting differential or 'shortfall' be compared to the shortfall experienced by nonhandicapped children." The District Court's definition arose from its assumption that the responsibility for "giv[ing] content to the requirement of an 'appropriate education'" had "been left entirely to the [federal] courts and the hearing officers."

A divided panel of the United States Court of Appeals for the Second Circuit affirmed. The Court of Appeals "agree[d] with the [D]istrict [C]ourt's conclusions of law," and held that its "findings of fact [were] not clearly erroneous." 632 F.2d 945, 947 (1980).

We granted certiorari to review the lower courts' interpretation of the Act. Such review requires us to consider two questions: What is meant by the Act's requirement of a "free appropriate public education"? And what is the role of state and federal courts in exercising the review granted by 20 U.S.C. § 1415? We consider these questions separately.

III

A

This is the first case in which this Court has been called upon to interpret any provision of the Act. As noted previously, the District Court and the Court of Appeals concluded that "[t]he Act itself does not define 'appropriate education,'" 483 F.Supp., at 533, but leaves "to the courts and the hearing officers" the responsibility of "giv[ing] content to the requirement of an 'appropriate education.'" See also 632 F.2d, at 947. Petitioners contend that the definition of the phrase "free appropriate public education" used by the courts below overlooks the definition of that phrase actually found in the Act. Respondents agree that the Act defines "free appropriate public education," but contend that the statutory definition is not "functional" and thus "offers judges no guidance in their consideration of controversies involving 'the identification, evaluation, or educational placement of the child or the provision of a free appropriate public education.'" The United States, appearing as *amicus curiae* on behalf of respondents, states that "[a]lthough the Act includes definitions of a 'free appropriate public education' and other related terms, the statutory definitions do not adequately explain what is meant by 'appropriate.'"

We are loath to conclude that Congress failed to offer any assistance in defining the meaning of the principal substantive phrase used in the Act. It is beyond dispute that, contrary to the conclusions of the courts below, the Act does expressly define "free appropriate public education":

> "The term 'free appropriate public education' means *special education* and *related services* which (A) have been provided at public expense, under public supervision and direction, and without charge, (B) meet the standards of the State educational agency, (C) include an appropriate preschool, elementary, or secondary school education in the State involved, and (D) are provided in conformity with the individualized education program required under section 1414(a)(5) of this title." § 1401(18) (emphasis added).

"Special education," as referred to in this definition, means "specially designed instruction, at no cost to parents or guardians, to meet the unique needs of a handicapped child, including classroom instruction, instruction in physical education, home instruction, and instruction in hospitals and institutions." § 1401(16). "Related services" are defined as "transportation, and such developmental, corrective, and other supportive services ... as may be required to assist a handicapped child to benefit from special education." § 1401(17).

Like many statutory definitions, this one tends toward the cryptic rather than the comprehensive, but that is scarcely a reason for abandoning the quest for legislative intent.

* * *

According to the definitions contained in the Act, a "free appropriate public education" consists of educational instruction specially designed to meet the unique needs of the handicapped child, supported by such services as are necessary to permit the child "to benefit" from the instruction. Almost as a checklist for adequacy under the Act, the definition also requires that such instruction and services be provided at public expense and under public supervision, meet the State's educational standards, approximate the grade levels used in the State's regular education, and comport with the child's IEP. Thus, if personalized instruction is being provided with sufficient supportive services to permit the child to benefit from the instruction, and the other items on the definitional checklist are satisfied, the child is receiving a "free appropriate public education" as defined by the Act.

* * *

Noticeably absent from the language of the statute is any substantive standard prescribing the level of education to be accorded handicapped children. Certainly the language of the statute contains no requirement like the one imposed by the lower courts—that States maximize the potential of handicapped children "commensurate with the opportunity provided to other children." That standard was expounded by the District Court without reference to the statutory definitions or even to the legislative history of the Act.

* * *

B

* * *

(ii)

Respondents contend that "the goal of the Act is to provide each handicapped child with an equal educational opportunity." We think, however, that the requirement that a State provide specialized educational services to handicapped children generates no additional requirement that the services so provided be sufficient to maximize each child's potential "commensurate with the opportunity provided other children."

* * *

(iii)

Implicit in the congressional purpose of providing access to a "free appropriate public education" is the requirement that the education to which access is provided be sufficient to confer some educational benefit upon the handicapped child. It would do little good for Congress to spend millions of dollars in providing access to a public education only to have the handicapped child receive no benefit from that education. The statutory definition of "free appropriate public education," in addition to requiring that States provide each child with "specially designed instruction," expressly requires the provision of "such ... supportive services ... as may be required to assist a handicapped child *to benefit* from special education." § 1401(17) (emphasis added). We therefore conclude that the "basic floor of opportunity" provided by the Act consists of access to specialized instruction and related services which are individually designed to provide educational benefit to the handicapped child.

The determination of when handicapped children are receiving sufficient educational benefits to satisfy the requirements of the Act presents a more difficult problem. The Act requires participating States to educate a wide spectrum of handicapped children, from the marginally hearing-impaired to the profoundly retarded and palsied. It is clear that the benefits obtainable by children at one end of the spectrum will differ dramatically from those obtainable by children at the other end, with infinite variations in between. One child may have little difficulty competing successfully in an academic setting with non-handicapped children while another child may encounter great difficulty in acquiring even the most basic of self-maintenance skills. We do not attempt today to establish any one test for determining the adequacy of educational benefits conferred upon all children covered by the Act. Because in this case we are presented with a handicapped child who is receiving substantial specialized instruction and related services, and who is performing above average in the regular classrooms of a public school system, we confine our analysis to that situation.

* * *

C

When the language of the Act and its legislative history are considered together, the requirements imposed by Congress become tolerably clear. Insofar as a State is required to provide a handicapped child with a "free appropriate public education," we hold that it satisfies this requirement by providing personalized instruction with sufficient support services to permit the child to benefit educationally from that instruction.

* * *

IV

A

As mentioned in Part I, the Act permits "[a]ny party aggrieved by the findings and decision" of the state administrative hearings "to bring a civil action" in "any State court of competent jurisdiction or in a district court of the United States without regard to the amount in controversy." § 1415(e)(2). The complaint, and therefore the civil action, may concern "any matter relating to the identification, evaluation, or educational placement of the child, or the provision of a free appropriate public education to such child." § 1415(b)(1)(E). In reviewing the complaint, the Act provides that a court "shall receive the record of the [state] administrative proceedings, shall hear additional evidence at the request of a party, and, basing its decision on the preponderance of the evidence, shall grant such relief as the court determines is appropriate." § 1415(e)(2).

The parties disagree sharply over the meaning of these provisions, petitioners contending that courts are given only limited authority to review for state compliance with the Act's procedural requirements and no power to review the substance of the state program, and respondents contending that the Act requires courts to exercise *de novo* review over state educational decisions and policies. We find petitioners' contention unpersuasive, for Congress expressly rejected provisions that would have so severely restricted the role of reviewing courts. In substituting the current language of the statute for language that would have made state administrative findings conclusive if supported by substantial evidence, the Conference Committee explained that courts were to make "independent decision[s] based on a preponderance of the evidence."

But although we find that this grant of authority is broader than claimed by petitioners, we think the fact that it is found in § 1415, which is entitled "Procedural safeguards," is not without significance. When the elaborate and highly specific procedural safeguards embodied in § 1415 are contrasted with the general and somewhat imprecise substantive admonitions contained in the Act, we think that the importance Congress attached to these procedural safeguards cannot be gainsaid. It seems to us no exaggeration to say that Congress placed every bit as much emphasis upon compliance with procedures giving parents and guardians a large measure of participation at every stage of the administrative process, see, *e.g.,* §§ 1415(a)–(d), as it did upon the measurement of the resulting IEP against a substantive standard. We think that the congressional emphasis upon full participation of concerned parties throughout the development of the IEP, as well as the requirements that state and local plans be submitted to the Secretary for approval, demonstrates the legislative conviction that adequate compliance with the procedures prescribed would in most cases assure much if not all of what Congress wished in the way of substantive content in an IEP.

Thus the provision that a reviewing court base its decision on the "preponderance of the evidence" is by no means an invitation to the courts to substitute their own notions of sound educational policy for those of the school authorities which they review. The very importance which Congress has attached to compliance with certain procedures in the preparation of an IEP would be frustrated if a court were permitted simply to set state decisions at nought. The fact that § 1415(e) requires that the reviewing court "receive the records of the [state] administrative proceedings" carries with it the implied requirement that due weight shall be given to these proceedings.

* * *

Therefore, a court's inquiry in suits brought under § 1415(e)(2) is twofold. First, has the State complied with the procedures set forth in the Act? And second, is the individualized educational program developed through the Act's procedures reasonably calculated to enable the child to receive educational benefits? If these requirements are met, the

State has complied with the obligations imposed by Congress and the courts can require no more.

B

In assuring that the requirements of the Act have been met, courts must be careful to avoid imposing their view of preferable educational methods upon the States. The primary responsibility for formulating the education to be accorded a handicapped child, and for choosing the educational method most suitable to the child's needs, was left by the Act to state and local educational agencies in cooperation with the parents or guardian of the child.

We previously have cautioned that courts lack the "specialized knowledge and experience" necessary to resolve "persistent and difficult questions of educational policy." *San Antonio Independent School Dist. v. Rodriguez*, 411 U.S., at 42, 93 S.Ct., at 1301. We think that Congress shared that view when it passed the Act. As already demonstrated, Congress' intention was not that the Act displace the primacy of States in the field of education, but that States receive funds to assist them in extending their educational systems to the handicapped. Therefore, once a court determines that the requirements of the Act have been met, questions of methodology are for resolution by the States.

* * *

VI

Applying these principles to the facts of this case, we conclude that the Court of Appeals erred in affirming the decision of the District Court. Neither the District Court nor the Court of Appeals found that petitioners had failed to comply with the procedures of the Act, and the findings of neither court would support a conclusion that Amy's educational program failed to comply with the substantive requirements of the Act. On the contrary, the District Court found that the "evidence firmly establishes that Amy is receiving an 'adequate' education, since she performs better than the average child in her class and is advancing easily from grade to grade." 483 F.Supp., at 534. In light of this finding, and of the fact that Amy was receiving personalized instruction and related services calculated by the Furnace Woods school administrators to meet her educational needs, the lower courts should not have concluded that the Act requires the provision of a sign-language interpreter. Accordingly, the decision of the Court of Appeals is reversed, and the case is remanded for further proceedings consistent with this opinion.

So ordered.

* * *

[The concurring opinion of Mr. Justice Blackmun is omitted].

JUSTICE WHITE, with whom JUSTICE BRENNAN and JUSTICE MARSHALL join, dissenting.

In order to reach its result in this case, the majority opinion contradicts itself, the language of the statute, and the legislative history. Both the majority's standard for a "free appropriate education" and its standard for judicial review disregard congressional intent.

* * *

I

I agree that the language of the Act does not contain a substantive standard beyond requiring that the education offered must be "appropriate." However, if there are limits not evident from the face of the statute on what may be considered an "appropriate education," they must be found in the purpose of the statute or its legislative history.

* * *

The majority opinion announces a different substantive standard, that "Congress did not impose upon the States any greater substantive educational standard than would be necessary to make such access meaningful." *Ante,* at 3043. While "meaningful" is no more enlightening than "appropriate," the Court purports to clarify itself. Because Amy was provided with *some* specialized instruction from which she obtained *some* benefit and because she passed from grade to grade, she was receiving a meaningful and therefore appropriate education.

This falls far short of what the Act intended. * * * The basic floor of opportunity is as the courts below recognized, intended to eliminate the effects of the handicap, at least to the extent that the child will be given an equal opportunity to learn if that is reasonably possible. Amy Rowley, without a sign-language interpreter, comprehends less than half of what is said in the classroom—less than half of what normal children comprehend. This is hardly an equal opportunity to learn, even if Amy makes passing grades.

* * *

The issue before us is what standard the word "appropriate" incorporates when it is used to modify "education." The answer given by the Court is not a satisfactory one.

II

The Court's discussion of the standard for judicial review is as flawed as its discussion of a "free appropriate public education." According to the Court, a court can ask only whether the State has "complied with the procedures set forth in the Act" and whether the individualized education program is "reasonably calculated to enable the child to receive educational benefits." *Ante,* at 3051. Both the language of the Act and the legislative history, however, demonstrate that Congress intended the courts to conduct a far more searching inquiry.

* * *

There is no doubt that the state agency itself must make substantive decisions. The legislative history reveals that the courts are to consider, *de novo,* the same issues.

* * *

Thus, the Court's limitations on judicial review have no support in either the language of the Act or the legislative history. * * * I respectfully dissent.

POLK v. CENTRAL SUSQUEHANNA INTERMEDIATE UNIT 16

United States Court of Appeals, Third Circuit, 1988.
853 F.2d 171.

BECKER, CIRCUIT JUDGE.

This appeal requires that we examine the contours of the "free appropriate public education" requirement of the Education of the Handicapped Act, as amended, 20 U.S.C. §§ 1401–1461, (1982) (EHA), as it touches on the delivery of physical therapy, which is a "related service" under the EHA. Ronald and Cindy Polk are parents of Christopher Polk, a child with severe mental and physical impairments. They claim that defendants, the local school district and the larger administrative Intermediate Unit (which oversees special education for students in a five-county area) violated the EHA because they failed to provide Christopher with an adequate program of special education. Specifically, plaintiffs contend that defendants' failure to provide direct "hands-on" physical therapy from a licensed physical therapist once a week has hindered Christopher's progress in meeting his educational goals.

The district court granted summary judgment in favor of defendants. The court held that because Christopher derived "*some* educational benefit" from his educational program, the requirements of the EHA, as interpreted by the Supreme Court in *Board of Education v. Rowley* have been met.

We will reverse the district court's grant of summary judgment for two reasons. First, we discern a genuine issue of material fact as to whether the defendants, in violation of the EHA procedural requirement for *individualized* educational programs, have refused, as a blanket rule, to consider providing handicapped students with direct physical therapy from a licensed physical therapist. Second, we conclude that the district court applied the wrong standard in evaluating the appropriateness of the child's education. Although the district court relied upon language from a recent Supreme Court case, it took that language out of context and applied it beyond the narrow holding of the Supreme Court's opinion. More specifically, we believe that the district court erred in evaluating this severely handicapped child's educational program by a standard under which even trivial advancement satisfied the substantive provisions of the EHA's guarantee of a free and appropriate education. There is evidence in the record that would support a finding that the program prescribed for Christopher afforded no more than trivial progress. We will therefore reverse and remand for further proceedings consistent with this opinion.

* * *

II.   FACTS & PROCEDURAL HISTORY

Christopher Polk is severely developmentally disabled. At the age of seven months he contracted encephalopathy, a disease of the brain similar to cerebral palsy. He is also mentally retarded. Although Christopher is fourteen years old, he has the functional and mental capacity of a toddler. All parties agree that he requires "related services" in order to learn. He receives special education from defendants, the Central Susquehanna Intermediate Unit #16 (the IU) and Central Columbia Area School District (the school district). Placed in a class for the mentally handicapped, Christopher has a full-time personal classroom aide. His education consists of learning basic life skills such as feeding himself, dressing himself, and using the toilet. He has mastered sitting and kneeling, is learning to stand independently, and is showing some potential for ambulation. Christopher is working on basic concepts such as "behind," "in," "on," and "under," and the identification of shapes, coins, and colors. Although he is cooperative, Christopher finds such learning difficult because he has a short attention span.

Although the record is not clear on this point, until 1980, the defendants apparently provided Christopher with direct physical therapy from a licensed physical therapist. Since that time, however, under a newer, so-called consultative model, Christopher no longer receives direct physical therapy from a physical therapist. Instead, a physical therapist (one of two hired by the IU) comes once a month to train Christopher's teacher in how to integrate physical therapy with Christopher's education. Although the therapist may lay hands on Christopher in demonstrating to the teacher the correct approach, he or she does not provide any therapy to Christopher directly, but uses such interaction to teach the teacher. Plaintiffs do not object to the consultative method per se, but argue that, to meet Christopher's individual needs, the consultative method must be supplemented by direct ("hands on") physical therapy.

In support of this position, plaintiffs adduced evidence that direct physical therapy from a licensed physical therapist has significantly expanded Christopher's physical capacities. In the summer of 1985, Christopher received two weeks of intensive physical therapy from a licensed physical therapist at Shriner's Hospital in Philadelphia. According to Christopher's parents, this brief treatment produced dramatic improvements in Christopher's physical capabilities. A doctor at Shriner's prescribed that Christopher receive at least one hour a week of direct physical therapy. Because the defendants were unwilling to provide direct physical therapy as part of Christopher's special education program, the Polks hired a licensed physical therapist, Nancy Brown, to work with Christopher at home. At the time of the hearing, she was seeing Christopher twice a week.

Plaintiffs acknowledge that the school program has benefited Christopher to some degree, but argue that his educational program is not appropriate because it is not individually tailored to his specific needs, as the EHA requires. Moreover, throughout all of the administrative and judicial proceedings that we now describe, plaintiffs have maintained that to comply with the EHA the defendants must provide, as part of Christopher's "free appropriate public education," one session a week with a licensed physical therapist.

Plaintiffs first challenged Christopher's IEP before a Commonwealth of Pennsylvania Department of Education Hearing Officer. At that hearing and in later depositions, the administrator of the IU, Christopher's teachers, the IU's physical therapy consultant, Christopher's current private physical therapist and his therapist from Shriner's all testified concerning Christopher's capabilities and educational needs. The Hearing Officer found that Christopher was benefiting from his education, and that his education was appropriate.

After exhausting administrative remedies to their dissatisfaction, the Polks brought suit in the district court for the Middle District of Pennsylvania.

* * *

[T]he district court granted summary judgment for the defendants. Relying on the Supreme Court's decision in *Rowley,* 458 U.S. at 206–07, 102 S.Ct. at 3050–51, the court held that the provisions of EHA had been met because Christopher had received *some* benefit from his education. This appeal followed.

Plaintiffs present two arguments on appeal. First, they submit that the defendants violated EHA's procedural requirements because Christopher's program is not truly individualized. Plaintiffs rely, in this regard, on the defendants' failure to provide direct ("hands on") physical therapy from a licensed physical therapist to *any* of the children in the intermediate unit (a fact they learned during Christopher's due process hearing before the state examiner). This failure, they contend, is evidence that the defendants have an inflexible rule prohibiting direct therapy and that such a rigid rule conflicts with the EHA's mandate of providing *individualized* education. Plaintiffs argue that genuine questions of material fact exist as to the defendants' willingness to provide direct physical therapy under any circumstances, and that such disputes preclude summary judgment.

Second, plaintiffs assert that Christopher's education is inadequate to meet his unique needs. They claim that the district court found Christopher's education appropriate only because it applied an erroneous legal standard in judging the educational benefit of Christopher's program.

III.   ROLE OF PHYSICAL THERAPY IN PROVIDING A FREE
APPROPRIATE PUBLIC EDUCATION UNDER THE EHA

For some handicapped children, the related services provided by the EHA serve as important facilitators of classroom learning.

* * *

For children like Christopher with severe disabilities, related services serve a dual purpose. First, because these children have extensive physical difficulties that often interfere with development in other areas, physical therapy is an essential prerequisite to education. For example, development of motor abilities is often the first step in overall educational development.[5]

As we explained in *Battle v. Pennsylvania,* 629 F.2d 269, 275 (3d Cir.1980), *cert. denied,* 452 U.S. 968, 101 S.Ct. 3123, 69 L.Ed.2d 981 (1981), in discussing children with severe emotional disturbances:

> Where basic self-help and social skills such as toilet training, dressing, feeding and communication are lacking, formal education begins at that point. If the child masters these fundamentals, the education moves on to more difficult but still very basic language, social and arithmetic skills, such as counting, making change, and identifying simple words.

Id. at 275.

Second, the physical therapy itself may form the core of a severely disabled child's special education. This court has recognized that "[t]he educational program of a handicapped child, particularly a severely and profoundly handicapped child ... is very different from that of a non-handicapped child. The program may consist largely of 'related services' such as physical, occupational, or speech therapy." In Christopher's case, physical therapy is not merely a conduit to his education but constitutes, in and of itself, a major portion of his special education, teaching him basic skills such as toileting, feeding, ambulation, etc.

IV.   THE PLAINTIFFS' PROCEDURAL CLAIM (THAT CHRISTOPHER'S
EDUCATIONAL PLAN WAS NOT INDIVIDUALIZED)

As we noted above, the plaintiffs have offered to prove that the defendants never genuinely considered Christopher's unique needs because of a rigid policy of providing only consultative physical therapy. They adduced evidence during cross examination at the state administrative hearing that none of the 65 children in defendants' intermediate unit whose IEPs call for physical therapy actually receive direct physical therapy. The plaintiffs also contend that, since the adoption of the consultative model, this rigid policy has precluded the defendants from recognizing Christopher's individual needs in violation of the EHA. Plaintiffs submit that the district court did not recognize the force of

---

5. Physical therapy is essential for a child like Christopher because, in order to learn basic skills, he must learn to use his muscles properly. A key function of physical therapy is to normalize tonic reflex patterns....

this procedural argument, and hence erred in granting summary judgment when a genuine issue of material fact existed as to the willingness of the defendants to provide direct physical therapy to any child.

The defendants respond that it is, and always has been, their position that direct therapy would be provided, if needed. The therapist who consults monthly with Christopher's teacher testified before the Department of Education hearing examiner that she would provide therapy treatment directly if she determined that such therapy were appropriate. The previous physical therapy consultant and the administrator of the IU similarly claimed in testimony before the hearing examiner that direct physical therapy would be provided, if needed, but that such a case has never arisen for Christopher nor for any other student in the Unit.

Critical to resolution of this question are the Act's procedural protections. To repeat, the centerpiece of the procedural scheme is the IEP.

* * *

This system of procedural protection only works if the state devises an *individualized* program and is willing to address the handicapped child's "unique needs."

* * *

In our view, a rigid rule under which defendants refuse even to consider providing physical therapy, as did the rule struck down in *Battle,* would conflict with Christopher's procedural right to an individualized program. Drawing all reasonable inferences in favor of the non-moving party, we believe that a genuine dispute exists over whether the defendants would consider, under any circumstances, offering direct physical therapy, and that this dispute is over material facts, precluding summary judgment. Concomitantly, we believe that plaintiffs should be given an opportunity to continue their discovery into this question because the existence of a rigid rule prohibiting such therapy would violate the EHA. Therefore, we will reverse and remand the district court's decision for inquiry into whether defendants possess a rigid policy prohibiting the provision of direct physical therapy to children in the IU.

V.　Plaintiffs' Substantive Claim (That the Court Misapplied the Legal Standard for Evaluating Appropriate Education)

A.　*The Supreme Court's Opinion in Rowley*

We begin our discussion of the substantive protections of the EHA with the Supreme Court's opinion in *Board of Education v. Rowley,* 458 U.S. 176, 102 S.Ct. 3034, 73 L.Ed.2d 690 (1982), because the parties' arguments are so closely tied to that case; only in the context of *Rowley* can we intelligently present the parties' contentions and the district court's opinion.

* * *

Although the tenor of the *Rowley* opinion reflects the Court's reluctance to involve the courts in substantive determinations of appropriate education and its emphasis on the *procedural* protection of the IEP process, it is clear that the Court was not espousing an entirely toothless standard of substantive review. Rather, the *Rowley* Court described the level of benefit conferred by the Act as "meaningful." 458 U.S. at 192, 102 S.Ct. at 3043. As the Court explained:

> By passing the Act, Congress sought primarily to make public education available to handicapped children. But in seeking to provide such access to public education, Congress did not impose upon the States any greater substantive educational standard than would be necessary to make such access *meaningful.*

Id. (emphasis added). After noting the deference due to states on questions of education and the theme of *access* rather than a guarantee of any particular standard of benefit, the Court acknowledged that:

> Implicit in the congressional purpose of providing access to a "free appropriate public education" is the requirement that the education to which access is provided be sufficient to confer some educational benefit upon the handicapped child.

* * *

The preceding quotation demonstrates that the Supreme Court in *Rowley* did not abdicate responsibility for monitoring the substantive quality of education under the EHA. Instead, it held that the education must "provide educational benefit." The Court thus recognized that the substantive, independent judicial review envisioned by the EHA was not a hollow gesture. Instead, courts must ensure "a basic floor of opportunity" that is defined by an *individualized* program that confers benefit.

Finally, it is important to note that, notwithstanding *Rowley*'s broad language, the Court indicated that its holding might not cover every case brought under the EHA. Indeed, *Rowley* was an avowedly narrow opinion that relied significantly on the fact that Amy Rowley progressed successfully from grade to grade in a "mainstreamed" classroom.

* * *

Although we do not argue that *Rowley* "contradicts itself," *id.* at 212, 102 S.Ct. at 3053 (White, J., dissenting), we nevertheless note the tension in the *Rowley* majority opinion between its emphasis on procedural protection (almost to the exclusion of substantive inquiry) and its substantive component quoted and discussed *supra.* This tension is unresolved in the *Rowley* case itself because the facts of the case (including Amy Rowley's quite substantial benefit from her education) did not force the Court to confront squarely the fact that Congress cared about the quality of special education. In the case *sub judice,* however, the question of how much benefit is sufficient to be "meaningful" is inescapable. Therefore we must examine the Act's notion of "benefit" and apply a standard that is faithful to congressional intent and consistent with *Rowley.*

B.   EHA Requires More than a De Minimis Benefit

We hold that the EHA calls for more than a trivial educational benefit. That holding rests on the Act and its legislative history as well as interpretation of *Rowley.*

1.

The opinion of the district court, anchored to the "some benefit" language of *Rowley,* 458 U.S. at 200, 102 S.Ct. at 3047, explained its holding as follows:

> The fact that Christopher would advance more quickly with intensive therapy rather than the therapy he now receives does not make the School District's program for Christopher defective. Programs need only render some benefit; they need not maximize potential.... The Supreme Court has determined that the Act is primarily a procedural statute and does not impose a substantive duty on the state to provide a student with other than *some* educational benefits. Increased muscle tone may well fall outside of the scope of the requirement that Christopher receive some educational benefits from the program in which he is enrolled.

Plaintiffs argue on appeal that the district court applied the wrong standard in measuring the educational benefit of Christopher's program and that the case should be remanded for further proceedings consistent with the correct standard, one that requires more than a *de minimis* benefit. Defendants rejoin that *Rowley*'s announcement of a "some benefit" test precludes judicial inquiry into the substantive education conferred by the Act, so long as the handicapped child receives any benefit at all. Noting that Christopher's parents acknowledge that he derives some benefit from his education, defendants submit that the inquiry is over and that the district court's summary judgment must be affirmed.

* * *

This court recently has had occasion to interpret and apply the *Rowley* standard in the context of a severely impaired child. In *Board of Education v. Diamond,* 808 F.2d 987, 991 (3d Cir.1986), we expressly rejected the argument that when the Supreme Court in *Rowley* referred to "some benefit," it meant any benefit at all, even if the child nevertheless regressed. The case involved a child, Andrew Diamond, with severe physical, neurological, and emotional handicaps. Despite evidence that Andrew's learning skills were deteriorating and his behavior was becoming counterproductive, the state resisted transferring Andrew from his placement in a day program to a placement in a residential program. As a result, Andrew's parents put him in a residential program and paid for it themselves.

After a due process hearing, the school board was ordered to place Andrew in an appropriate residential setting. The school board filed an action in federal court seeking a day placement for Andrew. The district court, however, endorsed the residential placement and ordered the school district to reimburse Andrew's parents for the expenses incurred when paying for his residential placement themselves.

In *Diamond,* we thus confronted and rejected the very argument that the defendants make here:

> The School District's legal argument is that it is obliged by governing law to provide no more for Andrew Diamond than will be "of benefit" to him. The governing law, however, clearly imposes a higher standard.

Id. at 991. After observing that "the *Rowley* standard of enabling one to achieve passing marks and advance from grade to grade probably is not achievable for Andrew," *id.,* the court observed:

> But *Rowley* makes it perfectly clear that the Act requires a plan of instruction under which educational *progress* is likely. The School District's "of benefit" test is offered in defense of an educational plan under which educational regression actually occurred. Literally the School Board's plan might be conceived as conferring some benefit to Andrew in that less regression might occur under it than if Andrew Diamond had simply been left to vegetate. The Act, however, requires a plan likely to produce progress, not regression or trivial educational advancement.

Id. (emphasis in original). The teaching of *Diamond* is that, when the Supreme Court said "some benefit" in *Rowley,* it did not mean "some" as opposed to "none." Rather, "some" connotes an amount of benefit greater than mere trivial advancement.

Defendants seek to distinguish *Diamond,* arguing that *Diamond* was a more egregious case, whereby regression had occurred under the state's educational plan (there has been no regression here). Although we acknowledge that this distinction has some force, and that *Diamond* does indeed stand for the proposition that a child who is regressing (and whose regression can be reversed by reasonable means) is not receiving sufficient "benefit" under the Act, we believe that *Diamond* can and should be read more expansively.

Indeed, defendants' distinction of *Diamond,* if carried to its logical conclusion, would arguably render that case more expansive because progress for some severely handicapped children may require optimal benefit. As we noted in *Battle,* 629 F.2d at 269, severely handicapped children (unlike normal children) have a strong tendency to regress. A program calculated to lead to non-regression might actually, in the case of severely handicapped children, impose a greater burden on the state than one that requires a program designed to lead to more than trivial progress. The educational progress of a handicapped child (whether in life skills or in a more sophisticated program) can be understood as a continuum where the point of regression versus progress is less relevant than the conferral of benefit. We note that it is therefore possible to construe *Diamond* 's holding not solely as an issue of progress or regression but also as requiring that any educational benefit be more than *de minimis.*

* * *

Obviously, this court is in no position to determine the factual question whether the treatment the defendants currently provide for Christopher is appropriate. We are, however, obligated to correct errors of law on appeal, and we hold that the district court applied the wrong standard in granting summary judgment for defendants when it allowed for the possibility of only *de minimis* benefit.

* * *

We recognize the difficulty of measuring levels of benefit in severely handicapped children. Obviously, the question whether benefit is *de minimis* must be gauged in relation to the child's potential. However, we believe that the extent of the factual dispute concerning the level of benefit Christopher received from his educational program precludes summary judgment under the standard that we announce today. The judgment of the district court will therefore be reversed and the case remanded for further proceedings consistent with this opinion.

Questions and Comments

1. *The "some benefit" standard. Rowley* holds that, to meet the requirements of the IDEA, education must be of "some benefit" to the child. One of the grounds on which the Third Circuit relied in reversing the district court in *Polk* was the lower court's failure to apply this standard. What was the "test" employed by the district court? Is the Court of Appeals' articulation of the *Rowley* standard correct? The parents of Polk conceded that the child was deriving "some benefit from his education." Why wasn't this concession dispositive? How are the services Christopher (Polk) was receiving "less" than those received by Amy (Rowley)? Won't both Christopher and Amy "advance" without the services they each requested?

What *should* be the standard for evaluating whether the free appropriate education requirement of the IDEA is met? The Third Circuit opinion in *Polk* refers negatively to the "de minimis benefit" standard, which it believed to be less rigorous than *Rowley's* "some benefit" standard. More demanding than the some-benefit standard, at least as far as the Supreme Court is concerned, is the test devised by the district court in *Rowley*, which required that the child be provided "an opportunity to achieve [his or her] full potential commensurate with the opportunity provided to other children." See also *In re Conklin*, 946 F.2d 306, 320–21 (4th Cir. 1991)(summarizing state statutes, some of which adopt this standard). Perhaps most demanding of all is the test announced in *B.G. v. Cranford Board of Education*, 702 F.Supp. 1140 (D.N.J.1988), which explicitly adopted, as a matter of state law, a higher standard than required by *Rowley*. There, the court noted that the state of New Jersey by law requires school boards "to provide educational services according to how the student can *best* achieve success in learning." Id. at 1148. The court found that this standard required a residential placement of an emotionally disturbed child. The school district's day school placement of the child "though perhaps sufficient to satisfy the minimum federal standards under *Rowley,* is insufficient and inconsistent with New Jersey's requirements that B.G. be afforded a program that assures him the fullest opportunity to develop his intellectual capacities." Id. at 1157.

How do these various IDEA standards compare to *Youngberg v. Romeo* and other caselaw dealing with the right to treatment for those who are institutionalized (see pp. 1116–24)?

2. *Related services.* As *Polk* indicates, the IDEA obligates the state to provide not only a free appropriate education but also "related services." According to the statute, these are services "required to assist a child with a disability to benefit from special education," including "developmental, corrective, and other supportive services ... psychological services ... therapeutic recreation, social work services, counselling services [and] rehabilitation counselling and medical services [the latter to be provided 'for diagnostic and evaluation purposes only].'" 20 U.S.C. 1401(17). In *Irving Independent School District v. Tatro*, 468 U.S. 883, 104 S.Ct. 3371, 82 L.Ed.2d 664 (1984), the Supreme Court interpreted this provision to require, consistent with *Rowley*, "only those services necessary to aid a handicapped child to benefit from a special education."

In determining what "necessary" might mean in this context, consider *T.G. v. Board of Education of Piscataway,* 576 F.Supp. 420 (D.N.J.1983), where parents of an emotionally disturbed child placed him in a residential facility "to provide him with the controls and attention necessary for social and environmental development" and then requested reimbursement for the cost of the placement. The school board denied the claim on the grounds that " 'psychotherapy' other than that necessary for diagnostic or evaluative purposes was not a 'related service' for which a local school district would be responsible under the mandate of the Act." Id. at 422. In granting summary judgment for the parent-claimant the court held that psychotherapy provided to an emotionally disturbed child is a related service under the Act since "the therapy was designed as an essential service to allow [the child] to simply benefit from the educational program planned for him." Id. at 424. See also, *Kruelle v. New Castle County School District*, 642 F.2d 687 (3d Cir.1981) (holding that 24–hour care in a residential setting was necessary to allow a child with profound mental retardation to learn). But see *Field v. Haddonfield Bd. of Educ.*, 769 F.Supp. 1313, 1326–27 (D.N.J. 1991), which held that a substance abuse program is not a related service even though "successful completion of a substance abuse program can be expected to increase the effectiveness of the child's education program," and the school in this case required the plaintiff to undergo such a program before he could return to school.

Note that, while the IDEA clearly includes "psychological services" in the related services category, it also states that medical services need be provided at state expense only for "diagnostic and evaluation purposes." In *Tatro*, the Supreme Court appeared to interpret the latter language to mean that if the medical services could readily be performed by a school nurse they would generally be related services for purposes of the Act, whereas if they could only be provided by a licensed physician they would usually not be. See also, *Cedar Rapids Comm. School Dist. v. Garret F.*, 526 U.S. 66, 119 S.Ct. 992, 143 L.Ed.2d 154 (1999)(affirming *Tatro's* "bright-line test" between physician-provided and non-physician-provided medical services). The *Tatro* Court concluded that it was reasonable to believe that Congress included the exception in connection with medical services to "spare schools from an obligation to provide a service that might well prove unduly expensive and beyond the range of their competence." Id. at 892. Lower courts have also indicated that, in considering the scope of medical services exception, "it is appropriate to take into account the risk involved [in the medical procedure] and the liability factor of the school district inherent in providing a service of a medical nature." See *Neely v. Rutherford County School*, 68 F.3d 965, 971 (6th Cir.1995).

Does this reasoning exclude the administration of psychotropic medication from the IDEA's related services requirement? Therapy of the type provided in *T.G.* or *Kruelle*? Substance abuse treatment of the type sought in *Field*? Should the answers to these questions depend, as it apparently does after *Tatro* and *Garret F.*, upon whether the service must be provided by a psychiatrist as opposed to a non-physician? At the school or somewhere else? Compare *Babb v. Knox Cty. School System*, 965 F.2d 104 (6th Cir. 1992)(school district must pay for all institutional services provided a teenager who, since at least the age of 13, "was suffering from a fairly severe degree of psychopathology.... [and] exhibit[ed] a highly ideational/schizoid personality style that is marked by underlying rage, paranoid misinterpretation of interpersonal situations, hyper-vigilance, affective reactivity, impulsive acting out of unconscious issues, intense splitting, suspiciousness, and withdrawal into fantasy") with *Tice v. Botetourt Cty. School Bd.*, 908 F.2d 1200 (4th Cir.1990)(differentiating between institutional medical services and institutional psychological and counseling services that are "educational") and *Clovis Unified School Dist. v. California Office of Admin. Hearings*, 903 F.2d 635 (9th Cir.1990)(child hospitalized primarily for "medical, psychiatric" reasons and therefore school not liable). If these types of services are *not* excluded medical services, does the IDEA in essence provide a right to state-paid psychiatric treatment for all disabled children up to age 21 (the point at which IDEA benefits cease)?

3. *Definition of disability.* Rowley and Polk were clearly disabled. But most of the resources currently expended under the IDEA are for children who are only moderately impaired. Similar to controversy over the definition of disability under the Americans with Disabilities Act (see Chapter 12), a debate has erupted over the proper definition of disability for purposes of the IDEA. Under the Act, the disability must be (1) an enumerated impairment which (2) adversely affects educational performance and (3) creates a need for special education and related services. The enumerated mental impairments most likely to cause controversy are "learning disabilities" and "emotional disturbance." Proof of a learning disability can consist of a discrepancy between IQ and achievement, but may also rely on a finding

that the child does not make sufficient progress when provided with re-search-based educational interventions. 20 U.S.C. § 1414(b)(6). "Emotional disturbance" is defined in the relevant regulations as a condition persisting "over a long period of time and to a marked degree that adversely affects a child's educational performance" which is characterized by: (1) an inability to learn that cannot be explained by intellectual, sensory, or health factors; (2) an inability to build or maintain satisfactory interpersonal relationships with peers and teachers; (3) inappropriate types of behavior or feelings under normal circumstances; (4) a general pervasive mood of unhappiness or depression; or (5) a tendency to develop physical symptoms or fears associated with personal or school problems. 34 C.F.R. § 300.8(C)(4)(i)(A).

Some courts have equated the term "educational performance" in the above regulation with "academic performance" and thus have held that if a student is able to achieve satisfactory grades, perform the required class-room work, or demonstrate the ability to learn in any respect, he or she does not possess a qualifying impairment regardless of other performance difficulties in school. See, e.g., *Doe ex rel. Doe v. Bd. of Educ.*, 753 F.Supp. 65, 70 (D. Conn. 1990) (finding student who was hospitalized for depression and aggression ineligible where grades were satisfactory before and after hospitalization). Others have required that the adverse impact be substantial. See, e.g., *Ashli C. ex rel. Sidney C. v. State of Hawaii*, 2007 WL 247761, at *9 (D. Haw., 2007) (holding that "adverse effect" language requires evidence of more than a "minimal" impact on education).

If a student is able to obtain A's and B's despite "emotional distur-bance" or a "learning disability," why should special accommodations be made? Consider these comments:

> Children with less severe impairments are likely to have the best opportunity for meaningful integration into mainstream classrooms. Many children with learning disabilities, for example, can succeed in general education when provided with additional individualized instruc-tion or alternative methods of delivery that often enhance the learning opportunities of other children in the classroom. Limiting the reach of the IDEA to only those with serious impairments threatens to transform special education into a place rather than a set of services. Because children with more significant impairments may be less likely to secure an appropriate education in an integrated setting, the severity-linked identification of disability becomes irretrievably associated with a self-contained classroom separate and apart from the general school popula-tion.

* * *

> Tying assistance to academic failure and impaired functioning creates perverse incentives to emphasize the significance of a child's impairment in his life. Because eligibility is all or nothing, parents and students are encouraged to characterize a child's functioning as negatively as possible to the eligibility team. They may be reluctant to share a child's strengths and abilities with educators out of fear that the same will result in a refusal of services. This characterization is damaging both to a parent's perception of his child and the child's perception of himself to the extent that he is involved in the evaluation process. Children with

disabilities will increasingly be viewed as a bundle of problems to solve rather than as individuals with strengths and weaknesses in need of educational redress. The moral foundation of supporting these children is no longer the educational system's failure to meet their needs, but instead the extent of the children's internal impairments. The resources and educational services schools allocated to this population look more like benevolent charity and less like the equitable distribution of resources to all children in society. The medical model of disability, eroded by the passage of EAHCA, is resurrected as the dominant paradigm in American special education.

* * *

It is important to recognize that the advancement of people with disabilities will not be achieved by conceding that the stigma attached to this status is so great that any reasonable person would do anything to avoid such a label, including foregoing services designed to foster educational success. It is in such concessions that the imagery of disability as an unnatural and pathetic state is reinforced and entrenched. It is only by normalizing the concept of impairment, rather than restricting disability status to the most severely impaired, that the stigma of disability will be reduced. If students capable of even modest academic success are deemed insufficiently "special" to qualify for assistance, this will not occur. It is not the legal identification process itself that harms the student, but rather the negative imagery of disability that is communicated by teachers, administrators and fellow students in the wake of labeling.

Wendy F. Hensel, "Sharing the Short Bus: Eligibility and Identity under the IDEA," 58 Hastings L.J. 1147, 1181–82, 1187, 1196 (2007).

4. *Costs.* One's perspective on the scope of the "appropriate education," "related services" and "disabled" requirements might depend upon the financial burdens these requirements place on school districts. According to one report based on 1996 data, because of technological advances allowing more disabled children to survive birth and more fine-tuned diagnostic procedures, the number of "special education" students has skyrocketed since the 1970s (to 1 out of 8 children, or 5.4 million). Spending on special education doubled between 1970 and 1996 to $30 billion, and comprised nearly a quarter of the school budget in some jurisdictions. The IDEA was meant to cover 40% of these costs, but in 1996 federal spending on special education was only 7%. Although every state now has its own version of the IDEA, most don't pick up much more of the cost, which means that localities may have to foot as much as 75% of the special education bill. In one South Dakota county, for instance, a quarter of the local school district's 80% increase in budget for 1992 (roughly $125,000) was due to costs associated with one autistic student. Sam Allis, *The Struggle to Pay for Special Ed.*, TIME, November 4, 1996, at 82–83.

Can parents be asked to defray at least part of the costs? In *Parks v. Pavkovic,* 557 F.Supp. 1280 (N.D.Ill.1983), affirmed 753 F.2d 1397 (7th Cir.1985), the state of Illinois was enjoined from requiring parents to pay a portion of their mentally disabled child's institutional living expenses. Illinois law sought to assess "responsible relative liability" against the parents of children receiving services from the Illinois Department of Mental Health and Developmental Disabilities. The court held that such an assessment, as to children placed in residential facilities for educational reasons, violates the Act's mandate to states to provide a *free* appropriate public education. In *School Comm. of Town of Burlington v. Department of Educ. of Mass.*, 471 U.S. 359, 105 S.Ct. 1996, 85 L.Ed.2d 385 (1985), the Supreme Court held the school district even had to reimburse parents for the costs of *private* placement subsequently found to be more appropriate than the public school placement advocated by the school district. However, if the parents place their child in a private facility unilaterally, without working with the state to produce an IEP, reimbursement may not be required. See, e.g., *Tucker v. Calloway County Bd. of Educ.*, 136 F.3d 495 (6th Cir.1998).

Some states have tried to reduce costs in other ways as well, not always with success:

> Massachusetts, convinced that schools were over-identifying students with disabilities and too lax in containing the costs associated with special education, changed its state funding formula in the early 1990s. Rather than allocating funds based on actual enrollment of special needs students in a district, the state instead based funding "on a preset percentage of children in special education set at a rate lower than the state average" and "allocated less than half of what would be required to pay for services for these students." Eligibility, moreover, was changed to require not only the presence of a disability, but also a "determination that a child was not making effective progress in regular education." The legislature believed that these disincentives would cause districts to more rigorously police eligibility and placement decisions.

> Despite the financial disincentives imposed by the legislature, the number of children in special education in the state declined by less than 1% of the student population over the next decade. The funding available to serve their educational needs, on the other hand, indisputably declined as a result of the revised formula. A study evaluating the shift in funding concluded that the rise in special education eligibility experienced in the past and predicted for the future did not flow from lax enforcement of eligibility standards, but instead from a variety of social, medical and economic sources outside the control of school districts.

Hensel, supra, at 1186. More is said about the relevance of costs to coverage under the IDEA in the next section.

5. *Procedures.* As *Rowley* and *Polk* note, the primary mechanism for implementing the IDEA is the Individualized Education Plan (IEP). The IEP is supposed to be the product of a multidisciplinary team composed of a professional who is knowledgeable about the child's suspected disability (e.g., an occupational or physical therapist or school psychologist), as well as the child's teacher and parents and, "whenever appropriate," the child. The team must rely on multiple sources; the IDEA specifically provides that "intelligence tests may not form the only basis for an evaluation," nor should placement decisions "be based on tests alone, but should include at least one other evaluation source, such as a teacher's observation of the child's classroom performance." 20 U.S.C. § 1412(a)(6)(B). The 2004 reau-

thorization of the Act made clear that the IEP need only be revised once a year, unless the parties agree otherwise, and must provide annual goals that are "measurable" (consistent with the results-oriented provisions of the No Child Left Behind Act of 2001). Thus the IEP must include sections on (1) the child's present level of educational performance; (2) measurable annual goals; (3) the special education and related services to be provided to the child; (4) the extent, if any, to which the child will not participate with nondisabled children in the regular classroom; (5) any individual modifications in the administration of assessments that are needed for the child to participate in an assessment; (6) the projected dates for the beginning and duration of services; (7) needed transition services at applicable ages; and (8) how the child's progress toward the annual goals will be measured. See Gary Melton et al., Psychological Evaluations for the Courts: A Handbook for Mental Health Professionals and Lawyers 569 (3d ed. 2007).

If the parents are dissatisfied with the IEP process they can ask for an independent evaluation at school expense or go directly to a hearing; even if the parents lose at this hearing, they may request an independent evaluation. If the parents lose in the administrative process, they can take the issue to the courts. 20 U.S.C. §§ 1414(e)(f); 1414(a)(2). The Supreme Court has held that the parents bear the burden of proof in such proceedings, *Schaffer ex rel. Schaffer v. Weast*, 546 U.S. 49, 126 S.Ct. 528, 163 L.Ed.2d 387 (2005), and must bear the cost of non-attorney expert fees, *Arlington Cent. Sch. Dist. v. Murphy*, 548 U.S. 291, 126 S.Ct. 2455, 165 L.Ed.2d 526 (2006), although attorney's fees are picked up by the state if the parents prevail. In *Dellmuth v. Muth*, 491 U.S. 223, 242, 109 S.Ct. 2397, 2402, 105 L.Ed.2d 181 (1989), the Court also limited, on Eleventh Amendment grounds, the ability of private litigants to obtain money damages from the state. Some lower courts have held that even injunctive relief from the state is not available under the IDEA. See *Pace v. Bogalusa City Sch. Bd.*, 325 F.3d 609 (5th Cir. 2003). Of course, school districts, which are not agencies of the state, may still be enjoined and sued for damages under the IDEA. Chapter Twelve (pp. 1280–82) describes the eleventh amendment defense in more detail.

B. MAINSTREAMING

In enacting the predecessor to the IDEA in 1975, Congress signaled a clear preference for the educational "mainstreaming" of handicapped children. The statute specifically permitted a placement in a special class or school only when the nature or severity of the handicap is such that regular classroom education cannot be achieved satisfactorily. 20 U.S.C. § 1412(5)(B). Although this language was already relatively strong, the 1990 amendments to the Act again emphasized that "mainstreaming" is a priority.

The original preference for "mainstreaming" was a response to the tendency of school districts to warehouse handicapped children in ill-equipped special classrooms or schools. Congress' 1990 reiteration of mainstreaming's priority was probably a reaction to research showing that, even after passage of the IDEA, most of the children covered by the Act were still being educated in separate classes (albeit usually on a regular school campus). For instance, one study found that 74% of all eligible children received their education in "pull-out" classes. See, e.g., Alan Gartner & Dorothy Lipsky, *Beyond Special Education: Toward a Quality System for All Students*, 57 HARV. EDUC. REV. 367 (1987). In another district, only between 3% and 7% of the students with disability were assigned to regular academic classes, with mainstreaming occurring only in such subjects as art, music, and physical education. Janet Sansone & Naomi Zigmond, *Evaluating Mainstreaming through an Analysis of Students' Schedules*, 52(5) EXCEPTIONAL CHILDREN 452 (1986).

BOARD OF EDUC., SACRAMENTO CITY UNIFIED SCHOOL DIST. v. HOLLAND

Eastern District, California, 1992.
786 F.Supp. 874.

LEVI, DISTRICT JUDGE

[I]

... Rachel Holland is a nine year old girl who is moderately mentally retarded. She has an I.Q. of 44 and on academic testing functions at about the level of a four year old child.... Rachel attended a variety of special education programs provided by the District from 1985 until 1989. While Rachel was in special education classes provided by the District, she spent a small part of each day with nonhandicapped children. For the period from 1987 through 1989, Rachel received no more than approximately one hour per day of integration with a regular class. Her parents repeatedly sought, with little success, to increase the amount of time Rachel spent in regular classrooms. In the fall of 1989, the Hollands requested that Rachel be placed full-time in a regular classroom for the 1989–90 school year. The District rejected this request and offered only special education placements for Rachel. Later, after mediation, the District proposed a placement for Rachel that included some integration into a regular classroom. The proposed placement would have divided Rachel's time between a regular class for nonacademic activities—such as art, music, lunch, and recess—and a special education class of handicapped children for all academic subjects. This would have required moving Rachel at least six times each day between the two classes. The Hollands rejected the District's proposals and entered Rachel in a regular kindergarten class at the Shalom School, a private school. Rachel has remained at the Shalom School in regular classes and is now in second grade. She is assisted by a part-time aide who sits by her in the classroom.

Although unable to agree on a placement for Rachel, the District and the Hollands, through mediation, agreed on an Individualized Education Program for Rachel. The IDEA requires such a program, known as an IEP, for each handicapped child and requires that it be reviewed at least annually. See 20 U.S.C. § 1401(19). Because of the dispute between the District and the Hollands, Rachel's IEP has not been revised since January 1990. Rachel's 1990 IEP stresses language and communication goals. The agreed objectives include: speaking in four or five word sentences; repeating instructions of complex tasks; initiating and terminating conversations; verbally stating her name, address, and telephone number; participating in a personal safety program with classmates; developing a 24–word sight vocabulary; counting to 25; printing her first and last name and the alphabet; playing cooperatively; participating in lunch without teacher supervision; identifying upper and lower case letters and sounds associated with them; and following her schedule of daily activities.

The Hollands appealed the District's placement decision to a state hearing officer, as provided by the IDEA. See 20 U.S.C. § 1415(b)(2). The District's position at the hearing, as here, was that Rachel is too severely handicapped to benefit from a full time placement in a regular class.

* * *

II

The Individuals with Disabilities Education Act, which governs this lawsuit, provides federal funds to states for the education of handicapped children. *Board of Educ. v. Rowley*, 458 U.S. 176, 179, 102 S.Ct. 3034, 3037, 73 L.Ed.2d 690 (1982). If a state elects to receive these funds, the Act requires that the state adopt certain procedures and practices in the education of the handicapped. The IDEA requires that each handicapped child be provided a free appropriate education, and be educated "to the maximum extent appropriate" with children who are not handicapped. 20 U.S.C. 1412(1) and (5); see 20 U.S.C. 1401(a)(1) (broadly defining "handicapped"). The free appropriate education requirement is satisfied if "personalized instruction is being provided with sufficient support services to permit the child to benefit from the instruction, and other items of the definitional checklist are satisfied." Rowley, 458 U.S. at 189, 102 S.Ct. at 3042.

The second requirement, that each child be educated with non-handicapped children to the maximum extent appropriate, is the basis of the dispute in this case. The Act requires each state receiving federal funds to establish

> procedures to assure that, to the maximum extent appropriate, handicapped children ... are educated with children who are not handicapped and that special classes, separate schooling, or other removal of handicapped children from the regular educational environment occurs only when the nature or severity of the handicap is such that education in regular classes with the use of supplementary aids and services cannot be achieved satisfactorily.

20 U.S.C. § 1412(5)(B). The placement of handicapped children in regular classrooms "to the maximum extent appropriate" is sometimes referred to as "mainstreaming" or as placement in the "least restrictive environment." See 34 C.F.R. § 300.550. The Act "has a strong preference for mainstreaming" which rises to the level of a rebuttable pre-

sumption. *Daniel R.R. v. State Bd. of Educ.*, 874 F.2d 1036, 1044–45 (5th Cir.1989). The Act also views each handicapped child as having unique needs entitled to individualized consideration. See 20 U.S.C. § 1400(c), 1401(a)(16) & (19). Thus, the decision as to whether any particular child should be educated in a regular classroom setting, all of the time, part of the time, or none of the time, is necessarily an inquiry into the needs and abilities of one child, and does not extend to a group or category of handicapped children, as the District suggests. See *Daniel R.R.*, 874 F.2d at 1048 ("our analysis is an individualized, fact-specific inquiry").

III

In considering whether the District has proposed a placement for Rachel that complies with the Act, the court must determine what is meant by the requirement that handicapped children be mainstreamed "to the maximum extent appropriate." Because the Act does not define this requirement, cases interpreting the Act guide the court's analysis. The federal appellate courts have recognized the following factors as relevant to determining if a placement is appropriate: (1) the educational benefits available to the child in a regular classroom, supplemented with appropriate aids and services, as compared to the educational benefits of a special education classroom; (2) the non-academic benefits to the handicapped child of interaction with nonhandicapped children; (3) the effect of the presence of the handicapped child on the teacher and other children in the regular classroom; and (4) the costs of supplementary aids and services necessary to mainstream the handicapped child in a regular classroom setting. *Greer v. Rome City Sch. Dist.*, 950 F.2d 688, 697 (11th Cir.1991); *Barnett v. Fairfax County Sch. Bd.*, 927 F.2d 146, 153–54 (4th Cir.), cert. denied, 502 U.S. 859, 112 S.Ct. 175, 116 L.Ed.2d 138 (1991); *Daniel R.R.*, 874 F.2d at 1048–50; *Roncker v. Walter*, 700 F.2d 1058 (6th Cir.), cert. denied, 464 U.S. 864, 104 S.Ct. 196, 78 L.Ed.2d 171 (1983).

As to the first factor, if the child's disabilities are so severe that he or she will receive little or no academic benefit from placement in a regular education class, then mainstreaming may not be appropriate. *DeVries v. Fairfax County Sch. Bd.*, 882 F.2d 876, 879 (4th Cir.1989) (disparity between cognitive levels of handicapped 17–year old and non-handicapped peers so great that 17–year old would be simply "monitoring" regular classes). However, the Act's requirement of integration, based on recognition of the non-academic value of such integration, is not overcome by a showing that a special education placement may be academically superior to placement in a regular classroom. *Roland v. Concord School Comm.*, 910 F.2d 983, 993 (1st Cir.1990), cert. denied, 499 U.S. 912, 111 S.Ct. 1122, 113 L.Ed.2d 230 (1991) (citing *Roncker*, 700 F.2d at 1063); *Norton Sch. Comm. v. Massachusetts Dept. of Educ.*, 768 F.Supp. 900, 910 (D.Mass.1991). The Act's presumption in favor of mainstreaming requires that a handicapped child be educated in a regular classroom if the child can receive a satisfactory education there, even if it is not the best academic setting for that child. Further, in considering the relative educational benefits available in integrated and non-integrated settings, the school district must demonstrate that it has considered "whether supplemental aids and services would permit satisfactory education in the regular classroom." *Greer*, 950 F.2d at 696. Only if the child cannot receive a satisfactory education in a regular education class, even if appropriate support services are offered, should the child be placed in a special education class. See *Roncker*, 700 F.2d at 1063.

The second factor addresses the significant non-academic benefits a handicapped child may receive from exposure to nonhandicapped peers. This factor reflects the fundamental purpose of the IDEA's mainstreaming requirement. A handicapped child may benefit from language and behavior models provided by nonhandicapped children. See *Daniel R.R.*, 874 F.2d at 1049 ("[T]he language and behavior models available from nonhandicapped children may be essential or helpful to the handicapped child's development. In other words, although a handicapped child may not be able to absorb all of the regular education curriculum, he may benefit from nonacademic experiences in the regular education environment."); accord, *Greer*, 950 F.2d at 697; *Liscio v. Woodland Hills Sch. Dist.*, 734 F.Supp. 689, 702 (W.D.Pa.), aff'd w/o op., 902 F.2d 1561 (3d Cir.1990) (partial integration appropriate where child "benefits from his interaction with non-handicapped peers ... and enjoys such interaction"). Moreover, the non-academic benefits of mainstreaming a child are closely related to the academic benefits. See *Greer*, 950 F.2d at 697. For example, a child may be better able to learn academic subjects because of improved self-esteem and increased motivation due to placement in regular education.

The third factor addresses the possible negative effects of placing a handicapped child in a regular classroom. The child may be disruptive to other children or may unreasonably occupy the teacher's time to the detriment of other students. *Daniel R.R.*, 874 F.2d at 1049. If other children are disadvantaged by the presence of the handicapped child, mainstreaming is not appropriate. Id. When evaluating the burden that would be created by placing a handicapped child in a regular education class, the school district must consider all reasonable means to minimize the demands on the teacher:

> A handicapped child who merely requires more teacher attention than most other children is not likely to be so disruptive as to significantly impair the education of other children. In weighing this factor, the school district must keep in mind its obligation to consider supplemental aids and services that could accommodate a handicapped child's need for additional attention.

Greer, 950 F.2d at 688. A teacher's aide can minimize the burden on the teacher if the handicapped child is not disruptive but needs special assistance. This factor weighs against placing a handicapped child in regular education only if, after taking all reasonable steps to reduce the burden to the teacher, the other children in the class will still be deprived of their share of the teacher's attention.

Finally, a school district may properly consider cost as a factor in making placement decisions.

> The school district must balance the needs of each handicapped child against the needs of other children in the district. If the cost of educating a handicapped child in a regular classroom is so great that it would significantly impact upon the education of other children in the district, then education in a regular classroom is not appropriate.

Greer, 950 F.2d at 697; see *Barnett*, 927 F.2d at 154; *Roncker*, 700 F.2d at 1063 (cost a factor because excessive spending on one handicapped child may deprive other handicapped children). Only where the cost of placing a handicapped child in regular education will significantly affect other children in the district will this factor weigh against placement in a regular classroom.

In addition to the four factors discussed above, the District urges the court to consider the extent of curriculum modification as a distinct factor. But modification of the curriculum for a handicapped child, even dramatic modification, has no significance in and of itself. The IDEA, in its provision for the IEP process, contemplates that the academic curriculum may be modified to accommodate the individual needs of handicapped children. Curriculum modification becomes significant only if it bears upon the factors already noted. For example, modification of the curriculum may place undue burdens on the teacher both because to modify the curriculum is time consuming and to teach, in effect, two classes in one room could prove impossible. Also, a drastically modified curriculum could deprive the handicapped child of that sense of belonging to a regular class that is important to the achievement of nonacademic benefit.

IV

The District has the burden of demonstrating that its proposed placement of Rachel in a regular classroom for slightly less than half of the day provides mainstreaming to "the maximum extent appropriate" for Rachel.[6] As discussed below, three of the four factors favor mainstreaming, and on the fourth, cost, the District has not met its burden.

---

6. The statutory presumption in favor of mainstreaming has been construed as imposing a burden on the school district to prove that a child cannot be mainstreamed. Davis v. District of Columbia Bd. of Educ., 530 F.Supp. 1209, 1211 (D.D.C.1982) (school district has burden of proving that placement is appropriate).

This burden is explicit in 45 C.F.R. § 84.34, a regulation which implements the Rehabilitation Act of 1973, designed to prevent discrimination against people with handicaps in any program receiving federal funding. "A recipient [of federal funds] shall place a handicapped person in the regular educational environment ... unless it is demonstrated by the recipient that the education of the person in the regular environment with the use of supplementary aids and services cannot be achieved satisfactorily." Although this regulation is not promulgated under the IDEA, it reflects the same strong preference for mainstreaming. Moreover, the District also bears the burden of proof because it seeks to overturn the decision of the hearing officer.

A. *Educational Benefits to Rachel.*

The first factor, the comparative educational benefits to placement in regular or special education classes, weighs in favor of placing Rachel in a regular classroom. The Holland witnesses credibly testified that all of Rachel's goals and objectives could be achieved either in the regular class with some curriculum modification, or through supplementary aids and services. Most of Rachel's IEP goals relate to communication, which the Holland witnesses testified could best be taught by exposure to other children. The District's proffered testimony was focussed primarily on Rachel's educational limitations, but did not establish that the educational opportunities available through special education were superior or equal to those available in a regular education setting.

The bulk of the evidence presented by the District related to Rachel's performance on achievement and aptitude testing conducted by the California Diagnostic Center, and observation of Rachel at school by members of the Diagnostic Center team that tested Rachel. According to the Diagnostic Center witnesses, Rachel has made no progress toward her 1990 IEP goals and derives little academic benefit from regular class placement. These witnesses further suggest that supplemental aids and services are ineffective. By contrast, the Hollands' witnesses testified that Rachel had made significant academic strides at the Shalom School. They suggest that her motivation to learn stems from the regular classroom placement and that she is learning language and other skills from modelling the behavior of her non-handicapped peers. The California Department of Education agrees with the Hollands that Rachel benefits academically from placement in a regular education class.

It is evident that the contrary assessments of Rachel's academic progress are founded in conflicting educational philosophies. The Diagnostic Center witnesses do not believe that a child with Rachel's I.Q. can be effectively educated in a regular classroom.[7] They believe that Rachel's education at this point should focus on functional skills, such as handling money, doing laundry, and using public transportation. Conversely, the Holland experts believe that all handicapped children, even children with much greater handicaps than Rachel, are best educated in regular classrooms. They believe that it is a mistake to limit Rachel's learning opportunities to functional skills.

These sharply different points of view have led the experts to different evaluations of the progress Rachel has made since placement in a regular class at the Shalom School in 1989. One example illustrates how differing educational philosophies may color perceptions. During the November 1991 assessment, one of the Diagnostic Center witnesses observed Rachel in Hebrew class. She was holding the book upside down. The witness drew the conclusion that Rachel was deriving no benefit

---

7. "The perception that a segregated institution is academically superior for a handicapped child may reflect no more than a basic disagreement with the mainstreaming concept. Such a disagreement is not, of course, any basis for not following the Act's mandate." *Roncker,* 700 F.2d at 1063 (citing *Campbell v. Talladega City Bd. of Educ.,* 518 F.Supp. 47, 55 (N.D.Ala.1981)).

from inclusion in the class. One of the Holland witnesses observed the same incident. This witness saw that another child helped Rachel right the book and find her place. From this incident, the witness concluded that Rachel had positive interaction with her peers that would be important to her future ability to live in society.

The court suggests no criticism of these witnesses. But because of the radically different points of view from which they start, their observations on Rachel's academic progress are by no means objective. Nonetheless, the court finds more credible the Holland witnesses' testimony concerning Rachel's academic progress. First, these witnesses have more background in evaluating handicapped children placed in regular classrooms, and they had greater opportunity to observe Rachel over an extended period of time in normal circumstances. Moreover, it appears that for much of the formalized testing by the Diagnostic Center, Rachel was uncomfortable and unhappy. Finally, to the extent that the Holland witnesses have a preference for mainstreaming, it is a preference shared by Congress and embodied in the IDEA.

Because of the conflict among the experts as to Rachel's academic progress, the testimony of her current teacher is all the more important. The District concedes that Nina Crone, Rachel's second grade teacher, is an experienced, skillful teacher. She has no partisan involvement in this controversy. Crone testified that Rachel is a full member of the second grade class. She participates in all activities. For the class as a whole, Crone's major areas of emphasis are socialization, behavior and communication. These are the same areas of emphasis in Rachel's IEP. Crone testified that Rachel was making progress on her IEP goals. For example, Crone noted that Rachel is learning one-to-one correspondence in counting. She can recite the English and Hebrew alphabets, and her communication abilities and sentence length are also improving. Crone testified that Rachel is in many ways a typical second grader. She is eager to participate in class activities and is very motivated. She has become more self-confident and independent. Crone's testimony is consistent with the testimony of Rachel's kindergarten teacher at the Shalom School. See hearing officer's op. at 5–6.

The District offered no persuasive evidence that Rachel would receive educational benefits in special education classes that are equal to or greater than those available in special education classes. Although the District's witnesses testified that many of Rachel's IEP goals could best be implemented in a special education setting, there is no empirical evidence to support this assertion. Rachel made very little progress while in special education in kindergarten. Her special education teacher testified that Rachel had an extremely slow rate of learning, poor social skills, and interacted better with adults than children. When Rachel was shuttled into a regular education class for an informal mainstreaming program, she was treated as an outsider by the non-handicapped children and derived little benefit from her short exposure to these children. The program currently proposed by the District mirrors in part the deficiencies of the previous program. The proposed program would move

Rachel out of the regular class whenever academic subjects were being taught. Rachel would be moved in and out of class at least six times per day. Such a program would mark Rachel as an outsider, depriving her of the primary benefit of mainstreaming.

In short, the District has failed to meet its burden of establishing that Rachel would not receive academic benefits in regular classes and has failed to demonstrate that placement in special classes will provide equal or greater educational benefit to Rachel. Based on the record below and the supplemental evidence presented at the hearing, the court finds that Rachel receives substantial academic benefits in regular education. The court finds that all of Rachel's IEP goals could be implemented in a regular education setting with some modification to the curriculum and with the assistance of a part-time aide.

B. Non-academic Benefits to Rachel.

As discussed above, a handicapped child may derive significant non-academic benefits from education with nonhandicapped peers. The District's evidence tended to show that Rachel is not learning from exposure to other children and that she is isolated from her classmates. The Hollands' evidence supported the conclusion that Rachel has developed her social and communication skills as well as her self-confidence from her placement in regular education. As before, these differing evaluations in large part reflect the predisposition of the evaluators. The court finds the testimony by Rachel's current teacher and Rachel's mother the most credible as to the non-academic benefits Rachel derives from her placement in a regular classroom. Perhaps the strongest evidence that Rachel is gaining incidental benefits from being mainstreamed is her excitement about school and her improved self-confidence. The two witnesses who testified to Rachel's positive attitude, her mother and her teacher, are in a far better position to know and understand Rachel's emotional well-being and social development than the District's witnesses, who evaluated Rachel primarily by using standardized testing techniques. Although Rachel's mother cannot be considered an objective observer, she has had the opportunity to compare Rachel's attitude toward school when she was in special education and since she has been in regular education. She testified that since Rachel was placed in a regular class, she has been excited and enthusiastic about learning. Rachel relishes the new friendships that she has developed at the Shalom School. Because of the evidence that Rachel is developing socially from her full-time placement in a regular education class, this factor weighs in favor of placing Rachel in a regular class.[8]

---

8. Rachel is currently in second grade. The District asserts that Rachel should be placed in fourth grade next year so she can model age appropriate behavior. However, Dr. Sailor testified that although Rachel should be educated with children near her age, it is not necessary that there be an exact match. Rachel is no more than two years older than the children with whom she is now placed. This age difference is not so pronounced that she is learning inappropriate behavior, or is not perceived as part of the class.

C. Effect on the Teacher and Other Children.

The third factor—effect on others in the class—has two aspects. The first is whether there is detriment to the other students because the handicapped child is disruptive, distracting, or unruly. There has been no evidence presented to this court that Rachel is a discipline problem at school or distracts other children. The witnesses, including the District's, were in agreement that Rachel is an agreeable child who follows directions and is well-behaved. When Rachel works separately with her aide, it is not a distraction for the other children. The second consideration is whether the handicapped child would take up so much of the teacher's time that the other students would suffer from lack of attention. The most germane evidence on this point comes from Rachel's second grade teacher, who testified that she does not find that Rachel's presence interferes with her ability to teach the other children. Rachel's teacher testified that she was initially apprehensive about her ability to teach Rachel and the rest of the class. Now that she has had experience with Rachel, she finds that Rachel's assignment to her class is not burdensome.

Because there is no evidence of detriment to other children in Rachel's regular education classroom, this factor also weighs in favor of placing Rachel in a regular education program.

D. Cost

The question of how much it would cost to place Rachel in a regular education class with the necessary support services was vigorously contested by the District on one hand and by the California Department of Education and the Hollands on the other. According to the District witnesses, the placement that the Hollands are requesting for Rachel would cost $109,000 per year. This cost estimate is based on a full-time aide for Rachel, and also attributes to Rachel alone the cost of school-wide training programs that would benefit other students.

The District has painted an exaggerated, hyperbolic picture of what it would cost to educate Rachel in a regular classroom with appropriate support services. For example, the District claims that it would cost over $80,000 to provide school-wide sensitivity training. Yet the District does not establish that such training is necessary. And even if it is, the California Department of Education provided evidence that such training may be had for free. Nor is it appropriate to assign the total cost to Rachel when other handicapped children will benefit. Similarly, the evidence does not suggest that Rachel requires a full-time aide.[9]

---

9. The District asserts that the Hearing Officer's proposed placement in a regular second grade class with a part-time aide violates California law requiring that handicapped children receive instruction on their IEP goals from specially credentialed teachers. This argument misconceives California's credentialing requirements. Although Rachel's educational program must be supervised by an appropriately credentialed professional, there is no requirement that she learn academic subjects only from a special education credentialed teacher. Furthermore, even if California did require that handicapped children be taught only by specially credentialed teachers, it would conflict with the IDEA's mainstreaming requirement favoring education by regular

In reality the cost comparison is between placing Rachel in a special class with a full-time special education teacher and two full-time aides, with approximately 11 other children, with placing her in a regular class with a part-time aide. The District has provided no evidence of this cost comparison, presumably because the difference is modest. To the extent that the special class has fewer than 12 children, and that the cost of a special education teacher exceeds that of an aide, the difference in cost will be reduced. Moreover, the California Department of Education provides free in-service training programs to assist schools that wish to fully integrate handicapped students.

The District also argues that it will lose significant funding from the state if Rachel does not spend at least 51% of her time in special education classes. Ordinarily, state funding is allocated according to a formula that is based in part on how much time a child spends in a special education class. If Rachel were moved out of special education class, the District claims it would lose funding equivalent to one teacher and three aides. However, the California Department of Education witness testified that waivers are available from the state if a school district seeks to adopt a program that does not fit neatly with funding guidelines. If a school district receives a waiver, it will not lose any funding because it places handicapped students in regular classes. The District has not applied for such a waiver. According to the California Department of Education's evidence, the District will incur little additional cost by providing full-time placement in regular education classes among the continuum of options offered to handicapped children.

Furthermore, the IDEA provides funding for the specific purpose of educating handicapped children, and envisions that those monies will be used in part to provide the supplemental aids and services that make mainstreaming possible. The funding provisions suggest that the IDEA foresees some possible increased costs due to mainstreaming. Those increased costs are permissible so long as they are not of a magnitude that will affect other programs or other handicapped children

In short, the court concludes that the cost of placing Rachel full-time in a regular class, as opposed to placing her in a special class for handicapped children, is modest if there is any additional cost at all. By inflating the costs, and failing to address the true comparison, the District does not meet its burden of proving that regular placement would burden the District funds or adversely affect services available to other children. Because the District has offered no persuasive or credible evidence in support of its claim that educating Rachel in a regular education classroom with appropriate services would be significantly more expensive than educating her in the District's proposed setting, this factor does not weigh against mainstreaming Rachel.

teachers. Where federal law conflicts with state law, federal law prevails.

Furthermore, Cal.Educ.Code § 56101 provides that a school district can request a waiver of any provision of the Education Code necessary to implement a student's IEP. The District could apply for a waiver of the credentialing requirement, if there were one, in order to educate Rachel in a regular class.

V

For the reasons discussed, the court finds that the appropriate placement for Rachel Holland, under the Individuals with Disabilities Education Act, is in a regular second grade classroom, with some supplemental services, as a full-time member of that class.

Children change, the educational demands on them change, and Rachel may change.[10] If Rachel does not flourish under this placement in the future, then adjustments should be made. The IDEA foresees such adjustments at the annual IEP review. But the weight of the evidence suggest that this is the appropriate placement now for Rachel Holland.

The decision of the hearing officer is affirmed.

IT IS SO ORDERED.

Questions and Comments

1. *The definition of "mainstreaming".* Mainstreaming can be a relative term. Practically speaking, there are a variety of possible placements for children with disabilities: state institutions; county "center" schools which are full segregated; self-contained, segregated classrooms at certain regular schools; self-contained classrooms in the child's neighborhood school; a split between the latter and regular classrooms (with certain classes like art and music taking place in the latter); and regular classrooms. Some courts reserve the term "mainstreaming" only for the final option. See, e.g., *Thomas v. Cincinnati Bd. of Educ.*, 918 F.2d 618, 627 (6th Cir.1990). Most, however, consider any movement from the beginning of the list toward the end as a move toward "mainstreaming"; further, the regulations under the IDEA require states to provide a continuum of placement options. See 34 C.F.R. § 300.551.

2. *Determining when mainstreaming should occur.* The courts have developed several methods of operationalizing the mainstreaming inquiry. Compare *Roncker v. Walter*, 700 F.2d 1058 (6th Cir.1983) to *Daniel R.R. v. State Bd. of Educ.*, 874 F.2d 1036 (5th Cir.1989). See generally, Stacey Gordon, "Making Sense of the Inclusion Debate Under IDEA," 2006 B.Y.U. Educ. L.J. 189. The four-factor test developed in *Holland*, which was affirmed and adopted by the Ninth Circuit in *Sacramento City Unified School Dist. v. Rachel H.*, 14 F.3d 1398 (9th Cir.1994), purports to combine the factors found in the other tests. Because the *Holland* test represents a composite of the thinking of several circuits, it will be used as an organizing framework for these notes, beginning with the "educational benefit" factor.

3. *Educational benefit.* How do you evaluate the educational (as opposed to non-academic) benefits of Rachel's mainstream placement? Assume that, although both placements would meet *Rowley's* some benefit test, the school district is correct in its argument that Rachel would do better

---

10. See [Lou] Brown, *How Much Time Should Students with Severe Intellectual Disabilities Spend in Regular Education Classrooms and Elsewhere?*, TASH, 1991 Vol. 16, No. 1, at 46 ("How much time should be spent in regular classes? Enough to ensure that the student is a member, not a visitor. A lot, if the student is engaged in meaningful activities. Quite a lot if she is young, but less as she approaches 21. There is still a lot we do not know.").

academically in a special education class where one-on-one and small group instruction is more likely to occur than in a regular school placement. Does this fact matter, in light of the preference for mainstreaming in the IDEA? See note 8 in *Holland*.

Consider in this regard the fact that, in many cases involving the mainstreaming issue, the role of the parties is reversed. School districts prefer mainstreaming as a cost-saving measure, while parents often want segregated placement on the ground that it will provide superior services. For instance, *Kerkam v. McKenzie*, 862 F.2d 884, 889 (D.C.Cir.1988), the parents of a child with severe mental disability wanted to place him in a residential facility in a different state, while the school district determined that a day placement at a local school would be appropriate. While admitting that there was "little doubt" that the child would make "less progress" in the school district's program, the D.C. Circuit stated that "*Rowley* precludes our taking that factor into account so long as the public-school alternative confers some educational benefit." In *Swift II v. Rapides Parish Public School System*, 812 F.Supp. 666 (W.D.La.1993), the parents of a child with several behavioral disorders who had been hospitalized on at three occasions for altercations at school were denied a nearby residential placement on the ground that the school's program could still provide some benefit. On similar facts the court in *Hall v. Shawnee Mission School Dist.*, 856 F.Supp. 1521 (D.Kan.1994), concluded that "such a [residential] placement is not mandated by IDEA, and in fact may have been more than the district could legally choose in light of IDEA's mainstreaming goal." In all of these cases, the school's option consisted of placement in a segregated classroom. Is this placement really "less restrictive" than a residential placement?

4. *Non-academic benefit.* In *Daniel R.R.*, supra, the court stated that "[a]cademic achievement is not the only purpose of mainstreaming. Integrating a handicapped child into a nonhandicapped environment may be beneficial in and of itself." 874 F.2d at 1049. *Holland* alludes to several specific "non-academic benefits" that might come from mainstreaming, in particular increased self-confidence and other psychosocial skills that develop from interaction with those who do not have disability. Other such benefits might be closer proximity to family (compared to placement in a residential facility) and facilitation of the child's transition to his or her community once school ends. All of these potential benefits could be grouped under the rubric of "group integration." In this regard, consider the following excerpt:

> The rationale behind group integration is as follows: only if the mentally disabled become familiar to and interact with the rest of society will they have any chance at successful assimilation into the community. Otherwise, "irrational prejudices," to use the Supreme Court's language in *Cleburne* [*v. City of Cleburne*, see pp. 1312–20], will persist and even those mentally disabled persons who are qualified will be discriminated against in subtle ways that can make it difficult for them to recover fully or function to the best of their ability.

> The mentally disabled have often been compared in this regard to minorities. The Supreme Court's decision in *Brown v. Board of Education* was based, not so much on proof that schools for blacks were inherently unequal in quality to schools for whites, but on the notion

that separate education of blacks would symbolize continued diminishment of their status and prevent them from being taken seriously as members of society. Analogously, so the argument goes, the mentally disabled should be educated and treated in the community with the rest of the populace, or prejudices against them will be perpetuated and their position in society will remain precarious.

Unfortunately, when the focus is mentally disabled persons who are committable or who require special educational services, it is easy to harbor doubts about the validity of the thesis that familiarity breeds acceptance. As Professor Minow has argued,[11] discrimination based on perceived differences usually does not depend upon the extent to which those who are different are physically integrated with the rest of the population. Just as segregation can stigmatize the mentally disabled by marking them as different, incautious integration can stigmatize the disabled by making painfully obvious their difficulties. The deaf child who needs an interpreter, the emotionally disturbed child who receives "counselling," and the mentally retarded child who attends special classes clearly become more conspicuous and very possible more alien to the rest of society when their needs are met by the public schools instead of a segregated institution. The number of instances in which communities have attempted to remove group homes from their midst suggests that outpatient treatment may produce the same result.

Ultimately, Minow suggests this "dilemma of difference" can be overcome through integration, but only if differences are treated as aspects of the community's identity rather than as evidence of inequality or lower status. For example, rather than singling out the deaf child who has been mainstreamed by providing her an interpreter or requiring her to attend special classes after regular hours, the entire class could be taught sign language. This approach, Minow asserts, would be effective in "making the hearing-impaired child's difference no longer signify stigma or isolation while still responding to that difference as an issue for the entire community." As another example, Minow suggests that all students, not just those who are handicapped, spend different days or portions of different days in different settings, with different mixes of children and teachers. As she states, "a real mix of special classes could modulate the implicit hierarchy of such extra classes, and diminish the implication that difference resides in the unusual student rather than in all the students."

The problem with Minow's approach is that, as she readily admits, it can be extremely hard to implement. If we do not create programs that treat the differences of the mentally disabled as one type of difference among many rather than as a special problem area, then we are left with the dilemma that Minow describes. Under such circumstances, the community-first notion may not be better than institutional programs at producing effective assimilation of the mentally disabled.[12] Separate but

---

11. Martha Minow, *Learning to Live with the Dilemma of Difference: Bilingual and Special Education*, 48 LAW & CONTEMP. PROBS. 257 (1985).

12. Most of the research indicates that unless integration of the type described by Minow takes place, mainstreaming is conceptually and practically problematic. Tay-

equal institutions may make more sense, assuming the institutions are indeed "equal" in quality.

Christopher Slobogin, "*Treatment of the Mentally Disabled: Rethinking the Community–First Idea*," 69 Neb. L. Rev. 413, 430–32 (1990).

How much weight should be given to the extent to which a placement provides an opportunity for interaction with non-handicapped children? In *School District of Kettle Moraine v. Grover*, 755 F.Supp. 243 (E.D.Wis. 1990) the parents wanted their 16 year-old child with Downs Syndrome to be placed in a segregated school for those with mental retardation rather than in a special education class. They asserted that most of the child's disabled friends from her previous school would be matriculating at the segregated school, that the integrated environment at the regular school might be hostile and insensitive to their daughter and thus interfere with her education, and that the Special Olympics program at the segregated school would be superior to what the integrated school would offer. They also noted that integration at the regular school would only occur in art, physical education, chorus, and marketing and that education at the regular school was more regimented that its segregated counterpart. The court denied their request, leaning heavily on the school district's experts, who testified that the child's "socialization needs could be met only at [the integrated school] because only that school would provide [her] with any opportunities to interact with age-appropriate non-handicapped peers," opportunities which were "essential for her social development." Id. at 247.

Is mainstreaming the only way to satisfy a particular child's socialization needs? If so, and if age-appropriateness is important, should a disabled child who has been mainstreamed in a regular classroom be automatically promoted through each grade so as to enable interaction with others of the same age? See, e.g., *Mavis v. Sobol*, 839 F.Supp. 968, 974 (N.D.N.Y. 1993)(child with moderate retardation advanced through sixth grade so as not to be "too far removed from her chronological peers").

If placement outside the regular school system is the only means of meeting the some benefit test, does the "non-academic benefit" of being close to one's original community and family dictate that placement be in one's own community? In *Todd D. v. Andrews*, 933 F.2d 1576 (11th Cir. 1991), the district court upheld a decision by the local school district's and the state to place the child in an out-of-state psychiatric facility, given the lack of such a facility in Georgia; the court opined that failing to do so would place on the state "the obligation to establish facilities in every community of Georgia in which a handicapped child preparing for discharge resides." Id. at 1581. The Eleventh Circuit reversed the district court's holding, which it

lor, *Caught in the Continuum: A Critical Analysis of the Principle of the Least Restrictive Environment*, 13 J.A. SEVERAL HANDICAPPED 41 (1988) (arguing that the least restrictive environment idea is outmoded and should be replaced by a policy of "integration", meaning the elimination of social, cultural, economic, and administrative barriers to community integration and encouragement of relationships between people with developmental disabilities and nondisabled people); *see also*, . . . J. GERHART & A. WEISHAHN, THE HANDICAPPED STUDENT IN THE REGULAR CLASSROOM 90 (2d ed. 1980) (if more than physical integration is not achieved, handicapped students may become "more severely and directly stigmatized, stereotyped and rejected" than if they had stayed in their segregated classrooms).

characterized as a conclusion that Todd D. "need not be placed in a facility in proximity to his home community." Id. at 1584. It pointed to federal regulations providing that in determining the least restrictive educational environment the agency is required to consider the proximity of the facility to the child's home. 34 C.F.R. § 300.552 (1989). It also noted that Todd D.'s IEP specifically called for "transition" into the Georgia community in the county in which he lived. Id. at 1582. Thus, the district court's holding "is clearly not in line with [the Act's] requirement that each handicapped child's IEP be crafted to meet that child's individual needs.... Todd must ... be placed at a facility close enough to his home community to allow implementation of his transition goals." Id. The Eleventh Circuit went on to hold that if the county did not have such facilities, the state was ultimately obligated under the statute to provide them. Id. at 1582–83.

Does *Todd D.* create a statutory right to force creation of community services for children covered by the IDEA? Compare this case to *Lelsz v. Kavanagh's* treatment of the argument that the Constitution requires creation of less restrictive alternatives for institutionalized persons (see pp. 1165–72) and to *Olmstead v. L.C.'s* treatment of a similar argument under the Americans with Disabilities Act (see pp. 1178–85).

5. *Effects on the class.* The district court in *Holland* found that neither Rachel's presence or the presence of an aide had a negative effect on the class. Given the fact that Rachel was not able to learn the same material as the rest of the class, at least as readily, isn't it inevitable that the teacher will spend more time with her, to the detriment of the other students? Or if the aide picks up the slack, isn't that in tension with the IDEA's requirement that instruction be by regular teachers (see note 11 of the opinion)?

In some cases involving assaultive behavior and the like, the disabled child is clearly disruptive and the school may seek to have the student suspended (temporarily) or expelled (permanently). Under Supreme Court case law construing the due process clause, the typical disruptive student may be suspended for ten days after being allowed to tell his or her side of the story; if expulsion is sought, more process, including counsel and an impartial hearing officer, is required, although the suspension may continue pending the proceeding. *Goss v. Lopez,* 419 U.S. 565, 95 S.Ct. 729, 42 L.Ed.2d 725 (1975). In *Kaelin v. Grubbs,* 682 F.2d 595 (6th Cir.1982), the court held that this procedure would be inadequate where disabled students are concerned. According to the court, "one of the principal features of the [Act] is the concept of individualized educational planning for handicapped children. This concept would be eviscerated if school officials could expel handicapped children using traditional expulsion procedures." Id. at 602. Thus, it held that any change in placement must take place through the IEP process, which is considerably more elaborate than the usual expulsion process. See, e.g., *Hemberger v. Labrae Bd. of Educ.,* No. 96–T–5567, 1997 WL 772939 (Ohio Ct. App., Dec. 5, 1997)(overturning summary judgement for school which, after two hearings, had expelled a 13 year-old disabled child found with a loaded pistol in his gym bag, because a due process hearing pursuant to the IDEA had not been held to determine whether child had attention-deficit hyperactivity disorder and was entitled to supplementary aids). In *Honig v. Doe,* 484 U.S. 305, 108 S.Ct. 592, 98 L.Ed.2d 686 (1988), the Supreme Court appeared to concur with the position adopted in *Kaelin* with respect to expulsions (although it held that suspensions did not require special process). The Court added that, in view of the IDEA's "stay put" provision, 20 U.S.C. § 1415(e)(3), which requires keeping the child in his or her current placement pending review of changes in placement, the typical practice of barring school access to suspended students pending the outcome of the expulsion proceeding was also inappropriate, unless the parents consent or the school can show that keeping the child in school "is substantially likely to result in injury either to himself or herself, or to others." Id. at 327.

The differential treatment between disabled and non-disabled children considered for expulsion occasioned the following comment, which may be generally applicable to administration of the IDEA:

> It is the unfortunate plight of the school administrator to be responsible for the administration of the special education paradigm when he is imbued with the norms and philosophies of another. By training and inclination, the administrator views rules as tautological, gaining their meaning from their mere existence and the need for order. To create multiple exceptions to these rules for handicapped students is to challenge the entire structure within which rules operate. He is forced to operate two systems within the same school: one based on rules and structure, the other on standards and flexibility. Faced with administrative schizophrenia, he may attempt to resolve the problem by asserting the norms of the dominant system over those of the subordinate system. When he does, he conflicts with the statute and litigation results.

Kevin Hill, "Legal Conflicts in Special Education: How Competing Paradigms in the Education for All Handicapped Children Act Create Litigation," 64 Det. C.L.Rev. 129, 153 (1986). Perhaps partly for this reason, in the 2004 amendments to the IDEA the scope of the stay-put provision was narrowed by giving the local education agency the authority to immediately remove a child who has inflicted "serious bodily injury" to an interim placement for not more than 45 days. 20 U.S.C. § 1415(k)(3)-(4).

6. *Costs.* The district court in *Holland* states that "only where the cost of placing a handicapped child in regular education will significantly affect other children in the district will this factor weigh against placement in a regular classroom." Is it fair to say that mainstreaming Rachel will not have a significant effect on the resources available to other children? Whatever the answer to this question, much of the foregoing material—dealing with the need to provide (and create?) residential treatments to the need for special hearings—suggests that the IDEA as a whole is a very expensive proposition. Thus, there is a real tension between the goals of the IDEA, which is based on the premise that expenditure of resources should be individualized, and the goals of the traditional school system, which generally allocate expenditures by category.

Professor Bartlett suggests that these competing concerns can be reconciled (albeit while still expending considerably more on children with disabilities than other children) through following the "program parity" concept in allocating resources:

> Program parity requires that educational needs be identified for every child and programs hypothesized to satisfy those needs. Resource avail-

ability would then determine what portion of a child's needs could be met, and schools would adjust programs so that each child would be afforded the same portion (or relative deprivation) as others. The purpose of this standard is to ensure that in allocating scarce resources, some students are not favored over others. More precisely, the standard ensures that decisionmakers do not disfavor members of certain targeted groups and make them absorb more than their fair share of the effects of resource scarcity.

The concept of program parity begins with the identification of 'first-rate' educational programs. A first-rate educational program is not one for which improvements cannot be imagined, but rather one that is reasonably comprehensive and which adopts the highest standards of practice among professionals in the field. There is reason to believe that such programs can be identified, at least in general categories. Theoretically, one could begin this process by defining an optimal program, and work down from there in parallel fashion for all educational programs. [The concept would then require that children with disabilities receive the same level of program within their hierarchy of programs that children without disabilities receive].

* * *

The program parity model ... mediates the tension between the need-based framework for determining educational services for the handicapped and the merit-based framework of public education. Program parity recognizes that there are differences in need and ability that will justify different treatment, but compels evenhanded consideration of the interests of both. Differences in ability between the handicapped and nonhandicapped justify neither a lower level of attention, because of the inability of the handicapped to demonstrate the same levels of "innate" ability, nor compensation for the handicapped so extensive as to eliminate as far as educationally possible the effects of that handicap without regard to resource limitations. Instead, it requires school districts to offer services based on need to the handicapped on a par with services to others whose positions in the system will still be based on merit. Merit thus retains its established place in the public education system without compromising the need-based rationale for allocating resources to the handicapped.

Katharine T. Bartlett, "The Role of Cost in Educational Decisionmaking for the Handicapped Child," 48(2) L. & Contemp. Probs. 7, 38–43 (1985). Is the program parity concept consistent with *Rowley*?

II. SOCIAL SECURITY DISABILITY BENEFITS

A number of public programs and many private insurance plans provide compensation to persons who become disabled. Eligibility for the benefits provided by these programs is likely to turn on a determination that a disabling physical or mental impairment exists. The determination process can be complex to administer, especially in cases of psychiatric disabilities. In these cases, the determination of disability will in large part rest on the evaluator's interpretations of sometimes subtle symptoms.

This section focuses on two disability benefits programs, Social Security Disability Insurance ("SSDI") and Supplemental Security Income ("SSI"). Both of these programs were created by the federal Social Security Act and are administered by the Social Security Administration ("SSA"). SSDI and SSI provide valuable financial benefits on their own terms. SSDI and SSI are also important because, as discussed further in Section IV of Chapter 1, they are respectively linked to Medicare and Medicaid eligibility.

Social Security Disability Insurance ("SSDI") is paid to disabled persons who have been employed and have therefore made tax payments to the Social Security system. Eligibility for SSDI (and the amount of the SSDI payment) is therefore based on the claimant's work and earnings history. In contrast, the Supplement Security Income Program ("SSI") program is a benefit available to "aged, blind, and disabled individuals" whose income and resources fall below a certain level. Eligibility is based not on work history but on present level of financial need. The procedures and criteria used to determine whether an individual is disabled are the same under both SSI and SSDI. For a comprehensive discussion of the SSI and SSDI programs, see Matthew Diller, "Entitlement and Exclusion: The Role of Disability in the Social Welfare System," 44 UCLA L. Rev. 361 (1996).

While the discussion in this section addresses the specific application of SSI and SSDI, many of these same issues will be encountered in the administration of any program that awards benefits to those whose disability is grounded on a psychiatric impairment. The case that follows illustrates some of the complex problems, evidentiary and otherwise, involved in making mental disability determinations.

A. PROBLEMS IN THE DETERMINATION OF DISABILITY

CHRISTENSEN v. BOWEN

United States District Court, Northern District of California, 1986.
633 F.Supp. 1214.

ORDER

CONTI, DISTRICT JUDGE.

Plaintiff brings this action pursuant to section 205(g) of the Social Security Act ("Act"), 42 U.S.C. section 405(g), to obtain judicial review of a "final decision" of the Secretary of Health and Human Services ("Secretary"), denying his claim for disability insurance benefits ("DIB").

In order to be affirmed on appeal, the Secretary's findings must be supported by substantial evidence and the Secretary must have applied the proper legal standards in denying plaintiff's claims. If the Secretary's findings are not supported by substantial evidence *or* are based upon a legal error, the Secretary's denial of benefits must be set aside. Substantial evidence is defined as "such relevant evidence as a reasonable mind might accept as adequate to support a conclusion," and it must be based on the record as a whole.

An individual is disabled under the Act if he is unable to,

"engage in any substantial gainful activity by reason of any medically determinable physical or mental impairment which can be expected to result in death or which has lasted or can be expected to last for a continuous period of not less than twelve months."

42 U.S.C. section 423(d)(1)(A). The impairment must be "of such severity that the claimant is not only unable to do his previous work but cannot, considering his age, education, and work experience, engage in any other kind of substantial gainful work which exists in the national economy." 42 U.S.C. section 423(d)(2)(A). The claimant has the initial burden of establishing that he is unable to do his previous work, but once the claimant has made such a showing the burden shifts to the Secretary to come forward with specific findings showing that there is other substantial gainful activity that the claimant can perform. *Bonilla v. Secretary of HEW,* 671 F.2d 1245, 1246 (9th Cir.1982); *Hall v. Secretary of HEW,* 602 F.2d 1372, 1375 (9th Cir.1979). Under the "medical-vocational guidelines" ("grids") promulgated by the Secretary, *see* Appendix 2 of Subpart P, 20 C.F.R. section 404.1501 *et seq.,* a claimant will be found capable of "other substantial gainful employment" if he meets certain age, educational, skill and exertional requirements.

While the medical-vocational guidelines provide some evidence of a claimant's ability to engage in substantial gainful work, however, it is well established that they are not of themselves sufficient to meet the Secretary's burden of proving nondisability. In *Lightfoot v. Mathews,* for example, this court held that a disability claimant's capacity to work "must be assessed in terms of age, education, work experience and impairments," and that "[t]his requires a finding of capacity to work which is expressed in specific kinds of jobs ... not simply in terms of catch-all categories." 430 F.Supp. 620, 621 (N.D.Cal.1977). Similarly, in *Hall v. Secretary of HEW,* the Ninth Circuit Court of Appeals stated that the Secretary must "come forward with specific findings showing that the claimant has the physical and mental capacity to perform specified jobs," and that "the better method to demonstrate this is through the testimony of a vocational expert," although such testimony "would not be required when the availability of work is established by other reliable evidence." 602 F.2d 1372, 1377 (9th Cir.1979). * * *

I. Background.

Plaintiff in this case filed an application for DIB on November 17, 1983, alleging inability to work since May 6, 1983. The application was denied initially and on reconsideration by the Social Security Administration ("SSA"). Accordingly, plaintiff filed for a hearing before an administrative law judge ("ALJ") pursuant to 42 U.S.C. § 405(b). On March 7, 1985, the ALJ determined that plaintiff retained the residual functional capacity to perform work that did not involve high levels of stress, and therefore was not disabled. The Appeals Council affirmed the ALJ's findings on April 23, 1985, whereupon plaintiff filed the present action with this court.

Plaintiff is a 56–year old male who has a Bachelor's degree from Sacramento State College. His work history consists of 36 years of uninterrupted employment with Sears Roebuck Company as an operating superintendent and operating manager. When he last worked, he was responsible for the hiring, firing and discipline of 380 employees, in addition to the implementation of budgetary guidelines from Sears headquarters in Chicago. He worked a minimum of 10 hours per day and sometimes worked as many as 12 to 16 hours per day.

Plaintiff's alleged disability began in May 1983. At that time he consulted Dr. Thomas Ball for symptoms of significant work-induced stress, including severe depression, crying spells, suicidal tendencies, chronic fatigue, loss of appetite and a decreased sexual drive. Pursuant to the recommendations of Dr. Ball and plaintiff's work supervisor, plaintiff took a leave of absence from his job for a five-week period. Plaintiff returned to work on July 5, 1983. He continued to experience serious mental problems, including illegible handwriting, speaking with hesitation, difficulty in composing his thoughts, and a fear of leaving his office. Consequently, plaintiff again left work at Sears on August 7, 1983, and has not worked since.

Dr. Ball continued to treat plaintiff throughout 1983 and 1984. Dr. Ball prescribed Adapin, Xanax, and Halcion. In a report dated June 25, 1984, Dr. Ball indicated that plaintiff's "domestic activities" were unaffected by his mental condition, with the exception of sleeping difficulties, and that plaintiff's capacity to cope with the pressures of ordinary work seemed to be average. He noted, however, that plaintiff had no inclination to return to the stressful circumstances of his previous managerial position, but felt himself more capable of functioning in a work situation that was primarily physical. In a subsequent report dated September 11, 1984, Dr. Ball prescribed plaintiff's psychiatric symptoms as few, mild, and "not incapacitating."

In a consultative psychiatric evaluation dated August 14, 1984, Kathryn H. Knutsson, M.D. gave the following impression:

> This patient could benefit from appropriate anti-depressant medication and talking type of psychotherapy. He is bottled up within himself; is very self-critical. If he is able to learn new skills he would be able to work on for many years. When I saw him on 12/20/83 he was obviously not ready to return to work.

In a report dated September 17, 1984, Robert C. Burr, M.D., stated:

> He seems to have many of the anal-compulsive character traits often seen in people who are predisposed to depression. At present he

seems to be able to function adequately as long as he is placed in a sheltered environment in which very little is actually required of him. The idea of returning to the competitive work world seems to produce instant anxiety.

Mr. Christensen is obviously doing better than he did when he was still working at Sears in the summer of 1983. He does not appear to have recovered to the point where he could return to work.

Tr. at 189 (emphasis added). Donald L. Tasto, Ph.D., also conducted a consultative psychological evaluation of Mr. Christensen. In his report dated January 10, 1985, Dr. Tasto stated:

I think that, *because of his memory problems, concentration difficulties and fatigability, Mr. Christensen is presently unable to hold a job with much responsibility or one that requires much stamina, ability to recall, or intense concentration.* I think it is an unanswered question at this point as to whether he will be able to handle something more demanding in the future. It is quite possible his symptoms will change as he changes his use of medication. *This issue aside, I do not think that Mr. Christensen will ever be able to return to a job with a high degree of stress like he had when working for Sears.* Whether or not his intellectual capabilities return as a result of changing medication usage, I think *his capability to deal with stress has been permanently reduced and he, therefore, must be precluded from any job where stress is more than moderate and periodic.*

(emphasis added). The most recent assessment of residual functional capacity was rendered by Bradley M. Greenblott, M.D. In his report dated February 8, 1985, Dr. Greenblott concluded:

At the present time, Mr. Christensen is clearly totally temporarily disabled from a psychiatric standpoint. *He is unable to tolerate even minimal stress, and can in no way handle competitive employment.* I do not believe that he is capable of re-training programs at the present time. The extent of his depression does not allow for this.

Tr. at 224 (emphasis added).

In rejecting the above findings and conclusions regarding plaintiff's residual functional capacity, the ALJ stated that plaintiff's disability claim was not supported by "... the reported clinical findings and laboratory test results." Tr. at 16. Specifically, the ALJ found that the conclusions of Drs. Knutsson and Burr regarding plaintiff's inability to return to his previous work were unsupported by clinical findings which indicated, *inter alia*, that plaintiff's memory was intact, that his intelligence was average, that he exhibited no psychotic symptoms, that he was able to engage in certain leisure activities, and that there were some indications of improvement in his overall mental condition. The ALJ cited no clinical findings, however (and the record reveals none), which indicated that plaintiff was able to engage in any forms of employment which involved even minimal amounts of stress. Rather, the ALJ merely noted that Dr. Burr's report "... *does not rule out* other, less stressful forms of substantial gainful activity." Tr. at 17 (emphasis added). The ALJ did not address the findings of Drs. Tasto and Greenblott, and made no findings whatsoever regarding plaintiff's ability to engage in other types of work based on plaintiff's age, education, prior work experience and residual functional capacity.

* * *

Plaintiff's motion for summary judgment is three-pronged. First, he argues that inasmuch as the ALJ's decision gave little or no weight to the specific clinical findings of Drs. Knutsson, Burr, Tasto, and Greenblott, quoted above, his determination of non-disability was not supported by substantial evidence. Second, plaintiff contends that the ALJ committed legal error by failing to follow the Secretary's own policy promulgations regarding the evaluation of chronic mental impairments. Finally, plaintiff argues that since the ALJ himself conceded that plaintiff could not return to his former employment, the Secretary bears the burden of proof regarding what specific jobs plaintiff can perform. Plaintiff contends that the Secretary has not met that burden. For the reasons set forth below, the court agrees with plaintiff.

As noted above, substantial evidence means that a finding is supported by "more than a mere scintilla. It means such relevant evidence as a reasonable mind might accept as adequate to support a conclusion."

* * *

Applying these principles to the present case, the court concludes that Dr. Ball's findings to the effect that plaintiff's impairments were "not incapacitating" when considered together with the findings of the four remaining doctors who examined plaintiff and emphatically concluded to the contrary, does not constitute substantial evidence sufficient to support a finding of nondisability.

Plaintiff's second argument is that the ALJ erred both in giving improper weight to the findings of Drs. Knutsson, Burr, Tasto and Greenblott, and in failing to follow the Secretary's own policy promulgations regarding the evaluation of chronic mental impairments.

In support of this argument, plaintiff notes that the ALJ evidently rejected the findings of the aforementioned doctors on the ground that they were not supported by "... the reported clinical findings and laboratory test results." Plaintiff correctly points out that objective demonstrability is not the correct standard to be applied in evaluating evidence of mental disorders. As the court stated in *Lebus v. Harris,*

> Courts have recognized that a psychiatric impairment is not as readily amenable to substantiation by objective laboratory testing as is a medical impairment and that consequently, the diagnostic techniques employed in the field of psychiatry may be somewhat less tangible than those in the field of medicine. In general, mental disorders cannot be ascertained and verified as are most physical

illnesses, for the mind cannot be probed by mechanical devices in order to obtain objective clinical manifestations of mental illness. A strict reading of the statutory requirement that an impairment be 'demonstrable by medically acceptable clinical and laboratory diagnostic techniques,' 42 U.S.C. §§ 423(d)(3), 1382c(a)(3)(C), is inappropriate in the context of mental illness. Rather, when mental illness is the basis of a disability claim, clinical and laboratory data may consist of the diagnoses and observations of professionals trained in the field of psychopathology. The report of a psychiatrist should not be rejected simply because of the relative imprecision of the psychiatric methodology or the absence of substantial documentation, unless there are other reasons to question the diagnostic technique.

526 F.Supp. 56, 60 (N.D.Cal.1981) (extensive citations omitted).

Were the findings of Drs. Knutsson, Burr, Tasto, and Greenblott properly considered under the *Lebus* standard, plaintiff argues, the ALJ would have found plaintiff's impairments to be of listed severity under either the original or the revised criteria. Assuming, *arguendo,* that plaintiff's impairments were not of listed severity, however, plaintiff contends that the ALJ failed to follow the Secretary's own policy promulgations regarding evaluation of mental impairments which are of less than listed severity. The court agrees with plaintiff.

Social Security Ruling 85–16 ("SSR 85–16"), which became effective on April 1, 1985, some three weeks prior to the Appeals Council's final decision in this case, states in pertinent part as follows:

> For impairments of listing severity, inability to perform substantial gainful activity (SGA) is presumed from prescribed findings. However, with mental impairments of lesser severity, such inability must be demonstrated through a detailed assessment of the individual's capacity to perform and sustain mental activities which are critical to work performance. *Conclusions of ability to engage in SGA are not to be inferred from the fact that the mental disorder is not of listing severity.*

* * *

> Reports from psychiatrists and other physicians, psychologists, and other professionals working in the field of mental health should contain the individual's medical history, mental status evaluation, psychological testing, diagnosis, treatment prescribed and response, prognosis, a description of the individual's daily activities, and a medical assessment describing ability to do work-related activities. These *reports may also contain other observations and opinions or conclusions on such matters as the individual's ability to cope with stress, the ability to relate to other people, and the ability to function in a group or work situation.*

> *Medical documentation can often give clues as to functional limitation. For example, evidence that an individual is markedly*

withdrawn or seclusive suggests a greatly reduced capacity for close contact and interaction with other people. The conclusion of reduced RFC in this area can then be applied to all steps of vocational assessment. For example, when the vocational assessment establishes that the claimant's past work has been limited to work requiring close contact and interaction with other people, the preceding assessment would indicate that the claimant would be unable to fulfill the requirements of his or her past work. Therefore, the determination of disability in this instance would depend on the individual's capacity for other work.

SSR 85–16 (C.E.1985) (emphasis added).

Upon a review of the record, the court finds that had the evidence of plaintiff's inability to cope with even minimal stress much less competitive employment been evaluated in accordance with the factors listed in SSR 85–16, a finding of inability to engage in past relevant work would have been mandated. Since the ALJ erroneously failed to apply these factors to the evidence before him, his decision must also be set aside on this ground.

Finally, plaintiff argues that when he met his initial burden of establishing his inability to do his previous work as a retail supervisor, the burden shifted to the Secretary to show that he was capable of other types of work, and that the Secretary did not meet this burden. Here again, the court agrees with plaintiff.

In his memorandum of decision, the ALJ found that,

> [w]hile the claimant's depressive symptoms might be exacerbated by a return to the level of responsibilities and pressures involved in his most recent work for Sears, he could perform other supervisory, managerial, or even lower level work without the unusually high level of stresses and pressures described in his past work.

Such a generalized finding, however, does not satisfy the requirement, under the law of this Circuit, that the Secretary make specific findings showing that there is other substantial gainful activity that the claimant can perform. As the Ninth Circuit stated in *Hall v. Secretary of Health, Education & Welfare,*

> [a] general statement that a claimant may engage in "sedentary" work, without testimony by a vocational expert who can identify specific jobs, absent other reliable evidence of the claimant's ability to engage in other occupations, does not satisfy the substantial evidence test.
>
> It is incumbent on the Secretary *at a minimum,* to come forward with specific findings showing that the claimant has the physical *and mental* capacity to perform *specified* jobs, taking into consideration the requirements of the job as well as the claimant's age, education and background.

602 F.2d 1372, 1377 (9th Cir.1979) (emphasis added).

* * *

Since the Secretary has failed to meet this burden, and has not given any reasons for its failure, the court finds that reversal is warranted on this ground as well.

III. Conclusion.

In accordance with the foregoing, * * * plaintiff's motion for summary judgment is granted.

Questions and Comments

1. *Individualized determinations vs. administrative efficiency.* As suggested by the principal case, the procedure for determining whether a claimant is disabled is complex and individualized. In fact, although the *Christensen* court does not specifically address each step, Social Security Act regulations specify a five-step procedure to be followed for each SSDI or SSI claimant. The claimant bears the burden of proof with respect to the first four steps. The agency bears the burden of proof on the fifth step. In *Christensen*, the court held that the agency had not met its burden of proof on the fifth step.

Under the five-step procedure, the Social Security Administration ("SSA") must first determine whether the claimant is engaged in a "substantial gainful activity." If he is, benefits are denied. If he is not engaged in such an activity, the process then moves to the second step, which decides whether the claimant's condition is "severe"—in other words, one that significantly limits his physical or mental ability to do basic work activities. If the impairment is not severe, benefits are denied. If the impairment is severe, the third step determines whether the claimant's impairments meet or equal certain specific impairments acknowledged by the SSA to be of sufficient severity to preclude any gainful employment. If the claimant's condition meets or equals these "Listed Impairments," he is conclusively presumed to be disabled and entitled to benefits. (Note that the medical criteria defining the Listed Impairments are set higher than the statutory standard; a claimant suffering from a Listed Impairment is incapable of performing *any* gainful activity, not just "substantial gainful activity." The reason for this is that the Listed Impairments are supposed to operate as a conclusive presumption of disability, obviating the need for any individualized inquiry.) If the claimant's impairment is not listed, the process moves to the fourth step, which is an individualized assessment of the claimant's "residual functional capacity" (RFC). If the claimant's RFC permits him to perform his prior work, benefits are denied. If the claimant is not capable of performing his prior work, the inquiry moves to the fifth step, where a decision is made as to whether the claimant, in light of his RFC, age, education, and work experience, has the capacity to perform other work in the national economy. See generally 20 CFR §§ 404.1520, 416.920. If he does not, then benefits are granted.

Courts have rejected attempts by the SSA to circumvent this individualized, multi-step process. In *City of New York v. Heckler*, 742 F.2d 729 (2d

Cir.1984), aff'd *Bowen v. City of New York*, 476 U.S. 467, 106 S.Ct. 2022, 90 L.Ed.2d 462 (1986), the Second Circuit rejected an informal SSA policy which presumed that those whose mental impairments were not as severe as the Listed Impairments retained an RFC sufficient to perform at least unskilled work. The practical effect of the presumption had been to end the five-step process for most claimants at step three.

Admittedly, however, the balance has not always been struck in favor of individualization. In *Bowen v. Yuckert*, 482 U.S. 137, 107 S.Ct. 2287, 96 L.Ed.2d 119 (1987), the claimant challenged step two of the five-step review procedure, arguing that, under the language of the Social Security Act, a determination of severity could not be made without consideration of the claimant's age, education, or work experience. The Court upheld the challenged regulation, noting that it increased "the efficiency and reliability of the evaluation process by identifying at an early stage those claimants whose medical impairments are so slight that it is unlikely they would be found to be disabled even if their age, education, and experience were taken into account." Section B, *infra*, discusses questions of individualization in the context of childrens' eligibility for SSI.

2. *The "objective medical evidence" requirement.* The language in the Social Security Act governing evidence of disability reads as follows:

"Section 423(d)

* * *

(3) For purposes of this subsection, a "physical or mental impairment" is an impairment that results from anatomical, physiological, or psychological abnormalities which are demonstrable by medically acceptable clinical and laboratory diagnostic techniques.

* * *

(5)(A) An individual shall not be considered to be under a disability unless he furnishes such medical and other evidence of the existence thereof as the Secretary may require. An individual's statement as to pain or other symptoms shall not alone be conclusive evidence of disability as defined in this section; there must be medical signs and findings, established by medically acceptable clinical or laboratory diagnostic techniques, which show the existence of a medical impairment that results from anatomical, physiological, or psychological abnormalities which could reasonably be expected to produce the pain or other symptoms alleged and which, when considered with all evidence required to be furnished under this paragraph (including statements of the individual or his physician as to the intensity and persistence of such pain or other symptoms which may reasonably be accepted as consistent with the medical signs and findings), would lead to a conclusion that the individual is under a disability. Objective medical evidence of pain or other symptoms established by medically acceptable clinical or laboratory techniques (for example, deteriorating nerve or muscle tissue) must be considered in reaching a conclusion as to whether the individual is under a disability . . . ."

In the case of psychiatric disorders, the questions that arise are: What constitutes "medically acceptable clinical or laboratory diagnostic techniques"? What is the meaning of the phrase "[o]bjective medical evidence of pain and other symptoms . . . must be considered in reaching a conclusion as to whether the individual is under a disability"? It is noteworthy that the court in *Christensen* did not attempt to wrestle with the meaning of this language. Had the issue been confronted, how might or should the court have construed the phrase "objective medical evidence?"

Lebus v. Harris, quoted by the court in the principal case, was decided prior to a 1984 amendment to Section 423(d)(5)(A). At the time *Lebus* was decided the operative provisions of the Act read as follows:

"Section 423(d)

* * *

(3) For purposes of this subsection, a "physical or mental impairment" is an impairment that results from anatomical, physiological, or psychological abnormalities which are demonstrable by medically acceptable clinical and laboratory diagnostic techniques.

* * *

(5)(A) An individual shall not be considered to be under a disability unless he furnishes such medical and other evidence of the existence thereof as the Secretary may require."

Did the language added by the 1984 amendment serve at all to clarify the meaning of these provisions? Did the courts in *Lebus* and *Christensen* essentially read these evidentiary provisions out of the Act?

3. *Special problems confronting the claimant with mental disability.* The Social Security Act and its implementing regulations place the burden of making a *prima facie* showing of disability on the claimant. This burden may be particularly difficult for those whose disability is grounded upon a psychiatric disorder. However, some courts have shown an inclination not to distinguish the conditions of those with *mental* handicaps from those of the *physically* handicapped. For instance, in *Tusson v. Bowen,* 675 F.Supp. 1032 (E.D.La.1987), aff'd 847 F.2d 284 (5th Cir.1988), the issue concerned a limitation on the award of *retroactive* benefits to a claimant who had failed, because of a mental disability, to file an earlier claim. The claimant in *Tusson* filed for disability benefits in 1982. Following an initial denial, the Administrative Law Judge to whom the matter had been appealed found Tusson to have been disabled since 1977, or 5 years before his initial application for benefits. In challenging the statutory 12 month limitation on the award of retroactive benefits, the claimant argued that:

"A person suffering from severe mental problems, which prevent him from making applications, should be given the opportunity of having his benefits begin at the same time that the disability began so that he is given equal protection under law as provided others, who although disabled but not to the point that they are unable to file, are capable of making an application with the administration."

In reviewing the claimant's contention that the application of the statutory limitations on the award of retroactive benefits violated his constitutional rights, the court held:

> "Even assuming that Tusson's interest in retroactive benefits is cognizable under the Due Process Clause, the twelve-month limitation does not violate due process principles. The loss of retroactive benefits by an individual whose mental impairment prevents a timely application suggests unfairness, but a considered analysis reveals otherwise.

> The issue of whether the twelve-month limit on retroactive benefits applies where the failure to file for benefits arises from mental impairment was recently addressed in *Yeiter v. Secretary of Health & Human Services,* 818 F.2d 8 (6th Cir.1987), *cert. denied,* 484 U.S. 854, 108 S.Ct. 160, 98 L.Ed.2d 115. In *Yeiter,* the court found that 42 U.S.C. § 423(b) does not violate the Due Process Clause because some person acting in behalf of the mentally impaired person could have filed an application. An application for benefits can be filed not only by the claimant, but also by a guardian, a person responsible for the care of the claimant, or the manager or principle officer of an institution caring for the claimant. 20 C.F.R. § 404.612(c). The court assumed that "[a] person who is mentally incapacitated and totally unable to care for himself or herself will ordinarily be in the care of someone. That person responsible for the claimant's care will have a strong incentive to file for benefits." * * * Ordinarily, a mentally impaired person will have a caretaker of some kind but, of course, that will not always be true. Indeed, in the case at bar, Tusson was not in the care of a guardian or some other person. He was capable of taking care of most of his needs, but relied on family members for special needs.

* * *

> The fact that *some* mentally impaired persons cannot rely on others to file their application does not render the twelve-month limitation fundamentally unfair, arbitrary, or unreasonable.

> "Whether wisdom or unwisdom resides in the scheme of benefits set forth in Title II, it is not for us to say. The answer to such inquiries must come from Congress, not the courts. Our concern here, as often, is with power, not with wisdom." (Citation omitted). Particularly when we deal with a withholding of a noncontractual benefit under a social welfare program such as this, we must recognize that the Due Process Clause can be thought to interpose a bar only if the statute manifests a patently arbitrary classification, utterly lacking in rational justification. *Flemming v. Nestor,* 363 U.S. 603, 610–611, 80 S.Ct. 1367, 1373, 4 L.Ed.2d 1435 (1960). "Congress faces an unusually difficult task in providing for the distribution of benefits under the Social Security Act." *Bowen v. Owens,* 476 U.S. 340, 106 S.Ct. 1881, 1885, 90 L.Ed.2d 316 (1986). In 1958, Congress provided for retroactive payments for a twelve-month period "[t]o avoid penalizing disabled workers who do not timely file applications for disability benefits." S.Rep. No. 2388, 85th Cong., 2d Sess. 4, *reprinted in* 1958 U.S.Code Cong. & Admin.News 4218, 4221–22. Thus, Congress decided to give claimants a year's grace to become aware of and file for benefits. Congress' decision that the

grace period should terminate at twelve months is not so arbitrary or irrational as to violate due process.

With respect to Tusson's equal protection claim, a challenged statutory classification is presumed valid if it serves a rational means of furthering a legitimate legislative end. *Mathews v. De Castro,* 429 U.S. 181, 185, 97 S.Ct. 431, 434, 50 L.Ed.2d 389 (1976). The Court notes that the twelve-month limit applies evenhandedly to all claimants; mentally incompetent claimants are not treated differently from other claimants. The legislative purpose for not creating an exception for the mentally impaired is clear. Application of the twelve-month period to all claimants helps to preserve the fiscal integrity of the social security trust fund. Even if the volume of such claims as Tusson's were low enough to allay concerns for financial integrity, an ever-growing corpus of government funds would need to be set aside for late-filers to insure that ample funds would be available when claimed. The Court realizes that some mentally impaired people, who are entitled to disability benefits but who cannot file for themselves or rely on others to do so, may not receive benefits to which they would be entitled upon a timely filing. However, as the Supreme Court has recognized, legislation "does not offend the Constitution simply because [it] 'is not made with mathematical nicety or because in practice it results in some inequality.' " *Mathews,* 97 S.Ct. at 434.

Accordingly, this Court finds no violation of the Equal Protection Clause.

The district court's analysis suggests that, when the group which is impacted negatively is the mentally disabled, a minimally rational legislative scheme can withstand equal protection scrutiny. As discussed further in Chapter 12, Section V, the district court's analysis is in accord with recent Supreme Court pronouncements on the constitutional status of individuals with disabilities.

4. *The treating physician rule.* In the *Christensen* case, the plaintiff's treating physician was the only medical expert who thought that the plaintiff's symptoms were mild. In 1991, the Commissioner of Social Security adopted regulations approving and formalizing a rule under which administrative law judges are supposed to give more weight to opinions from treating sources than from other examinations, such as consultative examinations. 20 C.F.R. § 404.1527(d)(2). The regulations note that the treating physician is "most able to provide a detailed, longitudinal picture" of the medical impairment. Do you think the Christensen court gave sufficient weight to the opinion of the treating psychiatrist?

5. *Eligibility of substance abusers, alcoholics.* A 1996 amendment to the Social Security Act excludes from eligibility for disability benefits those for whom alcoholism or drug addiction is the major basis on which they could claim to be disabled. 42 U.S.C. § 423(D)(2)(C). As a consequence of the amendment, an estimated 200,000 individuals have lost cash and associated medical benefits. Approximately 50,000 individuals have lost SSI eligibility and approximately 150,000 individuals have lost SSDI eligibility. Although the SSA had estimated that most of those who lost eligibility would be able to reestablish their benefits on other bases, only about 34% of former

beneficiaries have been able to reestablish benefits. See Interim Report of Lewin Group, Policy Evaluation of Effect of Legislation Prohibiting the Payment of Disability Benefits to Individuals Whose Disability is Based on Drug Addiction or Alcoholism.

The legislative effort to preclude substance abusers from eligibility was influenced by reports that many drug or alcohol addicted recipients of disability payments used a substantial percentage of this money on drugs or alcohol. See, e.g., Andrew Shaner et al., "Disability Income, Cocaine Use, and Repeated Hospitalization Among Schizophrenic Cocaine Abusers: A Government–Sponsored Revolving Door?" 333 New Engl. J. Med 777 (1995). Although the Social Security Administration was required to ensure that drug addicted and alcoholic beneficiaries participated in treatment programs, these requirements were not enforced. See General Accounting Office, Social Security: Disability Benefits for Drug Addicts and Alcoholics are Out of Control (Feb. 1994) (GAO/T–HEHS–94–1010). Moreover, although payments were not made to the beneficiaries directly but rather to representative payees, many of these payees apparently enabled beneficiaries to purchase drugs and alcohol. See, e.g., Rising Costs of Social Security's Disability Programs: Hearing Before the Subcomm. on Social Security and Family Policy of the Committee on Finance of the Senate, 104th Cong. 2 (1995) (statement of Sen. Cohen); Exploring Means of Achieving Higher Rates of Treatment and Rehabilitation Among Alcoholics and Drug Addicts Receiving Federal Disability Benefits: Joint Hearing Before the Subcomms. on Social Security and Human Resources of the House Comm. on Ways and Means, 103d Cong. 3–4 (1994). Do you think eliminating payments to substance abusers was the appropriate response to these problems? Could systems have been set up to monitor the use of disability payments by substance abusers?

Notably, the Social Security Independence and Program Improvements Act, which was passed in 1994, did attempt a more limited response. The Act strengthened the representative payee and treatment requirements and also placed a 36–month time limit on payments. The 1994 Act was soon superseded, however.

5. *Disability determination review.* The SSA requires determinations of disability to be reviewed by the state agency every three years in order to determine whether recipients are eligible for continued payment of benefits. However, there are two exceptions to this requirement. First, where a disability has been found to be permanent, that determination may be reviewed "at such times as the Secretary determines to be appropriate." Second, the Secretary may waive the three-year review requirement for a particular state and instead require the state to review an "appropriate number" of cases. Determinations of the appropriate number of cases depend upon the state's backlog of pending reviews, projected number of new applications, and staffing levels. See 42 U.S.C. § 421(I). Significantly, the disability review is not a de novo determination of disability. Rather, Congress has specified that the Social Security Administration be prohibited from redetermining claims in the absence of an initial finding that the recipient's medical condition has improved. 42 U.S.C § 423(f).

6. *The impact of the ADA on disability benefits programs.* As discussed further in Chapter 12, Section II, the Americans with Disabilities Act of 1990

("ADA") seeks to integrate individuals with disabilities into the workforce. In fact, the ADA requires employers to provide disabled individuals with those "reasonable accommodations" that will enable such individuals to discharge the essential responsibilities of the jobs that they seek. Some commentators have suggested that the disability benefits programs, which tend to segregate individuals with disabilities from the workforce, are therefore at odds with the philosophy of the ADA. See, e.g., Matthew Diller, "Dissonant Disability Policies: The Tensions Between the Americans with Disabilities Act and Federal Disability Benefit Programs," 76 Tex. L. Rev. 1003 (1998); Edward D. Berkowitz, Implications for Income Maintenance Policy, in Implementing the Americans with Disabilities Act (Jane West ed., 1996), at 195. For further discussion of the relationship between disability benefits law and anti-discrimination law, pp. 1253–65.

Proposals for returning SSI and SSDI recipients to the workforce employ both the carrot and the stick. These proposal include everything from time limits on disability benefits to rehabilitation and counseling services for those who seek to return to work. Another important mechanism for returning disability recipients to work involves ensuring continuity of health insurance coverage. Concerns about losing Medicare or Medicaid coverage are very prominent among disabled individuals who want to work. See, e.g., National Council on Disability, Removing Barriers to Work: Action Proposals for the 105th Congress and Beyond 17 (1997).

The work incentive programs currently in place have had little success in returning SSI and SSDI recipients to the workforce. The incentives operate as follows. Under the SSDI program, benefits recipients can work for a trial period of up to nine months. The Social Security Administration will continue to pay benefits during this time and will also not view work (done)during this time as evidence of a lack of disability. See 20 C.F.R. § 404.1592(a). The SSI program includes a complicated scheme under which recipients can continue to qualify for "special" SSI benefits even when they have earnings above the threshold that would otherwise lead to termination from the program. See 20 C.F.R. § 416.260. For a detailed discussion of the work incentive programs, see James R. Sheldon, Jr. Work Incentives for Persons with Disabilities Under the Social Security and SSI programs, 28 Clearinghouse Rev. 236 (1994).

B. CHILDREN AND DISABILITY

The SSI program assists not only disabled low-income adults but also disabled low-income children. In the last decade, the procedures for evaluating children for SSI eligibility have undergone considerable change. This section describes and analyzes these changes.

Prior to 1990, the determination of SSI eligibility for children was made through a much-abbreviated version of the five-step process used for determining adult eligibility. (For a discussion of this five-step process, p. 1240). The procedure for determining the eligibility of children did not include the individualized determination represented by the fourth and fifth steps of the adult process. Rather the inquiry for children was terminated at the third step: a child qualified for benefits only if he was "not doing any substantial gainful activity" and his impairment matched or was medically equal to one of the specific "Listed Impairments."

In the 1990 case *Sullivan v. Zebley*, 493 U.S. 521, 110 S.Ct. 885, 107 L.Ed.2d 967 (1990), the Supreme Court struck down this procedure. The Court's analysis emphasized the statutory language that was in effect at the time. Under this language, a child was considered to be disabled if "if he suffer[ed] from any . . . impairment of comparable severity" to one that would render an adult "unable to engage in any substantial activity." *Id.* at 529 (citing 42 U.S.C. § 1382c(a)(3)(A) (1982 ed.)). The Court reasoned that because the method for determining child disability did not include any individualized inquiry similar to the inquiry for adults, it did not meet a statutory standard, in the Court's view, that required child claimants "to receive benefits whenever their impairments were of 'comparable severity' to ones that would qualify an adult for benefits under the individualized, functional analysis contemplated by the statute and provided to adults. . . ." *Id.* at 539. According to the Court, the difficulties caused by the lack of an individualized approach were exacerbated by the fact that the Listed Impairments identified by the Social Security Administration's regulations were set at a level of severity higher than that prescribed by the statute and also did not include a large number of childhood impairments. *Id.*

The Social Security Administration ("SSA") responded to the *Sullivan v. Zebley* decision by issuing a set of regulations that allowed for an "individualized functional assessment" ("IFA") of each child claimant's disability. Under these regulations, if the child was not engaged in any substantial gainful activity and also had a severe impairment, the decisionmaker had to determine whether the impairment met or equaled one of the "Listed Impairments." 20 C.F.R. § 416.924(e). If one of the Listed Impairments was met or equaled, the child was deemed disabled. *Id.* If none of the Listed Impairments was met or equaled, the evaluation would proceed to the final step. Under this step, an IFA would be made to determine whether the claimant had an impairment or impairments of comparable severity to those which would prevent any adult from engaging in substantial gainful activity. *See id.* § 416.924(f).

After the IFA requirement was put into place, the number of children who qualified as disabled increased substantially: while only 296,300 children received SSI disability payments in 1989, by 1993 the number had increased to 770,500. Moreover, among children who qualified through the new IFA provision, about 44% had a mental illness or serious emotional disorder. As of 1995, the children's SSI program served almost 1 million children with severe disabilities. Children with mental retardation were the single largest group, representing about 42% of all children enrolled. Another 25% of child SSI recipients had other mental disorders. The remaining 33% had physical disabilities.

The IFA provision generated much controversy. In particular, critics alleged that parents were coaching their children to fake mental disorders. These criticisms led to audits of the program by the SSA, the HHS

Office of the Inspector General, and the General Accounting Office. The investigators criticized various aspects of the children's SSI program, but they did not confirm allegations of widespread fraud.

Nonetheless, in 1996, as part of the Personal Responsibility and Work Opportunity Reconciliation Act, Pub.L.No. 104–193, 110 Stat. 2105, ("PRWORA"), Congress moved to eliminate IFAs by amending the underlying statutory standard for evaluating child disability. The new statutory standard for evaluating children's disability claims, found at 42 U.S.C. § 1382c(a)(3)(C), reads as follows:

> An individual under the age of 18 shall be considered disabled ... if that individual has a medically determinable physical or mental impairment, which results in marked and severe functional limitations, and which can be expected to result in death or which has lasted and can be expected to last for a continuous period of not less than 12 months.

The SSA's new regulations implement the statutory mandate by eliminating the IFA. The new regulations provide that if a child's impairments do not meet, medically equal, or functionally equal in severity a "Listed Impairment," the child is not disabled. 20 C.F.R. § 416.924(d)(2)(1997).

The PRWORA legislation also limits children's eligibility for SSI in several other respects. It eliminates maladaptive behavior as a medical criterion to be evaluated in determining which mental impairments should be included in the "Listed Impairments." In addition, the PRWORA brings the standard for reviewing children's eligibility for benefits in line with the adult standard: the SSA must review the eligibility of all children on the rolls at least once every three years, unless a child's condition is considered unlikely to improve.

As a consequence of the elimination of the IFA, the federal government sent letters to 264,000 parents notifying them that their children's eligibility for disability benefits was being reviewed. As of July 1997, the SSA had completed the majority of the reviews. About 42% of children whose cases had been reviewed had been found ineligible.

Given the new emphasis on Listed Impairments, one important question involves how the SSA determines "functional equivalence" to the Listed Impairments. In September 2000, the SSA issued guidance on this question. See 65 FR 54747, September 11, 2000. This guidance became effective as of January 2001. The functional equivalence standard looks at six areas of function in children: acquiring and using information; attending and completing tasks; interacting and relating with others; moving about and manipulating objects; caring for yourself; and health and physical being. It then asks whether the child suffers from "extreme" limitations in one area or "marked" limitation in two areas.

Chapter Twelve

PROTECTION AGAINST DISCRIMINATION

Table of Sections

I. ANTI–DISCRIMINATION LAW: AN OVERVIEW

The two major laws that protect individuals with mental disabilities (as well as individuals with physical disabilities) against discrimination are the Americans with Disabilities Act of 1990 ("ADA") and the Rehabilitation Act of 1973. The Rehabilitation Act bars discrimination in programs that are operated or funded by the federal government. The later-enacted ADA is much broader and bars discrimination in a wide variety of non-federal programs, both public and private. Significantly, the language of the ADA as well as its legislative history demonstrate that it should be interpreted consistently with the Rehabilitation Act. This parallel interpretation is important because case law under the Rehabilitation Act can inform the analysis of the more recently enacted ADA.

Sections 501 and 503 of the Rehabilitation Act impose employment-related affirmative action obligations on the federal government and on federal contractors. Section 504 of the Rehabilitation Act extends beyond employment and more generally bars discrimination by federally-operated/funded institutions against an "otherwise qualified" individual with a disability "by reason of his or her disability." 29 U.S.C. § 794(a). The ADA extends this protection "on the basis of disability" to the following areas that are highly relevant to persons with mental disabilities: non-federal employers that have more than 15 employees (Title I), public services and programs provided by state and local governments (Title II), and "public accommodations" (Title III), a broadly defined category that includes everything from private educational institutions to insurance offices and the "professional office of a health care provider." 42 U.S.C. § 12181(7)(F).

Both the Rehabilitation Act and the ADA cover individuals who have "a physical or mental impairment which substantially limits one or more . . . major life activities," who have "a record of such impairment," or who are "regarded as having such an impairment." 29 U.S.C. § 706(8)(B) (Rehabilitation Act); 42 U.S.C. § 12102(2) (ADA). The provisions covering those who have a record of impairment or are regarded as having an impairment "are intended to protect people who may be victimized by myths, fears, and stereotypes about certain mental or physical conditions," misperceptions which "are especially common with mental disabilities." See John Parry, Mental Disabilities and the Americans with Disabilities Act: A Practitioner's Guide to Employment, Insurance Treatment, Public Access, and Housing, American Bar Association 12 (1994). However, certain conditions, such as the current use of illegal drugs, are excluded from coverage under both the ADA and the Rehabilitation Act.

Under the ADA and the Rehabilitation Act, discrimination encompasses not only programs or acts that explicitly treat individuals with disabilities disparately but also programs or acts that are facially neutral but have a disparate impact on such individuals. However, under the Supreme Court's jurisprudence, a plaintiff's ability to bring a disparate impact claim may be quite limited. See *Alexander v. Choate*, 469 U.S. 287, 105 S.Ct. 712, 83 L.Ed.2d 661 (1985) (holding that even though Medicaid limitation on inpatient hospital care coverage disproportionately affected persons with disabilities, it did not violate Rehabilitation Act because such persons still had "meaningful access"). In addition, under both statutes, a central question for the discrimination analysis is whether the person alleging discrimination is a "qualified individual with a disability." This question, in turn, requires the court to make two inquiries. First, the court must inquire into whether the individual in fact has a disability. The statutes' definition of a specific class of individuals who have disabilities, and are therefore protected, signals an important difference between civil rights statutes that protect against race and sex-based discrimination and those that protect against disability-based discrimination. In the context of laws that target race or sex, all individuals are covered: there is no need to prove that one has a particular race or sex. Second, the court must inquire into whether the individual is nonetheless qualified—that is, whether, with reasonable accommodation or modification of the program in question, the person can meet the program's "essential eligibility requirements." Reasonable accommodations or modifications are those that can be undertaken without causing "undue burden" to the program or activity in question.

The focus on "qualified" individuals with disabilities signals an important difference between the law governing disability-based discrimination and other types of anti-discrimination law. While discrimination on the basis of characteristics such as race is presumptively illegal, disability-based discrimination is only illegal if the individual targeted is "qualified." On the other hand, unlike members of other protected minority groups, individuals with disabilities can, through the reasonable accommodation requirement, demand that resources be directed towards them. But see Christine Jolls, "Anti-discrimination and Accommodation," 114 Harv. L. Rev. 642 (2001) (arguing that the disparate impact strand of traditional anti-discrimination liability can resemble the reasonable accommodation requirement). Under both the ADA and the Rehabilitation Act, the challenged program or activity must bear the cost of the reasonable accommodation.

Another significant feature of the law governing disability-based discrimination is the ambiguity of its central terms: perhaps needless to say, concepts such as "disability," "qualified individual with a disability" and "reasonable accommodation" leave much room for interpretation. For years after the passage of the ADA, litigation over these central terms percolated in the lower federal courts. In the last few years, the Supreme Court has resolved many of these interpretive questions, largely in a manner that narrows the scope of the ADA. For example, the Court has held that the threshold determination of disability should take into account any corrective or mitigating measures that can be taken to address the impairment. *Sutton v. United Air Lines, Inc.*, 527 U.S. 471, 119 S.Ct. 2139, 144 L.Ed.2d 450 (1999). The Court has also given employers greater discretion in determining whether an individual is qualified, *Chevron U.S.A. Inc. v. Echazabal*, 536 U.S. 73, 122 S.Ct. 2045, 153 L.Ed.2d 82 (2002) and has limited the scope of the reasonable accommodation requirement. *US Airways, Inc. v. Barnett*, 535 U.S. 391, 122 S.Ct. 1516, 152 L.Ed.2d 589 (2002). These cases are discussed further in Section II.

Further, the Court has significantly limited the remedies available under the ADA to private plaintiffs who sue state defendants. In *Board of Trustees of the University of Alabama v. Garrett*, 531 U.S. 356, 121 S.Ct. 955, 148 L.Ed.2d 866 (2001), the Court held that state government employees are barred by the 11th Amendment from suing for monetary damages under Title I. Although this inability to recover damages does not apply where constitutional rights violations are arguably at stake, see *Tennessee v. Lane*, 541 U.S. 509, 124 S.Ct. 1978, 158 L.Ed.2d 820 (2004) (Title II suit involving access to the courts) and *United States v. Georgia*, 546 U.S. 151, 126 S.Ct. 877, 163 L.Ed.2d 650 (2006) (Title II suit involving violations of Eighth and Fourteenth Amendments), the number of ADA cases involving violations of constitutional rights is likely to be small. Limitations on the ability to secure monetary damages against state defendants are likely to bolster the significance of those cases that can be brought under the Rehabilitation Act. In such cases, where federal funding is involved, most courts have held that states have waived their sovereign immunity and that monetary damages are available.

In general, ADA plaintiffs have been among the least successful classes of federal litigants. See Sharona Hoffman, "Settling the Matter: Does Title I of the ADA Work?" 59 Ala. L.Rev. 305 (2008) (discussing plaintiff win rates in Title I cases of 3%). Some commentators have argued that this lack of success in the courts indicates that the ADA may have been "enacted ahead of its time, in that much of the country is not yet ready to embrace the precepts on which the ADA is premised." Bonnie P. Tucker, "The ADA's Revolving Door: Inherent Flaws in the Civil Rights Paradigm," 62 Ohio St.L.J. 335, 337 (2001). Even these commentators note, however, that the terms of the ADA are sufficiently ambiguous that they leave the ADA open to narrow court interpretations. *Id.* Additionally, empirical studies of cases litigated to a final outcome have many limitations. The largest of these is selection bias. The evidence indicates that parties claiming ADA violations in employment cases are sometimes able to secure significant settlements, whether at the administrative (EEOC) stage or at the litigation stage. See Hoffman, supra.

This chapter discusses the ADA in three contexts important for individuals with mental disabilities: employment, postsecondary education, and the licensing activities of state government agencies. Depending on whether federal funds are involved, employment discrimination claims are governed either by the Rehabilitation Act or by Title I of the ADA. Congress has granted the Equal Employment Opportunity Commission ("EEOC") authority to issue interpretive regulations covering employment under Title I of the ADA. 42 U.S.C.§ 12116 (1994). As for postsecondary education, it may be governed by a variety of different statutes: the Rehabilitation Act governs postsecondary institutions that receive federal funding; Title II of the ADA governs postsecondary institutions that are supported by state government funding; and Title III of the ADA governs private postsecondary institutions. The Justice Department is charged with promulgating regulations that implement Titles II and III of the ADA. 42 U.S.C. § 12134(a); *id.* § 12186(b) (Title III).

A fourth important context for anti-discrimination law is housing. Housing differs from employment, postsecondary education, and state licensing in that the ADA and the Rehabilitation Act are not central to the anti-discrimination analysis. Although Titles II and III of the ADA do cover limited classes of housing, the most important anti-discrimination statute is the Fair Housing Act ("FHA"). Significantly, however, the legal analysis under the FHA is quite similar to that under the ADA and the Rehabilitation Act. The chapter concludes with a discussion of disability-based anti-discrimination law in the context of housing. (A final important context for anti-discrimination analysis, the context of insurance coverage for mental health care, is discussed in Chapter 1, Section IV).

II. EMPLOYMENT OPPORTUNITIES

Many employment discrimination claims brought under the ADA and Rehabilitation Act allege discrimination on the basis of emotional or psychiatric impairment. For example, during the period from 1997–2007, 6.7% of ADA complaints filed with the EEOC claimed depression as the relevant disability, 2.1% claimed bipolar disorder, and 2.6% claimed anxiety disorder. EEOC, ADA Charge Data by Impairments/Bases— Receipts, available at www.eeoc.gov/stats/ada-receipts.html. The significance of such claims is underscored by data suggesting that people with mental impairments have much lower employment rates than the general population and also have lower employment rates than people with physical disabilities.

A. CONDITIONS GIVING RISE TO COVERAGE UNDER ANTI-DISCRIMINATION LAW

A threshold question that must be addressed with respect to every employment discrimination claim (and, indeed, with respect to any claim of discrimination under the ADA) is whether the claimant's condition is a covered disability. The claimant has the burden of proof on this threshold question. As noted earlier, the ADA and Rehabilitation Act define "disability" in a rather ambiguous fashion, as any "physical or mental impairment which substantially limits one or more . . . major life activities." Giving content to this definition poses a substantial challenge. The challenge is particularly acute in the context of mental disorders. With mental disorders, there is often disagreement even among experts as to the appropriate diagnostic category for any given individual. In addition, mental disorders can be highly variable, at least in terms of the symptomatology in evidence at any particular time.

In the context of employment, the EEOC has promulgated interpretive regulations that attempt to clarify the terms central to the anti-discrimination analysis. EEOC regulations note, for example, that a mental impairment includes "[a]ny mental or psychological disorder, such as mental retardation, organic brain syndrome, emotional or mental illness, and specific learning disabilities." 29 C.F.R. § 1630.2(h)(2). The term "major life activities" includes such functions as "caring for oneself, performing manual tasks, walking, seeing, hearing, speaking, breathing, learning, and working." *Id.* § 1630.2(I); *see also* 29 C.F.R. § 1613.703(c) (Rehabilitation Act regulations). Finally, the regulations identify in some detail the situations in which a mental disorder can be considered to "substantially limit" a major life activity. In general, the impairment must either leave the individual in question unable to perform the life activity or must significantly restrict the "condition, manner or duration" under which the individual can perform the activity. *Id.* § 1630.2(j)(1)(i,ii). In addition, the regulations suggest that the duration or expected duration of the impairment, as well as its "nature and severity," must be significant. *Id.* § 1630.2(j)(2).

The EEOC regulations also specify what "substantial limitation" means with respect to the particular major life activity of working. It means that the individual must be "significantly restricted in the ability to perform either a class of jobs or a broad range of jobs in various classes as compared to the average person having comparable training, skills, and abilities." The regulations emphasize that the "inability to perform a single, particular job does not constitute a substantial limitation in the major life activity of working." *Id.* § 1630.2(j)(3)(i).

The following case illustrates both the application of the EEOC regulations and the variability of mental disorder.

WITTER v. DELTA AIRLINES, INC., ET AL.

United States District Court, N.D. Georgia, 1997.
966 F.Supp. 1193.

ORDER

ORINDA D. EVANS, DISTRICT JUDGE.

This civil case alleging violations of the Americans with Disabilities Act (ADA), as amended, 42 U.S.C. §§ 12101–12213, the Age Discrimination in Employment Act (ADEA), as amended, 29 U.S.C. §§ 621–624, and state tort law is before the court on Defendants' motion for summary judgment and Plaintiff's motion for leave to file additional deposition excerpts in opposition to summary judgment. * * *

The following relevant facts are undisputed unless otherwise noted. Plaintiff has been employed as a pilot by Defendant Delta since 1967. Defendant Delta requires that its pilots meet the physical requirements for a Federal Aviation Administration (FAA) Class I Medical Certificate.

In February 1992, Plaintiff was involved in a domestic dispute with his wife. (Witter Depo. at 59–61). During this dispute, Plaintiff yelled at his wife and threatened to commit suicide. (Witter Depo. at 60). As a result of this incident, Plaintiff was incarcerated in the DeKalb County, Georgia Jail. (*Id.* at 67).

Plaintiff was sent to Parkwood Hospital for psychiatric evaluation. (*Id.* at 67–68). After eight days, at Parkwood, Plaintiff was transferred to Anchor hospital apparently at Defendant Delta's request. (*Id.* at 68–69). Among those who apparently saw plaintiff at Anchor was Wes Anderson, Defendant Delta's System Manager for Flight Operations Administration, and Shand Gause who was Plaintiff's chief pilot at the time. (Anderson Depo. at 85). According to Plaintiff, Gause told him that if he did not voluntarily consent to treatment at Anchor, he would be fired. (Witter Aff. at 3). After the February 1992 incident, Plaintiff voluntarily grounded himself because he believed that he was not medically fit to fly. (Witter Aff. at 4).

Plaintiff's FAA Class I Medical Certification was due to expire in June 1992. In May 1992, Plaintiff contacted the Air Line Pilots Association (ALPA) to inquire about the best way to renew his certification. (Witter Aff. at 5). Plaintiff was apparently told that the recertification would take some time. (*Id.*).

At this time, Plaintiff's sick leave was running out, and he would only be eligible for disability payments from Defendant Delta if he had a formal denial of his medical certification. (*Id.*). Dr. William Whaley, an FAA certified air medical examiner (AME) in Atlanta apparently agreed to help Plaintiff with this situation. (Pl.Exhs.119, 120). On June 12, 1992, Plaintiff was seen by Dr. Walter Hill to whom Whaley had referred him. (D–001529 et seq.). Hill diagnosed Plaintiff as suffering from bipolar disorder and found Plaintiff unfit to fly. (*Id.*). Relying on this report Whaley formally denied Plaintiff's medical certification.

During the fall of 1992, Plaintiff was seen by an FAA psychiatrist, Barton Pakull. Pakull determined that while Plaintiff had a "characterological problem that might be considered a personality disorder," he should nonetheless be issued Class I Medical Certification. (D–001556—58). The recommendation of certification, however, was issued with the "limitation that [Plaintiff] submit semi-annual update psychiatric reports." (D001558). Plaintiff received his FAA medical certificate in February 1993, and on March 1, 1993 presented the certificate to Jack Kelly who was Defendant Delta's Chief Pilot in Atlanta. (Witter Depo. at 89; Witter Aff. at 6).

Defendant Delta decided that Plaintiff should be further evaluated by Defendant Berry who was associated with Defendant Preventative & Aerospace Medicine Consultants, P.A. (PAMC). Defendant Berry is board certified in aerospace medicine and has been designated by the FAA as a senior AME. The decision to refer Plaintiff to Defendant Berry was apparently based on the felony charge pending against Plaintiff from the February 1992 incident and the fact that Plaintiff had spent time under psychiatric evaluation. (Anderson Depo. at 85).

Defendant Berry examined Plaintiff on June 2, 1993. (Pl.Exh. 86). Defendant Berry also referred Plaintiff to Dr. Louis A. Faillace, a psychiatrist and Dr. Edward J. McLaughlin, a psychologist. (D–001321). Defendant Berry reported their findings and his own in a July 1993 report which was submitted to Defendant Delta. Defendant Berry concluded that Plaintiff suffered from an Adjustment Disorder with Mixed Emotional Features. (D–001324). In his report, Defendant Berry noted:

> In returning Capt. Witter to the cockpit, the major concern is the possibility of a recurrence of this type of behavior reaction, especially while flying. . . . If it did occur again, even in the cockpit, I do not believe that it would be incapacitating from a safety point of view. Capt. Witter's basic personality may make him a difficult person with whom to work. However, he does not have a psychiatric

disorder at the present time. If any future unusual behavior indicates the occurrence of another adjustment disorder, Capt. Witter should be grounded permanently. Until then, he is qualified to fly.

(*Id.*). Based on this report, Plaintiff returned to regular line operations in August 1993. (Witter Depo. at 98).

In November 1993, Plaintiff flew a European rotation. (*Id.* at 99). The flight crew for the rotation consisted of Plaintiff, First Officer Jeffrey Berlin, and Second Officer John Sweeney. (Dollarhide Depo. at 25). During the rotation, Plaintiff and the other two crew members did not get along. (*Id.*, Witter Depo. at 100). According to Plaintiff, the crew members had a "personality conflict," and Berlin and Sweeney refused to follow his instructions. (Witter Depo. at 99–100).

As a result of this situation, Plaintiff and the other two crew members filed reports with David Dollarhide, who was Defendant Delta's chief pilot at LaGuardia Airport in New York City. Dollarhide, apparently at the recommendation of Gause, arranged for the flight crew to attend a Cockpit Resource Management ("CRM") session on February 14, 1994. It was apparently Gause's intention that he and Witter have a personal counseling session after the CRM and that Plaintiff would be given a choice of either seeking professional help or leaving flight status. (Gause Depo. at 52–53).

The flight crew apparently were unable to resolve their differences during the CRM session. (Anderson Depo. at 153). Gause interviewed Witter after the CRM, and Dollarhide met with Plaintiff the next day. (Pl.Exh. 6). Plaintiff was told that he was the center of the problem, that a letter would be put in his file to that effect, and that he would get a line check when he arrived in Frankfurt on his next rotation. (*Id.*).

Gause and Anderson telephoned Defendant Berry the day after the CRM to discuss with him whether Plaintiff's behavior during his November 1993 rotation was of the type which Defendant Berry mentioned could lead to grounding in his 1993 report. (Berry Depo. at 182). Defendant Berry and Faillace reviewed the reports concerning Plaintiff's November 1993 rotation and they were of the opinion that Plaintiff required further evaluation. (Berry Depo. at 192–93; Faillace Depo. at 116–18). Defendant Berry recommended that Plaintiff be grounded pending this further evaluation. (Berry Depo. at 198).

Defendant Berry and Faillace interviewed Plaintiff about the events of November 1993. (Berry Depo. at 227–229; Faillace Depo at 122). In addition, Berry also interviewed Berlin and Sweeney. (Berry Depo. at 201–202). Both Berlin and Sweeney apparently told Berry that Plaintiff would get very angry at them when they made suggestions and that they believed Plaintiff was a danger in the cockpit. (Pl.Exh. 91). Plaintiff told Defendant Berry that the problems resulted from the fact that his crewmates were totally ignoring him and acting on their own. (Id.). Plaintiff also indicated that Berlin and Sweeney were difficult to work with because they were younger pilots. (Id.). Furthermore, Plaintiff had suspicions of a plot against him and that he thought that Berlin and Sweeney's placement on his crew may have been intentional. (Id.).

Faillace also interviewed Plaintiff in March 1994. Like Defendant Berry, Faillace noted that Plaintiff indicated that there might be a plot against him. (D–001310). In addition, Faillace concluded that Plaintiff reacts to criticism with feelings of rage and that Plaintiff has a grandiose sense of self importance. (D–001311). Based on his interview, Faillace concluded,

> When Mr. Witter is under extreme stress, his basic underlying narcissistic personality flaws become apparent. He also has a significant affective component with some features of Cyclothymia. When stressed, he exhibits significant symptoms of Narcissistic Personality Disorder.(D–001310).

McLaughlin was also consulted by Defendant Berry, although he never interviewed Plaintiff or Berlin or Sweeney. McLaughlin concurred that when Plaintiff is under stress it becomes clear that he has a personality disorder with narcissistic, self-centered characteristics. (D–001313). Defendant Berry eventually diagnosed Plaintiff as suffering from Narcissistic Personality Disorder and possible Cyclothymia and memorialized this diagnosis in an April 1994 report. (P1.Exh. 91). Based on this report, Defendant Delta grounded Plaintiff.

Defendant Berry felt that, as a Delta medical consultant, he had the authority to send copies of the report to interested third parties. (Berry Depo. at 95). As such, Defendant Berry sent copies of his 1993 and 1994 reports on Plaintiff to the FAA. (Berry Depo. at 96). Defendant Berry also discussed Plaintiff's medical condition with representatives of ALPA. (Id.).

The FAA convened a panel of six psychiatrists to review Plaintiff's case. (Berry Depo. at 247–48). In June 1994, the FAA panel concluded that Plaintiff should not be granted a Class I Medical Certification due to the fact that he was suffering from a personality disorder. (Witter Depo. at 134). In December 1994, Pakull, the FAA's Chief Psychiatrist, agreed with the panel's finding that Plaintiff should not be certified. (Def's.Exh. 21). Plaintiff's Class I Medical Certification was not renewed by the FAA in February 1995.

Plaintiff subsequently appealed this decision to the National Transportation Safety Board (NTSB). The NTSB overturned the FAA's decision and restored Plaintiff's Class I Medical Certification. Defendant Delta, however, has apparently refused to reinstate Plaintiff to flight status without further medical evaluation.

* * *

Plaintiff's first claim against Defendant is a claim under the ADA. In order to make out a prima facie case under the ADA, Plaintiff bears the burden of showing three things: (1) that he has a disability; (2) that he is a qualified individual; and (3) that he was subjected to unlawful discrimination because of his disability. *Morisky v. Broward County*, 80

F.3d 445, 447 (11th Cir.1996). The court concludes that Plaintiff fails to meet this test because he is not disabled within the meaning of the ADA.

Under the ADA, a person is considered disabled if he: (1) suffers from a mental or physical impairment that substantially limits one or more of his major life activities; (2) has a record of such impairment; or (3) is regarded as having such an impairment. 42 U.S.C. § 12102(2). In this case, Plaintiff claims that he is disabled for purposes of the statute because he suffers from a mental impairment that substantially limits his major life activity of working or alternatively because he was regarded by Defendant Delta as suffering from such an impairment.

The regulations promulgated under the ADA deal extensively with the meaning of disability. As to the concept of substantial limitation, the regulations indicate that in deciding whether a particular condition is substantially limiting, the court should consider: "(i) the nature and severity of the impairment; (ii) the duration or expected duration of the impairment; and (iii) the permanent or long-term impact, or the expected permanent or long-term impact resulting from the impairment." 29 C.F.R. § 1630.2(j)(2). Additionally, the regulations note that with regard to claims that a condition is a disability because it substantially limits the life activity of working,

> The term substantially limits means significantly restricted in the ability to perform either a class of jobs or a broad range of jobs in various classes as compared to the average person having comparable training, skills, and abilities. The inability to perform a single, particular job does not constitute a substantial limitation in the major life activity of working.

29 C.F.R. § 1630.2(j)(3)(ii).

Finally, the regulations set out three factors which the court may consider in looking at the question of whether a plaintiff is substantially limited from working. These three factors are,

> (A) The geographical area to which the individual has reasonable access; (B) The job from which the individual has been disqualified because of an impairment, and the number and types of jobs utilizing similar training, knowledge, skills or abilities, within that geographical area, from which the individual is also disqualified because of the impairment (class of jobs); and/or (C) The job from which the individual has been disqualified because of an impairment, and the number and types of other jobs not utilizing similar training, knowledge, skills or abilities, within that geographical area, from which the individual is also disqualified because of the impairment (broad range of jobs in various classes).

29 C.F.R. § 1630.2(j)(3)(ii).

Plaintiff claims that he is disabled under the ADA because his condition rendered him unable to be a commercial airline pilot. Despite this condition, under the regulations Plaintiff is not substantially limited in the life activity of working. First, the court notes that Plaintiff's psychological condition does not appear to be exceptionally severe as it only appears to be a serious condition when Plaintiff is under stress or pressure. Second, the long-term impact of Plaintiff's psychological condition does not appear great as the NTSB has found that his Class I Medical Certification should be returned.

Furthermore, the factors enumerated under 29 C.F.R. § 1630.2(j)(3)(ii), point to the same conclusion. First, Plaintiff is a resident of DeKalb County, Georgia which is part of the metropolitan Atlanta area. (Amended Complaint at 1). Plaintiff thus lives in a community with substantial job opportunities.

Second, Plaintiff's condition did not disqualify him completely from the class of jobs which utilize similar training, skills, knowledge and ability. While the loss of his Class I Medical Certification rendered Plaintiff unable to pilot an aircraft, Plaintiff recognizes that, "Delta has pilots such as Anderson, Gause and David Greenberg[1] in management, and in flight training and administration. It is inconceivable that an employer the size of Delta could not accommodate, and derive benefit from, the non-flying services of a senior captain with 27 years of flight experience." (Pl. response to Defs. mtn. for summary judgment at 27). While Plaintiff's comments refer only to Defendant Delta, the court takes judicial notice of the fact that the metropolitan Atlanta area is served by Hartsfield Atlanta International Airport which is one of the busiest airports in the country. It thus stands to reason that there would be several jobs within this geographic area which Plaintiff would be qualified to do and which would utilize his unique training, skills, ability, knowledge. Thus, this factor also points toward finding Plaintiff nondisabled.

Finally, while Plaintiff's condition may have made it impossible for him to fly a commercial aircraft, Plaintiff has made no argument that he is in any way impaired from holding any other job. Consideration of the third factor set out under 29 C.F.R. § 1630.2(j)(3)(ii), therefore also leads to the conclusion that Plaintiff is not disabled.

The analysis of the disability issue, however, is not yet complete because Plaintiff contends that he should be considered disabled under ADA since Defendant Delta regarded him as having an impairment that substantially limited his life activity of working. Plaintiff claims that he was regarded as disabled under 29 C.F.R. § 1630.2(*l*)(3). Under this section, a person can be regarded as having a disabling impairment if he "has none of the impairments defined in ... this section but is treated by a covered entity as having a substantially limiting impairment."

Thus, if Plaintiff was treated by Defendant Delta as having a disability that impaired his life activity of working, then Plaintiff would be considered disabled under the ADA. The record clearly shows that Defendant Delta considered Plaintiff's mental condition a substantial limitation on his ability to act as a commercial airline pilot. The court,

---

1. Greenberg is Defendant Delta's vice president of flight operations.

however, finds that this treatment is not tantamount to treating Plaintiff as being substantially limited in his major life activity of working. This conclusion flows from the above discussion that impairment of Plaintiff's ability to be a commercial airline pilot is not substantial impairment of Plaintiff's life activity of working. Accordingly, since Plaintiff cannot prove that he was disabled within the meaning of the ADA, summary judgment for Defendants is appropriate on Plaintiff's ADA claim.

[The court's discussion of the plaintiff's other claims is omitted.]

* * *

Questions and Comments

1. *Variability of mental disorder/psychiatric diagnosis.* The *Witter* case illustrates well how the symptomatology of a mental disorder can vary: several of the psychiatrists who examined Witter noted that he appeared to show "significant symptoms of Narcissistic Personality Disorder" *only* when stressed. In holding that Witter's condition was not severe enough to render him disabled within the meaning of the ADA, the court relied in part on this psychiatric finding. Do you agree with the court's reasoning?

The variability of Witter's symptomatology may also explain the differing diagnoses reached by the various psychiatrists who examined him. As the court's recitation of the facts points out, before the determination of Narcisstic Personality Disorder was ultimately made, Witter was diagnosed as suffering from everything from bipolar disorder to "Adjustment Disorder with Mixed Emotional Features."

2. *Pre-employment inquiries as to disability.* Under the ADA, an employer may not ask a job applicant questions about whether the applicant has a disability and/or about the nature or severity of the disability. Rather, at the pre-employment stage, the employer is restricted to inquiries into the ability of an applicant to perform job-related functions. 42 U.S.C. § 12112(d)(2)(A,B). Similarly, under a regulation promulgated pursuant to the Rehabilitation Act, employers that receive federal funds "may not make pre-employment inquiry of an applicant as to whether the applicant is a handicapped person or as to the nature or severity of a handicap"; they may inquire only "into an applicant's ability to perform job related functions." 45 C.F.R. § 84.14(a). A similar prohibition which applies to federal employers is contained in 29 C.F.R. § 1613.706. For a strong critique of the prohibition on pre-employment inquiries, see Richard Epstein, "The Legal Regulation of Genetic Discrimination: Old Responses to New Technologies," 74 B.U. L. Rev. 1 (1994).

Should employers be able to ask broader questions than might normally be allowed under the ADA or Rehabilitation Act when the position involved is a particularly sensitive one? For example, because stability and judgment would seem to be essential to the job-related functions of a law enforcement official, should applicants for such a position be questioned broadly about their prior treatment for mental disorder? For consideration of these issues in the context of professional licensing and certification, *see* Section III, *infra.*

Note: The Supreme Court on the Definition of Disability

During the years after the passage of the ADA, appellate courts reached varying conclusions regarding whether the determination of disability should be made with or without reference to the availability of mitigating measures (e.g. corrective medical devices and medications). *Compare Chandler v. City of Dallas*, 2 F.3d 1385 (5th Cir.1993), *cert. denied*, 511 U.S. 1011, 114 S.Ct. 1386, 128 L.Ed.2d 61 (1994) (arguing that mitigating measures should be taken into account) with *Harris v. H & W Contracting Co.*, 102 F.3d 516 (11th Cir.1996) (reaching the opposite conclusion). In total, however, 8 of 9 appellate courts that addressed the issue determined that the determination of disability should be made *without* reference to mitigating measures.

In a trio of cases decided in 1999, the Supreme Court addressed this issue. See *Sutton v. United Air Lines*, 527 U.S. 471, 119 S.Ct. 2139, 144 L.Ed.2d 450 (1999), *Murphy v. United Parcel Service*, 527 U.S. 516, 119 S.Ct. 2133, 144 L.Ed.2d 484 (1999), and *Albertsons, Inc. v. Kirkingburg*, 527 U.S. 555, 119 S.Ct. 2162, 144 L.Ed.2d 518 (1999). In each case, the Court held that, in order to qualify under the ADA, an individual had to be disabled even once mitigating measures were taken into account. The main case, *Sutton*, was a lawsuit by two severely myopic twin sisters who were denied positions as commercial airline pilots because they did not meet respondent's minimum vision requirement, which was uncorrected visual acuity of 20/100 or better. With corrective lenses, however, the sisters had vision of 20/20 or better.

In a majority opinion authored by Justice O'Connor, the Court ruled against the twin sisters. According to the majority, the language in three provisions of the ADA required taking mitigating measures into account and hence led to the conclusion that the sisters did not have a disability within the meaning of the ADA. First, the ADA's use of the term "substantially limits" in its "present indicative verb form" indicated that the language was "properly read as requiring that a person be presently—not potentially or hypothetically—substantially limited in order to demonstrate a disability ..." Second, the ADA's requirement that a individualized determination be made to determine whether an individual has a disability argued in favor of judging individuals in their corrected or mitigated state. Third, the ADA's findings (enacted as part of the statute) that "some 43,000,000 American have one or more physical or mental disabilities ..." reflected an understanding that those whose impairments are largely corrected by medication or medical devices are not disabled within the meaning of the ADA.

The majority also addressed the petitioners' argument that they should be covered by the ADA because they were "regarded as" having a disability by the respondent. See 42 U.S.C. § 12101(2)(C) (covering this class of individuals). According to the petitioners, because the respondent did not think that they were capable of being global airline pilots, they were seen by the respondent as being substantially limited in the major life activity of working. The majority rejected the petitioners' contention, holding that the position global airline pilot was a single job, not a class of jobs, and that there were other positions utilizing petitioners' skills, "such as regional pilot and pilot instructor to name a few" that were available to them.

Justice Stevens, joined by Justice Breyer, dissented. The dissent argued that determining disability by taking into account mitigating measures would penalize individuals who, by virtue of their determination and hardiness, compensated for their disabilities. Moreover, if Congress were concerned only with the corrected or mitigated status of a person's impairment, there would be no reason to include within the protected class those individuals who were once disabled but had now fully recovered. Yet the ADA, by covering those who had a history of disability, clearly covered those individuals. The dissent also emphasized that both the Senate and House reports on the ADA stated that "whether a person has a disability should be assessed without regard to the availability of mitigating measures, such as reasonable accommodations or auxiliary aids."

Like *Sutton*, the *Murphy* case involved an individual with a condition—high blood pressure—that could be corrected through medication. Hence the *Murphy* Court determined that Murphy was not disabled under the first prong of the ADA's disability determination. The Court also held that Murphy was not "regarded as" having a disability by the defendant (United Parcel Service) because the defendant's exclusion of individuals with high blood pressure from mechanic jobs that required driving a commercial vehicle did not exclude Murphy from all jobs as a mechanic. The final case in the trilogy, *Albertson's Inc.*, involved a plaintiff with monocular vision. The Court stated that the Ninth Circuit had been "too quick" to find that this monocular vision substantially limited the major life activity of seeing because it had not taken into account the manner in which the plaintiff's brain had adapted to the condition.

Questions and Comments

1. *Substantial limitation on the major life activity of working.* *Witter*, *Sutton*, and *Murphy* all address the question of what constitutes a substantial limitation on the major life activity of working. They do so either directly and/or through the lens of whether the plaintiff is regarded by the defendant as having a substantial limitation on the major life activity of working. In each case, the court determines that, in order to be substantially limited with respect to working, an individual has to be excluded not just from one job but from a class of jobs available to individuals with comparable skills and training. Is the *Witter* court correct in arguing that a position in management or in flight training and administration would utilize the plaintiff's particular skills and training? Similarly, is the *Sutton* Court correct in arguing that a job as a regional airline pilot or flight instructor would utilize the plaintiffs' particular skills and training? With respect to the latter question, should it matter that pilots at regional airlines earn significantly less that international pilots? In the *Murphy* case, the UPS regula-

tions excluded the plaintiff from driving any commercial vehicle. Should it matter that millions of jobs require the ability to drive a commercial vehicle?

Working is not the only "major life activity" in which the Supreme Court has set a high threshold for what constitutes "substantial limitation." In *Toyota Motor Manufacturing, Kentucky, Inc. v. Williams*, 534 U.S. 184, 122 S.Ct. 681, 151 L.Ed.2d 615 (2002) the Court held that the major life activity of performing manual tasks must include tasks that are "central to most people's daily lives." The respondent's carpal tunnel syndrome did not substantially limit her from performing tasks central to daily life and hence did not qualify her for coverage under the ADA. The Court also rejected the idea that an individual's inability to perform the manual tasks associated with her particular job is sufficient to qualify as a substantial restriction on the ability to perform manual tasks.

Lower courts have interpreted *Toyota* to apply to a wide range of major life activities and to require that the major life activity in question be "severely restricted." See, e.g., *EEOC v. Sears, Roebuck & Co.*, 417 F.3d 789 (7th Cir. 2005); *Fenney v. Dakota, Minn. & E.R.R. Co.*, 327 F.3d 707 (8th Cir. 2003); *DePrisco v. Delta Air Lines, Inc.*, 90 Fed.Appx. 790 (6th Cir. 2004); *Holt v. Grand Lake Mental Health Ctr., Inc.*, 443 F.3d 762 (10th Cir. 2006); *Greenberg v. BellSouth Telecomms., Inc.*, 498 F.3d 1258 (11th Cir. 2007).

2. *Is "interacting with others" a major life activity?* The *Toyota* Court also held that major life activities have to be "of central importance to daily life." In ADA cases involving mental disability, the major life activity at issue is often characterized as some version of interacting or socializing with others. Courts have split on the question of whether interacting with others is in fact a major life activity. While the First, Fourth, and Eighth Circuits have questioned whether the "ability to get along with others" is a major life activity, see *Soileau v. Guilford of Me., Inc.*, 105 F.3d 12, 15 (1st Cir. 1997); *Davis v. Univ. of N.C.*, 263 F.3d 95 (4th Cir. 2001); *Amir v. St. Louis Univ.*, 184 F.3d 1017 (8th Cir. 1999), the Ninth Circuit has held that it is. *McAlindin v. County of San Diego*, 192 F.3d 1226 (9th Cir. 1999). In a recent case, the Second Circuit stated that although it accepted the view that interacting with others was a major life activity, it had a more parsimonious view than did the district court of what rendered an individual (in that case, a woman with bipolar disorder) "substantially limited" in that activity. *Jacques v. DiMarzio, Inc.*, 386 F.3d 192 (2d Cir. 2004).

3. *Deference to agency regulations and interpretations.* Under *Chevron U.S.A., Inc. v. Natural Resources Defense Council*, 467 U.S. 837, 104 S.Ct. 2778, 81 L.Ed.2d 694 (1984), and its progeny, courts are obliged to give deference to "reasonable" agency interpretations of ambiguous statutory language in cases where Congress has given the agency authority to interpret that language, and the agency acts via rulemaking or formal adjudication in rendering its interpretation. In *Sutton*, the Court suggested in dicta that *Chevron* deference should not be given to EEOC and DOJ regulations that interpret such generally applicable terms as "disability." According to the Court, no agency has been given authority by Congress to interpret terms that apply to the ADA generally rather than to specific Titles of the statute. The *Sutton* Court also suggested that interpretive guidance by the

EEOC and DOJ stating that the determination of disability should be made without reference to mitigating measures was contrary to the unambiguous language of the ADA.

4. *Normative approaches to defining disability.* Numerous commentators have argued (contra the *Sutton* majority) that the central terms used in the ADA—terms like disability and the related concepts of substantial limitation and major life activity—do not have a single plain meaning. These commentators have suggested different normative principles that could be used to define the class of persons with disabilities. For example, disability could be defined in a manner that encompassed only the most disadvantaged: this approach could be seen as implementing John Rawls's principle of preferential treatment of those individuals who are worst off. See Chapter 1, Section IV. According to some disability rights scholars, the Supreme Court's parsimonious approach to defining disability under the ADA is a reflection of a belief that only this "truly disabled" group deserves to be protected. Bonnie P. Tucker, "The Supreme Court's Definition of Disability Under the ADA: A Return to the Dark Ages," 52 Ala.L.Rev. 321 (2000).

The disability scholar Samuel Bagenstos has articulated an alternate normative principle. Under this principle, the class of disabled persons subject to protection from discrimination would be larger but would still encompass only those individuals who are systematically subject to stigma on the basis of their impairment. According to Bagenstos, a stigma-based approach is arguably in accord with the outcomes (if not the reasoning) in some of the Supreme Court's disability cases, particularly *Sutton* and *Murphy*: in the modern era, where corrective lenses and high blood pressure medication are readily available, few individuals with myopia or elevated blood pressure are stigmatized. See generally Samuel R. Bagenstos, "Subordination, Stigma, and 'Disability,'" 86 Va.L.Rev. 397 (2000). Bagenstos also argues that an approach based on stigma would implement an alternative component of John Rawls's model of distributive justice—the idea that all individuals should be given fair equality of opportunity. *Id.* at 461. But see Matthew Diller, "Judicial Backlash, the ADA, and the Civil Rights Model," 21 Berkeley J. Emp. & Lab.L. 19 (2000) (arguing that the Supreme Court's definition-of-disability cases provide many individuals with disabilities only very narrow access to the job market and hence undermine equality of opportunity).

Finally, note that one suggested normative approach would reject the ADA model of attempting to define a limited class subject to its protection: on this view, anyone who had a mental or physical impairment of any sort (or was seen as having such an impairment) would be protected from irrational discrimination. See Robert L. Burgdorf, Jr., "Substantially Limited Protection from Disability Discrimination: The Special Treatment Model and Misconstructions of the Definition of Disability," 42 Vill.L.Rev. 409 (1997) (advocating this approach). Under Burgdorf's approach, cases like *Sutton*—where a plaintiff could be considered disabled enough to be rejected from a job but not disabled enough to challenge the rejection—would not arise.

Which of these normative approaches to defining disability do you find most appealing? Which might be the most feasible for the court system (and/or society as a whole) to implement?

B. QUALIFICATION AND REASONABLE ACCOMMODATION

Once a claimant has proved that he is "disabled" within the meaning of the anti-discrimination laws, he must then prove that he is a "qualified individual with a disability"—that is, someone who, "with or without reasonable accommodation, can perform the essential functions of the employment position that such individual holds or desires." 42 U.S.C. § 12111(8) (ADA); 29 C.F.R. § 1613.702(f); 45 C.F.R. § 84.3K; (Rehabilitation Act regulations respectively governing federal employers and entities that receive federal funds). As a practical matter, it may be difficult for a plaintiff to prove that, despite the fact that he suffers from a significant disability, he is nonetheless qualified for the employment in question. If, however, the plaintiff can prove these claims, the burden then shifts to the defendant "to either rebut those claims or establish that the reasonable accommodation required would create an undue hardship." *Dutton v. Johnson County Board of County Commr's*, 859 F.Supp. 498, 505 (D.Kan.1994).

As is obvious from the definition of the term "qualified individual with a disability," qualification and reasonable accommodation are part of the same inquiry. However, as the case set out below reveals, it is difficult to apply the two concepts simultaneously. In the *EEOC v. Amego* case, the First Circuit attempts to separate the two inquiries: it first asks whether the claimant is qualified without reasonable accommodation; only after it has answered this first question in the negative does the court explicitly look at reasonable accommodation. *Amego* also poses interesting questions, discussed in the notes that follow the case, regarding how such vague terms as qualification and reasonable accommodation should be interpreted in the context of specific facts.

EQUAL EMPLOYMENT OPPORTUNITY COMMISSION v. AMEGO, INC.

United States Court of Appeals, First Circuit, 1997.
110 F.3d 135.

Lynch, Circuit Judge.

Amego, Inc., is a small not-for-profit organization which cares for severely disabled people suffering from autism, retardation, and behavioral disorders. It serves twenty-five to thirty clients, including six in a residential program in Mansfield, Massachusetts, where Ann Marie Guglielmi was employed as a Team Leader. The Team Leader position required her to be responsible for the care of these disabled clients, including the responsibility of administering vital medications to them. After an unresolved investigation of improprieties in the administering of medication to patients at a related facility, Amego learned that other staff felt Guglielmi was not performing her job adequately and was putting patients at risk. Amego also learned that Ms. Guglielmi had twice attempted to commit suicide within the previous six weeks by overdosing on medications. This, Amego decided, meant that Guglielmi could not safely dispense medications, an essential job function, and that there was no other job reasonably available to her. Her employment was thus terminated.

The Equal Employment Opportunity Commission ("EEOC") sued Amego on behalf of Guglielmi under the Americans with Disabilities Act ("ADA"), 42 U.S.C. § 12101 et seq. The district court entered summary judgment against the EEOC, holding that the EEOC had not made out a prima facie case that Guglielmi was an otherwise "qualified" individual, that an accommodation could be reasonably made, and that there was discrimination "because of" her disability.

The EEOC appeals and argues that the question of whether an employee poses a significant risk to other individuals in the workplace is an affirmative defense on which the employer bears the burden of proof and is thus not part of the plaintiff's burden that the employee is qualified. Those issues of qualification and risk, the EEOC says, are matters for the jury to resolve at trial and may not be resolved on summary judgment. The EEOC also invites this court to hold that "adverse employment action taken because of conduct related to a disability is tantamount to action taken because of a disability itself" for purposes of the ADA.

We affirm the judgment of the district court.

I.

The following facts are undisputed.

Founded in 1972 by parents of autistic individuals, Amego receives public funding and is licensed by two state agencies. A condition of licensing is that Amego provide conditions that ensure the safety and well-being of its clients. Amego maintains a very low client-to-staff ratio, usually one staff member to two clients. One particularly aggressive client required supervision by three staff members, eighteen hours a day.

Amego has a policy of not rejecting those who seek its help. Most of its clients engage in aggressive and self-injuring behavior, including self-mutilation. Many have been rejected by, or discharged from, other agencies. Most clients are on prescription medications, and in June of 1992, all clients at the Mansfield residence, save one, were receiving prescription medications.

Consistent with its philosophy of attempted integration, Amego provides its clients with access to community activities on a regular basis. Residential clients are transported daily to the Day Treatment Program, where they frequently are taken by direct care staff to stores, bowling alleys, banks, and the like.

In September 1990, Amego hired Guglielmi as a Behavior Therapist. She was then about 21 years old and did not represent herself to have any disability. In January 1991, she was diagnosed as bulimic and clinically depressed; however, she did not tell her employer about these conditions until after her first suicide attempt, over a year after the diagnosis. She was prescribed Prozac in 1991, but it only partially alleviated the depression. She stopped taking the drug in April. In the fall of 1991, she started living with her boyfriend, David Andrade, who worked at a different Amego residence. That relationship was fraught with problems. Andrade used cocaine; Guglielmi, however, says she did not confirm her suspicions of that until late June 1992. In early 1992, she started seeing a social worker, Margaret Posever, for bimonthly therapy sessions.

Earlier, in July 1991, Guglielmi was promoted to the position of Team Leader at the Mansfield residence. The essential functions of that position included: supervising the day-to-day implementation of individual clinical, educational, and vocational programs and data collection for all programs; serving as a role model for staff in all areas of client programming, client services, and professional practice; assessing staff performance, providing additional training, support, and counseling as appropriate; ensuring that Amego's policies and procedures on clients' rights were implemented and documented; responding appropriately in crisis situations; and administering and documenting the use of prescribed medications.

On March 4, 1992, Guglielmi received a performance evaluation which said she was an "exceptional" Team Leader. The evaluation was based on her performance through January 1992. In the spring of 1992, Guglielmi applied for promotion to the position of Program Coordinator for the Mansfield residence. The promotion instead went to Kristen Stone. Stone assumed her new responsibilities on May 4, 1992.

That same day, Guglielmi deliberately took an overdose of nonprescription sleeping pills which she had purchased for that purpose. After taking the pills, she told Andrade what she had done; he took her to the emergency room. She was transferred to a psychiatric hospital and released later that evening. She told health care workers that she attempted suicide because she was upset by problems in her relationship with her boyfriend, her failure to receive the promotion, and other work-related stress. She was readmitted to the psychiatric hospital on May 6, 1992, and stayed there until May 12 because of concerns about her safety. On the day of her readmission to the hospital—two days after her suicide attempt—Guglielmi was not able to "contract for safety" with her therapist Posever. Guglielmi told Posever that even if she were to so contract, her mood was in such flux that she could not be sure she would not hurt herself anyway. A week after returning to work, and again two weeks later, she told Posever that she felt suicidal.

When Guglielmi returned to work on May 13, she told her supervisor only that she had been hospitalized for bulimia and depression. She did not say that she had attempted suicide. She asked her supervisor to modify her work schedule so that she could attend therapy twice or thrice weekly. Her supervisor agreed to this accommodation. However, Guglielmi stopped going to the therapy sessions after a few weeks.

On May 21, 1992, Guglielmi began seeing Dr. Kenneth Levin for psychopharmacological treatment. He diagnosed her as suffering from bulimia and major depression, prescribed Prozac and trazodone, and saw her to monitor her use of medication. Prozac was one of the medications regularly administered to Amego's clients. On June 4, 1992, she told Dr. Levin that she had experienced periodic feelings of increased depression, including a period when she contemplated overdosing. She assured Dr. Levin that if such thoughts recurred, she would not act on them but would inform her boyfriend or a health care provider. She did not keep her word.

On June 13, Guglielmi deliberately overdosed again, this time using her prescription medications, Prozac and trazadone, as well as aspirin. After taking the overdose, she called the Plainville police, who took her to the hospital. She was released on June 15, 1992. She told her health care providers that she was not really depressed when she overdosed but wanted to provoke a reaction from her boyfriend. When Guglielmi returned to work on June 17, she again did not tell her employer that she had attempted suicide.

On the day Guglielmi returned to work, the Executive Director of Amego, Caryn Driscoll, and the Director of Administrative Services, Karen Seal, met with David Andrade about his job performance problems. During this meeting, Andrade mentioned rumors that clients were being drugged at the Fales Road residence. He worked at that location regularly, and Guglielmi worked there occasionally. Around that time, Driscoll learned that Klonopin, one of the medications prescribed for clients, was either missing or was being used at an accelerated rate at the Fales Road residence. Some cocaine users take Klonopin as an antidote, to calm them down from the effects of cocaine.

Amego investigated and found that four of the clients at the Fales Road residence (two of whom should not have had Klonopin at all) had blood levels of Klonopin which were too high. Amego asked any employees who had pertinent information to step forward. Guglielmi did so and was interviewed on June 26 by Driscoll, Amego's Human Rights Officer, and a private investigator. During the interview, Guglielmi focused on her relationship with Andrade, who she feared might be targeted in the investigation. She said that she was suffering from bulimia and depression and revealed for the first time her two recent suicide attempts. In an attempt to explain Andrade's performance issues, she said that he had helped her when she attempted suicide two times by overdosing on both prescription and over-the-counter drugs.

Earlier, on June 5, a shift supervisor at the Mansfield residence, Chester Millet, had noticed that the medication log was missing. He conducted a thorough search, including behind the medication cabinet, and did not find it. Guglielmi also helped look for it. On the same day of her interview with Driscoll, June 26, Guglielmi reported that she had found the missing medication log. She said the log had been behind the medication cabinet, between the cabinet and the wall. Millet told Driscoll that he had previously looked there and had not seen it. Although Driscoll did not initially consider Guglielmi under suspicion for the improper drugging of patients at Fales Road, she and other staff members found the discovery of the book by Guglielmi to be peculiar. A review of the medication log showed that the supply of drugs on hand at the Mansfield residence was excessive. It was not possible to determine from the log whether medications were missing.

On June 26, Driscoll spoke with the Plainville police about her concerns about the drugging of patients at Fales Road. The police told Driscoll that they found pills, initially thought to be Klonopin, in Guglielmi's apartment on the night they responded to her suicide call.

Around June 28, Driscoll received a call from Carlos Andrade, an Amego employee and David Andrade's brother. He told her that staff members felt Guglielmi's job performance was suffering and had asked him to do something about it. He reported that staff members were uncomfortable with her job performance, that she was erratic in behavior, had mood swings, seemed to be focussed on her personal problems, that she was seen walking outside and crying, that she was heard fighting on the phone with David Andrade, and that she was self-absorbed and unable to concentrate on her job.

Carlos Andrade also passed on that Millet, the shift supervisor and one of the most senior staff members at the Mansfield residence, was concerned that Guglielmi had suddenly handed him the drug log, saying that she had found it in the residence when he had searched everywhere for it. Driscoll confirmed Carlos Andrade's report with Millet, who had never before complained about another employee. Carlos Andrade felt that Guglielmi was not performing her job safely and was putting clients at risk. Driscoll knew there was no way to prevent Guglielmi from having access to medication while she worked at Amego.

A few days later, on July 1, Driscoll informed Guglielmi in writing that she was temporarily removed from her position as Team Leader and would be reassigned to perform clerical and other light duties. The letter stated that the fact that Guglielmi's recent hospitalizations were the result of deliberate overdoses of prescription medications raised "concerns about [her] ability to perform [her] present job functions including medication ordering, dispensing and shift supervision." The letter also indicated that Amego's Safety Committee would meet to determine whether Guglielmi could perform her job, or another available job, with or without accommodations. Driscoll said that the Committee should seek medical information from Guglielmi's treating physician.

In an attempt to obtain a professional opinion on Guglielmi's ability to resume her duties, Driscoll sent a letter to Posever on July 1 asking whether Guglielmi could perform eleven duties that a Team Leader would need to perform, set forth on a checklist. The letter came back to

Amego on July 8 with a check in the "yes" column for each job duty. Only Guglielmi had signed the bottom of the checklist.

Driscoll called Posever to ask if the checklist accurately reflected Posever's opinion that Guglielmi could complete the duties or whether the list merely reflected Guglielmi's own opinion. Posever told Driscoll she was not a medical doctor, that the checklist did not represent a medical competency evaluation as to each specific job duty, nor was it a guarantee regarding each duty. It was rather that, based on her discussions with Guglielmi and her knowledge of her work and treatment history, Posever had no reason to think Guglielmi could not perform those duties. Posever's checking "yes" was based on her observations of Guglielmi's demeanor and on Guglielmi's statement that she felt comfortable giving out psychotropic medications at work, even in light of her suicide attempts. Driscoll appeared dissatisfied with the response and pressed for a more definitive opinion, which Posever declined to give. Later, Driscoll told Guglielmi that Posever's response was inadequate.

On July 22, Driscoll sent Dr. Levin a letter requesting his opinion as to whether Guglielmi could perform the eleven functions of her job and enclosing the checklist. In a letter dated July 27, 1992, Dr. Levin wrote that Guglielmi was no longer on prescription medication. He concluded: "My understanding is that she has consistently performed her regular job responsibilities conscientiously and I see no difficulty with her returning to her regular position." There was no checklist with the letter Amego received. Driscoll viewed Dr. Levin's conclusions as largely being based on what Guglielmi said she could do and her representation that she had no performance problems. But Driscoll knew from staff complaints that Guglielmi had a range of performance problems. And Driscoll knew Dr. Levin had not checked with anyone at Amego about whether Guglielmi was in fact performing well. Driscoll told Guglielmi that Dr. Levin's letter did not adequately deal with the job functions issue.

Driscoll was also concerned that the parents of Amego's charges would feel that their children would be put at risk by being in the care of someone who abused prescription drugs. The parents, she felt, would contact one of the state agencies which licensed Amego.

On July 21, the Safety Committee met. The Committee was comprised of four administrators: Seal, the Director of Administrative Services; Amego's Health Coordinator, who was a nurse; the Staff Development Coordinator; and the Administrative Assistant/Workers' Compensation Coordinator. The Committee found that Guglielmi was not in fact performing her job duties conscientiously or performing them well. The Committee concluded that Guglielmi could not safely perform the Team Leader position and that there was no Amego position that could be modified to accommodate her.

On July 27, 1992, Amego's Board of Directors was informed of the recommendation of the Safety Committee and, after additional discussion, concluded that there was no alternative position that could accommodate Guglielmi. The following day Driscoll informed Guglielmi that her employment was terminated. Amego says its core concern was that Guglielmi could not meet the essential job function of handling prescription medication.

II.

The district court entered summary judgment for Amego, finding that the EEOC had failed to meet its burden under the ADA of showing that Guglielmi was qualified for the position of Team Leader and that Amego could have made a reasonable accommodation. The district court also found that the EEOC had failed to meet its burden of showing that Amego had discriminated against Guglielmi "because of" a disability.

* * *

For summary judgment purposes, the parties do not dispute that Guglielmi was a disabled person within the meaning of the ADA. It is also undisputed that an essential function of the Team Leader position is to administer and monitor the medication of Amego's clients. The written job description provides that this is an essential job function, and the EEOC concedes that Team Leaders have access to locked medicine cabinets containing large quantities of drugs and are expected to administer medications to clients.

This case initially turns on whether the EEOC has met its burden of showing that Guglielmi was a "qualified" person. Amego's position is that it terminated Guglielmi's employment because she showed by her conduct—by behavior leading co-workers to have concerns about whether she was a risk to clients and by her two attempts to commit suicide using prescription and non-prescription drugs—that she could not reasonably be trusted to meet her responsibilities as to medications. Although the qualification analysis could be understood to subsume the concept of reasonable accommodation, we think it analytically sounder to treat the two topics separately.

* * *

QUALIFICATION/DIRECT THREAT UNDER TITLE I OF THE ADA

* * *

The general rule of the ADA is that an employer shall not "discriminate against a qualified individual with a disability because of the disability...." 42 U.S.C. § 12112(a). It is generally accepted that, in a Title I case, the plaintiff bears the burden of showing she is a "qualified" individual. *See Jacques*, 96 F.3d at 511. A qualified individual is one who can perform the essential functions of the job held. *See* 29 C.F.R. § 1630.2(m). The statute also says that "the term 'qualification standards' may include a requirement that an individual shall not pose a direct threat to the health or safety of other individuals in the workplace." 42 U.S.C. § 12113(b). It defines "direct threat" as meaning "a significant risk to the health or safety of others that cannot be eliminated by reasonable accommodation." 42 U.S.C. § 12111(3). The rub is that the language about "qualification standards" under Title I appears in a section of the statute entitled "Defenses." 42 U.S.C. § 12113(a) ("It may be a defense to a charge of discrimination under [the ADA] that an alleged application of qualification standards . . . has been shown to be job-related.") The EEOC argues that the employer bears the burden of proof on this affirmative defense.

The EEOC argues further that whenever an issue of threats to the safety or health of others is involved in a Title I case, it must be analyzed under the "direct threat" provision of § 12113(b) as an affirmative defense. Specifically, the EEOC contends that the § 12113(b) provision that qualification standards may include a requirement that an individual not be a direct threat is to be read in the context of the defense set out in § 12113(a). The EEOC supports its position by noting that § 12113 is captioned "Defenses." Thus, the EEOC says, the district court erred in considering the matter of whether Guglielmi posed a threat to the safety of Amego's clients as a matter of "qualification," on which plaintiff bears the burden. Amego contends that the risks posed to others may be considered as part of the qualified individual analysis, and that the specific discussion of a direct threat defense in § 12113 does not preclude the consideration of safety risks in other prongs of the ADA analysis.

* * *

The EEOC stakes out a position which is far too broad. This is not a case where a person who can perform all essential job functions nonetheless poses a risk to others. The district court did not, we believe, commit error in considering risk posed to others under the category of "qualification," where the risk is expressly associated with performance of an essential job function.

The precise issue here concerns the employer's judgment that Guglielmi could not be trusted to handle the medication-related functions of her job. In this case, a failure to perform an essential function—overseeing and administering medication—would necessarily create a risk to others. That a failure to perform a job function correctly creates a risk to others does not preclude the ability to perform that function from being a job qualification. The position argued by the EEOC would lead to the anomalous result that there is a lesser burden of proving qualifications on a plaintiff where the job involves the care of others, and necessarily entails risk to others, than when the job does not. We do not believe Congress intended to weaken the burden on plaintiffs to show they are qualified in such circumstances.

In such cases, where the employee is responsible for ensuring the safety of others entrusted to his or her care, other courts, without discussion of the point the EEOC raises, have simply considered the risk question to be part of the "qualified" analysis. *See, e.g., Doe v. University of Maryland Med. Sys. Corp.,* 50 F.3d 1261, 1265 (4th Cir.1995); *Altman v. New York City Health and Hosp. Corp.,* 903 F.Supp. 503, 509–

10 (S.D.N.Y.1995); *Mauro v. Borgess Med. Ctr.*, 886 F.Supp. 1349, 1352–53 (W.D.Mich.1995).

* * *

Appropriateness of Summary Judgment

The EEOC argues that a jury question is presented, in any event, as to whether the evidence showed Guglielmi was qualified. This is not, we think, a close question.

We set the context. Guglielmi did not meet her burden of demonstrating that she is qualified. There is in this record no suggestion that the employer has applied its standards differentially. The EEOC presents no evidence that the employer has ever found a similarly situated employee to be qualified to handle the essential medication function. Instead, the EEOC attempts to derive from its disagreement with Amego over whether Guglielmi is qualified an inference that the employer's different assessment is based on disability discrimination. However, where, as here, no evidence of animus is present, courts may give reasonable deference to the employer's assessment of what the position demands. *See Doe v. New York Univ.*, 666 F.2d 761, 776 (2d Cir. 1981)(finding that, in case involving mentally ill applicant to medical school, "considerable judicial deference must be paid to the evaluation made by the institution itself, absent proof that its standards and its application of them serve no purpose other than to deny an education to handicapped persons"); *cf. Southeastern Community College*, 442 U.S. at 406, 99 S.Ct. at 2367 (supporting reasonable deference to the decisions made by administrators of federally funded programs so long as no evidence is presented of discriminatory intent with regard to the handicapped person).

* * *

It was eminently reasonable for Amego to be concerned about whether Guglielmi could meet her responsibilities, and also reasonable for it to conclude that the risk was too great to run. The employer's judgment here about the risks of future behavior by an employee is based on past behavior and reasonable indicia of future behavior.

First, the nature of the risk was such that it was extremely difficult to guard against. The clients were particularly vulnerable to abuse or neglect. The mechanisms to insure that they were properly treated with regard to their medications, other than having trustworthy staff, were not obvious. Amego had just learned that, despite its normal procedures, four patients at the Fales Road residence were overly medicated and that it could not determine whether any medications were missing. Testing the clients' blood to determine whether they had received the correct dosage level, or indeed the correct drugs, has to be considered an extraordinary step, and not a safeguard which could routinely be taken. Additionally, the severity of the risk, i.e., the potential harm to third parties, *Arline*, 480 U.S. at 288, 107 S.Ct. at 1131, is great. The potential outcomes of administering the wrong medication to a client are obvious and extreme.

Second, there were performance issues which enhanced the likelihood that the clients could be harmed unless steps were taken. Amego received complaints, from other staff members, that Guglielmi was unable to focus on her job and was a risk to patients. The situation was serious enough that staff members sent an emissary to management, asking that something be done. The peculiarity of Guglielmi finding the missing medication log at a place which had been searched earlier would reasonably give Amego pause. Amego had reason to fear that Guglielmi would take medications from Amego. When the police came to her apartment on the night of her second suicide attempt, they found pills they believed to be Klonopin. Klonopin is taken by cocaine users, and management suspected the man with whom Guglielmi lived of being a cocaine user and of drugging Amego clients.

Third, other measures had not eliminated the risk of Guglielmi mishandling medication. Amego knew that, despite counselling and medication, Guglielmi had attempted suicide a second time using medication and that she would have access to Prozac at work, one of the drugs used in this second attempt. The EEOC says that Amego should have had greater confidence in Guglielmi because she no longer had a prescription for drugs after the second attempt. There is cold comfort in that: this fact increased the likelihood that Guglielmi would use the drugs available to her at work for a third attempt. Amego also knew that despite its provision of a work schedule accommodation, Guglielmi soon stopped going to the therapy sessions she said she wanted to attend after her first suicide attempt. Amego knew that by concealing her suicide attempts Guglielmi had misled them about the nature of her previous absences from work.

Fourth, when Amego sought reassurance from Guglielmi's health care providers, the responses were not confidence-building. Posever, the social worker, neither responded to the substance of the request for information nor signed her name to the checklist. After receiving the checklist, Driscoll telephoned Posever. Posever explicitly declined to give a psychiatric medical opinion. Dr. Levin, the psychopharmacologist, gave a brief response which Amego could reasonably understand to be unresponsive to its concerns and to be based on Guglielmi's own assessment of her ability to do the work.

* * *

Reasonable Accommodation

The EEOC argues that Amego was required to move Guglielmi from the Team Leader position to a Behavior Therapist position as a reasonable accommodation. If the Behavior Therapist position required no responsibility with respect to medication, there would be more force to the EEOC's position. *See Hurley–Bardige v. Brown*, 900 F.Supp. 567, 570 (D.Mass.1995)(finding that there is "no per se rule against transfers as reasonable accommodations"). But the position did entail that responsibility.

Although medication-related duties are not specifically mentioned in the Behavior Therapist job description, the ability to handle, administer, and document medication was inherently part of the Behavior Therapist's function, as listed in Amego's job description, of "implementing individual clinical and educational programs."

All Behavior Therapists receive training in the administration of medications. Behavior Therapists accompany clients on frequent off-site trips into the community and must dispense medications to clients at appropriate times without supervision. When no Shift Supervisors or Team Leaders are present, the Behavior Therapists must dispense medications at the residences. Behavior Therapists also accept deliveries of client medications in Amego's facilities. Keys to the medicine cabinet are easily accessible to Behavior Therapists.

There is no material factual dispute; only the legal implications of these facts are in true dispute. Medication-related duties of the Behavior Therapist position are essential, and not marginal, to the position. While the amount of time a Behavior Therapist spends dispensing medication is not great, the consequences of getting it wrong are quite great indeed.

There was no accommodation that Amego could make to the Behavior Therapist position that would not cause it undue hardship. See 42 U.S.C. §§ 12112(b)(5)(A), 12111(9). To retain Guglielmi while eliminating all of Guglielmi's medication-related duties, it would have been necessary to hire another Behavior Therapist to be paired with her to ensure that she would never be left alone with a client who needed medication. Amego might also have needed an additional supervisor to ensure that Guglielmi did not have access to client medications. The expense of hiring these additional staff would be too great for a small nonprofit like Amego to be reasonably expected to bear. *See Vande Zande v. Wisconsin Dep't of Admin.*, 44 F.3d 538, 542 (7th Cir. 1995)(holding that employer may prove undue hardship by establishing that the costs of the proposed accommodation are excessive in relation either to its benefits or to the employer's financial health or survival).

* * *

Another possible option, rearranging Guglielmi's assignment to clients so that she was never with a client who required medication, would obviously be difficult since, at the time of Guglielmi's employment, only one client at the Mansfield residence did not take medication. Assigning Guglielmi to that one client would disrupt Amego's crucial one-staff-member-to-two-clients ratio, or result in the need for an additional Behavior Therapist. Both options would alter the basic operations of Amego and go beyond the scope of a reasonable accommodation. *See Reigel v. Kaiser Found. Health Plan*, 859 F.Supp. 963, 973 (E.D.N.C. 1994).

[The court's discussion of the EEOC's argument that "action taken because of conduct related to a disability is tantamount to action because of a disability itself" is omitted.]

* * *

The entry of summary judgment for Amego, Inc. is affirmed.

Questions and Comments

1. *Analysis of qualification/direct threat.* The *Amego* court concludes that because one of the Guglielmi's job responsibilities involved ensuring the safety of others, the fact that she was herself a safety risk rendered her unqualified. If Guglielmi's responsibilities had *not* involved caring for others, should she nonetheless have had to prove that she did not pose a safety risk? Or, in that case, should the argument that Guglielmi posed a safety risk have been an affirmative defense, with respect to which Amego had the burden of proof? See Ann Hubbard, "Understanding and Implementing the ADA's Direct Threat Defense," 95 Nw. U.L.Rev. 1279 (2001) (arguing that assertions that a plaintiff creates a threat of violence should be treated as an affirmative defense with respect to which the employer has the burden of proof).

2. *Qualification and Addiction to Illegal Drugs.* Although the definition of disability includes drug addiction or alcoholism that substantially limits one or more major life activities, see, e.g., *Thompson v. Davis,* 282 F.3d 780, 784 (9th Cir.2002), the ADA specifically states the any employee or applicant who is *currently* engaged in the illegal use of drugs is not a "qualified individual with a disability." 42 U.S.C. § 12114(a).

3. *Danger to health or safety of person with disability.* The language of the ADA does not speak directly to the question of whether an employer can assert danger to the health or safety of the disabled person *herself* as an affirmative defense in discrimination actions. An EEOC regulation that permits this defense, 29 CFR § 1630.15(b)(2) (2001), was, however, recently upheld as reasonable by the Supreme Court in the case *Chevron U.S.A. Inc. v. Echazabal,* 536 U.S. 73, 122 S.Ct. 2045, 153 L.Ed.2d 82 (2002). The Court argued that the broad language of the ADA's affirmative defense provision (Section 12113), which allows employers to set qualification standards that are "job-related and consistent with business necessity," coupled with the authority Congress specifically delegated to the EEOC to interpret Title I of the ADA, gave the agency significant discretion in specifying such standards. Moreover, the fact that under Section 12113(b), qualification standards *could* include a requirement "that an individual shall not pose a direct threat to the health or safety of *other individuals* in the workplace" (emphasis added) did not mean that Congress intended to preclude employers from considering the health or safety of the disabled person *herself.* In addition, according to the Court, the EEOC regulation did not promote the "kind of workplace paternalism the ADA was meant to outlaw." In the Court's view, what Congress meant to outlaw was blanket refusal to give opportunities to individuals with disabilities based on "untested and pretextual stereotypes." Congress did not mean to outlaw the "particularized inquiry into the harms the employee would probably face" required by the EEOC regulation.

4. *Reasonable accommodation*. Although the *Amego* court purports to perform its initial analysis of Guglielmi's qualifications without reference to the issue of reasonable accommodation, this initial analysis does emphasize certain steps that Amego had already taken, such as modifying Guglielmi's schedule so she could attend therapy twice or thrice weekly. The court notes that these steps "had not eliminated the risk of Guglielmi mishandling medication." Arguably, Amego's modification of Guglielmi's work schedule was a reasonable accommodation. Indeed, under EEOC enforcement guidelines issued in March 1997, suggested reasonable accommodations include such changes as different working hours and reassignment to different tasks.

Under Title I of the ADA, private employers bear the cost of reasonable accommodation. Was the decision to place these costs on private employers a good idea? What unintended policy consequences might the decision have? For an argument that reasonable accommodations should be funded through general taxation rather than private employers, see Scott A. Moss and Daniel A. Malin, Note, "Public Funding for Disability Accommodations: A Rational Solution to Rational Discrimination," 33 Harv. C.R.-C.L. L. Rev. 197 (1998).

In *U.S. Airways v. Barnett*, 535 U.S. 391, 122 S.Ct. 1516, 152 L.Ed.2d 589 (2002) the Supreme Court suggested that it may take a conservative view of what employers need to do to fulfill the reasonable accommodation requirement. In that case, the Court held that an employer's showing that a requested accommodation conflicts with seniority rules is ordinarily sufficient to show, as a matter of law, that the accommodation is not reasonable. Lower courts have also taken a parsimonious view of what is required to meet the reasonable accommodation requirement, suggesting that only those accommodations that yield benefits in excess of their costs should be considered reasonable. See, e.g., *Vande Zande v. Wisconsin Dep't of Administration*, 44 F.3d 538 (7th Cir.1995). According to the *Vande Zande* court, a focus on cost-benefit analysis is consistent with the ADA's purpose of saving society the costs of welfare dependency by individuals with disabilities: "The savings will be illusory if employers are required to expend many more billions in accommodation than will be saved by enabling disabled people to work." Id. at 543. See also Samuel R. Bagenstos, "The American with Disabilities Act as Welfare Reform," 44 Wm. & Mary L.Rev. 921 (2003) (observing that many supporters of the proposed ADA "argued that the statute was necessary to reduce the high societal costs of dependency . . .") For arguments that the reasonable accommodation requirement, and the ADA more generally, may be efficient, see J.H. Verkerke, "Is the ADA Efficient?," 50 U.C.L.A. Rev. 903 (2003) (arguing that disability discrimination law can combat problems of incomplete and asymmetric information that would otherwise arise through the presence of individuals with disabilities in the labor market); Amy Wax, "Disability, Reciprocity, and 'Real Efficiency': A Unified Approach," 44 Wm. & Mary L.Rev. 1421 (2003) (arguing that ADA is efficient so long as one assumes some imperfections in labor markets and that society will feel obliged provide basic support to those who cannot support themselves through no fault of their own).

While the ADA may be efficient for society as a whole, its reasonable accommodation requirement does impose a cost on employers and could therefore discourage the hiring of individuals with disabilities. One recent empirical study suggests that decreases in the employment rates of these individuals after the enactment of the ADA are in fact attributable to the law's imposition of an accommodation requirement. Christine Jolls and J.J. Prescott, "Disaggregating Employment Discrimination: The Case of Disability Discrimination," available at www.ssrn.com/abstract_580741. On the other hand, at least one study, conducted at Sears, Roebuck, & Co.between 1993 and 1995, indicates that the cost of accommodating workers with mental and behavioral disorders may be low. At Sears, Roebuck these workers represented only 7% of the population requesting accommodation; in addition, the average cost of accommodation for each of these workers was negligible. See Terry Carter, "Unhappy to Oblige," ABA Journal 36, July 1997 (summarizing study results). Similarly, according to one commentator, the majority of workplace disability cases involve disabilities triggered by aspects of the workplace environment that could readily have been remedied. See Susan Stefan, "You'd Have to Be Crazy To Work Here": Worker Stress, the Abusive Workplace, and Title I of the ADA, 31 Loy. L.A.L. Rev. 795 (1998). Note that requests for telecommuting as an accommodation have not fared well in the courts. See, e.g., *Vande Zande*, supra (employer did not have to allow telecommuting to accommodate an employee with pressure ulcers); *Mason v. Avaya Communications*, 357 F.3d 1114 (10th Cir. 2004) (rejecting a requirement of telecommuting for an employee with posttraumatic stress disorder).

5. *Reasonable accommodation for those "regarded as" having a disability*. Individuals can qualify for ADA protection not only by virtue of a current disability but also if they are "regarded as" having a disability or if they have a "record" of a disability. The appellate courts are currently split as to whether employers must accommodate individuals who are regarded as having a disability. While the Fifth, Sixth, and Ninth Circuits have held that such employees are not entitled to accommodation, the Third, Tenth, and Eleventh Circuits have held that they are entitled. In rejecting an accommodation requirement, the Ninth Circuit acknowledged that the plain language of the ADA does not draw distinctions between the three mechanisms for proving disability. The court nonetheless argued that if "regarded as" employees were entitled to accommodation, "it would do nothing to encourage those employees to educate employers of their capabilities, and do nothing to encourage the employers to see their employees' talents clearly." *Kaplan v. City of North Las Vegas*, 323 F.3d 1226 (9th Cir. 2003). Is the Ninth Circuit's argument persuasive?

6. *Undue hardship*. Title I of the ADA provides that the following factors must be weighed in determining whether a particular accommodation should be considered an undue hardship: the nature and cost of the accommodation; the overall financial resources of the facility; the number of persons employed at the facility; the effect on expenses and resources, or the impact otherwise of such accommodation upon the operation of the facility; the overall financial resources of the covered entity; the overall size of the business of a covered entity; the number, type, and location of its facilities; and the type of operations of the covered entity including the composition, structure, and functions of the workforce of such entity; the geographic separateness, administrative, or fiscal relationship of the facility in question to the covered entity. 42 U.S.C. § 12111(10)(B). On which of these factors did the court focus in making its determination that Guglielmi could not be

reasonably accommodated as a Behavior Therapist? Do you think these factors provide enough guidance to courts?

7. *Relationship between anti-discrimination law and disability law.* Sometimes claimants who file anti-discrimination lawsuits under the ADA or the Rehabilitation Act also file claims for disability benefits under the Supplementary Security Income ("SSI") or Supplemental Security Disability Insurance ("SSDI") programs. In order to receive benefits under SSI or SSDI, the claimant must prove that he or she is unable to "engage in *any* substantial gainful activity by reason of any medically determinable mental or physical impairment . . ." 42 U.S.C. § 423(d)(1)(A) (emphasis added). (For further discussion of the SSI and SSDI programs, see Chapter 11, Section II(A) *supra*.) In the years immediately following passage of the ADA, some appellate courts determined that individuals who claimed complete inability to work in order to secure benefits under SSI or SSDI were judicially estopped from then claiming that they were "qualified" for the purposes of the ADA or Rehabilitation Act. See *McNemar v. Disney Store, Inc.*, 91 F.3d 610 (3d. Cir.1996); *Hindman v. Greenville Hosp. Sys.*, 947 F.Supp. 215 (D.S.C.1996), *aff'd* 133 F.3d 915 (4th Cir.1997). Other courts declined to establish a per se rule of judicial estoppel but nonetheless established a rebuttable presumption in favor of summary judgment for the employer. See *Cleveland v. Policy Mgmt. Sys. Corp.*, 120 F.3d 513 (5th Cir.1997); *Dush v. Appleton Elec. Co.*, 124 F.3d 957 (8th Cir.1997). A third set of appellate decisions rejected the judicial estoppel argument altogether on the grounds that the disability benefits determination did not take into account the question of reasonable accommodation. See *Talavera v. School Board of Palm Beach County*, 129 F.3d 1214 (11th Cir.1997); *Swanks v. Washington Metro. Area Transit Auth'y*, 116 F.3d 582 (D.C.Cir.1997). Thus, an individual who, without reasonable accommodation, was unable to work could make a legitimate claim for disability benefits. With reasonable accommodation, this same person could also legitimately claim that he was "qualified" for the purposes of ADA protection.

In *Cleveland v. Policy Management Systems Corp.*, 526 U.S. 795, 119 S.Ct. 1597, 143 L.Ed.2d 966 (1999), the Supreme Court addressed the division among the circuits. The Court held that the receipt of SSDI did not preclude an ADA claim or result in a strong presumption against the success of such a claim. Following several of the lower courts, the Supreme Court noted that Social Security Administration ("SSA") does not take into account the possibility of reasonable accommodation when determining SSI or SSDI eligibility. In addition, an individual may qualify for SSI or SSDI under the SSA's administrative rules, which create a variety of simplifying assumptions regarding eligibility but, nonetheless, "due to special individual circumstances, be capable of performing the essential functions of her job." Finally, an individual's condition may change over time, so that a statement about her disability at the time of application for SSI or SSDI benefits does not necessarily reflect her capacities at the time of employment.

C. PROCEDURES AND REMEDIES

Title I of the ADA specifically incorporates by reference the procedural requirements set forth in Title VII of the Civil Rights Act of 1964. *See* 42 U.S.C. § 12117 (Title I ADA provision incorporating section

2000e–5 of Title VII). As a consequence, individuals claiming discrimination by employers under Titles I must exhaust administrative remedies before bringing judicial action. The administrative procedure involves filing a charge of discrimination with the EEOC within 180 days of the alleged violation. If the EEOC either dismisses the charge or declines to file a civil action, the individual may thereafter file an action on his own behalf in federal district court. 42 U.S.C. § 2000e–5. These procedural requirements also apply to employees bringing claims under the Rehabilitation Act. See, e.g., *Davoll v. Webb*, 943 F.Supp. 1289, 1297–98 (D.Colo. 1996) (collecting cases).

The remedies available under Title I of the ADA are also based on Title VII. Thus, pursuant to the Civil Rights Act of 1991, employees bringing Title I claims may seek not only reinstatement and back pay but also compensatory and punitive damages. 42 U.S.C. § 1981a. Compensatory and punitive damages are only recoverable, however, in cases that claim intentional discriminations. Moreover, in order to recover punitive damages, the claimant must prove that the employer "engaged in a discriminatory practice with malice or with reckless indifference to the federally protected rights of an aggrieved individual." 29 U.S.C. § 1981a(b)(1).

Finally, there are certain limits on the amounts of compensatory and punitive damages that can be recovered. The limits, which apply to the sum of compensatory and punitive damages, vary according to the total numbers of employees the employer has. Thus, for employers who have fewer that 100 employees, the damages may total no more than $50,000. At the other end of the spectrum, employers with more than 500 employees may be liable for damages of up to $300,000. *Id.* § 1981(b) (3).

Note: Title I Suits Against State Government Defendants

In *Board of Trustees of the University of Alabama v. Garrett*, 531 U.S. 356, 121 S.Ct. 955, 148 L.Ed.2d 866 (2001), the Supreme Court issued a 5–4 opinion holding that state government employees are barred by the 11th amendment from suing for monetary damages under Title I of the ADA. The *Garrett* decision extends to the ADA a line of federalism jurisprudence in which the Supreme Court has held, 5–4 (with Justices Rehnquist, Scalia, O'Connor, Kennedy, and Thomas in the majority) that 11th Amendment immunity applies to states in suits brought under federal law for monetary damages and that Congress' ability to abrogate such immunity is limited. According to this jurisprudence, Congress may not abrogate state sovereign immunity based upon its Article I powers. Moreover, even when Congress acts pursuant to its powers under Section 5 of the 14th amendment, it may only enact legislation that exhibits "congruence and proportionality between the injury to be prevented or remedied and the means adopted to that end." Id. at 365 (citing *City of Boerne v. Flores*, 521 U.S. 507, 520, 117 S.Ct. 2157, 138 L.Ed.2d 624 (1997)).

The *Garrett* majority emphasized that the disabled are not a suspect class for purposes of 14th Amendment equal protection analysis. Given this fact, the injury to be prevented or remedied is discrimination that fails rational basis review. According to the *Garrett* majority, prior to the enactment of the ADA, there was insufficient evidence that state governments had shown a pattern of clearly irrational discrimination against the disabled in employment. Moreover, evidence of discrimination by local government units could not be used to support abrogation of state sovereign immunity. In addition, even if Congress had found a pattern of unconstitutional (i.e. irrational) disability-based discrimination by the states, the rights and remedies created by the ADA against state employers, particularly the affirmative requirement of reasonable accommodation, raised questions of "congruence and proportionality."

Writing for the dissent, Justice Breyer emphasized that the majority was applying to Congress an elevated evidentiary standard that was generally applied only to judges. As he noted, "[t]he problem with the Court's approach is that neither the "burden of proof" that favors States nor any other rule of restraint applicable to *judges* applies to *Congress* when it exercises its 5 power." (emphasis in original). See also Robert C. Post and Reva B. Siegel, "Protecting the Constitution from the People: Juricentric Restrictions on Section Five Power," 78 Ind.L.J. 1 (2003) (noting that "*Garrett* imposes a substantial and improper burden on congressional power to enforce civil rights" and arguing that, as a historical matter, the Court understood Congress' Section 5 power as extending to conduct that would not violate the Court's own interpretation of Section 1 of the Fourteenth Amendment).

The *Garrett* decision mention that some remedies may still be available under the ADA to state employees who face disability-based discrimination. For example, state employees can sue individual state officials (as contrasted with state institutions) for prospective injunctive relief under the *Ex Parte Young* doctrine. In addition, Title I standards can be enforced by the United States in actions for money damages. The inability of employees to secure monetary damages nonetheless diminishes the likelihood that they will file suit under the ADA. In addition, there is some question regarding whether, as a statutory matter, the remedial scheme set up by the ADA precludes suits for injunctive relief against individual state officials.

To the extent that the state government employer receives federal government funding under the Rehabilitation Act, it may be vulnerable to suits for monetary damages under the Rehabilitation Act. The Supreme Court has recognized that Congress may "condition its grant of funds to States upon their taking certain actions that Congress could not require them to take." See College Savings Bank v. Florida Prepaid Postsecondary Education Expense Board, et al., 527 U.S. 666, 686, 119 S.Ct. 2219, 144 L.Ed.2d 605 (1999). Such actions include a waiver of sovereign immunity. Moreover, most lower courts (and, arguably, the Supreme Court, see *Lane v. Pena*, 518 U.S. 187, 116 S.Ct. 2092, 135

L.Ed.2d 486 (1996)) have held that the language of Section 2000d–7 of the Rehabilitation Act, which speaks directly to the sovereign immunity question, makes it clear that states waive sovereign immunity when they agree to accept funds under the Act. See *Duncan v. Washington Metropolitan Area Transit Authority*, 214 F.R.D. 43, 47 (2003) (holding that Section 2000d–7 provision is a "valid and unambiguous waiver" of sovereign immunity and citing various decisions by Ninth, Sixth, Eighth, Fourth, and Fifth Circuits that have relied on *Lane* or Section 2000d–7 to reach the same holding). But see *Garcia v. S.U.N.Y. Health Sciences Center*, 280 F.3d 98 (2d Cir.2001) (finding no waiver of sovereign immunity through acceptance of Rehabilitation Act funds).

In contrast with Title I of the ADA, the language of the Rehabilitation Act is silent as to the availability of monetary damages. 29 U.S.C. § 794a(a)(2). However, the Rehabilitation Act imports the remedial scheme of Title VI of the Civil Rights Act, and the Supreme Court has held that monetary damages are available under Title VI. *Alexander v. Sandoval*, 532 U.S. 275, 277–80, 121 S.Ct. 1511, 149 L.Ed.2d 517 (2001). In addition to relying on the Rehabilitation Act, it is possible that plaintiffs suing for monetary damages could rely directly on constitutional equal protection guarantees. However, as noted earlier (and as discussed further in Section V), individuals with disabilities are not a suspect class. Thus these guarantees could only be invoked if the defendant's behavior was clearly irrational.

The *Garrett* Court did not rule on the question of whether sovereign immunity barred suits against state defendants for monetary damages under Title II, which applies to non-employment cases. As discussed further in Parts III and IV, several recent Supreme Court cases have allowed Title II suits for monetary damages to proceed in circumstances where a constitutional right was arguably at issue.

D. SPECIAL PROBLEMS: AFFIRMATIVE ACTION PROGRAMS

Section 501 of the Rehabilitation Act of 1973 requires each federal agency to promulgate "an affirmative action program plan for the hiring, placement, and advancement of individuals with handicaps...." 29 U.S.C. § 791(b). The agency is to include within the plan "a description of the extent to which and methods whereby the special needs of employees with handicaps are being met." *Id.* This affirmative action requirement is, however, fairly narrow: it extends only to federal agencies and not to entities receiving federal funds. (Notably, the ADA does not have an affirmative action requirement.) As is clear from the case that follows, the Rehabilitation Act allows private causes of action for alleged violations of Section 501.

Persons given indefinite appointments under subsection (h), on the other hand, are former patients of the mental institution who no longer are disabled at the time of their appointment, but whose well-being favors their employment at the institution with which they are familiar. Some of those individuals might have qualified initially for appointment in the competitive service by taking and passing the usual examination, and any of them could have obtained such competitive permanent positions after appointment by following that course. Indeed, a number of former patients of St. Elizabeth's, originally appointed under subsection (h), have done precisely that and now hold permanent appointments in the classified service with the accompanying rights and benefits. Although the appellees might have obtained a classified position after their appointment by taking and passing the same competitive examination that other nondisqualified persons routinely take, they have not attempted to do so.

The appellees' position is that because they perform the same work as other employees who occupy identical positions in the competitive service, they are entitled to the same benefits the other employees have, and that the denial of those benefits illegally discriminates against them on the basis of their former mental disability. The different treatment of the appellees from the other employees performing the same work, however, results not from the former mental disability of the appellees but from the fact that they were appointed without having to comply with the requirements for the competitive service. In order to achieve the benefits from employment in an environment with which they had become familiar and in which they were comfortable, the government permitted the appellees to obtain their positions without taking and passing the competitive examination that other employees were required to take to obtain the same jobs.

In my view, the government justifiably treated these two categories of employees differently in not giving to the appellees all the civil service protections and benefits of the employees who obtained their positions through the competitive examination process. The difference in the nature of their appointments warranted the different rights and benefits given to each category.

* * *

As a policy matter, the result reached in the present case is commendable. My difficulty with that result is that I do not think it reflects a proper use of judicial power. Congress has given the President broad discretion by regulation to administer the laws regulating government employment and therefore to determine the bases for appointments to positions in the executive branch and to define the rights and benefits of employees so appointed. 5 U.S.C. § 3301 (1982). The President in turn has delegated this authority to the Office of Personnel Management. * * * If the type of appointment under subsection (h) and the rights and benefits of employees appointed under that subsection are to be changed,

I think such changes must come from the Office of Personnel Management and not from the courts.

Questions and Comments

1. *The scope of the affirmative action requirement.* Neither Section 501 nor the implementing regulations prescribes how agencies should design affirmative action plans. Given this lack of textual authority, did the majority go beyond its authority in finding a Section 501 violation? What are the likely long term effects of decisions such as *Allen v. Heckler*? Do decisions like these make it more or less likely that agencies will adopt affirmative action programs?

2. *Remedies for Section 501 violations.* The Rehabilitation Act gives courts broad power to remedy Section 501 violations. It provides that courts may fashion remedies for Section 501 violations that "take into account the reasonableness of any necessary workplace accommodation, and the availability of alternatives therefor or other appropriate relief in order to achieve an equitable and appropriate remedy." 29 U.S.C. § 794a(a)(1).

3. *Section 501 and the qualification requirement.* Courts have held that Section 501 can be used to challenge not only the validity of an agency's affirmative action plan but also employment decisions more generally. See, e.g., *Langon v. Department of Health and Human Services*, 959 F.2d 1053 (D.C.Cir.1992); *Fuller v. Frank*, 916 F.2d 558 (9th Cir.1990). In particular, regulations issued under Section 501 impose on government employers obligations very similar to those imposed under Section 504. These regulations provide that the governmental employer must "make reasonable accommodation to the known physical or mental limitations of a qualified handicapped applicant or employee unless the agency can demonstrate that the accommodation would impose an undue hardship on the operation of its program." 29 C.F.R. § 1613.704(a). Could the *Allen* plaintiffs have brought suit under this alternate Section 501 theory?

4. *Disabled v. "recovered" employees.* The dissent emphasizes that (while persons covered by) subsections (t) and (u) of the regulations concerning excepted positions are disabled at the time they are hired, persons covered by subsection (h) are not disabled at the time they are hired. The dissent claims that for this reason a distinction can be drawn between the treatment of subsection (h) employees and subsection (t) and (u) employees. Is this reasoning compelling?

III.   POSTSECONDARY EDUCATION

The Individuals with Disabilities Education Act ("IDEA"), discussed in Chapter 11, Section I, provides special educational benefits at the elementary and secondary school level. At the postsecondary level, there is no comparable statute that specifically mandates special benefits for individuals with disabilities: Rather than mandating benefits, the ADA and the Rehabilitation Act require postsecondary educational institutions to make accommodations for students with disabilities, both mental and physical. The IDEA has, nonetheless had a significant effect on postsecondary education. Since its passage in 1976, it has led to many more disabled children being diagnosed and provided with special educational services; as a consequence, the number of disabled applicants to postsecondary educational institutions has increased substantially. The proportion of students claiming a mental disability has increased at a particularly significant rate. While 16.1% of entering college freshmen with disabilities reported a learning disability in 1988, by 2001 that percentage had more than doubled, to 40.1%. See American Council on Education, College Freshmen with Disabilities: A Biennial Statistical Profile (2001). Dyslexia (reading disorder) is the most common cognitive impairment that college students report; they also report such disorders as dyscalculia (difficulty with math), dysgraphia (difficulty with writing), anxiety disorders, and attention deficit-hyperactivity disorder.

As noted earlier, depending on how the postsecondary educational institution is funded, one or more of the following anti-discrimination provisions may be applicable: Section 504 of the Rehabilitation Act, Title II of the ADA, or Title III of the ADA. Each statutory provision prohibits the educational institution from denying services or programs to qualified disabled students or from adopting program eligibility criteria that tend to screen out qualified disabled students.

One of the most important issues that arises in the application of anti-discrimination law to educational institutions is the scope of the reasonable accommodation requirement. Under Titles II and III of the ADA, for example, an accommodation is not reasonable under two circumstances: one, if it would cause undue hardship (the same limitation as in Title I); and two, if it would cause a "fundamental alteration" of the service or program in question. *See* 28 C.F.R. §§ 35.130(b)(7), 35.164 (regulations interpreting Title II); 28 C.F.R. §§ 36.302(a), 36.303(a) (regulations interpreting Title III). As the case set out below illustrates, the educational context is somewhat unique in that courts often defer to the professional judgment of educators with respect to what would be "unreasonable."

WYNNE v. TUFTS UNIVERSITY SCHOOL OF MEDICINE

United States Court of Appeals, First Circuit, 1992.
976 F.2d 791.

SELYA, CIRCUIT JUDGE.

This appeal requires us to revisit a longstanding dispute between Tufts University School of Medicine and Steven Wynne, a former student. On a previous occasion, we vacated the district court's entry of summary judgment in Tufts' favor. *See Wynne v. Tufts Univ. School of Medicine*, 932 F.2d 19 (1st Cir.1991) (en banc). After further proceedings, the district court again entered summary judgment for the defendant. This time around, on an augmented record, we affirm.

BACKGROUND

The facts pertinent to Wynne's banishment from the groves of academe are chronicled in our earlier opinion and need not be fully rehearsed. A succinct summary suffices.

Wynne matriculated at Tufts in 1983. He failed eight of fifteen first-year courses. Although academic guidelines provided for dismissal after five course failures, the dean granted Wynne a special dispensation and allowed him to repeat the first year of medical school. Over the summer of 1984, Wynne underwent neuropsychological testing at Tufts' instance and expense. The results, described in detail in our earlier opinion, *id.* at 21, showed cognitive deficits and weaknesses in processing discrete units of information. However, no differential diagnosis of dyslexia or any other particularized learning disability was made at this time.

During Wynne's second tour of the first-year curriculum, Tufts arranged to supply him with tutors, counsellors, note-takers, and other aids. This time, he passed all but two courses: pharmacology and biochemistry. Tufts still did not expel Wynne. Instead, it permitted him to take make-up examinations in these two subjects. He passed pharmacology but failed biochemistry. That ended the matter. Wynne was dismissed in September, 1985.

PRIOR PROCEEDINGS

In his court case, Wynne alleged that he was learning-disabled and that Tufts had discriminated against him on the basis of his handicap. In short order, Wynne refined his claim to allege that his disability placed him at an unfair disadvantage in taking written multiple-choice examinations and that Tufts, for no good reason, had stubbornly refused to test his proficiency in biochemistry by some other means. Eventually, the district court granted summary judgment in Tufts' favor on the ground that Wynne, because of his inability to pass biochemistry, was not an "otherwise qualified" handicapped person within the meaning of section 504 of the Rehabilitation Act of 1973, 29 U.S.C. § 794 (1988), as explicated by the relevant caselaw.

On appeal, a panel of this court reversed. That opinion was withdrawn, however, and the full court reheard Wynne's appeal. We concluded that, in determining whether an aspiring medical student meets section 504's "otherwise qualified" prong, it is necessary to take into account the extent to which reasonable accommodations that will satisfy the legitimate interests of both the school and the student are (or are not) available and, if such accommodations exist, the extent to which the institution explored those alternatives. *See Wynne*, 932 F.2d at 24–26 (citing, *inter alia*, *School Bd. of Nassau County v. Arline*, 480 U.S. 273, 107 S.Ct. 1123, 94 L.Ed.2d 307 (1987)). Recognizing the unique considerations that come into play when the parties to a Rehabilitation Act case are a student and an academic institution, particularly a medical school training apprentice physicians, we formulated a test for determining whether the academic institution adequately explored the availability of reasonable accommodations:

If the institution submits undisputed facts demonstrating that the relevant officials within the institution considered alternative means, their feasibility, cost and effect on the academic program, and came to a rationally justifiable conclusion that the available alternatives would result either in lowering academic standards or requiring substantial program alteration, the court could rule as a matter of law that the institution had met its duty of seeking reasonable accommodation. In most cases, we believe that, as in the qualified immunity context, the issue of whether the facts alleged by a university support its claim that it has met its duty of reasonable accommodation will be a purely legal one. Only if essential facts were genuinely disputed or if there were significantly probative evidence of bad faith or pretext would further fact finding be necessary.

Id. at 26 (citation and internal quotation marks omitted). Because the summary judgment record did not satisfactorily address this issue,[2] we vacated the judgment and remanded for further proceedings, leaving the district court "free to consider other submissions [and] to enter summary judgment."

Following remand, Tufts filed a renewed motion for summary judgment accompanied by six new affidavits. The plaintiff filed a comprehensive opposition supported, inter alia, by his own supplemental affidavit. The court below read the briefs, heard oral argument, reviewed the parties' updated submissions, and determined that Tufts had met its burden under Wynne. In the lower court's view, the expanded record clearly showed that Tufts had evaluated the available alternatives to its current testing format and had reasonably concluded that it was not practicable in this instance to depart from the standard multiple-choice format. Accordingly, the court again entered summary judgment in Tufts' favor. This appeal ensued.

ISSUES

The principal issue on appeal is whether, given those facts not genuinely in dispute, Tufts can be said, as a matter of law, either to have provided reasonable accommodations for plaintiff's handicapping condition or to have demonstrated that it reached a rationally justifiable conclusion that accommodating plaintiff would lower academic standards or otherwise unduly affect its program. There is also a secondary issue: whether plaintiff has advanced significantly probative evidence sufficient

---

2. Tufts had filed only a single affidavit touching upon this issue. Scrutiny of that affidavit, signed by the dean, revealed the following shortcomings: "There is no mention [in the dean's affidavit] of any consideration of possible alternatives, nor reference to any discussion of the unique qualities of multiple choice examinations. There is no indication of who took part in the decision [not to deviate from multiple choice examinations] or when it was made." *Wynne*, 932 F.2d at 28. Because we thought that a party seeking summary judgment should proffer more than "the simple conclusory averment of the head of an institution," we declined to accept the dean's affidavit as a sufficient basis for shortstopping the litigation thereon "if [an expanded record] meet[s] the standard we have set forth". *Id.* at 28.

to ground a finding that Tufts' reasons for not making further accommodations were pretextual or asserted in bad faith.

* * *

DISCUSSION

We have carefully reviewed the amplitudinous record and are fully satisfied that the district court did not err in granting summary judgment. Fairly read, the record presents no genuine issue as to any material fact. Because this case has consumed so many hours of judicial time, we resist the temptation to wax longiloquent. Instead, we add only a few decurtate observations embellishing what the en banc court previously wrote and remarking the significance of the new materials adduced below.

First: Following remand, Tufts satisfactorily filled the gaps that wrecked its initial effort at summary judgment. The expanded record contains undisputed facts demonstrating, in considerable detail, that Tufts' hierarchy "considered alternative means" and "came to a rationally justifiable conclusion" regarding the adverse effects of such putative accommodations. *Wynne*, 932 F.2d at 26. Tufts not only documented the importance of biochemistry in a medical school curriculum, but explained why, in the departmental chair's words, "the multiple choice format provides the fairest way to test the students' mastery of the subject matter of biochemistry." Tufts likewise explained what thought it had given to different methods of testing proficiency in biochemistry and why it eschewed alternatives to multiple-choice testing, particularly with respect to make-up examinations. In so doing, Tufts elaborated upon the unique qualities of multiple-choice examinations as they apply to biochemistry and offered an exposition of the historical record to show the background against which such tests were administered to Wynne. In short, Tufts demythologized the institutional thought processes leading to its determination that it could not deviate from its wonted format to accommodate Wynne's professed disability. It concluded that to do so would require substantial program alterations, result in lowering academic standards, and devalue Tufts' end product—highly trained physicians carrying the prized credential of a Tufts degree.

To be sure, Tufts' explanations, though plausible, are not necessarily ironclad. For instance, Wynne has offered evidence that at least one other medical school and a national testing service occasionally allow oral renderings of multiple-choice examinations in respect to dyslexic students. But, the point is not whether a medical school is "right" or "wrong" in making program-related decisions. Such absolutes rarely apply in the context of subjective decisionmaking, particularly in a scholastic setting. The point is that Tufts, after undertaking a diligent assessment of the available options, felt itself obliged to make "a professional, academic judgment that [a] reasonable accommodation [was] simply not available." *Wynne*, 932 F.2d at 27–28. Phrased another way, Tufts decided, rationally if not inevitably, that no further accommodation could be made without imposing an undue (and injurious) hardship on the academic program. With the diligence of its assessment and the justification for its judgment clearly shown in the augmented record, and with the fact of the judgment uncontroverted, the deficiency that spoiled Tufts' original effort at brevis disposition has been cured.

Second: The undisputed facts show that Tufts neither ignored Wynne nor turned a deaf ear to his plight. To the contrary, the defendant (a) warned Wynne in 1983 that he was failing biochemistry and suggested he defer his examination (a suggestion that Wynne scotched); (b) arranged for a complete battery of neuropsychological tests after Wynne failed eight courses in his freshman year; (c) waived the rules and permitted Wynne to repeat the first-year curriculum; (d) furnished Wynne access to tutoring, taped lectures, and the like; (e) allowed him to take untimed examinations; and (f) gave him make-up examinations in pharmacology and biochemistry after he again failed both courses. Given the other circumstances extant in this case, we do not think that a reasonable factfinder could conclude that Tufts, having volunteered such an array of remedial measures, was guilty of failing to make a reasonable accommodation merely because it did not also offer Wynne, unsolicited, an oral rendering of the biochemistry examination.

Third: Reasonableness is not a constant. To the contrary, what is reasonable in a particular situation may not be reasonable in a different situation—even if the situational differences are relatively slight. *Cf., e.g., United States v. Rodriguez–Morales*, 929 F.2d 780, 785 (1st Cir. 1991) (concluding that "reasonableness has a protean quality"), *cert. denied*, 502 U.S. 1030, 112 S.Ct. 868, 116 L.Ed.2d 774 (1992); *Sierra Club v. Secretary of the Army*, 820 F.2d 513, 517 (1st Cir.1987) (paraphrasing Emerson and observing that "reasonableness 'is a mutable cloud, which is always and never the same.'"). Ultimately, what is reasonable depends on a variable mix of factors.

In the section 504 milieu, an academic institution can be expected to respond only to what it knows (or is chargeable with knowing). This means, as the Third Circuit has recently observed, that for a medical school "to be liable under the Rehabilitation Act, [it] must know or be reasonably expected to know of [a student's] handicap." *Nathanson v. Medical College of Pa.*, 926 F.2d 1368, 1381 (3d Cir.1991). A relevant aspect of this inquiry is whether the student ever put the medical school on notice of his handicap by making "a sufficiently direct and specific request for special accommodations." *Id.* at 1386. Thus, we must view the reasonableness of Tufts' accommodations against the backdrop of what Tufts knew about Wynne's needs while he was enrolled there.

Several factors are entitled to weight in this equation, including the following: (a) Wynne was never diagnosed as dyslexic while enrolled at Tufts; (b) the school gave him a number of special dispensations and "second chances"—including virtually every accommodation that he seasonably suggested; (c) Wynne had taken, and passed, multiple-choice examinations in several courses; and (d) he never requested, at any time prior to taking and failing the third biochemistry exam, that an oral rendering be substituted for the standard version of the multiple-choice test. Under these circumstances, we do not believe a rational factfinder could conclude that Tufts' efforts at accommodation fell short of the reasonableness standard.

Fourth: Wynne's allegations of pretext do not raise prohibitory doubts about the reasonableness of Tufts' attempted accommodations or about the honesty of its assessment of alternatives to multiple-choice examinations vis-a-vis the school's educational plan. When pretext is at issue in a discrimination case, it is a plaintiff's duty to produce specific facts which, reasonably viewed, tend logically to undercut the defendant's position. *See, e.g., Villanueva v. Wellesley College*, 930 F.2d 124, 127 (1st Cir.), *cert. denied*, 502 U.S. 861, 112 S.Ct. 181, 116 L.Ed.2d 143 (1991); *Mack*, 871 F.2d at 181. The plaintiff may neither "rest[ ] merely upon conclusory allegations, improbable inferences, and unsupported speculation," *Medina-Munoz v. R.J. Reynolds Tobacco Co.*, 896 F.2d 5, 8 (1st Cir.1990), nor measurably bolster his cause by hurling rancorous epithets and espousing tenuous insinuations. *See Mesnick*, 950 F.2d at 826; *Yerardi's Moody St. Restaurant & Lounge, Inc. v. Board of Selectmen*, 932 F.2d 89, 92 (1st Cir.1991).

Here, Wynne's charges comprise more cry than wool. They consist of unsubstantiated conclusions, backed only by a few uncoordinated evidentiary fragments. More is required to forestall summary judgment. *See Wynne*, 932 F.2d at 26.

CONCLUSION

We need go no further. In our earlier opinion, we recognized the existence of a statutory obligation on the part of an academic institution such as Tufts to consider available ways of accommodating a handicapped student and, when seeking summary judgment, to produce a factual record documenting its scrupulous attention to this obligation. *Id.* at 25–26. Of course, the effort requires more than lip service; it must be sincerely conceived and conscientiously implemented. We think that Tufts, the second time around, has cleared the hurdle that we envisioned: the undisputed facts contained in the expanded record, when considered in the deferential light that academic decisionmaking deserves, *id.* at 25, meet the required standard.

We add a final note of caution. Although both parties to this litigation invite us to paint with a broad brush, we decline their joint invitation. The issue before us is not whether a medical student, authoritatively diagnosed as a dyslexic and known to the school to be so afflicted, is ever entitled, upon timely request, to an opportunity to take an examination orally. Rather, we are limited to the idiosyncratic facts of Wynne's case. The resulting record presents a narrower, easier issue— and we believe that the district court resolved that issue correctly.

Affirmed.

Questions and Comments

1. *Deference to academics and educators.* Deference to the decisionmaking of academics and educators is a longstanding judicial principle. The Supreme Court has noted that "[w]hen judges are asked to review the substance of a genuinely academic decision ... they should show great respect for the faculty's professional judgment." *Regents of Univ. of Mich. v. Ewing*, 474 U.S. 214, 227, 106 S.Ct. 507, 88 L.Ed.2d 523 (1985); see also *Halasz v. University of New England*, 1992 WL 404581 (D.Me.1992) (deferring to university decision to mandate a higher GPA for students in school's special learning disability program than for other students); *Doe v. New York University*, 666 F.2d 761 (2d Cir.1981) (deferring to medical school decision that applicant with history of mental illness and antisocial behavior was not qualified to reenter medical school). Arguably, however, blind deference can mean that the court is abdicating the responsibility it has to enforce anti-discrimination law. Do you think that the *Wynne* court's refusal to look into whether what Tufts had done was "right" or "wrong" constituted an abdication of its responsibility?

Some commentators have argued that courts are more willing to defer to academic decisionmaking in cases involving students with mental disabilities than in cases involving students with physical disabilities. See Bonnie Poitras Tucker, Application of the Americans with Disabilities Act (ADA) and Section 504 to Colleges and Universities, 23 J.C. & U.L. 1, 39 (1996). Can you think of any reasons why this might be the case?

2. *Admissions testing and admissions.* Entities that give standardized examinations for admission to postsecondary institutions are governed by Title III of the ADA and are thus subject to anti-discrimination requirements. *See* 42 U.S.C. § 12189 ("Any person that offers examination or courses related to applications, licensing, certification, or credentialing for secondary or post-secondary education, professional, or trade purposes shall offer such examinations or courses in a place and manner accessible to persons with disabilities ... "). Thus, virtually without exception, standardized testing programs provide accommodations for students with learning disabilities. Because testing programs provide this accommodation, educational institutions can use standardized test scores as a criterion for admission without running afoul of the anti-discrimination laws. In addition, the Department of Education's Office of Civil Rights ("OCR"), which has responsibility for investigating complaints of discrimination brought under the Rehabilitation Act and Title II, has taken the position that educational institutions are not required to lower their admissions standards in order to accommodate applicants with disabilities. See Laura Rothstein, "Higher Education and Disabilities: Trends and Developments," 27 Stetson L.Rev. 119, 122 (1997) (collecting cases).

One controversy that remains in the area of admissions testing concerns the practice of "flagging" the scores of those who take standardized tests under nonstandard conditions. In the case of the Scholastic Aptitude Test ("SAT"), the scores of all those who receive any sort of accommodation are flagged. In the case of the Law School Admission Test ("LSAT"), only the scores of those who receive extended time are flagged. The Department of Education's OCR has taken the position that educational institutions may not ignore or devalue the scores of applicants who take tests under nonstandard conditions. See, e.g., *SUNY Health Science Ctr. at Brooklyn–College of Med.*, 5 Nat'l Disability Rep. (LRP Publications) ¶ 77 (OCT Aug. 18, 1993). For an argument that the practice of flagging scores nonetheless violates the ADA and the Rehabilitation Act, see Kristan S. Mayer, Note, "Flagging Nonstandard Test Scores in Admissions to Institutions of Higher Education," 59 Stan. L. Rev. 469 (1998).

3. *Cost of reasonable accommodation.* Reasonable accommodations for students with learning or other mental disabilities range from the relatively inexpensive to the quite expensive. Inexpensive accommodations include additional time for examinations, changes in examination format, reduced course loads, and course substitutions. More expensive accommodations include the provision of taped texts, notetakers, and readers for course materials and exams. See Bonnie Poitras Tucker, "Application of the American with Disabilities Act (ADA) and Section 504 To Colleges and Universities," 23 J.C. & U.L. 1, 16–25 (1996) (summarizing accommodations considered by courts and suggested by applicable regulations). Postsecondary educational institutions are required to pay for all reasonable accommodations. They may not impose a surcharge on disabled students or require such students to demonstrate a lack of ability to pay. See *United States v. Board of Trustees for University of Alabama*, 908 F.2d 740 (11th Cir.1990).

4. *Definition of disability.* As with employment, the threshold question of whether an individual has a disability cognizable under the ADA often arises in higher education cases. After the Supreme Court decision in *Sutton v. United Airlines*, (discussed in Section II(A)) it is clear that the analysis must take into account mitigating measures that the student has taken. See, e.g., *Betts v. Rector and Visitors of the University of Virginia*, 18 Fed.Appx. 114, 118 (4th Cir. 2001) (noting this point). Moreover, in cases where the mental disability being claimed is a learning disability, most courts have held that the student must be limited in the activity of learning as compared with the general population, not just other students. Thus, in the *Betts* case, the court agreed that Betts had a learning impairment. However, given his superior IQ and the coping mechanisms he had developed to mitigate his learning impairment, he was not substantially limited in his ability to learn in comparison with the general population. See also *Price v. National Board of Medical Examiners*, 966 F.Supp. 419 (S.D.W.Va. 1997) (noting that a student with average intellectual ability and an impairment such as dyslexia that allowed him to learn only at the tenth percentile of the general population would be considered disabled under the ADA, but that a student with a superior IQ whose dyslexia caused her to learn only as well as the average person would not be considered disabled).

At a conceptual level, the issue of what constitutes a learning disorder, as contrasted with low intellectual ability, is not entirely clear. Learning disorders such as reading disorder are typically diagnosed when the person's reading ability is substantially below that predicted by his predicted intelligence. (See DSM–IV diagnostic criteria for reading disorder in Chapter 1, Appendix.) But some commentators have argued that recent studies show that poor readers with low IQ scores process words in the same manner as poor readers with high IQs. Moreover, there is no neuroanatomical difference between the two groups. In other words, there is no clear scientific proof that low IQ causes poor reading in one group while dyslexia causes it in the other group. See Karla K. Struebing et al., "Validity of IQ–Discrepancy Classifications of Reading Disabilities: A Meta–Analysis," 39 Am.Educ. Res.J. 469 (2002).

The increasing number of students claiming mental disabilities has generated much controversy. Critics have charged that institutions of higher education may be succumbing to pressures to grant accommodations to students who are clearly not entitled to receive them. Suzanne Wilhelm, "Accommodating Mental Disabilities in Higher Education: A Practical Guide to ADA Requirements," 32 J.L & Educ.217 (2003) (discussing case of *Guckenberger v. Boston University*, 957 F.Supp. 306 (D.Mass.1997), in which court found that several of students who had received accommodations lacked sufficient documentation). This creates an unfair system in which certain students are improperly given advantages and thus have a greater likelihood of success. Mark Kelman & Gillian Lester, Jumping the Queue: An Inquiry into the Legal Treatment of Students With Learning Disabilities (1997). Some critics also blame the DSM–IV for creating overly broad diagnostic categories that can then serve as the basis for learning disability claims (discussing attention deficit-hyperactivity disorder and oppositional disorder). See, e.g., Ruth Shalit, "Defining Disability Down: Why Johnny Can't Read, Write, or Sit Still," The New Republic, August 25, 1997. (For a general discussion of the charge that DSM–IV creates overly broad diagnostic categories, see Chapter 1.)

In cases where the court rejects the contention that the plaintiff's learning impairment substantially limits a major life activity, it may nonetheless find that the plaintiff is protected by the ADA because it finds that the defendant regarded the plaintiff as having such an impairment. For example, in the *Betts* case, the court ultimately determined that because the defendant had provided Betts with a large variety of accommodations, it regarded Betts as having a disability. What sorts of incentives does this line of reasoning create for educational institutions?

5. *Remedies*. Depending on the type of educational institution involved, a challenge to its practices may be brought under Title II of the ADA, Title III of the ADA, or under the Rehabilitation Act. Title III of the ADA, which could be invoked against any private university, incorporates the public accommodations provisions of the Civil Rights Act of 1964 and hence does not include monetary damages among the available remedies. As for Title II, which could be invoked against state universities, it incorporates the remedial scheme of Title VI of the Civil Rights Act. Under Supreme Court case law interpreting Title VI, *see Alexander v. Sandoval*, 532 U.S. 275, 121 S.Ct. 1511, 149 L.Ed.2d 517 (2001), monetary damages may be available.

Under the ADA, by contrast, the availability of monetary damages against state universities is much less clear. Many lower courts have held that the reasoning of the Supreme Court decision in *Board of Trustees of Univ. of Ala. v. Garrett*, 531 U.S. 356, 121 S.Ct. 955, 148 L.Ed.2d 866 (2001) (see discussion in Section II above), also bars Title II suits for monetary damages against state institutions. See, e.g., *Garcia v. S.U.N.Y. Health Sciences Center of Brooklyn*, 280 F.3d 98 (2d Cir.2001); *Reickenbacker v. Foster*, 274 F.3d 974 (5th Cir.2001). Two recent Supreme Court cases,

Tennessee v. Lane, 541 U.S. 509, 124 S.Ct. 1978, 158 L.Ed.2d 820 (2004) and United States v. Georgia, *546 U.S. 151, 126 S.Ct. 877, 163 L.Ed.2d 650 (2006), do indicate that Title II suits that could be construed to allege denials of constitutional rights will pass muster. But the scope of these cases is relatively narrow. Even the* Lane *case, a 5–4 ruling that carves out a broader exception to sovereign immunity than does the unanimous opinion in* United States v. Georgia, *requires that the Title II protection being sought have some connection to a right of constitutional dimension (in the* Lane *case the right of access of courts).*

Thus neither Title III nor Title II is likely to be a promising mechanism for securing monetary damages against universities. However, many universities, both public and private, do receive federal funding under the Rehabilitation Act, however. Moreover, as discussed in Section II, most courts have held that monetary damages are available under the Rehabilitation Act and that acceptance of Rehabilitation Act funds constitutes a waiver of sovereign immunity.

IV.   LICENSING AND CERTIFICATION PROGRAMS

Regulations promulgated under Title II of the ADA extend its anti-discrimination requirements to the licensing activities of state agencies. See 28 C.F.R. § 35.130(b)(6). Traditionally, state agencies with authority over medical licensing or bar admission have, as part of the admissions process, inquired as to the applicant's mental health history. Such inquiry has been deemed relevant to protecting the public from the hazards of practitioners whose mental condition might impair their ability to provide competent services. With the enactment of the ADA, inquiries pertaining to mental health history have been the subject of numerous court challenges. The case below provides a comprehensive overview of this area.

CLARK v. VIRGINIA BOARD OF BAR EXAMINERS

United States District Court, E.D. Virginia, 1995.
880 F.Supp. 430.

MEMORANDUM OPINION

CACHERIS, CHIEF JUDGE.

The issue before the Court is whether a question appearing on the Virginia Board of Bar Examiners' "Applicant's Character and Fitness Questionnaire" addressing an applicant's history of mental or emotional disorders violates the Americans with Disabilities Act, 42 U.S.C. §§ 12101 et seq. (1994). Following a preamble explaining that the Virginia Board of Bar Examiners is concerned only with "severe forms of mental or emotional problems," Question 20(b) asks: "Have you within the past five (5) years been treated or counselled for any mental, emotional or nervous disorders?" If Question 20(b) is answered affirmatively, applicants must then give specific treatment information pursuant to Question 21.

For the reasons set forth below, the Court finds that Question 20(b) is framed too broadly and violates the Plaintiff's rights under the Americans with Disabilities Act. Accordingly, judgment is entered in favor of the Plaintiff and the Virginia Board of Bar Examiners is enjoined from requiring that future applicants answer Question 20(b).

I. FINDINGS OF FACT

Plaintiff Julie Ann Clark brings this action against the Virginia Board of Bar Examiners (the "Board") to have Question 20(b) stricken from the Board's "Applicant's Character and Fitness Questionnaire" (the "Questionnaire") because it violates the Americans with Disabilities Act (the "ADA"). The Board maintains that Question 20(b) is posed appropriately and is necessary to identify applicants with mental disabilities that would seriously impair their ability to practice law and protect their clients' interests. The Court, after reviewing the evidence, authorities and arguments of counsel, makes the following findings of fact.

A. The Parties to the Case

Plaintiff Julie Ann Clark, a resident of Virginia, graduated from George Mason University Law School in June of 1993. She is currently employed as a children's program specialist at the Bazelon Center for Mental Health Law. * * * Ms. Clark suffers from a condition previously diagnosed as "major depression, recurrent". Plaintiff's Exhibit 68(a). * * * This condition, which occurred a few years ago, affected her for thirteen months.

The Virginia Board of Bar Examiners, an entity created under the authority of Virginia Code § 54.1–3919 (1994), is responsible for the examination of applicants for licenses to practice law in Virginia. Under Va.Code § 54.1–3925.1(A), the Board must determine, prior to licensing, that each applicant is a "person of honest demeanor and good moral character, is over the age of eighteen and possesses the requisite fitness to perform the obligations and responsibilities of a practicing attorney at law." The Board makes this determination "from satisfactory evidence produced by the applicant in such form as the board may require." *Id.* As a precondition to licensure, the Board requires that applicants answer all of the questions contained in its Questionnaire, including Question 20(b).

* * *

B. Application for Admission to the Virginia State Bar

On or about December 13, 1993, Plaintiff completed the Questionnaire and filed it with the Board. Plaintiff declined to answer Questions 20(b) and 21 of the Questionnaire on the grounds that they violated Title II of the ADA. Question 20(b) and 21, and the preamble introducing these questions, read as follows:

The Board is required to assess effectively the fitness of each applicant to perform the obligations and responsibilities of a practicing attorney at law. In this regard, a lawyer's chemical dependency or untreated or uncontrolled mental or emotional disorders may result in injury to the public. Questions 20 and 21 request information essential to the Board's assessment. The members of the Board recognize that stress of law school, as well as other life factors, frequently result in applicants seeking psychiatric or psychological counseling. The Board encourages you to obtain counseling or treatment if you believe that you may benefit from it. Because generally only severe forms of mental or emotional problems will trigger an investigation or impact on bar admission decisions, your decision to seek counseling should not be colored by your bar application....

* * *

20. (b) Have you within the past five (5) years, been treated or counselled for a mental, emotional or nervous disorders?

* * *

21. If your answer to question 20(a), (b) or (c) is yes, complete the following that apply:

(a) Dates of treatment or counseling;

(b) Name, address and telephone number of attending physician or counselor or other health care provider;

(c) Name, address and telephone number of hospital or institution;

(d) Describe completely the diagnosis and treatment and the prognosis and provide any other relevant facts. You may attach letters from your treating health professionals if you believe this would be helpful.

See Pl.Ex. 1 (emphasis in original).

On February 8, 1994, the Board advised Ms. Clark that her refusal to provide relevant information would prevent her from taking the bar examination. Pursuant to agreement of counsel, the Board subsequently agreed to allow Ms. Clark to sit for the February bar examination without answering Questions 20(b) and 21 of the Questionnaire. However, the Board indicated that it would not grant her a license until she completed the Questionnaire.

Ms. Clark took the Virginia bar examination on February 22 and 23, 1994 and passed it. She completed all of the application procedures with the exception of answering Questions 20(b) and 21. The Board concedes that, but for her refusal to answer Questions 20(b), it has no reason to believe that Ms. Clark lacks the requisite character and fitness to practice law in Virginia. Pl.Ex. 6. As the only thing preventing Ms. Clark's licensure is her refusal to answer Question 20(b), the issue of whether Question 20(b) violates the ADA is properly framed for the Court.

* * *

D. Battle of the Experts

Plaintiff maintains that Question 20(b) must be rejected because it is overbroad and is ineffectual in identifying those applicants unfit to practice law. Plaintiff offered the testimony of Dr. Howard V. Zonana, Director of the Law and Psychiatric Division and Professor of Clinical Psychology at the Yale University School of Medicine, to support its contention that there is no correlation between past mental health counseling and fitness to practice law. Dr. Zonana testified that Question 20(b) elicits information that, unlike evidence of past behavior, is unrelated to applicants' present ability to practice law and has little or no predictive value. According to Dr. Zonana, there is little evidence to support the ability of bar examiners, or even mental health professionals, to predict inappropriate or irresponsible future behavior based on a person's history of mental health treatment. Dr. Zonana believes that evidence of past behavior, as elicited by the Board's other "characterological" questions, provides the best indicator of an applicant's present ability to function and work. See Record at 84–87.

The credibility of Dr. Zonana's position is supported by its consistency with the position of the American Psychiatric Association (the "APA"). According to the APA, psychiatric history should not be the subject of applicant inquiry because it is not an accurate predictor of fitness.

In support of maintaining Question 20(b), the Board offered the testimony of Dr. Charles B. Mutter, a psychiatrist, assistant professor of Psychiatry and Family Medicine at the University of Miami School of Medicine, and member of the Florida Board of Bar Examiners from 1989 to 1993. Dr. Mutter, drafter of a question similar to Question 20(b) included in Florida's bar application, testified that Question 20(b) is appropriate as posed. He stated that attorneys, as protectors of clients' rights and assets, hold a special position of trust with the public which must be safeguarded with mental health pre-screening. Record at 171–72. Further, Dr. Mutter insisted that broad mental health questions are essential for collecting complete information regarding applicants' fitness to practice law. Narrower mental health questions, in Dr. Mutter's view, are inadequate because they allow applicants to filter their responses and provide self-promoting answers. Id. at 177.

Dr. Mutter's immoderate position, however, is unsupported by objective evidence and is discordant with a contemporary understanding of mental health questions under the ADA. For one, Dr. Mutter was unable point to any evidence proving a correlation between mental health questions and an inability to practice law. * * * Accordingly, the Court finds that, although both doctors have impressive curricula vitarum, Dr.

Zonana's position is more credible and persuasive than that of Dr. Mutter.

E. Need for Inquiry into Mental Health

The Court accepts that an attorney's uncontrolled and untreated mental or emotional illness may result in injury to clients and the public. This conclusion is supported by the recent cases of acute mental disability among lawyers which have resulted in license suspensions by the Virginia State Bar. See Def.Ex. 8–15. Dr. Zonana acknowledged that there are many mental illnesses which may adversely affect, or even preclude, a person's ability to practice law. See Record at 48–58. He also indicated that, while responses to behavioral questions are better indicators of mental health, inquiry into an applicant's mental health is necessary for a complete evaluation of their fitness to practice law. Id. at 62–66. Thus, it is clear from the facts before the Court that, at some stage in the application proceeding, some form of mental health inquiry is appropriate.

F. Efficiency of Question 20(b)

Assuming that a mental health question is allowed under the ADA, the Court must determine whether Question 20(b) is a permissible mental health inquiry. Although characterological questions elicit useful information about past behaviors likely to shed light on applicants' fitness, the Board insists that it is necessary to probe applicants' mental health with Question 20(b). Conversely, Ms. Clark maintains that the question is objectionable because it is intrusive without being effective.

According to testimony presented by both Plaintiff and Defendant, approximately twenty percent of the population suffers from some form of mental or emotional disorder at any given time. See Record at 30 and 213–214. However, despite reviewing some 2000 applications per year, the Board has received only forty-seven affirmative answers to its mental health questions in the past five years. This affirmative response rate, or "hit" rate, of less than one percent is far below the expected rate of twenty percent. The Board has presented no evidence to suggest, nor is there any reason to believe, that bar applicants are not reflective of the general population. Thus, the great discrepancy between the Board's hit rate and the reported percentage of persons suffering from mental impairment indicates that Question 20(b) is ineffective in identifying applicants suffering from mental illness.

Notwithstanding its receipt of forty-seven affirmative responses, the Board has never denied a license on the basis of prior mental health counseling. Pl.Ex. 5. Although the Virginia State Bar has suspended attorneys for mental disability, see Def. Ex. 8–15, the Board is unable to point to a single instance where an affirmative answer to Question 20(b) has prevented licensure. Thus, based on the Board's own experience, Question 20(b) has failed to serve its purpose of preventing the licensure of applicants lacking the fitness to practice law.

G. Deterrent Effect

In addition to being ineffectual, Plaintiff argues that Question 20(b) has a deterrent effect which inhibits applicants from getting necessary mental health counseling or treatment. Plaintiff presented the deposition testimony of Dean Paul M. Marcus, Acting Dean and Professor of Law at the Marshall–Wythe School of Law at the College of William and Mary, and Philip P. Frickey, Professor of Law at the University of Minnesota Law School, on the deterrent effect of broad mental health questions, like Question 20(b). Drawing on his experience counseling law students as both a teacher and administrator, Dean Marcus concluded that questions such as Question 20(b) deter law students from seeking counseling or treatment from which they might otherwise benefit. Similarly, Professor Frickey stated that broad mental health questions like Question 20(b) have a strong negative effect upon many law students, often discouraging them from seeking beneficial mental health counseling. Pl.Ex. 69.

* * *

H. Data from other Jurisdictions and Authorities

* * *

In the wake of the passage of the ADA, which became effective for public entities in January 1992, the inclusion of mental health questions on bar applications has gained new significance. At least eight states, including Connecticut, Florida, Maine, Minnesota, New York, Pennsylvania, Rhode Island and Texas, have recently altered their mental health questions in light of potential or actual litigation under the ADA.

The changes in these states are reflected in similar adjustments in the policies of the American Bar Association ("ABA") and the NCBE [National Commission of Bar Examiners], two leading national legal organizations. In August 1994, the House of Delegates of the American Bar Association ("ABA") adopted a recommendation that:

> when making character and fitness determinations for the purpose of bar admission, state and territorial bar examiners, in carrying out their responsibilities to the public to admit only qualified applicants worthy of the public trust, should consider the privacy concerns of bar admission applicants, tailor questions concerning mental health and treatment narrowly in order to elicit information about current fitness to practice law, and take steps to ensure that their processes do not discourage those who would benefit from seeking professional assistance with personal problems and issues of mental health from doing so.

Proposal 110, A.B.A. House of Delegates (August 9, 1994). While not the most strongly worded admonition, the resolution represents an acknowledgement of the changing atmosphere under the ADA.

Recently, the NCBE has acted to change the mental health questions on its character and fitness questionnaire. Formerly, questions 28 and 29 of the NCBE's character and fitness application asked, respectively: "Have you ever been treated or counseled for any mental, emotional or nervous disorder or condition?" and "Have you ever voluntarily entered or been involuntarily admitted to an institution for treatment of a mental, emotional or nervous disorder or condition?" These questions formed the basis for many states' mental health questions, including Virginia. As of February 17, 1995, the NCBE altered its mental health questions to limit their scope and to more sharply focus on chronic mental conditions which affect the ability to practice law. While the actions of the NCBE and ABA are not binding on the states, they signify the substantial impact the ADA is having on the formulation of mental health inquiries.

II. Conclusions of Law

Title II of the Americans with Disabilities Act prohibits discrimination against disabled persons by public entities. 42 U.S.C. §§ 12101 et seq. (1994). It provides that "no qualified individual with a disability shall, by reason of such disability, be excluded from participation in or be denied the benefits of the services, programs, or activities of a public entity, or be subject to discrimination by such entity." 42 U.S.C. § 12132. A "public entity" is defined as "any department, agency ... or other instrumentality of a State ... government." 42 U.S.C. § 12131(1)(B). The Virginia Board of Bar Examiners concedes that it is a public agency within this definition.

A "qualified individual with a disability" is defined as "[a]n individual with a disability who, with or without reasonable modification to rules, policies, or practices ... meets the essential eligibility requirements for the receipt of services or participation in programs or activities provided by the public entity." 42 U.S.C. § 12131(2). Under regulations promulgated by the Department of Justice, pursuant to 42 U.S.C. § 12134, "disability" is further defined as "a physical or mental impairment that substantially limits one or more of the major life activities of such individual; a record of such impairment; or being regarded as having such an impairment." 28 C.F.R. § 35.104. "Major life activities" include "functions such as caring for one's self, performing manual tasks, walking, seeing, hearing, speaking, breathing, learning, and working." *Id.*

The Court finds, based on the affidavit Plaintiff filed under seal, that Ms. Clark is a person with a disability or, alternatively, a person with a past record of impairment within the meaning of the ADA. 42 U.S.C. § 12102(2); 28 C.F.R. § 35.104. Further, Ms. Clark has shown that she can meet the essential eligibility requirements of practicing law and is "a qualified person with a disability" under the ADA. 42 U.S.C. § 12131(2); 28 C.F.R. § 35.104. While Defendant argues that Ms. Clark is not an "otherwise qualified individual" because she failed to answer Question 20(b), this argument begs the question of whether Question 20(b) must be answered at all.

An applicant may not meet the essential eligibility requirements, however, where they "pose[ ] a direct threat to the health or safety of others." 28 C.F.R. pt. 35, app. A at 446. A determination that a person poses a "direct threat" must be based not on generalizations or stereotypes, but on:

> an individualized assessment, based on reasonable judgment that relies on current medical evidence or on the best available objective evidence to determine: the nature, duration, and severity of the risk; the probability that potential injury will actually occur; and whether reasonable modification of policies, practices and procedures will mitigate the risk.

Id. at 446. The Board has presented no evidence to suggest that all or most of the applicants answering Question 20(b) affirmatively threaten the health or safety of the public. Nor is there any evidence that the Board engaged in any individualized assessment in formulating Question 20(b) as called for by 28 C.F.R. pt. 35, app. A at 446. Absent a showing that Ms. Clark would pose a direct threat to the health or safety of others, the Court finds that Ms. Clark meets all of the "essential eligibility requirements" for admission to the bar of the Commonwealth of Virginia.

In addition to the general provisions of Title II, public entities are specifically prohibited from acting discriminatorily in administering licensing programs. 28 C.F.R. § 35.130(b)(6). This regulation provides:

> A public entity may not administer a licensing or certification program in a manner that subjects qualified individuals with disabilities to discrimination on the basis of disability, nor may a public entity establish requirements for the programs or activities of licensees or certified entities that subject qualified individuals with disabilities to discrimination on the basis of disability. . . .

28 C.F.R. § 35.130(b)(6). Further, 28 C.F.R. § 35.130(b)(8) forbids a public entity from:

> impos[ing] or apply[ing] eligibility criteria that screen out or tend to screen out any individual with a disability or any class of individuals with disabilities from fully and equally enjoying any service, program, or activity, unless such criteria can be shown to be necessary for the provision of the service, program or activity being offered.

Id. As a public licensing agency, the Board must comply with the strict requirements of 28 C.F.R. §§ 35.130(b)(6) and (8) in probing applicants' mental health histories.

In assessing the propriety of Question 20(b), the Court is faced with two issues: (1) whether the Board has established requirements or imposed eligibility criteria that subject qualified individuals to discrimination on the basis of their disability, and (2) whether such requirements or criteria are necessary to the Board's licensing function.

A. Question 20(b) Subjects Qualified Individuals with a Disability to Discrimination on the Basis of that Disability

To find a violation of the ADA, the Court first must determine whether the Board, in posing Question 20(b), subjects persons with disabilities to discrimination on the basis of their disability. While it is not clear that Question 20(b) "screens out" potential applicants, it is clear that Question 20(b) imposes an additional burden on applicants with disabilities to satisfy additional eligibility criteria. *See Ellen S. v. Florida Board of Bar Examiners*, 859 F.Supp. 1489, 1494 (S.D.Fla.1994) (Florida's mental health questions "discriminate against Plaintiffs by subjecting them to additional burdens based on their disability."); *Medical Society of New Jersey v. Jacobs*, 1993 WL 413016, * 7 (D.N.J.1993) (mental health questions imposed extra burdens on qualified persons with disabilities in violation of ADA); *In re Applications of Underwood and Plano*, No. BAR–93–21, 1993 WL 649283 at * 2 (Me.1993) (requirement that applicants answer mental health questions discriminates on the bases of disability and imposes eligibility criteria that unnecessarily screen out individuals with disabilities).

Unlike other applicants, those with mental disabilities are required to subject themselves to further inquiry and scrutiny. The Court finds that this additional burden discriminates against those with mental disabilities. Thus, to avoid violating the ADA, the Board must show that Question 20(b) is necessary to the performance of its licensing function.

B.   Necessity of Imposing Question 20(b)

"The practice of law is not a matter of grace, but of right for one who is qualified by his learning and his moral character." *Baird v. State Bar of Arizona*, 401 U.S. 1, 8, 91 S.Ct. 702, 707, 27 L.Ed.2d 639 (1971). It is generally accepted that a state can set high standards of qualification and, to this end, may investigate an applicant's character and fitness to practice law. *See Schware v. Board of Bar Examiners of New Mexico*, 353 U.S. 232, 239, 77 S.Ct. 752, 756, 1 L.Ed.2d 796 (1957); *Martin-Trigona v. Underwood*, 529 F.2d 33, 38 (7th Cir.1975); *Hawkins v. Moss*, 503 F.2d 1171, 1175 (4th Cir.1974). It is equally clear that all states have set qualifications of moral character as preconditions for admission to the practice of law, with the burden of demonstrating good character borne by the applicant. *See Konigsberg v. State Bar of California*, 366 U.S. 36, 41 n. 4, 81 S.Ct. 997, 1002 n. 4, 6 L.Ed.2d 105 (1961). While the Board's broad authority to set licensing qualifications is well established, such authority is subject to the requirements of the ADA.

1.   Duty to assess the character and fitness of applicants

The Board is charged with a statutory duty to find, prior to licensure, that each applicant has the "requisite fitness to perform the obligations and responsibilities of a practicing attorney at law." Va.Code § 54.1–3925.1. As part of this duty, the Board must identify those people who suffer from mental conditions which would severely affect or impair their ability to practice law.

The Board contends that, in fulfilling this duty, it is necessary to ask Question 20(b) to uncover all of the skeletons hidden in each applicant's psychological closet. Further, the Board opines that its ability to investigate applicants' character and fitness is limited by inadequate resources and time constraints. According to the Board, Question 20(b) is necessary because it enables the Board to identify potentially unfit applicants with the limited resources and time available to it. While the Court recognizes that the Board has limited resources with which to discharge its duty under Va.Code § 54.1–3925.1, the Court finds such limitations do not make Question 20(b) "necessary" under the ADA.

2. Decisions in other jurisdictions

Other courts, considering broad mental health questions similar to Question 20(b), have concluded that such inquiries would violate Title II of the ADA. *See Ellen S.*, 859 F.Supp. at 1494 (court stated, in dicta, that licensing board's broad inquiry into applicants' mental health would violate Title II); *Medical Society of New Jersey v. Jacobs*, 1993 WL 413016 (court concluded, in dicta, that licensing agency's question "have you ever suffered or been treated for any mental illness or psychiatric problem" violates ADA); *Underwood*, No. BAR–93–21, 1993 WL 649283 at * 2 (bar examiner's inquiry into diagnosis and treatment for emotional, nervous or mental disorders, and accompanying medical authorization form, violates ADA). "Although it is certainly permissible for the Board of Bar Examiners to fashion other questions more directly related to behavior that can affect the practice of law without violating the ADA, the questions and medical authorization objected to here are contrary to the ADA" *Underwood*, 1993 WL 649283 at * 2 (emphasis in original). While not binding authority, these cases offer persuasive guidance in the evaluation of Question 20(b) under the ADA.

In support of maintaining Question 20(b), the Board relies on *Applicants v. Texas State Board of Bar Examiners*, No. 93 CA 740SS, 1994 WL 776693 (W.D.Tex.1994), which upheld the right of the Texas Board of Bar Examiners to inquire into an applicant's mental history. Unlike Question 20(b), however, the questions considered in *Texas State Board of Bar Examiners* were addressed only to specific behavioral disorders found relevant to the practice of law.[3] Further, the *Texas State Board of Bar Examiners* court noted that the mental health question used by the Texas Board of Bar Examiners before 1992, which asked "[h]ave you within the last ten (10) years . . . [b]een examined or treated for any mental, emotional or nervous conditions," was "revised . . . to comply with the ADA." Id. at 4. Hence, the *Texas State Board of Bar Examiners* decision has limited application and does not support the breadth of inquiry posed by the Board.

* * *

3. The *Texas State Board of Bar Examiners* court reviewed question 11 of the bar application which asked:

(a) Within the last ten years, have you been diagnosed with or have you been treated [for] bipolar disorder, schizophrenia, paranoia, or any other psychotic disorder?

(b) Have you, since attaining the age or eighteen or within the last ten years, whichever is shorter, been admitted to a hospital or other facility for the treatment of bipolar disorder, schizophrenia, paranoia, or any other psychotic disorder?

The *Texas State Board of Bar Examiners* court concluded that these inquiries did not violate the ADA because they narrowly addressed only those disorders relevant to the practice of law. *Id.* at 24.

III. CONCLUSION

On the basis of the record produced at trial, the Court easily reaches the conclusion that question 20(b) is too broad and should be rewritten to achieve the Board's objective of protecting the public. Question 20(b)'s broadly worded mental health question discriminates against disabled applicants by imposing additional eligibility criteria. While certain severe mental or emotional disorders may pose a direct threat to public safety, the Board has made no individualized finding that obtaining evidence of mental health counseling or treatment is effective in guarding against this threat.

In fact, the Board presented no evidence of correlation between obtaining mental counseling and employment dysfunction. Question 20(b), while offering little marginal utility in identifying unfit applicants, has strong negative stigmatic and deterrent effects upon applicants. Both Drs. Zonana and Mutter acknowledged this deterrent effect and testified that past behavior is the best predictor of present and future mental fitness. Thus, the Board has failed to show that Question 20(b) is necessary to the performance of its duty to license only fit bar applicants.

As the Court's job in this case is to decide whether 20(b) complies with the ADA, not to draft a question that would comply with the ADA, the Court will refrain from offering any dictum guidance. The imposition of Question 20(b) by the Board violates the ADA. 42 U.S.C. § 12132; 28 C.F.R. §§ 35.130(b)(6) and (8). While the licensure of attorneys implicates issues of public safety, the Board has failed to show that Question 20(b), as posed, is necessary to the Board's performance of its licensing function. Accordingly, judgment is entered for the Plaintiff and the Virginia Board of Bar Examiners is enjoined from requiring that future applicants answer Question 20(b) of the Questionnaire.

* * *

Questions and Comments

1. *State bar inquiry into mental health.* Approximately one-third of all state bar examiners ask questions as broadly worded as the question that was challenged in the *Clark* case. Most other states either: 1) ask no mental health questions; 2) ask only about hospitalization or institutionalization; 3) ask only about specific diagnoses; or 4) ask applicants if they have any mental disorder which they believe will affect their ability to practice law.

2. *American Psychiatric Association ("APA") guidelines for medical licensing.* The APA suggests that medical licensing boards and regulatory agencies should adhere to the following guidelines for mental health inquiry:

> 1) Prior psychiatric treatment is, per se, not relevant to the question of current impairment. It is not appropriate or informative to ask about past psychiatric treatment in the context of understanding current functioning. A past history of work impairment, but not simply of past treatment or leaves of absence, may be gathered.

2) The salient concern is always the individual's current capacity to function and/or current impairment. Only information about current impairing disorder affecting the capacity to function as a physician, and which is relevant to present practice, should be disclosed on application forms. Types of impairment may include emotional or mental difficulties, physical illness, or dependency upon alcohol or other drugs.

3) Applicants must be informed of the potential for public disclosure of any information they provide on applications.

3. *Licensing examinations and the determination of disability.* Courts have held that the requirements of the ADA also extend to professional licensing examinations. Indeed, *both* Title II and Title III of the ADA appear to apply to state agencies administering such examinations. Thus, in administering such examinations, state agencies must reasonably accommodate test takers who can prove that they are disabled within the meaning of the ADA. As discussed in Section III, in the case of learning disabilities, making the threshold determination of disability can be quite challenging. Under both the relevant Department of Justice regulations and most courts decisions, the appropriate reference population against whom the plaintiff should be compared is the general population. See *Price et al. v. The National Board of Medical Examiners*, 966 F.Supp. 419 (S.D.W.Va.1997) (declining to find a group of medical student plaintiffs who claimed that they suffered from attention deficit disorder disabled because they were not substantially limited in the major life activity of learning as compared with "the average person in the general population.") Whether the plaintiff is in fact substantially limited when compared with the general population may depend, however, on how the court defines the major life activity in question. For example, in *Bartlett v. New York State Board of Law Examiners*, 2001 WL 930792 (S.D.N.Y. 2001), the court determined that the relevant major life activity in question was reading and that, with respect to this activity, the plaintiff was substantially limited in reference to the general population. In contrast, if the major life activity had been defined as learning more generally, the plaintiff's ability to complete college and graduate school without formal accommodation might have cast doubt on her claim of disability. In addition, courts may reach different conclusions on the threshold disability question depending on whether they focus primarily on outcome measures or on the process by which the plaintiff conducts the major life activity. Compare *Gonzales v. National Bd. of Med. Exam'rs*, 225 F.3d 620 (6th Cir.2000) (focusing on outcome measures, such as test scores, to determine that plaintiff did not have a reading disability) with *Bartlett* (holding that plaintiff had a reading disability despite her average performance, without formal accommodation on the LSAT and other standardized tests, by focusing on the fact that the plaintiff used a test strategy that minimized the need for reading).

4. *Remedies Available Against State Licensing Agencies.* Given the Supreme Court's recent decisions on sovereign immunity, discussed at length in Sections II and III, it is likely that only injunctive relief will be available against state licensing board defendants.

V. HOUSING

A. CONSTITUTIONAL PROTECTIONS

CITY OF CLEBURNE, TEXAS v. CLEBURNE LIVING CENTER

Supreme Court of the United States, 1985.
473 U.S. 432, 105 S.Ct. 3249, 87 L.Ed.2d 313.

Justice White delivered the opinion of the Court.

A Texas city denied a special use permit for the operation of a group home for the mentally retarded, acting pursuant to a municipal zoning ordinance requiring permits for such homes. The Court of Appeals for the Fifth Circuit held that mental retardation is a "quasi-suspect" classification and that the ordinance violated the Equal Protection Clause because it did not substantially further an important governmental purpose. We hold that a lesser standard of scrutiny is appropriate, but conclude that under that standard the ordinance is invalid as applied in this case.

I

In July 1980, respondent Jan Hannah purchased a building at 201 Featherston Street in the city of Cleburne, Texas, with the intention of leasing it to Cleburne Living Center, Inc. (CLC), for the operation of a group home for the mentally retarded. It was anticipated that the home would house 13 retarded men and women, who would be under the constant supervision of CLC staff members. The house had four bedrooms and two baths, with a half bath to be added. CLC planned to comply with all applicable state and federal regulations.

The city informed CLC that a special use permit would be required for the operation of a group home at the site, and CLC accordingly submitted a permit application. In response to a subsequent inquiry from CLC, the city explained that under the zoning regulations applicable to the site, a special use permit, renewable annually, was required for the construction of "[h]ospitals for the insane or feeble-minded, or alcoholic [*sic*] or drug addicts, or penal or correctional institutions."[4]

---

4. The site of the home is in an area zoned "R–3," an "Apartment House District." App. 51. Section 8 of the Cleburne zoning ordinance, in pertinent part, allows the following uses in an R–3 district:

"1. Any use permitted in District R–2.

"2. Apartment houses, or multiple dwellings.

"3. Boarding and lodging houses.

"4. Fraternity or sorority houses and dormitories.

"5. Apartment hotels.

"6. Hospitals, sanitariums, nursing homes or homes for convalescents or aged, *other than for the* insane or *feeble-minded* or alcoholics or drug addicts."

"7. Private clubs or fraternal orders, except those whose chief activity is carried on as a business.

"8. Philanthropic or eleemosynary institutions, other than penal institutions.

"9. Accessory uses customarily incident to any of the above uses. . . ." *Id.,* at 60–61 (emphasis added).

The city had determined that the proposed group home should be classified as a "hospital for the feeble-minded." After holding a public hearing on CLC's application, the City Council voted 3 to 1 to deny a special use permit.

CLC then filed suit in Federal District Court against the city and a number of its officials, alleging, *inter alia,* that the zoning ordinance was invalid on its face and as applied because it discriminated against the mentally retarded in violation of the equal protection rights of CLC and its potential residents. The District Court found that "[i]f the potential residents of the Featherston Street home were not mentally retarded, but the home was the same in all other respects, its use would be permitted under the city's zoning ordinance," and that the City Counsel's decision "was motivated primarily by the fact that the residents of the home would be persons who are mentally retarded." Even so, the District Court held the ordinance and its application constitutional. Concluding that no fundamental right was implicated and that mental retardation was neither a suspect nor a quasi-suspect classification, the court employed the minimum level of judicial scrutiny applicable to equal protection claims. The court deemed the ordinance, as written and applied, to be rationally related to the city's legitimate interests in "the legal responsibility of CLC and its residents, . . . the safety and fears of residents in the adjoining neighborhood," and the number of people to be housed in the home.

The Court of Appeals for the Fifth Circuit reversed, determining that mental retardation was a quasi-suspect classification and that it should assess the validity of the ordinance under intermediate-level scrutiny. Because mental retardation was in fact relevant to many legislative actions, strict scrutiny was not appropriate. But in light of the history of "unfair and often grotesque mistreatment" of the retarded, discrimination against them was "likely to reflect deep-seated prejudice." In addition, the mentally retarded lacked political power, and their condition was immutable. The court considered heightened scrutiny to be particularly appropriate in this case, because the city's ordinance withheld a benefit which, although not fundamental, was very important to the mentally retarded. Without group homes, the court stated, the retarded could never hope to integrate themselves into the community. Applying the test that it considered appropriate, the court held that the ordinance was invalid on its face because it did not substantially further any important governmental interests. The Court of Appeals went on to hold that the ordinance was also invalid as applied.

* * *

II

The Equal Protection Clause of the Fourteenth Amendment commands that no State shall "deny to any person within its jurisdiction the equal protection of the laws," which is essentially a direction that all persons similarly situated should be treated alike. *Plyler v. Doe,* 457 U.S. 202, 216, 102 S.Ct. 2382, 2394, 72 L.Ed.2d 786 (1982). Section 5 of the

Amendment empowers Congress to enforce this mandate, but absent controlling congressional direction, the courts have themselves devised standards for determining the validity of state legislation or other official action that is challenged as denying equal protection. The general rule is that legislation is presumed to be valid and will be sustained if the classification drawn by the statute is rationally related to a legitimate state interest.

* * *

The general rule gives way, however, when a statute classifies by race, alienage, or national origin. These factors are so seldom relevant to the achievement of any legitimate state interest that laws grounded in such considerations are deemed to reflect prejudice and antipathy—a view that those in the burdened class are not as worthy or deserving as others. For these reasons and because such discrimination is unlikely to be soon rectified by legislative means, these laws are subjected to strict scrutiny and will be sustained only if they are suitably tailored to serve a compelling state interest. Similar oversight by the courts is due when state laws impinge on personal rights protected by the Constitution.

Legislative classifications based on gender also call for a heightened standard of review. That factor generally provides no sensible ground for differential treatment. "[W]hat differentiates sex from such nonsuspect statuses as intelligence or physical disability ... is that the sex characteristic frequently bears no relation to ability to perform or contribute to society." Rather than resting on meaningful considerations, statutes distributing benefits and burdens between the sexes in different ways very likely reflect outmoded notions of the relative capabilities of men and women. A gender classification fails unless it is substantially related to a sufficiently important governmental interest. Because illegitimacy is beyond the individual's control and bears "no relation to the individual's ability to participate in and contribute to society," official discriminations resting on that characteristic are also subject to somewhat heightened review.

* * *

We have declined, however, to extend heightened review to differential treatment based on age. . . .

* * *

III

Against this background, we conclude for several reasons that the Court of Appeals erred in holding mental retardation a quasi-suspect classification calling for a more exacting standard of judicial review than is normally accorded economic and social legislation. First, it is undeniable, and it is not argued otherwise here, that those who are mentally retarded have a reduced ability to cope with and function in the everyday world. Nor are they all cut from the same pattern: as the testimony in this record indicates, they range from those whose disability is not immediately evident to those who must be constantly cared for. They are thus different, immutably so, in relevant respects, and the States' interest in dealing with and providing for them is plainly a legitimate one. How this large and diversified group is to be treated under the law is a difficult and often a technical matter, very much a task for legislators guided by qualified professionals and not by the perhaps ill-informed opinions of the judiciary. Heightened scrutiny inevitably involves substantive judgments about legislative decisions, and we doubt that the predicate for such judicial oversight is present where the classification deals with mental retardation.

Second, the distinctive legislative response, both national and state, to the plight of those who are mentally retarded demonstrates not only that they have unique problems, but also that the lawmakers have been addressing their difficulties in a manner that belies a continuing antipathy or prejudice and a corresponding need for more intrusive oversight by the judiciary.

* * *

Third, the legislative response, which could hardly have occurred and survived without public support, negates any claim that the mentally retarded are politically powerless in the sense that they have no ability to attract the attention of the lawmakers. Any minority can be said to be powerless to assert direct control over the legislature, but if that were a criterion for higher level scrutiny by the courts, much economic and social legislation would now be suspect.

Fourth, if the large and amorphous class of the mentally retarded were deemed quasi-suspect for the reasons given by the Court of Appeals, it would be difficult to find a principled way to distinguish a variety of other groups who have perhaps immutable disabilities setting them off from others, who cannot themselves mandate the desired legislative responses, and who can claim some degree of prejudice from at least part of the public at large. One need mention in this respect only the aging, the disabled, the mentally ill, and the infirm. We are reluctant to set out on that course, and we decline to do so.

Doubtless, there have been and there will continue to be instances of discrimination against the retarded that are in fact invidious, and that are properly subject to judicial correction under constitutional norms. But the appropriate method of reaching such instances is not to create a new quasi-suspect classification and subject all governmental action based on that classification to more searching evaluation. Rather, we should look to the likelihood that governmental action premised on a particular classification is valid as a general matter, not merely to the specifics of the case before us. Because mental retardation is a characteristic that the government may legitimately take into account in a wide range of decisions, and because both State and Federal Governments have recently committed themselves to assisting the retarded, we will not presume that any given legislative action, even one that disadvantages retarded individuals, is rooted in considerations that the Constitution will not tolerate.

Our refusal to recognize the retarded as a quasi-suspect class does not leave them entirely unprotected from invidious discrimination. To withstand equal protection review, legislation that distinguishes between the mentally retarded and others must be rationally related to a legitimate governmental purpose. This standard, we believe, affords government the latitude necessary both to pursue policies designed to assist the retarded in realizing their full potential, and to freely and efficiently engage in activities that burden the retarded in what is essentially an incidental manner. The State may not rely on a classification whose relationship to an asserted goal is so attenuated as to render the distinction arbitrary or irrational.

* * *

IV

We turn to the issue of the validity of the zoning ordinance insofar as it requires a special use permit for homes for the mentally retarded. We inquire first whether requiring a special use permit for the Featherston home in the circumstances here deprives respondents of the equal protection of the laws. If it does, there will be no occasion to decide whether the special use permit provision is facially invalid where the mentally retarded are involved, or to put it another way, whether the city may never insist on a special use permit for a home for the mentally retarded in an R–3 zone. This is the preferred course of adjudication since it enables courts to avoid making unnecessarily broad constitutional judgments.

The constitutional issue is clearly posed. The city does not require a special use permit in an R–3 zone for apartment houses, multiple dwellings, boarding and lodging houses, fraternity or sorority houses, dormitories, apartment hotels, hospitals, sanitariums, nursing homes for convalescents or the aged (other than for the insane or feebleminded or alcoholics or drug addicts), private clubs or fraternal orders, and other specified uses. It does, however, insist on a special permit for the Featherston home, and it does so, as the District Court found, because it would be a facility for the mentally retarded. May the city require the permit for this facility when other care and multiple-dwelling facilities are freely permitted?

It is true, as already pointed out, that the mentally retarded as a group are indeed different from others not sharing their misfortune, and in this respect they may be different from those who would occupy other facilities that would be permitted in an R–3 zone without a special permit. But this difference is largely irrelevant unless the Featherston home and those who would occupy it would threaten legitimate interests of the city in a way that other permitted uses such as boarding houses and hospitals would not. Because in our view the record does not reveal any rational basis for believing that the Featherston home would pose any special threat to the city's legitimate interests, we affirm the judgment below insofar as it holds the ordinance invalid as applied in this case.

The District Court found that the City Council's insistence on the permit rested on several factors. First, the Council was concerned with the negative attitude of the majority of property owners located within 200 feet of the Featherston facility, as well as with the fears of elderly residents of the neighborhood. But mere negative attitudes, or fear, unsubstantiated by factors which are properly cognizable in a zoning proceeding, are not permissible bases for treating a home for the mentally retarded differently from apartment houses, multiple dwellings, and the like.

* * *

Second, the Council had two objections to the location of the facility. It was concerned that the facility was across the street from a junior high school, and it feared that the students might harass the occupants of the Featherston home. But the school itself is attended by about 30 mentally retarded students, and denying a permit based on such vague, undifferentiated fears is again permitting some portion of the community to validate what would otherwise be an equal protection violation. The other objection to the home's location was that it was located on "a five hundred year flood plain." This concern with the possibility of a flood, however, can hardly be based on a distinction between the Featherston home and, for example, nursing homes, homes for convalescents or the aged, or sanitariums or hospitals, any of which could be located on the Featherston site without obtaining a special use permit. The same may be said of another concern of the Council—doubts about the legal responsibility for actions which the mentally retarded might take. If there is no concern about legal responsibility with respect to other uses that would be permitted in the area, such as boarding and fraternity houses, it is difficult to believe that the groups of mildly or moderately mentally retarded individuals who would live at 201 Featherston would present any different or special hazard.

Fourth, the Council was concerned with the size of the home and the number of people that would occupy it. The District Court found, and the Court of Appeals repeated, that "[i]f the potential residents of the Featherston Street home were not mentally retarded, but the home was the same in all other respects, its use would be permitted under the city's zoning ordinance." Given this finding, there would be no restrictions on the number of people who could occupy this home as a boarding house, nursing home, family dwelling, fraternity house, or dormitory. The question is whether it is rational to treat the mentally retarded differently. It is true that they suffer disability not shared by others; but why this difference warrants a density regulation that others need not observe is not at all apparent. At least this record does not clarify how, in this connection, the characteristics of the intended occupants of the Featherston home rationally justify denying to those occupants what would be permitted to groups occupying the same site for different purposes. Those who would live in the Featherston home are the type of individuals who, with supporting staff, satisfy federal and state standards for group housing in the community; and there is no dispute that the home would meet the federal square-footage-per-resident requirement for facilities of this type. In the words of the Court of Appeals, "[t]he City never justifies its apparent view that other people can live under such 'crowded' conditions when mentally retarded persons cannot."

In the courts below the city also urged that the ordinance is aimed at avoiding concentration of population and at lessening congestion of the streets. These concerns obviously fail to explain why apartment houses, fraternity and sorority houses, hospitals and the like, may freely locate in the area without a permit. So, too, the expressed worry about fire hazards, the serenity of the neighborhood, and the avoidance of danger to other residents fail rationally to justify singling out a home such as 201 Featherston for the special use permit, yet imposing no such restrictions on the many other uses freely permitted in the neighborhood.

The short of it is that requiring the permit in this case appears to us to rest on an irrational prejudice against the mentally retarded, including those who would occupy the Featherston facility and who would live under the closely supervised and highly regulated conditions expressly provided for by state and federal law.

The judgment of the Court of Appeals is affirmed insofar as it invalidates the zoning ordinance as applied to the Featherston home. The judgment is otherwise vacated, and the case is remanded.

It is so ordered.

JUSTICE STEVENS, with whom THE CHIEF JUSTICE joins, concurring.

* * *

Every law that places the mentally retarded in a special class is not presumptively irrational. The differences between mentally retarded persons and those with greater mental capacity are obviously relevant to certain legislative decisions. An impartial lawmaker—indeed, even a member of a class of persons defined as mentally retarded—could rationally vote in favor of a law providing funds for special education and special treatment for the mentally retarded. A mentally retarded person could also recognize that he is a member of a class that might need special supervision in some situations, both to protect himself and to protect others. Restrictions on his right to drive cars or to operate hazardous equipment might well seem rational even though they deprived him of employment opportunities and the kind of freedom of travel enjoyed by other citizens. "That a civilized and decent society expects and approves such legislation indicates that governmental consideration of those differences in the vast majority of situations is not only legitimate but also desirable."

Even so, the Court of Appeals correctly observed that through ignorance and prejudice the mentally retarded "have been subjected to a history of unfair and often grotesque mistreatment." 726 F.2d 191, 197 (C.A.5 1984). The discrimination against the mentally retarded that is at issue in this case is the city's decision to require an annual special use permit before property in an apartment house district may be used as a group home for persons who are mildly retarded. The record convinces me that this permit was required because of the irrational fears of neighboring property owners, rather than for the protection of the mentally retarded persons who would reside in respondent's home.

Although the city argued in the Court of Appeals that legitimate interests of the neighbors justified the restriction, the court unambiguously rejected that argument. *Id.*, at 201. In this Court, the city has argued that the discrimination was really motivated by a desire to protect the mentally retarded from the hazards presented by the neighborhood. Zoning ordinances are not usually justified on any such basis, and in this case, for the reasons explained by the Court, I find that justification wholly unconvincing. I cannot believe that a rational member of this disadvantaged class could ever approve of the discriminatory application of the city's ordinance in this case.

Accordingly, I join the opinion of the Court.

JUSTICE MARSHALL, with whom JUSTICE BRENNAN and JUSTICE BLACKMUN join, concurring in the judgment in part and dissenting in part.

* * *

I share the Court's criticisms of the overly broad lines that Cleburne's zoning ordinance has drawn. But if the ordinance is to be invalidated for its imprecise classifications, it must be pursuant to more powerful scrutiny than the minimal rational-basis test used to review classifications affecting only economic and commercial matters.

* * *

In light of the importance of the interest at stake and the history of discrimination the retarded have suffered, the Equal Protection Clause requires us to do more than review the distinctions drawn by Cleburne's zoning ordinance as if they appeared in a taxing statute or in economic or commercial legislation. The searching scrutiny I would give to restrictions on the ability of the retarded to establish community group homes leads me to conclude that Cleburne's vague generalizations for classifying the "feeble-minded" with drug addicts, alcoholics, and the insane, and excluding them where the elderly, the ill, the boarder, and the transient are allowed, are not substantial or important enough to overcome the suspicion that the ordinance rests on impermissible assumptions or outmoded and perhaps invidious stereotypes.

* * *

In light of the scrutiny that should be applied here, Cleburne's ordinance sweeps too broadly to dispel the suspicion that it rests on a bare desire to treat the retarded as outsiders, pariahs who do not belong in the community. The Court, while disclaiming that special scrutiny is necessary or warranted, reaches the same conclusion. Rather than striking the ordinance down, however, the Court invalidates it merely as applied to respondents. I must dissent from the novel proposition that "the preferred course of adjudication" is to leave standing a legislative Act resting on "irrational prejudice", thereby forcing individuals in the group discriminated against to continue to run the Act's gauntlet.

The Court appears to act out of a belief that the ordinance might be "rational" as applied to some subgroup of the retarded under some circumstances, such as those utterly without the capacity to live in a community, and that the ordinance should not be invalidated *in toto* if it is capable of ever being validly applied. But the issue is not "whether the city may never insist on a special use permit for the mentally retarded in an R–3 zone." The issue is whether the city may require a permit pursuant to a blunderbuss ordinance drafted many years ago to exclude all the "feeble-minded," or whether the city must enact a new ordinance carefully tailored to the exclusion of some well-defined subgroup of retarded people in circumstances in which exclusion might reasonably further legitimate city purposes.

* * *

Invalidating on its face the ordinance's special treatment of the "feebleminded," in contrast, would place the responsibility for tailoring and updating Cleburne's unconstitutional ordinance where it belongs: with the legislative arm of the City of Cleburne. If Cleburne perceives a legitimate need for requiring a certain well-defined subgroup of the retarded to obtain special permits before establishing group homes, Cleburne will, after studying the problem and making the appropriate policy decisions, enact a new, more narrowly tailored ordinance. That ordinance might well look very different from the current one; it might separate group homes (presently treated nowhere in the ordinance) from hospitals, and it might define a narrow subclass of the retarded for whom even group homes could legitimately be excluded. Special treatment of the retarded might be ended altogether. But whatever the contours such an ordinance might take, the city should not be allowed to keep its ordinance on the books intact and thereby shift to the courts the responsibility to confront the complex empirical and policy questions involved in updating statutes affecting the mentally retarded. A legislative solution would yield standards and provide the sort of certainty to retarded applicants and administrative officials that case-by-case judicial rulings cannot provide. Retarded applicants should not have to continue to attempt to surmount Cleburne's vastly overbroad ordinance.

Questions and Comments

1. *Impact of an "invalid as applied" holding.* What is the practical significance of a holding which invalidates the ordinance as applied to the Cleburne Living Center (CLC) but leaves the regulatory scheme in place?

Are there any circumstances under which the city of Cleburne might legally deny a permit to applicants seeking to establish a group home for the developmentally disabled? For a general analysis of the *Cleburne* case and a proposal for an alternate approach to the analysis of laws distinguishing on the basis of mental capacity, see Martha Minow, "When Difference Has Its Home: Group Homes For The Mentally Retarded, Equal Protection and Legal Treatment of Difference," 22 Harv.C.R.–C.L. L.Rev. 111 (1987).

2. *Anti-discrimination legislation.* Amendments to the Fair Housing Act ("FHA") enacted in 1988 make it "unlawful to discriminate in the sale or rental or otherwise make unavailable or deny a dwelling to any buyer or renter because of a handicap . . ." 42 U.S.C. § 3604(f)(1). As discussed in the section that follows, zoning ordinances of the type adopted by the city of Cleburne are now frequently challenged under the FHA.

3. *People with mental retardation as a quasi–suspect class.* Because rational basis review is rarely used to strike down legislative enactments, commentators writing immediately following the *Cleburne* decision suggested that the Court was really using a heightened form of scrutiny. See, e.g., Laurence H. Tribe, American Constitutional Law (2nd ed. 1988), § 16–3, at 1444–46. However, the Supreme Court's 2001 decision in *Garrett* (discussed in Section II) makes it abundantly clear that individuals with disabilities, mental or physical, are not entitled to any form of heightened scrutiny. Even earlier, in *Heller v. Doe*, 509 U.S. 312, 113 S.Ct. 2637, 125 L.Ed.2d 257 (1993), a case involving the state of Kentucky's involuntary commitment procedures, a majority of the Court had applied ordinary rational basis review to uphold distinctions that tended to make it easier to commit people with mental retardation than people with mental illness generally. The *Heller* case did not, however, squarely address the substantive standard of review question. Rather, the majority rejected the argument that heightened scrutiny applied on the procedural ground that this claim had not been properly presented. For further discussion of the *Heller* case, see pp. 896–903.

B. LEGISLATIVE PROTECTIONS

Two federal laws now protect persons suffering from a physical or mental disability from discrimination in housing. The more comprehensive of these is the FHA. The other is the ADA, specifically Titles II and III.

The FHA bans discrimination based on mental or physical disability in most areas of the housing market, public and private. The scope of the Act extends to all sales, as well as rentals, of multi-family housing; only transactions between private persons involving single family units are not covered by the FHA. The FHA's definition of discrimination encompasses both disparate treatment and disparate impact claims. The FHA also requires those "reasonable modifications" or "reasonable accommodations" that are necessary to order to provide disabled persons with equal access to housing. 42 U.S.C. § 3604(f)(3)(A),(B). This reasonable accommodation mandate has been interpreted rather narrowly by the courts, however. For example, in *Salute v. Stratford Greens Garden Apts.*, 136 F.3d 293 (2d Cir.1998), the Second Circuit held that a landlord's refusal to accept Section 8 low-income housing vouchers did not violate the FHA's mandate to provide reasonable accommodation. Under the FHA, victims of discriminatory housing practices may recover actual and punitive damages. 42 U.S. § 3613(c)(1).

Titles II and III of the ADA have similar legal standards for protection against discrimination. They apply, however, only to limited classes of housing. Title II covers housing sponsored or operated by state, county, or local authorities. Title III covers housing which falls under the broad heading of "public accommodations"; this heading includes inns, motels, hotels, halfway houses, and homeless shelters. See John Parry, American Bar Association Commission on Mental and Physical Disability Law, Mental Disabilities and the Americans with Disabilities Act: A Practitioner's Guide to Employment, Insurance, Treatment, Public Access to Housing 65 (1994).

Because of its broader scope, in particular its coverage of all multi-family housing, the materials which follow will focus on the key provisions of the FHA.

1. *FHA Coverage*

The coverage of the FHA largely parallels that of the ADA and Rehabilitation Act. Under the FHA, "handicapped" persons are: 1) those who have physical or mental impairments that substantially limit their major life activities; 2) those who have a record of such impairments; or 3) those who are regarded as having such impairments. 42 U.S.C. § 3602(h). Persons undergoing treatment for drug or alcohol abuse are covered. The FHA excludes from coverage those who are actively using illegal drugs or who constitute a "direct threat to the health and safety of other individuals or whose tendency would result in substantial physical damage to the property of others." 42 U.S.C. § 3604(f)(9). There is little case law giving content to the "direct threat" provision. In one state court case, however, the court held that a child molester posed a "direct threat to the health or safety of other individuals" such that the molester could not qualify for protection under the FHA. *Stout v. Kokomo Manor Apartments*, 677 N.E.2d 1060 (Ind.Ct.App.1997).

2. *FHA Enforcement*

Under the FHA, private parties may bring judicial actions seeking damages or injunctive relief. 42 U.S.C. § 3613. As a consequence, for example, providers and operators of group community-based residences or rehabilitation facilities have the right to challenge zoning and land use laws which have a disparate impact on those protected by the Act. Private parties may also file complaints with the Secretary of Housing and Urban Development. The Secretary is responsible for investigating the allegedly discriminatory practice. If the Secretary finds evidence of illegal discrimination, the complainant (or respondent) then has the option of proceeding either administratively or judicially. *See* 42 U.S.C. §§ 3610, 3612. If the illegality involves a state or local zoning or land use regulation, however, the Secretary is required by the FHA to refer the matter to the Attorney General. 42 U.S.C. § 3610(g)(2)(C). As a consequence, to date, most enforcement actions brought by the Attorney General have focused on discriminatory zoning practices.

A court that finds an FHA violation is empowered to award either injunctive relief (in the form of a permanent or temporary injunction) or monetary damages. The court may also assess a civil penalty, in an amount not exceeding $50,000 for the first violation and not exceeding $100,000 for any subsequent violation. 42 U.S.C. § 3614(d)(1).

3. *Zoning and Land Use Regulations*

Local zoning and land use control regulations have served to deter, and at times prohibit, the establishment of community treatment programs for people with mental disabilities, whether residential or otherwise. In some cases (as in the *Cleburne* case discussed in the preceding section), these laws have been drafted or applied with the intent of excluding treatment or rehabilitation facilities from particular neighborhoods. More commonly, however, zoning laws and ordinances have been neutral on their face. They have not targeted particular types of residential facilities; rather they have simply banned anything but single family residences and have had limitations on the number of unrelated persons who could live in a particular single family residence. Though neutral on their face, these laws have had a disparate impact on those individuals with a disability who need residential treatment or rehabilitative services.

Where a patent or overt discriminatory purpose can be established, adjudication is relatively simple. If, for example, the record showed that a local authority which had discretion to issue permits for multi-person residences granted them to sorority or fraternity houses but specifically did not grant them to residential facilities for the disabled, then an FHA violation would be established. Alternatively, if a local authority failed to enforce zoning ordinances *except* in the case of residential facilities for the disabled, such behavior would violate the FHA. See *United States v. Borough of Audubon, New Jersey*, 797 F.Supp. 353 (D.C.N.J.1991).

A more complicated issue is presented by a zoning or land use regulation that is facially neutral (and is enforced in a neutral fashion) but which through its operation precludes the operation of group homes or residences that serve people with mental illness—for example, a regulation which bars more than a specified number of unrelated persons from occupying a structure or residence. The case set out below involves this type of regulation.

OXFORD HOUSE, INC. v. TOWN OF BABYLON

United States District Court, E.D. New York, 1993.
819 F.Supp. 1179.

AMENDED ORDER

WEXLER, DISTRICT JUDGE.

Pursuant to the Fair Housing Act, 42 U.S.C. § 3601 et seq. ("FHA"), Oxford House, Inc. ("Oxford House") and Gary and Geri

Erichson ("the Erichsons"), plaintiffs in the above referenced action, seek to enjoin the Town of Babylon ("Town" or "defendant") from evicting persons with handicaps (also referred to as "plaintiffs") from their residence at 73 East Walnut Avenue, East Farmingdale, New York. Now before the Court is plaintiffs' motion for partial summary judgment pursuant to Rule 56 of the Federal Rules of Civil Procedure on the ground that the Town violated the Fair Housing Act because its proposed eviction of plaintiffs has a disparate impact on persons with handicaps; or, in the alternative, because the Town failed to make reasonable accommodations in its zoning ordinances as may have been necessary to afford plaintiffs an equal opportunity to enjoy housing in the Town. For the reasons discussed below, plaintiffs' motion for partial summary judgment is granted.

I. BACKGROUND

Oxford House was founded in 1975 by a group of men who were recovering from drug and/or alcohol addiction. Today there are 375 individual "Oxford Houses" which are operated on the same premise as the original. * * * [The court then describes how the Oxford House at issue in this case was set up.] The house is owned by the Erichsons, and is located in a residential district in the Town, which is zoned for single family dwellings only.

Shortly after the lease was signed, neighbors complained to Town officials that recovering alcoholics were living in their community. On September 3, 1991, a Town meeting was held to discuss the new residents. This was followed by a letter from the Town Attorney to the representatives of Oxford House, alleging that the house in East Farmingdale was in violation of the Multiple Dwelling Code because the residents were not a family.[5] On or about September 6, 1991, Oxford House requested that the Town make a reasonable accommodation in the application of its zoning ordinance so that the residents could continue living there. The Town has never responded.

On or about September 17, 1991, the Town Board authorized the Town attorney to commence appropriate litigation, including injunctive relief and contempt proceedings, to evict the residents of the East Farmingdale Oxford House. That same day, plaintiffs filed this action to enjoin the Town from carrying out its resolution.

* * *

II. DISCUSSION

* * *

5. The Town of Babylon Multiple Dwelling Code § 153–13 states that a family is one or more persons related by blood, marriage, or adoption. It may also be a number of unrelated persons, not exceeding four, who are not related by blood, marriage or adoption. The East Farmingdale Oxford House accommodates from five to eight individuals.

B.   Overview of the Fair Housing Act

Under the FHA, it is unlawful to discriminate in the sale or rental, or to otherwise make unavailable or deny a dwelling to any buyer or renter because of a handicap. 42 U.S.C. § 3604(f)(1). A person is handicapped if he or she has a mental or physical impairment. 42 U.S.C. § 3602(h). It is well established that individuals recovering from drug or alcohol addiction are handicapped under the FHA. * * * A plaintiff can establish a violation under the FHA by proving the disparate impact of a practice or policy on a particular group, *Huntington Branch, NAACP v. Town of Huntington*, 844 F.2d 926, 933 (2d Cir.), *aff'd*, 488 U.S. 15, 109 S.Ct. 276, 102 L.Ed.2d 180 (1988), or by showing that the defendant failed to make reasonable accommodations in rules, policies, or practices so as to afford people with disabilities an equal opportunity to live in a dwelling. 42 U.S.C. § 3604(f)(3)(B). Once an FHA violation is established, the plaintiff is entitled to injunctive relief. *Southern Management Corp.*, 955 F.2d at 923.

C.   Plaintiff's Claim that the Town's Zoning Ordinance Has a Disparate Impact on People with Handicaps

To establish a prima facie case under the disparate impact analysis, a plaintiff must prove that the challenged practice "actually or predictably" results in discrimination. *Huntington Branch, NAACP*, 844 F.2d at 933. Once the plaintiff establishes a prima facie case, the burden shifts to the defendant to prove that "its actions furthered, in theory and in practice, a legitimate, bona fide governmental interest and that no alternative would serve the interest with less discriminatory effect." *Id.* at 936 (citing *Resident Advisory Bd. v. Rizzo*, 564 F.2d 126, 148–49 (3d Cir.1977)), *cert. denied*, 435 U.S. 908, 98 S.Ct. 1457, 55 L.Ed.2d 499 (1978).

In the end, the court must balance the plaintiff's showing of discriminatory impact against the defendant's justifications for its conduct. *Huntington Branch, NAACP*, 844 F.2d at 936. When conducting this balance, two factors weigh heavily in the plaintiffs' favor: (1) evidence of discriminatory intent on the part of the defendant; and (2) evidence that the plaintiff is seeking only to require a municipal defendant to eliminate an obstacle to housing rather than suing to compel it to build. *Id.*

Plaintiffs in the present case have set forth evidence to establish that the Town's proposed eviction actually or predictably results in discrimination. The Town asserts that the Oxford House facility is not permitted at 73 East Walnut Avenue because the residents are not a "family" or the "functional and factual equivalent of a natural family." Under § 213–1 of the Town Code, a "family" is a group of persons related by "kinship, adoption, blood or marriage." The "functional and factual equivalent of a natural family" is defined as a "single housekeeping unit" bearing the same characteristics as a biological family, including a stable non-transient existence. The Town maintains that because plaintiffs are transients, they do not function as a family unit, and can therefore be evicted pursuant to the Town Code.

Applying § 213–1 of the Town Code to evict plaintiffs would discriminate against them because of their handicap. Recovering alcoholics or drug addicts require a group living arrangement in a residential neighborhood for psychological and emotional support during the recovery process. As a result, residents of an Oxford House are more likely than those without handicaps to live with unrelated individuals. Moreover, because residents of an Oxford House may leave at any time due to relapse or any other reason, they cannot predict the length of their stay. Therefore, a finding of a violation of the Town Code leading to the town's eviction of plaintiffs from a dwelling due to the size or transient nature of plaintiffs' group living arrangement actually or predictably results in discrimination.

Once the plaintiff establishes a prima facie case, the burden shifts to the defendant to prove that its actions furthered a legitimate governmental interest and that there were no less discriminatory alternatives. *Huntington Branch, NAACP*, 844 F.2d at 936. Defendant in the present case asserts that the ordinance is designed to keep boarding houses, rooming houses, multiple family dwellings, and other similar arrangements out of residential neighborhoods. The Town contends that it enforces the ordinance against all violators; the enforcement of the ordinance furthers a legitimate governmental interest in maintaining the residential character of the areas zoned for single family dwellings; and any discriminatory effect it may have on plaintiffs is due to plaintiffs' transiency and failure to live as a family, not because of their handicap.

Although a town's interest in zoning requirements is substantial, *see Village of Belle Terre v. Boraas*, 416 U.S. 1, 94 S.Ct. 1536, 39 L.Ed.2d 797 (1974), the Court finds that evicting plaintiffs from the East Farmingdale Oxford House is not in furtherance of that interest. Five Town officials testified that the Town has received no substantial complaints from plaintiffs' neighbors within the past year. Furthermore, the house is well maintained and does not in any way burden the Town or alter the residential character of the neighborhood. The presence of the East Farmingdale Oxford House in a single family, residential district does not undermine the purpose of the Town's zoning ordinance. Therefore, defendant cannot justify evicting plaintiffs as being in furtherance of its asserted governmental interest.

Even if the Town's proposed enforcement of its zoning ordinance advances a legitimate governmental interest, the Court nevertheless finds that plaintiffs' showing of discriminatory effect far outweighs the Town's weak justifications. Although the plaintiff is not required to prove discriminatory intent in order to show discriminatory effect, in balancing disparate impact against a governmental interest, evidence of such intent weighs heavily in the plaintiff's favor. *Huntington Branch NAACP*, 844 F.2d at 936. Plaintiffs in the present case have set forth substantial evidence to indicate that the Town had the intent to evict them because they were recovering alcoholics.

On September 3, 1991, a public meeting was held to discuss the East Farmingdale Oxford House. So many neighbors came to the meeting that Supervisor Pitts suspended the normal rules. (Excerpts from Regular Town Board Meeting of September 3, 1991, p. 1 (hereafter "Town Board Meeting")). These neighbors were "hostile" to it, (Deposition of Supervisor Pitts, p. 12), expressing their fears regarding the safety of children and senior citizens. (Town Board Meeting, pp. 1, 3–5). No one from the community or the Town Board spoke in favor of the East Farmingdale Oxford House. (Plaintiffs' Exhibit B, p. 30).

* * *

After the Town meeting, the Town attorney sent a letter to Oxford House asserting that plaintiffs did not comport with the definition of a "family" in the Multiple Dwelling Code. (Plaintiffs' Exhibit G). Next, the Town alleged that the East Farmingdale Oxford House violated the Town Code because it was a "boarding house or the house of transients." (Resolution No. 716, Plaintiffs' Exhibit A). The Town presently contends that plaintiffs are in violation of the Town Code because they are not a "family" or the "functional and factual equivalent of a natural family." The statements made at the Town Board meeting, in conjunction with the shifting bases for eviction asserted by the Town, indicates that the Town wants to evict plaintiffs because they are recovering alcoholics.

Furthermore, in *Huntington Branch, NAACP*, the court held that where the plaintiff was not suing to require the municipal defendant to build housing, but rather to remove an obstacle to housing, the defendant needs to establish a more substantial justification for its conduct. *Huntington Branch, NAACP*, 844 F.2d at 936. Plaintiffs in the present case merely seek to require the Town to permit them to continue to use housing which already exists. This is another factor which weighs heavily in plaintiffs' favor. Accordingly, because there is no genuine issue of material fact as to whether the Town's conduct actually or predictably has a discriminatory effect on plaintiffs due to their handicap, and the showing of discriminatory effect far outweighs defendant's justifications for its predisposition, plaintiffs' motion for partial summary judgment is granted.

D. Plaintiffs' Claim that the Town Failed to Make Reasonable Accommodations Necessary to Permit Handicapped Persons to Use and Enjoy a Dwelling

Even if the Town's proposed eviction of plaintiffs does not have a disparate impact on handicapped persons, the Court nevertheless finds that defendant's conduct constituted discrimination as it is defined in 42 U.S.C. § 3604(f)(3)(B). Under the FHA, it is a discriminatory practice to refuse to make "a reasonable accommodation in rules, policies, practices, or services when such accommodation may be necessary to afford [a handicapped] person equal opportunity to use and enjoy a dwelling." 42 U.S.C. § 3604(f)(3)(B). Courts have unanimously applied the reasonable accommodations requirement to zoning ordinances and other land use regulations and practices. *See, e.g., Township of Cherry Hill*, 799 F.Supp. at 462–63; *Horizon House Developmental Services, Inc. v. Town of Upper Southampton*, 804 F.Supp. 683, 699–70 (E.D.Pa.1992); *Stewart B. McKinney Foundation, Inc. v. Town Plan & Zoning Comm'n of the Town of Fairfield*, 790 F.Supp. 1197, 1221 (D.Conn.1992); *United States v. Village of Marshall*, 787 F.Supp. 872, 878 (W.D.Wis.1991); *Oxford House–Evergreen v. City of Plainfield*, 769 F.Supp. 1329, 1344–45 (D.N.J. 1991); *United States v. Commonwealth of Puerto Rico*, 764 F.Supp. 220, 224 (D.P.R.1991).

In the present case, plaintiffs requested that the Town modify the definition of a "family" as it was applied to them. Plaintiffs have demonstrated that as recovering alcoholics and drug addicts, they must live in a residential neighborhood because an Oxford House "seeks to provide a stable, affordable, and drug-free living situation so as to increase the likelihood that a person will stay sober." (Plaintiffs' statement ¶ 6). In *Township of Cherry Hill*, the court held that the location of the houses in a drug-free, single family neighborhood played a crucial role in an individual's recovery by "promoting self-esteem, helping to create an incentive not to relapse, and avoiding the temptations that the presence of drug trafficking can create." *Township of Cherry Hill*, 799 F.Supp. at 450. This Court finds that reasoning persuasive. Because an Oxford House cannot exist in a single family, residential district under the Town Code, a modification of the definition of a "family" in plaintiffs' situation is warranted so that they may have the same opportunity to rent a house as do persons without handicaps.

Plaintiffs have also established that the requested accommodation was reasonable. An accommodation is reasonable under the FHA if it does not cause any undue hardship or fiscal or administrative burdens on the municipality, or does not undermine the basic purpose that the zoning ordinance seeks to achieve. *Township of Cherry Hill*, 799 F.Supp. at 463–66; *Village of Marshall*, 787 F.Supp. at 878; *City of Plainfield*, 769 F.Supp. at 1344–45. Because one of the purposes of the reasonable accommodations provision is to address individual needs and respond to individual circumstances, courts have held that municipalities must change, waive, or make exceptions in their zoning rules to afford people with disabilities the same access to housing as those who are without disabilities. *Horizon House*, 804 F.Supp. at 699. *See also Township of Cherry Hill*, 799 F.Supp. at 461–63; *Village of Marshall*, 787 F.Supp. at 878; *Commonwealth of Puerto Rico*, 764 F.Supp. at 224.

As discussed above, the East Farmingdale Oxford House has no adverse effect on the residential character of the neighborhood that the Town Code seeks to preserve. Moreover, neither the operation of the house nor the residents themselves have caused any financial or administrative burdens on the Town. (Pitts Deposition, p. 37). Consequently, the Court finds that the requested accommodation was reasonable and defendant's failure to make such accommodation was discriminatory conduct. Accordingly, even if the Court did not find that defendant's conduct had a disparate impact on plaintiffs, there is nevertheless no genuine issue of material fact with regard to defendant's violation of 42 U.S.C. § 3604(f)(3)(B), and plaintiffs' motion for partial summary judgment would be granted on this ground as well.

III. CONCLUSION

Accordingly, for the foregoing reasons, plaintiffs' motion for partial summary judgment pursuant to Rule 56 of the Federal Rules of Civil Procedure is granted and defendant is enjoined from taking any further steps to evict plaintiffs from the East Farmingdale Oxford House.

SO ORDERED.

In FHA-based challenges to regulations limiting the number of unrelated persons who can live together, defendants sometimes invoke the FHA exemption for "reasonable local, State, or Federal restrictions regarding the maximum number of occupants permitted to occupy a dwelling." 42 U.S.C. § 3607(b)(1). In the case set out below, the Supreme Court resolved a conflict between the Eleventh and Ninth Circuits on the scope of this exemption.

CITY OF EDMONDS v. OXFORD HOUSE, INC.

Supreme Court of the United States, 1995.
514 U.S. 725, 115 S.Ct. 1776, 131 L.Ed.2d 801.

JUSTICE GINSBURG delivered the opinion of the Court.

The Fair Housing Act (FHA or Act) prohibits discrimination in housing against, inter alios, persons with handicaps. Section 3607(b)(1) of the Act entirely exempts from the FHA's compass "any reasonable local, State, or Federal restrictions regarding the maximum number of occupants permitted to occupy a dwelling." 42 U.S.C. § 3607(b)(1). This case presents the question whether a provision in petitioner City of Edmonds' zoning code qualifies for § 3607(b)(1)'s complete exemption from FHA scrutiny. The provision, governing areas zoned for single-family dwelling units, defines "family" as "persons [without regard to number] related by genetics, adoption, or marriage, or a group of five or fewer [unrelated] persons." Edmonds Community Development Code (ECDC) § 21.30.010 (1991).

The defining provision at issue describes who may compose a family unit; it does not prescribe "the maximum number of occupants" a dwelling unit may house. We hold that § 3607(b)(1) does not exempt prescriptions of the family-defining kind, i.e., provisions designed to foster the family character of a neighborhood. Instead, § 3607(b)(1)'s absolute exemption removes from the FHA's scope only total occupancy limits, i.e., numerical ceilings that serve to prevent overcrowding in living quarters.

I

In the summer of 1990, respondent Oxford House opened a group home in the City of Edmonds, Washington for 10 to 12 adults recovering from alcoholism and drug addiction. The group home, called Oxford

House–Edmonds, is located in a neighborhood zoned for single-family residences. Upon learning that Oxford House had leased and was operating a home in Edmonds, the City issued criminal citations to the owner and a resident of the house. The citations charged violation of the zoning code rule that defines who may live in single-family dwelling units. The occupants of such units must compose a "family," and family, under the City's defining rule, "means an individual or two or more persons related by genetics, adoption, or marriage, or a group of five or fewer persons who are not related by genetics, adoption, or marriage." Edmonds Community Development Code (ECDC) § 21.30.010. Oxford House–Edmonds houses more than five unrelated persons, and therefore does not conform to the code.

Oxford House asserted reliance on the Fair Housing Act, 102 Stat. 1619, 42 U.S.C. § 3601 et seq., which declares it unlawful "[t]o discriminate in the sale or rental, or to otherwise make unavailable or deny, a dwelling to any buyer or renter because of a handicap of . . . that buyer or a renter." § 3604(f)(1)(A). The parties have stipulated, for purposes of this litigation, that the residents of Oxford House–Edmonds "are recovering alcoholics and drug addicts and are handicapped persons within the meaning" of the Act. App. 106.

Discrimination covered by the FHA includes "a refusal to make reasonable accommodations in rules, policies, practices, or services, when such accommodations may be necessary to afford [handicapped] person[s] equal opportunity to use and enjoy a dwelling." § 3604(f)(3)(B). Oxford House asked Edmonds to make a "reasonable accommodation" by allowing it to remain in the single-family dwelling it had leased. Group homes for recovering substance abusers, Oxford urged, need 8 to 12 residents to be financially and therapeutically viable. Edmonds declined to permit Oxford House to stay in a single-family residential zone, but passed an ordinance listing group homes as permitted uses in multifamily and general commercial zones.

Edmonds sued Oxford House in the United States District Court for the Western District of Washington seeking a declaration that the FHA does not constrain the City's zoning code family definition rule. Oxford House counterclaimed under the FHA, charging the City with failure to make a "reasonable accommodation" permitting maintenance of the group home in a single-family zone. The United States filed a separate action on the same FHA-"reasonable accommodation" ground, and the two cases were consolidated. Edmonds suspended its criminal enforcement actions pending resolution of the federal litigation.

On cross-motions for summary judgment, the District Court held that ECDC § 21.30.010, defining "family," is exempt from the FHA under § 3607(b)(1) as a "reasonable . . . restrictio[n] regarding the maximum number of occupants permitted to occupy a dwelling." App. to Pet. for Cert. B–7. The United States Court of Appeals for the Ninth Circuit reversed; holding § 3607(b)(1)'s absolute exemption inapplicable, the Court of Appeals remanded the cases for further consideration of the claims asserted by Oxford House and the United States. *Edmonds v. Washington State Building Code Council*, 18 F.3d 802 (1994).

The Ninth Circuit's decision conflicts with an Eleventh Circuit decision declaring exempt under § 3607(b)(1) a family definition provision similar to the Edmonds prescription. *See Elliott v. Athens*, 960 F.2d 975 (1992). We granted certiorari to resolve the conflict, 513 U.S. 959, 115 S.Ct. 417, 130 L.Ed.2d 332 (1994), and we now affirm the Ninth Circuit's judgment.

II

The sole question before the Court is whether Edmonds' family composition rule qualifies as a "restrictio[n] regarding the maximum number of occupants permitted to occupy a dwelling" within the meaning of the FHA's absolute exemption. 42 U.S.C. § 3607(b)(1). In answering this question, we are mindful of the Act's stated policy "to provide, within constitutional limitations, for fair housing throughout the United States." § 3601. We also note precedent recognizing the FHA's "broad and inclusive" compass, and therefore according a "generous construction" to the Act's complaint-filing provision. *Trafficante v. Metropolitan Life Ins. Co.*, 409 U.S. 205, 209, 212, 93 S.Ct. 364, 366–367, 368, 34 L.Ed.2d 415 (1972). Accordingly, we regard this case as an instance in which an exception to "a general statement of policy" is sensibly read "narrowly in order to preserve the primary operation of the [policy]." *Commissioner v. Clark*, 489 U.S. 726, 739, 109 S.Ct. 1455, 1463, 103 L.Ed.2d 753 (1989).

A

Congress enacted § 3607(b)(1) against the backdrop of an evident distinction between municipal land use restrictions and maximum occupancy restrictions.

Land use restrictions designate "districts in which only compatible uses are allowed and incompatible uses are excluded." D. Mandelker, Land Use Law § 4.16, pp. 113–114 (3d ed.1993) (hereinafter Mandelker). These restrictions typically categorize uses as single-family residential, multiple-family residential, commercial, or industrial.

Land use restrictions aim to prevent problems caused by the "pig in the parlor instead of the barnyard." *Village of Euclid v. Ambler Realty Co.*, 272 U.S. 365, 388, 47 S.Ct. 114, 118, 71 L.Ed. 303 (1926). In particular, reserving land for single-family residences preserves the character of neighborhoods, securing "zones where family values, youth values, and the blessings of quiet seclusion and clean air make the area a sanctuary for people." *Village of Belle Terre v. Boraas*, 416 U.S. 1, 9, 94 S.Ct. 1536, 1541, 39 L.Ed.2d 797 (1974); *see also Moore v. City of East Cleveland*, 431 U.S. 494, 521, 97 S.Ct. 1932, 1947, 52 L.Ed.2d 531 (1977) (Burger, C.J., dissenting) (purpose of East Cleveland's single-family zoning ordinance "is the traditional one of preserving certain areas as family residential communities"). To limit land use to single-family residences, a municipality must define the term "family"; thus family composition rules are an essential component of single-family residential use restrictions.

Maximum occupancy restrictions, in contradistinction, cap the number of occupants per dwelling, typically in relation to available floor space or the number and type of rooms. *See, e.g.*, Uniform Housing Code § 503(b) (1988) * * * These restrictions ordinarily apply uniformly to all residents of all dwelling units. Their purpose is to protect health and safety by preventing dwelling overcrowding. *See, e.g.*, BOCA Code §§ PM–101.3, PM–405.3, PM–405.5 and commentary; Abbott, Housing Policy, Housing Codes and Tenant Remedies, 56 B.U.L.Rev. 1, 41–45 (1976).

We recognized this distinction between maximum occupancy restrictions and land use restrictions in *Moore v. City of East Cleveland*, 431 U.S. 494, 97 S.Ct. 1932, 52 L.Ed.2d 531 (1977). In *Moore*, the Court held unconstitutional the constricted definition of "family" contained in East Cleveland's housing ordinance. East Cleveland's ordinance "select[ed] certain categories of relatives who may live together and declare[d] that others may not"; in particular, East Cleveland's definition of "family" made "a crime of a grandmother's choice to live with her grandson." *Id.*, at 498–499, 97 S.Ct., at 1935 (plurality opinion). In response to East Cleveland's argument that its aim was to prevent overcrowded dwellings, streets, and schools, we observed that the municipality's restrictive definition of family served the asserted, and undeniably legitimate, goals "marginally, at best." *Id.*, at 500, 97 S.Ct., at 1936 (footnote omitted). Another East Cleveland ordinance, we noted, "specifically addressed ... the problem of overcrowding"; that ordinance tied "the maximum permissible occupancy of a dwelling to the habitable floor area."

Section 3607(b)(1)'s language—"restrictions regarding the maximum number of occupants permitted to occupy a dwelling"—surely encompasses maximum occupancy restrictions. But the formulation does not fit family composition rules typically tied to land use restrictions. In sum, rules that cap the total number of occupants in order to prevent overcrowding of a dwelling "plainly and unmistakably," *see A.H. Phillips, Inc. v. Walling*, 324 U.S. 490, 493, 65 S.Ct. 807, 808, 89 L.Ed. 1095 (1945), fall within § 3607(b)(1)'s absolute exemption from the FHA's governance; rules designed to preserve the family character of a neighborhood, fastening on the composition of households rather than on the total number of occupants living quarters can contain, do not.

B

Turning specifically to the City's Community Development Code, we note that the provisions Edmonds invoked against Oxford House, ECDC §§ 16.20.010 and 21.30.010, are classic examples of a use restriction and complementing family composition rule. These provisions do not cap the number of people who may live in a dwelling. In plain terms, they direct that dwellings be used only to house families. Captioned "USES," ECDC § 16.20.010 provides that the sole "Permitted Primary Us[e]" in a single-family residential zone is "[s]ingle-family dwelling units." Edmonds itself recognizes that this provision simply "defines those uses permitted in a single family residential zone." Pet. for Cert. 3.

A separate provision caps the number of occupants a dwelling may house, based on floor area:

> "Floor Area. Every dwelling unit shall have at least one room which shall have not less than 120 square feet of floor area. Other habitable rooms, except kitchens, shall have an area of not less than 70 square feet. Where more than two persons occupy a room used for sleeping purposes, the required floor area shall be increased at the rate of 50 square feet for each occupant in excess of two." ECDC § 19.10.000 (adopting Uniform Housing Code § 503(b) (1988)).

This space and occupancy standard is a prototypical maximum occupancy restriction.

Edmonds nevertheless argues that its family composition rule, ECDC § 21.30.010, falls within § 3607(b)(1), the FHA exemption for maximum occupancy restrictions, because the rule caps at five the number of unrelated persons allowed to occupy a single-family dwelling. But Edmonds' family composition rule surely does not answer the question: "What is the maximum number of occupants permitted to occupy a house?" So long as they are related "by genetics, adoption, or marriage," any number of people can live in a house. Ten siblings, their parents and grandparents, for example, could dwell in a house in Edmonds' single-family residential zone without offending Edmonds' family composition rule.

Family living, not living space per occupant, is what ECDC § 21.30.010 describes. Defining family primarily by biological and legal relationships, the provision also accommodates another group association: five or fewer unrelated people are allowed to live together as though they were family. This accommodation is the peg on which Edmonds rests its plea for § 3607(b)(1) exemption. Had the City defined a family solely by biological and legal links, § 3607(b)(1) would not have been the ground on which Edmonds staked its case. See Tr. of Oral Arg. 11–12, 16. It is curious reasoning indeed that converts a family values preserver into a maximum occupancy restriction once a town adds to a related persons prescription "and also two unrelated persons."

Edmonds additionally contends that subjecting single-family zoning to FHA scrutiny will "overturn Euclidian zoning" and "destroy the effectiveness and purpose of single-family zoning." Brief for Petitioner 11, 25. This contention both ignores the limited scope of the issue before us and exaggerates the force of the FHA's antidiscrimination provisions. We address only whether Edmonds' family composition rule qualifies for § 3607(b)(1) exemption. Moreover, the FHA antidiscrimination provisions, when applicable, require only "reasonable" accommodations to afford persons with handicaps "equal opportunity to use and enjoy" housing. §§ 3604(f)(1)(A) and (f)(3)(B).

* * *

The parties have presented, and we have decided, only a threshold question: Edmonds' zoning code provision describing who may compose a "family" is not a maximum occupancy restriction exempt from the FHA under § 3607(b)(1). It remains for the lower courts to decide whether Edmonds' actions against Oxford House violate the FHA's prohibitions against discrimination set out in §§ 3604(f)(1)(A) and (f)(3)(B). For the reasons stated, the judgment of the United States Court of Appeals for the Ninth Circuit is

Affirmed.

JUSTICE THOMAS, with whom JUSTICE SCALIA and JUSTICE KENNEDY join, dissenting.

Congress has exempted from the requirements of the Fair Housing Act (FHA) "any reasonable local, State, or Federal restrictions regarding the maximum number of occupants permitted to occupy a dwelling." 42 U.S.C. § 3607(b)(1) (emphasis added). In today's decision, the Court concludes that the challenged provisions of petitioner's zoning code do not qualify for this exemption, even though they establish a specific number—five—as the maximum number of unrelated persons permitted to occupy a dwelling in the single-family neighborhoods of Edmonds, Washington. Because the Court's conclusion fails to give effect to the plain language of the statute, I respectfully dissent.

I

Petitioner's zoning code reserves certain neighborhoods primarily for "[s]ingle-family dwelling units." Edmonds Community Development Code (ECDC) § 16.20.010(A)(1) (1991), App. 225. To live together in such a dwelling, a group must constitute a "family," which may be either a traditional kind of family, comprising "two or more persons related by genetics, adoption, or marriage," or a nontraditional one, comprising "a group of five or fewer persons who are not [so] related." § 21.30.010, App. 250. As respondent United States conceded at oral argument, the effect of these provisions is to establish a rule that "no house in [a single-family] area of the city shall have more than five occupants unless it is a [traditional kind of] family." Tr. of Oral Arg. 46. In other words, petitioner's zoning code establishes for certain dwellings "a five-occupant limit, [with] an exception for [traditional] families." *Ibid.*

To my mind, the rule that "no house . . . shall have more than five occupants" (a "five-occupant limit") readily qualifies as a "restrictio[n] regarding the maximum number of occupants permitted to occupy a dwelling." In plain fashion, it "restrict[s]"—to five—"the maximum number of occupants permitted to occupy a dwelling." To be sure, as the majority observes, the restriction imposed by petitioner's zoning code is not an absolute one, because it does not apply to related persons. *See ante*, at 1782. But § 3607(b)(1) does not set forth a narrow exemption only for "absolute" or "unqualified" restrictions regarding the maximum number of occupants. Instead, it sweeps broadly to exempt any restrictions regarding such maximum number. It is difficult to imagine what broader terms Congress could have used to signify the categories or kinds of relevant governmental restrictions that are exempt from the FHA.

* * *

I would apply § 3607(b)(1) as it is written. Because petitioner's zoning code imposes a qualified "restrictio[n] regarding the maximum number of occupants permitted to occupy a dwelling," and because the statute exempts from the FHA "any" such restrictions, I would reverse the Ninth Circuit's holding that the exemption does not apply in this case.

II

The majority's failure to ask the right question about petitioner's zoning code results from a more fundamental error in focusing on "maximum occupancy restrictions" and "family composition rules." *See generally ante*, at 1780–1781. These two terms—and the two categories of zoning rules they describe—are simply irrelevant to this case.

A

As an initial matter, I do not agree with the majority's interpretive premise that "this case [is] an instance in which an exception to 'a general statement of policy' is sensibly read 'narrowly in order to preserve the primary operation of the [policy].' " *Ante*, at 1780 (quoting *Commissioner v. Clark*, 489 U.S. 726, 739, 109 S.Ct. 1455, 1463, 103 L.Ed.2d 753 (1989)). Why this case? Surely, it is not because the FHA has a "policy"; every statute has that. Nor could the reason be that a narrow reading of § 3607(b)(1) is necessary to preserve the primary operation of the FHA's stated policy "to provide ... for fair housing throughout the United States." 42 U.S.C. § 3601. Congress, the body responsible for deciding how specifically to achieve the objective of fair housing, obviously believed that § 3607(b)(1)'s exemption for "any ... restrictions regarding the maximum number of occupants permitted to occupy a dwelling" is consistent with the FHA's general statement of policy. We do Congress no service—indeed, we negate the "primary operation" of § 3607(b)(1)—by giving that congressional enactment an artificially narrow reading. *See Rodriguez v. United States*, 480 U.S. 522, 526, 107 S.Ct. 1391, 1393, 94 L.Ed.2d 533 (1987) (per curiam) ("[I]t frustrates rather than effectuates legislative intent simplistically to assume that whatever furthers the statute's primary objective must be law"); *Board of Governors, FRS v. Dimension Financial Corp.*, 474 U.S. 361, 374, 106 S.Ct. 681, 689, 88 L.Ed.2d 691 (1986) ("Invocation of the 'plain purpose' of legislation at the expense of the terms of the statute itself ... , in the end, prevents the effectuation of congressional intent").

* * *

B

I turn now to the substance of the majority's analysis, the focus of which is "maximum occupancy restrictions" and "family composition rules." The first of these two terms has the sole function of serving as a label for a category of zoning rules simply invented by the majority: rules that "cap the number of occupants per dwelling, typically in relation to available floor space or the number and type of rooms," that "ordinarily apply uniformly to all residents of all dwelling units," and that have the "purpose ... to protect health and safety by preventing dwelling overcrowding." *Ante*, at 1780–1781. The majority's term does bear a familial resemblance to the statutory term "restrictions regarding the maximum number of occupants permitted to occupy a dwelling," but it should be readily apparent that the category of zoning rules the majority labels "maximum occupancy restrictions" does not exhaust the category of restrictions exempted from the FHA by § 3607(b)(1). The plain words of the statute do not refer to "available floor space or the number and type of rooms"; they embrace no requirement that the exempted restrictions "apply uniformly to all residents of all dwelling units"; and they give no indication that such restrictions must have the "purpose ... to protect health and safety by preventing dwelling overcrowding." *Ibid.*

Of course, the majority does not contend that the language of § 3607(b)(1) precisely describes the category of zoning rules it has labeled "maximum occupancy restrictions." Rather, the majority makes the far more narrow claim that the statutory language "surely encompasses" that category. *Ante*, at 1781. I readily concede this point. But the obvious conclusion that § 3607(b)(1) encompasses "maximum occupancy restrictions" tells us nothing about whether the statute also encompasses ECDC § 21.30.010, the zoning rule at issue here. In other words, although the majority's discussion will no doubt provide guidance in future cases, it is completely irrelevant to the question presented in this case.

* * *

The majority fares no better in its treatment of "family composition rules," a term employed by the majority to describe yet another invented category of zoning restrictions. Although today's decision seems to hinge on the majority's judgment that ECDC § 21.30.010 is a "classic exampl[e] of a ... family composition rule," *ante*, at 1782, the majority says virtually nothing about this crucial category. Thus, it briefly alludes to the derivation of "family composition rules" and provides a single example of them. Apart from these two references, however, the majority's analysis consists solely of announcing its conclusion that "the formulation [of § 3607(b)(1)] does not fit family composition rules." *Ante*, at 1781. This is not reasoning; it is ipse dixit.

* * *

In sum, it does not matter that ECDC § 21.030.010 describes "[f]amily living, not living space per occupant," *ante*, at 1782, because it is immaterial under § 3607(b)(1) whether § 21.030.010 constitutes a "family composition rule" but not a "maximum occupancy restriction." The sole relevant question is whether petitioner's zoning code imposes "any ... restrictions regarding the maximum number of occupants permitted to occupy a dwelling." Because I believe it does, I respectfully dissent.

Questions and Comments

1. *The defendant's burden.* In FHA-based challenges, once the plaintiff has established a prima facie case, the burden of proof shifts to the defendant. In disparate impact challenges of the type brought in the *Town of Babylon* case, the nature of the defendant's burden is clear. As the *Town of Babylon* court noted, the defendant must prove that "its actions further, in theory and in practice, a legitimate, bona fide governmental interest and that no alternative would serve the interest with less discriminatory effect." By contrast, in disparate treatment challenges, the nature of the defendant's burden is not so clear. Some courts have applied a rational basis standard, holding that if the discriminatory statute or policy is rationally related to a legitimate government objective, it should be upheld. *See, e.g., Oxford House–C v. City of St. Louis*, 77 F.3d 249, 252 (8th Cir.1996); *Familystyle of St. Paul, Inc. v. City of St. Paul, Minnesota*, 728 F.Supp. 1396 (D.Minn. 1990), *aff'd* 923 F.2d 91 (8th Cir.1991). Other courts have argued that such use of constitutional equal protection analysis is misplaced when the plaintiff's challenge is based on a federal statute and not on the Fourteenth Amendment. *See, e.g., Bangerter v. Orem City Corporation*, 46 F.3d 1491 (10th Cir.1995). The *Bangerter* court determined that facially discriminatory treatment of the mentally disabled was justified only if (1) it was based on specific concerns about safety or (2) it actually benefitted the disabled. What *should* the defendant's burden in disparate treatment cases be? Should it be higher or lower than in disparate impact cases?

2. *Spacing requirements.* Ordinances that require facilities for the mentally handicapped to be located at least a certain distance apart from one another have been the subject of FHA-based challenges. These challenges have had mixed success. In *Familystyle of St. Paul v. City of St. Paul*, 923 F.2d 91 (8th Cir.1991), the 8th Circuit held that a state statute and local zoning ordinance which required that homes for the mentally disabled be located at least a quarter of a mile apart did not violate the FHA. According to the court, the ordinance furthered Minnesota's deinstitutionalization policy, which called for all persons with mental illness to live in settings that "maximize community integration and opportunities for acceptance." *Id.* at 93. By contrast, in *Larkin v. State of Michigan Department of Social Services*, 89 F.3d 285 (6th Cir.1996), the court struck down a 1500–foot spacing requirement. The court reasoned that "integration is not a sufficient justification for maintaining permanent quotas under the FHA ..." *Id.* at 291. While the *Familystyle* court applied a rational basis test to evaluate the defendant's justifications for its discriminatory treatment, the *Larkin* looked at whether the defendant could demonstrate that its discriminatory treatment was " 'warranted by the unique and specific needs and abilities of those handicapped persons' to whom the regulations apply." *Id.* at 290 (citation omitted).

Appendix A

SELECTED DIAGNOSES FROM DSM–IV–TR*

DISORDERS USUALLY FIRST DIAGNOSED IN INFANCY, CHILDHOOD OR ADOLESCENCE

Mental Retardation

A. Significantly subaverage intellectual functioning: an IQ of approximately 70 or below on an individually administered IQ test (for infants, a clinical judgment of significantly subaverage intellectual functioning).

B. Concurrent deficits or impairments in present adaptive functioning (i.e., the person's effectiveness in meeting the standards expected for his or her age by his or her cultural group) in at least two of the following areas: communication, self-care, home living, social/interpersonal skills, use of community resources, self-direction, functional academic skills, work, leisure, health, and safety.

C. The onset is before age 18 years.

Code based on degree of severity reflecting level of intellectual impairment:

Mild Mental Retardation:	IQ level 50–55 to approximately 70
Moderate Mental Retardation:	IQ level 35–40 to 50–55
Severe Mental Retardation:	IQ level 20–25 to 35–40
Profound Mental Retardation:	IQ level below 20 or 25
Mental Retardation, Severity Unspecified:	when there is strong presumption of Mental Retardation but the person's intelligence is untestable by standard tests

* Reprinted with permission of American Psychiatric Association.

Attention-Deficit/Hyperactivity Disorder

A.   Either (1) or (2):

(1) six (or more) of the following symptoms of **inattention** have persisted for at least 6 months to a degree that is maladaptive and inconsistent with developmental level:

Inattention

(a) often fails to give close attention to details or makes careless mistakes in schoolwork, work, or other activities.

(b) often has difficulty sustaining attention in tasks or play activities.

(c) often does not seem to listen when spoken to directly.

(d) often does not follow through on instructions and fails to finish schoolwork, chores, or duties in the workplace (not due to oppositional behavior or failure to understand instructions).

(e) often has difficulty organizing tasks and activities.

(f) often avoids, dislikes, or is reluctant to engage in tasks that require sustained mental effort (such as schoolwork or homework).

(g) often loses things necessary for tasks or activities (e.g., toys, school assignments, pencils, books, or tools).

(h) is often easily distracted by extraneous stimuli.

(i) is often forgetful in daily activities.

(2) six (or more) of the following symptoms of **hyperactivity-impulsivity** have persisted for at least 6 months to a degree that is maladaptive and inconsistent with developmental level:

Hyperactivity

(a) often fidgets with hands or feet or squirms in seat.

(b) often leaves seat in classroom or in other situations in which remaining seated is expected.

(c) often runs about or climbs excessively in situations in which is inappropriate (in adolescents or adults, may be limited to subjective feeling of restlessness).

(d) often has difficulty playing or engaging in leisure activities quietly.

(e) is often "on the go" or often acts as if "driven by a motor".

(f) often talks excessively.

Impulsivity

(g) often blurts out answers before questions have been completed.

House–Edmonds, is located in a neighborhood zoned for single-family residences. Upon learning that Oxford House had leased and was operating a home in Edmonds, the City issued criminal citations to the owner and a resident of the house. The citations charged violation of the zoning code rule that defines who may live in single-family dwelling units. The occupants of such units must compose a "family," and family, under the City's defining rule, "means an individual or two or more persons related by genetics, adoption, or marriage, or a group of five or fewer persons who are not related by genetics, adoption, or marriage." Edmonds Community Development Code (ECDC) § 21.30.010. Oxford House–Edmonds houses more than five unrelated persons, and therefore does not conform to the code.

Oxford House asserted reliance on the Fair Housing Act, 102 Stat. 1619, 42 U.S.C. § 3601 et seq., which declares it unlawful "[t]o discriminate in the sale or rental, or to otherwise make unavailable or deny, a dwelling to any buyer or renter because of a handicap of . . . that buyer or a renter." § 3604(f)(1)(A). The parties have stipulated, for purposes of this litigation, that the residents of Oxford House–Edmonds "are recovering alcoholics and drug addicts and are handicapped persons within the meaning" of the Act. App. 106.

Discrimination covered by the FHA includes "a refusal to make reasonable accommodations in rules, policies, practices, or services, when such accommodations may be necessary to afford [handicapped] person[s] equal opportunity to use and enjoy a dwelling." § 3604(f)(3)(B). Oxford House asked Edmonds to make a "reasonable accommodation" by allowing it to remain in the single-family dwelling it had leased. Group homes for recovering substance abusers, Oxford urged, need 8 to 12 residents to be financially and therapeutically viable. Edmonds declined to permit Oxford House to stay in a single-family residential zone, but passed an ordinance listing group homes as permitted uses in multifamily and general commercial zones.

Edmonds sued Oxford House in the United States District Court for the Western District of Washington seeking a declaration that the FHA does not constrain the City's zoning code family definition rule. Oxford House counterclaimed under the FHA, charging the City with failure to make a "reasonable accommodation" permitting maintenance of the group home in a single-family zone. The United States filed a separate action on the same FHA-"reasonable accommodation" ground, and the two cases were consolidated. Edmonds suspended its criminal enforcement actions pending resolution of the federal litigation.

On cross-motions for summary judgment, the District Court held that ECDC § 21.30.010, defining "family," is exempt from the FHA under § 3607(b)(1) as a "reasonable . . . restrictio[n] regarding the maximum number of occupants permitted to occupy a dwelling." App. to Pet. for Cert. B–7. The United States Court of Appeals for the Ninth Circuit reversed; holding § 3607(b)(1)'s absolute exemption inapplicable, the Court of Appeals remanded the cases for further consideration of the genuine issue of material fact with regard to defendant's violation of 42 U.S.C. § 3604(f)(3)(B), and plaintiffs' motion for partial summary judgment would be granted on this ground as well.

III. CONCLUSION

Accordingly, for the foregoing reasons, plaintiffs' motion for partial summary judgment pursuant to Rule 56 of the Federal Rules of Civil Procedure is granted and defendant is enjoined from taking any further steps to evict plaintiffs from the East Farmingdale Oxford House.

SO ORDERED.

In FHA-based challenges to regulations limiting the number of unrelated persons who can live together, defendants sometimes invoke the FHA exemption for "reasonable local, State, or Federal restrictions regarding the maximum number of occupants permitted to occupy a dwelling." 42 U.S.C. § 3607(b)(1). In the case set out below, the Supreme Court resolved a conflict between the Eleventh and Ninth Circuits on the scope of this exemption.

CITY OF EDMONDS v. OXFORD HOUSE, INC.

Supreme Court of the United States, 1995.
514 U.S. 725, 115 S.Ct. 1776, 131 L.Ed.2d 801.

JUSTICE GINSBURG delivered the opinion of the Court.

The Fair Housing Act (FHA or Act) prohibits discrimination in housing against, inter alios, persons with handicaps. Section 3607(b)(1) of the Act entirely exempts from the FHA's compass "any reasonable local, State, or Federal restrictions regarding the maximum number of occupants permitted to occupy a dwelling." 42 U.S.C. § 3607(b)(1). This case presents the question whether a provision in petitioner City of Edmonds' zoning code qualifies for § 3607(b)(1)'s complete exemption from FHA scrutiny. The provision, governing areas zoned for single-family dwelling units, defines "family" as "persons [without regard to number] related by genetics, adoption, or marriage, or a group of five or fewer [unrelated] persons." Edmonds Community Development Code (ECDC) § 21.30.010 (1991).

The defining provision at issue describes who may compose a family unit; it does not prescribe "the maximum number of occupants" a dwelling unit may house. We hold that § 3607(b)(1) does not exempt prescriptions of the family-defining kind, i.e., provisions designed to foster the family character of a neighborhood. Instead, § 3607(b)(1)'s absolute exemption removes from the FHA's scope only total occupancy limits, i.e., numerical ceilings that serve to prevent overcrowding in living quarters.

I

In the summer of 1990, respondent Oxford House opened a group home in the City of Edmonds, Washington for 10 to 12 adults recovering from alcoholism and drug addiction. The group home, called Oxford

(h) often has difficulty awaiting turn.

(i) often interrupts or intrudes on others (e.g., butts into conversations or games).

B. Some hyperactive-impulsive or inattentive symptoms that caused impairment were present before age 7 years.

C. Some impairment from the symptoms is present in two or more settings (e.g., at school [or work] and at home).

D. There must be clear evidence of clinically significant impairment in social, academic, or occupational functioning.

E. The symptoms do not occur exclusively during the course of a Pervasive Developmental Disorder, Schizophrenia, or other Psychotic Disorder and are not better accounted for by another mental order (e.g., Mood Disorder, Anxiety Disorder, Dissociative Disorder, or a Personality Disorder).

SCHIZOPHRENIA AND OTHER PSYCHOTIC DISORDERS

SCHIZOPHRENIA

A. *Characteristic symptoms:* Two (or more) of the following each present for a significant portion of time during a 1–month period (or less if successfully treated):

(1) delusions.

(2) hallucinations.

(3) disorganized speech (e.g., frequent derailment or incoherence).

(4) grossly disorganized or catatonic behavior.

(5) negative symptoms, i.e., affective flattening, alogia, or avolition.

Note: Only one Criterion A symptom is required if delusions are bizarre or hallucinations consist of a voice keeping up a running commentary on the person's behavior or thoughts, or two or more voices conversing with each other.

Paranoid Type

A type of Schizophrenia in which the following criteria are met:

A. Preoccupation with one or more delusions or frequent auditory hallucinations.

B. None of the following is prominent: disorganized speech, disorganized or catatonic behavior, or flat or inappropriate affect.

Disorganized Type

A type of Schizophrenia in which the following criteria are met:

A. All of the following are prominent:

(1) disorganized speech.

(2) disorganized behavior.

(3) flat or inappropriate affect.

B.   The criteria are not met for Catatonic Type.

Catatonic Type

A type of Schizophrenia in which the clinical picture is dominated by at least two of the following:

(1) motoric immobility as evidenced by catalepsy (including waxy flexibility) or stupor.

(2) excessive motor activity (that is apparently purposeless and not influenced by external stimuli).

(3) extreme negativism (an apparently motiveless resistance to all instructions or maintenance of a rigid posture against attempts to be moved) or mutism.

(4) peculiarities of voluntary movement as evidenced by posturing (voluntary assumption of inappropriate or bizarre postures), stereotyped movements, prominent mannerisms, or prominent grimacing.

(5) echolalia or echopraxia.

Undifferentiated Type

A type of Schizophrenia in which symptoms that meet Criterion A are present, but the criteria are not met for the Paranoid, Disorganized, or Catatonic Type.

Schizoaffective Disorder

A.   An uninterrupted period of illness during which, at some time, there is either a Major Depressive Episode, a Manic Episode, or a Mixed Episode [see below for criteria for these diagnoses] concurrent with symptoms that meet Criterion A for Schizophrenia.

B.   During the same period of illness, there have been delusions or hallucinations for at least 2 weeks in the absence of prominent mood symptoms.

Delusional Disorder

A.   Nonbizarre delusions (i.e., involving situations that occur in real life, such as being followed, poisoned, infected, loved at a distance, or deceived by spouse or lover, or having a disease) of at least 1 month's duration.

B.   Criterion A for Schizophrenia has never been met. **Note:** Tactile and olfactory hallucinations may be present in Delusional Disorder if they are related to the delusional theme.

Specify type (the following types are assigned based on the predominant delusional theme):

Erotomanic Type: delusions that another person, usually of higher status, is in love with the individual.

Grandiose Type: delusions of inflated worth, power, knowledge, identity, or special relationship to a deity or famous person.

Jealous Type: delusions that the individual's sexual partner is unfaithful.

Persecutory Type: delusions that the person (or someone to whom the person is close) is being malevolently treated in some way.

Somatic Type: delusions that the person has some physical defect or general medical condition.

Mixed Type: delusions characteristic of more than one of the above types but no one theme predominates.

Unspecified Type

Brief Psychotic Disorder

A.   Presence of one (or more) of the following symptoms:

(1) delusions.

(2) hallucinations.

(3) disorganized speech (e.g., frequent derailment or incoherence).

(4) grossly disorganized or catatonic behavior.

Note: Do not include a symptom if it is a culturally sanctioned response pattern.

B.   Duration of an episode of the disturbance is at least 1 day but less than 1 month, with eventual full return to premorbid level of functioning.

MOOD DISORDERS

Major Depressive Episode

A.   Five (or more) of the following symptoms have been present during the same 2–week period and represent a change from previous functioning; at least one of the symptoms is either (1) depressed mood or (2) loss of interest or pleasure.

Note: Do not include symptoms that are clearly due to a general medical condition, or mood-incongruent delusions or hallucinations.

(1) depressed mood most of the day, nearly every day, as indicated by either subjective report (e.g., feels sad or empty) or observation made by others (e.g., appears tearful).

Note: In children and adolescents, can be irritable mood.

(2) markedly diminished interest or pleasure in all, or almost all, activities most of the day, nearly every day (as indicated by either subjective account or observation made by others)

(3) significant weight loss when not dieting or weight gain (e.g., a change of more than 5% of body weight in a month), or decrease or increase in appetite nearly every day.

Note: In children, consider failure to make expected weight gains.

(4) insomnia or hypersomnia nearly every day.

(5) psychomotor agitation or retardation nearly every day (observable by others, not merely subjective feelings of restlessness or being slowed down).

(6) fatigue or loss of energy nearly every day.

(7) feelings of worthlessness or excessive or inappropriate guilt (which may be delusional) nearly every day (not merely self-reproach or guilt about being sick).

(8) diminished ability to think or concentrate, or indecisiveness, nearly every day (either by subjective account or as observed by others).

(9) recurrent thoughts of death (not just fear of dying), recurrent suicidal ideation without a specific plan, or a suicide attempt or a specific plan for committing suicide.

Manic Episode

A. A distinct period of abnormally and persistently elevated, expansive, or irritable mood, lasting at least 1 week (or any duration if hospitalization is necessary).

B. During the period of mood disturbance, three (or more) of the following symptoms have persisted (four if the mood is only irritable) and have been present to a significant degree:

(1) inflated self-esteem or grandiosity.

(2) decreased need for sleep (e.g., feels rested after only 3 hours of sleep).

(3) more talkative than usual or pressure to keep talking.

(4) flight of ideas or subjective experience that thoughts are racing.

(5) distractibility (i.e., attention too easily drawn to unimportant or irrelevant external stimuli).

(6) increase in goal-directed activity (either socially, at work or school, or sexually) or psychomotor agitation.

(7) excessive involvement in pleasurable activities that have a high potential for painful consequences (e.g., engaging in unrestrained buying sprees, sexual indiscretions, or foolish business investments).

Mixed Episode

A.   The criteria are met both for a manic Episode and for a Major Depressive Episode (except for duration) nearly every day during at least a 1–week period.

Dysthymic Disorder

A.   Depressed mood for most of the day, for more days than not, as indicated either by subjective account or observations by others, for at least 2 years.

Note: In children and adolescents, mood can be irritable and duration must be at least 1 year.

B.   Presence, while depressed, of two (or more) of the following:

(1) poor appetite or overeating.

(2) insomnia or hypersomnia.

(3) low energy or fatigue.

(4) low self-esteem.

(5) poor concentration or difficulty making decisions.

(6) feelings of hopelessness.

ANXIETY DISORDERS

Panic Attack

A discrete period of intense fear or discomfort, in which four (or more) of the following symptoms developed abruptly and reached a peak within 10 minutes:

(1) palpitations, pounding heart, or accelerated heart rate.

(2) sweating.

(3) trembling or shaking.

(4) sensations of shortness of breath or smothering.

(5) feeling of choking.

(6) chest pain or discomfort.

(7) nausea or abdominal distress.

(8) feeling dizzy, unsteadly, lightheaded, or faint.

(9) derealization (feelings of unreality) or depersonalization (being detached from oneself).

(10) fear of losing control or going crazy.

(11) fear of dying.

(12) paresthesias (numbness or tingling sensations).

(13) chills or hot flushes.

Social Phobia

A.   A marked and persistent fear of one or more social or performance situations in which the person is exposed to unfamiliar people or to possible scrutiny by others. The individual fears that he or she will act in a way (or show anxiety symptoms) that will be humiliating or embarrassing.

Note: In children, there must be evidence of the capacity for age-appropriate social relationships with familiar people and the anxiety must occur in peer settings, not just in interactions with adults.

B.   Exposure to the feared social situation almost invariably provokes anxiety, which may take the form of a situationally bound or situationally predisposed Panic Attack.

Note: In children, the anxiety may be expressed by crying, tantrums, freezing, or shrinking from social situations with unfamiliar people.

C.   The person recognizes that the fear is excessive or unreasonable.

Note: In children, this feature may be absent.

D.   The feared social or performance situations are avoided or else are endured with intense anxiety or distress.

E.   The avoidance, anxious anticipation, or distress in the feared social or performance situation(s) interferes significantly with the person's normal routine, occupational (academic) functioning, or social activities or relationships, or there is marked distress about having the phobia.

Post-Traumatic Stress Syndrome (see pp. 557–58 for DSM criteria).

Dissociative Identity Disorder

A.   The presence of two or more distinct identities or personality states (each with its own relatively enduring pattern of perceiving, relating to, and thinking about the environment and self).

B.   At least two of these identities or personality states recurrently take control of the person's behavior.

C.   Inability to recall important personal information that is too extensive to be explained by ordinary forgetfulness.

D.   The disturbance is not due to the direct physiological effects of a substance (e.g., blackouts or chaotic behavior during alcohol intoxication) or a general medical condition (e.g., complex partial seizures).

IMPULSE–CONTROL DISORDERS NOT ELSEWHERE CLASSIFIED

Intermittent Explosive Disorder

A.   Several discrete episodes of failure to resist aggressive impulses that result in serious assaultive acts or destruction of property.

B. The degree of aggressiveness during the episodes is grossly out of proportion to any precipitating psychosocial stressors.

Kleptomania

A. Recurrent failure to resist impulses to steal objects that are not needed for personal use or for their monetary value.

B. Increasing sense of tension immediately before committing the theft.

C. Pleasure, gratification, or relief at the time of committing the theft.

D. The stealing is not committed to express anger or vengeance and is not in response to a delusion or a hallucination.

Pathological Gambling (see p. 451 for DSM criteria).

PERSONALITY DISORDERS

A Personality Disorder is an enduring pattern of inner experience and behavior that deviates markedly from the expectations of the individual's culture, is pervasive and inflexible, has an onset in adolescence or early adulthood, is stable over time, and leads to distress or impairment. The Personality Disorders ... are listed below. [Full criteria are provided only for a few disorders.]

Paranoid Personality Disorder is a pattern of distrust and suspiciousness such that others' motives are interpreted as malevolent.

Schizoid Personality Disorder is a pattern of detachment from social relationships and a restricted range of emotional expression.

Schizotypal Personality Disorder is a pattern of acute discomfort in close relationships, cognitive or perceptual distortions, and eccentricities of behavior.

Antisocial Personality Disorder is a pattern of disregard for, and violation of, the rights of others.

Borderline Personality Disorder is a pattern of instability in interpersonal relationships, self-image, and affects, and marked impulsivity.

Histrionic Personality Disorder is a pattern of excessive emotionality and attention seeking.

Narcissistic Personality Disorder is a pattern of grandiosity, need for admiration, and lack of empathy.

Avoidant Personality Disorder is a pattern of social inhibition, feelings of inadequacy, and hypersensitivity to negative evaluation.

Dependent Personality Disorder is a pattern of submissive and clinging behavior related to an excessive need to be taken care of.

Obsessive-Compulsive Personality Disorder is a pattern of preoccupation with orderliness, perfectionism, and control.

Schizoid Personality Disorder

A. A pervasive pattern of detachment from social relationships and a restricted range of expression of emotions in interpersonal settings, beginning by early adulthood and present in a variety of contexts, as indicated by four (or more) of the following:

(1) neither desires nor enjoys close relationships, including being part of a family.

(2) almost always chooses solitary activities.

(3) has little, if any, interest in having sexual experiences with another person.

(4) takes pleasure in few, if any, activities.

(5) lacks close friends or confidants other than first-degree relatives.

(6) appears indifferent to the praise or criticism of others.

(7) shows emotional coldness, detachment, or flattened affectivity.

B. Does not occur exclusively during the course of Schizophrenia, a Mood Disorder With Psychotic Features, another Psychotic Disorder, or a Pervasive Developmental Disorder and is not due to the direct physiological effects of a general medical condition.

Schizotypal Personality Disorder

A. A pervasive pattern of social and interpersonal deficits marked by acute discomfort with, and reduced capacity for, close relationships as well as by cognitive or perceptual distortions and eccentricities of behavior, beginning by early adulthood and present in a variety of contexts, as indicated by five (or more) of the following:

(1) ideas of reference (excluding delusions of reference).

(2) odd beliefs or magical thinking that influences behavior and is inconsistent with subcultural norms (e.g., superstitiousness, belief in clairvoyance, telepathy, or "sixth sense"; in children and adolescents, bizarre fantasies or preoccupations).

(3) unusual perceptual experiences, including bodily illusions.

(4) odd thinking and speech (e.g., vague, circumstantial, metaphorical, overelaborate, or stereotyped).

(5) suspiciousness or paranoid ideation.

(6) inappropriate or constricted affect.

(7) behavior or appearance that is odd, eccentric, or peculiar.

(8) lack of close friends or confidants other than first-degree relatives.

(9) excessive social anxiety that does not diminish with familiarity and tends to be associated with paranoid fears rather than negative judgments about self.

B.   Does not occur exclusively during the course of Schizophrenia, a Mood Disorder With Psychotic Features, another Psychotic Disorder, or a Pervasive Developmental Disorder.

Antisocial Personality Disorder

A.   There is a pervasive pattern of disregard for and violation of the rights of others occurring since age 15 years, as indicated by three (or more) of the following:

(1) failure to conform to social norms with respect to lawful behaviors as indicated by repeatedly performing acts that are grounds for arrest.

(2) deceitfulness, as indicated by repeated lying, use of aliases, or conning others for personal profit or pleasure.

(3) impulsivity or failure to plan ahead.

(4) irritability and aggressiveness, as indicated by repeated physical fights or assaults.

(5) reckless disregard for safety of self or others.

(6) consistent irresponsibility, as indicated by repeated failure to sustain consistent work behavior or honor financial obligations.

(7) lack of remorse, as indicated by being indifferent to rationalizing having hurt, mistreated, or stolen from another.

B.   The individual is at least age 18 years.

C.   There is evidence of Conduct Disorder with onset before age 15 years.

D.   The occurrence of antisocial behavior is not exclusively during the course of Schizophrenia or a Manic Episode.

Borderline Personality Disorder

A pervasive pattern of instability of interpersonal relationships, self-image, and affects, and marked impulsivity beginning by early adulthood and present in a variety of contexts, as indicated by five (or more) of the following:

(1) frantic efforts to avoid real or imagined abandonment.

Note: Do not include suicidal or self-mutilating behavior covered in Criterion 5.

(2) a pattern of unstable and intense interpersonal relationships characterized by alternating between extremes of idealization and devaluation.

(3) identity disturbance: markedly and persistently unstable self-image or sense of self.

(4) impulsivity in at least two areas that are potentially self-damaging (e.g., spending, sex, substance abuse, reckless driving, binge eating).

Note: Do not include suicidal or self-mutilating behavior covered in Criterion 5.

(5) recurrent suicidal behavior, gestures, or threats, or self-mutilating behavior.

(6) affective instability due to a marked reactivity of mood (e.g., intense episodic dysphoria, irritability, or anxiety usually lasting a few hours and only rarely more than a few days).

(7) chronic feelings of emptiness.

(8) inappropriate, intense anger or difficulty controlling anger (e.g., frequent displays of temper, constant anger, recurrent physical fights).

(9) transient, stress-related paranoid ideation or severe dissociative symptoms.

Narcissistic Personality Disorder

A pervasive pattern of grandiosity (in fantasy or behavior), need for admiration, and lack of empathy, beginning by early adulthood and present in a variety of contexts, as indicated by five (or more) of the following:

(1) has a grandiose sense of self-importance (e.g., exaggerates achievements and talents, expects to be recognized as superior without commensurate achievements).

(2) is preoccupied with fantasies of unlimited success, power, brilliance, beauty, or ideal love.

(3) believes that he or she is "special" and unique and can only be understood by, or should associate with, other special or high-status people (or institutions).

(4) requires excessive admiration.

(5) has a sense of entitlement, i.e., unreasonable expectations of especially favorable treatment or automatic compliance with his or her expectations.

(6) is interpersonally exploitative, i.e., takes advantage of others to achieve his or own ends.

(7) lacks empathy: is unwilling to recognize or identify with the feelings and needs of others.

(8) is often envious of others or believes that others are envious of him or her.

(9) shows arrogant, haughty behaviors or attitudes.

Dependent Personality Disorder

A pervasive and excessive need to be taken care of that leads to submissive and clinging behavior and fears of separation, beginning by early adulthood and present in a variety of contexts, as indicated by five (or more) of the following:

(1) has difficulty making everyday decisions without an excessive amount of advice and reassurance from others.

(2) needs others to assume responsibility for most major areas of his or her life.

(3) has difficulty expressing disagreement with others because of fear of loss of support or approval.

Note: Do not include realistic fears of retribution.

(4) has difficulty initiating projects or doing things on his or her own (because of a lack of self-confidence in judgment or abilities rather than a lack of motivation or energy).

(5) goes to excessive lengths to obtain nurturance and support from others, to the point of volunteering to do things that are unpleasant.

(6) feels uncomfortable or helpless when alone because of exaggerated fears of being unable to care for himself or herself.

(7) urgently seeks another relationship as a source of care and support when a close relationship ends.

(8) is unrealistically preoccupied with fears of being left to take care of himself or herself.

Appendix B

EXCERPTS FROM TRANSCRIPT TRIAL OF JOHN W. HINCKLEY, JR.

Dr. William R. Carpenter, Jr., Defense Witness

Direct Examination by Defense Attorney Vincent Fuller

Q. [Would you describe the basis for your] diagnos[is] of the defendant's mental illness, mental disease?

A. ... Delusion is a technical term that refers to the development of a false belief, and a false belief that is not shared by others and is not readily shaken by evidence to the contrary ... And it is not simply that it is false that makes it a delusion because people have many false beliefs. But it is false, it is not shared by others, and evidence that would show that it is not, in fact, accurate doesn't shake the belief that the person has. So I use the term "delusion" because it will be important to understand that as a technical judgment that I have made that relates to this withdrawal from reality and the development of the relationship, for example, with Jodie Foster, as it developed over time, took on a quality of a delusion and became delusional. So it was not that it was only a fantasy and a fantasy that became an obsession. It was both of those things. But [he] also developed in that context false beliefs that were not shaken by evidence to the contrary and that, in fact, he was basing many actions of his life on. So that I did conclude that he had developed delusions.

There is another technical term that is important in diagnosis and a symptom that can appear in several different diagnostic categories and that term is "ideas of reference." And this is a technical term that means that a person's mental state is such that they will interpret in a highly personal and idiosyncratic way—that is, a personal and unusual way—what may be common-place events. [M]y conclusion that he had the symptom and manifestation of ideas of reference [comes] from any different examples, some as trivial as like walking down a street and a newspaper blowing across his leg and his giving it some unusual significance or importance that had some actual meaning to him, not just to an event. [Another example is the] personalized quality of when President

1353

Reagan was smiling and waving in the crowd in the vicinity where he was, the belief that it had a personal connection.

MR. FULLER: Your Honor, I had the witness [look at] what has been marked Exhibit–15.... Can you identify that document, Doctor?

A. Yes. The document, N–15, is a letter that John Hinckley wrote to Jodie Foster [in New Haven] when he was in his hotel room after having seen President Reagan's itinerary, made his plan to go to the Hilton and then he sat down and wrote a letter to her addressed—[that is]—put her name on the envelope for the letter. This [was] not actually mailed, but he prepared it that morning, the morning of the 30th before going to the Hilton.

Q. Without reading the letter, can you just summarize the substance of it?

A. Yes. He says to her that is going to assassinate President Reagan, that there is a definite possibility that he will be killed in his attempt to do that. He described to her how he has tried to gain her attention and affection.... That time is running out on him. That he is not able to wait any longer to make her understand the importance of this and that he hopes in sacrificing his own life or his own freedom in what he refers to as an "historic deed" that he will finally gain her respect and love.

Q. Is there a time written on that document, N?

A. The date is 3/30/81, and the time is 12:45 p.m.

Q. And shortly after that, Mr. Hinckley left for the Hilton Hotel?

A. Yes.

Q. And have you reviewed with Mr. Hinckley his thought processes that he was experiencing when he arrived at the Hilton Hotel up to and through the actual shooting?

A. Yes, I have.

Q. ... First, recite what you learned from Mr. Hinckley regarding his thought processes.

A. Yes. Picking up then after he has prepared the letter, has loaded his weapon, he goes to the Hilton. What is on his mind is to see if he can in fact make an assassination attempt on Reagan; not knowing that that is possible, to decide whether or not to stay overnight again in Washington before going to New Haven or going on to New Haven then.

He is seeing two possible outcomes both now and in the immediate further, either the outcome of the assassination attempt and what happens to him in that process or, and what he assumes to be at least a termination of his freedom and a wish for termination of his life, and the other outcome being to proceed on to New Haven, which has been his primary plan during this period of time, to either kill himself or to kill Jodie Foster and himself. So those are the things that are on his mind.

When he arrives at the Hilton he said that he was surprised at how easy it was to get in the vicinity of where President Reagan would be. He had a sense there was something lapsed about the security, but was able to get in the vicinity, and when President Reagan arrived was fairly close to him as he went into the Hilton.

He said that, on his way in, ... President Reagan looked at him and smiled and waved and his own interpretation of that was something highly personal, that he felt that President Reagan was looking at him and smiling and waving.

President Reagan went on into the Hilton. John Hinckley left, left that location, walked up into the lobby of the Hilton and spent some time resting, trying to decide what to do.

He at that point assumed that President Reagan would be ... there for 45 minutes or an hour or so, some period of time, and he was debating whether to wait and see if he could get close to him as he departed, [or] whether he should go back to the hotel. There was still this issue about whether to go to New Haven, whether to stay overnight in Washington.

He walks back out of the hotel in what he estimates to be about 15 minutes later, goes back to the spot where he had been before and would have been, as he describes it, one or two minutes, but in a very quick period of time he is surprised that President Reagan's party is coming out again and as he comes out he has the experience of time moving very quickly, that is, that there is only a moment before President Reagan [will] walk to his limousine and be out of the area, that he is there, is able to do it. [He] feels that President Reagan is about to turn again in his direction, and before the President has an opportunity to do that, he beings shooting.

Q. Doctor, how do you interpret Mr. Hinckley's mental state in those moments, those few moments before the actual shooting?

A. Well, his mental state is predominantly one of despair, depression, and a sense of the end of things. In terms of his own, as he can weigh and value things, the thing that is most important to him is to terminate his own existence and to find a way to do that. The suicidal aspects and self-destructiveness of this are foremost in his mind.

At the same time the wish for realization of this relationship with Jodie Foster is on his mind in terms of how his doing that act will unite him with Jodie Foster.

There are the primary things that are on his mind. There is a quickening of the time perspective at the moment that President Reagan is coming out and the sense of something highly personal in the encounter between the two.

... I can explain this by ... showing contrast and similarity to a previous experience. Remember that some months ago there had been a series of Jodie Foster films on TV in a short period of time, that he had sensed that they had been put there in some personal way in relationship to him, as a particular symptom or manifestation of illness that we see in some forms of illness. He had that same kind of highly personalized sense of when the President presumably waved and smiled to a crowd of people that he personalized on it and this [was] taking place in a very compacted time frame.

Cross Examination by Assistant U.S. Attorney Roger Adelman

Q. You have heard, have you not, the tapes of Mr. Hinckley talking to Jodie Foster; right?

A. Yes.

Q. Now, Mr. Hinckley told you that he went up there because he admired Miss Foster, he was interested in her; right?

A. Well, those two things are true. That doesn't quite capture what was on his mind about Miss Foster, but it is true that part of what was on his mind included admiration and an interest.

Q. Right. And he was in a way obsessed with her?

A. He was more than obsessed. I mean he was *obsessed* with her.

Q. Was he delusional about her?

A. Yes; he had developed delusional expectations of that relationship by that time.

Q. Now wait a minute. Are you telling this jury then that when Mr. Hinckley was up there on the telephone with Miss Foster and her roommates, that he was delusional?

A. He had delusions at that time, yes.

Q. What delusion did he have during the telephone calls that this jury heard? Name those delusions for us, please.

A. Oh, the whole, the basis of being there, including making the telephone calls, was based on delusional function that he had in relationship to Jodie Foster. . . .

He, by then, had come to believe that the only salvation that he had, the only way he could extricate himself from this life was through union with her.

He had come to believe that a union with her was in some sense ordained, that he was being propelled in that direction. He had taken it as a message to him that a number of her films had been shown on television during the time prior to that as the purpose—the purpose of that was a personal purpose, to spur him onward to activity in this regard.

He believed if he could make contact with her, that they could become an extraordinary couple.

He believed that he had some responsibilities toward her in terms of protecting her.

He believed that he could be made whole again in some sense in terms of the wretched existence and experiences that he was having.

[All] of these things . . . are called a delusion because there are many components of false belief, and they are false beliefs that could not be readily shaken by evidence to the contrary, and they are beliefs upon which he is basing his activity, his plans, his actions. In pursuing them he then makes telephone calls, and the delusions that are present during that whole period of time, including the telephone calls, are the type of thing I am saying.

This type of delusional formation would not [be expected] to interfere with ordinary activities like purchasing tickets or purchasing food or being able to make telephone calls.

There is considerable evidence that he did not have the kind of incoherence of thinking, the scattering of thoughts . . . that can be an aspect of schizophrenia, and lead in certain periods of time during a person's life to much more incoherent activity. Those have never been present, to my knowledge, in John Hinckley. . . .

The delusional formation—and of course this is very common to process schizophrenia—people can have long-term delusional formations at the same time they can be going to work everyday. They can be conducting their life outside of hospitals. They can be looking after families. So it is not an incompatibility with many areas of functioning that appears ordinary and accomplishes ordinary tasks, but the whole basis for [his] being there and making the telephone calls is [his] delusions. . . .

Q. What you are saying is that nobody, including you, has ever found any observable delusions in this person, Mr. Hinckley: right?

A. Say that again.

Q. You are telling us in that long response there that nobody observed active delusions in Mr. Hinckley, right? Or manifestations?

A. A delusion is a mental process and it is not possible to have direct access to observe it. . . . You learn about delusions from learning about the person, what their beliefs are, and then by trying to see whether or not there are behaviors and impacts and effects on the person's life that are consistent with those beliefs.

   . . .

[Q.] Now you mentioned in your testimony [that] Mr. Hinckley, as part of this delusional system at the time of the shooting, had an idea of reference about Mr. Reagan, that Mr. Reagan was waving at him, just him alone; is that right?

A. Yes, he personalized that experience and that would be an example of an idea of reference.

Q. You have examined and have read the report of the government doctors, that is to say, Drs. Cavanaugh, Dietz, and Rappeport, have you not?

A.   Yes. [The witness is shown a portion of the report summarizing statements by the defendant.]

Q.   [Reading:] "He said that although he felt the President had looked right at him, he did not feel any message other than 'hello' was being communicated. He added: 'I was probably the only one he could see, so that is probably why he picked me out.'" Did you see that passage in this report before you testified today?

A.   Yes.

Q.   Mr. Hinckley reports to these doctors that there was no idea of reference at all, he just saw the President wave at him; right?

A.   He thinks that the President has picked him out and I don't know that there is any evidence that President Reagan had singled him out.

Q.   But he pointed out in the next sentence: "I was probably the only one he could see"; so that is probably why he picked him out.

A.   That seems to me unlikely, that of the people there the only person he could see was John Hinckley, and in his description of the events to me, it was my inference that it was a highly personalized experience. This is a phenonmen[on] that he has experienced on a number of other occasions, so it has some compatibility with the longitudinal view, and it is strange to me to think the only person President Reagan could see would be John Hinckley, and ... it strains my credulity to think President Reagan singled out John Hinckley and smiled and said hello to him personally.

Dr. Park Elliott Dietz, Government Witness

Direct Examination by Mr. Adelman

[A] ... On June 7, 1981, in exploring possible evidence of ideas of reference, I asked Mr. Hinckley specifically about what he thought was happening when the President looked at him, and he said that he did not feel that any message other than "hello" was being communicated. He said he "was probably the only one he could see, so that is probably why he picked me out."

Q.   What does that show you?

A.   Well, had this been an example of an idea of reference or delusion[al] thinking, I believe that Mr. Hinckley would have said that the President meant to convey something to him personally, or that the President meant in some way to communicate "now was the time," or the President had some message to convey, or that this was "meant for him." None of those things were said.

He said that he believed the President meant to communicate "hello," and probably he was the only one that the President could see, which I took to [reflect] the fact that most of the other people there were cameramen who had cameras in front of their faces, so John Hinckley's face would be one of the few faces visible at the time.

Q. All right.

A. Also on June 7, 1981, I made note of another comment that Mr. Hinckley had made about the same incident in which he said, "He waved across the street and then waved to us, meaning other people where I was, and to cameramen and all, and then they rushed him inside, and when he waved to us I felt he was looking right at me, and I waved back. I was kind of startled but maybe it was just my imagination."

Q. Was that an idea of reference?

A. That was a statement that led me to inquire further about it. Hi[s] saying "Maybe it was just my imagination" leaves doubt.

Q. When you explored, what did you find and what did you conclude?

A. I found that he thought probably the President couldn't see anybody else and didn't intend to communicate anything other than "hello."

I would point out one other thing, and that is that these comments about the President waving are things that [were said] in June 1981. There is an earlier account, as I've mentioned before, of the events of March 30, and that is the account in the file at Butner [the federal mental hospital]. Dr. Johnson got an account of the events of March 30, and the relevant quotation from that period reads as follows: "President got out and waved. John waved back."

Q. What is the significance of that?

A. Well, that says nothing that would even suggest an idea of reference.

Q. Do you draw any conclusions from the fact that 2½ months later he told you about the special significance of the waving?

A. Well, in order to draw conclusions from that I have to make inferences, and so far I've tried to keep my testimony to the facts and not to inference.

Q. Are there a number of inferences that can be made from that?

A. Yes, I think there are.

Q. Is manipulation one of the inferences, one of the many that could be made from this incident?

A. That is one of the possibilities.

Q. Can you determine from all of your evaluation of the case, including interviews of Mr. Hinckley, as to whether, in fact, he had a delusion as to Miss Foster?

A. I made such a determination.

Q. What did you determine?

A. That he has not had a delusion about Jodie Foster.

Q. Now why do you have that view?

A.   From talking to him about it. You see, my first thought when I heard about this case prior to being personally involved, just based on media accounts, was that this sounded like a case that I happened to be particularly interested in, a type of case in which individuals do have a delusion of a relationship that isn't true. In fact, I had conducted a library search on the topic before getting any of the materials on the case just out of interest, because from the media accounts one would have thought that that is what this was about, that Hinckley would have had a delusional belief about Jodie Foster.

In talking to him, in learning the facts and learning about his actions and what else went on, it became clear that there is no delusion about Jodie Foster and there was no delusion about Jodie Foster. He recognized throughout that the relationship was one-sided—his care for her, his love for her—but that it was not reciprocated and that it was not likely to be reciprocated.

Q.   All right. This might be a useful time to turn to that matter of Jodie Foster, if we can.

THE COURT: Are you saying that in the absence of a return of interest there is no delusional pattern as far as he is concerned?

THE WITNESS: Well, there are other kinds of delusions, Your Honor, but delusional relationships in which a person has the delusion of a love relationship with someone else have to be two ways. There has to be a view that the other person somehow shares the relationship.

THE COURT: Could you give an example of that?

THE WITNESS: Surely. The young woman who is in love with a movie star from Hollywood and believes that every time a plane flies overhead it is his sending her a message of love. She writes him fan mail and then she gets answers because a plane flies over and she thinks it means he is saying, "Yes, I love you. Thank you for your letter."

These cases are reported with some frequency in the literature. We see it in both women and men—the delusion of relationship with another individual. For example, cases I have seen, Your Honor, include a young man who had the delusion that a particular woman might like him, loved him, and that he loved her. Now he may have loved her, but she didn't even know who he was. One day he broke into her apartment and he thought that she was being held hostage there. Well, that fellow is fine in every other area of his life, but he had a true delusion about his relationship with this woman, and she didn't even know him.

BY MR. ADELMAN:

Q.   Now could you compare that description you gave to the Court with Mr. Hinckley with respect to whether or not in your view he had a delusion as to Miss Foster?

A.   In my opinion he did not have a delusion about Miss Foster.

Q.   What is the reason or reasons that you say that? What is the evidence?

A.   Well, let me tell you the evidence.

First of all, the development of his interest in Miss Foster took a perfectly natural course. He had seen her in movies. He saw her on television. He saw more of her movies. He became interested in her through that medium, and this is the first time he had become interested that way in a movie star. There was nothing special about the way he regarded seeing her in the movies. It is just that he was attracted to her and thought she would be a good person.

When he narrates his efforts to contact Jodie Foster by telephone, Mr. Hinckley has consistently narrated them to me in a manner indicating he understood that she was not really available to him. For example, in the very first interview we had with him, this is on May 30th, he said he felt that part of his fascination with Jodie Foster is that she was unattainable, out of reach, unapproachable.

He speculated that he knew all along that it wasn't going to work out, and that even when he went to New Haven, intending to introduce himself to her, he knew it wouldn't work.

Q.   Why does that show it was not a delusion in your opinion?

A.   Well, part of what would make this kind of belief system a delusion—and it is not even a belief system—what would render these ideas delusional would be a fixed false belief.

Q.   Did he have a fixed false belief?

A.   No, he didn't have a fixed belief, and it is hard to find evidence that he had a false belief. He had unrealistic hopes.

Q.   What is that called besides—

A.   That is called being a dreamer.

Q.   Is being a dreamer a manifestation of serious mental disorder?

A.   No, it isn't.

[Q.] Did you learn in the course of your evaluation of Mr. Hinckley's goals for that day?

A.   Yes, I did.

Q.   Can you tell us what they were and what significance each of them has as far as your evaluation of his criminal responsibility is concerned?

A.   [D]uring the first interview that I had occasion to speak to Mr. Hinckley personally, . . . Mr. Hinckley was asked if he had thought that after he carried out his plan assassination, that Jodie Foster would know about him, and his response on that date was to smile and to say "Yeah, it worked."

Q.   Now, have you explored that with him either then or [in] other interviews?

A.   Yes. I will give you other examples of exploring that question.

On June 7, 1981, I interviewed Mr. Hinckley, and I asked him if he had been trying to impress Jodie Foster, and he said, "Well, it is a combination of things: To impress her, almost to traumatize her. That is the best word. To link myself with her for almost the rest of history, if you want to go that far."

I asked how he thought Jodie Foster would view him. He said, "I would have preferred for her to feel good about me, but going this way it is kind of hard for her to feel good about me."

I then asked him if he had been trying to communicate something to Jodie Foster, and he said that he had been trying to communicate something to the effect of, "Now you will appreciate how much I cared for you. I went to this extent. Now do you appreciate it?" . . . I asked a follow-up to that, which was whether he thought he had accomplished that goal, and he said, "You know, actually, I accomplished everything on a grand scale." I asked him if he really meant that because that statement struck me as an extraordinary one, and he said, "Actually, I accomplished exactly what I wanted to accomplish, without exception."

Q. Now, with that as a goal or a series of goals, could you explain the significance of that [to] your evaluation of Mr. Hinckley and to whatever mental disorders you found that he has and to the general question of criminal responsibility. What does that mean in this case?

A. Well, from my general evaluation of Mr. Hinckley, what that statements means to me is that he did, indeed, intend to make an impression upon Jodie Foster; that he understood that the impression he would make . . . with an act of this sort was a traumatic one, not likely to win affection, but one which would indeed impress upon her who he is and cause her to remember him; that he undertook the shootings of March 30 with [that] as a goal he had in mind. I believe there were other goals, but that is one he has articulated in writing, and that he believes he accomplished that goal which shows that his goal was indeed reasonable since he accomplished it.

Q. Does it show he was schizophrenic?

A. No, it doesn't.

Q. . . . Does the fact that he had this particular goal show he suffered from a particular mental disorder?

A. That fact does not show that, no.

Q. Explain that to the jury.

A. Well, this goal certainly seems like a very odd one, and when I first heard that that was the goal—prior to my involvement in this case—I was impressed with what an odd and, in the lay sense, "crazy" thing such a goal would be.

After having the opportunity to evaluate Mr. Hinckley, to interview all of these other people, to review all of the facts, that goal makes sense. He had felt rejected by Jodie Foster as early as September, after his first efforts to contact her, and, as he later described, he was angry about what she had done, that is, that she had not responded to his calls as he hoped. To win her attention, to be able to impress upon her, here is John Hinckley who loves her, to make her remember him, was a goal for which he was willing to sacrifice a great deal. But it was not entirely a sacrifice, as I will show, because in addition to winning her attention, he wished to have fame and notoriety.

Q. Is that a separate goal?

A. Well, they are linked in this way, but it is a goal that I will show separate evidence for.

Q. All right. Do you have anything more to say about the goal insofar as it relates to a serious mental disorder?

A. Only to say that my first impression without the facts was that that could well reflect a serious mental disorder.

Q. Where do you stand today?

A. That is does not.

Q. Why?

A. Because I have had the opportunity to obtain the facts, to speak with him, and to determine that indeed that was a goal that developed out of his experiences in life and which he feels he has accomplished. . . .

Q. You mentioned the goal f–I believe it is—fame?

A. He displayed a considerable concern with the media, as I will show . . . [a]nd he indicated his interest in assassination through not only the things I have referred to already, but comparisons he made between himself and other assassins.

Q. Does the fact he had the goal or purpose or whatever of fame show that he had a serious mental disorder?

A. No, the goal of becoming famous is not limited to those who are mentally disordered. In Mr. Hinckley's case, it does relate to [the] narcissistic personality disorder that I have diagnosed.

Q. Briefly, why is that?

A. That is because with narcissistic personality disorders, the view of one's self as special and more important than others may translate itself into a concern with becoming both the center of attention and famous to the extent of wanting to be in the media, wanting to be in history books. . . .

Cross Examination by Mr. Fuller

Q. You . . . discussed yesterday, doctor, a motive on Mr. Hinckley's part that you described as a desire for fame, is that correct?

A. That is correct.

Q. And I believe you described that as being a quality of a narcissistic personality disorder?

A. Well, to be precise about it, the quality of narcissistic personality disorder includes a preoccupation with fantasies of unlimited success and fame and other kinds of glory.

Q. But what I am saying is the idea of desiring fame, you have put into the cluster of features that go to make up a narcissistic personality disorder, is that correct?

A. Well, I didn't put it there. It is there as one of the listed diagnostic features. Of course there are people interested in fame who don't suffer from any disorder at all, but in this instance I think the desire for fame is related to that disorder.

Q. I didn't mean to imply that you wrote DSM–III and put that particular characteristic under the heading "Narcissistic Personality Disorder." But I do mean to ask, is it not so that you have identified that feature as one which you observed in Mr. Hinckley as supporting your diagnosis of his suffering from a narcissistic personality disorder?

A. Yes, it is. Of course it is also the case that part of his concern with fame may have nothing to do with personality disorder. It is hard to know how much of that concern comes from this personality feature and how much of it is independent of it.

Q. And is it fair to characterize this idea of fame [as] an idea of grandiosity?

A. Well, it is a grandiose concern and a grandiose preoccupation if one continues it to the point of fantasizing unlimited success, unlimited fame, and so on. It is not a grandiose delusion, which is another matter altogether.

Q. If it were a grandiose delusion, it then, of course, would it not, become a personality feature associated with the disease of schizophrenia?

A. Yes. Well, yes. Grandiose delusions are often found in schizophrenia as well as in other disorders, and that is when a person believes that they already are successful or famous or has a delusion—of being Napoleon or Jesus Christ—examples of grandiose delusions.

Q. Well, there are other grandiose delusions short of thinking you are Napoleon, are there not?

A. Yes, there are.

Q. . . . There is quite an array of the delusions that might go into delusions of grandiosity?

A. Yes, indeed. I have heard many of them.

Dr. William T. Carpenter, Jr., Defense

Witness Direct Examination by Mr. Fuller

Q. . . . Doctor, I believe I had asked you whether you had an opinion as to whether at the time of the shooting on March 30, 1981 the defendant, as a result of the mental disease you described, lacked the substantial capacity to appreciate the wrongfulness of his conduct.

. . .

A. Yes, . . . I do think that he had—lacked substantial capacity to appreciate the wrongfulness of his conduct.

Q. Would you in your own terms elaborate on that and explain to the jury what you mean when you say he "lacked capacity to appreciate the wrongfulness of his conduct"?

A. Yes. In forming an opinion about his ability to appreciate wrongfulness, I tried to look at three components of that, the components in real life that are merged together, but found it useful to try to think of each separately.

The first was whether [at] a purely intellectual level that what he did was illegal. And it is my opinion on a purely intellectual level that he didn't know that he had that knowledge, that those were illegal acts.

The ability to reason that is implied in appreciation: I think appreci-ation of wrongfulness would mean that a person had an ability to reason about it, to think about it, to understand the consequences, to draw inferences about the acts and their meaning. And reasoning processes, which involve both the intellectual component and the emotional compo-nent. It is part of what goes together in our reasoning about any issue. That in this regard I believe Mr. Hinckley lacked substantial capacity to appreciate.

The reason for this opinion is that it is an understanding of the very reasoning process he was going through in preparation for and in carrying out the acts, that in his own mind, his own reasoning, the predominant reasoning had to do with two major things, the first of which was the termination of his own existence; the second of which was to accomplish this union with Jodie Foster through death, after life, whatever. But these were the major things that were dominating his reasoning about it. The magnitude of importance to him in weighing and in his reasoning of accomplishing these aims was far greater than the magnitude of the events per se. And in that regard it was not only his mind. He was not able to—he was not reasoning about the legality issue itself.

On the more emotional side appreciation, which would have to do with some—with the feelings, the emotional appreciation or understand-ing of the nature of the events, the consequences, he also had an impairment in that regard. And the impairment there was that the emotional consequences of the acts that he conducted were in his experience solely in terms of the inner world he had constructed. The meaning of this to the victims of the act was not on his mind. I don't mean to be crass about this, but in his mental state the effect of this on the President [and] on any other victims was trivial, that they—in his mental state they were bit players who were there in a way to help him to accomplish the two major roles [on] which his reasoning was taking place and were not in and of themselves important to this.

So that I do think that he had a purely intellectual appreciation that it was illegal. Emotionally he could give no weight to that because other factors weighed far heavier in his emotional appreciation.

And as these two things come together in his reasoning process, his reasoning processes were dominated by the inner state—by the inner drives that he was trying to accomplish in terms of the ending of his own life and in terms of the culminating relationship with Jodie Foster.

It was on that basis that I concluded that he did lack substantial capacity to appreciate the wrongfulness of his acts.

Q.   In considering his cognitive awareness, doctor, does that include an element of reason as well?

A.   . . . You see, reason is where the purely emotional and purely cognitive parts don't take place independent of each other. They come together and that is around the reasoning.

The cognitive part, just for clarity of thinking about it, [consider an] analogy that might help explain what I am thinking about there. If one were in a medical emergency, rushing someone to the hospital and you asked the true/false question . . . "Are you aware that the speed you are going is breaking the law?" There would be a cognitive appreciation, but in their reasoning around what they are doing, because of the emotional importance of what is going on, this cognitive appreciation would not be having a major impact on their reasoning about what they are doing.

So in my view the purely intellectual and purely emotional doesn't exist independent of each other, but they come together in the reasoning. And it is the impact on his reasoning that I have tried to describe predominantly in understanding his impairment in his ability to appreciate wrongfulness.

MR. FULLER: I have no further questions, Your Honor.

Cross Examination by Mr. Adelman

. . .

Q.   He made a decision not to shoot [President] Carter [in Dayton on October 2]?

A.   He made a decision to leave his gun behind, to go without the gun, to see if he could get more into the frame of mind by getting in the proximity of President Carter to do it.

Q.   He made a decision to leave the gun at the hotel?

A.   Yes.

Q.   Because he knew it was wrong to carry a gun into the streets, particularly near the President of the United States?

A.   He didn't leave it in the room because he was concerned with the wrongfulness of carrying it in the presence of the President.

Q. Can't you infer that he knew on that day that he knew that carrying a gun out on the streets of Dayton was wrong? Yes or no.

A. He in that purely intellectual sense has always known that carrying a gun like that was wrong, was illegal. But what I'm saying is it is not because of that consideration that he left the gun behind. He left the gun behind for other reasons, not because he was mindful. I don't think he was concerned with the legality of it one way or the other. He was concerned with other things he was trying to accomplish for himself and it met his needs at that point to go without the gun, trying to see how close he could [get]—and see if he could get himself into a different state of mind.

THE COURT: Namely what?

THE WITNESS: He wanted—he had on his mind ... the despair he felt as he left New Haven and his inability to make a simple and successful encounter of Jodie Foster. He was now trying to get himself back into a frame of mind where he felt more competent, more able, more effective in life [and he] found himself doing this by taking on the Travis Bickle parallel.

He felt he could accomplish this—and he did have suicidal thoughts at the time—through the stalking of President Carter. In that context he then is trying to psych himself up to get the impulses more intense, trying to prompt himself to be able to take action on them, so that he had, if you will, the mental scenario in place.

There was not the intensive impulsivity that could lead to his taking action and he was doing things to increase the likelihood.

Q. That is your explanation for what he did and didn't do in Dayton?

Dr. Park Elliott Dietz, Government Witness

Direct Examination by Mr. Adelman

Q. [L]et me ask you ... whether at the time of the criminal conduct on March 30, 1981, the defendant, as a result of mental disease or defect, lacked substantial capacity to appreciate the wrongfulness of his conduct?

A. I ... made a determination on that point.

Q. What is that determination?

A. That determination is that on March 30, 1981, Mr. Hinckley, as a result of mental disease or defect, did not lack substantial capacity to appreciate the wrongfulness of his conduct.

Q. Can you tell us [t]he evidence that you have evaluated and set forth that indicates that Mr. Hinckley was on that day able to appreciate the wrongfulness of his conduct?

A.   The answer is yes, I can provide some of the evidence. I will summarize. I will need to summarize a bit to do that because I have already presented some of the evidence to that effect.

Let me begin by saying that the evidence of Mr. Hinckley's ability to appreciate wrongfulness on March 30, 1981 has a background. That background includes long-standing interest in fame and assassinations. It includes study of the publicity associated with various crimes. It includes extensive study of assassinations. It includes choice of Travis Bickle as a major role model, a subject I will tell you about when I describe "Taxi Driver." It includes his choice of concealable handguns for his assassination plans, and his recognition that the 6.5 rifle he purchased was too powerful for him to handle. It includes his purchase of Devastator exploding ammunition on June 18, 1980. It includes multiple writings about assassination plans.

Q.   Continue.

A.   Now on that backdrop we see specific behaviors involved in Mr. Hinckley's pursuit of the President. His purchase of guns in Lubbock, Texas, in September of 1980 may or may not have been made after a decision to stalk President Carter. I say "may or may not" because there is a late-coming piece of evidence to the effect that Mr. Hinckley may have considered or actually stalked President Carter in March of 1980. He never mentioned that to me. He never mentioned that to my colleagues. I believe he mentioned that very recently to Dr. Goldman, as recently as during the trial.

Laying that aside, since I have no way to determine if that is true that he stalked or considered stalking in March 1980, I know that he had made the decision by the time that he went to—that he left Lubbock, Texas, for Dayton, Ohio, to stalk and shoot President Carter. We can tell you more about that stalking, but his stalking of President Carter in Dayton for which he tried to "psych himself up," as he put it, and stalking of President Carter in Nashville when he tried to "psych himself up," as he put it, are all part of the backdrop—are all part of the evidence that goes to show he understood on March 30th what assassination was, how it was carried out, and the consequences of assassination, which he knew from his study of the subject.

When he traveled to Dallas to purchase guns in October '80 after his arrest in Nashville, he was replacing his arsenal, which had been confiscated by the police there. He made the decision to switch his target from President Carter to President-elect Reagan after the November 4, 1980, election. He concealed successfully all of his stalking from his parents, from his brother, from his sister, from his brother-in-law, and from Dr. Hopper, including hiding his weapons, hiding his ammunition, and misleading them about his travels and his plans. This concealment indicates that he appreciated the wrongfulness of his plans, of his stalking behavior, throughout that entire time period and is further evidence of his appreciation of the wrongfulness on March 30, 1981.

Mind you, no single piece of evidence is determinative here. I am providing you with example of kinds of evidence that, taken together, make up an opinion about his appreciation of wrongfulness on March 30th, and these are examples of some of those pieces of evidence.

He purchased a highly concealable, .38 caliber revolver the day after Reagan's inauguration. He indicated that he became interested in President Reagan's whereabouts in March of 1981 before he had even begun his trip to Washington, D.C. He said he had become interested in the President's whereabouts.

When we get closer to the events of March 30th his decision on that day to, as he put it, "check out the scene" and to see how close he could get at the Hilton indicates that his decision to go to the Hilton Hotel reflected his thoughts about committing assassination on that day. He wanted to know how close he could get. Could he get within range? Could he get a clear shot?

He wrote a letter, having made his decision, to Jodie Foster, and we discussed that today already. In that letter to Jodie Foster, he indicated he was going to attempt to get Reagan and he indicates his knowledge that he could be killed by the Secret Service in the attempt. That is an indication that he understood and appreciated the wrongfulness of his plans because the Secret Service might well shoot someone who attempted to kill the President.

His decision to load his revolver with exploding ammunition before he left room 312 at the Park Central Hotel: Again, decisionmaking reflecting a choice of the use of explodable bullets which would have maximum effect on the victim, and understanding of the damage that he might bring upon other people.

His concealment of his revolver in his right pocket because he shoots right-handed: A decision to have his revolver where he could quickly draw it and understanding of the damage that he might bring upon other people.

His waiting until he had a clear shot at the President before drawing his gun: He didn't draw his gun when the President first arrived at the Hilton Hotel, as I have indicated before, because he didn't have a clear shot when the presidential motorcade first arrived. The limousine was farther away, and there was a curve in the wall between Mr. Hinckley and where the President entered the building. His waiting until the President came within his accurate range before drawing his gun reflects an appreciation of the behavior he was about to engage in and its purpose: its purpose was to shoot the President of the United States.

His reflection about his decision to draw the gun: I have referred before to his saying that he thought to himself "Should I?" reflecting on a moral decision he was to make.

And his decision to draw the gun at the very moment he did because of the circumstances which at that time favored a successful assassination: He viewed the situation as having poor security. He saw that the range was close and within the distance with which he was accurate, and at the precise moment that he chose to draw his revolver there was a diversion of attention from him. The Secret Service and the others in the presidential entourage looked the other way just as he was pulling the gun.

Finally, his decision to proceed to fire, thinking that others had seen him, as I have mentioned before, indicates his awareness that others seeing him was significant because others recognized that what he was doing and about to do were wrong.

Dr. William T. Carpenter, Jr., Defense Witness

Direct Examination by Mr. Fuller

Q. [B]ased upon your diagnosis of Mr. Hinckley's mental existence—of the mental disease of Mr. Hinckley on March 30, 1981, do you have an opinion whether at the time of the shooting, which occurred on that date, Mr. Hinckley, as a result of mental disease lacked substantial capacity to [conform] his conduct to the requirements of the law?

A. Yes, I have an opinion about that.

Q. Would you please tell us what that opinion is?

A. Yes. The fact that he had, in my opinion, that he had the illness that I have described to you does not indicate whether at any particular moment he would have had a substantial incapacity to conform his conduct to the requirements of the law. I reach, in my own opinion, I reach the conclusion that he did have a substantial incapacity at the time. The basis for that view deals, of course, with the whole background of psychotic development in his illness that I have described.

And then, more particularly for the point of time in question, was the driven quality to his experiences, the frantic activity that he had become involved in, his determination to end his own life, to terminate this existence that he was experiencing made, foremost in his own mind, actions that would terminate his own life. He experienced the lack of the anchoring, the two anchors that I described [treatment, which had failed, and the loss of parental support], potentially holding him somewhat in contact with reality so that by the time March 30th had arrived he was so dominated, in my opinion, by the inner state that he had developed over a period of time that his actions and the requirement for actions were so extensively determined by this inner state that he was, in my opinion, not able to [conform] his conduct to the outside requirements, to the legal requirements or social requirements of conduct, so that things at that point were completely out of balance for him and it was the driven quality of his inner state that was foremost in determining [is] actions.

And for that reason I reach the opinion that he did have a substantial incapacity in his ability to conform his conduct to the requirements of the law.

Dr. Park Elliott Dietz, Government Witness

Direct Examination by Mr. Adelman

Q. [L]et me ask you formally, if you determined whether at the time of the criminal conduct on March 30, 1981, the defendant Hinckley, as a result of mental disease or defect, lacked substantial capacity to conform his conduct to the requirements of the law?

A. I did make such a determination

Q. What determination did you make?

A. That on March 30, 1981, as a result of mental disease or defect, Mr. Hinckley did not lack substantial capacity to conform his conduct to the requirements of the law.

. . .

Q. . . . Can you give us the evidence, some of the evidence which underlies your answer?

A. Yes, I can . . . Among the reasons, the pieces of evidence, for my opinion that Mr. Hinckley was able to conform his conduct on March 30, 1981, are, again, the background. I have reviewed for you some of the evidence that he was capable of deliberation, of planning, that he had backed out in the past despite his efforts to "psych himself up."

This background indicates that in the past he had conformed his behavior, that he had had the ability to do so and had, in fact, done so. He hadn't drawn a gun in Dayton, perhaps because he didn't carry one with him. He hadn't drawn a gun in Nashville, and at Blair House in Washington he hadn't shot. He says he thought to himself on those occasions that he could do it another time. His ability to control his conduct on those dates to conform to the requirements of the law is part of the background for how it is that we know that he had that ability on March 30th.

At no point has Mr. Hinckley stated to me that he had a compulsion or a drive to assassinate or to commit other crimes.

Now, specific examples of evidence:

First of all, his decisionmaking ability itself was [intact] on March 30th. He was able to make other decisions on that date. He decided where to go for breakfast, what to eat. He decided to buy a newspaper, to shower. He made personal decisions of that sort. He was not a man incapable on that day of making decisions about his life, about which of these relatively minor things to do.

He deliberated and made a decision to survey the scene at the Hilton Hotel. There was no voice commanding him to do that. There was no drive within him pushing him to do that. He decided, as he tells us, to go to the Hilton to check out the scene to see how close he could get.

We know from the facts that he chose his bullets, that he loaded his revolver. He has never said that a voice commanded him to choose the shiniest bullets or that he had, for some other reason, to choose these.

He indicated that he chose them randomly. And we know that is not so. He chose the exploding [Devastator] bullets. This reflects decisionmaking and choice. He is controlling his conduct, is taking the time to write the "Jodie letter" to explain that he had a deliberate reason for carrying it out. A man driven by passion, by uncontrollable forces, is not often inclined to take the time to write a letter to explain what this is about. He did. And he claims he spent 20 to 35 minutes writing that letter.

He concealed the weapon not only from Mrs. Kondeah [the maid at the hotel], but from people in the hotel lobby, from taxi drivers, from people at the scene at the Hilton, until the moment he chose to draw his weapon. That ability to conceal his weapon is further evidence of his conforming his conduct, that is, he recognized that [w]aving a gun would be behavior likely to attract attention, and did not wave the gun. He concealed it.

His ability to wait, when he did not have a clear shot of the President on the President's way into the Hilton is further evidence of his ability to conform his behavior. A man driven, a man out of control, would not have the capacity to wait at that moment for the best shot.

His lack of desperation that day, and his recognition that he had other options: I haven't told you all the evidence of that yet, but he has indicated on a number of occasions what some of his options were. He considered going to New Haven, Connecticut. He considered going back to his hotel and going to sleep. These are options. He chose which option to carry out.

He says that he gave consideration to not firing after he had pulled the gun, and of course he said that he deliberated whether to pull the gun.

These choices, his description of deliberation, of decisionmaking, indicate that he was conforming his conduct to his own wishes, that he had the ability to control, to think, to decide, and that he did so. He controlled his conduct. He decided what to do, and he carried out his goals.

His having waited for the very moment to pull his gun and seizing that moment to fire the six shots, again indicates not a man who is willed, but a man who chooses the precise moment when his opportunity for assassination is best.

He took aim at the President, not, as he says, no aiming. He is seen in the videotapes in a combat crouch with a two-handed hold on the gun, the gun pointed toward the President, tracking the President's movements. These are organized acts. These are not disorganized random motions. These are specifically designed, organized acts.

Those are examples of the evidence supporting Mr. Hinckley having had the capacity to conform his conduct on March 30.

Index

References are to Pages

PRIVACY, INVASION OF
See also Confidential Communications, HIPPA
Hospitalized patients, 326–332, 1154–1155
Right to refuse and, 979–980

PRIVILEGE AGAINST SELF–INCRIMINA-TION
Civil commitment, 842–849
Competency to waive, 1072–1084
Criminal cases, 511–528
MDSO cases, 842–849

PROCEDURES
Commitment
    Adult mentally ill, 815–849
    Adversarial Rights, 825–832
    Decisionmakers, 820–825
    Developmentally disabled, 896–904
    Impact of, 801–803
    Insanity acquittees, 881
    Minors, 906–922
    Prisoners, 884–889
    Standard of proof, 815–820
    Therapeutic effect of, 803–806
Competency to be executed, 1094–1095
Competency to proceed, 1020–1027
Evaluation
    See Psychiatric Examination
Individualized treatment plan, 1144–1147, 1151–1152
Guardianship, 780, 947–948
Release from hospital, 849–857
Right to refuse, 853–854
Voluntary patients, 857–868

PSYCHIATRIC EXAMINATION
Liability for wrongful diagnosis, 334–340
Privilege against self-incrimination, application of, 511–525
Right to,
    Civil commitment, 840–841
    Criminal cases, 500–511
Right to counsel at, 525–527
State access to results, 510–511, 520–524
Testimonial privilege associated with,
    In civil cases, 360–387
    In criminal cases, 387–414, 510–511, 524–525
    Third party information, reliance on, 528–533
Warnings prior to, 520–524

PSYCHIATRIC RECORDS
See Confidential Communications, Rights of Patients
Patient right of access, 417–419

PSYCHIATRISTS
As expert witnesses, 493–499
Confidentiality requirement
    See Confidential Communications
Licensing, requirements for, 49–51, 83–84
Prescription function, 51–52, 112–119

PSYCHIATRISTS—Cont'd
Training and education, 49–51, 108–110

PSYCHOANALYSTS
Medication, utilization of, 48
Professional organizations, 51
Theoretical orientation, 10, 33–34
Training, 51, 109–110

PSYCHOLOGISTS
As expert witnesses, 493–499
Confidentiality requirement
    See Confidential Communications
Disciplinary proceedings
    See Regulation of Professions
Ethical standards, 89–96
Freedom of choice laws, 108
Licensing and certification, 84–86
Prescription privilege, 112–122
Psychiatrist supervision requirement, 102–109
Testimonial privilege
    See Testimonial Privilege
Title licensing, 85–86
Training, 53–54

PSYCHOSURGERY
Description, 32
Regulation, 991–999

PSYCHOTHERAPY
See also Negligence, Recovered Memory Therapy, Treatment
Mental Health Parity Act of 1996, 61–62
Outcome studies, 45–48
Schools of, 32–34, 47–48
Treatment, methods and approaches, 24–25, 33–34, 36–42, 140–145

RECOVERED MEMORY THERAPY
See also Negligence
Generally, 148–151
Hypnosis, use in, 150–151
Litigation against therapist, 151–155
Multiple Personality disorder, 149–151

REGULATION OF PROFESSIONS (ADMIN-ISTRATIVE)
See also Psychiatric Social Workers, Psychiatrists, Psychologists
Certification distinguished from licensing, 84–86
Disciplinary proceedings, 88–89
Licensing requirements, 81–85

REHABILITATION ACT OF 1973
Affirmative action programs, 1282–1290
Employment, 1253–1290
Overview, 1249–1253
Postsecondary education, 1290–1300

REIMBURSEMENT FOR HOSPITAL COSTS
Generally, 1163–1164

RESEARCH AND EXPERIMENTATION
See also Informed Consent

TREATMENT—Cont'd
Psychotherapies, 32–42
Right to, 1111–1131. See also Rights of Patients, Treatment
Right to refuse, 963–1003
Selection of therapist, economic factors influencing, 55–59
Types, 22–42

VAGUENESS DOCTRINE
Guardianship, 947
Parens patriae commitment, 779–780
Police power commitment, 734–736

VOLUNTARY PSYCHIATRIC HOSPITAL-IZATION

VAGUENESS DOCTRINE—Cont'd
See also Developmentally Disabled, Minors
Generally, 857–863
Informed consent doctrine, application of, 861–863
Mandatory notice provisions, 866–867
Non-protesting admissions, 863–864
Release, 866–868
Voluntariness, definition of, 862–863

†